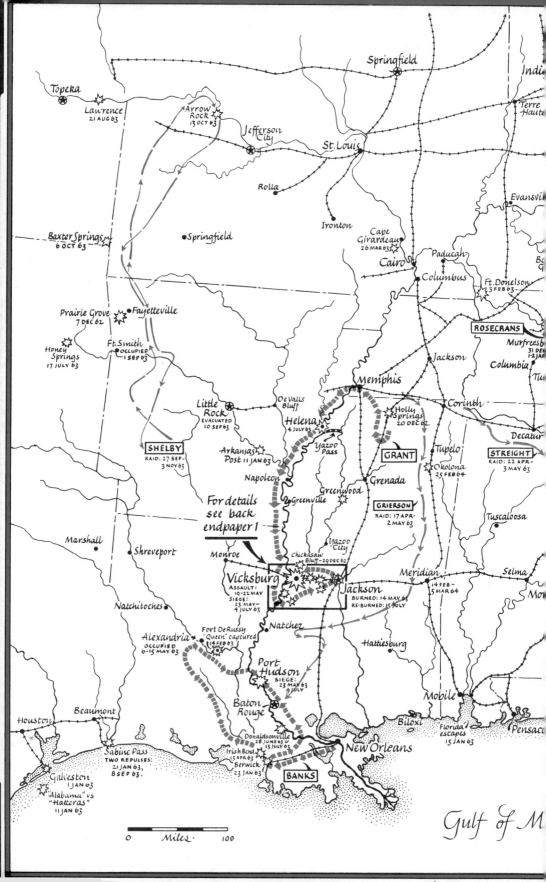

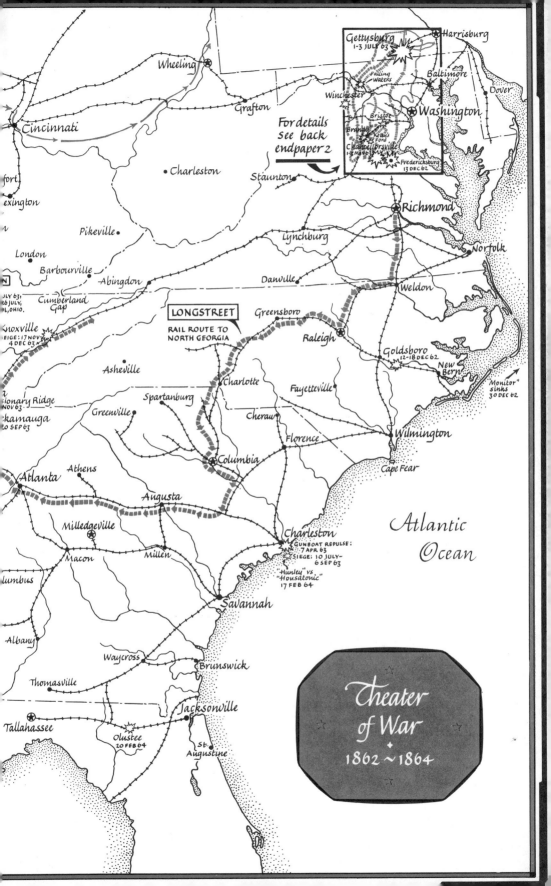

Wheeling

Cincinnati

fort

exington

Charleston

London

Barbourville

Pikeville

Abingdon

Cumberland
Gap

JLY 63;
26 JULY,
L, OHIO.

Knoxville
SIEGE: 17 NOV–
4 DEC 63

ionary Ridge
NOV 63

kamauga
0 SEP 63

Athens

Atlanta

Milledgeville

Macon

lumbus

Albany

Thomasville

Tallahassee

Grafton

Staunton

Lynchburg

Danville

LONGSTREET
RAIL ROUTE TO
NORTH GEORGIA

Greensboro

Raleigh

Asheville

Charlotte

Spartanburg

Greenville

Cheraw

Columbia

Augusta

Millen

Fayetteville

Florence

Savannah

Waycross

Brunswick

Jacksonville

Olustee
20 FEB 64

St.
Augustine

For details
see back
endpaper 2

Gettysburg
1–3 JULY 63

Harrisburg

Falling
Waters

Winchester

Bristol

Branch

Kelly's
Ford

Chancellorsville
1–3 MAY 63

Baltimore

Washington

Dover

Richmond

Norfolk

Weldon

Goldsboro
12–18 DEC 62

New
Bern

"Monitor"
sinks
30 DEC 62

Wilmington

Cape Fear

Charleston
GUNBOAT REPULSE:
7 APR 63
SIEGE: 10 JULY–
6 SEP 63

"Hunley" vs.
"Housatonic,"
17 FEB 64

Fredericksburg
13 DEC 62

*Atlantic
Ocean*

*Theater
of War
✦
1862 ~ 1864*

The Civil War
A Narrative

*Happy Reading
Clyde!*

*Roger, Beth + Jen
Thompson
1994*

ALL THESE WERE HONOURED IN THEIR GENERATIONS

AND WERE THE GLORY OF THEIR TIMES

THERE BE OF THEM

THAT HAVE LEFT A NAME BEHIND THEM

THAT THEIR PRAISES MIGHT BE REPORTED

AND SOME THERE BE WHICH HAVE NO MEMORIAL

WHO ARE PERISHED AS THOUGH THEY HAD NEVER BEEN

AND ARE BECOME AS THOUGH THEY HAD NEVER BEEN BORN

AND THEIR CHILDREN AFTER THEM

BUT THESE WERE MERCIFUL MEN

WHOSE RIGHTEOUSNESS HATH NOT BEEN FORGOTTEN

WITH THEIR SEED SHALL CONTINUALLY REMAIN

A GOOD INHERITANCE

AND THEIR CHILDREN ARE WITHIN THE COVENANT

THEIR SEED STANDETH FAST

AND THEIR CHILDREN FOR THEIR SAKES

THEIR SEED SHALL REMAIN FOR EVER

AND THEIR GLORY SHALL NOT BE BLOTTED OUT

THEIR BODIES ARE BURIED IN PEACE

BUT THEIR NAME LIVETH FOR EVERMORE

Ecclesiasticus xliv

THE
Civil War
A Narrative

★ ★

FREDERICKSBURG
to MERIDIAN

★ ★

By SHELBY FOOTE

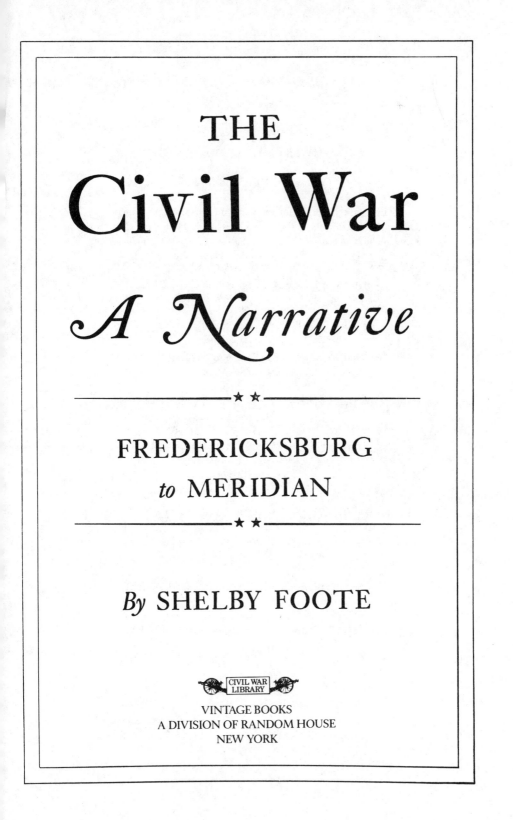

CIVIL WAR
LIBRARY

VINTAGE BOOKS
A DIVISION OF RANDOM HOUSE
NEW YORK

First Vintage Books Edition, September 1986

Library of Congress Cataloging-in-Publication Data

Foote, Shelby.
The Civil War, a narrative.

Includes bibliographies and indexes.
Contents: v. 1. Fort Sumter to Perryville—
v. 2. Fredericksburg to Meridian—
v. 3. Red River to Appomattox.
1. United States—History—Civil War, 1861–1865.
I. Title.
E468.F7   1986   973.7   86-40135
ISBN: 0-394-74623-6 (v. 1) (pbk.)
0-394-74621-X (v. 2) (pbk.)
0-394-74622-8 (v. 3) (pbk.)
0-394-74913-8 (3 vol. boxed set)

Manufactured in the United States of America

C9876543210

CONTENTS

★ ✗ ☆

I

II

III

☆ I ☆

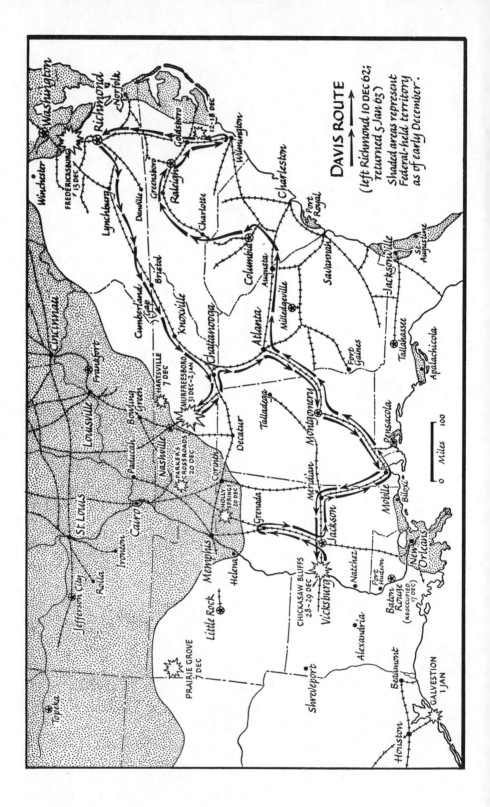

DAVIS ROUTE →

(left Richmond 10 DEC 62; returned 5 Jan '63)
Shaded areas represent
Federal-held territory
as of early December.

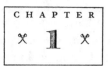
The Longest Journey

★ ✗ ☆

"AFTER AN ABSENCE OF NEARLY TWO YEARS," Jefferson Davis told the legislators assembled under the golden dome of his home-state capitol on the day after Christmas, 1862 — twenty months and two weeks, to the day, since the guns of Charleston opened fire on Sumter to inaugurate the civil war no one could know was not yet halfway over — "I again find myself among those who, from the days of my childhood, have ever been the trusted objects of my affection, those for whose good I have ever striven and whose interests I have sometimes hoped I may have contributed to subserve.... I left you to assume the duties which have devolved upon me as the representative of the new Confederacy. The responsibilities of this position have occupied all my time, and have left me no opportunity for mingling with my friends in Mississippi or for sharing in the dangers which have menaced them. But, wherever duty may have called me, my heart has been with you, and the success of the cause in which we are all engaged has been first in my thoughts and prayers."

In February of the year before, he had left for Montgomery, Alabama, to assume his role as President of the newly established provisional government, believing, as he said now, "that the service to which I was called could be but temporary." A West Pointer and an authentic hero of the Mexican War, he had considered his primary talent — or, as he termed it, his "capacity" — to be military. He had thought to return to the duty he found congenial, that of a line officer in the service of his state, "to lead Mississippians in the field, and to be with them where danger was to be braved and glory won.... But it was decided differently. I was called to another sphere of action. How, in that sphere, I have discharged the duties and obligations imposed on me, it does not become me to constitute myself the judge. It is for others to decide that question. But, speaking to you with that frankness and that confidence with which I have always spoken to you, and which partakes of the nature of thinking aloud, I can say with my hand upon my heart that whatever I have done has been done with the sincere purpose of promoting the noble cause in which we are engaged. The period which has elapsed since I left you is short; for the time which may appear long in the life of a man is short in the history of a nation. And in that short period remarkable changes have been wrought in all the circumstances by which we are sur-rounded."

Remarkable changes had indeed been wrought, and of these the most immediately striking to those present, seated row on row beneath him or standing close-packed along the outer aisles, was in the aspect of the man who stood before them, tall and slender, careworn and oracular, in a mote-shot nimbus of hazy noonday sunlight pouring down from the high windows of the hall. When they had seen him last on this same ros-trum, just short of twenty-three months ago this week, he had not ap-peared to be within a decade of his fifty-two years of age. Now, though, he was fifty-four, and he looked it. The "troubles and thorns innumera-ble" which he foretold on his arrival in Montgomery to take the oath of office, back in the first glad springtime of the nation, had not only come to pass; they had also left their marks — as if the thorns, being more than figurative, had scored his brow and made of him what he had never seemed before, a man of sorrows. The gray eyes, one lustrous, the other sightless, its stone gray pupil covered by a film, were deeply sunken above the jut of the high cheekbones, and the thin upper lip, indicative of an iron will and rigid self-control, was held so tightly against the teeth, even in repose, that you saw their shape behind it. The accustomed ge-niality was there, the inveterate grace and charm of manner, along with the rich music of the voice, but the symptoms of strain and overwork were all too obvious. These proceeded, it was said, not only from having had to await (as he was awaiting even now) the outcome of battles in which he could have no active part, whatever his inclination, but also, it was added, from a congenital inability to relegate authority, including the minor paperwork which took up such a disproportionate share of his existence.

Other changes there were, too, less physical and therefore less im-mediately obvious, but on closer inspection no less profound. In this case, moreover, the contrast between now and then was emphasized by mutu-ality, involving others besides Davis. It was two-sided; reciprocal, so to speak. Arriving in Jackson to accept his appointment as commander of Mississippi troops after his farewell to the Senate in January of what had presently turned out to be the first year of the conflict some men had still believed could be avoided, he had been met at the station by Gover-nor J. J. Pettus, whom he advised to push the procurement of arms. "We shall need all and many more than we can get," he said, expressing the conviction that blood would soon be shed. "General, you overrate the risk," the governor protested, and Davis replied: "I only wish I did." So

thoroughly had this prediction been fulfilled in the past twenty months —
Kentucky and Missouri irretrievably gone, along with most of Tennessee and the northwest quarter of Virginia, New Orleans fallen, Nashville
and Memphis occupied, and North Mississippi itself aswarm with bluecoats — that now it was Governor Pettus who was calling for reassurance, and calling for it urgently, from the man to whom he previously
had offered it so blandly.

"You have often visited the army of Virginia," he wired Richmond in early December. "At this critical juncture could you not visit
the army of the West? Something must be done to inspire confidence."

By way of reinforcement for this plea there came a letter from
Senator James Phelan, whose home lay in the path of the invaders. "The
present alarming crisis in this state, so far from arousing the people,
seems to have sunk them in listless despondency," he wrote. "The spirit
of enlistment is thrice dead. Enthusiasm has expired to a cold pile of
damp ashes. Defeats, retreats, sufferings, dangers, magnified by spiritless
helplessness and an unchangeable conviction that our army is in the hands
of ignorant and feeble commanders, are rapidly producing a sense of settled despair. . . . I imagine but one event that could awaken from its waning spark the enthusiastic hopes and energy of Mississippians. Plant your
own foot upon our soil, unfurl your banner at the head of the army, tell
your own people that you have come to share with them the perils of this
dark hour. . . . If ever your presence was needed as a last refuge from an
'Iliad of woes,' this is the hour. It is not a point to be argued. [Only] you
can save us or help us save ourselves from the dread evils now so immi-
nently pending."

Flattering as this was, in part — especially the exhortation to "unfurl your banner," which touched the former hero of Buena Vista where
his inclination was strongest and his vanity was most susceptible — the
senator's depiction of regional gloom and fears, tossed thus into the balance, added weight to the governor's urgent plea that the Commander in
Chief undertake the suggested journey to his homeland and thereby refute in the flesh the growing complaint that the authorities in Richmond
were concerned only for the welfare of the soldiers and civilians in Virginia, where if anywhere the war was being won, rather than for those in
the western theater, where if anywhere the war was being lost. Not that
the danger nearest the national capital was slight. Major General Ambrose Burnside, a month in command of the Army of the Potomac as
successor to Major General George McClellan, who had been relieved
for a lack of aggressiveness, was menacing the line of the Rappahannock with a mobile force of 150,000 men, backed by another 50,000 in
the Washington defenses. To oppose this host General Robert E. Lee
had something under 80,000 in the Army of Northern Virginia moving
toward a concentration near Fredericksburg, where the threat of a crossing seemed gravest, midway of the direct north-south hundred-mile line

connecting the two capitals. That the battle, now obviously at hand, would be fought even closer to the Confederate seat of government appeared likely, for Davis wrote Lee on December 8: "You will know best when it will be proper to make a masked movement to the rear, should circumstances require you to move nearer to Richmond."

Something else he said in this same letter. Hard as it was for him to leave the capital at a time when every day might bring the battle that would perhaps decide his country's fate, he had made up his mind to heed the call that reached him from the West. "I propose to go out there immediately," he told Lee, "with the hope that something may be done to bring out men not heretofore in service, and to arouse all classes to united and desperate resistance." After expressing the hope that "God may bless us, as in other cases seemingly as desperate, with success over our impious foe," he added, by way of apology for not having reviewed the Virginian's army since it marched northward on the eve of Second Manassas: "I have been very anxious to visit you, but feeble health and constant labor have caused me to delay until necessity hurries me in the opposite direction." He sent the letter by special courier that same December 8; then, two days later, he himself was off.

He left incognito, aboard a special car and accompanied by a single military aide, lest his going stir up rumors that the capital was about to be abandoned in the face of the threat to the line of the Rappahannock. His planned itinerary was necessarily roundabout: not only because the only direct east-west route was closed to him by the Federal grip on the final hundred miles of the Memphis & Charleston Railroad, but also because he had decided to combine the attempt to restore morale among the distraught civilians of the region, as suggested by Governor Pettus and Senator Phelan, with a personal inspection of the two main armies charged with the defense of the theater bounded east and west by the Blue Ridge Mountains and the Mississippi River. The Army of Tennessee, the larger of the two, northwest of Chattanooga and covering that city by pretending to threaten Nashville, was under General Braxton Bragg; the other, the Army of Mississippi under Lieutenant General John C. Pemberton, covered Vicksburg. Both were menaced by superior forces, or combinations of forces, under Major Generals William S. Rosecrans and Ulysses S. Grant, and Davis had lately appointed General Joseph E. Johnston to co-ordinate the efforts of both armies in order to meet the double menace by operating on interior lines, much as Lee had done for the past six months in Virginia, on a smaller scale but with such success as had won for Confederate arms the admiration of the world.

Johnston's was the more difficult task, albeit one on which the survival of the nation was equally dependent. Whether it could be performed — specifically, whether it could be performed by Johnston — remained to be seen. So far, though, the signs had appeared to the general himself to be anything but promising. Pemberton was falling back

under pressure from Grant in North Mississippi, and Bragg's preparations for the defense of Middle Tennessee, though they had not yet been
tested by Federal pressure, did not meet with the new commander's approval when he inspected them this week. In fact, he found in them full
justification for a judgment he had delivered the week before, when he
first established headquarters in Chattanooga. "Nobody ever assumed a
command under more unfavorable circumstances," he wrote to a friend
back East. "If Rosecrans had disposed our troops himself, their disposition could not have been more unfavorable to us."

    Davis did not share the Virginian's gloom; or if he did he did not
show it as he left Richmond, December 10, and rode westward through
Lynchburg and Wytheville and across the state line to Knoxville, where,
beginning his attempt to bolster civilian morale by a show of confidence, he made a speech in which he characterized "the Toryism of East
Tennessee" as "greatly exaggerated." Joined by Lieutenant General
Edmund Kirby Smith, the department commander whose march north
in August and September had cleared the region of bluecoats and delivered Cumberland Gap, but whose strength had been reduced by
considerably more than half in the past month as a result of orders to reinforce Bragg in the adjoining department, the President reached Chattanooga by nightfall and went at once to pay a call on Johnston.

    He found him somewhat indisposed, waiting in his quarters.
Short of stature, gray and balding, a year older than Davis despite the fact
that he had been a year behind him at West Point, the general had a
high-colored, wedge-shaped face, fluffed white side whiskers, a grizzled
mustache and goatee, eyes that crinkled attractively at their outer corners when he smiled, and a jaunty, gamecock manner. Mrs Johnston, in
attendance on her husband, was able to serve their visitor a genuine cup
of coffee: the "real Rio," she reported proudly to a friend next day,
describing the event. She claimed nonetheless the saddest heart in Chattanooga. Whatever Davis might have accomplished elsewhere on this
arduous first day of the journey he had undertaken "to arouse all
classes to united and desperate resistance," he obviously had had little
success in her direction. "How ill and weary I feel in this desolate land,"
she added in the letter to her friend in the Old Dominion, which she so
much regretted having left, "& how dreary it all looks, & how little
prospect there is of my poor husband doing ought than lose his army.
Truly a forlorn hope it is."

    The general himself was far from well, suffering from a flare-
up of the wound that had cost him his Virginia command, six months
ago at Seven Pines, and from a weariness brought on by his just-
completed inspection of the Army of Tennessee. So Davis, postponing
their strategy conference until such time as he would be able to see for
himself the condition of that army, left next day for Bragg's head-

quarters at Murfreesboro, ninety miles away and only thirty miles from Nashville.

It was a two-day visit, and unlike Johnston he was heartened by what he saw. Serenaded at his hotel by a large and enthusiastic crowd, he announced that he entertained no fears for the safety of Richmond, that Tennessee would be held to the last extremity, and that if the people would but arouse themselves to sustain the conflict, eventual if not immediate foreign intervention would assure a southern victory and peace on southern terms. His listeners, delighted by a recent exploit beyond the northern lines by Colonel John H. Morgan, did not seem to doubt for a moment the validity of his contentions or predictions. Whatever dejection he might encounter in other portions of the threatened region, he found here an optimism to match his own. The thirty-seven-year-old Morgan, with four small regiments of cavalry and two of infantry — just over 2000 men in all, most of them Kentuckians like himself — had crossed the icy Cumberland by starlight, in order to strike at dawn on Sunday, December 7, a Union force of equal strength in camp at Hartsville, forty miles upstream from Nashville. Another enemy force, three times his strength, was camped nine miles away at Castalian Springs, within easy hearing distance of his guns, but had no chance to interfere. After less than an hour of fighting, in which he inflicted more than 300 casualties at a cost of 125, Morgan accepted the surrender of Colonel Absalom B. Moore of Illinois. By noon he was back across the Cumberland with 1762 prisoners and a wagon train heavily loaded with captured equipment and supplies, riding hard for Murfreesboro and the cheers that awaited him there. "A brilliant feat," Joe Johnston called it, and recommended that Morgan "be appointed brigadier general immediately. He is indispensable."

Davis gladly conferred the promotion in person when he arrived, receiving from Morgan's own hands in return one of the three sets of enemy infantry colors the cavalryman had brought home. A formal review of one corps of the Army of Tennessee next day, followed that evening by a conference with Bragg and his lieutenants, was equally satisfying, fulfilling as it did the other half of the President's double-barreled purpose. "Found the troops there in good condition and fine spirits," he wired the Secretary of War on December 14, after his return to Chattanooga the night before. "Enemy is kept close in to Nashville, and indicates only defensive purposes."

This last had led to a strategic decision, made on the spot and before consultation with Johnston. As Davis saw it, comparing Pemberton's plight with Bragg's, the Mississippi commander was not only more gravely threatened by a combination of army and naval forces, above and below the Vicksburg bluff; he was also far more heavily outnumbered, and with less room for maneuver. Practically speaking, despite the assurance lately given the serenaders, the loss of Middle Tennessee would mean no more than the loss of supplies to be gathered in the region; whereas the loss of Vicksburg would mean the loss of the Mississippi River throughout its length, which in turn would mean the loss of Texas, West Louisiana, Arkansas, and the last tenuous hope for the recovery of Missouri. Consequently, in an attempt to even the odds — east and west, that is; North and South the odds could never be evened, here or elsewhere — Davis decided to reinforce Pemberton with a division from Bragg. When the latter protested that this would encourage Rosecrans to attack him, he was informed that he would have to take his chances, depending on maneuver for deliverance. "Fight if you can," Davis told him, and if necessary "fall back beyond the Tennessee."

Bragg took the decision with such grace as he could muster; but not Johnston. When Davis returned to Chattanooga with instructions for the transfer to be ordered, the Virginian protested for all he was worth against a policy which seemed to him no better than robbing Peter to pay Paul. Both western armies, he declared, were already too weak for effective operations; to weaken either was to invite disaster, particularly in Tennessee, which he referred to as "the shield of the South." But in this matter the President was inflexible. Apparently reasoning that if the general would not do the job for which he had been sent here — a balancing and a taking of calculated risks in order to make the most of the advantage of operating on interior lines — then he would do it for him, Davis insisted that the transfer order be issued immediately. This Johnston did, though with a heavy heart and still protesting, convinced that he would be proved right in the end.

Whatever Davis's reaction was on learning thus that one of his two ranking commanders was opposed to availing himself of the one solid advantage strategically accruing to the South, he had other worries to fret him now: worries that threatened not a long-range but an immediate collapse, not of a part but of the whole. On his return from Murfreesboro he heard from the War Department that the national capital was menaced from two directions simultaneously. A force of undetermined strength was moving inland from coastal North Carolina against Goldsboro and the vital Weldon Railroad, and Burnside was across the Rappahannock. "You can imagine my anxiety," Davis wrote his wife, chafed by distance and the impossibility of being in two places at once. "If the necessity demands, I will return to Richmond, though already there are indications of a strong desire for me to visit the further West, expressed in terms which render me unwilling to disappoint the expectation." Presently, however, his anxiety was relieved. The Carolina invasion, though strongly mounted, had been halted at the Neuse, well short of the vital supply line, and Lee had inflicted another staggering defeat on the main northern army, flinging it back across the Rappahannock. Davis was elated at the news, but Johnston's reaction was curiously mixed. "What luck some people have," he said. "Nobody will ever come to attack me in such a place."

After a day of rest and conferences, political as well as military, Davis left Chattanooga late on the afternoon of December 16, accompanied by Johnston, who would be making his first inspection of the western portion of his command. However, with the Memphis & Charleston in Federal hands along the Tennessee-Mississippi line, their route at first led south to Atlanta, where they spent the night and Davis responded to another serenade. Continuing south to Montgomery next morning, he spoke at midday from the portico of the Alabama capitol, where he had delivered his first inaugural a week after being notified of his unexpected election to head the newly established Confederate States of America. That was nearly two years ago. Whatever thoughts he had as to the contrast between now and then, as evidenced by the demeanor of the crowd that gathered to hear him, he kept to himself as he and Johnston rode on that night to Mobile, where he spoke formally for the second time that day. Next morning, December 19, they reached Jackson, but having agreed to return for a joint appearance before the Mississippi legislature on the day after Christmas, they only stayed for lunch and left immediately afterwards for Vicksburg.

This too was a two-day visit, and mainly they spent it inspecting the town's land and water defenses, which had been extended northward a dozen miles along a range of hills and ridges overlooking the Yazoo and its swampy bayous — Chickasaw Bluffs, the range was called, or sometimes Walnut Hills — and southward about half that far to Warrenton, a hamlet near the lower end of the tall red bluff dominating the eastern shank of the hairpin bend described at this point by a whim of the Mississippi. To an untrained eye the installations might look stout indeed, bristling with guns at intervals for nearly twenty miles, but Johnston was not pleased by what he saw. To his professional eye, they not only left much to be desired in the way of execution; their very conception, it seemed to him, was badly flawed. Nor was he any slower to say so now than he had been eight months ago at Yorktown, in a similar situation down the York-James peninsula from Richmond. "Instead of a fort requiring a small garrison," which would leave the bulk of available troops free to maneuver, he protested, the overzealous engineers had made the place into "an immense intrenched camp, requiring an army to hold it." Besides, scattered as they were along the high ground north and south "to prevent the bombardment of the town, instead of to close the navigation of the river to the enemy," the batteries would not be able to concentrate their fire against naval attack. In these and other matters Johnston expressed his discontent. Davis, a professional too, could see the justice in much of this, and though he did not order the line contracted, he moved to strengthen it by wiring the

War Department of the "immediate and urgent necessity for heavy guns and long-range fieldpieces at Vicksburg."

Two bits of news, one welcome, one disturbing, reached them here in the course of their brief visit. The first was that a Federal iron-clad, the *Cairo*, had been sunk up the Yazoo the week before, the result of an experiment with torpedoes by Commander Isaac N. Brown, builder and skipper of the *Arkansas*, which single-handedly had raised the midsummer naval siege by an all-out attack on the two enemy fleets before she steamed downriver to her destruction in early August. The other news was that Major General Nathaniel P. Banks, whose troops were escorted upriver from New Orleans by the deep-draft fleet under Rear Admiral David G. Farragut, had reoccupied Baton Rouge, abandoned three months before by his predecessor, Major General Benjamin F. Butler. Whatever comfort the bluff's defenders found in the mishap encountered by the Yankees in their probe of the Yazoo was more than offset by the news that they were approaching in strength from the opposite direction. Johnston, for one, was convinced that, in addition to the 9000-man division already on the way from Bragg, another 20,000 troops would be required if Vicksburg and Port Hudson, another strong point on another bluff three hundred miles downriver, were to be held against the combined forces of Grant and Banks. What was more, he thought he knew just where to get them: from the adjoining Transmississippi Department, commanded by Lieutenant General Theophilus H. Holmes.

"Our great object is to hold the Mississippi," Johnston told Davis. In this connection, he firmly believed "that our true system of warfare would be to concentrate the forces of the two departments" — his and Holmes's — "on this side of the Mississippi, beat the enemy here, then reconquer the country beyond it, which [the Federals] might have gained in the meantime."

Davis had already shown his appreciation of this "true system" by recommending, a month before he left Richmond and two weeks before Johnston himself had been assigned to the western command, that Holmes send reinforcements eastward to assist in the accomplishment of the "great objective." Since then, unfortunately, and by coincidence on the December 7 of Morgan's victory at Hartsville, the Arkansas army under Major General Thomas C. Hindman, the one mobile force of any size in the department beyond the river, had fought and lost the Battle of Prairie Grove, up in the northwest corner of the state. This altered considerably Holmes's ability to comply with the request. However, instead of pointing out this and other drawbacks to Johnston's argument — 1) that to lose the Transmississippi temporarily might be to lose it permanently, as a result of losing the confidence of the people of the region; 2) that the Confederacy, already suffering from the strictures of the Federal blockade, could not afford even a brief stoppage of the flow of supplies from Texas and the valleys of the Arkansas and the Red; and 3) that the transfer east of men in gray would result in a proportional transfer of men in blue, which would lengthen rather than shorten the odds on both sides of the river unless the blow was delivered with unaccustomed lightning speed — Davis was willing to repeat the recommendation in stronger terms. Accordingly, on this same December 21, he wrote to Holmes in Little Rock, apprising him of the growing danger and urging full co-operation with Johnston's plan as set forth in that general's correspondence, which was included. It was a long letter, and in it the President said in part: "From the best information at command, a large force is now ready to descend the Mississippi and co-operate with the army advancing from Memphis to make an attack upon Vicksburg. Large forces are also reported to have been sent to the lower Mississippi for the purpose of ascending the river to attempt the reduction of Port Hudson. . . . It seems to me then unquestionably best that you should reinforce Genl Johnston." After reminding Holmes that "we cannot hope at all points to meet the enemy with a force equal to his own, and must find our security in the concentration and rapid movement of troops," Davis closed with a compliment and an admonition: "I have thus presented to you my views, and trusting alike in your patriotism and discretion, leave you to make the application of them when circumstances will permit. Whatever may be done should be done with all possible dispatch."

Johnston's enthusiasm on reading the opening paragraphs of the letter, which was shown to him before it was given to a courier bound for Little Rock, was considerably dampened by the close. Judging perhaps by his own reaction the week before, when he protested against the detachment of a division from Bragg for this same purpose, he did not share the President's trust in the "patriotism and discretion" Holmes was expected to bring to bear, and he noted regretfully that, despite the final suggestion as to the need for haste, "circumstances" had been left to govern the application of what Davis called his "views."

Two days later, moreover, the general's gloom was deepened when they returned to Jackson and proceeded north a hundred miles by rail to Grenada, where Pemberton had ended his southward retreat in the face of Grant's advance and had his badly outnumbered field force hard at work in an attempt to fortify the banks of the Yalobusha River while his cavalry, under Major General Earl Van Dorn, probed for Grant's rear in an attempt to make him call a halt, or anyhow slow him down, by giving him trouble along his lengthening supply line. Here as at Vicksburg, Johnston found the intrenchments "very extensive, but slight — the usual defect of Confederate engineering." Nor was he pleased to discover, as he said later, that "General Pemberton and I advocated opposite modes of warfare." He would have continued the retreat to a better position farther south, hoping for a stronger concentration; but as usual Davis discounted the advantage of withdrawal and sided with the commander who was opposed to delaying a showdown.

Christmas Day they returned to Jackson, which gave the President time for an overnight preparation of the speech he would deliver tomorrow before his home-state legislature. This was not so large a task as might be thought, despite the fact that he would speak for the better part of an hour. In general, what he would say here was what he had been saying for more than two weeks now, en route from Virginia, through Tennessee, Georgia, and Alabama, and elsewhere already in Mississippi. His overnight task was mainly one of consolidating his various impromptu responses to serenades and calls for "remarks" from station platforms along the way, albeit with added emphasis on his home ties and the government's concern for the welfare of the people in what he called "the further West."

That was why he began by addressing his listeners as "those who, from the days of my childhood, have ever been the trusted objects of my affection," and adding: "Whatever fortunes I may have achieved in life have been gained as a representative of Mississippi, and before all I have labored for the advancement of her glory and honor. I now, for the first time in my career, find myself the representative of a wider circle of interest, but a circle of which the interests of Mississippi are still embraced. . . . For, although in the discharge of my duties as President of the Confederate States I had determined to make no distinction between the various parts of the country — to know no separate state — yet my heart has always beat more warmly for Mississippi, and I have looked on Mississippi soldiers with a pride and emotion such as no others inspired."

Flanked on the rostrum by Governor Pettus and Senator Phelan, he waited for the polite applause to subside, then launched at once into an excoriation of the northern government: not only its leaders but also its followers, in and out of the armies of invasion.

"I was among those who, from the beginning, predicted war . . . not because our right to secede and form a government of our own was not indisputable and clearly defined in the spirit of that declaration which rests the right to govern on the consent of the governed, but because I saw that the wickedness of the North would precipitate a war upon us. Those who supposed that the exercise of this right of separation could not produce war have had cause to be convinced that they had credited their recent associates of the North with a moderation, a sagacity, a morality they did not possess. You have been involved in a war waged for the gratification of the lust of power and aggrandizement, for your conquest and your subjugation, with a malignant ferocity and with a disregard and a contempt of the usages of civilization entirely unequaled in history. Such, I have ever warned you, were the characteristics of the northern people. . . . After what has happened during the last two years, my only wonder is that we consented to live for so long a time in association with such miscreants and have loved so much a government rotten to the core. Were it ever to be proposed again to enter into a Union with such a people, I could no more consent to do it than to trust myself in a den of thieves. . . . There is indeed a difference between the two peoples. Let no man hug the delusion that there can be renewed association between them. Our enemies are a traditionless and homeless race. From the time of Cromwell to the present moment they have been disturbers of the peace of the world. Gathered together by Cromwell from the bogs and fens of the north of Ireland and England, they commenced by disturbing the peace of their own country; they disturbed Holland, to which they fled; and they disturbed England on their return. They persecuted Catholics in England, and they hung Quakers and witches in America."

He spoke next of the conscription act, defending it against its critics; reviewed the recent successes of Confederate arms, sometimes against odds that had amounted to four to one; recommended local provision for the families of soldiers in the field; urged upon the legislators "the necessity of harmony" between the national government and the governments of the states; then returned to a bitter expression of his views as to the contrast between the two embattled peoples.

"The issue before us is one of no ordinary character. We are not engaged in a conflict for conquest, or for aggrandizement, or for the settlement of a point of international law. The question for you to decide is, Will you be slaves or will you be independent? Will you transmit to your children the freedom and equality which your fathers transmitted to you, or will you bow down in adoration before an idol baser than ever was worshipped by Eastern idolators? Nothing more is necessary than the mere statement of this issue. Whatever may be the personal sacrifices involved, I am confident that you will not shrink from them whenever the question comes before you. Those men who now assail us, who have been associated with us in a common Union, who have inherited a government which they claim to be the best the world ever saw — these men, when left to themselves, have shown that they are incapable of preserving their own personal liberty. They have destroyed the freedom of the press; they have seized upon and imprisoned members of state legislatures and of municipal councils, who were suspected of sympathy with the South; men have been carried off into captivity in distant states without indictment, without a knowledge of the accusations brought against them, in utter defiance of all rights guaranteed by the institutions under which they live. These people, when separated from the South and left entirely to themselves, have in six months demonstrated their utter incapacity for self-government. And yet these are the people who claim to be your masters. These are the people who have determined to divide out the South among their Federal troops. Mississippi they have devoted to the direst vengeance of all. 'But vengeance is the Lord's,' and beneath His banner you will meet and hurl back these worse than vandal hordes."

Having attempted thus to breathe heat into what Senator Phelan had called "a cold pile of damp ashes," Davis spoke of final success as certain. "Our people have only to be true to themselves to behold the Confederate flag among the recognized nations of the earth. The question is only one of time. It may be remote, but it may be nearer than many people suppose. It is not possible that a war of the dimensions that this one has assumed, of proportions so gigantic, can be very long protracted. The combatants must soon be exhausted. But it is impossible, with a cause like ours, that we can be the first to cry, 'Hold, enough.' " He spoke of valor and determination, of his pride in the southern fighting man, and assured his listeners that the Confederacy could accomplish its own salvation. This last led him into a statement unlike any he had made before:

"In the course of this war our eyes have often been turned abroad. We have expected sometimes recognition, and sometimes intervention, at the hands of foreign nations; and we had a right to expect it. Never before in the history of the world have a people so long a time maintained their ground, and shown themselves capable of maintaining their national existence, without securing the recognition of commercial nations. I know not why this has been so, but this I say: 'Put not your trust in princes,' and rest not your hopes on foreign nations. This war is ours; we must fight it out ourselves. And I feel some pride in knowing that, so far, we have done it without the good will of anybody."

When the applause that echoed this had died away he defined what he believed to be the "two prominent objects in the program of the enemy. One is to get possession of the Mississippi River, and to open it to navigation, in order to appease the clamors of the [Northwest] and to utilize the capture of New Orleans, which has thus far rendered them no service. The other is to seize upon the capital of the Confederacy, and hold this but as proof that the Confederacy has no existence." The fourth full-scale attempt to accomplish the latter object had just been frustrated by Lee at Fredericksburg, he informed the legislature, "and I believe that, under God and by the valor of our troops, the capital of the Confederacy will stand safe behind its wall of living breasts." As for the likelihood that the Unionists might accomplish the first-mentioned object, Davis admitted that this had caused him grave concern, and was in fact the reason for his present visit.

"This was the land of my affections," he declared. "Here were situated the little of worldly goods I possessed." He had, he repeated, "every confidence in the skill and energy of the officers in command. But when I received dispatches and heard rumors of alarm and trepidation and despondency among the people of Mississippi; when I heard, even, that people were fleeing to Texas in order to save themselves from the enemy; when I saw it stated by the enemy that they had handled other states with gloves, but Mississippi was to be handled without gloves — every impulse of my heart dragged me hither, in spite of duties which might have claimed my attention elsewhere. When I heard of the sufferings of my own people, of the danger of their subjugation by a ruthless foe, I felt that if Mississippi were destined for such a fate, I would wish to sleep in her soil." However, now that he had seen for himself the condition of the army and the people of his homeland, "I shall go away from you with a lighter heart . . . anxious, but hopeful."

In closing he spoke as a man who had kept a vigil through darkness into dawn, so that now he stood in sunlight. "I can, then, say with confidence that our condition is in every respect greatly improved over what it was last year. Our armies have been augmented; our troops have been instructed and disciplined. The articles necessary for the support of our troops and our people, and from which the enemy's blockade has cut us off, are being produced by the Confederacy. . . . Our people have learned to economize and are satisfied to wear homespun. I never see a woman dressed in homespun that I do not feel like taking off my hat to her, and although our women never lose their good looks, I cannot help thinking that they are improved by this garb. I never meet a man dressed in homespun but I feel like saluting him. I cannot avoid remarking with how much pleasure I have noticed the superior morality of our troops and the contrast which in this respect they present to the invader. On their valor and the assistance of God I confidently rely."

The applause that followed had begun to fade, when suddenly it swelled again, provoked and augmented by loud calls for "Johnston! Johnston!" At last the general rose and came forward, modestly acknowledging the cheers, which were redoubled. When they subsided he spoke with characteristic brevity and the self-effacement becoming to a soldier. "Fellow citizens," he said. "My only regret is that I have done so little to merit such a greeting. I promise you, however, that hereafter I shall be watchful, energetic, and indefatigable in your defense." That was all; but it was enough. According to one reporter, the applause that burst forth as he turned to resume his seat was "tremendous, uproarious, and prolonged." Apparently the general was more popular than the Chief Executive, even in the latter's own home state.

Despite this evidence of enthusiastic support from the civilians of the region, now that he had completed his military inspection Johnston was more dissatisfied than ever with the task which had been thrust into his hands. His command, he told Davis as soon as they were alone, was "a nominal one merely, and useless. . . . The great distance between the Armies of Mississippi and Tennessee, and the fact that they had different objects and adversaries, made it impossible to combine their action." The only use he saw for his talents, he continued in a subsequent account of the interview, was as a substitute commander of one of the armies, "which, as each had its own general, was not intended or desirable." In short, he told the President, he asked to be excused from serving in a capacity "so little to my taste."

Davis replied that distance was precisely the factor which had caused Johnston to be sent here. However far apart the two armies were, both were certainly too far from Richmond for effective control to be exercised from there; someone with higher authority than the two commanders should be at hand to co-ordinate their efforts and "transfer troops from one army to another in an emergency." Unpersuaded, still perturbed, the general continued to protest that, each being already "too weak for its object," neither army "could be drawn upon to strengthen the other," and with so much distance between the two, even "temporary transfers" were "impracticable." In point of fact, he could see nothing but ultimate disaster resulting from so unorthodox an arrangement. Once more Davis disagreed. Johnston was not only here; he was *needed* here. He must do the best he could. Or as the general put it, his "objections were disregarded."

On this discordant note the two men parted, Johnston to establish a new headquarters in the Mississippi capital and Davis to visit his eldest brother Joseph at his new plantation near Bolton, on the railroad west of Jackson. Their previous holdings on Davis Bend, just below Vicksburg — Joseph's, called The Hurricane, and his own, called Brierfield — had been overrun and sacked by Butler's men during their abortive upriver thrust, made in conjunction with Farragut's fleet the previous summer: which, incidentally, was why Davis had used the past tense in reference to "the little of worldly goods I possessed," and which, in part, was also why he referred to the Federals as "worse than vandal hordes."

In the course of his two-day visit with his septuagenarian brother, good news reached him on December 27 which seemed to indicate that Johnston's unwelcome burden already had been made a good deal lighter than he had protested it to be. Grant's army in North Mississippi was in full retreat; Van Dorn had broken loose in its immediate rear and burned its forward supply base at Holly Springs, capturing the garrison in the process, while Brigadier General Nathan Bedford Forrest, even farther in the northern commander's rear, was wrecking vital supply lines and creating general havoc all over West Tennessee. The following day, however, on the heels of these glad tidings, came word that Vicksburg itself was under assault by Major General William Tecumseh Sherman, who had come downriver from Memphis with the other half of Grant's command, escorted by Rear Admiral David Porter's ironclad fleet, and was storming the Chickasaw Bluffs. With the main body off opposing Grant, this was the worst of all possible news, short of the actual capture of the place; but on the 29th the President's anxiety was relieved and his spirits lifted by word that Sherman's repulse had been accomplished as effectively and as decisively, against even longer odds, as Burnside's had been at Fredericksburg two weeks before. What was more, the means by which it had been done went far toward sustaining Davis's military judgment, since the victory had been won in a large part by two brigades from the division he had recently detached, under protest, from the Army of Tennessee.

Vicksburg, then, had been delivered from the two-pronged pressure being applied from the north. If Bragg could do even partly as well in keeping Rosecrans out of Chattanooga, and if the garrison at Port Hudson could stop Banks and Farragut in their ascent of the Mississippi, the multiple threats to the western theater would have been smashed all round, or anyhow blunted for a season, despite the dire predictions made only that week by its over-all commander. One thing at any rate was certain. The President's long train ride back to Richmond would be made in a far more genial atmosphere, militarily speaking, than he had encountered at successive stops in the course of the outward journey.

He left Jackson on the last day of the year, and after speaking again that evening from a balcony of the Battle House in Mobile, received while retracing in reverse his route through Alabama and Georgia a double — indeed, a triple — further measure of good tidings. "God has granted us a happy New Year," Bragg wired from Murfreesboro. Rosecrans had ventured out of his intrenchments to attack the Army of Tennessee, which had then turned the tables with a dawn assault, jackknifing the Union right against the Union left. Not only was Chattanooga secure, but from the sound of the victorious commander's dispatch, Nashville itself might soon be recovered. "The enemy has yielded his strong position and is falling back," Bragg exulted. "We occupy whole field and shall follow him."

The pleasure Davis felt at this — augmented as it was by information that John Morgan had outdone himself in Kentucky on a Christmas raid, wrecking culverts, burning trestles, and capturing more than two thousand men, while Forrest and Van Dorn were returning safely from their separate and equally spectacular raids, the former after escaping a convergence designed for his destruction at Parker's Crossroads, deep inside the enemy lines — was raised another notch by word that a Federal reconnaissance force, sent upriver by Banks from Baton Rouge, had turned tail at the unexpected sight of the guns emplaced on Port Hudson's bluff and steamed back down without offering a challenge. And when this in turn was followed by still a third major item in the budget of good news, the presidential cup ran over. Major General John B. Magruder, recently arrived to take command of all the Confederates in Texas, had improvised a two-boat fleet of "cotton-clads" and had retaken Galveston in a New Year's predawn surprise attack, destroying one Yankee deep-water gunboat and forcing another to strike its colors. With the surrender of the army garrison in occupation of the island town, Texas was decontaminated. The only bluecoats still on her soil were Magruder's prisoners.

Leaving Mobile, Davis again visited Montgomery and Atlanta, but passing through the latter place he proceeded, not north to Chattanooga, but eastward to Augusta, where he spent the night of January 2. Next morning he entered South Carolina for the first time since the removal of the government to Richmond, back in May, and after a halt for a speech in Columbia, the capital, went on that night across the state line to Charlotte. At noon the following day he spoke in Raleigh, the North Carolina capital, then detoured south to Wilmington, the principal east coast port for blockade-runners, where he received the first really disturbing military news that had reached him since he left Virginia, nearly a month before. Instead of "following" the defeated Rosecrans, as he had said he would do, Bragg had waited a day before resuming the offensive, and then had been repulsed; whereupon, having been informed that the enemy had been reinforced — and bearing in mind, moreover, the Commander in Chief's recent advice: "Fight if you can, and fall back [if you must]" — he fell back thirty miles to a better defensive position on Duck River, just in front of Tullahoma and still protecting Chattanooga, another fifty-odd miles in his rear. As at Perryville, three months ago, he had won a battle and then retreated. Not that Murfreesboro was not still considered a victory; it was, at least in southern eyes. Only some of the luster had been lost. Davis, however, placing emphasis on the odds and the fact that Chattanooga was secure, counted it scarcely less a triumph than before. In response to a Wilmington serenade, tendered just after he received word that Bragg had fallen back, he spoke for a full hour from his hotel balcony. Employing what one hearer called "purity of diction" and a "fervid eloquence" to match the enthusiasm of the torchlight serenaders, he characterized recent events as a vindication of the valor of southern arms, and even went so far as to repeat the words he had spoken to a similar crowd from a Richmond balcony on the jubilant morrow of First Manassas: "Never be humble to the haughty. Never be haughty to the humble."

That was a Sunday. Next day, January 5, he covered the final leg of his long journey, returning to Richmond before dark. He was weary and he looked it, and with cause, for in twenty-five days he had traveled better than twenty-five hundred miles and had made no less than twenty-five public addresses, including some that had lasted more than an hour. However, his elation overmatched his weariness, and this too was with cause. He knew that he had done much to restore civilian morale by appearing before the disaffected people, and militarily the gains had been even greater. Though mostly they had been fought against odds that should have been oppressive, if not completely paralyzing, of the several major actions which had occurred during his absence from the capital or on the eve of his departure — Prairie Grove and Hartsville, Fredericksburg and Goldsboro, Holly Springs and Chickasaw Bluffs, Galveston and Murfreesboro — all were resounding victories except the first and possibly the last. Taken in conjunction with the spectacular Christmas forays of Morgan and Forrest, the torpedoing of the *Cairo* up the Yazoo River, and Grant's enforced retreat in North Mississippi, these latest additions to the record not only sustained the reputation Confederate arms had gained on many a field during the year just passed into history; they also augured well for a future which only lately had seemed dark. Defensively speaking, indeed, the record could scarcely have been improved. Of the three objectives the Federals had set for themselves, announcing them plainly to all the world by moving simultaneously against them as the year drew to a close, Vicksburg had been disenthralled and Chattanooga remained as secure as Richmond.

Davis himself had done as much as any man, and a good deal more than most, to bring about the result that not a single armed enemy soldier now stood within fifty air-line miles of any one of these three vital cities. It was therefore a grateful, if weary, President who was met by his wife and their four children on the steps of the White House, late that Monday afternoon of the first week of the third calendar year of this second American war for independence.

✗ 2 ✗

Of all these various battles and engagements, fought in all these various places, Fredericksburg, the nearest to the national capital, was the largest — in numbers engaged, if not in bloodshed — as well as the grandest as a spectacle, in which respect it equaled, if indeed it did not outdo, any other major conflict of the war. Staged as it was, with a curtain of fog that lifted, under the influence of a genial sun, upon a sort of natural amphitheater referred to by one of the 200,000 participants, a native of the site, as "a champaign tract inclosed by hills," it quite fulfilled the volunteers' early-abandoned notion of combat as a picture-book affair. What was more, the setting had been historical long before the armies met there to add a bloody chapter to a past that had been peaceful up to now. John Paul Jones had lived as a boy in the old colonial town that gave its name and sacrificed the contents of its houses to the battle. Hugh Mercer's apothecary shop and James Monroe's law office were two among the many points of interest normally apt to be pointed out to strangers by the four thousand inhabitants, most of whom had lately been evacuated, however, by order of the commander of the army whose looters would presently take the place apart and whose corpses would find shallow graves on its unwarlike lawns and in its gardens. Here the widowed Mary Washington had lived, and it was here or near here that her son was reported to have thrown a Spanish silver dollar across the Rappahannock. During the battle itself, from one of the dominant hills where he established his forward command post, R. E. Lee would peer through rifts in the swirling gunsmoke in an attempt to spot in the yard of Chatham, a mansion on the heights beyond the river, the old tree beneath whose branches he had courted Mary Custis, granddaughter of the woman who later married the dollar-flinging George and thus became the nation's first first lady.

Yet it was Burnside, not Lee, who had chosen the setting for the impending carnage. Appointed to succeed his friend McClellan because of that general's apparent lack of aggressiveness after the Battle of Antietam, he had shifted the Army of the Potomac eastward to this point where the Rappahannock, attaining its head of navigation, swerved suddenly south to lave the doorsteps of the town on its right bank. Washington lay fifty miles behind him; Richmond, his goal, lay fifty miles ahead. Mindful of the President's admonition that his plan for eluding Lee in order to descend on the southern capital would succeed "if you move very rapidly, otherwise not," he had indeed moved rapidly; but, as it turned out, he had moved to no avail. Though he had successfully given Lee the slip, the pontoons he had requisitioned in advance from Harpers Ferry, altogether necessary if he was to cross the river, did not reach the Fredericksburg area until his army had been massed in jump-off positions for more than a week; by which time, to his confoundment, Lee had the opposite ridges bristling with guns that were trained on the prospective bridge sites. Burnside was so profoundly distressed by this turn of events that he spent two more weeks looking down on the town from the left-bank heights, with something of the intentness and singularity of purpose which he had displayed, back in September at Antietam, looking down at the little triple-arched bridge that ever afterwards bore his name as indelibly as if the intensity of his gaze had etched it deep into the stone. Meanwhile, by way of increasing his chagrin as Lee's butternut veterans clustered thick and thicker on the hills across the way, it was becoming increasingly apparent, not only to the northern commander but also to his men, that what had begun as a sprint for Richmond had landed him and them in coffin corner.

He had troubles enough, in all conscience, but at least they were not of the kind that proceeded from any shortage of troops. Here opposite Fredericksburg, ready to execute his orders as soon as he could decide what those orders were going to be, Burnside had 121,402 effectives in his six corps of three divisions each. Organized into three Grand Divisions of two corps each, these eighteen divisions were supported by 312 pieces of artillery. Nor was that all. Marching on Dumfries, twenty miles to the north, were two more corps with an effective strength of 27,724 soldiers and 97 guns. In addition to this field force of nearly 150,000 men, supported by more than 400 guns, another 52,000 in the Washington defenses and along the upper Potomac were also included in his nominal command; so that his total "present for duty" during this second week of December — at any rate the first part of it, before the butchering began — was something over 200,000 of all arms. He did not know the exact strength of the rebels waiting for him beyond the town and at other undetermined positions downriver, but he estimated their strength at just over 80,000 men.

In this — unlike McClellan, who habitually doubled and sometimes even tripled an enemy force by estimation — he was not far off. Lee had nine divisions organized into two corps of about 35,000 each, which, together with some 8000 cavalry and artillery, gave him a total of 78,511 effectives, supported by 275 guns. He had, then, not quite two thirds as many troops in the immediate vicinity as his opponent had. By ordinary, as he had lately told the Secretary of War, he thought it preferable, considering the disparity of force, "to attempt to baffle [the enemy's] designs by maneuvering rather than to resist his advance by main force." However, he found his present position so advantageous — naturally strong, though not so formidable in appearance as to rule out the possibility of an attempted assault — that he was determined to hold his ground, despite the odds, in the belief that the present situation contained the seeds of another full-scale Federal disaster.

Except for two detached brigades of cavalry, his whole army was at hand. So far, though, he had effected the concentration of only one corps, leaving the other spread out downstream to guard the crossings all the way to Port Royal, twenty miles below. The first corps, five divisions under Lieutenant General James Longstreet — "Old Peter," his men called him, adopting his West Point nickname; Lee had lately dubbed him "my old warhorse" — was in position on the slopes and crest of a seven-mile-long range of hills overlooking the mile-wide "champaign tract" that gave down upon the town and the river, its flanks protected right and left by Massaponax Creek and the southward bend of the Rappahannock. Forbidding in appearance, the position was even more formidable in fact; for the range of hills — in effect, a broken ridge — was mostly wooded, affording concealment for the infantry, and the batteries had been sited with such care that when Longstreet suggested the need for another gun at a critical point, the artillery commander replied: "General, we cover that ground now so well that we comb it as with a fine-tooth comb. A chicken could not live on that field when we open on it."

The other corps commander, Lieutenant General Thomas Jonathan Jackson — "Old Jack" to his men, redoubtable "Stonewall" to the world at large — had three of his four divisions posted at eight-mile in-

tervals downstream, one on the south bank of Massaponax Creek, one
at Skinker's Neck, and one near Port Royal, while the fourth was held
at Guiney Station, on the Richmond, Fredericksburg & Potomac Railroad, eight miles in rear of Longstreet's right at Hamilton's Crossing.
Despite the possibility that Burnside might swamp Longstreet with a
sudden assault, outnumbering him no less that three-to-one, Lee accepted the risk of keeping the second corps widely scattered in order to
be able to challenge the Union advance at the very outset, whenever and
wherever it began. Jackson, on the other hand, would have preferred
to fight on the line of the North Anna, a less formidable stream thirty
miles nearer Richmond, rather than here on the Rappahannock, which
he believed would be an effective barrier to pursuit of the beaten Yankees when they retreated, as he was sure they would do, under cover of
their superior artillery posted on the dominant left-bank heights. "We
will whip the enemy, but gain no fruits of victory," he predicted.

In point of fact, whatever validity Jackson might have as a
prophet, Lee not only accepted the risk of a sudden, all-out attack on
Longstreet; he actually preferred it. Though he expected the crossing to
be attempted at some point downriver, in which case he intended to challenge it at the water's edge, it was his fervent hope that Burnside could
be persuaded — or, best of all, would persuade himself — to make one
here. In that case, Lee did not intend to contest the crossing itself with
any considerable force. The serious challenge would come later, when
the enemy came at him across that open, gently undulating plain. He had
confidence that Old Peter, securely intrenched along the ridge, his guns
already laid and carefully ranged on check points, could absorb the
shock until the two closest of Stonewall's divisions could be summoned.

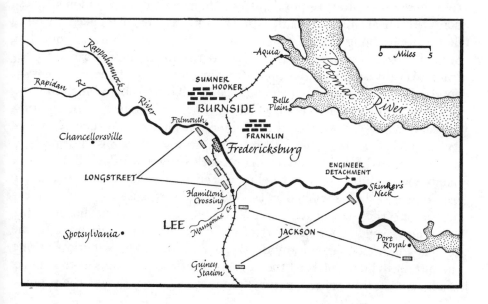

Their arrival would give the Confederate infantry the unaccustomed numerical wealth of six men to every yard of their seven-mile line: which Lee believed would be enough, not only to repulse the Federals, but also to enable the graybacks to launch a savage counterstroke, in the style of Second Manassas, that would drive the bluecoats in a panicky mass and pen them for slaughter against the unfordable river, too thickly clustered for escape across their pontoon bridges and too closely intermingled with his own charging troops for the Union artillery to attempt a bombardment from the opposite heights. It was unlikely that Burnside would thus expose his army to the Cannae so many Southerners believed was overdue. It was, indeed, almost too much to hope for. But Lee did hope for it. He hoped for it intensely.

Burnside, too, was weighing these possibilities, and it seemed to him also that the situation was heavy with the potentials of disaster: much more so, in fact, than it had been before he shifted his army eastward in November from the scene of Pope's late-August rout. Though so far he had escaped direct connection with a military fiasco, he had not been unacquainted with sudden blows of adversity in the years before the war. Once as a newly commissioned lieutenant on his way to the Mexican War he had lost his stake to a gambler on a Mississippi steamboat, and again in the mid-50's he had failed to get a government contract for the manufacture of a breech-loading rifle he had invented and put his cash in after leaving the army to devote full time to its promotion, which left him so broke that he had to sell his sword and uniforms for money to live on until his friend McClellan gave him a job with the land office of a railroad, where he prospered. Between these two financial upsets, he had received his worst personal shock when a Kentucky girl, whom he had wooed and finally persuaded to accompany him to the altar, responded to the minister's final ceremonial question with an abrupt, emphatic "No!" Hard as they had been to take, these three among several lesser setbacks had really hurt no one but himself, nor had they seriously affected the thirty-eight-year-old general's basically sunny disposition. But now that he had the lives of two hundred thousand men dependent on his abilities, not to mention the possible outcome of a war in which his country claimed to be fighting for survival, he did not face the likelihood of failure with such equanimity as he had shown in those previous trying situations. Formerly a hearty man, whose distinctive ruff of dark brown whiskers described a flamboyant double parabola below a generous, wide-nostriled nose, a pair of alert, dark-socketed eyes, and a pale expanse of skin that extended all the way back to the crown of his head, he had become increasingly morose and fretful here on the high left bank of the Rappahannock. "I deem it my duty," he had advised his superiors during the interim which followed the nonarrival of the pontoons at the climax of his rapid cross-country march, "to say that I cannot make the promise of probable success with the faith that I did when I supposed that all the parts of the plan would be carried out."

This was putting it rather mildly. Yet, notwithstanding his qualms, he had evolved a design which he believed would work by virtue of its daring. His balloons were up, despite the blustery weather, and the observers reported heavy concentrations of rebels far downstream. He had intended to throw his bridges across the river at Skinker's Neck, ten miles beyond Lee's immediate right, then march directly on the railroad in the southern army's rear, thus forcing its retreat to protect its supply line. However, the balloon reports convinced him that Lee had divined his purpose, and this — plus the difficulty of concealing his preparations in that quarter, which led him to suspect that he would be doing nothing more than side-stepping into another stalemate — caused him to shift the intended attack back to the vicinity of Fredericksburg itself, where he could use the town to mask the crossing. It was a bold decision, made in the belief that, of all possible moves, this was the one his opponent would be least likely to suspect until it was already in execution: which, as he saw it from the Confederate point of view, would be too late. The troops below were Jackson's, the renowned "foot cavalry" of the Army of Northern Virginia, but a good part of them were as much as twenty miles away. By the time they arrived, if all went as Burnside intended, there would be no other half of their army for them to support; he would have crushed it, and they would find that what they had been hastening toward was slaughter or surrender.

Accordingly, early on December 9, a warning order went out for Grand Division commanders to report to army headquarters at noon, by which time they were to have alerted their troops, supplied each man with sixty rounds of ammunition, and begun the issue of three days' cooked rations. They would have the rest of today to get ready, he told them, and all of tomorrow. Then, in the predawn darkness of Thursday, December 11, the engineers would throw the six bridges by which the infantry and cavalry would cross for the attack, followed at once by such artillery as had been assigned to furnish close-up support. The crossing would be made in two general areas, one directly behind the town and the other just below it, with three bridges at each affording passage for the left and right Grand Divisions, commanded respectively by Major Generals William B. Franklin and Edwin V. Sumner. The center Grand Division, under Major General Joseph Hooker, would lend weight to the assault by detaching two of its divisions to Franklin and the other four to Sumner, giving them each a total of approximately 60,000 men, including cavalry and support artillery. Burnside's intention — not unlike McClellan's at Antietam, except that the flanks were reversed — was for Franklin's column to attack and carry the lower end of the ridge on which the Confederates were intrenched, then wheel and sweep northward along it while the enemy was being held in place by attacks delivered simultaneously by Sumner on the right. It was simple enough, as all such designs for destruction were meant to be. In fact, Burnside apparently considered it so readily comprehensible as to require little or no incidental explanation when the three generals reported to him at noon.

One additional subterfuge he would employ, but that was all. The engineers at Skinker's Neck, assisted by a regiment of Maine axmen, would be kept at work felling trees and laying a corduroy approach down to the riverbank at that point, as if for the passage of infantry with artillery support. The sound of chopping, along with the glow of fires at night, would help to delude the rebels in their expectation of a crossing there. However, even this was but a strengthening of the original subterfuge, the shifting of the main effort back upstream, on which the ruff-whiskered general based his belief, or at any rate his hope, that he would find Lee unprepared and paralyze him with his daring.

That was a good deal more than any of the northern commander's predecessors had been able to do, but Burnside's gloom had been dispelled; his confidence had risen now to zenith. As he phrased it in a dispatch telegraphed to Washington near midnight, outlining his attack plan and divulging his expectations, "I think now that the enemy will be more surprised by a crossing immediately in our front than in any other part of the river. The commanders of Grand Divisions coincide with me in this opinion, and I have accordingly ordered the movement. . . . We hope to succeed."

Lee was indeed surprised, though not unpleasantly. Already a firm believer in the efficacy of prayer, he might have seen in this development a further confirmation of his faith. Nor was the surprise as complete as Burnside had intended. On Wednesday night, December 10, a woman crept down to the east bank of the Rappahannock and called across to the gray pickets that the Yankees had drawn a large issue of cooked rations — always a sign that action was at hand. Then at 4.45 next morning, two hours before dawn, two guns boom-boomed the prearranged signal that the enemy was attempting a crossing here in front of Fredericksburg. At once the Confederate bivouacs were astir with men turning out of their blankets to take the posts already assigned them along the ridge overlooking the plain that sloped eastward to the old colonial town, still invisible in the frosty darkness.

In it there was one brigade of Mississippi infantry, bled down to 1600 veterans under Brigadier General William Barksdale, a former congressman with long white hair and what one of his soldiers called "a thirst for battle glory." He had had his share of this in every major engagement since Manassas, but today was his best chance to slake that thirst; for Lee, being unwilling to subject the town to shelling, had left to these few Deep South troops the task of contesting the crossing — not with any intention of preventing it, even if that had been possible in the face of all those guns on the dominant heights, but merely to make it as costly to the Federals as he could. Barksdale received the assignment gladly, posting most of his men in stout brick houses whose rear walls, looking out upon the river, they loopholed so as to draw their beads with a minimum of distraction in the form of return fire from the men they would be dropping when the time came. Shortly after midnight, hearing sounds of preparation across the way — the muffled tread of soldiers on the march, the occasional whinny of a horse or bray of a mule, the clank of trace-chains, and at last the ponderous rumble of what he took to be pontoons being brought down from the heights — he knew the time was very much at hand. After sending word of this to his superiors, he saw to it that the few remaining civilians, mostly women and children, with a sprinkling of old men, either hastened away to the safety of the hills or else took refuge in their cellars.

He was in no hurry to open fire, preferring not to waste ammunition in the darkness. Long before daylight, however, his men could hear the Federal engineers at work: low-voiced commands, the clatter of lumber, and at intervals the loud crack of half-inch skim ice as another pontoon was launched. This last drew closer with every repetition as the bridge was extended, unit by six-foot unit, across the intervening four hundred feet of water. At last, judging by the sound that the pontoniers had reached midstream, the waiting riflemen opened fire. They aimed necessarily by ear, but the result was satisfactory. After the first yelp of pain there was the miniature thunder of boots on planks, diminishing as the runners cleared the bridge; then silence, broken presently by the boom-boom of the two guns passing the word along the ridge that the Yanks were coming.

Soon they returned to the bridge-end, working as quietly as possible since every sound, including even the squeak of a bolt, was echoed by the crack of rifles from the western bank. It was perilous work, but it was nothing compared to the trouble brought by a misty dawn and a rising sun that began to burn the fog away, exposing the workers to aimed shots from marksmen whose skill was practically superfluous at a range of two hundred feet. A pattern was quickly established. The pontoniers would rush out onto the bridge, take up their tools, and work feverishly until the fire grew too hot; whereupon they would drop their tools and run the gauntlet back to bank. Then, as they got up their nerve again, their officers would lead or chevy them back onto the bridge, where the performance would be repeated. This went on for hours, to the high delight of the Mississippians, who jeered and hooted as they shot and waited, then shot and waited to shoot some more.

By 10 o'clock the northern commander's patience had run out.

The movement was already hours off schedule; Longstreet's signal guns had announced Lee's alertness, and Jackson's lean marchers might well be on the way by now. Rifle fire having proved ineffective against the snipers behind the brick walls of the houses along the riverbank, Burnside ordered his chief of artillery, Brigadier General Henry Hunt, to open fire with the 147 heavy-caliber guns posted on Stafford Heights, frowning down on the old town a hundred feet below. The response was immediate and uproarious, and it lasted for more than an hour, Hunt having instructed his gun crews to maintain a rate of fire of one shot every two minutes. Seventy-odd solid shot and shells a minute were thrown until 5000 had been fired. During all that time, a correspondent wrote, "the earth shook beneath the terrific explosions of the shells, which went howling over the river, crashing into houses, battering down walls, splintering doors, ripping up floors."

As a spectacle of modern war it was a great success, and it was also quite successful against the town. It wrecked houses, setting several afire; it tore up cobblestones; it shook the very hills the armies stood on. But it did not seem to dampen the spirits or influence the marksmanship of the Mississippians, who rose from the rubble and dropped more of the pontoniers, driving them again from the work they had returned to during the lull that followed the bombardment. When Barksdale sent a message asking whether he should have his men put out the fires, Longstreet replied: "You have enough to do to watch the Yankees." Back at Lee's observation post, the sight of what the Union guns had done to the Old Dominion town so riled the southern commander that he broke out wrathfully against the cannoneers and the officers who had given them orders to open fire. "Those people delight to destroy the weak and those who can make no defense," he said hotly. "It just suits them!" However, when he sent to inquire after the welfare of Barksdale's men and to see if there was anything they wanted, that general sent back word that he had everything he needed. But he added, "Tell General Lee that if he wants a bridge of dead Yankees, I can furnish him with one."

It was well past noon by now. Hunt, admitting that his guns could never dislodge the rebels, suggested that infantry use the pontoons as assault boats in order to get across the river and pry the snipers out of the rubble with bayonets. A Michigan regiment drew the duty, supported by two others from Massachusetts, and did it smartly, establishing a bridgehead in short order. During the street fighting, which used up what was left of daylight, the bridges were laid and other regiments came to their support. Barksdale's thirst was still unslaked, however. When he received permission to withdraw, he declined and kept on fighting, house to house, until past sundown. Not till dusk had fallen was he willing to call it a day, and even then he had trouble persuading some of his men to agree. This was particularly difficult in the case of the rear-guard company, whose commander somehow discovered in the course of the engagement that the Federal advance was being led by a Massachusetts company whose commander had been his classmate at Harvard. The Mississippi lieutenant called a halt and faced his men about, determined to whip his blue-clad friend then and there, until his colonel had him placed in arrest in order to continue the withdrawal. It was 7 o'clock by the time the last of Barksdale's veterans crossed the plain to join their admiring comrades on the ridge, leaving Fredericksburg to the bluecoats they had been fighting for fifteen hours.

Not until well after dark did Lee order Jackson to bring his two nearest divisions to Longstreet's support, and not even then did he summon the other two from Port Royal and Skinker's Neck, where the Maine axmen on the opposite bank had kindled campfires around which they were resting from their daylong chopping. Pleased though he was with the day's work — his eyes had lighted up at each report that a new attempt to extend the bridge had been defeated — Lee simply could not believe that his hopes had been so completely fulfilled that the enemy was concentrating everything for an attack against the ridge where his guns had been laid for weeks now and his infantry was disposed at ease in overlapping lines of battle.

Across the way, on Stafford Heights, Burnside too was pleased. Despite delays that had been maddening, he had his six bridges down at last (the three lower ones, below the town, had been down since noon, but he had hesitated to use them so long as the Fredericksburg force of unknown strength was in position on their flank) and his army was assembled for the crossing. Besides, he had received balloon reports at sundown informing him that the other half of the rebel army was still in its former positions down the river, with no signs of preparation for a move in this direction. The delay, it seemed, had cost him nothing more than some nervous twinges and a few expendable combat engineers; Lee might be caught napping yet. So confidently did the ruff-whiskered general feel next morning, when observers reported Jackson's troops still in position at Skinker's Neck and Port Royal, twenty miles away, that he decided he could afford to spend another day assembling his army on the west bank of the Rappahannock for the assault across the empty plain and against the rebel ridge.

Fog shrouded the entire valley while the long blue lines of men came steeply down to the riverbank and broke step as they crossed the swaying bridges. On the heights above, the Union guns fired blindly over their heads, in case the Confederates attempted to challenge the crossing. They did not. At noon, however, the fog lifted; Lee, with a close-up view of the bluecoats massed in their thousands beyond the plain, saw at once that this was no feint, but a major effort. He sent for Jackson's other two divisions, instructing them to begin their long marches immediately in order to arrive in time for the battle, which he now saw would be fought tomorrow. Beyond that he could do no more.

Though he was outnumbered worse than three-to-two, and knew it, he was in good spirits as he rode on a sundown inspection of his lines. Returning to headquarters, he seemed pleased that the Federals on the flat were about to charge him. "I shall try to do them all the damage in our power when they move forward," he said.

Down in the town, meanwhile, the Union soldiers had been having themselves a field day. Cavalrymen ripped the strings from grand pianos to make feed troughs for their horses, while others cavorted amid the rubble in women's lace-trimmed underwear and crinoline gowns snatched from closets and bureau drawers. Scarcely a house escaped pillage. Family portraits were slashed with bayonets; pier glass mirrors were shattered with musket butts; barrels of flour and molasses were dumped together on deep-piled rugs. It was all a lot of fun, especially for the more fortunate ones who found bottles of rare old madeira in the cellars. Gradually, though, the excitement paled and the looters began to speculate as to why the rebs had made no attempt to challenge the crossing today, not even with their artillery. Some guessed it was because they had no ammunition to spare, others that they were afraid of retaliation by "our siege guns." One man had a psychological theory: "General Lee thinks he will have a big thing on us about the bombardment of this town. He proposes to rouse the indignation of the civilized world, as they call it. You'll see he won't throw a shell into it. He is playing for the sympathies of Europe." Still another, a veteran private, had a different idea. "Shit," he said. "They *want* us to get in. Getting out won't be quite so smart and easy. You'll see."

★ ★ ★

They would see; but not just yet. Day broke on a fog so thick that the sun, which rose at 7.17 beyond the Union left, could not pierce it, but rather gave an eerie, luminous quality to the mist that swathed the ridge where Lee's reunited army awaited the challenge foretold by sounds of preparation on the invisible plain below; "an indistinct murmur," one listener called it, "like the distant hum of myriads of bees."

Longstreet held the Confederate left. Four of his five divisions were on line, commanded north to south by Major Generals Richard Anderson, Lafayette McLaws, George Pickett, and John Bell Hood; the fifth and smallest, a demi-division under Brigadier General Robert Ransom, was in reserve. Jackson, on the right, had posted Major General A. P. Hill's large division along his entire front, backed by a second line of two close-packed divisions under Brigadier Generals William Taliaferro and Jubal Early, which in turn was supported by Major General D. H. Hill's division, just arrived from Port Royal after an all-night march. Major General J. E. B. Stuart's cavalry guarded the flank, extending it southward from Hamilton's Crossing to Massaponax Creek. Since this end of the ridge was considerably lower than the other, and consequently much less easy to defend, Lee had assigned five miles of the line to Longstreet and only two to Jackson, who thus had no less than ten men to every yard of front and could distribute them in depth. It was no wonder, then, that he replied this morning to a staff officer's expression of qualms about the enemy strength and the lowness of the ridge in this direction: "Major, my men have sometimes failed to take a position, but to defend one, never! I am glad the Yankees are coming."

Lee and Longstreet stood on an eminence known thereafter as Lee's Hill because that general had set up his forward command post here, about midway of Longstreet's line, with an excellent view — or at any rate what would be an excellent view, once the curtain of fog had lifted — of the lines in both directions, including most of Jackson's line to the south, as well as of Fredericksburg and the snow-pocked plain where the blue host was massing under cover of their guns on Stafford Heights, preparing even now to give the lower ridge across the way a long-range pounding. Today as yesterday, however, the southern commander was in good spirits. Tall and comely — nothing less, indeed,

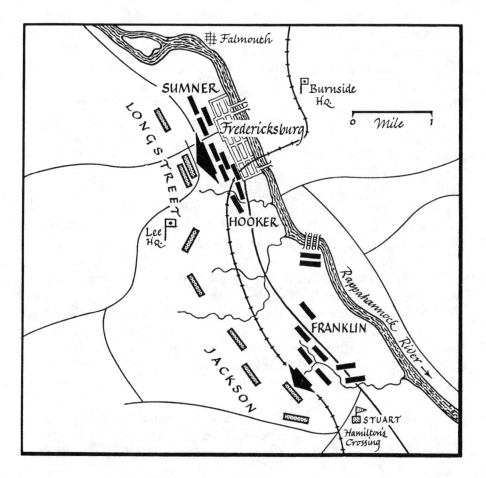

than "the handsomest man in Christendom," according to one who saw him there this morning — neatly dressed, as always, with only the three unwreathed stars on the collar of his thigh-length gray sack coat to show his rank, he gave no sign of nervousness or apprehension. Above the short-clipped iron-gray beard and beneath the medium brim of a sand-colored planter's hat, his quick brown eyes had a youthfulness which, together with the litheness of his figure and the deftness of his movements, disguised the fact that he would be fifty-six years old next month.

His companion seemed to share his confidence, if not his handsomeness of person, though he too was prepossessing of appearance. A burly, shaggy man, six feet tall, of Dutch extraction and just past forty-one, Longstreet gave above all an impression of solidity and dependability. His men's great fondness for him was based in part on their knowledge of his concern for their well-being, in and out of combat. Yesterday, for example, when some engineers protested to him that the gun crews were ruining their emplacements by digging them too deep, Old Peter would not agree to order them to stop. "If we only save the finger of a man, that's good enough," he told the engineers, and the cannoneers kept digging. Often phlegmatic, this morning he was in an expansive mood: especially after he and Lee were joined by the third-ranking member of the army triumvirate, who came riding up from the south. It was Jackson, but a Jackson quite unlike the Stonewall they had known of old. Gone were the mangy cadet cap and the homespun uniform worn threadbare since its purchase on the eve of the Valley Campaign, through the miasmic nightmare of the Seven Days, the suppression of the "miscreant Pope" at Cedar Mountain and Second Manassas, the invasion of Maryland and the hard fight at Sharpsburg. Instead he wore a new cap bound with gold braid, and more braid — "chicken guts," Confederate soldiers irreverently styled the stuff — looped on the cuffs and sleeves of a brand-new uniform, a recent gift from Jeb Stuart. Even his outsized boots were brightly polished. For all his finery, he looked as always older than his thirty-eight years. His pale blue eyes were stern, his thin-lipped mouth clamped forbiddingly behind the scraggly dark-brown beard; but this had not protected him from the jibes of his men, who greeted him with their accustomed rough affection as he rode among them. "Come here, boys!" they yelled. "Stonewall has drawed his bounty and bought hisself some new clothes." Others shook their heads in mock dismay at seeing him tricked out like some newly commissioned quartermaster lieutenant. "Old Jack will be afraid for his clothes," they said, doleful amid the catcalls, "and will not get down to work."

He had ridden all this way, exposing himself to all that raillery, for a purpose which he was quick to divulge. Turning aside Longstreet's banter, he muttered that the finery was "some doing of my friend Stuart,

I believe," and passed at once to the matter that had brought him here. He wanted permission to attack. If his men surged down the ridge and onto the plain before the fog had lifted, he explained, they would be hidden from the guns on Stafford Heights and could fling the startled bluecoats into the river. Lee shook his head. He preferred to have the superior enemy force worn down by repeated charges and repulses, in the style of Second Manassas, before he passed to the offensive. Stonewall had his answer. As he turned to leave, Longstreet began to bait him again. "General, do not all those multitudes of Federals frighten you?" Old Peter's humor was heavy-handed, but Jackson had no humor at all. "We shall see very soon whether I shall not frighten *them*," he said as he put one foot in the stirrup. But Longstreet kept at him. "Jackson, what are you going to do with all those people over there?" Stonewall mounted. "Sir, we will give them the bayonet," he said, and he turned his horse and rode away.

By 10 o'clock the fog had begun to thin. It drained downward, burned away by the sun, layer by upper layer, so that the valley seemed to empty after the manner of a tub when the plug is pulled. Gradually the town revealed itself: first the steeples of two churches and the courthouse, then the chimneys and rooftops, and finally the houses and gardens, set upon the checkerboard of streets. Dark lines of troops flowed steadily toward two clusters, one within the town, masked by the nearer buildings, the other two miles down the Richmond Stage Road, which ran parallel to the river and roughly bisected the mile-wide plain. Already the more adventurous Federal batteries had opened, arching their shells through sunlit rifts in the thinning mist, but the Confederates made no reply until 10.30 when Lee passed the word: "Test the ranges on the left." Longstreet's guns began to roar from Marye's Heights, the tall north end of the long ridge, directly opposite the center of the town, where the first of the two clusters of blue-clad men was thickening. All the fog was gone by now, replaced by brilliant sunlight. The drifting smoke made shifting patterns on the plain. High over Stafford Heights, where the long-range guns were adding their deeper voices to the chorus of the Union, two of Burnside's big yellow observation balloons bobbed and floated, the men in their swaying baskets looking down on war reduced to miniature.

First blood was drawn in a brief dramatic action staged in front of the Confederate right. Here the fog had rolled away so rapidly that the scene was exposed as if by the sudden lift of a curtain, showing a three-division Federal corps advancing westward in long lines so neatly dressed that watchers on the ridge could count the brigades and regiments — ten of the former, forty-six of the latter, plus eleven batteries of artillery — each with its attendant colors rippling in the sunlight. From Lee's Hill, the southern commander was surprised to see two horse-drawn guns, toy-sized in the distance, go twinkling out to the old stage road and go into position in the open, within easy range of the left flank of the 18,000 Federals, which was thrown into some disorder and came to a milling halt as the two guns began to slam their shots endwise into the blue ranks, toppling men like tenpins.

They had been brought into action by Stuart's chief of artillery, twenty-four-year-old Major John Pelham of Alabama, who in his haste to join the southern army had left West Point on the eve of graduation in '61. He had often done daring things, similar to this today, but never before with so large an audience to applaud him. As the men of both armies watched from the surrounding heights, he fired so rapidly that one general involved in the blue confusion estimated his strength at a full battery. Four Union batteries gave him their undivided attention, turning their two dozen guns against his two. One, a rifled Blakely, was soon disabled and had to be sent to the rear, but Pelham kept the other barking furiously, a 12-pounder brass Napoleon, and shifted his position each time the enemy gunners got his range. The handsome young major was in his glory, wearing bound about his cap, at the request of a British army observer, a necktie woven of red and blue, the colors of the Grenadier Guards. When Stuart sent word for him to retire, Pelham declined, though he had lost so many cannoneers by then that he himself was helping to serve the gun. "Tell the general I can hold my ground," he said. Three times the order came, but he obeyed only when his caissons were nearly empty. Back at Hamilton's Crossing, he returned the smoke-grimed necktie-souvenir to the English visitor, blushing with pleasure and embarrassment at the cheers. Lee on his hill took his glasses down, smiling as he exclaimed: "It is glorious to see such courage in one so young!"

While the Federals remained halted on the plain, recovering the alignment Pelham had disturbed, their artillery began to pound the lower ridge in earnest, probing the woods in an attempt to knock out Jackson's hidden batteries before the battle passed to the infantry. The Confederate gunners made no reply, being under orders not to disclose their positions until the enemy came within easy range. At last he did, and the graybacks got their revenge for the punishment they had had to accept in silence. When the advance came within 800 yards, all of Stonewall's guns cut loose at once. The blue flood stopped, flailed ragged along its forward edge, and then reversed its flow.

The Union guns resumed the argument, having spotted their targets by the smoke that boiled up through the trees, but the infantry battle now shifted northward to where the bluecoats had been massing under cover of the town. At 11.30 they emerged and began to surge across the plain toward Marye's Heights, less than half a mile away. A thirty-foot spillway, six feet deep, lay athwart their path, however, and the rebel gunners caught them close-packed as they funneled onto three bridges whose planks had been removed but whose stringers had been left in place, apparently to lure them across in single file. "Hi! Hi! Hi!" the Federals yelled as they pounded over, taking their losses in order to gain the cover of a slight roll or "dip" of ground that hid them from the guns on the heights beyond.

"It appeared to us there was no end of them," a waiting cannoneer observed. But Longstreet was not worried; he had a surprise in store for them. Along the base of Marye's Heights ran a road, flanked by stone walls four feet high, which Brigadier General T.R.R. Cobb had had his Georgians deepen, throwing the spoil over the townward wall, to add to its effectiveness as a breastwork and to hide it from the enemy. This was the advance position of the whole army, and as such it might be outflanked or enfiladed. However, when Cobb was given permission to fall back up the hill in case that happened, he replied grimly in the spirit of Barksdale and Pelham: "Well, if they wait for me to fall back, they will wait a long time."

Presently he got the chance to begin to prove his staunchness; for the Federals leaped to their feet in the swale and made a sudden rush, as if they intended to scale the heights whose base was only 400 yards away. High up the slope the guns crashed, darting tongues of flame, and the Georgians along the sunken road pulled trigger. It was as if the charging bluecoats had struck a trip wire. When the smoke of that single rifle volley rolled away, all that were left in front of the wall were writhing on the ground or scampering back to safety in the swale. After a wait, they rose and came forward again, deploying as they advanced. This time the reaction was less immediate, since they knew what to expect; but it was no different in the end. The guns on the slope and the rifles down along the wall broke into a clattering frenzy of smoke and flame, and more men were left writhing as others fell back off the blasted plain and into the swale. Again they rose. Again, incredibly, they charged. They came forward, one of them afterwards recalled, "as though they were breasting a storm of rain and sleet, their faces and bodies being only half turned to the storm, with their shoulders shrugged." Another observed that "everybody, from the smallest drummer boy on up, seemed to be shouting to the full extent of his capacity." Like the first and second, except that more men fell because it lasted longer, this third charge broke in blood and pain before a single man got within fifty yards of the wall. The survivors flowed back over the roll of earth and into the "dip," where reinforcements were nerving themselves for still a fourth attempt.

"They are massing very heavily and will break your line, I am afraid," Lee told Longstreet. But Old Peter did not believe it. He was ready for the whole Yankee nation, provided it would come at him from the direction this portion of it had done three times already, and he said so: "General, if you put every man now on the other side of the Potomac in that field to approach me over that same line, and give me plenty of ammunition, I will kill them all before they reach my line. Look to your right; you are in some danger there," he said. "But not on my line."

It was true; Lee's line was in considerable danger southward. While Sumner's men were charging the sunken road, repeatedly and headlong, taking their losses, Franklin was taking stock of the situation as Pelham's brass Napoleon and Jackson's masked batteries had left it when they disrupted his first and second advances. Both had been tentative, at best, but now he believed he knew what he had to deal with. However, as in Pleasant Valley preceding the battle on Antietam Creek, he was inclined to be circumspect: an inclination which had not been lessened here on the Rappahannock by Burnside's instructions that, once he was over the river "with a view to taking the heights," he was to be "governed by circumstances as to the extent of your movements." Further instructions had arrived this morning, warning him to keep his attack column "well supported and its line of retreat open." Accordingly, before going forward for the third time, he took care to protect the flank in Stuart's direction. The attack was delivered by the same corps, commanded by Major General John F. Reynolds, whose three divisions were under Major General George G. Meade and Brigadier Generals Abner Doubleday and John Gibbon. Doubleday was ordered to wheel left, guarding the bruised flank (sure enough, Pelham came out promptly and began to pound him) while the other two went forward in an attempt to storm the ridge. Gibbon, on the right, got as far as the railroad embankment, where he ran into murderous point-blank fire, was himself wounded, and had to be brought out on a stretcher. He was followed shortly by his men, who were not long in discovering that the Johnnies had drawn them into a trap.

That left Meade, whose division was the smallest of the three. Out of 60,000 soldiers available for the intended assault on the Confederate right, Franklin managed to get only these 4500 Pennsylvanians into slugging contact with the enemy, but they did what they could to make up in spirit for what they lacked in weight. Charging first to the railroad, then beyond it, they struck a boggy stretch of ground, about 500 yards in width, which A. P. Hill had left unmanned in the belief that it was impenetrable. It was not. Meade's troops slogged through it, burst upon and scattered a second-line brigade of startled rebels, and were still driving hard toward the accomplishment of Franklin's assignment — that is, to get astride the lower ridge and then sweep northward along it, dislodging men and guns as he went — when they themselves were struck in front and on both flanks by a horde of screaming graybacks.

These were Early's men, from over on the right. Told that Hill's line had been pierced, they came on the run, hooting as they passed the fugitives: "Here comes old Jubal! Let old Jubal straighten out that fence!" Then they struck. The Pennsylvanians were driven back through the boggy gap and out again across the open fields, where the pursuers stabbed vengefully at their rear and Confederate guns to the left and right tore viciously at their flanks. Unsupported, heavily outnumbered, thrown off balance by surprise, they paid dearly for their daring; more than a third of the men who had gone in did not come out again. There was no safety for the survivors until they regained the cover of their artillery, which promptly drove the pursuers back with severe losses and shifted without delay to the rebel batteries, blanketing them so accurately with shellbursts that the fire drew an indirect compliment from Pelham himself, who happened to be visiting this part of the line at the time. "Well, you men stand killing better than any I ever saw," he remarked as he watched the cannoneers being knocked about.

At any rate, the break had been repaired, the line restored. Lee on his hill had seen it all, the penetration and repulse on Jackson's front, coincident with the bloody disintegration of the third attack on Longstreet. The ground in front of both was carpeted blue with the torn bodies of men who had challenged unsuccessfully the integrity of his line. Beyond the river, Stafford Heights were ablaze with guns whose commanding elevation and heavier metal enabled them to rake the western ridge almost at will. Even now, one of them put a large-caliber shell into the earth at the southern commander's feet, but it did not explode. A British observer saw "antique courage" in Lee's manner as he turned to Longstreet, lowering his glasses after a long look at the blasted plain where still more Federals were massing to continue their assault over the mangled remains of comrades who had tried before and failed. "It is well that war is so terrible," the gray-bearded general said. "We should grow too fond of it."

If the assault was to be resumed after the comparative lull that settled over the field about 3.30, following the double failure at opposite ends of the line, it would have to be launched against that portion of the ridge where Longstreet's men were ranked four-deep in the sunken road, their rifles cocked and primed for firing at whatever came at them across the fields beyond their breast-high wall of stone and dirt. To the south, Franklin had shot his bolt with Meade's quick probe of the hole in Jackson's front: in reaction to which he was not unlike a man who has managed to salvage a good part of one hand after groping about in the dark and finding a bear trap. There might be other holes, for all he knew, but after that one costly venture the commander of the left Grand Division seemed less concerned about finding than he was about avoiding them. Whoever might deliver another attack, it was not going to be Franklin. That left Sumner and Hooker. Burnside sent them instructions to continue the assault with their right and center

Grand Divisions, in hopes that the Confederates along the ridge could be breached or budged or somehow thrown into confusion as a prelude to their downfall.

Sumner, a crusty veteran of forty-four years' service, nearly forty of which had been spent accomplishing the slow climb from second lieutenant to colonel, was altogether willing, despite his heavy losses up to now. So was Hooker, whose nickname was "Fighting Joe." Shortly before 4 o'clock, the men crouched in the swale caught sight of what they thought was their best chance to storm the ridge. A whole battalion of rebel artillery began a displacement from the slopes of Marye's Heights. Quickly the word passed down the Union line; men braced themselves for the order to charge. It came and they surged forward, followed this time by several batteries, which ventured out to within 300 yards of the fuming wall, adding the weight of their metal to the attack but losing cannoneers so fast that the guns could only be served slowly. As it turned out, this was worse than ever. The artillery displacement they had spotted was not the beginning of a retreat, as they had supposed, but a yielding of the position to a fresh battalion, which arrived with full caissons in time to aid in contesting this fourth assault. Down in the sunken road, Tom Cobb had been hit by a sharp-shooter firing from the upper story of a house on the edge of town; he had bled to death by now; but his men were still there, reinforced by several regiments of North Carolinians from Ransom's reserve division. Shoulder to shoulder along the wall, they loosed their volleys, then stepped back to reload while the rank behind stepped up to fire. So it went, through all four ranks, until the first had reloaded and taken its place along the wall, which flamed continuously under a mounting bank of smoke as if the defenders were armed with automatic weapons. This attack, like the three preceding it, broke in blood. The Federals fell back, leaving the stretch of open ground between the swale and a hundred yards of the wall thick-strewn with corpses and writhing men whose cries could be heard above the diminishing clatter of musketry.

While the carnage was being continued here ("Oh, great God!" a division commander groaned in anguish from his lookout post in the cupola of the courthouse. "See how our men, our poor fellows, are falling!") Jackson was burning to take the offensive against the inactive bluecoats at the other end of the line: so much so, indeed, that according to one observer "his countenance glowed, as from the glare of a great conflagration." If all those thousands of Federals on the plain could not be persuaded to approach the ridge, he ached to go down after them. "I want to move forward," he said impatiently; "to attack them — drive them into the river yonder," and as he spoke he threw out his arm, by way of lending emphasis to his words. The risk was great, he knew, for a repulse would expose his men to annihilation by the guns on the opposite heights. But at last, out of urgency, he devised a plan by which he hoped to nullify his prediction that the Confederates would "gain no fruits" from their victory. If the counterstroke were preceded by a bombardment, he believed, the enemy might be so stunned that the sudden charge across the plain might be made without undue sacrifice of life, and if it were launched just at sundown he could withdraw under cover of darkness in case it failed.

So conceived, it was so ordered. However, the almanac put sunset at 4.34; there was little time for preparation. Word was passed to the four divisions assigned to the attack, and as they got ready for the jump-off Stonewall's batteries went forward, out into the open, to begin their work of stunning or confusing the enemy. Instead, it was they who were stunned and confused, and in short order. Beyond the river, Stafford Heights seemed to buck and jump in flame and thunder as the guns on the crest redoubled their fire at the sight of these easy targets down below. Jackson quickly recalled his badly pounded artillerymen and canceled the attack, which he now saw would be shattered as soon as the infantry emerged from the woods. At that, the demonstration was not without its effect: especially on Franklin, who had already notified Burnside that "any movement to my front is impossible at present. . . . The truth is, my left is in danger of being turned. What hope is there of getting reinforcements across the river?" Of his eight divisions, only three had been employed offensively, and one whole corps of 24,000 men, the largest in the army, saw no action at all; yet he was asking after reinforcements. At the height of Jackson's abortive demonstration, orders came from Burnside for Franklin to take the offensive, but he declined. He was in grave danger here, he repeated. Besides, there was no time; the sun was down behind the western ridge.

Sunset did not slow the tempo of the fighting to the north, where a fifth major assault on Marye's Heights had been repulsed in much the same manner as all the others, though the officers in charge had attempted a somewhat different approach. Their instructions were for the men to veer northward when they left the swale and thus confront the sunken road from the right, which perhaps would enable them to lay down an enfilade as they gained the flank and bore down at an angle. But it did not work out that way. As the men went forward, attempting to bear off to the right, they encountered a marsh that forced them back to the left and a repetition of the direct approach to the stone wall, which seemed thus to draw them like a magnet. From behind it, all this while, the rebels — many of whom were shoeless, without overcoats or blankets to protect them from the penetrating mid-December chill — taunted the warmly clad Federals coming toward them in a tangle-footed huddle after their encounter with the bog: "Come on, blue belly! Bring them boots and blankets! Bring 'em hyar!" And they did bring them, up to within fifty yards of the flame-stitched wall at any rate. There the forward edge of the charge was frayed and broken, the survivors crawling or running to regain the protection of the swale, which by now they were convinced they never should have left.

Sumner had done his best, or worst but the carnage was by no means over. Hooker's men had crossed the river, under orders to continue the assault, and the commander of one of his divisions, Brigadier General Andrew Humphreys, believed he knew a way to get his troops up to and over the wall, so they could come to grips with the jeering scarecrows in the sunken road. While they were deploying in the dusk he rode among them, telling them not to fire while they were charging. It was obvious by now, he said, that firing did the rebels little damage behind their ready-made breastwork; it only served to slow the attack and expose the attackers to more of the rapid-fire volleys from beyond the wall. The object was to get there fast — much as a man might hurry across an open space in a shower of rain, intending to be as dry as possible when he reached the other side — then rely on the bayonet to do the work that would remain to be done when they got there.

They went forward in the twilight, stumbling over the human wreckage left by five previous charges. Prone men, wounded and unwounded, called out to them not to try it; some even caught at their legs as they passed, attempting to hold them back; but they ignored them and went on, beckoned by voices that mocked them from ahead, calling them blue-bellies and urging them to bring their boots and blankets within reach. Humphreys sat his horse amid the bullets, a slim veteran of aristocratic mien. He had left West Point in '31, two years behind R. E. Lee, and his record in the peacetime army had been a good one; yet his advancement since then, it was said, had been delayed because of suspicions aroused by his prewar friendship with Jefferson Davis. Now he was out to prove those suspicions false. As he watched he saw the stone wall become "a sheet of flame that enveloped the head and flanks of the column." Its formations unraveled by sudden attrition, the charge was brought to a stumbling halt about forty yards from the wall. For a moment the Federals hung there, beginning to return the galling fire; but it was useless, and they knew it. Despite the shouts and pleas of their officers — including Humphreys, who remained mounted yet incredibly went unhit — the men turned and stumbled back through the gathering darkness. Or anyhow the survivors did, having added a thousand casualties to the wreckage that cluttered the open slope, ghastly under the pinkish yellow flicker of muzzle-flashes still rippling back and forth along the crest of the stone wall.

"The fighting is about over," a Union signal officer reported at 6 o'clock from the heights across the way; "only an occasional gun is heard."

It was over, as he said, but not as the result of instructions from Burnside. Hooker was the one who finally called a halt to the carnage.

"Finding that I had lost as many men as my orders required me to lose," he later declared in his official report, "I suspended the attack."

Burnside himself took a much less gloomy view of the state of affairs when he crossed the river late that night for an inspection of the front. Unquestionably a great deal of blood had been shed — far more, in fact, than he would know until he received the final casualty returns — but he had little doubt that a continuation of today's work would break Lee's line tomorrow. At any rate he was determined to try it, and he sent out orders to that effect, alerting his front-line commanders. Recrossing the Rappahannock at 4 o'clock in the morning, he got off a wire to Washington: "I have just returned from the field. Our troops are all over the river. We hold the first ridge outside the town, and 3 miles below. We hope to carry the crest today."

★   ★   ★

Once more Lee had divined his opponent's purpose. "I expect the battle to be renewed at daylight," he wired Richmond, three hours after the final assault had failed, and this opinion was reinforced within another three hours by the capture, shortly before midnight, of a courier bearing orders to Burnside's front-line commanders for tomorrow's continuation of the attack. But Sunday's dawn, December 14, brought only the soup-thick fog of yesterday, without the familiar hum of preparation from down on the curtained plain. Indeed, even after the rising sun had burned away the mist, the only change apparent to the eye was in the lines along the western ridge. Expecting a turning movement, Lee had instructed his men to improve their fortifications in order to free all but a comparative handful for action on the flanks. So well had they plied their tools, these soldiers who six months ago had sneered at digging as cowardly work "unfit for a white man" and in derision had dubbed their new commander "the King of Spades," that Lee remarked with pleasure at the sight: "My army is as much stronger for these new intrenchments as if I had received reinforcements of 20,000 men."

No longer in need of prodding, or even suggestion, they kept digging. As the sun rose higher, so did the parapets. But the observers on Lee's Hill discerned no corresponding activity among the Federals on the plain, portions of whose forward edge were carpeted solid blue with the thick-fallen dead and wounded. The only sign of preparation was that the near ends of the east-west streets of Fredericksburg had been barricaded, as if in expectation of receiving, not delivering, an attack. The morning wore on. Noon came and went: then afternoon: and still no sign that the bluecoats were about to launch the assault that had been ordered in the dispatch captured the night before. As the shadows lengthened, Lee turned at last to Longstreet, who had been acquainted with the northern commander in the peacetime army. "General," he said, "I am losing faith in your friend General Burnside."

He was by no means alone in this, although the principal loss of faith in Old Peter's friend had occurred within the luckless commander's own ranks. Refreshed by a short sleep, and still convinced that he would break Lee's line by continuing yesterday's headlong tactics, Burnside had risen early that morning, only to be confronted by Sumner, who had been five years in the army before his present chief was born. He was known to be no quitter; in fact, so pronounced was his fondness for personal combat, Burnside had ordered the old man to remain at his left-bank headquarters yesterday, lest he get himself killed leading charges. Today, though, he was quite unlike himself in this respect.

"General," he said, obviously unstrung by all he had seen the day before, if only from a distance, "I hope you will desist from this attack. I do not know of any general officer who approves of it, and I think it will prove disastrous to the army."

Burnside was taken aback, having expected to encounter a different spirit. However, as he later wrote, "Advice of that kind from General Sumner, who had always been in favor of an advance whenever it was possible, caused me to hesitate." To his further dismay, he found his other Grand Division commanders of the same opinion. Franklin did not surprise him greatly in this regard — ironically, that general had served him on the left at Fredericksburg in much the same fashion as he himself had served McClellan on the left at Antietam — but when Hooker, the redoubtable Fighting Joe, was even more emphatic than Sumner in advising no renewal of the attack, he knew the thing was off. His first reaction was one of frantic despair. He had a wild impulse to place himself at the head of his old corps and lead an all-out, all-or-nothing charge against the sunken road, intending to break Lee's line or else be broken by it. Dissuaded from this, he retired to his tent, bitter with the knowledge that all yesterday's blood had been shed to no advantage: except to the rebels, who would be facing that many fewer men next time the two armies came to grips. A corps commander, Major General W. F. Smith, followed him into the tent and found him pacing back and forth, distracted. "Oh, those men! Oh, those men!" he was saying. What men? Smith asked, and Burnside replied: "Those men over there," pointing across the river, where portions of the plain were carpeted blue: "I am thinking of them all the time!"

Sunset closed a day that had witnessed nothing more than a bit of long-range firing on one side and a great deal of digging on the other. Such spectacle as there was, and it was much, came after nightfall. A mysterious refulgence, shot with fanwise shafts of varicolored light, predominantly reds and blues — first a glimmer, then a spreading glow, as if all the countryside between Fredericksburg and Washington were afire — filled a wide arc of the horizon beyond the Federal right. It was the aurora borealis, seldom visible this far south and never before seen by most of the Confederates, who watched it with amazement. The Northerners might make of it what they chose by way of a portent (after all, these were the *Northern* Lights) but to one Southerner it seemed "that the heavens were hanging out banners and streamers and setting off fireworks in honor of our great victory."

As if to rival this gaudy nighttime aerial display, morning brought a terrestrial phenomenon, equally amazing in its way. The ground in front of the sunken road, formerly carpeted solid blue, had taken on a mottled hue, with patches of startling white. Binoculars disclosed the cause. Many of the Federal dead had been stripped stark naked by shivering Confederates, who had crept out in the darkness to scavenge the warm clothes from the bodies of men who needed them no longer.

That afternoon, as a result of a request by Burnside for a truce during which he could bury his dead and relieve such of his wounded as had survived two days and nights of exposure without medicine for their hurts or water for their fever-parched throats, the men of both armies had a nearer view of the carnage. No one assigned to one of the burial details ever forgot the horror of what he saw; for here, close-up and life-size, was an effective antidote to the long-range, miniature pageantry of Saturday's battle as it had been viewed from the opposing heights. Up close, you heard the groans and smelled the blood. You saw the dead. According to one who moved among them, they were "swollen to twice their natural size, black as Negroes in most cases." They sprawled "in every conceivable position, some on their backs with gaping jaws, some with eyes as large as walnuts, protruding with glassy stare, some doubled up like a contortionist." Here, he wrote — approaching incoherency as the memory grew stronger — lay "one without a head, there one without legs, yonder a head and legs without a trunk; everywhere horrible expressions, fear, rage, agony, madness, torture; lying in pools of blood, lying with heads half buried in mud, with fragments of shell sticking in oozing brain, with bullet holes all over the puffed limbs."

Not even amid such scenes as this, however, did the irrepressible rebel soldier's wry sense of humor — or anyhow what passed for such; mainly it was a biting sense of the ridiculous — desert him. One, about to remove a shoe from what he thought was a Federal corpse, was surprised to see the "corpse" lift its head and look at him reproachfully. "Beg pardon, sir," the would-be scavenger said, carefully lowering the leg; "I thought you had gone above." Another butternut scarecrow, reprimanded by a Union officer for violating the terms of the truce by picking up a fine Belgian rifle that had been dropped between the lines, looked his critic up and down, pausing for a long stare at the polished boots the officer was wearing. "Never mind," he said dryly. "I'll shoot you tomorrow and git them boots."

So he said. But as the thing turned out, neither he nor anyone else was going to be doing any shooting on that field tomorrow: not unless the Confederates started shooting at each other. Night brought a storm of sleet and driving rain, with a hard wind blowing eastward off the ridge and toward the river. When the fog of December 16 rolled away, the plain was empty. A hurried and red-faced investigation disclosed the fact that not a single live, unwounded Federal remained on the west bank of the Rappahannock. Covered by darkness, the sound of their movements drowned by the howling wind, the bluecoats had made a successful withdrawal in the night, taking up their pontoons after such a good job of salvaging equipment that one signal officer proudly reported that he had not left a yard of wire behind.

Burnside was distressed that a campaign which had opened so auspiciously should have so ignominious a close. What was more, reports of the battle were appearing by now in the northern papers, and the correspondents, ignoring the general's plea that they not treat "the affair at Fredericksburg" as a disaster, pulled out all the descriptive stops and figuratively threw up their hands in horror at the bungling and the bloodshed. An account in the New York *Times* so infuriated Burnside that he summoned the reporter to his tent and threatened to run him through with his sword. By ordinary a mild-natured man, he was souring under the goads of criticism, such as those made by two of his own colonels: one that he and his men had been committed piecemeal — "handed in on toasting forks," he phrased it — and the other that the defeat had been "owing to the heavy fire in front and an excess of enthusiasm in the rear." Nor was his temper soothed when he read such comments as the following, from an Ohio journal: "It can hardly be in human nature for men to show more valor, or generals to manifest less judgment, than were perceptible on our side that day."

In truth, the casualties were staggering: especially by contrast. The Federals had lost 12,653 men, the Confederates well under half as many: 5309. The latter figure was subsequently adjusted to 4201, just under one third of the former, when it was found that more than a thousand of those reported missing or wounded had taken advantage of the chance at a Christmas holiday immediately after the battle.

Longstreet was not unhappy with the results, despite the bloodless withdrawal. Suffering fewer than 2000 casualties, he had inflicted about 9000, and he was looking forward to a repetition of the tactics which had made this exploit possible. But Jackson, whose losses were not much less than his opponent's on the right, was far from satisfied, even though 11,000 stands of arms had been gleaned from the field after the departure of the Yankees. "I did not think a little red earth would have frightened them," he said. "I am sorry they are gone. I am sorry that I fortified." Lee agreed, saying of Burnside and the punishment that general had absorbed: "Had I divined that was to have been his only effort, he would have had more of it."

That evening he wrote his wife, "They went as they came — in the night. They suffered heavily as far as the battle went, but it did not go far enough to satisfy me." His anger had been aroused by the evidence of rabid vandalism he saw when he rode into Fredericksburg that afternoon. So had Jackson's. "What can we do?" a staff officer asked helplessly when he saw how thoroughly the Federals had taken the town apart. "Do?" Stonewall replied promptly. "Why, shoot them."

The stern-lipped Jackson's ire would never cool (later he expanded this remark; "We must do more than defeat their armies," he said. "We must destroy them") but Lee's was influenced considerably by the advent of the season of the Nativity. On Christmas Day he wrote his wife: "My heart is filled with gratitude to Almighty God for His unspeakable mercies with which He has blessed us in this day, for those He has granted us from the beginning of life, and particularly for those He has vouchsafed us during the past year. What should have become of us without His crowning help and protection? Oh, if our people would only realize it and cease from vain self-boasting and adulation, how strong would be my belief in final success and happiness to our country! But what a cruel thing is war; to separate and destroy families and friends, and mar the purest joys and happiness God has granted us in this world; to fill our hearts with hatred instead of love for our neighbors, and to devastate the fair face of this beautiful world. I pray that, on this day when only peace and good-will are preached to mankind, better thoughts may fill the hearts of our enemies and turn them to peace." But he added a sort of postscript in a letter to his youngest daughter, remarking that he was "happy in the knowledge that General Burnside and his army will not eat their promised Christmas dinner in Richmond today."

✗ 3 ✗

Near the far end of the thousand-mile-long firing line that swerved and crooked its way between North and South — westward across northern Virginia, East and Middle Tennessee, North Mississippi, central Arkansas, and thence on out to Texas — Theophilus Holmes, with less rank and not one half as many soldiers in a department better than twenty times as large, had troubles which, in multiplicity at any rate, made Lee's seem downright single. From his Transmississippi headquarters in Little Rock the lately appointed North Carolinian looked apprehensively north and west and south; he was threatened from all those quarters; while from the east he was being jogged by repeated pleas and suggestions from Johnston and the President, not to mention such comparatively minor figures as Pemberton and the Secretary of War, that he send his hard-pressed and outnumbered troops to the aid of his fellow department commander on the opposite bank of the big river that ran between them. A grim-featured man, deaf as a post, at fifty-seven Holmes was the oldest of the Confederate field commanders. Moreover, his rigidity of face, indicative of arteriosclerosis, was matched by a rigidity of mind which augured ill in a situation that called for nothing so much as it called for flexibility.

By way of compensation for this drawback, he had under him three major generals whose outstanding characteristic, individually and collectively, was the very flexibility he lacked. John Magruder, Richard Taylor, and Thomas Hindman, respectively in charge of Texas, West Louisiana, and Arkansas, were remarkable men, battle tested and of proved resourcefulness. In this regard the last was not the least accomplished of the three. A prewar Helena lawyer, thirty-four years old, Hindman had preceded his present chief to his home state, and within six months of his arrival in late May, stepping into the vacuum left by Van Dorn's April crossing of the Mississippi with all the men and weapons that could be salvaged from the defeat at Elkhorn Tavern, had created and equipped, by strict enforcement of the new conscription act and the establishment of factories and foundries where none had been before, an army of 20,000 recruits, armed and uniformed more or less in accordance with regulations and supported by 46 guns. This in itself was about as close to a miracle of improvised logistics as any general ever came in the whole war, but Hindman expected to accomplish a great deal more before he was through. Dapper, jaunty, dandified, addicted to patent leather boots and rose-colored kidskin gloves, frilled shirt fronts and a rattan cane, perhaps by way of compensation for his Napoleonic five feet two of height, he was accustomed to getting what he wanted, whether it was a fine brick house, a seat in Congress, or a wife whose father had sought to keep her from him by locking her away in a convent: all of which he had won, despite the odds, by extending his credit, demolishing opponents from the stump, and scaling the convent wall. What he had in mind just now, though, was not only the scourging of all bluecoats from the soil of Arkansas — including Helena, where the Federal commander of the force in occupation had taken over the fine brick house for his headquarters — but also the recovery of Missouri.

Arriving in mid-August to find the diminutive Arkansan already far along with his plans, Holmes had been infected by his enthusiasm and had approved his preparations for a counterinvasion. It was gotten under way at once. By October Hindman's advance, a combined command of cavalry and Indians, was across the Missouri border, but suffered a repulse at the hands of a superior Union force under Brigadier

General John M. Schofield, in command of three divisions styled the Army of the Frontier. The Indians scattered like chaff before a fan, and the cavalry fell back to the security of the Boston Mountains, skirmishing as they went. Hindman, coming forward to Fort Smith with the main body, was not discouraged by this turn of events. Indeed, as he saw it, the Federals were being lured to their destruction in the wilds of northwest Arkansas. Accordingly, he crossed the Arkansas river and concentrated his infantry at Van Buren. All he wanted, he told Holmes, was a chance to hit the Yankees with something approaching equal strength, after which he would "move into Missouri, take Springfield, and winter on the Osage at least."

Presently he got that chance, and at odds considerably better than he had dared even to hope for. Schofield, believing in mid-November that hostilities had ended for the winter, left the largest of his three divisions near Fayetteville under Brigadier General James G. Blunt, with the assignment of blocking the path of another Confederate incursion, and withdrew to Springfield with the other two, which he placed under Brigadier General Francis J. Herron while he himself took off on sick leave. Hindman, with a mobile force of 11,500 men and 22 guns, was preparing to take advantage of this chance to strike at Blunt, who had 7000 men and 20 guns, when word came from Holmes (who by now had received instructions from the Secretary of War, urging the necessity for reinforcing Vicksburg) for him to return posthaste to Little Rock with all his men, in preparation for an eastward march across the Mississippi. Hindman protested for all he was worth. To fall back would cost him heavily in desertions, he knew, since many of his conscripts were natives of the region through which they would be retreating. Besides, he told Holmes, "to withdraw without fighting at all would . . . so embolden the enemy as to insure his following me up." Without waiting for a reply he put his army in motion on December 3, intending to precede the retrograde movement with an advance and a victory that would leave the Federals in no condition to pursue. Slogging next day through the brushy Boston Mountains, the highest and most rugged section of the Ozark chain, he printed and distributed an address to his soldiers, designed to steel their arms for the strike at Blunt. "Remember that the enemy you engage has no feeling of mercy or kindness toward you," he told them. "His ranks are made up of Pin Indians, free negroes, Southern tories, Kansas jayhawkers, and hired Dutch cut-throats. These bloody ruffians have invaded your country; stolen and destroyed your property; murdered your neighbors; outraged your women; driven your children from their homes, and defiled the graves of your kindred. If each man of you will do what I have here urged upon you, we will utterly destroy them."

Blunt now had his troops in bivouac about twenty miles southwest of Fayetteville, near the hamlet of Cane Hill, from which he had

driven the grayback cavalry that week. When he got word that Hindman was across the Arkansas with an estimated 25,000 men he reacted
according to his nature, rejecting the notion of retreat. A Maine-born
Kansan who had practiced medicine en route in Ohio, he was a militant
abolitionist and a graduate of the border wars. Round-faced, stocky,
pugnacious in manner, he was thirty-six years old and no part of his
training had prepared him for running from rebels, whatever their numbers. Determined to hold his ground, he wired for reinforcements and
began to organize his position for defense.

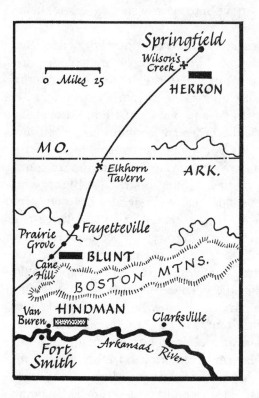

The trouble with this was
that the only reinforcements
available were the two small divisions under Herron, a scant 6000
men with 22 guns, and they were
back near Springfield, well over
a hundred miles away, whereas
Hindman's camp at Van Buren
was little more than a third that
distance from Cane Hill, so that
the chances were strong that the
rebels would arrive before the reinforcements did. However, this
was leaving two factors out of
account. The first was that Hindman's route of march lay through
the mountains; his men would be
climbing and descending about
as much as they would be advancing along the rugged trails.
The other factor was Frank Herron. An adopted Iowan, already
in command of two divisions at
the age of twenty-five, he intended to accomplish a great deal more in
the way of fulfilling his military ambitions before returning to civilian
life as head of the Dubuque bank established for him by his wealthy
Pennsylvania parents. Just now, more than anything, he wanted a chance
to command those two divisions in actual battle, and he got it much
sooner than he had expected. At 8 o'clock on the morning of December
3 — by which hour, unknown to him or Blunt, Hindman had put his
army on the road for its trek across the Boston Mountains — Herron
received the summons from Cane Hill, one hundred and thirty miles
from his present camp on the somber fields where the Battle of Wilson's
Creek had been fought and lost by Nathaniel Lyon, almost a year and a
half ago. Drums and bugles sounded assembly and the men fell in to receive instructions for the march. It would be made without tents or bag-

gage, they were told, except for knapsacks which would be hauled in wagons. By noon they were headed south, and before they stopped at dawn next morning, slogging at route step down the pike, they had made twenty miles. After a short rest they were off again. Across the state line on December 5, munching hardtack and raw bacon as they walked, they skirted the granite slopes of Pea Ridge and saw the nine-months-old scars on the Elkhorn Tavern, where Van Dorn had come to grief. At midnight the following day, having covered better than one hundred blistering miles of road, the head of the column entered Fayetteville, where the weary marchers slept in the streets, sprawled around fires they kindled and fed by ripping pickets from front-yard fences. Another twenty miles tomorrow and they would be at Cane Hill with Blunt, ready for whatever came at them from beyond the mountains whose foothills they could presently see by the glimmer of dawn on Sunday, December 7.

The first sign they had that they were not going to make it — at least not on schedule — came later that morning, twelve miles down the pike, when they encountered long-range cannonfire as they were approaching Illinois Creek. Soon they saw that the Confederates had drawn a line of battle around the hilltop village of Prairie Grove, a couple of miles beyond the creek, blocking the path of the road-worn bluecoats eight miles short of their goal. Herron shook out a regiment of skirmishers and advanced them to the protection of the creekbank, where to his horror he discovered that his men were so weary that once they were off their feet they promptly dropped to sleep with rebel shells and bullets whistling and twittering over their heads. Undaunted, he built up his firing line and put his batteries in position, partly by way of returning the hostile fire, but mostly by way of letting Blunt know from the racket that he had arrived, or almost arrived, and needed help. The trouble was, with all those graybacks swarming in his front, he was not even sure that Blunt and his men were still in existence. For all he knew, Hindman might have gobbled them up while he himself was on the march from Wilson's Creek.

Hindman had not gobbled up Blunt; he had gone around him. Approaching Cane Hill late the afternoon before, after a march across the shoulder of the mountains in weather so cold that water froze in the men's canteens and icicles tinkled on the beards of the horses, he had put his troops in position for a dawn attack, only to learn that Herron was on the way, already approaching Fayetteville with a force which, once it was joined to Blunt's, would give the Federals the advantage of numbers, both in men and guns. In command of a brigade at Shiloh, where he had been wounded and commended for gallantry, Hindman decided to profit from the example of that battle by preventing what had caused its loss, the arrival of Buell after Grant had been pushed to the edge of desperation. That is, he would strike at the reinforcements first, then turn on the main body. Accordingly, he built up the campfires along his outpost line, left a skeleton brigade of cavalry to keep up the bluff next morning, and set off after moonset on a circuitous march with 10,000 men to intercept and defeat the blue column hurrying southward out of Fayetteville. That was how it came about that Herron encountered long-range cannonfire at the crossing of Illinois Creek and the bristling line of battle at Prairie Grove, eight miles short of a junction with Blunt at Cane Hill.

Blunt had spent the morning in constant expectation of being swamped by the rebels maneuvering boldly to his front, apparently in overwhelming numbers. Near noon, however, hearing the sudden boom of guns from across the hills to his left rear, he realized that he had been outflanked; whereupon he fell back hastily to Rhea's Mills, six miles north, in order to protect his trains. Finding them secure he turned southeast in the direction of the booms and at 4 o'clock reached Prairie Grove, where he came upon the battle still in full swing after nearly five hours of doubtful contest. Two rounds from his lead battery announced his arrival — announced it all too emphatically, in fact, for both shots landed among Herron's skirmishers, causing them to think that they were being flanked by their foes instead of being supported by their friends. Herron had been holding his own despite the weariness of his foot-sore men. Two charges against the ridge had failed, breaking in blood against the rim of the rebel horseshoe line, but Hindman had had no better luck in attempting a counterattack with his green conscripts, who fell apart whenever he ordered them forward. The fighting continued, left and right, muzzle flashes stabbing the early darkness. Despite their superiority of numbers, especially in guns — 42 to 22, now that the Union forces were united — Blunt's fresh troops could make no more of a penetration of the rebel line than Herron's weary ones had been able to achieve. Gradually the firing died to a sputter. Then it stopped. The battle was over.

Losses in killed, wounded, and missing totaled 1317 for the Confederates and 1251 for the Federals. Of the latter only 333 were from Blunt's command, indicating how much heavier a proportion of the conflict Herron's men had borne, despite the fact that both laid claim to a lion's share in having brought the victory about. Hindman's only claim in that respect was the not inconsiderable one that he had managed to hold his ground throughout the fighting. Whether he had also accomplished his main objective — to shock the enemy into immobility, escaping pursuit while he fell back southward in compliance with the previous orders from Holmes — would soon be known; for he retreated that night under cover of darkness, wrapping the iron tires of his gun and caisson wheels with blankets to muffle the sound of his withdrawal. The ruse worked, and so did another he tried next morning. Not only did Blunt not hear him go, but at dawn he also granted a request for a truce, which Hindman sent forward under a white flag, to allow for tending the wounded and burying the dead. Discovering presently that the Confederate main body had departed in the night, Blunt canceled the truce, on grounds that the rebels were gleaning abandoned arms from the field, and prepared to follow. By that time, however, Schofield was on the scene. Up from his sickbed and furious that his army had been committed to battle in his absence, he censured both commanders: Blunt for not withdrawing to meet the reinforcements hurrying toward him, and Herron for attacking with troops so badly blown that some of them were found dead on the field, not from wounds but from exhaustion and exposure after their long march from Wilson's Creek. If Schofield's purpose in this was to prevent his subordinates' advancement by discrediting their valor, that purpose failed. By way of showing its appreciation for a victory won by northern arms as the year drew to a close — a victory which presently shone the brighter by contrast with the several full-scale disasters that developed elsewhere along the thousand-mile-long firing line before the month was out — the government promptly awarded major general's stars not only to Blunt but also to Herron, who then succeeded Lew Wallace as the youngest man to hold that rank in the U.S. Army. Moreover, as soon as these promotions came through, both men would outrank their present commander.

Hindman's discomfort was considerably increased in late December, when Schofield finally unleashed his cavalry for a forced march against the Confederates who, down to about 4000 men as a result of straggling and desertions, had taken sanctuary behind the Arkansas River. Three days after Christmas the blue riders struck Van Buren, destroying five steamboats at the wharf and all of the supplies of corn and bacon Hindman had gathered over the months in order to keep his army from starvation. Once more he was thrown into dispirited retreat, losing still more soldiers as he went. The Federals withdrew to Fayetteville, and thence on back to comfortable winter quarters in Missouri, but now there was no question of Hindman's returning to Little Rock with the prospect of marching his army to the relief of Vicksburg. Practically speaking he had no army. So much of it as did not lie in shallow graves at Prairie Grove was scattered over northern Arkansas, hiding from conscription agents in Ozark coves and valleys.

Thus it was that the battle lost in northwest Arkansas had repercussions far beyond the theater it was fought in. Holmes had opposed the eastward transfer from the start, protesting that the march led through a region barren of supplies and would require no less than thirty days. "Solemnly, under the circumstances," he had informed the Adjutant General earlier that month, "I regard the movement ordered as equivalent to abandoning Arkansas." All the same, against his better judgment, he had been preparing to go along with the plan. But now, with Hindman's army practically out of existence and only the local reserves to protect Little Rock itself against an advance from occupied Helena, he had what he considered the best of specific reasons for declining to comply with the government's wishes. On December 29, the day after Schofield's cavalry hit Van Buren, he wrote Johnston in reply to the correspondence the President had forwarded from Vicksburg during his inspection of that place the week before: "My information from Helena is to the effect that a heavy force of the enemy has passed down the Mississippi on transports. . . . Thus it seems very certain that any force I can now send from here would not be able to reach Vicksburg, and if at all not before such a reinforcement would be useless, while such a diversion would enable the enemy to penetrate those portions of the Arkansas Valley where the existence of supplies of subsistence and forage would afford them leisure to overrun the entire state and gradually reduce the people to . . . dependence."

★ ★ ★

It was bad enough that the Yankees were steaming down the Mississippi, but they were also steaming up it — simultaneously. Banks had reoccupied Baton Rouge in mid-December and now was giving every sign that he intended to continue the northward penetration, shortening the stretch of river necessarily rebel-held if Holmes was to keep open the supply lines vital to the feeding and reinforcement, if not indeed to the survival, of all the armies of the South. Since the loss of the armed ram *Arkansas*, three months back, the Confederacy had had no vestige of a navy with which to oppose this two-pronged challenge designed for her riving and destruction; the threat would have to be stopped, if at all, not on the river itself, but from its banks. On the east bank the responsibility was Pemberton's, and to help him meet it he had two stout high-ground bastions one hundred air-line miles apart, commanding bends of the river at Vicksburg and Port Hudson. On the west bank it was Richard Taylor's, who had nothing: not only no lofty fortresses bristling with heavy-caliber guns emplaced to blow the Union ironclads out of the water, but also no army. In fact, on his arrival from Virginia in late August, he had found that his total force consisted of two troops of home-guard cavalry, a scattering of guerillas hidden from friends and foes in the moss-hung swamps and bayous, and a battalion of mounted infantry just arrived from Texas — in all, fewer than 2000 effectives for the defense of the whole Department of Louisiana. Nonetheless, Holmes had confidence that this second of his three major generals would be ingenious and tireless in his efforts to reduce the nearly immeasurable odds, and this confidence was not misplaced.

Commander of a division used as shock troops by Stonewall Jackson throughout the Shenandoah Valley campaign, Taylor had been one of the stars of that amazing chapter in military history, and had found in that experience ample compensation for his lack of formal training in the art of war. Gripped on the eve of the Seven Days by a strange paralysis of the legs, which seemed to portend the close of a promising career and a denial of any further share in winning his country's independence, this son of Zachary Taylor had recovered in time to receive his present assignment, together with a promotion, from his brother-in-law Jefferson Davis. Happy over what in fact would be a home-coming, for he had commanded Louisianians in the Valley and had spent his antebellum years on a Louisiana plantation, he came West with an enthusiasm that was only slightly dampened by the discovery of conditions in his new department, as of August 20, when he established headquarters in Alexandria. Undismayed by the shortage of soldiers, which kept him from any immediate accomplishment of big things — such as the retaking of New Orleans, which was very much a part of his plans for the future — he decided to be content at first with small ones. Within two weeks of his arrival he mounted a surprise attack that captured a four-gun battery and two companies of infantry at Bayou des Allemands, a Federal post near his plantation home, fifty miles downriver from Donaldsonville and less than half that far above New Orleans. If he could not retake the Crescent City just yet, he could at least draw near it — and profitably, too.

Slight though it was, this first success gained locally by Confederate arms in the four months since the fall of the South's first city was heartening indeed to the people of the district. Not even the recapture of the post in late October, when the resurgent Louisianians were driven away by a Federal amphibious force that included four regiments of infantry and a quartet of light-draft gunboats, detracted from the brilliance of that first strike. What was more, Taylor was planning others of still larger scope. Denied access to the Lafourche, that fertile region lying between the Mississippi and the Atchafalaya, he moved into the Teche country, which lay between the Atchafalaya basin and the Gulf of Mexico, and here, despite the fact that his government, as he said, "had no soldiers, no arms or munitions, and no money within the limits of the district," he set about the task of raising, equipping, and training the army with which he hoped, in time, not only to capture but also to hold the series of fortified posts that blocked the path between him and his goal, New Orleans. Meanwhile, intent on preventing further enemy penetrations, he had to disperse what forces he had in order to meet threats from all directions. With few trained subordinates and almost no telegraph or railway lines, the problem of central control was well-nigh insoluble. However, now that December had come on and the year drew toward a close, Taylor went far toward solving it. By using relays of fast-stepping mules and an ambulance in which he could sleep while traveling, the thirty-six-year-old general managed to employ what might have been his immobile hours for visits to the various scattered points in his large department. "Like the Irishman's bird," he subsequently wrote, "I almost succeeded in being in two places at the same time."

In this respect, as well as in several others, he was easily distinguishable from his opposite number, the newly arrived commander of all the Union forces in the region. Ten years Taylor's senior, of humbler birth but with much larger accomplishments in public life, having been a three-term governor of Massachusetts and speaker of the national House of Representatives, Nathaniel Banks was nothing like the Irishman's bird and had nothing like his opponent's nighttime mobility — though the fact was, he had perhaps an even greater need for it if he was to carry out the multiple assignment given him by his superiors when he set out from Hampton Roads on his voyage down and around the coast to relieve his fellow Bay State politician, Benjamin Butler, as military ruler of New Orleans and commander of the Department of the Gulf. Vicksburg and Mobile were his primary objectives, he was told, and after the fall of the former place had opened the Mississippi to Union traffic throughout its length he was to move up the Red in order to gain control of northern Louisiana and, eventually, Texas. It was a large order, particularly for a general who not only had not a single battlefield victory to his credit, but rather had been whipped twice already in open contest — once at Winchester, in the Shenendoah Valley, and again at Cedar Mountain, both times by Stonewall Jackson, whose lean marchers had captured so many of his supplies that they had dubbed him "Commissary" Banks — but he apparently had no doubt that it could be filled and that he was the man to fill it. He docked at New Orleans, December 14, and took over formally next day from Butler, who issued an address to his army — "I greet you, my brave comrades, and say farewell!" it began, and ended: "Farewell, my comrades! Again, Farewell!" — and promptly departed for Washington to take the government to task for having made what seemed to him an improvident substitution.

Banks wasted no time on speeches. On the day he took command he issued orders for one of the divisions he had brought along to proceed at once upriver, without unloading from its transports, and to reoccupy Baton Rouge, which Butler had abandoned after repulsing an all-out attack on the place in early August. Two days later, when the Louisiana capital fell without even a show of resistance, Banks was greatly pleased at having made so prompt and effective a beginning toward fulfilling his government's outsized expectations. Including the reinforcements still arriving after their long voyage from New York and Fort Monroe, he had 36,508 effectives in his department, exclusive of navy personnel, and he felt that these were ample for the accomplishment of his task. What was more, he reported that he had found in Farragut, who was to be his partner in continuing the bold upriver thrust, a sailor who was "earnest for work." After a conference with the Tennessee-born admiral he added that he was delighted with his enthusiasm and frankness, and that he looked forward to "a most satisfactory result from our mutual labors." Banks was feeling chipper, and he said so. "All the indications of our campaign are auspicious," he notified Washington on December 18, the day after the fall of Baton Rouge, "and I hope to make good the most sanguine expectations in regard to my expedition."

There were, however, two previously unsuspected matters for concern, one military, one civil, and both grave. The first was the presence, thirty-five miles above Baton Rouge, which in turn was a hundred miles above New Orleans, of the fortifications at Port Hudson. Neither his Washington superiors nor Banks himself, until he arrived, had known of the existence of any such obstacle south of Vicksburg, another 250 winding miles upstream; yet intelligence reports informed him now that the Confederates had no less than 12,000 troops in the place, strongly intrenched on the landward side and with 21 heavy guns emplaced on the high bluff, waiting to sink or blow sky high whatever came their way across the chocolate-colored surface of the river. This in itself, placing as it did a new complexion on the problem of ascent, was enough to give Banks pause. But the other concern, the civil one, was even more disturbing in its way, since it showed that the command of the department was going to be a far more complex occupation than he had supposed, early that month, when he set out from Virginia. Less than two weeks after his arrival, for example, he received a note from one C. A. Smith, commission agent for certain northern interests, and Andrew Butler, whose brother Ben had set him up in business when he took over as military ruler of New Orleans. "Dear Sir," it read. "If you will allow our commercial program to be [carried] out as projected previous to your arrival in this department, giving the same support and facilities as your predecessor, I am authorized on [receiving] your assent to place at your disposal $100,000."

In the course of his rise from bobbin boy to the top of the heap in Massachusetts politics Banks no doubt had encountered other offers of this nature, but hardly one that was made so blatantly or with such apparent confidence in his basic corruptibility. "It was no temptation," he told his wife. "I thank God every night that I have no desire for dishonest gains." All the same, he felt obliged to report to Washington "that as much, or more, attention has been given to civil than to military matters," including the training of his army, and that, in consequence, the troops were "not in condition for immediate service." Though he declared on Christmas Eve, "We hope to move up the river at the close of the week," he was still in New Orleans after New Year's, complaining that he was cramped by a shortage of siege artillery. "The enemy's works at Port Hudson have been in progress many months and are formidable," he explained. "Our light field guns would make no impression on them." In fact, having learned by now of the reverses lately suffered by the column supposed to be working its way southward out of Memphis while he moved northward from New Orleans, he was beginning to "feel some anxiety as to the defenses of this city. . . . The enemy is concentrating all available forces on the river, and in the event of disasters North will not fail to turn their attention to this quarter."

So it was that, now in January — while Taylor kept busy raising and training an army in the bayous, lulled to sleep each night in his ambulance by the clopping of hoofs as he traveled the moon-drenched roads of the Teche and dreamed of retaking the South's first city — Banks stayed where he was, bedeviled by itchy-handed speculators, made apprehensive by rebel successes upriver, and fretted by shortages while he continued his preparations for the upstream movement which he had assured his superiors in December would be launched without delay.

Another part of his assignment, albeit one that was no more than incidental, he had also placed in the way of execution, though so far on a scale that was small indeed. Its conception was provoked by the shortage of cotton for the textile mills of New England, 3,252,000 of whose 4,745,750 spindles had fallen idle by the middle of the year, with the result that production was down to less than one fourth of normal before its close. New Orleans having failed to yield more than a comparative handful of bales, the hungry manufacturers had cast their eyes on Texas. What they had in mind was conquest and colonization; they saw their chance to make of it what one observer called "another and a fairer Kansas," where Yankee know-how and industry, replacing the slovenly farming methods now employed, would produce more cotton in a single year than had previously been grown in all the history of the vast Lone Star expanse. That way, the idle spindles would be fed, the mill hands would return to work, and the owners would get rich. First, however, the army would have to clear the path for immigration, and in this connection Banks had in his entourage a Texas Unionist, Andrew Jackson Hamilton, upon whom the War Department, at the behest of the New England manufacturers, had conferred the rank of brigadier general, together with appointment as military governor of Texas. He would take office, preparing the way for the textile-sponsored "colonists," when and if Banks won control of some portion of the state for him to govern.

So far, all there was for him in this regard was Galveston harbor, seized two months ago by the navy and now being patrolled by gunboats of the West Coast Blockading Squadron, part of Farragut's command. Texas was far down on the list of Banks's assigned objectives; though his department had been enlarged to include that state, its occupation was scheduled to follow the opening of the Mississippi and the conquest of the Red River Valley in northwest Louisiana; but at Hamilton's urging he agreed to send a Massachusetts regiment to take and hold the island town at once, thus giving the newly appointed governor at least the shadow of a dry-land claim to his high title. Accordingly, an advance party of three companies left New Orleans on December 22, before they had had time for more than a hurried look at the sights of the city, and landed at Galveston on Christmas Eve. There, under the muzzles of the gunboats anchored in the harbor, they set to work barricading the wharf as a precaution against attack from the landward side while awaiting the arrival of the rest of the infantry by sea, together with attached units of cavalry and field artillery.

They had need for greater caution than they suspected, for this action brought them into immediate contact with the first in rank of Holmes's three major generals, John Magruder. Known to be unpredictable and tricky, he was also first in reputation; "Prince John" he had been called in the old army, partly because of his aristocratic manner and his fondness for staging amateur theatricals, partly too because of his flared mustache, luxuriant sideburns, gaudy clothes, and imperial six-feet-two of height. As flamboyant in the Transmississippi as he had been in his native Virginia — where, previous to becoming somewhat unstrung in the jangle of the Seven Days, he had put on such a show of strength with a handful of men that McClellan had been awed into immobility before Yorktown — his ache for distinction and love of flourish were no less pronounced in the Lone Star state. The difference here, eight months later, was that Magruder was thinking offensively. For some time now, in fact ever since his assignment to command the District of Texas, Arizona, and New Mexico on October 10, five days after the Union flotilla steamed in and put Galveston under its guns, he had had it in mind not only to liberate the island town, less than fifty miles southeast of his Houston headquarters, but also to sink or capture the warships riding insolently at anchor in the harbor. So far as Prince John was concerned, the addition of those three companies of Massachusetts infantry, now barricading the wharf against attack, only fattened the prize within his grasp and added to the glory about to be won.

Nor was his plan for making a naval assault deterred by his lack of anything resembling a navy. If he had none then he would build one, or at any rate improvise one, and he did so in short order. Workmen off the Houston docks piled bales of cotton around the paddle boxes and decks of the *Bayou City*, a two-story side-wheel Mississippi steamboat, and the stern-wheeler *Neptune*, a smaller vessel. The former was armed with a rifled 32-pounder, located forward of her stacks, and the latter's bow was faced with railroad iron to stiffen her punch as a ram.

Their crews were army volunteers, including some 300 riflemen stationed about the decks as sharpshooters. These two "cotton-clads" would stage the naval assault, descending Buffalo Bayou to come booming down on the five Union gunboats, *Westfield, Harriet Lane, Owasco, Clifton,* and *Sachem,* which had a combined displacement of over 3000 tons and mounted a total of 28 guns, mostly heavy. For the land attack there were in all about 500 men; Texans under Colonel Tom Green, who had led them at Valverde, they were survivors of Brigadier General Henry Sibley's nightmare expedition up the Rio Grande, back in the spring. Magruder divided them into three assault columns, taking the center one himself. By New Year's Eve his preparations were complete. He gave the signal and the attack got under way, bringing in the new year with a bang.

Crossing from the mainland by the unguarded bridge, he struck the barricade shortly after midnight — only to find that his scaling ladders were too short. All he could do was work his men up close and keep exchanging shots with the defenders, who had turned out at the first alarm and were laying down a heavy fire. Everything depended now on the untried two-boat navy. The first the Federals knew of its existence was when lookouts on the *Westfield,* Commander W. B. Renshaw's flagship, spotted two ungainly-looking steamboats, apparently overloaded with cotton bales, driving hard toward the anchored flotilla. Attempting to take evasive action, the *Westfield* went aground on Pelican Island Bar, removed from the fight as effectively as if she had been sunk. Aboard the *Bayou City,* bearing down on the *Harriet Lane,* the gun captain of the 32-pounder shouted: "Well, here goes for a New Year's present!" and pulled the lanyard. The first shot missed, as did the second, and on the third the gun exploded at the breech, killing him and four of its crew; whereupon the *Neptune* came up, churning the water in her wake, and struck the *Lane* such a tremendous thump that she broke her own nose and had to run up on the flats to keep from sinking. Afloat as ashore, the battle seemed lost by mishap or miscalculation.

By now, however, the *Bayou City* had pulled up alongside the *Lane,* her upper-deck riflemen firing down on the rattled bluejackets while a boarding party swarmed over the bulwarks and began slashing at the survivors in the style of John Paul Jones. In the course of this melee the Union skipper was killed and his lieutenant ran up the white flag of surrender; observing which, the other three nearby captains did the same. Across the way, still hard aground, Renshaw saw that the *Westfield* was next on the rebel target list. Determined not to have her fall into enemy hands, he ordered the crew to abandon ship while he lowered into an open magazine a barrel of turpentine equipped with a slow fuze which he set and started before he turned to go. That was his last act on earth or water, for the fuze was defective or wrongly set.

Before he made it out of range, a flame-shot column of black smoke roared skyward and the *Westfield* blew apart, her wreckage enveloped in fire and steam.

Watching this abrupt disintegration of the naval support for the defenders of the wharf, the Texans in front of the barricade took heart and the Federals behind it were dejected; so much so, indeed, that the three Massachusetts companies, warned by a step-up in the firing that an assault was about to be launched, surrendered in a body. But the commanders of the gunboats *Clifton, Owasco,* and *Sachem,* claiming that this forcing of the issue ashore was in violation of the naval "truce" — for so they had considered it, they later affirmed by way of rebuttal to the outrage expressed by the rebels — hauled down their white flags and made a sudden run for open water. The Confederates, unable to pursue out into the Gulf, could do nothing but howl in protest at foul play. They had lost 143 killed and wounded. Including captives the Federals had lost about 600 soldiers and sailors: plus, of course, two gunboats and the town. At a single stroke, boldly conceived and boldly delivered, Magruder had cleared Texas of armed bluecoats. Nor did he intend to grant them another foothold. Moving his headquarters triumphantly to Galveston, he notified his government next day: "We are preparing to give them a warm reception should they return."

The navy might (and in fact did, the following week, withdrawing the 2000-ton screw steamer *Brooklyn* and six gunboats from the blockade squadron off Mobile and bringing them to Galveston, where they were careful however to maintain station well outside the harbor and thus beyond reach of another eruption of Magruder's cotton-clads) but Banks had no intention of returning, not even with a token force. He counted himself lucky that the whole Bay State regiment, together with its artillery and cavalry supports, had not landed in time to be gobbled up, and he brought the still-loaded transports back to New Orleans, turning a deaf ear to Would-Be-Governor Hamilton's disgruntled protestations. That gentleman and his party — a sizable group, characterized by one critic as "friends, patrons, and creditors," who had meant to be front runners in the intended Lone Star colonization — returned instead to Washington, complaining bitterly that they had been "deliberately and purposely humbugged."

Though Holmes of course was quick to congratulate Magruder, whose amphibious coup made the one bright spot in the entire Transmississippi as the new year came in, Hamilton's dejection and disgust were not matched by any corresponding elation on the part of the overall commander of the Confederate Far West. Though he had managed, on the face of it, to achieve a sort of balance within the limits of his department — defeat in northwestern Arkansas, stalemate in West Louisiana, victory in coastal Texas — he knew that it was precarious in nature, tenuous at best and, in consideration of the odds, most likely temporary.

Nor was the maintenance of that shaky balance only dependent on what occurred within the borders of the monster region. Cut off, Holmes and all those under him would be left as it were to wither on the vine; so that what happened beyond or along those borders was equally important, and this was true in particular as to what happened along the eastern border, the Mississippi itself, down which he had reported the "heavy force" of Union ironclads and transports steaming the week before past Helena. It was headed, according to his conjecture, for Vicksburg, the linchpin whose loss might well result in the collapse of the whole Confederate wagon.

⚔ 4 ⚔

Haste made waste and Grant knew it, but in this case the haste was unavoidable — unavoidable, that is, unless he was willing to take the risk of having another general win the prize he was after — because he was fighting two wars simultaneously: one against the Confederacy, or at any rate so much of its army as stood between him and the river town that was his goal, and the other against a man who, like himself, wore blue. That was where the need for haste came in, for the rival general's name was John McClernand. A former Springfield lawyer and Illinois congressman, McClernand was known to have political aspirations designed to carry him not one inch below the top position occupied at present by his friend, another former Springfield lawyer and Illinois congressman, Abraham Lincoln. Moreover, having decided that the road to the White House led through Vicksburg, he had taken pains to see that he traveled it well equipped, and this he had done by engaging the preliminary support, the active military backing, not only of his friend the President, but also of the Secretary of War, the crusty and often difficult Edwin M. Stanton. With the odds thus lengthened against him, Grant — when he belatedly found out what his rival had been up to — could see that this private war against McClernand might well turn out to be as tough, in several ways, as the public one he had been fighting for eighteen months against the rebels.

In the first place, he had not even known that he had this private war on his hands until it was so well under way that his rival had already won the opening skirmish. McClernand had gone to Washington on leave in late September, complaining privately that he was "tired of furnishing brains" for Grant's army. Arriving in the capital he appealed to Lincoln to "let one volunteer officer try his abilities." His plan was to return to his old political stamping ground and there, by reaching also into Indiana and Iowa, raise an army with which he would descend the Mississippi, capture Vicksburg, "and open navigation to New Orleans." Lincoln liked the sound of that and took him to see Stanton, who liked it too. McClernand left Washington in late October, armed with a confidential order signed by Stanton and indorsed by Lincoln, giving official sanction to his plan. By early November Grant was hearing rumors from upriver in Illinois: rumors which were presently reinforced by a dispatch from General-in-Chief Henry W. Halleck, whom the three former lawyers had not taken into their confidence. Memphis, which was in Grant's department, was to "be made the depot of a joint military and naval expedition on Vicksburg." Alarmed at hearing the rumors confirmed, Grant wired back: "Am I to understand that I lie still here while an expedition is fitted out from Memphis, or do you want me to push south as far as possible?" Halleck was something of a lawyer, too, though he now found himself at cross-purposes with the men who had not let him in on the secret. "You have command of all troops sent to your department," he replied, " and have permission to fight the enemy where you please."

Grant considered himself unleashed. Organizing his mobile force of about 40,000 effectives into right and left wings, respectively under Major General W. T. Sherman and Brigadier General C. S. Hamilton, with the center under Major General J. B. McPherson, he began to move at once, southward along the Mississippi Central Railroad from Grand Junction. Ordinarily he would have preferred to wait for reinforcements, but not now. "I feared that delay might bring McClernand," he later explained. Vicksburg was 250 miles away, and as he saw it the town belonged to the man who got there first. By mid-November he was in Holly Springs, where he set up a depot of supplies and munitions, then continued on across the Tallahatchie, leapfrogging his headquarters to Oxford while the lead division was fording the Yocknapatalfa, eight miles north of Water Valley, which was occupied during the first week of December. The movement had been rapid and well coordinated; so far, it had encountered only token resistance from the rebels, who were fading back before the advance of the bluecoats. Presently Grant discovered why. Pemberton — whose strength he considerably overestimated as equal to his own — was avoiding serious contact while seeking a tactical advantage, and at last he found it. He called a halt near Grenada, another twenty-five miles beyond Water Valley, and put his gray-clad troops to work improving with intrenchments a position of great natural strength along the Yalobusha. Approaching Coffeeville on December 5, midway between Water Valley and Grenada, the Federal cavalry was struck a blow that signified the end of easy progress. Still 150-odd miles from Vicksburg, Grant could see that the going was apt to be a good deal rougher and slower from here on.

Something else he could see as well, something that disturbed him even more. While he was being delayed in the piny highlands of north-central Mississippi, facing the rebels intrenched along the high-banked Yalobusha, McClernand might come down to Memphis, where advance contingents of his expedition were awaiting him already, and ride the broad smooth highway of the Mississippi River down to Vicksburg unopposed: in which case Grant would not only have lost his private war, he would even have helped his opponent win it by holding Pemberton and the greater part of the Vicksburg garrison in position, 150 miles away, while McClernand captured the weakly defended town with little more exertion than had been required in the course of the long boat ride south from Cairo. That was what rankled worst, the thought that he would have helped to pluck the laurels that would grace his rival's brow. But as he thought distastefully of this, it began to occur to him that he saw here the possibility of a campaign of his own along these lines. "You have command of all troops sent to your department," Halleck had told him, and presumably this included the recruits awaiting McClernand's arrival at Memphis. So Grant, still at his Oxford headquarters on December 8, sent a note to Sherman, whose command was at College Hill, ten miles away: "I wish you would come over this evening and stay tonight, or come in the morning. I would like to talk with you."

Sherman did not wait for morning. Impatient as always, he rode straight over, a tall red-haired man with a fidgety manner, concave temples, glittering hazel eyes, and a scraggly, close-cropped beard. "I never saw him but I thought of Lazarus," one observer was to write. A chain smoker who, according to another witness, got through each cigar "as if it was a duty to be finished in the shortest possible time," he was forty-two, two years older than the comparatively stolid Grant and once his military senior, too, until Donelson brought the younger brigadier fame and a promotion, both of which had been delayed for Sherman until Shiloh, where he fought under — some said, saved — his former junior. He felt no resentment at that. In fact, he saw Grant as "the coming man in this war." But he had never had better reason for this belief than now at Oxford, when he was closeted with him and heard his plan for the sudden capture of Vicksburg with the help of a kidnaped army.

As usual in military matters, geography played a primary part in determining what was to be done, and how. Various geographic factors made Vicksburg an extremely difficult nut to crack. First there was the bluff itself, the 200-foot red-clay escarpment dominating the hairpin bend of the river at its base, unscalable for infantry and affording the guns emplaced on its crest a deadly plunging fire — as Farragut, for one, could testify — against whatever naval forces moved against or past it. As for land forces, since they could not scale the bluff itself, even if they had been able to approach it from the front, their only alternative was to come upon it from the rear; that is, either to march overland down the Mississippi Central to Grenada, as Grant was now attempting to do, and thence along the high ground lying between the Yazoo and the Big Black Rivers, or else debark from their transports somewhere short of the town and make a wide swing east, in order to approach it from that direction. However, the latter was nearly impossible, too, because of another geographic factor, the so-called Yazoo-Mississippi alluvial delta. This incredibly fertile, magnolia-leaf-shaped region, 200 miles in length and 50 miles in average width, bounded east and west by the two rivers that gave it its compound name, and north and south by the hills that rose below and above Memphis and Vicksburg, was nearly roadless throughout its flat and swampy expanse, was subject to floods in all but the driest seasons, and — except for the presence of a scattering of pioneers who risked its malarial and intestinal disorders for the sake of the richness of its forty-foot topsoil, which in time, after the felling of its big trees and the draining of its bayous, would make it the best cotton farmland in the world — was the exclusive domain of moccasins,

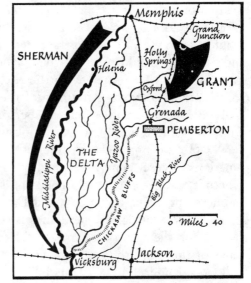

bears, alligators, and panthers. It was, in short, impenetrable to all but the smallest of military parties, engaged in the briefest of forays. An army attempting to march across or through it would come out at the other end considerably reduced in numbers and fit for nothing more strenuous than a six-month rest, with quinine as the principal item on its diet. Anyhow, Grant did not intend to try it that way. He had his eye fixed on the mouth of the Yazoo, twelve miles above Vicksburg, and it seemed to him that an amphibious force could ascend that river for a landing on the southeast bank, which would afford the troops a straight shot at the town on the bluff. True, there were hills here, too — the Walnut Hills, they were called, the beginning of the long ridge known as the Chickasaw Bluffs, which lay along the left bank of the Yazoo, overlooking the flat morass of the delta — but they were by no means as forbidding as the heights overlooking the Mississippi, a dozen miles below. It was Grant's belief that determined men, supported by the guns of the fleet, could swarm over these comparatively low-lying hills, brushing aside whatever portion of the weakened garrison tried to stop them, and be inside the town before nightfall of the day they came ashore.

That was why he had sent for Sherman, who seemed to him the right man for the job. Sherman happily agreed to undertake it, and Grant gave him his written orders that same evening. He was to return at once to Memphis with one of his three divisions, which he would combine with McClernand's volunteers, already waiting there. This would give him 21,000 troops, and to these would be added another 12,000 to be picked up at Helena on the way downriver, bringing his total strength to four divisions of 33,000 men, supported by Porter's fleet. Grant explained that he himself would continue to bristle aggressively along the line of the Yalobusha "so as to keep up the impression of a continuous move," and if Pemberton fell back prematurely he would "follow him even to the gates of Vicksburg," in which event he and Sherman would meet on the Yazoo and combine for the final dash into the town. Delighted with the prospect, Sherman was off next day for Memphis, altogether mindful of the need for haste if he was to forestall both McClernand and Pemberton. "Time now is the great object," he wired Porter. "We must not give time for new combinations."

He did not make it precisely clear whether these feared "combinations" were being designed in Richmond or in Washington — whether, that is, they threatened the successful prosecution of Grant's public or his private war. By mid-December, however, Grant's worries in regard to the latter were mostly over. Sherman was in Memphis, poised for the jump-off, and McClernand's men had become organic parts of the army the redhead was about to take downriver. There was still one danger. McClernand outranked him; which meant that if he arrived before Sherman left, he would assume command by virtue of seniority. But Grant considered this unlikely. Sherman was thoroughly aware of the risk and would be sure to avoid the consequences. Besides, with Halleck's telegram in his files as license for the kidnap operation, Grant felt secure from possible thunder from on high. "I doubted McClernand's fitness," he later wrote, "and I had good reason to believe that in forestalling him I was by no means giving offense to those whose authority to command was above both him and me."

The arrival of a telegram from Washington on the 18th, instructing him to divide his command (now and henceforward to be called the Army of the Tennessee) into four corps, with McClernand in charge of one of those assigned to operations down the Mississippi — which meant of course that, once he joined it, he would be in charge of the whole column by virtue of his rank, unless Grant himself came over and took command along the river route — did not disturb the plans Grant had described in a letter home, three days ago, as "all complete for weeks to come," adding: "I hope to have them all work out just as planned." Sherman was ready to leave, he knew, and in fact would be gone tomorrow, before McClernand could possibly arrive from Illinois. Blandly he wired his new subordinate word of the Washington order, which dispelled McClernand's illusion that his command was to be an independent one. Instructing him to come on down to Memphis, Grant even managed to keep a straight face while remarking: "I hope you will find all the preliminary preparations completed on your arrival and the expedition ready to move."

★   ★   ★

McClernand found no such thing, of course. All he found when at last he reached Memphis on December 29 were the empty docks his men had departed from, ten days ago under Sherman, and Grant's telegram, delayed eleven days in transmission. Nor did Grant's own plans, "all complete for weeks to come," work out as he had intended and predicted. In both cases — entirely in the former and largely in the latter — the cause could be summed up in three two-syllable nouns: Nathan Bedford Forrest.

"He was the only Confederate cavalryman of whom Grant stood in much dread," a friend of the Union general's once remarked. Then he told why. "Who's commanding?" Grant would ask on hearing that gray raiders were on the prowl. If it was some other rebel chieftain he would shrug off the threat with a light remark; "but if Forrest was in command he at once became apprehensive, because the latter was amenable to no known rules of procedure, was a law unto himself for all military acts, and was constantly doing the unexpected at all times and places."

Grant's apprehensions were well founded as he looked back over his shoulder in the direction of his main supply base at Columbus, Kentucky; or, more specifically, since the far-off river town was adequately garrisoned against raiders, as he traced on the map the nearly two hundred highly vulnerable, not to say frangible, miles of railroad which were his sole all-weather connection with the munitions and food his army in North Mississippi required if it was to continue to shoot and eat. Without that base and those railroads, once he had used up the reserve supplies already brought forward and stored at Holly Springs, his choice would lie between retreat on the one hand and starvation or surrender on the other. Just now, moreover, the reason his apprehensions were so well founded was that Forrest was looking — and not only looking, but moving — in that direction, too: as Grant learned from a dispatch received December 15 from Jackson, Tennessee, a vital junction about midway of his vulnerable supply line. "Forrest is crossing [the] Tennessee at Clifton," the local commander wired. Four days later, Jackson itself was under attack by a mounted force which the Federal defenders estimated at 10,000 men, with Forrest himself definitely in charge.

Pemberton had begun it by appealing to Bragg in late November for a diversion in West Tennessee, which he thought might ease the pressure on his front, and Bragg had responded by sending Forrest instructions to "throw his command rapidly over the Tennessee River and precipitate it upon the enemy's lines, break up railroads, burn bridges, destroy depots, capture hospitals and guards, and harass him generally." Receiving these orders December 10 at Columbia, forty miles south of Nashville, Forrest was off next day with four regiments of cavalry and a four-gun battery, 2100 men in all, mostly recruits newly brigaded under his command and mainly armed with shotguns and flintlock muskets. Four days later and sixty miles away, he began to cross the Tennessee at Clifton on two flatboats which he had built for the emergency and which he afterwards sank in a nearby creek in case he needed them coming back. Deep in enemy country, with the bluecoats warned of his crossing while it was still in progress, he encountered on the 18th, near Lexington, two regiments of infantry, a battalion of cavalry, and a section of artillery, all under Colonel Robert G. Ingersoll, who had been sent out to intercept him. The meeting engagement was brief and decisive. Falling back on the town, Ingersoll took up what he thought was a good defensive position and was firing rapidly with his two guns at the rebels to his front, when suddenly he "found that the enemy were pouring in on all directions." The fight ended quite as abruptly as it had begun. "If he really believed that there is no hell," one grayback later said of the postwar orator-agnostic, "we convinced him that there was something mightily like it." Captured along with his two guns and 150 of his men, while the rest made off "on the full run" for Jackson, twenty-five miles to the west, Ingersoll greeted his captors with aplomb: "Is this the army of your Southern Confederacy for which I have so diligently sought? Then I am your guest until the wheels of the great Cartel are put in motion."

Following hard on the heels of the fugitives, who he knew would stumble into Jackson with exaggerated stories of his strength, Forrest advanced to within four miles of the place and began to dispose his "army" as if for assault, maneuvering boldly along the ridge-lines and beating kettledrums at widely scattered points to keep up the illusion, or, as he called it, "the skeer." It worked quite well. Convinced that he was heavily outnumbered, though in fact he had about four times as many troops inside the town as the Confederates had outside it, Brigadier General Jeremiah Sullivan prepared to make a desperate house-to-house defense. All next day the rebel host continued to gather, waxing bolder hour by hour. When dawn of the 20th showed the graybacks gone, Sullivan took heart and set out after them, pushing eastward — into emptiness, as it turned out, for Forrest had swung north. Today in fact, having thrown the Federal main body off his trail, he began in earnest to carry out his primary assignment, the destruction of the sixty miles of the Mobile & Ohio connecting Jackson and Union City, up near the Kentucky line. The common complaint of army commanders, that cavalry could seldom be persuaded to get down off their horses for the hard work that was necessary if the damage to enemy installations was to be more than temporary, was never leveled against Forrest's men.

Besides forcing the surrender of the several blue garrisons in towns along the line, they tore up track, burned crossties and trestles, and wrecked culverts so effectively that this stretch of the M&O was out of commission for the balance of the war. In Union City on Christmas Eve, resting his troopers after their four-day rampage with axes and sledges, Forrest reported by courier to Bragg that, at a cost so far of 22 men, he had killed or captured more than 1300 of the enemy, "including 4 colonels, 4 majors, 10 captains, and 23 lieutenants." That he considered this no more than a respectable beginning was shown by his closing remark: "My men have all behaved well in action, and as soon as rested a little you will hear from me in another quarter."

His problem now, after paroling his captives and sending them north to Columbus to spread bizarre reports of his strength — reports that were based on bogus dispatches, which he had been careful to let them overhear while their papers were being made out at his headquarters — was, first, what further damage to inflict and, second, how to get back over the river intact before the various Federal columns, still chasing phantoms all over West Tennessee, converged on him with overwhelming numbers. The first was solved on Christmas Day, when he marched southeast out of Union City and spent the next two days administering to the Nashville & Northwestern the treatment already given the M&O. Reaching McKenzie on the 28th in an icy, pelting rain, he headed south across the swampy bottoms of the swollen Obion River, and now began his solution of the second part of his problem. Instead of trying to make a run for the Tennessee, with the chance of being caught half-over and hamstrung, he decided to brazen out the game by thrusting in among the Federals attempting a convergence, and by vigorous blows, struck right or left at whatever came within his reach, stun them into inaction or retreat, while he continued his movement toward the security of Middle Tennessee.

The fact was, he had little to fear from the direction of Columbus. Brigadier General Thomas A. Davies, commander of the 5000 bluecoats gathered there, had been so alarmed by demonstrations within ten miles of the town on Christmas Eve, as well as by the parolees coming in next day with reports of 40,000 infantry on the march from Bragg, that he had spiked the guns at New Madrid and Island Ten, throwing the powder into the Mississippi to keep it out of rebel hands, and now was concentrating everything in order to protect the $13,000,000 worth of supplies and equipment being loaded onto steamboats at the Columbus wharf for a getaway in case Forrest broke his lines. Conditions were scarcely better, from the Union point of view, 250 miles downriver at Memphis, where the citizens had become so elated over rumors that their former alderman was coming home, along with thousands of his troopers, that Major General S. A. Hurlbut, perturbed by their reaction and the fact that his garrison was down to a handful since the departure of

Sherman, telegraphed Washington: "I hold city by terror of heavy guns bearing upon it and the belief that an attack would cause its destruction." Grant, however, was of a different breed. He was thinking not of his safety, but of the possible destruction of Forrest and his men. "I have directed such a concentration of troops that I think not many of them will get back to the east bank of the Tennessee," he informed a subordinate. Nor was this opinion ill-founded. One superior blue force was coming south from Fort Henry, another north from Corinth, and both were now much closer to the Clifton crossing than Forrest was. So, for that matter, were Jere Sullivan and his three brigades, two of which were back by now from their goose chase east of Jackson and headed north. Undiscouraged by his lack of luck so far, he believed he knew just where the raiders were, and he intended to bag them. "I have Forrest in a tight place," he wired Grant on December 29. "My troops are moving on him from three directions, and I hope with success."

Forrest was indeed in a tight place, and that place was about to get tighter. Emerging from the flooded Obion bottoms, which he had crossed by an abandoned causeway, he paused on December 30 to let Sullivan's unsuspecting lead brigade go by him, then resumed his march past Huntingdon and toward Clarksburg, nearing which place on the morning of the last day of the year he encountered the other brigade, forewarned and drawn up to meet him at Parker's Crossroads. By way of precaution he had sent four companies to guard the road from Huntingdon and warn him in case the lead brigade turned back, and now, secure in the belief that his rear was well protected against surprise, he settled down to a casualty-saving artillery duel with the blue force to his front. It lasted from about 9 o'clock until an hour past noon, by which time he had captured three of the enemy guns and 18 wagonloads of ammunition and had driven the skirmishers back on their supports. He had in fact ceased firing, in response to several white flags displayed along the Union line, and was sending in his usual demand for "unconditional surrender to prevent the further effusion of blood," when an attack exploded directly in his rear. For the first last only time in his career, Forrest was completely surprised in battle. His reaction was immediate. Quickly resuming the fight to his front, he simultaneously charged rearward, stalling the surprise attackers with blows to the head and flanks, and withdrew sideways before his opponents recovered from the shock. It was smartly done — later giving rise to the legend that his response to a staff officer's flustered question, "What shall we do? What shall we do?" was: "Charge both ways!" — but not without sacrifice. The captured guns were abandoned, along with three of his own, for lack of horses to draw them, as well as the 18 wagonloads of ammunition. Three hundred men who had been fighting afoot were taken, too, while trying to catch their mounts, which had bolted at the sudden burst of gunfire from the rear. Sullivan, coming up from behind Jackson with his third brigade next day, was elated. "Forrest's army completely broken up," he wired Grant. "They are scattered over the country without ammunition. We need a good cavalry regiment to go through the country and pick them up."

So he said. But while he and his three brigades were waiting for that "good regiment," Forrest and his troopers were riding hard for the Tennessee and eluding the columns approaching cautiously from Corinth and Fort Henry. All in high spirits on New Year's Day — except possibly the captain who by now had been verbally blistered for taking yesterday's rear-guard companies up the wrong road and thus permitting the Federals to march past him unobserved — they reached Clifton about midday, raised the sunken flatboats, and were across the icy river before dawn. The basis for their high spirits was a sense of accomplishment. They had gone out as green recruits, miserably armed, and had returned within less than three weeks as veterans, equipped with the best accouterments and weapons the U.S. government could provide. In the course of a brief midwinter campaign, which opened and closed with a pontoonless crossing of one of the nation's great rivers, and in the course of which they more than made up in recruits for what they lost in battle or on the march, they had killed or paroled as many men as they had in their whole command and had kept at least ten times their number of bluecoats frantically busy for a fortnight. Besides the estimated $3,000,000 they had cost the Federals in wrecked installations and equipment, they had taken or destroyed 10 guns and captured 10,000 rifles and a million badly needed cartridges. Above all, they had accomplished their primary assignment by cutting Grant's lifeline, from Jackson north to the Kentucky border. They saw all this as Forrest's doing, and it was their pride, now and for all the rest of their lives — whether those lives were to end next week in combat or were to stretch on down the years to the ones they spent sunning their old bones on the galleries of crossroads stores throughout the Deep and Central South — that they had belonged to what in time would be known as his Old Brigade.

Pemberton was highly pleased, not only with the results of this cavalry action outside the limits of his department, but also with another which had been carried out within those limits and which he himself had designed as a sort of companion piece or counterpart to the raid-in-progress beyond the Tennessee line. Both had a profound effect on the situation he had been facing ever since he called a halt and began intrenching along the Yalobusha, preparatory to coming to grips with Grant's superior army: so profound an effect, indeed, that it presently became obvious that if he and Grant were to come to grips, it would be neither here nor now. Like that of the first, the success of this second horseback exploit — which in point of fact was simultaneous rather than sequential, beginning later and ending sooner — could also be summed up in three nouns, though in this case the summary was even briefer, since all three were single-syllabled: Earl Van Dorn.

"Buck" Van Dorn, as he had been called at West Point and by his fellow officers in the old army, had leaped at the chance for distinction, not only because it was part of his nature to delight in desperate ventures, but also because he was badly in need just now of personal re-

demption. After a brilliant pre-Manassas career in Texas, he had been called to Virginia, then reassigned to Arkansas, where his attempt at a double envelopment had been foiled disastrously at Elkhorn Tavern. Crossing the Mississippi after Shiloh, he had suffered an even bloodier repulse at Corinth in October, which gave him so evil a reputation in his home state that a court had been called to hear evidence of his bungling. Although he was cleared by the court, the government soon afterwards promoted Pemberton over the head upon which the public was still heaping condemnations. The accusation that he was "the source of all our woes," Senator Phelan wrote President Davis, was "so fastened in the public belief that an acquittal by a court-martial of angels would not relieve him of the charge." Van Dorn was depressed, but he was not without hope. A court-martial of angels was one thing; a brilliant military exploit, characterized by boldness and attended by great risk, was quite another. So when Pemberton summoned him to army headquarters and gave him his assignment — an all-out raid on Grant's communications and supply lines, including the great depot lately established at Holly Springs — the diminutive Mississippian saw in it the opportunity to retrieve his reputation and bask once more in the warmth of his countrymen's affection. Always one to grasp the nettle danger, he embraced the offered chance without delay.

He left Grenada on December 18 with 3500 cavalry, heading east at first to skirt Grant's flank, then north as if for a return to Corinth. Next day, however, he turned west beyond New Albany and came thundering into Holly Springs at dawn, December 20. The Federal commander there, Colonel R. C. Murphy, had been placed in a similar uncomfortable position in September at Iuka, which he had abandoned without a fight or even destruction of the stores to keep them from falling into enemy hands. Grant had forgiven him then because of his youth and inexperience, and now he was given another chance to prove his mettle. He did no better. In fact, despite advance warning that a heavy column of graybacks was moving in his direction, he did far worse. This time, he lost not only the stores in his charge but also the soldiers, 1500 of whom were captured and paroled on the spot by the jubilant rebels, caracoling their horses at the sight of the mountains of food and equipment piled here for Grant's army. "My fate is most mortifying," he reported that night amid the embers which were all that remained of the million-dollar depot of supplies. "I have done all in my power — in truth, my force was inadequate."

Grant reacted "with pain and mortification" at the news of his loss and ordered Murphy dismissed from the service, as of "the date of his cowardly and disgraceful conduct." With Forrest loose on the railroad north of Jackson that same day, and his own wife spared embarrassment at Holly Springs only because she had left to join him in Oxford the day before, Grant began to design combinations of forces in North Mississippi, not unlike those already sent out after Forrest in West Tennessee, to accomplish Van Dorn's destruction before he could return to safety behind the Yalobusha. "I want those fellows caught, if possible," he said.

The trouble with this was that by the time the various columns could be put in motion Van Dorn was no longer in North Mississippi. Instead of racing for home, and perhaps into the arms of superior forces already gathering in his rear, he pushed on northward into Tennessee. Before he left his native state, however, the commander of a small outpost at Davis Mill, twenty miles north of Holly Springs and just south of the Tennessee line, gave him — and, incidentally, Murphy — a lesson in how well an "inadequate" force could hold its own against "overwhelming" numbers. His name was Colonel W. H. Morgan and he had less than 300 men for the defense of a point made critical by the presence of a trestle by which the Mississippi Central crossed Wolf River. Hearing that the raiders were coming his way, he converted an old sawmill into a blockhouse, reinforcing its walls with cotton bales and crossties, and a nearby Indian mound into a moated earthwork, both of which covered the railroad approach with converging fire. About noon of the 21st, the Confederates came up and launched a quick assault, which was repulsed. After a two-hour long-range skirmish, finding the fire too hot for a storming party to reach and ignite the trestle, let alone cross the river, the attackers sent forward, under a flag of truce, a note asking whether the defenders were ready to surrender. Morgan replied with what he later termed "a respectful but decided negative," and the Confederates withdrew, leaving 22 dead and 30 wounded on the field, along with another 20 prisoners who had ventured up too close to be able to pull back without exposing themselves to slaughter. Morgan's loss was 3 men slightly wounded.

Except for the further damage it did to his former opinion that one Southerner was worth ten Yankee hirelings in a scrap, Van Dorn was not greatly disturbed by this tactical upset. In the course of his approach to the fight, and even while it was in progress, he had done the railroad enough damage to be able to afford to let the trestle go. Bypassing Morgan's improvised blockhouse, he crossed upstream and pushed on northward between Grand Junction and LaGrange, where he tore up sections of the Memphis & Charleston for good measure. Near Bolivar on the 23rd, he circled Middleburg, still ripping up track and wrecking culverts, and headed back south on Christmas Eve, riding through Van Buren and Saulsbury to re-enter Mississippi. South of Ripley on Christmas Day, he had a brush with one of the converging Union colums, but pressed on without delay, through Pontotoc and thence on back to Grenada, which he reached by midafternoon of December 28. He had carried out his mission in fine style, destroying Grant's reserve supplies of food, forage, and munitions. What was more, at least from a particular point of view, he had refurbished his tarnished reputation. Households which formerly had mentioned his name only with frowns of disapproval or downright scowls of condemnation now drank his health with shouts of joy and praised him to the skies.

Pemberton, then, was delighted at the manner in which Van Dorn had achieved redemption; but not Grant, who paid the bill which thus was added to all that Forrest was costing him simultaneously. With Columbus in a panic, Memphis cowed by heavy guns, his communications disrupted, and his supply line almost a continuous wreck from Holly Springs north to the Kentucky border, he was stymied and he knew it. Van Dorn having destroyed his supplies on hand and Forrest having made it impossible for him to bring up more, he could neither move forward nor stand still. There was no way he could go but back, and this he proceeded to do, meanwhile solving the problem of immediate subsistence by sending out "all the wagons we had, under proper escort, to collect and bring in all supplies of forage and food from a region of fifteen miles east and west of the road from our front back to Grand Junction." At the news of this, the broad smiles caused by Van Dorn's coup faded from the faces of the people around Oxford. Their former mocking question, "What will you do now?" was changed to: "What are *we* to do?" Grant replied that he had done his best to feed his soldiers from their own northern resources, but now that these had been cut off "it could not be expected that men, with arms in their hands, would starve in the midst of plenty." In short, as he said later, "I advised them to emigrate east, or west, fifteen miles and assist in eating up what we left."

To his amazement — for he had thought the pickings would be slim and had lately advised his government that an army could not "subsist itself on the country except in forage"; "Disaster would result in the end," he had predicted — the wagons returned heavy-laden with hams, corn on the cob, field peas and beans, sweet and Irish potatoes, and fowls of every description, accompanied by herds of beef on the hoof. "It showed that we could have subsisted off the country for two months instead of two weeks without going beyond the limits designated," he subsequently wrote, adding: "This taught me a lesson."

The knowledge thus gained might prove to be of great use in the future, but for the present one thing still bothered him beyond all others. This was the thought that, putting it baldly, he was leaving his friend Sherman in the lurch. He had promised to hold Pemberton in position, 150 miles from Vicksburg, while Sherman was storming its thinly held defenses; yet Pemberton was already hurrying troops in that direction, as Grant knew, and might well arrive in time to smother the attackers in the Yazoo bottoms. However, there was little Grant could do about it now, except depend on Sherman to work out his own salvation. Out of touch as he was, because of his ruptured communications, Grant did not even know whether Sherman had left Memphis yet — or, if so, whether he was still in command of the river expedition; McClernand, in event of delay, might have arrived in time to take over. All Grant could do was send a courier to Memphis with a message addressed to "Commanding Officer Expedition down Mississippi," advising him, whoever he was, "that farther advance by this route is perfectly impracticable" and that he and his men were falling back, while Pemberton did likewise. Whether this would arrive in time to forestall disaster, he did not know.

★ ★ ★

Sherman was already downriver, and so far his only thought of disaster had been the intention to inflict it. "You may calculate on our being at Vicksburg by Christmas," he wrote Grant's adjutant on December 19, the day he left Memphis. "River has risen some feet, and all is now good navigation. Gunboats are at mouth of Yazoo now, and there will be no difficulty in effecting a landing up Yazoo within twelve miles of Vicksburg." Two days later at Helena, where he picked up his fourth division, he received from upriver his first intimation that Grant might be having trouble in the form of rebel cavalry, which was reported to have captured Holly Springs. If this was so, then Sherman's first letter most likely had not got through to Oxford; nor would a second. Nevertheless, he refused to be disconcerted, and wrote again. "I hardly know what faith to put in such a report," he said, "but suppose whatever may be the case you will attend to it."

All was indeed "good navigation" for the fifty-odd army transports and the 32,500 soldiers close-packed on their decks, steaming rapidly toward their destiny below, as well as for the naval escort of three ironclads, two wooden gunboats, and two rams. But for the rest of Porter's fleet — three ironclads and two "tinclads," so called because their armor was no more than musket-proof — the going had been less easy. Sent downriver two weeks before, they had succeeded in clearing the Yazoo from its mouth upstream to Haines Bluff, where a stout Confederate battery defined the limit of penetration, 23 winding miles from the point of entrance. This had not been accomplished without cost, however, for the defenses were in charge of Isaac Brown, and Brown was known to be hungry for vengeance because of the recent loss above Baton Rouge of the steam ram *Arkansas,* which he had built up this same river the summer before and with which he had charged and sundered the two flotillas then besieging Vicksburg. He had no warship now, but he had notions about torpedoes, five-gallon whiskey demijohns packed with powder, fuzed with artillery friction tubes, and each suspended a few feet below a float on the muddy surface. On December 12 the five-boat Union reconnaissance squadron appeared up the Yazoo, shelling the banks and fishing up Brown's torpedoes as it advanced. Approaching Haines Bluff, the ironclad *Cairo* made contact with one of the glass demijohns at five minutes before noon, and at 12.03 she was out of sight, all but the tips of her stacks, in thirty feet of water.

Celerity and good discipline made it possible for the crew to abandon ship within the allowed eight minutes. No lives were lost, but the *Cairo*'s skipper, Lieutenant Commander T. O. Selfridge, Jr., a young man with a lofty forehead and luxuriant sideburns, was greatly disturbed by the loss of his boat and the possible end of his career as well, depending on the admiral's reaction to the news. Steaming back down the Yazoo aboard one of the tinclads, he found Porter himself at the mouth of the river, just arrived from Memphis, and stiffly requested a court of inquiry. "Court!" the admiral snorted. "I have no time to order courts. I can't blame an officer who puts his ship close to the enemy. Is there any other vessel you would like to have?" Without waiting for an answer he turned abruptly to the flag captain standing beside him on the bridge. "Breese, make out Selfridge's orders to the *Conestoga.*"

Porter was like that, when he chose to be. Just short of fifty and rather hard-faced, with a hearty manner and a full dark beard, he had been given his present assignment, together with the rank of acting rear admiral, over the heads of eighty seniors. For the present, though, despite this cause for self-congratulation, the heartiness and bluster were cover for worry. Most of his old sailors had broken down, with the result that his heavy boats were half-manned, while ten light-draft vessels were laid up for lack of crews, and he was complaining to Washington that a draft of new men, lately arrived from New York, were "all boys and very ordinary landsmen." Characteristically, however, in a letter written this week to Sherman, after protesting of these and other matters, including a shortage of provisions, fuel, medicines, and clothing — not to mention the loss of the *Cairo* — he closed by observing: "I expected that the government would send men from the East, but not a man will they send or notice my complaints, so we will have to go on with what we have."

Reaching Milliken's Bend, on the west bank of the Mississippi ten miles above the mouth of the Yazoo, Sherman landed a brigade on Christmas Day and sent it out to wreck a section of the railroad connecting Vicksburg and Monroe, Louisiana. Next morning, while the brigade was returning, its mission accomplished, the rest of the armada proceeded downstream, entered the Yazoo, and steamed up its intricate channel. A light gunboat and an ironclad led the way, followed by twenty transports, each with two companies of riflemen charged with returning the fire of snipers. Then came another ironclad and twenty more transports, similarly protected. So it went, to the tail of the 64-boat column, until a landing was made at Johnson's Farm, on the Vicksburg shore of the Yazoo ten miles above its mouth. Alertness had paid off, or else it had been unnecessary. "Some few guerilla parties infested the banks," Sherman explained, "but did not dare to molest so strong a force as I commanded." It occurred to some of his soldiers, though, that the rebels were going to let geography do their fighting for them. Wide-eyed as the Illinois and Indiana farmboys were in this strange land, that seemed altogether possible. First there had been the big river itself — or himself; the Old Man, natives called the stream, taking their cue from the Indians, who had named it the Father of Waters — the tawny, mile-wide Mississippi, so thick with silt that recruits could almost believe the steamboat hands who solemnly assured them that if you drank its water for as much as a week "you will have a sandbar in you a mile long." Then had come the smaller stream, with its currentless bayous and mazy sloughs, whose very name was the Indian word for death. And now there was this, the land itself, spongelike under their feet as they came ashore, desolate as the back side of the moon and brooded over by cypresses and water oaks with long gray beards of Spanish moss. North was only a direction indicated by a compass — if a man had one, that is, for otherwise there was no north or south or east or west; there was only the brooding desolation. If this was the country the rebs wanted to take out of the Union, the blue-coated farmboys were ready to say good riddance.

The molestation Sherman had said the Confederates did not dare to attempt began the following day, December 27, against the navy. Commander William Gwin, a veteran of all the river fights since Fort Henry, took his ironclad *Benton* upstream to shell out some graybacks lurking in the woods on the left flank, but got caught in a narrow stretch of the river and was pounded by a battery on the bluffs. Three of the more than thirty hits came through the *Benton*'s ports, cutting her crew up badly, and Gwin, who refused to take cover in the shot-proof pilothouse — "A captain's place is on the quarterdeck," he protested when urged to step inside — was mortally wounded by an 8-inch solid that took off most of his right arm and breast, exposing the ribs and lung in a sudden flash of white and scarlet. Meanwhile the army was having its share of opposition, too, as it floundered about in the Yazoo bottoms and tried to get itself aligned for the assault on the Walnut Hills. The four division commanders, Brigadier Generals A. J. Smith, M. L. Smith, G. W. Morgan, and Frederick Steele, were in the thick of things next morning, dodging bullets like all the rest, when suddenly their number was reduced to three by a sniper who hit the second Smith in the hip joint and retired him from the campaign.

These two high-placed casualties only added to a confusion that was rife enough already. Johnson's Farm, which was little more than a patch of cleared ground in the midst of swampy woods, was separated from the hills ahead by a broad, shallow bayou, a former bed of the Yazoo, and hemmed in on the flanks by two others, Old River Bayou on the right and Chickasaw Bayou on the left. All three looked much alike to an unpracticed eye, so that there was much consequent loss of direction, misidentification of objectives, and countermarching of columns. A bridge ordered constructed over the shallow bayou to the front was built by mistake over one of the others, too late to be relaid. Whole companies got separated from their regiments and spent hours ricocheting from one alien outfit to another. As a result of all this, and more, it was Monday morning, December 29, before the objectives could be assigned and pointed out on the ground instead of on the inadequate maps. Sherman's plan for overrunning the hilltop defenses was for all four divisions to make "a show of attack along the whole front," but to concentrate his main effort at two points, half a mile apart, which seemed to him to afford his soldiers the best chance for a penetration. One of these was in front of Morgan's division, and when Sherman pointed it out to him and told him what he wanted, Morgan nodded positively. "General, in ten minutes after you give the signal I'll be on those hills," he said.

His timing was a good deal off. Except for one brigade, which "took cover behind the [opposite] bank, and could not be moved forward," as Sherman later reported in disgust, Morgan not only did not reach "those hills," he did not even get across the bayou, in ten or any other number of minutes after the signal for attack was given by the batteries all along the Federal line. Presently, however, it was demonstrated that, all in all, this was perhaps the best thing to have done in the situation in which their red-headed commander had placed them. A brigade of Steele's division, led by Brigadier General Frank Blair, Jr., a former Missouri congressman and brother of the Postmaster General, got across in good order and excellent spirits, only to encounter a savage artillery crossfire that sent it staggering back, leaving 500 killed, wounded, and captured at the point where it had been struck. One regiment kept going but was stopped by the steepness of the bluff and a battery firing directly down the throats of the attackers. With their hands they began to scoop out burrows in the face of the nearly perpendicular hillside, seeking overhead cover from enemy riflemen who held their muskets out over the parapet and fired them vertically into the huddled, frantically digging mass below. Indeed, so critical was their position, as Sherman later said, "that we could not recall the men till after dark, and then one at a time." He added, in summation of the day's activities: "Our loss had been pretty heavy, and we had accomplished nothing, and had inflicted little loss on our enemy."

"Pretty heavy" was putting it mildly, as he would discover when he found time for counting noses, but the rest of this estimation was accurate enough. Federal losses reached the commemorative figure 1776, of whom 208 were killed, 1005 were wounded, and 563 were captured or otherwise missing. The Confederates lost 207 in all: 63 killed, 134 wounded, and 10 missing.

Unwilling to let it go at that — "We will lose 5000 men before we take Vicksburg," he had said, "and may as well lose them here as anywhere else" — Sherman decided to reload Steele's division aboard transports and move it upstream for a diversionary strike in the vicinity of Haines Bluff, which might induce the defenders to weaken their present line. Porter was no less willing than before. Moreover, by way of disposing of Brown's remaining torpedoes, he conceived the idea of using one of the rams to clear the path. "I propose to sent her ahead and explode them," he explained. "If we lose her, it does not matter much." Colonel Charles R. Ellet, youthful successor to his dead father as commander of the former army vessels, did not take to this notion of a sacrificial ram. With Porter's consent, he added a 45-foot boom extending beyond the prow and equipped it with pulleys and cords and hooks for fishing up the floats and demijohns. Ram and transports set out by the dark of the moon on the last night of the year, while Sherman alerted his other three divisions for a second all-out assault on the Walnut Hills as soon as they heard the boom of guns upstream. What came instead, at 4 a.m. on New Year's Day, was a note from Steele, explaining that the boats were fog-bound and could not proceed. So Sherman called a halt and took stock. He had been waiting all this time for some word from Grant, either on the line of the Yalobusha or here on the Yazoo, but there had been nothing since the rumor of the fall of Holly Springs. From Vicksburg itself, ten air-line miles away, its steeples visible from several points along his boggy front, he had been hearing for the past three days the sound of trains arriving and departing. It might be a ruse, as at Corinth back in May. On the

other hand, it might signify what it sounded like: the arrival from
Grenada or Mobile or Chattanooga, or possibly all three, of reinforcements for the rebel garrison. Also, rain had begun to fall by now in
earnest, and looking up he saw watermarks on the trunks of trees "ten
feet above our heads." In short, as he later reported, seeing "no good
reason for remaining in so unenviable a position any longer," he "became
convinced that the part of wisdom was to withdraw."

Withdraw he did, re-embarking his soldiers the following day
and proceeding downriver without delay. There was more room on the
decks of the transports now, and Sherman was low in spirits: not
because he was dissatisfied with his direction of the attempt — "There
was no bungling on my part," he wrote, "for I never worked harder or
with more intensity of purpose in my life" — but because he knew that
the journalists, whom he had snubbed at every opportunity since their
spreading of last year's rumors that he was insane, would have a field
day writing their descriptions of his repulse and retreat. Presently he
was hailed by Porter, who signaled him to come aboard the flagship.
Sherman did so, rain-drenched and disconsolate.

"I've lost 1700 men," he said, "and those infernal reporters will
publish all over the country their ridiculous stories about Sherman being
whipped."

"Pshaw," the admiral replied. "That's nothing; simply an epi-
sode of the war. You'll lose 17,000 before the war is over and think
nothing of it. We'll have Vicksburg yet, before we die. Steward! Bring
some punch."

When he got the red-head settled down he gave him the unwelcome news that McClernand was at hand, anchored just inside the
mouth of the Yazoo and waiting to see him. Sherman, who could keep as
straight a face as his friend Grant when so inclined, afterwards remarked
of his rival's sudden but long-expected appearance on the scene: "It was
rumored he had come down to supersede me."

McClernand, too, had news for him when they met later that
day. Grant was not coming down through Mississippi; he had in fact
been in retreat for more than a week, leaving Pemberton free to concentrate for the defense of Vicksburg. Sherman suggested that this
meant that any further attempt against the town with their present force
was hopeless. Indeed, in the light of this disclosure, he began to consider
himself most fortunate in failure, even though it had cost him a total of
1848 casualties for the whole campaign. "Had we succeeded," he reasoned, "we might have found ourselves in a worse trap, when General
Pemberton was at full liberty to turn his whole force against us."

Dark-bearded McClernand agreed that the grapes were sour, at
least for now. Next day, January 3, he and Sherman withdrew their
troops from the Yazoo and rendezvoused again at Milliken's Bend,
where McClernand took command.

"Well, we have been to Vicksburg and it was too much for us and we have backed out," Sherman wrote his wife from the camp on the west bank of the Mississippi. Reporting by dispatch to Grant, however, he went a bit more into detail as to causes. "I attribute our failure to the strength of the enemy's position, both natural and artificial, and not to his superior fighting," he declared; "but as we must all in the future have ample opportunities to test this quality, it is foolish to discuss it."

Pemberton would have agreed that it was foolish to discuss it, not for the reason his adversary gave, but because he considered the question already settled. The proof of the answer, so far as he was concerned, had been demonstrated in the course of the past two weeks, during which time he had stood off and repulsed two separate Union armies, each superior in numbers to his own. What was more, he had gained new confidence in his top commanders: in Van Dorn, whose lightning raid, staged in conjunction with Forrest's in West Tennessee, had abolished the northward menace: in the on-the-spot Vicksburg defenders, Major General Martin L. Smith and Brigadier General Stephen D. Lee, who with fewer than 15,000 soldiers, most of whom had arrived at the last minute from Grenada, had driven better than twice as many bluecoats out of their side yard, inflicting in the process about nine times as many casualties as they suffered: and in himself, who had engineered the whole and had been present for both repulses. Not that he did not expect to have to fight a return engagement. He did. But he considered that this would be no more than an occasion for redemonstrating what had been proved already.

"Vicksburg is daily growing stronger," he wired Richmond soon after New Year's. "We intend to hold it."

✕ 5 ✕

Rosecrans too was aware that haste made waste, but unlike Grant he was having no part of it. In reply to Halleck's frequent urgings that he move against Bragg and Chattanooga without delay — it was for this, after all, that he had been appointed to succeed his fellow Ohioan, Don Carlos Buell, whose characteristic attitude had seemed to his superiors to be one of hesitation — he made it clear that he intended to take his time. He would move when he got ready, not before, and thus, as he put it, avoid having to "stop and tinker" along the way. His policy, he explained in a series of answers to the telegraphic nudges, was "to lull [the rebels] into security," then "press them up solidly" and "endeavor to make an end of them." When Halleck at last lost patience altogether, informing the general in early December that he had twice been asked to designate a successor for him — "If you remain one more week in

Nashville," he warned, "I cannot prevent your removal" — Rosecrans set his heels in hard and bristled back at the general-in-chief: "I need no other stimulus to make me do my duty than the knowledge of what it is. To threats of removal or the like I must be permitted to say that I am insensible."

"Old Rosy" the men called him, not only because of his colorful name, but also because of his large red nose, which one observer classified as "intensified Roman." He was a tall, hale man, a heavy drinker but withal an ardent Catholic; he carried a crucifix on his watch chain and a rosary in his pocket, and he so delighted in small-hours religious discussions that he sometimes kept his staff up half the night debating such fine points as the distinction between profanity, which he freely employed, and blasphemy, which he eschewed. One such discussion achieved marathon proportions, going on for ten nights running, and though this was hard on the staff men, who missed their sleep, Rosecrans considered the problem solved beforehand by the fact that, like himself, they were all blond; "sandy fellows," he remarked upon occasion, were "quick and sharp," and, being more industrious by nature than brunets, required less rest — although he, for his own part, often slept till noon on the day following one of the all-night sessions devoted to eschatology or the question of how many angels could stand tiptoe on a pinpoint. Like Bardolph, whom he so much resembled in physiognomy, he could swing rapidly from gloom to equanimity or from abusiveness to affability. The bristly reply to Halleck was characteristic, for he would often flare up on short notice; but he was likely to calm down just as fast. All of a sudden, on the heels of an outburst of temper, he would be all smiles and congeniality, stroking and cajoling the very man he had been reviling a moment past, and if this was sometimes confusing to those around him, it was also a rather welcome relief from the dour and noncommittal Buell. Rosecrans was forty-three, two years younger than his present opponent Bragg, who had graduated five years ahead of him at West Point, where each had stood fifth in his class. Sometimes he seemed older than his years, sometimes not, depending on his mood, but in general he was liked and even admired, especially by the volunteers, who found him approachable and amusing. For instance, he would stroll through the camps after lights-out, and if he saw a lamp still burning in one of the tents he would whack on the canvas with the flat of his sword. The response, if not blasphemous, would at any rate be profane and abusive. Prompt to apologize when they saw the red-nosed face of their general appear through the tent flap, the soldiers would explain that they had thought he was some rowdy prowling around in the dark. He took it well, including the muffled laughter that followed the extinguishing of the lamp on his departure, and the result was a steady growth of affection between him and the men of the army which Halleck was protesting he was slow to commit to battle.

That army's present over-all strength was 81,729 effectives, divided like Grant's into Left Wing, Center, and Right Wing, commanded respectively by Major Generals T. L. Crittenden, George Thomas, and Alexander McCook, all veterans of the bloody October fight at Perryville, Kentucky, under Buell. By mid-December — Halleck having more or less apologized for the previous nudgings by explaining that they had not been intended as "threats of removal or the like," but merely as expressions of the President's "great anxiety" over the fact that, Middle Tennessee being the Confederacy's only late-summer gain which had not been erased, pro-Southern members of the British parliament, scheduled to convene in January, might find in this apparent stalemate persuasive arguments for the intervention France was already urging — Rosecrans became more optimistic, despite the drouth which kept the Cumberland River too shallow for it to serve as a dependable supply line. "Things will be ripe soon," he assured his nervous superiors on the 15th, and followed this dispatch with another, put on the wire within an hour: "Rebel troops say they will fight us. . . . Cumberland still very low; rain threatens; will be ready in a few days."

The few days stretched on to Christmas, and still he had not moved. By then, however, he had received encouraging reports from scouts and spies beyond the rebel lines. In the first place, Morgan and Forrest were on the prowl, and though normally this would have been considered alarming information, in this case it was not so, for the former was now so far in his rear as not to be able to interfere with any immediate action south or east of Nashville, while the latter was clean outside his department. Whatever harm they might do in Kentucky and West Tennessee (which, as it turned out, was considerable) Rosecrans could wish them Godspeed, so long as they kept their backs in his direction. Moreover, he had learned of the visit to Murfreesboro by Jefferson Davis and the subsequent detachment of one of Bragg's six divisions to Pemberton. Now if ever was the time to strike, and the Union commander was ready. Orders went out Christmas Day for the advance to begin next morning in three columns: Crittenden on the left, marching down the Murfreesboro turnpike through La Vergne and paralleling the Nashville & Chattanooga Railroad; McCook in the middle, cross-country through Nolensville; Thomas on the right, due south through Brentwood, then eastward across McCook's rear to take his rightful position in the center. Each of the three "wings" was well below its normal three-divisional strength because of guard detachments. Thomas, for example, had left a whole division on garrison duty at Nashville, in case Morgan or Forrest turned back or some other pack of raiders struck in that direction while the main body was attending to Bragg, and Crittenden and McCook were almost equally reduced by piecemeal detachments on similar duty elsewhere along the lines of supply and communication. The result was that Rosecrans had barely

44,000 troops in his three columns — Crittenden 14,500, Thomas — 13,500, McCook 16,000 — or only a little more than half of his total effective strength. But he was not ruffled by this reduction of the numerical odds in his favor; he knew that he was still a good deal stronger than his opponent. What was more, his deliberate preparations had paid off. Not only would he be free of the necessity to "stop and tinker" for lack of engineering equipment; he had within reach "the essentials of ammunition and twenty days' rations." Thus he had notified Washington on Christmas Eve, while planning the movement of his eight attack divisions, and he added in regard to the enemy, thirty miles southeastward down the pike: "If they meet us, we shall fight tomorrow; if they wait for us, next day."

It was neither "tomorrow" nor the "next day" — which was in fact the day he actually got started. Nor was it the day after that, or the day after that, or even the day after that. Still, Rosecrans was not unduly perturbed. Delay had already gained him much, including the loss by the Confederates of one infantry division and two brigades of cavalry; further delay might gain him more. Such was not the case, as it turned out, but what fretted him most just now was the slashing efficiency of the cavalry retained by Bragg, which cost the advancing Federals portions of their wagon train, as well as isolated detachments of their own horsemen assigned to protect the flanks and rear of the main body, slogging forward in three columns. As these drew near Murfreesboro on the 29th and 30th, consolidating at last to form a continuous line of battle along the west bank of the south fork of Stones River, two miles short of the town, they began to encounter infantry resistance, spasmodic at first and then determined, which seemed to promise fulfillment of the vow Rosecrans had passed along to Halleck two weeks before: "Rebel troops say they will fight us." However, he had followed this with a vow of his own, which he also believed was moving toward fulfillment: "If we beat them, I shall try to drive them to the wall."

Bragg had 37,713 effectives, well under half as many as his opponent, but he had them all at hand, with the result that the attackers were only about fifteen percent stronger than the defenders. Not that he considered himself committed to the tactical defensive. If the opportunity arose he intended to hit Rosecrans first, and hard. By way of preparation, however, he wanted him within reach, and therefore he gave his outpost commanders instructions to offer the advancing blue columns no more than a token resistance. "General Bragg sent us word not to fight them too much, but to let them come on," one gray cavalryman afterwards recalled.

In the course of the four-day Federal approach march — which was impeded, but not "too much," by the nearly 4000 troopers under

Brigadier General Joseph Wheeler — Bragg assembled his 34,000 infantry at Murfreesboro, the center of the wide arc along which his five divisions had been disposed so as to cover the roads out of Nashville. Lieutenant General Leonidas Polk's two-division corps was there already, and Lieutenant General William J. Hardee's came in on December 28 from Triune, fifteen miles west. With the arrival next day of Major General John McCown's division from Readyville, a dozen miles east, the concentration was complete, and the army formed for combat astride Stones River, which was fordable at practically all points because of the drouth. Hardee was on the right, northwest of the town and with a bend of the river to his front; Polk was on the left, due west of the town and with another bend of the river to his rear; McCown was in reserve behind the center, which

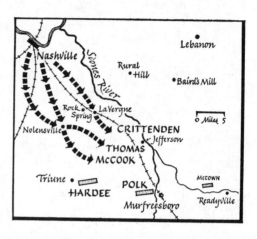

was pierced by the Nashville turnpike and the Nashville & Chattanooga Railroad, pointing arrow-straight in the direction from which Rosecrans was expected. Except for Wheeler's horsemen, who, now that the consolidation of the infantry had been effected with time to spare, were turned loose with a vengeance on the flanks and rear of the still approaching Federals, the Confederates settled down to wait for the opening of the battle everyone knew was about to be fought.

Many of them — particularly the officers, whose opportunities were larger in this respect — were still suffering from the aftereffects of a Christmas which they had celebrated with the fervor of men who knew only too well that the chances were strong that it would be their last. "I felt feeble," a Georgia lieutenant wrote in his diary the morning after, "but, being anxious to be with my men, reported for duty." Things had been that way for weeks now. Murfreesboro, a former state capital named for a colonel in the Revolution, was a lively place whose citizens, decidedly pro-rebel no matter which army happened to be in occupation, afforded their gray-clad defenders entertainments and amusements of all kinds, including horse races, balls, whist parties, and midnight gatherings in their parlors. President Davis's visit, two weeks before, had been the occasion for much rejoicing and pride, but all agreed that the social high point of the season had been the marriage on December 14, the day after the President's departure, of John Morgan and a local belle. Spirited in her defense of all things southern, when she heard some northern officers disparaging the raider during the Union occupation the previous summer, she told them off so roundly that one of the bluecoats asked her name. "It's Mattie Ready now," she said. "But by the grace of God one day I hope to call myself the wife of John Morgan." Hearing the story, the widower cavalryman came to call on her as soon as the town was again in southern hands, and in due time — for the young lady was apparently as skilled in her brand of tactics as the colonel was in his — they became engaged. Because of the size of the guest list, which included Bragg and his ranking commanders, Morgan's fellow officers and kinsmen from Kentucky, and a host of civilians invited from round about by the bride's family, the wedding was held in the courtroom of the Murfreesboro courthouse, Leonidas Polk officiating and wearing over the uniform of a Confederate lieutenant general the vestments of an Episcopal bishop. Thus it was that Mattie Ready, by the grace of God, became Mrs John Hunt Morgan.

Within a week, apparently not content with his exploit at Hartsville earlier that month, the bridegroom was off on what would be known as his Christmas Raid, a twofold celebration of his marriage and the brigadier's commission recently handed him by the President himself. His goal, assigned by Bragg, was Rosecrans' supply line, specifically the Louisville & Nashville Railroad north of Bowling Green, with particular attention to be paid to the great trestles at Muldraugh's Hill. He left Alexandria, thirty miles northeast of Murfreesboro, on December 21 with 2500 horsemen, crossed the Cumberland the following day, and re-entered his home state the day after that. Passing through Glasgow on the 24th, he forded the Green on Christmas Day, skirmishing as he went and taking prisoners by the hundreds, and struck suddenly north of Munfordville to lay siege to the Federal garrison at Elizabethtown, which surrendered on the 27th, opening the way to Muldraugh's Hill, where the garrison also surrendered. After burning the trestles, enormous structures five hundred feet long and eighty feet tall, he continued east through Bardstown to Springfield, then turned south, skirting heavily garrisoned Lebanon and fighting off pursuers for a getaway through Campbellsville, Columbia, and Burkesville, to reach Smithville, Tennessee, on January 5, fifteen miles southeast of his starting point at Alexandria. In two weeks, having covered better than 400 miles, he had fought four engagements and numerous skirmishes. At a total cost of 2 men killed and 24 wounded, plus about 300 stragglers — victims not of enemy guns but of the weather, which was bitter, and of confiscated bourbon — he had destroyed the vital railroad trestles and four important bridges, along with an estimated $2,000,000 in Union stores, and had torn up more than twenty miles of L&N track, while capturing and paroling 1887 enemy soldiers.

Joe Wheeler, West Point '59, was not to be outdone by Morgan or Forrest, who were his subordinates as a result of Bragg's appointment of the twenty-six-year-old Georgian as commander of all the cavalry in the Army of Tennessee. Unleashed on the night of December 29, after screening the concentration of the gray infantry in his rear and delaying the advance of the blue columns to his front, he rode north on the Lebanon pike with 2000 troopers, then swung west to Jefferson, where he attacked a brigade of infantry on the march and gobbled up a 20-wagon segment of Crittenden's supply train. At La Vergne by noon, halfway to Nashville and well in the Union rear, he captured and burned McCook's whole train of 300 wagons, packed with stores valued by Wheeler at "many hundred thousands of dollars," and paroled 700 prisoners, including the teamsters and their escort. "The turnpike, as far as the eye could reach, was filled with burning wagons," a Federal officer reported when he rode through the town next morning and surveyed the ruin the graybacks left behind. "The country was over-spread with disarmed men [and] broken-down horses and mules. The streets were covered with empty valises and trunks, knapsacks, broken guns, and all the indescribable débris of a captured and rifled army train." Wheeler and his horsemen were over the southwest horizon by then, having taken two more trains, one at Rock Spring and another at Nolensville. Beyond there, more prisoners were paroled while the weary raiders snatched a few hours' sleep before swinging back into their saddles and heading east for Murfreesboro to rejoin the infantry drawn up along Stones River. Completing his two-day circuit of Rose-crans — in the course of which he had captured more than a thousand men, destroyed all or parts of four wagon trains, brought off enough rifles and carbines to arm a brigade, remounted all of his troopers who needed fresh horses, and left a train of devastation along both flanks and around the rear of the entire Union army — Wheeler made contact with Bragg's left at 2 a.m. on the last day of the year, in time for a share in the battle which was now about to open.

A certain amount of reshuffling had occurred during his absence. Rosecrans, coming forward with his main body on the 30th while Wheeler was clawing at his flanks and rear, put his three corps in line, left to right, Crittenden and Thomas and McCook, the first opposite Hardee, the second opposite Polk, and the third — the largest of the three — opposite nothing more than a thin line of skirmishers extend-ing the rebel left. Because of skillful screening by the gray cavalry during the approach march, the Federal commander was not aware of the opportunity he had created for a lunge straight into Murfreesboro around the Confederate flank; but Bragg was, and he moved at once to correct his dispositions, shifting McCown's reserve division from its post behind the center to a position on Polk's left, extending his line of battle southward to meet the threat. Rosecrans meanwhile was plan-ning and issuing orders for an attack. His intention was to execute a right wheel, sending Crittenden forward on the north, with instructions to pivot on the left of Thomas, who would also move forward in sequence to assist in the capture of the town, cutting the rebels off from their supplies and setting them up for annihilation. McCook was thus to serve as anchor man. "If the enemy attacks you," Rosecrans told him, "fall back slowly, refusing your right, contesting the ground inch by inch. If the enemy does not attack you, you will attack him, not vigorously but warmly." As an added piece of deception, McCook was ordered about 6 p.m. to build a line of fires beyond his right, simulating a prolongation of his line so as to draw Bragg's attention away from the main effort at the far end of the field.

The southern commander was indeed deceived, and quite as thoroughly as Rosecrans had intended, but his reaction was something different from what the northern commander had hoped for. Or, rather, it was what he had hoped for, only more so. When Bragg observed the fires and heard sounds of movement on the Federal right, not only did he take the bait, but he proceeded, so to speak, to run away with it. Devising an offensive of his own to meet what he conceived to be a new threat to his left, he instructed Hardee, whose two divisions were under Major Generals John C. Breckinridge and Patrick R. Cleburne, to leave the former posted where it was, guarding the river crossings on the right, and move the latter southward to a position in support of McCown, who had been shifted earlier that day. Hardee himself was to come along, moreover, and take command of these two divisions on the left for a slashing assault on the Federals seemingly massed in that direction. Bragg's plans called for a right wheel by both corps on the west bank of Stones River, with the pivot on Polk's right division near the Nashville pike, the brigades attacking in rapid sequence from left to right, obliquing northward as they advanced, in order to throw the bluecoats back against the stretch of river whose crossings were covered by Breckinridge's guns and infantry.

Just before tattoo, while this additional shift was being completed under cover of darkness and orders were going out for the assault next morning, the military bands of both armies began to play their respective favorite tunes. Carrying sweet and clear on the windless wintry air, the music of any one band was about as audible on one side of the line as on the other, and the concert thus became something of a contest, a musical bombardment. "Dixie" answered the taunting "Yankee Doodle"; "Hail Columbia" followed "The Bonnie Blue Flag." Finally, though, one group of musicians began to play the familiar "Home Sweet Home," and one by one the others took it up, until at last all the bands of both armies were playing the song. Soldiers on both sides of the battle line began to sing the words, swelling the chorus east and west, North and South. As it died away on the final line — "There's no-o place like home" — the words caught in the throats of men, who, bluecoat and butternut alike, would be killing each other tomorrow in what already gave promise of being one of the bloodiest battles in that fratricidal war.

★ ★ ★

As at First Manassas, a year and a half ago, both commanders had identical plans of battle: in this case, an advance on the left to strike the enemy right. Here as there, if they had moved simultaneously, the two armies might have grappled and swung round and round, like a pair of dancers clutching each other and twirling to the accompaniment of cannon. So it might have been, but it was not. For one thing, the lines were closer together on the south than on the north, and there was no natural obstacle such as the river to delay the Confederate attack in its initial stages. For another, with his usual attention to preparatory matters, Rosecrans had told his generals to advance as soon as possible after breakfast; whereas Bragg, with less concern for the creature comforts, had called for a dawn assault, and that was what he got.

McCown went forward in the steely twilight before sunrise, Cleburne following 400 yards behind. Between them they had 10,000 men and McCook had 16,000, but the latter were still preparing breakfast when the rebel skirmishers, preceding a long gray double line of infantry extending left and right, shoulder to shoulder as far as the eye could reach, broke through the cedar thickets and bore down on them, yelling. Coming as it did, with all the advantage of surprise, the charge was well-nigh irresistible. A Tennessee private later recalled that his brigade, in the front rank of the attackers, "swooped down on those Yankees like a whirl-a-gust of woodpeckers in a hail storm." The fact was, in this opening phase, everything went so smoothly for the aggressors that even their mistakes seemed to work to their advantage. When McCown, who had had little combat experience, having been left behind in command of Knoxville during the invasion of Kentucky, drifted wide because he neglected to oblique to the right as instructed, Pat Cleburne, whose soldierly qualities had grown steadily since Shiloh despite the wounds he had taken at Richmond and Perryville, moved neatly forward into the gap without even the need to pause for alignment. Advancing on this extended front the two divisions swept everything before them, their captures including several front-line batteries taken before the cannoneers could leap to their posts and get a round off. Such knots of bluecoats as managed to form for individual resistance in clumps of cedar or behind outcroppings of rock, finding themselves suddenly outflanked on the left or right, cried as they had cried under Buell twelve weeks before: "We are sold! Sold again!" and broke for the rear, discarding their weapons as they ran.

McCook's three divisions, on line from right to left under Brigadier Generals R. W. Johnson, Jefferson Davis, and Philip Sheridan, caught the full force of the initial assault. Johnson and Davis were under personal clouds, the former because he had been captured by Morgan early that month and exchanged on the eve of battle, the latter because of his assassination of Major General William Nelson in a Lousiville hotel lobby back in September; but they had little chance to earn redemption here. Johnson's division, on the far right of the army, practically disintegrated on contact, losing within the opening half-hour more than half its members by sudden death, injury, or capture. Davis, next in line, fared scarcely better, though most of his men at least had time to put up a show of resistance before falling back, dribbling skulkers as they went. That left Sheridan. As pugnacious here as he had been at Perryville, where he first attracted general attention, the bandy-legged, bullet-headed Ohioan was determined to yield no ground except under direct pressure, and only then when that pressure buckled his knees. "Square-shouldered, muscular, wiry to the last degree, and as nearly insensible to hardship and fatigue as is consistent with humanity" — thus a staff man saw him here, on the eve of his thirty-second birthday — he rode his lines, calling on his men to stand firm while the storm of battle drew nearer, then broke in fury against his front.

Polk's corps, with its two divisions under Major Generals J. M. Withers and Benjamin Cheatham, had taken up the assault by now, and it was Withers who struck Sheridan first — and suffered the first Confederate repulse. The Federals were in a position described by one of its defenders as "a confused mass of rock, lying in slabs, and boulders interspersed with holes, fissures, and caverns which would have made progress over it extremely difficult even if there had been no timber." But there was timber, a thick tangle of cedars whose trunks "ran straight up into the air so near together that the sunlight was obscured." Fighting here, with all that was happening on the right or left hidden from them "except as we could gather it from the portentous avalanches of sound which assailed us from every direction," Sheridan's men repulsed three separate charges by Withers. Then Cheatham came up. A veteran of Mexico and all the army's battles since Belmont, where he had saved the day, Cheatham was forty-two, a native Tennessean, and had earned the distinction of being the most profane man in the Army of Tennessee, despite the disadvantage in this respect of having as his corps commander the distinguished and watchful Bishop of Louisiana. "Give 'em hell, boys!" he shouted as he led his division forward. Polk, who was riding beside him, approved of the intention if not of the unchurchly language. "Give them what General Cheatham says, boys!" he cried. "Give them what General Cheatham says!"

That was what they gave them, though they received in return a goodly measure of the same. Sheridan, down to his last three rounds and having lost the first of his three brigade commanders, his West Point classmate Brigadier General Joshua Sill — he would lose the other two before the day was over — fell back under knee-buckling pressure from Cheatham in front and Cleburne on the flank, abandoning eight guns in the thicket for lack of horses to draw them off. He then replenished his ammunition and took a position back near the Nashville turnpike, facing south and east alongside Brigadier General J. S. Negley's division, one of the two belonging to Thomas, who had been forced to give ground during the struggle. It was now about 10 o'clock; Bragg's initial objectives had been attained, along with the capture of 28 guns and no less than 3000 soldiers. The enemy right had been driven three miles and the center had also given way, until now the Union line of battle resembled a half-closed jackknife, most of it being at right angles to its original position. Bragg was about to open the second phase, intending to break the knife at the critical juncture of blade and handle; after which would come the third phase, the mop-up.

Rosecrans meanwhile had used to good advantage the interlude afforded him by Sheridan's resistance, though it was not until the battle had been raging for more than an hour that he realized he was face to face with probable disaster. For some time, indeed, having joined Crittenden on the left so as to supervise the opening attack, he assumed that what was occurring on the right — the uproar being considerably diminished by distance and acoustical peculiarities — was in accordance with his instructions to McCook, whereby Bragg had been deceived

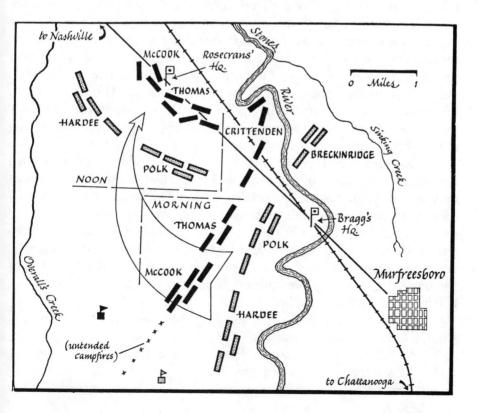

into stripping the flank about to be assaulted, in order to bolster the flank beyond which the untended campfires had been kindled the night before. One of Crittenden's divisions was already crossing Stones River, and he was preparing to follow with the other two. Not even the arrival of a courier from McCook, informing Rosecrans that he was being assailed and needed reinforcements, changed the Federal commander's belief in this regard.

"Tell General McCook to contest every inch of ground," he told the courier, repeating his previous instructions. "If he holds them we will swing into Murfreesboro with our left and cut them off." To his staff he added, with apparent satisfaction: "It's working right."

Discovering presently, however, that it was "working" not for him but for Bragg, who was using his own battle plan against him and had got the jump in the process — with the result that McCook, far from being able to conduct an inch-by-inch defense, had lost control of two of his three divisions before he was able to conduct a defense that was even mile-by-mile — Rosecrans reacted fast. To one observer he seemed "profoundly moved," but that was putting it rather mildly. Even his florid nose "had paled and lost its ruddy luster," the officer added, the glow apparently having been transferred to his eyes, which "blazed with sullen fire." Canceling the advance on the left, he told Crittenden to send the two uncrossed divisions of Brigadier Generals John Palmer and Thomas Wood to reinforce the frazzled right. Brigadier General Horatio Van Cleve's division was to be recalled from the opposite bank of the river and sent without delay after the others, except for one brigade which would be left to guard against a crossing, in case the rebels tried to follow up the withdrawal in this quarter. Crittenden passed the word at once, and: "Goodbye, General," Wood replied as he set out in the direction of the uproar, which now was swelling louder as it drew nearer. "We'll all meet at the hatter's, as one coon said to another when the dogs were after them."

Rosecrans had no time for jokes. His exclusive concern just now was the salvation of his army, and it seemed to him that there was only one way for this to be accomplished. "This battle must be won," he said. He intended to see personally to all the dispositions, especially on the crumbling right, but first he needed a feeling of security on the left — if for no other purpose than to be able to forget it. Accordingly, accompanied by his chief of staff, he rode to the riverbank position of the one brigade Van Cleve had left behind to prevent a rebel crossing, and inquired who commanded.

"I do, sir," a colonel said, stepping forward. He was Samuel W. Price, a Union-loyal Kentuckian.

"Will you hold this ford?" Rosecrans asked him.

"I will try, sir," Price replied.

Unsatisfied, Rosecrans repeated: "Will you hold this ford?"

"I will die right here," the colonel answered stoutly.

Still unsatisfied, for he was less interested in the Kentuckian's willingness to lay down his life than he was in his ability to prevent a rebel crossing, the general pressed the question a third time: "Will you hold this ford?"

"Yes, sir," Price said.

"That will do," Rosecrans snapped, and having at last got the answer he wanted, turned his horse and galloped off.

As he drew near the tumult of battle, which by now was approaching the turnpike on the right, he received another shock in the form of a cannonball which, narrowly missing him, tore off the head of his chief of staff, riding beside him, and so bespattered Rosecrans that whoever saw him afterwards that morning assumed at first sight that he was badly wounded. "Oh, no," he would say, in response to expressions of concern. "That is the blood of poor Garesché." However, this did nothing to restrict or slow his movements; he would not even pause to change his coat. "At no one time, and I rode with him during most of the day," a signal officer afterwards reported, "do I remember of his having been one half-hour at the same place." To Crittenden, whose troops he was using as a reserve in order to shore up the line along the turnpike, he "seemed ubiquitous," and to another observer he appeared "as firm as iron and fixed as fate" as he moved about the field, rallying panicked men and hoicking them into line. "This battle must be won," he kept repeating.

Arriving in time to meet Sheridan, who had just been driven back, he directed him to refill his cartridge boxes from the ammunition train and to fall in alongside Negley and Major General Lovell Rousseau, commanding Thomas's other division. As a result of such stopgap improvisations, adopted amid the confusion of retreat, there was much intermingling of units and a resultant loss of control by division and corps commanders. Some of Crittenden's brigades were on the right with McCook, who had set up a straggler line along which he was doing what he could to rally the remnants of Johnson and Davis, and some of McCook's brigades were on the left with Crittenden, who was nervously making his dispositions on unfamiliar ground. Between them, with his two divisions consolidated and supported by Van Cleve, George Thomas was calm as always, whatever the panic all around him. Where his left joined Crittenden's right there was a salient, marking the point where the half-closed knife blade joined the handle, and within this angle, just east of the pike and on both sides of the railroad, there was a slight elevation inclosed by a circular four-acre clump of cedars, not unlike the one Sheridan had successfully defended against three separate all-out rebel assaults that morning. Known locally as the Round Forest, this tree-choked patch of rocky earth was presently dubbed "Hell's Half-Acre" by the soldiers; for it was here that Bragg seemed most determined to score a breakthrough, despite the heavy concentration of artillery of all calibers which Rosecrans had massed on the high ground directly in its rear.

He struck first, and hard, with a brigade of Mississippians from Withers. They surged forward across fields of unpicked cotton, yelling as they had yelled at Shiloh, where they had been the farthest to advance, and were staggered by rapid-fire volleys from fifty guns ranked hub to hub on the high ground just beyond the clump of dark-green trees. At that point-blank range, one cannoneer remarked, the Federal batteries "could not fire amiss." Deafened by the uproar, the Confederates plucked cotton from the fallen bolls and stuffed it in their ears. Still they came on — to be met, halfway across, by sheets of musketry from the blue infantry close-packed under cover of the cedars; whereupon, some regiments having lost as many as half a dozen color-bearers, the Mississippians wavered and fell back, leaving a third of their number dead or wounded in the furrows or lying crosswise to the blasted rows. Next to try it, about noon, was a Tennessee brigade from Cheatham, which lately had helped throw Sheridan out of a similar position. They charged through the rattling dry brown stalks, yelling with all the frenzy of those who had come this way before, but with no better luck. They too were repulsed, and with even crueler losses. More than half of the men of the 16th Tennessee were casualties, while the 8th Tennessee lost 306 out of the 424 who had started across the fields in an attempt to drive the bluecoats out of the Round Forest.

Bragg was by no means resigned, as yet, to the fact that this could not be done. Though he had no reserves at hand — McCown and Cleburne were still winded from their long advance, around and over the original Federal right, and Withers and Cheatham had just been fought to a frazzle by the newly established left — the five-brigade division of Breckinridge, the largest in the army, was still posted beyond the river, having contributed nothing to the victory up to this point except the shells its batteries had been throwing from an east-bank hill which the former Vice President had been instructed to hold at all costs, as "the key to the position." So far, he had had no trouble doing this, despite an early-morning cavalry warning that a large body of enemy troops had crossed the river well upstream and was headed in his direction. This was of course Van Cleve's division, whose advance had been spotted promptly, but whose subsequent withdrawal had gone unnoticed or at any rate unreported; so that when Bragg's order came, about 1 o'clock, for him to leave one brigade to guard the right while he marched to the support of Polk and Hardee with the other four, Breckinridge was alarmed and sent back word that it was he who needed reinforcements; the enemy, in heavy force, was moving upon him even now, intending to challenge his hold on "the key to the position." Bragg's reply was a peremptory repetition of the order, which left the Kentuckian no choice except to obey. He sent two brigades at 2 o'clock, and followed with the other two himself, about an hour later.

That way, they came up piecemeal, and piecemeal they were fed into the hopper. The Federals, allowed an hour or more in which to improve their dispositions in the Round Forest and replenish the ammunition for the guns posted just behind it, caught the third wave of attackers much as they had caught the first and second, naked in the open fields, with devastating effect. Here again there was no lack of valor. One defender said of the charge that it was "without doubt the most daring, courageous, and best-executed attack which the Confederates made on our line between pike and river." But it broke in blood, as the others had done, and the survivors fell back across the fields, leaving their dead and wounded behind with the dead and wounded Tennesseans and Mississippians. Again there was a lull, until about 4 o'clock, when the last two brigades arrived from Breckinridge and the fourth gray wave rolled out across the fields of cotton.

"The battle had hushed," a Union brigadier reported, "and the dreadful splendor of this advance can only be conceived, as all descriptions must fall vastly short." While the attackers moved forward, "steadily, and, as it seemed, to certain victory," he added, "I sent back all my remaining staff successively to ask for support, and braced up my own lines as perfectly as possible." The bracing served its purpose; for though the defenders suffered heavily, too — it was here that Sheridan lost the third of his three brigade commanders — the charge was repulsed quite as decisively as the others. The sun went down at 4.30 and the racket died away. After eleven hours of uproar, a mutual hush fell over the glades and copses, and the brief winter twilight faded into the darkness before moonrise.

Bragg's losses had been heavy — about 9000 — but he had reason to believe that the enemy's, which included several thousand prisoners, had been much heavier. Moreover, in thus reversing the usual casualty ratio between attacker and defender, he had not only foiled the attempt to throw him out of his position covering Murfreesboro and Chattanooga; he had overrun the original Union position at every point where he had applied pressure, driving major portions of the blue line as far as three miles backward and taking guns and colors in abundance as he went. By all the logic of war, despite their stubborn stand that afternoon in the Round Forest, the Federals were whipped, and now they would have to accept the consequences. As Bragg saw it, they had little choice in this respect. They could stay and suffer further reverses, amounting in the end to annihilation; or they could retreat, hoping to find sanctuary in the Nashville intrenchments. Perhaps because it was the one he himself would have chosen, he believed the latter course to be the one Rosecrans was most likely to adopt. At any rate, this opinion seemed presently to have been confirmed by the arrival of outpost reports informing him that long lines of wagons had been heard rumbling through the darkness behind the Union lines and along the Nashville pike. Elated by this apparent chance to catch the northern army strung out on the roads and ripe for slaughter, Bragg prepared to follow in the morning. Proudly reviewing today's accomplishments while anticipating tomorrow's, he got off a wire to Richmond before he went to bed: "The enemy has yielded his strong position and is falling back. We occupy whole field and shall follow him.... God has granted us a happy New Year."

He was mistaken, at least in part. The rumble of wagons, northwestward along the turnpike, had not signified an attempt on the part of the Federal commander to save his trains before the commencement of a general retreat, but rather was the sound made by a long cavalcade of wounded — part of today's total of about 12,000 Union casualties — being taken back to the Tennessee capital for treatment in the military hospitals established there as another example of foresight and careful preparation. Not that Rosecrans had given no thought to a withdrawal. He had indeed. In fact, in an attempt to make up his mind as to the wisdom of retreating, he was holding a council of war to debate the matter and share the responsibility of the decision, even as Bragg was composing his victory message. It was a stormy night, rain beating hard on the roof of the cabin which Rosecrans had selected the day before as his headquarters beside the Nashville pike, never suspecting that the battle line would be drawn today practically on its doorstep. All three of his corps commanders were present, along with a number of their subordinates, and all presented a rather bedraggled aspect, "battered as to hats, tousled as to hair, torn as to clothes, and depressed as to spirits." An adjutant in attendance described them thus, and added: "If there was a cheerful-expressioned face present I did not see it."

After a long silence, broken only by the drumming of rain on shingles, Rosecrans began the questioning, addressing the several generals in turn, clockwise as they sat about the room. "General McCook, have you any suggestions for tomorrow?" Smooth-shaven and round-faced, the thirty-one-year-old McCook was somewhat more subdued tonight than he had been on the night after Perryville — where, as here, his had been the corps that was surprised and routed — but he showed by his reply that at least a part of his rollicking nature still remained. "No," he said. "Only I would like for Bragg to pay me for my two horses lost today." Others were gloomier and more forthright, advising retreat as the army's best way out its predicament. Characteristically, George Thomas had fallen asleep in his chair before the discussion got well under way. When the word "retreat" came through to him, he opened his eyes. "This army doesn't retreat," he muttered, and fell back into the sleep he had emerged from. The discussion thus interrupted was resumed, but it led to no clear-cut decision before the council broke up and the commanders returned to their units. Except for incidental tactical adjustments, specifically authorized from above, they would hold their present positions through tomorrow, unless they received alternate instructions before dawn.

Still undecided, Rosecrans rode out for a midnight inspection of his lines, in the course of which he looked out across the fields and saw an alarming sight. On the far side of Overall's Creek, which crossed the turnpike at right angles and covered his right flank and rear, firebrands were moving in the night. The explanation was actually simple: Federal cavalrymen, suffering from the cold, had disobeyed orders against kindling fires and were carrying brands from point to point along the outpost line: but Rosecrans, never suspecting that his orders would be flaunted in this fashion, assumed that they were rebels. "They have got entirely in our rear," he said, "and are forming line of battle by torchlight!" With retreat no longer even a possibility, let alone an alternative — or so at any rate he thought — he returned at once to army headquarters and, adopting the dramatic phraseology of the Kentucky colonel which he had rejected that morning beside the upper Stones River ford, sent word for his subordinates to "prepare to fight or die."

Except for the surgeons and the men they worked on, blue and gray, whose screams broke through the singing of the bone saws, both sides were bedded down by now amid the wreckage and the corpses, preparing to sleep out as best they could the last night of the year. Simultaneously, from a balcony of the Mobile Battle House, Jefferson Davis lifted the hearts of his listeners with a review of recent Confederate successes, unaware that even as he spoke the list was about to be lengthened by John Magruder, whose two-boat navy of cotton-clads was steaming down Buffalo Bayou to recapture Galveston. Lee's Army of Northern Virginia still occupied the field of its two-weeks-old long-odds victory on the southwest bank of the Rappahannock, and the Federal invaders from coastal North Carolina were back beneath the shelter of their siege guns, licking the wounds they had suffered in their repulse along the Neuse. In North Mississippi, where Van Dorn was resting his troopers after their exploits in Holly Springs and beyond the Tennessee line, Grant was in retreat on Memphis, while Sherman, three hundred winding miles downriver, was counting his casualties under Chickasaw Bluff and preparing to give it one more try before falling back down the Yazoo to meet the general whose army he had kidnaped and depleted to no avail. Forrest and Morgan, the former moving east from Parker's Crossroads, the latter riding south through Campbellsville, both having eluded their pursuers, were returning in triumph from disruptive raids on their respective home regions in West Tennessee and Kentucky. In all these scattered theaters, where so recently the Confederacy had seemed at best to be approaching near-certain disaster, fortune had smiled on southern arms; yet nowhere did her smile seem broader than here, southeast of Nashville and northwest of vital Chattanooga, where Bragg with such alacrity had snatched up the gage flung down by Rosecrans and struck him smartly with it, first on the flank, a smashing blow, and then between the eyes. Now both rested from their injuries and exertions. Wrapped in their blankets, those who had them, the soldiers of both armies huddled close to fires they had kindled against orders. The waxing moon set early and the wind veered and blew coldly from the north; the screams of the wounded died away with the singing of the bone saws. Unlike the night before, on the eve of carnage, there were no serenades tonight, no mingled choruses of "Home Sweet Home," for even the bandsmen had fought in this savage battle, and expected to have to fight again tomorrow, bringing in the new year as they had ushered out the old.

★ ★ ★

So they thought; but they were wrong, at least so far as the schedule was concerned. Though there were tentative skirmishes, fitful exchanges of artillery fire, and some readjustment of the tactical dispositions on both sides, New Year's Day saw nothing like the carnival of death that had been staged on New Year's Eve. In point of fact, the two armies were rather like two great jungle cats who, having fought to mutual exhaustion, were content — aside, that is, from the more or less secret hope on the part of each that the other would slink away — to eye one another balefully, limiting their actions to licking their wounds and emitting only occasional growls and rumbles, while storing up strength to resume the mortal contest.

Considerably surprised, in the light of last night's cavalry reports of a withdrawal, to find the enemy not only still there, but still there in line of battle, Bragg sent Polk forward about midmorning to discover what effect a prod would have. He soon found out. Though the troops moved unopposed into the Round Forest, which Rosecrans had ordered evacuated so as to straighten out his line, and which in turn gave validity to the bishop's subsequent claim that "the opening of the new year found us masters of the field," Polk encountered resistance just beyond it too stiff to permit his men to emerge from the woods on the far side. All he had gained for his pains were more blue corpses, along with the unwelcome task of digging their graves in order to rid his nostrils of their stench. Likewise, on the Union left, Rosecrans advanced Van Cleve's division — now under Colonel Samuel Beatty; Van Cleve had caught a bullet in the leg — beyond Stones River, retracing the route it had taken the previous morning by moving today into the vacuum created by the withdrawal of Breckinridge the afternoon before, and occupied a hill overlooking the ford. These were the only major read-adjustments, North or South, though the Federals were reinforced by a brigade arrived from Nashville, accompanied as one officer said by "an army of stragglers" picked up along the pike. For the most part, the soldiers on both sides roved the field, looking for fallen comrades among the wounded and the slain. The search for food was even more intensive, and for once, as a result of Wheeler's depredations in the course of his prebattle ride around the Union forces, the Yankees were worse off in this respect than the rebels. One brigade commander later recorded that he made his supper off a piece of raw pork and a few crackers he found in his pocket. No food had ever tasted sweeter, he declared. Even so high-ranking an officer as Crittenden was not exempt from want, but as he went to bed, complaining of hunger pangs, he was delighted to hear his orderly say he could get him "a first-rate beefsteak." The Kentuckian accepted the offer gladly, and presently, when the promised meal was brought, consumed it with gusto — only to learn next morning that the "beefsteak" had been cut from a horse that had been killed in the battle. "I didn't know this at the time I ate it," he afterwards explained, somewhat ruefully.

Day ended; night came down. Although Rosecrans had no apparent notion of resuming the offensive, or indeed any definite plan at all beyond holding onto the ground he had fallen back to, he was pleased to have had this day-long opportunity to consolidate his forces and recover in some measure from the shock to his army and his nervous system. Bragg on the other hand seemed to have no more of a plan than his opponent. Convinced that he had won a victory, he apparently did not know what to do with it beyond setting various details to work collecting the arms and matériel scattered about the field and paroling the thousands of captives he had taken the day before. What he mainly wanted, still, was for the enemy to admit defeat by retreating, and thus substantiate his claim; then he would follow, as he had promised in his wire to Richmond, hoping to catch the blue mass in motion on the pike and tear its flanks and rear, which now were inaccessible to him beyond the guns parked hub to hub behind the long lines of close-spaced bayonets weaving in and out of the cedar brakes and among the gray outcroppings of rock that scarred the landscape. The prospect was altogether grim. After nightfall, however, he was again encouraged by cavalry reports that well-guarded Federal trains were in motion on the roads leading back to Nashville. If this meant what Bragg hoped it did, that the Unionists were finally admitting they were whipped and were preparing to retire, bag and baggage, he would be up and after them tomorrow.

Tomorrow's dawn showed the prospect unimproved. Whatever might be moving along the rearward roads, the bayonets defining the Union front glinted quite as close-spaced as ever and the guns frowned every bit as grim. In fact, as Bragg conducted a personal in-

spection of his lines that morning, combining with it a long-range bin-
ocular reconnaissance of the enemy position, he began to perceive that,
despite his bloodless occupation of the Round Forest, which increased
his claim to the honors of the field, it was his own army which was in the
graver danger as a result of yesterday's tactical readjustments. The advance of Van Cleve's division, which put it in possession of the
hill just east of the river, gave him particular concern. Artillery emplaced on that height could fire across the stream and enfilade Polk's
flank if he attempted to advance. With this in mind, Bragg decided the
enemy guns must be dislodged. Accordingly he sent for Breckinridge,
whose troops had returned to their east-bank position north of Murfreesboro, along a ridge about a mile short of the hill overlooking the
ford. When the former Vice President reached army headquarters, under a large sycamore that stood alongside the Nashville pike just west of
the wrecked bridge that had spanned Stones River, Bragg told him what
he wanted. He was going to resume the offensive by sending Polk forward, he explained. First, though, he wanted Van Cleve's men flung off
the dominant height. This was admittedly a tough assignment, he continued, but to protect the attackers from the added strain of having to
repulse a counterattack, he was directing that the movement be made
less than an hour before sundown, which would give the Federals no
time to reorganize or bring up reinforcements before dark. Then next
morning Polk could jump off, not only with his flank secure, but also
with the enemy mouse-trapped out of position to his front.

　　Breckinridge, who was not yet forty-two despite his distinguished prewar career in national politics — a hearty-looking man
with a prominent forehead, somewhat bulging eyes, a plump but firm
jaw, and the swooping dark mustache of a Sicilian brigand, he was a
leading contender among the many candidates for the title of the handsomest general in the southern army — protested at once and for all he
was worth. The hill was well-nigh impregnable, he said, and Van
Cleve's division had now been reinforced by two brigades from Palmer;
besides which, he added, guns from the main Union line across the river
would tear his flank as he advanced, thus exposing his men to the very
horror he would be sparing Polk's if he was successful, which was
doubtful. Warming to the subject, he took up a stick and began to draw
in the soft dirt a map that emphasized the difficulty of the terrain. Bragg
stopped him in mid-sketch. The Kentuckian had delayed the battle two
days ago with similar protests which had turned out to be ill-founded,
and the army commander was having no more of that. "Sir," Bragg
said curtly, "my information is different. I have given the order to attack the enemy in your front and expect it to be obeyed."

　　That was that, and Breckinridge returned to his troops, most of
whom were Bluegrass natives like himself, exiles from their homeland
since midwinter nearly a year ago; "my poor orphans," he sometimes

called them, jokingly but not without an undertone of sadness and homesickness. Rejoining them he sought out his friend Brigadier General William Preston — now commanding one of his brigades, but formerly chief of staff to his brother-in-law Albert Sidney Johnston, who had died in his arms at Shiloh — to whom he now addressed himself concerning the assignment he had just been given. "General Preston," he said, speaking formally and with a tone that strangely combined dejection and determination, "this attack is made against my judgment and by the special orders of General Bragg. Of course we all must try to do our duty and fight the best we can. But if it should result in disaster and I be among the slain, I want you to do justice to my memory and tell the people that I believed this attack to be very unwise and tried to prevent it." And having thus unburdened his mind he ordered his five brigades to form for the assault.

Across the way, Crittenden was inspecting his dispositions along the west bank of Stones River, accompanied by his chief of artillery Captain John Mendenhall, when he looked over the ford near the base of the occupied hill beyond and saw the graybacks forming in heavy columns along the ridge to the south, obviously preparing for a blow at Beatty, who commanded not only Van Cleve's division but also the two brigades of reinforcements which had joined him that morning. It was now about 3.30; the sun was within an hour of the landline. According to Mendenhall, "The general asked me if I could not do something to relieve Colonel Beatty with my guns." The Indiana-born West Pointer could indeed, and he moved to do so promptly. Assembling within the next half hour a total of 58 pieces of various calibers, he stationed 37 of these on the crest of a west-bank hill, cradled by a bend of the stream and overlooking the opposite bank, and placed the other 21 along its eastern base for flat-trajectory fire that would catch the rebel columns end-on as they charged across the rolling slopes beyond the river. Then he waited; but not for long.

The five Confederate brigades, with a total effective strength of 4500 men, started down off their sheltering ridge at 4 o'clock, moving steadily across the valley which lay between them and the hill from whose crest Beatty's cannoneers and riflemen soon took them under fire. As at Baton Rouge five months ago, where they had fought in isolation while the rest of Bragg's army was preparing to set out for their native Bluegrass, the Kentuckians did not falter as they swung down the long slope of the intervening valley, crossed its floor, and began to climb the other side. Halfway up the face of the hill, taking heavier losses now at closer range, they fired their first volleys and then, beginning to yell, broke into a run for the crest. The bluecoats did not wait for them, but whirled and fled from the threat of contact, and the attackers came on after them, yelling now with shrill screams of triumph as they topped the rise and pursued the defenders down the rearward slope.

However, they could not close the gap created by the quick retreat, and this gave Mendenhall the chance he had been waiting for all this time, to shoot at his foes without injuring his friends. At the signal "Fire!" his 58 double-shotted guns began to roar in chorus, flinging more than a hundred rounds a minute against the flank of the butternut mass across the way. "Thinned, reeling, broken under that terrible hail" — thus one reporter described the instantaneous effect — the graybacks milled in confusion, scarcely knowing at first what had struck them. When they saw what it was, they attempted to change front to the left and move against the fuming hill beyond the ford; but to no avail. "The very forest seemed to fall before our fire," one Federal observer wrote — without exaggeration, for men in the gray ranks were actually crushed under fallen limbs that were torn from the trees by exploding shells when they tried to find shelter in a patch of woods — "and not a Confederate reached the river." Shattered, they changed front again to the left, of one accord, and ran for the ridge that had marked their line of departure. A Union colonel, watching this sudden turn of events, was the amused witness of a double, simultaneous retreat. "It was difficult to say which was running away the more rapidly," he later reported, "the division of Van Cleve to the rear, or the enemy in the opposite direction."

Breckinridge watched his men come stumbling back through the dusk that followed sunset of the brief winter day. They had been gone just seventy minutes in all, and of their number 1700 had fallen: which meant that better than one man out of every three who descended the slope did not return unhurt. As their commander, who had protested the slaughter in advance and done what he could to prevent it, watched them close ranks to fill the gaps as they formed their line behind their own ten guns on the ridge, his eyes filled with tears. "My poor orphans! My poor orphans!" he exclaimed.

The lament for the fallen need not have been limited to the Confederate right, nor indeed to either side of the line of battle; for the overall Federal losses had been even heavier. According to final reports and computations, in two days of conflict — the day-long struggle of the 31st and the sunset repulse on the 2d — only a dozen less than 25,000 casualties had been suffered by the two armies. (Which, incidentally, indicated something of the fury of western fighting. With fewer than half as many troops involved, the butcher bill at Murfreesboro, Tennessee, was more than one-third greater than the one presented at Fredericksburg, Virginia, three weeks back.) The South lost 1294 killed, 7945 wounded, and 2500 captured or missing, a total of 11,739. The North lost 1730 killed, 7802 wounded, and 3717 captured or missing, a total of 13,249. The over-all total thus was 24,988: which was to say, and more could scarcely *be* said, that the battle had been bloodier than Shiloh or Sharpsburg.

At any rate, though neither commander yet recognized the fact, the carnage was over. Polk, who had learned of the sunset assault only just before it was launched, when Bragg came to his headquarters for a better view of the action across the river, had protested almost as vehemently as Breckinridge had done, but with no more success; Bragg's mind was quite made up. And now that the attack had met with predicted disaster, the blue defenders returned to the abandoned hill in greater strength than ever, reinforced by another whole division. Tactically, all was as it had been before the assault was launched, only more so; Polk would be less able to advance tomorrow than he had been today. Whether the enemy was under a similar disadvantage he did not know, but his two division commanders were not only doubtful that such was the case, they were also doubtful that their troops were in any fit condition to block the way: as was shown by a letter they wrote, shortly after midnight, and sent through channels to Bragg. "We deem it our duty to say to you frankly," Cheatham and Withers declared, "that, in our judgment, this army should be promptly put in retreat. . . . We do fear great disaster from the condition of things now existing, and think it should be averted if possible." Polk added his endorsement to the unusual document: "I greatly fear the consequences of another engagement at this place in the ensuing day. We could now, perhaps, get off with some safety and some credit, if the affair is well managed," and forwarded it to Bragg. Waked at 2 a.m., the grim-faced commander sat up in bed and read the letter halfway through, then stopped and told the aide who had disturbed his sleep: "Say to the general we shall maintain our position at every hazard."

When he rose at daylight, however, he began to discover how great that hazard was. Rain was falling steadily and the river was rising fast, threatening to isolate the two wings of his army. Moreover, unlike the previous ones, this morning's cavalry reports gave no hint of signs in the night that the enemy was considering withdrawal, but rather informed him that another fresh brigade of reinforcements had just arrived on the Union right, accompanying a train of supplies from the Tennessee capital. By now, too, his staff had found time to study the papers captured when McCook's headquarters were overrun, which indicated an effective strength of nearly 70,000 bluecoats to his front. This gave Bragg pause, and having paused he wavered. At 10 o'clock that morning he sent for Polk and Hardee, who found him in a different frame of mind from the one he had shown eight hours ago, when he was roused out of sleep to read the letter advising retreat. With the enemy heavily reinforced, as he believed and later wrote in his report, "Common prudence and the safety of my army, upon which even the safety of our cause depended, left no doubt on my mind as to the necessity of my withdrawal from so unequal a contest." The retrograde movement got under way that night, January 3, and was conducted with such skill that not even a rear-guard action was fought with the unsuspecting Federals, who seemed no more anxious to pursue than Bragg had been to stay. He himself went to Winchester, fifty miles southeast, planning to establish a new line along Elk River. Polk was instructed to fall back on Shelbyville, Hardee on Tullahoma, respectively twenty-three and thirty-five miles from Murfreesboro, but when the former reached his goal and reported that the bluecoats had not ventured beyond Stones River, Bragg ordered Hardee to stop at Wartrace, on line with Polk. Returning at once to establish headquarters at Tullahoma, on the railroad about midway between Nashville and Chattanooga, he began to organize a new defensive position along the Duck, whose rich valley offered much in the way of subsistence and adequate camp sites, including level fields for the daily hours of close-order drill in which he placed great store as a disciplinarian.

His pride in his army and its conduct during the battle — which was in a way a coda to the Kentucky excursion, launched soon after he took command at Tupelo, Mississippi, back in June — was expressed in his report, where he listed with satisfaction the capture of 6273 prisoners and enemy colors in abundance, along with 31 cannon and 6000 small arms, as well as "a large amount of other valuable property, all of which was secured and appropriated to proper uses." Moreover, he declared by way of final proof of moral superiority over his antagonist, "the army retired to its present position behind Duck River without giving or receiving a shot." Within the ranks of that army, however, though the men agreed that they had won a victory, there were fewer signs of elation. The retreat was made in wretched weather, and as they plodded southward through the mud, alternately drenched with rain and pelted with sleet, bent beneath the weight of their sodden packs, it seemed to them that the Perryville technique — fight; win; fall back — had been repeated. "What does he fight battles for?" they grumbled, beginning to discern a discouraging pattern to their efforts under Bragg. Similarly at home, as one civilian diarist recorded, "It was small surcease to the sob of the widow and the moan of the orphan that 'the retreat to Tullahoma was conducted in good order.'"

Rosecrans, on the other hand — who had not made a single offensive move since the explosive attack on his right wing at dawn of the 31st, who had allowed a foe he claimed was beaten to withdraw from his immediate front without so much as a threat of molestation, and who was so cautious in pursuit that his eventual movement to the east bank of Stones River, from which he had withdrawn on the night of January 3 lest the rising waters expose his troops to destruction in detail, amounted to practically no pursuit at all — was praised not only by those below and above him in the army, but also by the public at large, including the Ohio legislature, which tendered him before the month was out a resolution of thanks "for the glorious victory resulting in the capture of Murfreesboro and the defeat of the rebel forces at that place." Cheered by his soldiers as he rode among them, he received equally gratifying responses to the dispatches by which he announced his victory to the authorities in Washington. "God bless you, and all of you," the President replied, and the Secretary of War (who had said of Rosecrans' appointment at the outset, "Well, you have made your choice of idiots. Now you can await the news of a terrible disaster") was quite expansive, wiring: "The country is filled with admiration of the gallantry and heroic achievement of yourself and the officers and troops under your command. . . . There is nothing you can ask within my power to grant to yourself or your noble command that will not be cheerfully given." Even Halleck, who had prodded and nudged him for weeks beyond endurance, eventually joined the chorus of praise, though not before he had waited a few days for verification in Confederate newspapers smuggled across the border. "Rebel accounts fully confirm your telegrams from the battlefield," he wired, and added: "You and your brave army have won the gratitude of your country and the admiration of the world. . . . All honor to the Army of the Cumberland — thanks to the living and tears for the lamented dead."

Bragg, he knew, was playing a cagey game at Tullahoma ("We shall fight him again at every hazard if he advances, and harass him daily if he does not," the terrible-tempered general was telling his superiors even now) but Rosecrans was firm in his intentions and had already reverted to the use of vigorous phrases he had been employing two weeks back, on the eve of battle. "We shall press them as rapidly as our means of traveling and subsistence will permit," he notified Stanton on January 5. Next day, though he was still at Murfreesboro, he boldly repeated words he had used at Nashville in mid-December: "I now wish to press them to the wall."

★ ★ ★

When Davis returned to Richmond that same January 5, to be met on the portico of the White House by his wife and their four children — three sons and a daughter, stair-stepped at two-year intervals so that their ages ranged from just past one to almost eight — Mrs Davis, observing that her husband was near exhaustion, insisted that he retire at once to rest from the exertions of his journey. Presently, however, they heard the thump and blare of drums and horns and the cheers of a crowd that had gathered in front of the house to welcome him back with a serenade. Weary though he was, and despite his desire to be alone with his family — "Every sound is the voice of my child and every child renews the memory of a loved one's appearance," he had written home from Tennessee, "but none can equal their charms, nor can any compare with my own long-worshipped Winnie" — he felt that he could not ignore the shouts of the crowd or fail to acknowledge the courtesy being tendered.

The cheers were redoubled as the big front door swung ajar once more and the President came out onto the steps. Captain J. B. Smith's Silver Band played "Listen to the Mocking Bird" and several other airs which the crowd enjoyed while waiting for the speech they had come to hear. Davis did not disappoint them. Carried forward perhaps by a sort of verbal secondary inertia, he spoke as he had been speaking now for more than three weeks, to similar crowds and with similar words, in the course of his nearly three-thousand-mile trip to "the further West" and back.

"I am happy to be welcomed on my return to the capital of the Confederacy — the last hope, as I believe, for the perpetuation of that system of government which our forefathers founded — the asylum of the oppressed, and the home of true representative liberty." His voice, as he thus began, showed the strain to which it had been exposed, but as usual it gathered strength as he continued, reverting to the deeds of olden days in the Old Dominion, where the earlier Revolution had been proclaimed and, finally, won. Now once more, he told these latter-day Virginians, "anticipating the overthrow of that government which you had inherited, you assumed to yourselves the right, as your fathers had done before you, to declare yourself independent, and nobly have you advocated the assertion which you have made. Here, upon your soil, some of the fiercest battles of the Revolution were fought, and upon your soil it closed by the surrender of Cornwallis. Here again are men of every state; here they have congregated, linked in the defense of a most sacred cause. They have battled, they have bled upon your soil, and it is now consecrated by blood which cries for vengeance against the insensate foe of religion as well as of humanity, of the altar as well as of the hearthstone." Thus he repeated the bitterness he had voiced in his home state, ten days ago. Nor, with first-hand accounts of the sack of Fredericksburg now added to the list of northern depredations — not the least of them being the recently issued Emancipation Proclamation, which, as he saw it, incited the slaves to the murder of their masters — had that reaction been tempered by second thought. Rather, the bitterness had increased: as he now showed. "It is true," he told his listeners, "you have a cause which binds you together more firmly than your fathers were. They fought to be free from the usurpations of the British crown, but they fought against a manly foe. You fight against the offscourings of the earth."

Applauded, he passed on to a brief review of recent Confederate successes in the field, which he predicted would bring discord to northern councils, and then returned to his condemnation, not only of the conduct of the Federal armies of invasion, but also of the men who had sent them South. "Every crime which could characterize the course of demons has marked the course of the invader . . . from the burning of defenseless towns to the stealing of silver forks and spoons." In this last he had particular reference to Ben Butler, known as "Beast" Butler and "Spoons" Butler as a result of his alleged brutality and deftness in the exercise of his authority in command of the occupation of New Orleans, and Davis made the charge explicit, asserting that the Massachusetts general had "exerted himself to earn the excoriations of the civilized world, and now returns [to Washington] with his dishonors thick upon him to receive the plaudits of the only people on earth who do not blush to think he wears the human form. . . . They have come to disturb your social organization on the plea that it is a military necessity. For what are they waging war? They say to preserve the Union. Can they preserve the Union by destroying the social existence of a portion of the South? Do they hope to reconstruct the Union by striking at everything which is dear to man? — by showing themselves so utterly disgraced that if the question was proposed to you whether you would combine with hyenas or Yankees, I trust every Virginian would say: 'Give me the hyenas.' "

"Good! Good!" his listeners cried, and there was laughter. They wanted more along these lines.

But Davis spoke calmly now, as if to refute the charge made by his critics that he was cold in his attitude toward the people, unconcerned for their welfare, and anxious to avoid commingling with them — as if, indeed, he had brought back East from his journey West an increased awareness of the warmth and strength proceeding from contact with those who looked to him for leadership not only as their President but also as a man. "My friends, constant labor in the duties of office, borne down by care, and with an anxiety which has left me scarcely a moment for repose, I have had but little opportunity for social intercourse among you. I thank you for this greeting, and hope the time may come soon when you and I alike, relieved of the anxieties of the hour, may have more of social intercourse than has heretofore existed." Flushed with confidence as a result of the victories won by the nation's armies in the course of his trip, he added: "If the war continues we shall only grow stronger and stronger as each year rolls on. Compare our condition today with that which existed one year ago. See the increasing power of the enemy, but mark that our own has been proportionately greater, until we see in the future nothing to disturb the prospect of the independence for which we are struggling. One year ago, many were depressed and some were despondent. Now deep resolve is seen in every eye; an unconquerable spirit nerves every arm. And gentle woman, too;

who can estimate the value of her services in this struggle? . . . With such noble women at home, and such heroic soldiers in the field, we are invincible."

He waited for the applause to die away, and then concluded his remarks, once more on a personal note. "I thank you, my friends, for the kind salutation tonight; it is an indication that at some future time we shall be better acquainted. I trust we shall all live to enjoy some of the fruits of the struggle in which we are engaged. My prayers are for your individual and collective welfare. May God prosper our cause, and may we live to give to our children untarnished the rich inheritance which our fathers gave us. Good night!"

Unhappy New Year

★ ✗ ☆

NEW YEAR'S 1863 WAS FOR ABRAHAM LINCOLN perhaps the single busiest day of his whole presidential life, and it came moreover at dead center of what was perhaps his period of deepest gloom and perplexity of spirit. Not only was there political division within his party, and even within his own official family, but with the possible exception of Rosecrans, whose battle was in mid-career and appeared worse than doubtful, all his hand-picked commanders had failed him utterly, through enemy action or their own inaction, in his hopes for a multifaceted early-winter triumph in which he himself had assigned them the parts they were to play in putting a quick end to rebellion. One by one, sometimes two by two, they had failed him. Burnside and his fellow generals on the Rappahannock, having blundered into defeat at Fredericksburg, were engaged in a frenzy of backbiting such as not even the highly contentious Army of the Potomac had ever known before. Grant, according to the New York *Times*, remained "stuck in the mud of northern Mississippi, his army of no use to him or anybody else." Banks, caught in a toil of imported New Orleans cotton speculators, was stymied by a previously unsuspected fort on the Mississippi, two hundred and fifty miles downstream from his assigned objective. And McClernand, from whom the Commander in Chief had perhaps expected most, was apparently the worst off of all. He not only had done nothing with his army; the last Lincoln had heard from him, he could not even find it.

Nor had these and other failures of omission and commission gone unnoticed by the country at large, the voters and investors on whose will and trust the prosecution of the war depended. The Democrats, still on the outside looking in, but with substantial gains in the fall elections to sharpen their appetite for more, had seen to that: especially Ohio Representative Clement L. Vallandigham, who was savagely pointing out, from the vantage point of his seat in Congress, the administration's errors. "Money you have expended without limit," he told Republicans in the House, "and blood poured out like water. Defeat, debt, taxation, and sepulchers — these are your only trophies." Others, less violent but no less earnest, including his disaffected former allies, were accusing the President in a similar vein; so that now, perhaps, with his own critics crying out against him, he could feel more sympathy for James K. Polk than he had felt when he spoke against him in Congress, fifteen years ago this month, in the midst of another war. "I more than suspect already," the youthful Lincoln had declared from a seat in the rear of the House, "that he is deeply conscious of being in the wrong; that he feels the blood of this war, like the blood of Abel, is crying to heaven against him; that originally having some strong motive . . . to involve the two countries in a war, and trusting to escape scrutiny by fixing the public gaze upon the exceeding brightness of military glory . . . he plunged into it and has swept on and on, till, disappointed in his calculation . . . he now finds himself he knows not where. . . . His mind, tasked beyond its power, is running hither and thither, like some tortured creature on a burning surface, finding no position on which it can settle down and be at ease. . . . He is a bewildered, confounded, and miserably perplexed man. God grant he may be able to show there is not something about his conscience more painful than all his mental perplexity!"

The words rebounded from the target, boomeranged down the years, and came back in other forms to strike the sender. Orestes Brownson, the prominent Boston author and former transcendentalist, wrote of Lincoln: "His soul seems made of leather, and incapable of any grand or noble emotion. Compared with the mass of men, he is a line of flat prose in a beautiful and spirited lyric. He lowers, he never elevates you. You leave his presence with your enthusiasm dampened, your better feelings crushed, and your hopes cast to the winds. You ask not, can this man carry the nation through its terrible struggles? but can the nation carry this man through them, and not perish in the attempt?" Brownson was of no uncertain mind where Lincoln was concerned. "He is thickheaded; he is ignorant; he is tricky, somewhat astute, in a small way, and obstinate as a mule. . . . He is wrong-headed, the attorney not the lawyer, the petty politician not the statesman, and, in my belief, ill-deserving of the soubriquet of Honest. I am out of all patience with him," he added, rather anticlimactically, and inquired: "Is there no way of inducing him to resign, and allow Mr Hamlin to take his place?" Senator William Pitt Fessenden, a Maine Republican high in the party's councils, replied in somewhat the same vein when told that he should be a member of the cabinet in order to be at Lincoln's elbow and give the nation the full benefit of his advice. "No friend of mine should ever wish to see me there," he answered. "You cannot change the President's character or conduct. He remained long enough in Springfield, surrounded by toadies and office-seekers, to persuade himself that he was specially chosen by the Almighty for this crisis, and well chosen. This conceit has never yet been beaten out of him, and until it is, no human wisdom can be of much avail. I see nothing for it but to let the ship of state drift along, hoping that the current of public opinion may bring it safely into port." Similarly, a Boston philanthropist, railroad magnate J. M. Forbes, convinced that Lincoln was badly off the track, was asking: "Can nothing be done to reach the President's ear and heart? I hear he is susceptible to religious impressions; shall we send our eloquent divines to talk to him, or shall we send on a deputation of mothers and wives, or can we, the conservators of liberty, who have elected him, combine with Congress in beseeching him to save the country?"

In point of fact, one such group of "eloquent divines" as Forbes suggested did come to call on Lincoln at this time, protesting with considerable heat the lack of progress in the war; but he gave them little satisfaction beyond a brief, short-tempered lecture comparing the administration's predicament to that of a tightrope walker in mid-act. "Gentlemen," he told them, "suppose all the property you were worth was in gold, and you had put it in the hands of Blondin to carry across the Niagara River. Would you shake the cable or keep shouting out to him, 'Blondin, stand up a little straighter!' 'Blondin, stoop a little more!' 'Go a little faster'; 'Lean a little more to the north'; 'Lean a little more to the south'? No. You would hold your breath as well as your tongue, and keep your hands off until he was safe over. The government is carrying an immense weight. Untold treasures are in their hands. They are doing the very best they can. Don't badger them. Keep silence, and we'll get you safe across." The visit, he said afterwards, made him "a little shy of preachers" for a time. "But the latchstring is out," he added, "and they have the right to come here and preach to me if they will go about it with some gentleness and moderation."

Gentleness and moderation were easier to prescribe than they were to practice. An infinitely patient man, he was beginning to lose patience: with the result that some who formerly had complained that he lacked firmness were now protesting that he had assumed the prerogatives of a dictator, spurning their counsels and high-handedly overruling their objections. It was true in some respects. His accustomed tact sometimes failed him under pressure nowadays, and he gave short answers, though rarely without the saving grace of humor, the velvet glove that softened the clutch of the iron hand. This was evident, for example, in a clash with Secretary of the Treasury Salmon P. Chase about this time. An economist came to Lincoln with a plan for issuing greenbacks. Lincoln heard him out, liked the notion, but told him: "You must go to Chase. He is running that end of the machine." The man left, then presently returned, saying that the Secretary had dismissed him with the objection that the proposal was unconstitutional. Lincoln grimaced. "Go back to

Chase," he said, "and tell him not to bother himself about the Constitution. Say that I have that sacred instrument here at the White House, and am guarding it with great care."

Such brusque, not to say cavalier, treatment of his highly respected Treasury chief was prologue to an even rougher handling of that dignitary in mid-December, when he tripped him neatly from behind as he tried a sprint up several rungs of the political ladder. This was a time of crisis and division, in the cabinet as in the nation at large. One member, Secretary of the Interior Caleb Blood Smith, who had received his appointment as the result of a convention bargain, was leaving to accept a judgeship Lincoln had offered him in his native Indiana; his post would go to John Palmer Usher, another Hoosier, at present the Assistant Secretary. The other six members were split on the question of whether to admit West Virginia as a state under an act just passed by Congress, divorcing Virginia's northwest counties from the Old Dominion and validating the rump government set up in Charleston during the Sumter furor. Three cabinet officers — Chase, Stanton, and Secretary of State William H. Seward — wanted Lincoln to sign the bill, converting slave soil into free soil by the stroke of a pen, and incidentally adding good Republican votes on whatever questions Congress might decide needed settling in the future; while three others — Secretary of the Navy Gideon Welles, Attorney General Edward Bates, and Postmaster General Montgomery Blair — recommended that he veto it, on grounds that the act was in a sense a ratification of secession. Though he could not reconcile their views, Lincoln quickly solved the problem to his own approximate satisfaction. "The division of a state is dreaded as a precedent," he reasoned. "But a measure made expedient by a war is no precedent for times of peace. It is said that the admission of West Virginia is secession, and tolerated only because it is *our* secession. Well, if we call it by that name, there is still difference enough between secession against the Constitution and secession in favor of the Constitution." On the last day of the year, though he did so with a wry face, he signed the bill. West Virginia would become in June a full-fledged state of the Union, the thirty-fifth, not discounting the eleven who had no representation in Congress pending the settlement of their claim to have abolished their old ties.

Seward and Chase had voted together on the issue, but that was rare. In general they were diametrically opposed, as they had been in the old days when they were rivals for the office which, by a fluke, had gone to Lincoln. Chase, who was jealous of Seward's position as the President's chief adviser, wanted not only the seat closest to the one at the head of the table, but also, as time would show, the principal seat itself. In this connection, noting the way the wind blew, he had aligned himself with the radicals in Congress, the so-called Jacobins who had come to see Seward as the stumbling block in the way of adoption of their notions as to how the war should be fought and the country run, just as Chase had come to see him as a hurdle that would have to be removed or overleaped if he was to fulfill his own ambitions. By way of undoing their common adversary, he fanned the flames of the radicals' hatred by reporting Seward's every private opposition to their aims (the New Yorker, for example, had delayed the promulgation of the Preliminary Emancipation Proclamation by advising Lincoln to wait for a more propitious season before releasing it to the world; than which, indeed, there could be no crime greater in radical eyes) as well as by giving them a blow-by-blow account of every cabinet crisis, omitting nothing that served to thicken the atmosphere of discord and indecision. So it was that at last, on December 17 — four days after the Fredericksburg fiasco, which seemed to them to prove emphatically that the prosecution of the war was in quite the wrong hands — all but one of the thirty-two Republican senators met in secret caucus on Capitol Hill and passed unanimously the following resolution, by way of advice to the leader of their party: *"Resolved, that . . . the public confidence in the present administration would be increased by a change in and partial reconstruction of the cabinet."* It was Seward they were after, Seward alone, and lest there be any doubt on that score a committee of nine was appointed to present the resolution to Lincoln and explain to him just what it was they meant.

The one abstaining senator was New York's Preston King, who went at once to Seward and warned his former senatorial colleague that the Jacobins, "thirsty for a victim" in the wake of recent misfortunes, had selected his neck for the ax. Seward reacted fast when he learned thus of the resolution about to be presented. "They may do as they please about me," he said, "but they shall not put the President in a false position on my account." Accordingly he took a sheet of paper, and having scrawled a few words across it —"Sir, I hereby resign from the office of Secretary of State, and beg that my resignation be accepted immediately" — sent it forthwith to the White House. Lincoln was shocked. "What does this mean?" he asked as he put on his hat and set out for Seward's house, which was just across the street. Seward explained what had happened, along with what was about to happen, and added that he personally would be glad to get from under the burden of official duties and political harassment. "Ah yes, Governor," Lincoln said, shaking his head. "That will do very well for you, but I am like the starling in Sterne's story. 'I can't get out.'" He pocketed the resignation and went sadly back across the White House lawn.

At any rate, next morning when the committee spokesman called, he knew what to expect. He set the time for the presentation at 7 o'clock that evening; he would receive the full committee then. This was a crisis, not only for Lincoln but also for the nation, and he knew it. "If I had yielded to that storm and dismissed Seward," he said later, "the thing would have all slumped over one way, and we should have been left with a scant handful of supporters." Knowing what had to be done was a quite different thing, however, from knowing how to do it. Ben Wade of Ohio, George W. Julian of Indiana, Zachariah Chandler of Michigan: these and others like them were men of power and savage purpose, accomplished haters who would be merciless in revenging even an imagined slight, let alone an outright rebuff. Whatever Lincoln did had better be done without incurring their personal enmity. Besides, he not only had to avoid their anger; he also needed their support. What he required just now was someone to draw their wrath, someone to serve him much as a billygoat serves the farmer who places him in a barnlot to draw fleas. By evening, not without a certain sense of political and even poetical justice, he had chosen the someone. All that remained was to make him serve, and that could be done quite simply by branding him, in the eyes of all, for what he was.

The nine committeemen were prompt; Lincoln received them in his office. By way of a beginning, seventy-one-year-old Jacob Collamer of Vermont, who had been elected spokesman, read the resolution and followed it with a paper which summed up the conclusions reached in caucus the day before. The war should be prosecuted vigorously; cabinet members should be "cordial, resolute, unwavering" in their devotion to the principles of the Republican majority; the cabinet itself, once it had been stripped and rebuilt so as to contain only such stalwarts, should have a larger voice in the running of the government. Wade rose next, a vigorous man with "burning" eyes and bulldog flews, protesting hotly that the President had "placed the direction of our military affairs in the hands of bitter and malignant Democrats." He spoke at length, going somewhat afield from the central issue, and was followed by Fessenden, who agreed that the war was "not sufficiently in the hands of its friends," then brought the discussion back on target by charging specifically "that the Secretary of State [is] not in accord with the majority of the cabinet and [has] exerted an injurious influence upon the conduct of the war." Others had their say along these lines, also at considerable length, but Lincoln kept his temper and said little. After three hours of listening, however, he suggested that the meeting adjourn until the following night. The senators agreed. Alone at last, he saw clearly, as he presently remarked, that if he let these men have their way "the whole government must cave in; it could not stand, could not hold water; the bottom would be out."

He knew what to do and, by now, how to do it; but he was saddened. "What do those men want?" he asked his friend Senator Orville Browning of Illinois next day. "I hardly know, Mr President," Browning replied, "but they are exceedingly violent...." Lincoln knew well enough what they wanted, though, and he said so: "They wish to get rid of me — and I am sometimes half disposed to gratify them." Browning protested, but Lincoln shook his head. "We are now on the brink of destruction," he said. "It appears to me the Almighty is against us, and I can hardly see a ray of hope." Again Browning protested. Though he was not a member of the committee, he had attended the caucus and had voted for the resolution: which, he explained defensively, "was the gentlest thing that could be done. We had to do that, or worse." The trouble he said was Seward. While he personally had a high regard for the Secretary, others were saying that the New Yorker had the President under his thumb. "Why should men believe a lie," Lincoln broke in, "an absurd lie, that could not impose on a child, and cling to it and repeat it in defiance of all evidences to the contrary?" His sadness deepened. "The committee is to be up to see me at 7 o'clock. Since I heard last night of the proceedings of the caucus I have been more distressed than by any event of my life."

If this was so, it did not show in his manner when he welcomed the committeemen that evening for a second round of grievance presentations. Before the discussion got under way, however, he announced to the assembled senators that he had thought it fitting to have the cabinet officers — minus Seward, of course, since even aside from the fact that his resignation was pending, that would have been too indelicate — present to answer the charge that there was discord among them and that the President seldom followed or even asked for their advice. Whereupon the door opened and the six gentlemen in question filed into the room. Lincoln had invited them at the cabinet meeting that morning, after telling them of the matter afoot and of Seward's submission of his resignation. Mostly they had welcomed the chance to confront their accusers, although two of their number — Chase in particular — had protested that they "knew of no good that could come of an interview." In the end, however, the two — the other was Bates — had been obliged to go along with the majority. Now here they were, face to face with critics whose accusations were based, at least in part, on information supplied in private by Chase in order to curry favor with them. Already he was squirming, as if the fleas had jumped at the sight of his large, handsome person: but the worst was still to come.

If Chase and some of the senators were embarrassed by the confrontation, Lincoln certainly was not. He began the proceedings by reading aloud yesterday's bill of particulars, admitting as he went along that he had not consulted the cabinet on all affairs of state or war, and that he had not always followed their advice, even when he had sought it; but in the main, he said, he had valued and used their abilities, individually and collectively. As for discord, he did not think it reasonable to expect seven such independent-minded men to agree on every issue that came before them; but here again, he said, he thought they worked together mainly as a unit, and certainly he himself had no complaint. He paused, then turned to the six cabinet members present, beginning to poll them one by one. Did they or did they not agree with his statement of the case? They did; or so they said, one by one; until he came to Chase. Chase, as it turned out, also agreed, though not without considerable hemming and hawing by way of preamble. He would never have come to the meeting, he said, if he had known he was "to be arraigned." He seemed angry. He seemed to feel that he was being "put upon"— as indeed he was. In the end, with Wade and the others watching balefully, he admitted that matters of prime importance had usually come before the cabinet, though perhaps "not so fully as might be desired," and that there had been "no want of unity in the cabinet, but a general acquiescence in public measures." Thus he wound up, and the Jacobins watched him cold-eyed, contrasting what he said now, in the presence of Lincoln and his colleagues, with what he had said in private. The President did not prolong his suffering. Having more or less settled these two points of contention, he shifted the talk to the question of Seward, defending his chief minister against yesterday's charges, and then began to poll the committeemen on their views. At that point Fessenden recoiled. "I do not think it proper," he said, "to discuss the merits or demerits of a member of the cabinet in the presence of his associates." Chase was quick to agree. "I think the members of the cabinet should withdraw," he said. In solemn procession they did so, some amused, some disgruntled, and one, at least, discredited in the eyes of men whose favor he had sought.

Like Simon Cameron a year ago, the Treasury chief had learned the hard way what it meant to tangle with Lincoln. Cameron was in Russia now, a victim of political decapitation, and Chase was determined to avoid such punishment. He would forestall the headsman by submitting, however regretfully, his resignation. This was exactly what Lincoln wanted: as was shown next morning, December 20, when he came into his office and found Chase, Welles, and Stanton grouped around the fire. Chase began to complain of yesterday's damage to his dignity. It had affected him most painfully, he said, for it seemed to indicate a lack of confidence. In fact — he hesitated — he had written out his resignation at home the night before.... Lincoln's reaction to this was not at all what the Secretary had expected. His expression was one of downright joy.

"Where is it?" he said eagerly.

"I brought it with me," Chase replied, taking a letter from his inside coat pocket.

"Let me have it," Lincoln said, and he put out a long arm.

Chase drew back, but not in time. Lincoln already had hold of the paper, and the Secretary suffered the added shock of having it snatched from his grasp. Reading it quickly through, Lincoln laughed; "a triumphal laugh," Welles called it in his diary. "This cuts the Gordian knot," he exclaimed. "I can dispose of this subject now without difficulty. I see my way clear." Stanton, who had been guilty of some of the same backstairs maneuvers — though he did not know whether the President suspected him, or what he might do if he did — remarked stiffly that he was prepared to tender his resignation, too. But Lincoln already had what he had been working toward. "You may go to your department," he said gaily. "I don't want yours. This"— he held up Chase's letter —"is all I want; this relieves me; the case is clear; the trouble is ended. I will detain neither of you longer."

His satisfaction was obvious, amounting to delight. What he had had in mind all along, and had achieved through skillful handling, was a balance: Chase's resignation against Seward's, which the Jacobins were still urging him to accept. Now, however, with Chase's inseparably included —"If one goes, the other must," he presently notified the senators; "they must hunt in couples"— they would be much less insistent; for, whatever their disgust with the Treasury chief's performance the day before, they still believed that he could be useful to them within the administration's private councils. Lincoln himself described the situation with a metaphor out of his boyhood in Kentucky, where he had seen farmers riding to market with a brace of pumpkins lodged snugly in a bag, one at each end in order to make a balanced load across the horse's withers. "Now I can ride," he said. "I have got a pumpkin in each end of my bag." Accordingly, he sent polite, identical notes to the two ministers, declining to accept their resignations and requesting them to continue as members of his official family. Seward, who had watched the maneuvers with amusement from a seat behind the scene, agreed at once; but Chase held off, still suffering from the fleabites, which were no less painful for being figurative. "I will sleep on it," he said. However, after a day of meditation and prayer — for it was a Sunday and he was intensely religious, spending a good part of each Sabbath on his knees — he agreed to remain at his post, as Lincoln had confidently expected.

Here was a case of double salvation, in more ways than one. Within the confines of his office in the White House, Lincoln had planned and fought a three-day battle as important to the welfare of the nation, and the progress of the war through united effort, as many that raged in the open field with booming guns and casualties by the thousands. In addition to retaining the services of Seward and Chase, both excellent men at their respective posts, he had managed to turn aside the wrath of the Jacobins without increasing their bitterness toward himself or incurring their open hatred, which might well have been fatal. Nor was that all. Paradoxically, because of the way he had gone about it, in avoiding the disruption of his cabinet he had achieved within it a closer harmony than had obtained before. This was partly because of the increased respect his actions earned him, but it was also because of the effect the incident had on the two ministers most intimately concerned. For all his loyalty to Lincoln through the storm, Seward had not previously abandoned the notion that he was the man directly in line for his job. Now, though, with all but one of the senators in his own party having expressed a desire to see him removed from any connection with the executive branch of the government, the presidential itch was cured. From that hour, his devotion to his duties was single-minded and his loyalty acquired an added zeal. So much could hardly be said for Chase, exactly, but he too had been sobered, and his ambition taken down a notch, by the cold-eyed looks the radical leaders had given him while he squirmed. It was no wonder, then, that Lincoln indulged in self-congratulation when he reviewed the three-day maneuver. "I do not see how I could have done better," he remarked.

    Few would disagree with this assessment, even among the frock-coated politicians he had bested, whether senators or members of his cabinet. In point of fact, whatever shocks they had suffered along the way, there should have been little surprise at the outcome; for the matter had been essentially political, and politics (or statesmanship, if you will, which he once defined as the art of getting the best from men who all too often were intent on giving nothing better than their worst) was a science he had mastered some time back. The military art was something else. Whether Lincoln would ever do as well as Commander in Chief of the nation's armies as he had done as its Chief Executive was more than doubtful — particularly in the light of current testimony as to the condition of the largest of those armies, still on the near bank of the Rappahannock attempting to recover from the shock of its mid-December blood bath.

    "Exhaustion steals over the country. Confidence and hope are dying," the Quartermaster General wrote privately this week to its commander. "The slumber of the army since [the attack at Fredericksburg] is eating into the vitals of the nation. As day after day has gone, my heart has sunk and I see greater peril to our nationality in the present condition of affairs than I have seen at any time during the struggle." Complaints were heard from below as well as above, and though these were not addressed to Burnside personally, accusing fingers were leveled in his direction and even higher. "Our poppycorn generals kill men as Herod killed the innocents," a Massachusetts private declared, and a Wisconsin major called this winter "the Valley Forge of the war." A bitterness was spreading through the ranks. "Alas my poor country!" a New York corporal wrote home. "It has strong limbs to march and meet the foe, stout arms to strike heavy blows, brave hearts to dare. But the brains, the brains — have we no brains to use the arms and limbs and eager hearts with cunning? Perhaps Old Abe has some funny story to tell, appropriate to the occasion. . . . Mother, do not wonder that my loyalty is growing weak," he added. "I am sick and tired of disaster and the fools that bring disaster upon us."

    There was a snatch of doggerel, sung to the tune of the old sea chanty "Johnny, Fill up the Bowl," making the rounds:

Abram Lincoln, what yer 'bout?
Hurrah! Hurrah!
Stop this war. It's all played out.
Hurrah! Hurrah!
Abram Lincoln, what yer 'bout?
Stop this war. It's all played out.
We'll all drink stone blind:
Johnny, fill up the bowl!

Veterans in the Army of the Potomac took up the refrain, "all played out," and made it their own. Once they had pretended cynicism as a cover for their greenness and their fears, but now they felt they had earned it and they found the phrase descriptive of their outlook through this season of discontent. "The phrensy of our soldiers rushing to glory or death has, as our boys amusingly affirm, *been played out*," a regimental chaplain wrote. "Our battle-worn veterans go into danger when ordered, remain as a stern duty so long as directed, and leave as soon as honor and duty allow." Case-hardened by their recent experience over the river, particularly in the repeated fruitless assaults on the stone wall at the base of Marye's Heights, they had no use for heroic postures or pretensions nowadays. When they saw magazine illustrations showing mounted officers with drawn sabers leading smartly aligned columns of troops unflinchingly through shellbursts, they snickered and jeered and whooped their motto: "All played out!"

Lincoln already knew something of this, but he learned a good deal more on December 29 when two disgruntled brigadiers hurried from Falmouth to Washington on short-term passes, intending to warn their congressmen of what they believed was imminent disaster. Burnside was planning to recross the Rappahannock any day now, having issued three days' cooked rations the day after Christmas, along with orders for the troops to be held in readiness to move on twelve hours' notice. What alarmed the two brigadiers — John Newton and John Cochrane, the latter a former Republican congressman himself — was that the army, which they were convinced was in a condition of near-mutiny, would come apart at the seams if it was called upon to repeat this soon the tragic performance it had staged two weeks ago in the same arena, and therefore they had come to warn the influential Bay State senator Henry Wilson, chairman of the Senate Military Committee, in hopes that he could get the movement stopped. In the intensity of their concern, as they discovered when they reached the capital, they had failed to take into account the fact that Congress was in recess over the holidays; Wilson had gone home. Undeterred, they went to see the Secretary of State, a former political associate of Cochrane's. When Seward heard their burden of woes he took them straight to the President, to whom — though they were somewhat daunted now, never having intended to climb this high up the chain of command — they repeated, along with hasty assurances that the basis for their admittedly irregular visit was patriotism, not hope for advancement, their conviction that if the Army of the Potomac was committed to battle in its present discouraged state it would be utterly destroyed. Not only would it be unable to hold the line of the Rappahannock; it would not even be able to hold the line of the river from which it took its name. Lincoln, who had known nothing of the pending movement, and scarcely more of the extent of the demoralization Cochrane and Newton claimed was rampant, was infected with their fears and got off a wire to Burnside without delay: "I have good reason for saying that you must not make a general movement without first letting me know of it."

Burnside, though his infantry had already been alerted for a downstream crossing while his cavalry was in motion for a feint upstream —"a risky expedition but a buster," one trooper called the plan — promptly complied with the President's telegram by canceling the movement, but he was angered and saddened by the obvious lack of confidence on the part of his superiors. The army, too — whatever its gladness over the postponement of another blood bath — was aggrieved as it filed back into its camps, feeling mistrusted and mistrustful. "Such checks destroy the enthusiasm of any army," the same trooper dolefully protested.

Yet it was at this point, near the apparent nadir of its self-confidence and pride, with disaffection evident in all of its components, from the commander down to the youngest drummer boy, that the one truly imperishable quality of this army first began to be discerned, like a gleam that only shone in darkness. If men could survive the unprofitable slaughter of Fredericksburg — the patent bungling, the horror piled on pointless horror, and the disgust that came with the conclusion that their comrades had died less by way of proving their love for their country than by way of proving the ineptness of their leaders — it might well be that they could survive almost anything. There were those who saw this. There were those who, unlike Newton and Cochrane, did not mistake the vociferous reaction for near-mutiny, who knew that griping was not only the time-honored prerogative of the American soldier, from Valley Forge on down, but was also, in its way, a proof of his basic toughness and resilience. "The more I saw of the Army of the Potomac," one correspondent wrote from the camps around Falmouth, "the more I wondered at its invincible spirit, which no disaster seemed able to destroy." A *Harper's Weekly* editor perhaps overstated the case —"All played out!" the soldiers who read it doubtless jeered — but was also thinking along these lines in an issue that came out about this time: "Like our forefathers the English, who always began their wars by getting soundly thrashed by their enemies, and only commenced to achieve success when it was thought they were exhausted, we are warming to the work with each mishap."

Lincoln thought so, too, what time he managed to shake off the deep melancholy that was so much a part of his complex nature. He probed and, probing, he considered what emerged. As of the first day of the year which was opening so inauspiciously, the Union had 918,211 soldiers under arms, whereas the Confederacy had 446,622, or a good deal less than half as many. At several critical points along the thousand-mile line of division the odds were even longer — out in Middle Tennessee, for instance, or down along the Rappahannock — and the troubled Commander in Chief found solace in brooding on the figures, even those that reached him from the field of Fredericksburg. "We lost fifty percent more men than did the enemy," a member of the White House staff remarked after hearing his chief discuss the outcome of the fighting there, "and yet there is sense in the awful arithmetic propounded by Mr Lincoln. He says that if the same battle were to be fought over again, every day, through a week of days, with the same relative results, the army under Lee would be wiped out to the last man, [while] the Army of the Potomac would still be a mighty host. The war would be over, the Confederacy gone." There was error here. Northern losses in the battle had exceeded southern losses, not by fifty, but by considerably better than one hundred percent. And yet there was validity in Lincoln's premise as to the end result, and especially was there validity in the conclusion the staff man heard him draw: "No general yet found can face the arithmetic, but the end of the war will be at hand when he shall be discovered."

Scott and McDowell, Pope and McClellan, and now Burnside: none of these was the killer he was seeking. Already he saw that this search was perhaps after all the major problem. All else — while, like Blondin, Lincoln threaded his way, burdened by untold treasures — was, in a sense, a biding of time until the unknown killer could be found. Somewhere he existed, and somewhere he would find him, this unidentified general who could face the grim arithmetic being scrawled in blood across these critical, tragic pages of the nation's history.

★ ★ ★

These and other matters were much on the President's mind when he woke on January 1. After an early-morning conference with Burnside, who had come up from Falmouth to ask in person just what the Commander in Chief's "good reason" had been for not allowing him to handle his own army as he saw fit, Lincoln spent the usual half hour with his barber, then got into his best clothes and went downstairs for the accustomed New Year's White House reception. For three hours, beginning at 11 o'clock, it was "How do you do?" "Thank you." "Glad to see you." "How do you do?" as the invited guests — high government officials, members of the diplomatic corps, and other important dignitaries, foreign and domestic — having threaded their way through the crowd of uninvited onlookers collected on the lawn, alighted from their carriages, came into the parlor, and filed past Lincoln for handshakes and refreshments. At 1 o'clock the long ordeal was over; he went back upstairs to his office for the day's — or, some would say, the century's — most important business, the signing of the Emancipation Proclamation.

Throughout the ninety-nine days since September 23, when the preliminary announcement of intention had been made, there had been much speculation as to whether he would issue or withdraw the final proclamation. Some were for it, some against. His friend Browning, for example, reflecting the view of constituents in the President's home state, thought it "fraught with evil, and evil only." The senator believed that the "useless and mischievous" document would serve "to unite and exasperate" the South, and to "divide and distract us in the North." Lincoln himself, if only by his neglect of the subject while the hundred days ticked off, had seemed to see the point of this objection. In his December message to Congress he had barely mentioned the projected edict, but had reverted instead to his original plan for compensated emancipation, a quite different thing indeed. Alarmed by this apparent failure of nerve, Abolitionists looked to their hero Senator Charles Sumner of Massachusetts, who went to Lincoln three days after Christmas for a straight talk on the matter. He found him hard at work on the final draft of the proclamation, writing it out in longhand. "I know very well that the name connected with this document will never be forgotten," Lincoln said, by way of explanation for his pains, and Sumner returned to his own desk to reassure a qualmish friend in Boston: "The President says he would not stop the Proclamation if he could, and he could not if he would. . . . Hallelujah!"

So it was. Seward brought the official copy over from the State Department, where a skilled penman had engrossed it from Lincoln's final draft, just completed the night before. All it lacked was the President's signature. He dipped his pen, then paused with it suspended over the expanse of whiteness spread out on his desk, and looked around with a serious expression. "I never in my life felt more certain that I was doing right," he said, "than I do in signing this paper. But I have been receiving calls and shaking hands since 9 o'clock this morning, till my arm is stiff and numb. Now this signature is one that will be closely examined, and if they find my hand trembled they will say, 'He had some compunctions.' But anyway it is going to be done." Slowly and carefully he signed, not the usual *A. Lincoln*, but his name in full: *Abraham Lincoln*. The witnesses crowded nearer for a look at the result, then laughed in relief of nervous tension; for the signature, though "slightly tremulous," as Lincoln himself remarked, was bold and clear. Seward signed next, the quick, slanting scrawl of the busy administrator, and the great seal was affixed, after which it went to its place in the State Department files (where it later was destroyed by fire) and in the hearts of men, where it would remain forever, though some of them had doubted lately that it would even be issued.

★ ★ ★

It was one thing to claim that by the stroke of a pen the fetters had been struck from the limbs of five million slaves and that their combined worth of more than a billion dollars was thereby automatically subtracted from enemy assets. It was quite another, however, to translate the announcement into fact, especially considering its peculiar limitations. All of Delaware, Maryland, Kentucky, Tennessee, and Missouri were exempt by specific definition within the body of the edict, along with those portions of Virginia and Louisiana already under Federal control. Lincoln himself explained that the proclamation had "no constitutional or legal justification, except as a military measure. The exemptions were made because the military necessity did not apply to the exempted localities." He freed no slave within his reach, and whether those beyond his reach would ever be affected by his pronouncement was dependent on the outcome of the war, which in turn depended on the southward progress of his armies. Just now that progress, East and West — once more with the possible exception of Middle Tennessee, where the issue remained in doubt — was negligible at best and nonexistent for the most part. Nor did the signs in either direction give promise of early improvement. Here in the East, in fact, if this morning's conference with Burnside was any indication of what to expect, the outlook was downright bleak.

The ruff-whiskered general had arrived in a state of acute distress, obviously fretted by more than the discomforts of his all-night ride from Falmouth, and Lincoln was distressed in turn to see him so. He liked Burnside — almost everyone did, personally — for his courage, for his impressive military bearing, and for what one subordinate called his "single-hearted honesty and unselfishness." All these qualities he had, and Lincoln, with a feeling of relief after weeks of trying to budge the balky McClellan, had chosen him in expectation of aggressiveness. The Indiana-born Rhode Islander had certainly given him that at Fredericksburg, in overplus indeed, but with a resolution so little tempered by discretion that critics now were remarking that he waged war in much the same way some folks played the fiddle, "by main strength and awkwardness." He himself was the first to admit his shortcomings. He had done so from the start, and recently in testimony given under oath before a congressional committee he had taken on his shoulders the whole blame for the late repulse. This was in a way disarming; it had the welcome but unfamiliar sound of natural modesty, so becoming in a truly capable man. However, there were those who saw it merely as further proof of his unfitness for the job he had accepted under protest. Burnside, they said, had not only admitted his incompetency; he had sworn to it.

When he opened the New Year's conference by asking what lay behind the telegram advising him not to move against the enemy without notifying Washington beforehand, Lincoln told him of the interview with the two brigadiers, in which they had stated that the army lacked confidence in its commander and was in no fit shape to be committed. Bristling at this evidence of perfidy from below, Burnside demanded to know their names, but Lincoln declined to divulge them for fear of the reprisal which he now saw would be visited upon their heads. This further increased the general's depression. It might well be true, he said, that his army had no faith in him; certainly not a single one of his senior commanders had approved of the movement he had canceled at Lincoln's suggestion. In fact, he added, plunging deeper into gloom, "It is my belief that I ought to retire to private life." When Lincoln demurred, Burnside's spirits rose a bit: enough, at least, to allow a sudden shift to the offensive. However low his own stock might have fallen, he said earnestly, he wanted the President to know that in his opinion neither Stanton's nor Halleck's was any higher. A man was apt to be a poor judge of his own usefulness and the loyalty of his subordinates, but of one thing he was sure. Neither the Secretary of War nor the general-in-chief had the confidence of the army — or of the country either for that matter, he quickly added, though he admitted that Lincoln was probably better informed on this latter point than he was. At any rate it was his belief that they too should be removed. . . . Lincoln expressed no opinion as to whether he could spare Stanton or Halleck, but he assured the unhappy Burnside that he valued his services highly. He urged him to return at once to his command and do the best he could, as he was sure he had done invariably in the past. Burnside replied that his plan was still to cross the Rappahannock, somewhere above or below Fredericksburg, and attack the rebels on their own ground. Lincoln said that was what he wanted, too, but prudence sometimes had to be applied, especially when risky ventures were involved. Whereupon, having secured this approval, however qualified, the general took his leave, apparently in a somewhat better frame of mind.

Still the fact remained that he was returning to his army with the intention of requiring it to pursue a course of action which, by his own admission, did not have the approval of the ranking subordinates who would be charged with its execution. The situation was, to say the least, loaded with possibilities of disaster. Here, Lincoln saw, was where the general-in-chief would fit into the picture; here was where Halleck could begin to perform the principal duty for which he had been summoned to the capital almost six months ago. He could go down to Falmouth for a first-hand look at the lay of the land and a talk with the disaffected corps commanders, then come back and submit his recommendations as to whether Burnside should be given his head or halted and replaced. Accordingly, before going upstairs to dress for the New Year's reception, Lincoln took out a sheet of paper and wrote the owl-eyed general a letter explaining what it was he wanted him to do. "If in such a difficulty as this you do not help," he wrote, "you fail me precisely in the point for which I sought your assistance." The tone was somewhat tart, doubtless because Lincoln was irked at having to ask for what should have been forthcoming as a matter of course, and he added: "Your military skill is useless to me, if you will not do this."

The letter was forwarded through Stanton, who gave it to Halleck that same morning at the reception. "Old Brains," as he was called, was taken aback. Twice already in this war he had ventured into the field — one occasion was the inchworm advance on Corinth, back in May, when all he got for his pains was an empty town, plus the guffaws that went with being hoodwinked; the other was his trip to see McClellan down on the York-James peninsula, shortly after his arrival East in late July, when he ordered the withdrawal that had permitted Lee to concentrate against Pope with such disastrous results on the plains of Manassas — and he was having no more of such exposure to the jangle of alarums and excursions. He prized the sweatless quiet of his office, where he could scratch his elbows in seclusion and ponder the imponderables of war. Lincoln's letter was a wrench, not so much because of what it said — which was, after all, little more than a definition of Halleck's duties — but because of the way it said it. The fact that his chief had thought it necessary to put the thing on record, in black and white, instead of making the suggestion verbally, which would have left no blot, seemed to him to indicate a lack of confidence. His reaction was immediate and decisive. As soon as the reception was over he went to his office, wrote out his resignation, and sent it at once to the Secretary of War.

Lincoln heard of this development from Stanton late that afternoon, following the signing of the Emancipation Proclamation. Saddened though he was by the general's reaction, which deprived him, as he said, of the professional advice he badly needed at this juncture, he still did not want to lose the services of Old Brains, such as they were. To mollify the offended man he recalled the letter that same day and put it away in his files with the indorsement: "Withdrawn, because considered harsh by General Halleck." He was pleased when the general then agreed to remain at his post, even though he amounted, as Lincoln subsequently remarked, to "little more . . . than a first-rate clerk." The fact was, in spite of his objection to what he called "Halleck's habitual attitude of demur," he valued his opinions highly, especially those on theoretical or procedural matters. "He is a military man, has had a military education. I brought him here to give me military advice." So Lincoln defended him, and added: "However you may doubt or disagree [with] Halleck, he is very apt to be right in the end." Then too, since he knew something of the unfortunate general's sufferings from hemorrhoids, which made him gruff as a sore-tailed bear and caused him to be avoided by all who could possibly stay beyond his reach, Lincoln's sympathy was aroused. Once when he was asked why he did not get rid of so unpleasant a creature, he replied: "Well, the fact is the man has no friends. [He] should be taken care of."

All in all, it had been a wearing day, and as Lincoln went to bed that night (having attended to several other less important matters, such as the complaint made to him by "an old lady of genteel appearance" that, despite previous assurances to the contrary, her boarding house near the corner of Tenth and E Streets was about to be commandeered by the War Department; "I know nothing about it myself," he wrote Stanton, "but promised to bring it to your notice") he might well have slept the sleep of nervous exhaustion: unless, that is, he was kept awake by an aching right hand, which had been squeezed and pumped by more than a thousand people in the course of this busy New Year's, or by the knowledge that from now on — or at any rate until he found the man who, as he said, could "face the arithmetic"— he would have to continue to act as his own general-in-chief, as in fact he had been doing all along, leaving the West Pointer who occupied the post at present to act as little more than a clerk, albeit a first-rate one.

In the days that followed hard on this, the one touch of relief in a prevailing military gloom was the news that Bragg had retreated from Stones River and that Rosecrans had taken Murfreesboro. Lincoln would have preferred a bolder pursuit, but he was grateful all the same for what he got. "I can never forget, while I remember anything," he told Rosecrans some months later, looking back, "that at about the end of last year, and beginning of this, you gave us a hard-earned victory which, had there been a defeat instead, the nation could scarcely have lived over." The law of diminishing utility obtained here in reverse; by contrast, this one glimmer swelled to bonfire proportions. All else was blackness — even afloat, where up to now the salt-water navy (so long at least as it had kept to its proper medium and stayed out of the muddy Mississippi) had suffered not a single major check in all the more than twenty months since the opening shots were fired at Sumter. Now suddenly all the news was bad and the checks frequent: not only at Galveston, where Magruder's cotton-clads had wrecked and panicked the Union warships, driving them from the bay, but also at other points along and off the rebel shore, before and after that disaster.

The first of these several naval wounds was self-inflicted, so to speak, or at any rate was not the result of enemy action. This did not make it any less painful or sad, however, for though the loss amounted to only one ship, that one was the most famous in the navy. Under tow off stormy Hatteras, with waves breaking over her deck and starting the oakum from her turret seam, the little ironclad *Monitor* — David to the *Merrimac*'s Goliath in Hampton Roads almost ten months ago — foundered and went to the bottom in the first hour of the last day of the year, taking four of her officers and a dozen of her crew down with her. This was hard news for the North, and close on its heels came word of what happened in Galveston harbor the following day. By way of reaction, the squadron commander at Pensacola ordered the 24-gun screw steamer *Brooklyn* and six gunboats to haul off from the blockade of Mobile and proceed at once to Texas to retrieve the situation. They arrived on January 8, but found there was little they could do except resume the blockade outside the harbor and engage in long-range shelling of the island town, now fast in rebel hands. They kept this up for three days, with little or no profit, until on January 11 they were handed another jolt.

About an hour before sundown the *Brooklyn*'s lookout spotted a bark-rigged vessel, apparently a merchantman, approaching from the south. When she saw the blockaders she halted as if surprised, and the Union flag officer, finding her manner suspicious, ordered the 10-gun sidewheel steamer *Hatteras* to heave her to for investigation of her papers. As the gunboat approached, she drew off and the chase began. It was a strange business. She ran awkwardly, despite the trimness of her lines, and though she managed to maintain her distance, on through twilight into a moonless darkness relieved only by the stars, the blockader had no difficulty in keeping her within sight. At last she hove to, as if exhausted, her sails furled. The *Hatteras* closed to within a hundred yards, stopped dead, and put a boat out. Before the boarding party reached her, however, a loud clear voice identified the vessel: "This is the Confederate States steamer *Alabama;* FIRE!" and a broadside lurched her sideways in the water, striking the *Hatteras* hard amidships so that she too recoiled, as if in horror. Ten guns to eight, the Federal outweighed her adversary by one hundred tons, but the advantage of surprise was decisive. Though she promptly returned the fire, the fight was brief. Within thirteen minutes, her walking beam shot away and her magazine flooded, she hoisted the signal for surrender.

"Have you struck?"

"I have."

"Cease fire! Cease fire!"

Within another six minutes she was on the bottom, thirty-fifth on the list of vessels taken, sunk, or ransomed by Captain Raphael Semmes, who would add another thirty-six to the list before the year was out.

He had read in captured Boston newspapers that the 30,000-man expedition under Banks was scheduled to rendezvous off Galveston on January 10 for the conquest of Texas, and he had shown up the following day, intending to get among the transports under cover of darkness, just outside the bar, and sink them left and right. When he saw the gunboats shelling the town, however, he knew it had been retaken, and he seized the opportunity to realize his life's ambition to stage a hand-to-hand fight with an enemy warship, provided he could lure one into pursuit and single combat: which he had done, fluttering just beyond her reach like a wounded bird until, having her altogether to himself, he turned and pounced. He was proud of the outcome of this "first yardarm engagement between steamers at sea," but just now his problem was to get away before his victim's friends, warned of the hoax by the flash and roar of guns, came up to avenge her. Pausing long enough to pick up the 118 survivors — about as many as he had in his whole crew, whose only casualty was a carpenter's mate with a cheek wound — he doused his lights and made off through the night. The *Brooklyn* and the other gunboats, arriving shortly thereafter, saw no sign of the *Hatteras* until dawn showed bits of her wreckage tossed about by the waves. By that time the *Alabama* was a hundred miles away, running hard for Jamaica, where Semmes and his crew — that "precious set of rascals," as he called them, being known in turn as "Old Beeswax" because of the needle-sharp tips to his long black mustache — would parole their captives and celebrate their exploit. Chagrined, the Union skippers turned back to resume their fruitless shelling of the island, bitterly conscious of the fact that instead of redeeming the late Galveston disaster, as they had intended, they had enlarged it.

Word of this no sooner reached Washington than it was followed, four days later, by news that was potentially even worse. At Mobile, where the departure of the *Brooklyn* and her consorts had weakened the cordon drawn across the entrance to the bay, the other famous Confederate raider *Florida* had been bottled up since early September, when she slipped in through the blockade with her crew and captain, Commander John N. Maffitt, down with yellow fever. By now they were very much up and about, however: as they proved on the night of January 15, when they steered the rebel cruiser squarely between two of the largest and fastest ships in the blockade squadron and made unscathed for the open sea, leaving her frantic pursuers far behind. Within ten days she had captured and sunk three U.S. merchantmen, the first of more then twenty she would take before midsummer, in happy rivalry with her younger sister the *Alabama*. Secretary Welles had been so furious over her penetration of the cordon, four months back, that he had summarily dismissed the squadron commander from the navy, despite the fact that he was a nephew of Commodore Edward Preble of *Constitution* fame; but this repetition of the exploit, outward bound, was seen by some as a reflection on the Secretary himself and a substantiation of the protest a prominent New Yorker had made to Lincoln, on the occasion of the Connecticut journalist's appointment, that if he would "select an attractive figurehead, to be adorned with an elaborate wig and luxuriant whiskers, and transfer it from the prow of a ship to the entrance of the Navy Department, it would in my opinion be quite as serviceable . . . and less expensive."

Nor was this by any means the last bad news to reach the Department from down on the Gulf before the month was out. On January 21, at the end of the week that had opened with the *Florida*'s escape, John Magruder staged in Texas — apparently, like Browning's thrush, lest it be thought that the first had been no more than a fine careless rapture — a re-enactment of the previous descent on the Union flotilla in Galveston harbor. This time the scene was Sabine Pass, eighty miles to the east, and once more two cotton-clad steamboats were employed, with like results. The *Morning Light*, a sloop of war, and the schooner *Velocity*, finding themselves unable to maneuver in all the confusion, struck their flags and surrendered 11 guns and more than a hundred seamen to the jubilant Confederates who had come booming down the pass with a rattle of small arms and a caterwaul of high-pitched rebel yells. Next day the blockade was re-established by gunboats sent over from the flotilla cruising off Galveston, but there was little satisfaction in the fact, considering the increase of tension in the wardrooms and on lookout stations. However, a lull now followed, almost as if the crowing rebels were giving the bluejackets time to digest the three bitter pills administered in the course of the past three weeks.

For Lincoln there was no such lull, nor did there seem likely to be one so long as the present commander of the Army of the Potomac remained at his post. He had chosen Burnside primarily as a man of action, and however far the ruff-whiskered general had fallen short of other expectations, from the day of his appointment he had never done less than his fervent best to measure up to this one. The Fredericksburg fight, pressed despite a snarl-up of preparatory matters which had turned it into something quite different from what had been intended at the outset, was an instance of that determination to be up and doing, and Lincoln was in constant trepidation that a similar sequence of snarl-ups — the canceled year-end maneuver, for example — presaged a similar disaster. The signs were unmistakably there.

Four days after the New Year's conference Burnside informed the President that he still intended to attempt another Rappahannock crossing, and had in fact alerted his engineers, although his generals practically unanimously remained opposed to the movement. Inclosed with the note was his resignation; Lincoln could either sustain him or let him return to civilian life. Another letter went to Halleck this same day. "I do not ask you to assume any responsibility in reference to the mode or place of crossing," Burnside wrote, "but it seems to me that, in making so hazardous a movement, I should receive some general directions from you as to the advisability of crossing at some point, as you are necessarily well informed of the effect at this time upon other parts of the army of a success or a repulse." However, this attempt to wring a definite personal commitment from the general-in-chief was no more productive than Lincoln's had been. Halleck — described by a correspondent as resembling "an oleaginous Methodist parson in regimentals," with a "large, tabular, Teutonic" face — replied on January 7, administering an elementary textbook strategy lecture. He had always been in favor of an advance, he said, but he cautioned Burnside to "effect a crossing in a position where we can meet the enemy on favorable or even equal terms. . . . If the enemy should concentrate his forces at the place you have selected for a crossing, make it a feint and try another place. Again, the circumstances at the time may be such as to render an attempt to cross the entire army not advisable. In that case theory suggests that, while the enemy concentrates at that point, advantages can be gained by crossing smaller forces at other points, to cut off his lines, destroy his communication, and capture his rear guards, outposts, &c. The great object is . . . to injure him all you can with the least injury to yourself. . . . As you yourself admit, it devolves upon you to decide upon the time, place, and character of the crossing which you may attempt. I can only advise that an attempt be made, and as early as possible. Very respectfully, your obedient servant, H. W. Halleck, General-in-Chief."

Burnside had asked for "general directions." What he got was very general advice. Tacked onto it, however, was a presidential indorsement in which, after urging him to "be cautious, and do not understand that the Government or the country is driving you," Lincoln added: "I do not yet see how I could profit by changing the command of the Army of the Potomac, and if I did, I should not do it by accepting the resignation of your commission." The "yet" might well have given Burnside pause, but at any rate he had a sort of left-handed reply to his ultimatum demanding that the President either fire or sustain him. He prepared therefore to go ahead with his plan for an upstream crossing, beyond Lee's left, and a southward march to some rearward point athwart the Confederate lines of supply and communication. This time he intended to guard against failure by feeling his way carefully beforehand. After originally selecting United States Ford as the bridgehead, a dozen miles above Fredericksburg, he rejected it when a cavalry reconnaissance showed the position well covered by Confederate guns, and selected instead Banks Ford, which was not only less heavily protected but was also less than half as far away. By January 19 his preparations were complete. Next morning his soldiers assembled under full packs for the march, stood there while a general order was read to them, and set out with its spirited phrases ringing in their ears: "The commanding general announces to the Army of the Potomac that they are about to meet the enemy once more. . . . The auspicious moment seems to have arrived to strike a great and mortal blow to the rebellion, and to gain that decisive victory which is due to the country."

It took several hours for so many men to clear their camps, but once this had been done the march went well — indeed, auspiciously — until midafternoon, when a slow drizzle began. For a time it seemed no more than a passing shower, but the sun went down behind a steely curtain of true rain, which was pattering steadily by nightfall. All night it fell; by morning it was drumming without letup. Looking out from their sodden bivouacs, in which they could find not even enough dry twigs for boiling coffee, the soldiers could hardly recognize yesterday's Virginia. "The whole country was an ocean of mud," one wrote. "The roads were rivers of deep mire, and the heavy rain had made the ground a vast mortar bed." Presently, as the troops fell in coffeeless to resume the march in a downpour that showed no sign of slacking, broad-tired wagons loaded with big pontoons (despite all Burnside's precautions against snarl-ups, the pontoniers had been late in getting the word) churned the roads to near-impassability. Their six-mule teams were doubled and even tripled, but to small avail. Then long ropes were attached to the cumbersome things, affording hand-holds for as many as 150 men at a time, but this still did no real good according to a correspondent who watched them strain and fail: "They would flounder through the mire for a few feet — the gang of Lilliputians with their huge-ribbed Gulliver — and then give up breathlessly." Guns were even more perverse. Whole regiments pulled them along with the help of prolonges, leaving deep troughs in the roadbed to mark their progress, but if they stopped for a breather, without first putting brush or logs under the axle, the gun would begin to sink and, what was worse, would keep on sinking until only its muzzle showed, and the men would have to dig it out with shovels. "One might fancy that some new geologic cataclysm had overtaken the world," a reporter declared, surveying the desolation, "and that he saw around him the elemental wrecks left by another Deluge." When Burnside himself, trailing a gaudy kite-tail of staff officers, came riding through this waste of mired confusion, one irreverent teamster whose mules and wagon were stalled like all the rest called out to him across the sea of mud: "General, the auspicious moment has arrived!"

He was undaunted, even in the face of this. Though the rain was still coming down steadily, without a suggestion of a pause, and though most of his soldiers were thinking, as one recalled, that "it was no longer a question of how to go forward, but how to get back," Burnside no more had it in mind to quit now than he had had six weeks ago, when he had kept throwing some of these same men against the fuming base of Marye's Heights. Today was finished but there was still tomorrow, and he gave orders that the march would be re-

sumed at dawn. However, in an attempt to raise the dejected spirits of
the troops, he directed that a ration of whiskey be issued to all ranks.
Somehow the barrels were brought up in the night and the distribution
made next morning. The result, in several cases — for the officers poured
liberally and the stuff went into empty stomachs — was spectacular. For
example, rival regiments from Pennsylvania and Massachusetts promptly
decided the time had come for them to settle a long-term feud, and
when a Maine outfit stepped in to try and stop the scuffle, the result
was the biggest three-sided fist fight in the history of the world. Meanwhile, from grandstand seats on the crests of hills across the way, the
rebels were enjoying all of this enormously. Pickets jeered from the
south bank of the Rappahannock, and one butternut cluster went so far
as to hold up a crudely lettered placard: THIS WAY TO RICHMOND, un-
derlined with an arrow pointing in the opposite direction. Finally, about
noon, even Burnside saw the hopelessness of the situation. He gave orders and the long, bedraggled files of men faced painfully about. The
Mud March — so called in the official records — was over.

It was over, that is for most of them, except for the getting back
to camp and the consequences. For some, though, it was over then and
there; they kept slogging northward, right on out of the war. Desertion
reached an all-time high. Sick lists had never been so long. Morale
hit an all-time low. "I never knew so much discontent in the army before," an enlisted diarist wrote. "A great many say that they 'don't
care whether school keeps or not,' for they think there is a destructive
fate hovering over our army." This reaction was by no means limited to
the ranks, and what was more the men in higher positions were specific
in their placement of the blame. "I came to the conclusion that Burnside
was fast losing his mind," Franklin was presently saying, and Hooker
was even more emphatic in the expression of his views. Without limiting his criticism to the luckless army commander, whom he considered
merely inept, he told a newsman that the President was an imbecile,
not only for keeping Burnside on but also in his own right, and that the
administration itself was "all played out." What the country needed,
Fighting Joe declared, and the sooner the better, too, was a dictator.
... Much of this reached army headquarters in one form or another,
and Burnside's thin-stretched patience finally snapped under the double
burden of abuse and ridicule. Early next evening, January 23, while his
troops were still straggling forlornly back to their camps, he wired
Lincoln: "I have prepared some very important orders, and I want to
see you before issuing them. Can I see you alone if I am at the White
House after midnight?"

In mud and fog and darkness he left headquarters about 9
o'clock in an ambulance, lost the road, found it, then lost it again, bumping into dead mules, stalled caissons, and other derelicts of the late
lamented march. Finally, near midnight, he arrived at the Falmouth rail-

head, two miles from his starting point, only to learn that the special locomotive he had ordered held had given him up and chuffed away on other business. He took a lantern and set out down the track to meet it coming back, flagged and boarded it, and at last got onto a steamer at Aquia Landing. It was midmorning before he was with Lincoln at the White House, but the orders he brought for his perusal were no less startling for having been delayed. What Burnside was suggesting — in fact *ordering*, "subject to the approval of the President" — was the immediate dismissal of four officers from the service and the relief of six from further duty with the Army of the Potomac. The first group was headed by Joe Hooker, who was referred to as "a man unfit to hold an important commission during a crisis like the present, when so much patience, charity, confidence, consideration, and patriotism are due from every soldier in the field." Next came Brigadier General W.T.H. Brooks, a division commander accused of "using language tending to demoralize his command." The other two, lumped together in one paragraph, were Newton and Cochrane, whose names Burnside had learned simply by checking the morning reports to see what general officers had been on pass at the time of their late-December conference with Lincoln. These four were to be cashiered. The six who were to be relieved were two major generals — Franklin and W. F. Smith, Newton's and Cochrane's corps commander — three brigadiers (including, by some strange oversight, Cochrane, who supposedly had just been cashiered) and one lieutenant colonel, a lowly assistant adjutant who was apparently to be struck by an incidental pellet from the blast that was to bring down all those other, larger birds.

Burnside left the order with the startled President, telling him plainly to make a choice between approving it or accepting its author's resignation from command of an army that included such a set of villains. The order was dated the 23d, a Friday. Lincoln took what was left of Saturday to think the matter over. Then on Sunday, January 25, the ruff-whiskered general got his answer in the form of a general order of Lincoln's own, directing: 1) that Burnside be relieved of command, upon his own request; 2) that Sumner be relieved, also upon his own request; 3) that Franklin be relieved, period; and 4) "that Maj. Gen. J. Hooker be assigned to the command of the Army of the Potomac."

This last was a hard thing for the departing commander to accept. He had planned to blow up Hooker, but instead he had blown himself up, and Hooker into his place. It was hard, too, for Sumner and for Franklin; the fact that both were the new commander's seniors necessitated their transfer after long association with the eastern army. Lincoln did not so much regret having to sidetrack Franklin, whose lack of aggressiveness at South Mountain and Fredericksburg was notorious, but he was sorry to have to offend the superannuated Sumner, who had saved the day at Fair Oaks and fought well on every field until his soul was sickened by the slaughter at Antietam. Nor had he hurt without regret the normally good-natured Burnside, whose forthright honesty in admission of faults and acceptance of blame was so different from what was ordinarily encountered. However, what there had been of hesitation was mainly based on what Lincoln knew of Fighting Joe himself, who was next in line for the assignment. He had heard from others beside Burnside of Hooker's infidelity to his chief, and also of his excoriation of the Washington authorities. In fact, when the *Times* reporter who had talked recently with Hooker came to Lincoln on this Sunday and told him of what the general had said about the administration's shortcomings and the need for a dictator, Lincoln showed no trace of surprise. "That is all true; Hooker does talk badly," he admitted. But he decided, all the same, that Hooker was what the army and the country needed in the present crisis — a fighter who, unlike Burnside, had self-confidence and a reputation for canniness. "Now there is Joe Hooker," Lincoln had remarked a short time back. "He can fight. I think that is pretty well established."

And so it was. Without consulting Halleck or Stanton or anyone else, and despite the admitted risk to the national cause and the incidental injury to Burnside and Sumner, he made his choice and acted on it. However, before the new commander had been two days at his post, Lincoln sent for him and handed him a letter which was calculated to let him know how much he knew about him, as well as to advise him of what was now expected:

> General:
> I have placed you at the head of the Army of the Potomac. Of course I have done this upon what appear to me to be sufficient reasons, and yet I think it best for you to know that there are some things in regard to which I am not quite satisfied with you. I believe you to be a brave and a skillful soldier, which of course I like. I also believe you do not mix politics with your profession, in which you are right. You have confidence in yourself, which is a valuable if not an indispensable quality. You are ambitious, which, within reasonable bounds, does good rather than harm; but I think that during General Burnside's command of the army you have taken counsel of your ambition and thwarted him as much as you could, in which you did a great wrong to the country and to a most meritorious and honorable brother officer. I have heard, in such way as to believe it, of your recently saying that both the army and the government needed a dictator. Of course it was not for this, but in spite of it, that I have given you the command. Only those generals who gain successes can set up dictators. What I now ask of you is military success, and I will risk the dictatorship. The government will support you to the utmost of its ability, which is neither more nor less than it has done and will do for all commanders. I much fear that the spirit which you have aided to infuse into the army, of criticising their commander and withhold-

ing confidence from him, will now turn upon you. I shall assist you
as far as I can to put it down. Neither you nor Napoleon, if he were
alive again, could get any good out of an army while such a spirit
prevails in it.

And now, beware of rashness. Beware of rashness, but with energy
and sleepless vigilance go forward and give us victories.

Yours very truly

A. LINCOLN

✕ 2 ✕

McClernand, conferring with Sherman at Milliken's Bend on the day
after his arrival from upriver — it was January 3; the two were aboard
the former Illinois politician's headquarters boat, the *Tigress,* tied up to
bank twenty-odd miles above Vicksburg — did not blame the red-
haired Ohioan for the repulse suffered earlier that week at Chickasaw
Bluffs; Sherman, he said in a letter to Stanton that same day, had "probably done all in the present case anyone could have done." The fault
was Grant's, and Grant's alone. Grant had designed the operation and
then, taking off half-cocked in his eagerness for glory that was rightfully another's, had failed to co-operate as promised, leaving Sherman to
hold the bag and do the bleeding. So McClernand said, considerably em-
bittered by the knowledge that a good part of the nearly two thousand
casualties lost up the Yazoo were recruits he had been sending down
from Cairo for the past two months, only to have them snatched from
under him while his back was turned. "I believe I am superseded.
Please advise me," he had wired Lincoln as soon as he got word of
what was afoot. But permission to go downriver had not come in time
for him to circumvent the circumvention; the fighting was over before
he got there. He took what consolation he could from having been
spared a share in a fiasco. At least he was with his men again — what
was left of them, at any rate — and ready to take over. "Soon as I shall
have verified the condition of the army," he told Stanton, "I will assume
command of it."

He did so the following day. Christening his new command "The
Army of the Mississippi" in nominal expression of his intentions, or at
any rate his hopes, he divided it into two corps of two divisions each,
the first under George Morgan and the second under Sherman —
which, incidentally, was something of a bitter pill for the latter to swallow, since he believed a large share of the blame for the recent failure up
the Yazoo rested with Morgan, who had promised that in ten minutes
he would "be on those hills," but who apparently had forgot to wind
his watch. However that might be, McClernand now had what he had
been wanting all along: the chance to prove his ingenuity and demonstrate his mettle in independent style. His eyes brightened with an-

ticipation of triumph as he spoke of "opening the navigation of the Mississippi," of "cutting my way to the sea," and so forth. For all the expansiveness of his mood, however, the terms in which he expressed it were more general than specific; or, as Sherman later said, "the *modus operandi* was not so clear."

In this connection — being anxious, moreover, to balance his recent defeat with a success — the Ohioan had a suggestion. During the Chickasaw Bluffs expedition the packet *Blue Wing,* coming south out of Memphis with a cargo of mail and ammunition, had been captured by a Confederate gunboat that swooped down on her near the mouth of the Arkansas and carried her forty miles up that river to Arkansas Post, an outpost established by the French away back in 1685, where the rebels had constructed an inclosed work they called Fort Hindman, garrisoned by about 5000 men. So long as this threat to the main Federal supply line existed, Sherman said, operations against Vicksburg would be subject to such harassment, and it was his belief that, by way of preamble to McClernand's larger plans — whatever they were, precisely — he ought to go up the Arkansas and abolish the threat by "thrashing out Fort Hindman."

McClernand was not so sure. He had suffered no defeat that needed canceling, and what was more he had larger things in mind than the capture of an obscure and isolated post. However, he agreed to go with Sherman for a discussion of the project with Porter, whose cooperation would be required. They steamed downriver and found the admiral aboard his headquarters boat, the *Black Hawk,* anchored in the mouth of the Yazoo. It was late, near midnight; Porter received them in his nightshirt. He too was not so sure at first. He was short of coal, he said, and the ironclads, which would be needed to reduce the fort, could not burn wood. Presently, though, as Sherman continued to press his suit, asking at least for the loan of a couple of gunboats, which he offered to tow up the river and thus save coal, Porter — perhaps reflecting that he had on his record that same blot which a victory would erase — not only agreed to give the landsmen naval support; "Suppose I go along myself?" he added. Suddenly, on second thought, McClernand was convinced: so much so, indeed, that instead of merely sending Sherman to do the job with half the troops, as Sherman had expected, he decided it was worth the undivided attention of the whole army and its commander, whose record, if blotless, was also blank. With no minus to cancel, this plus would stand alone, auspicious, and make a good beginning as he stepped off on the road that led to glory and the White House.

He took three days to get ready, then (but not until then) sent a message by way of Memphis to notify Grant that he was off — one of his purposes being, as he said, "the counteraction of the moral effect of the failure of the attack near Vicksburg and the reinspiration of the forces repulsed by making them the champions of new, important, and successful enterprises." He left Milliken's Bend that same day, January 8, his 30,000 soldiers still aboard their fifty transports, accompanied by 13 rams and gunboats, three of which were ironclads and packed his Sunday punch. By way of deception the flotilla steamed past the mouth of the Arkansas, then into the White, from which a cutoff led back into the bypassed river. Late the following afternoon the troops began debarking three miles below Fort Hindman, a square bastioned work set on high ground at the head of a horseshoe bend, whose dozen guns included three 9-inch Columbiads, one to each riverward casemate, and a hard-hitting 8-inch rifle. A good portion of the defending butternut infantry, supported by six light pieces of field artillery, occupied a line of rifle-pits a mile and a half below the fort, but these were quickly driven out when the gunboats forged ahead and took them under fire from the flank. Late the following afternoon, when the debarkation had been completed and the four divisions were maneuvering for positions from which to launch an assault, the ironclads took the lead. The *Louisville*, the *De Kalb*, and the *Cincinnati* advanced in line abreast to within four hundred yards of the fort, pressing the attack bows on, one to each casemate, while the thinner-skinned vessels followed close behind to throw in shrapnel and light rifled shell. It was hot work for a time as the defenders stood to their guns, firing with precision; the *Cincinnati*, for example, took eight hits from 9-inch shells on her pilot house alone, though Porter reported proudly that they "glanced off like peas against glass"; the only naval casualties were suffered from unlucky shots that came in through the ports. When the admiral broke off the fight because of darkness, the fort was silent, apparently overwhelmed. But when Sherman, reconnoitering by moonlight, drew close to the enemy outposts he could hear the Confederates at work with spades and axes, drawing a new line under cover of their heavy guns and preparing to continue to resist despite the long numerical odds. Crouched behind a stump in the predawn darkness of January 11 he heard a rebel bugler sound what he later called "as pretty a reveille as I ever listened to."

Shortly before noon he sent word that he was ready. His corps was on the right, Morgan's on the left; both faced the newly drawn enemy line which extended across the rear of the fort, from the river to an impassable swamp one mile west. McClernand, having established a command post in the woods and sent a lookout up a tree to observe and report the progress of events, passed the word to Porter, who ordered the ironclads forward at 1.30 to renew yesterday's attack. Sherman heard the clear ring of the naval guns, the fire increasing in volume and rapidity as the range was closed. Then he and Morgan went forward, the troops advancing by rushes across the open fields, "once or twice falling to the ground," as Sherman said, "for a sort of rest or pause." As they approached the fort they saw above its parapet the pennants of the ironclads, which had smothered the heavy guns by now and were giving the place a close-up pounding. Simultaneously, white flags began to break out all along the rebel line. "Cease firing! Cease firing!" Sherman cried, and rode forward to receive the fort's surrender.

But that was not to be: not just yet, at any rate, and not to Sherman. Colonel John Dunnington, the fort's commander, a former U.S. naval officer, insisted on surrendering to Porter, and Brigadier General Thomas J. Churchill, commander of the field force, did not want to surrender at all. As Sherman approached, Churchill was arguing with his subordinates, wanting to know by whose authority the white flags had been shown. (He had received an order from Little Rock the night before, while there was still a chance to get away, "to hold out till help arrives or until all dead" — which Holmes later explained with the comment: "It never occurred to me when the order was issued that such an overpowering command would be devoted to an end so trivial.") One brigade commander, Colonel James Deshler of Alabama, a fiery West Pointer in his late twenties — "small but very handsome," Sherman called him — did not want to stop fighting even now, with the Yankees already inside his works. When Sherman, wishing as he said "to soften the blow of defeat," remarked in a friendly way that he knew a family of Deshlers in his home state and wondered if they were relations, the Alabamian hotly disclaimed kinship with anyone north of the Ohio River; whereupon the red-headed general changed his tone and, as he later wrote, "gave him a piece of my mind that he did not relish." However, all this was rather beside the point. The fighting was over and the butternut troops stacked arms. The Federals had suffered 31 navy and 1032 army casualties, for a total of 140 killed and 923 wounded. The Confederates, on the other hand, had had only 109 men hit; but that left 4791 to be taken captive, including a regiment that marched in from Pine Bluff during the surrender negotiations.

McClernand, who had got back aboard the *Tigress* and come forward, was tremendously set up. "Glorious! Glorious!" he kept exclaiming. "My star is ever in the ascendant." He could scarcely contain himself. "I had a man up a tree," he said. "I'll make a splendid report!"

Grant by now was in Memphis. He had arrived the day before, riding in ahead of the main body, which was still on the way under McPherson, near the end of its long retrograde movement from Coffeeville, northward through the scorched wreckage of Holly Springs, then westward by way of Grand Junction and LaGrange. Having heard no word from Sherman, he knew nothing of his friend's defeat downriver — optimistic as always, he was even inclined to credit rumors that the Vicksburg defenses had crumbled under assault from the Yazoo —

until the evening of his arrival, when he received McClernand's letter from Milliken's Bend informing him of the need for "reinspiration of the forces repulsed."

This was something of a backhand slap, at least by implication — McClernand seemed to be saying that he would set right what Grant had bungled — but what disturbed him most was the Illinois general's expressed intention to withdraw upriver for what he called "new, important, and successful enterprises." For one thing, if Banks was on the way up from New Orleans in accordance with the instructions for a combined assault on Vicksburg, it would leave him unsupported when he got there. For another, any division of effort was wrong as long as the true objective remained unaccomplished, and Grant said so in no uncertain terms next morning when he replied to McClernand's letter: "I do not approve of your move on the Post of Arkansas while the other is in abeyance. It will lead to the loss of men without a result. . . . It might answer for some of the purposes you suggest, but certainly not as a military movement looking to the accomplishment of the one great result, the capture of Vicksburg. Unless you are acting under authority not derived from me, keep your command where it can soonest be assembled for the renewal of the attack on Vicksburg. . . . From the best information I have, Milliken's Bend is the proper place for you to be, and unless there is some great reason of which I am not advised you will immediately proceed to that point and await the arrival of reinforcements and General Banks' expedition, keeping me fully advised of your movements."

He expressed his opinion more briefly in a telegram sent to Halleck that afternoon: "General McClernand has fallen back to White River, and gone on a wild-goose chase to the Post of Arkansas. I am ready to reinforce, but must await further information before knowing what to do." The general-in-chief replied promptly the following morning, January 12: "You are hereby authorized to relieve General Mc-Clernand from command of the expedition against Vicksburg, giving it to the next in rank or taking it yourself."

Grant now had what he wanted. Formerly he had moved with caution in the prosecution of his private war, by no means sure that in wrecking McClernand he would not be calling down the thunder on his own head; but not now. Halleck almost certainly would have discussed so important a matter with Lincoln before adding this ultimate weapon to Grant's arsenal and assuring him that there would be no restrictions from above as to its use. In short, Grant could proceed without fear of retaliation except from the victim himself, whom he outranked. However, two pieces of information that came to hand within the next twenty-four hours forestalled delivery of the blow. First, he learned that Port Hudson was a more formidable obstacle than he had formerly supposed, which meant that it was unlikely that Banks's upriver thrust would reach Vicksburg at any early date. And, second, he received next day from McClernand himself the "splendid report" announcing the fall of Arkansas Post and the capture of "a large number of prisoners, variously estimated at from 7000 to 10,000, together with all [their] stores, animals, and munitions of war." Not only was the urgency for a hookup with Banks removed, but to proceed against McClernand now would be to attack a public hero in his first full flush of victory; besides which, Grant had also learned that the inception of what he had called the "wild-goose chase" had been upon the advice of his friend Sherman, and this put a different complexion on his judgment as to the military soundness of the expedition. All that remained was to play the old army game — which Grant well knew how to do, having had it played against him with such success, nine years ago in California, that he had been nudged completely out of the service. When the time came for pouncing he would pounce, but not before. Meanwhile he would wait, watching and building up his case as he did so.

This did not mean that he intended to sit idly by while McClernand continued to gather present glory; not by a long shot. Four days later, January 17 — McClernand having returned as ordered to the Mississippi, awaiting further instructions at Napoleon, just below the mouth of the Arkansas — Grant got aboard a steamboat headed south from the Memphis wharf. Before leaving he wired McPherson, who had called a halt at LaGrange to rest his troops near the end of their long retreat from Coffeeville: "It is my present intention to command the expedition down the river in person."

★   ★   ★

Banks was going to be a lot longer in reaching Vicksburg than Grant knew, and more was going to detain him than the guns that bristled atop the bluff at Port Hudson. After a sobering look at this bastion he decided that his proper course of action, before attempting a reduction of that place or a sprint past its frowning batteries, would be a move up the opposite bank of the big river, clearing out the various nests of rebels who otherwise would interfere with his progress by harassing his flank as he moved upstream. Brigadier General Godfrey Weitzel, a twenty-eight-year-old West Pointer who already had been stationed in that direction by Ben Butler, was reinforced by troops from the New Orleans and Baton Rouge garrisons and told to make the region west of those two cities secure from molestation. He built a stout defensive work at Donaldsonville, commanding the head of Bayou La Fourche, and threw up intrenchments at Brashear City, blocking the approach from Berwick Bay. Then, crossing the bay with his mobile force on January 13, he entered and began to ascend the Teche, accompanied by three gunboats. This brought him into sudden contact next morning with Richard Taylor, who fought briefly and fell back, sinking the armed steamer *Cotton* athwart the bayou as he did so, corking it against farther penetration. Weitzel, who had lost 33 killed and wounded, including one of the navy skippers picked off by a sniper, reported proudly as he withdrew: "The Confederate States gunboat *Cotton* is one of the things that were. . . . My men behaved magnificently. I am recrossing the bay."

As a successful operation — the first of what he intended would be many — this was unquestionably gratifying to Banks, who made the most of it in reporting the action to Washington as a follow-up to the bloodless reoccupation of the Louisiana capital. Yet even as he tendered his thanks to Weitzel for "the skillful manner in which he has performed the task confided to him," he could also see much that was foreboding in this small-scale expedition up the Teche. For one thing, the rebels were very much there, though in what numbers he did not know, and for another they would fight, but only as it suited them, choosing the time and place that gave them the best advantage, fading back into the rank undergrowth quite as mysteriously as they had appeared, and then moving forward again as the bluecoats withdrew from what Taylor himself, who knew all its crooks and byways, called "a region of lakes, bayous, jungle, and bog." How long it might take to clear such an army of phantoms from the district, or whether indeed it could ever be done, Banks could not tell. By mid-January, however, he had decided that it would have to be done. His expectations, described in mid-December as "most sanguine," were tempered now by prudence and better acquaintance with the peculiar factors involved. He perceived that they would have to be refashioned to conform to a different schedule before he attempted the reduction of Port Hudson and the eventual link-up with Grant in front of Vicksburg, all those devious hundreds of miles up the tawny Mississippi.

In Northwest Arkansas and South Missouri things were not going much better for John Schofield, who had risen from a sickbed to resume command of his army on the morrow of Prairie Grove. They could in fact be said to be going a good deal worse, so far at least as personal vexation was concerned. He had won a battle (or anyhow Blunt and Herron had, with the result that they were about to be promoted over his head) and had followed it up with a lunge at Van Buren, resulting in the destruction of Hindman's stores, before withdrawing to Fayetteville; but he had no sooner regained the presumed security of this pro-Union district, where he expected to enjoy in comparative relaxation his belated but welcome promotion to major general, than he was distracted by a series of explosions in his rear. First, Hindman unleashed his cavalry under Brigadier General John S. Marmaduke, a Missouri-born West Pointer, for an all-out raid on the main Federal supply base at Springfield, a hundred miles north of the point where Schofield was in the

process of drawing his lines facing south. On New Year's Eve Marmaduke left Lewisburg, on the north bank of the Arkansas River midway
across the state, and reached his objective one week later at the head of
2300 horsemen, many of them picked up along the way and added to the
original brigade of veterans under Colonel J. O. Shelby, who had led
them on every field since Wilson's Creek. Attacking on January 8 the
raiders burned the Springfield depot of supplies and withdrew eastward
45 miles to strike at Hartville on the 11th, with similar results after savage fighting, then turned south through a gale of sleet and snow,
gobbling up enemy detachments as they went, and recrossed the White
River at Batesville on January 25.

Casualties in the two main fights had been about 250 on each
side, in addition to which Marmaduke not only had captured and paroled
more than 300 of the enemy in the course of the raid, for the most
part turning them loose in bitter weather without their outer garments
— "In winter," one observer remarked, "the overcoat-bearing Federal
was esteemed especially for his pelt" — but also had destroyed vital reserve supplies and refitted his troopers with arms and equipment greatly
superior to the ones they had carried northward. All this came out of
Schofield's pocket, so to speak, but that was by no means the most
painful aftereffect of the operation. Major General Samuel Curtis, promoted to command of the department as a result of his Pea Ridge victory back in March, took alarm and ordered the Army of the Frontier
withdrawn from Fayetteville to protect the penetrated region across
the state line in its rear, abolishing at a stroke the hard-won gains of
Prairie Grove. Schofield protested, to no avail; Missouri soon had greater
need than ever for on-the-spot protection, Marmaduke's excursion having served to bring the guerillas out of hiding and onto the highways,
along which new recruits hastened to join the bands reassembling under such leaders as George Todd, David Pool, William C. Anderson,
called "Bloody Bill," and William C. Quantrill. Enrolling was a simple
process. All a recruit had to do was answer "Yes" to the question: "Will
you follow orders, be true to your fellows, and kill all those who
serve and support the Union?"

In the wake of this sudden activity, in effect not unlike the upset-
ting of a beehive, came violent dissension in the ranks of the Union leaders.
Curtis, a former Iowa Republican congressman and abolitionist, represented the radical faction, while Schofield, with the support of Governor
Hamilton R. Gamble, became the champion of conservative views. Militarily, as well, the two generals were divergent in opinion. Curtis wanted
to hold all available troops within the borders of the state in order to
use them in putting down troublemakers of all sorts, armed or unarmed; Schofield on the other hand believed in taking the offensive
against the Confederates to his front in Arkansas. At length, as the situation grew more tense between the two, Lincoln was appealed to as ar-

bitrator. He backed the department commander, ordering Schofield east
of the Mississippi and leaving the hero of Pea Ridge in full control.
However, the storm of protest which followed this decision gave
promise of greater trouble than ever, and caused him to seek a different solution. Transferring Curtis out to Kansas, where his political views
would be more in accord with those of the majority of the people,
Lincoln appointed as the new commander of the Department of Missouri old Edwin V. Sumner, lately relieved of duty with the Army of
the Potomac. But this did not work either; Sumner died en route. . . .
It was March 21. Breaking his journey at Syracuse, New York, the old
soldier lay in a coma, as if in belated reaction to the horror of Antietam,
where he had begun to lose the grip that had been strong enough to
save the day at Fair Oaks. "The Second Corps never lost a flag or a
cannon!" he suddenly cried out. When his aide came over he opened
his eyes. "That is true; never lost one," he said weakly. At sixty-six he
was nearing the end of forty-four years of army service, and except for
his long sharp nose he resembled a death's-head. The aide raised him to a
more comfortable position on the bed and poured him a glass of wine,
prescribed by the doctor to keep up his strength. Sumner took a sip,
saying across the rim of the glass by way of a toast: "God save my
country, the United States of America," then dropped the glass and died.
. . . Lincoln, receiving the news of Sumner's death, decided that Schofield was probably the best man to take charge in Missouri after all. In
reassigning him to duty there, however, he thought it proper to give
him some advice on how to proceed among people who were engaged in
what he called "a pestilent factional quarrel among themselves." It was,
he said in the accents of Polonius, "a difficult role, and so much greater
will be the honor if you perform it well. If both factions, or neither,
shall abuse you, you will probably be about right. Beware of being
assailed by one and praised by the other."

The trouble with this, as advice, was that it was the counsel of
perfection, since the only way a man could avoid factions, being cham-
pioned on the one hand and excoriated on the other, was to stay out of
Missouri in the first place. Schofield, a rather plump New York West
Pointer who wore a long thin growth of curly whiskers in partial
compensation for the fact that he was already balding at the age of
thirty-two, was quite aware of this, of course, but promised to do his
best in that regard. At the same time, however — it was late spring by
then, well up in May — he had to forgo his plans for an offensive into
Arkansas, not only because of guerilla troubles within his department
(they continued to grow worse as time went by, until at last they exceeded in horror the wildest nightmares Curtis or anyone else, except
possibly Bill Anderson and Quantrill — not to mention old John Brown
— had ever had) but also because he lacked the troops, Missouri having
become in effect a recruiting ground for the support of operations far

down the big river that laved its eastern flank. Schofield could only give what he had promised, his best, and if this was not a great deal, under the nearly impossible circumstances it was enough.

He could take consolation, however, in the fact that the Confederates to the south were quite as bedeviled as he himself was, though in a different way: with the result that throughout this unhappy season, when so much of military importance was moving inexorably toward a climax on the east flank of the theater, they were no more able to assume the offensive than Schofield was. Not only were they suffering from an even more acute shortage of troops, but a sequence of rapid-fire shifts in command, beginning at the very top, quite paralyzed whatever movements they might otherwise have undertaken.

Not that the shifts were avoidable. It had in fact already become apparent that Holmes had been given a good deal more than he could handle. In mid-January, a week after his return to Richmond from his western journey, Davis sent for Kirby Smith, whom he admired, and assigned him to command the newly created Department of West Louisiana and Texas, intending in this way to relieve Holmes of the task of co-ordinating the efforts of Taylor and Magruder. "Am I thus to be sent into exile?" Smith asked wistfully. Not yet thirty-nine, he ranked second among the nation's seven lieutenant generals, and Lee himself had lately said that he would be pleased to have him as a corps commander, alongside Longstreet and Jackson. Davis explained that the assignment, far from amounting to exile, was as important as any in the whole Confederacy, since his main duty "would be directed to aiding in the defense of the Lower Mississippi and keeping that great artery of the West effectually closed to Northern occupation or trade." Acquiescing, Smith set out in early February, only to learn en route that his command had been enlarged to include the entire Transmississippi. In the light of this he arranged with Pemberton for the transfer of Major General Sterling Price, who was much admired in the Far West and had formerly been governor of Missouri, the scene of his early victories at Wilson's Creek and Lexington. It was hoped that Price would repeat them presently, although a sadly large proportion of the men with whom he had won them were buried now in shallow graves around Corinth and Iuka, and the survivors, few as they were in number, were too badly needed around Vicksburg to be allowed to recross the river. How he would replace them Smith did not know, for the region had been stripped of troops, first by Van Dorn, who had brought them east after his defeat at Elkhorn Tavern, and then by Hindman, who, by stringent enforcement of the conscription laws, had raised the army which he had taken across the Boston Mountains and then returned with no more than a comparative handful. Smith soon found his worst fears confirmed. "The male population remaining are old men, or have furnished substitutes," he reported, "are lukewarm, or are wrapped up in speculation and money-making."

Crossing at Port Hudson, he ascended Red River in a steamboat Richard Taylor had waiting for him by prearrangement, and on March 7 at Alexandria, Louisiana, he assumed command of all troops west of the Mississippi. What he encountered first-off gave his Regular Army nature quite a shock. "There was no general system, no common head," he later reported; "each district was acting independently." It was necessary, he said, to "begin *de novo* in any attempt at a general systematizing and development of the department resources." Accordingly he set out at once on a preliminary tour of inspection, which only served to increase his first dismay. Conferring with Holmes at Little Rock — the North Carolinian now had charge of the subdepartment including Arkansas, Missouri, and Indian Territory — he found him anxiously awaiting the arrival of Price to command the army remnant left by Hindman, who had resigned in a huff at having been superseded by Holmes on the occasion of that officer's step-down from command of the whole theater. Price arrived before the end of the month, yet there was little he could do until he got his men in condition to fight, which obviously would not be soon. Smith meantime established his headquarters at Shreveport. He considered it "a miserable place with a miserable population," but it had the virtue of central location, at the head of navigation of Red River and on the direct route between Texas and Richmond. Here he set to work, laying the groundwork for organization of the enormous region which in time would be known as Kirby-Smithdom. He worked long hours and did not spare himself or his subordinates; but spring had come, and so had Banks and Grant, before his command — which included, in all, about 30,000 soldiers between the Mississippi and the Rio Grande, fewer even than Bragg had in the Duck River Valley or Pemberton had at Vicksburg and Port Hudson — was in any condition to offer them anything more than a token resistance.

★　★　★

After an all-night boat ride down the Mississippi, from Memphis past the mouth of the Arkansas, Grant reached Napoleon on January 18 to find McClernand, Porter, and Sherman awaiting his arrival with mixed emotions — mixed, that is, so far as McClernand's were concerned; Porter and Sherman were united, if by nothing more than a mutual and intense dislike of the congressman-turned-commander. To them, Grant came as something of a savior, since he outranked the object of their scorn. To McClernand, on the other hand, he seemed nothing of the sort; McClernand plainly suspected another attempt to steal his thunder, if not his army. He had enlarged his Arkansas Post exploit by sending a pair of gunboats up White River to drive the rebels from St Charles and wreck their installations at De Valls Bluff, terminus of the railroad running east from Little Rock toward Memphis. It was smartly done, accomplishing at the latter place the destruction of the depot and some rolling stock, as well as the capture of two 8-inch guns which the flustered garrison was trying to load aboard the cars for a getaway west. Still at Fort Hindman while this was in progress, McClernand received Grant's curt and critical letter ordering him back to the Mississippi at once, and he bucked it along to Lincoln with a covering letter of his own.

"I believe my success here is gall and wormwood to the clique of West Pointers who have been persecuting me for months," he wrote, imploring his friend and fellow-townsman not to "let me be clandestinely destroyed, or, what is worse, dishonored, without a hearing." He asked, "How can General Grant at a distance of 400 miles intelligently command the army with me?" and answered his own question without a pause: "He cannot do it. It should be made an independent command, as both you and the Secretary of War, as I believe, originally intended."

Grant was about to get in some licks of his own in this regard, if not through out-of-channels access to Lincoln — whom he had not only never met, but had never even seen, despite the fact that both had gone to war from Illinois — then at any rate through Halleck, which was the next-best thing. For the present he merely conferred with the three officers, collectively and singly, and ordered the return of the whole expedition to Milliken's Bend for a renewal of the drive on Vicksburg by the direct route. By now, however, as a result of his talk with these men who had been there, he was beginning to see that the only successful approach, after all, might have to be roundabout. "What may be necessary to reduce the place I do not yet know," he wired the general-in-chief, "but since the late rains [I] think our troops must get below the city to be used effectually."

He spent the night ashore at Napoleon, whose partial destruction by incendiaries the day before caused Sherman to declare that he was "free to admit we all deserve to be killed unless we can produce a state of discipline when such disgraceful acts cannot be committed unpunished." One solution, he decided, would be "to assess the damages upon the whole army, officers included," but no such drastic remedy was adopted. The following morning Grant saw the transports and their escort vessels steam away south, in accordance with his orders, and returned that evening to Memphis. Next day, January 20, he sent Halleck a long dispatch explaining the tactical situation as he saw it and announcing that, by way of a start, he intended to try his hand at redigging the canal across the base of the hairpin bend in front of Vicksburg, abandoned the previous summer by Butler's men when the two Union fleets were sundered and repulsed by the rebel warship *Arkansas*, now fortunately at the bottom of the river. Grant suggested that, in view of the importance of the campaign he was about to undertake, it would be wise to combine the four western departments, now under Banks, Curtis, Rosecrans, and himself, under a single over-all commander in order to assure co-operation. "As I am the senior department commander in the West," he wrote — apparently unaware that Banks was nine months his senior and in point of fact had been a major general before Grant himself was even a brigadier — "I will state that I have no desire whatever for such combined command, but would prefer the command I now have to any other than can be given." From which disclaimer he passed at once to the subject of John McClernand: "I regard it as my duty to state that I found there was not sufficient confidence felt in General Mc-Clernand as a commander, either by the Army or Navy, to insure him success. Of course, all would co-operate to the best of their ability, but still with a distrust. This is a matter I made no inquiries about, but it was thrust upon me." (As a later observer pointed out, there was "a touch of artfulness" in this; Grant "elevated Sherman and Porter to speak for entire branches of the service, then sought audiences with them so that the issue might be forced upon him!") However, he continued, "as it is my intention to command in person, unless otherwise directed, there is no special necessity of mentioning this matter; but I want you to know that others besides myself agree in the necessity of the course I had already determined upon pursuing."

His belief that Old Brains was on his side was strengthened the following day by a quick reply to his suggestion that "both banks of the Mississippi should be under one command, at least during the present operations." "The President has directed that so much of Arkansas as you may desire to control be temporarily attached to your department," Halleck wired. "This will give you control of both banks of the river." Pleased to learn of Lincoln's support, even at second hand, Grant kept busy with administrative and logistical matters preparatory to his departure from Memphis at the earliest possible date. McPherson was marching in from LaGrange with two divisions to accompany him downriver; these 14,979, added to the 32,015 already there, would give him an "aggregate present" of 46,994 in the vicinity of Vicksburg, with more to follow, not only from his own Department of the Tennessee, which included a grand total of 93,816 of all arms, but also from the Department of Missouri, now under Curtis and later under Schofield. On January 25 he received further evidence of Lincoln's interest in the campaign for control of the Lower Mississippi, whose whimsical habit of carving itself new channels the Chief Executive knew from having made two flatboat voyages down it to New Orleans as a youth. "Direct your attention particularly to the canal proposed across the point," Halleck urged. "The President attaches much importance to this."

Grant himself was about ready to embark by now, wiring the general-in-chief this same day: "I leave for the fleet . . . tomorrow." Last-minute details held him up an extra day, but on the 27th he was off. "The work of reducing Vicksburg will take time and men," he had told Halleck the week before, "but can be accomplished."

Sherman was already hard at work on the project which had drawn Lincoln's particular attention, and with his present arduous endeavor — in effect a gigantic wrestling match with Mother Nature herself, or at any rate with her son the Father of Waters — added to his previous bloody experience up the Yazoo, he could testify as to the validity of Grant's long-range observation that the conquest of Vicksburg would "take time and men." In fact, he was inclined to think it might require so much of both commodities as to prove impossible. Both were expendable in the ordinary sense, but after all there were limits. He was discouraged, he wrote his senator brother John this week, by the lack of substantial progress by Union arms, East and West, and by the unexpected resilience of the Confederates, civilian as well as military: "Two years have passed and the rebel flag still haunts our nation's capital. Our armies enter the best rebel territory and the wave closes in behind. The utmost we can claim is that our enemy respects our power to do them physical harm more than they did at first; but as to loving us any more, it were idle even to claim it. . . . I still see no end," he added, "or even the beginning of the end."

Perhaps the senseless burning of Napoleon the week before was on his mind or conscience, but the truth was he had enough on his hands to distress him here and now. The rain continued to come down hard — even harder, perhaps, than it was falling along the Rappahannock, where Burnside's Mud March was coming to its sticky close and the soldiers were composing a parody of a bedtime prayer:

> *Now I lay me down to sleep*
> *In mud that's many fathoms deep.*
> *If I'm not here when you awake*
> *Just hunt me up with an oyster rake*

— with the result that Sherman's men, in addition to having to widen and deepen the old canal, which was little more than a narrow ditch across the base of the low-lying tongue of land, had to work day and night at throwing up a levee along its right flank in order not to be washed away by water from the flooded bayous in their rear. Besides, even if the river could be persuaded to scour out a new channel along this line and thus "leave Vicksburg out in the cold," as Sherman said, it would be no great gain so far as he could see. The Confederates would merely shift their guns southward along the bluff to command the river at and below the outlet, leaving the shovel-weary Federals no better off than before. So he told his brother. And Porter, watching his red-haired friend slosh around in the mud and lose his temper a dozen times a day — "half sailor, half soldier, with a touch of the snapping turtle," he called him — once more found it necessary to bolster Sherman's spirits with hot rum and rollicking words. "If this rain lasts much longer we will not need a canal," he ended a note to the unhappy general on January 27. "I think the whole point will disappear, troops and all, in which case the gunboats will have the field to themselves."

Next day, however, Grant arrived, and Porter, reporting the fact to Welles, could say: "I hope for a better state of things."

✕ 3 ✕

The word *shoddy* was comparatively new, having originated during the present century in Yorkshire, where it was used in reference to almost worthless quarry stone or nearly unburnable coal. Crossing the ocean to America it took on other meanings, at first being used specifically to designate an inferior woolen yarn made from fibers taken from worn-out fabrics and reprocessed, then later as the name for the resultant cloth itself. "Poor sleezy stuff," one of Horace Greeley's *Tribune* reporters called it, "woven open enough for sieves, and then filled with shearmen's dust," while *Harper's Weekly* used even harsher words in referring to it as "a villainous compound, the refuse and sweepings of the shop, pounded, rolled, glued, and smoothed to the external form and gloss of cloth, but no more like the genuine article than the shadow is to the substance." Thoroughly indignant, the magazine went on to tell how "soldiers, on the first day's march or in the earliest storm, found their clothes, overcoats, and blankets scattering to the wind in rags or dissolving into their primitive elements of dust under the pelting rain."

It followed that the merchants and manufacturers who supplied the government with such cloth became suddenly and fantastically rich in the course of their scramble for contracts alongside others of their kind, the purveyors of tainted beef and weevily grain, the sellers of cardboard haversacks and leaky tents. No one was really discomforted by all this — so far, at least, as they could see — except the soldiers, the Union volunteers whose sufferings under bungling leaders in battles such as Fredericksburg and Chickasaw Bluffs were of a nature that made their flop-soled shoes and tattered garments seem relatively unimportant, and the Confederate jackals who stripped the blue-clad corpses after the inevitable retreat. If the generals were unashamed, were hailed in fact as heroes after such fiascos, why should anyone else have pangs of conscience? The contractors asked that, meanwhile raking in profits that were as long as they were quick. The only drawback was the money itself, which was in some ways no more real than the sleazy cloth or the imitation leather, being itself the shadow of what had formerly been substance. With prosperity in full swing and gold rising steadily, paper money declined from day to day, sometimes taking sickening drops as it passed from hand to hand. All it seemed good for was spending, and they spent it. Spending, they rose swiftly in the social scale, creating in the process a society which drew upon itself the word that formerly had been used to describe the goods they bartered — "shoddy" — and upon their heads the scorn of those who had made their money earlier and resented the fact that it was being debased. One such was Amos Lawrence, a millionaire Boston merchant. "Cheap money makes speculation, rising prices, and rapid fortunes," Lawrence declared, "but it will not make patriots." He wanted hard times back again. Closed factories would turn men's minds away from gain; then and only then could the war be won. So he believed. "We must have Sunday all over the land," he said, "instead of feasting and gambling."

For the present, though, all that was Sunday about the leaders of the trend which he deplored was their clothes. They wore on weekdays now the suits they once had reserved for wear to church, and as they prospered they bought others, fine broadcloth with nothing shoddy about them except possibly what they inclosed. So garbed, and still with money to burn before it declined still further, the feasters and gamblers acquired new habits and pretensions, with the result that the disparaging word was attached by the New York *World* not only to the new society, but also to the age in which it flourished:

The lavish profusion in which the old southern cotton aristocracy used to indulge is completely eclipsed by the dash, parade, and magnificence of the new northern shoddy aristocracy of this period. Ideas of cheapness and economy are thrown to the winds. The individual who makes the most money — no matter how — and spends the most money — no matter for what — is considered the greatest man. To be extravagant is to be fashionable. These facts sufficiently account for the immense and brilliant audiences at the opera and the theatres, and until the final crash comes such audiences undoubtedly will continue. The world has seen its iron age, its silver age, its golden age, and its brazen age. This is the age of shoddy.

The new brown-stone palaces on Fifth Avenue, the new equipages at the Park, the new diamonds which dazzle unaccustomed eyes, the new silks and satins which rustle overloudly, as if to demand attention, the new people who live in the palaces, and ride in the carriages, and wear the diamonds and silks — all are shoddy.... They set or follow the shoddy fashions, and fondly imagine themselves à la mode de Paris, when they are only à la mode de shoddy. They are shoddy brokers on Wall Street, or shoddy manufacturers of shoddy goods, or shoddy contractors for shoddy articles for a shoddy government. Six days in the week they are shoddy business men. On the seventh day they are shoddy Christians.

Nor were journalists and previously wealthy men the only ones to express a growing indignation. Wages had not risen in step with the rising cost of food and rent and other necessities of life, and this had brought on a growth of the trade-union movement, with mass meetings held in cities throughout the North to protest the unequal distribution of advantages and hardships. (Karl Marx was even now at work on *Das Kapital* in London's British Museum, having issued with Friedrich Engels *The Communist Manifesto* fifteen years ago, and Lincoln himself had said in his first December message to Congress: "Labor is prior to, and independent of, capital. Capital is only the fruit of labor, and could never have existed if labor had not first existed. Labor is the superior of capital, and deserves much the higher consideration.") One such meeting, held about this time at Cooper Union, filled the building to capacity while hundreds of people waited outside for word to be passed of what was being said within by delegates on the rostrum; whatever it was was being received with cheers and loud applause, along with a sprinkling of hisses and vehement boos. A representative of the hatters, one McDonough Bucklin, believed that the war was being used by the rich as an excuse for increased exploitation of the poor. As Bucklin put it, "The machinery is forging fetters to bind you in perpetual bondage. It gives you a distracted country with men crying out loud and strong for the Union. Union with them means no more nor less than that they want the war prolonged that they may get the whole of the capital of the country into their breeches pocket and let it out at a percentage that will rivet the chain about your neck." It was the old story: "Every day the rich are getting richer, the poor poorer." Apparently at this point Bucklin got carried away, for a *World* reporter noted that "the speaker made some concluding remarks strongly tainted with communism, which did not meet with general approval."

And yet, for all the offense to the sensibilities of the Boston millionaire, who had made his pile in a different time, as well as to those of the New York journalist, whose indignation was one of the tools he used in earning a living, and the labor delegate, who after all was mainly concerned with the fact that he and his hatters were not getting what he considered a large fair slice of the general pie, much of the undoubted ugliness of the era — the Age of Shoddy, if you will — was little more than the manifest awkwardness of national adolescence, a reaction to growing pains. Unquestionably the growth was there, and unquestionably, too — despite the prevalent gaucherie, the scarcity of grace and graciousness, the apparent concern with money and money alone, getting and spending — much of the growth was solid and even permanent. The signs were at hand for everyone to read. "Old King Cotton's dead and buried; brave young Corn is king," was the refrain of a popular song written to celebrate the bumper grain crops being gathered every fall,

of which the ample surpluses were shipped to Europe, where a coincidental succession of drouths — as if the guns booming and growling beyond the Atlantic had drawn the rain clouds, magnet-like, and then discharged them empty — resulted in poor harvests which otherwise would
have signaled the return of Old World famine. More than five million
quarters of wheat and flour were exported to England in 1862, whereas
the total in 1859 had been less than a hundred thousand. In the course of
the conflict the annual pork pack nearly doubled in the northern states,
and the wool clip more than tripled. Meanwhile, industry not only kept
pace with agriculture, it outran it. In Philadelphia alone, 180 new factories were established between 1862 and 1864 to accommodate labor-
saving devices which had been invented on the eve of war but which now
came into their own in response to the accelerated demands of the boom
economy of wartime: the Howe sewing machine, for example, which
revolutionized the garment industry, and the Gordon McKay machine
for stitching bootsoles to uppers, producing one hundred pairs of shoes in
the time previously required to finish a single pair by hand. All those
humming wheels and clamorous drive-shafts needed oil; and got it, too,
despite the fact that no such amounts as were now required had
even existed before, so far at least as men had suspected a short while
back; for within that same brief three-year span the production of pe-
troleum, discovered in Pennsylvania less than two years before Sumter,
increased from 84,000 to 128,000,000 gallons. The North was fighting
the South with one hand and getting rich with the other behind its back,
though which was left and which was right was hard to say. In any
case, with such profits and progress involved, who could oppose the
trend except a comparative handful of men and women, maimed or
widowed or otherwise made squeamish, if not downright unpatriotic,
by hard luck or oversubscription to Christian ethics?

A change was coming upon the land, and upon the land's inhabitants; nor was the change merely a dollars-and-cents affair, as
likely to pass as to last. Legislation which had long hung fire because of
peacetime caution and restraints imposed by jealous Southerners, now
departed, came out of the congressional machine about as fast as proponents could feed bills into the hopper. Kansas had become a state and
Colorado, Dakota, and Nevada were organized as Territories before
the war was one year old, with the result that no part of the national area
remained beyond the scope of the national law. Wherever a man went
now the law went with him, at least in theory, and this also had its effect. Helping to make room on the eastern seaboard for the nearly
800,000 immigrants who arrived in the course of the conflict — especially from Ireland and Germany, where recruiting agents were hard at
work, helping certain northern states to fill their quotas — no less
than 300,000 people crossed the prairies, headed west for Pike's Peak or
California, Oregon or the new Territories, some in search of gold as in

the days of '49 and others to farm the cornlands made available under the Homestead Act of 1862, whereby a settler could stake off a claim to a quarter-section of public land and, upon payment of a nominal fee, call those 160 acres his own; 15,000 such homesteads were settled thus in the course of the war, mostly in Minnesota, amounting in all to some 2,500,-000 acres. In this way the development of the Far West continued, despite the distraction southward, while back East the cities grew in wealth and population, despite the double drain in both directions. Nor were the cultural pursuits neglected, and these included more than attendance of the opera as a chance to show off the silks and satins whose rustling had disturbed the *World* reporter. Not only did university enrollments not decline much below what could be accounted for by the departure of southern students, but while the older schools were expanding their facilities with the aid of numerous wartime bequests, fifteen new institutions of higher learning were founded, including Cornell and Swarthmore, Vassar and the Massachusetts Institute of Technology. Campus life was not greatly different as a whole, once the undergraduates and professors grew accustomed to the fact that armies were locked in battle from time to time at various distances off beyond the southern horizon. Interrupted in 1861, for example, the Harvard-Yale boat races were resumed three years later in the midst of the bloodiest season of the war, and not a member of either crew volunteered for service in the army or the navy.

The draft, passed in early January as if in solution of the problem of Fredericksburg losses, hardly affected anyone not willing to be affected or else so miserably poor in these high times as not to be able to scrape up the $300 exemption fee as often as his name or number came up at the periodic drawings, in which case it might be said that he was about as well off in the army as out of it, except for the added discomfort of being drilled and possibly shot at. Large numbers of men from the upper classes, whether recently arrived at that level or established there of old, went to the expense of hiring substitutes (usually immigrants who were brought over by companies newly formed to supply the demand, trafficking thus in flesh to an extent unknown since the stoppage of the slave trade, and who were glad of the chance to earn a nest egg, which included the money they got from the men whose substitutes they were, plus the bounty paid by that particular state to volunteers — minus, of course, the fee that went to the company agent who had got them this opportunity in the first place) not only because it meant that the substitute-hirer was done with the problem of the draft for the duration, but also because it was considered more patriotic. All the same, the parody *We Are Coming, Father Abraham, Three Hundred Dollars More* was greeted with laughter wherever it was heard; for there was no stigma attached to the man who stayed out of combat, however he went about it short of actual dodging or desertion.

"In the vast new army of 300,000 which Mr Lincoln has ordered to be raised," one editor wrote, marveling at this gap disclosed in the new prosperity, "there will not be *one* man able to pay $300. Not one! Think of that!"

Washington itself was riding the crest of the wave thrown up by the boom, its ante-bellum population of 60,000 having nearly quadrupled under pressure from the throng of men and women rushing in to fill the partial vacuum created by the departure of the Southerners who formerly had set the social tone. Here the growing pains were the worst of all, according to Lincoln's young secretary John Hay, who wrote: "This miserable sprawling village imagines itself a city because it is wicked, as a boy thinks he is a man when he smokes and swears." In this instance Hay was offended because he and the President, riding back from the Soldiers Home after an interesting talk on philology — for which, he said, Lincoln had "a little indulged inclination" — encountered "a party of drunken gamblers and harlots returning in the twilight from [*erased*]." The fact was, the carousers might have been returning from almost any quarter of the city; for the provost marshal, while unable to give even a rough estimate of the number of houses of prostitution doing business here beside the Potomac, reported 163 gambling establishments in full swing, including one in which a congressman had lately achieved fame by breaking the bank in a single night and leaving with $100,000 bulging his pockets. It was a clutch-and-grab society now, with a clutch-and-grab way of doing business, whether its own or the government's, though it still affected a free and easy manner out of office hours. Nathaniel Hawthorne, in town for a look-round, found that the nation's pulse could be taken better at Willard's Hotel, especially in the bar, than at either the Capitol or the White House. "Everybody may be seen there," he declared. "You exchange nods with governors of sovereign states; you elbow illustrious men, and tread on the toes of generals; you hear statesmen and orators speaking in their familiar tones. You are mixed up with office-seekers, wire pullers, inventors, artists, poets, editors, army correspondents, attachés of foreign journals, long-winded talkers, clerks, diplomats, mail contractors, railway directors, until your own identity is lost among them. You adopt the universal habit of the place, and call for a mint julep, a whiskey skin, a gin cocktail, a brandy smash, or a glass of pure Old Rye; at any hour all these drinks are in request."

Not that there were no evidences of war aside from the uniforms, which were everywhere, and the personal experience of wounds or bereavement. There were indeed. War was the central fact around which life in Washington revolved, and what was more there were constant reminders that war was closely involved with death in its more unattractive forms. Although men with wrecked faces and empty sleeves or trouser-legs no longer drew the attention they once had drawn, other signs were not so easily ignored. Under huge transparencies boasting their skill at embalming, undertakers would buttonhole you on the street and urgently guarantee that, after receiving payment in advance, they would bring you back from the place where you caught the bullet "as lifelike as if you were asleep," the price being scaled in accordance with your preference for rosewood, pine, or something in between. One section of the city ticked like an oversized clock as the coffinmakers plied their hammers, stocking their shops against the day of battle, the news of which would empty their storerooms overnight and step up the tempo of their hammers in response to the law of supply and demand, as if time itself were hurrying to keep pace with the rush of events. In the small hours of the night, when this cacophonous ticking was stilled, men might toss sleepless on their beds, with dread like a presence in the room and sweat breaking out on the palms and foreheads even of those who knew the horror only by hearsay; but the outward show, by daylight or lamplight, was garish. Pennsylvania Avenue was crowded diurnally, to and beyond its margins of alternate dust and mud, and the plumes and sashes of the blue-clad officers, setting off the occasional gaudy splash of a Zouave, gave it the look of a carnival midway. This impression was heightened by the hawkers of roasted chestnuts and rock candy, and the women also did their part, contributing to the over-all effect the variegated dresses and tall hats that had come into fashion lately, the latter burdened about their incongruously narrow brims "with over-hanging balconies of flowers."

A future historian described them so, finding also in the course of her researches that the ladies "were wearing much red that season." Magenta and Solferino were two of the shades; "warm, bright, amusing names," she called them, derived from far-off battlefields "where alien men had died for some vague cause." Search as she might, however, she could find no shade of red identified with Chickasaw Bluffs, and it was her opinion that the flightiest trollop on the Avenue would have shrunk from wearing a scarlet dress that took its name from Fredericksburg.

★   ★   ★

Across the Atlantic, unfortunately for Confederate hopes of official acceptance into the family of nations, the Schleswig-Holstein problem, unrest in Poland, and the rivalry of Austria and Prussia gave the ministries of Europe a great deal more to think about than the intricacies of what was called "the American question." Aware that any disturbance of the precarious balance of power might be the signal for a general conflagration, they recalled Voltaire's comment that a torch lighted in 1756 in the forests of the new world had promptly wrapped the old world in flames. Russia, by coincidence having emancipated her serfs in the same year the western conflict began, was pro-Union from the start, while France remained in general sympathetic to the South; but neither could act without England, and England could not or would not intervene, being herself divided on the matter. The result, aside from occasional fumbling and inopportune attempts at mediation — mostly on the part of Napoleon III, who had needs and ambitions private and particular to himself — was that Europe, in effect, maintained a hands-off policy with regard to the blood now being shed beyond the ocean.

The double repulse, at Sharpsburg and Perryville, of the one Confederate attempt (so far) to conquer a peace by invasion of the North did not mean to Lord Palmerston and his ministers that the South would necessarily lose the war; far from it. But it did convince these gentlemen that the time was by no means ripe for intervention, as they had recently supposed, and was the basis for their mid-November rejection of a proposal by Napoleon that England, France, and Russia join in urging a North-South armistice, accompanied by a six-month lifting of the blockade. The result, if they had agreed — as they had been warned in no uncertain terms by Seward in private conversations with British representatives overseas — would have been an immediate diplomatic rupture, if not an outright declaration of war: in which connection the London *Times* remarked that "it would be cheaper to keep all Lancashire in turtle and venison than to plunge into a desperate war with the Northern States of America, even with all Europe at our back." No one knew better than Palmerston the calamity that might ensue, for he had been Minister at War from 1812 to 1815, during which period Yankee privateers had sunk about 2500 English ships, almost the entire marine. At that rate, with all those international tigers crouched for a leap in case the head tiger suffered some crippling injury, England not only could not afford to risk the loss of a sideline war; she could not even afford to win one.

Besides, desirable though it was that the flow of American cotton to British spindles be resumed — of 534,000 operatives, less than a quarter were working full time and more than half were out of work entirely; including their dependents, and those of other workers who lost their jobs in ancillary industries, approximately two million people were without means of self-support as a result of the cotton famine — the over-all economic picture was far from gloomy. In addition to the obvious example of the munitions manufacturers, who were profiting handsomely from the quarrel across the way, the linen and woolen industries had gained an appreciable part of what the cotton industry had lost, and the British merchant marine, whose principal rival for world trade was being chased from the high seas by rebel cruisers, was prospering as never before, augmented by more than seven hundred American vessels which transferred to the Union Jack in an attempt to avoid capture or destruction. And though there were those who favored intervention on the side of the South as a means of disposing permanently of a growing competitor, if by no other way then by assisting him to cut himself in two — the poet Matthew Arnold took this line of reason even further, speaking of the need "to prevent the English people from becoming, with the growth of democracy, *Americanized*" — the majority, even among the hard-pressed cotton operatives, did not. The Emancipation Proclamation saw to that, and Lincoln, having won what he first had feared was a gamble, was quick to press the advantage he had gained. When the workingmen of Manchester, the city hardest hit by the cotton famine, sent him an address approved at a meeting held on New Year's Eve, announcing their support of the North in its efforts to "strike off the fetters of the slave," Lincoln replied promptly in mid-January, pulling out all the stops in his conclusion: "I know and deeply deplore the sufferings which the workingmen at Manchester and in all Europe are called upon to endure in this crisis. . . . Under these circumstances, I cannot but regard your decisive utterance upon the question as an instance of sublime Christian heroism which has not been surpassed in any age or in any country. It is, indeed, an energetic and reinspiring assurance of the inherent power of truth and of the ultimate and universal triumph of justice, humanity, and freedom. I do not doubt that the sentiments you have expressed will be sustained by your great nation, and, on the other hand, I have no hesitation in assuring you that they will excite admiration, esteem, and the most reciprocal feelings of friendship among the American people. I hail this interchange of sentiment, therefore, as an augury that whatever else may happen, whatever misfortune may befall your country or my own, the peace and friendship which now exist between the two nations will be, as it shall be my desire to make them, perpetual."

Palmerston could have made little headway against the current of this rhetoric, even if he had so desired. In point of fact he did not try. Having resisted up to now the efforts of Confederate envoys to rush him off his feet — which they had done their best to do, knowing that it was their best chance to secure European intervention: aside, that is, from such happy accidents as the *Trent* affair, which unfortunately after a great deal of furor had come to nothing — he would have little trouble in keeping his balance from now on. Napoleon, across the Channel, was another matter. Practically without popular objection to restrain him, he continued to work in favor of those interests which, as he saw them, coincided with his own. Through the prominent Paris banking firm, Erlanger et Cie — whose president's son had lately married Matilda Slidell, daughter of the Confederate commissioner — a multi-million-dollar loan to the struggling young nation across the Atlantic was arranged, not in answer to any plea for financial assistance (it had not occurred to the Southerners, including John Slidell, despite the recent matrimonial connection, that asking would result in anything more than a Gallic shrug of regret) but purely as a gesture of good will. So the firm's representatives said as they broached the subject to Secretary of State Judah P. Benjamin in Richmond, having crossed the ocean for that purpose. However, being bankers — and what is more, French bankers — they added that they saw no harm in combining the good-will gesture with the chance to turn a profit, not only for the prospective buyers of the bonds that would be issued, but also for Erlanger et Cie. Then came the explanation, which showed that the transaction, though ostensibly a loan, was in fact little more than a scheme for large-scale speculation in cotton. Each 8% bond, which the firm would obtain at 70 for sale at approximately 100, was to be made exchangeable at face value, not later than six months after the end of the war, for New Orleans middling cotton at 12¢ a pound. There was the catch; for cotton was worth twice that much already, and was still rising. Benjamin, who was quite as sharp as the visiting bankers or their chief — Erlanger was a Jew and so was he; Erlanger was a Frenchman and so was he, after a manner of speaking, being Creole by adoption — saw through the scheme at once, as indeed anyone but a blind man would have done; but he also saw its propaganda value, which amounted at least to financial recognition of the Confederacy as a member of the family of nations. After certain adjustments on which he insisted, though not without exposing himself to charges of ingratitude for having looked a gift horse in the mouth — the original offer of $25,000,000 was scaled down to $15,000,000 and the interest rate to 7%, while the price at which the firm was to secure the bonds was raised to 77 — the deal was closed.

That was in late January, and at first all went well. Issued in early March at 90 — which gave Erlanger a spread of 13 points, plus a 5% commission on all sales — the bonds were enthusiastically oversubscribed and quickly arose to 95½. But that was the peak. Before the month was out they began to fall, and they kept falling, partly because of the influence of U.S. foreign agents who, basing their charge on the fact that Jefferson Davis himself had been a prewar advocate of the repudiation of Mississippi state bonds, predicted vociferously that the Southerners, if by some outside chance they won the war, would celebrate their victory by repudiating their debts. This had its effect. As the price declined, the alarmed Parisian bankers brought pressure on James M. Mason, the Confederate commissioner in London, to bull the market by using the receipts of the first installment for the purchase of his government's own bonds. Reluctantly, with the agreement of Slidell, he consented and, before he was through, put $6,000,000 into the attempt. But even this caused no more than a hesitation. When the artificial respiration stopped, the decline resumed, eventually pausing of its own accord at a depth of 36 before the bonds went off the board entirely. By that time, however, Erlanger et Cie was well in the clear, with a profit of about $2,500,000: which was more than the Confederacy obtained in all from a bond issue for which it had pledged six times that amount in capital and 7% in interest. The real losers, though, were the individual purchasers, mostly British admirers of the Confederacy, who left to their descendants the worthless scroll-worked souvenirs of a curious chapter in international finance.

As a fund-raising device the experiment was nearly a total failure — for the Confederates, that is, if not for the French bankers — but it did provide an additional incentive for Napoleon, who had taken considerable interest in the transaction, to hope for a southern victory. On February 3, after the bond issue had been authorized but before it had begun, the Emperor had his minister at Washington, Henri Mercier by name, present an offer of mediation, suggesting that representatives of the North and South meet on neutral soil for a discussion of terms of peace. The reaction to this was immediate and negative, at least on the part of the North. Seward replied that the Federal government had not the slightest notion of abandoning its efforts to save the Union, and certainly not by any such relinquishment of authority as the French proposal seemed to imply. This was seconded emphatically by Congress on March 3, when both houses issued a joint resolution denouncing mediation as "foreign interference" and reaffirming their "unalterable purpose" to suppress a rebellion which had for its object the tearing of the fabric of the finest government the world had ever known. In short, all that came of this latest effort by Napoleon to befriend the South was a further reduction of his possible influence. And Palmerston, watching the outcome from across the Channel, was more than ever convinced that no good could proceed from any such machinations. Dependent as his people were on U.S. grain to keep them from starvation, with Canada liable to seizure as a hostage to fortune and the British merchant marine exposed to being crippled if not destroyed, it seemed to him little short of madness to step into an argument which was after all a family affair. "Those who in quarrels interpose, Are apt to get a bloody nose," he intoned, falling back on doggerel to express his fears.

A. Dudley Mann, third in the trio of Confederate commissioners in Europe, had opened the year by complaining to his government that "the conduct of [England and France] toward us has been extremely shabby" and deploring their lack of spirit in the face of "the arrogant pretensions of the insolent Washington concern." Now in mid-March, as the third spring of the war began its green advance across the embattled South, all those thousands of miles away, Slidell in Paris was becoming increasingly impatient with Napoleon, whose avowed good will and favors never seemed to lead to anything valid or substantial, and Mason in London was lamenting bitterly that he had "no intercourse, unofficial or otherwise, with any member of the [British] Government." It was his private opinion, expressed frequently to Benjamin these days, that instead of continuing to put up with snubs and rebuffs, he would do better to come home.

★ ★ ★

If he had come home to Virginia now — as he did not; not yet — he would have done well to brace himself for the shock of finding it considerably altered from what it had been when he left it, a year and a half ago, to begin his aborted voyage on the *Trent*. That was perhaps the greatest paradox of all: that the Confederacy, in launching a revolution against change, should experience under pressure of the war which then ensued an even greater transformation, at any rate of the manner in which its citizens pursued their daily rounds, than did the nation it accused of trying to foist upon it an unwanted metamorphosis, not only of its cherished institutions, but also of its very way of life.

That way of life was going fast, and some there were, particularly among those who could remember a time when a society was judged in accordance with its sense of leisure, who affirmed that it was gone already. Nowhere was the change more obvious than in Richmond. Though the city was no longer even semi-beleaguered, as it had been in the time of McClellan, the outer fortifications had been lengthened and strengthened to such an extent that wags were saying, "They ought to be called fiftyfications now." Within that earthwork girdle, where home-guard clerks from government offices walked their appointed posts in their off hours, an ante-bellum population of less than 40,000 had mushroomed to an estimated 140,000, exclusive of the Union captives and Confederate wounded who jammed the old tobacco warehouses converted to prisons and hospitals. Yet the discomfort to which the older residents objected was not so much the result of the quantity of these late arrivers as it was of their quality, so to speak, or lack of it. "Virginians regarded the newcomers much as Romans would regard the First Families of the Visigoths," a diarist wrote. In truth, they had provocation far beyond the normal offense to their normal snobbery. Tenderloin districts such as Locust Alley, where painted women helped furloughed men forget the rigors of the field, and Johnny Worsham's gambling hell, directly across from the State House itself, had given the Old Dominion capital a reputation for being "the most corrupt and licentious city south of the Potomac." A Charlestonian administered the unkindest cut, however, by writing home that he had come to Richmond and found an entirely new city erected "after the model of Sodom and New York." According to another observer, an Englishman with a sharper ear for slang and a greater capacity for shock, the formerly decorous streets were crowded now with types quaintly designated as pug-uglies, dead rabbits, shoulder-hitters, "and a hundred other classes of villains for whom the hangman has sighed for many a long year."

Richmond saw and duly shuddered; but there was grimmer cause for shuddering than the wrench given its sense of propriety by the whores and gamblers who had taken up residence within its gates. As new-mounded graves spread over hillsides where none had been before, the population of the dead kept pace with the fast-growing population of the living. Though the Confederates in general lost fewer men in battle than their opponents, the fact that they had fewer to lose gave the casualty lists a greater impact, and it was remarked that "funerals were so many, even the funerals of friends, that none could be more than sparsely attended." Even more pitiful were the dying; Richmonders had come to know what one of them called "the peculiar chant of pain" that went up from a line of springless wagons hauling wounded over a rutted road or a cobbled street. You saw the maimed wherever you looked. For the city's hospitals — including the one on Chimborazo Heights, which had 150 buildings and was said to be the largest in the world — were so congested during periods immediately following battles that men who had lost an arm three days before had to be turned out, white-faced and trembling from shock and loss of blood, to make room for others in more urgent need of medical attention. It was up to the people to take them into their houses for warmth and food, and this they did, though only by the hardest, for both were dear and getting further beyond their means with every day that passed.

A gold dollar now was worth four in Confederate money, and even a despised $1 Yankee greenback brought $2.50 in a swap. Of coined money there was none, and in fact there had never been any, except for four half-dollars struck in the New Orleans mint before the fall of that city caused the government to abandon its plans for coinage. Congress's first solution to the small-change problem had been to make U.S. silver coins legal tender up to $10, along with English sovereigns, French napoleons, and Spanish and Mexican doubloons, but presently a flood of paper money was released upon the country, bills of smaller denominations being known as "shinplasters" because a soldier once had used a fistful to cover a tibia wound. Sometimes, as depreciation continued, that seemed about all they were good for. A War Department official, comparing current with prewar household expenses — flour, then $7, now $28 a barrel; bacon, then 20¢, now $1.25 a pound; firewood, then $3 or $4, now $15 a cord — found, as many others were finding, that he could not make ends meet; "My salary of $3000 will go about as far as $700 would in 1860." Wool and salt, drugs and medicines, nails and needles were scarcely to be had at any price, though the last were often salvaged from sewing kits found in the pockets of dead Federals. Dress muslin was $6 to $8 a yard, calico $1.75, coal $14 a cartload, and dinner in a first-class hotel ran as high as $25 a plate. In addition to genuine shortages, others were artificial, the result of transportation problems. Items that were plenteous in one part of the country might be as rare as hen's teeth in another. Peaches selling for 25¢ a dozen in Charleston, for instance, cost ten, fifteen, even twenty cents apiece in Richmond nowadays. For men perhaps the worst shock was the rising price of whiskey. As low as 25¢ a gallon in 1861, inferior stuff known variously as bust-head, red-eye, and tangle-foot now sold for as high as $35 a gallon. For women, on the other hand, the main source of incidental distress was clothes, the lack of new ones and the unsuitability of old ones through wear-and-tear and changing styles, although the latter were of necessity kept to a minimum. "Do you realize the fact that we shall soon be without a stitch of clothes?" a young woman wrote to a friend in early January. "There is not a bonnet for sale in Richmond. Some of the girls smuggle them, which I for one consider in the worst possible taste." Apparently ashamed to have let her mind turn in this direction at this time, she hastened to apologize for her flightiness, only to fall into fresh despair. "It seems rather volatile to discuss such things while our dear country is in such peril. Heaven knows I would costume myself in coffee-bags if that would help, but having no coffee, where would I get the bags?"

One provident source of amusement and delivery from care was the theater, which was popular as never before, though it did not escape the censure of the more respectable. "The thing took well, and money flowed into the treasury," a manager afterwards recalled, "but often had I cause to upbraid myself for having fallen so low in my own estimation, for I had always considered myself a gentleman, and I found that in taking control of this theatre and its vagabond company I had forfeited my claim to a respectable stand in the ranks of Society." A prominent Baptist preacher's complaint from his pulpit that "twenty *gentlemen* for the chorus and the ballet" might be more useful to their country in the army, where they could do more than "mimic fighting on the stage," met with the approval of his congregation; but the S.R.O. signs continued to go up nightly beside the ticket windows. When the Richmond Theatre burned soon after New Year's, an entirely new building was promptly raised on the old foundations. Opening night was greeted with an "Inaugural Poem" by Henry Timrod, concluding:

> *Bid Liberty rejoice! Aye, though its day*
> *Be far or near, these clouds shall yet be red*
> *With the large promise of the coming ray.*
> *Meanwhile, with that calm courage which can smile*
> *Amid the terrors of the wildest fray*
> *Let us among the charms of Art awhile*
>   *Fleet the deep gloom away;*
> *Nor yet forget that on each hand and head*
> *Rest the dear rights for which we fight and pray.*

If the production itself — Shakespeare's *As You Like It;* "but not as *we* like it," one critic unkindly remarked — left much to be desired in the way of professional excellence, Richmonders were glad to have found release "among the charms," and even the disgruntled reviewer was pleased to note "that the audience evinced a disposition at once to stop all rowdyism." For example, when the callboy came out from behind the curtain to fasten down the carpet, certain ill-bred persons began to yell, "Soup! Soup!" but were promptly shushed by those around them.

An even better show, according to some, was presented at the Capitol whenever Congress was in session, though unfortunately — or fortunately, depending on the point of view — these theatricals were in general unavailable to the public, being conducted behind closed doors. It was not so much what occurred in the regular course of business that was lively or amusing (for, as was usual with such bodies, there was a good deal more discussion of what to do than there was of doing. One member interrupted a long debate as to a proper time for adjournment by remarking, "If the House would adjourn and not meet any more, it would benefit the country." Others outside the legislative assembly agreed, including a Deep South editor who, learning that Congress had spent the past year trying without success to agree on a device for the national seal, suggested "A terrapin *passant*," with the motto "Never in haste"); it was what happened beside the point, so to speak, that provided the excitement. In early February the Alabama fire-eater William L. Yancey, opposing the creation of a Confederate Supreme Court — which, incidentally, never came into being because of States Rights obstructionists — so infuriated Benjamin H. Hill of Georgia, a moderate, that he threw a cutglass inkstand at the speaker and cut his cheek to the bone. As Yancey, spattered with blood and ink, started for him across the intervening desks, Hill followed up with a second shot, this time a heavy tumbler, which missed, and the sergeant-at-arms had to place both men in restraint and remove them from the chamber. Less fortunate was the chief clerk, shot to death on Capitol Square two months later by the journal clerk, who was angry at having been accused of slipshod work by his superior. The killer was sentenced to eighteen years in the penitentiary, but nothing at all was done to a woman who appeared one day on the floor of the House and proceeded to cowhide a Missouri congressman. She too was a government clerk, but it developed that her wrath had been aroused by information that Congress, in connection with enforcement of the Conscription Act, was about to require all clerks to divulge their ages. Deciding that the woman was demented, the House voted its confidence in the unlucky Missourian, who apparently had been selected at random. No such vote was ever given Jefferson Davis's old Mississippi stump opponent Henry S. Foote, who worked hard to deserve the reputation of being the stormiest man in Congress. He fought with his fists, in and out of the chamber, and was always ready to fall back on dueling pistols, with which he had had considerable experience. An altercation with an expatriate Irishman and a Tennessee colleague, who struck Foote over the head with an umbrella and then dodged nimbly to keep from being shot, caused all three to be brought into the Mayor's Court and placed under a peace bond. Another three-sided argument occurred in the course of a congressional hearing in which a Commissary Department witness was so badgered by Foote that the two came to blows. Foote tore off his adversary's shirt bosom, and when Commissary General Lucius B. Northrop came to the witness's assistance Foote knocked him into a corner. According to some who despised Colonel Northrop, asserting that he was attempting to convert the southern armies to vegetarianism, this was Foote's one real contribution to the Confederate war effort. But he was by no means through providing excitement. In the course of a speech by E. S. Dargan of Alabama, Foote broke in to call him a "damned rascal," which so infuriated the elderly congressman that he went for the Mississippian with a knife. Foote avoided the lunge, and then — Dargan by now had been disarmed and lay pinned to the floor by colleagues — stepped back within range and, striking an attitude not unworthy of Edwin Booth, whose work he much admired, hissed at the prostrate Alabamian: "I defy the steel of the assassin!"

All this was part and parcel of the revolution-in-progress, and if much of it was scandalous and distasteful, most Confederates could take that too in stride, along with spiraling prices and increasing scarcities. A native inclination toward light-heartedness served them well in times of strain. What the newcomers to Richmond lacked in tone they more than made up for in gaiety. Practically nothing was exempt from being laughed at nowadays, not even the sacred escutcheon of Virginia, whose motto *Sic semper tyrannis*, engraved below the figure of Liberty treading down Britannia, was freely rendered as "Take your foot off my neck!" Officers and men on leave and furlough from the Rappahannock line opened Volume I, "Fantine," of Victor Hugo's *Les Misérables*, which had come out in France the year before, and professed surprise at finding that it was not about themselves, "Lee's Miserables, Faintin'." One whose spirits never seemed to falter was Judah Benjamin, who remarked in this connection that it was "wrong and useless to disturb oneself and thus weaken one's energy to bear what was foreordained." This hedonistic fatalist went his way, invariably smiling, whether in attendance at government councils or at Johnny Worsham's green baize tables across the way. He once assured Varina Davis that with a glass of McHenry sherry, of which she had a small supply, and beaten biscuits made of flour from Crenshaw Mills, spread with a paste made of English walnuts from a tree on the White House grounds, "a man's patriotism became rampant." She found him amusing, an ornament to her receptions, and an excellent antidote to the FFV's who currently were condemning her as "disloyal to the South" because of a rumor that she had employed a white nurse for her baby.

The easy laughter was infectious, though some could hear it for what it was, part of an outward pose assumed at times to hide or hold back tears. What was happening behind the mask — not only Benjamin's, but the public's at large — no one could say for certain. Presently, however, there were signs that the mask was beginning to crack, or at any rate slip, and thus disclose what it had been designed to cover. When the President proclaimed March 5 another "day of fasting and prayer," this too was not exempt from unregenerate laughter; "Fasting in the midst of famine!" some remarked sardonically. Then, just short of one month later, on Holy Thursday — Easter came on April 5, a week before the second anniversary of Sumter — a demonstration staged on the streets of the capital itself gave the authorities cause to question whether all was as well concerning public morale here in the East as they had supposed, especially among those citizens who could not enjoy the relaxations afforded by such places as Johnny Worsham's, where a lavish buffet was maintained for the refreshment of patrons at all hours. The Holy Thursday demonstration, at least at the start, was concerned with more basic matters: being known, then and thereafter, as the Bread Riot.

Apparently it began at the Oregon Hill Baptist church, where Mary Jackson, a huckster with "straight, strong features and a vixenish eye," harangued a group of women who had gathered to protest the rising cost of food. Adjourning to Capitol Square they came under the leadership of a butcher's Amazonian assistant, Minerva Meredith by name. Six feet tall and further distinguished by a long white feather that stood up from her hat and quivered angrily as she tossed her head, she proposed that they move on the shops to demand goods at government prices and to take them by force if this was refused. As she spoke she took from under her apron, by way of emphasis, a Navy revolver and a Bowie knife. Brandishing these she set out for the business section at the head of a mob which quickly swelled to about three hundred persons, including the children some of the women had in tow. "Bread! Bread!" they shouted as they marched. Governor John Letcher, who had watched from his office as the demonstration got under way, had the mayor read the Riot Act to them, but they hooted and surged on past him, smashing plate-glass windows in their anger and haste to get at the goods in the shops on Main and Cary. It was obvious that they were after more than food, for they emerged with armloads of shoes and clothes, utensils and even jewelry, which some began to pile in to handcarts they had thought to bring along. Governor Letcher sent for a company of militia and threatened to fire on the looters when it arrived, but the women sneered at him, as they had done at the mayor, and went on with their vandalism. Just then, however, those on the outer fringes of the mob saw a tall thin man dressed in gray homespun climb onto a loaded dray and begin to address them sternly. They could not hear what he was saying, but they saw him do a strange thing. He took money from his pockets and tossed it in their direction. Whereupon they fell silent and his voice came through: "You say you are hungry and have no money. Here is all I have. It is not much, but take it." His pockets empty of all but his watch, he took that out too, but instead of throwing it at them, as he had done the money, he stood with it open in his hand, glancing sidelong at the militia company which had just arrived. "We do not desire to injure anyone," he said in a voice that rang clear above the murmur of the crowd, "but this lawlessness must stop. I will give you five minutes to disperse. Otherwise you will be fired on."

Recognizing the President — and knowing, moreover, that he was not given to issuing idle threats — the mob began to disperse, first slowly, then rapidly as the deadline approached. By the time the five minutes were up, there was no one left for the soldiers to fire at. Davis put his watch back in his pocket, climbed down off the dray, and returned to his office. Outwardly calm, inwardly he was so concerned that he did something he had never done before. He made a special appeal to the Richmond press, requesting that it "avoid all reference directly or indirectly to the affair," and ordered the telegraph company to "permit nothing relative to the unfortunate disturbance . . . to be sent over the telegraph lines in any direction for any purpose." He feared the reaction abroad, as well as in other parts of the South, if it became known that the streets of the Confederate capital had been the scene of a riot that had as its cause, if only by pretense, a shortage of food. Two days later, however, the *Enquirer* broke the story by way of refuting defeatist rumors that were beginning to be spread. Identifying the rioters as "a handful of prostitutes, professional thieves, Irish and Yankee hags, gallows birds from all lands but our own," the paper denounced them for having broken into "half a dozen shoe stores, hat stores and tobacco houses and robbed them of everything but bread, which was just the thing they wanted least."

This one attempt at suggesting censorship was as useless as it was ineffective: Richmond was by no means the only place where such disturbances occurred in the course of Holy Week. Simultaneously in Atlanta a group of about fifteen well-dressed women entered a store on Whitehall Street and asked the price of bacon. $1.10 a pound, they were told: whereupon their man-tall leader, a shoemaker's wife "on whose countenance rested care and determination," produced a revolver with which she covered the grocer while her companions snatched what they wanted from the shelves, paying their own price or nothing. From there they proceeded to other shops along the street, repeating the performance until their market baskets were full, and then went home. A similar raid was staged at about the same time in Mobile, as well as in other towns and cities throughout the South. Presently countrywomen took their cue from their urban sisters. North Carolina experienced practically an epidemic of demonstrations by irate housewives. Near Lafayette, Alabama, a dozen such — armed, according to one correspondent, with "guns, pistols, knives, and tongues" — attacked a rural mill and seized a supply of flour, while a dozen more came down out of the hills around Abingdon, Virginia, and cowered merchants into handing over cotton yarn and cloth; wagon trains were stopped at gunpoint and robbed of corn near Thomasville and Marietta, Georgia. All these were but a few among the many, and there were those who saw in this ubiquitous manifestation of discontent the first crack in the newly constructed edifice of government. If the Confederacy could not be defeated from without, then it might be abolished from within; for the protests were not so much against shortages, which were by no means chronic at this stage, as they were against the inefficiency which resulted in spiraling prices. These observers saw the demonstrations, in fact — despite the recent successes of southern arms, both East and West — as symptoms of war weariness, the one national ailment which could lead to nothing but defeat. The new government could survive, and indeed had survived already, an assortment of calamities; but that did not and could not include the loss of the will to fight, either by the soldiers in its armies or by the people on its home front.

No one saw the danger more clearly than the man whose principal task — aside, that is, from his duties as Commander in Chief, which now as always he placed first — was to do all he could to avert it. Recently he had undertaken a 2500-mile year-end journey to investigate and shore up crumbling morale, with such apparent success that on his return he could report to Congress, convening in Richmond for its third session on January 12, that the state of the nation, in its civil as well as in its military aspect, "affords ample cause for congratulation and demands the most fervent expression of our thankfulness to the Almighty Father, who has blessed our cause. We are justified in asserting, with a pride surely not unbecoming, that these Confederate States have added another to the lessons taught by history for the instruction of man; that they have afforded another example of the impossibility of subjugating a people determined to be free, and have demonstrated that no superiority of numbers or available resources can overcome the resistance offered by such valor in combat, such constancy under suffering, and such cheerful endurance of privation as have been conspicuously displayed by this people in the defense of their rights and liberties." Moreover, he added, flushed by the confidence his words had generated: "By resolute perseverance in the path we have hitherto pursued, by vigorous efforts in the development of all our resources for defense, and by the continued exhibition of the same unfaltering courage in our soldiers and able conduct in their leaders as have distinguished the past, we have every reason to expect that this will be the closing year of the war."

Since then, despite continued successful resistance by the armies in the field, symptoms of unrest among civilians had culminated in the rash of so-called Bread Riots, the largest of which had occurred in the capital itself and had been broken up only by the personal intervention of the Chief Executive. Two days later — on April 10, just short of three months since his confident prediction of an early end to the conflict — Davis issued, in response to a congressional resolution passed the week before, a proclamation "To the People of the Confederate States." Observing that "a strong impression prevails throughout the country that the war . . . may terminate during the present year," Congress urged the people not to be taken in by such false hopes, but rather to "look to prolonged war as the only condition proffered by the enemy short of subjugation." The presidential proclamation, issued broadcast across the land, afforded the people the unusual opportunity of seeing their President eat his words, not only by revoking his previous prediction, but by substituting another which clearly implied that what lay ahead was a longer and harder war than ever.

Though "fully concurring in the views thus expressed by Congress," he began with the same boldness of assertion as before. "We have reached the close of the second year of the war, and may point with just pride to the history of our young Confederacy. Alone, unaided, we have met and overthrown the most formidable combination of naval and military armaments that the lust of conquest ever gathered together for the subjugation of a free people. . . . The contrast between our past and present condition is well calculated to inspire full confidence in the triumph of our arms. At no previous period of the war have our forces been so numerous, so well organized, and so thoroughly disciplined, armed, and equipped as at present." Then he passed to darker matters. "We must not forget, however, that the war is not yet ended, and that we are still confronted by powerful armies and threatened by numerous fleets. . . . Your country, therefore, appeals to you to lay aside all thoughts of gain, and to devote yourselves to securing your liberties, without which those gains would be valueless. . . . Let fields be devoted exclusively to the production of corn, oats, beans, peas, potatoes, and other food for man and beast; let corn be sown broadcast for fodder in immediate proximity to railroads, rivers, and canals, and let all your efforts be directed to the prompt supply of these articles in the districts where our armies are operating. . . . Entertaining no fear that you will either misconstrue the motives of this address or fail to respond to the call of patriotism, I have placed the facts fully and frankly before you. Let us all unite in the performance of our duty, each in his own sphere, and with concerted, persistent, and well-directed effort . . . we shall maintain the sovereignty and independence of these Confederate

States, and transmit to our posterity the heritage bequeathed to us by our fathers."

As usual, the people responded well for the most part to a clear statement of necessity. But there were those who reacted otherwise. The Georgia fire-eater Robert Toombs, for example, who had left the cabinet to join the army on the day of First Manassas and then had left the army to re-enter politics after his one big day at Sharpsburg, petulantly announced that he was increasing his plantation's cotton acreage. Nor were opposition editors inclined to neglect the opportunity to launch the verbal barbs they had been sharpening through months of increasing dissatisfaction. "Mr Davis is troubled by blindness," the Mobile *Tribune* told its subscribers, "is very dyspeptic and splenetic, and as prejudiced and stubborn as a man can well be, and not be well."

Thus did the Confederacy enter upon its third year of war.

✕ 4 ✕

Disenchantment was mainly limited to civilians, but it was by no means limited to the sphere of civilian activities. Illogically or not — that is, despite the lopsided triumphs at Fredericksburg and Chickasaw Bluffs, the flood-reversing coups at Holly Springs and Galveston, the brilliant cavalry forays into Kentucky and West Tennessee, and the absence of anything resembling a clear-cut defeat east of the Mississippi — there was a growing impression that victory, on field after field, brought little more than temporary joy, which soon gave way to sobering realizations. The public's reaction was not unlike that of a boxer who delivers his best punch, square on the button, then sees his opponent merely blink and shake his head and bore back in. People began to suspect that if the North could survive Fredericksburg and the Mud March, Chickasaw Bluffs and the loss of the *Cairo* to a demijohn of powder, it might well be able to survive almost anything the South seemed able to inflict. A whole season of victories apparently had done nothing to bring peace and independence so much as one day closer. Howell Cobb of Georgia could say, not altogether in jest, "Only two things stand in the way of an amicable settlement of the whole difficulty: the Landing of the Pilgrims and Original Sin," while the Richmond *Examiner* could simultaneously call attention to the chilling fact that, aside from Sumter, "[Lincoln's] pledge once deemed foolish by the South, that he would 'hold, occupy, and possess' all the forts belonging to the United States Government, has been redeemed almost to the letter."

Fredericksburg had been hailed at the outset as the turning point of the war. Presently, however, as Lee and his army failed to find a way to follow it up, the triumph paled to something of a disappointment. In time, paradoxically, the more perceptive began to see that it had indeed

been a turning point, though in a sense quite different from the one originally implied; for no battle East or West, whether a victory or a defeat,
showed more plainly the essential toughness of the blue-clad fighting
man than this in which, judging by a comparison of the casualties inflicted and received, he suffered the worst of his several large-scale drub-
bings. But this was an insight that came gradually and only to those who
were not only able but also willing to perceive it. Murfreesboro was
more immediately disappointing in respect to Confederate expectations,
and no such insight was required. Here the contrast between claims and
accomplishments was as stark as it was sudden. First it was seen to be a
much less brilliant victory than the southern commander had announced
before his guns had hushed their growling. Then it was seen to be
scarcely a victory at all. It was seen, in fact, to have several of the aspects
of a typical defeat: not the least of which was the undeniable validity of
the Federal claim to control of the field when the smoke had cleared. "So
far the news has come in what may be called the classical style of the
Southwest," the *Examiner* observed caustically near the end of the first
week in January, having belatedly learned of Bragg's withdrawal.
"When the Southern army fights a battle, we first hear that it has gained
one of the most stupendous victories on record; that regiments from Mississippi, Texas, Louisiana, Arkansas, &c. have exhibited an irresistible and
superhuman valor unknown in history this side of Sparta and Rome. As
for their generals, they usually get all their clothes shot off, and replace
them with a suit of glory. The enemy, of course, is simply annihilated.
Next day more dispatches come, still very good, but not quite as good as
the first. The telegrams of the third day are invariably such as make a
mist, a muddle, and a fog of the whole affair."

No mist, muddle, or fog could hide Bragg from the ire aroused
when the public learned the premature and insubstantial basis for his wire
announcing that God had granted him and them a Happy New Year.
What saved him from the immediate consequences of their anger was his
adversary Rosecrans, who, despite his recent promise to "press [the reb-
els] to the wall," not only refused to follow up the victory he claimed,
but resisted with all his strength — as he had done through the months
preceding the march out of Nashville, pleading the need to lay in "a couple of millions of rations"— the efforts by his superiors to prod him into
motion. Crittenden, who had commanded the unassailed left wing
throughout the first day's fight and then repulsed his fellow-Kentuckian
Breckinridge on the second, stated the case as it appeared to many in the
Union ranks: "The battle was fought for the possession of Middle Tennessee. We went down to drive the Confederates out of Murfreesboro,
and we drove them out. They went off a few miles and camped again.
And we, although we were the victors, virtually went into hospital for
six months before we could march after them again." He added, by way
of developing a theory: "As in most of our battles, very meager fruits

resulted to either side from such partial victories as were for the most part won. Yet it was a triumph. It showed that in the long run the big purse and the big battalions — both on our side — must win; and it proved that there were no better soldiers than ours."

Rosecrans disagreed with much of this critique, particularly the remark that the army had gone "into hospital," but he not only subscribed to Crittenden's opinion about the big purse and the big battalions, he also took it a step further by insisting that the last ounce be wrung from the advantage. What good were riches, he seemed to be asking, unless they were at hand? When he swung the purse he wanted it to be heavy. "I believe the most fatal errors of this war have begun in an impatient desire of success, that would not take time to get ready," he protested in mid-February, by way of reply to Halleck's continuous urging. So the general-in-chief changed his tack. "There is a vacant major generalcy in the Regular Army," he wired on March 1, "and I am authorized to say that it will be given to the general in the field who first wins an important and decisive victory." The implication was that Rosecrans had better get to Chattanooga before Grant got to Vicksburg; but Old Rosy did not react at all in the way that had been intended. "As an officer and a citizen, I feel degraded to see such auctioneering of honor," he replied. "Have we a general who would fight for his own personal benefit, when he would not for honor and the country? He would come by his commission basely in that case, and deserve to be despised by men of honor." Halleck in turn resented this show of righteous indignation, and said so, which only served to increase their differences. Rosecrans was convinced by now that all of Washington was against him: especially Stanton, who had promised, in the first flush of excitement over the news of a hard-fought triumph, to withhold "nothing ... within my power to grant," but who lately had bridled at filling the balky commander's many requisitions and requests, including one that his latest promotion be predated so as to give him rank over Grant and all the other western generals. Finally he protested to the President himself, who gave him little satisfaction beyond assurances of admiration. "I know not a single enemy of yours here," Lincoln wrote, and added: "Truth to speak, I do not appreciate this matter of rank on paper as you officers do. The world will not forget that you fought the battle of Stones River, and it will never care a fig whether you rank Gen. Grant on paper, or he so ranks you."

By then it was mid-March. The bloody contest, ten weeks back, had done much to increase Old Rosy's appreciation of the dangers involved in challenging the rebs on their own ground. The rest of March went by, and all of April. Still he would not budge. May followed. Still he would not move until he was good and ready, down to the final nail in the final horseshoe. As June came on, approaching the end of the six-month term which Crittenden said the army spent "in hospital," Rosecrans made a virtue of his immobility, claiming that by refraining from driving Bragg southward he was preventing him from co-operating with Pemberton against Grant. Besides, he added, he had held a council of war at which it had been decided to "observe a great military maxim, not to risk two great and decisive battles at the same time." He thought it best to wait till Vicksburg fell or Grant abandoned the effort to take it, whereupon he himself would advance against Bragg and Chattanooga. Halleck by now was fairly frantic. A master of maxims, he fired one back at Rosecrans: "Councils of war never fight." But this had no more effect than the earlier proddings had done; Old Rosy stayed exactly where he was. If Bragg would only leave him alone, he would gladly return the favor, at any rate until he was good and ready to advance. Just when that would be he would not say.

He might have taken some measure of consolation, amid the prod-dings, from the fact that his opponent's troubles quite overmatched his own. The difference was that Rosecrans' woes came mainly from above, whereas Bragg's came mainly from below. As a result, the latter were not only more widely spread, they were also frequently sharper barbed. His harsh discipline in camp, unbalanced by conspicuous victories in the field, and his reputation as a commander who invariably retreated after battle, whether his troops won or lost, had resulted in bitter censure from all sides, civil as well as military, in and out of the newspapers. Rid-ing one day near his Tullahoma headquarters, soon after his withdrawal behind Duck River, he encountered a man wearing butternut garb and requested information about the roads. When this had been given, the general thanked him and, unable to tell from his clothes whether the man was a soldier or a civilian — the kindest thing that could be said about dress in the Army of Tennessee was that it was informal — asked if he belonged to Bragg's army. "Bragg's army?" the countryman replied, scowling at the grim-faced man on horseback. "Bragg's got no army. He shot half of them himself, up in Kentucky, and the other half got killed at Murfreesboro."

Bragg laughed and rode on, curbing for once his terrible temper. But the experience rankled under pressure of newspaper criticisms leveled at him while his troops were getting settled along their new defensive line: particularly the charge, widely printed and reprinted, that he had pulled out of Murfreesboro against the advice of his lieutenants. This was patently untrue, as he could prove by the note from Cheatham and With-ers, urging immediate retreat, which he had rejected, at least at first, despite Polk's indorsement of their plea. Accordingly, he decided to make an issue of it, addressing on January 11 a letter to his chief subordi-nates. "It becomes necessary for me to save my fair name," he wrote, and "stop the deluge of abuse which [threatens to] destroy my usefulness and demoralize this army." He asked them to acquit him of the fabrication that he had gone against their wishes in ordering a retreat, which in point of fact "was resisted by me for some time after [it was] advised by my corps and division commanders. . . . Unanimous as you were in council in verbally advising a retrograde movement," he added, "I cannot doubt that you will cheerfully attest the same in writing." So far, he was on safe ground. Unwilling to let it go at that, however, he closed with something of a flourish: "I desire that you will consult your subordinate commanders and be candid with me. . . . I shall retire without a regret if I find I have lost the good opinion of my generals, upon whom I have ever relied as upon a foundation of rock."

.   This last was what opened the floodgates. Though none could fail to exonerate him from the specific charge that he had originated the notion of retreat, his closing statement that he would retire if he found that he had lost their good opinion presented the generals with a once-in-a-lifetime opportunity, which they did not neglect. Hardee, after pointing out that neither he nor his division commanders had proposed a withdrawal, though they had made no objection once the decision had been announced, replied that he had consulted his subordinates, as requested, and found them "unanimous in the opinion that a change in the command of this army is necessary. In this opinion I concur." He had "the highest regard for the purity of your motives, your energy, and your personal character," he told Bragg, but he was "convinced, as you must feel, that the peril of the country is superior to all personal considerations." His lieutenants replied in a similar vein. "I have consulted with my brigade commanders," Cleburne wrote, "and they unite with me in personal regard for yourself . . . but at the same time they see, with regret, and it has also met my observation, that you do not possess the confidence of the army in other respects in that degree necessary to secure success." Breckinridge was as forthright, and what was more — the officers and men of his division having found Bragg's report of the recent battle so disparaging to themselves and their dead comrades that they had urged their chief to challenge him to a duel — took perhaps the greatest satisfaction of all in seizing the present chance to sit in judgment. "Acting with the candor which you invoke," the former Vice President replied, "[my brigade commanders] request me to say that, in their opinion, the conduct of the military operations in front of Murfreesboro made it necessary for our army to retire." Lest the irony of this be lost, he passed at once to a summation. "They also request me to say that while they entertain the highest respect for your patriotism, it is their opinion that you do not possess the confidence of the army to an extent which will enable you to be useful as its commander. In this opinion I feel bound to state that I concur."

Polk was away on leave at the time, visiting his refugee family in North Carolina, and in his absence Cheatham and Withers merely replied with an acknowledgment that they had made the original suggestion to withdraw. When the bishop returned at the end of the month he found the army a-buzz with talk of this latest development. Since there was some difference of opinion as to whether Bragg had really intended to call down all this thunder on his head, Polk wrote to ask whether his chief had meant for him to answer both questions — 1) as to who was responsible for bringing up the subject of retreat, and 2) as to whether the army commander had lost the confidence of his subordinates — or only the first. Bragg by now had had quite enough "candid" responses to the second question, and stated that he had only wanted to get an opinion on the inception of the retreat; "The paragraph relating to my supercedure was only an expression of the feeling with which I should receive your replies." In that case, Polk responded, he believed the original battlefield note would suffice as a documentary answer. He was content to let the matter drop. But learning presently that Hardee and his officers felt that he had dodged the issue, thereby leaving them in the position of insubordinate malcontents, he decided to write directly to his friend the President, attaching the rather voluminous correspondence he had had with Bragg. "I feel it my duty to say to you," he told Davis, "that had I and my division commanders been asked to answer, our replies would have coincided with those of the officers of the other corps. . . . My opinion is he had better be transferred." The best place for him, Polk believed, was Richmond, where "his capacity for organization and discipline, which has not been equaled among us, could be used by you at headquarters with infinite advantage to the whole army. I think, too," he added, "that the best thing to be done in supplying his place would be to give his command to General Joseph E. Johnston. He will cure all discontent and inspire the army with new life and confidence. He is here on the spot, and I am sure will be content to take it."

Davis was quite aware that Johnston was at Tullahoma, having ordered him there two weeks ago, when Bragg's circular, together with the replies of Hardee and his lieutenants, first landed on the presidential desk. "Why General Bragg should have selected that tribunal, and have invited its judgment upon him, is to me unexplained; it manifests, however, a condition of things which seems to me to require your presence." So Davis wrote Johnston, who was engaged at the time in an inspection of the Mobile defenses, instructing him to proceed at once to Bragg's headquarters and determine "whether he had so far lost the confidence of the army as to impair his usefulness in his present position. . . . You will, I trust, be able, by conversation with General Bragg and others of his command, to decide what the best interests of the service require, and to give me the advice which I need at this juncture. As that army is part of your command," the President added, knowing the Virginian's meticulosity in such matters, "no order will be necessary to give you authority there, as, whether present or absent, you have a right to direct its operations and do whatever else belongs to the general commanding."

However, Johnston's squeamishness went further than Davis reckoned. He found much that was improper in the conduct of an inquiry which might result in the displacement of the officer under investigation by the one who was doing the investigating. Besides, he had a high regard for the grim-faced North Carolinian's abilities. "Bragg has done wonders, I think," he wrote privately. "No body of troops has done more in proportion to numbers in the same time." Accordingly on February 3, ten days after his arrival, although "incessant rain has permitted me to see but a fourth of the troops as yet," he reported them "in high spirits, and as ready as ever for fight." He found his confidence in Bragg not only unshaken but "confirmed by his recent operations, which, in my opinion, evince great vigor and skill." In short: "It would be very unfortunate to remove him at this juncture, when he has just earned, if not won, the gratitude of the country." He would report more fully, Johnston said, when he had completed his inspection. Meanwhile, "I respectfully suggest that, should it appear to you necessary to remove General Bragg, no one in this army or engaged in this investigation ought to be his successor." Nine days later, his final report buttressed his first impression. He had found the men "well clothed, healthy, and in good spirits," which gave "positive evidence of General Bragg's capacity to command.... To me it seems that the operations of this army in Middle Tennessee have been conducted admirably. I can find no record of more effective fighting in modern battles than that of this army in December, evincing great skill in the commander and courage in the troops." He had heard, he said in closing, that Polk and Hardee had advised their present chief's removal and his own appointment to the command; but "I am sure that you will agree with me that the part I have borne in this investigation would render it inconsistent with my personal honor to occupy that position.... General Bragg should not be removed."

With that, he left for Chattanooga. Davis replied that he was "truly gratified at the language of commendation which you employ in relation to General Bragg," but he considered it "scarcely possible," in the light of Polk's and Hardee's formal disapproval, "for [Bragg] to possess the requisite confidence of the troops." He still thought Johnston should take over, and he could not see that this involved any breach of military etiquette. Johnston was already in command, by rank and title, whenever he was on the scene; "The removal of General Bragg would only affect you so far as it deprived you of his services." However, Davis assured him, "You shall not be urged by me to any course which would wound your sensibility of views of professional propriety." In early March, Johnston having made no reply to this, the Secretary of War added his pleas to those of the Commander in Chief. It was his opinion that Bragg should be "recalled altogether," but if Johnston's conscience would not permit this, then he suggested that he keep him at hand, "as an organizer and disciplinarian," in the post of assistant commander. "Let me urge you, my dear general," Seddon wrote, "to think well, in view of all the great interests to our beloved South ... and, if possible, make the sacrifice of your honorable delicacy to the importance of the occasion and the greatness of our cause." When Johnston still did not reply — he was back in Mobile by now, though Davis and Seddon supposed he was still in Chattanooga — the matter was taken out of his hands by a wire from Richmond, which reached him on March 12: "Order General Bragg to report to the War Department here for conference. Assume yourself direct charge of the army in Middle Tennessee."

Perhaps Davis and Seddon had decided that what Johnston had been wanting all along, and even hinting at, was for them to *order* him to the post in spite of his objections; that way, the conditions of honor would be met, since he would have done all he could to avoid the outcome. If so, they were wrong. Johnston really did not want the command. The fact was, he did not want the larger one he had already — his duties, he said disparagingly, were those of an "inspector general"— despite the President's and the Secretary's insistence that it was the most important post in the Confederacy. If that was the case, Lee should have it as a reward for his recent accomplishments; then "with great propriety," Johnston wrote in confidence to a friend, he himself could return to his native Virginia and resume command of the army he had lost at Seven Pines, "where the Yankee bullets found me." Now it looked as if that hope was going up in smoke. He was ordered to Middle Tennessee, with no alternative to compliance except submission of his resignation.

So it seemed. When he returned to Tullahoma on March 19, however, he found a way — still on grounds of sparing offense to what Seddon had called his "honorable delicacy"— at least to delay what he had sought all this time to avoid. Bragg's wife was down with typhoid, despaired of by the doctors, and her husband had given over his official duties in order to be at her bedside round the clock. It was therefore no more than normal courtesy, under the circumstances, for Johnston to carry out that portion of the orders which required him to take command of the army; but as for increasing the distracted general's present woes by instructing him to report at once to Richmond, that was manifestly impossible, Johnston wired the authorities, "on account of Mrs Bragg's critical condition." Besides, he added, the country was "becoming practicable" now that the rains had slacked and the roads were drying; "Should the enemy advance, General Bragg will be indispensable here." Apparently he intended to take the Secretary's earlier suggestion that he keep the unpopular general at hand as his assistant. But presently even this went by the board. By the time Mrs Bragg had recovered sufficiently from her illness to permit her husband's return to active duty, Johnston himself was bedridden, suffering from a debility brought on by a flare-up of his wounds. "General Bragg is therefore necessary here," he notified Richmond on April 10. "If conference with him is still desirable, might not a confidential officer visit him, for the purpose, in Tullahoma?"

★ ★ ★

That was that; Bragg remained at his post by default, so to speak. Meanwhile — principally by courtesy of Rosecrans, who, though the methods employed to avoid compliance were quite different in each case, would no more be budged by his superiors than Johnston would be influenced by his — the Army of Tennessee enjoyed, throughout the opening half of the year, the longest period of inaction afforded any considerable body of Confederates in the whole course of the war. Polk's corps was on the left at Shelbyville, Hardee's on the right at Wartrace, with cavalry extending the long defensive line westward to Columbia and eastward to McMinnville, seventy air-line miles apart. Breastworks protected by abatis were thrown up along the critical center, and behind them, once the countryside emerged from the quagmires created by the late winter and early spring rains — which had afforded one self-styled etymologist the opportunity to remark that the name of the little railroad town where Bragg had his headquarters was derived from the conjunction of two Greek words: *tulla*, meaning "mud," and *homa*, meaning "more mud" — the infantry enjoyed the foison of the lush Duck River Valley and indulged in such diversions as attending church services and revival meetings (Bragg set an example here by allowing himself to be baptized in an impressive ceremony) or chuck-a-luck games and cockfights, depending on individual inclinations. The army's effective strength had risen by now to almost 50,000 of all arms, including better than 15,000 cavalry, who passed the time in a quite different manner by probing at Rosecrans' flanks and rear and harassing his front.

Joe Wheeler got things off to a rousing start on January 13 with a strike at Harpeth Shoals, midway between Nashville and Clarksville, where he captured or sank four loaded packets and one lightly armored gunboat, taking them under fire from the bank, and thus effectively suspended the flow of goods up the Cumberland River, the main Federal supply line. But this accomplishment was more than offset, another fifty miles downstream, by the repulse he suffered on February 3 when he launched an ill-conceived and poorly co-ordinated assault on an outnumbered but stout blue garrison at Dover, two weeks short of the anniversary of the fall of adjacent Fort Donelson to Grant. Bedford Forrest, who had not only lost some of his best men but had also had two fine horses shot from under him in the course of attacks which he had advised against making in the first place, was so incensed by Wheeler's handling of the affair that he bluntly told the young commander that he would resign from the army before he would fight again under his direction. The discouraged graybacks limped back to Columbia, the western tip of Bragg's long crescent. Meanwhile, far out the opposite horn, Morgan was doing no better, if indeed as well. With two of his regiments de-

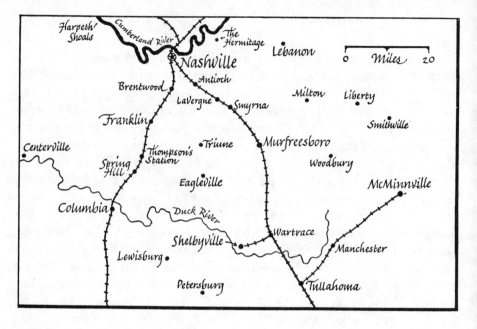

tached to stir up excitement in Kentucky, he too suffered a bloody repulse at the hands of an inferior force on March 20 at Milton, fifteen
miles northeast of Murfreesboro, and still another, two weeks later, at
nearby Liberty, which resulted in his being driven in some confusion back
on his base at McMinnville. Perhaps the best that could be said for all
these various affairs, at any rate from the Confederate point of view, was
that they all occurred within the Union lines and therefore served, victories and defeats alike, to keep Rosecrans off balance by increasing his native caution and apprehensiveness. "Their numerous cavalry goads and
worries me," he had informed Washington at the outset, "but I will try
to be equal to them."

     This was going to be more difficult than he knew. Even as he
wrote, Earl Van Dorn, the South's ranking major general — ordered
north by Johnston over Pemberton's frantic protest at thus being practically stripped of cavalry despite the skill he recently had shown in handling that arm — was on the way from Mississippi with two divisions of
horsemen, all thirsty for more of the glory they lately had tasted when
they threw a whole Yankee army into retreat from Holly Springs. In
this respect, their leader was the thirstiest man among them. After the
Transmississippi disasters and the Corinth fiasco, which had resulted,
amid wholesale condemnation, in his being superseded as commander of
his home state forces, his bad luck had suddenly turned good, and he was
eager to take further advantage of the switch. Presently, soon after his
arrival on February 22 at Columbia, where he assumed responsibility for
protecting the left horn of Bragg's crescent while Wheeler protected the
right, Rosecrans gave the diminutive Mississippian just the chance he had
been seeking ever since his return to his first love, cavalry. The Federal

plan was for a convergence of two infantry columns, one out of Murfreesboro under Phil Sheridan, the other out of Franklin, directly south of Nashville, under Colonel John Coburn; they would unite at Spring Hill, a dozen miles north of Columbia, then move together against that place, foraging as they went. Coburn set out on March 4, with just under 3000 of all arms. Van Dorn was waiting for him next morning at Thompson's Station, just above the intended point of convergence, with twice as many men — including Forrest, who had been transferred in consideration of his vow to serve no more under Wheeler. The result was a sudden and stunning victory, cinched by Forrest, who came in on the flank and rear while Van Dorn maintained pressure against the front, and a bag of 1221 prisoners, including Coburn, whose artillery and cavalry, along with one of his infantry regiments assigned to guard the forage train, had fled at the first detection of the odds. His thirst unslaked, Van Dorn sent his captives south and turned east to tackle Sheridan, intending thus to sweep the board of all available opponents, but found that the other column had taken warning from the boom of guns and pulled back out of danger.

Rosecrans too had taken alarm, and though his present-for-duty strength now stood at 80,124, as compared to Bragg's 49,068, he began to suspect that he was outnumbered. "I am not, as you know, an alarmist," he wired Halleck on the day after Coburn's defeat, "but I do not think it will do to risk as we did before." He reinforced the threatened quarter, causing the rebel horsemen to pull back. But when the blue tide once more receded, Van Dorn returned again, cutting and slashing, left and right, and playing all the while on Rosecrans' fears. On March 24, having leapfrogged his headquarters to Spring Hill, he sent Forrest against Brentwood (ten miles north of Federal-held Franklin) where a garrison of about 800 Wisconsin and Michigan infantry protected army stores and a stockaded railroad bridge across the Little Harpeth River. Forrest appeared before the place next morning, demanding an unconditional surrender. "Come and take us," Colonel Edward Bloodgood replied stoutly, until he saw the graybacks preparing to do just that: whereupon he changed his mind and hauled down his flag. Setting fire to the stockade and packing the stores for removal along with his captives, Forrest sent one regiment up the Nashville pike to spread the scare in that direction — which it did, penetrating the southern environs of the city and riding within plain sight of the capitol tower — while the main body, after pausing to fight a confused rear-guard action provoked by a blue column that moved up from Franklin, made its getaway eastward before turning south to safety. In a general order issued on the last day of the month, Bragg expressed the "pride and gratification" he felt as a result of the "two brilliant and successful affairs recently achieved by the forces of the cavalry of Major General Van Dorn."

Unwilling to rest on his laurels now that fortune's smile was broadening still further, Van Dorn moved on April 10 against Franklin itself. A forced reconnaissance, he called it afterwards, though the defenders insisted that it had been an all-out attempt to take the place by storm. In support of the former contention was the fact that casualties were fewer than a hundred on each side; anyhow, he disengaged and withdrew when he found that the Union commander, Major General Gordon Granger, had been reinforced to a strength of about 8000. Back at Spring Hill, he continued to design projects for the discomfiture of the enemy, assisting Bragg to hold onto the fruitful region despite the odds which favored a Federal advance. On through April he labored, and into May, though apparently not so exclusively as to require him to abandon other pursuits; for at 10 o'clock on the morning of May 7, Dr George B. Peters, a local citizen, walked into headquarters, where Van Dorn was hard at work at his desk, and shot him in the back of the head with a pistol. He died about 2 o'clock that afternoon, by which time the assassin was safe within the Union lines, having ridden off in the buggy he had left parked outside while he stepped indoors to carry out his project. The accepted explanation was that the doctor had chosen this emphatic means to protest the general's attention to his young wife, though there were some who claimed that he had done the shooting for political reasons. At any rate, that was the end of the saga of Buck Van Dorn. Fortune's smile had turned out fickle after all, and they buried him in Columbia next day.

Wheeler had got back in stride by then with a double blow at Rosecrans' rail supply lines on April 10, the day Van Dorn tested the Franklin defenses and found them strong. The first was scored northeast of Nashville, beyond Andrew Jackson's Hermitage, by secretly posting guns along the near bank of a bend that took the Cumberland River within 500-yard range of the Louisville & Nashville tracks. After a wait of two hours, Wheeler reported, "a very large locomotive came in view, drawing eighteen cars loaded with horses and other stock." Though the target was moving his marksmanship was excellent, according to a Federal brigadier. "The first shot knocked off the dome of the locomotive, the next went through the boiler, one shot broke out a spoke in one of the driving-wheels." When the engine stalled in a cloud of steam, the gunners continued to pump shells into the cars, scattering bluecoats, horses, and cattle in all directions. Meanwhile, on the Nashville & Chattanooga side of the Tennessee capital, another group of Wheeler's men rode into Antioch, where they ambushed and derailed a train by spreading the tracks and took from the wreckage about seventy Union captives — including twenty officers, three of whom were members of Rosecrans' staff — along with some forty Confederates en route to Ohio prison camps, $30,000 in greenbacks, and a large mail containing much useful information. Loaded with booty, the raiders got away eastward to join their friends, who by now had ridden back past the Hermitage after their shooting-gallery fun on the Cumberland. Wheeler's total cost for both accomplishments was one man wounded.

He was cheered all round and greeted with smiles on his return, for both actions had a somewhat comic tinge. But the loudest cheers and the broadest smiles were reserved for Bedford Forrest, who began to win his *nom de guerre* "the Wizard of the Saddle" with an exploit which took him, through the closing days of April and the opening days of May, into parts of three states and across the northern width of Alabama. He was drawn in that direction by a Federal project which got under way, by coincidence on that same April 10, with the embarkation at Nashville of an expedition designed to sever Bragg's main supply line, the Western & Atlantic Railroad, between Atlanta and Chattanooga. This had been attempted once before, a year ago this week, but had resulted in the Great Locomotive Chase and the capture of the twenty-two spies who tried it. The new plan, while perhaps equally daring, was of a quite different nature. Taking a page from the book the rebel cavalry fought by — particularly John Morgan and Forrest himself — Colonel Abel D. Streight, New-York-born commander of a regiment of Hoosier infantry, proposed to Rosecrans that a large body of men, say 2000, be mounted for a quick but powerful thrust, into and out of the South's vitals. Rosecrans, who so often had been on the receiving end of this kind of thing, was delighted at the prospect of turning the tables, and his delight increased when Streight removed his final objection by agreeing to mount the men on mules instead of horses, of which there was a shortage; mules, he said, were not only more sure-footed, they were also more intelligent. (Which was true, so far as it went, though that was by no means all of the story. Mules had other, less admirable qualities: as he would presently discover.) At any rate, Rosecrans gave his approval to the project, designated Streight as commander, and assigned him three more regiments of Ohio, Indiana, and Illinois infantry, together with two companies of North Alabama Unionists — a breed of men who were known to their late compatriots as "homemade Yankees," but who were expected to prove invaluable as guides through a region unfamiliar to everyone else in the flying column — and a requisition for some nine hundred quartermaster mules. This would mount only about half of the troops, but Rosecrans explained that the rest could secure animals by commandeering them from rebel sympathizers while on the way to their starting point in the northeast corner of Mississippi.

So Streight got his men and mules aboard the transports and steamed next morning down the Cumberland to unload at Palmyra, on the left bank just around the bend from Clarksville, for a stock-gathering march to Fort Henry, where they again met the transports for the long ride south up the Tennessee to Eastport, Mississippi. That was the true starting point, tactically speaking, but Streight — a broad-chested man of soldierly appearance, just past forty, with a tall forehead, light-colored eyes, a fleshy, powerful-looking nose, and a dark, well-trimmed beard framing a wide, determined mouth exposed below a clean-shaven upper lip — had already encountered complications well outside the original margin he had allowed for error. For one thing, after waiting to pick up rations and forage on the Ohio, the navy did not turn up at Fort Henry on time, with the result that he did not reach Eastport until April 19, three days behind schedule. For another, a delayed check disclosed that a large proportion of the quartermaster mules were sadly afflicted with distemper, while many others were unbroken colts, not over two years old. This last exposed a further drawback; for he found that his converted infantrymen, as one of them remarked, "were at first very easily dismounted, frequently in a most undignified and unceremonious manner." Practice might improve the men's equestrian skill, but the mules were going to remain a problem. About five hundred had been commandeered on the course of the overland march, which more than made up for the hundred-odd who died of sickness and exhaustion while en route; but this gain was canceled on the evening of his arrival at Eastport. Returning to headquarters about midnight from a conference with Brigadier General Grenville M. Dodge, who had brought a 7500-man column over from Corinth to serve as a screen for the raiders' departure, he learned that some four hundred of the creatures — naturally the most intelligent of the lot — had escaped from their crudely built corrals and now were scattered about the countryside, disrupting the stillness of the night and mocking his woes with brays that had the sound of fiendish laughter. Two more days were spent here in rounding them up; half of them, that is, for the rest were never recovered. However, Dodge made up the difference with animals out of his pack train, and Streight at last got started in earnest, moving eastward across Bear Creek on the morning of April 22.

Five days behind schedule, but still protected from inquisitive eyes by the screen Dodge's troops had drawn along the south bank of the Tennessee River, he reached Tuscumbia late on the 24th and called a final two-day rest halt before resuming the march at 11 p.m. of the 26th, his force reduced to 1500 by a rigid inspection in which the surgeons culled such men as they judged unfit for the rigorous work ahead. All next day, and the next, as the column moved south to Russellville, then eastward to Mount Hope, rain and mud held its progress to a crawl and 300 of the fledgling troopers were reconverted to infantry because their mounts were too weak to carry anything heavier than a saddle. On the 29th, however, the sun broke through, giving "strong hopes of better times," as Streight declared in his last rearward message, and he began to pick up speed, along with replacements for his ailing mules. Thirty-five miles he made that day, clearing Moulton to make camp that night at the western foot of Day's Gap, a narrow defile piercing a lofty ridge that signaled the advent of the Appalachians. At this point, with the tactically dangerous flatlands left behind, he was about halfway to his first objective: Rome, Georgia, where the Confederacy had a cannon foundry and machine shops for the Western & Atlantic, whose main line was barely a half-day's ride beyond. Starting early next morning, the last day of April, Streight rode at the head of the column toiling upward through the gap. "The sun shone out bright and beautiful as spring day's sun ever beamed," his adjutant later recalled, "and from the smouldering camp-fires of the previous night the mild blue smoke ascended in graceful curves and mingled with the gray mist slumbering on the mountain tops above." There was in fact much that was dreamlike and idyllic about the scene —"well calculated to inspire and refresh the minds of our weary soldiers," the admiring lieutenant phrased it — until suddenly, without previous intimation of a transition, as Streight and the forward elements of the column neared the crest, the dream shifted kaleidoscopically into nightmare. From downhill, in the direction of last night's camp, the deep-voiced booms of guns, mixed in with the tearing rattle of musketry, abruptly informed him that he was under attack.

It was Forrest. A week ago today — the day after Streight left Eastport — he had received at Spring Hill, Tennessee, orders from Bragg to proceed south to the Florence-Tuscumbia region and assist the inadequate local defense units to oppose the force moving eastward under Dodge. He left next morning, April 24, and thirty-six hours later had his 1577-man brigade at Brown's Ferry, Alabama, ninety miles away. Leaving one of his three regiments to guard the north bank of the Tennessee in case Dodge decided to strike in that direction, he ferried the others across on the 26th and moved west through Courtland to Town Creek, which he reached in time to challenge a Federal crossing. The long-range skirmish continued until dusk of the following day, when Forrest received word from a scout that a mounted column estimated at 2000 men had left Mount Hope that morning, headed east. This was the first he had heard of Streight's existence, but he decided at once that this was the major threat, not the larger force immediately to his front. Accordingly, leaving Dodge to the local defenders and the regiment already posted beyond the river, he took off southward at dawn of the 29th for Moulton, which Streight had cleared six hours before. At midnight, having covered fifty miles of road with just over a thousand horsemen and eight guns, he went into bivouac, four miles short of Streight's camp at Day's Gap, in order to give his saddle-weary troopers some rest for tomorrow, and soon after sunrise was banging away at the Federal rear.

In the course of the three-day running fight which followed, the pursued had certain definite advantages. The first was a superiority of numbers, although Streight's enjoyment of this was considerably diminished by the fact that he did not know he had it. All the same, the numerical odds were with him, three to two, whether he knew it or not, and what was more they grew as he moved eastward past well-stocked farms untouched by war till now. When his mules gave out, as they frequently did, he could remount his men by seizing others; whereas for Forrest, coming along in the raiders' clean-swept wake, a broken-down horse meant a lost rider. Another tactical advantage accruing to the blue commander was that whenever he chose to make a stand he could not only select the terrain best suited for defensive fighting, he could also lay small-scale ambushes by which a rear-guard handful could shock the pursuers with surprise fire, forcing them to halt and deploy, then hurry ahead to rejoin the main body before the attack was delivered. Streight was altogether aware of this advantage, and used it first within three miles of the point where he heard the opening boom of guns. Selecting a position along a wooded ridge, with a boggy creek protecting his left and a steep ravine his right, he sent back word for the rear-guard Alabama Unionists, still skirmishing in Day's Gap, to retreat on the run through the newly drawn line and thus draw the graybacks into ambush. It worked to perfection. As the pursuers rode fast to overtake the home-made Yankees, the waiting bluecoats rose from the underbrush and shattered the head of the column with massed volleys. When reinforcements came up to repeat the attempt, this time advancing a section of artillery to counterbalance the two 12-pounder mountain howitzers firing rapidly from the ridge, the defenders followed up a second repulse with a counterattack and captured both of the guns, then drew off, leaving the rebels rocked back on their heels.

Forrest was thrown into a towering rage by the loss of his guns and the fact that the raiders had won first honors and drawn first blood — including that of his brother, Captain William Forrest, who had led his company of scouts in the charge and had been unhorsed by a bullet that broke his thigh — but by the time he got his troopers back into line for a third attack, the bluecoats had pulled out. He pushed on, closing again on their rear at Crooked Creek, where Streight again formed line of battle, six miles beyond the first. Here, from about an hour before dark until 10 o'clock that night, the two forces engaged in a fire fight. Determined to give the raiders no rest, Forrest kept forcing the issue by moonlight, and his orders, though brief, were conclusive: "Shoot at everything blue and keep up the scare." Finally, with one flank about to crumple, Streight "resumed the march," leaving the two captured guns behind him, spiked. At midnight, then again two hours later, he laid ambushes, but Forrest kept crowding him and did not call a halt till daylight, when he paused long enough to water and feed the horses and give the weaker ones an opportunity to catch up. Streight meanwhile pushed on to the outskirts of Blountsville, which he reached about midmorning of May Day, having covered forty-three miles over mountain roads since the skirmishing began soon after sunrise yesterday. However, before his men could finish feeding their weary mounts, Forrest once more was driving in the pickets, and the two commands went through the town in a whirl of dust and gunsmoke, shooting at one another over the ears of their horses or the cruppers of their mules.

So it went, all that day and the next, eastward another fifty miles, then northeastward along the near bank of the Coosa River, with Streight making stands behind the east fork of the Black Warrior River and Big Will's Creek, laying ambushes in the heavily wooded valley off the southern end of Lookout Mountain, and burning the only bridge across Black Creek, just short of Gadsden. Forrest kept the pressure on, however. He got over the last-named obstacle by using a ford that was shown him, under fire from the opposite bank, by a sixteen-year-old farm girl, Emma Sanson — in appreciation of whose courage he took time and pains to leave an autograph note of thanks:

> *Hed Quaters in Sadle*
> *May 2 1863*
> *My highest regardes to miss Ema Sanson for hir Gallant con-*
> *duct while my posse was skirmishing with the Federals across*
> *Black Creek near Gadesden Allabama.*
> *N. B. Forrest*
> *Brig Genl Comding N. Ala —*

and pressed on after the blue raiders, engaging them in another running fight through Gadsden and beyond, where they soon were forced to make another stand. He had the advantage of singleness of purpose, plus the chance to give his men a breather when he chose, pursuing as it were in shifts, some resting while others kept up the chase; whereas Streight not only had to keep fending off the myriad and apparently inexhaustible graybacks hot on his trail — a profitless business at best — but also had to keep pushing on toward the accomplishment of his mission in North Georgia. After nearly three days of riding and fighting, and two nights without rest, his men were falling asleep on muleback and even in line of battle whenever he called a halt to lay another ambush or defend another opportune position, and now that his pursuers had avoided delay at Black Creek, thanks to Emma Sanson, he faced another sleepless night. "It now became evident to me," he later reported, "that our only hope was in crossing the river at Rome and destroying the bridge, which would delay Forrest a day or two and give us time to collect horses and mules and allow the command a little time to sleep, without which it was impossible to proceed."

Accordingly, when he reached Turkeytown, eight miles beyond Gadsden, he selected two hundred of the best-mounted men and sent them ahead to seize the bridge across the Oostanaula River at Rome and hold it until the main body came up. At sunset, four miles farther along, he formed again for battle "as it was impossible to continue the march through the night without feeding and resting." In the course of the preliminary skirmish, however, he discovered that much of the men's

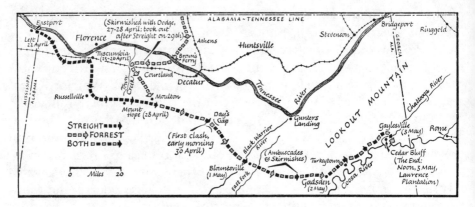

ammunition had been ruined by dampness and abrasion. Instead of risking another general engagement under these circumstances, he decided to disengage — "unobserved, if possible" — and lay another ambush in a thicket half a mile ahead. When Forrest detected the ruse and began to move out on the flank, Streight had to pull back and make a run for it in the dusk, beginning another horrendous night march with men who by now had the look of somnambulists and mules that were "jaded, tender-footed, and worn out." But the worst development, so far, was encountered when they reached the Cedar Bluff ferry across the Chattooga River, just above its confluence with the Coosa. The 200-man detail had passed this way a short while back, headed for Rome, but had neglected to post a guard: with the result that some citizens had spirited the ferryboat away, leaving Streight with the sort of problem he had been leaving Forrest all along.

Yet he was nothing if not persevering. Turning left, he plodded wearily through the darkness along the west bank of the Chattooga, intent on reaching a bridge near Gaylesville, half a dozen miles upstream. Whereupon — while Forrest was giving his troopers a few hours' sleep: all but one squadron, which he instructed to stay on the trail of the raiders and "devil them all night" — Streight and his muleback soldiers entered the worst of their several Deep South nightmares. The way led through extensive "choppings" where the timber had been cut and burned to furnish charcoal for nearby Round Mountain Furnace, which in turn supplied the Rome foundry with pig iron. Though the raiders succeeded in wrecking part of the smelting plant — the one substantial blow they struck in the course of their long ride across Alabama — they paid a high price in the extra miles they covered in order to bring it within reach. Lost in a maze of wagon trails, segments of the blue column were scattered about the choppings until daylight showed them the way back to the river and then to the bridge, which they crossed and burned in their wake. Wobbly with fatigue, animals and men alike, they staggered along the opposite bank, again to the vicinity of Cedar Bluff, then turned eastward five more miles to the Lawrence plantation, which they reached about 9 a.m. The Georgia line was only five miles ahead, with Rome barely another fifteen miles beyond, but Streight had no choice except to drop from exhaustion or halt for rest and food. He had no sooner begun the distribution of rations, however, than the graybacks once more were driving in his pickets.

Forrest had swum the Chattooga at sunup, using long ropes to drag two of his guns across, submerged on the sandy bottom. Down to six hundred men by now, he was outnumbered worse than two to one and knew it, even if Streight did not. All along he had had to avoid the obvious maneuver of circling the flank of the blue column in order to block its path; for in that case, goaded by desperation, the Federals might have run right over him, swamping his line with the sheer weight of numbers. Even now, in fact, though his troopers were considerably refreshed by the sleep they had enjoyed while the bluecoats were stumbling around in the choppings south of Gaylesville, he preferred not to risk a pitched battle if he could accomplish his purpose otherwise. So he did as he had done before, in similar circumstances: sent forward, under a flag of truce, an officer with a note demanding immediate surrender "to stop the further and useless effusion of blood."

Streight, who had had to wake his men to put them into line of battle — where they promptly fell asleep again, with bullets whistling overhead — replied that he was by no means ready to give up, but that, sharing Forrest's humane views as to unnecessary bloodshed, he was willing to parley. He insisted further, when the guns fell silent and the two commanders met between the lines, that he would not even consider laying down his arms unless his opponent would prove that he had an overwhelming superiority of numbers. Forrest declined to show his hand in any such manner; but all the while, acting under previous instructions, the officer in charge of the section of artillery kept bringing his two guns over a distant rise in the road, then back under cover and over the rise again, producing for the benefit of Streight, who had been placed so as to watch all this over Forrest's shoulder, the appearance of a stream of guns arriving at intervals to bolster the rebel line. "Name of God!" Streight cried at last. "How many guns have you got? There's fifteen I've counted already." Forrest looked around casually. "I reckon that's all that has kept up," he said. So Streight went back to his own lines for a conference with his regimental commanders, most of whom, as he later reported, "had already expressed the opinion that, unless we could reach Rome and cross the river before the enemy came up with us again, we should be compelled to surrender." At this juncture, a messenger arrived from the 200-man detail sent ahead the night before and reported that the bridge across the Oostanaula was strongly held by rebel troops in Rome. That did it; Streight returned and announced his willingness to surrender. Forrest replied, "Stack your arms right along there, Colonel, and march your men away down that hollow."

The total bag, including the 200-man detail picked up on the way into Rome that same Sunday afternoon as it returned from its fruitless mission, was 1466 bluecoats, and though they had been feared as would-be conquerors — a fear which had thrown the Rome citizenry into such a panic of feverish activity that the Federal scouts, observing from across the Oostanaula, had mistaken the milling for preparedness — they were welcomed and fed generously as captives. Forrest's own entrance was the occasion for the presentation of a horseshoe wreath of flowers, hailing him as the town's deliverer, and a fine saddle horse, which helped to make up for the two that had been shot from under him in the course of the long chase. Then began a famous celebration, attended by what one matron called "just a regular wholesale cooking of hams and shoulders and all sorts of provisions" to relieve the hunger pangs of the gray heroes. Nor were the prisoners excluded from this bounty; "We were quite willing to feed the Yankees when they had no guns," she added. But the Roman holiday was cut short on the night of May 5 by the arrival of word that another column of blue raiders had left Tuscumbia that afternoon, headed southeast for Jasper and possibly Montgomery. Forrest and his men were back in the saddle next morning. Riding once more through Gadsden the following day, they learned that the rumor was groundless, Dodge having returned to Corinth; so they swung north, recovering the third regiment en route, to resume their accustomed work in Tennessee. On May 10, however — another Sunday — Forrest was handed orders from Bragg, instructing him to have his brigade continue its present march but for him to report in person to army headquarters, where he would receive, along with a recommendation for promotion to major general, appointment to the command Van Dorn had vacated three days ago, when he came under the Spring Hill doctor's pistol.

⚔ 5 ⚔

Along toward sunset of January 28, completing a 400-mile overnight trip from Memphis down the swollen, tawny, mile-wide Mississippi, a stern-wheel packet warped in for a west-bank landing at Young's Point, just opposite the base of the long hairpin bend in front of Vicksburg and within half a dozen air-line miles of the guns emplaced along the lip of the tall clay bluff the city stood on. First off the steamboat, once the deck hands had swung out the stageplank, was a slight man, rather stooped, five feet eight inches in height and weighing less than a hundred and forty pounds, who walked with a peculiar gait, shoulders

hunched "a little forward of the perpendicular," as one observer remarked, so that each step seemed to arrest him momentarily in the act
of pitching on his face. He had on a plain blue suit and what the same
reporter called "an indifferently good 'Kossuth' hat, with the top battered in close to his head." Forty years old, he looked considerably older,
partly because of the crow's-feet crinkling the outer corners of his eyes
— the result of intense concentration, according to some, while others
identified them as whiskey lines, plainly confirming rumors of over-
indulgence and refuting the protestations of friends that he never
touched the stuff — but mainly because of the full, barely grizzled, light
brown beard, close-cropped to emphasize the jut of a square jaw and
expose a mouth described as being "of the letterbox shape," clamped
firmly shut below a nose that surprised by contrast, being delicately
chiseled, and blue-gray eyes that gave the face a somewhat out-of-
balance look because one was set a trifle lower than the other. Wearing
neither sword nor sash, and indeed no trappings of rank at all, except for
the twin-starred straps of a major general tacked to the weathered
shoulders of his coat, he was reading a newspaper as he came down the
plank to the Louisiana shore, and he chewed the unlighted stump of a
cigar, which not only seemed habitual but also appeared to be a more
congruous facial appendage than the surprisingly aquiline nose.

"There's General Grant," an Illinois soldier told a comrade as
they stood watching this unceremonious arrival.

"I guess not," the other replied, shaking his head. "That fellow
don't look like he has the ability to command a regiment, much less an
army."

It was not so much that Grant was unexpected; he had a habit of
turning up unannounced at almost any time and place within the limits
of his large department. The trouble was that he bore such faint resemblance to his photographs, which had been distributed widely ever
since Donelson and which, according to an acquaintance, made him look
like a "burly beef-contractor." In person he resembled at best a badly
printed copy of one of those photos, with the burliness left out. Conversely, the lines of worry — if his friends were right and that was what
they were — were more pronounced, as was perhaps only natural when
he had more to fret about than the discomfort of holding still for a
camera. Just now, for instance, there was John McClernand, who persisted in considering the river force a separate command and continued
to issue general orders under the heading, "Headquarters, Army of the
Mississippi." Before Grant had been downriver two days he received a
letter from McClernand, noting "that orders are being issued directly
from your headquarters directly to army corps commanders, and not
through me." This could only result in "dangerous confusion," McClernand protested, "as I am invested, by order of the Secretary of War, indorsed by the President, and by order of the President communicated to

you by the General-in-Chief, with the command of all the forces operating on the Mississippi River. . . . If different views are entertained by
you, then the question should be immediately referred to Washington,
and one or the other, or both of us, relieved. One thing is certain; two
generals cannot command this army, issuing independent and direct orders to subordinate officers, and the public service be promoted."

Grant agreed at least with the final sentence — which he later
paraphrased and sharpened into a maxim: "Two commanders on the
same field are always one too many" — but he found the letter as a whole
"more in the nature of a reprimand than a protest." The fact was, it approached outright insubordination, although not quite close enough to
afford occasion for the pounce Grant was crouched for. "I overlooked
it, as I believed, for the good of the service," he subsequently wrote. By
way of reply, instead of direct reproof, he issued orders announcing that
he was assuming personal command of the river expedition and instructing all corps commanders, including McClernand, to report henceforth
directly to him; McClernand's corps, he added by way of a stinger,
would garrison Helena and other west-bank points well upriver. Outraged at being the apparent victim of a squeeze play, the former congressman responded by asking whether, "having projected the Mississippi
River expedition, and having been by a series of orders assigned to the
command of it," he was thus to be "entirely withdrawn from it." Grant
replied to the effect that he would do as he saw fit, since "as yet I have
seen no order to prevent my taking command in the field." McClernand
acquiesced, as he said, "for the purpose of avoiding a conflict of authority
in the presence of the enemy," but requested that the entire matter be
referred to their superiors in Washington, "not only in respect for the
President and Secretary, under whose authority I claim the right to
command the expedition, but in justice to myself as its author and actual
promoter." Grant accordingly forwarded the correspondence to Halleck, saying that he had assumed command only because he lacked confidence in McClernand. "I respectfully submit the whole matter to the
General-in-Chief and the President," he ended his indorsement. "Whatever the decision made by them, I will cheerfully submit to and give a
hearty support."

In bucking all this up to the top echelon Grant was on even safer
ground than he supposed. Just last week McClernand had received, in
reply to a private letter to Lincoln charging Halleck "with wilful contempt of superior authority" because of his so-far "interference" in the
matter, "and with incompetency for the extraordinary and vital functions with which he is charged," a note in which the President told him
plainly: "I have too many *family* controversies (so to speak) already on
my hands to voluntarily, or so long as I can avoid it, take up another.
You are now doing well — well for the country, and well for yourself
— much better than you could possibly be if engaged in open war with

General Halleck. Allow me to beg that tor your sake, for my sake, and for the country's sake, you give your whole attention to the better work." So it was: McClernand already had his answer before he filed his latest appeal. Lincoln would not interfere. The army was Grant's, and would remain Grant's, to do with as he saw fit in accomplishing what Lincoln called "the better work."

His problem was how best to go about it. Now that he had inspected at first hand the obstacles to success in this swampy region, much of which was at present under water and would continue to be so for months to come, he could see that the wisest procedure, from a strategic point of view, "would have been to go back to Memphis, establish that as a base of supplies, fortify it so that the storehouses could be held by a small garrison, and move from there along the line of the [Mississippi & Tennessee] railroad, repairing as we advanced to the Yalo-busha," from which point he would have what he now so gravely lacked: a straight, high-ground shot at the city on the rebel bluff. So he wrote, years later, having gained the advantage of hindsight. For the present, however, he saw certain drawbacks to the retrograde movement, which in his judgment far outweighed the strictly tactical advantages. For one thing, the November elections had gone against the party that stood for all-out prosecution of the war, and this had turned out to be a warning of future trouble, with the croakers finding encouragement in the reverse. There was the question of morale, not only in the army itself, but also on the home front, where even a temporary withdrawal would be considered an admission that Vicksburg was too tough a nut to crack. At this critical juncture, both temporal and political, with voluntary enlistment practically at a standstill throughout much of the North and the new conscription laws already meeting sporadic opposition, such a discouragement might well prove fatal to the cause. "It was my judgment at the time," Grant subsequently wrote, "that to make a backward movement as long as that from Vicksburg to Memphis, would be interpreted, by many of those yet full of hope for the preservation of the Union, as a defeat, and that the draft would be resisted, desertions ensue, and the power to capture and punish deserters lost. There was nothing left to be done but to *go forward to a decisive victory*. This was in my mind from the moment I took command in person at Young's Point."

In his own mind at least that much was settled. He would stay. But this decision only brought him face to face with the basic problem, as he put it, of how "to secure a footing upon dry ground on the east side of the river, from which the troops could operate against Vicksburg ... without an apparent retreat." Aside from a frontal assault, either against the bluff itself or against the heights flanking it on the north — which Sherman, even if he had done nothing more last month, had proved would not only be costly in the extreme but would also be fruit-

less, and which Grant said "was never contemplated; certainly not by
me" — the choice lay between whether to cross upstream or down,
above or below the rebel bastion. One seemed about as impossible as the
other. Above, the swampy, fifty-mile-wide delta lay in his path, practically roadless and altogether malarial. Even if he were able to slog his
foot soldiers across it, which was doubtful, it was worse than doubtful whether he would be able to establish and maintain a vital supply
line by that route. On the other hand, to attempt a crossing below
the city seemed even more suicidal, since this would involve a run past
frowning batteries, not only at Vicksburg itself, but also at Warrenton
and Grand Gulf, respectively seven and thirty-five miles downriver.
Armored gunboats — as Farragut had demonstrated twice the year before, first up, then down, with his heavily gunned salt-water fleet —
might run this fiery gauntlet, taking their losses as they went, but brittle-
skinned transports and supply boats would be quite another matter, considering the likelihood of their being reduced to kindling in short order,
with much attendant loss of life and goods.... In short, the choice
seemed to lie between two impossibilities, flanking a third which had
been rejected before it was even considered.

Two clear advantages Grant had, however, by way of helping to
offset the gloom, and both afforded him comfort under the strain. One
was the unflinching support of his superiors; the other was an ample supply of troops, either downstream with him or else on call above. "The
eyes and hopes of the whole country are now directed to your army,"
Halleck presently would tell him. "In my opinion, the opening of the
Mississippi River will be to us of more advantage than the capture of
forty Richmonds. We shall omit nothing which we can do to assist you."
Already, before Grant left Memphis, Old Brains had urged him: "Take
everything you can dispense with in Tennessee and [North] Mississippi.
We must not fail in this if within human power to accomplish it." His
total effective strength within his department, as of late January, was
approximately 103,000 officers and men, and of these, as a result of abandoning railroads and other important rear-area installations, Grant had
been able to earmark just over half for the downriver expedition: 32,000
in the two corps under McClernand and Sherman, already at hand, and
15,000 in McPherson's corps, filing aboard transports southbound from
Memphis even now. In addition to these 47,000 — the official total,
"present for duty, equipped," was 46,994 — another 15,000 were standing by under Hurlbut, who commanded the fourth corps, ready to follow McPherson as soon as they got the word. Just now, though, there
not only was no need for them; there actually was no room. Because of
the high water and the incessant rain overflowing the bayous, there was
no place to camp on the low-lying west bank except upon the levee,
with the result that the army was strung out along it for more than fifty
miles, north and south, under conditions that were anything but healthy.

As morale declined, the sick-lists lengthened; desertions were up; funerals were frequent. "Go any day down the levee," one recruit wrote home, "and you could see a squad or two of soldiers burying a companion, until the levee was nearly full of graves and the hospitals still full of sick. And those that were not down sick were not well by a considerable." Pneumonia was the chief killer, with smallpox a close second. Some regiments soon had more men down than up. The food was bad. Paymasters did not venture south of Helena, which increased the disaffection, and the rumor mills were grinding as never before. When the mails were held up, as they frequently were, it was reported from camp to camp, like a spark moving along a fifty-mile train of powder, that the war was over but that the news was being kept from the troops "for fear we could not be held in subjection if we knew the state of affairs." They took out at least a share of their resentment on such rebel property as came within their reach. "Farms disappear, houses are burned and plundered, and every living animal killed and eaten," Sherman informed his senator brother. "General officers make feeble efforts to stay the disorder, but it is idle." Then when the mail came through at last they could read in anti-administration newspapers of the instability and incompetence of the West Pointers responsible for their welfare, including Sherman — "He hates reporters, foams at the mouth when he sees them, snaps at them; sure symptoms of a deep-seated mania" — and the army commander himself: "The confidence of the army is greatly shaken in General Grant, who hitherto undoubtedly depended more upon good fortune than upon military ability for success."

The wet season would continue for months, during which all these problems would be with him. As Grant said in retrospect, "There seemed to be no possibility of a land movement before the end of March or later." Yet "it would not do to lie idle all this time. The effect would be demoralizing to the troops and injurious to their health. Friends in the North would have grown more and more insolent in their gibes and denunciations of the cause and those engaged in it." So he launched (or rather, continued) what he called "a series of experiments," designed not only "to consume time," but also to serve the triple purpose of diverting "the attention of the enemy, of my troops, and of the public generally." Two failures were already behind him in his campaign against Vicksburg: the advance down the Mississippi Central and the assault on the Chickasaw Bluffs, both of which had ended in retreat. Now there followed five more failures, bringing the total to seven. Looking back on them later he was to say — quite untruthfully, as the record would show — that he had "never felt great confidence that any of the experiments resorted to would prove successful," though he had always been "prepared to take advantage of them in case they did."

The third of these seven "experiments" — the attempt, by means of a canal across the base of the tongue of land in front of Vicksburg, to divert the channel of the river and thus permit the column of warships, transports, and supply boats to bypass the batteries on the bluff — had been in progress ever since the return of the army from Arkansas Post, but Sherman, who had assigned a thousand men a day to the digging job, was not sanguine of results. "The river is about full and threatens to drown us out," he was complaining as he sloshed about in a waste of gumbo, with the rain coming down harder every week. "The ground is wet, almost water, and it is impossible for wagons to haul stores from the river to camp, or even horses to wallow through." Conversely, as if to preserve a balance of optimism, Grant's expectations rose with the passage of time. In early March he wired Halleck: "The canal is near completion. . . . I will have Vicksburg this month, or fail in the attempt." But this was the signal for disaster. "If the river rises 8 feet more, we would have to take to the trees," Sherman had said, and presently it did. The dam at the upper end of the cut gave way, and the water, instead of scouring out a channel — as had been expected, or anyhow intended — spread all over the lower end of the peninsula, forcing the evacuation of the troops from their flooded camps, with the resultant sacrifice of many horses and much equipment. "This little affair of ours here on Vicksburg Point is labor lost," Sherman reported in disgust, announcing the unceremonious end of the third experiment.

But Grant already had a fourth in progress. Fifty-odd miles above Vicksburg, just west of the river and south of the Arkansas line, lay Lake Providence, once a bend of the Mississippi but long since abandoned by the Old Man in the course of one of his cataclysmic whims. Though the lake now was land-locked, separated moreover from the river by a levee, Bayou Baxter drained it sluggishly westward into Bayou Macon, which in turn flowed into the Tensas River, just over a hundred winding miles to the south. Still farther down, the Tensas joined the Ouachita to form the Black, and the Black ran into the Red, which entered the Mississippi a brief stretch above Port Hudson. Despite its roundabout meandering, a distance of some 470 miles, this route seemed to Grant to offer a chance, once the levee had been breached to afford access to Lake Providence and the intricate system of hinterland bayous and rivers, for a naval column to avoid not only the Vicksburg batteries but also those below at Warrenton and Grand Gulf. Accordingly, two days after his arrival at Young's Point, he sent an engineer detail to look into the possibilities indicated on the map, and the following week, in early February, he went up to see for himself. It seemed to him that "a little digging" — "less than one-quarter," he said, of what Sherman had done already on the old canal — "will connect the Mississippi and Lake, and in all probability will wash a channel in a short time." If so, the way would be open for a bloodless descent, at the end of which he would join Banks for a combined attack on Port Hudson, and once that final bastion had been reduced the Confederacy would

have been cut in two and the Great Lakes region would have recovered its sorely missed trade connection with the Gulf. Impressed by this vista, Grant sent at once for McPherson to come down with a full division and get the project started without delay. "This bids fair to be the most practicable route for turning Vicksburg," he told him in the body of the summons.

He could scarcely have assigned the task to an officer better prepared to undertake it. McPherson, who was thirty-three and a fellow Ohioan, had been top man in the West Point class of '53 and had returned to the academy as an engineering instructor; he also had worked on river and harbor projects in the peacetime army, and had served at the time of Shiloh, when he was a lieutenant colonel, as chief engineer on Grant's staff. His advancement since then had been rapid, though not without some grousing, on the part of line officers he had passed on his way up the ladder, that a man who had never led troops in a major action should be given command of a corps. Sherman, on the other hand, considered him the army's "best hope for a great soldier," not excepting Grant and himself; "if he lives," he added. A bright-eyed, pleasant-faced young man, alternately bland and impulsive, McPherson came quickly down from Memphis with one of his two divisions and set to work at once. Without waiting for the levee to be cut, he horsed a small towboat overland, launched it on the lake, and got aboard for a reconnaissance — with the result that his high hopes took a sudden drop. The Bayou Baxter outlet led through an extensive cypress brake, and what could be found of its channel, which was but little at the present flood stage, was badly choked with stumps and snags that threatened to knock or rip the bottom out of whatever came their way. He put his men to work with underwater saws, but it was clear that at best the job would be a long one, if not impossible. Besides, Grant now saw that, even if a passage could be opened in time to be of use, he would never be able to get together enough light-draft boats to carry his army down to the Red River anyhow. McPherson and his staff meanwhile enjoyed something of a holiday, taking a regimental band aboard the little steamer for moonlight excursions, to and from the landing at one of the lakeside plantation houses which turned out to have a well-stocked cellar. Soldiers too found relaxation in this quiet backwater of the war, mainly in fishing, what time they were not taking turns on the underwater saws. By early March it was more or less obvious that nothing substantial was going to come of this fourth attempt to take or bypass Vicksburg, but Grant declared, later and rather laconically: "I let the work go on, believing employment was better than idleness for the men."

All seven of these experiments, four of which by now had gone by the board, anticipated some degree of co-operation from the navy. For the most part, indeed, they were classically amphibious, depending as much on naval as on army strength and skill. But if Porter, whatever his other shortcomings — one acquaintance called him "by all odds the greatest humbug of the war" — was not the kind of man to withhold needed help, neither was he the kind to be satisfied with a supporting role if he saw even an outside chance at stardom. And he believed he saw one now: had seen it, in fact, from the outset, and had already made his solo entrance on the stage. One of the two main reasons for attempting the reduction of Vicksburg and Port Hudson — in addition, that is, to opening a pathway to New Orleans and the Gulf — was to choke off rebel traffic along and across the nearly three hundred miles of river that flowed between them, particularly that segment of it tangent to the mouth of Red River, the main artery of trade connecting the goods-rich Transmississippi's far-west region with the principal Confederate supply depots in Georgia and Virginia. To accomplish this, the admiral perceived, it would not be absolutely necessary to capture either of the two bastions anchoring opposite ends of the long stretch of river. All that was needed, really, was to control what lay between them, and this could be done by sending warships down to knock out whatever vestiges of the rebel fleet remained and to establish a sort of internal blockade by patrolling all possible crossings. In early February, accordingly, while Sherman's men were still digging their way across soggy Vicksburg Point and Grant was steaming upriver for a preliminary look at cypress-choked Lake Providence, Porter gave orders which put his plan in the way of execution.

First off, this would require a run past the batteries on the bluff, and he gave the assignment to the steam ram *Queen of the West,* which had done it twice before, back in July, in an unsuccessful attempt to come to grips with the *Arkansas.* She was one of the navy's best-known vessels, having led the ram attack at the Battle of Memphis, where she had been commanded by her designer and builder, Colonel Charles Ellet, Jr., who had died of the only wound inflicted on a Northerner in that one-sided triumph. His son, nineteen-year-old Colonel Charles R. Ellet — who, as a medical cadet, had gone ashore in a rowboat, accompanied by three seamen, to complete the Memphis victory by raising the Stars and Stripes over the post office — had succeeded his uncle, Brigadier General A. W. Ellet, who had succeeded the first Ellet as commander of the ram fleet, as skipper of the *Queen.* Patched up from the two poundings she had taken from Vicksburg's high-perched guns, and fitted out now with guns of her own for the first time — previously she had depended solely on her punch — she made her run at daybreak, February 4, taking an even dozen hits, including two in the hull but none below the water line, and pulled up at a battery Sherman had established on the west bank, just around the bend, for the protection of his diggers. Above the town, two nights later, Porter set adrift a barge loaded with 20,000 bushels of coal, which made it downstream on schedule and without mishap, apparently not having been spotted by the lookouts on the bluff. "This gives the ram nearly coal enough to last a month," the admiral proudly informed Secretary Welles, "in which time she can commit great havoc, if no accident happens to her."

Though at first it seemed an unnecessary flourish — he knew the rebels had nothing afloat to match the *Queen* — that final reservation was prophetic. Setting out on the night of February 10, accompanied by an ex-Confederate steamboat, the *DeSoto*, which had been captured by the army below Vicksburg, Ellet began his career as a commerce raider in fine style, slipping past the Warrenton batteries undetected and going to work at once on enemy shipping by destroying skiffs and flatboats on both banks. He burned or commandeered hundreds of bales of cotton, taking some aboard for "armoring" the wheelhouse, destroyed supply trains heavily loaded with grain and salt pork being sent to collection points, and in reprisal for a sniper bullet, which struck one of his sailors in the leg, burned no less than three plantation houses, together with their outbuildings, apparently undismayed even when one planter's daughter sang "The Bonny Blue Flag" full in his face as the flames crackled. His greatest single prize, however, was the corn-laden packet *Era No. 5*, which he captured after passing Natchez and entering the Red River. But at that point, or just beyond it — seventy-five miles from the mouth of the river and with Alexandria in a turmoil less than half that far ahead — he and the *Queen* ran out of luck. On Valentine's Day, approaching Gordon's Landing, where a battery of guns had been reported, the ram stuck fast on a mud flat and was taken suddenly under fire by enemy gunners who yelled with delight at thus being offered a stationary target at a range of four hundred yards. In short order the boat's engine controls were smashed, her escape-pipe shot away, her boiler fractured. As she disappeared in hissing clouds of steam — one survivor later claimed to have avoided scalding his lungs because "I had sufficient presence of mind to cram the tail of my coat into my mouth" — officers and men began to tumble bales of cotton over the rail, then leap after them into the river, clinging to them in hope of reaching the *DeSoto* or the *Era*, a mile below. By now it was every man for himself, including the wounded, and the youthful skipper was not among the last to abandon the *Queen* in favor of a downstream ride astride a bale of cotton.

Picked up by the *DeSoto*, Ellet and the others were alarmed to discover that in the excitement she had unshipped both rudders and become unmanageable; so they set her afire and abandoned her, too, in favor of the more recently captured *Era*. Their career as raiders had lasted just four days. From now on, their only concern was escape, which seemed unlikely because of reports that the Confederates had at Alexandria a high-speed steamboat, the *William H. Webb*, which would surely be after them as soon as the news arrived upriver. She mounted only one gun, they had heard, and would never have dared to tackle the *Queen*, but now the tables were more or less turned; the pursuers became the pursued. "With a sigh for the poor fellows left behind, and a hope that our enemies would be merciful," a survivor wrote, "the prow of the *Era* was turned toward the Mississippi." They made it by daylight, after a race through stormy darkness unrelieved except for blinding flashes of lightning, and started north up the big river, heaving overboard all possible incidentals, including rations, in an attempt to coax more speed from their unarmed boat. Next morning, February 16, just below Natchez, with the *Webb* reportedly closing fast on their stern, they were startled to see an enormous, twin-stacked vessel bearing down on them from dead ahead. Their dismay at the prospect of being ground between two millstones was relieved, however, when the lookout identified her as the *Indianola*. The latest addition to the ironclad fleet and the pride of the Federal inland-waters navy, she mounted two great 11-inch smoothbores forward and a pair of 9-inch rifles amidships, casemated between her towering sidewheel-boxes, while for power she boasted four engines, driving twin screws in addition to her paddles, and she had brought two large barges of coal along, one lashed to starboard and one to port, to insure a long-term stay on the previously rebel-held 250-mile stretch of river above Port Hudson. Porter had sent her down past the Vicksburg batteries three nights ago, intending for her to support the *Queen* and thus, as he said, "make matters doubly sure."

Learning from Ellet that the *Queen* had been lost, Lieutenant Commander George Brown, captain of the *Indianola*, decided at once to proceed downriver, accompanied by the *Era*. Presently they sighted the *Webb*, in hot pursuit, and once more the tables were turned; for the *Webb* took one quick look at the iron-clad monster and promptly made use of her superior speed to withdraw before coming within range of those 11-inch guns, two short-falling shots from which only served to hurry her along, as one observer said, "for all the world like a frightened racehorse." Brown gave chase as far as the mouth of Red River, up which the rebel vessel disappeared, but there he called a halt, Porter having warned him not to venture up that stream without an experienced pilot, which he lacked. While Brown continued on patrol, guarding against a re-emergence of the *Webb*, Ellet took off northward in the *Era* with the unpleasant duty of informing Porter that he had lost the *Queen*. Two days later, still on patrol at the mouth of the Red, Brown received astounding news. The Confederates had resurrected the *Queen of the West*, patching up her punctured hull and repairing her fractured steam drum. Even now, in company with the skittish *Webb* and two cottonclad boats whose upper decks were crowded with sharpshooters, she was preparing to come out after the *Indianola*. Brown thought it over and decided to retire.

He would have done better to leave without taking time to think it over; the fuze was burning shorter than he knew. However, he was in for a fight in any event because of the two coal barges, which he knew would decrease his upstream speed considerably, but which he was determined to hold onto, despite the fact that the *Indianola*'s bunkers were chock-full. Partly this decision was the result of his ingrained peacetime frugality, but mostly it was because he wanted to have plenty of fuel on hand in case Porter complied with his request, forwarded by Ellet, that another gunboat be sent downriver as a replacement for the *Queen*. Brown left the mouth of the Red on Saturday, February 21, and stopped for the night at a plantation landing up the Mississippi to take on a load of cotton bales, which he stacked around the ironclad's low main deck to make her less vulnerable to boarders. Next morning he was off again in earnest, all four engines straining to offset the drag of the two barges lashed alongside. He did not know how much of a head start he had, but he feared it was not enough. In point of fact, it was even less than he supposed; for the four-boat Confederate flotilla, including the resurrected *Queen*, set out after him at about the same hour that Sunday morning, ninety miles astern of the landing where the *Indianola* had commandeered the cotton. The race was on.

It was not really much of a race. Major Joseph L. Brent, commanding the quartet of rebel warships, each of which was in the charge of an army captain, could have overtaken Brown at almost anytime Tuesday afternoon, the 24th, but he preferred to wait for darkness, which would not only make the aiming of the ironclad's big guns more difficult but would also give the Grand Gulf batteries a chance at her as she went by. Held to a crawl though she was by the awkward burden of her barges, the *Indianola* got past that danger without mishap; but Brown could see the smoke from his pursuers' chimneys drawing closer with every mile as the sun declined, and he knew that he was in for a fight before it rose again. He also knew by now that no reinforcing consort was going to join him from the fleet above Vicksburg, in spite of which he held doggedly to his barges, counting on them to give him fender protection from ram attacks. As darkness fell, moonless but dusky with starlight, he cleared for action and kept half of his crew at battle stations: "watch and watch," it was called. At 9.30 he passed New Carthage, which put him within thirteen miles of the nearest west-bank Union battery, but by that time the rebel boats were in plain sight. Abreast of Palmyra Island, heading into Davis Bend — so called because it flowed past the Confederate President's Brierfield Plantation — Brown swung his iron prow around to face his pursuers at last, thus bringing his heavy guns to bear and protecting his more vulnerable stern.

As the *Queen* and the *Webb* came at him simultaneously, the former in the lead, he fired an 11-inch shell point-blank at each. Both missed, and the *Queen* was on him, lunging in from port with such force that the barge on that side was sliced almost in two. Emerging unscathed from this, except for the loss of the barge, which was cut adrift to sink, the *Indianola* met the *Webb* bows on, with a crash that knocked most of both crews off their feet and left the Confederate with a gash in her bow extending from water line to keelson, while the Federal was comparatively unhurt. Nevertheless the *Webb* backed off and struck again, crushing the remaining barge so completely as to leave it hanging by the lashings. Meanwhile the *Queen*, having run upstream a ways to gain momentum, turned and came charging down, striking her adversary just abaft the starboard wheelhouse, which was wrecked along with the rudder on that side, and starting a number of leaks along the shaft. Likewise the *Webb*, having gained momentum in the same fashion, brought her broken nose down hard and fair on the crippled ironclad's lightly armored stern, starting the timbers and causing the water to pour in rapidly. All this time the *Indianola* had kept throwing shells into the smoky darkness, left and right, but had scored only a single hit on the *Queen*, which did no considerable damage to the boat herself though it killed two and wounded four of her crew. Brown, having done his worst with this one shot, was now in a hopeless condition, scarcely able to steer and with both of his starboard engines flooded. After waiting a while in midstream until the water had risen nearly to the grate-bars of the ironclad's furnaces, planning thus to avoid her capture by making sure that she would sink, he ran her hard into the more friendly west bank and hauled down his colors just as the two cottonclads came alongside, crowded with yelling rebels prepared for boarding. Quickly they leaped down and attached two ropes by which the steamers could haul the *Indianola* across the river to the Confederate-held east bank, barely making it in time for her to sink in ten feet of water. As soon as they got their prisoners ashore they went to work on the captured dreadnought, intending to raise her, as they had raised the *Queen of the West* the week before, for service under the Stars and Bars.

Though he had heard the heavy nighttime firing just downriver, Porter did not know for certain what had happened until two days later, when a seaman who had escaped from the *Indianola* during her brief contact with the western bank came aboard his flagship *Black Hawk* and gave him an eyewitness account of the tragedy. Coming as it did on the heels of news of the loss of the *Queen* — which in turn had been preceded, two months back, by the destruction of the *Cairo* — the blow was hard, especially since it included the information that the *Queen* had been taken over by the enemy and had played a leading part in the defeat of her intended consort, which was now about to be used in the same manner as soon as the rebels succeeded in getting her afloat. What made it doubly hard, for Porter at any rate, was the contrast between his present gloom and his recent optimism. "If you open the Father of Waters," Assistant Navy Secretary G. A. Fox had wired the acting rear admiral in response to reports of his progress just two weeks ago, "you will at once be made an admiral; besides we will try for a ribboned star. . . . Do your work up clean," Fox had added, "and the public will never be in doubt who did it. The flaming army correspondence misleads nobody. Keep cool, be very modest under great success, as a contrast to the soldiers." At any rate, such strain as there had been on Porter's modesty was removed by the awareness that all he had really accomplished so far — aside from the capture of Arkansas Post, which had had to be shared with the army — was the loss of three of his best warships, two of which were now in enemy hands. What filled his mind just now was the thought of what this newest-model ironclad, the former pride of the Union fleet, could accomplish once she went into action on the Confederate side. Supported as she would be by the captured ram, she might well prove invincible in an upstream fight. In fact, any attempt to challenge her en masse would probably add other powerful units to the rebel flotilla of defected boats, since any disabled vessel would be swept helplessly downstream in such an engagement. Far from opening the Father of Waters, and gaining thereby a ribboned star and the permanent rank of admiral, Porter could see that he would be more likely to lose what had been won by his predecessors. Besides, even if he had wanted to launch such an all-out attack, he had no gunboats in the vicinity of Vicksburg now; they had been sent far upriver to co-operate in another of Grant's ill-fated amphibious experiments.

Porter was inventive in more ways than one, however, and his resourcefulness now stood him in good stead. If he had no available ironclad, then he would build one — or anyhow the semblance of one. Ordering every man off the noncombatant vessels to turn to, he took an old flat-bottomed barge, extended its length to three hundred feet by use of rafts hidden behind false bulwarks, and covered it over with flimsy decking to support a frame-and-canvas pilothouse and two huge but empty paddle-wheel boxes. A casemate was mounted forward, with a number of large-caliber logs protruding from its ports, and two tall smokestacks were erected by piling barrels one upon another. As a final realistic touch, after two abandoned skiffs were swung from unworkable davits, the completed dummy warship was given an all-over coat of tar. Within twenty-four hours, at a reported cost of $8.63, the navy had what appeared, at least from a distance, to be a sister ship of the *Indianola*. Belching smoke from pots of burning tar and oakum installed in her barrel stacks, she was set adrift the following night to make her run past the Vicksburg batteries. They gave her everything they had, but to no avail; her black armor seemingly impervious to damage, she glided unscathed past the roaring guns, not even deigning to reply. At daybreak she grounded near the lower end of Sherman's canal, and the diggers pushed her off again with a cheer. As she resumed her course downriver, the *Queen of the West*, coming up past Warrenton on a scout, spotted the dark behemoth in the distance, bearing down with her guns run out and her deck apparently cleared for action. The ram spun on her heel and sped back to spread the alarm: whereupon — since neither the *Queen* nor the broken-nosed *Webb* was in any condition for another fight just yet — all four of the Confederate vessels made off southward to avoid a clash with this second ironclad. Aboard the *Indianola*, still immobile and now deserted by her new friends, the lieutenant in charge of salvage operations was for holding onto her and fighting it out, despite repeated orders for him to complete her destruction before she could be recaptured. At a range of about two miles, the dreadnought halted as if to look the situation over before closing in for the bloody work she was bent on. Still the lieutenant held his ground until nightfall, when he decided to comply with the instructions of his superiors. After heaving the 9-inch rifles into the river, he laid the 11-inch smoothbores muzzle to muzzle and fired them with slow matches. When the smoke from this had cleared, he came back and set fire to what was left, burning the wreckage to the water line and ending the brief but stormy career of the ironclad *Indianola*.

Next morning, seeing the black monster still in her former position, some two miles upriver — one observer later described her as "terrible though inert" — a party of Confederates went out in a rowboat to investigate. Drawing closer they recognized her for the hoax she was, and saw that she had come to rest on a mudbank. Nailed to her starboard wheelhouse was a crudely lettered sign. "Deluded people, cave in," it read.

"Then, too," Grant added, continuing the comment on his reasons for keeping McPherson's men sawing away at the underwater stumps and snags clogging the Bayou Baxter exit from Lake Providence even after he knew that, in itself, the work was unlikely to produce anything substantial, "it served as a cover for other efforts which gave a better prospect of success." What he had in mind — in addition, that is, to Sherman's canal, which was not to be abandoned until March — was a fifth experimental project, whose starting point was four hundred tortuous miles upriver from its intended finish atop the Vicksburg bluff. In olden days, just south of Helena and on the opposite bank, a bayou had afforded egress from the Mississippi; Yazoo Pass, it was called, because it connected eastward with the Coldwater River, which flowed south into the Tallahatchie, which in turn combined with the Yalobusha, farther down, to form the Yazoo. Steamboats once had plied this route for trade with the planters of the delta hinterland. In fact, they still steamed up and down this intricate chain of rivers, but only by entering from below, through the mouth of the Yazoo River; for the state of Mississippi had sealed off the northern entrance, five years before the war, by constructing across the mouth of Yazoo Pass a levee which served to keep the low-lying cotton fields from going under water with every rise of the big river. Now it was Grant's notion that perhaps all he needed to do, in order to utilize this old peacetime trade route for his wartime purpose, was cut the levee and send in gunboats to provide cover for transports, which then could be unloaded on high ground — well down the left bank of the Yazoo but short of Haines Bluff, whose fortifications blocked an ascent of that river from below — and thus, by forcing the outnumbered defenders to come out into the open for a fight which could only result in their defeat, take Vicksburg from the rear. Accordingly, at the same time he ordered McPherson down from Memphis to Lake Providence, he sent his chief topographical engineer, Lieutenant Colonel James H. Wilson, to inspect and report on the possibility of launching such an attack by way of Yazoo Pass.

Wilson, described by a contemporary as "a slight person of a light complexion and with rather a pinched face," was enthusiastic from the start. An Illinois regular, only two years out of West Point and approaching his twenty-sixth birthday, he recently had been transferred from the East, where he had served as an aide to McClellan at Antietam, and he had approached his western assignment with doubts, particularly in regard to Grant, whose "simple and unmilitary bearing," as the young man phrased it, made a drab impression by contrast with the recent splendor of Little Mac, whose official family had included an Astor and two genuine French princes of the blood. But in this case familiarity bred affection; Wilson soon was remarking that his new commander was "a most agreeable companion both on the march and in camp." What drew him more than anything, however, was the trust Grant showed in sending him to take charge of the opening phase of this fifth and latest project for the reduction of the Gibraltar of the West. After a bit of preliminary surveying and shovel work, he wasted no time. On the evening of February 3 — while Ellet prepared to take the *Queen* past the Vicksburg bluff at daybreak and Grant himself was about to head upriver for a first-hand look at Lake Providence — Wilson mined and blew the levee sealing the mouth of Yazoo Pass. The result was altogether spectacular, he reported, "water pouring through like nothing else I ever saw except Niagara." After waiting four days for the surface level to equalize, east and west of the cut, he boarded a gunboat, steamed "with great ease" into Moon Lake, a mile beyond, and "ran down it about five miles to where the Pass leaves it." Hard work was going to be involved, he wrote Grant's adjutant, but he was confident of a large return on such an investment. Grant was infected at once with the colonel's enthusiasm. Wilson already had with him a 4500-man division from Helena; now a second division was ordered to join him from there. Presently, when he reported that he had got through to the Coldwater, McPherson was told to be prepared to follow with his whole corps. "The Yazoo Pass expedition is going to prove a perfect success," Grant informed Elihu B. Washburne, his home-state Representative and congressional guardian angel.

Hard work had been foreseen, and that was what it took. Emerging from Moon Lake, Wilson found the remaining twelve-mile segment of the pass sufficiently deep but so narrow in some places that the gunboat could not squeeze between giant oaks and cypresses growing on opposite banks. These had to be felled with axes, a patience-testing business but by no means the most discouraging he encountered. Warned of his coming, the Confederates had brought in working parties of slaves from surrounding plantations and had chopped down other trees, some of them more than four feet through the bole, so that they lay athwart the bayou, ponderous and apparently immovable. Undaunted, Wilson borrowed navy hawsers long enough to afford simultaneous handholds for whole regiments of soldiers, whom he put to work snaking the impediments out of the way. They did it with such ease, he later remarked, that he never afterwards wondered how the Egyptians had lifted the great stones in place when they built the Pyramids; enough men on a rope could move anything, he decided. Still, he had no such span of time at his disposal as the Pharaohs had had, and this was at best a time-consuming process. February was almost gone before he reached the eastern end of the pass. South of there, however, he expected to find clear sailing. The Coldwater being "a considerable stream," he reported, vessels of almost any length and draft could be sent from the Mississippi into the Tallahatchie in just four days. And so it proved when a ten-boat flotilla, including two ironclads, two steam rams, and six tinclads — the 22 light transports were to come along behind — tried it during the first week in March. In fact, it was not until the warships were more than a hundred miles down the winding Tallahatchie, near its junction with the Yalobusha, that Wilson realized he was in for a great deal more trouble, and of a kind he had not encountered up to now.

The trouble now was the rebels themselves, not just the various obstructions they had left in his path before fading back into the swamps and woods. Five miles above Greenwood, a hamlet at the confluence of the rivers, they had improvised on a boggy island inclosed by a loop of the Tallahatchie a fort whose parapets, built of cotton bales and reinforced with sandbags, were designed not only to deflect heavy projectiles but also to keep out the river itself, which had gone well past the flood stage when the Yankees blew the levee far upstream. Fort Pemberton, the place was called, and it had as its commander a man out of the dim Confederate past: Brigadier General Lloyd Tilghman, who had fought against Grant and the ironclads under similar circumstances at Fort Henry, thirteen months ago. Exchanged and reinstated, he was determined to wipe out that defeat, though the odds were as long and the tactical situation not much different. His immediate superior, Major General W. W. Loring, was also a carry-over from the past, and as commander of the delta subdepartment he intended to give the Federals even more trouble than he had given Lee and Jackson in Virginia the year before, which was considerable. A third relic on the scene was the former U.S. ocean steamer *Star of the West,* whose name had been in the scareheads three full months before the war, when the Charleston batteries fired on her for attempting the relief of Sumter. Continuing on to Texas, she had been captured in mid-April by Van Dorn at Indianola and was in the rebel service as a receiving-ship at New Orleans a year later, when Farragut provoked her flight up the Mississippi and into the Yazoo to avoid recapture. Here above Greenwood she ended her days afloat, but not her career, for she was sunk in the Tallahatchie alongside Fort Pemberton, blocking the channel and thus becoming an integral part of the outer defenses of Vicksburg. Three regiments, one from Texas and two from Mississippi, were all the high command could spare for manning the breastworks and the guns, which included one 6.4-inch rifle and half a dozen smaller pieces. This was scarcely a formidable armament with which to oppose 11-inch Dahlgrens housed in armored casemates, but on March 11 — while northward a long column of approaching warships and transports sent up a winding trail of smoke, stretching out of sight beyond the heavy screen of woods — the graybacks were a determined crew as they sighted their guns up the straight stretch of river giving down upon the fort.

Lieutenant Commander Watson Smith, who had charge of the ten-boat Union flotilla, was by now in a state of acute distress; he had never experienced anything like this in all his years afloat. Coming through Yazoo Pass into the Coldwater and down the Tallahatchie, all of which were so narrow in places that the gunboats had to be warped around the sharper bends with ropes, one tinclad had shattered her wheel and was out of action, while another had lost both smokestacks. All the rest had taken similar punishment in passing over rafts of driftwood or under projecting limbs that came sweeping and crashing along their upper works. The most serious of these mishaps was suffered when the *Chillicothe,* one of the two ironclads, struck a snag and started a plank in her bottom, which had to be held in place by beams shored in from the deck above. Smith's distress was greatly increased this morning, however, when this same unlucky vessel, at the head of the column, rounded the next-to-final bend leading down to the Yazoo and was struck hard twice on the turrets by high-velocity shells from dead ahead. She pulled back to survey the damage and fortify with cotton bales, then came on again that afternoon, accompanied by the other ironclad, the *De Kalb.* She got off four rounds at 800 yards and was about to fire a fifth — the loaders had already set the 11-inch shell in the gun's muzzle and were stripping the patch from the fuze — when a rebel shell came screaming through the port; both projectiles exploded on contact, killing 2 and wounding 11 of the gun crew. The two ironclads withdrew under urgent orders from Smith, whose distress had increased to the point where, according to Porter's subsequent report, he was showing "symptoms of aberration of mind."

Twice more, on the 13th and the 16th — without, however, attempting to close the range — the ironclads tried for a reduction of the fort at the end of that tree-lined stretch of river, as straight and uncluttered as a bowling alley: with similar results. Unable to maneuver in the narrow stream, the two boats took a terrible pounding, but could do little more than bounce their big projectiles off the resilient enemy parapet. The infantry, waiting rearward in the transports, gave no help at all; for the flooded banks made debarkation impossible, and any attempt at a small-boat attack — even if such boats had been available, which they were not — would have been suicidal. By the time the third day's bombardment was over, both ironclads were badly crippled; the *De Kalb* had lost ten of her gun-deck beams and her steerage was shot to pieces, while the luckless *Chillicothe* had more of her crew felled by armor bolts driven inward, under the impact of shells from the hard-hitting enemy rifle, to fly like bullets through the casemate. On March 17, in an apparent moment of lucidity, Smith ordered the flotilla to withdraw. Everyone agreed that this was the wisest course: everyone but Wilson, who complained hotly to Grant that the issue had not been pressed. "To let one 6½-inch rifle stop our navy. Bah!" he protested, and put the blame on "Acting Rear Admiral, Commodore, Captain, Lieutenant-Commander Smith" and the other naval officers. "I've talked with them all and tried to give them backbone," he said, "but they are not confident."

Returning up the Coldwater two days later — while Loring and Tilghman were celebrating the repulse in victory dispatches sent downriver to Vicksburg — the disconsolate Federals met the second Helena division on its way to reinforce them under Brigadier General Isaac Quinby, who outranked all the brass at hand and was unwilling to retreat without so much as a look at what stood in the way of an advance. So the expedition turned around and came back down again. Stopping short of the bend leading into the bowling alley, the men aboard the transports and gunboats slapped at mosquitoes and practiced their marksmanship on alligators, while Quinby conducted a boggy twelve-day reconnaissance which finally persuaded him that Smith had been right in the first place. Besides, even Wilson was convinced by now that the game was not worth the candle, for the rebels had brought up another steamboat which they were "either ready to sink or use as a boarding-craft and ram," and it seemed to the young colonel that they were "making great calculations 'to bag us' entire." He agreed that the time had come for a final departure. This began on April 5 and brought the Yazoo Pass experiment to a close. Being, as he said, "solicitous for

my reputation at headquarters," Wilson ended a letter to Grant's adjutant with a request for the latest staff gossip, and thought to add:
"Remember me kindly to the general."

His fears, though natural enough in an ambitious young career
officer who had failed in his first independent assignment, were groundless. For unlike Porter, who no sooner learned the details of the Tallahatchie nightmare than he relieved Watson Smith of duty with the fleet
and sent him North — where presently, by way of proving that his
affliction had been physical as well as mental, he died in a delirium of
fever and chagrin — Grant did not hold the collapse of this fifth experiment against his subordinate, but rather, when Wilson returned at last
to Young's Point after an absence of more than two months, welcomed
him back without reproach into the fold. By then the army commander
had a better appreciation of the problems that stood in the way of an
amphibious penetration of the delta, having been involved simultaneously in a not unsimilar nightmare of his own. In point of fact, however,
no matter how little he chose to bring it to bear, Porter had even
greater occasion for such charity, since he had been more intimately
involved, not only as the author but also as the on-the-scene director of
this latest fiasco, the sole result of which had been the addition of a sixth
to the sequence of failures designed for the reduction of Vicksburg.

Left with time more or less on his hands after the downriver loss
of two of his best warships, and being anxious moreover to offset the
damage to his reputation with an exploit involving something less flimsy
than a dummy ironclad, the admiral pored over his charts and made
various exploratory trips up and down the network of creeks and
bayous flowing into the Yazoo River below Haines Bluff, whose guns he
had learned to respect back in December. Five miles upstream from its
junction with the Mississippi, the Yazoo received the sluggish waters of
Steele Bayou, and forty miles up Steele Bayou, Black Bayou connected eastward with Deer Creek, which in turn, at about the same upstream distance and by means of another bayou called Rolling Fork,
connected eastward with the Sunflower River. That was where the pay-
off came within easy reach; for the Sunflower flowed into the Yazoo,
fifty miles below, offering the chance for an uncontested high-ground
landing well above the Haines Bluff fortifications, which then could be
assaulted from the rear or bypassed on the way to the back door of
Vicksburg. Though the route was crooked and the distance great —
especially by contrast; no less than two hundred roundabout miles
would have to be traversed by the column of gunboats and transports in
order to put the troops ashore no more than twenty air-line miles above
their starting point — Porter was so firmly convinced he had found the
solution to the knotty Vicksburg problem that he called at Young's
Point and persuaded Grant to come aboard the Black Hawk for a demonstration. Steaming up the Yazoo, the admiral watched the tree-fringed

north bank for a while, then suddenly to his companion's amazement signaled the helm for a hard turn to port, into brush that was apparently impenetrable. So far, high water had been the curse of the campaign, but now it proved an asset. As the boat swung through the leafy barrier, which parted to admit it, the leadsman sang out a sounding of fifteen feet — better than twice the depth the ironclads required. Formerly startled, Grant was now convinced, especially when Porter informed him that they were steaming above an old road once used for hauling cotton to the river. Practically all the lower delta was submerged, in part because of the seasonal rise of the rivers, but mostly because of the cut Wilson had made in the levee, four hundred miles upstream at Yazoo Pass; a tremendous volume of water had come down the various tributaries and had spread itself over the land. It was Porter's contention, based on limited reconnaissance, that as a result all those creeks and bayous would be navigable from end to end by vessels of almost any size, including the gunboats and transports selected to thread the labyrinth giving down upon the back-door approach to Vicksburg. Infected once more with contagious enthusiasm, Grant returned without delay to Young's Point, where he issued orders that same night for the army's share in what was known thereafter as the Steele Bayou expedition.

Sherman drew the assignment, along with one of his two divisions of men who just that week had been flooded out of their pick-and-shovel work on the doomed canal, and went up the Mississippi to a point where a long bend swung eastward to within a mile of Steele Bayou. On the afternoon of March 16, after slogging across this boggy neck of land, he made contact with the naval units, which had come up by way of the Yazoo that morning. As soon as he got his troops aboard the waiting transports the column resumed its progress northward, five ironclads in the lead, followed by four all-purpose tugs and a pair of mortar boats which Porter, not knowing what he might encounter in the labyrinth ahead, had had "built for the occasion." With his mind's eye fixed on permanent rank and the ribboned star Fox had promised to try for, the admiral was taking no chances he could avoid. All went well — as he had expected because of his preliminary reconnaissance — until the gunboats approached Black Bayou, where the unreconnoitered portion of the route began. This narrow, four-mile, time-forgotten stretch of stagnant water was not only extremely crooked, it was also filled with trees. Porter used his heavy boats to butt them down, bulldozer style, and hoisted them aside with snatch blocks. This was heavy labor, necessarily slow, and as it progressed the column changed considerably in appearance. Overhead branches swept the upper decks of the warships, leaving a mess of wreckage in the place of boats and woodwork. Occasionally, too, as Porter said, "a rude tree would throw Briarean arms" around the stacks of the slowly passing vessels, "and knock their bonnets sideways." After about a mile of this, Sherman's men were put to work with ropes and axes, clearing a broader passage for the transports, while the sturdier ironclads forged ahead, thumping and bumping their way into Deer Creek, where they resumed a northward course next morning.

But this was worse in several ways, one of them being that the creek was even narrower than the bayou. If the trees were fewer, they were also closer together, and vermin of all kinds had taken refuge in them from the flood; so that when one of the gunboats struck a tree the quivering limbs let fall a plague of rats, mice, cockroaches, snakes, and lizards. Men were stationed about the decks with brooms to rid the vessels of such unwelcome boarders, but sometimes the sweepers had larger game to contend with, including coons and wildcats. These last, however, "were prejudiced against us, and refused to be comforted on board," the admiral subsequently wrote, "though I am sorry to say we found more Union feeling among the bugs." To add to the nightmare, Deer Creek was the crookedest stream he had ever encountered: "One minute an ironclad would apparently be leading ahead, and the next minute would as apparently be steering the other way." Along one brief stretch, less than half a mile in length, the five warships were steaming in five quite different directions. Moreover, this was a region of plantations, which meant that there were man-made obstacles such as bridges, and though these gave the heavy boats no real trouble — they could plow through them as if they were built of matchsticks — other impediments were more disturbing. For example, hearing of the approach of the Yankees, the planters had had their baled cotton stacked along both creekbanks and set afire in order to keep it out of the hands of the invaders: with the result that, from time to time, the gunboats had to run a fiery gauntlet. The thick white smoke sent the crews into spasms of coughing, while the heat singed their hair, scorched their faces, and blistered the paint from the vessels' iron flanks.

So far, despite the crowds of field hands who lined the banks to marvel at the appearance of ironclads where not even flat-bottomed packets had ventured before, Porter had not seen a single white man. He found this odd, and indeed somewhat foreboding. Presently, however, spotting one sitting in front of a cabin and smoking a pipe as if nothing unusual were going on around him, the admiral had the flagship stopped just short of another bridge and summoned the man to come down to the landing; which he did — a burly, rough-faced individual, in shirt sleeves and bareheaded; "half bulldog, half bloodhound," Porter called him. When the admiral began to question him he identified himself as the plantation overseer. "I suppose you are Union, of course?" Porter said. "You all are so when it suits you." "No, by God, I'm not, and never will be," the man replied. "As to the others, I know nothing about them. Find out for yourself. I'm for Jeff Davis first, last, and all the time. Do you want any more of me?" he added; "for I am not a loquacious man at any time." "No, I want nothing more with you," Porter said. "But I am going to steam into that bridge of yours across the stream and knock it down. Is it strongly built?" "You may knock it down and be damned," the overseer told him. "It don't belong to me." Catching something in his accent, Porter remarked: "You're a Yankee by birth, are you not?" "Yes, damn it, I am," the man admitted. "But that's no reason I should like the institution. I cut it long ago." And with this he turned on his heel and walked away. Porter had the skipper ring "Go ahead fast," and the ironclad smashed through the bridge about as easily as if it had not been there. When he looked back, however, to see what impression this had made on the overseer, he saw him seated once more in front of the cabin, smoking his pipe, not having bothered even to turn his head and watch. Deciding that the fellow "was but one remove from a brute," Porter was disturbed by the thought that "there were hundreds more like him" lurking somewhere in the brush. At any rate, he fervently hoped that Sherman's men — particularly one regiment, which had the reputation of being able to "catch, scrape, and skin a hog without a soldier leaving the ranks" — would "pay the apostate Yankee a visit, if only to teach him good manners."

Under the circumstances, even aside from the necessary halts, half a mile an hour was the best speed the ironclads could make on this St Patrick's Day. Nightfall overtook them a scant eight miles from the morning's starting point. Twelve miles they made next day, but the increased speed increased the damage to the boats, including the loss of all the skylights to falling debris, and when they stopped engines for the night, Porter heard from up ahead the least welcome of all sounds: the steady chuck of axes, informing him that the rebels were warned of his coming. He wished fervently for Sherman, whose men were still at work in Black Bayou, widening a pathway for their transports, and consoled himself with the thought that the red-haired general would be along eventually; "there was only one road, so he couldn't have taken the wrong one." For the present, however, he did what he could with what he had, sending the mortar boats forward in the darkness; and when their firing stopped, so had the axes. Next morning, March 19, he pushed on. Despite the delay involved in hoisting the felled trees aside, he made such good progress that by nightfall he was within half a mile of the entrance to Rolling Fork. At daybreak he steamed north again, but the flagship had gone barely two hundred yards when, just ahead and extending all the way across the creek, the admiral saw "a large green patch . . . like the green scum on ponds." He shouted down from the bridge to one of the admiring field hands on the bank: "What is that?" "It's nuffin but willers, sah," the Negro replied, explaining that in the off season the plantation workers often went out in skiffs and canoes to cut the willow wands for weaving baskets. "You kin go through dat lak a eel."

That this last was an overstatement — based on a failure to realize that, unlike skiffs and canoes, the gunboats moved *through* rather than *over* the water, and what was more had paddle wheels and overlapping plates of armor — Porter discovered within a couple of minutes of giving the order to go ahead. Starting with a full head of steam, the ironclad made about thirty yards before coming to a dead stop, gripped tightly by the willow withes, not unlike Gulliver when he woke to find himself in Lilliputian bonds. The admiral called for hard astern; but that was no good either; the vessel would not budge. Here was a ticklish situation. The high creekbanks rendered the warships practically helpless, for their guns would not clear them even at extreme elevation. Not knowing what he would do if the Confederates made a determined boarding attack, Porter fortified a nearby Indian mound with four smoothbore howitzers and put the flagship's crew over the side with knives and hooks and orders to cut her loose, twig by twig. It was slow work; "I wished ironclads were in Jericho," he later declared. Just then his wish seemed about to be fulfilled. The shrill shrieks of two rifle shots, which he recognized as high-velocity Whitworths, were followed at once by a pair of bursts, abrupt as blue-sky thunder and directly over the mound. Suddenly, in the wake of these two ranging shots — within six hundred yards of Rolling Fork and less than ten miles from clear sailing down the broad and unobstructed Sunflower River — two six-gun rebel batteries were firing on the outranged smoothbores from opposite directions, and the naval commander was shocked to see his cannoneers come tumbling down the rearward slope of the mound, seeking cover from the rain of shells. Continuing to hack at the clinging willows, he got his mortars into counterbattery action and, with the help of half a dollar, persuaded a "truthful contraband" (so Porter termed him later, but just then he called him Sambo; which drew the reply, "My name aint Sambo, sah. My name's Tub") to attempt to get a message through to Sherman and his soldiers, wherever downstream they might be by now. "Dear Sherman," the note began: "Hurry up, for Heaven's sake."

Tub reached Sherman on Black Bayou late that night, having taken various short cuts, and Sherman started northward before daylight, accompanied by all the troops on hand. Retracing the messenger's route through darkness, they carried lighted candles in their hands as they slogged waist-deep through swamps and canebrakes. "The smaller drummer boys had to carry their drums on their heads," the general afterwards recalled, "and most of the men slung their cartridge boxes around their necks." All the following day they pushed on, frequently losing their way, and into darkness again. At dawn Sunday, March 22, they heard from surprisingly close at hand the boom of Porter's mortars, punctuated by the sharper crack of the Whitworths. Presently they encountered rebels who had got below the ironclads and were felling trees to block their escape downstream. Sherman chased them from their work and pushed on. Soon he came within sight of the beleaguered flotilla, but found it woefully changed in appearance. After finally managing to extricate the willow-bound flagship with winches, Porter had unshipped the rudders of all five gunboats and was steaming backward down the narrow creek, fighting as he went. He had not only heard the sound of axes in his rear; what was worse, he had suddenly realized that the Confederates might dam the creek upstream with cotton bales and leave him stranded in the mud. The arriving bluecoats ran the snipers off — they were not actually so numerous as they seemed; just industrious — and came up to find the admiral on the deck of the flagship, directing the retreat from behind a shield improvised from a section of smokestack. "I doubt if he was ever more glad to meet a friend than he was to see me," Sherman later declared. For the present, though, he asked if Porter wanted him to go ahead and "clean those fellows out" so the navy could resume its former course. "Thank you, no," the admiral said. He had had enough, and so had Sherman, who complained hotly that this was "the most infernal expedition I was ever on." As Porter subsequently put it, "The game was up, and we bumped on homeward."

All the way downstream, from Deer Creek through Black Bayou, the sailors took a ribbing from the soldiers who stood along the banks to watch them go by, in reverse and rudderless. "Halloo, Jack," they would call. "How do you like playing mud turtle?" "Where's all your masts and sails, Jack?" "By the Widow Perkins, if Johnny Reb hasn't taken their rudders away and set them adrift!" But an old forecastleman gave as good as he got. "Dry up!" he shouted back at them. "We wa'n't half as much used up as you was at Chickasaw Bayou." So it went until the gunboats regained Steele Bayou and finally the mouth of the Yazoo, where they dropped anchor — those that still had them — and were laid up for repairs. Within another week they were supplied with new chimneys and skylights and woodwork; they glistened with fresh coats of paint, and according to Porter, "no one would have supposed we had ever been away from a dock-yard." By then, too, the officers had begun to discuss their share in this sixth of Grant's Vicksburg failures with something resembling nostalgia. There was an edge of pride in their voices as they spoke of the exploit, and some even talked of being willing to go again. But they did so, the admiral added, much "as people who have gone in search of the North Pole, and have fared dreadfully, wish to try it once more."

. . .

Despite the high hopes generated during the preliminary re-connaissance up Steele Bayou, Grant was no more discouraged by this penultimate failure, reported in no uncertain terms by a disgusted Sherman, than he had been by the preceding five. Now as before, he already had a successive experiment in progress, which served to distract the public's attention and occupy his mind and men. Besides, for once, he had good news to send along to Washington with the bad — the announcement of the first real success achieved by Federal arms on the river since his arrival in late January — although his pleasure in reporting it was considerably diminished by the fact that it had been accomplished not in his own department but in Banks's, not by the army but by the navy, and not by Porter but by Farragut.

Banks himself had been having troubles that rivaled Grant's, if not in number — being limited by a lack of corresponding ingenuity and equipment in his attempts to come to grips with the problem — then at any rate in thorniness. Port Hudson was quite as invulnerable to a frontal assault as Vicksburg, so that here too the solution was restricted to two methods: either to attack the hundred-foot bluff from the rear or else to go around it. He worked hard for a time at the latter, seeking a route up the Atchafalaya, into the Red, and thence into the Mississippi, fifty miles above the Confederate bastion. At first this appeared to be ready-made for his use, but it turned out to be impractical on three counts. 1) He had only one gunboat designed for work on the rivers; 2) a large portion of the Atchafalaya basin was under water as a result of breaks in the neglected levees; and 3) he became convinced that to leave the rebel garrison alive and kicking in his rear would be to risk, if not invite, the recapture of New Orleans. This last was so unthinkable that it no sooner occurred to him than he abandoned all notion of such an attempt. As for attacking Port Hudson from the rear, he perceived that this would be about as risky as attacking it from the front. Knowing nothing of Grant's success or failure upriver, except the significant fact that something must have happened to delay him, Banks did not know but what the Confederates would be free to concentrate against him from all directions, including the north, as soon as he got his troops ashore; which would mean, at best, that he would lose his siege train in a retreat from superior numbers, and at worst that he would lose his army. Thus both methods of approaching a solution to the problem seemed to him likely to end in disaster; he did not know what to do, at least until he could get in touch with Grant upstream. Consequently, he did nothing.

This reverse approach, with its stress on what the enemy might do to him, rather than on what he intended to do to the enemy, had not been Grant's way of coming to grips with the similar problem, some three hundred miles upstream; nor was it Farragut's. The old sea dog —

approaching sixty-two, he was Tennessee-born and twice married, both times to Virginians, which had caused some doubt as to his loyalty in the early months of the war — had surmounted what had seemed to be longer odds below New Orleans the year before, and he was altogether willing to try it again, "army or no army." In early March, when he received word that the rebels, by way of reinforcing their claim to control of the whole Red River system, along with so much of the Mississippi as ran between Vicksburg and Port Hudson, had captured the steam ram *Queen of the West,* he took the action as a challenge to personal combat; especially when they emphasized it by sinking and seizing the ironclad *Indianola,* which for all he knew was about to join the *Queen* in defying the flag she once had flown. He promptly assembled his seven wooden ships off Profit's Island, seven miles below Port Hudson, intending to take them past the fortified heights for a showdown with the renegade boats upriver. He had with him the three heavy sloops-of-war *Hartford, Richmond,* and *Monongahela,* the old sidewheeler *Mississippi,* and three gunboats. All were ocean-going vessels, unarmored but mounting a total of 95 guns, mostly heavy — the flagship *Hartford* alone carried two dozen 9-inch Dahlgrens — with which to oppose the 21 pieces manned by the Confederates ashore. This advantage in the weight of metal would be offset considerably, however, by the plunging fire of the guns on the hundred-foot bluff and by the five-knot current, which would hold the ships to a crawl as they rounded the sharp bend at its foot. In an attempt to increase the speed and power of his slower and larger ships, Farragut gave instructions for the three gunboats to be lashed to the unengaged port sides of the three sloops; the *Mississippi,* whose paddle boxes would not allow this, would have to take her chances unassisted. It was the admiral's hope that the flotilla would steam past undetected in the moonless darkness, but a greenhorn chaplain, watching the gun crews place within easy reach "little square, shallow, wooden boxes filled with sawdust, like the spittoons one used to see in country barrooms," was shocked to learn that the contents were to be scattered about the deck as "an absorbent" to keep the men from slipping in their own blood, when and if the guns began to roar and hits were scored. At 9.30 p.m. March 14, the prearranged signal — two red lights described by the same impressionable chaplain as "two distinct red spots like burning coals" — appeared just under the stern of the flagship in the lead, and the run began.

At first it went as had been planned and hoped for. Undetected, unsuspected, the *Hartford* led the way up the long straight stretch of river leading due north into the bend that would swing the column west-southwest; she even cleared the first battery south of town, her engines throbbing in the darkness, her pilot hugging the east bank to avoid the mudflat shallows of the point across the way. Then suddenly the night was bright with rockets and the glare of pitch-pine bonfires

ignited by west-bank sentinels, who thus not only alerted the gun crews
on the bluff, but also did them the service of illuminating their targets
on the river down below. The fight began as it were in mid-crescendo.
Still holding so close to the east bank that the men on her deck could
hear the shouts of the enemy cannoneers, the flagship opened a rolling
fire which was taken up in turn by the ships astern. The night was misty
and windless; smoke settled thick on the water, leaving the helmsmen
groping blindly and the gunners with nothing to aim at but the
overhead muzzle flashes. In this respect the *Hartford* had the advantage,
steaming ahead of her own smoke, but even she had her troubles, being
caught by the swift current and swept against the enemy bank as she
turned into the bend. Helped by her gunboat tug, she backed off and
swung clear, chugging upstream at barely three knots, much damaged
about her top and spars, but with only three men hit. Attempting to follow, the *Richmond* was struck by a plunging shot that crashed into her
engine room and caromed about, cracking both port and starboard
safety valves and dropping her boiler pressure below ten pounds. Too
weak to make headway, even with the assistance of the gunboat lashed
to her flank, she went with the current and out of the fight, leaking steam
from all her ports, followed presently by the *Monongahela*, which suffered the same fate when her escort's rudder was wedged by an unlucky
shot, one of her own engines was disabled by an overheated crankpin,
and her captain was incapacitated by a shell that cut the bridge from
under him and pitched him headlong onto the deck below. Between
them, the two sloops and their escorts lost 45 killed and wounded before
they veered out of range downriver. But the veteran frigate *Mississippi*
— Commodore Matthew Perry's flagship, ten years ago, when he
steamed into Tokyo Bay and opened Japan to the Western world —
took the worst beating of the lot, not only from the Confederates on the
bluff, but also from the gunners on the *Richmond*, who, not having gotten the word that the sloop had turned in the opposite direction, fired
at the flashes of the side-wheeler's guns as they swept past her. Blind in
the smoke, pounded alike by friend and foe, the pilot went into the
bend and put the ship hard to larboard all too soon: with the result that
she ran full tilt onto the mudflats across the way from the fuming bluff.
Silhouetted against the glare of bonfires and taking hit after hit from
the rebel guns, she tried for half an hour to pull loose by reversing her
engines, but to no avail. Her captain ordered her set afire as soon as the
crew — 64 of whom were casualties by now — could be taken off in
boats, and it was only through the efforts of her executive, Lieutenant
George Dewey, that many of her wounded were not roasted, including
a badly frightened ship's boy he found hiding under a pile of corpses.
Burning furiously, the *Mississippi* lightened before dawn and drifted off
the flats of her own accord, threatening to set the other repulsed vessels afire as she passed unmanned among them and piled up at last on the

head of Profit's Island, where she exploded with what an observer called "the grandest display of fireworks I ever witnessed, and the costliest."

It had been quite a costly operation all around. Thirty-five of the flotilla's 112 casualties were dead men — only two less than had been killed in the venture below New Orleans by a force almost three times as large — and of the seven ships that had attempted to run Port Hudson, one was destroyed and four had been driven back disabled. As a box score, this gave the Confederates ample claim to the honors of the engagement; but the fact remained that, whatever the cost, Farragut had done what he set out to do. He had put warships north of the bluff on the Mississippi, and he was ready to use them to dispute the rebel claim to control of the 250 miles of river below Vicksburg. Dropping down at dawn to just beyond range of Port Hudson's upper batteries, he fired the prearranged three-gun signal to let the rest of the flotilla know that he was still afloat, then set out upriver and anchored next morning off the mouth of the Red, up which he learned that the renegade *Queen* and the fast-steaming *Webb* had taken refuge after their flight from Porter's dummy ironclad. Both were too heavily damaged, as a result of their ram attacks on the *Indianola,* to be able to fight again without extensive repairs. So he heard; but he was taking no chances. Lowering the *Hartford*'s yards to the deck, he lashed them there and carried a heavy anchor chain from yard tip to yard tip, all the way round, to fend off attackers. Still unsatisfied, he improvised water-line armor by lashing cypress logs to the sides of the vessel and slung hawsers from the rigging, thirty feet above the deck, with heavy netting carried all the way down to the rail to frustrate would-be boarders. Then, accompanied by her six-gun escort *Albatross,* the *Hartford* — whose own builders would scarcely have recognized her, dressed out in this manner — set out northward, heading for Vicksburg in order to open communications with the upper fleet.

Passing Grand Gulf on March 19 the two ships came under fire that cost them 2 more killed and 6 more wounded, almost three times the number they had lost five nights ago; otherwise they encountered no opposition between Port Hudson and the point where they dropped anchor next morning, just beyond range of the lower Vicksburg batteries. Porter was up Steele Bayou, but conferring that afternoon with Grant and A. W. Ellet, the ram fleet commander, Farragut asked that he be reinforced by units from the upper flotilla. Ellet volunteered to send two of his boats, the *Switzerland* and the *Lancaster,* respectively under C. R. Ellet, the former captain of the *Queen,* and his uncle Lieutenant Colonel J. A. Ellet. They made their run at first light, March 25. The *Lancaster* was struck repeatedly in her machinery and hull, but she made it downstream, where a week's patchwork labor would put her back in shape to fight again. Not so the *Switzerland;* she received a shell in her boilers and others which did such damage to her hull that she went to pieces and sank, affording her nineteen-year-old skipper another ride on a bale of cotton. Unperturbed, Grant reported her loss as a blessing in disguise, since it served to reveal her basic unfitness for combat: "It is almost certain that had she made one *ram* into another vessel she would have closed up like a spy-glass, encompassing all on board."

In point of fact, whatever the cost and entirely aside from his accustomed optimism, he and all who favored the Union cause had much to be joyful about. As a result of this latest naval development, which would establish a blockade of the mouth of the Red and deny the rebels the use of their last extensive stretch of the Mississippi, Farragut had cut the Confederacy in two. The halves were still unconquered, and seemed likely to remain so for no one knew how long, but they were permanently severed one from the other. When the *Hartford* and the *Albatross* passed Port Hudson and were joined ten days later below Vicksburg by the steam ram *Lancaster*, the cattle and cereals of the Transmississippi, together with the goods of war that could be smuggled in through Mexico from Europe, became as inaccessible to the eastern South as if they were awaiting shipment on the moon.

This was not to say, conversely, that the Mississippi was open throughout its length to Federal commerce or even to Federal gunboats; that would not be the case, of course, until Vicksburg and Port Hudson had been taken or abolished. Continuing his efforts to accomplish this end, or anyhow his half of it, Grant was already engaged in the seventh of his experiments — which presently turned out to be the seventh of his failures. Work on the canal across the base of Vicksburg Point having been abandoned, he sent an engineering party out to find a better site for such a project close at hand. Receiving a report that a little digging south of Duckport, just above Young's Point, would give the light-draft vessels access to Roundaway Bayou, which entered the main river at New Carthage, well below the Vicksburg and Warrenton batteries, Grant gave McClernand's men a turn on the picks and shovels. For once, however, he had no great hope that much would come of the enterprise, even if it went as planned — only the lightest-draft supply boats would be able to get through; besides, there would still be the Grand Gulf batteries to contend with — and for once he was right. Even this limited success depended on a rise of the river; whereupon the river, perverse as always, began to fall, leaving Grant with a seventh failure on his hands.

"This campaign is being badly managed," Cadwallader Washburn, a brigadier in McPherson's corps, informed his congressman brother Elihu in Washington. "I am sure of it. I fear a calamity before Vicksburg. All Grant's schemes have failed. He knows that he has got to do something or off goes his head. My impression is that he intends to attack in front." (Washburn's fears were better founded than he knew. Grant had just written a long letter to Banks, reviewing his lack of progress up to now, and in it he had stated flatly: "There is nothing left for me but to collect my strength and attack Haines Bluff. This will necessarily be attended with much loss, but I think it can be done." On April Fools' Day, however, accompanying Porter up the Yazoo for a reconnaissance of the position, he decided that such an attack "would be attended with immense sacrifice of life, if not defeat," and abandoned the notion, adding: "This, then, closes out the last hope of turning the enemy by the right.") Nor were others, farther removed from the scene of action, more reticent in giving their opinion of the disaster in store for the Army of the Tennessee. For example Marat Halstead, editor of the *Cincinnati Commercial,* addressed his friend the Secretary of the Treasury on the matter: "You do once in a while, don't you, say a word to the President, or Stanton, or Halleck, about the conduct of the war? Well, now, for God's sake say that Genl Grant, entrusted with our greatest army, is a jackass in the original package. He is a poor drunken imbecile. He is a poor stick sober, and he is most of the time more than half drunk, and much of the time idiotically drunk.... Grant will fail miserably, hopelessly, eternally. You may look for and calculate his failures, in every position in which he may be placed, as a perfect certainty. Don't say I am grumbling. Alas! I know too well I am but feebly outlining the truth." Alarmed, Chase passed the letter on to Lincoln with the reminder that the *Commercial* was an influential paper, and the indorsement: "Reports concerning General Grant similar to the statements made by Mr Halstead are too common to be safely or even prudently disregarded." Lincoln read it with a sigh. "I think Grant has hardly a friend left, except myself," he told his secretary, and when a delegation came to protest Grant's alleged insobriety he put these civilians off with the remark, "If I knew what brand of whiskey he drinks I would send a barrel or so to some other generals." About this time a Nebraska brigadier, in Washington on leave from Vicksburg, called on the President and the two men got to talking. "What I want, and what the people want, is generals who will fight battles and win victories," Lincoln said. "Grant has done this, and I propose to stand by him."

The evidence was conflicting. Some said the general never touched a drop; others declared that he was seldom sober; while still others had him pegged as a spree drinker. "He tries to let liquor alone but he cannot resist the temptation always," a Wisconsin brigadier wrote home. "When he came to Memphis he left his wife at LaGrange, and for several days after getting here was beastly drunk, utterly incapable of doing anything. Quinby and I took him in charge, watching him day and night and keeping liquor away from him." According to this witness, the bender was only brought to an end when "we telegraphed to his wife and brought her on to take care of him." On the other hand, Mary Livermore — later famous as a suffragette — led a Sanitary Commission delegation down to Young's Point to investigate the rumors, and it was her opinion that the general's "clear eye, clean skin, firm flesh, and steady nerves . . . gave the lie to the universal calumnies then current concerning his intemperate habits." Still unsatisfied, Stanton sent the former Brook Farm colonist and Greeley journalist Charles Dana down the Mississippi, ostensibly as an inspector of the pay service, but actually as a spy for the War Department. He arrived in early April, became in effect a member of the general's military family, and soon was filing reports that glowed with praise not only of Grant but also of Sherman and McPherson, declaring that in their "unpretending simplicity" the three Ohioans were "as alike as three peas." McClernand did not fare so well in these dispatches; for if Dana acquired a fondness for the army commander's friends, he also developed a dislike for his enemies. Later he summed up his findings by describing Grant as "the most modest, the most disinterested, and the most honest man I ever knew, with a temper that nothing could disturb and a judgment that was judicial in its comprehensiveness and wisdom. Not a great man except morally; not an original or brilliant man, but sincere, thoughtful, deep, and gifted with courage that never faltered."

Aside from the rhetoric here included, practically all of the general's soldiers would have agreed with this assessment of his character and abilities, even though it was delivered in the wake of seven failures. "Everything that Grant directs is right," one declared. "His soldiers believe in him. In our private talks among ourselves I never heard a single soldier speak in doubt of Grant." According to a New York reporter, this was not only because of "his energy and disposition to do something," it was also because he had "the remarkable tact of never spoiling any mysterious and vague notions which [might] be entertained in the minds of the privates as to the qualities of the commander-in-chief. He confines himself to saying and doing as little as possible before his men." Another described him as "a man who could be silent in several languages," and it was remarked that, on the march, he was more inclined to talk of "Illinois horses, hogs, cattle, and farming, than of the business actually at hand." In general he went about his job, as one observer had stated at the outset, "with so little friction and noise that it required a second look to be sure he was doing anything at all." One of his staff officers got the impression that he was "half a dozen men condensed into one," while a journalist, finding him puzzling in the extreme because he seemed to amount to a good deal more than the sum of all his parts, came up with the word "unpronounceable" as the one that described him best. Grant, he wrote, "has none of the soldier's bearing about him, but is a man whom one would take for a country merchant or a village lawyer. He had no distinctive feature; there are a thousand like him in personal appearance in the ranks. . . . A plain, unpretending face, with a comely, brownish-red beard and a square forehead, of short stature and thick-set. He is we would say a good liver, and altogether an unpronounceable man; he is so like hundreds of others as to be only described in general terms." The soldiers appreciated the lack of "superfluous flummery" as he moved among them, "turning and chewing restlessly the end of his unlighted cigar." They almost never cheered him, and they did not often salute him formally; rather, they watched him, as one said, "with a certain sort of familiar reverence." Present discouragements were mutual; so, someday, would be the glory. Somehow he was more partner than boss; they were in this thing together. "Good morning, General," "Pleasant day, General," were the usual salutations, more fitting than cheers or hat-tossing exhibitions; "A pleasant salute to, and a good-natured nod from him in return, seems more appropriate." All these things were said of him, and this: "Here was no McClellan, begging the boys to allow him to light his cigar on theirs, or inquiring to what regiment that exceedingly fine-marching company belonged. . . . There was no nonsense, no sentiment; only a plain business man of the republic, there for the one single purpose of getting that command over the river in the shortest time possible."

Yet the fact remained that he and they were into their third month of camping almost within the shadow of the Vicksburg bluff, and all they had accomplished so far was the addition of five to their previous two failures; they were still not "over the river." However, as the flood waters receded, defining the banks of the bayous and even the network of greasy-looking roads hub deep in mud, there were rumors that Grant was evolving an entirely new approach to the old problem. "As one after another of his schemes fail," Congressman Washburne heard from his brigadier brother — who had dropped the final euphonious "e" from his surname, presumably as superfluous baggage for a soldier — "I hear that he says he has a plan of his own which is yet to be tried [but] in which he has great confidence." Just what this was Grant would not say, either to subordinates or superiors, but his staff observed that he spent long hours in the former ladies' cabin of his headquarters boat the *Magnolia*, blueing the air with cigar smoke as he pored over maps and tentative orders, not so much inaccessible ("I aint got no business with you, General," they heard one caller tell him; "I just wanted to have a little talk with you, because folks will ask me if I did") as removed, withdrawn behind a barrier of intense preoccupation. After several days of this, McPherson came into the cabin one evening, glass in hand, and stood facing Grant across the work-littered desk. "General, this won't do," he said. "You are injuring yourself. Join us in a few toasts, and throw this burden off your mind." Mrs Livermore, for one, would have been horrified, but what followed would have quickly reassured her. Grant looked up, smiled, and replied that whiskey was not the answer; if McPherson really wanted to help him, he said, he could give him a dozen cigars and leave him alone. McPherson did so, and Grant returned to brooding over his papers, still seeking a way to come to grips with the Confederates in their hilltop citadel.

Death of a Soldier

★ ✗ ☆

PIERRE GUSTAVE TOUTANT BEAUREGARD WAS as flamboyant by nature as by name, and over the course of the past two years this quality, coupled all too often with a readiness to lay down the sword and take up the pen in defense of his reputation with the public, had got him into considerable trouble with his superiors, who sometimes found it difficult to abide his Creole touchiness off the field of battle for the sake of his undoubted abilities on it. Called "Old Bory" by his men, though he was not yet forty-five, the Hero of Sumter had twice been relieved of important commands, first in the East, where he had routed McDowell's invasion attempt at Manassas, then in the West, where he had saved his badly outnumbered army by giving Halleck the slip at Corinth, and now he was back on the scene of his first glory in Charleston harbor. Here, as elsewhere, he saw his position as the hub of the wheel of war. Defying Union sea power, Mobile on the Gulf and Wilmington, Savannah, and Charleston on the Atlantic remained in Confederate hands, and of these four it was clear at least to Beauregard that the one the Federals coveted most was the last, variously referred to in their journals as "the hotbed of treachery," "the cradle of secession," and "the nursery of disunion." Industrious as always, the general was determined that this proud South Carolina city should not suffer the fate of his native New Orleans, no matter what force the Yankees brought against it. Conducting frequent tours of inspection and keeping up as usual a voluminous correspondence — a steady stream of requisitions for more guns and men, more warships and munitions, nearly all of which were returned to him regretfully unfilled — he only relaxed from his duties when he slept, and even then he kept a pencil and a note pad under his pillow, ready to jot down any notion that came to him in the night. "Carolinians and Georgians!" he exhorted by proclamation. "The hour is at hand to prove your devotion to your country's cause. Let all able-bodied men, from the seaboard to the mountains, rush to arms. Be not exacting in the choice of weapons; pikes and scythes will do for exterminating your enemies, spades and shovels for protecting your friends. To arms, fellow citizens! Come share with us our dangers, our brilliant success, or our glorious death."

Two approaches to Charleston were available to the Federals. They could make an amphibious landing on one of the islands or up one of the inlets to the south, then swing northeastward up the mainland to move upon the city from the rear; or they could enter through the harbor itself, braving the massed batteries for the sake of a quick decision, however bloody. Twice already they had tried the former method, but both times — first at Secessionville, three months before Beauregard's return from the West in mid-September, and again at Pocotaligo, one month after he reassumed command — they had been stopped and flung back on their naval support before they could gather momentum. This time he thought it probable that they would attempt the front-door approach, using their new flotilla of vaunted ironclads to spearhead the attack. If so, they were going to find they had taken on a good deal more than they expected; for the harbor defenses had been greatly improved during the nearly two years that had elapsed since the war first opened here. Fort Moultrie, Castle Pinckney, and Fort Sumter, respectively on Sullivan's Island, off the mouth of the Cooper River, and opposite the entrance to the bay, had not only been strengthened, each in its own right, but now they were supported by other fortifications constructed at intervals along the beaches and connected by a continuous line of signal stations, making it possible for a central headquarters, itself transferrable, to direct and consolidate their fire. First Beauregard, then Pemberton, and now Beauregard again — both accomplished engineers and artillerists, advised moreover by staffs of specialists as expert as themselves — had applied all their skill and knowledge to make the place as nearly impregnable as military science and Confederate resources would allow. A total of seventy-seven guns of various calibers now frowned from their various embrasures, in addition to which the harbor channels were thickly sown with torpedoes and other obstructions, such as floating webs of hemp designed to entangle rudders and snarl propellers. Not content with this, the sad-eyed little Creole had not hesitated to dip into his limited supply of powder in order to improve the marksmanship of his cannoneers with frequent target practice. Like his idol Napoleon he believed in a lucky star, but he was leaving as little as possible to chance; for which reason he had set marker buoys at known ranges in the bay, with the corresponding elevations chalked on the breeches of the guns. As a last-ditch measure of desperation, to be employed if all else failed, he encouraged the organization of a unit known as the Tigers, made up of volunteers whose assignment was to hurl explosives down the smokestacks of such enemy ships as managed to break through the ring of fire and approach the fortress walls or the city docks. The ironclads might indeed be invincible; some said so, some said not; but one thing was fairly certain. The argument was likely to be settled on the day their owners tested them in Charleston harbor.

This was not to say that Beauregard had abandoned all notion of assuming the offensive, however limited his means. He had at his disposal two homemade rams, the *Palmetto State* and the *Chicora*, built with funds supplied by the South Carolina legislature and the Ladies' Gunboat Fair. The former mounted an 80-pounder rifle aft and an 8-inch shell gun on each broadside, while the latter had two 9-inch smoothbores and four rifled 32-pounders. Both were balky and slow, with cranky, inadequate engines and armor improvised from boiler plate and railroad iron, but as January drew to a close the general was determined to put them to the test by challenging the blockade squadron off the Charleston bar. Orders were handed Flag Officer Duncan Ingraham on the 30th, instructing him to make the attempt at dawn of the following day. Beauregard meanwhile had in mind a more limited offensive of his own, to be launched against the 9-gun screw steamer *Isaac Smith*, which had been coming up the Stono River almost nightly to shell the Confederate camps on James and John's islands. That night he lay in wait for her with batteries of field artillery, allowed her to pass unchallenged, then took her under fire as she came back down. The opening volley tore off her stack, stopped her engines, riddled her lifeboats, and killed eight of her crew. Her captain quickly surrendered himself and his ship and the 94 survivors, including 17 wounded. Repaired and rechristened, the *Smith* became the *Stono* and served under that name as part of Charleston's miniature defense squadron, the rest of which was already on its way across the bay, under cover of darkness, in accordance with Ingraham's orders to try his hand at lifting the Union blockade.

Palmetto State and *Chicora*, followed by three steam tenders brought along to tow them back into the harbor in case their engines failed, were over the bar and among the wooden-walled blockaders by first light. Mounting a total of one hundred guns, the Federal squadron included the 1200-ton sloop-of-war *Housatonic*, two gunboats, and seven converted merchantmen. A lookout aboard one of these last, the 9-gun steamer *Mercedita*, was the first to spot the misty outline of an approaching vessel. "She has black smoke!" he shouted. "Watch, man the guns! Spring the rattle! Call all hands to quarters!" This brought the captain out on deck, clad only in a pea jacket. When he too spotted the stranger, nearer now, he cupped his hands about his mouth and called out: "Steamer, ahoy! You will be into us! What steamer is that?" It was the *Palmetto State*, but for a time she did not deign to answer. Then: "Halloo!" her skipper finally replied, and with that the ram put her snout into the quarter of the *Mercedita* and fired her guns. Flames went up from the crippled steamer. "Surrender," the rebel captain yelled up, "or I'll sink you!" The only answer was a cloud of oily smoke shot through with steam. "Do you surrender?" he repeated. This brought the reply, "I can make no resistance; my boiler is destroyed!" "Then do you surrender?" "Yes!" So the *Palmetto State* backed off, withdrawing her snout, and turned to go to the help of the *Chicora*, which meanwhile had been serving the 10-gun sidewheel steamer *Keystone State* in much the same fashion. Riddled and aflame, the Federal hauled down her flag to signify surrender, then ran it up again and limped out to sea as the two rams moved off in the opposite direction. At the far end of the line, the *Housatonic* and the gunboats held their station, thinking the racket had been provoked by a blockade runner venturing out. By full daylight the two improvised ironclads were back in Charleston harbor, their crews accepting the cheers of a crowd collected on the docks.

Beauregard was elated by the double coup. Quick to claim that the blockade had been lifted, at least for a time, he took the French and Spanish consuls out to witness the truth of his words that "the outer harbor remained in the full possession of the two Confederate rams. Not a Federal sail was visible, even with spyglasses." Next day the blockaders were back again, presumably too vigilant now to permit him to risk another such attempt, but he did not admit that this detracted in the slightest from the brilliance of the exploit. He bided his time, still improving his defenses for the all-out attack which he believed was about to be launched. "Already six monitors . . . are in the waters of my department, concentrating about Port Royal, and transports with troops are still arriving from the North," he reported in mid-March. "I believe the drama will not much longer be delayed; the curtain will soon rise." Three more weeks went past before his prediction was fulfilled. Then on Monday, April 6, the day after Easter — it was also the first anniversary of Shiloh and within a week of the second anniversary of the opening of the war in this same harbor — not six but nine brand-new Union ironclads, some single- and some double-turreted, crossed the Charleston bar and dropped anchor in the channel, bringing their great 15-inch guns to bear on the forts and batteries Beauregard had prepared for their reception. The curtain had indeed risen.

Rear Admiral Samuel Du Pont had the flag. It was he who, back in early November of 1861, had conceived and executed the elliptical attack on Port Royal, thereby giving the North its first substantial victory of the war, and it was hoped by his superiors — his desk-bound superiors in Washington, that is, for he had no superiors afloat — that he would repeat the triumph here in Charleston harbor. Son of a wealthy New York importer and nephew of an even wealthier Delaware powder maker, the admiral was approaching sixty, a hale, well-set-up aristocrat with a dignified but genial manner and a growth of luxuriant whiskers describing a bushy U about his chops and under his clean-shaven mouth and chin, all of which combined to give at least one journalist the impression that he was "one of the stateliest, handsomest, and most polished gentlemen I have ever seen." Gideon Welles admired him, too; up to a point. "He is a skillful and accomplished officer," the Secretary confided in his diary. "Has a fine address, [but] is a courtier with perhaps too much finesse and management." This edge of mistrust was returned by the man who was its object. It seemed to Du Pont, whose enthusiasm had been tempered by close association, that the Navy Department was suffering from an affliction which might have been diagnosed as "ironclads on the brain."

This had not always been the case, particularly in the days when John Ericsson was trying to persuade the brass to give him authority for construction of the *Monitor*. Grudgingly, despite grave objections, they had finally let him go ahead with a contract which stipulated that he would not be reimbursed in case of failure. But after Hampton Roads and the draw engagement that put an end to the overnight depredations of the *Merrimac*, the Department not only reversed itself, but went all-out in the opposite direction. Ericsson received an order for half a dozen sister ships of the one already delivered, and other builders were engaged for the construction of twenty-one more, of various shapes and sizes. Assistant Secretary Fox was especially enthusiastic, informing Du Pont that after he had used the new-fangled warships to reduce Charleston he was to move on to Savannah, then send them down to the Gulf to give Mobile the same treatment. Ironclads were trumps, according to Fox. He told Ericsson he had not "a shadow of a doubt as to our success, and this confidence arises from a study of your marvelous vessels." The Swede was less positive. "The most I dare hope is that the contest will end without loss of that prestige which your ironclads have conferred upon the nation abroad," he replied, adding the reminder: "A single shot may sink a ship, while a hundred rounds cannot silence a fort." Unwilling to have his confidence undermined or his ebullience lessened, Fox assured a congressional committee that the monitors (such was the generic name, adopted in honor of the first of what was intended to be a long line of invincible vessels) could steam into southern harbors, flatten the defenses, and emerge unscathed. His only note of caution was injected into a dispatch addressed to Du Pont. "I beg of you," he pleaded, "not to let the Army spoil it." He wanted the show to be all Navy, with the landsmen merely standing by to be ferried in to pick up the pieces when the smoke cleared. In late March, having gained nothing from nudging Porter with the promise of a ribboned star and permanent promotion, he informed Du Pont that it was up to him to make up for the reverses lately suffered in the West: "Farragut has had a setback at Port Hudson and lost the noble old *Mississippi*. It finally devolves upon you by great good fortune to avert the series of disasters that have fallen upon our Navy. That you will do it most gloriously I have no misgivings whatever."

In point of fact, Du Pont by this time had misgivings enough for them both. What was more, these doubts were shared by a majority of his ironclad skippers — and with cause. Near the mouth of the Ogeechee River, just beyond the Georgia line, the Confederates had constructed as part of the Savannah defenses a 9-gun earthwork called Fort McAllister, which Du Pont decided to use as a sort of test range to determine how well the monitors would do, offensively and defensively, under fire. He gave the reduction assignment to the *Montauk,* which meant that he was giving the best he had; for her captain was Commander John L. Worden, who had skippered the *Monitor* in her fight with the *Merrimac.* Worden made his first attack on January 27 and, after expending all his ammunition in a four-hour bombardment, withdrew undamaged despite repeated hits scored by the guns of the fort, which was not silenced. Returning February 1 he tried again, with like results. Neither the ship nor the fort had done much damage to the other, aside from the concussive strain on the eardrums of the *Montauk*'s crew from the forty-six hits taken on her iron decks and turret. A third attack, February 27, was more fruitful, although not in the way intended. Finding the rebel cruiser *Nashville* aground beyond Fort McAllister, Worden took her under long-range fire with his 11- and 15-inch guns, set her ablaze, and had the satisfaction of watching her destruction when her magazine exploded. Struck only five times by the guns of the fort, the ironclad pulled back without replying, well satisfied with her morning's work, only to run upon a torpedo which blew such a hole in her bottom that she had to be beached in the mud at the mouth of the river. While she was undergoing repairs that soon restored her to full efficiency, three more monitors came down from Port Royal on March 3 and tried their hand with an eight-hour bombardment of the fort: with similar results. Neither silenced or seriously damaged the other, and the ironclads withdrew to try no more.

Fruitless though the experiment had been in positive results — aside, that is, from the fortunate interception of the *Nashville* — a lesson had been learned, on the negative side, as to the capabilities of the monitors. "Whatever degree of impenetrability they might have," Du Pont reported, "there was no corresponding degree of destructiveness as against forts." He felt much as one sailor had felt on a test run. "Give me an oyster-scow!" the man had cried. "Anything — only let it be of wood, and something that will float over instead of under the water." Most of the captains were of a similar mind, and when they looked beyond the present to the impending future, their doubts increased. If these vaunted engines of destruction could not humble a modest 9-gun sand fort, what could they hope to accomplish against multi-gunned bastions like Sumter and Moultrie? They asked the question and shook their heads. "I do not feel as sure as I could wish," one skipper admitted, while another was more positive in expressing his reservations. "I begin to rue the day I got into the iron clad business," he wrote home.

Still, orders were orders, and as April came in Du Pont completed his final preparations for the attack. In addition to his flagship the *New Ironsides,* a high-bulwarked 3500-ton frigate whose ponderous armor and twenty heavy guns mounted in broadside made her the most powerful battleship in the world, he had eight low-riding monitors, mounting one or two guns each in revolving turrets: which meant that, in all, he would be opposing 77 guns ashore with 33 afloat. These odds were rather evened by the fact that the naval guns, in addition to being mounted on moving targets, which made them far more difficult to hit, were heavier in caliber and threw about an equal weight of metal. Other odds were irreducible, however, one being that in order to reach the city from the sea his ships would have to steam for seven winding miles in a shoal-lined channel, much of which had been fiendishly obstructed and practically all of which was exposed to the plunging fire of forts whose gun crews had been anticipating for months this golden opportunity to disprove the claim that monitors were indestructible. On April 2, despite increasing doubts and reservations, Du Pont left Port Royal and reached Edisto Island, twenty-odd miles below the entrance to Charleston harbor, before nightfall. There the ships were cleared for action, the exposed armor of their decks and turrets covered over with slippery untanned hides and their bulwarks slopped with grease to lessen the "bite" of enemy projectiles. (That at least was the hoped-for effect, when the vessels should come under fire. The more immediate result, however, was that they stank fearfully under the influence of the Carolina sun.) On the 5th — Easter Sunday — they cleared North Edisto and crossed the Charleston bar next morning. Du Pont had intended to attack at once, but finding the weather hazy, which as he said "prevent[ed] our seeing the ranges," he decided to drop anchors and wait for tomorrow, in hopes that it would afford him better visibility. (It would also afford the same for the gunners in the forts; but Du Pont was not thinking along these lines, or else he would have made a night attack.) Finally, against his better judgment — and after much prodding from above, including jeers that he had "the slows" and taunts that identified him as a sea-going McClellan, overcautious and too mindful of comparative statistics — he was going in.

Tomorrow — April 7 — brought the weather he thought he wanted, and soon after noon the iron column started forward, the nine ships moving in single file, slowly and with a certain ponderous majesty not lost on the beholders in the forts. Originally the admiral had intended to lead the way in the flagship, but on second thought he decided to take the center position from which "signals could be better made to both ends of the line," so that the resultant order of battle was *Weehawken, Passaic, Montauk, Patapsco; New Ironsides; Catskill, Nantucket, Nahant, Keokuk.* There was an exasperating delay of about an hour when the lead monitor's heavy anchor chain became entangled with the bootjack raft designed to protect her bow from torpedoes; then the column resumed its forward motion, passing Morris Island in an ominous silence as the rebel cannoneers on Cummings Point held their fire. As the ships approached the inner works, however, the Confederate and Palmetto flags were hoisted over Sumter and Moultrie, while bands on the parapets struck up patriotic airs and the guns began to roar in salute. Captain John Rodgers of the *Weehawken,* spotting the rope obstructions dead ahead, commanded the helmsman to swing hard to starboard in order to avoid becoming entangled in the web and immobilized under the muzzles of guns whose projectiles were already hammering the monitor like an anvil. This was well short of the point at which Du Pont had intended to open fire, however, and the result was that the whole line was thrown into confusion by the abrupt necessity, confronting each ship in rapid sequence, of avoiding a collision with the ship ahead. Moreover, as the *Weehawken* turned she encountered a torpedo which exploded directly under her. "It lifted the vessel a little," Rodgers later reported, "but I am unable to perceive that it has done us any damage."

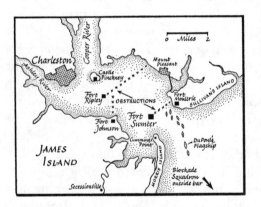

Aboard the flagship, with her deeper draft, the confusion was at its worst. When she lost headway she had to drop her anchor to keep from going aground, and as she hung there, trying to get her nose into the tide, she received two disconcerting butts from two of the monitors astern as they swept past in response to her signal to move up and join the action. Hoisting anchor at last, the *Ironsides* chugged forward a short distance, only to have to drop it again in order to avoid piling up on a shoal. This brought her, unbeknownst, directly over a huge submerged torpedo which the Confederates had fashioned by packing an old boiler with explosives and connecting it to an observation post ashore, to be used to detonate the charge at the proper time. Now the proper time was very much at hand; the rebel electrician later said that if he himself had been allowed to spot the Yankee flagship he could not have placed her more precisely where he wanted her. However, his elation quickly faded, turning first to dismay and then to disgust, when the detonating mechanism failed time after time to send a spark to the underwater engine of destruction. Meanwhile, happily unaware that he and his ship were in mortal danger of being hoisted skyward in sudden flame and smoke, Du Pont signaled the monitors to "disregard motions of commander in chief" and continue to press the attack without his help. The *Ironsides,* as one of her surgeons complained, was as completely out of the fight as if she had been moored to a dock in the Philadelphia Navy Yard, but this did not prevent her taking long-range punishment from the rebel guns. Presenting if not the closest, then at any rate the largest and least mobile target in the harbor, she was struck no less than ninety-five times in the course of the engagement. Despite the din, according to one of her officers, "the sense of security the iron walls gave to those within was wonderful, a feeling akin to that which one experiences in a heavy storm when the wind and hail beat harmlessly against the windows of a well-protected house."

No such feeling was experienced by the crews of the monitors, the officer added; "for in their turrets the nuts that secured the laminated plates flew wildly, to the injury and discomfiture of the men at the guns." Up closer, they were harder hit. "The shots literally rained around them," a correspondent wrote, "splashing the water up thirty feet in the air, and striking and booming from their decks and turrets." The flagship was a mile from Sumter, the nearest monitors about half that far, but the captain of the twin-turreted *Nahant* quickly found what it would cost to close the range. "Mr Clarke, you haven't hit anything yet," he protested to the ensign in charge of the 15-inch gun, which was throwing its 420-pound shells at seven-minute intervals. When the young man replied, "We aint near enough, Captain," the skipper went into a rage. "Not near enough? God damn it," he cried, "I'll put you near enough! Starboard your helm, Quartermaster!" As the ship came about, a rebel projectile slammed against the sight-slit, killing the helmsman and mangling the pilot. "Retire! Retire!" the captain shouted. Others caught it as hard or harder, with similar results: smokestacks perforated, turrets jammed, decks ripped up, guns knocked out of action. The only effect on the enemy a journalist could see, examining the brick northeast face of Sumter through his glasses, was that of "increasing pock marks and discolorations on the walls, as if there had been a sudden breaking out of cutaneous disease." But there was no corresponding slackening of fire from within the fort, whose cannoneers were jubilant over the many hits they scored. Frenzied at being kept from a share in the fun of pummeling the ironclads, Confederates locked in the Moultrie guardhouse screamed above the roar of the bombardment: "For God's sake, let us come out and go to the guns!"

After peering through the drifting smoke for about two hours, Du Pont was told that it was nearly 5 o'clock. "Make signal to the ships to drop out of fire," he said quietly. "It is too late to fight this battle tonight. We will renew it early in the morning." Below decks, when the

gun captains received word of this decision, they sent up an urgent request that they be allowed to fire at least one broadside before retiring.
It was granted, and as the *Ironsides* turned to steam down the channel
an eight-gun salvo was hurled at Moultrie, the only shots she fired in
the course of the engagement. This brought the total to an even 150
rounds expended by the flotilla, and of these 55 were scored as hits. The
Confederates, on the other hand, had fired 2209, of which no less than
441 had found their mark, despite the fact that the targets had not only
been comparatively small, and moving, but had also been mostly submerged. That this was remarkably effective shooting Du Pont himself
began to appreciate when the retiring monitors came within hailing distance of the flagship and he got a close-up look at their condition. The
first to approach was the *Keokuk*, limping badly. Last in and first out,
she had ventured nearest to Sumter's 44 guns, and she had the scars of
90 point-blank hits to prove it. She was "riddled like a colander," one
witness remarked, "the most severely mauled ship one ever saw." That
night, in fact, she keeled over and sank at her anchorage off Morris Island. Others also had been roughly handled; *Weehawken* had taken 53
hits, *Nantucket* 51, *Patapsco* 47, *Nahant* 36, *Passaic* 35, *Catskill* 20, and
Montauk 14. In general, the damage suffered was in inverse ratio to the
individual distance between them and the rebel guns, and none had been
closer than 600 yards.

The admiral's intention to "renew [the battle] early in the
morning" was modified by the sight of his crippled monitors. Five of the
eight were too badly damaged to be able to engage if ordered, and of
these five, one would sink before the scheduled time for action. Equally
conclusive were the reports and recommendations of the several captains
when they came aboard the flagship that evening. "With your present
means," John Rodgers advised, "I could not, if I were asked, recommend a renewal of the attack." The redoubtable Worden was no less
emphatic. "After testing the weight of the enemy's fire, and observing
the obstructions," he reported, "I am led to believe that Charleston cannot be taken by the naval force now present, and that had the attack
been continued [today] it could not have failed to result in disaster."
This gave Du Pont pause, and pausing he reflected on the risks. Here
was no New Orleans, where the problem had been to run the fleet
through a brief, furious gauntlet of fire in order to gain a safe haven
above the forts and place a defenseless city under the muzzles of its
guns; this was Charleston, whose harbor, in the words of a staff officer, "was a *cul-de-sac*, a circle of fire not to be passed." The deeper you
penetrated the circle, the more you were exposed to destruction from its
rim. Moreover, as the admiral saw the outcome, even if he pressed the
attack "in the end we shall retire, leaving some of our ironclads in the
hands of the enemy, to be refitted and turned against our blockade with
deplorable effect." This last was unthinkable — though he thought about

it in his cabin all night long. By daybreak he had made up his mind. "I have decided not to renew the attack," he told his chief of staff. "We have met with a sad repulse; I shall not turn it into a great disaster."

Next afternoon he recrossed the bar. "I attempted to take the bull by the horns, but he was too much for us," he admitted to the army commander whose troops had been standing by to pick up the pieces. By the end of the week the flotilla again was riding at anchor inside Port Royal, swarmed over by armorers hammering the vessels back into shape. The admiral knew the reaction in Washington would be severe, coming as it did on the heels of such great expectations, but he also knew that he had the support of his monitor captains, who stood, as one of them said, "like a wall of iron" around his reputation, agreeing with his chief of staff's opinion that "Admiral Du Pont never showed greater courage or patriotism than when he saved his ships and men, and sacrificed himself to the clamor and disappointment evoked by his defeat." In point of fact, however, part of the expressed disappointment, if not the outright clamor, occurred within the fleet itself. A chief engineer was clapped in arrest for complaining in his ship's mess that the attack had not been pressed to the victory point, and at least one junior officer remarked wryly that "the grim sort of soul like Farragut was lacking." Welles and Fox, though hot enough at the outcome and in no doubt at all as to where the blame lay, were considerably hampered in their criticisms by the political necessity for delay in bringing the matter out into the open with the publication of the adverse battle reports. After all, it was they — especially Fox — who had announced that the monitors were irresistible, and contracts already had been signed for the delivery of eighteen more of the expensive naval monsters. Two weeks after the repulse, Welles was attempting to shrug it off by telling his diary: "I am by no means confident that we are acting wisely in expending so much strength and effort on Charleston, a place of no strategic importance."

The grapes had soured for him; but not for Beauregard. The Louisiana general's only regrets were that the boiler-torpedo had not gone off beneath the *Ironsides* and that the Yankees had slunk away without attempting a renewal of the assault, which he felt certain would have been even more decisively repulsed. In a congratulatory address to his troops, his enthusiasm knew no bounds. He spoke of "the stranded, riddled wreck" of the *Keokuk*, whose big guns now were part of the harbor defenses, and of the ignominious flight of "her baffled coadjutors," whose defeat had reinspired world-wide confidence in the ultimate and glorious triumph of the Confederate cause. In his official report to Richmond, though — for he had recently confided to a friend that, from now on, he was adopting a more restrained style in his dispatches, in order to counteract a rumor that he was prone to exaggerate his accomplishments — the little Creole, with his bloodhound eyes, his swarthy face, and his hair brushed forward in lovelocks at the temples, contented himself for the most part with factual observations. "It may be accepted, as shown," he wrote, "that these vaunted monitor batteries, though formidable engines of war, after all are not invulnerable or invincible, and may be destroyed or defeated by heavy ordnance, properly placed and skillfully handled." However, in the glow and warmth of congratulations being pressed upon him, including one that he had made Sumter "a household word, like Salamis and Thermopylae," he could not resist the temptation to add a closing flourish to the report: "My expectations were fully realized, and the country, as well as the State of South Carolina, may well be proud of the men who first met and vanquished the iron-mailed, terribly armed armada, so confidently prepared and sent forth by the enemy to certain and easy victory."

✕ 2 ✕

Though he grew snappish at the first report that the fleet had been repulsed — "Hold your position inside the bar near Charleston," he instructed Du Pont in a message sent posthaste down the coast; "or, if you shall have left it, return to it, and hold it till further orders" — Lincoln was in a better frame of mind for the reception of bad news than he had been for months. The reason for this was that he had just returned from a five-day Easter vacation combined with a highly satisfactory inspection of the Army of the Potomac, whose tents were pitched along the Rappahannock in the vicinity of Falmouth. The visit was a heartening experience, not only because it showed him that the condition of the troops was excellent, but also because it abolished his main previous doubt as to the fitness of the man he had appointed as their commander. After saying, "Now there is Joe Hooker. He can fight. I think that is pretty well established," Lincoln had added: "But whether he can 'keep tavern' for a large army is not so sure." If the trip down the bay had done nothing else, it had reassured the President on that score. Fighting Joe had taken hold with a vengeance, and the results were plain to see on the faces and in the attitude of the men. Fredericksburg and the Mud March, though the letters of the former were embroidered on the rippling blue of their regimental colors, were no longer even a part of their vocabulary.

Hooker could indeed keep tavern. Within a week of his assumption of command he jolted the commissary department by ordering the issue of rations expanded to include fresh vegetables and soft bread; he supervised a thorough cleanup of the unsanitary camps, shrinking the overlong sick lists in the process, and he instituted a liberal system of furloughs which, combined with a tightening of security regulations, did much to reduce desertion. "Ah! the furloughs and vegetables he gave!" one infantryman still marveled years later. "How he did understand the road to the soldier's heart!" In the midst of all this welcome reform, army paymasters came down from Washington with bulging satchels and surprised the troops with six months' back pay. It was no wonder another veteran recalled that "cheerfulness, good order, and military discipline at once took the place of grumbling, depression, and want of confidence." Idleness, that breeder of discontent, was abolished by a revival of the old-time grand reviews, with regiment after regiment swinging past the reviewing stand so that when the men executed the command "eyes right" they saw their chieftain's clean-shaven face light up with pleasure at seeing their appearance improved by their diurnal spit-and-polish preparations. Unit pride, being thus encouraged, increased even more when Hooker, expanding the use of the so-called Kearny patch — a device improvised by the late Phil Kearny, about this time last year, to identify the men of his division in the course of their march up the York-James peninsula — ordered the adoption of corps insignia of various shapes, cut from red, white, or blue cloth, thus indicating the first, second, or third division, and stitched to the crown of the caps of the troops, so that he and they could tell at a glance what corps and division a man was gracing or disgracing, on duty or off. Moreover, after the gruff and dish-faced Pope and the flustered and fantastically whiskered Burnside, Hooker himself, by the force of his personality and the handsomeness of his presence, infused some of the old McClellan magnetism into the reviving army's ranks. "Apollo-like," a Wisconsin major called the forty-eight-year-old Massachusetts-born commander, and a visiting editor wrote of him as "a man of unusually handsome face and elegant proportions, with a complexion as delicate and silken as a woman's." Another remarked, along this same line, that the general looked "as rosy as the most healthy woman alive."

Some claimed that this glow, this rosiness, had its origin in the bottle (the men themselves apparently took pride in the assertion;

> *"Joe Hooker is our leader —*
> *He takes his whiskey strong!"*

they sang as they set off on practice marches) while other dissenters from the prevalent chorus of praise, although admitting that the general was "handsome and picturesque in the extreme," directed attention to what one of them called his "fatally weak chin." Still others believed they detected inner flaws, below the rosy surface. "He could play the best game of poker I ever saw," a former West Coast intimate recollected, "until it came to the point when he should go a thousand better, and then he would flunk." But the harshest judgment of all came from a cavalry officer, Charles F. Adams, Jr. According to this son of the ambassador to England, the new commander was "a noisy, low-toned intriguer" under whose influence army headquarters became "a place to which no self-respecting man liked to go, and no decent woman could go. It was a combination of barroom and brothel." Young Adams' own "tone" was exceptionally high, which made him something less than tolerant of the weakness of others — particularly the weaknesses of the flesh, from which he himself apparently was exempt — but in support of at least a part of the accusation was the fact that, from this time on, the general's surname entered the language as one of the many lower-case slang words for prostitute. As for the rest, however, a friend who was with him almost daily insisted that Hooker had gone on the wagon the day he took command. Headquarters might have some of the aspects of a barroom, as Adams said, but according to this observer the general himself did not imbibe.

The fact was, it did indeed appear that he as well as the army had experienced a basic change of character. Much of his former bluster was gone; he had even acquired a dislike for his *nom-de-guerre*, though perhaps this was largely because the story was beginning to get around that he had come by it as the result of an error made in a New York composing room during the Peninsula Campaign, when a last-minute dispatch arrived from the front with additional news involving his division. "Fighting — Joe Hooker," the follow-up was tagged, indicating that it was to be added to what had gone before, but the typesetter dropped the dash and it was printed as a separate story, under the resultant heading. The nickname stuck despite the general's objections. "Don't call me Fighting Joe," he said. "[It] makes the public think that I am a hot-headed, furious young fellow, accustomed to making furious and needless dashes at the enemy." Nor was this the only change in Hooker. All his military life, at West Point, in Mexico, and in the peacetime army — from which he had resigned in 1853, after sixteen years of service, in order to take up California farming and civil engineering, only to fail at both so utterly that when news came that the war had begun his friends had to pass the hat to get up money for his fare back East — he had been quick to resent the authority and criticize the conduct of his superiors. Just recently, he had sneered at the President and the Cabinet as a flock of bunglers and had asserted that what the country needed was a dictator, making it more or less clear that the man he had in mind for the job was himself. Now, though, all that had gone by the board. He had not even resented Lincoln's "beware of rashness. Beware of rashness" letter, calling him to account for his derogations while appointing him to command the army. Soon afterwards, in the privacy of his tent, Hooker read the letter to a journalist, only taking exception to the charge that he had "thwarted" Burnside. "The President is mistaken. I never thwarted Burnside in any way, shape, or manner," he broke off reading to say — though even now he could not resist adding: "Burnside was pre-eminently a man of deportment. He fought the battle of Fredericksburg on his deportment; he was defeated on his deportment; and he took his deportment with him out of the Army of the Potomac, thank God." He returned to the letter, and when he had finished reading it he folded it and put it back into his breast pocket, as if to emphasize the claim that he had taken it to heart. "That is just such a letter as a father might write to his son," he mused aloud, and the reporter thought he saw tears beginning to mist the general's pale blue-gray eyes. "It is a beautiful letter," Hooker went on, "and although I think he was harder on me than I deserved, I will say that I love the man who wrote it." Again he paused. Then he said, "After I have got to Richmond I shall give that letter to you to have published."

This last, variously phrased as "When I get to Richmond" or "After we have taken Richmond," cropped up more frequently in his talk as the spirit and strength of his army grew, and it was one of the few things that struck Lincoln unfavorably when he arrived for his Easter visit. "If you get to Richmond, General —" he remarked at their first conference, only to have Hooker break in with "Excuse me, Mr President, but there is no 'if' in this case. I am going straight to Richmond if I live." Lincoln let it pass, though afterwards he said privately to a friend: "That is the most depressing thing about Hooker. It seems to me that he is over-confident." Presently, however, as the inspection tour progressed, he began to see for himself that the general's ready assurance was solidly based on facts and figures. Even after the detachment of Burnside's old corps — which took with it, down the coast to Newport News, whatever resentment its members might be feeling as a result of the supersession of their former chief — Hooker still had seven others, plus a newly consolidated corps of cavalry, including in all no less than twenty divisions of infantry and three of horsemen, here on the Rappahannock, with a present-for-duty total of 133,450 effectives, supported by seventy batteries of artillery with a total of 412 guns. Across the way, the Confederates had less than half as many men and a good deal less than half as many guns, and Hooker not only knew the approximate odds, he was also preparing to take advantage of them. On the eve of Lincoln's arrival he had put his corps commanders on the alert by ordering all surplus baggage sent to the rear, and he had warned the War Department to have siege equipment ready for shipment to him in front of the rebel capital. In addition to 10,000 shovels, 5000 picks, 5000 axes, and 30,000 sandbags, he wanted authentic maps of the Richmond defenses, to be used in laying out saps and parallels, and he requested that a flotilla of supply boats be kept standing by at all times, ready to deliver 1,500,000 rations up the Pamunkey River as soon as the army got that far. He did not say "if," he said "as soon as," and when this was repeated at Falmouth on Easter Sunday Lincoln shook his head in some perplexity. He admired determination and self-reliance, especially in a military man, but he also knew there was such a thing as whistling in the dark. He had known men — John Pope, for one — who assumed those qualities to hide their doubts, not only from their associates but also from themselves. In fact, the louder a man insisted that there was no room for doubt in his make-up, the more likely he was to belong to the whistler category, and Lincoln feared that Hooker's brashness might be assumed for some such purpose. "It is about the worst thing I have seen since I have been down here," he remarked.

Most of what he saw he found encouraging, however. He agreed with Hooker's estimation of the army as "the finest on the planet," and he particularly enjoyed the temporary relief the visit afforded him from the day-to-day pressure of White House paperwork and the importunities of favor-seekers. Not that he was entirely delivered from the latter. Now that the career officers had him where they could get at him, out of channels and yet with no great strain on their ingrained sense of propriety, they did not neglect the opportunity. Even so stiff a professional as Meade, whose testiness had caused his troops to refer to him as "a God-damned old goggle-eyed snapping turtle," could not resist the chance to curry favor, difficult though he found it to unbend. "In view of the vacant brigadiership in the regular army," he wrote his wife, "I have ventured to tell the President one or two stories, and I think I have made decided progress in his affections." But this was all comparatively mild and even enjoyable — even the stories — in contrast to what the Chief Executive had left behind, and presently would be returning to, in Washington. What was more, his wife and younger son, who accompanied him on the outing, appeared to enjoy it every bit as much as he did. Mary Lincoln responded happily to the all-too-rare opportunity of being with her husband, in and out of office hours, and playing the role of First Lady in a style she considered fitting. Riding one day through a camp of Negro refugees, who crowded about the presidential carriage and lifted their children overhead for a look at the Great Emancipator, she asked her husband how many of "those piccaninnies" he supposed were named Abraham Lincoln. "Let's see," he calculated. "This is April, 1863. I should say that of all those babies under two years of age perhaps two thirds have been named for me." Mrs Lincoln, who enjoyed the notion — it was fairly customary in her native Bluegrass for slaves to name their offspring for the master — smiled. But ten-year-old Tad had an entirely different notion of what was fun. He wanted to see some real, live rebels. And Lincoln obliged him. Proceeding one blustery morning to Stafford Heights, they looked across the Rappahannock and down into the ruined streets of Fredericksburg, where the army had staged its two-day carnival before crossing the "champaign tract" to be brought up short in front of the sunken road at the foot of Marye's Heights, and to Tad's delight they saw floating from the eaves of one of the town's few unwrecked houses the Stars and Bars. Nearby, moreover, alongside a tall scorched chimney like a monument erected to commemorate a home, stood two sentinels: genuine, armed graybacks, though one of them —

perversely, as if to lessen Tad's pleasure — wore a light-blue U. S. Army overcoat. Their voices faint with distance, they began yelling across the river at the Yankee spectators, something about Fort Sumter and the ironclads being "licked," which brought an officer out of one of the Fredericksburg bomb-proofs to investigate the shouting. He took out his binoculars, beginning to sweep the opposite heights, and when he spotted the presidential group he paused, adjusted the focus, and peered intently. Whether or not he recognized the tall form, made still taller by the familiar stovepipe hat, they never knew; but at any rate he seemed to. He lowered the glasses and struck an attitude of dignity, then removed his wide-brimmed hat, made a low, formal bow, and retired.

For the Confederates across the way — less than 60,000 in all, including the punctilious officer and the two sentinels, one of whom had been lucky enough to scavenge a Yankee overcoat to put between him and the chill of Virginia's early spring — there had been no corresponding improvement, but rather a decline, in the quantity as well as the quality of the supplies provided by their government. The basic daily ration at this time consisted of a quarter-pound of bacon, often rancid, and eighteen ounces of cornmeal, including a high proportion of pulverized cob, supplemented about every third day by the issue of ten pounds of rice to each one hundred men, along with an occasional few peas and a scant handful of dried fruit when it was available, which was seldom. "This may give existence to the troops while idle," Lee complained to the War Department, "but [it] will certainly cause them to break down when called upon for exertion." Scurvy had begun to appear, and though he attempted to combat this by sending out details to gather sassafras buds, wild onions, and such antiscorbutics — together with other, more substantial windfalls, unofficial and in fact illegal; "Ah, General," he chided Hood, "when you Texans come about, the chickens have to roost mighty high" — Lee felt, as he said, "painfully anxious lest the spirit and efficiency of the men should become impaired, and they be rendered unable to sustain their former reputation or perform the service necessary for our safety."

Yet their morale was as high as ever, if not higher: not only because they managed to forget, or at least ignore, their hunger pangs by staging regimental theatricals and minstrel shows, attending the mammoth prayer meetings which were a part of the great religious revival that swept like wildfire through the army at this time, and organizing brigade-size snowball battles which served much the same purpose on this side of the river as Hooker's grand reviews were serving on the other; but also because they could look back on a practically uninterrupted series of victories which they had grounds for believing would be continued, whatever the odds. In the ten months Lee had been in command of the Army of Northern Virginia, including the past three spent in winter quarters, they had fought no less than thirteen battles, large and small, and in all but one of these — South Mountain, where they had been outnumbered ten to one — they had maintained the integrity of their position from start to finish, and in all but one other — Sharpsburg, where the odds were never better than one to three and mostly worse — they had dominated the field when the smoke cleared. Although they had generally assumed the more costly tactical role of the attacker, they had inflicted more than 70,000 casualties, at a cost of less than 50,000 of their own, and had captured about 75,000 small arms while losing fewer than one tenth as many. In guns, the advantage was greatest of all in this respect; losing 8, they had taken 155. ("I declare," a North Carolina private said as his Federal captors were taking him rearward through their lines. "You-uns has got about as many of them 'U.S.' guns as we have.") The over-all result was confidence, in Lee and in themselves, and a pride that burned fiercely despite privation and grim want. One Confederate, writing home, expressed amazement at the contrast between the army's bedraggled appearance in camp and its efficiency in combat. He marveled at the spirit of his companions, "so ragged, slovenly, sleeveless, without a superfluous ounce of flesh upon their bones, with wild matted hair, in mendicants' rags — and to think when the battle-flag goes to the front how they can and do fight!" Nor was praise of Lee's scarecrow heroes limited to those who stood in his army's ranks. An exchanged Union officer, returning to his own lines this spring after a term spent beyond them as a captive, put his first-hand observations on the record in a letter home. "Their artillery horses are poor, starved frames of beasts, tied to their carriages and caissons with odds and ends of rope and strips of raw hide; their supply and ammunition trains look like a congregation of all the crippled California emigrant trains that ever escaped off the desert out of the clutches of the rampaging Comanche Indians. The men are ill-dressed, ill-equipped, and ill-provided, a set of ragamuffins that a man is ashamed to be seen among, even when he is a prisoner and can't help it. And yet they have beaten us fairly, beaten us all to pieces, beaten us so easily that we are objects of contempt even to their commonest private soldiers, with no shirts to hang out the holes of their pantaloons, and cartridge-boxes tied around their waists with strands of rope."

Lee himself could silence grousing with a jest. "You ought not to mind that," he reassured a young officer who complained about the toughness of some biscuits; "they will stick by you the longer." He referred in much the same tone of levity to the threats made by his new opponent, who had no sooner taken charge of the blue army than he began showing signs of living up to his nickname, Fighting Joe. "General Hooker is obliged to do something," the gray commander wrote home in early February. "I do not know what it will be. He is playing the Chinese game, trying what frightening will do. He runs out his guns, starts wagons and troops up and down the river, and creates an excitement generally. Our men look on in wonder, give a cheer, and all again subsides *in statu quo ante bellum.*" When nothing came of all this show of force before the month was out, Lee expressed a wry impatience. "I owe Mr F. J. Hooker no thanks for keeping me here," he told his wife. "He ought to have made up his mind long ago what to do." At the same time, though, he was warning subordinates that the bluecoats would "make every effort to crush us between now and June, and it will require all our strength to resist them." His confidence, while as firm as that of the men he led, did not cause him to ignore the present odds or the fact that if they continued to lengthen they would stretch beyond endurance. Within a month of the destructive but fruitless repulse of the Federal host that ventured across the river in mid-December, he made his warning explicit in a dispatch to the Secretary of War. "More than once have most promising opportunities been lost for want of men to take advantage of them, and victory itself has been made to put on the appearance of defeat because our diminished and exhausted troops have been unable to renew a successful struggle against fresh numbers of the enemy. The lives of our soldiers are too precious to be sacrificed in the attainment of successes that inflict no loss upon the enemy beyond the actual loss in battle." And he added, with a new note of bitterness which had come with the sack of Fredericksburg and the issuance of the Emancipation Proclamation: "In view of the vast increase of the forces of the enemy, of the savage and brutal policy he has proclaimed, which leaves us no alternative but success or degradation worse than death, if we would save the honor of our families from pollution [and] our social system from destruction, let every effort be made, every means be employed, to fill and maintain the ranks of our armies, until God in his mercy shall bless us with the establishment of our independence."

Instead of an increase, what followed hard on the heels of this appeal was a drastic reduction of his fighting strength, beginning January 14 with the detachment of D. H. Hill to contest the further invasion of the crusty Tarheel general's home state, presaged by the Federals' mid-December advance on Goldsboro. Lee himself went to Richmond two days later to confer with Davis on this and other problems, but had to hurry back to the Rappahannock on the 18th — the eve of his fifty-sixth birthday — when the high-level council of war was disrupted by news that Burnside's army was astir in its camps around Falmouth. As it turned out, all that came of this was the Mud March and Joe Hooker's elevation; Lee detached Robert Ransom's demi-division, which had played a leading role in Longstreet's defense of the sunken road the month before, and sent it south to North Carolina, as he had agreed to do at the interrupted strategy conference. Shortly afterwards, however, word came that Burnside's old corps had boarded transports at Aquia Landing and steamed down Chesapeake Bay to Hampton Roads. It seemed likely that these men were being returned to the scene of their year-old triumph below Norfolk, with instructions to extend their conquest eastward to the Weldon Railroad, Lee's vital supply connection with the factories and grainfields of Georgia and the Carolinas, or to Petersburg, whose fall would give them access to the back door of the capital itself. This two-pronged menace could not be ignored, whatever risk might be involved in attempting to contest it by a further weakening of the Rappahannock line. On February 15 the dismemberment of Longstreet's corps was resumed. Pickett's division was hastened south to Richmond; Hood's followed two days later, accompanied by Old Peter himself, who was charged with the defense of the region beyond the James. These two divisions combined with the troops already there would give him 44,000 men in all, whereas the Federals had 55,000 on hand, exclusive of the corps that presumably was about to join them from Hampton Roads. It was at best a chancy business for the Confederates, north and south of their threatened capital; for even if these blue reinforcements arrived, as was expected momentarily, the command on the south side of the James would be no worse outnumbered than the one on the south side of the Rappahannock, now that more than a fourth of the latter's strength had been subtracted in favor of the former. All Lee could do in this extremity was urge Longstreet to be ready to hurry northward, if possible — that is, if he could find a way to disengage without inviting the destruction of his command or the capture of Richmond — as soon as he got word that Hooker had left off playing the Chinese game and was on the move in earnest. "As our numbers will not admit of our meeting [the enemy] on equality everywhere," the gray commander wrote his detached lieutenant in mid-March, "we must endeavor, by judicious dispositions, to be enabled to make our troops available in any quarter where they may be needed [and] after the emergency passes in one place to transfer them to any other point that may be threatened."

With fewer First Corps troops on hand than had departed, he was down to 58,800 effectives and 170 guns, to be used in opposing a good deal better than twice as many of both. He was almost precisely aware of his opponent's numerical preponderance, not only because of information he received from spies beyond the northern lines, but also because he read the northern papers, one of which was quite specific on the point. Quoting Hooker's medical director, this journal showed 10,777 men on the current sick list, and then went on to state that the sick-well ratio was 67.64 per 1000. By computation Lee arrived at a figure close to 160,000. (Awesome though this total was, it was even a bit low. In late March the Federal commander, lumping teamsters, cooks, and other extra-duty personnel with all the rest, reported an "aggregate present" of 163,005.) Against such odds, and with the knowledge that Hooker would choose the time and place of attack, Lee's only hope for salvation was superior generalship — his own and that of his chief subordinates — coupled with the valor of his soldiers and the increased efficiency of his army. To help achieve this last, he reorganized the artillery into battalions of four four-gun batteries each, four of which battalions were attached to each of the two corps, with two more in general reserve. His hope was that this arrangement, besides strengthening the close-up support of the infantry on the defensive, would provide the "long arm" with a flexibility that would permit a more rapid massing of fire from several quarters of the field at once, either for counter-battery work or for softening an enemy position as a prelude to attack. Whether such measures would produce the desired effect remained to be seen in combat, but another innovation required no testing, its effectiveness being apparent even to a casual eye. This was a legacy left by Longstreet on his departure beyond the James: left, indeed, not only to the Army of Northern Virginia, but also to military science, since in time it would be recognized as perhaps the Confederacy's main contribution to the art of war, which was never the same thereafter.

In mid-January, while Lee was away on his brief trip to Richmond, Old Peter had been left in command on the Rappahannock by virtue of his seniority. His corps, still intact at the time, occupied the northern half of the position, from Hamilton's Crossing to Banks Ford, five miles above Fredericksburg, while Jackson's occupied the rest, from Massaponax Creek down to Port Royal, twenty miles below the town. Lee had no sooner left than Longstreet invited Stonewall to inspect the First Corps defenses, and what the grim Virginian saw when he arrived

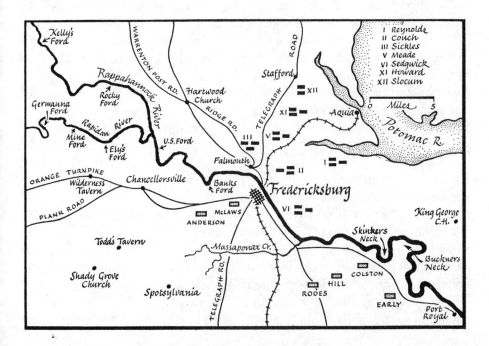

was in the nature of a revelation. Located so as to dominate the roads
and open ground, the fieldworks had been designed for use by a skeleton
force which could hold them against a surprise attack until supports
came up from the reserve. There was nothing new about that; Lee had
conceived and used intrenchments for the same purpose on the Peninsula, nearly a year ago. The innovation here involved was the traversed
trench. Formerly such works had been little more than long, open
ditches, with the spoil thrown forward to serve as a parapet, which gave
excellent protection from low-trajectory fire from dead ahead but were
vulnerable to flank attack and the lateral effect of bursting shells. To offset these two disadvantages — particularly the latter, intensified by the
long-range rifled cannon of the Federals, firing from positions well beyond the reach of most Confederate batteries — Longstreet's engineers
had broken the long ditches into quite short, squad-sized rifle trenches,
staggered in depth, disposed for mutual support, and connected by trav-
erses which could be utilized against flank attacks and afforded solid protection from all but direct artillery hits. Jackson took a careful look,
then returned to his own lines, where the dirt began at once to fly anew.
From such crude beginnings, fathered by the necessity for defending a
fixed position against a greatly superior foe, grew the highly intricate
field fortifications of the future. Presently the whole Rappahannock
line, from Banks Ford to Port Royal, was thus protected throughout
its undulant, winding, 25-mile length, and when Old Peter left next
month with more than half of his men, so well had he and they designed
and dug, Lee did not find it necessary to reinforce the two-division remnant by shifting troops from Jackson. "The world has never seen such a
fortified position," a young Second Corps artillerist declared some weeks
later. "The famous lines at Torres Vedras could not compare with them.
... They follow the contour of the ground and hug the bases of the hills
as they wind to and from the river, thus giving natural flanking arrangements, and from the tops of the hills frown the redoubts for sunken
batteries and barbette batteries *ad libitum,* far exceeding the number of
our guns; while occasionally, where the trenches take straight across the
fields, a redoubt stands out defiantly in the open plain to receive our
howitzers." Hooker might, as Lee said, "make every effort to crush [the
defenders] between now and June," but he was going to find it a much
harder job, from here on out, if he tried anything like the approach his
predecessor had adopted in December.

On the face of it, that seemed unlikely; Hooker did not resemble
Burnside in manner any more than he did in looks. Clearly, if he continued to develop along the lines he had followed so far, Lee was going
to have a far thornier problem on his hands, even aside from the lengthened numerical odds, than any he had overcome in frustrating the two
all-out offensives that had succeeded his repulse of McClellan, within
sight and sound of Richmond, nine months back. The new chieftain's re-

organization of his mounted force was a case in point; "Hooker *made*
the Federal cavalry," an admiring trooper later declared. Formerly par-
celed out, regiment by regiment, to infantry commanders whose handling of them had been at best inept, whether in or out of combat, the
three divisions — 11,500 strong, with about 13,000 horses — were
grouped into a single corps under Brigadier General George Stoneman,
a forty-year-old West Pointer, all of whose previous service had been
with the mounted arm, before and during the present war, except for a
brief term as an infantry corps commander, in which capacity he had
won a brevet for gallantry at Fredericksburg. His current rank was one
grade below that of the other seven heads of corps; Hooker was withholding promotion until Stoneman proved that he could weld his inherited conglomeration of horsemen into an effective striking force.
That was his basic task, and he seemed well on the way toward pushing
it to fulfillment, helped considerably by the fact that, after nearly two
years in the saddle, the early blue-jacket volunteers — formerly sneered
at by their fox-hunt-trained opponents as "white-faced clerks and
counter jumpers" who scarcely knew the on side from the off — were
becoming seasoned troopers, no longer mounted on crowbait nags
fobbed off on the government by unprincipled contractors, but on
strong-limbed, sound-winded, well-fed animals who, like their riders,
had learned the evolutions of the line and had mastered the art of survival in all weathers.

This improvement came moreover at a time of crisis for the gray
cavalry on the opposite bank of the Rappahannock. Not only was there
a critical shortage of horses in the Army of Northern Virginia; there
was also the likelihood that those on hand, survivors for the most part
of a year of hard campaigning, would die for lack of forage. This second danger increased the threat implicit in the first. So clean had the region been swept of fodder that such few remounts as could be found
outside the immediate theater of war could not be brought northward.
For example, four hundred artillery horses procured that winter in
Georgia had to be kept in North Carolina because they could not be
foraged with the army, all but a dozen of whose batteries had already
been withdrawn from the lines in order to save the animals from starvation. A man could subsist, at least barely, on a couple of pounds of food
a day, whereas a horse required about ten times that amount, and this
was a great deal more than the rickety single-track railroad from
Richmond could bring forward, even if that much grain had been available there. The result was that the cavalry's activity was severely limited. Brigadier General Wade Hampton's brigade, for instance — the
first of Stuart's three, which contained in all about 5000 men — had
staged three highly successful small-scale raids, deep in the Federal rear
at Dumfries and Occoquan, immediately before and after the Battle of
Fredericksburg, returning with some 300 captives and their mounts,

mostly unwary vedettes picked up in the course of the gray column's advance by starlight, together with a sizeable train of mule-drawn wagons loaded with captured stores, including 300 pairs of badly needed boots — a real windfall. But the end result of these three coups was that Hampton's underfed horses were so utterly broken down by their exertions that the whole brigade had to be sent south to recover, thus weakening Lee still further at a time when he expected Hooker to make up his mind to come booming over the river any day.

Stuart chafed under the restriction thus imposed. His one exploit this winter was an 1800-trooper raid on Fairfax Courthouse, fifteen miles from the Federal capital, beginning the day after Christmas and ending New Year's Day; but all it earned him — in contrast to the enormously successful forays by Forrest and Morgan, launched simultaneously in the West — was 200 mounted prisoners, 20 wagons, and the contents of a dozen sutler stalls; which scarcely made up for the wear and tear of the long ride. Though as usual he made the most of the adventure in his report, it was followed by two months spent in winter quarters, where he was obliged to give less attention to the fast-developing enemy cavalry than to the problem of finding forage for his hungry horses. In such surroundings, though he sought diversion for himself and his men in regimental balls and serenades, the plumed hat, red-lined cape, and golden spurs lost a measure of their glitter, at least in certain eyes. "Stuart carries around with him a banjo player and a special correspondent," one high-ranking fellow officer remarked. "This claptrap is noticed and lauded as a peculiarity of genius, when in fact it is nothing else but the act of a buffoon to attract attention." Down to two brigades after Hampton's departure — one under W. H. F. Lee, called "Rooney," and the other under Fitzhugh Lee, respectively the commanding general's son and nephew — Jeb was obliged to take his pleasure at second hand, from the occasional exploits of subordinates and even ex-subordinates. Among the latter was Captain John S. Mosby, a former cavalry scout who had been given permission in January to recruit a body of partisans for operations in the Loudoun Valley, part of a region to be known in time as "Mosby's Confederacy," so successful were he and his Rangers in bedeviling and defeating the bluecoats sent there to capture or destroy him. Twenty-eight years old and weighing barely 125 pounds, the slim, gray-eyed Virginian first attracted wide attention by his capture, at Fairfax on a night in early March, of Brigadier General E. H. Stoughton, a Vermont-born West Pointer, together with two other officers, 30 men, and 58 horses. Mosby, who at present had fewer men than that in his whole command, entered the general's headquarters, stole upstairs in the darkness, and found the general himself asleep in bed. Turning down the covers, he lifted the tail of the sleeper's nightshirt and gave him a spank on the behind.

"General," he said, "did you ever hear of Mosby?"

"Yes," Stoughton replied, flustered and half awake; "have you caught him?"

"He has caught you," Mosby said, by way of self-introduction, and got his captive up and dressed and took him back through the lines, along with virtually all of his headquarters guard, for delivery to Fitzhugh Lee the following morning at Culpeper.

Fitz Lee, a year younger than the clean-shaven Mosby, though he disguised the fact behind an enormous shovel beard that outdid even Longstreet's in length and thickness, could appreciate a joke as well as the next man, and in this case he could appreciate it perhaps a good deal better, since he and the captive Vermonter had been schoolmates at the Point. Besides, he was in an excellent frame of mind just now, having returned the week before from a similar though less spectacular exploit involving still another fellow cadet of his and Stoughton's: New York-born Brigadier General W. W. Averell, who commanded the second of Stoneman's three divisions. Young Lee was sent by his uncle to investigate a rumor that Hooker was about to repeat McClellan's strategy by transferring his army to the Peninsula. Crossing the Rappahannock well upstream at Kelly's Ford on February 24, Lee's 400-man detachment pushed on to the Warrenton Post Road, then down it, penetrating the blue cavalry screen to the vicinity of Hartwood Church, eight miles short of Falmouth. Here the graybacks encountered their first serious opposition in the form of the 3d Pennsylvania Cavalry, Averell's old regiment before his promotion to divisional command. Lee promptly charged and routed the Keystone troopers, capturing 150 of them at a cost to himself of 14 killed and wounded. Then, having secured the information he had come for — Hooker, whose headquarters were a scant half-dozen miles away by now, obviously was planning no such move as had been rumored — Lee successfully withdrew without further incident, leaving behind him a note for his former schoolmate, whose entire division had been turned out, along with two others of infantry, in a vain attempt to intercept the raiders and avenge the defeat of one of its best regiments. The note was brief and characteristic. "I wish you would put up your sword, leave my state, and go home," Fitz told his old friend, adding in reference to the speed with which the bluecoats had retreated when attacked: "You ride a good horse, I ride a better. Yours can beat mine running." The close was in the nature of a challenge. "If you won't go home, return my visit and bring me a sack of coffee."

Averell returned the visit within three weeks, and he took care to bring along a sack of coffee in his saddlebags. What was more, he repaid the call in force, splashing through the shallows of Kelly's Ford on the morning of March 17 with 3000 troopers. Lee had fewer than 1000 at the time, but his pickets put up such a scrap at the crossing that Averell, though he was pleased to have captured about two dozen of them in the skirmish, persuaded himself that it would be wise to leave a third of his force there to protect his rear, thereby of his own accord reducing the odds to only a little better than two to one. Also, being aware of his old schoolmate's impulsive nature, he halted about midmorning, less than a mile beyond the river, dismounted his men, and took up a strong defensive position behind a stone wall crossing a pasture on the farm of a family named Brooks. Sure enough, at noon Lee came riding hard from Culpeper and attacked without delay, his lead regiment charging dragoon-style, four abreast. The result, as the defenders poured a hot fire from behind their ready-made breastworks, was a quick and bloody repulse. Averell cautiously followed it up, but was struck again, one mile north, with like results. While the blue riders held their ground, the Confederates crossed Carter's Run and reassembled; whereupon the two commands settled down to long-range firing across the creek, relieving the monotony from time to time with limited charges and counter-

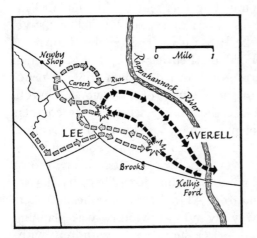

charges which did nothing to alter the tactical stalemate. This continued until about 5.30, when Averell, having learned from captured rebels that Stuart and his crack artillerist Pelham were on the field, decided that the time had come for him to recross the Rappahannock. "My horses were very much exhausted. We had been successful so far. I deemed it proper to withdraw." So he stated later in his report. However, before terminating the requested "visit" he took care to observe the amenities by leaving the sack of coffee Lee had asked for, together with a note: "Dear Fitz. Here's your coffee. Here's your visit. How do you like it? Averell."

The truth was, Fitz did not much like it. Though he could, and did, claim victory on grounds that he had remained in control of the field after the enemy withdrew, this was not very satisfactory when he considered that the Federals could make the same claim with regard to every similar Confederate penetration, including his own recent raid on Hartwood Church and Stuart's dazzling "rides" the year before. Then too, there was the matter of casualties. Suffering 133, Lee had inflicted only 78, or not much over half as many. If this was a victory, it was certainly a strange one. But there was more that was alarming about this St Patrick's Day action: much more, at least from the southern point of view. For the first time on a fair field of fight — the two-to-one odds were not unusual; moreover, they had been the source of considerable underdog glory in the past — Confederate cavalry had fallen back repeatedly under pressure from Federal cavalry. Nothing could have demonstrated better the vast improvement of this arm of the Union war machine, especially when it was admitted that only Averell's lack of the true aggressive instinct, which twice had left the rebel horsemen unmolested while they reformed their broken ranks, had kept the blue troopers from converting both repulses into routs. Unquestionably, this proof that the Federal cavalry had come of age, so to speak, meant future trouble for the men who previously had ridden around and through and over their awkward opponents almost at will. . . . Nor was that all either. This light-hearted exchange of calling cards, accompanied in one case by the gift of a pound of coffee, had its more immediate somber consequences, too. After all, a man who died on this small field was every bit as dead as a man who died in the thunderous pageantry of Fredericksburg, and his survivors were apt to be quite as inconsolable in their sorrow. They might possibly be even more inconsolable, since their grief did not take into account the battle or skirmish itself, but rather the identity of the man who fell. What made Kelly's Ford particular in this respect was that it produced one casualty for whom the whole South mourned.

One of Averell's reasons for withdrawing had been the report that Stuart was on the field. It was true, so far as it went; Jeb was there, but he had brought no reinforcements with him, as Averell supposed; he had come to Culpeper on court-martial business, and thus happened to be on hand when the news arrived that bluecoats were over the river. Similarly, the day before, John Pelham had left cavalry headquarters to see a girl in Orange, so that he too turned up in time to join Fitz Lee on the ride toward Kelly's Ford; "tall, slender, beautifully proportioned," a friend called the twenty-three-year-old Alabamian, and "as grand a flirt as ever lived." With his own guns back near Fredericksburg — including the brass Napoleon with which he had held up the advance of a whole Federal division for the better part of an hour — he was here supposedly as a spectator, but anyone who knew him also knew that he would never be content with anything less than a ringside seat, and would scarcely be satisfied even with that, once the action had been joined. And so it was. When the first charge was launched against the stone wall, the young major smiled, drew the sword which he happened to be wearing because he had gone courting the night before, and waved it gaily as he rode hard to overtake the van. "Forward! Forward!" he cried. Just then, abrupt as a clap of blue-sky thunder, a shell burst with a flash and a roar directly overhead. Pelham fell. He lay on his back, full length and motionless, his blue eyes open and the smile still on his handsome face, which was unmarked. Turning him over, however, his companions found a small, deep gash at the base of his skull, just above the hair line, where a fragment of the shell had struck and entered. When Stuart, who had ridden to another quarter of the field, heard that his young chief of artillery was dead he bowed his head on his horse's neck and wept. "Our loss is irreparable," he said.

Others thought so, too: three girls in nearby towns, for instance, who put on mourning. Word spread quickly throughout the South, and men and women in far-off places, who had known him only by reputation, received with a sense of personal bereavement the news that "the gallant Pelham" had fallen. Robert Lee, who had attached the adjective to the young gunner's name in his report on their last great battle, made an unusual suggestion to the President. "I mourn the loss of Major Pelham," he wrote. "I had hoped that a long career of usefulness and honor was still before him. He has been stricken down in the midst of both, and before he could receive the promotion he had richly won. I hope there will be no impropriety in presenting his name to the Senate, that his comrades may see that his services have been appreciated, and may be incited to emulate them." Davis promptly forwarded the letter, with the result that Pelham was promoted even as he lay in state in the Virginia capitol. For once, the Senate had acted quickly, and the dead artillerist, who just under two years ago had left West Point on the eve of graduation in order to go with his native state, went home to Alabama as Lieutenant Colonel Pelham.

At this time of grief, coupled with uncertainty as to the enemy's intentions, Lee fell ill for the first time in the war. A throat infection had settled in his chest, giving him pains that interfered with his sleep and made him testy during his waking hours. By the end of March his condition was such that his medical director insisted that he leave his tent and take up quarters in a house at Yerby's, on the railroad five miles south of Fredericksburg. He did so, much against his wishes, and complained in a home letter that the doctors were "tapping me all over like an old steam boiler before condemning it." After the manner of most men unfamiliar with sickness, he was irritable and inclined to be impatient with those around him at such times (which in turn provoked his staff into giving him the irreverent nickname "the Tycoon") but he never really lost the iron self-control that was the basis of the character he presented to the world. Once, for example, when he was short with his adjutant over some administrative detail, that officer drew himself up with dignity and silently defied his chief; whereupon Lee at once got hold of himself and said calmly, "Major Taylor, when I lose my temper don't let it make you angry." Nor did his illness detract in any way from the qualities which, at the time of his appointment to command, had led an acquaintance to declare: "His name might be Audacity. He will take more desperate chances, and take them quicker, than any other general in this country, North and South." Confirmation of these words had come in the smoke and flame of the Seven Days, in the fifty-mile march around Pope with half of an outnumbered army, and in the bloody defense of the Sharpsburg ridge with his back to a deep river. Yet nothing gave them more emphasis than his reaction now to the early-April news that Burnside's old corps, after lingering all this time at Newport News, was proceeding west to join its old commander, who had been assigned to head the Department of the Ohio. This signified trouble for Johnston and Bragg in Tennessee, since it probably meant that these troops would reinforce Rosecrans. At Charleston, moreover, Beauregard even now was under what might well be an irresistible attack by an ironclad fleet, with thousands of bluecoats waiting aboard transports for the signal to steam into the blasted harbor and occupy the city. Lee's reaction to this combination of pressures, sick though he was, and faced with odds which he knew were worse than two to one here on the Rappahannock, was to suggest that, if this bolstering of the Union effort down the coast and in the West indicated a lessening of the Union effort in the East, the Army of Northern Virginia should swing over to the offensive. "Should Hooker's army assume the defensive," he wrote the Secretary of War on April 9, "the readiest method of relieving the pressure on General Johnston and General Beauregard would be for this army to cross into Maryland." The wretched condition of the roads, plus the cramping shortage of provisions and transportation, made such a move impossible at present, he added; "But this is what I would recommend, if practicable."

Such audacity, though ingrained and very much a part of the nature of the man, was also based on the combat-tested valor of the soldiers he commanded. He knew there was nothing he could ask of them that they would not try to give him, and he believed that with such a spirit they could not fail; or if they failed, it would not be their fault. "There never were such men in an army before," he said this spring. "They will go anywhere and do anything if properly led." And if his admiration for them was practically boundless, so too was his concern. "His theory, expressed upon many occasions," a staff officer later wrote, "was that the private soldiers — men who fought without the stimulus of rank, emolument, or individual renown — were the most meritorious class of the army, and that they deserved and should receive the utmost respect and consideration." Not one of them ever appealed to him without being given a sympathetic hearing, sometimes in the very heat of battle, and he turned down a plan for the formation of a battalion of honor because he did not believe there would be room in its ranks for all who deserved a place there. Quite literally, nothing was too good for them in the way of reward, according to Lee, and this applied without reservation. To him, they all were heroes. One day he saw a man in uniform standing near the open flap of his tent. "Come in, Captain, and take a seat," he said. When the man replied, "I'm no captain, General; I'm nothing but a private," Lee told him: "Come in, sir. Come in and take a seat. You ought to be a captain."

.   .   .

Lincoln apparently felt much the same way about the enlisted men in blue. One correspondent observed that at the final Grand Review, staged on the last full day of his Falmouth visit, "the President merely touched his hat in return salute to the officers, but uncovered to the men in the ranks." Seated upon a short, thick-set horse with a docked tail, the tall civilian in the stovepipe hat and rusty tailcoat presented quite a contrast to the army commander, who wore a dress uniform and rode his usual milk-white charger. A Maine soldier noticed Hooker's "evident satisfaction" as the long blue files swung past in neat array, and spoke of "the conscious power shown on his handsome but rather too rosy face," whereas another from Wisconsin remarked that "Mr Lincoln sat his cob perfectly straight, and dressed as he was in dark clothes, it appeared as if he was an exclamation point astride of the small letter *m*." He seemed oddly preoccupied with matters far removed from the present martial business of watching the troops pass in review. This was shown to be the case when he turned without preamble to Major General Darius N. Couch, the senior corps commander, and asked: "What do you suppose will become of all these men when the war is over?" Couch was somewhat taken aback; his mind had not been working along those lines; but he said later, "It struck me as very pleasant that somebody had an idea that the war would sometime end."

Four days of intimate acquaintance with the Army of the Potomac had indicated to Lincoln, despite the blusterous symptoms of overconfidence on the part of the man beside him on the big white horse — despite, too, the rumored repulse of the ironclads at Charleston, the loss of the Union foothold on Texas, the upsurge of guerillas in Missouri, the apparent stalemate in Middle Tennessee, and Grant's long sequence of failures in front of Vicksburg — that the end of the war might indeed be within reach, once Hooker decided the time had come for a jump-off. Morale had never been higher, the Chief Excutive found by talking with the troops in their renovated camps and hospitals. Moreover, the reorganizational shake-up seemed to have brought the best men to the top. Sumner and Franklin were gone for good, along with the clumsy Grand Division arrangement which had accomplished little more than the addition of another link to the overlong chain of command, and of the seven major generals now at the head of the seven infantry corps, less than half — Couch, Reynolds, and Henry W. Slocum had served in the same capacity during the recent Fredericksburg fiasco, while the remaining four were graduates of the hard-knocks school of experience and therefore could be presumed to have achieved their current eminence on merit. Daniel E. Sickles, the only nonregular of the lot, had taken over from Stoneman after that officer's transfer to the cavalry; Meade had succeeded Dan Butterfield, who had moved up to the post of army chief of staff; John Sedgwick had inherited the command of W. F. Smith, now in charge of Burnside's old corps on its way out to Ohio; Oliver O. Howard, who had lost an arm last year on the Peninsula, had replaced Sigel when that general, already miffed because Hooker had been promoted over his head, resigned in protest because his corps, being next to the smallest of the seven, was incommensurate with his rank. Lincoln had known most of these men before, but in the course of the past four days he had come to know them better, with the result that he felt confident, more confident at any rate than he had felt before, as to the probable outcome of a clash between the armies now facing each other across the Rappahannock. In fact his principal admonition, in a memorandum which he prepared in the course of his visit — perhaps on this same April 9 of the final Grand Review, while Lee was recommending to his government that the Army of Northern Virginia swing over to the offensive in order to break up the menacing Federal combinations — was that "our prime object is the enemy's army in front of us, and is not . . . Richmond at all, unless it be incidental to the main object." Having observed from Stafford Heights the strength of the rebel fortifications, he did not think it would be wise to "take the disadvantage of attacking [Lee] in his intrenchments; but we should continually harass and menace him, so that he shall have no leisure or safety in sending away detachments. If he weakens himself, then pitch into him."

One further admonition he had, and he delivered himself of it the following morning as he sat with Hooker and Couch before departing for Aquia Landing, where the steamer was waiting to take him and his party back to Washington. "I want to impress upon you two gentlemen," he said, "in your next fight, put in all your men." He pronounced the last five words with emphasis, perhaps recalling that in the December fight a good half of the army had stood idle on the left while the conflict wore toward its bloody twilight finish on the right, and then he was off to join his wife and son for the boat ride up the Potomac. Although the trip unquestionably had done him good, providing him with a rare chance to relax, it was after all no more than an interlude in the round of administrative cares, a brief recess from the importunities of men who sought to avail themselves of the power of his office. When a friend remarked that he was looking rested and in better health as a result of his visit to the army, Lincoln replied that it had been "a great relief to get away from Washington and the politicians. But nothing touches the tired spot," he added.

⚹ 3 ⚹

Longstreet, on his own at last — at least in a manner of speaking — was finding no such opportunities for glory beyond the James as his fellow corps commander Jackson had found the year before, on detached service out in the Shenandoah Valley. There Stonewall had not only added a brisk chapter to military history and several exemplary paragraphs to future tactics manuals, but had also earned for himself, according to admirers, the one thing his senior rival, according to detractors, wanted more than anything on or off the earth: a seat among the immortals in Valhalla. However, this southside venture, being a different kind of thing, seemed quite unlikely to be productive of any such reward. Designed less for the gathering of laurels than for the gathering of the hams and bacon which for generations had made and would continue to make the Smithfield region famous, it was aimed at satisfying the hunger of the stomach, rather than the hunger of the soul. What was more, throughout his ten weeks of "independent" command, Old Peter was obliged to serve three masters — Davis, Seddon, and Lee — who saddled him with three separate, simultaneous, and sometimes incompatible assignments: 1) the protection of the national capital, threatened by combinations of forces superior to his own, 2) the gathering of supplies in an area that had been under Federal domination for nearly a year, and 3) the disposition of his troops so as to be able to hurry them back to the Rappahannock on short notice. To these, there presently was added a fourth, the investment of Suffolk, which had more men within its fortifications than he could bring against them. The wonder, under such conditions as obtained, was not that he failed in part, but that he succeeded to any degree at all in fulfilling these divergent expectations.

In Richmond itself there had been no talk of failure at the outset, only a feeling of vast relief as the battle-hardened divisions of Hood and Pickett arrived to block the approach of blue forces reported to be gathering ominously, east and southeast of the city, beyond the rim of intrenchments mainly occupied by part-time defenders recruited in the emergency from the host of clerks and other government workers who had escaped conscription up to now. One of these, an industrious diarist, influenced perhaps by a far-fetched sense of rivalry — or perhaps by the fact that in the past six months, since Lee's army had set out northward after Pope, he had forgot what a combat soldier looked like — thought the First Corps veterans "pale and haggard" when he saw them on February 18, slogging through snow deposited calf-deep in the streets by a heavy storm the night before. Four days later, however, Seddon wrote Lee that their "appearance, spirit, and cheerfulness afforded great satisfaction," not only to the authorities but also to the fretful populace. "General Longstreet is here," the Secretary added, "and under his able guidance of such troops no one doubts as to the entire security of the capital." On February 25 he appointed the burly Georgian commander of the Department of Virginia and North Carolina, which was created by combining the three departments of Richmond, Southern Virginia, and North Carolina, respectively under Major Generals Arnold Elzey, Samuel G. French, and D. H. Hill, together with the independent Cape Fear

River District under Brigadier General W. H. C. Whiting, who was charged with protecting Wilmington from attack by land or water. Longstreet's total number of men present for duty, including those in the two divisions he brought with him, plus Ransom's demi-division forwarded earlier, was 44,193 of all arms, mostly scattered about the two states in ill-equipped and poorly administered garrisons of defense. Already outnumbered by the Federals on hand — whose current strength of 50,995 effectives he considerably overestimated — he was alarmed by reports, received on the day he assumed command, that transports were arriving daily in Hampton Roads, crowded to the gunwales with reinforcements for the intended all-out drive on Richmond. So far, they had unloaded an estimated "40,000 or 50,000" troops at Newport News, he wired Lee, and there were rumors that Joe Hooker himself had been seen at Fort Monroe, presaging the early arrival of the balance of the Army of the Potomac.

In such alarming circumstances, and schooled as he had been in strategy under Lee, Old Peter reasoned that the time had come for him to attack, if only by way of creating a diversion. As he put it, "We are much more likely to succeed by operating ourselves than by lying still to await the enemy's time for thorough preparations before he moves upon us." However, it was in the attempted application of this commendable principle that his troubles really began; for it was then that he came face to face with the fact that the exercise of independent command, especially in the armies of the Confederacy, involved a good deal more than a knowledge of tactics and logistics. Like him, his three ranking subordinates were West Pointers in their early or middle forties, and like him, too, they had their share of temperamental peculiarities — as he discovered when he issued instructions for a joint attack on New Bern. Held by the Federals for nearly a year now, the town had been the base for their mid-December advance against the Wilmington & Weldon Railroad, sixty miles away at Goldsboro, and it was Longstreet's belief that an attack on both banks of the Neuse River, farther down, would pinch off the blue garrison and expose it to capture or destruction. His plan was for Hill to move against the place with his whole command, reinforced by one of Whiting's two brigades, which would give him about 14,000 men in all. Hill was altogether willing, having recently excoriated the Yankee invaders by calling upon his infantry to "cut down to 6 feet by 2 the dimensions of the farms which these plunderers propose to appropriate." But Whiting was not, even though the brigade asked for was Ransom's, detached from the First Corps and forwarded to him only the month before. In response to Longstreet's call for "half your force and as many more as can be spared from the Wilmington garrison," along with one of his three long-range Whitworth guns, Whiting — a brilliant thirty-nine-year-old Mississippian who, three years after Old Peter had finished near the bottom of the

West Point class of '42, had not only graduated at the top of his class, but had done so with the highest marks any cadet had ever made — promptly wrote: "I perceive you are not acquainted with this vicinity. ... So far from considering myself able to spare troops from here, I have applied for and earnestly urged that another brigade be sent here immediately. The works here are by no means completed and I need the services of every man I can raise."

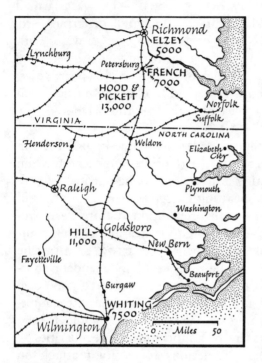

The result was that Hill moved against New Bern without the help of Whiting's men or the loan of the precious long-range gun, and though he converted what was to have been an attack into a demonstration — it was March 14, the anniversary of the fall of the town to the Federals as a follow-up of their capture of Roanoke Island — even that was repulsed decisively when the defenders towed gunboats up the river from Pamlico Sound and opened a scorching fire against the Confederates on both banks, inflicting 30-odd casualties at a cost of only 6. Back in Goldsboro two days later, Hill was furious. "The spirit manifested by Whiting has spoiled everything," he protested in his report. As he saw it, the proper correction for this was for the government to keep its word that he would be given command of all the troops in the state, including those at Wilmington, in which case he would be able to bend the fractious Whiting to his will. "I have received nothing but contemptuous treatment from Richmond from the very beginning of the war," he complained hotly, "but I hope they will not carry matters so far as to perpetuate a swindle." Longstreet, receiving his caustic friend's report, sought to protect him from the wrath of their superiors. "I presume that this was not intended as an official communication," he replied, "and have not forwarded it. I hope that you will send up another account of your trip." Hill neither insisted that the document stand nor offered to withdraw it, but he declined to submit a new or expurgated account of what Old Peter referred to as his "trip."

For all his obstreperous ways of protesting the injustice he saw everywhere around him, Hill was only one among the many when it came to presenting his chief with problems. Arnold Elzey, in charge of the Richmond defenses north of the James, had only recently returned to duty after a long and painful convalescence from the face wound he had suffered at Gaines Mill. A Marylander, he originally had had the last name Jones, but had dropped it in favor of his mother's more distinctive maiden name. Erratic and moody, perhaps because of his disfigurement and the internal damage to his mouth which made his words scarcely intelligible, he was said to be drinking heavily — a particular yet not uncommon type among the casualties of war, injured as much in pride as in body. At any rate, neither he nor his command could be counted on for anything more than the desperate last-ditch resistance that was his and their assignment. Moreover, Longstreet had no high opinion of the abilities of Sam French, who was charged with the defense of Petersburg, that vital nexus of rail supply lines connecting Virginia and the deeper South. A New-Jersey-born adoptive Mississippian and a veteran of the Mexican War, French had attained high rank without distinction in the field of the present conflict, and Old Peter had the usual combat officer's prejudice in this and other such cases he encountered when he crossed the James. Because of Lee's policy of quietly getting rid of men he found unsatisfactory, not by cashiering them but by transferring them to far or adjoining theaters where he considered their shortcomings would cost their country less, Longstreet might have thought he was back with the old Army of the Potomac, as it had been called before the advent of Lee and its transfiguration into the Army of Northern Virginia, so familiar were the faces of many of the officers he found serving under him when he took over his new department. All too many of those faces reflected failure, and all too many others identified men who were inexperienced in combat.

Not that there appeared to be any considerable need for such experience just now. Foraging operations were in full swing, with commissary details scouring the countryside and sending back long trains of wagons heavily loaded with hams and bacon, side meat, salted fish, and flour and cornmeal, all of which were plenteous in the region. Increasingly, as the Federals failed to press their rumored drive on Richmond, the removal of such badly needed stores was becoming the prime concern of the department commander and his troops.

On March 17 their work was interrupted by a dispatch from Lee. Bluecoats were over the Rappahannock at Kelly's Ford; Longstreet was to hurry north with Hood and Pickett to help drive them back. Before he could obey, however, the order was countermanded. The threat had been no more than a cavalry raid; the enemy troopers had retired. Old Peter returned to his foraging duties with new zeal. Now that the nearer counties had been picked clean, he wanted to move eastward into those beyond the Blackwater and Chowan Rivers, out of reach for the past year because of the Union occupation. He figured that if the Yankees could be driven back within their works and held there for a reasonable length of time, his commissary agents — unhampered by the enemy and aided by the citizens of those regions, who had remained intensely loyal to the Confederacy through long months when they might have thought themselves forsaken — would be able to effect a quick removal of the stores. However, this was at best a risky business for him to undertake. He would not only have to keep his two most effective divisions ready to disengage on short notice, in order to be able to speed them north on call from Lee; he would also have to detail a considerable portion of his force for commissary duties behind the lines if he was to accomplish the main purpose underlying his reason for advancing in the first place. In short, with these two disadvantages added to the fact that he was outnumbered before he even began, he would be reversing the required two-to-one numerical ratio between the two parties engaged in siege operations. But he decided to give the thing a try in any event, for the sake of all those thousands of slabs of bacon and barrels of herring awaiting removal from areas previously inaccessible to the soldiers who were fighting here and elsewhere for their eventual deliverance from the blue forces now in occupation.

He made his plans accordingly. Hood and Pickett would join French for a movement against Suffolk, which would serve the double purpose of bringing the fertile Blackwater-Chowan watersheds within the grasp of his commissary agents and of blocking the path of a Federal drive on Petersburg from the lower reaches of the James. Nor was that all. Hill — reinforced at last by Ransom's brigade, pried loose from Whiting over that general's violent protest that he was being stripped of two thirds of his infantry on the eve of an all-out assault on Wilmington by the ironclad fleet Du Pont was assembling at Port Royal — would move simultaneously against Washington, North Carolina, the Tar River gateway to a region which was lush with agricultural produce and gave access to the fisheries of upper Pamlico Sound. This lower movement under Hill, while equally rich in foraging possibilities, was more in the nature of a diversion, favoring the main effort against Suffolk, which would be under Longstreet's personal direction. It was Old Peter's hope that the Unionists, being threatened in two places at once, would not only be prevented from strengthening either at the expense of the other, but would also be thrown off balance by the expectation of additional strikes, all down the long perimeter of their coastal holdings. Though he made it clear at the outset, to his superiors as well as to his subordinates, that both advances were intended to be no more than demonstrations, staged primarily to drive the bluecoats within their works so that his foraging details would be free to scour the area unmolested, he did not overlook the possibility of taking advantage of any opening the enemy might afford. Food for Lee's soldiers was his main concern, but he intended to draw blood, too — despite the numerical odds — whenever and wherever the tactical risk appeared slight enough to justify grasping the nettle. "The principal object of the expedition was to draw out supplies for our army," he reminded the War Department after the movement against Suffolk was under way. "I shall confine myself to this unless I find a fair opportunity for something more."

Hill took off first, however, advancing so rapidly from Goldsboro that on March 30 he had Washington invested before the Federal department commander, Major General John G. Foster, had a chance to reinforce its 1200-man garrison. With ten times that many troops on hand, the Confederates would have little trouble keeping the defenders penned up, but Hill did not believe their capture would be worth the casualties he would suffer in an assault. Consequently, while his foragers were busily rounding up hogs and cattle, he continued to hover about the place, making threatening gestures from time to time in the face of highly accurate fire from gunboats anchored off the town. His chief worry was that Foster — one of Burnside's three aggressive brigadiers in last year's smashing attack on Roanoke Island — would order an advance against his rear by the Union force at New Bern, only thirty miles away. As the siege progressed through the first week in April he vibrated with alternate emotions of jubilation and despair, much to the confusion of Longstreet, who scarcely knew what to make of his lieutenant's fluctuant dispatches. "Up to the 2d instant," he replied from Petersburg on April 7, apparently in something of a daze, "you gave me no reason to hope that you could accomplish anything. . . . Then came your letter of the 2d, which was full of encouragement and hope. . . . After your letter of the 2d came one of the 4th, which I believe was more desponding than your previous letters. . . . Your letter of the 5th revives much hope again." Old Peter was understandably confused, but in point of fact Hill was doing much better than he knew or would admit. Not only were large quantities of supplies moving swiftly back to Goldsboro for forwarding to Richmond and the Rappahannock line, but Foster was reacting exactly as the Confederates had hoped he would do to their pretense of great strength and earnestness. Drawing in his horns in expectation of being struck next at almost any point in his department, he left Hill's commissary agents a clear field for exploitation. "I am confident," he warned Halleck on Easter Sunday, "that heavy operations will be necessary in this state, and that the most desperate efforts are and will continue to be made to drive us from the towns now occupied."

At any rate Longstreet's main concern was centered presently on matters closer at hand than Hill's pendulum swings from gloom to elation down on the banks of the Tar. On April 9 — the day Lee recommended an advance into Maryland as the best Confederate strategy for contesting the over-all Union menace, East and West, and also the day Hooker staged the last of the Grand Reviews in honor of Lincoln's Falmouth visit — First Corps troops moved out of their camps near Petersburg and took up the march southeastward in the direction of the

lower Blackwater crossings less than twenty miles from Suffolk, which
the Federals had been fortifying ever since they occupied it formally in
September. Two divisions were quartered there now, under Major General John J. Peck and Brigadier General George W. Getty, with a combined total of 21,108 effectives. Hood, Pickett, and French had 20,192
between them; but Peck, estimating the rebel strength at "40,000 to
60,000 men," reacted much as Foster had done, ten days ago, to Hill's
advance on Washington. Calling in all his detachments from the surrounding countryside, he skirmished briefly along the Blackwater to
gain time for a concentration, then fell back on Suffolk, where he buttoned himself up tightly. While his troops were at work improving the
intrenchments, he notified his superiors at Fort Monroe and Washington that he was prepared to fight to the last man, despite the enemy's
"great preponderance of artillery as well as other branches." Longstreet
moved up deliberately. On April 11 he invested the town, taking the
bluecoats under fire from the opposite bank of the Nansemond River
while extending his right southward all the way to Dismal Swamp. Behind this long, concave front, which he held with a minimum number of
men in order to provide details for his all-important foraging operations,
commissary officers were soon busy purchasing everything in sight that
a man could eat or wear. Long trains of wagons, piled high with goods
and forage, soon were grinding westward amid a din of cracking
whips, ungreased axles, and teamster curses. After unloading at newly
established dumps along the Petersburg & Norfolk Railroad, they returned eastward, rattling empty across the muddy landscape, for new
loads. Day and night, to Longstreet's considerable satisfaction — as well
as to that of the hungry men on the Rappahannock, whose rations improved correspondingly — the shuttle work continued. Supplies appeared inexhaustible in this region scarcely touched by war till now.

Meanwhile, by way of keeping up the bluff, the troops on line
were demonstrating noisily, as if in preparation for an assault on the blue
intrenchments across the way. Although the duty was mostly dull, there
were occasional incidents that provided all the excitement a man could
want, and more. For instance, there was the affair at Fort Huger, an
old Confederate redoubt constructed originally as part of the Suffolk defenses but abandoned by the Federals when they took over. As it turned
out, they showed wisdom by this action. On April 16, French moved
five guns and three companies of infantry into the fort on the far left
of his line, intending to deny enemy gunboats the use of the adjoining
Nansemond River. Three nights later, however, six companies of Connecticut infantry crossed the river, a quarter of a mile upstream, and
swooped down in a surprise attack that captured the works, along with
all five of the guns and 130 officers and men. Joined before dawn by the
other four companies of their regiment, they held the place all the following day and returned to their own lines after dark, taking along the

captured men and guns. Longstreet had scarcely had time to absorb the news of this setback when he heard from Hill that the Washington siege had been abandoned on the same day Fort Huger was occupied by French. Two weeks had sufficed for the removal of most of the stores from the region; so that when, at the end of that span, the Federals succeeded in running in two ships to replenish the supplies of the garrison, Hill decided the time had come for him to withdraw. Back at Goldsboro before the week was out, he praised his troops for their "vigilance on duty and good behavior everywhere." His scorn he reserved for home-guarders, especially those of lofty rank, whose avoidance of combat duty he blamed for his lack of the strength required to drive the detested Yankees not only "into their rat holes at New Bern and Washington," but into Pamlico Sound as well. "And such noble regiments they have," he sneered at these stay-at-home Tarheel warriors. "Three field officers, four staff officers, ten captains, thirty lieutenants, and one private with a misery in his bowels. . . . When our independence is won, the most trifling soldier in the ranks will be more respected, as he is now more respectable, than an army of these skulking exempts."

Longstreet accepted vexation far more philosophically. Even the overrunning of Fort Huger, though it showed, as he said, "a general lack of vigilance and prompt attention to duties," did not arouse his ire. "Many of the officers were of limited experience," he concluded his report of the affair, "and I have no doubt acted as they thought best. I do not know that any of them deserve censure. This lesson, it is hoped, will be of service to us all." Others reacted differently as the Suffolk siege wore on. Hood, for example, had small use for this buttoned-up style of warfare. "Here we are in front of the enemy again," he wrote Lee toward the end of April. "The Yankees have a very strong position, and of course they increase the strength of their position daily. I presume we shall leave here so soon as we gather all the bacon in the country." Boyishly the Kentucky-born Texan added: "When we leave here it is my desire to return to you. If any troops come to the Rappahannock please don't forget me." Thirty-one and a bachelor, Hood was bored. But that could scarcely be said of his fellow division commander Pickett. This thirty-eight-year-old widower, a handsome if rather doll-faced man with long chestnut curls which he anointed regularly with perfume, was in the full flush of a sunset love affair with a southside girl not half his age. LaSalle Corbell was her name; he styled her "the charming Sally" — his dead wife had been called Sally, too — and wrote her ardent letters signed "Your Soldier" despite the fact that he saw her almost nightly, riding up to her home at Chuckatuck by twilight and back to his lines before the first red glow of dawn. When Longstreet at last began to frown on this inattentiveness to duty, not to mention the abuse of horse-flesh, Pickett tried to persuade the corps adjutant, Major G. Moxley Sorrel, to give him permission to take off without Old Peter's knowledge.

Sorrel, who did not approve of what he called "such carpet-knight do-ings in the field," declined to accept the responsibility for what might happen in Pickett's absence, and referred him back to Longstreet. "But he is tired of it and will refuse," the ringleted Virginian protested. "And I must go; I must see her. I swear, Sorrel, I'll be back before anything can happen in the morning." Sorrel still said no; but recalling the scene years later he added that "Pickett went all the same. Nothing could hold him back from that pursuit."

Increasingly, as spring wore on and the end of the campaign drew near — he himself had set a May 3 closing date by notifying Rich-mond on April 19 that two more weeks would suffice for draining the region of its stores — Longstreet grew dissatisfied: not so much with what he had done, which was after all considerable, as with the thought of what he had not done. While it was true that he had carried out, prac-tically to the letter, his difficult triple assignment — that is, he had kept the Yankees out of Petersburg, he had secured enormous quantities of previously inaccessible supplies, and he had kept his First Corps troops on the alert for a swift return to Lee — it was also painfully true that he had accomplished nothing that would compare in tactical brilliance with even the smallest battlefield victory scored by Jackson out in the Valley a year ago. As a result, the taking of Suffolk, along with its thou-sands of bluecoats and tons of matériel, began to appeal to him more and more as a fitting end to these two months of detached service. More-over, as the notion grew more attractive in his mind's eye, it also began to appear more feasible to his military judgment, despite the fact that the Federals inside the place were stronger now, by some 9000 rein-forcements brought in from Hampton Roads, than they had been at the outset. There were several ways of assessing this last, however, and one was that the grandeur of the triumph would be in direct ratio to the plumpness of the prize. Accordingly, Old Peter wrote to Lee, telling him what he had in mind and asking if he could not be sent the rest of his corps in order to assure the success of his assault on the blue intrench-ments. Foreseeing objections — as well he might — he suggested that Lee, if need be, could fall back to the line of the Annas, though it was his own conviction that one corps would be able to stand fast on the Rappa-hannock in the event of an attack. Lee replied on April 27 that Hooker was far too strong, and just now far too active, for him to consider a further weakening of his army. In fact, he countered by asking his lieu-tenant if he could spare him any of the troops in North Carolina. But he certainly did not veto the proposal for ending the southside siege with an assault. "As regards your aggressive movement upon Suffolk," he wrote, "you must act according to your good judgment. If a damaging blow could be struck there or elsewhere of course it would be advan-tageous." He added some doubts as to whether the game would be worth the candle in this case, but Longstreet could see in the letter a relaxation of the urgency for keeping his First Corps divisions practically uncommitted in order to have them ready to hurry north on short notice. Consequently, while his foraging crews kept busy, hauling out the last of the precious wagonloads of hogs and corn and herring, he turned his thoughts to tactical details of the assault that would cap the climax by adding the one element — glory — so far lacking in a campaign already productive of much else.

Three days later, however — April 30 — his plans were shattered by a wire from Adjutant General Cooper in Richmond, quoting a dispatch just received from Lee. Hooker was over the Rappahannock in great strength, above as well as below Fredericksburg, Lee had announced, "and it looks as if he was in earnest." Cooper's instructions to Longstreet were brief and to the point: "Move without delay your command to this place to effect a junction with General Lee."

Longstreet inquired by telegraph whether this meant that he was to abandon his wagons, still scattered about on foraging operations, and risk a quick withdrawal of his men, which would bring out the Federals hot on his heels. By no means, Cooper replied on May Day. What had been intended was for him "to secure all possible dispatch without incurring loss of trains or unnecessary hazard of troops." Having thus avoided going off half-cocked, Old Peter turned to the always difficult task of designing a disengagement. After the wagons had been called in and sent rearward, orders were issued on May 2 for all the troops to withdraw from the intrenchments the following evening and retire westward under cover of darkness, burning bridges and felling trees in their wake to discourage pursuit. This came off on schedule, and after some sharp skirmishing by rear-guard elements, the whole command was across the Blackwater by sundown of the 4th. Leaving French to defend that line, Hood and Pickett moved to Petersburg next day. Dawn of the 6th found them on the march for the James, leg-weary but eager, and Longstreet himself was in Richmond before noon, making preparations to speed both divisions northward by rail for a share in the great battle reportedly still raging along the near bank of the Rappahannock. All this ended the following day, however, when he received a wire from Lee: "The emergency that made your presence so desirable has passed for the present, so far as I can see, and I desire that you will not distress your troops by a forced movement to join me, or sacrifice for that purpose any public interest that your sudden departure might make it necessary to abandon."

✕ 4 ✕

"Go forward, and give us victories," Lincoln had written, and that was what Hooker had in mind when he crossed the Rappahannock. Nor was that all. "I not only expected victory," he would recall when the smoke had cleared, "I expected to get the whole [rebel] army." That this had indeed been his intention was confirmed by his chief of staff, who also declared in retrospect that the real purpose of the campaign had been "to destroy the army of General Lee where it then was." Earlier, on the eve of committing what he called "the finest body of soldiers the sun ever shone on," Fighting Joe had expressed his resolution in terms that were even more expansive. "My plans are perfect," he announced, "and when I start to carry them out, may God have mercy on Bobby Lee; for I shall have none."

Just what those plans were he was not saying, even to those whose task it would be to translate them into action. In point of fact, however, they were influenced considerably by the man who had preceded him in command. In addition to having demonstrated the folly of launching headlong attacks against prepared intrenchments — intrenchments which, incidentally, had been enormously strengthened and extended since December — Burnside had explored, at least on paper, several other approaches to the problem of how to prise the rebels loose from their works and come to grips with them in the open, where the advantage of numbers would be likely to decide the issue in favor of the Union. Now he had departed, taking "his deportment with him out of the Army of the Potomac, thank God," but Hooker could remember how the lush-whiskered general had stressed the need for secrecy and then proceeded to talk with all and sundry about his plans, with the result that his opponent's only surprise had been at his foolhardiness. So the new commander, who, by ordinary, was anything but a close-mouthed man, profited in reverse from his predecessor's example. He kept his plans to himself.

Not that he did not have any; he did, indeed, and he did not care who knew it, so long as the particulars remained hidden. These too had been inherited, however, for the most part. Originally, like Burnside on the eve of his bloody mid-December commitment, Hooker had planned to cross the Rappahannock well below Fredericksburg; but this had two serious disadvantages. It would uncover the direct route to Washington, which he knew would distress Lincoln, and it would have to be announced to the Confederates in advance by the laying of pontoons. Upstream, on the other hand, the river narrowed and was comparatively shallow. There were fords in that direction — Banks Ford, five miles above the town, and United States Ford, seven miles farther west — behind which he could mass and conceal his troops in order to send them splashing across in a rush that would smother the south-bank gray outpost detachments, thus forcing Lee to face about and meet his assailants without the advantage of those formidable intrenchments. This had been Burnside's intention in the campaign that ground to a soggy halt in January, but Hooker, by waiting for the advent of fair weather, had greatly

reduced the likelihood of the movement's coming to any such premature and ignominious end. Besides, there would be tactical embellish-
ments, designed to increase the Federal chances for an all-out victory.

Principal among these was a plan for taking advantage of the recently demonstrated improvement of the blue cavalry. With Stoneman
outnumbering Stuart better than three to one — just over 11,500 sabers
opposed to just under 3500 — it was Hooker's belief that if his troopers
crossed the river in strength they would be able to have things pretty
much their own way in the Confederate rear. Damage to Lee's communications and supply lines, coupled with strikes at such vital points as
Gordonsville and Hanover Junction, might throw him into sudden retreat; in which case the Federal infantry, coming down on the run from
the upstream crossings, would catch him in flight, strung out on the
roads leading southward, and destroy him. No one so far in this war had
been able to throw Lee into such a panic, it was true, but the reason for
this might be that no one had dared to touch him where he was tender.
At any rate Hooker thought it worth a try, and he had his adjutant general draw up careful instructions for Stoneman. His entire corps, less one
brigade but accompanied by all 22 of its guns, was to cross Rappahannock Bridge, thirty miles above Fredericksburg, not later than 7 a.m.
on April 13, "for the purpose of turning the enemy's position on his left,
throwing the cavalry between him and Richmond, isolating him from his
supplies, checking his retreat, and inflicting on him every possible injury
which will tend to his discomfiture and defeat." Lest there be any doubt
that the cavalry chief was to be vigorous in his treatment of the fleeing
Lee, the adjutant then broke into what might one day have become the
model for a pregame Rockne pep talk: "If you cannot cut off from his
column large slices, the general desires that you will not fail to take small
ones. Let your watchword be fight, fight, fight, bearing in mind that
time is as valuable to the general as rebel carcasses."

Stoneman and his 10,000 chosen troopers, along with their 22
guns and a train of 275 wagons containing enough additional food and
forage to sustain them for nine days beyond the lines, were poised for a
crossing at the specified hour. One brigade had already forded the river
a few miles above Rappahannock Bridge, with instructions to come
sweeping down and clear out the rebel horsemen watching from across
the way. But as the three divisions stood to their mounts, awaiting the
order that would send them about their task of cutting slices large and
small from Lee's retreating column, rain began to patter and then to
drum, ominously reminiscent of the downpour that had queered the
Mud March. Now as then, roads became quagmires and the river began
to swell, flooding the fords and tugging at the shaky pilings of the
bridge. Stoneman decided to wait it out. Recalling the brigade that had
crossed, he wired headquarters that his rolling stock was stalled. Hooker
replied that he was to shuck his guns and wagons and proceed without

them. Stoneman said he would, and set dawn of the 15th as his new jump-off time. Then the wire went dead. Hooker, having promised to keep the President posted on the progress of the movement, struck an optimistic note in a dispatch sent to Washington on that date: "I am rejoiced that Stoneman had two good days to go up the river, and was able to cross it before it had become too much swollen. If he can reach his position [deep in the enemy rear] the storm and mud will not damage our prospects." Lincoln was not so sure. It was his belief, he replied within the hour, that "General S. is not moving rapidly enough to make the expedition come to anything. He has now been out three days, two of which were unusually fair weather, and all three without hindrance from the enemy, and yet he is not 25 miles from where he started. To reach his point he still has 60 to go, another river (the Rapidan) to cross, and will be hindered by the enemy. By arithmetic, how many days will it take him to do it? . . . I greatly fear it is another failure already."

His fears were confirmed the following day when a courier reached Falmouth with a letter from upstream. "I cannot say what has been the state of affairs away from this vicinity," Stoneman wrote, "but here, at the hour of my last dispatch, the condition of things may be judged of when I tell you that almost every rivulet was swimming, and the roads next to impassable for horses or pack-mules. . . . The railroad bridge has been partly carried away by the freshet. The river is out of its banks, and was still on the rise a few hours ago. . . . My dispatch [setting a new date for the crossing] was based upon the expectation that we were to be favored with a continuation of fair weather. It certainly was not predicated upon the expectation of being overtaken by one of the most violent rainstorms I have ever been caught in." There was much else by way of explanation and excuse, including the news that three men and several horses had been drowned that morning while attempting to cross what had been a nearly dry stream bed the day before. But the gist of the long letter came about midway: "The elements seem to have conspired to prevent the accomplishment of a brilliant cavalry operation."

Hooker was disappointed. He told Stoneman to stay where he was, keep up his reserve supply of rations, and be ready to take off southward "as soon as the roads and rivers will permit." However, the rain showed no sign of a real letup. For nearly two weeks it kept falling, with only a few fair days mixed in to mock the army's immobility, and all this time Hooker was champing at the bit, anxious to put his troops in motion for the kill. As the days went by, his bitterness increased. He began to doubt that Stoneman and the cavalry were up to carrying out the mission he had assigned them; he began, in fact, to see room for improvement in the plans he had called perfect. Since he had the Confederates outnumbered better than two to one — as he knew by reports from the excellent intelligence service he had established as part of his staff — he had a rare chance to attack them, front and back, with separate columns each of which would be superior to the gray mass clamped between them. Instead of 10,000 cavalry, he would put 60,000 infantry and artillery in Lee's immediate rear, blocking his retreat while the other 60,000 pounded his front and the troopers far in his rear slashed at his lines of supply and communication. Isolated and surrounded, prised out of his intrenchments and grievously outnumbered, Lee would be pulverized; Hooker would "get the whole army." It was a pleasant thing to contemplate, not only because of its classic tactical simplicity, but also because it would involve what might be called poetic justice, a turning of the tables on the old fox who so often had divided his own army, but without the advantage of numbers, in hopes of destroying the very soldiers who now were about to destroy him.

What was more, as Hooker pored over his maps to plan the logistical details of the proposed envelopment, he found that the terrain seemed made to order for just such a maneuver. Banks Ford was stoutly defended from across the way, the rebels having honeycombed the dominant south-bank heights with trenches that formed the left-flank anchor of their line, and U. S. Ford was guarded nearly as heavily by an intrenched outpost detachment; besides which, the recent rains had swollen them both well past wading depth, so that his previous design to seize them in a sudden, splashing rush was now impractical. On the other hand Kelly's Ford, fifteen miles above the junction of the Rappannock and the Rapidan, which occurred just over a mile above U. S. Ford, was lightly held, unfortified, and comparatively shallow. Although crossing there would call for a long approach march and would involve another river crossing when the column reached the Rapidan, the advantages greatly outweighed the drawbacks. For one thing, Kelly's Ford was far enough out beyond the enemy flank to give hope that, with luck, the march and perhaps both crossings could be accomplished before the rebs knew what was afoot, and for another it would afford a covered approach, along excellent roads traversing a wooded region known locally as the Wilderness, to within striking distance of the Confederate rear. Moreover, as the column moved eastward along the south bank of the Rappahannock it would uncover both U.S. and Banks Fords, which would not only shorten considerably its lines of supply and communication, thereby making it possible for the two halves of the blue army to reinforce each other quickly if an emergency arose in either direction, but would also give the flankers, in the case of the Banks Ford defenses, control of high ground that dominated much of the present rebel line of fortifications; Lee would be obliged to come out into the open, whether he wanted to or not. All this sounded fine to Hooker. Admittedly he was about to engage in the risky business of dividing his army in the presence of the enemy, but Lee had proved on more than one occasion that the profits more than justified the risk, even though he had done so with the numerical odds against him; whereas with Hooker it would be the other way around. It was this last that gave him substantial reason to hope for the Cannae which so far, and for all his vaunted skill in battle, had eluded Lee.

Translating theory into action, Fighting Joe sent orders on April 26 for the corps of Slocum, Howard, and Meade to march for Kelly's Ford at sunrise the following morning. They were to be in position there not later than 4 p.m. of the 28th, at which time they were to head south for the Rapidan, cross that river at Ely's and Germanna Fords, and take the roads leading southeast to the Orange Turnpike, then proceed due east along it to a position covering a crossroads hamlet called Chancellorsville, eight miles west of Lee's line and less than half that far from the ragged eastern rim of the Wilderness. Couch — minus Gibbon's division, which could not be moved just yet because its Falmouth camp was in plain view of the enemy on Marye's Heights — was to march at dawn of the 29th to a position in the rear of Banks Ford and stand ready to throw pontoons for a crossing as soon as Slocum's advance flanked the rebels out of the trenches across the way. Meanwhile, with 60,000 Federal soldiers marching against the Confederate rear, the corps of Sedgwick, Reynolds, and Sickles, aggregating another 60,000, would move down to the riverbank south of Fredericksburg, near the point of Frank-

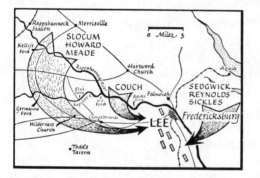

lin's crossing in December, where they would establish a west-bank bridgehead on the 29th for the purpose of demonstrating against Lee's front, thus distracting his attention from what would be going on behind him and keeping him in doubt as to where the heaviest blow would fall. Stoneman would add to the confusion by

striking first at the Virginia Central Railroad, then eastward along it to the Richmond, Fredericksburg & Potomac, where he was to harass and slow down the gray army if it attempted to escape the jaws of the blue vise by falling back on its threatened capital. Still mindful of the need for secrecy, Hooker enjoined the generals with the upstream column to regard the "destination of their commands as strictly confidential." Apparently his left hand was to be kept from knowing what his right hand was about, but he lifted the veil a little by telling Sedgwick, who was in charge of the downstream column, to carry the enemy works "at all hazards" in case Lee detached "a considerable part of his force against the troops operating . . . west of Fredericksburg." Whether the main attack would be delivered against the enemy's front or his rear — that is, by Sedgwick's 60,000 or by Slocum's — remained to be seen. At the critical moment, probably on the 30th but certainly by May Day, Hooker would ride to Chancellorsville, make his estimate of the situation, and then, like an ambidextrous boxer, swing with either hand for the knockout.

The upstream march began on schedule Monday, April 27, despite a slow drizzle that threatened to undo the good which three days of fair weather had done the roads. Slogging toward Hartwood Church and Morrisville, where they would turn off south for Kelly's Ford, the veterans chanted as they trudged:

> *"The Union boys are moving on the left and on the right,*
> *The bugle call is sounding, our shelters we must strike;*
> *Joe Hooker is our leader, he takes his whiskey strong,*
> *So our knapsacks we will sling, and go marching along."*

Sweating under fifty to sixty pounds of weight, which included eight days' rations, a pair of blankets, a thick wool overcoat, and forty rounds of ammunition each, they interpreted the word "sling" as they saw fit, shedding knapsacks by the roadside to be gleaned by civilian scavengers — "ready finders," the army called them — who moved in their wake and profited from their prodigality. Hooker's administrative sensibilities were offended by the waste, but he was consoled by the fact that the march was otherwise orderly and rapid in spite of the showers, which fortunately left off before midday without softening the roads. In response to a wire that afternoon from a fretful Lincoln — "How does it look now?" — he managed to be at once reticent and reassuring: "I am not sufficiently advanced to give an opinion. We are busy. Will tell you all soon as I can, and have it satisfactory." Riding next day up to Morrisville, through rain that had come on again to slow the march and throw it several hours behind schedule, he was pleased all the same to note that the column had turned south for the Rappahannock, and he sent an aide ahead with a message urging Slocum to make up for lost time: "The general desires that not a moment be lost until our troops are established at or near Chancellorsville. From that moment all will be ours."

He sounded buoyant, and presently he had cause for feeling even more so. By dusk the head of the flanking column was approaching Kelly's Ford, and Hooker received word from his chief of staff at Falmouth that Couch had his two divisions in position behind Banks Ford, as ordered, and was improving the waiting time by extending the telegraph to U.S. Ford, in case that proved to be a better point for crossing. Sedgwick had been delayed by the rain, Butterfield added, but he had his three corps on the march and would begin throwing five pontoon bridges across the river below Fredericksburg on schedule in the morning. Moreover, though the weather had been too gusty to permit spy-glass observation from the bobbing gondolas of Professor T. S. C. Lowe's two balloons, the ruse of leaving Gibbon's division in its exposed camp seemed to have worked as intended; Lowe reported that, from what he could see, the Confederate trenches "appeared to be occupied as usual," indicating that Lee almost certainly had no intimation that the various Federal columns were on the move for positions from which to accomplish his destruction. All this was about as encouraging as could be, but Hooker, being painfully familiar with the tricks of the old fox across the way, was leaving as little as possible to chance. He wired Lowe to send a balloon up anyhow, despite the wind and darkness, "to see where the enemy's campfires are," not forgetting to add: "Someone acquainted with the position and location of the ground and of the enemy's forces should go up."

By the time the Professor — the title was complimentary; his official designation was "Chief of Aeronauts, Army of the Potomac," and his basic uniform was a voluminous linen duster — got a balloon up into the windy night for a look at the rebel campfires, Howard's corps was over the Rappahannock, crossing dry-shod on a pontoon bridge just completed by the engineers, and had taken up a position on the south bank to guard against a surprise attack while the other two corps were crossing. Slocum came over at dawn, followed by Meade, who struck out southeastward for Ely's Ford; then Howard fell in behind Slocum, who had already headed south for Germanna Ford. Behind all three came Stoneman, a full day late and complaining bitterly that the alert order had not allowed him time to call in his 10,000 horsemen from their camps around Warrenton. He set out for Raccoon Ford, ten miles west of Germanna, for a descent on the Virginia Central in the vicinity of Louisa Courthouse, leaving Hooker a single 1000-man brigade of three slim regiments to accompany the infantry on the march and another 500 troopers to guard the deserted north-bank camps and installations. The foot soldiers pushed ahead, stepping fast but warily now; for it was here in the V of the rivers that Pope, for all his bluster, had nearly come to grief in August. Neither column encountered any real difficulty, however, in the course of its daylong hike to the Rapidan. Nor did Slocum's run into much trouble after it got there. His advance guard, splashing its way through the chest-deep water, surprised a drowsy 100-man rebel detachment at Germanna, capturing a number of graybacks before they knew what was upon them. Finding timbers collected here on the south bank for the construction of a bridge, the jubilant bluecoats set to work and put them to use in short order, with the result that the rest of their corps, and all of Howard's, made a second river crossing without having to wet their socks.

Meade's troops had no such luck. Though he too encountered no opposition in the V, his march to Ely's was longer than Slocum's to Germanna, and he found no bridge materials awaiting him at its end.

Coming down to the ford at sunset the advance guard plunged across the cold, swift-running Rapidan, chased off the startled pickets on the opposite bank, and set to work building fires to light the way for the rest of the corps approaching the crossing in the dusk. Regiment by regiment the three road-worn divisions entered the foam-flecked, scrotum-tightening water and emerged to toil up the steep south bank, which became increasingly slippery as the slope was churned to gumbo by the passage of nearly 16,000 soldiers, all dripping wet from the armpits down. Once across, they gathered about the fires for warmth, some in good spirits, some in bad, each arriving cluster somewhat muddier than the one before, but all about equally wet and cold. By midnight the last man was over. Low in the east, the late-risen moon, burgeoning toward the full, had the bruised-orange color of old gold, and while all around them the whippoorwills sang plaintively in the moon-drenched woods, the men lay rolled in their blankets, feet to the fire, catching snatches of sleep while awaiting the word to fall back into column. Meade had them on the go again by sunup of the last day of April, still marching southeast, but now through an eerie and seemingly God-forsaken region; the Wilderness, it was called, and they could see why. Mostly a tangle of second-growth scrub oak and pine, choked with vines and brambles that would tear the clothes from a man's back within minutes of the time he left the road, it was interrupted briefly at scattered points by occasional small clearings whose abandoned cabins and sag-roofed barns gave proof, if such was needed, that no amount of hard work could scratch a living from this jungle. To make matters worse, rebel cavalry slashed at the column from time to time, emerging suddenly from ambush, then back again, apparently for the purpose of taking prisoners who would identify their units. Meade did not like the look of things any better than the men did. He rode with the van and set a rapid pace, wanting to get them out of here, and for once they were altogether willing. Chancellorsville was less than half a dozen miles from the ford, and though it was still a good three miles short of open country where he could deploy his troops and bring his guns to bear, he remembered that Hooker had said that once the flankers were "established" in that vicinity, "all will be ours."

Arriving about an hour before noon, still without having encountered anything more than token resistance from the enemy cavalry and none at all from the famed, hard-marching rebel infantry, he found that for all its grand-sounding name the crossroads hamlet — if it could be called even that — consisted of nothing more than a large, multi-chimneyed brick-and-timber mansion, with tall slim pillars across its front supporting a double-decked veranda, and three or four outbuildings scattered about the quadrants of the turnpike intersection. There was, however, a hundred-acre clearing, which seemed expansive indeed after what he had just emerged from and would re-enter when he moved on, and there were also four ladies, of various ages and in bright spring dresses, who likewise were a relief of sorts despite their show of pique at having to receive unwelcome guests. At any rate, Meade's spirits rose as he waited for Slocum and Howard, whose troops had the longer march today. Much that he previously had not understood, mainly because of Hooker's refusal to give out details of his plan — "It's all right" had been his usual and evasive reply to questions from commanders of all ranks — suddenly became much clearer to Meade, now that he was within a half-day's march of Lee's rear without its having cost him anything more than the handful of men gobbled up by the graybacks in the course of his plunge through the heart of the Wilderness. Now that he believed he saw the whole design, his dourness gave way to something approaching exaltation. By 2 o'clock, when Slocum arrived at the head of his two-corps column, Meade was fairly beside himself. "This is splendid, Slocum," he cried, displaying an exuberance that seemed all the more abandoned because it was so unlike him; "hurrah for Old Joe! We are on Lee's flank and he doesn't know it."

What he wanted now, he added with no slackening of enthusiasm, was to push on eastward without further delay, at least another couple of miles before nightfall, "and we'll get out of this Wilderness." Slocum felt much the same way about it. But while they talked a courier arrived with a dispatch signed by Butterfield, relaying an order from Hooker: "The general directs that no advance be made from Chancellorsville until the columns are concentrated. He expects to be at Chancellorsville tonight."

Somewhat crestfallen, and nearly as puzzled now as he had been before he saw what he had believed was the light, Meade went about the business of getting his troops into bivouac. Slocum and Howard were doing the same when presently, at about 4.30 and true to his word, Fighting Joe himself came riding up on his big white horse, cheered lustily by the men along the roadside, and explained the logic behind the restraining order. The easterly advance along the turnpike had already flanked the rebels out of their U.S. Ford defenses, permitting Couch to sidle upstream for a crossing there instead of at Banks Ford, where the defenders were still in occupation; he was on the march for Chancellorsville even now, and Gibbon had been alerted to join him from Falmouth with his third division. This would put four whole corps in the Confederate rear, as had been intended from the start, but the northern commander had it in mind to do even more by way of cinching the victory already within reach. Sedgwick's bridgehead having been established across the river below Fredericksburg with a minimal resistance from the rebels on the heights — who thus were clamped securely between two superior Union forces which now could reinforce each other, rapidly and at will, by way of U.S. Ford — Hooker had decided to summon Sickles from the left to add the weight of his corps to the blow about to be delivered against the more vulnerable enemy rear. His arrival to-night or tomorrow morning would bring the striking force up to a strength of 77,865 effectives within the five corps. With three regiments of cavalry added, along with several batteries detached from the artillery reserve, engineer troops, and headquarters personnel, the total would reach about 80,000 of all arms, who then could be flung in mass against Lee's rear to accomplish his destruction with a single May Day blow.

Meade was considerably reassured; he saw in fact, or believed he saw, a brighter light than ever. A rare attention to detail — pontoons in place on time, road space properly allotted to columns on the march, surprise achieved through ruse and secrecy — had made possible, at practically no cost at all, one of the finest maneuvers in military history. Now this same attentiveness, with regard to the massing of troops for the ultimate thrust, would also make possible one of the grandest victories. Sure enough, Couch arrived before nightfall and went into bivouac a mile north of the crossroads; Sickles sent word that he was on the way. Once more careful planning had paid off. A New York *Herald* correspondent who had accompanied the flankers shared the pervading optimism. "It is rumored that the enemy are falling back toward Richmond," he wrote, "but a fight tomorrow seems more than probable. We expect it, and we also expect to be victorious." Hooker expected it, too, because he knew the rumor to be untrue. Sedgwick, from his low-lying, close-up position south of Fredericksburg, and Professor Lowe, from the gondola of one of his big yellow balloons riding high over Stafford Heights, had both assured him that the Confederates still occupied the ridge beyond the town. Reynolds, in fact, had reported to headquarters this afternoon that he believed some of the troops in his front had just arrived from Richmond: which brought the reply, "General Hooker hopes they are from Richmond, as the greater will be our success."

His spirits were high, and so were those of his men, who cheered him to the echo, especially when a congratulatory order was read to them that evening in their camps around Chancellorsville: "It is with heartfelt satisfaction that the commanding general announces to the army that the operations of the last three days have determined that our enemy must either ingloriously fly, or come out from behind his defenses and give us battle on our own ground, where certain destruction awaits him."

★ ★ ★

Battle on his "own ground" — setting aside for the moment the question of whether any part of the Old Dominion could ever properly be so termed in relation to the man Lee called Mr F. J. Hooker — was exactly what Stonewall Jackson had been aching to give him for the past three months. "We must make this campaign an exceedingly active one," the Virginian declared as spring approached. "Only thus can a weaker country cope with a stronger. It must make up in activity what it lacks in strength." Fredericksburg, for all its one-sided tactical brilliance, had been a strategic disappointment to him, and he hoped to compensate for this in the great battle he knew would be fought as soon as the Federals decided the time had come for them to attempt another Rappahannock crossing. "My trust is in God," he said quietly, seated one day in his tent and musing on the future. But then, anticipating the hour when the blue host would venture within his reach, his patience broke its bounds and he rose bristling from his chair, eyes aglow. "I wish they would come!" he cried.

These past three months had been perhaps the happiest of his military life. In fact, despite his eagerness to interrupt any or all of them with bloodshed, February, March, and April, following as they did his thirty-ninth birthday in late January, had been idyllic, at least by Jacksonian standards. Aside from administrative concerns, such as the usual spate of court-martials and the preparation of battle reports, grievously neglected up to now because he had been too busy fighting to find time for writing — the total was fourteen full-scale battles in the previous eight months, with the reduction and capture of Harpers Ferry added for good measure — his principal occupation was prayer and meditation, relieved from time to time by evenings of unaccustomed social pleasure. His quarters, an office cottage on the grounds of a Moss Neck estate, were comfortable to the point of lavishness, which prompted Jeb Stuart to express mock horror at the erstwhile Presbyterian deacon's evident fall from spirituality, and Lee himself, in the course of a particularly fine meal featuring oysters, turkey, and a waiter decked out in a fresh white apron, taunted the high-ranking guests and their host with the remark that they were merely playing at being soldiers; they should come and dine with him, he said, if they wanted to see how a real soldier lived. Stonewall took the raillery and the chiding in good part, at once flustered and delighted. But the best of the idyl came at its close. The last nine days, beginning April 20, were spent with the wife he had not seen in just over a year and the five-month-old daughter he had never seen at all.

He had moved by then, back into his tent near Hamilton's Crossing, which did much to reduce the Calvinistic twinges. "It is rather a relief," he said, "to get where there will be less comfort in a room." But for the occasion of the long-anticipated visit he accepted the hospitality of the Yerby house, in which Lee had stayed for a time under doctor's orders, and was given a large room, with no less than three beds, where he could be alone with his wife and get to know the baby. Outside duty hours, the couple took walks in the woods and along the heights overlooking the Fredericksburg plain whose December scars were beginning to be grassed over. It was the happiest of times for them both. The days went by in a rush, however, for there in full view across the way were the enemy guns and the yellow observation balloons, reminders that the idyl was likely to have a sudden end. And so it was. Dawn, Wednesday, April 29; booted feet on the stairs and a knock at the bedroom door; "That looks as if Hooker were crossing," Jackson said. He drew on some clothes and went out, was gone ten minutes, and then returned to finish dressing. The visit was over, he told Anna as he buckled on his sword. He would come back if he could, but if he could not he would send an aide to see her to the train. After a last embrace, and a last long look at the baby, he was gone. Presently the staff chaplain arrived to tell her the general would not be coming back. While she was packing she began hearing the rattle of musketry from down by the river. It grew louder behind her, all the way to Guiney Station, where she boarded an almost empty train for Richmond.

Lee expressed even less surprise when an aide sent by Jackson came into his tent before sunup to give him the news. Still abed, Lee said teasingly: "Captain, what do you young men mean by waking a man out of his sleep?" Hooker had thrown his pontoons near the site of the lower December crossing, the aide replied; he was over the river in force. "Well, I thought I heard firing," Lee said, "and I was beginning to think it was time some of you young fellows were coming to tell me what it was all about. You want me to send a message to your good general, Captain? Tell him that I am sure he knows what to do. I will meet him at the front very soon."

Shortly afterwards, peering through rifts in the early morning fog, he saw for himself that the Federals had one bridge down and others under construction, all near the point now known as Franklin's Crossing, just over a mile below the town. They did not attempt an advance across the plain, but seemed content to stay within their bridgehead, at least for the present, covered by the long-range guns on Stafford Heights. Resisting the temptation to attack while the build-up was in progress, Lee decided to make his defense along the ridge, as he had done in December. Accordingly, he told Jackson to bring up the rest of his corps from below, and ordered the reserve artillery to leave its rearward camps and move forward into line. In notifying Richmond of these developments, although he knew it was unlikely that the two detached divisions would arrive in time for a share in the battle now shaping up, he requested that Longstreet be alerted for a return from Suffolk as soon as possible. Before noon, the situation was complicated by a dispatch from Stuart, informing Lee that a blue force of about 14,000 infantry and six guns had crossed at Kelly's Ford and appeared to be headed for Gordonsville. This was corrected a few hours later, however, when the cavalry commander sent word that the enemy column had turned in the direction of Ely's and Germanna Fords; so far, Jeb added, he had taken prisoners from three different Union corps, though he did not say whether he

thought all three were present in full strength. In reaction, Lee sent instructions for Stuart to move eastward at once and thus avoid being cut
off from headquarters. This would leave the Federal cavalry free to
operate practically unmolested against his lines of supply; yet, bad as
that was, it was by no means as bad as having to fight blind when he and
the greatly superior Federal main body came within grappling distance
of each other, here on Marye's Heights or elsewhere. Just after sundown
a third courier arrived to report the bluecoats across both Rapidan fords.
Though Lee still had no reliable information as to the strength of this
flanking column, it was clear by now that some part of Hooker's
army — a considerable part, for all he knew — was in the Confederate
rear and moving closer, hour by hour. Whatever its strength, the threat
it offered was too grave to be ignored. Nor did he ignore it. Two brigades of Richard Anderson's division were already at U.S. Ford;
Lee instructed him to draw them in and move the others rearward to
meet them in the vicinity of Chancellorsville, where the roads leading
south and east from Ely's and Germanna Fords came together, "taking
the strongest line you can and holding it to the best advantage." To Mc-
Laws, who commanded Longstreet's other remaining division, went orders alerting him for a possible westward march, in case it turned out
that Anderson was not strong enough to stop the blue columns last reported to be moving in his direction. Anderson pulled out of the line
at 9 o'clock, and after a three-hour march through driving rain informed
headquarters that his division was concentrated near Chancellorsville by
midnight. Knowing that his rear was protected at least to this extent, Lee
turned in to rest for tomorrow.

Morning of the 30th disclosed a total of five bridges spanning the
river below Fredericksburg. Though the bluecoats had enlarged their
west-bank foothold, they showed no disposition to advance. In fact,
they were intrenching their perimeter — as if in expectation, not of delivering, but of receiving an attack. Jackson, for one, was eager to give
it to them, whereas Lee preferred to draw them farther away from their
heavy guns on Stafford Heights. Both men thus reacted as they had
done to the similar situation in December; but this time Lee offered to
defer to his lieutenant's judgment. "If you think you can effect anything," he said, "I will give orders for the attack." While Stonewall went
about conducting a more thorough examination of the bridgehead, preparatory to moving against it, Lee received another cavalry report that
the Federals were advancing eastward from Germanna Ford, along the
Orange Turnpike, while a substantial train of wagons and artillery was
across Ely's Ford with a heavy infantry escort, following in the wake of
the column that had crossed at that point the night before. A little later
— it was now past noon — Anderson sent word that he had taken up a
good defensive position east of Chancellorsville, along the near fringe of
the Wilderness, and was preparing to resist the blue advance. So far, all

he had seen of the enemy were cavalry outriders, he added, but he thought he was going to need support when the infantry came up. Lee replied at 2.30 that Anderson was to dig in where he was, providing hasty fortifications not only for his own division but also for McLaws', which was on call to join him in case it was needed. "Set all your spades to work as vigorously as possible," Lee urged, and sent him some engineers to assist in drawing his line, as well as a battalion of artillery from the reserve. Then he turned back to see how Jackson was doing.

The fact was, Jackson was not doing so well, at least by his own interpretation. A careful reconnaissance had shown the enemy bridgehead to be stronger than he had supposed; he regretfully admitted that an assault would be unwise. Lee took out his binoculars for a better look at the bluecoats massed on the plain below and on the heights beyond the river. He took his time, evaluating reports while he peered. There was by now much disagreement among his officers as to whether Hooker was planning to deliver his heaviest blow from upstream or down. Presently, however, Lee returned the glasses to their case and snapped it shut with a decisive gesture. "The main attack will come from above," he said.

Having made this estimate of the situation he proceeded to act on it with an urgency required by the fact that a farther advance by the Federals approaching his rear would put them between him and Richmond, in which case he would have no choice except to retreat. He might have to do so anyhow, under the menace of Hooker's skillful combinations, but he was determined, now as always, to yield no ground he saw any chance of holding. His decision, then — announced in orders which he retired to his tent to write and issue soon after nightfall — was to turn on the rearward Union column with a preponderance of his badly outnumbered army, leaving a skeleton force to defend his present position against a possible frontal assault by the blue mass on the plain. Early's division of Jackson's corps drew the latter assignment, reinforced by a brigade from McLaws, whose other three brigades were to proceed at once to join Anderson in the intrenchments he was digging four miles east of Chancellorsville. Jackson was to follow McLaws with his remaining three divisions "at daylight tomorrow morning . . . and make arrangements to repulse the enemy." This would give Lee a total of 45,000 troops, plus Stuart when he came up, to block the path of the enemy columns moving eastward through the Wilderness, and barely 10,000, including the artillery reserve, to hold the Fredericksburg ridge, which by tomorrow would have become his rear. The risks were great, but perhaps no greater than the odds that led him to accept them. At any rate, if it came to a simultaneous fight in both directions, he would have the advantage of interior lines, even though he would have gained it by inviting annihilation.

McLaws pulled back at midnight, leaving Barksdale's Mississippians behind for a possible repetition of their mid-December exploit. Early spread his lone division all up and down the five-mile stretch of in-trenchments from Marye's Heights to Hamilton's Crossing, mindful of Lee's admonition that he was to keep up a bristling pretense of strength and aggressive intentions. Jackson, told to move at daylight, was on the march by 3 a.m. Riding ahead of his troops he arrived soon after sunrise at Tabernacle Church, the left-flank anchor of Anderson's newly estab-lished line, which McLaws was busy extending northward to the vicinity of Duerson's Mill, covering Banks Ford. His instructions were to "make arrangements to repulse the enemy," and to Stonewall this meant, quite simply, to attack him. If he had no orders to proceed beyond this point, neither did he have any to remain here. Besides, there was no enemy in sight except an occasional scampering blue horseman in brief silhouette against the verdant background of the Wilderness. Before he could re-pulse the enemy he would have to find him, and the obvious way to find him would be to go where he was — reportedly, four miles dead ahead at Chancellorsville. So he told Anderson and McLaws to leave off digging and get their men in motion. He would go forward with them. If they ran into trouble up ahead, and it was clear by now that trouble was what they definitely were going to find in that direction, his three divisions would soon be up to lend support.

It was about 11 o'clock of a fine May Day morning by the time they got their troops into march formation and set out, preceded by clouds of skirmishers. The advance was by two main roads, the turn-pike on the right and the plank road on the left; McLaws took the former, Anderson the latter, accompanied by Jackson himself. Almost as soon as they entered the green hug of the Wilderness, McLaws made contact with the enemy advancing on the turnpike. At 11.20 the first gun of the meeting engagement boomed. Then others began to roar in that direction. Jackson's instructions were for both divisions to keep pushing west until they ran into something solid. Presently he received a dispatch from Stuart, who was near at hand. "I will close in on the flank," Jeb wrote, "and will help all I can when the ball opens. . . . May God grant us victory." Stonewall replied, "I trust that God will grant us a great victory." But he added, by way of showing what he had in mind to reinforce his trust: "Keep closed on Chancellorsville."

★   ★   ★

Hooker too had started forward at 11 o'clock, so that the meeting engagement occurred about midway between Chancellorsville and Tab-ernacle Church. Sickles having come up that morning, the northern com-mander was set to throw a five-corps Sunday punch. This was no time for wild blows, however, and he made his preparations with the same concern for detail as before. Slocum would advance along the plank road on the right, supported by Howard; Meade would take the left, along the turnpike, supported by Couch; Sickles would remain in general reserve, on call to add the extra weight that might be needed in either direction. Nor was Fighting Joe committing the amateur's gaffe of forgetting he had another hand to box with. Orders had gone the previous evening to Sedgwick: "It is not known, of course, what effect the advance will have upon the enemy, and the general commanding directs that you observe [Lee's] movements with the utmost vigilance, and, should he expose a weak point, attack him in full force and destroy him." This was made even more specific by instructions sent to Sedgwick as the advance got under way. No matter whether the rebels weakened their Fredericksburg line or not, he was "to threaten an attack in full force at 1 o'clock and to continue in that attitude until further orders. Let the demonstration be as severe as can be," Hooker added, "but not an attack," unless of course the enemy afforded a real opening, in which case the earlier instructions would obtain and Sedgwick would go for a left-hand knockout.

Slocum and Meade stepped off smartly, much encouraged by a circular prescribing the order of march and closing: "After the movement commences, headquarters will be at Tabernacle Church." It sounded as if Hooker meant business this time. Also it made considerable tactical sense, for the turnpike and the plank road, after branching off from one another at Chancellorsville, converged near that objective. Out of the woods at last, the two lead corps would be concentrated for the final lunge, supported by Howard, Couch, and Sickles, who would follow close behind. For more than half the distance, however, these two main Wilderness arteries diverged: with the result that as the two columns moved eastward, hemmed in by the dense jungle of stunted trees and brambly underbrush, they lost contact with each other. As an additional complication, Meade had one division on the pike and two on the River Road, which curved northward to outflank the rebel intrenchments at Banks Ford; so that here, too, contact was quickly lost. Two miles from its crossroads starting point, out of touch with Slocum on the right and the rest of its own corps on the left, the division on the turnpike came under fire from enemy skirmishers as it plodded up a long slope whose crest would bring the eastern rim of the Wilderness in view. It so happened that this division, commanded by Major General George Sykes, could lay substantial claims to being the sturdiest in the Army of the Potomac, two of its three brigades being composed exclusively of U.S. regulars, while the third was made up of battle-hardened New York volunteers who had stood fast on Henry Hill and thereby saved the fleeing remnant of Pope's army from utter destruction at Bull Run. As steady now as then, they went smoothly into attack formation and drove the rebel skirmishers back to the crest of the low ridge. There, however, they came upon the Confederate main body, long gray lines of infantry supported by clusters of guns that broke into a roar at the sight of bluecoats. Calling a halt, Sykes sent back word that he was badly in need of help. Then, as the gray mass started forward, overlapping both of his open flanks, he began a rearward movement down the pike, dribbling casualties as he went. What would be known as the Battle of Chancellorsville had opened.

Couch was already coming up with Major General Winfield S. Hancock's division, which he threw into the line at once to stabilize the situation preparatory to resuming the advance. Before this last could be accomplished, however, a courier arrived with orders from Hooker: "Withdraw both divisions to Chancellorsville." Couch was amazed. Here he was, as he later said, with "open country in front and the commanding position," yet his chief was telling him to retire. Sykes and Hancock were equally puzzled. They too wanted to push ahead in accordance with the original instructions. With their approval, Couch sent an aide to inform Hooker that the situation was under control and the troops were about ready to continue their drive along the pike. Off to the right, a mounting bank of smoke and the rumble of guns told them that Slocum was likewise engaged and seemed to be holding his own, while Meade's other two divisions apparently had encountered no resistance at all on the left. But within half an hour the aide returned with a peremptory repetition of the order: Pull back to Chancellorsville without delay. Couch considered outright disobedience. Brigadier General G. K. Warren, chief engineer of the army, urged him to adopt just such a course while he himself rode back to explain its advantages to Hooker. He spurred rearward; but as soon as he left, Couch's West-Point-inculcated instinct for obedience took over. Complying with the order to retire, he withdrew the two divisions, first Sykes, then Hancock. The disengagement had been completed, except for two rear-guard regiments still in line, when a third message arrived from Hooker: "Hold on until 5 o'clock." Evidently Warren had stated his case persuasively, but Couch by now was disgusted. "Tell General Hooker he is too late," he replied testily. "The enemy are already on my right and rear. I am in full retreat."

In point of fact, his right was more seriously threatened than he knew. Slocum, followed as closely by Anderson as Couch himself was being followed by McLaws, had already fallen back down the plank road in accordance with similar instructions from headquarters. Meade too was backtracking by now, but unpursued, having encountered nothing substantial in the way of resistance on the left. As a result he was even more astounded than Couch had been at receiving the order to withdraw. Within sight of Duerson's Mill, he had been within easy reach of Banks Ford, control of which would shorten greatly the lines of supply and communication between the army's divided wings. To be told to fall back under such circumstances, with clear going to his front and his lines extending along the crest of the eastward rise, was more exasperating than anything he had encountered up to now. Once again Hooker had built up his hopes only to dash them with a peremptory order which not only called for a halt, as before, but also insisted on a retirement. Meade was furious. "If he thinks he can't hold the top of a hill, how does he expect to hold the bottom of it?" the Pennsylvanian stormed as he complied with the instructions to fall back.

That was about 2 o'clock. All three corps commanders were hard put to understand what had come over Fighting Joe in the scant three hours since they had set out from the crossroads they now were under orders to return to. At the outset, with the announcement that his headquarters would be leapfrogged four miles forward while the movement was in progress, he had seemed confident of delivering a knockout blow. Then suddenly, at the first sputter of musketry on the turnpike, he had abandoned all his aggressive intentions and ordered everything back for a defense of Chancellorsville, deep in the Wilderness. Why? They did not know, but already they were beginning to formulate theories which they and others down the years would enlarge on. For one thing, that excellent intelligence section back at Falmouth was hard at work, forwarding information disturbing enough to jangle the nerves of the steadiest man alive. According to one rebel deserter, brought in for interrogation the night before, Longstreet's whole corps had left Suffolk, presumably by rail, and had "gone to Culpeper," which would place it directly in rear of the Union flanking column and scarcely a day's march away. The prisoner added "that Lee said it was the only time he should fight equal numbers," which if true was alarming in the extreme, considering all the old fox had been able to accomplish with inferior numbers in the past. Another deserter — "from New York state originally; an intelligent man," Butterfield commented — avowed that Hood's division was already with Lee; he knew this, he said, because he had "asked the troops as they passed along." One of the two informers must be lying, at least so far as Longstreet's location was concerned. Indeed, both might be lying; it was not unusual for the Confederates to send out bogus "deserters" to confuse an opponent with misleading information. But the fact was, Lee was not reacting to his present predicament at all as he ought to be doing if he was heavily outnumbered. He was reacting, in fact, as if the numerical advantage was with him even more than either deserter claimed. And just what that reaction was Hooker had learned shortly after Meade and Slocum left him. Until that time, Professor Lowe's balloons had been fogbound high over Stafford Heights, but all of a sudden the weather faired, permitting the aeronaut to tap out a steady flow of information regarding the panorama now spread out before his eyes. He could see various rebel columns in motion, he wired Hooker at 11 o'clock, but the largest of these was "moving on the road toward Chancellorsville." This tallied with the intelligence summation forwarded shortly thereafter by Butterfield. Completing his tabulation of the Confederate order of battle, the chief of staff declared: "Anderson, McLaws, A. P. Hill, and Hood would, therefore, be in your front."

It also explained — all too clearly — the sudden clatter of musketry and the boom of guns, first down the turnpike, then down the plank road, not long after the two columns set out eastward through the forest. In part, as well, it accounted for Hooker's reaction, which in effect was a surrendering of the initiative to Jackson, who plunged deeper into the Wilderness in pursuit. But there was a good deal more to it than this: a good deal more that was no less valid for being less specific. Perhaps Hooker at last had recalled Lincoln's admonition, "Beware of rashness." Perhaps at this critical juncture he missed the artificial stimulus of whiskey, which formerly had been part of his daily ration but which he had abjured on taking command. Perhaps he mistrusted his already considerable accomplishment in putting more than 70,000 soldiers in Lee's immediate rear, with practically no losses because he had met practically no resistance. It had been altogether too easy; Lee must have wanted him where he was, or at any rate where he had been headed before he called a halt and ordered a pull-back. Or perhaps it was even simpler than that. Perhaps he was badly frightened (not physically frightened: Hooker was never that: but morally frightened) after the manner of the bullfighter Gallo, who, according to Hemingway, "was the inventor of refusing to kill the bull if the bull looked at him in a certain way." This Gallo had a long career, featuring many farewell performances, and at the first of these, having fought the animal bravely and well, when the time came for killing he faced the stands and made three eloquent speeches of dedication to three distinguished aficionados; after which he turned, sword in hand, and approached the bull, which was standing there, head down, looking at him. Gallo returned to the barrera. "You take him, Paco," he told a fellow matador; "I don't like the way he looks at me." So it was with Hooker, perhaps, when he heard that Lee had turned in his direction and was, so to speak, looking at him. Lowe had signaled at noon that the rebels were "considerably diminished" on the heights behind Fredericksburg. Consequently, at 2 o'clock, Fighting Joe wired Butterfield: "From character of information have suspended attack. The enemy may attack me — I will try it. Tell Sedgwick to keep a sharp lookout, and attack if can succeed." In effect, now that Lee had turned his attention westward, Hooker was telling Sedgwick: "You take him, Paco. I don't like the way he looks at me."

None of this perturbation showed in his manner, however, when the returning generals confronted him at the Chancellor house, which he had taken over as his headquarters. "It's all right, Couch; I've got Lee just where I want him," he said expansively. "He must fight me on my own ground." Couch had a cold eye for this blusterous performance. "The retrograde movement had prepared me for something of the kind," he wrote years later, "but to hear from his own lips that the ad-

vantages gained by the successive marches of his lieutenants were to cul-
minate in fighting a defensive battle in that nest of thickets was too
much. . . . I retired from his presence with the belief that my commanding general was a whipped man."

Whether or not this was the case remained to be seen. For the
present, the order was for the army to intrench itself along lines prescribed with the usual attention to detail. On the map they resembled a
double-handled dipper. Couch and Slocum, with two divisions each in
the vicinity of Chancellorsville — Gibbon had stayed at Falmouth
after all — formed the cup, bulging south of the crossroads to include
some comparatively high ground known as Fairview. The cup was just
over a mile wide at the rim, tapering slightly toward the base, and just
under a mile deep. Sickles' three divisions were in reserve, poised for a
leap into the cup or a quick march out either of the handles, which were
between two and three miles long and extended generally northeast and
due west. Meade's three divisions connected the eastern lip of the cup
with the Rappahannock, his left resting on a bend of the river south of
U. S. Ford, which thus was covered. Howard's three divisions, the dipper's western handle, extended out the turnpike past Wilderness Church,
where the plank road came in from the southwest, and thus presumably
could block the approach of an enemy moving up from that direction.
The troops worked into the night with picks and shovels, intrenching
the six-mile line from flank to flank. At 2 a.m. Couch, Slocum, and Howard reported themselves satisfied that their respective sectors could be
held against assault. Advantageously disposed along Mineral Spring
Run, a small boggy creek that covered his front and rendered his position doubly secure, Meade had reported the same thing earlier. Hooker,
with his accustomed thoroughness, seemed to have allowed for all even-
tualities before he retired to a bedroom in the crossroads mansion to
sleep and store up strength for whatever tomorrow was going to bring.

He hoped it would bring an all-out Confederate attack; or so at
least he had been saying, all afternoon and evening. "The rebel army is
now the legitimate property of the Army of the Potomac," he announced to the officers gathered about him in the May Day sunshine on
the Chancellor veranda. The fact that nearly all of his cavalry had ridden well beyond his reach, while nearly all of Lee's was in what Hooker
called "my immediate presence," did not seem to him a cause for alarm,
but rather an advantage, "which I trust will enable Stoneman to do a
land-office business in the interior. I think the enemy in his desperation
will be compelled to attack me on my own ground. . . . I am all right."
Thus he wired the Washington authorities, thinking that such information, besides relieving the President's concern, might "have an important bearing on movements elsewhere." If the other Union armies would
only keep step with this one, the war would soon be over and done with
— won. As the daylight hours wore on and his intrenchments were ex-

tended, still with no full-scale rebel assault, his show of confidence reached its zenith. He feared nothing and he wanted it known; not even the artillery of heaven. "The enemy is in my power," he exulted, "and God Almighty cannot deprive me of them." In the late afternoon he issued another circular for the encouragement of subordinates: "The major general commanding trusts that a suspension in the attack today will embolden the enemy to attack him."

✗ 5 ✗

Lee and Jackson met at sundown, on the plank road just over a mile southeast of Chancellorsville, for the purpose of deciding how best to go about giving Hooker what he claimed he wanted. They began their conference on the road itself, at the junction where a trail came in from Catharine Furnace, a rural ironworks on Lewis Creek a mile and a half to the west, but they withdrew presently into a nearby clump of pines when a Federal sharpshooter began ranging in on them from a perch in a tree just up the road, beyond the line along which Anderson's and Slocum's pickets were keeping up a rackety contention. Seated side by side on a log, the two men continued their discussion in the May Day twilight, the gray-bearded elder impeccably dressed as always, his neat gray tunic devoid of trappings except for the three unwreathed stars on each side of the turned-down collar, and the younger wearing the rather gaudy uniform which had provoked such hoots and catcalls on the day of Fredericksburg. Reconnoitering on the right this afternoon, Lee had found the terrain unpromising, hemmed in as it was by a bend of the Rappahannock, and the few heavily wooded approaches well guarded by troops already dug in along the far side of a marsh. To attempt to come to grips with them in that quarter, he said, would be to invite destruction. How about the center and the left? Jackson had not been far to the west, but he had made a long-range examination of the enemy lines in front of Chancellorsville itself and had found the bluecoats disposed three-deep, hard at work with picks and shovels, and supported by many batteries of artillery. However, he was inclined to believe that the question of how to get at Hooker, here in the Wilderness tomorrow, was largely academic. The ease with which he had repulsed the advancing Union columns today made him suspect that their recoil was prelude to a withdrawal. "By tomorrow morning there will not be any of them on this side of the river," he declared.

Lee shook his head. So far he had deferred to Stonewall's judgment, but not in this. Though he too was puzzled by his opponent's sudden, turtle-like reaction to moderate pressure, he was convinced that Hooker was planning to make his main effort right here. Anyhow, even if that were not the case, they must prepare to deal with him tomorrow

on even the outside chance that he would still be in his present intrenched position. Without quite giving over his belief that dawn would
show the forest empty to their front, Jackson could not disagree with
the logic of Lee's contention; besides which, he found the prospect so attractive as to overrule his inclination to think that it would not be offered. For him, as for his commander, to "deal with" Hooker meant to
attack him. But how? And where? One possibility was that the Federal
center might not appear as stout to a close-up view as it had seemed from
a distance. The two generals accordingly dispatched an engineer officer
from each of their staffs to go take a look at the intrenchments there and
report on what they saw.

While this night reconnaissance was in progress, and while Lee
and Jackson continued to speculate on ways of bringing the blue
army's current excursion to a violent close, Jeb Stuart came jingling up
from Catharine Furnace in fulfillment of his promise to "help all I can
when the ball opens." Glad as he was to see his friend Stonewall decked
out in the handsome uniform he had given him, he deferred comment in
favor of some interesting information which had just come to hand. According to Fitzhugh Lee, who had ridden west to scout it, Hooker's
right flank was "in the air" on the Orange Turnpike, wide open to attack
from that direction. Though this was news of a kind to set both him and
his chief lieutenant on tremble, the southern commander suppressed his
excitement to ask whether roads were available for a covered approach
to that critical point by troops in large numbers. Stuart replied that he
did not know but he would do what he could to find out, and with that
he swung back onto his horse and rode off westward, his red-lined cape
and cinnamon whiskers glistening in the light of the new-risen moon.

From this time on, Lee and Jackson gave little attention to anything but the possibility of launching the suggested flank attack. When
the two engineers returned to announce that the Union center was too
strongly intrenched to be assaulted, Lee received the anticlimactic report with a nod and kept peering at a map spread on his knees; he peered
so intently, indeed, that he seemed to be trying to make it give him information which it did not contain. "How can we get at those people?"
he asked, half to himself and half to Jackson, who replied in an equally
distracted manner, as he too searched the map for roads that were not
on it: "You know best. Show me what to do, and we will do it." Finally, Lee traced a fingertip westward along the map from their present
location, as if to sketch in an ideal route past the front of the enemy position, then northward to intersect the turnpike, where the latter veered
abruptly east to address the Union flank end-on. In naval parlance, he was
crossing Hooker's T. That would be the movement, he said; Jackson
would lead it and Stuart would cover his march. Smiling, Jackson stood
erect and saluted. "My troops will move at 4 o'clock," he said. In his
eagerness, he not only seemed unable to remain seated, he also seemed to

have forgotten his prediction that Hooker would clear out before sunup. Lee checked him with a reminder. If there was any doubt about this next morning, he said, Jackson could open from an exposed position with a couple of guns, then judge by the response as to whether the blue army was still behind its Wilderness fortifications.

There was much to be done between now and sunrise: especially by Jackson, to whom Lee had left the choice of a route, the composition of the force to be employed, and the decision as to when and in what manner the flank attack would be delivered. But what both men needed for the present, at the close of a strenuous day and on the eve of what promised to be an even more strenuous morrow, was a few hours' sleep: again especially Jackson, who had demonstrated on several occasions — the Seven Days, for one — that without at least a minimum of profound rest he would be reduced to a state of somnambulism. They lay down where they were, in separate quarters of the grove, spreading their saddle blankets on the pine needles for a bed and using their saddles for a pillow. Both were soon asleep, but Lee was wakened presently by an officer he had sent to look into conditions on the turnpike to the north. "Ah, Captain, you have returned, have you?" he said, and he sat up slowly. "Come here and tell me what you have learned on the right." It was the same young man from Jackson's staff who had wakened him two mornings ago to tell him Hooker was crossing; J. P. Smith was his name, a divinity student before the war. He hesitated, in awe of the general whose massive features and gray beard looked so imposing in the moonlight, but as he leaned forward the seated man put an arm about his shoulder and drew him down by his side while he finished his report. Lee thanked him and then, still retaining his grip, began to chide him by saying that he regretted that Smith and the other "young men about General Jackson" had not done a better job today of locating and silencing an enemy battery that had held up the advance. Young men nowadays, he declared in the accents of Nestor, were a far remove from the young men of his youth. The captain, seeing, as he later said, that the general "was jesting and disposed to rally me," broke away from the hold Lee tried to retain on his shoulder. As he moved off through the moonlit pines he could hear the Virginian laughing heartily there in the Wilderness where many men now sleeping would be laid in their graves tomorrow and the next day and the next, blue and gray alike, as a result of instructions he had given just before he himself lay down, in apparently excellent spirits, to rest for what he knew was coming with the dawn.

When Lee woke he saw the gaunt figure of Jackson bending over a small fire a courier had built. Rising, he joined him and the two sat on a couple of hardtack boxes the Federals had left behind the day before. It was already past 4 o'clock, the hour set for the column to move out, but Jackson explained that he was awaiting the return of his staff chaplain, who once had had a church hereabouts and was familiar with the region. For this reason he had sent him, together with a skilled cartographer, to explore the roads leading west from Catharine Furnace and then north to the plank road, up which he expected to make his strike. The two sat talking, warming their hands at the meager fire, until the glimmer of dawn showed the staff officers returning from their scout. Major Jedediah Hotchkiss, the cartographer, approached the generals and spread his map on another hardtack box which he placed between them. It was obvious from his manner, before he said a word, that he had found the route he had been seeking, and as he spoke he traced it on the map: first due west to the furnace, then due south, away from the enemy, along a trail that gradually turned back west to enter the Brock Road, which ran northward to the plank road and the turnpike. However, he explained that the column must not turn north at this point, since that would bring it within sight of a Federal signal station at Fairview, but south again for a short distance to another road leading north and paralleling the Brock Road, which it rejoined a couple of miles above in some heavy woods just short of its junction with the plank road. That way, practically the entire route — some ten miles in length from their present position and firm enough throughout to support wagons and artillery — would be screened from the eyes of enemy lookouts. Completing his exposition, Hotchkiss looked from one to another of the generals, both of whom kept their eyes fixed on the map for what seemed to him an inordinately long time. Finally Lee spoke, raising his head to look at his lieutenant: "General Jackson, what do you propose to do?" Jackson put out his hand and retraced, with a semicircular motion of his wrist, the route just drawn. "Go around here," he said. Lee kept looking at him. "What do you propose to make this movement with?" he asked, and Jackson promptly replied: "With my whole corps."

Now there was a pause while Lee absorbed the shock the words had given him. "What will you leave me?" he asked. The question was rhetorical; he already knew the answer. But Jackson answered it anyhow, as readily as before. "The divisions of Anderson and McLaws." This meant that he would have better than 30,000 soldiers off to the rear and on the flank, necessarily out of contact with the enemy and the rest of his own army for most of the day, while Lee would be left with scarcely half as many troops planted squarely across the path of a greatly superior blue host which might resume its forward movement at any minute. However, having weighed the odds — which had to include the by no means improbable chance that Hooker might learn what was afoot and react accordingly — the southern commander made and announced his decision. "Well, go on," he said.

While they talked the sun had reddened the east, and now it broke clear, fiery above the treetops back toward Fredericksburg, where Early was facing odds almost as long as Lee's would be when the flanking column left. Jackson informed his chief that the march would be led by D. H. Hill's old division, now under Brigadier General Robert Rodes; next would come his own old division, commanded by its senior brigadier, Raleigh Colston; A. P. Hill's division would bring up the rear. He would take all his artillery with him, dispersed along the column, and depend on Stuart to cover his advance. Lee took notes on this, then retired to write the necessary orders while his lieutenant went about making preparations to move out. As Jackson rode past one brigade camp the lounging veterans rose to cheer him, but seeing what one of them later called "battle in his haste and stern looks," they merely gazed at him and wondered what exertion he was about to require of them. The preliminary dispositions were a time-consuming business, involving the extraction of some units already committed, but at last they were completed. Shortly before 8 o'clock, the lead regiment — Georgians who had fought under him in every battle since McDowell, the prologue to the Valley Campaign, which had opened exactly a year ago today with his descent through Brown's Gap to put his troops aboard the cars for Staunton — turned off the plank road and set out westward for Catharine Furnace and Hooker's right. Though he was four hours behind the starting time he had set the night before, Stonewall did not appear to be disturbed by the delay. He was alert but not impatient, one observer remarked, and spoke tersely "as though all were distinctly formed in his mind and beyond all question." Under the lowered bill of his cap, the battle light was already shining fiercely in his pale blue eyes.

Lee came up and joined him at the turn-off where the sniper had tried to draw a bead on them at sunset. Both mounted — Lee on Traveller, a tall dapple gray, and Jackson on stocky, ox-eyed Little Sorrel — they spoke briefly against a background of skirmish fire which had begun to sputter along the two-mile front now occupied exclusively by Anderson and McLaws, with just over 15,000 troops between them. Nothing in Lee's manner showed the strain involved in gambling that his opponent, whether or not he became aware in the meantime of what was happening in his front and on his flank, would not exploit his five-to-one numerical advantage by launching an all-out attack — frontal or otherwise; either would be about equally destructive — before the widely divided Confederate wings were reunited. Moreover, Lee was proceeding not only on the assumption that Jackson could gain and strike the Union flank before the bluecoats recovered from their current puzzling lethargy, here in the Wilderness or back in front of Marye's Heights; he was also proceeding on the belief, or at any rate the hope, that Hooker would be completely unstrung by the explosion on his right. Nothing less would serve. For if Hooker could absorb and then recover from the shock, he might still take the offensive against the outnumbered and divided graybacks to the west and south, or signal eastward for an assault upon the thinly held Fredericksburg ridge in Lee's immediate rear. This was, in short, the longest gamble of a career which had been crowded with risks throughout the eleven months since Lee first took command at Seven Pines. Now, their brief conversation ended, the two men parted, the elder to stay, the other to go. As they did so, the dark-bearded younger general raised his arm and pointed west, in the direction he was headed. Lee nodded, and Stonewall rode off into the forest, out of sight.

Fighting Joe had been up for hours, conducting a flank-to-flank inspection of his lines. "How strong! How strong!" he marveled as he examined the hastily improvised but elaborate fortifications: particularly those out on the right, where so many of the regiments were composed of foreign-born troops who performed such labor with Germanic thoroughness and a meticulous attention to detail rivaling Hooker's own. Wherever he went this morning, tall in the saddle and rosy-looking, flushed with confidence and trailing a kite-tail of staff officers behind his big white high-stepping horse, the soldiers cheered him lustily, delighted to see their commander sharing with them the rigors of the field. His mood was as expansive as before; more so, in fact; and with cause. For he had received, the night before, a report from a trusted operative just in from Richmond, who not only had documentary evidence that Lee was receiving barely 59,000 daily rations, but also reported that the southern commander could hope for no reinforcements except from Longstreet, both of whose divisions — despite the contrary fabrications passed on by yesterday's rebel deserters — were still in front of Suffolk. This last was confirmed by Peck himself, who wired that he had taken prisoners from Hood and Pickett that same day. In reaction, Hooker's last move before retiring had been to direct that Reynolds' corps be detached from Sedgwick and sent to join him here at Chancellorsville. When it arrived — as it should do before long, the summons having been issued at 1.55 this morning — he would have better than 90,000 men on hand to repulse the attack Lee seemed to be preparing to deliver against the bulging center of the Union line. If the old fox really believed what he was rumored to have said the day before, that this "was the only time he should fight equal numbers," he was in for a large surprise. What Fighting Joe was planning was Fredericksburg in reverse, with Lee in the role of Burnside, and himself in the role of Lee: except that this time, when the attackers were exhausted and bled white as a result of their attempts to storm his fortifications, he would be in a position to swing over to the offensive that had been impossible for the Confederates, back in December, because of their numerical inferiority and the guns on Stafford Heights. Hereabouts there were no heights for Lee to mass his guns on, only the blinding and restricting thickets, and Hooker had men aplenty for the delivery of an all-out counterattack and the administration of the

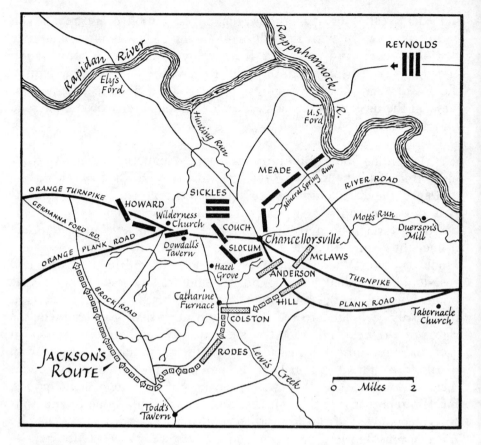

windup *coup de grâce* which would end the final spasmodic twitch of the dying rebel army.

He was in excellent spirits when he got back to headquarters at 9 o'clock to find a courier waiting for him from Brigadier General David Birney, commander of a division Sickles had sent out to some unoccupied high ground southwest of Fairview — Hazel Grove, it was called on the map — for a look at what the graybacks might be up to. According to the information brought back by the courier, they were up to a great deal. Hazel Grove afforded a clear but limited view of Catharine Furnace, less than one mile south, and the advancing bluecoats had spotted a rebel column moving due south of there along a stretch of road that disappeared into the woods. Apparently endless, the column included infantry, artillery, wagons, and ambulances; Birney thought it must signify an important development in the enemy's plans. Hooker agreed. In fact, after referring to his map, which showed that the road in question veered west beyond the screen of trees, he believed he knew just what that development was. The Confederates were in retreat, probably on Gordonsville, where Stoneman must have struck by now, severing one of their two main supply lines. However, on the off-chance that Lee was attempting at this late date to come up with something out of his bag of tricks, Hooker decided it would be wise to warn Howard of what was going on, and he sent him a message advising him to be vigilant in protecting the western flank: "We have good reason to suppose that the enemy is moving to our right. Please advance your pickets for purposes of observation as far as may be safe to obtain timely information of their approach." He might have followed to see for himself that his instructions were carried out, but presently a dispatch arrived from Howard, sent before his own had been received, stating that he too had sighted the rebel column "moving westward on a road parallel with this," and adding, of his own accord: "I am taking measures to resist an attack from the west." It was clear that Howard required no supervision to assure that he did his duty; he had performed it before he was even told what it was, thereby leaving Hooker free to concentrate on the question of pursuit.

In this connection he thought again of Sedgwick, who had been kept by a faulty telegraph connection from getting yesterday's instructions until the hour was too late for an attack. First Sickles and now Reynolds had been detached from the downstream force, but Sedgwick's was the largest corps in the army. With Gibbon's division still available at Falmouth, he had close to 30,000 effectives, plus the support of the long-range guns on Stafford Heights, and though Professor Lowe had reported earlier that a hard wind was bumping him around so much he could not use his telescope, the headquarters intelligence section informed Hooker that only Early's division remained on the Fredericksburg ridge. Accordingly, he directed Butterfield to pass the word along to Sedgwick and authorize him to attack if there was "a reasonable expectation of success." Meanwhile Hooker kept his staff busy preparing orders designed to put the whole army on Lee's trail if he still appeared to be in retreat next morning. A circular issued at 2.30 instructed corps commanders to load up with forage, provisions, and ammunition so as "to be ready to start at an early hour tomorrow." By the time this was distributed, reports had begun to come in from Sickles, who had been given permission at noon to advance with two divisions to investigate the movement Birney had spotted from Hazel Grove. He sent back word that he had pierced the rebel column near Catharine Furnace, capturing men and wagons, but that practically all of it had moved westward beyond his reach by now. Hooker took fire at this, his confidence soaring: Lee was unquestionably in full retreat, intending to follow the heavily escorted train with the Confederate main body. At 4.30 the jubilant Federal commander wired Butterfield to order Sedgwick to throw his entire force across the river, "capture Fredericksburg and everything in it, and vigorously pursue the enemy." Previous instructions had been discretionary, and so were these; but Hooker made it clear that a fine opportunity lay before him. "We know that the enemy is fleeing, trying to save his trains," he added. "Two of Sickles' divisions are among them."

As might have been expected with the rebel column filing through the woods to the army's front, there was a good deal of excitement along the outpost lines. Couriers and even unit commanders began to turn up at the Chancellor house with frantic, sometimes near-hysterical warnings of an impending flank attack. Staff officers had all they could do to keep some of them — especially one persistent artilleryman with the lowly rank of captain, who claimed to have ridden out and seen the graybacks massing — from bothering Hooker himself with their perturbations. When these men finally could be made to understand that the high command was already aware of the alleged danger and had taken steps to meet it in case it developed, they returned to their units, most of them feeling rather sheepish at having presumed to believe they knew more than their superiors. Others, however, remained unconvinced: particularly those through whose ranks the rebel prisoners had been taken rearward after their capture near Catharine Furnace. They were Georgians, hale-looking men in neat butternut clothes, and for the most part they seemed cheerful enough, considering their plight. They had come over, they replied to taunts, to help "eat up them eight-day rations." But some were surly and in no mood to be chided. Told by a bluecoat, "We'll have every mother's son of you before we go away," one snapped back: "You'll catch hell before night." Another was more specific as to how calamity was to be visited upon them, and by whom. "You think you've done a big thing just now," he said, "but wait till Jackson gets around on your flank." This seemed to its hearers well worth passing on to headquarters, but when they went there to report it they were told to return to their outfits; Lee was in retreat, no matter what the butternut captives said, and Hooker was making plans even now for an orderly pursuit.

Far out on the right flank, as the shadows lengthened toward 5 o'clock and beyond, Howard's men were taking it easy. They had seen no action so far in the campaign, but that was much as usual; they had seen little real action anywhere in the war, save for a great deal of marching and countermarching, and were in fact a sort of stepchild corps, collectively referred to by the rest of the army as "a bunch of Dutchmen." Indeed, nothing demonstrated more conclusively Hooker's lack of concern for his western flank than the fact that he had posted these men here. Mostly New Yorkers and Pennsylvanians, large numbers of them were immigrants, lately arrived and scarcely able to speak English; "Hessians," their enemies called them, with a contempt dating back to the days of the Revolution. Schurz, Steinwehr, and Schimmelfennig were three of their generals, while their colonels had names such as Von

Gilsa, Krzyzanowski, Einsiedel, Dachrodt, and Schluemback. Howard himself was by no means popular with them, despite his sacrifice of an arm to the cause and a record of steady progress up the ladder of command. After his maiming, a year ago at Fair Oaks, he had returned to lead a brigade at Antietam and a division at Fredericksburg, both with such distinction that now — to the considerable displeasure of men whose proudest boast had been "I fights mit Sigel" and who rather illogically put the blame for their hero's departure on his successor — he had a corps. He had had it, in fact, exactly a month today; but in his anxiety to make good he not only had borne down hard on discipline, he also had tried to influence the out-of-hours activities of his troops by distributing religious tracts among them. The latter action was resented even more than the former, for many of the men were freethinkers, lately emerged from countries where the church had played a considerable part in attempting their oppression, and they drew the line somewhere short of being preached at, prayed over, or uplifted. The result of all this, and more, was that army life was not a happy one for them or their commander, whose ill-concealed disappointment at their reaction to his attempt to play the role of Christian Soldier only served to increase their mistrust and dislike of him, empty sleeve and all.

Today was one of the better days, however, with a minimum of work, no drill whatsoever, and a maximum of rest. Extended for more than a mile along the turnpike west of Dowdall's Tavern, an oversized cabin just east of the junction where the plank road came in from the southwest, they lounged behind the elaborate southward-facing breastworks Hooker himself had admired. Like his chief, Howard was convinced that he was onto the rebel strategy, which seemed to him to be designed to cover a retreat with a pretense of strength and boldness. He too rejected various cries of wolf, including those from an outpost major who sent back a stream of frantic messages from beyond the flank, all patterned after the first at 2.45: "A large body of the enemy is massing in my front. For God's sake make disposition to receive him!" At the outer end of the intrenched line, two guns were posted hub-to-hub on the pike itself, facing west, and two regiments of infantry — not over 900 men in all — were disposed at right angles to the road, strung out northward from the point where the guns were posted. These two regiments and guns were all the flank protection Howard had provided after notifying Hooker that he was "taking measures to resist an attack from the west," but he considered them ample, since nothing could approach him from that direction except along the turnpike, covered by the two guns, or through a tangle of second-growth timber and briery underbrush which he had pronounced impenetrable. Moreover, there was a half-mile stretch of unoccupied ground between his left and Slocum's right, marking the former position of his one reserve brigade, which had been detached in the midafternoon and still had not returned from its mission of guarding Sickles' flank in the course of his advance from Hazel Grove. This gap was critical. Though it went unnoticed, or at any rate unfilled, it meant that if anything struck Howard a hard enough blow from the west, he would be in much the same predicament as a man attempting to sit on a chair he did not know had been removed.

That, or something like that, was what happened. Not long after 5 o'clock, with some regiments already eating supper and others lounging about while waiting for it, their rifles neatly stacked, the troops at the far end of the line were alarmed and then amused to see large numbers of deer break out of the thickets to the west and come bounding toward them, accompanied by droves of rabbits darting this way and that in the underbrush, as if pursued by invisible beaters. The men cheered and hallooed, waving their caps at the startled forest creatures, until presently something else they heard and saw froze the laughter in their throats. Long lines of men in gray and butternut, their clothes ripped to tatters by the briers and branches, were running toward them through the "impenetrable" thickets. They were screaming as they came on, jaws agape, and their bayonets caught angry glints from the low-angled sun pouring its beams through the reddened treetops and over their shoulders.

★ ★ ★

For all its explosive force, its practically complete surprise, and its rapid gathering of momentum, Stonewall's flank attack was launched with only about two hours of daylight left for the accomplishment of the destruction he intended. One of the two main reasons for this tardiness was that the start itself had been late, and the other was that the finish was delayed by an extension of the march. Between these two untoward extremes, however, all went smoothly, despite attempted enemy interruptions. The roads, described by one of the marchers as "just wet enough to be easy to the feet and free from dust," were narrow but firm, so that the column was elongated but its progress was not impeded. Like his men, who were enthused by a sense of adventure before they had even had time to guess what the adventure was going to be, Jackson was in excellent spirits, and though he did not push them to the limit of their endurance as he had done so often in the past, being concerned for once to conserve their energy for the work that lay ahead, he took care to deal with emergencies in a manner that would not hold up the main body. For instance, when the head of the column came under fire from a section of guns just north of Catharine Furnace, he detached the lead regiment of Georgians, with instructions for them to block a possible infantry probe at that point, and had the remaining units double-time across the clearing, being willing to suffer whatever incidental losses this involved rather than to burn more daylight by taking a roundabout route. Similarly A. P. Hill, whose division did not clear the starting point until well after 11 o'clock, dropped off his two rear brigades to assist the hard-pressed Georgians — forty of them had been captured and most of the rest were about to be captured — in fending off an infantry attack launched by the Federals just as he was approaching the furnace about noon, and forged ahead with his other four brigades. Far in the lead and quite unmindful of his rear, which he left to look out for itself after making the original provision, Jackson kept the main body on the go. "Press forward. Press forward," he urged his subordinate commanders. Including 1500 attached cavalry and 2000 artillerymen in support of his 70 regiments of infantry, Stonewall had better than 31,000 effectives in the column, and his only regret was that he did not have more. "I hear it said that General Hooker has more men than he can handle," he remarked in the course of the march. "I should like to have half as many more as I have today, and I should hurl him into the river!"

His eyes glowed at the thought, and presently they had occasion to blaze even more fiercely, not only at a thought, but also at what was actually spread before them. About 2 o'clock, as he approached the Orange Plank Road — the intended objective, up which he expected to turn the column northeastward for an attack that would strike the Orange Turnpike just west of Dowdall's Tavern, where Hooker's flank presumably was anchored — he was met by Fitz Lee, who approached from the opposite direction, drew rein alongside Little Sorrel, and announced with a barely suppressed excitement that explained his lack of ceremony: "General, if you will ride with me, halting your column here out of sight, I will show you the enemy's right." The two officers, accompanied by a single courier so as not to increase the risk of detection, rode past the plank road intersection, then turned off eastward through the trees to a little hill which they climbed on horseback. From the summit, parting the curtain of leaves, Stonewall saw what had provoked the excitement Lee would still be feeling, years later, when he came to write about it: "What a sight presented itself before me! Below, and but a few hundred yards distant, ran the Federal line of battle . . . with abatis in front and long lines of stacked arms in the rear. Two cannon were visible in the part of the line seen. The soldiers were in groups in the rear, laughing, smoking, probably engaged, here and there, in games of cards and other amusements indulged in while feeling safe and comfortable, awaiting orders. In rear of them were other parties driving up and butchering beeves." As he observed the peaceful scene, Jackson's mind was on a different kind of butchery. According to Lee, "his eyes burned with a brilliant glow, lighting his sad face. His expression was one of intense interest; his face was colored slightly with the paint of the approaching battle, and radiant in the success of his flank movement."

The salient fact was that Hooker's flank was as completely "in the air" as had been reported the night before, but that an attack up the plank road, such as had been intended, would strike it at an angle, about midway, rather than end-on; which would not do. Correction of this, however, called for a two-mile extension of the march in order to get beyond the farthest western reach of the Union intrenchments and approach them on the perpendicular. That meant a further delay of at least an hour, to which of course would be added the time required to form the three divisions for assault. With the sun already well past the overhead — by now, in fact, the hands of his watch were crowding 2.30 — there might not be enough daylight left for the execution of his plans. But Jackson did not hesitate beyond the few minutes it took him to make a careful examination of what was spread before his eyes. Seeing his lips moving as he looked at the enemy soldiers down below, Lee assumed that he was praying. If this was so, there was no evidence of it in his voice as he turned to the courier and snapped out an order for him to take back to the head of the column, halted on the Brock Road to await instructions: "Tell General Rodes to move across the plank road, halt when he gets to the old turnpike, and I will join him there." The courier took off. Jackson turned for a final look at the lounging bluecoats, disposed as they were for slaughter, then "rode rapidly [back] down the hill, his arms flapping to the motion of his horse, over whose head it seemed, good rider as he was, he would certainly go." Lee saw him thus; then he too turned and followed, somewhat chagrined that he had not received the thanks he had expected in return for making a discovery which not only would save many Confederate lives but also had made possible what gave promise of being the most brilliant tactical stroke of Stonewall's career.

Jackson had already forgotten him, along with practically everything else preceding the moment when his mind became fixed on what he was going to do. Retracing his horse's steps back down the Brock Road he passed Rodes, who had his men slogging northward for the turnpike, and returned to the plank road intersection, where he met and detached Colston's lead brigade — his own old First Manassas outfit, the Stonewall Brigade — to advance a short distance up the plank road and take position at a junction where the road from Germanna Ford came in from the northwest. With his rear and right flank thus screened and protected, he took a moment to scrawl a note briefly explaining the situation to Lee, who he knew must be fretting at the delay. "I hope as soon as practicable to attack," he wrote, and added: "I trust that an ever kind Providence will bless us with great success." The note was headed, "Near 3 p.m."; time was going fast. He hurried northward to the turnpike, overtook Rodes, and gave him the instructions he had promised. Rodes accordingly moved eastward on the pike for about a mile — unopposed and apparently unobserved, although this brought

him within 1000 yards of the western knuckle of Howard's intrenchments — then formed his division along a low, north-south ridge. Four
brigades were in line, two to the right and two to the left, extending
about a mile in each direction from the turnpike, which would be the
guide for the assault. The fifth brigade took position behind the extreme
right, and Colston's remaining three brigades prolonged this second line
northward, 200 yards in rear of the first. Jackson's orders were that the
charge would be headlong. Under no circumstances was there to be even
a pause in the advance. If a first-line brigade ran into trouble, it was to
call for help from the brigade in its immediate rear, without taking time
to notify either division commander. The main thing, he emphasized as
he spoke to his subordinates in turn, was to keep rolling, to keep up the
pressure and the scare.

Maneuvering the stretched-out column off the road and into a
compact mass, like a fist clenched for striking, was a time-consuming
business, however, especially when it had to be done in woods so dense
that visibility scarcely extended beyond the limits of a single regiment.
Also there was the problem of fatigue. Though by ordinary standards
the march had been neither long nor hard — an average dozen miles in
an average eight hours — none of the troops had had anything to eat
since breakfast, and many of them had not had even that. Hunger made
them trembly. Moreover, there had been a tormenting shortage of water all along the way, and the men were spitting cotton as they filed into
position to await the signal that would send them plunging eastward
through the thickets to their front. They knew now, for certain, what
they had only assumed before: Hooker's flank lay dead ahead and they
were about to strike it. But the waiting was long. It was 4.30 by the time
Colston had formed in rear of Rodes, and Hill was not yet off the road.
Another half hour sufficed to get Little Powell's two leading brigades
into position in rear of Colston's left, while the center two were coming
forward on the turnpike; but the last two were miles back down the
road, delayed by their rear-guard action at Catharine Furnace. Jackson
waited as long as he could, watch in hand. Rodes stood beside him, waiting too; he was a V.M.I. graduate, just past his thirty-fourth birthday,
and like his chief a former professor of mathematics. Tall and slender, a
Virginia-born Alabamian with a tawny mustache that drooped below
the corners of his mouth, he had fought well in almost every major battle since First Manassas, taking time off only for wounds, but he
would be leading a division in combat for the first time today. At 5.15 —
an hour and a half before sundown — Jackson looked up from his
watch. His proposed third line was not half formed, but he and the sun
could wait no longer.

"Are you ready, General Rodes?"

"Yes sir."

"You can go forward then."

He spoke calmly, almost matter-of-factly; yet what followed within the next quarter hour approximated pandemonium. Crashing through the half-mile screen of brush and stunted trees, whose thorns and brittle, low-hanging limbs quickly stripped the trail-blazing skirmishers near-naked, the long lines of Confederates broke suddenly into the clear, where the sight of the enemy brought their rifles to their shoulders and the quavering din of the rebel yell from their throats; "that hellish yell," one bluecoat called it, though Jackson himself had once referred to the caterwaul as "the sweetest music I ever heard." He was getting his fill of such music now. All across the nearly two-mile width of his front, the woods and fields resounded with it as the screaming attackers bore down on the startled Federals, who had just risen to whoop at the frightened deer and driven rabbits. Now it was their turn to be frightened — and driven, too. For the Union regiments facing west gave way in a rush before the onslaught, and as they fled the two guns they had abandoned were turned against them, hastening their departure and increasing the confusion among the troops facing south behind the now useless breastworks they had constructed with such care. These last, looking over their shoulders and seeing the fugitives running close-packed on the turnpike immediately in their rear, took their cue from them and began to pull out, too, in rapid succession from right to left down the long line of intrenchments, swelling the throng rushing eastward along the road. Within twenty minutes of the opening shots, Howard's flank division had gone out of military existence, converted that quickly from organization to mob. The adjoining division was sudden to follow the example set. Not even the sight of the corps commander himself, on horseback near Wilderness Church, breasting the surge of retreaters up the turnpike and clamping a stand of abandoned colors under the stump of his amputated arm while attempting to control his skittish horse with the other, served to end or even slow the rout. Bareheaded and with tears in his eyes, Howard was pleading with them to halt and form, halt and form, but they paid him no mind, evidently convinced that his distress, whether for the fate of his country or his career or both, took no precedence over their own distress for their very lives. Some in their haste drew knives from their pockets and cut their knapsack straps as they ran, unburdening themselves for greater speed without taking the time to fumble at buckles, lest they be overtaken by the horde of tatterdemalion demons stretching north and south as far as the eye could follow and screaming with delight at the prospect of carnage.

Jackson was among the pursuers, riding from point to point just in rear of the crest of the wave, exultant. "Push right ahead," he told his brigadiers and colonels, and as he spoke he made a vigorous thrusting gesture, such as a man would make in toppling a wall. When a jubilant young officer cried, "They are running too fast for us. We can't keep up with them!" he replied sternly: "They never run too fast for me, sir. Press them, press them!" It was 6.30 by now; the sun was down behind the rearward treetops. Dowdall's Tavern lay dead ahead, and from the east the answering thunder of guns and clatter of musketry told Stonewall that Lee had heard or learned of the attack and was applying pressure to keep the tottering Union giant off balance, even though he could scarcely hope to break through the endless curve of fortifications south and east of Chancellorsville. Here to the west, on the other hand, whenever a clump of bluecoats more stalwart than their fellows tried to make a stand, they found themselves quickly outflanked on the left and right by the overlapping lines of the attackers, and they had to give way in a scramble to avoid being surrounded. Every time Jackson heard the wild yell of victory that followed such collapses he would lift his head and smile grimly, as if in thanks to the God of battle. Conversely, whenever he came upon the bodies of his own men, lying where panicky shots had dropped them, he would frown, draw rein briefly, and raise one hand as if blessing the slain for their valor. A staff officer later remarked, "I have never seen him so well pleased with the progress and results of a fight."

On through sundown his pleasure was justified by continuing success, and presently it was increased. By 7 o'clock, with darkness settling fast in the clearings and the woods already black, his triumph over Howard was complete as the Federals gave way around Dowdall's Tavern and began their flight across the reserveless gap that yawned between them and the rest of the blue army. On the right, just south of the turnpike, there was a meeting engagement with a column of Union cavalry, which resulted in its repulse, and enemy guns were booming on Fairview Heights, firing blind to discourage pursuit, but Jackson did not believe there was anything substantial between him and the loom of forest screening Chancellorsville itself, just over a mile ahead. The only deterrent beyond his control was the darkness, and soon there was not even that. As if in response to a signal from the southern Joshua, the full moon came up, huge and red through the drifting smoke, then brightened to gold as it rose to light the way for pursuit. Many times in the past Stonewall had ached to launch a night attack; now he not only had the chance, he believed it was downright necessary if he was to prevent the enemy from recovering from the shock and attempting to turn the tables on the still-divided Confederates. Two immediate objectives he had in mind. One was to strike deep in Hooker's rear, cutting him off from U.S. Ford so as to prevent his escape across the Rappahannock, and the other was to reunite with Lee for a combined assault on the bluecoats who thus would be hemmed in for slaughter. It was more or less obvious by now that Rodes and Colston had done their worst, at least for the present; they would need a breathing spell in which to regain control of their troops, hopelessly mingled in a single

wave that was already ebbing because of exhaustion; but Hill's four brigades were still intact, available as a reserve, and Jackson was determined
to use them for a moonlight advance along the pike and up the roads
leading northeastward to the single river crossing in Hooker's rear. Soon
he found Little Powell and gave him his instructions. There was no studied calmness about him now, such as there had been three hours ago
when he told Rodes he could go forward. His excitement was evident to
everyone he met, and his sense of urgency was communicated with
every word he spoke, including those in the orders he gave Hill: "Press
them! Cut them off from the United States Ford, Hill. Press them!"

Hooker by then was doing all he could to avert disaster, but for
the better part of an hour after the first wave of attackers struck and
crumpled the tip of his western wing — three miles from the Chancellor
gallery where he sat chatting amiably with members of his staff — he
had been under the tactical disadvantage of not even knowing that he
had been surprised. Because of acoustic peculiarities of the terrain and
the cushioning effect of brush and trees, the roar of battle reached him
but faintly and indirectly. He and his aides supposed that the racket, such
as it was, came from down around Catharine Furnace, a couple of miles
to the south, and were exchanging conjectures as to the havoc Sickles
must be making among Lee's trains in that direction. Just before sundown, however, one of the officers strolled out to the road and casually
gazed westward. "My God — here they come!" the others heard him
shout. Then they saw for themselves what he meant. A stumbling herd
of wild-eyed men, the frantic and apparently unstoppable backwash of
Howard's unstrung corps, was rushing eastward, filling the pike from
shoulder to shoulder. Fighting Joe reacted fast. At hand was Sickles'
third division — his own in the days before his elevation to corps and
army command — left in reserve when the other two moved south;
Hooker ordered it to wheel right and stem the rout. "Receive them on
your bayonets! Receive them on your bayonets!" he cried, not making
it clear whether he meant the demoralized Dutchmen or the rebels
somewhere in their rear, as he rode westward through the failing light
and into the teeth of the storm.

At Hazel Grove, sealed off from the uproar which by now was
just over a mile away, a regiment of Pennsylvania cavalry received at
about this same time, between sunset and moonrise, orders to join Howard near Wilderness Church. With no suggestion of urgency in the message and no hint that a clash had occurred, let alone a retreat, the troopers mounted and set out northwestward on a trail too narrow for anything more than a column of twos. They rode at a walk, talking casually
among themselves, their weapons sheathed, until they approached the
turnpike: at which point the major in command barely had time to cry,
"Draw sabers! Charge!" before they ran spang into a whole Confederate

division moving eastward through darkness that all of a sudden was stitched with muzzle flashes and filled with yells and twittering bullets. One side was about as startled as the other. The riders managed to hack their way out of the melee, though by the time they reassembled in the moonlight back near Chancellorsville a good many saddles had been emptied and a number of troopers had been captured, along with their unmanageable horses.

For blue and gray alike, whether mounted or afoot, the meeting engagement had some of the qualities of a nightmare too awful to be remembered except in unavoidable snatches. But for other Union soldiers, east of there, such an experience would have been counted almost mild in comparison with the one they blundered into a few hours later, in which blue was pitted not only against gray, but also against blue. Down around Catharine Furnace, deep in enemy territory, Dan Sickles knew nothing of what had been happening until well past sundown, when he heard the roar of batteries massed on the heights at Hazel Grove and Fairview, far in his rear. Informed at last of the enemy flank attack, which placed his two divisions precariously between the superior halves of the rebel army and thus exposed him to the danger of being pinched off and surrounded, he pulled hurriedly back to Hazel Grove — unhindered, so far, but by no means out of the trap whose jaws seemed likely to snap shut at any moment. By now it was past 9 o'clock, and except for occasional bellows by the 22 guns posted here and the 34 at Fairview, the firing had died to a mutter. Placing one division on the left and the other on the right of a trail leading northward through the forest, Sickles prepared to continue his march to the comparative safety of the turnpike. He had scarcely set out, however, before the two columns lost the trail and drifted apart, one veering east and the other west, with the result that they ran into horrendous trouble in both directions. The division on the left angled into a line of Confederates, alert behind hastily improvised intrenchments, while the one on the right stumbled into a similar line along which one of Slocum's divisions was deployed. Both broke into flames on contact, and a three-sided fight was in progress as suddenly as if someone had thrown a switch. Caught in what a participant called "one vast square of fire," Sickles' troops milled aimlessly, throwing bullets indiscriminately east and west. Shouts of "Don't fire! We're friends!" brought heavier volleys from both sides of the gauntlet, and consternation reached a climax when rival batteries started pumping shell and canister into the frantic mass hemmed thus between the lines. Somehow, though, despite the darkness and confusion, Sickles finally managed to effect a withdrawal southward, in the direction he had come from. By midnight he had what was left of his two divisions back at Hazel Grove, where the men bedded down to wait for daylight, barely four hours off, and restore their jangled nerves as best they could.

Elsewhere along his contracted line — albeit the contraction had been accomplished more by Jackson's efforts than his own — Hooker saw to it that the rest of his army did likewise. He did not know what tomorrow was going to bring, but he intended to be ready for it. And in point of fact he had cause for confidence. Reynolds was over the river by now; his three divisions were available as a reserve. Even Howard's three, or anyhow a good part of them, had managed to reassemble in the vicinity of U.S. Ford, where they were brought to a halt after ricocheting northward off Lee's intrenchments east of Chancellorsville. Meade's three had been unaffected by the turmoil across the way. Couch and Slocum, under cover of the 56-gun barrage from Hazel Grove and Fairview, had adapted their four divisions to the altered situation, along with the one Sickles had left behind. Moreover, another brigade of cavalry was at hand, Averell having been called in from near Rapidan Station, where Stoneman had dropped him off, ostensibly to check Stuart's pursuit but actually, since there was no pursuit, to play little or no part in the southward raid. His total loss, after three days in enemy country, was 1 man killed and 4 wounded; Hooker was furious and relieved him on the spot. "If the enemy did not come to him, he should have gone to the enemy," Fighting Joe protested with unconscious irony. Apparently he could not see that this applied in his own case. He still depended on Sedgwick for the delivery of any blow that was to be struck, repeating in greater detail at 9 p.m. the instructions sent him earlier in the day. This time they were peremptory; Sedgwick was to "cross the Rappahannock at Fredericksburg on the receipt of this order." Leaving Gibbon to hold the town, he was to march at once on Chancellorsville and "attack and destroy any force he may fall in with on the road." This would bring him promptly into contact with Lee's rear, "and between us we will use him up.... Be sure not to fail." The pattern was unchanged. Now as before, Gallo-Hooker was leaving the confrontation of the bull to Paco-Sedgwick, while he himself stood fast behind the barrera to cheer him on.

　　　Lulled by what one insomniac called "the weird, plaintive notes of the whippoorwills," who would not let even a battle the size of this one cancel their serenade to the full, high-sailing moon, the army slept. From point to point the Wilderness was burning — "like a picture of hell," a cavalryman said of the scene as he viewed it from a hilltop — but the screams of the wounded caught earlier by the flames had died away, together with the growl and rumble of the guns. It was midnight and the Army of the Potomac took its rest.

　　　Though the Army of Northern Virginia was doing the same, west and south of the now one-handled Union dipper, it did so in an atmosphere of tragedy out of all ratio to the success it had scored today. Not only had Stonewall's plan for continuing the eastward drive by moonlight been abandoned, but Stonewall himself had been taken rearward, first on a stretcher and then in an ambulance, to a hospital tent near Wilderness Tavern, where even now, as midnight came and went, surgeons were laying out the probes and knives and saws they would use in their fight to save his life. Intimations of national tragedy, intensified by a sense of acute personal loss, pervaded the forest bivouacs as the rumor spread that Jackson had been wounded.

After telling Hill to bring his men forward in order to resume the stalled pursuit, he had proceeded east along the turnpike in search of a route that would intercept the expected blue retreat to U.S. Ford. As he and several members of his staff rode past the fringe of Confederate pickets, taking a secondary road that branched off through the woods on the left, they began hearing the sound of axes from up ahead, where the Federals were trimming and notching logs for a new line of breastworks. "General, don't you think this is the wrong place for you?" an officer asked. Jackson did not agree. "The danger is all over," he said. "The enemy is routed. Go back and tell A. P. Hill to press right on." Presently, though, with the ring of axes much nearer at hand, he drew rein and listened carefully. Then he turned and rode back the way he had come, apparently satisfied that the bluecoats, for all their frenzy of preparation, would be unable to resist what he intended to throw at them as soon as Hill got his troops into position. Soon he came upon Little Powell himself, riding forward with his staff to examine the ground over which he expected to advance, and the two parties returned together. To the pickets crouched in the brush ahead — North Carolinians whose apprehensiveness had been aroused by the meeting engagement, a short while ago, with the saber-swinging Pennsylvanians over on the turnpike — the mounted generals and their staffs, amounting in all to nearly a score of horsemen, must have had the sound of a troop of Union cavalry on the prowl or the advance element of a wave of attackers. At any rate that was the premise on which they acted in opening fire. "Cease firing! Cease firing!" Hill shouted, echoed by one of Jackson's officers: "Cease firing! You are firing into your own men!" Fortunately, no one had been hit by the sudden spatter of bullets, but the Tarheel commander believed he saw through a Yankee trick. "Who gave that order?" he cried. "It's a lie! Pour it into them, boys!" The boys did just that. Not only the pickets but the whole front-line battalion opened fire at twenty paces and with such devastating effect that the bodies of no less than fourteen horses were counted later in the immediate area.

Little Sorrel was not among them, having returned by then to the allegiance from which Stonewall had removed him, nearly two years ago, with his capture at Harpers Ferry. Frightened by the abrupt first clatter of fire from the pickets crouched in the brush ahead, he whirled and made a rearward dash through the woods. Jackson managed to turn him, though he could not slow him down, and was coming back west, his right arm raised to protect his face from low-hanging branches, when the second volley crashed. Once more Little Sorrel whirled and scampered toward the enemy lines, completely out of control now because his rider had been struck by three of the bullets, two in the left arm, which hung useless at his side, and one through the palm of the upraised hand, which he lowered and used as before, despite the pain, to turn the fear-crazed animal back toward his own lines. There one of the surviving officers, dismounted by the volley, caught hold of the horse's bridle and brought him to a stop, while another came up and braced the general in the saddle. He seemed dazed. "Wild fire, that, sir; wild fire," he exclaimed as he sat staring into the darkness lately stitched with muzzle flashes. All around them they could hear the groans and screams of injured men and horses. "How do you feel, General?" one of the officers asked, with the simplicity of great alarm, and Jackson replied: "You had better take me down. My arm is broken." They did so, finding him already so weak from shock and bleeding that he could not lift his feet from the stirrups. Freed at last of the restraining weight, Little Sorrel turned and ran for the third time toward the Union lines, and this time he made it. Meanwhile the two staffers laid the general under a tree. While one went off in search of a surgeon and the other was doing what he could to staunch the flow of blood from an artery severed in the left arm, just below the shoulder, Jackson began muttering to himself, as if in disbelief of what had happened. "My own men," he said.

That was about 9.30; the next two hours were a restless extension of the nightmare as Federal batteries at Fairview began firing, the gunners having spotted the moonlit confusion just over half a mile away. Presently the second of Jackson's two attendant staff officers returned through the storm of bursting shells with a regimental surgeon, who administered first aid and ordered the general taken rearward on a stretcher. This had to be done under artillery fire so intense that the bearers were forced to stop and lie flat from time to time, as much for Jackson's protection as their own. On several such occasions they almost dropped him, and once they did, hard on the injured arm, which made him groan with pain for the first time. At last they found an ambulance and got him back to the aid station near Wilderness Tavern, where his medical director, Dr Hunter McGuire, took one look at "the fixed, rigid face and the thin lips, so tightly compressed that the impression of the teeth could be seen through them," and ordered the patient prepared for surgery. "What an infinite blessing... blessing... blessing," Stonewall murmured as the chloroform blurred his pain. Then McGuire removed the shattered left arm, all but a two-inch stump. Coming out of the anesthetic, half an hour later — it was now about 3 o'clock in the morning — Jackson said that during the operation he had experienced "the most delightful music," which he now supposed had been the singing of the bone-saw. At that point, however, he was interrupted by a staff officer just arrived from the front. Tragedy had succeeded tragedy.

Hill had been incapacitated, struck in both legs by shell fragments, and had called on Jeb Stuart to take command instead of Rodes, the senior infantry brigadier, who until today had never led anything larger than a brigade. Stuart had come at a gallop from Ely's Ford, altogether willing. Knowing little of the situation and almost nothing of Stonewall's plans, however, he had sent to him for instructions or advice. Jackson stirred, contracting his brow at the effort. For a moment the light of battle returned to his eyes. Then it faded; his face relaxed. Even the exertion of thought was too much for him in his weakened condition. "I don't know — I can't tell," he stammered. "Say to General Stuart he must do what he thinks best."

Stuart would do that anyhow, of course, and so would Lee, who was informed at about this same time of the progress of the flank attack and the climactic wounding of his chief lieutenant. "Ah, Captain," he said; he shook his head; "Any victory is dearly bought which deprives us of the services of General Jackson, even for a short time." When the officer started to give him further details of the accident Lee stopped him. "Ah, don't talk about it. Thank God it is no worse." He was quick to agree, however, when the young man expressed the opinion that it had been Stonewall's intention to continue the attack. "Those people must be pressed today," Lee said decisively, and he put this into more formal language at once in a note to Stuart: "It is necessary that the glorious victory thus far achieved be prosecuted with the utmost vigor, and the enemy given no time to rally. . . . Endeavor, therefore, to dispossess them of Chancellorsville, which will permit the union of the army."

★ ★ ★

Hooker did not wait for Stuart or anyone else to dispossess him of Chancellorsville. He dispossessed himself. After establishing in the predawn darkness a secondary line of defense — a formidable V-shaped affair, with Reynolds deployed along Hunting Run, Meade at the southern apex, where the roads from Ely's and U.S. Fords came together in rear of army headquarters, and the fragments of Howard reassembled in Meade's old position along Mineral Spring Run, so that the flanks were anchored, right and left, on the Rapidan and the Rappahannock — he rode forward at first light, past the works still held by Couch and Slocum around Fairview, to confer in person with Sickles. Despite last night's horrendous experience of being mauled by foes and friends, Sickles had got his nerve back and was all for holding his ground; but Hooker would not hear of it, and ordered him to withdraw at once. It was this well-intentioned readjustment, designed to tidy up his lines and consolidate his defenses south of the vital crossroads, which resulted in his dispossession. Hazel Grove turned out to be the key to the whole advance position, since rebel artillery posted there could enfilade the intrenchments around Fairview, which in turn were all that covered Chancellorsville itself. The result was that everything south of the improvised V came suddenly unglued, and Hooker was left, scarcely twelve hours after his apparent delivery from the first, with a possible second disaster on his hands.

Stuart's advance, south of the turnpike and into the rising sun, coincided with Sickles' withdrawal, the final stages of which became a rout as the graybacks swarmed into Hazel Grove and overran the tail of the blue column. Immediately behind the first wave of attackers came the guns, 30 of them slamming away from the just-won heights at the Federals massed around Fairview, while another 30 assailed the western flank from a position near Howard's former headquarters, back out the pike, and 24 more were roaring from down the plank road to the southeast. Lee's midwinter reorganization of the Confederate long arm, for increased flexibility in close-up support, was paying short-term dividends this morning. Caught in the converging fire of these 84 guns, along with others west and south, the troops of Couch and Slocum were infected by the panic Sickles' men brought out of the smoke at Hazel Grove. North of the pike, sheltered by the breastworks Jackson had heard them constructing the night before, the bluecoats held fast against repeated assaults by the rebel infantry, but they were galled by the crossfire from batteries whose shots were plowing the fields around the crossroads in their rear and smashing their lines of supply and communication. Not even the Chancellor mansion, converted by now into a hospital as well as a headquarters by surgeons who took doors off their hinges and propped them on chairs for use as operating tables, was safe from the bombardment — as Hooker himself discovered presently, in a most emphatic manner. Shortly after 9 o'clock he was standing on the southwest veranda, leaning against one of the squat wooden pillars, when a solid projectile struck and split it lengthwise. He fell heavily to the floor, stunned by the shock. His aides gathered round and took him out into the yard, where they laid him on a blanket and poured a jolt of brandy down his throat. Revived by this first drink in weeks, Fighting Joe got up, rather wobbly still, and walked off a short distance, calling for his horse. It was well that he did, for just after he rose a second cannonball landed directly on the blanket, as if to emphasize the notion suggested by the first that the war had become an intensely personal matter between the Union commander and the rebel gunners who were probing for his life. He mounted awkwardly, suffering from a numbness on the side of his body that had been in contact with the shattered pillar, and rode for the rear, accompanied by his staff.

Despite the fact that he would succeed to command of the army in the event that its present chief was incapacitated, Couch knew nothing of Hooker's precipitate change of base until about 10 o'clock, when he received a summons to join him behind Meade's lines, where the apex of the secondary V came down to within a mile of the Chancellor house. Though he had his hands quite full just then — it was during the past half hour that the lines around Fairview had begun to come unglued in earnest — Couch told Hancock to take charge, and set out rearward in the wake of his chief, whom he found stretched out on a cot in a tent beside the road to U.S. Ford. "Couch, I turn the command of the army over to you," the injured general said, raising himself on one elbow as he spoke. However, his next words showed that he did not really mean what he had said. Whether or not he had control of himself at this point was open to question, but there was no doubt that he intended to retain control of the army. "You will withdraw it and place it in the position designated on this map," he added, indicating a field sketch with the V drawn on it to show where the new front lines would run. Couch perhaps was relieved to hear that he would not be given full control, along with full responsibility — "If he is killed, what shall I do with this disjointed army?" he had asked himself as soon as he heard that Hooker had been hurt — but others were hoping fervently that he would take charge; for he was known to be a fighter. "By God, we'll have some fighting now," a colonel said stoutly as Couch emerged from the tent. Meade looked inquiringly at his friend, hoping to receive at last the order for which he had been waiting all morning: Go in. Instead, Couch shook his head by way of reply and relayed Hooker's instructions for a withdrawal.

In any event, such instructions were superfluous by now except as they applied to Hancock, whose division was the only one still maintaining, however shakily, its forward position in a state that even approached cohesiveness. The choice, if the army's present disjointed condition allowed for any choice at all, lay not in whether or not to withdraw, as Hooker expressly directed, but in whether or not to counterattack and thus attempt to recover what had been lost by the retreat already in progress; which manifestly would be difficult, if not downright impossible, since the Confederates had just seized the heights at Fairview and with them domination of the open fields across which the troops of Sickles, Couch, and Slocum were streaming to find sanctuary within the line of breastworks to the north. Hancock's rear-guard division was having to back-pedal fast to keep from being cut off or overrun by a horde of butternut pursuers who were screaming as triumphantly now, and with what appeared to be equally good cause, as they had done when they bore down on Howard's startled Dutchmen yesterday. While Stuart pressed eastward, making his largest gains on the south side of the turnpike, Lee had been pushing north and west up the plank road and reaching out simultaneously to the left, past Catharine Furnace, for the anticipated hookup. It was his belief that the best and quickest way to accomplish the reunion of the two wings of his army would be to uncover Chancellorsville, after which it was his intention to launch a full-scale joint assault that would throw Hooker back against the Rappahannock and destroy him.

For a time it looked as if that might indeed be possible in the ten full hours of daylight still remaining. Never before, perhaps, had the Army of Northern Virginia fought with such frenzy and exaltation, such apparent confidence in its invincibility under Lee. Accompanied by the roar of artillery from the dominant heights, McLaws and Anderson moved steadily westward up the turnpike and the plank road, while Rodes, Colston, and Henry Heth — the senior brigadier in Hill's division — plunged eastward along both sides of the turnpike, cheered on by Stuart, who rode among them, jaunty in his red-lined cape, hoicking them up to the firing line and singing at the top of his voice some new words set to a familiar tune: "Old Joe Hooker, won't you come out the Wilderness?" All advanced rapidly toward the common objective, east and west, as the bluecoats faded back from contact. Shortly before 10.30 the two wings came together with a mighty shout in the hundred-acre clearing around the Chancellor mansion, which had been set afire by the bombardment. Lee rode forward from Hazel Grove, past Fairview, on whose crown two dozen guns had been massed to tear at the rear of the retreating enemy columns, and then into the yard of the burning house, formerly headquarters of the Union army, where the jubilant Confederates, recognizing the gray-bearded author of their victory, tendered him the wildest demonstration of their lives. "The fierce soldiers with their faces blackened with the smoke of battle, the wounded crawling with feeble limbs from the fury of the devouring flames, all seemed possessed with a common impulse," a staff man later wrote. "One long, unbroken cheer, in which the feeble cry of those who lay helpless on the earth blended with the strong voices of those who still fought, rose high above the roar of battle and hailed the presence of the victorious chief. He sat in the full realization of all that soldiers dream of — triumph. . . . As I looked upon him in the complete fruition of the success which his genius, courage, and confidence in his army had won," the officer added, "I thought that it must have been from such a scene that men in ancient times rose to the dignity of gods."

In the midst of this rousing accolade a courier arrived with a dispatch from Jackson, formally reporting that the extent of his wounds had compelled him to relinquish command of his corps. Lee had not known till now of the amputation, and the news shook him profoundly. His elation abruptly replaced by sadness, he dictated in reply an expression of regret. "Could I have directed events," he told his wounded lieutenant, "I would have chosen for the good of the country to be disabled in your stead," and added: "I congratulate you upon the victory, which is due to your skill and energy." This done, he returned to the business at hand. He had, as he said, won a victory; but if it was to amount to much more than the killing, as before, of large numbers of an enemy whose reserves were practically limitless, the present advantage would have to be pressed to the point at which Hooker, caught in the coils of the Rappahannock and with the scare still on him, would have to choose between slaughter and surrender. Before this could be accomplished, however, or even begin to be accomplished by a resumption of the advance, the attackers themselves would have to be reorganized and realigned for the final sweep of the fields and thickets stretching northward to the river. Lee gave instructions for this to be done as quickly as possible, and while waiting got off a dispatch to Davis in Richmond. "We have again to thank Almighty God for a great victory," he announced.

His hope was that he would be sending another announcement of an even greater victory by nightfall. But just as he was about to order the attack, a courier on a lathered horse rode in from the east with news of a disaster. At dawn that morning, with a rush across the pontoon bridge they had thrown under cover of darkness, the Federals had occupied Fredericksburg. Sedgwick then had feinted at the thinly held defenses on the ridge beyond the town, first on the far left and then the right, by way of distracting attention from his main effort against the center. This too had been repulsed, not once but twice, before the weight of numbers told and the bluecoats swarmed up and over Marye's Heights. In accordance with previous instructions designed for such a crisis, Early had withdrawn southward to protect the army's trains at Guiney Station; but Sedgwick had not pursued in that direction. Instead, he had moved — was moving now — due west along the plank road, which lay open in Lee's rear. This was the worst of all possible threats, and the southern commander had no choice except to meet it at this worst of all possible times. Postponing the assault on Hooker, he detached McLaws to head eastward and delay Sedgwick, if possible, while Anderson extended his present right out the River Road to prevent a junction of the two Union forces in case Sedgwick managed to sidestep McLaws or brush him out of the way. By now it was close to 3 o'clock. Holding Rodes and Heth in their jump-off positions, Lee ordered Colston to move up the Ely's Ford Road in order to establish and maintain contact with Hooker, who might be emboldened by this new turn of events. "Don't engage seriously," Lee told Colston, "but keep the enemy in check and prevent him from advancing. Move at once."

Now as before, he was improvising, dividing his badly outnumbered army in order to deal with a two-pronged menace. While McLaws swung east to throw his 7000 soldiers in the teeth of Sedgwick's 20,000 or more, Lee would endeavor to hold Hooker's 80,000 in position with his own 37,000. When and if he managed to stabilize the situation — as Jackson had done, two days ago, with the advance beyond Tabernacle Church — he would decide which of the two enemy wings to leap at, north or east. Meanwhile, as usual, he was prepared to take advantage of any blunder his opponents might commit, and he was determined to recover the initiative. Above all, he kept his head and refused to take counsel of his fears. When an excited officer, alarmed by the threat to the army's rear, arrived with a lurid eyewitness account of the loss of Marye's Heights, Lee cut him short. "We will attend to Mr Sedgwick later," he said calmly.

What with the relentless depletion of his forces, siphoned off westward at the rate of a corps a day for the past two days, and the spate of discretionary orders, generally so delayed in transmission that the conditions under which they had been issued no longer obtained by the time they came to hand, John Sedgwick — "Uncle John" to his troops, a fifty-year-old bachelor New Englander with thirty years of army service, including West Point, the Mexican War, the Kansas border troubles, and frontier Indian uprisings, in all of which he had shown a good deal more of plodding dependability than of flash — had difficulty in maintaining the unruffled disposition for which he was beloved. Even the peremptory dispatch received last night, after the uproar subsided in the thickets across the way, had left him somewhat puzzled. Hooker told him to "cross the Rappahannock at Fredericksburg on receipt of this order," which was clear enough, so far as the words themselves went; but what did it mean? Surely the army commander knew he was already across the Rappahannock, and in fact had been across it for the past three days. ... Deciding that it meant what it ought to mean, he told Gibbon, whose division was still at Falmouth, to cross the river at dawn and seize the west-bank town, preparatory to joining in the attack Sedgwick was planning to launch against the fortified ridge with his other three divisions. He had not taken part in the December battle, having been laid up with three wounds received at Antietam, but he knew well enough what Burnside had encountered on this ground. For a time, indeed, it appeared that Sedgwick was going to do no better, despite his usual methodical preparations. After feinting on the left and right, he sent ten regiments in mass against the sunken road at the foot of the heights where so many men had come to grief, five months ago, when two of Longstreet's divisions held this section of the line. Now, however, so well had the feints misled the defenders, all that were there were two slim regiments and sixteen guns. Even so, the first two assaults were bloodily repulsed. As the bluecoats dropped back into the swale for a breather, preparatory to giving the thing another try, the colonel of a Wisconsin regiment made a short speech to the men who would lead the third assault. "When the signal *forward* is given you will advance at double-quick," he told them. "You will not fire a gun and you will not stop until you get the order to halt." He paused briefly, then added: "You will never get that order."

The Badgers gulped, absorbing the shock of this, then cheered and went in fast, the other nine regiments following close on their heels. Beyond the stone wall to their front, Barksdale's two Mississippi regiments turned loose with everything they had, attempting to shatter the head of the column of assault, while four batteries of the Washington Artillery, a crack New Orleans outfit, broke into a frenzied roar on the ridge beyond. The attackers took their losses and kept going, over the wall and among the defenders with the bayonet, then across the sunken road and up the slope of Marye's Heights with scarcely a pause, staring directly into the muzzles of the flaming guns on the crest. These too were taken in a rush as the cannoneers got off a final volley and broke for the rear. Within half an hour, and at a cost of no more than 1500 casualties, Sedgwick had his flags aflutter on ground that Burnside had spent 6300 men for no more than a fairly close-up look at, back in December. The bluecoats went into a victory dance, hurrahing and thumping each other on the back in celebration of their triumph; whereas the Confederates, several hundred of whom had been captured, were correspondingly dejected or wrathful, depending on the individual reaction to defeat. One cannoneer, who had managed to get away at the last moment, just as the Union wave broke over his battery, was altogether furious. "Guns be damned!" he replied hotly when a reserve artillerist twitted him by asking where his guns were. "I reckon now the people of the Southern Confederacy are satisfied that Barksdale's Brigade and the Washington Artillery can't whip the whole damned Yankee army!"

Having broken Jubal Early's line and thrown him into retreat, Sedgwick would have enjoyed pursuing his West Point classmate down the Telegraph Road, but another classmate, Hooker himself, had forbidden this by insisting that he push westward without delay, so that between them, as Fighting Joe put it, they could "use up" Lee. Moreover, at 10 o'clock — less than an hour after being stunned by the split pillar, and at about the same time, as it turned out, that his forward defenses began to come unglued — Hooker had his adjutant send Sedgwick a dispatch reminding him of his primary mission: "You will hurry up your column. The enemy's right flank now rests near the plank road at Chancellorsville, all exposed. You will attack at once." This reached Sedgwick at about 11.30, amid the victory celebration on Marye's Heights, and he did what he could to comply. Leaving Gibbon to hold Fredericksburg in his rear, he began to prepare his other three divisions for the advance on Lee. It was a time-consuming business, however, to break up the celebration and get the troops into formation for the march. The lead division did not get started until 2 o'clock, and it was brought to a sudden halt within the hour, just over a mile from Marye's Heights, by the sight of Confederate skirmishers in position along a ridge athwart the road. Despite Hooker's assurance that Lee's flank was "all exposed," the graybacks seemed quite vigilant, and what was more they appeared to be present in considerable strength, with guns barking aggressively in support. Sedgwick was obliged to halt and deploy in the face of the resistance, at the cost of burning more daylight.

Slowly the rebels faded back, bristling as they went, leapfrogging their guns from ridge to ridge and flailing the pursuers all the time. Near Salem Church, a mile ahead and a mile short of the junction of the plank road and the turnpike, they stiffened. It was 4 o'clock by now; the day was going fast, and Sedgwick was still a good half-dozen miles from Chancellorsville. Without waiting for the others to come up, he sent the troops of his lead division forward on the run. At first they made headway, driving the graybacks before them, but then they encountered a heavy line of battle. Repulsed, they came streaming back across the fields. The second division was up by now, however, with the third not far behind, and between them they managed to check the pursuit, though by the time Sedgwick got them rallied and into attack formation the day was too far gone for fighting. Aware by now that he had run into something considerably stronger than a mere rear guard, he set up a perimetrical defense and passed the word for his 22,000 soldiers to bed down.

Today had been a hard day. Tomorrow gave promise of being even harder. He had set out to put the squeeze on Lee, but it had begun to seem to him that he was the one in danger now. All around him, south and east as well as west, he could hear enemy columns moving in the darkness. "Sedgwick scarcely slept that night," an observant soldier later recalled. "From time to time he dictated a dispatch to General Hooker. He would walk for a few paces apart and listen; then returning he would lie down again in the damp grass, with his saddle for a pillow, and try to sleep. The night was inexpressibly gloomy."

The night was inexpressibly gloomy, and he was in graver danger than he knew. All that had stood in his way at the outset, when he began his march from Marye's Heights, had been a single brigade of Alabamians, stationed for the past three days on outpost duty at Banks Ford, from which point their commander, Brigadier General Cadmus Wilcox, had shifted them, on his own initiative, when he learned that Early's defenses had been pierced. Determined to do what he could to protect Lee's unguarded rear, he had taken up a position athwart the plank road, spreading his men in the semblance of a stout line of skirmishers, and thus had managed to bluff Sedgwick into caution, delaying his advance until McLaws had had time to post his division near Salem Church and rock the charging bluecoats on their heels. As a result, when darkness ended the fighting here to the east of Chancellorsville, Lee had what he had been hoping for: a more or less stable situation and the opportunity, as he had said, to "attend to Mr Sedgwick." Early, he learned, had retreated only a couple of miles down the Telegraph Road, then had halted on finding that he was unpursued. Lee wrote him, just after sunset, that McLaws was confronting the Federals east of Salem Church; "If . . . you could come upon their left flank, and communicate with General McLaws, I think you would demolish them." A similar message went to McLaws, instructing him to co-operate with Early. "It is necessary to beat the enemy," Lee told him, "and I hope you will do it."

A dawn reconnaissance — Monday now: May 4 — showed Hooker's intrenchments well laid out and greatly strengthened overnight, the flanks securely anchored below and above the U.S. Ford escape hatch, and the whole supported by batteries massed in depth. While this discouraged attack, it also seemed to indicate that the Federals had gone entirely on the defensive in the region north of Chancellorsville. At any rate Lee proceeded on that assumption. Canceling a projected feeling-out of the enemy lines along Mineral Spring Run, he shifted half of Heth's division from the far left, beyond Colston and Rodes, to take up Anderson's position on the right, and ordered Anderson east to join with McLaws and Early in removing the threat to his rear. His plan, if daring, was simple enough. Stuart and the 25,000 survivors of Jackson's flanking column were given the task of keeping Hooker's 80,000 penned in their breastworks, while the remaining 22,000 Confederates disposed of Sedgwick, who had about the same number to the east. This last was now the main effort, and Lee decided to supervise it in person. Riding over to Salem Church at noon, he conferred with McLaws, who was awaiting Anderson's arrival before completing his dispositions for attack, and then proceeded east, skirting the southward bulge of Sedgwick's perimeter, to see Early. He found him on Marye's Heights, which he had reoccupied soon after sunrise, posting the remnant of Barksdale's brigade in the sunken road to resist another possible advance by Gibbon, who had retired into Fredericksburg. The plan of attack, as McLaws and Early had worked it out, was for Anderson to take up a position between them, confronting Sedgwick from the south, while they moved against him, simultaneously, from the east and west. The result, if all went well, would be his destruction. Lee gave his approval, though he saw that this would involve a good deal of maneuvering over difficult terrain, and rode back toward the center.

It was past 2 o'clock by now, and Anderson was not yet in position. Time was running out for Lee today, as it had done the day before for Sedgwick. Already he was finding what it cost him to be deprived even temporarily of the services of Jackson, of whom he would say before the week was over: "He has lost his left arm, but I have lost my right." More hours were spent examining the approaches and correcting the alignment of the columns so as to avoid collisions. While Anderson continued to balk, McLaws was strangely apathetic and Early floundered in the ravines across the way; it was 6 o'clock before all the troops were in position and the signal guns were fired. The fighting was savage

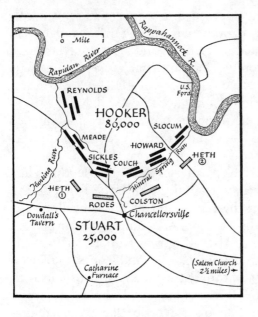

at scattered points, especially on Early's front, but McLaws got lost in a maze of thickets and scarcely made contact, either with the enemy or with Anderson, whose men added to the confusion by firing into each other as they advanced. Fog thickened the dusk and the disjointed movement lurched to a halt within an hour. Sedgwick had been shaken, though hardly demolished. Anxious to exploit his gains, such as they were, before the Federals reintrenched or got away across the river, Lee for the first time in his career ordered a night attack. While the artillery shelled Banks Ford in the darkness, attempting to seal off the exit, the infantry groped about in the fog, dog-tired, and made no progress. At first light, the skirmishers recovered their sense of direction, pushed forward, and found that the works to their front were empty; Sedgwick had escaped. Though his casualties had been heavy — worse than 4600 in all, including the men lost earlier — he had got his three divisions to safety across a bridge the engineers had thrown a mile below Banks Ford, well beyond range of the all-night interdictory fire.

Word came presently from Barksdale that Gibbon too had recrossed the river at Fredericksburg and cut his pontoons loose from the west bank. This meant that for the first time in three days no live, uncaptured bluecoats remained on the Confederate side of the Rappahannock except the ones intrenched above Chancellorsville; Lee had abolished the threat to his rear. Though he was far from satisfied, having failed in another of a lengthening sequence of attempts to destroy a considerable segment of the Union army, he had at least restored — and even improved — the situation that had existed yesterday, when he was preparing to give Hooker his undivided attention. Once more intent on destruction, he allowed the men of McLaws and Anderson no rest, but ordered them to take up the march back to Chancellorsville, intending for them to resume the offensive they had abandoned for Sedgwick's sake the day before. Stuart reported that the Federals, though still present in great strength behind their V, had made no attempt to move against him, either yesterday or so far this morning; yet Lee did what he could to hasten the march westward, not so much out of fear that Hooker would lash out at Stuart, whom he outnumbered better than three to one, as out of fear that he would do as Sedgwick had done and make his escape across the river before the Confederates had time to reconcentrate and crush him.

In point of fact, Lee's fears on the latter count were more valid than he had any way of knowing, not having attended a council of war held the night before at his opponent's headquarters. At midnight, while Sedgwick was beginning his withdrawal across the Rappahannock, Hooker had called his other corps commanders together to vote on whether they should do the same. Couch, Reynolds, Meade, Howard, and Sickles reported promptly, but Slocum, who had the farthest to come, did not arrive until after the meeting had broken up. Hooker put the question to them — remarking, as Couch would recall, "that his instructions compelled him to cover Washington, not to jeopardize the army, etc." — then retired to let them talk it over among themselves. Reynolds was much fatigued from loss of sleep; he lay down in one corner of the tent to get some rest, telling Meade to vote his proxy for attack. Meade did so, adding his own vote to that effect. Howard too was for taking the offensive; for unlike Meade and Reynolds, whose two corps had scarcely fired a shot, he had a reputation to retrieve. Couch on the other hand voted to withdraw, but made it clear that he favored such a course only because Hooker was still in charge. Sickles, whose corps had suffered almost as many casualties as any two of the other five combined, was in favor of pulling back at once, Hooker or no Hooker. Fighting Joe returned, was given the three-to-two opinion, and adjourned the council with the announcement that he intended to withdraw the army beyond the river as soon as possible. As the generals left the tent, Reynolds broke out angrily, quite loud enough for Hooker to overhear him: "What was the use of calling us together at this time of night when he intended to retreat anyhow?"

Their instructions were to cut whatever roads were necessary, leading from their present positions back to U.S. Ford, while the army engineers were selecting a strong inner line, anchored a mile above and a mile below the two pontoon bridges, for Meade's corps to occupy in covering the withdrawal. All were hard at work on their various assignments before dawn on the 5th, at which time Hooker crossed in person, accompanied by his staff. Then at noon, with the pull-back to the inner line completed, rain began to fall.

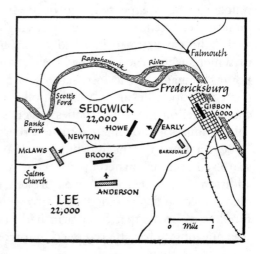

It fell in earnest, developing quickly into what one diarist called "a tremendous cold storm." By midnight the river had risen six feet, endangering the bridges and interrupting the retreat before more than a handful of regiments had reached the opposite bank. Cut off from Hooker, Couch believed he saw his chance. "We will stay where we are and fight it out," he announced. But peremptory orders arrived at 2 a.m. for the movement to be continued. One of the bridges was cannibalized to piece out the other, and the crossing was resumed. By midmorning Wednesday, May 6, it was completed. Except for the dead and missing, who would not be coming back, the army's week-long excursion south of the river had come full circle.

Lee was up by then, after being delayed by the storm the day before, but when his skirmishers pushed forward through the dripping woods they found the enemy gone. He lost his temper at the news and scolded the brigadier who brought it. "That is the way you young men always do," he fumed. "You allow those people to get away. I tell you what to do, but you won't do it!" He gestured impatiently. "Go after them, and damage them all you can!" But no further damage was possible; the bluecoats were well beyond his reach. At a cost of less than 13,000 casualties he had inflicted more than 17,000 and had won what future critics would call the most brilliant victory of his career, but he was by no means satisfied. He had aimed at total capture or annihilation of the foe, and the extent to which he had fallen short of this was, to his mind, the extent to which he had failed. Leaving a few regiments to tend the wounded, bury the dead, and glean the spoils abandoned by the Unionists on the field, he marched the rest of his army back through the rain-drenched Wilderness to Fredericksburg and the comparative comfort of the camps it had left a week ago, when word first came that the enemy was across the Rappahannock.

Back at Falmouth that evening, while his army straggled eastward in his wake, Hooker learned that Stoneman's raid, from which so much had been expected, had been almost a total failure. Intending, as he later reported, to "magnify our small force into overwhelming numbers," the cavalryman had broken up his column into fragments, none of which, as it turned out, had been strong enough to do more than temporary damage to the installations in Lee's rear. According to one disgusted trooper, "Our only accomplishments were the burning of a few canal boats on the upper James River, some bridges, hen roosts, and tobacco houses." Stoneman returned the way he had come, recrossing at Raccoon Ford on the morning of May 7, while other portions of his scattered column turned up as far away as Yorktown. His total losses, in addition to about 1000 horses broken down and abandoned, were 82 men killed and wounded and 307 missing. These figures seemed to Hooker to prove that Stoneman had not been seriously engaged, and it was not long before he removed him from command. However, his own casualties, while quite as heavy as anyone on his own side of the line could have desired — the ultimate total was 17,287, as compared to Lee's 12,821 — were equally condemning, though in a different way, since a breakdown of them indicated the disjointed manner in which he had fought and refrained from fighting the battle. Meade and Reynolds, for example, had lost fewer than 1000 men between them, while Sedgwick and Sickles had lost more than four times that number each. Obviously Lincoln's parting admonition, "Put in all your men," had been ignored. Hooker was quick to place the blame for his defeat on Stoneman, Averell, Howard, and Sedgwick, sometimes singly and at other times collectively. It was only in private, and some weeks later, that he was able to see, or at any rate confess, where the real trouble had lain. "I was not hurt by a shell, and I was not drunk," he told a fellow officer. "For once I lost confidence in Joe Hooker, and that is all there is to it."

In time that would become the registered consensus, but for the present many of his compatriots were hard put to understand how such a disaster had come about. Horace Greeley staggered into the *Tribune* managing editor's office Thursday morning, his face a ghastly color and his lips trembling. "My God, it is horrible," he exclaimed. "Horrible. And to think of it — 130,000 magnificent soldiers so cut to pieces by less than 60,000 half-starved ragamuffins!" An Episcopal clergyman, also in New York, could not reconcile the various reports and rumors he recorded in his diary that night. "It would seem that Hooker has beaten Lee, and that Lee has beaten Hooker; that we have taken Fredericksburg, and that the rebels have taken it also; that we have 4500 prisoners, and the rebels 5400; that Hooker has cut off Lee's retreat, and Lee has cut off Sedgwick's retreat, and Sedgwick has cut off everybody's retreat generally, but has retreated himself although his retreat was cut off. . . . In short, all is utter confusion. Everything seems to be everywhere, and everybody all over, and there is no getting at any truth." Official Washington was similarly confused and dismayed. When Sumner of Massachusetts heard that Hooker had been whipped, he flung up his hands and struck an attitude of despair. "Lost — lost," he groaned. "All is lost!" But the hardest-hit man of them all was Lincoln, whose hopes had had the longest way to fall. Six months ago, on the heels of Emancipation, he had foreseen clear sailing for the ship of state provided the helmsman kept a steady hand on the tiller. "We are like whalers who have been on a long chase," he told a friend. "We have at last got the harpoon into the monster, but we must now look how we steer, or with one flop of his tail he will send us all into eternity." Then had come Fredericksburg, and he had said: "If there is a worse place than Hell, I am in it." Now there was this, a still harder flop of the monster's tail, and Hooker and the Army of the Potomac had gone sprawling. Even before the news arrived, a White House caller had found the President "anxious and harassed beyond any power of description." Yet this was nothing compared to his reaction later in the day, when he reappeared with a telegram in his hand. "News from the army," he said in a trembling voice. The visitor read that Hooker was in retreat, and looking up saw that Lincoln's face, "usually sallow, was ashen in hue. The paper on the wall behind him was of the tint known as 'French gray,' and even in that moment of sorrow . . . I vaguely took in the thought that the complexion of the anguished President's visage was like that of the wall." He walked up and down the room, hands clasped behind his back. "My God, my God," he exclaimed as he paced back and forth. "What will the country say? What will the country say?"

Within the ranks of the army itself, slogging down the muddy roads toward Falmouth, the reaction was not unlike the New York clergyman's. "No one seems to understand this move," a Pennsylvania private wrote, "but I have no doubt it is all right." He belonged to Meade's corps, which had seen very little fighting, and he could not quite comprehend that what he had been involved in was a defeat. All he knew for certain was that the march back to camp was a hard one. "Most of the way the mud was over shoe, in some places knee deep, and the rain made our loads terrible to tired shoulders." Others knew well enough that they had taken part in a fiasco. "Go boil your shirt!" was their reply to jokes attempted by roadside stragglers. Turning the matter over in their minds, they could see that Hooker had been trounced, but they could not see that this applied to themselves, who had fought as well as ever — except, of course, the unregenerate Dutchmen — whenever and wherever they got the chance. Mostly, though, they preferred to ignore the question of praise or blame. "And thus ends the second attempt on the capture of Fredericksburg," a Maine soldier recorded when he got back to Falmouth. "I have nothing to say about it in any way. I have no opinions to express about the Gen'ls or the men nor do I wish to. I leave it in the hands of God. I don't want to think of it at all."

★ ★ ★

Unquestionably, this latest addition to the lengthening roster of Confederate victories was a great one. Indeed, considering the odds that had been faced and overcome, it was perhaps in terms of glory the greatest of them all; *Chancellorsville* would be stitched with pride across the crowded banners of the Army of Northern Virginia. But its ultimate worth, as compared to its cost, depended in large measure on the outcome of Stonewall Jackson's present indisposition. As Lee had said on Sunday morning, when he first learned that his lieutenant had been wounded, "Any victory is dearly bought which deprives us of the services of General Jackson, even for a short time."

So far — that is, up to the time when Hooker threw in the sponge and the northern army fell back across the Rappahannock — Dr McGuire's prognosis had been most encouraging and the general himself had been in excellent spirits, despite the loss of his arm. "I am wounded but not depressed," he said when he woke from the sleep that followed the amputation. "I believe it was according to God's will, and I can wait until He makes his object known to me." Presently, when Lee's midday note was brought, congratulating him on the victory, "which is due to your skill and energy," Jackson permitted himself the one criticism he had ever made of his commander. "General Lee is very kind," he said, "but he should give the praise to God." Next day, May 4, with Sedgwick threatening the army's rear, he was removed to safety in an ambulance. The route was south to Todd's Tavern, then southeast, through Spotsylvania Court House, to Guiney Station, where he had met his wife and child, two weeks ago today, to begin the idyl that had ended with the news that Hooker was on the march. All along the way, country people lined the roadside to watch the ambulance go by. They brought with them, and held out for the attendants to accept, such few gifts as their larders afforded in these hard times, cool buttermilk, hot biscuits, and fried chicken. Jackson was pleased by this evidence of their concern, and for much of the 25-mile journey he chatted with an aide, even responding to a question as to what he thought of Hooker's plan for the battle whose guns rumbled fainter as the ambulance rolled south. "It was in the main a good conception, sir; an excellent plan. But he should not have sent away his cavalry. That was his great blunder. It was that which enabled me to turn him, without his being aware of it, and to take him by the rear." Of his own share in frustrating that plan, he added that he believed his flank attack had been "the most successful movement of my life. But I have received more credit for it than I deserve. Most men will think that I had planned it all from the first; but it was not so. I simply took advantage of circumstances as they were presented to me in the providence of God. I feel that His hand led me."

By nightfall he was resting comfortably in a cottage on the Chandler estate near Guiney Station. He slept soundly, apparently free from pain, and woke next morning much refreshed. His wounds seemed to give him little trouble; primary intention and granulation were under way. All that day and the next, Tuesday and Wednesday, he rested easy, talking mainly of religious matters, as had always been his custom in times of relaxation. The doctor foresaw a rapid recovery and an early return to duty. Then — late Wednesday night and early Thursday morning, May 7 — a sudden change occurred. McGuire woke at dawn to find his patient restless and in severe discomfort. Examination showed that the general faced a new and formidable enemy: pneumonia. He was cupped, then given mercury, with antimony and opium, and morphine to ease his pain. From that time on, as the drugs took effect and the pneumonia followed its inexorable course, he drifted in and out of sleep and fuddled consciousness. His wife arrived at midday, having been delayed by Stoneman's raiders, to find him greatly changed from the husband she had left eight days ago. Despite advance warning, she was shocked at the sight of his wounds, especially the mutilated arm. Moreover, his cheeks were flushed, his breathing oppressed, and his senses numbed. At first he scarcely knew her, but presently, in a more lucid moment, he saw her anxiety and told her: "You must not wear a long face. I love cheerfulness and brightness in a sickroom." He lapsed into stupor, then woke again to find her still beside him. "My darling, you are very much loved," he murmured. "You are one of the most precious little wives in the world." Toward evening, he seemed to improve. Once at least, in the course of the night, he appeared to be altogether himself again. "Will you take this, General?" the doctor asked, bending over the bed with a dose of medicine. Stonewall looked at him sternly. "Do your duty," he said. Then, seeing the doctor hesitate, he repeated the words quite firmly: "Do your duty." Still later, those in the room were startled to hear him call out to his adjutant, Alexander Pendleton, who was in Fredericksburg with Lee: "Major Pendleton, send in and see if there is higher ground back of Chancellorsville! I must find out if there is high ground between Chancellorsville and the river. . . . Push up the columns; hasten the columns! Pendleton, you take charge of that. . . . Where is Pendleton? Tell him to push up the columns." In his delirium he was back on the field of battle, doing the one thing he did best in all the world.

All that day and the next, which was Saturday, he grew steadily worse; McGuire sent word to Fredericksburg and Richmond that recovery was doubtful. Lee could not believe a righteous cause would suffer such a blow. "Surely General Jackson will recover," he said. "God will not take him from us now that we need him so much." The editor of the Richmond *Whig* agreed. "We need have no fears for Jackson," he wrote. "He is no accidental manifestation of the powers of faith and courage. He came not by chance in this day and to this generation. He was born for a purpose, and not until that purpose is fulfilled will his great soul take flight." Jackson himself inclined to this belief that he would be spared for a specific purpose. "I am not afraid to die," he said in a lucid moment Friday. "I am willing to abide by the will of my Heavenly Father. But I do not believe I shall die at this time. I am persuaded the Almighty has yet a work for me to perform." On Saturday, when he was asked to name a hymn he would like to hear sung, he requested "Shew Pity, Lord," Isaac Watts's paraphrase of the Fifty-first Psalm:

> *"Shew pity, Lord; O Lord, forgive;*
> *Let a repenting rebel live —"*

This seemed to comfort him for a time, but night brought a return of suffering. He tossed sleepless, mumbling battle orders. Though these were mostly unintelligible, it was observed that he called most often on A. P. Hill, his hardest-hitting troop commander, and Wells Hawks, his commissary officer, as if even in delirium he strove to preserve a balance between tactics and logistics.

Sunday, May 10, dawned fair and clear; McGuire informed Anna Jackson that her husband could not last the day. She knelt at the bedside of the unconscious general, telling him over and over that he would "very soon be in heaven." Presently he stirred and opened his eyes. She asked him, "Do you feel willing to acquiesce in God's allotment if He will you to go today?" He watched her. "I prefer it," he said, and she pressed the point: "Well, before this day closes you will be with the blessed Savior in his glory." There was a pause. "I will be the infinite gainer to be translated," Jackson said as he dozed off again. He woke at noon, and once more she broached the subject, telling him that he would be gone before sundown. This time he seemed to understand her better. "Oh no; you are frightened, my child. Death is not so near. I may yet get well." She broke into tears, sobbing that the doctor had said there was no hope. Jackson summoned McGuire. "Doctor, Anna informs me that you have told her I am to die today. Is it so?" When McGuire replied that it was so, the general seemed to ponder. Then he said, "Very good, very good. It is all right." After a time he added, "It is the Lord's day; my wish is fulfilled. I have always desired to die on Sunday."

At 1.30 the doctor told him he had no more than a couple of hours to live. "Very good; it's all right," Jackson replied as before, but more weakly, for his breathing was high in his throat by now. When McGuire offered him brandy to keep up his strength, he shook his head. "It will only delay my departure, and do no good," he protested. "I want to preserve my mind, if possible, to the last." Presently, though, he was back in delirium, alternately praying and giving commands, all of which had to do with the offensive. Shortly after 3 o'clock, a few minutes before he died, he called out: "Order A. P. Hill to prepare for action! Pass the infantry to the front.... Tell Major Hawks —" He left the sentence unfinished, seeming thus to have put the war behind him; for he smiled as he spoke his last words, in a tone of calm relief. "Let us cross over the river," he said, "and rest under the shade of the trees."

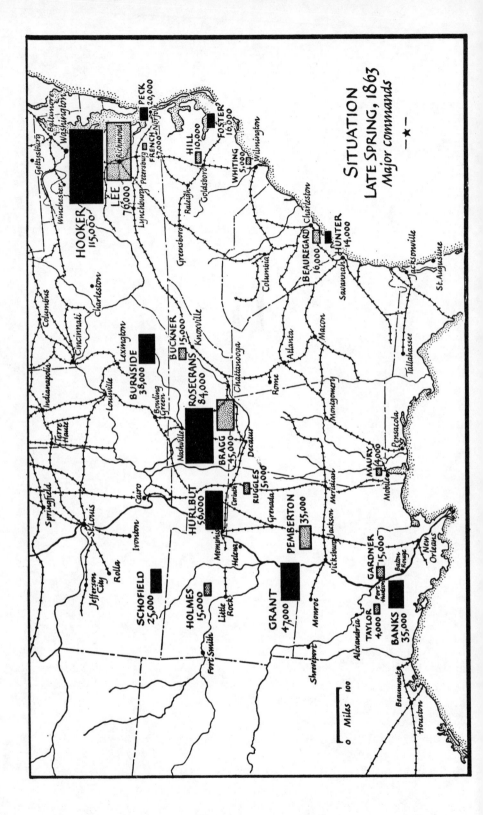

SITUATION
LATE SPRING, 1863
Major commands
— ★ —

HOOKER 115,000
LEE 76,000
PECK 20,000
FRENCH? 17,000 NOT?
HILL 10,000
FOSTER? 16,000
WHITING 5,000
BEAUREGARD 16,000
HUNTER 14,000
BUCKNER 15,000
BURNSIDE 38,000
ROSECRANS 84,000
BRAGG 45,000
RUGGLES 5,000
HURLBUT 56,000
PEMBERTON 35,000
MAURY 9,000
SCHOFIELD 25,000
HOLMES 15,000
GRANT 47,000
GARDNER 15,000
TAYLOR 4,000
BANKS 35,000

Baltimore, Washington, Gettysburg, Winchester, Columbus, Cincinnati, Charleston, Indianapolis, Terre Haute, Springfield, St. Louis, Ironton, Rolla, Jefferson City, Fort Smith, Beaumont, Houston, Shreveport, Alexandria, Monroe, New Orleans, Baton Rouge, Port Hudson, Little Rock, Helena, Memphis, Cairo, Nashville, Louisville, Bowling Green, Lexington, Knoxville, Chattanooga, Decatur, Corinth, Grenada, Jackson, Vicksburg, Meridian, Mobile, Pensacola, Montgomery, Rome, Atlanta, Macon, Columbia, Greensboro, Raleigh, Goldsboro, Wilmington, Charleston, Savannah, Tallahassee, Jacksonville, St. Augustine, Lynchburg, Petersburg, Richmond

0 Miles 100

The Beleaguered City

★ ✗ ☆

WHILE HOOKER WAS CROSSING THE RAPPA-
hannock, unaware as yet that he would come to grief within a week,
Grant, having caught what he believed was a gleam of victory through
the haze of cigar smoke in the former ladies' cabin of the *Magnolia,* was
putting the final improvisatorial touches to a plan of campaign that
would open, two days later, with a crossing of the greatest river of them
all. He too might come to grief, as two of his three chief lieutenants
feared and even predicted, but he was willing to risk it for the sake of
the prize, which had grown in value with every sore frustration. As
spring advanced and the roads emerged from the drowned lands adjacent to the Mississippi — although so far they were little more than
trails of slime through the surrounding ooze, not quite firm enough for
wagons nor quite wet enough for boats — the Illinois general, with
seven failures behind him in the course of the three months he had spent
attempting to take or bypass Vicksburg, reverted in early April to what
he had told Halleck in mid-January, before he left Memphis to assume
command in person of the expedition four hundred miles downriver:
"[I] think our troops must get below the city to be used effectively."

His plan, in essence, was to march his army down the Louisiana
bank to a position well south of the fortified bluff, then cross the river
and establish a bridgehead from which to assail the Confederate bastion
from the rear. The Duckport canal, designed to give his transports access to Walnut and Roundaway bayous, and thus allow them to avoid
exposure to the plunging fire of the batteries at Vicksburg and Warrenton, had failed; only one small steamer had got through before the
water level fell too low for navigation; but exploration of the route
had shown that, by bridging those slews that could not be avoided by
following the crests of levees flanking the horseshoe curves of the several bayous, it might be practicable to march dry-shod all the way from
Milliken's Bend to New Carthage, a west-bank hamlet about midway

between Warrenton and Grand Gulf, third of the rebel east-bank strongholds. In late March, by way of preparation, Grant had assigned McClernand the task of putting this route into shape for a march by his own corps as well as the two others, which would follow. This, if it worked, would get the army well south of its objective. Getting the troops across the river was quite another matter, however, depending as it did on the co-operation of the navy, which, as Grant said, "was absolutely essential to the success (even to the contemplation) of such an enterprise." For the navy to get below, in position to ferry the men across and cover the east-bank landing, it would have to run the batteries, and this had been shown in the past to be an expensive proposition even for armored vessels, let alone the brittle-skinned transports which would be required for the ferrying operation. Moreover, Porter was no more under Grant's command than Grant was under Porter's. The most Grant could do was "request" that the run be made. But that was enough, as it turned

out. The admiral — who had returned only the week before from the near-disastrous Steele Bayou expedition, considerably the worse for wear and with his boats still being hammered back into shape — expressed an instant willingness to give the thing a try, though not without first warning of what the consequences would be, not only in the event of initial failure but also in the event of initial success, so far at least as the navy was concerned. He could make a downstream run, he said, and in fact had proved it twice already with the ill-fated *Queen of the West* and the equally ill-fated *Indianola*, but his underpowered vessels could never attempt a slow-motion return trip, against the four-knot current, until Vicksburg had been reduced. "You must recollect that when these gunboats once go below we give up all hopes of ever getting them up again," he replied, wanting it understood from the start that this would be an all-or-nothing venture. Moreover: "If I do send vessels below, it will be the best vessels I have, and there will be nothing left to attack Haines Bluff, in case it should be deemed necessary to try it." Grant replied on April 2 that McClernand's men were already at work on the circuitous thirty-mile road down to New Carthage; he had no intention of turning back, even if that had been possible; and in any case Haines Bluff had cost the army blood enough by now. "I would,

Admiral, therefore renew my request to prepare for running the blockade at as early a day as possible."

Two days later he wrote Halleck: "My expectation is for a portion of the naval fleet to run the batteries of Vicksburg, whilst the army
moves through by this new route [to New Carthage]. Once there, I
will move either to Warrenton or Grand Gulf; most probably the latter.
From either of these points there are good roads to Vicksburg, and
from Grand Gulf there is a good road to Jackson and the Black River
Bridge without crossing the Black River." Much could be said for making the landing at either place. Warrenton, for example, was some fifteen
air-line miles closer to his objective. But he knew well enough that a
straight line was not always the surest connection between two military
points. A Grand Gulf landing, in addition to giving him access to Vicksburg's main artery of supply, would also afford him a chance to supple-
ment his own. By holding the newly established bridgehead with part
of his army and sending the balance downstream to assist in the reduction of Port Hudson by Banks, who presumably was working his way
upstream at the same time, he then would have an unbroken, all-weather
connection with New Orleans and would no longer be exclusively and
precariously dependent on what could be brought down from Memphis,
first by steamboat, then by wagon over the new road skirting the west-
bank complex of bayous across from the fortified bluff, and then again
by steamboat in order to get the supplies over the river and into the
east-bank bridgehead. Grant pondered the alternatives, and by April 11,
a week after the dispatch giving Halleck a brief statement of the problem,
he had made his choice: "Grand Gulf is the point at which I expect to
strike, and send an army corps to Port Hudson to co-operate with General Banks."

He did not know how Old Brains, whose timidity had been demonstrated in situations far less risky than this one, would react to a plan
of campaign that involved 1) exposing the irreplaceable Union fleet to
instantaneous destruction by batteries that had been sited on commanding and impregnable heights with just that end in mind, 2) crossing a
mile-wide river in order to throw his troops into the immediate rear of
a rebel force of unknown strength which, holding as it did the interior
lines, presumably could be reinforced more quickly than his own, and
3) remaining dependent all the while, or at least until the problematical
capture of Port Hudson, on a supply line that was not only tenuous to
the point of inadequacy, but was also subject to being cut by enemy intervention or obliterated by some accident of nature, by no means unusual at this season, such as a week of unrelenting rain, a sudden rise of
the river, and a resultant overflow that would re-drown the west-bank
lowlands and the improvised road that wound its way around and across
the curving bayous and treacherous morasses into which a wagon or a
gun could disappear completely, leaving no more trace than a man or a

mule whose bones had been picked clean by gars and crawfish. Whether Halleck would approve the taking of all these risks, Grant did not know; but he was left in no such doubt as to the reaction closer at hand. So far, of his three corps commanders, only his archrival McClernand had indicated anything resembling enthusiasm for the plan. Hard at work constructing makeshift bridges from materials found along the designated route to New Carthage, which he reached before mid-April, the former Illinois politician was in high spirits and predicted great results, for both the country and himself, because his corps had been assigned to lead the way. By contrast, though perhaps for the same reason — that is, because the nonprofessional McClernand had the lead — Sherman and McPherson, along with Dana and practically every member of Grant's own staff, considered the proposed operation not only overrisky and unwise, but also downright unmilitary. Sherman in fact was so alarmed at the prospect that he sat down and wrote Grant a long letter, insisting that the proper course would be for the army to return at once to Memphis and resume from there the overland advance along the Mississippi Central, abandoned in December. When his friend and chief replied that he had no intention of canceling his plans, Sherman had no choice except to go along with them, although he still did not approve. "I confess I don't like this roundabout project," he told one of his division commanders, "but we must support Grant in whatever he undertakes." He was loyal and he would remain so, but he also remained glum, writing home even as he ordered his men out of their camps at Milliken's Bend to join the movement: "I feel in its success less confidence than in any similar undertaking of the war."

Porter too had doubts as to the over-all wisdom of Grant's plan, as well as fears in regard to the specific risk the plan required the navy to assume, but he took no counsel of them aside from the more or less normal precautions the prospect of such exposure always prompted, as in the case of a farmer sending eggs to market in a springless wagon over a bumpy road. Unlike Sherman, he wrote no Cassandran letters and made no protest after his initial warning that once the fleet had gone below it could not come back up again until the batteries had been silenced in its rear. Instead, he kept busy preparing his crews and vessels for the passage of bluffs that bristled with 40-odd pieces of artillery, light and heavy, manned by cannoneers whose skill had improved with every chance to show it. By April 16 he was ready. Seven armored gunboats, mounting a total of 79 guns, were assigned to make the run, accompanied by three army transports, loaded with commissary stores instead of troops, and a steam ram captured the year before at Memphis when the Confederate flotilla was abolished in a brief half-morning's fight. At 9.30, two hours after dusk gave way to a starry but moonless night, the column cleared the mouth of the Yazoo, Porter leading aboard the flagship *Benton*.

The "run," so called, was in fact more creep than sprint, however, at least in its early stages; stealth was the watchword up and down the line of eleven boats steaming southward in single file on the dark chocolate surface of what one observer called "the great calm river, more like a long winding lake than a stream." Furnaces had been banked in advance, so as to show a minimum of smoke. All ports were covered and all deck lights doused, except for hooded lanterns visible only from dead astern for guidance. It was hoped that such precautions would hide the column from prying eyes. To reduce the likelihood of noise, which also might give the movement away, low speed was prescribed and exhaust pipes were diverted from the stacks to the paddle boxes, where the hiss of steam would be muffled. Pets and poultry were put ashore, moreover, lest a sudden mewing or cackling alert the rebel sentries. The admiral was leaving as little as possible to chance; but in the event of discovery he was prepared to shift at once from stealth to boldness. Coal-laden barges were lashed to the starboard flanks of the warships, leaving their port-side weapons free to take up any challenge from the high-sited batteries on the Mississippi shore, and water-soaked bales of hay were stacked around the otherwise unprotected boilers and pilot-houses of the transports. Instructed to maintain a fifty-yard interval, each helmsman was also told to steer a little to one side of the boat he followed, so as not to have to slow engines or change course to avoid a collision in case of a breakdown up ahead. Thus, though he wanted no trouble he could avoid, Porter was prepared to give as well as receive it in the event that his carefully woven veil of secrecy was ripped away. Passing Young's Point at about 10.30, the dark and silent column swung north as it approached the mouth of Sherman's abandoned canal, then rounded the final turn at 11 sharp, altering course again from north to south, and headed down the straightaway eastern shank of the hairpin bend that led past Vicksburg's dark and silent bluff. Ten minutes later all hell broke loose.

Grant was there to see the show, and he had his two families with him, one military and the other personal, the former consisting of his staff, the latter of his wife and their two sons, who had come downriver from Illinois to afford him a sort of furlough-in-reverse. Both were gathered tonight on the upper deck of the *Magnolia*, which was anchored three miles below Young's Point, just beyond range of the heaviest enemy guns, so that they watched as if from a box in a darkened theater, awaiting the raising of the curtain. The general and Mrs Grant occupied deck chairs near the starboard rail — front row center, as it were — with twelve-year-old Fred beside them; Ulysses Junior, who was ten, sat nearby in young Colonel Wilson's lap. Behind and on both sides of them stood twenty-odd men in uniform, staff officers and two high-ranking observers. One was Dana, who had been sent by Stanton to watch Grant, and the other was no less a personage than Adjutant General Lorenzo Thomas, who had arrived five days ago, five days after Dana, to watch them both. Or so it was said at any rate, so deep was the supposed mistrust the War Department felt. Just now though, whatever truth there was to the rumored assignment, there was a good deal more to watch than the unimpressive-looking department commander. First there was the passage of the hooded and muffled warships, disappearing northward in the direction of the bend that swung them south toward the rebel batteries; then a long wait in the blackness; then, eastward — across the narrow tongue of land called Vicksburg Point, beyond which the dark loom of bluff reared up to blot out the low-hanging stars — a sudden burgeoning incandescence, exposed as if by a rapid lifting of the awaited curtain. The show was on. It began, so to speak, in mid-crescendo as the guns came alive on the bluff and were replied to by those down on the brightly lighted river, growling full-throated, jarring the earth and water for miles around, and adding their muzzle flashes to the vivid illumination of the scene. "Magnificent, but terrible," Grant later called the sight. For the present, however, aside from ordering the younger boy to bed when he heard him whimper and saw him press his face against Wilson's chest in terror at the holocaust of flame and thunder, he said nothing. He merely smoked and watched the fireworks, holding all the while to his wife's hand. After ninety minutes of uproar, during which Dana tallied 525 shots fired by the Confederates, the bluff was once more dark and silent except for the reflection of fires still burning fitfully on the lower level where the boats had been. How much damage had been done and suffered, no one aboard the *Magnolia* could tell, although presently it was clear that some at least of the vessels had got past, for the Warrenton batteries came alive downstream, reproducing in miniature the earlier performance. Finally these too fell silent; which told the watchers exactly nothing, save that the final curtain had come down. Near and far, the fires burned out and the former blackness returned to the bluff and the river.

Unable to wait for word from below — news, perhaps, that the indispensable fleet had gone out of existence — Grant went ashore, got on his horse, and rode south under the paling stars, galloping along the crude and pot-holed road McClernand's corps had spent the past three weeks constructing. This was quite unlike the old Grant, who had never seemed in a hurry about anything at all. Something had come over him, here lately. "None who had known him the previous years could recognize him as being the same man," one officer observed. He had never seen the general ride at even a fast trot, let alone a gallop; but now, he said, "[Grant's] energies seemed to burst forth with new life," with the result that he rode at top speed practically all the time and "seemed wrought up to the last pitch of determination and energy." Shiloh and the long hot unproductive summer of 1862, the ill-wind fiasco near Iuka and the fruitless victory at Corinth, the period of indecision in

Memphis and the recent seven failures above Vicksburg, all were behind him now; he was launched at last on an all-or-nothing effort, a go-for-broke campaign, of which the passage of the batteries by the fleet was the first stage. If this failed, all failed; he would never get his troops across the mile-wide Mississippi. It was no wonder he rode fast.

Near New Carthage about midday he drew rein and breathed a sigh of relief at the sight of the fleet riding at anchor, apparently intact. Closer inspection showed that the boats had been knocked about considerably, however. All were damaged to various degrees, some in their hulls and others in their machinery. One was missing altogether: a transport, as it turned out, set afire by repeated hits and sunk to the accompaniment of cheers from the rebel batteries. But all the rest were seaworthy, or soon would be, after the completion of repairs already under way by bluejackets swarming over their ripped-up decks and pounded bulwarks. Porter and his captains were in excellent spirits, though they were frank to admit that last night's experience had been little short of horrendous. For one thing, all their precautions involving stealth and secrecy had availed them nothing. As they proceeded, dark and silent, down the straightaway eastern shank of the hairpin bend, Confederate sentries posted in skiffs on the river spotted them quickly; whereupon some rowed eastward to give the alarm to the Vicksburg cannoneers, while others, risking capture, crossed to the opposite bank, where they set fire to prepared stacks of pitch-soaked wood, as well as to the abandoned De Soto railroad station midway up the point. Quick-leaping flames floodlighted the approaching Yankee gunboats and the alerted rebel gunners promptly took these well-defined targets under fire. Another difficulty was that the prescribed low speed left the vessels to the mercy of the eddying current, which caught them alternately on the bow and quarter, swinging them broadside to the stream and in some cases even spinning them halfway around, so that they were obliged to come full circle under the plunging fire, as if responding to cruel encores that held them on the brightly lighted stage for further pelting by an irate audience. Clear at last, they played a brief epilogue at Warrenton, then swept on south to anchor above New Carthage in the predawn darkness. Assessing damages, Porter was grateful to discover that, despite a total of 68 hits received, the transport *Henry Clay* was the flotilla's only loss. Not a man had been killed, even aboard the missing boat, and only 13 — in this case a decidedly lucky number — had been wounded. Give him a couple of days in which to complete repairs, he said, and he would be quite ready to co-operate with the army.

Grant returned to Milliken's Bend, much pleased with the outcome, and prepared for another run within the week, this time by transports alone, in order to provide more ferries for the crossing. "If I do not underestimate the enemy," he wrote Halleck on April 21, "my force is abundant, with a foothold once obtained, to do the work." Next night six river steamers, loaded with rations, forage, and medical supplies, attempted the second run under instructions "to drop noiselessly down with the current . . . and not show steam until the enemy's batteries began firing, when the boats were to use all their legs." This was an all-army show, the steamers being army-owned and manned by army volunteers, since the civilian crews had balked at exposing their persons to what they had watched six nights ago from a safe distance. Now as then, Grant was there to see the show; an Illinois private later told how he "saw standing on the upper deck of his headquarters boat a man of iron, his wife by his side. He seemed to me the most immovable figure I ever saw." Then came the fireworks across the way, the sudden illumination and the uproar of the guns on the fuming bluff. Grant took it calmly, the soldier recalled; "No word escaped his lips, no muscle of his earnest face moved." Presently the batteries fell silent and word arrived from below that, now as before, only a single vessel had failed to survive the run — the steamer *Tigress*, McClernand's former headquarters boat, which Grant had ridden to Shiloh a year ago. Loaded with medicines and surgical equipment, she was hulled a dozen times or more and broke in two and sank, her skeleton crew floating downstream to safety on bits of wreckage. Once more not a man had been killed and the wounded were only a handful. Half the steamers had their engines permanently smashed, but that was no real drawback, since they would hold as many troops as ever and could be pushed or towed across the river as barges. As Grant saw it, this second run had been quite as successful as the first, and he was twice as pleased.

Belittling the loss of the *Tigress* and her cargo, which he said amounted to nothing more than "little extras for the men," he set off southward again on horseback to join Porter for a naval reconnaissance of Grand Gulf, designated as the point where the army would obtain a foothold once the navy had blasted its batteries out of existence. Porter was experiencing misgivings, and Grant, looking the place over from just beyond range of its guns on the 24th, saw that he had indeed given the navy a tough nut to crack. Its batteries were sited high, as at Donelson and Vicksburg, and what was more they seemed altogether ready for whatever came their way. "I foresee great difficulties in our present position," he informed Sherman on his return from the exploratory boat ride, "but it will not do to let these retard any movements." In this connection it seemed to him there might be a chance for an assault to succeed at last up the Yazoo, despite the previous fiasco. "It may possibly happen," he wrote Sherman, "that the enemy may so weaken his forces about Vicksburg and Haines Bluff as to make the latter vulnerable, particularly with a fall of water to give you an extended landing." However: "I leave the management of affairs at your end of the line to you," he added by way of making it clear that he was not definitely ordering an assault.

Monday, April 27, was Grant's forty-first birthday. It also marked the completion of his first-stage preparations for getting his troops across the river in order to come to grips with the rebels on dry ground, which was what he had been after from the start. By now all four divisions of McClernand's corps, having extended their march southward around Bayou Vidal and Lake Saint Joseph, were at Hard Times, Louisiana, the designated point of embarkation for the landing at Grand Gulf, five miles downstream. One of McPherson's divisions was also there and the other two were closing fast, while Sherman's three remained at Young's Point, on call to follow but held in place for the present so as to confuse the lookouts on the Vicksburg bluff. Seven warships and seven transports were available below, and though Porter was still troubled by misgivings — he thought his gunboats could suppress the Grand Gulf batteries, all right, but he warned that they might get so knocked about in the process that they would not be able to provide adequate cover for the crossing that would follow — Grant himself, as usual, expressed no doubt as to the outcome. He foresaw "great difficulties," but he did not admit that they were any occasion for delay. All he asked of the navy was that the rebel guns be silenced, after which there would be no need for cover. Before the anniversary was over, he sent McClernand word to go ahead: "Commence immediately the embarkation of your corps, or so much of it as there is transportation for."

The showdown was unquestionably at hand; but Grant was disclosing nothing he could avoid disclosing until the final moment. He had, in fact, devised three separate feints or demonstrations, two of them designed to mislead the enemy as to his chosen point of attack, well downstream, and a third whereby he hoped not only to distract his opponent by diverting his attention from front to rear, but also to add to his confusion, throughout this critical period, by disrupting the lines of supply and communication leading back into the interior of the state whose welfare and defense were the southern commander's assigned concern. Sherman was organically involved in two of these, one of which had already been accomplished during the first ten days of April. Lest Pemberton call in the troops disposed to guard against a penetration of the Delta, and thereby strengthen the Vicksburg garrison in time for the showdown fight now imminent, Fred Steele's division was sent a hundred miles up the Mississippi to Greenville, where the men went ashore and thrashed about for a week in the interior, giving the impression that they were merely the advance contingent for another major drive on the Gibraltar of the West. Having done so — to the extreme alarm of the local planters, who bemoaned the attendant loss of cotton, cattle, and Negroes, and the home-guard commanders, who called loudly for reinforcements — they got back aboard their transports and rejoined Sherman at Young's Point for a share in the second and more

important feint, this time against Haines Bluff. Grant had suggested it
in his letter of the 24th, after a look at the Grand Gulf defenses, but
now on his birthday he returned to the matter in more persuasive terms.
"The effect of a heavy demonstration in that direction would be good
so far as the enemy are concerned," he wrote Sherman from Hard Times,
where McClernand's men were preparing to embark, "but I am loth to
order it, because it would be hard to make our own troops understand
that only a demonstration was intended and our people at home would
characterize it as a repulse. I therefore leave it to you whether to
make such a demonstration."

In referring thus to the probable adverse reaction by "our people
at home," who of course would get their information from the papers,
many of which were hostile — particularly toward Sherman, who returned the hostility in full measure — Grant may or may not have intended to use psychology on his journalist-hating friend. But at any
rate it worked. "Does General Grant think I care what the newspapers
say?" Sherman exclaimed as soon as he read the letter. And despite his
growing antipathy for the strategy his superior had evolved ("I tremble
for the result," he wrote his wife that week; "I look upon the whole
thing as one of the most hazardous and desperate moves of this or any
other war") he replied at once with a pledge of full co-operation. "We
will make as strong a demonstration as possible," he declared. "The
troops will all understand the purpose and not be hurt by the repulse.
The people of the country must find out the truth as best they can;
it is none of their business. You are engaged in a hazardous enterprise,
and for good reason wish to divert attention; that is sufficient for me,
and it shall be done." Warming as he wrote, the red-haired general
bristled with contempt for public opinion. "The men have sense, and
will trust us. As to the reports in newspapers, we must scorn them, else
they will ruin us and our country. They are as much enemies to good
government as the secesh, and between the two I like the secesh best,
because they are a brave, open enemy and not a set of sneaking, croaking
scoundrels."

Accordingly, he spent the next two days in preparation, and on
the final day of April — previously designated by Lincoln, at the request
of Congress, "as a day of national humiliation, fasting, and prayer" because, in the words of the proclamation, the people had "forgotten God"
and become "too proud to pray" — set off up the Yazoo with ten regiments from Frank Blair's division, escorted by the flotilla remnant Porter had left behind, three gunboats, four tinclads, and three mortars,
under Lieutenant Commander K. R. Breese. Intent on making the
greatest possible show of strength, Sherman spread his troops over the
transport decks with orders for "every man [to] look as numerous as
possible." Short of Haines Bluff and near the scene of their December
repulse, the bluecoats went ashore; marching and countermarching, ban-

ners flying and bands playing for all they were worth in the boggy
woodland, they demonstrated in sight of the fortified line of hills, while
the gunboats closed to within point-blank range of the bluff itself. For
three hours the naval attack was pressed, as if in preparation for an infantry assault. However, the defenders clearly had their backs up; nor
was there anything wrong with their marksmanship. The overaged *Tyler*, a veteran of all the fights since Henry, retired early with a shot below the water line, and the other two hauled off at 2 p.m. roughly
handled, one having taken a total of forty-six hits. Sherman might have
let it go at that, but he was determined to play out the game to full advantage. May Day morning he wrote Grant: "At 3 p.m. we will open
another cannonade to prolong the diversion, and keep it up till after
dark, when we shall drop down to Chickasaw and go on back to camp."
The other two divisions, waiting at Young's Point under Steele and
Brigadier General James M. Tuttle, were alerted for the long march to
Hard Times, while Blair was told to keep up the pretense of attack until
darkness afforded cover for withdrawal, at which time he would "let
out for home," meaning Milliken's Bend, where he was to shield the
rear of the two divisions moving southward to join Grant. Meanwhile,
Sherman told him, "I will hammer away this p.m. because Major Row-
ley, [a staff observer] now here, says that our diversion has had perfect
success, great activity being seen in Vicksburg, and troops pushing up
this way. By prolonging the effort, we give Grant more chance." The
infantry continued to mass as if for attack, and the gunboats moved
again within range of Haines Bluff, keeping up the action until 8 o'clock
that evening. Then Blair's men got back aboard their transports and
withdrew, returning to the west bank of the Mississippi, followed by
the somewhat battered but undaunted ten-boat flotilla, which dropped
anchor off the mouth of the Yazoo. Steele and Tuttle took up the march
for Hard Times at first light next morning, accompanied by Sherman
himself, who sent a courier ahead with a full account of the two-day affair. Casualties had been negligible, he reported, afloat and ashore.
Whether matters had gone as well for Grant, far downriver at Grand
Gulf, he did not know; but he was satisfied that the feint from above had
held a considerable portion of the Vicksburg garrison in position north of
the city, away from the simultaneous main effort to the south. "We will
be there as soon as possible," he assured his friend and superior.

    Such were the first two of the three diversions intended to con-
fuse and distract the Confederate defenders in the course of this highly
critical span of time during which Grant was preparing to launch, and
indeed was launching, his main effort a good forty miles downriver from
the bluff that was his goal. Though both appeared to have exceeded
strategic expectations, the third, while altogether different in scope and
composition, was even more successful, and in fact was referred to afterwards by Sherman, who had no direct connection with the venture, as

nothing less than "the most brilliant expedition of the war." Grant was as usual more restrained in judgment, qualifying his praise by calling the exploit "one of the most brilliant," but he added that it would "be handed down in history as an example to be imitated."

In point of fact, it was itself an imitation. For two years now, in the West as in the East, the Federal cavalry had suffered from a well-founded inferiority complex; Stuart and Morgan and Forrest had quite literally ridden rings around the awkward blue squadrons and the armies in their charge. Now, perhaps, the time had come for them to emulate the example set by the exuberant gray riders. Hooker thought so, in Virginia, and so did Grant in Mississippi. Back in February he had suggested to Hurlbut, commanding in Memphis, that a cavalry force, "with about 500 picked men, might succeed in making [its] way south and cut the railroad east of Jackson, Miss. The undertaking would be a hazardous one," he added, "but would pay well if carried out. I do not direct that this shall be done, but leave it for a volunteer enterprise." A month later, in mid-March, his instructions were more specific. The conception had been enlarged, tripling the strength of the force to be employed, and the volunteer provision had been removed. Hurlbut was to have all "the available cavalry put in as good condition as possible in the next few weeks for heavy service. . . . The date when the expedition should start will depend upon movements here. You will be informed of the exact time for them to start." In early April the date was set and a leader chosen: Colonel Benjamin H. Grierson, of Grant's home state of Illinois. Hurlbut saw to it that the raiders got away on schedule, April 17, riding south out of La Grange, forty miles east of Memphis, into the dawn that saw Porter's battered gunboats drop anchor near New Carthage after their fiery run past the Vicksburg bluff. "God speed him," Hurlbut said of Grierson, who led the 1700-man column in the direction of the Mississippi line, "for he has started gallantly on a long and perilous ride. I shall anxiously await intelligence of the result."

The wait would necessarily be a long one. Before the raid was over, the blue riders would have covered more than six hundred miles of road and swamp, through hostile territory. At the outset, however, none of the troopers in the three regiments, two from Illinois and one from Iowa, nor of the cannoneers in the attached six-gun battery of 2-pounders, suspected that the warning order, "Oats in the nosebag and five days rations in haversacks, the rations to last ten days," was prelude to so deep a penetration. "We are going on a big scout to Columbus, Mississippi, and play smash with the railroads," one predicted. Only Grierson himself, riding at the head of the column, knew that the true objective was Pemberton's main supply line, the Southern Railroad east of Jackson, connecting Vicksburg with Meridian and thence with Mobile and the arsenals in Georgia and the East. Pennsylvania-born and just short of thirty-seven years of age, with a spade beard and an acquired mistrust of horses dating back to a kick received from a pony in childhood, which smashed one of his cheekbones, split his forehead, and left him scarred for life — he had protested his assignment to the cavalry in the first place, though to no avail; Halleck, who made the appointment, insisted that he looked "active and wiry enough to make a good cavalry-man" — Grierson eighteen months ago had been a music teacher and bandmaster at Jacksonville, Illinois, but all that was left to remind him or anyone else of that now was a jew's-harp he carried inside his blouse, along with a pocket compass and a small-scale map of the region he and his men would be traversing in the course of their strike at the railroad some two hundred air-line miles away. Riding where no bluecoat had ever been before, he could expect to be surrounded en route by small bodies of home guardsmen, who would outnumber him badly if they were consolidated, as well as by sizable detachments of regulars, horse and foot, which Pemberton would certainly send to oppose him, front and rear, once his presence and intention became known. Even if he succeeded in his mission — that is, reached and wrecked an appreciable stretch of the railroad between Jackson and Meridian, temporarily severing the one connection by which reinforcements could reach Vicksburg swiftly from outside Mississippi — he would then be deep in the heart of a land where every man's hand would be raised against him. One suggestion, included in his orders, was that he return to Tennessee by swinging east, then north through Alabama; another was that he plunge on south and west for a hookup with Grant in the vicinity of Grand Gulf, anticipating a successful crossing by McClernand and McPherson at that point, or else take sanctuary within Banks's outpost lines at Baton Rouge, which would give him about as far to go from the railroad south as he would have come already in order to reach it. In any case, whatever escape plan he adopted as a result of the unfolding course of events, the tactical requisites were vigilance, speed, boldness, and deception. Without any one of these four, he and his troopers, in the cavalry slang of the time, would be "gone up."

Across the Mississippi line by sunup, they made thirty miles the first day — a good average march for cavalry, though Grant himself covered nearly as great a distance before noon, galloping south from Milliken's Bend to check on the condition of Porter's gunboats at New Carthage — and called a halt that night just short of Ripley, which they passed through next morning, brushing aside the few startled gray militia they encountered, to camp beyond New Albany at sundown. On the third day, April 19, they continued due south through Pontotoc. Eighty miles from base, with rebel detachments no doubt alerted in his front and rear, Grierson began his fourth day with an inspection, culled out 175 victims of dysentery, chills and fever, and saddle galls — "the Quinine Brigade," the rejected troopers promptly dubbed themselves — and sent them back, under a staff major, with one of the 2-pounders and instructions to "pass through Pontotoc in the night, marching by fours, obliterating our tracks, and producing the impression that we have all returned." He himself continued south with the main body, to Houston and beyond. Deciding to throw a still larger tub to the Confederate whale, he detached Colonel Edward Hatch's regiment of Iowans next morning, along with another of the guns, and gave its commander orders to strike eastward for the Mobile & Ohio, inflicting what damage he could to that vital supply line before heading north in the wake of the Quinine Brigade, thus spreading the scare and increasing the impression that all the raiders were returning. Hatch, a transplanted New Englander hungry for fame and advancement — tomorrow would be his thirty-second birthday — now began a five-day adventure on his own. Though he did not succeed in breaking the well-guarded railroad to the east, he fought two severe skirmishes — one at the outset, a delaying action which allowed Grierson to get away southward, the other near the finish, which allowed his own getaway northward — burned several cotton-stocked warehouses in Okolona, and succeeded handsomely in his primary mission of drawing most of the North Mississippi home guardsmen pell-mell after him and away from Grierson. At a cost of ten men lost en route, he reported that he had inflicted ten times as many casualties on the enemy and "accumulated 600 head of horses and mules, with about 200 able-bodied negroes to lead them." Returning to La Grange on Sunday morning, April 26, he brought Hurlbut the first substantial news of the raiders' progress since their departure, nine days back.

The unavailable news was a good deal better; Grierson by then had not only reached his objective, he was already forty hours beyond it, having formulated and put into execution his tactics for escape. Relieved of the threat to his rear on the 21st by Hatch's decoy action south of Houston, he and his 1000 troopers — all Illinoisans now, including the fifty cannoneers with the four remaining guns — rode on past Starkville, where he detached one company for a strike at Macon, twenty-odd miles southeast on the M&O, then took up the march at dawn and cleared Louisville by sundown. Beyond Philadelphia on the 23d he called a halt at nightfall, and made an early start next morning in order to reach the Southern Railroad before noon. Preceded by scouts who seized the telegraph office and thus kept the alarm from being spread — "Butternut Guerillas," these outriders called themselves, for they wore Confederate uniforms, risking hanging for the advantage gained — the raiders burst into Newton Station, a trackside hamlet twenty-five miles west of Meridian and about twice as far east of Jackson, where they at once got down to the work for which they had ridden all this way. Two locomotives were captured and wrecked, along with three dozen freight cars loaded with ordnance and commissary supplies, including artillery ammunition on consignment for Vicksburg, which afforded a rackety fireworks display when set aflame. Meantime other details were ripping up miles of track and crossties, burning trestles and bridges, tearing down telegraph wires all the way to the Chunky River, and setting fire to a government building stocked with 500 small arms and a quantity of new gray uniforms. By 2 o'clock the destruction was complete; Grierson had his bugler sound the rally to assemble the smoke-grimed raiders, some of whom were showing the effects of rebel whiskey they had "res-cued" from the flames, then took his accustomed post at the head of the column and led them away from the charred and smoldering evidence of their efficiency as wreckers. Now as before, the march was south. They did not bivouac till near midnight, having covered a good fifty miles of road despite the arduous delay at Newton Station. Next day, April 25, was the easiest of the raid, however, since the blue raiders spent most of it on a plantation in the piny highlands just short of the Leaf River valley, resting their mounts, gorging themselves on smokehouse ham, and presuma-bly nursing their hangovers. Sunday followed, and while

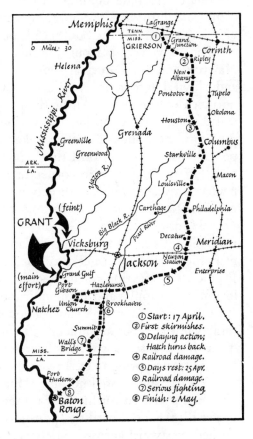

Hatch was riding into La Grange at the end of his five-day excursion through North Mississippi, the raiders turned west. In time, according to Grierson's calculations, this would bring them either to Grand Gulf, in case Grant had effected a crossing as planned, or to Natchez, which had been under intermittent Federal occupation for nearly a year.

Either place would afford refuge for his saddle-weary troopers if all went as he hoped and planned, but he knew well enough that the most dangerous part of the long ride lay before him. By now, doubtless, every grayback in the state would have learned of the presence of his two regiments at Newton Station two days ago, with the result that a considerable number of them must be hot on his trail or lying in wait for him in all directions. However, this had its compensations as well as its drawbacks. Scarcely less important than the temporary severing of Vicksburg's main supply line was the disruption of its defenses, preventing the hasty concentration of its outlying forces against Grant in the early stages of his river crossing. In point of fact, Grierson was more successful in this regard than he had any way of knowing. Orders flew thick and fast from Pemberton's headquarters in the Mississippi capital, directing all units within possible reach to concentrate on the capture of the ubiquitous blue column. An infantry brigade, en route from Alabama to reinforce Vicksburg, was halted at Meridian to protect that vital intersection of the Southern Railroad and the Mobile & Ohio, while another moved east from Jackson in the direction of the break at Newton Station. Forces at Panola and Canton, under James Chalmers and Lloyd Tilghman, were shifted to Okolona and Carthage to block the northern escape route. All of these troops, amounting to no less than a full division, not counting the various home-guard units caught up in the swirl, were thus effectively taken out of the play and removed from possible use at this critical time against either Grant or Grierson, who were off in the opposite corner of the map. Not that Pemberton was neglecting matters in that direction, at least so far as Grierson was concerned. Detachments of fast-riding cavalry were ordered eastward from Port Hudson and Port Gibson — the latter a scant half dozen miles from Grant's intended point of landing at Grand Gulf — in case the marauders tried for a getaway to the south or the southwest. In short, Pemberton's reaction to the widespread confusion in his rear and along his lines of supply and communication, while altogether commendable from a limited point of view, amounted to full co-operation with the raiders in the accomplishment of their secondary mission, which was to divert his attention, as well as his reserves, away from the point at which Grant was preparing to hurl two thirds of the blue army.

Grierson wasted no time. Monday, April 27 — Grant's birthday; Sherman prepared for his feint up the Yazoo, and McClernand was told to get his troops aboard the transports at Hard Times — the blue riders pushed westward across Pearl River, aided considerably by the capture of a ferryboat by scouts who masqueraded as Confederates. While the crossing was in progress the company detached five days ago near Starkville rejoined the main body, reporting that in addition to throwing a scare into the defenders of Macon, as instructed, it had also made a feint at Enterprise, twelve miles below Meridian, thus adding to the difficulties of the rebel high command's attempt to pinpoint the location of the invaders. Safely across the Pearl, the reunited 1000-man column pressed on west to Hazlehurst, where a string of boxcars was set afire on a siding of the New Orleans, Jackson & Great Northern Railroad. Flames spreading to a nearby block of buildings, the erstwhile incendiaries turned firemen and worked side by side with the citizens in preventing the loss of the whole town. At dusk, in a driving rain which had helped to contain the fire, the colonel ordered his troopers to remount. The march was west; Grand Gulf was only forty miles away and he hoped to make it there tomorrow, in case Grant had crossed the Mississippi. However, morning brought no indication that any part of the Army of the Tennessee was on this side of the river, so Grierson veered a bit to the south for Natchez, his alternate sanctuary, which was only twenty miles farther away than Grand Gulf. But that too was not to be. Beyond Union Church that afternoon, the raiders were enjoying a rest halt when they were charged by what one of them called "a crowd of graylooking horsemen galloping and shooting in a cloud of dust and smoke." The result at first was panic and the beginning of a rout, but presently they stiffened and repulsed the attackers, who turned out to be nothing more than a couple of understrength companies on the prowl. The colonel prepared to push on next day to Natchez, but was warned that night by one of the Butternut Guerillas, who had ridden ahead and struck up a conversation with a rebel outpost group, that seven companies of cavalry from Grand Gulf were planning to ambush him when he moved westward in the morning. So Grierson once more changed his plans, abandoning Natchez as his destination. Determined now to press on down to Baton Rouge, though this added another hundred miles to the distance his weary men would have to ride, he turned back east at dawn of April 29, avoiding the ambush laid so carefully in what was now his rear.

By early afternoon they were in Brookhaven, twenty-five miles east, astride the railroad they had crossed two days ago, twenty miles to the north, when the march was west. "There was much running and yelling" on the part of the startled citizens, Grierson later reported, "but it soon quieted into almost a welcome." Here, as at Hazlehurst on Monday, sparks from the burning railroad station and another string of boxcars set a section of the town ablaze, and the troopers once more turned firemen to help the natives keep the flames from spreading. Meantime, however, a wrecking crew kept busy tearing up track and burning crossties, thus abolishing the possibility of a locomotive pursuit by troops from Jackson. Back in the saddle, the raiders moved south along the railroad and made camp that night, eight miles below Brookhaven and just over a hundred miles from Baton Rouge. At Summit before sundown of the last day of April, the colonel spared the depot lest his men have to turn firefighters again to save the town, but there was another unfortunate — or fortunate, depending on the point of view — encounter with rebel spirits when the troopers uncovered a cache of rum in fifty-gallon barrels. Grierson broke up the binge, got the revelers mounted at last, drunk or sober, and pressed on south another half dozen miles before stopping for the night. Dawn of May Day completed two full weeks the men had spent in the saddle, with only a half day's rest aside from the minimal halts for sleep and food. Once more the march was west. "A straight line for Baton Rouge, and let speed be our safety," Grierson told his officers as the column was put in motion.

Speed there was — the raiders covered no less than seventy-five miles of road in the following twenty-eight hours — but there was fighting, too, the first and only serious opposition the main body encountered in the course of the long raid. Even so, it was not much. At Wall's Bridge, which spanned the Tickfaw River just north of the Louisiana line, three companies of Confederates from Port Hudson laid a noonday ambush that cost the leading Union company eight casualties. Grierson promptly brought his artillery to the front, shelled the opposite bank, and ordered a charge that not only cleared the bridge but threw the rebels into headlong flight. Riding south all night, with no time out for rest or food, the blue column reached and crossed the Amite River, the last unfordable stream this side of Baton Rouge, before the aroused graybacks could bar the way. Six miles short of the Louisiana capital next morning, his troopers reeling in their saddles from lack of sleep, Grierson called a halt at last. The men tumbled from their mounts and slept where they fell, along the roadside, but the colonel himself, as befitted a former music teacher with an ingrained mistrust of horses, was refreshing himself by playing the piano in the parlor of a nearby plantation house when a picket burst in with news that they were about to be overwhelmed and captured. A rebel force was approaching from the west, he said, with skirmishers out! Grierson, knowing better, rode out to meet the reported enemy, who turned out to be members of the garrison at Baton Rouge, sent to investigate an improbable-sounding rumor "that a brigade of cavalry from General Grant's army had cut their way through the heart of the rebel country, and were then only five miles outside the city." Somewhat restored by their naps, the men remounted and rode into the capital that afternoon. Cheered by spectators, civilians as well as soldiers, the two-mile-long procession of road-worn men and animals, so weathered and dust-caked that they could scarcely be distinguished from the prisoners and Negroes they had gathered along the way, wound slowly around the public square, then south out of town to a grove of magnolias two miles south, where they dismounted, unsaddled, and fell so soundly asleep that they could not be aroused to accept hot coffee.

They had cause for weariness, having covered more than six hundred miles in less than sixteen days, and for thankfulness as well: thankfulness that Pemberton had lost Van Dorn to Bragg three months before, along with nearly all his cavalry, and that it was Abel Streight and not themselves who had been made the prime concern of Bedford Forrest. Streight had left Fort Henry on the day they left La Grange, and was surrendering in East Alabama while Grierson's men, having caught up on their sleep at last, were enjoying their first midday meal in the magnolia grove just south of the Louisiana capital. Different circumstances might well have led to different results, including perhaps a reversal of their current roles as prisoners on the one hand and heroes on the other, but the fact remained that the Illinois troopers had dealt with conditions as they found them. And having done so, they had cause for pride. At a total cost of barely two dozen casualties — "3 killed, 7 wounded, 5 left on the route sick . . . and 9 men missing, supposed to have straggled" — they had "killed and wounded about one hundred of the enemy, captured and paroled over 500 prisoners, many of them officers, destroyed between fifty and sixty miles of railroad and telegraph, captured and destroyed over 3000 stand of arms, and other army stores and government property to an immense amount." So Grierson later reported, adding as if by afterthought, despite his continued mistrust of all equine creatures: "We also captured 1000 horses and mules."

Within three days the colonel was on a steamboat for New Orleans, where he was feted and presented with a horse by the admiring citizenry. "My dear Alice," he wrote his wife that night, "I like Byron have had to wake up one morning and find myself famous. Since I have been here it has been one continuous ovation." In early June, with his picture on the covers of both *Harper's Weekly* and *Leslie's Illustrated*, he was promoted to brigadier general. But perhaps the finest tribute of all came from a man by no means given to using superlatives, on or off the record. Assessing the value of the raid in its relation to the over-all campaign for the taking of Vicksburg, of which it was very much a part, Grant said flatly: "It was Grierson who first set the example of what might be done in the interior of the enemy's country without any base from which to draw supplies."

For the present, however, Grant at Hard Times had no more knowledge of Grierson's progress, across the way, than Grierson had had of Grant's while riding west from Hazlehurst. All the cavalryman learned for certain as he pressed on toward the river was that the army had not crossed as planned, which meant that something must have gone awry. Something had indeed. When the raiders turned back east from Union Church at dawn of April 29, avoiding the ambush laid in what had been their front, they missed hearing the guns of the attackers and defenders at Grand Gulf, less than thirty air-line miles away. It was just as well, for otherwise they might have been lured into what would have been a trap. Except for the rather negative advantage of proving that this was no place to attempt an east-bank landing, the attack was an utter failure, and an expensive one at that.

Porter's doubts had been increasing all week, ever since his April 22 reconnaissance of the stronghold on the bluff across the way. Though he had kept up a show of confidence in his talks with Grant, privately he was airing his misgivings in dispatches to his Washington superiors, not only by way of preparing them for bad news, but also by way of divesting himself in advance of any responsibility for the failure he saw looming. "I am quite depressed with this adventure," he wrote Fox, "which as you know never met with my approval." This last was something less than strictly true, though when he signaled the flotilla captains to move against Grand Gulf at 8 o'clock next morning, April 29, his forebodings soon turned out to have been well founded. The navy's task was to silence the rebel batteries, then cover the crossing by the transports bringing the army over to take the place by storm; but when four of the seven ironclads closed to within pistol shot of the 75-foot bluff — so at least it seemed to Grant, who watched the contest from aboard a tug — they were severely mauled. The flagship *Benton* took 70 hits, the *Tuscumbia* 81; the *Lafayette* took 45, the *Pittsburg* 35. The other three boats, *Carondelet, Mound City*, and *Louisville*, all veterans of the river war from its beginning, did their fighting at long range, lobbing shells into the blufftop works, and consequently suffered little damage. Even so, when Porter hoisted the pennant for the flotilla to drop back out of action at 12.30 — all but the *Tuscumbia*, which had been struck in her machinery and swept powerless downstream until she fetched up short against the Louisiana bank — a total of 75 casualties, including 18 dead, had been subtracted from its crews. By contrast, although time would disclose that they had lost 3 killed and 15 wounded, the defenders seemed unhurt behind their earthwork fortifications. Grand Gulf was as much a failure for the Union navy as Fort Donelson had been, just over a year ago. Porter frankly admitted as much. A crossing might be managed elsewhere, he told Grant, but not here, under the muzzles of those guns across the way.

Grant had not expected a repulse, but he was prepared for what he considered the outside chance of one. Now that a repulse had been encountered, an alternate plan was put into execution without delay. McClernand's men would debark at Hard Times, march south across the point of land to De Shroon's, a plantation landing some four miles downstream, and be ready before dawn to get back aboard the transports, which were to steal past Grand Gulf under cover of darkness, hugging the western bank while the gunboats re-engaged the batteries. All this went as planned, afloat and ashore. The navy lost only one man in its renewal of the duel with the blufftop cannoneers, and the army made its night march unobserved, to find the transports waiting unscathed in the predawn darkness at De Shroon's. "By the time it was light," Grant later wrote, "the enemy saw our whole fleet, ironclads, gunboats, river steamers, and barges, quietly moving down the river three miles below them, black, or rather blue, with National troops."

Accomplishing this he showed the flexibility that would characterize his planning throughout the various stages of the campaign which now was under way in earnest. Other characteristics he also showed. An officer was to remember seeing the general sitting his horse beside the road at a point where a narrow bridge had been thrown across a bog. "Push right along, men," he told the marchers, speaking in almost a conversational tone. "Close up fast and hurry over." The soldiers recognized him and were obviously pleased to see their commander sharing their exertions, but the officer noted that their only reply was to do as he directed. They did not cheer him; they just "hurried over." It was as if, in the course of the long winter of repeated failures, they had caught his quality of quiet confidence. Charles Dana, for one, had begun to think so. He had come down here three weeks ago to report on Grant's alleged bad habits. So far, though, he not only had detected none of these; he had never even heard him curse or seen him lose his temper. Dana was puzzled. "His equanimity was becoming a curious spectacle to me," the former journalist later recalled. Tonight, for example, riding beside the general along the dark road from Hard Times to De Shroon's, he saw Grant's horse stumble. "Now he will swear," he thought, half expecting to see the rider go tumbling over the animal's head; "For an instant his moral status was on trial." But Grant lost neither his balance nor his temper. "Pulling up his horse, he rode on, and, to my utter amazement, without a word or sign of impatience."

Nor did the night march across the point of land, from Hard Times to De Shroon's, put an end to the need for sudden improvisation. Having bypassed Grand Gulf — which he could not allow to remain alive for long, so close in his rear — Grant still was faced with the problem of where to effect a landing on the Mississippi bank, in order to return for a strike at the fortified bluff from its vulnerable landward flank. A look at the map suggested Rodney, another twelve miles downstream. But that would not only give the troops a considerable distance to march, and the defenders time to improve their position and call in reinforcements, it would also place the bluecoats on the far side of Bayou Pierre, which would have to be crossed when they turned back north. Yet to make a landing short of the point where the bayou flowed westward into the river, five miles below, might be to founder the army in some unmapped and unsuspected swamp. What was needed was a guide, a sympathetic native of the region, and Grant sent a detachment of soldiers across the river in a skiff, with instructions to bring back what he wanted. They returned before midnight with an east-bank slave who filled the bill. At first he had been unwilling to come, and in fact had had to be taken by force, but now that he found himself in the lamp-lighted headquarters tent, facing the Union commander across an unrolled chart, he turned co-operative. "Look here," Grant said. "Tell me where this road leads to — starting where you see my finger here on the map and running down that way." The Negro studied the problem, then shook his head. "That road fetches up at Bayou Pierre," he said. "But you can't go that way, 'cause it's plum full of backwater." The thing to do, he replied to further questions, was to go ashore at Bruinsburg, six miles below De Shroon's. This would still be south of Bayou Pierre, but at least it was only half as far as Rodney. Moreover, there was a good road leading from there to Grand Gulf by way of Port Gibson, which lay ten miles inland, well back from the trackless swamps and canebrakes of the river bottoms. At Bruinsburg, the captive slave explained, "you can leave the boats and the men can walk on high ground all the way. The best houses and plantations in all the country are there, sir, all along that road."

So Bruinsburg it was. By midmorning of this last day of April — while Sherman was launching his demonstration against Haines Bluff, fifty air-line miles to the north, and Grierson was pressing southward along the railroad below Brookhaven, the same distance to the east — all four of McClernand's divisions and one of McPherson's, some 23,000 men in all, had completed their debarkation and were slogging inland toward Port Gibson. "When this was effected," Grant declared years later, "I felt a degree of relief scarcely ever equaled since." Then he told why. "I was now in the enemy's country, with a vast river and the stronghold of Vicksburg between me and my base of supplies. But I was on dry ground on the same side of the river with the enemy. All the campaigns, labors, hardships, and exposures from the month of December previous to this time that had been made and endured were for the accomplishment of this one object."

✗ 2 ✗

For all his northern birth and starchy manner, which some continued to find personally distasteful, Pemberton by now had either sustained or won the confidence not only of his military superiors but also of the people of Mississippi, who came within his charge. His four-month sequence of successes in the face of threats from all points of the compass far outweighed their original prejudice against him. On May Day, for example — unaware that Sherman was knocking at Vicksburg's upper gate or that Grant, with half his army over the river, already was marching inland from below — an editor in the capital, where the department commander had his headquarters, was taking a sanguine view of the situation. "It would be idle to say that our state and country was not in a position of great peril," he declared. "Yet, strange as it may seem to our readers, we have never felt more secure since the fall of Donelson. The enemy will never reach Jackson; we are satisfied of that. . . . General Pemberton, assisted by vigilant and accomplished officers, is watching the movements of the enemy, and at the proper time will pounce upon him. Let us give the authorities all the assistance we can, and trust their superior and more experienced judgment as to the management of the armies. We know we have a force sufficient, if properly handled, not only to defeat but to rout and annihilate Grant if he ventures far from his river base." As for doubts as to the proper handling of this sufficient force: "Let any man who questions the ability of General Pemberton only think for a moment of the condition the department was in when he was first sent here. No general has evinced a more sleepless vigilance in the discharge of his duty, or accomplished more solid and gratifying results." Nor was this merely the opinion of one uninformed civilian. With reservations, Joe Johnston shared his view. Despite the gloom into which his inspection of the Vicksburg defenses had thrown him, back in December, the Virginian since had warmed to the Pennsylvanian as a result of his apparent skill in fending off the combinations designed for his destruction. In mid-March, reviewing the situation from three hundred miles away in Tennessee, he congratulated him handsomely. "Your activity and vigor in the defense of Mississippi must have secured for you the confidence of the people of Mississippi," he wrote, and added: "I have no apprehension for Port Hudson from Banks. The only fear is that the canal may enable Grant to unite their forces. I believe your arrangements at Vicksburg make it perfectly safe, unless that union should be effected."

Applause was one thing, assistance quite another: as Pemberton soon found out. Despite the denial of help from the vast department across the river, and despite the January transfer of three quarters of his cavalry to Middle Tennessee, he was so encouraged by the flooding of Grant's canal in March that he mistook the subsequent withdrawal of the diggers to Milliken's Bend for an abandonment by the Federals of their entire campaign. On April 11 he notified Johnston that the canal was no longer a danger, that Grant appeared to be pulling back to Memphis, and that he was therefore sending, as requested, a brigade to reinforce Bragg at Tullahoma. Five days later, however, with the blue army still in evidence on the opposite bank and Porter's gunboats preparing for their run past the batteries that night, he recalled the detached brigade, which by then was in northern Mississippi. "[Grant's] movement up the river was a ruse," he wired Johnston. "Certainly no more troops should leave this department." In fact, he said, it was he who stood in gravest need of help. Nothing came of that. Then on April 20, with Porter's ironclads riding at anchor near New Carthage, McClernand moving farther down the Louisiana bank, and Grierson on the rampage east of Grenada — "part and parcel of the formidable invasion preparing before my eyes" — Pemberton stepped up his plea for reinforcements: especially for the return of his 6000 troopers under Van Dorn, the loss of whom had left him three-fourths blind. "Heavy raids are making from Tennessee deep into this state," he warned. "Cavalry is indispensable to meet these expeditions. The little I have is . . . totally inadequate. Could you not make a demonstration with a cavalry force on their rear?" He protested that he had "literally no cavalry from Grand Gulf to Yazoo City, while the enemy is threatening to [cross] the river between Vicksburg and Grand Gulf, having now twelve vessels below

the former place." Johnston, obliged as he presently was to send Forrest
to Alabama after Streight, not only would not agree to make a demonstration against West Tennessee; he also declined to lessen the strength of
Bragg's mounted arm, which included Wheeler and Morgan as well as
Forrest and Van Dorn, despite the fact that Van Dorn was nominally
on loan from Pemberton. It turned out, moreover, that the Pennsylvanian's previous successes worked against him now. Matters had seemed
as dark several times before, in the course of the past four months, and
he had managed to survive without assistance; apparently Johnston believed he would do as well again. At any rate he was still of his former
opinion: "Van Dorn's cavalry is absolutely necessary to enable General
Bragg to hold the best part of the country from which he draws supplies."

In effect this amounted to signing Van Dorn's death warrant,
since it kept him within range of the Tennessee doctor's wife and her
husband's pistol. Pemberton was inclined to think that in the end it might
amount to much the same thing for Vicksburg, which Jefferson Davis
referred to as "the nailhead that held the South's two halves together."
For suddenly now the news grew more alarming. Two nights later,
April 22, five unarmored steamboats ran the batteries, obviously to provide the means for a crossing, somewhere below, by the bluecoats slogging down the western bank. Throughout the week that followed, Pemberton sent what little cavalry he had in pursuit of Grierson, whose
raiders were disrupting the interior of the state and playing havoc with
his lines of supply and communication. Then on April 29 word came
from Brigadier General John S. Bowen, commanding at Grand Gulf,
that the place was under heavy attack by gunboats attempting to soften
him up for an assault by infantry waiting in transports across the river at
Hard Times. Scarcely had the news arrived next morning that the ironclads had retired, severely battered, than Pemberton was notified that
Haines Bluff was under similar pressure to the north. By the time he
learned that this too had been beaten off, a follow-up message from
Bowen informed him that the Union fleet had slipped past Grand Gulf in
the darkness, transports and all, and was unloading soldiers in large
numbers at Bruinsburg, ten miles below. Then came word that the
Federals had resumed their pounding of Haines Bluff. Deciding that the
downriver threat was the graver of the two, Pemberton resolved to
reinforce Bowen, whom he instructed to contest the blue advance on
Port Gibson.

On May Day, with the issue still in doubt below — so he thought,
though it could scarcely be in doubt for long; the enemy strength was
reported at 20,000 men, while Bowen had considerably less than half
that many — he appealed once more to Johnston for assistance, bolstering his plea with a wire directly to the President. Davis replied that, in
addition to urging Johnston to send help from Tennessee, he was doing

all he could to forward troops from southern Alabama. Secretary Seddon, alerted to the danger, informed Pemberton that "heavy reinforcements" would start at once by rail from Beauregard in Charleston. Both messages were gratifying, communicating assurance of assistance from above. But all the harassed Vicksburg commander got from Johnston was advice. "If Grant's army lands on this side of the river," the Virginian replied from Tullahoma, "the safety of Mississippi depends on beating it. For that object you should unite your whole force."

A Georgia-born West Pointer, Bowen had left the old army after a single hitch as a lieutenant and had prospered as a St Louis architect before he was thirty, at which age he offered his sword to the newly formed Confederacy. Promoted to brigadier within ten months, he now was thirty-two and eager for further advancement, having spent more than a year in grade because of a long convalescence from a wound taken at Shiloh, where he led his brigade of Missourians with distinction. On the afternoon of April 30, marching his 5500 soldiers out of Grand Gulf and across Bayou Pierre to meet Grant's 23,000 moving inland from Bruinsburg after their downriver creep past his blufftop guns in the darkness, he carried proudly in his pocket a dispatch received last night from Pemberton, congratulating him on the repulse of Porter's ironclads: "In the name of the army, I desire to thank you and your troops for your gallant conduct today. Keep up the good work. . . . Yesterday I warmly recommended you for a major-generalcy. I shall renew it." Bowen had it very much in mind to keep up the good work. Despite the looming four-to-one odds and the changed nature of his task now that he and the blue invaders were on the same bank of the river, he welcomed this opportunity to deal with them ashore today as he had dealt with them afloat the day before. Four miles west of Port Gibson before nightfall, he put his men in a good defensive position astride a wooded ridge just short of a fork in the road leading east from Bruinsburg. Presently the Federals came up and his pickets took them under fire in the moonlight. Artillery deepened the tone of the argument, North and South, but soon after midnight, as if by mutual consent, both sides quieted down to wait for daylight.

McClernand opened the May Day fight soon after sunrise, advancing all four of his divisions under Brigadier Generals Peter Osterhaus, A. J. Smith, Alvin Hovey, and Eugene Carr. The road fork just ahead placed him in something of a quandary, lacking as he did an adequate map, but this was soon resolved by a local Negro who informed him that the two roads came together again on the near side of Port Gibson, his objective. He sent Osterhaus to the left as a diversion in favor of the other three commanders, who were charged with launching the main effort on the right. Grant came up at midmorning to find the battle in full swing and McClernand in some confusion, his heavily engaged columns being out of touch with each other because the two roads that wound along parallel ridges — "This part of Mississippi stands on edge" was how Grant put it — were divided by a timber-choked ravine that made lateral communication impossible. The result was that McClernand's right hand quite literally did not know what his left was doing, though the fact was neither was doing well at all. In his perplexity he called for help from McPherson, who supplied it by sending one brigade of Major General John A. Logan's division to the left and another to the right. "Push right along. Close up fast," the men heard Grant say as they went past the dust-covered general sitting a dust-covered horse beside the road fork. They did as he said, and arrived on the left in time to stall a rebel counterattack that had already thrown Osterhaus off balance, while on the right they added the weight needed for a resumption of the advance. Outflanked and heavily outnumbered on the road to the south, Bowen at last had to pull back to the outskirts of Port Gibson, where he rallied his men along a hastily improvised line and held off the blue attackers until nightfall ended the fighting.

 Casualties were about equal on both sides; 832 Confederates and 875 Federals had fallen or were missing. Bowen had done well and he knew it, considering the disparity of numbers, but he also knew that to fight here tomorrow, against lengthened odds and without the advantage of this morning's densely wooded terrain, would be to invite disaster. At sundown he notified Pemberton that he would "have to retire under cover of night to the other side of Bayou Pierre and await reinforcements." Pemberton, who had arrived in Vicksburg from Jackson by now, had already sent word that he was "hurrying reinforcements; also ammunition. Endeavor to hold your own until they arrive, though it may be some time, as the distance is great." At 7.30, having received Bowen's sundown message, he rather wistfully inquired: "Is it not probable that the enemy will himself retire tonight? It is very important, as you know, to retain your present position, if possible.... You must. however, of course, be guided by your own judgment. You and your men have done nobly." But Bowen by then had followed up his first dispatch with a second: "I am pulling back across Bayou Pierre. I will endeavor to hold that position until reinforcements arrive." He withdrew skillfully by moonlight, unpursued and unobserved, destroying the three bridges over the bayou and its south fork, northwest and northeast of Port Gibson, and took up a strong position on the opposite bank, covering the wrecked crossing of the railroad to Grand Gulf, which he believed would be Grant's next objective.

 But Grant did not come that way, at least not yet. Finding Port Gibson empty at dawn, he pressed on through and gave James Wilson a brigade-sized detail with which to construct a bridge across the south fork of Bayou Pierre, just beyond the town. Wilson was experienced in such work, having built no less than seven such spans in the course of the march from Milliken's Bend, and besides he had plenty of materials at hand, in the form of nearby houses which he tore down and cannibalized. By midafternoon the job was finished, "a continuous raft 166 feet long, 12 feet wide, with three rows of large mill-beams lying across the current, and the intervals between them closely filled with buoyant timber; the whole firmly tied together by a cross-floor or deck of 2-inch stuff." So Wilson later described it, not without pride, adding that he had also provided side rails, corduroy approaches over quicksand, and abutments "formed by building a slight crib-work, and filling in with rails covered by sand." Grant was impressed, but he did not linger to admire the young staff colonel's handiwork. The second of McPherson's three divisions having arrived that morning, he was given the lead today, with orders to march eight miles northeast to Grindstone Ford, which he reached soon after dark. He was prevented from crossing at once because the fine suspension bridge had been destroyed at that point, but Wilson was again at hand and had it repaired by daylight of May 3, when McPherson pressed on over. Near Willow Springs, two miles beyond the stream, he encountered and dislodged a small hostile force which retreated toward Hankinson's Ferry, six miles north, where the main road to Vicksburg crossed the Big Black River. Instructing McPherson to keep up the march northward in pursuit, Grant detached a single brigade to accompany him westward in the direction of Grand Gulf.

McClernand, coming along behind McPherson, whom he was ordered to follow north, was alarmed to learn what Grant had done, striking off on his own like that, and sent a courier galloping after him with a warning: "Had you not better be careful lest you may personally fall in with the enemy on your way to Grand Gulf?" But Grant was not only anxious to reach that place as soon as possible, and thus reestablish contact with the navy and with Sherman, who was on the march down the Louisiana bank; he also believed that Bowen, chastened by yesterday's encounter, would fall back beyond the Big Black as soon as he discovered that his position on Bayou Pierre had been turned upstream. And in this the northern commander was quite right. Reinforcements had reached Bowen from Jackson and Vicksburg by now, but they only increased his force to about 9000, whereas he reckoned the present enemy strength at 30,000, augmented as it was by a full division put ashore at Bruinsburg the night before. When he learned, moreover, that this host had bridged both forks of Bayou Pierre to the east of Port Gibson and was headed for the crossings of the Big Black, deep in his rear, he lost no time in reaching the decision Grant expected. At midnight, finding that his staff advisers "concurred in my belief that I was compelled to abandon the post at Grand Gulf," he "then ordered the evacuation, the time for each command to move being so fixed as to avoid any delay or confusion." The retrograde movement went smoothly despite the need for haste. Bringing off all their baggage — which Pemberton, when informed of their predicament, had authorized them to abandon lest it slow their march, but which Bowen declared he was "determined to and did save" — the weary veterans and the newly arrived reinforcements set off northward, leaving the blufftop intrenchments, which they had defended so ably against the ironclad assault four days ago, yawning empty behind them in the early morning sunlight.

Soon after they disappeared over the northern horizon Porter arrived with four gunboats, intending to launch a new attack. He approached with caution, remembering his previous woes and fearing a rebel trick, but when he found the Grand Gulf works abandoned he did not let that diminish his claim for credit for their reduction. "We had a hard fight for these forts," he wrote Secretary Welles, "and it is with great pleasure that I report that the Navy holds the door to Vicksburg." He announced that his fire had torn the place to pieces, leaving it so covered with earth and debris that no one could tell at a glance what had been there before the bombardment. "Had the enemy succeeded in finishing these fortifications no fleet could have taken them," he declared, quite as if he had subdued the batteries in the nick of time, and added: "I hear nothing of our army as yet; was expecting to hear their guns as we advanced on the forts."

He heard from "our army" presently with the arrival of its commander, who had got word of the evacuation while en route from Grindstone Ford and had ridden ahead of the infantry with an escort of twenty troopers. Grant was glad to see the admiral, but most of all — after seven days on a borrowed horse, with "no change of underclothing, no meal except such as I could pick up sometimes at other headquarters, and no tent to cover me" — he was glad to avail himself of the admiral's facilities. After a hot bath, a change of underwear borrowed from one of the naval officers, and a square meal aboard the flagship, he got off a full report to Halleck on the events of the past four days. "Our victory has been most complete, and the enemy thoroughly demoralized," he wrote. Bowen's defense of Port Gibson had been "a very bold one and well carried out. My force, however, was too heavy for his, and composed of well-disciplined and hardy men who know no defeat and are not willing to learn what it is." After this unaccustomed flourish he got down to the matter at hand. "This army is in the finest health and spirits," he declared. "Since leaving Milliken's Bend they have marched as much by night as by day, through mud and rain, without tents or much other baggage, and on irregular rations, without a complaint and with less straggling than I have ever before witnessed. . . . I shall not bring my troops into this place, but immediately follow the enemy, and, if all promises as favorable hereafter as it does now, not stop until Vicksburg is in our possession."

He was on his own, however, in a way he had neither intended nor foreseen. His plan had been to use Grand Gulf as a base, accumulating a reserve of supplies and marking time with Sherman and McPherson, so to speak, while McClernand took his corps downriver to cooperate with Banks in the reduction of Port Hudson, after which the two would join him for a combined assault on Vicksburg. But he found waiting for him today at Grand Gulf a three-week-old letter from Banks, dated April 10 and headed Brashear City — 75 miles west of New Orleans and equally far south of Port Hudson — informing him of a change in procedure made necessary, according to the Massachusetts general, by unexpected developments in western Louisiana which would threaten his flank and rear, including New Orleans itself, if he moved due north from the Crescent City as originally planned. Instead, he intended to abolish this danger with an advance up the Teche and the Atchafalaya, clearing out the rebels around Opelousas before returning east to Baton Rouge for the operation against Port Hudson with 15,000 men. He hoped to open this new phase of the campaign next day, he wrote, and if all went as planned he would return to the Mississippi within a month — that is, by May 10 — at which time he would be ready to co-operate with Grant in their double venture. . . . Reading the letter, Grant experienced a considerable shock. He had expected Banks to have twice as many troops already in position for a quick slash at Port Hudson, to be followed by an equally rapid boat ride north to assist in giving Vicksburg the same treatment. Now all that went glimmering. Some 30,000 men poorer than he had counted on being, he was on his own: which on second thought had its advantages, since the Massachusetts general outranked him and by virtue of his seniority would get the credit, from the public as well as the government, for the reduction of both Confederate strongholds and the resultant clearing of the Mississippi all the way to the Gulf. Grant absorbed the shock and quickly made up his mind that he was better off without him. Banks having left him on his own, he would do the same for Banks. "To wait for his co-operation would have detained me at least a month," he subsequently wrote in explanation of his decision. "The reinforcements would not have reached 10,000 men after deducting casualties and necessary river guards at all high points close to the river for over 300 miles. The enemy would have strengthened his position and been reinforced by more men than Banks could have brought. I therefore determined to move independently of Banks, cut loose from my base, destroy the rebel force in rear of Vicksburg, and invest or capture the city."

So much he intended, though he had not yet decided exactly how he would go about it. One thing he knew, however, was that the change of plans called for an immediate speed-up of the accumulation of supplies, preliminary to launching his all-out drive on the rebel citadel two dozen air-line miles to the north. A look at the Central Mississippi interior, with its lush fields, its many grazing cattle, and its well-stocked plantation houses — "of a character equal to some of the finest villas on

the Hudson," a provincial New York journalist called these last — had
convinced him that the problem was less acute than he had formerly
supposed. "This country will supply all the forage required for anything
like an active campaign, and the necessary fresh beef," he informed Halleck. "Other supplies will have to be drawn from Milliken's Bend. This
is a long and precarious route, but I have every confidence in succeeding
in doing it." Accordingly, he ordered this supply line shortened, as soon
as the river had fallen a bit, by the construction of a new road from
Young's Point to a west-bank landing just below Warrenton. "Everything depends upon the promptitude with which our supplies are forwarded," he warned. He had already directed that two towboats make
a third run past the Vicksburg guns with heavy-laden barges. "Do this
with all expedition," he told the quartermaster at Milliken's Bend, "in
48 hours from receipt of orders if possible. Time is of immense importance." Hurlbut was ordered to forward substantial reinforcements from
Memphis without delay, as well as to lay in a sixty-day surplus of rations,
to be kept on hand for shipment downriver at short notice. To Sherman,
hurrying south across the way, went instructions to collect 120 wagons
en route, load them with 100,000 pounds of bacon, then pile on all the
coffee, sugar, salt, and crackers they would hold. "It is unnecessary for
me to remind you of the overwhelming importance of celerity in your
movements," Grant told him, outlining the situation as he saw it now on
this side of the river: "The enemy is badly beaten, greatly demoralized,
and exhausted of ammunition. The road to Vicksburg is open. All we
want now are men, ammunition, and hard bread. We can subsist our horses
on the country, and obtain considerable supplies for our troops."

  With all this paper work behind him, he left Grand Gulf at midnight and rode eastward under a full moon to rejoin McPherson, who
had reached Hankinson's Ferry that afternoon and had already dispatched cavalry details to probe the opposite bank of the Big Black
River. From his new headquarters Grant kept stressing the need for
haste. "Every day's delay is worth 2000 men to the enemy," he warned
a supply officer, and kept goading him with questions that called for
specific answers: "How many teams have been loaded with rations and
sent forward? I want to know as near as possible how we stand in
every particular for supplies. How many wagons have you ferried over
the river? How many are still to bring over? What teams have gone
back for rations?" His impatience was such that he had no time for
head-shaking or regrets. Learning on May 5 that one of the two towboats
and all the barges had been lost the night before in attempting the moonlight run he had ordered, he dismissed the loss with the remark: "We
will risk no more rations to run the Vicksburg batteries," and turned
his attention elsewhere. This touch of bad luck was more than offset
the following day by news that Sherman had reached Hard Times, freeing McPherson's third division from guard duty along the supply route,

and was already in the process of crossing the river to Grand Gulf. The red-haired general was in excellent spirits, having learned that four newspaper reporters had been aboard the towboat that was lost. "They were so deeply laden with weighty matter that they must have sunk," he remarked happily, and added: "In our affliction we can console ourselves with the pious reflection that there are plenty more of the same sort."

One thing Grant did find time for, though, amid all his exertions at Hankinson's Ferry. On the 7th he issued a general order congratulating his soldiers for their May Day victory near Port Gibson, which he said extended "the long list of those previously won by your valor and endurance." He was proud of what they had accomplished so far in the campaign, he assured them, and proudest of all that they had endured their necessary privations without complaint. Then he closed on a note of exhortation. "A few days' continuance of the same zeal and constancy will secure to this army the crowning victory over the rebellion. More difficulties and privations are before us. Let us endure them manfully. Other battles are to be fought. Let us fight them bravely. A grateful country will rejoice at our success, and history will record it with immortal honor."

Pemberton at this stage was by no means "badly beaten." Neither was he "greatly demoralized," any more than Vicksburg's defenders were "exhausted of ammunition." Nor was the road to the city "open," despite Grant's suppositions in his May 3 note urging Sherman to hurry down to get in on the kill. It was true, on the other hand, that the southern commander had been acutely distressed by the news that the blue invaders were landing in force on the east bank of the river below Grand Gulf, for he saw only too clearly the dangers this involved. "Enemy movement threatens Jackson, and, if successful, cuts off Vicksburg and Port Hudson from the east," he wired Davis on May Day, before he knew the outcome of the battle for Port Gibson, and he followed this up next morning, when he learned that Bowen had withdrawn across Bayou Pierre, with advice to Governor Pettus that the state archives be removed from the capital for safekeeping; Grant most likely would be coming this way soon. Another appeal to Johnston for "large reinforcements" to meet the "completely changed character of defense," now that the Federals were established in strength on this side of the river, brought a repetition of yesterday's advice: "If Grant crosses, unite all your troops to beat him. Success will give back what was abandoned to win it."

If this proposed abandonment included Vicksburg, and presumably it did, Pemberton was not in agreement. He already had ordered all movable ordnance and ammunition sent to that place from all parts of the state, in preparation for a last-ditch fight if necessary, and he arrived in person the following day, about the same time Grant rode into Grand Gulf with a twenty-trooper escort. For all his original alarm, Pemberton felt considerably better now. Davis and Seddon had promised reinforcements from Alabama and South Carolina — 5000 were coming from Charleston by rail at once, the Secretary wired, with another 4000 to follow — and Sherman had withdrawn from in front of Haines Bluff, reducing by half the problem of the city's peripheral defense. Johnston moreover had agreed at last, now that Streight had been disposed of, to send some cavalry under Forrest to guard against future raids across the Tennessee line. Much encouraged, Pemberton telegraphed Davis: "With reinforcements and cavalry promised in North Mississippi, think we will be all right."

His new confidence was based on a reappraisal of the situation confronting him now that Bowen, with his approval, had fallen back across the Big Black River, which curved across his entire right front and center. Not only did this withdrawal make a larger number of troops available for the protection of a much smaller area; it also afforded him the interior lines, so that a direct attack from beyond the arc could be met with maximum strength by defenders fighting from prepared positions. Presumably Grant would avoid that, but Pemberton saw an even greater advantage proceeding from the concentration behind the curved shield of the Big Black. It greatly facilitated what he later called "my great object," which was "to prevent Grant from establishing a base on the Mississippi River, above Vicksburg." Until the invaders accomplished this they would be dependent for supplies on what could be run directly past the gun-bristled bluff, a risky business at best, or freighted down the opposite bank, along a single jerry-built road that was subject to all the ravages of nature. As Pemberton saw it, his opponent's logical course would be to extend his march up the left bank of the Big Black, avoiding the bloodshed that would be involved in attempting a crossing until he was well upstream, in position for an advance on Haines Bluff from the rear and the establishment there of a new base of supplies, assisted and protected by Porter's upper flotilla, which would have returned up the Yazoo to meet him. But the southern commander did not intend to stand idly by, particularly while the latter stages of the movement were in progress. "The farther north [Grant] advanced, toward my left, from his then base below, the weaker he became; the more exposed became his rear and flanks; the more difficult it became to subsist his army and obtain reinforcements." At the moment of greatest Union extension and exposure, the defenders — reinforced by then, their commander hoped, from all quarters of the Confederacy — would strike with all their strength at the enemy's flanks and rear, administering a sudden and stunning defeat to a foe for whom, given the time and place, defeat would mean disaster, perhaps annihilation. Such was the plan. And though there were obvious drawbacks — the region beyond the Big

Black, for example, would be exposed to unhindered depredations; critics would doubtless object, moreover, that Grant might adopt a different method of accomplishing his goal — Pemberton considered the possible consummation of his design well worth the risk. Having weighed the odds and assessed his opponent's probable intentions from his actions in the past, he was content to let the outcome test the validity of his insight into the mind of his adversary. "I am a northern man; I know my people," he was to say. Besides, he believed that the Federals, obliged to hold onto one base to the south while reaching out for another to the north, had little choice except to act as he predicted. It was true that in the interim they "might destroy Jackson and ravage the country," he admitted, "but that was a comparatively small matter. To take Vicksburg, to control the valley of the Mississippi, to sever the Confederacy, to ruin our cause, a base upon the eastern bank immediately above was absolutely necessary."

Whatever else was desirable in the conflict now about to be resumed, he knew he would need all the soldiers he could get for the close-up defense of the line on the Big Black. In this connection, at the same time he informed Richmond of the pending evacuation of Grand Gulf he requested permission to bring the so-far unthreatened garrison of Port Hudson north for a share in the coming struggle. "I think Port Hudson and Grand Gulf should be evacuated," he wired Davis on May 2, "and the whole force concentrated for defense of Vicksburg and Jackson." Accordingly, in conformity with Johnston's advice to "unite all your troops," he ordered Major General Franklin Gardner, commanding the lower fortress, to strip the garrison to an absolute minimum and move with all the rest of the men to Jackson; those remaining behind would follow as soon as Richmond confirmed his request for total evacuation. On May 7, however, Davis replied that he approved of the withdrawal from Grand Gulf, but that "to hold both Vicksburg and Port Hudson is necessary to a connection with the Trans-Mississippi." So Pemberton countermanded the order to Gardner. He was to return at once to Port Hudson "and hold it to the last. President says both places must be held."

Such discouragement as this occasioned had been offset in advance, at least in part, by the defeat three nights ago of Grant's third attempt to run supplies downriver past the Vicksburg batteries. The sunken towboat and the flaming barges — not to mention the four Yankee journalists, who had not drowned, as Sherman had so fervently hoped, but had been fished out of the muddy water as prisoners of war — were evidence of improvement in the marksmanship of the gunners on the bluff, although it had to be conceded that the brilliant moonlight gave them an advantage they had lacked before. Another encouragement came soon afterwards from Johnston, who replied on May 8 to a report in which Pemberton explained his preparations for defense: "Disposition of troops, as far as understood, judicious; can be readily concentrated against Grant's army." If this was guarded, it was also approving, which was something altogether new from that direction. Then next day came the best news of all: Johnston himself would be coming soon to Vicksburg to inspirit the men and lend the weight of his genius to the defense of the Gibraltar of the West. Acting under instructions from Davis, Seddon ordered the general to proceed from Tullahoma "at once to Mississippi and take chief command of the forces, giving to those in the field, as far as practicable, the encouragement and benefit of your personal direction." Johnston was suffering at the time from a flare-up of his Seven Pines wound, but he replied without apparent hesitation: "I shall go immediately, although unfit for service." He left Tennessee next morning, May 10, having complied with the Secretary's further instructions to have "3000 good troops" follow him from Bragg's army as reinforcements for Pemberton.

　　　Pemberton took new hope at the prospect of first-hand assistance from on high; now he could say, with a good deal more assurance than he had felt when he used the words the week before, "Think we will be all right." But there were flaws in the logic of his approach to the central problem, or at any rate errors in the conclusion to which that logic had led him. His assessment of Grant's intention was partly right, but it was also partly wrong: right, that is, in the conviction that what his opponent wanted and needed was a supply base above Vicksburg, but wrong as to how he would go about getting what he wanted. By now Grant had nine of his ten divisions across the Mississippi and had reached the final stage of his week-long build-up for an advance, though not in the direction Pemberton had supposed and planned for.

　　　McPherson had been shifted eight miles east to Rocky Springs, leaving Hankinson's Ferry to be occupied by Sherman, two of whose three divisions were with him, while McClernand was in position along the road between those two points. In connection with the problem of supply, Grant had been collecting all the transportation he could lay hands on, horses, mules, oxen, and whatever rolled on wheels, ever since the Bruinsburg crossing. The result was a weird conglomeration of vehicles, ranging from the finest plantation carriages to ramshackle farm wagons, with surreys and buckboards thrown in for good measure, all piled to the dashboards and tailgates with supplies — mainly crates of ammunition and hardtack, the two great necessities for an army on the move — constantly shuttling back and forth between the Grand Gulf steamboat landing and Rocky Springs, where Grant had established headquarters near McPherson. Sherman, being farthest in the rear, had a close-up view of vehicular confusion that seemed to him to be building up to the greatest traffic snarl in history, despite the fact that there was still not transportation enough to supply more than a fraction of the army's needs. It was his conclusion that Grant's headlong impatience to be up and off was plunging him toward a logistic disaster. By May 9 he could put up with it no longer. "Stop all troops till your army is partially supplied with wagons, and then act as quickly as possible," he advised his chief, "for this road will be jammed as sure as life if you attempt to supply 50,000 men by one single road." The prompt reply from Rocky Springs gave the redhead the shock of his military life. Previously he had known scarcely more of Grant's future plans than Pemberton knew from beyond the Big Black River, but suddenly the veil of secrecy was lifted enough to give him considerably more than a glimmer of what he had never suspected until now. "I do not calculate upon the possibility of supplying the army with full rations from Grand Gulf," Grant told him. "I know it will be impossible without constructing additional roads. What I do expect, however, is to get up what rations of hard bread, coffee, and salt we can, and make the country furnish the balance."

This clearly implied, if it did not actually state, that he intended to launch an invasion, much as Cortez and Scott had done in Mexico, without a base from which to draw supplies. And so he did. Back in December, returning through North Mississippi to Memphis after the destruction of his forward depot at Holly Springs, he had discovered that his troops could live quite easily off the country by the simple expedient of taking what they wanted from the farmers in their path. "This taught me a lesson," he later remarked, and now the lesson was about to be applied. Moreover, the success of Grierson, whose troopers had lacked for nothing in the course of a 600-mile ride that had "knocked the heart out of the state" — so Grant himself declared in passing along to Washington the news of the raid — was a nearer and more recent example of what might be accomplished along those lines. For his own part, in the course of his march from Bruinsburg through Port Gibson to Rocky Springs, he had observed that "beef, mutton, poultry, and forage were found in abundance," along with "quite a quantity of bacon and molasses." What was more, every rural commissary "had a run of stone, propelled by mule power, to grind corn for the owners and their slaves. All these [could be] kept running . . . day and night . . . at all plantations covered by the troops." He felt sure there would be enough food and forage of one sort or another for all his men and animals, leaving room in the makeshift train for ammunition and such hard-to-get items as salt and coffee, provided there were no long halts during which the local supplies would be exhausted. All that was required was that he keep his army moving, and that was precisely what he intended to do, from start to finish, for tactical as well as logistic reasons. His 45,000 effectives were roughly twice as many as Pemberton had behind the curved shield of the Big Black River; he was convinced that he could whip him in short order with a frontal attack. "If Blair were up now," he told Sherman, who was still awaiting the arrival of the division that had feinted at Haines Bluff, "I believe we could be in Vicksburg in seven days." But that would leave some 10,000 rebels alive in his rear at Jackson, which was connected by rail not only to Vicksburg but also to the rest of the Confederacy, so that reinforcements could be hurried there from Bragg and the East until they outnumbered him as severely as he had outnumbered Pemberton, thus turning the tables on him. His solution was to strike both north and east, severing the rail connection between Jackson and Vicksburg near the Big Black crossing, while simultaneously closing in on the capital. He would capture the inferior force at that place, if possible, but at any rate he would knock it out of commission as a transportation hub or a rallying point; after which he would be free to turn on Vicksburg unmolested, approaching it from the east and north, and thus either take the citadel by storm or else establish a base on the Yazoo from which to draw supplies while starving the cut-off defenders into surrender.

Sherman had much of this explained to him when he rode over to Rocky Springs that afternoon, in considerable perturbation, for what he called "a full conversation" with the army commander. But his doubts persisted, much as they had done after he had agreed to stage the Haines Bluff demonstration. "He is satisfied that he will succeed in his plan," he said of Grant in a letter urging Blair to hasten his crossing from Hard Times, "and, of course, we must do our full share." Though he would "of course" co-operate fully in carrying out his chief's design, he wanted it understood from the start — and placed indelibly on the record — that he was doing so with something less than enthusiasm and against his better judgment. Grant by now was accustomed to his lieutenant's mercurial ups and downs, and he did not let them discourage him or influence his thinking. The following day, May 10 — the Sunday Joe Johnston left Tullahoma for Jackson — he heard again from Banks, who informed him, in a letter written four days ago at Opelousas, that he was making steady progress up the Teche, clearing out the rebels on his flank, and expected to turn east presently for Port Hudson. "By the 25th, probably, and by the 1st certainly, we will be there," he promised. Convinced more than ever that he had done right not to wait for Banks, Grant replied that he was going ahead on his own. Previously he had told him nothing of his plans, not even that he would not be meeting him; but now he did, on the off-chance that Banks might be of assistance. "Many days cannot elapse before the battle will begin which is to decide the fate of Vicksburg," he wrote, "but it is impossible to predict how long it may last. I would urgently request, therefore, that you join me or send all the force you can spare to co-operate in the great struggle for opening the Mississippi River." Similarly, at this near-final moment, he got off a dispatch to the general-in-chief, announcing that he was leaving Banks to fend for himself against Port Hudson while the Army of the Tennessee cut loose from its base at Grand Gulf and plunged inland in order to come upon Vicksburg from the rear. "I knew well that Halleck's caution would lead him to disapprove of this course," he subsequently explained; "but it was the only one that gave any chance of success." Besides, such messages were necessarily slow in transmission, having to be taken overland from Hard Times to Milliken's Bend, then north by steamboat all the way to Cairo before they could be put on the wire, and Grant saw a certain advantage in this arrangement. "The time it would take to communicate with Washington and get a reply would be so great that I could not be interfered with until it was demonstrated whether my plan was practicable."

This done, he turned to putting the final touches to the plan he had evolved. McClernand would move up the left bank of the Big Black, guarding the crossings as he went, and strike beyond Fourteen Mile Creek at Edwards Station, on the railroad sixteen miles east of Vicksburg. McPherson would move simultaneously against Jackson, and Sherman would be on call to assist either column, depending on which ran into the stiffest resistance. On the 11th, Grant advanced all three to their jump-off positions: McClernand on the left, as near Fourteen Mile Creek as possible "without bringing on a general engagement," Sherman in the center, beyond Cayuga, and McPherson on the right, near Utica. "Move your command tonight to the next crossroads if there is water," Grant told McPherson, "and tomorrow with all activity into Raymond.... We must fight the enemy before our rations fail, and we are equally bound to make our rations last as long as possible."

Before dawn the following morning, May 12, they were off. The second phase of the campaign designed for the capture of Vicksburg was under way.

Advancing through a rugged and parched region, McClernand's troops found that the only way they could quench their thirst, aggravated by the heat of the day and the dust of the country roads, was to drive the opposing cavalry beyond Fourteen Mile Creek, which was held by a rebel force covering Edwards Station, some four miles to the north. By midafternoon they had done just that. "Our men enjoyed both the skirmish and the water," the commander of the lead division re-

ported. Sherman, coming up on the right, accomplished this same purpose by throwing "a few quick rounds of cannister" at the gray vedettes,
who promptly scampered out of range. Pioneers rebuilt a bridge the
Confederates had burned as they fell back, and several regiments crossed
the creek at dusk, establishing a bridgehead while the two corps went
into bivouac on the south bank, prepared to advance on Edwards in the
morning.

But that was not to be. McPherson, when within two miles of
Raymond at 11 o'clock that morning, had encountered an enemy force
of undetermined strength, "judiciously posted, with two batteries of artillery so placed as to sweep the road and a bridge over which it was
necessary to pass." This was in fact a single brigade of about 4000 men,
recently arrived from Port Hudson under Brigadier General John
Gregg, who had come out from Jackson the day before, under orders
from Pemberton to cover the southwest approaches to the capital. Informed that the Federals were moving on Edwards, over near the Big
Black River, he assumed that the blue column marching toward him
from Utica was only "a brigade on a marauding excursion," and he was
determined not only to resist but also, if possible, to slaughter the marauders. The result was a sharp and — considering the odds — surprisingly hot contest, in which seven butternut regiments took on a whole
Union corps. McPherson threw Logan's division against the wooded enemy position, only to have it bloodily repulsed. While the other two
were coming forward, Logan rallied in time to frustrate a determined
counterattack and follow it up with one of his own. By now, however,
having learned what it was he had challenged — and having suffered
514 casualties, as compared to McPherson's 442 — Gregg had managed
to disengage and was withdrawing through Raymond. Five miles to the
east, one third of the distance to Jackson, he met Brigadier General
W. H. T. Walker, who had marched out to join him with a thousand
men just arrived from South Carolina. Gregg halted and faced about,
ready to try his hand again; but there was no further action that day.
Entering Raymond at 5 o'clock, McPherson decided to stop for the
night. "The rough and impracticable nature of the country, filled with
ravines and dense undergrowth, prevented anything like an effective use
of artillery or a very rapid pursuit," he explained in a sundown dispatch
to the army commander.

Grant was seven miles away, at the Dillon plantation on Fourteen
Mile Creek with Sherman, and when he learned the outcome of the battle whose guns he had heard booming, five miles off at first, then fading
eastward into silence, he revised his over-all plan completely. Edwards
could wait. If Jackson was where the enemy was — and the determined
resistance at Raymond seemed to indicate as much — he would go after
him in strength; he would risk no halfway job in snuffing out a segment
of the rebel army concentrated near a rail hub that gave it access to

reinforcements from all quarters of the South. Accordingly, at 9.15 he sent orders assigning all three of his corps commanders new objectives for tomorrow and prescribing that each would begin his march "at daylight in the morning." McPherson would move against Clinton, on the railroad nine miles north, then eastward that same distance along the right-of-way to Jackson. Sherman would turn due east from his present bivouac at Dillon, swinging through Raymond so as to come upon the objective from the south. McClernand, after detaching one division to serve as a rear guard in the event that the Confederates at Vicksburg attempted to interfere by crossing the Big Black, would come along behind Sherman and McPherson, prepared to move in support of either or both as they closed in on the Mississippi capital. Such were Grant's instructions, and presently he had cause to believe that he had improvised aright. Two days ago McPherson had passed along a rumor that "some of the citizens in the vicinity of Utica say Beauregard is at or near Jackson." If the Charleston hero was there it was practically certain he had not come alone. And now there arrived a second dispatch from McPherson, headed 11 p.m. and relaying another rumor that heavy Confederate reinforcements were moving against him out of Jackson, intending to fight again at Raymond soon after sunup. He did not know how much fact there was in this, he added, but he would "try to be prepared for them." Grant had confidence in McPherson, especially when he was forewarned as he was now, and did not bother to reply. Besides, whether it was true or false that the rebels were marching in force to meet him west of their capital, he already had made provisions to counter such a threat by ordering all but one of his ten divisions, some 40,000 men in all, to move toward a convergence on that very objective "at daylight in the morning."

All three columns moved on schedule. By early afternoon McPherson was in Clinton, nine miles from Jackson, and Sherman was six miles beyond Raymond, about the same distance from the Mississippi capital. A lack of determined resistance seemed to indicate that last night's rumor of heavy reinforcements was in error, and this, plus reports from scouts that Pemberton had advanced in force to the vicinity of Edwards, caused Grant to modify his strategy again. McPherson was instructed to spend the rest of the day wrecking the railroad west of Clinton, then resume his eastward march at first light tomorrow, May 14, tearing up more track as he went. Sherman, half a dozen miles to the south, would regulate his progress so that both corps would approach the Jackson defenses simultaneously. McClernand, instead of following along to furnish unneeded support, would turn north at Raymond and march on Bolton Depot, eight miles west of Clinton, occupying a strong position in case Pemberton attempted a farther advance along the railroad toward his threatened capital. There was of course the possibility that the Confederate commander might lunge southward, across Fourteen Mile Creek, with the intention of attacking the Federal army's rear and severing its connection with Grand Gulf: in which case he would be removing himself from the campaign entirely, at least for the period of time required for him to discover that he had plunged into a vacuum. For Grant not only had no supply line; he had no rear,

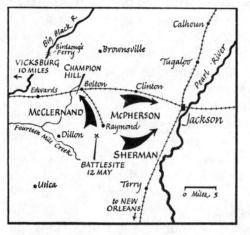

either, in the sense that Pemberton might suppose. Such rear as Grant had he had brought with him, embodied in McClernand, who now had orders to take up a position at Bolton, astride the railroad about midway between Vicksburg and Jackson, facing west. Moreover, once the capital had fallen and the blue army turned its attention back to its prime objective, the blufftop citadel forty-five miles away, what was now its rear would automatically become its front; McClernand, already in position for an advance, once more would take the lead, with Sherman and McPherson in support. For all the improvisatorial nature of his tactics, Grant, like any good chess player, was keeping a move or two ahead of the game.

By midmorning of May 14, slogging eastward under a torrential rain that quickly turned the dusty roads into troughs of mud, Sherman was within three miles of Jackson. At 10 o'clock, while peering through the steely curtain of the downpour to examine the crude fortifications to his front, he heard the welcome boom of guns off to the north; McPherson was on schedule and in place. While Sherman reconnoitered toward Pearl River for an opening on the flank, McPherson deployed for a time-saving frontal attack, to be launched astride the railroad. He waited an hour in the rain, lest the cartridge boxes of his troops be filled with water, like buckets under a tap, when they lifted the flaps to remove their paper-wrapped ammunition, and then at 11 o'clock, the rain having slacked to a drizzle at last, ordered his lead division forward across fields of shin-deep mud. The rebel pickets faded back to the shelter of their intrenchments, laying down a heavy fire that stopped the bluecoats in their tracks and flung them on their faces in the mud. By now it was noon. McPherson impatiently reformed his staggered line, having lost an even 300 men, and sent the survivors forward again. This time they found the rebel infantry gone. Only a handful of cannoneers had remained behind to serve the seven guns left on line and be captured by McPherson's jubilant soldiers. Sherman had the same experience, two miles to the south, except that he found ten guns in the abandoned works he had outflanked. Not only were his spoils thus greater than McPherson's; his casualties were fewer, numbering only 32. The Confederates, under Gregg and Walker, who had fallen back from east of Raymond the night before, had lost just over 200 men before pulling out of their trenches to make a hairbreadth getaway to the north. The Battle of Jackson was over, such as it was, and Grant had taken the Mississippi capital at a bargain price of 48 killed, 273 wounded, and 11 missing.

He was there to enjoy in person the first fruits of today's sudden and inexpensive victory. Sherman, riding in from the south — and noting with disapproval some "acts of pillage" already being committed by early arrived bluecoats under the influence "of some bad rum found concealed in the stores of the town" — was summoned by a courier to the Bowman House, Jackson's best hotel, where he found Grant and McPherson celebrating the capture of Jeff Davis's own home-state capital, the third the South had lost in the past two years. From the lobby they had a view, through a front window, of the State House where the rebel President had predicted, less than six months ago, that his fellow Mississippians would "meet and hurl back these worse than vandal hordes." Quick as the two generals had been to reach the heart of town, riding in ahead of the main body, they were slower than the army commander's young son Fred. His mother and brother had gone back North after the second running of the Vicksburg batteries, but Fred had stayed on to enjoy the fun that followed, wearing his father's dress sword and sash — which the general himself had little use for, and almost never wore — as badges of rank. Grant, an indulgent parent, later explained that the boy "caused no trouble either to me or his mother, who was at home. He looked out for himself and was in every battle of the campaign. His age, then not quite thirteen, enabled him to take in all he saw, and then to retain a recollection of it that would not be possible in more mature years." Fred's recollection of the capture of Jackson was saddened, however, by his failure to get a souvenir he badly wanted. He and a friendly journalist had seen from the outskirts of town a large Confederate flag waving from its staff atop the golden dome of the capitol. Mounted, they hurried ahead of the leading infantry column, tethered their horses in front of the big stone building, and raced upstairs — only to meet, on his way down, "a ragged, muddy, begrimed cavalryman" descending with the rebel banner tucked beneath his arm. For Fred, a good measure of the glory of Jackson's capture had departed, then and there.

Grant could sympathize with the boy's disappointment, but he had just been handed something considerably more valuable to him than the lost flag or even the seventeen guns that had been taken in the engagement that served as prelude to the occupation of the capital. Charles Dana arrived in mid-celebration with a dispatch just delivered by a courier from Grand Gulf. Signed by the Secretary of War and dated

May 5, it had been sent in response to a letter in which Dana had given him a summation of Grant's plan "to lose no time in pushing his army toward the Big Black and Jackson, threatening both and striking at either, as is most convenient. . . . He will disregard his base and depend on the country for meat and even for bread." Now Stanton replied:

> General Grant has full and absolute authority to enforce his own commands, to remove any person who, by ignorance, inaction, or any cause, interferes with or delays his operations. He has the full confidence of the Government, is expected to enforce his authority, and will be firmly and heartily supported; but he will be responsible for any failure to exert his powers. You may communicate this to him.

There was more here than met the eye. Stanton of course had authority over Halleck, so that if — or rather, as Grant believed from past experience, *when* — the time came for the general-in-chief to protest that Grant had disobeyed orders by abandoning Banks and striking out on his own, he would find — if indeed he had not found already — that Stanton, and presumably Lincoln as well, had approved in advance the course Grant had adopted. Nor was that all. Dana, having long since taken a position alongside the army commander in his private war against McClernand, had been keeping the Secretary copiously posted on the former congressman's military shortcomings, large and small, and feeling him out as to what the administration's reaction would be when Grant decided the time had come for him to swing the ax. Now the answer was at hand. Grant not only had "full and absolute authority" to sit in judgment; he would in fact be held "responsible for any failure to exert his powers" in all matters pertaining to what he considered his army's welfare and the progress of what Stanton called his "operations," whether against the rebels or McClernand.

It was no wonder then — protected as he now was from the wrath of his immediate superior, as well as from the machinations of his ranking subordinate — that he was in good spirits during the hotel-lobby victory celebration. All around him, meanwhile, the town was in a turmoil. "Many citizens [had] fled at our approach," one Federal witness later recalled, "abandoning houses, stores, and all their personal property, without so much as locking their doors. The Negroes, poor whites, and it must be admitted some stragglers and bummers from the ranks of the Union army, carried off thousands of dollars worth of property from houses, homes, shops and stores, until some excuse was given for the charge of 'northern vandalism,' which was afterwards made by the South. The streets were filled with people, white and black, who were carrying away all the stolen goods they could stagger under, without the slightest attempt at concealment and without let or hindrance from citizens or soldiers. . . . In addition . . . the convicts of the penitentiary, who had been released by their own authorities, set all the buildings connected with that prison on fire, and their lurid flames added to the holocaust elsewhere prevailing." He observed that "many calls were made upon [Grant] by citizens asking for guards to protect their private property, some of which perhaps were granted, but by far the greater number [of these petitioners] were left to the tender mercies of their Confederate friends."

After all, Grant had not brought his army here to protect the private property of men in revolution against the government that army represented; nor, for that matter, had it ever been his custom to deny his soldiers a chance at relaxation they had earned, even though that relaxation sometimes took a rather violent form. His purpose, rather, was to destroy all public property such as might be of possible comfort to the Confederacy. This applied especially to the railroads, the wrecking of which would abolish the Mississippi capital as a transportation hub, at least through the critical period just ahead. But that other facilities were not neglected was observed by a witness who testified that "foundries, machine shops, warehouses, factories, arsenals, and public stores were fired as fast as flames could be kindled." Sherman was the man for this work, Grant decided, and he gave him instructions "to remain in Jackson until he destroyed that place as a railroad center and manufacturing city of military supplies."

Meanwhile there was the campaign to get on with; Pemberton was hovering to the west, already on the near side of the Big Black, and beyond him there was Vicksburg, the true object of all this roundabout marching and such bloodshed as had so far been involved. McPherson was told to get his corps in hand and be prepared to set out for Bolton Depot at first light tomorrow to support McClernand, whose corps was no longer the army's rear guard, but rather its advance. Having attended to this, Grant joined Sherman for a little relaxation of his own; namely, a tour of inspection to determine which of the local business establishments would be spared or burned. In the course of the tour they came upon a cloth factory which, as Grant said later, "had not ceased work on account of the battle nor for the entrance of Yankee troops." Outside the building "an immense amount of cotton" was stacked in bales; inside, the looms were going full tilt, tended by girl operatives, weaving bolts of tent cloth plainly stamped C.S.A. No one seemed to notice the two generals, who watched for some time in amused admiration of such oblivious industry. "Finally," Grant said afterwards, "I told Sherman I thought they had done work enough. The operatives were told they could leave and take with them what cloth they could carry. In a few minutes cotton and factory were in a blaze."

This done, Grant returned to the Bowman House for his first

night's sleep on a mattress in two weeks. Joe Johnston, he was told, had occupied the same room the night before.

✗ 3 ✗

Johnston — not Beauregard, as rumor had had it earlier — had arrived at dusk the day before, at the end of a grueling three-day train ride from Tennessee by way of Atlanta, Montgomery, Mobile, and Meridian, only to find the Mississippi capital seething with reports of heavy Union columns advancing from the west. As night closed in, a hard rain began to fall, shrouding the city and deepening the Virginian's gloom still further: as was shown in a wire he got off to Seddon after dark. "I arrived this evening finding the enemy's force between this place and General Pemberton, cutting off communication. I am too late." To Pemberton, still on the far side of the Big Black, he sent a message advising quick action on that general's part. To insure delivery, three copies were forwarded by as many couriers. "I have lately arrived, and learn that Major General Sherman is between us, with four divisions, at Clinton," Johnston wrote. "It is important to re-establish communications, that you may be reinforced. If practicable, come up in his rear at once. To beat such a detachment would be of immense value. The troops here could co-operate. All the strength you can quickly assemble should be brought. Time is all important."

He had at Jackson, he presently discovered, only two brigades of about 6000 men with which to oppose the 25,000 Federals who were knocking at the western gates next morning. After a sharp, brief skirmish and the sacrifice of seventeen guns to cover a withdrawal, he retreated seven miles up the Canton road to Tugaloo, where he halted at nightfall, unpursued, and sent another message to Pemberton, from whom he had heard nothing since his arrival, informing him that the capital had been evacuated. He was expecting another "12,000 or 13,000" troops from the East, he said, and "as soon as [these] reinforcements are all up, they must be united to the rest of the army. I am anxious to see a force assembled that may be able to inflict a heavy blow upon the enemy.... If prisoners tell the truth, the force at Jackson must be half of Grant's army. It would decide the campaign to beat it, which can only be done by concentrating, especially when the remainder of the eastern troops arrive." He himself could do little or nothing until these men reached him, reducing the odds to something within reason, but he did not think that Pemberton should neglect any opportunity Grant afforded meanwhile, particularly in regard to his lines of supply and communication. "Can he supply himself from the Mississippi?" Johnston asked. "Can you not cut him off from it, and above all, should he be compelled to fall back for want of supplies, beat him?"

This last was in accord with Pemberton's own decision, already arrived at before the second message was received. The first, delivered by one of the three couriers that morning at Bovina Station, nine miles east of Vicksburg, had taken him greatly by surprise. He had expected Johnston to come to his assistance in defense of the line along or just in front of the Big Black; yet here that general was, requesting him "if practicable" to come to *his* assistance by marching against the enemy's rear at Clinton, some twenty miles away. Pemberton replied that he would "move at once with the whole available force," explaining however that this included only 17,500 troops at best, since the remaining 9000 under his command were required to man the Warrenton-Vicksburg-Haines Bluff defenses, as well as the principal crossings of the Big Black, which otherwise would remain open in his rear, exposing the Gibraltar of the West to sudden capture by whatever roving segment of the rampant blue host happened to lunge in that direction. "In directing this move," he felt obliged to add, by way of protest, "I do not think you fully comprehend the position Vicksburg will be left in; but I comply at once with your request."

So he said. However, when he rode forward to Edwards, where his mobile force of three divisions under Loring, Stevenson, and Bowen was posted four miles east of the Big Black, he learned that a Union column, reportedly five divisions strong — it was in fact McClernand's corps, with Blair attached as guard for the wagon train — was at Raymond, in position for a northward advance on Bolton. If Pemberton marched on Clinton, as Johnston suggested, ignoring this threat to his right flank as he moved eastward along the railroad, he would not only be leaving Vicksburg and the remaining two divisions under Major Generals M. L. Smith and John H. Forney in grave danger of being gobbled up while his back was turned; he would also be exposing his eastbound force to destruction at the hands of the other half of the Northern army. Perplexed by this dilemma, and mindful of some advice received two days ago from Richmond that he "add conciliation to the discharge of duty" — "Patience in listening to suggestions...is sometimes rewarded," Davis had added — he decided the time had come for him to call a council of war, something he had never done before in all his thirty years of military service. Assembling the general officers of the three divisions at Edwards Station shortly after noon, he laid Johnston's message before them and outlined the tactical problems it posed. Basically, what he had to deal with was a contradiction of orders from above. As he understood the President's wishes, he was not to risk losing Vicksburg by getting too far from it, whereas Johnston was suggesting a junction of their forces near Jackson, forty miles away, in order to engage what he called a "detachment" of four — in fact, five — divisions, without reference to or apparent knowledge of the five-division column now at Raymond, both of which outnumbered the Confederates at Edwards. Pemberton, on the other hand, did not strictly agree with either of his two superiors, preferring to await attack in a prepared position near or behind the Big Black River, with a chance of following up a repulse with a counterattack designed to cut off and annihilate the foe. These three views could not be reconciled, but neither did he consider that any one of them could be ignored; so that, like the nation at large, this Northerner who sided with the South was torn and divided against himself. That was his particular nightmare in this nightmare interlude of his country's history. According to an officer on his staff, the Pennsylvanian's trouble now and in the future was that he made "the capital mistake of trying to harmonize instructions from his superiors diametrically opposed to each other, and at the same time to bring them into accord with his own judgment, which was averse to the plans of both."

Nor was the council of much assistance to him in finding a way around the impasse. Though a majority of the participants favored complying with Johnston's suggestion that the two forces be united, they were obliged to admit that it could not be accomplished by a direct march on Clinton, which was plainly an invitation to disaster. Meanwhile Pemberton's own views, as he told Johnston later, "were strongly expressed as unfavorable to any advance which would remove me from my base, which was and is Vicksburg." Apparently he limited himself to this negative contention. But finally Loring — known as "Old Blizzards" since his and Tilghman's spirited repulse of the Yankee gunboats above Greenwood — suggested an alternate movement, southeast nine miles to Dillon, which he believed would sever Grant's connection with Grand Gulf and thus force him either to withdraw, for lack of supplies, or else to turn and fight at a disadvantage in a position of Pemberton's choice. Stevenson agreed, along with others, and Pemberton, though he disliked the notion of moving even that much farther from Vicksburg, "did not, however, see fit to put my own judgment and opinions so far in opposition as to prevent a movement altogether." He approved the suggestion, apparently for lack of having anything better to offer, and adjourned the council after giving the generals instructions to be ready to march at dawn. At 5.40, on the heels of the adjournment, he got off a message informing Johnston of his intentions. "I shall move as early tomorrow morning as practicable with a column of 17,000 men," he wrote, explaining the exact location of Dillon so that Johnston would have no trouble finding it on a map which was enclosed. "The object is to cut the enemy's communications and to force him to attack me, as I do not consider my force sufficient to justify an attack on the enemy in position or to attempt to cut my way to Jackson."

Johnston received this at 8.30 next morning, May 15, by which time he had withdrawn another three miles up the Canton road, still farther from the intended point of concentration at Clinton. Though the message showed that Pemberton had anticipated the Virginian's still unreceived suggestion that he attempt to "cut [Grant] off from [the Mississippi]," Johnston no longer favored such a movement. "Our being compelled to leave Jackson makes your plan impracticable," he replied, and repeated — despite Pemberton's objection to being drawn still farther from his base — his preference for an eastward march by the mobile force from Vicksburg: "The only mode by which we can unite is by your moving directly to Clinton, informing me, that [I] may move to that point with about 6000 troops. I have no means of estimating the enemy's force at Jackson. The principal officers here differ very widely, and I fear he will fortify if time is left him. Let me hear from you immediately."

Evidently Johnston believed that Grant was going to hole up in the Mississippi capital and thus allow him time to effect a junction between the Vicksburg troops and his own, including the "12,000 or 13,000" reinforcements expected any day now from the East. If so, he was presently disabused. A reply from Pemberton, written early the following morning but not delivered until after dark, informed him that the advance on Dillon — badly delayed anyhow by the need for building a bridge across a swollen creek — had been abandoned, in accordance with his wishes, and the direction of march reversed. It was Pemberton's intention, as explained in the message, to move north of the railroad, swing wide through Brownsville to avoid the mass of Federals reported to be near Bolton, and converge on Clinton as instructed. "The order of countermarch has been issued," he wrote, and followed a description of his proposed route with the words: "I am thus particular, so that you may be able to make a junction with this army."

The Vicksburg commander at last had abandoned his objections to what Johnston had called "the only mode by which we can unite." He was, or soon would be, moving east toward his appointed destination. But there was an ominous postscript to the message, written in evident haste and perhaps alarm: "Heavy skirmishing is now going on to my front."

What that portended Johnston did not know; but Grant did. Before he retired to the hotel room his adversary had occupied the night before the fall of Jackson, he received from McPherson one of the three copies of Johnston's message urging Pemberton to "come up in [Sherman's] rear at once." This windfall was the result of a ruse worked some months ago by Hurlbut, who banished from Memphis, with considerable fanfare, a citizen found guilty of "uttering disloyal and threatening sentiments," though he was in secret, as Hurlbut knew, a thoroughly loyal Union man. The expulsion, along with his continued expression of secessionist views after his removal to the Mississippi capital, won him the sympathy and admiration of the people there: so much so,

indeed, that he was one of the three couriers entrusted with copies of
Johnston's urgent message. He delivered it, however, not to Pemberton
but to McPherson, who passed it promptly along to Grant. "Time is all
important," the Virginian had written. Grant agreed. By first light next
morning, May 15, McPherson was marching west from the capital, leaving Sherman to accomplish its destruction while he himself moved toward a junction with McClernand, who had been instructed simultaneously by Grant: "Turn all your forces toward Bolton station, and
make all dispatch in getting there. Move troops by the most direct road
from wherever they may be on the receipt of this order."

McPherson's three divisions had seventeen miles to go, and Mc-
Clernand's four — five, including Blair — were variously scattered,
from Raymond back to Fourteen Mile Creek. Each corps got one division to Bolton by late afternoon — Hovey and Logan, in that order —
while the others camped along the roads at sundown. Carr and Osterhaus were three miles south, with A. J. Smith between them and Raymond, where Blair was. Brigadier Generals John McArthur and
Marcellus Crocker, commanding McPherson's other two divisions, were
bivouacked beside the railroad leading back to Clinton. Riding out from
Jackson to that point before nightfall, Grant ordered McClernand to
move on Edwards in the morning, supported by McPherson, but
warned him "to watch for the enemy and not bring on an engagement
unless he felt very certain of success." The fog of war, gathering again
to obscure the Confederate purpose, had provoked this note of caution;
but it was dispersed once more at 5 o'clock next morning, when two
Union-sympathizing employes of the Vicksburg-Jackson Railroad were
brought to Grant at Clinton. They had passed through Pemberton's
army in the night, they said, and could report that it was moving east
of Edwards with a strength of about 25,000 men. Though this was in
fact some 7500 high, it was still some 10,000 fewer than Grant had on
hand. But he was taking no unavoidable chances. Deciding to ignore
Johnston, who by now was a day's march north of Jackson at Calhoun
Station, he ordered Sherman to "put one division with an ammunition
train on the road at once, with directions to its commander to march
with all possible speed until he comes upon our rear." The remaining
division was to hurry its demolition work and follow along as soon as
might be. The orders to McClernand and McPherson were unaltered; all
that was changed by this second dispersal of the war fog was the weight
of the blow about to be delivered. Now that he knew Pemberton's
strength and had him spotted, Grant intended to hit him with everything he had.

At about the time the railroad men were telling all they knew,
McClernand started forward in high spirits. "My corps, again, led the
advance," he was to say proudly in a letter giving his friend Lincoln an
account of the campaign. Such was indeed the case. Three roads led

west from the vicinity of Bolton to a junction east of Edwards, and McClernand used all three: Hovey on the one to the north, Osterhaus and Carr on the one in the middle, and Smith on the one to the south. Blair followed Smith, and McPherson's three divisions followed Hovey. Rebel cavalry was soon encountered, gray phantoms who fired and scampered out of range while the blue skirmishers flailed the woods with bullets. Then at 7.30, five miles short of Edwards, Smith came upon a screen of butternut pickets and dislodged them, exposing a four-gun battery, which he silenced. He wanted to plunge on, despite the signs that the high ground ahead was occupied in strength, but McClernand told him to hold what he had till Blair came up to keep his exposed left flank from being turned. Immediately on the heels of this, a rattle of gunfire from the north signified that Osterhaus and Hovey had also come upon johnnies to their front. McClernand inspected the rebel position as best he could from a distance and, finding it formidable, decided to hang on where he was until the situation could be developed. Having obeyed Grant's instructions "to watch for the enemy," he was also mindful of the injunction "not [to] bring on an engagement unless he felt very certain of success." At this point, with his various columns a mile or two apart and facing a wooded ridge a-swarm with graybacks, he was not feeling very certain about anything at all. What he mainly felt was lonely.

Countermarching in obedience to the message received early that morning from Johnston, Pemberton had been warned by his outriders of the Union host advancing westward along the three roads from Bolton and Raymond. When this danger was emphasized by the "heavy skirmishing" mentioned in the postscript to his reply that he was moving north and east toward a junction at Clinton, he knew he had a fight on his hands, wanted or not, and to avoid the risk of being caught in motion, strung out on the road to Brownsville, he hastily put his troops in position for receiving the attack he knew was coming. Whether his choice of ground was "by accident or design," as Grant ungenerously remarked, there could be no doubt that Pemberton chose well. Just south of the railroad and within a broad northward loop of rain-swollen Baker's Creek, a seventy-foot eminence known as Champion Hill — so called because it was on a plantation belonging to a family of that name — caused the due-west road from Bolton to veer south around its flank, joining the middle road in order to cross a timbered ridge that extended southward for three miles, past the lower of the three roads along which the enemy was advancing. Pemberton placed Stevenson's division on the hill itself, overlooking the direct approach from Bolton, and Bowen's and Loring's divisions along the ridge, blocking the other two approaches. Here, in an opportune position of great natural strength, he faced as best he could the consequences of his reluctant and belated compliance with his superior's repeated suggestion that he abandon the security of his prepared lines, along and just in front of the Big Black, for an attack on the Federal "detachment" supposed to be at Clinton. Now, however, as the thing turned out, it was Pemberton who was about to be attacked, a dozen miles short of his assigned objective. And here, precisely midway between Vicksburg and Jackson, both of which were twenty-two miles away, was fought what at least one prominent western-minded historian was to call "the most decisive battle of the Civil War."

Grant did not much like the look of things when he came riding out from Bolton and reached the front, where the road veered south beyond the Champion house, to find Hovey exchanging long-range shots with the enemy on the tall hill just ahead. It seemed to him, as he said later, that the rebels "commanded all the ground in range." However, unlike McClernand on the two roads to the south, he was not content to hold his own while waiting for the situation to develop more or less of its own accord. Logan's division having arrived, he sent it to the right, to prolong the line and feel for an opening in that direction. This was about 10 o'clock; he preferred to wait for Crocker to come up and lend the weight of McPherson's second division to the attack. But Hovey by now was hotly engaged, taking punishment from the batteries on the height and protesting that he must either go forward or fall back. Grant unleashed him. A former Indiana lawyer, of whom it was said that he had taken to the army "just as if he expected to spend his life in it," Hovey drove straight up the steep acclivity to his front, flinging back successive Confederate lines, until he reached and seized the eleven guns that had been pounding him from near the crest. His men were whooping with delight, proud but winded, when they were struck in turn by a powerful counterattack launched from a fringe of woods along the crest. "We ran, and ran manfully," one among them declared, explaining how he and his fellows had been swept back from the captured guns and down the slope they had climbed. Reinforced by Crocker's lead brigade, which had just arrived under Colonel George Boomer, they managed to hang on at the foot of the hill; but only by the hardest. One officer called the fighting there "unequal, terrible, and most sanguinary." For half an hour, he said, the troops "on each side took their turn in driving and being driven."

It was obvious that Hovey, who had left about one third of his division lying dead or wounded on the hillside, could not hold out much longer unassisted. Then one of the survivors looked over his shoulder and saw the army commander speaking to the colonel in charge of Crocker's second brigade, which was coming forward along the road behind them. "I was close enough to see his features," the man was to recall. "Earnest they were, but sign of inward movement there was none." This was the Grant of Belmont, Donelson, and Shiloh, reacting to adversity here as he had reacted there. If the face was "cool and cal-

culating," the soldier observed, it was also "careful and half-cynical."
He could not catch the spoken words across the distance, but they were
as characteristic as the calm,
enigmatic mask or the habitual
cigar stump that was wedged
between its teeth. "Hovey's division and Boomer's brigade are
good troops," Grant was saying.
"If the enemy has driven them
he is not in good plight himself.
If we can go in again here and
make a little showing, I think he
will give way."

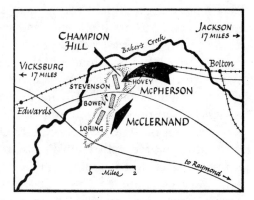

But it developed that a
good deal more than this one ad-
ditional brigade would have to join the melee at the base of Champion
Hill if Grant was to make what he called "a little showing." With Mc-
Pherson's third division still too far away to be of help in time, he had
to call on Logan, who had been sent to probe the rebel left. And this, as
Grant admitted later, was the salvation of Pemberton today. Logan had
ridden around the north end of the hill, where the terrain was more open
and gently rolling. He was sitting on horseback, surveying the scene,
when a private who had wandered on his own came up to him and remarked laconically, gesturing off to the right: "General, I've been over
the rise yonder, and it's my idea that if you'll put a regiment or two over
there you'll get on their flank and lick 'em easy." Logan took a look for
himself and saw that the man was right; Pemberton's left was "in the air"
and the way to his rear was practically unobstructed, including the single bridge over Baker's Creek by which he could fall back. Just then,
however, the order to return and support the hard-pressed Hovey was
received; Logan had to defer pressing the advantage the amateur tacti-
cian had discovered. Learning of this when it was too late to take full
advantage of the maneuver, Grant remarked with hindsight: "Had Mc-
Clernand come up with reasonable promptness, or had I known the
ground as I did afterwards, I cannot see how Pemberton could have escaped with any organized force."

The reference to McClernand was something more, this time,
than merely another point scored in the private war Grant waged on
paper against the former congressman from his home state. Pemberton,
observing the lack of enemy aggressiveness to the south, had reinforced
his staggered left by shifting troops northward from his center, which
was disposed along the ridge. Bowen brought them to Stevenson's assistance on the run, arriving just in time to launch the savage counterattack that drove Hovey's exultant soldiers back down the hill. Like
Grant, however, Pemberton was finding that he would need more than

this to keep up the pressure or even hold what he had won; so he sent for Loring. That general — referred to as "a scared turkey" by a member of Stonewall Jackson's staff during the Romney controversy, two Christmases ago, which had almost resulted in Jackson's retirement from the army and which had been settled only with Loring's transfer to the West — was already in a state of agitation because Bowen's departure had left him alone on the ridge, with four blue divisions in plain sight. When the summons came for him to follow Bowen he declined. It would be suicidal, he protested. All this time, the pressure against Stevenson was mounting, and when Logan added the weight of his division it became unsupportable. Old Blizzards moved at last, in response to repeated calls from Pemberton; but too late. He was scarcely in motion northward, about 4 o'clock, when the whole Confederate left flank gave way. Stevenson's men fell back in a panic, and though Pemberton managed to rally them with a personal appeal, the damage was done. The eleven retaken guns were lost again, this time for good, and Bowen's division — having, as one officer remarked, "sustained its reputation by making one of its grand old charges, in which it bored a hole through the Federal army" — now found itself unsupported and nearly surrounded; whereupon it "turned around and bored its way back again," following Stevenson's pell-mell flight down to Baker's Creek, where it formed a rear-guard line in an attempt to hold off the bluecoats until Loring too had made his escape across the stream. Darkness fell and there was still no sign of Loring. Bowen waited another two hours, still maintaining his position, then gave it up and crossed in good order, burning the bridge when his last man was safe on the west bank.

Casualties here, after three hours of skirmishing and four of actual battle, had been much the heaviest of the campaign. Grant had lost 2441 men, Pemberton 3624, including prisoners cut off in the retreat — plus 11 guns and, as it turned out, all of Loring's division. Finding his path along the ridge blocked by victorious Federals, he swung west, then back south, and after a brief skirmish in which Lloyd Tilghman was killed by a cannonball while covering the withdrawal, made a rapid getaway around McClernand's open flank. By the following evening he was in Crystal Springs, twenty-five miles south of Jackson, and two days later he was with Johnston at Canton, an equal distance north of the capital. Except for the loss of Tilghman, whose courage and ability had been proved at Fort Henry and Fort Pemberton, Loring's disappearance was more a source of mystery than regret for the army of which he had lately been a part, since he had contributed little to the battle except to assist in the show of strength that immobilized McClernand. Grant felt much the same way about McClernand, whose 15,000-man command — including Blair but not Hovey, who fought beyond McClernand's control and suffered almost half the army's casualties — had lost a total of 17 dead and 141 wounded in the course of what a brigade

commander with McPherson called "one of the most obstinate and murderous conflicts of the war." Despite the fact that not a single man had
been killed in three of the four divisions to the south, elation over the
victory scored by the three divisions to the north was tinged with sorrow at its cost. "I cannot think of this bloody hill without sadness and
pride," Hovey was to say, and an Illinois soldier, roaming the field
when the fighting was over, was struck by the thought that no moral
solution had been arrived at as a result of all the bloodshed. "There they
lay," he said of the dead and wounded all around him, "the blue and the
gray intermingled; the same rich, young American blood flowing out in
little rivulets of crimson; each thinking he was in the right."

Grant was more interested just now in military solutions, and he
believed he had reached one. "We were now assured of our position between Johnston and Pemberton," he subsequently declared, "without
a possibility of a junction of their forces." Others in his army believed
they saw an even more profitable outcome of the struggle on Champion
Hill. "Vicksburg must fall now," a participant wrote home that night;
"I think a week may find us in possession. It may take longer," he added
on second thought, "but the end will be the same."

While Pemberton's depleted army fell back through the darkness
to a position covering the Big Black crossing, eight miles to the west,
Grant let his soldiers sleep till dawn, by which time Wilson's engineers
had the bridge over Baker's Creek rebuilt, then took up the pursuit. Mc-
Clernand once more had the lead, though Blair was detached to rejoin
Sherman, who by now was close at hand with his other two divisions.
"We have made good progress today in the work of destruction," he
had written Grant the day before, as he prepared to leave the Mississippi
capital. "Jackson will no longer be a point of danger. The land is devas-
tated for thirty miles around." Next morning — Sunday, May 17 —
while Grant was crossing Baker's Creek to come to grips with Pemberton again, Sherman passed through Bolton and encountered other
signs of devastation. Seeing some soldiers drawing water from a well
in front of "a small hewn-log house" beside the road, he turned his horse
in at the gate to get a drink. The place had been rifled, its furnishings
wrecked and strewn about the yard, and though such acts of vandalism
were fairly common at this stage of the campaign — brought on, so to
speak, by an excess of skylark energy and delight that things were going
so well for the army of invasion — this one appeared to have been committed with an extra measure of glee and satisfaction. When Sherman had
one of the men hand him a book he saw lying on the ground beside the
well, he found out why. It was a copy of the United States Constitution,
with the name Jefferson Davis written on the title page. This was the
property the Confederate President's brother had secured for him the
year before, when Brierfield was occupied by Butler, and though in the

course of his December visit Davis had expressed the hope that he would be spared further depredations, it had not turned out that way. For him, as for his septuagenarian brother, the blue pursuit had been unrelenting. "Joe Davis's plantation was not far off," Sherman later recalled. "One of my staff officers went there, with a few soldiers, and took a pair of carriage horses, without my knowledge at the time. He found Joe Davis at home, an old man, attended by a young and affectionate niece; but they were overwhelmed with grief to see their country overrun and swarming with Federal troops."

Grant meanwhile was pushing west. About 7 o'clock he came upon Pemberton's new position — and found it even stronger, in some respects, than the one the rebels had occupied "by accident or design" the day before. This time, however, it was clearly by design. Not only had the position been prepared overnight for just such an emergency as the Confederates now faced; it was here, in fact, that Pemberton had wanted to do his fighting in the first place. The railroad bridge, which had been floored to provide for passage of his artillery and wagons, was at the apex of a horseshoe bend of the Big Black, whose high west bank afforded the guns emplaced along it an excellent field of fire out over the low-lying eastern bank and the mile-long line of rifle pits already dug across the open end of the horseshoe. Parapeted with bales of cotton brought from surrounding plantations, the line was a strong one, even without the concentric support of the guns emplaced to its rear, its front being protected by a shallow bayou that abutted north on the river and south on an impenetrable cypress brake. Whatever came at the men in these pits would have to come straight up the narrow railroad embankment, a suicidal prospect in the face of all that massed artillery, or across the rain-swollen bayou, beyond which open fields stretched for nearly half a mile, allowing the attackers little or no cover except for a single copse of woods about three hundred yards in front of the far left, where guns were also grouped in expectation. Still unaware that Loring had skedaddled, Pemberton held this intrenched bridgehead in hopes that Old Blizzards would show up in time for a share in the impending fight at the gates of Vicksburg, which was less than a dozen miles back down the road.

What showed up instead was the Yankees. One look at the position his opponent had selected — Pemberton, after all, was a trained engineer, with a reputation for skill in the old army — told Grant that he stood an excellent chance of suffering the bloodiest of repulses if he attempted a frontal attack. Fortunately, though, he had instructed Sherman to swing north of Edwards for a crossing at Bridgeport, five miles upstream; so that all Grant had to do here, for the present, was keep up a show of strength to hold Pemberton in place while Sherman got his three divisions over the river above and came down on his flank. But McClernand had other ideas. Troubled perhaps by his poor showing yesterday — though he would not hesitate presently to claim a lion's share of the credit for the Champion Hill success, on grounds that Hovey's division was from his corps — he moved vigorously today, sending Carr and Osterhaus, the Pea Ridge companions, respectively north and south of the railroad to confront the rebels crouched behind their cotton parapets. An assault was a desperate thing to venture against the dug-in Confederates and all those high-sited batteries in their rear, he knew, but he was quite as determined as Grant to "make a little showing," if not a big one. So was Brigadier General Michael Lawler, commanding Carr's second brigade, which had worked its way into the copse on the far right. A big man, over 250 pounds in weight and so large of girth that he had to wear his sword belt looped over one shoulder, Lawler was Irish, forty-nine years old, and lately an Illinois farmer. His favorite Tipperary maxim, "If you see a head, hit it," was much in his mind as he peered across the chocolate-colored bayou at the rebel intrenchments three hundred yards away. Many heads were visible there, inviting him to hit them, and at last he could bear it no longer. Stripped to his shirt sleeves because of the midday heat, he stood up, swinging his sword, and ordered his four regiments forward on the double. The bayou was shoulder-deep in places, but the Iowa and Wisconsin soldiers floundered straight across it in what a reporter called "the most perilous and ludicrous charge I witnessed during the war," and came mud-plastered up to the enemy line with a whoop, having suffered 199 casualties in the three minutes that had elapsed since they left the copse. The loss was small compared to the gain, however, for the rebels broke rearward, avoiding contact, only to find that the bridge had been set afire in their rear to keep the close-following bluecoats from surging across in their wake. Lawler's reward was 1200 prisoners — more men, he said, than he himself had brought into action — out of a final total of 1751 Confederates killed and captured, along with 18 guns, when the other brigades took fire from his example and rushed forward, breaking the gray line all down its length. Grant's losses were 276 killed and wounded, plus 3 missing, presumably left at the bottom of the bayou now in his rear.

Across the way, Pemberton had watched the disintegration of his skillfully drawn line and the quick subtraction of a brigade from his dwindling army. Neither was truly catastrophic; he still held the high west bank of the river, and the bridge the Federals might have used for a crossing was burning fiercely in the noonday sunlight; but he was depressed by the failure of his men to hold a position of such strength. If they would not stand fast here, where would they stand fast? Years later, a member of his staff was to say: "The affair of Big Black bridge was one which an ex-Confederate participant naturally dislikes to record." It was unpleasant to remember, and it had been even more unpleasant to observe. Presently, moreover, word came from upstream that Sherman had forced a crossing at Bridgeport, capturing the dozen pickets on duty at that point. There was nothing for it now but to continue the retreat or be outflanked. Pemberton gave the necessary orders and the westward march got under way, as it had done after yesterday's bloodier action, except that this time there would be no halt until Vicksburg itself was reached. Then what? He did not know how well his troops would fight with their backs to the wall, but this most recent action was not an encouraging example of their mettle. Some thirty hours ago he had had 17,500 effectives in his mobile force, and now he was down to a good deal less than half that many. In fact it was nearer a third, 5375 having been killed, wounded, or captured, while as many more had wandered off with Loring. As he rode westward, accompanied by his chief engineer, young Major Samuel Lockett, Pemberton's distress increased and his confidence touched bottom. "Just thirty years ago," he said at last, breaking a long and painful silence, "I began my military career by receiving my appointment to a cadetship at the U.S. Military Academy, and today — that same date — that career is ended in disaster and disgrace." Lockett tried to reassure the general by reminding him that two fresh divisions stood in the Vicksburg intrenchments, which had been designed to withstand repeated assaults by almost any number of men. Besides, he said, Joe Johnston would be reinforced at Canton in the event of a siege, and would come to the beleaguered city's relief with all the skill for which he was famous, North and South. "To all of which," the major recalled afterwards, "General Pemberton replied that my youth and hopes were the parents of my judgment; he himself did not believe our troops would stand the first shock of an attack."

A dispatch had already gone to Johnston that morning, announcing the results of yesterday's battle and warning that Haines Bluff would have to be abandoned if the Big Black position was outflanked or overrun. Accordingly, as the retreat got under way, orders were sent for the garrison on the Yazoo to fall back, all but two companies, who were to forward all stores possible and destroy the rest, "making a show of force until the approach of the enemy by land should compel them to retire." Provisions were much on Pemberton's mind, despite his dejection, and he issued instructions that, from Bovina on, "all cattle, sheep, and hogs belonging to private parties, and likely to fall into the hands of the enemy, should be driven within our lines." Similarly, corn was pulled from the fields along the way, "and all disposable wagons applied to this end." If it was to be a siege, food was likely to be as vital a factor as ammunition, and he did all he could in that respect. The march continued, accompanied by the lowing of cows, the bleating of sheep, and the squealing of pigs, steadily westward. For all the Confederates knew, Sherman might have moved fast around their flank and beaten them to the goal. Then up ahead, as Pemberton was to remember it years later, "the outlines of the hill city rose slowly through the heated dust — Vicksburg and security. Passing raddled fields turning colorless from the powdered earth that rose beneath their tramp, the gray soldiers slacked off the turnpikes along the high ground until they came inside the city's breastworks. As word carried down the crooked line of march that the race to Vicksburg had been won, the footsore remnants in the rear flooded down the pike."

Sunset made a red glory over the Louisiana bayous; "The sky faded to a cool green and it was dark." Pemberton and his aides worked through the night, seeing to the comfort of the troops who had fought today and yesterday, bivouacked now in rear of the intrenchments, and inspecting the front-line defenses manned by the two divisions which had remained in the city all this time. Dawn gave light by which to check the overlapping fields of fire commanded by the 102 guns, light and heavy, emplaced along the semicircular landward fortifications. Midmorning brought reports from scouts that the two companies left at Haines Bluff were on their way to Vicksburg, having complied with the order to hold out as long as possible. Heavy columns of Federals were close behind them, while other blue forces were hard on the march from Bovina. Before they arrived — as they presently did, to begin the investment — a messenger came riding in with a reply to yesterday's dispatch to Johnston, who had moved southwest from Canton to a position northeast of Brownsville. Pemberton's spirits had risen considerably since his confession of despair as he fell back from the Big Black the day before, but what his superior had to say was scarcely of a nature to raise them further. For one thing, the Virginian said nothing whatsoever about relief, either now or in the future. As he saw it, the choice had been narrowed to evacuation or surrender.

> May 17, 1863.
>
> LIEUTENANT GENERAL PEMBERTON:
>
> Your dispatch of today ... was received. If Haines Bluff is untenable, Vicksburg is of no value and cannot be held. If, therefore, you are invested at Vicksburg, you must ultimately surrender. Under such circumstances, instead of losing both troops and place, we must, if possible, save the troops. If it is not too late, evacuate Vicksburg and its dependencies, and march them to the northeast.
>
> Most respectfully, your obedient servant,
> J. E. JOHNSTON, General.

Even if Pemberton had wanted to follow this advice — which he did not, considering it in violation of orders from the Commander in Chief that the place be held at all costs — compliance was altogether beyond his means. Before he had time for more than brief speculation as to what effect these words might have on his chances of survival, Union guns were shelling his outer works. The siege had begun, and Grant was jockeying for positions from which to launch an all-out assault, intending to bring the three-week-old campaign, which had opened on his birthday, to the shortest possible end.

Yesterday's rout on the Big Black had seemed to indicate what the result of one hard smash at the rebel lines would be, and Grant's spirits had risen more or less in ratio to the droop of his opponent's. If roads could be found, he said as he watched the enemy abandon the high western bank, he intended to advance in three columns of one corps each, "and have Vicksburg or Haines Bluff tomorrow night." While Wilson and his engineers were collecting materials for replacing the burned railroad bridge, he rode up to Bridgeport and found Sherman hard at work laying India-rubber pontoons for a crossing in force. Soon after dark the first of his three divisions started over, their way lighted by pitch pine bonfires on both banks. Grant and his red-haired lieutenant sat on a log and watched the troops move westward over the Big Black, faces pale in the firelight and gun barrels catching glints from the flames as "the bridge swayed to and fro under the passing feet." Sherman was to remember it so. A water-colorist of some skill back in the days when there had been time for such diversions, he thought the present scene "made a fine war picture."

By daybreak all three divisions were across. Riding south to see whether McClernand and McPherson had done as well, Grant left instructions for Sherman to march northwest in order to interpose between Vicksburg and the forts on the Yazoo. By 10 o'clock this had been done. A detachment sent northward found Haines Bluff unoccupied, its big guns spiked, and made contact with the Union gunboats on the river below, signaling them to steam in close and tie up under the frowning bluff that had defied them for so long. Grant now had the supply base he wanted, north of the city. Presently he came riding up, to find his friend Sherman gazing down from the Walnut Hills at the Chickasaw Bayou region below, from which he had launched his bloody and fruitless assault against these heights five months ago. Up to now, the Ohioan had had his reservations about this eighth attempt to take or bypass Vicksburg, saying flatly, "I tremble for the result. I look upon the whole thing as one of the most hazardous and desperate moves of this or any other war." But now his doubts were gone, replaced by enthusiasm: as was shown when he turned to Grant, standing quietly by, and abruptly broke the silence.

"Until this moment I never thought your expedition a success," he said; "I never could see the end clearly until now. But this is a campaign. This is a success if we never take the town."

Grant shared his friend's enthusiasm, if not his verbal exuberance, with regard to a situation brought about by a combination of careful strategy, flawlessly improvised tactics, sudden marches, and hard blows delivered with such triphammer rapidity that the enemy had never been given a chance to recover the balance he lost when the blue army, feinting coincidentally at Haines Bluff, swarmed ashore at Bruinsburg, forty-five air-line miles away. At no time in the past three weeks, moreover, had the outlook been so bright as it was now. All three corps had crossed the Big Black, the final natural barrier between them and their goal, and were converging swiftly upon the hilltop citadel by three main roads so appropriate to their purpose that they might have been surveyed with this in mind. Sherman advanced from the northeast on the Benton road, McPherson from due east, along the railroad and the Jackson turnpike, and McClernand from the southeast on the Baldwin's Ferry road. By nightfall, after a few brief skirmishes along the ill-organized line of rebel outposts — invariably abandoned at the first suggestion of real pressure — the lead elements of all three columns were in lateral contact with each other and in jump-off positions for tomorrow's assault. Next morning, May 19, while they completed their dispositions, the men were in high spirits. They were in fact, like Sherman, "a little giddy with pride" at the realization of all they had accomplished up to now. In the twenty days since they crossed the Mississippi, they had marched 180 miles to fight and win five battles — Port Gibson, Raymond, Jackson, Champion Hill, Big Black River — occupy a Deep South capital, inflict over 7000 casualties at a cost of less than 4500 of their own, and seize no less than fifty pieces of

field artillery, not to mention two dozen larger pieces they found spiked in fortifications they outflanked. In all this time, they had not lost a gun or a stand of colors, and they had never failed to take an assigned objective, usually much more quickly than their commanders expected them to do. And now, just ahead, lay the last and largest of their objectives: Vicksburg itself, the ultimate prize for which the capture of all those others had served as prelude. Their belief that they would carry the place by storm, here and now, was matched by Grant, who issued his final orders before noon. "Corps commanders will push forward carefully, and gain as close position as possible to the enemy's works, until 2 p.m.; at [which] hour they will fire three volleys of artillery from all the pieces in position. This will be the signal for a general charge of all the army corps along the whole line." A closing sentence, intended to forestall the lapse of discipline that would attend a too-informal victory celebration, expressed the measure of his confidence that the assault would be successful, bringing the campaign to a triumphant close today: "When the works are carried, guards will be placed by all division commanders to prevent their men from straggling from their companies."

At the appointed hour, the guns boomed and the blue clots of troops rushed forward, shoulder to shoulder, cheering as they vied for the honor of being first to scale the ridge: whereupon, as if in response to the same signal, a long low cloud of smoke, torn along its bottom edge by the pinkish yellow stabs of muzzle flashes, boiled up with a great clatter from the rebel works ahead. The racket was so tremendous that no man could hear his own shouts or the sudden yelps of the wounded alongside him. What was immediately apparent, however, amid a confusion of sound so uproarious that it was as if the whole mad scene were being played in pantomime, was that the assault had failed almost as soon as it got started. Sherman, watching from a point of vantage near the north end of the line, put it simplest in a letter he wrote home that night: "The heads of the columns have been swept away as chaff thrown from the hand on a windy day." Others, closer up, had a more gritty sense of what had happened. Emerging into the open, an Illinois captain saw "the very sticks and chips, scattered over the ground, jumping under the hot shower of rebel bullets." Startled, he and his company plunged forward, tumbled into a cane-choked ravine at the base of the enemy ridge, and hugged the earth for cover and concealment. All up and down the line it was much the same for those who had not scattered rearward at the first burst of fire; once within point-blank musket range, there was little the attackers could do but try to stay out of sight until darkness gave them a chance to pull back without inviting a bullet between the shoulder blades. As they lay prone the fire continued, cutting the stalks of cane, one by one, so that "they lopped gently upon us," as if to assist in keeping them hidden. Through the remaining hours of daylight they stayed there, with bullets twittering just above the napes of their necks. Then they returned through the gathering dusk to the jump-off positions they had left five hours ago. Reaching safety after a hard run, the captain and other survivors of his company "stopped and took one long breath, bigger than a pound of wool."

Pemberton was perhaps as surprised as the bluecoats were at their abrupt repulse. In reporting to the President — the message would have to be smuggled out, of course, before it could be put on the wire for Richmond — that his army was "occupying the trenches around Vicksburg," he added proudly: "Our men have considerably recovered their morale." Meanwhile he strengthened his defenses and improved the disposition of his 20,000 effectives. M. L. Smith's division had the left, Forney's the center, and Stevenson's the right, while Bowen's was held in immediate reserve, under orders to be prepared to rush at a moment's notice to whatever point needed bolstering. There was a crippling shortage of intrenching tools, only about five hundred being on hand. "They were entirely inadequate," an engineer officer later declared, but "the men soon improvised wooden shovels [and used] their bayonets as picks." They had indeed "considerably recovered," now that they had stopped running, and they were hungry for revenge for the humiliations they had been handed, particularly day before yesterday on the Big Black River. If the Yankees would keep coming at them the way they had come this afternoon, the Confederates hoped they would keep it up forever.

In point of fact, that was pretty much what Grant had in mind. He had suffered 942 casualties and inflicted less than 200, thus coming close to reversing the Big Black ratio, but he still thought the ridge could be carried by assault. Conferring next morning with his corps commanders he found them agreed that this first effort had failed, in Sherman's words, "by reason of the natural strength of the position, and because we were forced by the nature of the ground to limit our attacks to the strongest part of the enemy line, viz., where the three principal roads entered the city." Nothing could be done about the first of these two drawbacks, but the second could be corrected by careful reconnaissance. Better artillery preparations would also be of help, it was decided, in softening up the rebel works; moreover, the navy could add the weight of its metal from the opposite side of the ridge, Porter having returned from a two-week expedition up the Red River to Alexandria, where he had met Banks coming north from Opelousas on May 6. Grant told McClernand, Sherman, and McPherson to spend today and tomorrow preparing "for a renewed assault on the 22d, simultaneously, at 10 a.m." Riding his line while the work was being pushed, he found the men undaunted by their repulse the day before, though they were prompt to let him know they were weary of the meat-and-vegetables diet on which they had been subsisting for the past three weeks. Turkey and sweet potatoes were fine as a special treat, it seemed, but such rich food had begun to pall as a regular thing. A private looked up from shoveling, recognized Grant riding by, and said in a pointed but conversational tone: "Hardtack." Others took up the call, on down the line, raising their voices with every repetition of the word, until finally they were shouting with all their might. "Hardtack! Hardtack!" they yelled as the army commander went past. "Hardtack! Hardtack!" Finally he reined in his horse and informed all those within earshot that the engineers were building a road from the Yazoo steamboat landing, "over which to supply them with everything they needed." At this, as he said later, "the cry was instantly changed to cheers." That night there was hardtack for everyone, along with beans, and coffee to wash it down. The soldiers woke next morning strengthened for the work that was now at hand.

For the first time in history, a major assault was launched by commanders whose eyes were fixed on the hands of watches synchronized the night before. This was necessary in the present case because the usual signal guns would not have been heard above the din of the preliminary bombardment, which included the naval weapons on both flanks, upstream and down, and six mortar boats already engaged for the past two days in what one defender contemptuously called "the grand but nearly harmless sport of pitching big shells into Vicksburg." All night the 13-inch mortars kept heaving their 200-pound projectiles into the checkerboard pattern of the city's streets and houses, terrifying citizens huddled under their beds and dining-room tables. ("Vertical fire is never very destructive of life," the same witness remarked. "Yet the howling and bursting shells had a very demoralizing effect on those not accustomed to them.") Then at dawn the 200 guns on the landward side chimed in, raising geysers of dirt on the ridge where the Confederates were intrenched and waiting. At 9.30, in compliance with Grant's request, Porter closed the range with four gunboats from below and took the lower water batteries under fire. He was supposed to keep this up until 10.30, half an hour past the scheduled time for the infantry assault to open, but since he could see no indication that the army had been successful in its storming attempt, he kept up the fire for an extra hour before dropping back downriver and out of range. One ironclad, the *Tuscumbia*, was severely battered and forced to retire before the others. Otherwise, though he reported that this was altogether the hottest fire his boats had yet endured, Porter suffered little damage in the bows-on fight, aside from a few men wounded. He could not see, however, that he had accomplished much in the way of punishing the defenders. Nor was there any evidence that the army had done any better.

As a matter of fact, the army had done a good deal worse, though not for lack of trying. At the appointed hour the men of all three corps rushed forward, the advance waves equipped with twenty-foot scaling ladders to be used against steep-walled strongpoints, of which there were many along the ridge ahead. "The rebel line, concealed by the parapet, showed no sign of unusual activity," Sherman observed from his point of vantage to the north, "but as our troops came in fair view, the enemy rose behind their parapet and poured a furious fire upon our lines.... For about two hours we had a severe and bloody battle, but at every point we were repulsed." It was much the same with McPherson and McClernand, to the south, who also lost heavily as a result of these whites-of-their-eyes tactics employed by the Confederates. At several points, left and right and center, individual groups managed to effect shallow penetrations, despite what an Illinois colonel called "the most murderous fire I ever saw," but were quickly expelled or captured by superior forces the enemy promptly brought to bear from his mobile reserve. Those bluecoats who crouched in the ravines and ditches at the base of the ridge, taking shelter there as they had done three days ago, were dislodged by the explosion in their midst of 12-inch shells which the defenders rolled downhill after lighting the fuzes. On McClernand's front a heavier lodgment was effected at one point, and the general, taking fire at the sight of his troops flaunting their banners on the rebel works, sent word to Grant that he had "part possession of two forts, and the stars and stripes are floating over them." If the other two corps "would make a diversion in my favor," he thought he could enlarge his gains and perhaps score an absolute break-through. At any rate, he earnestly declared, "a vigorous push ought to be made all along the line."

Grant was with Sherman when the message reached him. "I don't believe a word of it," he said. Sherman protested that the note was offi-cial and must be credited. Though he had just called off his own attack, admitting failure, he offered to renew it at once in the light of this appeal from McClernand. Grant thought the matter over, then told the redhead he "might try it again" at 3 o'clock, if no contrary orders reached him before that time. Riding south, he detached one of Mc-Pherson's divisions to support McClernand and authorized a resump-tion of the attack on the center as well. Promptly at 3, Sherman launched his promised second assault, but found it "a repetition of the first, equally unsuccessful and bloody." McPherson had the same un-pleasant experience. McClernand, still afire with hope, threw the bor-rowed division into the fray — though not in time to maintain, much less widen or deepen, the penetration of which he had been so proud. A whooping counterattack by Colonel T. N. Waul's Texas Legion killed or captured all but a handful of Federals at that point. By sundown the fir-ing had died to a sputter, and at nightfall the survivors crept back across the corpse-pocked fields to the safety of the lines they had left with such high hopes that morning. Some measure of their determination and valor was shown by a comparison of their losses today with those of three days ago. The previous assault had ended with two stands of col-ors left on the forward slope of the enemy ridge; this time there were five. Moreover, the casualties exceeded this five-two ratio. Less than a thousand men had fallen the time before, including 165 killed or miss-ing, whereas this time the figures went above three thousand — 3199, to be exact — with 649 in the killed-or-missing category. In other words, Grant had lost in the past three days almost as many soldiers as he had lost in the past three weeks of nearly continuous battle and maneuver which had brought him within sight of the ramparts of Vicksburg only to be repulsed.

He was furious. "This last attack only served to increase our cas-ualties without giving any benefit whatever," he wrote some twenty years later, still chagrined. Quick as ever to shift the blame for any set-back or evidence of shortcoming — at Belmont it had been overex-cited "higher officers"; at Donelson it had been McClernand; at Shiloh

it had been Prentiss and Lew Wallace, although the former most likely
had saved him from defeat; at Iuka it had been Rosecrans and the wind
— he notified Halleck, two days after the second Vicksburg repulse:
"The whole loss for the day will probably reach 1500 killed and
wounded. General McClernand's dispatches misled me as to the real
state of facts, and caused much of this loss. He is entirely unfit for the
position of corps commander, both on the march and on the battlefield.
Looking after his corps gives me more labor and infinitely more uneasiness than all the remainder of my department." And yet, on the day of
battle itself, he included that general's misleading claims in his own dispatch informing Halleck of the outcome. "Vicksburg is now completely
invested," he declared. "I have possession of Haines Bluff and the Yazoo;
consequently have supplies. Today an attempt was made to carry the
city by assault, but was not entirely successful. We hold possession,
however, of two of the enemy's forts, and have skirmishers close under
all of them. Our loss was not severe." As he wrote, his optimism grew;
for that was the reverse of the coin. He would no more admit discouragement than he would entertain self-blame. "The nature of the ground
about Vicksburg is such that it can only be taken by a siege," he judged,
but added: "It is entirely safe to us in time, I would say one week if the
enemy do not send a large army upon my rear."

    He did not regret having made the assaults; he only regretted
that they had failed. Besides, he subsequently explained, his high-spirited
troops had approached the gates of Vicksburg with a three-week cluster
of victories to their credit; they would never have settled down willingly to the tedium of siege operations unless they had first been given
the chance to prove that the place could not be taken by storm. Now
that this had been demonstrated, though at the rather excessive price of
4141 casualties, they took to spadework with a will, constructing their
own complex system of intrenchments roughly parallel to those of the
rebels, which in a few places were not much more than fifty yards away.
As they delved in the sandy yellow clay of the hillsides or drew their
beads on such heads as appeared above the enemy parapets, they were
encouraged by news of tangential victories, particularly on the part of
the navy, which was on a rampage now that the outlying Confederate
defenses had been abandoned. An expedition made up of the *DeKalb*
and three tinclads, all under Lieutenant Commander John Walker, had
been sent up the Yazoo on May 20, the day after the first assault, and returned on the 23d, the day after the second, to report that the rebels
had set their Yazoo City navy yard afire at the approach of the Union
vessels, the flames consuming three warships under construction on the
stocks, for an estimated loss of $3,000,000. This meant that there would
be no successor to the *Arkansas*, which was welcome news indeed. But
Porter was unsatisfied; he sent the expedition back upriver the next
morning. This time Walker steamed to within a dozen miles of Fort

Pemberton, destroying steamboats and sawmills as he went, then came back downstream to push 180 miles up the winding Sunflower River, where he caught and burned still more fugitive rebel steamboats. Returning this second time, he could report that these streams were no longer arteries of supply for the Confederates below the confluence of the Tallahatchie and the Yalobusha, nearly one hundred air-line miles from the beleaguered Vicksburg bluff.

Pemberton took the news of this without undue distress. After all, the Yazoo and the Sunflower were no longer of much interest to him; the Father of Waters was now his sole concern, and only about a dozen miles of that. "I have decided to hold Vicksburg as long as possible," he had replied to Johnston's last-minute dispatch urging evacuation, "with the firm hope that the Government may yet be able to assist me in keeping this obstruction to the enemy's free navigation of the Mississippi River. I still conceive it to be the most important point in the Confederacy." His outlook improved with the repulse of the first Federal assault, and on the eve of the second he was asking: "Am I to expect reinforcements? From what direction, and how soon? ... The men credit and are encouraged by a report that you are near with a large force. They are fighting in good spirits, and the reorganization is complete." After the second repulse, however, the defenders were faced with an unpleasant problem. For three days — six, in the case of those who had fallen in the first assault — Grant's dead and injured lay in the fields and ditches at the base of the Confederate ridge, exposed to the fierce heat of the early Mississippi summer. The stench of the dead, whose bodies were swollen grotesquely, and the cries of the wounded, who suffered the added torment of thirst, were intolerable to the men who had shot them down; yet Grant would not ask for a truce for burial or treatment of these unfortunates, evidently thinking that such a request would be an admission of weakness on his part. Finally Pemberton could bear it no longer. On the morning of May 25 he sent a message through the lines to the Union commander: "Two days having elapsed since your dead and wounded have been lying in our front, and as yet no disposition on your part of a desire to remove them being exhibited, in the name of humanity I have the honor to propose a cessation of hostilities for two hours and a half, that you may be enabled to remove your dead and dying men." To Pemberton's relief, Grant at last "acceded" to this proposal. At 6 p.m. all firing was suspended while the Federals came forward to bury the dead where they lay and bring comfort to such few men as had survived the three-day torture. This done, they returned through the darkness to their lines and the firing was resumed with as much fury as before.

In nothing was Grant more "unpronounceable" than in this. He would berate, and in at least one case attack with his fists, any man he saw abusing a dumb animal; he had, it was said to his credit, no stomach for suffering; he disliked above all to ride over a field where there had been recent heavy fighting; he would not eat a piece of meat until it had been cooked to a char, past any sign of blood or even pinkness. Yet this he could do to his own men, this abomination perhaps beyond all others of the war, without expressed regret or apparent concern. However, this too was the reverse of a coin, the other side of which was his singleness of purpose, his quality of intense preoccupation with what he called "the business," meaning combat. He took his losses as they came — they had, in fact, about been made up already with the arrival that week of a division of reinforcements from Memphis, and would be more than made up with the arrival, early the following week, of a second such division, while four more were being alerted even now for the trip downriver from Tennessee, Missouri, and Kentucky to bring his mid-June total to 71,000 effectives — for the sake of getting on with the job to which he had set his hand. Long ago in Mexico, during a lull in the war, he had written home to the girl he was to marry: "If we have to fight, I would like to do it all at once and then make friends." He felt that way about it still, and now that he was calling the turn, he wanted no interludes or delays; he wanted it finished, and he believed the finish was in sight. "The enemy are now undoubtedly in our grasp," he told Halleck the day before the burial truce. "The fall of Vicksburg and the capture of most of the garrison can only be a question of time."

This was not to say there would be no more setbacks and frustrations. There would indeed, war being the chancy thing it was, and Grant knew it: which perhaps was why he had dropped his prediction, made two days before, that the fall of the city would be accomplished within "I would say one week." And in fact there was one such mishap three days later, two days after the burial truce, this time involving the navy. In the course of drawing his lines for the siege, Sherman had begun to suspect, from the amount of artillery fire he drew, that the Confederates were shifting guns from their upper water batteries to cover the landward approaches, particularly on their far left. Requested by Grant to test the facts of the case, Porter on May 27 sent the *Cincinnati* to draw the fire of the guns "if still there," covering her movements with four other ironclads at long range. She started downriver at 7 o'clock in the morning, commanded by Lieutenant G. M. Bache, and by 10 the matter had been settled beyond doubt. Not only were the guns still there, but they sank the *Cincinnati*. Rounding to in order to open fire, she took a pair of solids in her shell room and a third in her magazine. As she tried to make an upstream escape, a heavy shot drove through her pilot house and her starboard tiller was carried away, along with all three flagstaffs. Hulled repeatedly by plunging fire, she began filling rapidly. Bache, with five of his guns disabled in short order, tried to get beyond range and tie the vessel up to the east bank before she sank, but could not make it. She went down in three fathoms of water, still within range of the enemy guns, and what remained of her crew had to swim for their lives. The total loss, aside from the *Cincinnati* herself, was 5 killed, 14 wounded, and 15 missing, presumed drowned.

Convinced that Bache and his crew had done their best under disadvantageous circumstances, Porter accepted the loss of the ironclad — the third since his arrival in early December — as one of the accidents of war, and did not relax on that account his pressure against the rebels beleaguered on their bluff. He already had the approval of Grant for his conduct of naval affairs. Replying to a message in which the admiral informed him that Banks, although he had wound up his West Louisiana campaign at last, would "not [be] coming here with his men. He is going to occupy the attention of Port Hudson, and has landed at Bayou Sara, using your transports for the purpose," Grant told Porter: "I am satisfied that you are doing all that can be done in aid of the reduction of Vicksburg. There is no doubt of the fall of the place ultimately, but how long it will be is a matter of doubt. I intend to lose no more men, but to force the enemy from one position to another without exposing my troops."

✗ 4 ✗

Banks had done a good deal more by now than merely "occupy the attention of Port Hudson." Crossing the Mississippi on the day after Grant's second repulse at Vicksburg, he completed his investment of the Louisiana stronghold on May 26, and next morning — simultaneous with the sinking of the *Cincinnati*, 240 winding miles upriver — launched his own all-out assault, designed to bring to a sudden and victorious end a campaign even more circuitous than Grant's. That general had covered some 180 miles by land and water before returning to his approximate starting point and placing his objective under siege, whereas Banks had marched or ridden about three times that far, as the thing turned out, to accomplish the same result. However, not only was the distance greater; the numerical odds had been tougher, at least at the start. Back in mid-March, when Farragut ran two ships past the fuming hundred-foot bluff, Banks had maneuvered on the landward side, only to discover that the defenders had more men inside the works than he had on the outside. This gave him pause, as well it might, and while he pondered the problem he learned that Grant, whom he had expected to join him in reducing Port Hudson as a prelude to their combined movement against Vicksburg, was stymied north of the latter place, involved in a series of canal and bayou experiments which seemed likely to delay him for some time. Thinking it over, Banks decided to accomplish his assignment on his own. If he could not take Port Hudson, he would do as Grant was trying to do upriver. He would go around it.

It was not only that he was disinclined to wait and share the glory, politically ambitious though he was. He also believed he could not, and with cause. Nearly half of the 35,000 troops in his department were nine-month volunteers whose enlistments would be expiring between May and August; they would have to be used before summer or not at all. However, there was about as much need for caution as there was for haste, since more than half of this total, long- and short-term men alike, were required to garrison Baton Rouge, New Orleans, and various other points along the Mississippi and the Gulf. As a result of these necessary smaller detachments, his five divisions were reduced to about 5000 men each. Three of the five were with him near Port Hudson, under Major General C. C. Augur and Brigadier Generals William Emory and Cuvier Grover, while the fourth was at New Orleans under Brigadier General Thomas W. Sherman. Leaving Augur to hold Baton Rouge, Banks set out downriver with the other two on March 25 to join Godfrey Weitzel, commanding his fifth division at Brashear City, near Grand Lake and the junction of the Atchafalaya River and Bayou Teche. Back in January, Weitzel had ascended the former stream for a few miles, intending to establish an alternate route, well removed from the guns of Port Hudson, from the mouth of Red River to the Gulf. In this he had failed, not so much because of interference from Richard Taylor's scratch command of swamp-bound rebels, which he had thrown into precipitate retreat, but mainly because he had found the Atchafalaya choked with brush at that season of the year. Banks believed that this time he would succeed, and he hoped to abolish Taylor as a continuing threat. He intended in fact to capture him, bag and baggage, having worked out his plans with that in mind.

Taylor had about 4000 troops between the Teche and the Atchafalaya, his flanks protected right and left by two captured Union warships, the gunboat *Diana* and the armed ram *Queen of the West*, the former having been ambushed and seized that week near Pattersonville, when she imprudently ventured up the bayou, and the latter having been brought down from the Red River the week before to prevent her destruction or recapture by Farragut after his run past Port Hudson. Banks had four Gulf Squadron gunboats with which he planned to neutralize these two turncoat vessels, and he intended to bag Taylor's entire land force by sending one division from his 15,000-man command across Grand Lake to land in the rear of the rebels while he engaged them in front with his other two divisions. Hemmed in and outnumbered nearly four to one, Taylor would have to choose between surrender and annihilation. On April 11, in accordance with his design, Banks moved Emory and Weitzel from Brashear across the Atchafalaya to Berwick, and while they were advancing up the left bank of the Teche next day, skirmishing as they went, Grover put his troops aboard transports, escorted by the quartet of gunboats, and set out across the lake for a landing on the western shore within a mile of Irish Bend, an eastward loop of the Teche, control of which would place him squarely athwart the only Confederate line of retreat. Despite some irritating delays, the maneuver seemed to be going as planned; the skirmishing continued in front and Grover got his division ashore six miles in the enemy rear; Banks anticipated a Cannae. But Taylor got wind of what was up and reacted fast. Leaving a handful of men to put up a show of resistance to the two blue divisions in his front, he swung rearward with the rest to attack Grover and if possible drive him into the lake. On the 13th heavy fighting ensued. The shoestring force managed to delude and delay Emory and Weitzel while the main body fell on Grover. Though the latter was not driven into the lake, he was held in check while Taylor withdrew up the Teche in the darkness, foiling the plans so carefully laid for his destruction. In three days of intermittent action the Federals had lost 577 killed and wounded, the Confederates somewhat less, although there was considerable disagreement between the two commanders, then and later, as to the number of prisoners taken on each side, Taylor afterwards protesting that Banks had claimed the capture of more men than had actually opposed him.

Whatever the truth of his claims in this regard, and despite his failure to bring off the Cannae he intended, there could be no doubt that Banks, after a season of rather spectacular defeats in Virginia at the hands of Stonewall Jackson, had won his first clear-cut victory in the field. And next day, when he received word that the *Diana* and the *Queen* had been destroyed — the former burned by the rebels, who could not take her with them up the narrow Teche, and the latter sunk by the four Union gunboats, who blew her almost literally out of the water as soon as she entered Grand Lake and came within their range — his elation knew no bounds. Moreover, two of the gunboats steamed forthwith up the Atchafalaya and found it open to navigation all the way to the mouth of the Red, fifty miles above Port Hudson. This meant that Banks had the bypass he had been seeking, though of course it would be of small practical use until Vicksburg had likewise been bypassed or reduced. Since there was no news that Grant had succeeded in any of his experimental projects in that direction, the Massachusetts general decided to explore some vistas he saw opening before him as a result of Taylor's defeat and withdrawal. Within two weeks New Orleans would have been returned to Federal control a solid year, and yet this principal seaport of the South had even less commerce with the outside world today than she had enjoyed in the days of the blockade runners, mainly because the rebel land forces had her cut off from those regions that normally supplied her with goods for shipment. One of the richest of these lay before him now: the Teche. Return of the Teche country to Union control, along with its vast supplies of cotton, salt, lumber, and foodstuffs, would restore New Orleans to her rightful place among the world's great ports and would demonstrate effectively, as one observer pointed out, "that the conquests of the national armies instead of destroying trade were calculated to instill new life into it." There was one drawback. Such a movement up the long riverlike bayou stretching north almost to Alexandria, even though unopposed, might throw him off his previously announced schedule, which called for a meeting with Grant at Baton Rouge on May 10 for a combined attack, first on Port Hudson and then on Vicksburg. But Banks decided the probable gains were worth the risk. Besides, May 10 was nearly a month away, and he hoped to have completed his conquest of the region before then. If not, then Grant could wait, just as he had kept Banks waiting all this time.

Eager for more victories now that he had caught the flavor, the former Bay State governor put his three divisions on the march up the right bank of the Teche without delay. Two days later — April 16: Porter's bluejackets were steeling themselves for their run past the Vicksburg batteries that night, and Grierson's troopers would ride out of La Grange the following morning — he entered New Iberia and pushed on next day to the Vermilion River, which branched southward from the Teche near Vermilionville. Finding Taylor's rear guard drawn up on the opposite bank to contest a crossing, the bluecoats forced it with a brief skirmish, rebuilt the wrecked bridge, and on April 20 marched into Opelousas, evacuated two days earlier by the Louisiana government

which had moved there a year ago when Farragut steamed upriver from New Orleans and trained his guns on Baton Rouge. Taylor did not challenge the occupation of this alternate capital, but continued to fall back toward Alexandria, having received from Kirby Smith at Shreveport, his Transmississippi headquarters, a message expressing "gratification at the conduct of the troops under your command" and congratulating Taylor for the skill he had shown "in extricating them from a position of great peril." Banks called a halt in order to rest his men for a few days and consolidate his gains, which were considerable. Conquest of the Teche had brought within his grasp large quantities of lumber, 5000 bales of cotton, many hogsheads of sugar, an inexhaustible supply of salt, and an estimated 20,000 head of cattle, mules, and horses. He later calculated the value of these spoils to have been perhaps as high as $5,000,000 and pointed out that even this liberal figure should be doubled, since the goods it represented had not only come into Federal hands but had also been kept from the Confederates beyond the Mississippi, for whom they had been in a large part intended. Nor was that all. There were human spoils as well. Back in New Orleans the year before, Ben Butler had begun to enlist freedmen and fugitive slaves in what he called his Corps d'Afrique; now Banks continued this recruitment in the Teche. Two such regiments were organized at Opelousas, with about 500 men in each. Styled the 1st and 3d Louisiana Native Guards, the former was composed of "free Negroes of means and intelligence," with colored line officers and a white lieutenant colonel in command, while the latter was made up largely of ex-slaves whose officers were all white. There was considerable speculation, in the army of which they were now a part, as to how they would behave in combat — when and if they were exposed to it, which many of their fellow soldiers thought inadvisable — but Banks was willing to abide the issue until it had been settled incontrovertibly under fire.

Taylor by now had reached the Red at Gordon's Landing, where the *Queen of the West* had been blasted and captured back in February, thirty miles below Alexandria. Renamed Fort De Russy, the triple-casemated battery had held the low bluff against all comers, and on May 4 its staunchness was proved again when it was attacked by the two gunboats that had come up the Atchafalaya from Grand Lake after sinking the *Queen*. Leading the way, however, was the *Albatross*, which had got past Port Hudson with Farragut in mid-March. She closed the range to five hundred yards and kept up a forty-minute bombardment, supported by the other two ships at longer range, before dropping back with eleven holes punched in her hull and most of her spars and rigging shot away. Fifty miles downriver next morning, having given up hope of reducing the fort on their own, the three ships met Porter — who, after completing the ferrying of Grant's two lead divisions across the Mississippi, had taken possession of Grand Gulf three days ago — coming up the Red with three of his ironclads, a steam ram, and a tug. This seemed quite enough for the task of reduction, but when he reached Fort De Russy late that afternoon, prepared to throw all he had at the place, he found it abandoned, its casemates yawning empty. Threatened from the rear by Banks, who had ended his Opelousas rest halt and resumed his northward march beyond the headwaters of the Teche, the garrison had retreated to avoid capture. Porter continued on to Alexandria next day, May 6, to find that Taylor had also fallen back from there. A couple of hours later, Banks marched in at the head of his three-division column. He was in fine spirits, still wearing his three-week-old aura of victory, and Porter was impressed — particularly by the outward contrast between this new general and the one he had been working alongside for the past four months around Vicksburg. "A handsome, soldierly-looking man," the admiral called the former Speaker of the House, "though rather theatrical in his style of dress." The impression was one of nattiness and sartorial elegance; Banks in fact was something of a military dude. "He wore yellow gauntlets high upon his wrists, looking as clean as if they had just come from the glove-maker; his hat was picturesque, his long boots and spurs were faultless, and his air was that of one used to command. In short, I never saw a more faultless-looking soldier."

Banks was about as proud as he was dapper, and with cause. His Negro recruits more than made up — in numbers at any rate, though it was true their combat value was untested — for the casualties he had suffered in the course of his profitable campaign up the Teche, and his present position at Alexandria gave him access to the entire Red River Valley, a region quite as rich as the one he had just traversed, and far more extensive. With elements already on the march for Natchitoches, fifty air-line miles upriver, and Taylor still fading back from contact, he saw more vistas opening out before him. He also realized, however, that they were unattainable just yet. "The decisive battle of the West must soon be fought near Vicksburg," Kirby Smith was telling a subordinate even now. "The fate of the Trans-Mississippi Department depends on it, and Banks, by operating here, is thrown out of the campaign on the Mississippi." The Massachusetts general agreed, although unwillingly, that he must first turn back east to resume his collaboration with Grant for the reduction of Vicksburg and Port Hudson. Then perhaps, with the Mississippi unshackled throughout its length, he would return up the Red to explore those new vistas stretching all the way to Texas. Grant meanwhile, having won the Battle of Port Gibson, crossed Bayou Pierre, and put his three divisions into jump-off positions for the advance on Jackson, was calling urgently for Banks to join him at once in front of Vicksburg; "But I must say, without qualifications," the latter replied on May 12, "that the means at my disposal do not leave me a shadow of a chance to accomplish it." Though he was "dying with a kind of vanishing hope to see [our] two armies acting together against the strong places of the enemy," he had "neither water nor land transportation to make the movement by the river or by land. The utmost I can accomplish," he told Grant, "is to cross for the purpose of operating with you against Port Hudson."

Once more having reached a decision he wasted no time. Two days later, ending a week's occupation in the course of which he sent no less than 2000 spoils-laden wagons groaning south, he began his withdrawal from Alexandria. The march prescribed was via Simmesport for a crossing at Bayou Sara, a dozen miles above Port Hudson, but Banks himself did not accompany the three divisions on their overland trek; he went instead by boat, first down the Red, then down the Atchafalaya to Brashear City, where he caught a train for New Orleans. With him rode the fifty-two-year-old Emory, whose health had failed in the field and who had been succeeded by Brigadier General Halbert Paine, fifteen years his junior and the only non-West Pointer in Banks's army with so much rank — aside from Banks himself, of course — though he could claim the distinction of having shared a law office with Lincoln's friend Carl Schurz before the war. In New Orleans, Banks gave Emory the task of defending the city with a stripped-down garrison left behind by Thomas Sherman, who was instructed to put most of his men aboard transports bound for Baton Rouge to join Augur for an advance on Port Hudson. As Banks planned it, the two divisions marching north from Baton Rouge would converge on the objective at the same time as the three marching south from Bayou Sara. For all the omnivorous reading he had done since his days as a bobbin boy in his home-state spinning mills, he may or may not have known that in thus intending to unite two widely divided columns on the field of battle he was attempting what Napoleon had called the most difficult maneuver in the book. If so, nonprofessional though he was, he showed no qualms beyond those normally involved in getting some 20,000 troops from one place — or in this case two places — to another. What was more, he brought it off. Advancing simultaneously north and south, the two bodies converged on schedule, May 25. Next day they completed their investment, and the following morning they launched an all-out assault on the 7000 rebels penned up inside Port Hudson.

Like Pemberton, who was nine years his senior, Franklin Gardner was a northern-born professional who married South — his father-in-law was ex-Governor Alexander Mouton, who presided over the legislative body that voted Louisiana out of the Union — then went with his wife's people when the national crisis forced a choice. New York born and Iowa raised, the son of a regular army colonel who had been Adjutant General during the War of 1812, he had graduated from West Point in the class of '43, four places above Ulysses Grant and one below Christopher Augur, whose division was part of the blue cordon now drawn around the bastion Gardner was defending. A brigadier at Shiloh and with Bragg in Kentucky, he had been promoted to major general in December, shortly before his fortieth birthday, and sent to command the stronghold Breckinridge had established at Port Hudson after being repulsed at Baton Rouge in August. By early April his strength had risen beyond 15,000 men, but it had since been whittled down to less than half that as a result of levies by the department commander, reacting to upriver pressure from Grant while Banks was off in the Teche. On May 4, in response to what turned out to be Pemberton's final call, Gardner set out for Jackson with all but a single brigade, only to receive on May 9 at Osyka, just north of the Mississippi line, a dispatch instructing him to return at once to Port Hudson and hold it "to the last," this being Pemberton's interpretation of the President's warning that "both Vicksburg and Port Hudson [are] necessary to a connection with Trans-Mississippi." Gardner did as he was told, and got back there barely ahead of Banks. His strength report of May 19 — the date of Grant's first assault on the Vicksburg intrenchments, 120 air-line miles upriver — showed an "aggregate present" of 5715 in his three brigades, plus about one thousand artillerists in the permanent garrison. That was also the date on a message Joe Johnston addressed to Gardner from north of the Mississippi capital, which had fallen on the day after his arrival the week before: "Evacuate Port Hudson forthwith, and move with your troops toward Jackson to join other troops which I am uniting. Bring all the fieldpieces that you have, with their ammunition and the means of transportation. Heavy guns and their ammunition had better be destroyed, as well as the other property you may be unable to remove." By the time the courier got there, however, he found a ring of Federal steel drawn tightly around the blufftop fortress. He could only report back to Johnston that Port Hudson, like Vicksburg 240 roundabout miles upriver, was besieged.

The Union navy had reappeared ahead of the Union army. On May 4, meeting Porter at the mouth of the Red, Farragut gave over his blockade duties from that point north and steamed back down the Mississippi to Port Hudson. For three days, May 8-10, he bombarded the bluff from above and below, doing all he could to soften it up for Banks, who was still at Alexandria. Upstream were the *Hartford* and the *Albatross*, patched up since her recent misfortune at Fort De Russy, while the downstream batteries were engaged by the screw sloops *Monongahela* and *Richmond*, the gunboat *Genesee*, and the orphaned ironclad *Essex*, which had been downriver ever since her run past Vicksburg the summer before. Coming overland down the western bank, Farragut conferred with Banks on his arrival from New Orleans, May 22. The rebels had given him shell for shell, he said, and shown no sign of weakening under fire, but he assured the general that the navy would continue to do its share until the place had been reduced. Banks thanked him and proceeded to invest the bluff on its landward side, north and east and south, depending on the fleet to see that the beleaguered garrison made no westward escape across the river and received no reinforcements or supplies from that direction. Assisted meanwhile by Grierson's well-rested troopers, who had ridden up from Baton Rouge with the column from the south, he drew his lines closer about the rebel fortifications. On May 26, with ninety guns in position opposing Gardner's thirty-one, he issued orders for a full-scale assault designed to take the place by storm next morning. Weitzel, Grover, and Paine were north of the Clinton railroad, which entered the works about midway, Augur and Sherman to the south. The artillery preparation would begin at daybreak, he explained, augmented by high-angle fire from the navy, and the five division commanders would "dispose their troops so as to annoy the enemy as much as possible during the cannonade by advancing skirmishers to kill the enemy's cannoneers and to cover the advance of the assaulting column." This was somewhat hasty and Banks knew it, but he had reasons for not wanting to delay the attempt for the sake of more extensive preparations. First, like Grant eight days ago at Vicksburg, he believed the rebels were demoralized and unlikely to stand up under a determined blow if it were delivered before they had time to recover their balance. Second, and more important still, he was anxious to wind up the campaign and return to New Orleans; Emory was already complaining that he was in danger of being swamped by an attack from Mobile, where the Confederates had some 5000 men — twice as many as he himself had for the defense of the South's first city — or from Brashear, to which Taylor was free to return now that Banks had left the Teche. This was indeed a two-pronged danger; in fact, despite the cited lack of transportation, it had been the real basis for the Massachusetts general's refusal to join Grant in front of Vicksburg. However, for all his haste, the special orders he distributed on the 26th for the guidance of his subordinates in next day's operation were meticulous and full. Attempting to forestall confusion by assigning particular duties, he included no less than eleven numbered paragraphs in the order, all of them fairly long except the last, which contained a scant half-dozen words: "Port Hudson must be taken tomorrow."

At first it appeared that the order would be carried out, final paragraph and all; but around midmorning, when the thunder of the preliminary bombardment subsided and Weitzel went forward according to plan, driving the rebel skirmishers handsomely before him, he found that this unmasked their artillery, which opened point-blank on his troops with murderous effect. The bluecoats promptly hit the dirt and hugged it while their own batteries came up just behind them and unlimbered, returning the deluge of grape and canister at a range of two hundred and fifty yards. Crouched under all that hurtling iron and lead from front and rear, the men were badly confused and lost what little sense of direction they had retained during their advance through a maze of obstructions, both natural and man-made. "The whole fight took place in a dense forest of magnolias, mostly amid a thick undergrowth, and among ravines choked with felled and fallen timber, so that it was difficult not only to move but even to see," a participant was to recall, adding that what he had been involved in was not so much a battle or a charge as it was "a gigantic bush-whack." Paine and Grover, moving out in support of Weitzel, ran into the same maelstrom of resistance, with the same result. So did Augur, somewhat later, when his turn came to strike the Confederate center just south of the railroad. But all was strangely quiet all this while on the far left. At noon Banks rode over to look into the cause of this inaction, and found to his amazement that Tom Sherman had "failed utterly and criminally to bring his men into the field." The fifty-two-year-old Rhode Islander was at lunch, surrounded by "staff officers all with their horses unsaddled." As usual, despite the multiparagraphed directive, someone — in this case about 3500 someones, from the division commander down to the youngest drummer — had not got the word. Nettled by the dressing-down Banks gave him along with peremptory orders to "carry the works at all hazards," Sherman got his two brigades aligned at last and took them forward shortly after 2 o'clock. He rode at their head, old army style; but not for long. A conspicuous target, he soon tumbled off his horse, and the surgeons had to remove what was left of the leg he had been shot in.

Command of the division passed to Brigadier General William Dwight, who had resigned as a West Point cadet ten years ago to go into manufacturing in his native Massachusetts at the age of twenty-one, but had returned to military life on the outbreak of the war. However, for all the youth and vigor which had enabled him to survive three wounds and a period of captivity after being left for dead on the field of Williamsburg a year ago next month, Dwight could do no more than Sherman had done already. His pinned-down men knew only too well that to attempt to rise, with all those guns and rifles trained on them from behind the red clay parapets ahead, would mean at best a trip back to the surgery where the doctors by now were sawing off their former commander's leg. To attempt a farther advance, either here or on the east, was clearly hopeless; yet Banks was unwilling to call it a day until he had made at least one more effort. Weitzel's division, which had opened the action that morning around to the north, had gained more ground than any of the other four, causing one observer to remark that if he had "continued to press his attack a few minutes longer he would probably have broken through the Confederate defense and taken their whole line in reverse." Now that the defenders were alert and had the attackers zeroed in, that extra pressure would be a good deal harder to exert, but Banks at any rate thought it worth a try. Orders were sent to the far right for a resumption of the assault, and were passed along to the colonel commanding the two regiments lately recruited in the Teche, the 1st and 3d Louisiana Native Guards. Held in reserve till now, they were about to receive their baptism of fire: a baptism which, as it turned out, amounted to total immersion. A Union staff officer who watched them form for the attack described what happened. "They had hardly done so," he said, "when the extreme left of the Confederate line opened on them, in an exposed position, with artillery and musketry and forced them to abandon the attempt with great loss." However, that was only part of the story. Of the 1080 men in ranks, 271 were hit, or one out of every four. They had accomplished little except to prove, with a series of disjointed rushes and repulses over broken ground and through a tangle of obstructions, that the rebel position could not be carried in this fashion. And yet they had settled one other matter effectively: the question of whether Negroes would stand up under fire and take their losses as well as white men. "It gives me pleasure to report that they answered every expectation," Banks wrote Halleck. "In many respects their conduct was heroic. No troops could be more determined or more daring."

Yet this was but a fraction of the day-long butcher's bill, which was especially high by contrast; 1995 Federals had fallen, and only 235 Confederates. In reaction, Banks told Farragut next day that Port Hudson was "the strongest position there is in the United States." Though he frankly admitted, "No man on either side can show himself without being shot," he was no less determined than he had been before the assault was launched. "We shall hold on today," he said, "and make careful examinations with reference to future operations." That morning — unlike Grant after his second repulse, five days earlier at Vicksburg — he had requested "a suspension of hostilities until 2 o'clock this afternoon, in order that the dead and wounded may be brought off the field." Gardner consented, not only to this but also to a five-hour extension of the truce when it was found that the grisly harvest required a longer time for gleaning. Meanwhile Banks was writing to Grant, bringing him up to date on events and outlining the problem as he saw it now. "The garrison of the enemy is 5000 or 6000 men," he wrote. "The works are what would ordinarily be styled 'impregnable.' They are surrounded by ravines, woods, valleys, and bayous of the most intricate and labyrinthic character, that make the works themselves almost inaccessible. It requires time even to understand the geography of the position. [The rebels] fight with determination, and our men, after a march of some 500 or 600 miles, have done all that could be expected or required of any similar force." A postscript added an urgent request: "If it be possible, I beg you to send me at least one brigade of 4000 or 5000 men. This will be of vital importance to us. We may have to abandon these operations without it." No such reinforcements would be coming either now or later from Grant, who had his hands quite full upriver; but Banks had no real intention of abandoning the siege. "We mean to harass the enemy night and day, and to give him no rest," he declared in a message to Farragut that same day, and he followed this up with another next morning: "Everything looks well for us. The rebels attempted a sortie upon our right last evening upon the cessation of the armistice, but were smartly and quickly repulsed." Two days later, May 31, when the admiral informed him that three Confederate deserters had stated that "unless reinforcements arrive they cannot hold out three days longer," Banks replied: "Thanks for your note and the cheering report of the deserters. We are closing in upon the enemy, and will have him in a day or two."

So he said. But presently a dispatch arrived from Halleck, dated June 3, which threatened to cut the ground from under the besieging army's feet. Like Grant, and perhaps for the same reasons, Banks had kept the general-in-chief in the dark as to his intentions until it was too late for interference, and Old Brains expressed incredulity at the second-hand reports of what had happened. "The newspapers state that your forces are moving on Port Hudson instead of co-operating with General Grant, leaving the latter to fight both Johnston and Pemberton. As this is so contrary to all your instructions, and so opposed to military principles, I can hardly believe it true." That it was true, however, was shown by a bundle of letters he received that same day from Banks, announcing his intention to move southeast from Alexandria. "These fully account for your movement on Port Hudson, which before seemed so unaccountable," Halleck wrote next morning. But he still did not approve, and he said so in a message advising Banks to get his army back on what the general-in-chief considered the right track. "I hope that you have ere this given up your attempt on Port Hudson and sent all your spare forces to Grant. . . . If I have been over-urgent in this matter, it has arisen from my extreme anxiety lest the enemy should concentrate all his strength on one of your armies before you could unite, whereas if you act together you certainly will be able to defeat him." Banks bristled at being thus lectured to. It irked him, moreover, that the authorities did not seem to take into account the fact that he was the senior general on the river. If any reproach for nonco-operation was called for, it seemed to him that it should have been aimed at Grant. "Since I have been in the army," he replied in mid-June, when the second message reached him, "I have done all in my power to comply with my orders. It is so in the position I now occupy. I came here not only for the purpose of co-operating with General Grant, but by his own suggestion and appointment." In time Halleck came round. "The reasons given by you for moving against Port Hudson are satisfactory," he conceded in late June. "It was presumed that you had good and sufficient reasons for the course pursued, although at this distance it seemed contrary to principles and likely to prove unfortunate." If this was not altogether gracious, Banks did not mind too much. He considered that he had already disposed of Halleck's bookish June 4 argument with a logical rebuttal, written by coincidence on the same day: "If I defend New Orleans and its adjacent territory, the enemy will go against Grant. If I go with a force sufficient to aid him, [bypassing Port Hudson,] my rear will be seriously threatened. My force is not large enough to do both. Under these circumstances, my only course seems to be to carry this post as soon as possible, and then to join General Grant. . . . I have now my heavy artillery in position, and am confident of success in the course of a week."

Here again he underestimated the rebel garrison's powers of resistance; Port Hudson was not going to fall within a month, much less a week. Gardner had drawn his semicircular lines with care, anchoring both extremities to the lip of the hundred-foot bluff overlooking the river, and had posted his troops for maximum effect, whatever the odds.

North of the railroad there were two main forts, one square, the other pentagonal, with a small redoubt between them, all three surrounded and tied together by a network of trenches, occupied by two brigades under Colonels I. G. W. Steedman and W. R. Miles. Brigadier General William Beall, a Kentucky-born West Pointer, had his brigade, which was as big as the other two combined, disposed to the south along a double line of bastions, the largest of which surmounted the crest of a ridge and was called the Citadel because it dominated all the ground in that direction. These various major works, together with their redans, parapets, ditches, and gun emplacements, were mutually supporting, so that an advance on one invited fire from those adjoining it. Banks had discovered this first, to his regret, while launching the May 27 assault. Since then, he had limited his activities mainly to long-range bombardments and the digging of lines of contravallation, designed to prevent a breakout and to protect his troops from sorties. After two weeks of this, in the course of which a considerable number of his men were dropped by snipers, he grew impatient and ordered a probing night action which he characterized as an endeavor "to get within attacking distance of the works in order to avoid the terrible losses incurred in moving over the ground in front." Informed that the sudden lunge was to be preceded by a twenty-hour bombardment, Farragut, whose ships by now were getting low on ammunition, protested mildly that he did not think the constant shelling did much good. "After people have been harassed to a certain extent, they become indifferent to danger, I think," he said. But he added: "We will do all in our power to aid you." That power was not enough, as it turned out. At 3 o'clock in the morning, June 11, the blue infantry crept quietly forward under cover of darkness — and found the defenders very much on the alert. Though some men got through the abatis and up to the hostile lines, once the alarm was sounded they were quickly driven back, while those who chose not to run the gauntlet to regain their jump-off positions were taken captive. Except for lengthening the Federal casualty lists and increasing Confederate vigilance in the future, the action had no effect on anything whatsoever, so far as Banks and his shovel-weary, sniper-harassed men could discern: least of all on the siege, which continued as before.

His spirits were revived, however, by a message received two days later from Dwight, who reported that he had interrogated a quartet of Confederate deserters and had learned from them that the garrison, reduced by sickness to 3200 infantry and 800 artillerymen, was down to "about five days' beef." There were "plenty of peas, plenty of corn," but "no more meal." Starvation was staring the rebels in the face. In fact, a Mississippi regiment was said to be in such low spirits that it "drove about 50 head of cattle out of the works about a week ago," intending thereby to hasten the inevitable end. In short, Dwight wrote, "The troops generally wish to surrender, and despair of relief." Next

morning, June 13, Banks decided to test the validity of this report. His
plan, as he explained it to Farragut, whose co-operation was requested,
was to "open a vigorous bombardment at exactly a quarter past eleven
this morning, and continue it for exactly one hour. . . . The bombardment will be immediately followed by a summons to surrender. If that
is not listened to, I shall probably attack tomorrow." The guns roared
on schedule, then stopped at the appointed time, and Banks sent forward
under a white flag his demand for instant capitulation. "Respect for the
usages of war, and a desire to avoid unnecessary sacrifice of life, impose
on me the necessity of formally demanding the surrender of the garrison of Port Hudson." That was the opening sentence of the page-long
"summons," and it was balanced by another very like it at the close: "I
desire to avoid unnecessary slaughter, and I therefore demand the immediate surrender of the garrison, subject to such conditions only as are
imposed by the usages of civilized warfare. I have the honor to be, sir,
very respectfully, your most obedient servant, *N. P. Banks*, Major General, Commanding." The Confederate reply was prompt and a good deal
briefer. "Your note of this date has just been handed to me, and in reply
I have to state that my duty requires me to defend this position, and
therefore I decline to surrender. I have the honor to be, sir, very respectfully, your most obedient servant, *Frank. Gardner*, Major General,
Commanding C. S. Forces."

Banks had said that if his demands were not "listened to" he
probably would launch a second full-scale assault next morning, all
along the line. At daybreak, following a vigorous one-hour cannonade
which apparently served little purpose except to warn the Confederates
he was coming, he did just that. When the smoke cleared it was found
that he had suffered the worst drubbing of the war, so far at least as a
comparison of the casualties was concerned. On the far left, Dwight
was misdirected by his guides, with the result that he was blasted into retreat before he even knew he was exposed. In the center, Augur and
Paine attacked with vigor and were bloodily repulsed when they struck
what turned out to be the strongest point of the enemy line, the priest-
cap near the Jackson road; Paine himself fell, badly wounded, and was
carried off the field. On the right, Grover and Weitzel were stopped in
midcareer when it was demonstrated that no man could clear the fire-
swept ridge along their front and live. "In examining the position afterward," a Union officer declared, "I found [one] grass-covered knoll
shaved bald, every blade cut down to the roots as by a hoe." By noon it
was apparent that the assault had failed in every sector. All that had
been accomplished was a reduction of the range for the deadly snipers
across the way, and the price exacted was far beyond the worth of a few
yards of shell-torn earth. There was hollow mockery, too, in the respective losses, North and South. The Federals had 1792 killed,

wounded, and missing subtracted from their ranks, while the Confederates had lost an over-all total of 47.

Four weeks of siege, highlighted by two full-scale assaults and one abortive night attack, had cost Banks more than 4000 casualties along his seven concave miles of front. His men, suspecting that they had inflicted scarcely more than one tenth as many casualties on the enemy, were so discouraged that the best he could say of them, in a note to Farragut that evening, was that they were "in tolerable good spirits." Presently, though, even this was more than he could claim. "The heat, especially in the trenches, became almost insupportable, the stenches quite so," a staff major later recalled. "The brooks dried up, the creek lost itself in the pestilential swamp, the springs gave out, and the river fell, exposing to the tropical sun a wide margin of festering ooze. The illness and mortality were enormous." Counting noses four days after the second decisive repulse, Banks reported that he was down to 14,000 effectives, including the nine-month volunteers whose enlistments were expiring. This too was a source of discontent, which reached the stage of outright mutiny in at least one Bay State regiment, and the reaction was corrosive. Men whose time was nearly up did not "feel like desperate service," Banks told Halleck, while those who had signed on for the duration did not "like to lead where the rest will not follow." Old Brains had a prescription for that, however. "When a column of attack is formed of doubtful troops," he answered, "the proper mode of curing their defection is to place artillery in their rear, loaded with grape and canister, in the hands of reliable men, with orders to fire at the first moment of disaffection. A knowledge of such orders will probably prevent any wavering, and, if not, one such punishment will prevent any repetition of it in your army."

This was perhaps reassuring, though in an unpleasant sort of way, since it showed the general-in-chief to be considerably more savage where blue rebels were concerned than he had ever been when his opponents wore butternut or gray. However, Banks had even larger problems than mutiny on his hands by then. Emory was crying havoc in New Orleans, which he protested was in grave danger of being retaken by the rebels any day now. "The railroad track at Terre Bonne is torn up. Communication with Brashear cut off," he notified Banks on June 20, adding: "I have but 400 men in the city, and I consider the city and the public property very unsafe. The secessionists here profess to have certain information that their forces are to make an attempt on the city." Five days later — by which date Port Hudson had been under siege a month — he declared that the rebels bearing down on him were "known and ascertained to be at least 9000, and may be more.... The city is quiet on the surface, but the undercurrent is in a ferment." "Something must be done for this city, and that quickly," he insisted four days later.

His anxiety continued to mount in ratio to his estimate of the number of graybacks moving against him, until finally he said flatly: "It is a choice between Port Hudson and New Orleans. . . . My information is as nearly positive as human testimony can make it that the enemy are 13,000 strong, and they are fortifying the whole country as they march from Brashear to this place, and are steadily advancing. I respectfully suggest that, unless Port Hudson is already taken, you can only save this city by sending me reinforcements immediately and at any cost." What was more, he said, the danger was not only from outside New Orleans. "There are at least 10,000 fighting men in this city (citizens) and I do not doubt, from what I see, that these men will, at the first appearance of the enemy within view of the city, be against us to a man. I have the honor to be &c. *W. H. Emory*, Brigadier General, Commanding."

But Banks had no intention of loosening his grip on the upriver fortress, which he believed — despite the nonfulfillment of all his earlier predictions — could not hold out much longer. Emory would have to take his chances. If it came to the worst and New Orleans fell, Farragut would steam down and retake it with the fleet that would be freed for action on the day Port Hudson ran up the white flag. Meanwhile the signs were good. On June 29, no less than thirty deserters stole out of the rebel intrenchments and into the Union lines, and though by now Banks knew better than to judge the temper of the garrison by that of such defectors, he was pleased to learn from those who arrived in the afternoon that their dinner had been meatless. In the future, they had been told, the only meat they would get would be that of mules. Judging by the adverse reaction of his own troops to a far more palatable diet, Banks did not think the johnnies would be likely to sustain their morale for long on that. However, one of the butternut scarecrows brought with him a copy of yesterday's *Port Hudson Herald*, which featured a general order issued the day before by Gardner, "assuring the garrison that General Johnston will soon relieve Vicksburg, and then send reinforcements here." The southern commander declared as well, Banks pointed out in passing the news along to Halleck, "his purpose to defend the place to the last extremity."

Confident none the less "of a speedy and favorable result" — so at least he assured the general-in-chief — Banks kept his long-range batteries at work around the clock, determined to give the Confederates no rest. The fire at night was necessarily blind, but that by day was skillfully directed by an observer perched on a lofty yardarm of the *Richmond*, tied up across the river from the bluff. He communicated by wigwag with a battery ashore, which also had a signalman, and the two kept up a running colloquy, not only to improve the marksmanship, but also to relieve the tedium of the siege.

"Your fifth gun has hit the breastwork of the big rifle four times. Its fire is splendid. Can dismount it soon."

"You say our fifth gun?"

"Yes, from the left." But the next salvo brought a shift of attention. "Your sixth gun just made a glorious shot. . . . Let the sixth gun fire 10 feet more to the left."

"How now about the fifth and sixth guns?"

"The sixth gun is the bully boy."

"Can you give it any directions to make it more bully?"

"Last shot was little to the right."

Just then, however, the cannoneers were forced to call a halt. "Fearfully hot here," the battery signalman explained. "Several men sunstruck. Bullets whiz like fun. Have ceased firing for a while, the guns are so hot. Will profit by your directions afterward." Presently they resumed firing, though with much less satisfactory results, according to the observer high in the rigging of the *Richmond*.

"Howitzer shell goes 6 feet over the guns every shot; last was too low, little too high again." Exasperated, he added: "Can't they, or won't they, depress that gun?"

"Won't, I guess. . . . Was that shot any better, and that?"

"Both and forever too high."

"We will vamose now. Come again tomorrow."

"Nine a.m. will do, will it not?"

"Yes; cease signaling."

✗ 5 ✗

The forces threatening New Orleans were no such host as Emory envisioned, but they were under the determined and resourceful Richard Taylor, who earlier, though much against his will, had struck at Grant's supposedly vital supply line opposite Vicksburg. "To break this would render a most important service," Pemberton had told Kirby Smith in early May, in one of his several urgent appeals for help across the way. Returning to Alexandria as soon as Banks pulled out, Taylor prepared to move at once back down the Teche, threaten New Orleans, and thereby "raise such a storm as to bring General Banks from Port Hudson, the garrison of which could then unite with General Joseph Johnston in the rear of General Grant." On May 20, however, before he could translate his plan into action, he received instructions from Smith directing him to march in the opposite direction. "Grant's army is now supplied from Milliken's Bend by Richmond, down the Roundaway and Bayou Vidal to New Carthage," the department commander explained, and if Taylor could interrupt the flow of supplies along this route, the

Federal drive on Vicksburg would be "checked, if not frustrated." He sympathized with Taylor's desire "to recover what you have lost in Lower Louisiana and to push on toward New Orleans," Smith added, "but the stake contended for near Vicksburg is the Valley of the Mississippi and the Trans-Mississippi Department; the defeat of General Grant is the *terminus ad quem* of all operations in the West this summer; to its attainment all minor advantages should be sacrificed." Taylor agreed as to the object, but not as to the method, much preferring his own. However, as he said later, "remonstrances were of no avail." He turned his back on New Orleans, at least for the present, and set out up the Tensas, where he was joined by a division of about 4000 men under Major General John G. Walker, a Missourian lately returned from Virginia, where he had commanded a division in Lee's army and was one of the many who could fairly be said to have saved the day at Sharpsburg.

Debarking June 5 on the east bank of the Tensas, some twenty-five miles west of Grant's former Young's Point headquarters, Taylor sent his unarmed transports back downstream to avoid losing them in his absence. Next day he surprised and captured a small party of Federals at Richmond, midway between the Tensas and the Mississippi, only to learn that Grant had established a new base up the Yazoo, well beyond the reach of any west-bank forces, and was no longer dependent on the one at Milliken's Bend. "Our movement resulted, and could result, in nothing," Taylor later admitted. All the same, he carried out his instructions by attacking, at dawn of the 7th, both Young's Point and Milliken's Bend, sending a full brigade against each. Like Banks, Grant had been recruiting Negroes, but since he intended to use them as laborers rather than as soldiers, he had given them little if any military training apart from the rudiments of drill. Surprised in their camps by the dawn attacks, they panicked and fled eastward over the levee to the protection of Porter's upstream flotilla. The gunboats promptly took up the quarrel, blasting away at the exultant rebels, and Taylor, observing that the panic was now on the side of the pursuers, ordered Walker to retire on Monroe, terminus of the railroad west of Vicksburg, while he himself went back down the Tensas and up the Red to Alexandria. Once there, he returned his attention to Banks and New Orleans, glad to have done with what he called "these absurd movements" against a supposedly vital supply line which in fact had been abandoned for nearly a month before he struck it.

Though the losses had been unequal — 652 Federals had fallen or were missing, as compared to 185 Confederates — Grant was not disposed to be critical of the outcome. Agreeing with Porter that the rebels had got "nothing but hard knocks," he was more laconic than reproachful in his mid-June report of the affair: "In this battle most of the troops engaged were Africans, who had little experience in the use of firearms. Their conduct is said, however, to have been most gallant, and I doubt not but with good officers they will make good troops." Anyhow, this was beyond the circle of his immediate attention, which was fixed on the close-up siege of Vicksburg itself. Six divisions had been added by now to his original ten, giving him a total of 71,000 effectives disposed along two lines, back to back, one snuggled up to the semicircular defenses and the other facing rearward in case Joe Johnston got up enough strength and nerve to risk an attack from the east. Three divisions arrived in late May and early June from Memphis, the first of which, commanded by Brigadier General Jacob Lauman, was used to extend the investment southward, while the other two, under Brigadier Generals Nathan Kimball and William Sooy Smith, made up a fourth corps under Washburn, now a major general, and were sent to join Osterhaus, who had been left behind to guard the Big Black crossings while the two assaults were being launched. Frank Herron, who at twenty-five had won his two stars at Prairie Grove to become the Union's youngest major general, arrived from Missouri with his division on June 11 and extended the line still farther southward to the river, completing Grant's nine-division bear hug on Pemberton's beleaguered garrison. The final two were sent by Burnside from his Department of the Ohio. Commanded by Brigadier Generals Thomas Welsh and Robert Potter, they constituted a fifth corps under Major General John G. Parke and raised the strength of the rearward-facing force to seven divisions. "Our situation is for the first time in the entire western campaign what it should be," Grant had written Banks in the course of the build-up. And now that it was complete, so was his confidence as to the outcome of the siege, which he expressed not only in official correspondence but also in informal talks with his officers and men. "Gen. Grant came along the line last night," an Illinois private wrote home. "He had on his old clothes and was alone. He sat on the ground and talked with the boys with less reserve than many a little puppy of a lieutenant. He told us that he had got as good a thing as he wanted here."

One item he would have liked more of was trained engineers. Only two such officers were serving in that capacity now in his whole army. However, as one of them afterwards declared, this problem was solved by the "native good sense and ingenuity" of the troops, Middle Western farm boys for the most part, who showed as much aptitude for such complicated work as they had shown for throwing bridges over creeks and bayous during the march that brought them here. According to the same officer, "Whether a battery was to be constructed by men who had never built one before, [or] a sap-roller made by those who had never heard the name . . . it was done, and after a few trials well done." Before long, a later observer remarked, "those who had cut wood only for stoves would be speaking fluently of gabions and fascines; men who had patiently smoothed earth so that radishes might grow better would be talking affectionately of terrepleins for guns." In all of this they were inspired by the same bustling energy and quick adaptability on the part of the generals who led them; for one thing that characterized Grant's army was the youth of its commanders. McClernand, who was fifty-one, was the only general officer past fifty. Of the twenty-one corps and division commanders assigned to the Army of the Tennessee in the course of the campaign, the average age was under forty. And that promotion had been based on merit was indicated by the fact that the average age of the nine major generals was as low as that of the dozen brigadiers; indeed, excepting McClernand, it was better than one year lower. Moreover, nine of these twenty-one men were older than Grant himself, and this too was part of the reason for his confidence in himself and in the army which had come of age, so to speak, under his care and tutelage. He considered it more than a match for anything the Confederates could bring against him — even under Joe Johnston, whose abilities he respected highly. One day a staff officer expressed the fear that Johnston was planning to fight his way into Vicksburg in order to help Pemberton stage a breakout; but Grant did not agree. "No," he said. "We are the only fellows who want to get in there. The rebels who are in now want to get out, and those who are out want to stay out. If Johnston tries to cut his way in we will let him do it, and then see that he don't get out. You say he has 30,000 men with him? That will give us 30,000 more prisoners than we now have."

This was not to say that the two repulsed assaults had taught him nothing. They had indeed, if only by way of confirming a first impression that the rebel works were formidable. One officer, riding west on the Jackson road, had found himself confronted by "a long line of high, rugged, irregular bluffs, clearly cut against the sky, crowned with cannon which peered ominously from embrasures to the right and left as far as the eye could see." Beyond an almost impenetrable tangle of timber felled on the forward slopes, "lines of heavy rifle pits, surmounted with head-logs, ran along the bluffs, connecting fort with fort, and filled with veteran infantry." The approaches, he said, "were frightful enough to appall the stoutest heart." Sherman agreed, especially after the two assaults which had cost the army more than four thousand casualties. "I have since seen the position at Sevastopol," he wrote years later, "and without hesitation I declare that at Vicksburg to have been the more difficult of the two." Skillfully constructed, well sited, and prepared for a year against the day of investment, the fortifications extended for seven miles along commanding ridges and were anchored at both extremities to the lip of the sheer 200-foot bluff, north and south of the beleaguered city. Forts, redoubts, salients, redans, lunets, and bastions had been erected or dug at irregular intervals along the line, protected by overlapping fields of fire and connected by a complex of trenches, which in turn were mutually supporting. There simply was no easy way to get at the defenders. Moreover, Grant's three-to-one numerical advantage was considerably offset, not only by the necessity for protecting his rear from possible attacks by the army Johnston was assembling to the east, but also by the fact that, because of the vagaries of the up-ended terrain, his line of contravallation had to be more than twice the length of the line he was attempting to confront. "There is only one way to account for the hills of Vicksburg," a Confederate soldier had said a year ago, while helping to survey the present works. "After the Lord of Creation had made all the big mountains and ranges of hills, He had left on His hands a large lot of scraps. These were all dumped at Vicksburg in a waste heap." One of Grant's two professional engineers was altogether in agreement, pronouncing the Confederate position "rather an intrenched camp than a fortified

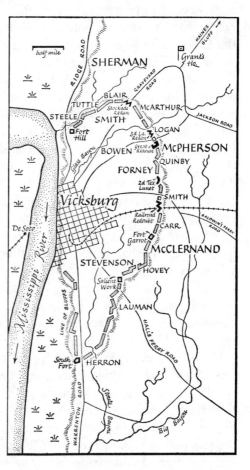

place, owing much of its strength to the difficult ground, obstructed by fallen trees to its front, which rendered rapidity of movement and *ensemble* in an assault impossible."

Yet even this ruggedness had its compensations. Although the hillsides, as one who climbed them said, "were often so steep that their ascent was difficult to a footman unless he aided himself with his hands," the many ravines provided excellent cover for the besiegers, and Grant had specified in his investment order: "Every advantage will be taken of the natural inequalities of the ground to gain positions from which to start mines, trenches, or advance batteries." With the memory of slaughter fresh in their minds as a result of their two repulses, the men dug with a will. Knowing little or nothing at the outset of the five formal stages of a siege — the investment, the artillery attack, the construction of parallels and approaches, the breaching by artillery or mines, and the final assault — they told one another that Grant, having failed to go over the rebel works, had decided to go under them instead. Fortunately the enemy used his artillery sparingly, apparently conserving ammunition for use in repelling major assaults, but snipers were quick to shoot at targets of opportunity: in which connection a Federal major was to recall that "a favorite amusement of the soldiers was to place a cap on the end of a ramrod and raise it just above the head-logs, betting on the number of bullets which would pass through it within a given time." Few things on earth appealed to them more, as humor, than the notion of some butternut marksman flaunting his skill when the target was something less than flesh and blood. Mostly, though, they dug and took what rest they could, sweating in their wool uniforms and cursing the heat even more than they did the snipers. Soon they were old hands at siege warfare. "The excitement . . . has worn away," a lieutenant wrote home from the trenches in early June, "and we have settled down to our work as quietly and as regularly as if we were hoeing corn or drawing bills in chancery."

Life in the trenches across the way — though the occupants did not call them that; they called them "ditches" — was at once more sedentary and more active. With their own 102 guns mostly silent and Grant's opposing 220 roaring practically all the time, they did nearly as much digging as the bluecoats, the difference being that they did it mainly in the same place, time after time, repairing damages inflicted by the steady rain of shells. Nor were they any less inventive. "Thunder barrels," for example — powder-filled hogsheads, fuzed at the bung — were found to be quite effective when rolled downhill into the enemy parallels and approaches. Similarly, such large naval projectiles as failed to detonate, either in the air or on contact with the ground, could be dug up, re-fuzed, and used in the same fashion to discourage the blue diggers on the slopes. However, despite such violent distractions, after a couple of weeks of spadework the two lines were within clod-tossing distance of each other at several points, and this resulted in an edgy sort of existence for the soldiers of both sides, as if they were spending their days and nights at the wrong end of a shooting gallery or in a testing chamber for explosives. "Fighting by hand grenades was all that was possible at such close quarters," a Confederate was to recall. "As the Federals had the hand grenades and we had none, we obtained our supply by using such of theirs as failed to explode, or by catching them as they came over the parapet and hurling them back."

Resistance under these circumstances implied a high state of morale, and such was indeed the case. Grant's heavy losses in his two assaults — inflicted at so little cost to the defenders that, until they looked out through the lifting smoke and saw the opposite hillsides strewn with the rag-doll shapes of the Union dead, they could scarcely believe a major effort had been made — convinced them that the Yankees could never take the place by storm. What was more, they had faith in "Old Joe" Johnston, believing that he would raise the siege as soon as he got his troops assembled off beyond the blue horizon, whereupon the two gray forces would combine and turn the tables on the besiegers. Until then, as they saw it, all that was needed was firmness against the odds, and they stood firm. Thanks to Pemberton's foresight, which included pulling corn along the roadside and driving livestock ahead of the army during its march from the Big Black, food so far was more plentiful inside the Confederate lines than it was beyond them. The people there were the first to feel the pinch of hunger; for the Federals, coming along behind the retreating graybacks, had consumed what little remained while waiting for roads to be opened to their new base on the Yazoo. "The soldiers ate up everything the folks had for ten miles around," a Union private wrote home. "They are now of necessity compelled to come here and ask for something to live upon, and they have discovered that they have the best success when the youngest and best-looking one in the family comes to plead their case, and they have some very handsome women here." This humbling of their pride did not displease him; it seemed to him no more than they deserved. "They were well educated and rich before their niggers ran away," he added, but adversity had brought them down in the world. "If I was to meet them in Illinois I should think they were born and brought up there."

Whether this last was meant as a compliment, and if so to whom, he did not say. But at least these people beyond the city's bristling limits were not being shot at; which was a great deal more than could be said of those within the gun-studded belt that girdled the bluff Vicksburg had been founded on, forty-odd years ago, by provision of the last will and testament of the pioneer farmer and Methodist parson Newitt Vick. In a sense, however, the bluff was returning to an earlier destiny. All that had been here when Vick arrived were the weed-choked ruins of a Spanish fort, around which the settlement had grown in less than two generations into a bustling town of some 4500 souls, mostly devoted to trade with planters in the lower Yazoo delta but also plagued by flatboat men on the way downriver from Memphis, who found it a convenient place for letting off what they called "a load of steam" that would not wait for New Orleans. As it turned out, though, the ham-fisted boatmen with knives in their boots and the gamblers with aces and derringers up their sleeves were mild indeed compared to what was visited upon them by the blue-clad host sent against them by what had lately been their government. Now the bluff was a fort again, on a scale beyond the most flamboyant dreams of the long-departed Spaniards, and the residents spent much of their time, as one of them said, watching the incoming shells "rising steadily and shiningly in great parabolic curves, descending with ever-increasing swiftness, and falling with deafening shrieks and explosions." The "ponderous fragments" flew everywhere, he added, thickening the atmosphere of terror until "even the dogs seemed to share the general fear. On hearing the descent of a shell, they would dart aside [and] then, as it exploded, sit down and howl in a pitiful manner." Children, on the other hand, observed the uproar with wide-eyed evident pleasure, accepting it as a natural phenomenon, like rain or lightning, unable to comprehend — as the dogs, for example, so obviously did — that men could do such things to one another and to them. "How is it possible you live here?" a woman who had arrived to visit her soldier husband just before the siege lines tightened asked a citizen, and was told: "After one is accustomed to the change, we do not mind it. But becoming accustomed: that is the trial." Some took it better than others, in or out of uniform. There was for instance a Frenchman, "a gallant officer who had distinguished himself in several severe engagements," who was "almost unmanned" whenever one of the huge mortar projectiles fell anywhere near him. Chided by friends for this reaction, he would reply: "I no like ze bomb: I cannot fight him back!" Neither could anyone else "fight him back," least of all the civilians, many of whom took refuge in caves dug into the hillsides. Some of these were quite commodious, with several rooms, and the occupants brought in chairs and beds and even carpets to add to the comfort, sleeping soundly or taking dinner unperturbed while the world outside seemed turned to flame and thunder. "Prairie Dog Village," the blue cannoneers renamed the city on the bluff, while from the decks of ironclads and mortar rafts on the great brown river, above and below, and from the semicircular curve of eighty-nine sand-bagged battery emplacements on the landward side, they continued to pump their steel-packaged explosives into the checkerboard pattern of its streets and houses.

Like the men in the trenches, civilians of both sexes and all ages were convinced that their tormentors could never take Vicksburg by storm, and whatever their fright they had no intention of knuckling under to what they called the bombs. For them, too, Johnston was the one bright hope of deliverance. Old Joe would be coming soon, they assured each other; all that was needed was to hold on till he completed his arrangements; then, with all the resources of the Confederacy at his command, he would come swooping over the eastern horizon and down on the Yankee rear. But presently, as time wore on and Johnston did not come, they were made aware of a new enemy. Hunger. By mid-June, though the garrison had been put first on half and then on quarter rations of meat, the livestock driven into the works ahead of the army back in May had been consumed, and Pemberton had his foragers impress all the cattle in the city. This struck nearer home than even the Union shells had done, for it was no easy thing for a family with milk-thirsty children to watch its one cow being led away to slaughter by a squad of ragged strangers. Moreover, the army's supply of bread was running low by now, and the commissary was directed to issue instead equal portions of rice and flour, four ounces of each per man per day, supplementing a quarter-pound of meat that was generally stringy or rancid or both. When these grains ran low, as they soon did, the experiment was tried of baking bread from dough composed of equal parts of corn and dried peas, ground up together until they achieved a gritty consistency not unlike cannon powder. "It made a nauseous composition," one who survived the diet was to recall with a shudder, "as the corn meal cooked in half the time the peas meal did, so the stuff was half raw. . . . It had the properties of india-rubber, and was worse than leather to digest." Soon afterwards came the crowning indignity. With the last cow and hog gone lowing and squealing under the sledge and cleaver, still another experiment was tried: the substitution of mule meat for beef and bacon. Though it was issued, out of respect for religious and folk prejudices, "only to those who desired it," Pemberton was gratified to report that both officers and men considered it "not only nutritious, but very palatable, and in every way preferable to poor beef." So he said; but soldiers and civilians alike found something humiliating, not to say degrading, about the practice. "The rebels don't starve with success," a Federal infantryman observed jokingly from beyond the lines about this time. "I think that if I had nothing to eat I'd starve better than they do." Vicksburg's residents and defenders might well have agreed, especially when mule meat was concerned. Even if a man refused to eat such stuff himself, he found it disturbing to live among companions who did not. It was enough to diminish even their faith in Joe Johnston, who seemed in point of fact a long time coming.

Though at the outset the Virginian had sounded vigorous and purposeful in his assurance of assistance, Pemberton himself by now had begun to doubt the outcome of the race between starvation and delivery. "I am trying to gather a force which may attempt to relieve you. Hold out," Johnston wrote on May 19, and six days later he made this more specific: "Bragg is sending a division. When it comes, I will move to you. Which do you think is the best route? How and where is the enemy encamped? What is your force?" Receiving this last on May 29 — the delay was not extreme, considering that couriers to and from the city had to creep by darkness through the Federal lines, risking capture every foot of the way — the Vicksburg commander replied as best he could to his superior's questions as to Grant's dispositions and strength. "My men are in good spirits, awaiting your arrival," he added. "You may depend on my holding the place as long as possible." After waiting nine days and receiving no answer, he asked: "When may I expect you to move, and in what direction?" Three more days he waited, and still there was no reply. "I am waiting most anxiously to know your intentions," he repeated. "I have heard nothing from you since [your dispatch of] May 25. I shall endeavor to hold out as long as we have anything to eat." Three days more went by, and then on June 13 — two weeks and a day since any word had reached him from the world outside — he received a message dated May 29. "I am too weak to save Vicksburg," Johnston told him. "Can do no more than attempt to save

you and your garrison. It will be impossible to extricate you unless you
co-operate and we make mutually supporting movements. Communicate your plans and suggestions, if possible." This was not only considerably less than had been expected in the way of help; it also seemed to
indicate that Johnston did not realize how tightly the Union cordon was
drawn about Vicksburg's bluff. In effect, the meager trickle of dispatches left Pemberton in a position not unlike that of a man who calls
on a friend to make a strangler turn loose of his throat, only to have
the friend inquire as to the strangler's strength, the position of his
thumbs, the condition of the sufferer's windpipe, and just what kind
of help he had in mind. So instead of "plans and suggestions," Vicksburg's
defender tried to communicate some measure of the desperation he and
his soldiers were feeling. "The enemy has placed several heavy guns in
position against our works," he replied on June 15, "and is approaching
them very nearly by sap. His fire is almost continuous. Our men have
no relief; are becoming much fatigued, but are still in pretty good spirits. I think your movement should be made as soon as possible. The enemy is receiving reinforcements. We are living on greatly reduced rations, but I think sufficient for twenty days yet."

Having thus placed the limit of Vicksburg's endurance only one
day beyond the Fourth of July — now strictly a Yankee holiday —
Pemberton followed this up, lest Johnston fail to sense the desperation
implied, with a more outspoken message four days later: "I hope you
will advance with the least possible delay. My men have been thirty-
four days and nights in the trenches, without relief, and the enemy
within conversation distance. We are living on very reduced rations,
and, as you know, are entirely isolated." He closed by asking bluntly,
"What aid am I to expect from you?" This time the answer, if vague,
was prompt. On June 23 a courier arrived with a dispatch written only
the day before. "Scouts report the enemy fortifying toward us and the
roads blocked," Johnston declared. "If I can do nothing to relieve you,
rather than surrender the garrison, endeavor to cross the river at the
last moment if you and General Taylor communicate." To Pemberton
this seemed little short of madness. Taylor had made his gesture against
Young's Point and Milliken's Bend more than two weeks ago; by now
he was all the way down the Teche, intent on menacing New Orleans.
But that was by no means the worst of Johnston's oversights, which
was to ignore the presence of the Union navy. The bluejacket gun
crews would have liked nothing better than a chance to try their marksmanship on a makeshift flotilla of skiffs, canoes, and rowboats manned
by the half-starved tatterdemalions they had been probing for at long
range all these weeks. Besides, even if the boats required had been available, which they were not, there was the question of whether the men
in the trenches were in any condition for such a strenuous effort. They
looked well enough to a casual eye, for all their rags and hollow-eyed

gauntness, but it was observed that they tired easily under the mildest exertion and could serve only brief shifts when shovel work was called for. The meager diet was beginning to tell. A Texas colonel reported that many of his men had "swollen ankles and symptoms of incipient scurvy." By late June, nearly half the garrison was on the sick list or in hospital. If Pemberton could not see what this meant, a letter he received at this time — June 28: exactly one week short of the date he had set, two weeks ago, as the limit of Vicksburg's endurance — presumed to define it for him in unmistakable terms. Signed "Many Soldiers," the letter called attention to the fact that the ration now had been reduced to "one biscuit and a small bit of bacon per day," and continued:

> The emergency of the case demands prompt and decided action on your part. If you can't feed us, you had better surrender us, horrible as the idea is, than suffer this noble army to disgrace themselves by desertion. I tell you plainly, men are not going to lie here and perish, if they do love their country dearly. Self-preservation is the first law of nature, and hunger will compel a man to do almost anything.... This army is now ripe for mutiny, unless it can be fed. Just think of one small biscuit and one or two mouthfuls of bacon per day. General, please direct your inquiries in the proper channel, and see if I have not stated the stubborn facts, which had better be heeded before we are disgraced.

★ ★ ★

"Grant is now deservedly the hero," Sherman wrote home in early June, adding characteristically — for his dislike of reporters was not tempered by any evidence of affection on their part, either for himself or for Grant, with whom, as he presently said, "I am a second self" — that his friend was being "belabored with praise by those who a month ago accused him of all the sins in the calendar, and who next will turn against him if so blows the popular breeze. Vox populi, vox humbug."

In point of fact, however, once the encompassing lines had been drawn, the journalists could find little else to write about that had not been covered during the first week of the siege. And it was much the same for the soldiers, whose only diversion was firing some fifty to one hundred rounds of ammunition a day, as required by orders. Across the way — though the Confederates lacked even this distraction, being under instructions to burn no powder needlessly — the main problem, or at any rate the most constant one, was hunger; whereas for the Federals it was boredom. "The history of a single day was the history of all the others," an officer was to recall. Different men had different ways of trying to hasten the slow drag of time. Sherman, for instance, took horseback rides and paid off-duty visits to points of interest roundabout, at least one of which resulted in a scene he found discomforting, even painful. Learning that the mother of one of his former Louisiana Academy cadets was refugeeing in the neighborhood — she had come all the way from Plaquemine Parish to escape the attentions of Butler and Banks, only to run spang into Grant and Sherman — he rode over to tender his respects and found her sitting on her gallery with about a dozen women visitors. He introduced himself, inquired politely after her son, and was told that the young man was besieged in Vicksburg, a lieutenant of artillery. When the general went on to ask for news of her husband, whom he had known in the days before the war, the woman suddenly burst into tears and cried out in anguish: "You killed him at Bull Run, where he was fighting for his country!" Sherman hastily denied that he had "killed anybody at Bull Run," which was literally true, but by now all the other women had joined the chorus of abuse and lamentation. This, he said long afterwards, "made it most uncomfortable for me, and I rode away."

Other men had other spare-time diversions. Grant's, it was said, was whiskey. Some denied this vehemently, protesting that he was a teetotaler, while some asserted that this only appeared to be the case because of his low tolerance for the stuff; a single glass unsteadied him, and a second gave him the glassy-eyed look of a man with a heavy load on. He himself seemed to recognize the problem from the outset, if only by the appointment and retention of John A. Rawlins as his assistant adjutant general. A frail but vigorous young man, with a "marble pallor" to his face and "large, lustrous eyes of a deep black," Rawlins at first had wanted to be a preacher, but had become instead a lawyer in Galena, where Grant first knew him. His wife had died of tuberculosis soon after the start of the war, and he himself would die of the same disease before he was forty, but the death that seemed to have affected him most had been that of his father, an improvident charcoal burner who had died at last of the alcoholism that had kept him and his large family in poverty all his life. Rawlins, a staff captain at thirty and now a lieutenant colonel at thirty-two, was rabid on the subject of drink. He was in fact blunt in most things, including his relationship with Grant. "He bossed everything at Grant's headquarters," Charles Dana later wrote, adding: "I have heard him curse at Grant when, according to his judgment, the general was doing something that he thought he had better not do." Observing this, many wondered why Grant put up with it. Others believed they knew. "If you hit Rawlins on the head, you'll knock out Grant's brains," they said. But they were wrong. Rawlins was not Grant's brain; he was his conscience, and a rough one, too, especially where whiskey was concerned. "I say to you frankly, and I pledge you my word for it," he had written eighteen months ago to Elihu Washburne, the general's congressional guardian angel, "that should General Grant at any time become an intemperate man or an habitual drunkard, I will notify you immediately, will ask to be removed from duty on his staff (kind as he has been to me) or resign my commission. For while there are times when I would gladly throw the mantle of charity over the faults of my friends, at this time and from a man of his position I would rather tear the mantle off and expose the deformity." Grant had cause to believe that Rawlins meant it. And yet, despite the danger to his career and despite what a fellow staffer called Rawlins' "insubordination twenty times a day," he kept him on, both for his own good and the army's.

Since writing to Washburne, however, the adjutant had either changed his mind about disturbing the mantle or else he had been singularly forgetful. Despite periodic incidents thereafter, in which Grant was involved with whiskey, Rawlins limited his remarks to the general himself, apparently in the belief that he could handle him. And so he could, except for lapses. Anyhow, there was never any problem so long as Mrs Grant was around; "If she is with him all will be well and I can be spared," he later confided to a friend. The trouble seemed in part sexual, as in California nine years ago, and it was intensified by periods of boredom, such as now. Three weeks of slam-bang fighting and rapid maneuver had given way to the tedium of a siege, and Mrs Grant had been six weeks off the scene. On June 5 Rawlins found a box of wine in front of the general's tent and had it removed, ignoring Grant's protest that he was saving it to toast the fall of Vicksburg. He learned, moreover, that the general had recently accepted a glass of wine from a convivial doctor. These were danger signs, and there were others that evening. Rawlins sat down after midnight and wrote Grant a letter. "The great solicitude I feel for the safety of this army leads me to mention, what I had hoped never again to do, the subject of your drinking. ... Tonight when you should, because of the condition of your health if nothing else, have been in bed, I find you where the wine bottle has just been emptied, in company with those who drink and urge you to do likewise, and the lack of your usual promptness and decision, and clearness in expressing yourself in writing conduces to confirm my suspicion." Rawlins himself had become rather incoherent by now, whether from anger or from sorrow; but the ending was clear enough. Unless Grant would pledge himself "[not] to touch a single drop of any kind of liquor, no matter by whom asked or under what circumstances," Rawlins wanted to be relieved at once from duty in the department. Grant, however, left early next morning — apparently before the letter reached him — on a tour of inspection up the Yazoo River to Satartia, near which he had posted a division in case Johnston came that way. The two-day trip, beyond the sight and influence of Rawlins, became a two-day bender.

Dana went with him, and on the way upriver from Haines Bluff they met the steamboat *Diligent* coming down. Grant hailed the vessel, whose captain was a friend of his, transferred to her, and had her turned back upstream for Satartia. Aboard was Sylvanus Cadwallader, a Chicago *Times* correspondent on the prowl for news. It was he who had ridden into Jackson with Fred Grant in mid-May, when they lost the race for the souvenir flag atop the capitol, and it was he who was to leave the only detailed eyewitness account of Grant on a wartime bender — specifically the two-day one which already was under way up the Yazoo. In some ways, for Cadwallader at least, it was more like a two-day nightmare. "I was not long in perceiving that Grant had been drinking," he wrote long afterwards, "and that he was still keeping it up. He made several trips to the bar room of the boat in a short time, and became stupid in speech and staggering in gait." The reporter of course had heard rumors of Grant's predilection, but this was the first time he had seen him show it to the extent of intoxication. Alarmed by the general's "condition, which was fast becoming worse," he tried to get the captain and a lieutenant aide to intervene. Neither would; so Cadwallader undertook to do it himself. He got Grant into his stateroom, locked the door, "and commenced throwing bottles of whiskey which stood on the table, through the windows, over the guards, into the river." Grant protested, to no avail; the reporter "firmly, but good-naturedly declined to obey," and finally got him quieted. "As it was a very hot day and the stateroom almost suffocating, I insisted on his taking off his coat, vest and boots, and lying down on one of the berths. After much resistance I succeeded, and soon fanned him to sleep."

But that was only the beginning. Shortly before dark, when the *Diligent* neared Satartia, she met two gunboats steaming down, and a naval officer came aboard to warn that it was not safe for the unarmed vessel to proceed. Dana — who later reported tactfully in his *Recollections* that "Grant was ill and went to bed soon after we started" — knocked on the stateroom door to ask whether the boat should turn back. Grant, he said, was "too sick to decide," and told him: "I will leave it to you." Now that he was awake, however, though still not "recovered from his stupor," Cadwallader said, the general took it into his head "to dress and go ashore," despite the naval officer's warning. Once more the reporter prevailed, and got him back to bed. While he slept, the *Diligent* returned downstream in the darkness to Haines Bluff. Next morning, according to Dana, Grant was "fresh as a rose, clean shirt and all, quite himself," when he came out to breakfast. "Well, Mr Dana," he observed, "I suppose we are at Satartia."

Cadwallader relaxed his guard, despite the 25-mile geographical error, presuming that "all necessity for extra vigilance on my part had passed," and was profoundly shocked to discover, an hour later, "that Grant had procured another supply of whiskey from on shore and was quite as much intoxicated as the day before." Again the reporter managed to separate the general from his bottle, only to have him insist on proceeding at once to Chickasaw Bayou. This would have brought them there "about the middle of the afternoon, when the landing would have been alive with officers, men, and trains from all parts of the army." Conferring with the captain as to the best means by which to avoid exposing Grant to "utter disgrace and ruin," Cadwallader managed to delay the departure so that they did not arrive until about sundown, when there was much less activity at the landing. As luck would have it, however, they tied up alongside a sutler boat whose owner "kept open house to all officers and dispensed free liquors and cigars generously." Alarmed at the possibilities of disaster, the reporter slipped hastily over the rail, warned the sutler of what was afoot, and "received his promise that the general should not have a drop of anything intoxicating on his boat." Back aboard the *Diligent*, Cadwallader helped the escort to unload the horses for the five-mile ride to army headquarters northeast of Vicksburg; but when this was done he looked around and could find no sign of Grant. Fearing the worst, he hurried aboard the sutler boat "and soon heard a general hum of conversation and laughter proceeding from a room opening out of the ladies' cabin." There he saw his worst fears realized. The sutler was seated at "a table covered with bottled whiskey and baskets of champagne," and Grant was beside him, "in the act of swallowing a glass of whiskey." Cadwallader once more intervened, insisting that "the escort was waiting, and it would be long after dark before we could reach headquarters." Grant came along, though he plainly resented the interruption. His horse was a borrowed one called Kangaroo "from his habit of rearing on his hind feet and making a plunging start whenever mounted." That was his reaction now; for "Grant gave him the spur the moment he was in the saddle, and the horse darted away at full speed before anyone was ready to follow." The road was crooked, winding among the many slews and bayous, but the general more or less straightened it out, "heading only for the bridges, and literally tore through and over everything in his way. The air was full of dust, ashes, and embers from campfires, and shouts and curses from those he rode down in his race." Cadwallader, whose horse was no match for Kangaroo, thought he had lost his charge for good. But he kept on anyhow, hoping against hope, and "after crossing the last bayou bridge three-fourths of a mile from the landing," caught up with him riding sedately at a walk. Finding that Grant had become "unsteady in the saddle" as a result of the drink or drinks he had had from the sutler, and fearing "discovery of his rank and situation," the reporter seized Kangaroo's rein and led him off into a roadside thicket, where he helped the general to dismount and persuaded him to lie down on the grass and get some sleep. While Grant slept Cadwallader managed to hail a trooper from the escort, whom he instructed to go directly to headquarters "and report at once to Rawlins — and no one else — and say to him that I want an ambulance with a careful driver."

Waking before the ambulance got there, Grant wanted to resume his ride at once, but the reporter "took him by the arm, walked him back and forth, and kept up a lively rather one-sided conversation, till the ambulance arrived." Then there was the problem of getting the general into the curtained vehicle, which he refused to permit until, as Cadwallader said, "we compromised the question by my agreeing to ride in the ambulance also, and having our horses led by the orderly." They reached headquarters about midnight to find the dark-eyed Rawlins and Colonel John Riggin, another staff officer, "waiting for us in the driveway." The reporter got out first, "followed promptly by Grant," who now gave him perhaps the greatest shock of the past two days. "He shrugged his shoulders, pulled down his vest, 'shook himself together,' as one just rising from a nap, and seeing Rawlins and Riggin, bid them good night in a natural tone and manner, and started to his tent as steadily as he ever walked in his life." Cadwallader turned to Rawlins, who was pale with rage — "The whole appearance of the man indicated a fierceness that would have torn me into a thousand pieces had he considered me to blame" — and said he was afraid, from what they had just seen, that the adjutant would think it was he, not Grant, who had been drinking. "No, no," Rawlins said through clenched teeth. "I know him, I know him. I want you to tell me the exact facts, and all of them, without any concealment. I have a right to know them, and I will know them."

He heard them all, from start to finish, but he never reported the incident to Washburne, any more than Dana did to the War Department, not only out of loyalty and friendship, but also perhaps on reflecting that if anything brought about Grant's removal, or even his suspension during an inquiry, command of the army would pass automatically to McClernand, whom they both despised. As for Cadwallader, despite assurances from Rawlins — "He will not send you out of the department while I remain in it," the adjutant told him — he spent an anxious night, "somewhat in doubt as to the view of the matter Gen. Grant would take next day," and "purposely kept out of his way for twenty-four hours to spare him the mortification I supposed he might feel." As it turned out, he need not have worried. "The second day afterward I passed in and out of his presence as though nothing unusual had occurred. To my surprise he never made the most distant allusion to [the matter] then, or ever afterward." From that time on, he said, it was "as if I had been regularly gazetted a member of his staff." Passes from Grant enabled the reporter to go anywhere he wanted; he could requisition transportation and draw subsistence from quartermaster and commissary authorities; his tent was always pitched near Grant's, and his dispatches often were sent in the official mail pouch; in short, he "constantly received flattering personal and professional favors and attentions shown to no one else in my position." All this was in return for his respecting a confidence which he kept for more than thirty years. In 1896, a seventy-year-old sheep raiser out in California, he wrote his memoirs, including an account of Grant's two-day trip up the Yazoo and back. For nearly sixty years they remained in manuscript, and when at last they were published, ninety years after the war was over, they were attacked and the writer vilified by some of the general's long-range admirers, who claimed that what Cadwallader called "this Yazoo-Vicksburg adventure" never happened.

At any rate, no harm had resulted from the army commander's two-day absence from headquarters, drunk or sober. The repulse of Taylor at Milliken's Bend and Young's Point by the gunboats, on the second day, increased Grant's confidence rather than his fretfulness, which in fact seemed to be cured. "All is going on here now just right," he wrote to a friend on June 15, and added: "My position is so strong that I feel myself abundantly able to leave it and go out twenty or thirty miles with force enough to whip two such garrisons." He had small use for Pemberton, characterizing him as "a northern man [who] got into bad company." Nor did he fear Joe Johnston. Though he respected his ability, he said he did not believe the Virginian could save Vicksburg without "a larger army than the Confederates now have at any one place." Next day, moreover, the watchful eye of former congressman Frank Blair enabled Grant to dispose of his third opponent, John McClernand, and thus wind up the private war he had been waging all this time. Scanning the columns of the Memphis *Evening Bulletin*, Blair spotted a congratulatory order McClernand had issued to his corps, claiming the lion's share of the credit for the victory he foresaw. Blair sent the clipping to Sherman, who forwarded it to Grant next day, calling it "a catalogue of nonsense" and "an effusion of vain-glory and hypocrisy . . . addressed not to an army, but to a constituency in Illinois." He also cited a War Department order, issued the year before, "which actually forbids the publication of all official letters and reports, and requires the name of the writer to be laid before the President of the United States for dismissal."

Grant had waited half a year for this, passing over various lesser offenses in hopes that one would come along which would justify charges that could not fail to stick. But now that he had it he still moved with deftness and precision, completing the adjustment of the noose. That same day, June 17, he forwarded the clipping to McClernand with a note: "Inclosed I send you what purports to be your congratulatory address to the Thirteenth Army Corps. I would respectfully ask if it is a true copy. If it is not a correct copy, furnish me one by bearer, as required both by regulations and existing orders of the Department." Next day McClernand acknowledged the validity of the clipping. "I am prepared to maintain its statements," he declared. "I regret that my adjutant did not send you a copy as he ought, and I thought he had." With the noose now snug, Grant sprang the trap: "Major General John A. McClernand is hereby relieved from command of the Thirteenth Army Corps. He will proceed to any point he may select in the state of Illinois and report by letter to Headquarters of the Army for orders." Grant signed the order after working hours, supposing that it would be delivered the following morning, but when James Wilson came in at midnight and heard what was afoot — there was bad blood between him and McClernand; the two had nearly come to blows a couple of weeks ago — he urged Rawlins to let him deliver the order in person, without delay, lest something come up — a rebel sortie at dawn, for example, which might enable McClernand to distinguish himself as he had done at Shiloh — to cause its suspension or cancellation. Rawlins agreed, and Wilson put on his dress uniform, summoned the provost marshal and a squad of soldiers, and set out through the darkness for McClernand's headquarters. Arriving about 2 o'clock in the morning, he demanded that the general be roused. Presently he was admitted to McClernand's tent, where he found the former congressman seated at a table on which two candles burned. Apparently he knew what to expect, for he too was in full uniform and his sword lay before him on the table. Wilson handed him the order, remarking that he had been instructed to see that it was read and understood. McClernand took it, adjusted his glasses, and perused it. "Well, sir, I am relieved," he said. Then, looking up at Wilson, whose expression did not mask his satisfaction, he added: "By God, sir, we are both relieved!"

   He did not intend to take this lying down, but he soon found that Grant had played the old army game with such skill that his opponent was left without a leg to stand on. "I have been relieved for an omission of my adjutant. Hear me," McClernand wired Lincoln from Cairo on his way to Springfield, their common home. From there he protested likewise to Halleck, suggesting the possible disclosure of matters that were dark indeed: "How far General Grant is indebted to the forbearance of officers under his command for his retention in the public service, I will not undertake to state unless he should challenge it. None know better than himself how much he is indebted to that forbearance." That might be, but it was no help to the general up in Illinois; Grant challenged nothing, except to state that he had "tolerat[ed] General McClernand long after I thought the good of the service demanded his removal." In time, there came to Springfield a letter signed "Your friend as ever, A. Lincoln," in which the unhappy warrior was told: "I doubt whether your present position is more painful to you than to myself. Grateful for the patriotic stand so early taken by you in this life-and-death struggle of the nation, I have done whatever has appeared practicable to advance you and the public interest together." However: "For me to force you back upon Gen. Grant would be forcing him to resign. I cannot give you a new command, because we have no forces except such as already have commanders." In short, the President had nothing to offer his fellow-townsman in the way of balm, save his conviction that a general was best judged by those "who have been with him in the field. . . . Relying on these," Lincoln said in closing, "he who has the right needs not to fear."

This was perhaps the unkindest cut of all, since McClernand knew only too well what was likely to happen to his reputation if judgment was left to Sherman and McPherson and their various subordinate commanders, including the army's two remaining ex-congressmen Blair and Logan. Among all these, and on Grant's staff, there was general rejoicing at his departure. Major General Edward O. C. Ord, who had fought under Grant at Iuka, had just arrived to take charge of a sixth corps intended to consist of the divisions under Herron and Lauman; instead, he replaced McClernand. Three days later, on June 22, Sherman was given command of the rearward line, which was strengthened by shifting more troops from in front of Vicksburg. "We want to whip Johnston at least 15 miles off, if possible," Grant explained. Steele succeeded Sherman, temporarily, and the siege went on as before. No less than nine approaches were being run, all with appropriate parallels close up to the enemy trenches, so that the final assault could be launched with the lowest possible loss in lives. Mines were sunk under rebel strongpoints, and on June 25 two of these were exploded on McPherson's front, the largest just north of the Jackson road. It blew off the top of a hill there, leaving a big, dusty crater which the attackers occupied for a day and then abandoned, finding themselves under heavy plunging fire from both flanks and the rear. The mine accomplished little, but contributed greatly to the legend of the siege by somehow lofting a Negro cook, Abraham by name, all the way from the Confederate hilltop and into the Federal lines. He landed more or less unhurt, though terribly frightened. An Iowa outfit claimed him, put him in a tent, and got rich charging five cents a look. Asked how high he had been blown, Abraham always gave the same answer, coached perhaps by some would-be Iowa Barnum. "Donno, massa," he would say, "but tink bout tree mile."

Mostly, though, the weeks passed in boredom and increasing heat, under whose influence the Confederates appeared to succumb to a strange apathy during the final days of June. A Federal engineer remarked that their defense "was far from being vigorous." It seemed to him that the rebel strategy was "to wait for another assault, losing in the meantime as few men as possible," and he complained that this had a bad effect on his own men, since "without the stimulus of danger ... troops of the line will not work efficiently, especially at night, after the novelty has worn off." Another trouble was that they foresaw the end of the siege, and no man coveted the distinction of being the last to die. Not that all was invariably quiet. Occasionally there were flare-ups, particularly where the trenches approached conjunction, and the snipers continued to take their toll. Though the losses were small, the suffering was great. "It looked hard," a Wisconsin soldier wrote, "to see six or eight poor fellows piled into an ambulance about the size of Jones's meat wagon and hustled over the rough roads as fast as the mules could trot and to see the blood running out of the carts in streams almost." Taunts were flung as handily as grenades, back and forth across the lines, the graybacks asking, "When are you folks going to come on into town?" and the bluecoats replying that they were in no hurry: "We are holding you fellows prisoner while you feed yourselves." There was much fraternization between pickets, who arranged informal truces for the exchange of coffee and tobacco, and the same Federal engineer reported that the enemy's "indifference to our approach became at some points almost ludicrous." Once, for example, when the blue sappers found that as a result of miscalculation a pair of approach trenches would converge just inside the rebel picket line, the two sides called a cease-fire and held a consultation at which it was decided that the Confederates would pull back a short distance in order to avoid an unnecessary fire fight. At one stage of the discussion a Federal suggested that the approaches could be redesigned to keep from disturbing the butternut sentries, but the latter seemed to think that it would be a shame if all that digging went to waste. Besides, one said, "it don't make any difference. You Yanks will soon have the place anyhow."

Grant thought so, too. By now, in fact — though he kept his soldiers burrowing, intending to launch his final assault from close-up positions in early July — he was giving less attention to Pemberton than he was to Johnston, off in the opposite direction, where Sherman described him as "vibrating between Jackson and Canton" in apparent indecision. Blair had reported earlier, on returning from a scout, that "every man I picked up was going to Canton to join him. The negroes told me their masters had joined him there, and those who were too old to go, or who could escape on any other pretext, told me the same story." This had a rather ominous sound, as if hosts were gathering to the east, but Grant was not disturbed. He had access, through the treacherous courier, to many of the messages that passed between his two opponents. He knew what they were thinking, what the men under them were thinking, and what the beleaguered citizens were thinking. He spoke of their expectations in a dispatch he sent Sherman on June 25, the day the slave Abraham came hurtling into the hands of the Iowans: "Strong faith is expressed by some in Johnston's coming to their relief. [They] cannot believe they have been so wicked as for Providence to allow the loss of their stronghold of Vicksburg. Their principal faith seems to be in Providence and Joe Johnston."

By then — the fortieth day of siege — it had been exactly a month since the man in whom Vicksburg's garrison placed its "principal faith" assured Pemberton: "Bragg is sending a division. When it joins I will come to you." The division reached him soon afterwards, under Breckinridge, and was combined with the three already at hand under

Loring, French, and Walker; Johnston's present-for-duty strength now totaled 31,226 men, two thirds of whom had joined him since his arrival in mid-May. But he found them quite deficient in equipment, especially wagons, and deferred action until such needs could be supplied. In the interim he got into a dispute with the Richmond authorities, protesting that he had only 23,000 troops, while Seddon insisted that the correct figure was 34,000. Finally the Secretary told him: "You must rely on what you have," and urged him to move at once to Pemberton's relief. But Johnston would not be prodded into action. "The odds against me are much greater than those you express," he wired on June 15, and added flatly: "I consider saving Vicksburg hopeless." Shocked by his fellow Virginian's statement that he considered his assignment an impossible one, Seddon took this to mean that Johnston did not comprehend the gravity of the situation or the consequences of the fall of the Gibraltar of the West, which in Seddon's eyes meant the probable fall of the Confederacy itself. It seemed to him, moreover, that the general — in line with his behavior a year ago, down the York-James peninsula — was moving toward a decision not to fight at all, and to the Secretary this was altogether unthinkable. "Your telegram grieves and alarms me," he replied next day. "Vicksburg must not be lost without a desperate struggle. The interest and honor of the Confederacy forbid it. I rely on you still to avert the loss. If better resources do not offer, you must hazard attack. It may be made in concert with the garrison, if practicable, but otherwise without; by day or night, as you think best." Still Johnston would not budge. "I think you do not appreciate the difficulties in the course you direct," he wired back, "nor the probabilities or consequences of failure. Grant's position, naturally very strong, is intrenched and protected by powerful artillery, and the roads obstructed. . . . The defeat of this little army would at once open Mississippi and Alabama to Grant. I will do all I can, without hope of doing more than aid to extricate the garrison." Fairly frantic and near despair over this prediction that the Father of Waters was about to pass out of Confederate hands, severing all practical connection with the Transmississippi and its supplies of men and food and horses, Seddon urged the general "to follow the most desperate course the occasion may demand. Rely upon it," he told him, "the eyes and hopes of the whole Confederacy are upon you, with the full confidence that you will act, and with the sentiment that it were better to fail nobly daring than, through prudence even, to be inactive. . . . I rely on you for all possible to save Vicksburg."

But no matter what ringing tones the Secretary employed, Johnston would not be provoked into what he considered rashness. "There has been no voluntary inaction," he protested; he simply had "not had the means of moving." By then it was June 22. Two days later he received a message from Pemberton, suggesting that he get in touch with Grant and make "propositions to pass this army out, with all its arms and equipages," in return for abandoning Vicksburg to him. Johnston declined, not only because he did not believe the proposal would be accepted, but also because "negotiations with Grant for the relief of the garrison, should they become necessary, must be made by you," he replied on June 27. "It would be a confession of weakness on my part, which I ought not to make, to propose them. When it becomes necessary to make terms, they may be considered as made under my authority." In other words, any time Pemberton wanted to throw in the sponge, it would be all right with Johnston. However, he prefaced this by saying that the Pennsylvanian's "determined spirit" encouraged him "to hope that something may yet be done to save Vicksburg," and two days later, June 29, "field transportation and other supplies having been obtained," he put his four divisions on the march for the Big Black, preceded by a screen of cavalry.

He had never been one to tilt at windmills, nor was he now. The march — or "expedition," as he preferred to call it — "was not undertaken in the wild spirit that dictated the dispatches from the War Department," he later explained, and added scornfully: "I did not indulge in the sentiment that it was better for me to waste the lives and blood of brave soldiers 'than, through prudence even,' to spare them." He never moved until he was ready, and then his movements were nearly always rearward. The one exception up to now had been Seven Pines, which turned out to be the exception that proved the rule, for it had cost him five months on the sidelines, command of the South's first army, and two wounds that were still unhealed a year later. Moreover, it had resulted in his present assignment, which was by no means to his liking, though his resultant brusqueness was reserved for those above him on the ladder of command, never for those below. To subordinates he was invariably genial and considerate, and they repaid him with loyalty, affection, and admiration. "His mind was clear as a bell," a staff officer had written from Jackson to a friend, two weeks ago, while the build-up for the present movement was still in progress. "I never saw a brain act with a quicker or more sustained movement, or one which exhibited a finer sweep or more striking power.... I cannot conceive surroundings more intensely depressing. Yet amidst them all, he preserved the elastic step and glowing brow of the genuine hero."

Desperation never rattled him; indeed, it had rather the opposite effect of increasing his native caution. And such was the case now as he approached the Big Black, beyond which Grant had intrenched a rearward-facing line. On the evening of July 1, Johnston called a halt between Brownsville and the river, and spent the next two days reconnoitering. Convinced by this "that attack north of the railroad was impracticable," he "determined, therefore, to make the examinations necessary for the attempt south of the railroad." On July 3, near Birdsong's Ferry, he wrote Pemberton that he intended "to create a diversion, and thus enable you to cut your way out if the time has arrived for you to do this. Of that time I cannot judge; you must, as it depends upon your condition. I hope to attack the enemy in your front [on] the 7th. . . . Our firing will show you where we are engaged. If Vicksburg cannot be saved, the garrison must."

Next morning, however, before he took up the march southward he noticed a strange thing. Today was the Fourth — Independence Day — but the Yankees over toward Vicksburg did not seem to be celebrating it in the usual fashion. On this of all days, the forty-eighth of the siege, the guns were silent for the first time since May 18, when the bluecoats filed into positions from which to launch their first and second assaults before settling down to the digging and bombarding that had gone on ever since; at least till now. Johnston and his men listened attentively, cocking their heads toward the beleaguered city. But there was no rumble of guns at all. Everything was quiet in that direction.

Stars in Their Courses

★ ✗ ☆

WHATEVER LACK OF NERVE OR INGENUITY
had been demonstrated in Mississippi throughout the long hot hungry
weeks that Vicksburg had shuddered under assault and languished under
siege, there had been no shortage elsewhere in the Confederate States of
either of these qualities on which the beleaguered city's hopes were hung.
Indeed, a sort of inverse ratio seemed to obtain between proximity
and daring, as if distance not only lent enchantment but also encouraged
boldness, so far at least as the western theater was concerned. A case in
point was Beauregard, 650 air-line miles away on the eastern seaboard.
Charleston's two-time savior was nothing if not inventive: especially
when he had time on his hands, as he did now. In mid-May, with the
laurels still green on his brow for the repulse of Du Pont's ironclad
fleet the month before, he unfolded in a letter to Joe Johnston — with
whom he had shared the triumph of Manassas, back in the first glad summer of the war, and to whom, under pressure from Richmond, he had
just dispatched 8000 of his men — a plan so sweeping in its concept that
the delivery of the Gibraltar of the West, whose plight had started him
thinking along these lines, was finally no more than an incidental facet of
a design for sudden and absolute victory over all the combinations
whereby the North intended to subjugate the South. According to his
"general views of the coming summer campaign," propounded in the
letter to his friend, Johnston would be reinforced by troops from all the
other Confederate commanders, who would stand on the defensive, east
and west, while Johnston joined Bragg for an all-out offensive against
the Union center, wrecking Rosecrans and driving the frazzled remnant of his army beyond the Ohio. Johnston would follow, picking up
10,000 recruits in Middle Tennessee and another 20,000 in Kentucky,
and if this threat to the Federal heartland had not already prompted a
withdrawal by the bluecoats from in front of Vicksburg, he could march
west to the Mississippi, above Memphis, "and thus cut off Grant's com-

munications with the north." When the besiegers moved upriver, as they would be obliged to do for want of supplies, Johnston would draw them into battle on a field of his choice, "and the result could not be doubtful for an instant." With Grant thus disposed of, the victorious southern Army of the Center, some 150,000 strong by then, could split in two, one half crossing the big river to assist Kirby Smith and Price in the liberation of Louisiana and Missouri, while the other half joined Lee in Virginia to complete "the terrible lesson the enemy has just had at Chancellorsville." Meanwhile, by way of lagniappe, a fleet of special torpedo boats would be constructed in England, from designs already on hand at Charleston, to steam westward across the Atlantic and "resecure" the Mississippi, upwards from its mouth. The war would be over: won.

Thus Beauregard. But after waiting five weeks and receiving no sign that his suggestions had been received, much less adopted, he felt, as he told another friend, "like Samson shorn of his locks." Time was slipping away, he complained in a postscript to his retained copy of the letter, despite the fact that "the whole of this brilliant campaign, which is only indicated here, could have been terminated by the end of June." On July 1 he heard at last from Johnston, though only on an administrative matter and without reference to his proposals of mid-May. Assuming that the original must have gone astray, he sent him at once a copy of the letter, together with the postscript stressing the need for haste in the adoption of the plan which he called brilliant. "I fear, though, it is now too late to undertake it," he admitted, and added rather lamely: "I hope everything will yet turn out well, although I do not exactly see how."

Nothing came of the Creole general's dream of reversing the blue flood, first in the center and then on the left and right; but others with easier access to the authorities in Richmond had been making similar, if less flamboyant, proposals all the while. Longstreet for example, on his way to rejoin Lee in early May, hard on the heels of Chancellorsville and the aborted Siege of Suffolk, outlined for the Secretary of War a plan not unlike Beauregard's, except that it had the virtue of comparative simplicity. It was Old Peter's conviction "that the only way to equalize the contest was by skillful use of our interior lines," and in this connection he proposed that Johnson give over any attempt to go directly to Pemberton's assistance and instead reinforce Bragg at Tullahoma, while Longstreet, with his two divisions now en route from Suffolk, moved by rail to that same point for that same purpose; Rosecrans would be swamped by overwhelming numbers, and the victors then could march for the Ohio. Grant's being the only force that could be used to meet this threat, his army would be withdrawn upriver and Vicksburg thereby would be relieved. . . . Seddon listened attentively. Though he liked the notion of using Hood and Pickett to break the enemy's grip on the Mississippi south of Memphis, he preferred the more direct and still simpler method of sending them to Jackson for a movement against Grant where he then was. However, this presupposed the approval of Lee: which was not forthcoming. Lee replied that he would of course obey any order sent him, but he considered the suggestion less than wise. "The adoption of your proposition is hazardous," he wired Seddon, "and it becomes a question between Virginia and the Mississippi." The date was May 10; Stonewall Jackson died that afternoon. But Lee suppressed his grief in order to expand his objections to the Secretary's proposal in a letter that same Sunday. He not only thought the attempt to rescue Pemberton by sending troops from Virginia unduly risky; he also considered it unnecessary. "I presume [the reinforcements] would not reach him until the last of this month," he wrote. "If anything is done in that quarter, it will be over by that time, as the climate in June will force the enemy to retire."

Seddon doubted that climate alone would be enough to cause the Federals to abandon, even for a season, their bid for source-to-mouth control of the Mississippi. Whatever Lee might think of Grant, the Secretary considered him "such an obstinate fellow that he could only be induced to quit Vicksburg by terribly hard knocks." In fact, that had been his objection to Longstreet's claim that a strike at Rosecrans would abolish the threat downriver; Grant might simply ignore the provocation and refuse to loosen his grip. Davis agreed. Moreover, he shared Seddon's reservations about Johnston, who had just been ordered to Jackson, as a deliverer of hard knocks. Between them, under pressure of the knowledge that something had to be done, and done quickly, now that the bluecoats were on the march in Pemberton's rear, the President and the Secretary decided that the time had come for a high-level conference to determine just what that something was to be. On May 14, the day Johnston abandoned the Mississippi capital to Union occupation, they summoned Lee to Richmond for a full discussion of the problem.

He arrived next day, which was one of sorrow and strain for the whole Confederacy; Stonewall Jackson was being buried, out in the Shenandoah Valley, and Joe Johnston was retreating to Canton while Grant turned west for a leap at Vicksburg from the rear. Davis and Seddon hoped that, face to face with Lee, they might persuade him to continue the risk of facing Hooker with a depleted army, so that Longstreet could join Johnston for a strike at Grant. However, they found him still convinced that such an attempt, undertaken for the possible salvation of Mississippi for a season, would mean the loss of Virginia forever; and that for him was quite unthinkable. "Save in defense of my native State, I never again desire to draw my sword," he had said two years ago, on the day he resigned from the U.S. Army. Apparently he still felt that way about it: with one refinement. His proposal now —

for he agreed that something drastic had to be done to reverse the blue flood of conquest in the center and on the far left of the thousand-mile Confederate line of battle — was that he launch a second invasion of the North. The first, back in September, had come to grief in Maryland because of a combination of mishaps, not the least of which had been McClellan's luck in finding the lost order issued by Lee when he snapped at the bait left dangling at Harpers Ferry. This time, though, he would profit by that experience. He would march without delay into Pennsylvania, deep in Washington's rear, where a victory might well prove decisive, not only in his year-long contest with the Army of the Potomac, in which he had never lost a major battle, but also in the war. It might or might not cause the withdrawal of Grant from in front of Vicksburg, but at least it would remove the invaders from the soil of Virginia during the vital harvest season, while at best it would accomplish the fall of the northern capital and thus encourage the foreign intervention which Davis long had seen as the key to victory over the superior forces of the Union. . . . The President and Seddon were impressed. Having heard Lee out, Davis asked him to return the following morning for a presentation of his views to the entire cabinet.

That too was a critical day for the young republic. Before it was over, Grant had thrown Pemberton into retreat from Champion Hill, continuing his lunge for the back door of Vicksburg, and Banks had ended his week-long occupation of Alexandria in order to move against Port Hudson. Lee spent most of it closeted with Davis and the cabinet at the White House, presenting his solution to the national crisis. He spoke not in his former capacity as military adviser to the President, and certainly not as general-in-chief — no such office existed in the Confederacy; Halleck's only counterpart was Davis, or at least a fraction of him — but rather as commander of the Department of Northern Virginia. Having rejected the notion of reinforcing Vicksburg — "The distance and the uncertainty of the employment of the troops are unfavorable," he told Seddon — Lee based his present advice on what was good or bad for his department and the soldiers in his charge. "I considered the problem in every possible phase," he subsequently explained, "and to my mind, it resolved itself into a choice of one of two things: either to retire to Richmond and stand a siege, which must ultimately have ended in surrender, or to invade Pennsylvania." Placed in that light, the alternatives were much the same as if the cabinet members were being asked to choose between certain defeat and possible victory. In fact, "possible" became *probable* with Robert E. Lee in charge of an invasion launched as the aftermath of Fredericksburg and Chancellorsville, triumphs scored against the same adversary and against longer odds than he would be likely to encounter when he crossed the Potomac with the reunited Army of Northern Virginia. Seddon and Benjamin, Secretary of the Treasury Christopher G. Memminger,

Attorney General Thomas H. Watts, and Secretary of the Navy Stephen R. Mallory all agreed with the gray-bearded general "whose fame," as one of them said, "now filled the world." They were not only persuaded by his logic; they were awed by his presence, his aura of invincibility. And this included Davis, who had seldom experienced that reaction to any man.

It did not include Postmaster General John H. Reagan. He was by no means persuaded by Lee, and such awe as he felt for any living man was reserved for Jefferson Davis, whom he considered self-made and practical-minded like himself. Born in poverty forty-five years ago in Tennessee, Reagan had been a schoolteacher and a Mississippi plantation overseer before he was eighteen, when he moved to Texas with all he owned tied up in a kerchief. Passing the bar, he had gone into Lone Star politics and in time won election to Congress, where service on the postal committee prepared him for his present assignment. In this he already had scored a singular triumph, unequaled by any American postmaster in the past seventy-five years or indeed in the next one hundred. Under Reagan's watchful eye, the Confederate postal department did not suffer an annual deficit, but yielded a clear profit. He accomplished this mainly by forcefulness and vigor, and now he employed these qualities in an attempt to persuade Davis and his fellow cabinet members that no victory anywhere, even in Washington itself, could offset the disaster that would result from the loss of the Mississippi. The only man present whose home lay beyond that river, he said plainly that he thought Lee was so absorbed in his masterful defense of Virginia that he did not realize the importance of the Transmississippi, which would be cut off from the rest of the country with the fall of Vicksburg. It had been claimed that Lee's advance might result in Grant's withdrawal to meet the challenge, but Reagan did not believe this for an instant. Grant was committed, he declared. The only way to stop him from accomplishing his object was to destroy him, and the only way to destroy him was to move against him with all possible reinforcements, including Longstreet's two divisions from Lee's army. As for the talk of co-operation expected from those with antiwar sentiments in the North — this too had been advanced as an argument for invasion; the peace movement had been growing beyond the Potomac — Reagan agreed with Beauregard as to "the probability that the threatened danger to Washington would arouse again the whole Yankee nation to renewed efforts for the protection of their capital." In short, he saw everything wrong with Lee's plan and everything right about the plan it had superseded. Grant was the main threat to the survival of the Confederacy, and it was Grant at whom the main blow must be aimed and struck.

Davis and the others heard both men out, and when the two had had their say a vote was taken. In theory, the cabinet could reject Lee's proposal as readily as that of any other department commander, Bragg or

Pemberton or Beauregard, for example, each of whom was zealous to protect the interests of the region for which he was responsible. But that
was only in theory. This was Lee, the first soldier of the Confederacy —
the first soldier of the world, some would assert — and this was, after
all, a military decision. The vote was five to one, in the general's favor.
Davis concurring, it was agreed that the invasion would begin at the
earliest possible date.

Pleased with the outcome and the confidence expressed, Lee
went that evening to pay his respects to a Richmond matron who had
done much to comfort the wounded of his army. As he took his leave,
it seemed to a young lady of the house — much as it had seemed earlier
to five of the six cabinet members — that he was clothed in glory. "It
was broad moonlight," she was to write years later, "and I recall the
superb figure of our hero standing in the little porch without, saying
a last few words, as he swung his military cape around his shoulders. It
did not need my fervid imagination to think him the most noble looking mortal I had ever seen. We felt, as he left us and walked off up the
quiet leafy street in the moonlight, that we had been honored by more
than royalty."

Again Reagan had a different reaction. Unable to sleep because of
his conviction that a fatal mistake had been made that day at the White
House, he rose before dawn — it was Sunday now, May 17; Pemberton
would be routed at high noon on the Big Black, and Johnston was advising the immediate evacuation of Vicksburg — to send a message urging Davis to call the cabinet back into session for a reconsideration of
yesterday's decision. Davis did so, having much the same concern for
Mississippi as Lee had for Virginia — his brother and sisters were
there, along with many lifelong friends who had sent their sons to help
defend the Old Dominion and now looked to him for deliverance from
the gathering blue host — but the result of today's vote, taken after
another long discussion, was the same as yesterday's: five to one, against
Reagan. Lee returned to the Rappahannock the following day, which
was the first of many in the far-off Siege of Vicksburg.

The problems awaiting him at Fredericksburg were multitudi-
nous and complex. Chancellorsville, barely two weeks in the past and
already being referred to as "Lee's masterpiece," had subtracted nearly
13,000 of the best men from his army. Of these, in time, about half
would be returning; but the other half would not. And of these last, as
all agreed, the most sorely missed was Jackson. "Any victory would be
dear at such a price," Lee declared. He found it hard to speak of him, so
deep was his emotion at the loss. "I know not how to replace him," he
said — and, indeed, he did not try. Instead he reorganized the army,
abandoning the previous grouping of the infantry into two corps, of
four divisions each, for a new arrangement of three corps, each with
three divisions. The new ninth division thus required was created by de-

taching two brigades from A. P. Hill's so-called Light Division, the largest in the army, and combining them with two brought up from Richmond and North Carolina; Henry Heth, Hill's senior brigadier, was given command, along with a promotion to major general. Similarly, one division was taken from each of the two existing corps — Anderson's from the First and what was left of Hill's from the Second — in order to fill out the new Third. The problem of appointing corps commanders was solved with equal facility. Longstreet of course would remain at the head of the First Corps, whose composition was unchanged except for the loss of Anderson; McLaws, Pickett, and Hood were in command of their three divisions, as before. The Second Corps went to Richard S. Ewell, Jackson's former chief subordinate, who opportunely returned to the army at this time, having recovered from the loss of a leg nine months ago at Groveton. A. P. Hill got the new Third Corps, which was scarcely a surprise; Lee had praised him weeks ago to Davis as the best of his division commanders, and moreover a good half of the troops involved had been under him all along. Promotion to lieutenant general went to both Ewell and Hill. Jubal Early kept the division he had led since Ewell's departure, and W. Dorsey Pender succeeded Hill, under whom he had served from the outset. He was promoted to major general, as was Robert Rodes, who was confirmed as commander of the division that had spearheaded the flank attack on Hooker. Major General Edward Johnson, returning to duty after a year-long absence spent healing the bad leg wound he had suffered at McDowell, the curtain raiser for Jackson's Valley Campaign, completed the roster of corps and division commanders by taking over the Second Corps division which had been temporarily under Colston. The artillery was reshuffled, too, and the general reserve abolished, so that each corps now had five battalions; William Pendleton, the former Episcopal rector, retained his assignment as chief of the army's artillery, though the title was merely nominal now that the reserve battalions had been distributed, and he remained a brigadier. Stuart, on the other hand, gained three new brigades of Virginia cavalry, brought in from various parts of the state in order to add their weight to the three he already had for the offensive. As a result of all these acquisitions, supplemented by volunteers and conscripts forwarded from all parts of the nation as replacements for the fallen, the army was almost up to the strength it had enjoyed before the subtractions of Fredericksburg and Chancellorsville. Approximately 75,000 effectives — in round figures, 5000 artillery, 10,000 cavalry, and 60,000 infantry — stood in its ranks. The infantry order of battle was as follows:

I. LONGSTREET	II. EWELL	III. A. P. HILL
McLaws	Early	Anderson
Pickett	Johnson	Heth
Hood	Rodes	Pender

The arrangement seemed pat and apt enough, but there were those who had objections no less sharp for being silent. Longstreet for instance, perhaps chagrined that Lee had not consulted him beforehand, resented Hill's promotion over the head of McLaws, whom he considered better qualified for the job. Aside from that, Old Peter was of the opinion that the post should have gone to Harvey Hill, on duty now in his home state of North Carolina. "His record was as good as that of Stonewall Jackson," the Georgian later wrote, "but, not being a Virginian, he was not so well advertised." There was, he thought, "too much Virginia" on the roster — and there were, in fact, apparent grounds for the complaint. Of the fifteen most responsible assignments in the army, ten were held by natives of the Old Dominion, including Lee himself, Ewell and Hill, Stuart, Early and Johnson, Pickett, Rodes and Heth, and Pendleton. Georgia had two, Longstreet and McLaws; Texas had Hood, South Carolina Anderson, and North Carolina, which furnished more than a quarter of Lee's troops, had only the newly promoted Pender; while Mississippi and Alabama, which furnished three brigades apiece, had no representative on the list at all.

Lee too saw possible drawbacks and shortcomings to the arrangement, though not with regard to the states his leading generals came from. His concern was rather with the extent of the reorganization, which placed two of his three corps and five of his nine divisions under men who previously had served either briefly or not at all in their present capacities. Moreover, though his brigadiers were the acknowledged backbone of his army, six of the thirty-seven brigades were under new commanders, and another half dozen were under colonels whom he considered unready for promotion. This troubled him, though not as much as something else. Always in his mind was the missing Jackson, whose death had been the occasion for the shake-up now in progress and of whom he said, "I never troubled myself to give him detailed instructions. The most general suggestions were all that he needed." Lee's proposed solution was characteristically simple. "We must all do more than formerly," he told one general. And this applied as much to himself as it did to anyone; especially as far as "detailed instructions" were concerned. The sustaining factor was the army itself, the foot soldiers, troopers, and cannoneers who had never failed him in the year since the last day of May, 1862, when Davis gave him the command amid the half-fought confusion of Seven Pines. He was convinced, he declared within ten days of the anniversary of his appointment, "that our army would be invincible if it could be properly organized and officered." Of the troops themselves, the rank and file who carried the South's cause on their bayonets, he had no doubts at all. "There never were such men in an army before," he said. "They will go anywhere and do anything if properly led."

Another known quantity, or at any rate an assumed one, was

James Longstreet. "My old warhorse," Lee had called him after Sharpsburg, a battle which Old Peter had advised against fighting — "General," he had said to Lee on entering Maryland, "I wish we could stand
still and let the damned Yankees come to us" — but which at least was
fought in the style he preferred, with the Confederates taking up a
strong defensive position against which the superior blue forces were
shattered, like waves against a rock. Fredericksburg, where his corps
had suffered fewer than 2000 casualties while inflicting about 9000, had
confirmed his predilection in that respect, and he considered Chancellorsville the kind of flashy spectacle the South could ill afford. Facing
what Lincoln called "the arithmetic," he perceived that four more such
battles, in which the Confederates were outnumbered two to one and
inflicted casualties at a rate of three for four, would reduce Lee's army
to a handful, while Hooker would be left with the number Lee had had
at the outset. Disappointed by the rejection of his proposal that he
take Hood and Pickett west for an assault on Rosecrans, the burly
Georgian listened with disapproval as Lee announced his intention to
launch an offensive in the East. He protested, much as Reagan had
done, but with no more success; Lee's mind was made up. So Longstreet contented himself with developing his theory — or, as he thought,
advancing the stipulation — that the proposed invasion be conducted
in accordance with his preference for receiving rather than delivering
attack when the two armies came to grips, wherever that might be. As
he put it later, quite as if he and Lee had been joint commanders of the
army, "I then accepted his proposition to make a campaign into Pennsylvania, provided it should be offensive in strategy but defensive in tactics, forcing the Federal army to give us battle when we were in strong
position and ready to receive them."

Lee heard him out with the courtesy which he was accustomed
to extend to all subordinates, but which in this case was mistaken for a
commitment. He intended no such thing, of course, and when he was
told years later that Longstreet had said he so understood him, he refused
to believe that his former lieutenant had made the statement. But Old
Peter had said it, and he had indeed received that impression at the time;
whereby trouble was stored up for all involved.

In any case, once Lee had completed the groundwork for his
plans, he wasted no time in putting them into execution. Four days
after his May 30 announcement of the army's reorganization, and just
one month after Chancellorsville, he started McLaws on a march up
the south bank of the Rappahannock to Culpeper, near which Hood
and Pickett had been halted on their return from Suffolk. Rodes
followed on June 4, and Early and Johnson the next day, leaving Hill's
three divisions at Fredericksburg to face alone the Union host across the
river. Hooker's balloons were up and apparently spotted the movement,

for the bluecoats promptly effected a crossing below the town. It was rumored that Lee had expressed a willingness to "swap queens," Richmond for Washington, in case Hooker plunged south while his back was turned. However, the validity of the rumor was not tested; Hill reported the bridgehead was nothing he could not handle, and Lee took him at his word. Riding westward in the wake of Longstreet and Ewell, he joined them at Culpeper on June 7.

Stuart had been there more than two weeks already, getting his cavalry in shape for new exertions, and two days before Lee's arrival he had staged at nearby Brandy Station a grand review of five of his brigades, including by way of finale a mock charge on the guns of the horse artillery, which lent a touch of realism to the pageant by firing blank rounds as the long lines of grayjackets bore down on them with drawn sabers and wild yells. Stirred or frightened by this gaudy climax, several ladies fainted, or pretended to faint, in the grandstand which Jeb had had set up for them along one side of the field. To his further delight, the army commander agreed to let him restage the show for his benefit on the day after his arrival, though he insisted that the finale be omitted as a waste of powder and horseflesh. Despite this curtailment, the performance was a source of pride to the plumed chief of cavalry, who, as Lee wrote home, "was in all his glory." It was something more, as well; for another result of this second review was that he still had most of his 10,000 troopers concentrated near Brandy on June 9 for what turned out to be the greatest cavalry battle of the war.

Thirty-nine-year-old Alfred Pleasonton, recently promoted to major general as successor to Stoneman, had eight brigades of cavalry, roughly 12,000 men, grouped in three divisions under Brigadier Generals John Buford, David Gregg, and Judson Kilpatrick. All were West Pointers, like himself, and all were of the new hell-for-leather style of horsemen who had learned to care more for results than they did for spit and polish. Buford, the oldest, was thirty-seven; Gregg was thirty; Kilpatrick was twenty-seven. Supported by two brigades of infantry, Pleasonton moved upriver from Falmouth on June 8, with six of his brigades, which gave him a mounted force equal in strength to Stuart's, and crossed at dawn next morning at Beverly and Kelly's fords, above and below Rappahannock Station. Instructed to determine what Lee was up to, there in the V of the rivers where Pope had nearly come to grief the year before, he got over under cover of the heavy morning fog and surprised the rebel pickets, who were driven back toward Brandy, five miles away, with the blue riders hard on their heels. And so it was that Stuart, who had pitched his headquarters tent on Fleetwood Hill overlooking the field where the two reviews were held, got his first sight of the Yankees at about the same time he received the first message warning him that they were over the river at Beverly Ford. Two of his present five brigades, under Rooney Lee and Brigadier General William E. Jones, were already in that direction, contesting the advance. Fitz Lee's brigade was seven miles north, beyond the Hazel River, and the other two, under Wade Hampton and Brigadier General Beverly Robertson, were in the vicinity of Kelly's Ford, where Pelham had fallen twelve weeks ago today. Stuart sent couriers to alert the brigades to the north and south, then rode forward to join the fight Lee and Jones were making, about midway between Beverly Ford and Fleetwood Hill. However, he had no sooner gotten the situation fairly well in hand on that quarter of the field than he learned that another enemy column of equal strength had eluded the pickets at Kelly's Ford and was riding now into Brandy Station, two miles in his rear. The result, as he regrouped his forces arriving from north and south to meet the double threat, was hard fighting in the classic style, headlong charges met by headlong countercharges, with sabers, pistols, and carbines employed hand to hand to empty a lot of saddles. He lost Fleetwood Hill, retook it, lost it again, and again retook it. Near sundown, spotting rebel infantry on the march from Brandy — his own infantry had been engaged only lightly — Pleasonton fell back the way he had come, effecting an orderly withdrawal. He had lost 936 men, including 486 taken prisoner, as compared to the Confederate total of 523, but he was well satisfied with his troopers and their day's work on the rebel side of the Rappahannock.

Stuart expressed an equal if not greater satisfaction. After all, he retained possession of the field, along with three captured guns, and had inflicted a good deal more damage than he had suffered: except perhaps in terms of pride. For there could be no denying that he had been surprised, on his own ground, or that the Yankees had fought as hard — and, for that matter, as well — as his own famed gray horsemen, at least one of whom was saying, even now, that the bluecoats had been successful because he and his fellows had been "worried out," all the preceding week, by the grand reviews Jeb staged out of fondness for "military foppery and display." One thing was clear to Stuart at any rate. Such exploits as he hoped to perform in the future, enhancing his already considerable reputation, were going to be more difficult to bring off than those he had accomplished in the days when the blue troopers were comparatively inept. Doubtless his solution was the same as the army commander's. "We must all do more than formerly," Lee had said, and for Jeb this meant more, even, than the two rides around McClellan.

Approaching the field of battle that afternoon, Lee experienced the double shock of learning that his normally vigilant chief of cavalry had suffered a surprise and of seeing his son Rooney being carried to the rear with an ugly leg wound. However, he did not let either development change his plans for the march northward; which were as follows. While Longstreet remained at Culpeper, in position to reinforce Hill in case Hooker tried to swamp him, Ewell would move into and down the

Shenandoah Valley, preceded by Stuart's sixth brigade of cavalry, en route from Southwest Virginia under Brigadier General Albert Jenkins. When Ewell reached the Potomac, he was to cross into Maryland and strike out for Pennsylvania without delay. Longstreet then would advance northward, east of the Blue Ridge, thus preventing Union penetration of the passes, while Hill marched west from Fredericksburg and followed Ewell down the Valley and over the Potomac, to be followed in turn by Longstreet, who would leave Stuart to guard the Blue Ridge passes until the combined advance of 60,000 butternut infantry into Pennsylvania caused the Washington authorities to call the Army of the Potomac northward across the river from which it took its name.

Lee's plan was a bold one, but it had worked well against Lincoln and McClellan in September and it seemed likely to work as well against Lincoln and Hooker nine months later. The most questionable factor was Ewell, whose corps would not only set the pace for the rest of the army, but would also be the first to encounter whatever trouble lay in store for the Confederates in the North. In effect, this meant that he was being required to march and fight with the same fervor and skill as his former chief and predecessor, and whether he could ever become another Jackson was extremely doubtful, especially since he was not even the same Ewell, either to the ear or eye, who had fought under and alongside the dead Wizard of the Valley. In partial compensation for the loss of his leg — though this seemed in fact to bother him very little, either on horseback or afoot — he had made two acquisitions. One was religion, which tempered his language, and the other was a wife, which tempered his whole outlook. Formerly profane, he now was mild in manner. Formerly of modest means, he now was wealthy, having won the hand of a rich widow who in her youth had rejected his suit in order to marry a man with the undistinguished name of Brown. Now that she and her extensive property were in his charge, Old Bald Head could scarcely believe his luck, and sometimes he forgot himself so far as to introduce her as "My wife, Mrs Brown." Whether this new, gentled Ewell would measure up to such high expectations was the subject of much discussion around the campfires of all three corps, particularly his own; but it soon appeared that all the worry had been for nothing. Out in the Valley, the scene of former military magic, his firm grasp of strategy and tactics, coupled with a decisiveness of judgment, a good eye, and an eagerness to gather all the fruits of sudden victory, made it seem to former doubters that another Stonewall had indeed been found to lead the Second Corps and inspire the army.

He moved northward on the day after Stuart's fight at Brandy Station, entered the Valley by way of Chester Gap, and on June 13, having divided his corps at Front Royal the day before, marched on Winchester with Early and Johnson while Rodes and the cavalry struck at Berryville. Major General Robert Milroy had 5100 bluecoats at the former place, and Ewell was out to get them, along with an 1800-man detachment at the latter, ten miles east. As it turned out, the Berryville force made its getaway due to blunders by Jenkins, who was unfamiliar with the kind of work expected of horsemen in Lee's army, but the success of the operation against Winchester more than made up for the disappointment. Warned to fall back, Milroy chose to stand his ground, much as Banks had done in a similar predicament the year before. That hesitation had led to Banks's undoing, and so now did it lead to Milroy's. Charged by Early on the 14th from the west, he retreated northeastward in the darkness, only to be intercepted at dawn by Johnson some four miles up the Harpers Ferry road at Stevenson's Depot, where he was routed. The Union general managed to escape with a couple of hundred of his troopers, but his unmounted men had no such luck in outrunning their pursuers, who gathered them up in droves. Johnson himself — called "Old Clubby" by his soldiers because he preferred to direct their combat maneuvers with a heavy walking stick instead of a sword — asserted happily that he had taken thirty prisoners "with his opera glass" before he ended his private chase by falling off his horse and into Opequon Creek. Milroy was presently removed from command by Lincoln, but that was a rather superfluous gesture, since practically all of his command had already been removed from him by Ewell. The total bag, in addition to the infliction of 443 casualties on the immediate field of battle, was 700 sick and 3358 able-bodied prisoners, 23 fine guns, and some 300 well-stocked wagons: all at a cost of 269 Confederate casualties, less than fifty of whom were killed. Ewell's triumph over Milroy was even greater than Jackson's had been over Banks on that same field: a fact that was not lost on the men of the Second Corps, whose final doubts as to the worth of their new commander were forgotten. Moreover, like Stonewall, Old Bald Head did not sit down to enjoy in leisure the spoils and glory he had won. Pushing Jenkins forward to the Potomac before sundown, he had Rodes follow on June 16 for a crossing at Williamsport, Maryland, where a halt was called to allow the other two divisions to catch up for a combined advance into Pennsylvania.

Lee had already put the other two corps in motion. On June 15, while Ewell was gathering prisoners in the woods and fields near Winchester, Longstreet started north from Culpeper, and Hill — who reported that Hooker had abandoned his west-bank bridgehead and withdrawn his army from its camps around Falmouth the day before, apparently for a concentration at or near Manassas, where he would stand athwart Lee's path in case the unpredictable Virginian launched a direct drive on Washington from Culpeper — left Fredericksburg, under instructions to follow Ewell's line of march to the Potomac. Two days later, Lee himself moved north, establishing headquarters at Berryville on the 19th, while Stuart fought a series of thunderous cavalry engagements at Aldie, Middleburg, and Upperville, in all of which he was successful at keeping his hard-riding blue opponents from discovering what was afoot beyond the mountains that screened the Valley from the Piedmont. Pleased with Jeb's recovery of his verve, the army commander listened with sympathy to the cavalry chief's suggestion that he leave two brigades of horsemen to plug the gaps of the Blue Ridge and move with the other three into Hooker's rear, the better to annoy and delay him when he started north across the Potomac. Lee approved, in principle, but warned that once it became clear that Fighting Joe was crossing the river, Stuart "must immediately cross himself and take his place on our right flank," where he would be needed to screen the northward advance and keep the invading army informed of the movements of the defenders. Aware of his former cadet's fondness for adventure at any price, Lee sent him written instructions on June 22, repeating the warning that he must not allow himself to be delayed in joining the rest of the column when the time came. Next day, when Stuart reported the bluecoats lying quiet in their camps north of Manassas and suggested that a crossing of the Potomac to the east of them by his three mobile brigades would help to mislead Hooker as to Lee's intentions, Lee followed his first message with a second, re-emphasizing the need for close observance of the Federals, but adding: "You will, however, be able to judge whether you can pass around their army without hindrance, doing them all the damage you can, and cross the river east of the mountains. In either case, after crossing the river, you must move on and feel the right of Ewell's troops, collecting information, provisions, etc." The dispatch ended on a note of caution. "Be watchful and circumspect in all your movements," Lee told Stuart.

Meanwhile the infantry was marching rapidly. By June 24, Ewell's main body had cleared Hagerstown and his lead division was at Chambersburg, twenty miles beyond the Pennsylvania line, with orders to press on to the Susquehanna. Presumably the North was in turmoil, having been warned that the penetration would be deep. "It is said," the Richmond *Whig* had reported the week before, "that an artificial leg ordered some months ago awaits General Ewell's arrival in the city of Philadelphia." Hill and Longstreet crossed the Potomac that same day, at Shepherdstown and Williamsport, and Lee himself made camp that night on the south bank, opposite the latter place, intending to cross over in the morning. Before he did so, however, he received from the President a reply to a letter written two weeks before, in which Lee had made certain admissions in regard to the present national outlook and had suggested some maneuvers he thought might be available to the Confederacy, not only on the military but also on the diplomatic front. "Our resources in men are constantly diminishing," he had written, "and the disproportion in this respect between us and our enemies, if they continue united in their efforts to subjugate us, is steadily augmenting." This being so, he thought the proper course would be to promote divi-

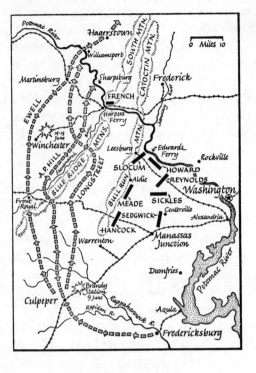

sion in the northern ranks by encouraging those who favored arbitration as a substitute for bloodshed. "Should the belief that peace will bring back the Union become general," Lee continued, "the war would no longer be supported, and that, after all, is what we are interested in bringing about. When peace is proposed to us, it will be time enough to discuss its terms, and it is not the part of prudence to spurn the proposition in advance, merely because those who wish to make it believe, or affect to believe, that it will result in bringing us back to the Union." If this was sly, it was also rather ingenuous, particularly in its assumption of such a contrast between the peoples of the North and South that the latter would be willing to resume fighting if negotiations produced no better terms than a restoration of the Union, whereas the former would be willing to concede the Confederacy's independence rather than have the war begin again. Perceiving the risk involved — after all, it might turn out the other way around — Davis contented himself with remarking that encouragement of the followers of the northern peace party was a commendable notion, especially now that a second invasion was being launched at them. Lee replied next morning, as he prepared to cross the Potomac, that he was "much gratified" by the President's approval of his views. He suggested, moreover, that Bragg at Tullahoma and Buckner at Knoxville take the offensive against the Union center and thus "accomplish something in Ohio." Beauregard, too, could share in the delivery of the all-out blow about to be struck for southern independence, Lee said, by bringing to Culpeper such troops as he could scrape together on the Seaboard for a feint at Washington. This "army in effigy," as Lee called it, would have at least a psychological effect, particularly with the Hero of Manassas at its head, since it probably would cause Lincoln to make Hooker leave a portion of his army behind when he started north to challenge the invaders of Pennsylvania. Of course, it was rather late for such improvisations, but Lee suggested them anyhow. "I still hope that all things will end well for us in Vicksburg," he said in closing, unaware that this was the day Grant exploded the mine that transferred the slave Abraham's allegiance to the Union. "At any rate, every effort should be made to bring about that result." And with that, having advanced such recommendations as he thought proper in connection with the supreme endeavor he was about to make with the Army of Northern Virginia, he mounted Traveler and rode in a heavy rain across the shallow Potomac.

This was the week of the summer solstice, and the land was green with promise as Lee rode northward, this day and the next. "It's like a hole full of blubber to a Greenlander!" Ewell had exclaimed as he passed this way the week before. Hill and Longstreet agreed, finding that his heavy requisitions of food and livestock had scarcely diminished the pickings all around. Marches were so rapid over the good roads that some outfits enjoyed "breakfast in Virginia, whiskey in Maryland, and supper in Pennsylvania." Struck by the contrast to the ravaged, fought-over region in which they had spent most of the past two years, the Confederates gazed wide-eyed at the lush fields and cattle and the prosperity of the citizens who tilled and tended them. A Texas private wrote home in amazement that the barns hereabouts were "positively more tastily built than two thirds of the houses in Waco." The sour looks of the natives had no repressive effect on the soldiers, who "would ask them for their names so we could write them on a piece of paper, so we told them, and put it in water as we knew it would turn to vinegar." Spirits were high all down the long gray column. "Och, mine con-tree!" the lean marchers called out to the stolid men along the roadside, or: "Here's your played-out rebellion!" The Pennsylvanians in turn were impressed by the butternut invaders, so different from their own well-turned-out militiamen, who had fallen back northward at the approach of Ewell's outriders the week before. "Many were ragged, shoe-less, and filthy," a civilian wrote, but all were "well armed and under perfect discipline. They seemed to move as one vast machine." Others found that the obvious admiration the rebels felt for this land of plenty did not necessarily mean that they preferred it to their homeland. The farms were too close together for their liking, and they complained of the lack of trees and shade, which made the atmosphere seem cramped and unfit for leisure. Even the magnificent-looking horses, the great Percherons and Clydesdales, turned out to be a disappointment in the end. Consuming about twice the feed, they could stand only about half the hardship required of what one artilleryman called "our compact, hard-muscled little horses. . . . It was pitiful later," he added, "to see these great brutes suffer when compelled to dash off at full gallop with a gun, after pasturing on dry broom sedge and eating a quarter of feed of weevil-eaten corn." Nor was the qualified reaction limited to those from whom it might have been expected. A housewife, questioning a Negro body servant who was attending his North Carolina master on the march, tested his loyalty by asking him if he was treated well, and she got a careful answer. "I live as I wish," he told her, "and if I did not,

I think I couldn't better myself by stopping here. This is a beautiful country, but it doesn't come up to home in my eyes."

Apparently Lee felt much the same way about it, for at Chambersburg on June 27 — he had arrived the day before and pitched his headquarters tent just east of town in a roadside grove called Shetter's Woods, where the townspeople came in normal times for picnics and such celebrations as the one planned for the Fourth of July, a week from now — he told "a true Union woman" who asked him for his autograph: "My only desire is that they will let me go home and eat my bread in peace." He said this despite the fact that his ride northward had in some ways resembled a triumphal procession, beginning with a gift of fresh raspberries just after he crossed the Potomac. Though Marylanders noted that he had aged considerably in the ten months since his previous visit, the gray commander on the iron-gray horse still impressed them as quite the handsomest man they had ever seen. "Oh, I wish he was ours!" a girl who was waving a Union flag exclaimed with sudden fervor as he passed through Hagerstown, and in Pennsylvania when a civilian whispered in awe as he rode by, "What a large neck he has," a nearby Confederate was quick with an explanation: "It takes a damn big neck to hold his head." The "perfect discipline" remarked on by civilians as the butternut columns wound past their houses and left them unmolested was the result of a decision Lee had made before leaving Virginia. "I cannot hope that Heaven will prosper our cause when we are violating its laws," he said. "I shall therefore carry on the war in Pennsylvania without offending the sanctions of a high civilization and of Christianity." Accordingly, he had instructed his commissary officers to meet all the necessities of the army by formal requisition on local authorities or by direct purchase with Confederate money. Exhorting his troops "to abstain with most scrupulous care from unnecessary or wanton injury to private property," he issued at Chambersburg today a general order commending them for their good behavior so far on the march. "It must be remembered that we make war only upon armed men," he told them, "and that we cannot take vengeance for the wrongs our people have suffered without lowering ourselves in the eyes of all whose abhorrence has been excited by the atrocities of our enemies, and offending against Him to whom vengeance belongeth, without whose favor and support our efforts must all prove in vain."

In part these words were written, and enforced, with an eye to the encouragement of the northern peace movement. Whether anything would come of that remained to be seen, but the effect on the men to whom the order was addressed was all that could have been desired. No army had ever marched better or with so little straggling. Longstreet and Hill had their two corps in bivouac at Chambersburg and Fayetteville, six miles east, and their men were in excellent spirits, well rested and far better shod and clad and fed than they had been when they were up this way the year before. Ewell by now was well along with his independent mission; Early was within half a dozen miles of York, and the other two divisions were at Carlisle, a short day's march from the Susquehanna and Harrisburg, which Ewell had been authorized to capture if it "comes within your means." This now seemed likely, and Lee was prepared to follow with the other two corps as soon as Stuart arrived to shield his flank and bring him news of what the Federals were up to on the far side of the Potomac. But there was the rub; Lee had heard nothing from Stuart in three days. This probably meant that Jeb and his picked brigades were off on the "ride" Lee had authorized on the 23d, but he seemed either to have ignored the admonition to "take his place on our right flank," which was highly improbable, or else to have run into unforeseen difficulties: which might mean almost anything, including annihilation, except that it was hard to imagine the irrepressible Stuart being caught in any box he could not get out of. Still, the strain of waiting was beginning to tell on Lee, who spent much of his time poring over a large-scale map of western Maryland and southern Pennsylvania which Stonewall Jackson had had prepared that winter, with just such a campaign as the present one in mind.

Another legacy from Jackson was a sixty-one-year-old West Pointer named Isaac Trimble, one of his favorite brigadiers, who reported for duty to Lee in Shetter's Woods today, having recovered at last from a leg wound received ten months ago. "Before this war is over," he had told Stonewall, "I intend to be a major general or a corpse." His promotion having come through in April, he had been slated for command of the division that had gone to Edward Johnson, but his injuries had been so slow to heal — in part, no doubt, because of his age — that it had been necessary to go ahead without him. There could be no question of his superseding Old Clubby, who had done so well at Winchester, yet Lee had no intention of losing the services of so hard a fighter as this veteran of all the Second Corps victories from First through Second Manassas, even though there was no specific command to give him that was commensurate with his rank. Ewell was moving against Harrisburg, Lee told Trimble; "go and join him and help him take the place." Before he left, however, Lee drew him into conversation about the terrain just beyond the mountains to the east. Trimble, who had been chief engineer of a nearby railroad before the war, replied that there was scarcely a square mile in that direction that did not contain excellent ground for battle or maneuver. Lee seemed pleased at that, and he told why. "Our army is in good spirits, not overfatigued, and can be concentrated in twenty-four hours or less." Not having heard from Stuart to the contrary — as he surely would have done if such had been the case — he assumed that the Federals were still on the far side of the Potomac, and he outlined for Trimble his plans for their destruction. "When they hear where we are, they will make forced

marches to interpose their forces between us and Baltimore and Philadelphia. They will come up, probably through Frederick, broken down
with hunger and hard marching, strung out on a long line and much
demoralized. When they come into Pennsylvania, I shall throw an overwhelming force on their advance, crush it, follow up the success, drive
one corps back on another, and by successive repulses and surprises, before they can concentrate, create a panic and virtually destroy the
army."

Stirred by this vision of the Army of the Potomac being toppled
like a row of dominoes, Trimble said that he did not doubt the outcome
of such a confrontation, especially since the morale of the Army of
Northern Virginia had never been higher than it was now. "That is, I
hear, the general impression," Lee replied, and by way of a parting gesture he laid his hand on the dead Jackson's map, touching the region
just east of the mountains that caught on their western flanks the rays
of the setting sun. "Hereabouts we shall probably meet the enemy and
fight a great battle," he said, "and if God gives us the victory, the war
will be over and we shall achieve the recognition of our independence."

One of the place names under his hand as he spoke was the college
town of Gettysburg, just over twenty miles away, from which no less
than ten roads ran to as many disparate points of the compass, as if it
were probing for trouble in all directions.

★ ★ ★

At sundown of that same June 27, as Trimble said goodbye to Lee
and left for Carlisle to join Ewell, a courier left Washington aboard a
special train for Hooker's headquarters, established just that afternoon at
Frederick. Though he thus was risking capture by rebel cavalry, which
was known to be on the loose, the documents he carried would admit
of no delay. In the past ten months, the army had fought four major battles under as many different commanders — Bull Run under Pope, Antietam under McClellan, Fredericksburg under Burnside, and Chancellorsville under Hooker — all against a single adversary, Robert Lee,
who could claim unquestionable victory in three out of the four: especially the first and the last, of which about the best that could be said
was that the Federal army had survived them. Now it was about to fight
its fifth great battle, and the import of the messages about to be delivered
was that it would fight it under still a fifth commander.

Not that Hooker had not done well in the seven weeks since
Chancellorsville. He had indeed: especially in the past few days, when
by dint of hard and skillful marching he managed to interpose his
100,000 soldiers between Lee and Washington without that general's
knowledge that the blue army had even crossed the river from which it
took its name. The trouble was that, despite his efforts to shift the
blame for the recent Wilderness fiasco — principally onto Stoneman

and Sedgwick and Howard's rattled Dutchmen — he could not blur a
line of the picture fixed in the public mind of himself as the exclusive
author of that woeful chapter. In early June, for example, the Chicago
Tribune defined its attitude in an editorial reprinted in papers as far away
as Richmond: "Under the leadership of 'fighting Joe Hooker' the glorious Army of the Potomac is becoming more slow in its movements,
more unwieldy, less confident of itself, more of a football to the enemy,
and less an honor to the country than any army we have yet raised."
There was much in this that was unfair — particularly in regard to slowness, a charge Hooker had refuted once and would refute again — but it
was generally known, in and out of army circles, that his ranking corps
commander, Darius Couch, had applied for and been granted transfer
to another department in order to avoid further service under a man he
judged incompetent. Moreover, this mistrust was shared to a considerable extent by the authorities in Washington. Stanton and Halleck had
never liked Joe Hooker, and Lincoln had sent him at the outset a letter
which made only too clear the doubts that had attended his appointment. These doubts had been allayed for a time by the boldness and
celerity of his movements preceding the May Day confrontation in the
Wilderness, when he came unglued under pressure and revived them.
Now they were back, and in force: as was shown by the day-to-day correspondence between himself and Lincoln, made voluminous by his determination to avoid all possible contact with Halleck, whom he regarded with reciprocal distaste.

On June 4, when Lowe's balloonists reported some Confederates
gone from their camps across the Rappahannock, Hooker interpreted this
as the opening movement of an offensive elsewhere, probably upriver,
and reasoned that the most effective way to stop it was to launch one of
his own, here and now. Next morning, after directing the establishment
of a west-bank bridgehead for this purpose, he wired Lincoln that he
thought his best move would be "to pitch into [Lee's] rear," and he
asked: "Will it be within the sphere of my instructions to do so?" Lincoln replied promptly, to the effect that it would not. He had, he said,
"but one idea which I think worth suggesting to you, and that is, in
case you find Lee coming to the north of the Rappahannock, I would by
no means cross to the south of it. . . . In one word, I would not take
any risk of being entangled upon the river, like an ox jumped half over
a fence and liable to be torn by dogs, front and rear, without a fair
chance to gore one way or kick the other." Halleck followed this up
with some advice of his own. "Lee will probably move light and rapidly," he warned. "Your movable force should be prepared to do the
same." Hooker did as he was told, alerting his troops for a sidling movement up the north bank, but he maintained the bridgehead, not only as a
possible means of learning what the enemy was up to, but also on the
off-chance that the authorities might decide to give him his head after

all. On June 10, hearing from Pleasonton that rebel infantry had been spotted in force at Brandy Station the day before, he showed that he too, though he considered the Washington defenses quite strong enough to withstand attack, was willing to risk a swap of queens in the presently deadly chess game. If Lee had taken a good part of his army west to Culpeper, Hooker wired Lincoln, "will it not promote the true interest of the cause for me to march to Richmond at once? . . . If left to operate from my own judgment, with my present information, I do not hesitate to say that I should adopt this course as being the most speedy and certain mode of giving the rebellion a mortal blow." Once more Lincoln was prompt in reply. Unlike Davis, who believed that the best defense of his capital was a threat to the enemy's, he was plainly horrified at this notion of removing the army from its present tactical position between Lee and Washington. Besides, he said, "If you had Richmond invested today, you would not be able to take it in twenty days; meanwhile your communications, and with them your army, would be ruined. I think Lee's army, and not Richmond, is your true objective point. If he comes toward the Upper Potomac, follow on his flank and on his inside track, shortening your lines whilst he lengthens his. Fight him, too, when opportunity offers. If he stays where he is, fret him and fret him."

Next morning Hooker began the movement north, conforming to the pattern set by Lee, but maintaining what Lincoln called the "inside track." This meant that he was required to keep between the Confederates and the capital in his rear, a limitation he found irksome. Moreover, though he knew the rebels had been reinforced for the campaign now fairly under way, his own army was far below the strength it had enjoyed when it marched on Chancellorsville. Nearly 17,000 men had fallen there, and an equal number of short-term enlistments had expired in the past six weeks. As a result of these subtractions, by no means offset by the trickle of recruits, barely 100,000 effectives left the familiar camps around Falmouth in the course of the next four days. To facilitate the march, which would be a hard one, he divided his army into two unequal wings, one led by John Reynolds, consisting of his own corps and those under Sickles and Howard, and the other by Hooker himself, consisting of those under Meade, Sedgwick, Slocum, and Hancock, who had succeeded Couch. "If the enemy should be making for Maryland, I will make the best dispositions in my power to come up with him," he assured Lincoln on June 14: only to receive from him a message sent at the same time. Foreseeing disaster in the present threat to Milroy, the Commander in Chief wanted something more from Fighting Joe than words of reassurance. "If the head of Lee's army is at Martinsburg and the tail of it on the Plank road between Fredericksburg and Chancellorsville," he wired, "the animal must be very slim somewhere. Could you not break him?" Strung out on the roads as he was by now, having abandoned the bridgehead he had held for more than a week, there was nothing Hooker could do for the present but keep marching, and that was what he did. Hancock's corps, the last to go, pulled out of Falmouth on June 15, the day that A. P. Hill left Fredericksburg and Ewell's lead division began its crossing of the Potomac. A simultaneous dispatch from Halleck, warning against "wanton and wasteful destruction of public property," snapped the string of Hooker's patience, and he got off an urgent wire to Lincoln: "You have long been aware, Mr President, that I have not enjoyed the confidence of the major general commanding the army, and I can assure you so long as this continues we may look in vain for success." This sounded as if he was saying he lacked confidence in himself, "the major general commanding the army," but it was Old Brains he meant, and Lincoln knew it. "To remove all misunderstanding," he replied, "I now place you in the strict military relation to General Halleck of a commander of one of the armies to the general-in-chief of all the armies. I have not intended differently, but as it seems to be differently understood, I shall direct him to give you orders and you to obey them."

The sting of this was somewhat relieved by a covering letter in which the Chief Executive explained that all he asked was "that you will be in such mood that we can get into our action the best cordial judgment of yourself and General Halleck, with my own poor mite added, if indeed he and you shall think it entitled to any consideration at all." However, it had begun to seem to Hooker that Lincoln's advice in regard to Lee — "fret him and fret him" — was also being applied in regard to himself, not only by the general-in-chief but also by the President, whose "poor mite" often made up in sharpness for what it lacked in weight. It seemed to Hooker that he was being goaded, and unquestionably he was. One after another his proposals had been dismissed as rash, or else they had been urged upon him only after subsequent instructions had placed his army in an attitude from which they could no longer be accomplished. Urgent appeals for reinforcements were rejected out of hand, as were others that his authority be extended to include the soldiers in the capital defenses. More and more, as the long hot days of hard and dusty marching went by, it came to seem to Fighting Joe that he commanded his army only in semblance, though it was clear enough at the same time that his was the head on which the blame would fall in event of the disaster he saw looming. Leapfrogging his headquarters northward, first to Dumfries and then to Fairfax, with no information as to what was occurring beyond his immediate horizon, he complained at last to Halleck, on June 24, that "outside of the Army of the Potomac I don't know whether I am standing on my head or feet." The next two days were spent crossing the Potomac at Edwards Ferry and effecting a concentration around Frederick. His plan was to strike westward into the Cumberland Valley, severing Lee's communica-

tions with Virginia, and for this he wanted the co-operation of the
10,000 men at Harpers Ferry, which was beyond the limits of his control, but which he thought should be evacuated before Lee turned and
gobbled up the garrison as he had done in September. On the evening of
June 26, believing that the authorities might have learned from that example — at least they had learned to post the troops on Maryland
Heights, occupation of which had permitted the Confederates to take
the place in short order the time before, along with some 12,000 men
and 73 cannon — Hooker wired Halleck: "Is there any reason why
Maryland Heights should not be abandoned after the public stores and
property are removed?" Halleck replied next morning: "Maryland
Heights have always been regarded as an important point to be held
by us, and much expense and labor incurred in fortifying them. I cannot approve their abandonment, except in case of absolute necessity."

Convinced that the garrison was "of no earthly account" on its
perch above the Ferry, Hooker decided to appeal through channels to
Stanton and Lincoln. "All the public property could have been secured
tonight," he wired back, "and the troops marched to where they
could have been of some service. Now they are but a bait for the rebels,
should they return. I beg that this may be presented to the Secretary of
War and His Excellency the President." While waiting for an answer, he
either decided the appeal should be strengthened or else he lost his head
entirely. Or perhaps, having taken all he could take from above, he really
wanted to get from under. At any rate, before the general-in-chief
replied, Fighting Joe got off a second wire to him, hard on the heels of
the first. "My original instructions require me to cover Harpers Ferry
and Washington," it read. "I have now imposed upon me, in addition,
an enemy in my front of more than my number. I beg to be understood,
respectfully, but firmly, that I am unable to comply with this condition
with the means at my disposal, and earnestly request that I may at once
be relieved from the position I occupy." This was sent at 1 p.m. The
long afternoon wore slowly away; the sun had set and night had fallen
before he received an answer addressed to "Major General Hooker,
Army of the Potomac." Whether the word *commanding* had been
omitted by accident or design he could not tell. Nor was the body of
the message at all conclusive on that point. "Your application to be relieved from your present command is received," Halleck told him. "As
you were appointed to this command by the President, I have no
power to relieve you. Your dispatch has been duly referred for Executive action."

The wire was headed 8 p.m. and that was where duplicity came
in. Halleck knew that the special train had left Washington half an hour
before that time, for the courier aboard it was Colonel James A. Hardie,
his own assistant adjutant general, and Old Brains himself had written
the documents he carried, one an order relieving Hooker of command

and the other a letter of instructions for his successor. Reaching Frederick well after midnight, Hardie did not wait for morning. Nor did he call first on Joe Hooker. Rather, he went directly to the tent of the man who would succeed him: George Meade.

This would come as something of a shock to the army, especially to Reynolds and Sedgwick, who ranked him, but no one was more surprised than Meade himself. His immediate reaction, on waking out of a sound sleep at 3 o'clock in the morning to find the staff officer standing beside his cot, was alarm. He thought he was about to be arrested. Sure enough, after a brief exchange of greetings, during which Meade wondered just what military sin he had committed, Hardie's first words were: "General, I'm afraid I've come to make trouble for you." And with that, changing the nature if not the force of the shock, he handed him Halleck's letter of instructions, which began: "You will receive with this the order of the President placing you in command of the Army of the Potomac."

Shortly before, in a letter to his wife, Meade had commented on "the ridiculous appearance we present of changing our generals after each battle," and only two days ago, amid rumors that Hooker was slated for removal, he had written her that he stood little chance of receiving the appointment, not only because he was outranked by two of his six fellow corps commanders, but also "because I have no friends, political or others, who press or advance my claims or pretensions." Yet now he had it, against all the odds, and with it a cluster of problems inherited on what was obviously the eve of battle. Partly, though — if he could believe what Halleck told him — these problems were reduced at the very outset. "You will not be hampered by any minute instructions from these headquarters," the letter read. "Your army is free to act as you may deem proper under the circumstances as they arise." His main duty would be to cover Washington and Baltimore. "Should General Lee move upon either of these places, it is expected that you will either anticipate him or arrive with him so as to give him battle." By way of stressing the fact that the new commander would have a free hand, Halleck added: "Harpers Ferry and its garrison are under your direct orders." Knowing the difficulties Hooker had encountered on this question, Meade could scarcely believe his eyes. "Am I permitted, under existing circumstances," he inquired by telegraph, later that same day, "to withdraw a portion of the garrison of Harpers Ferry, providing I leave sufficient force to hold Maryland Heights against a *coup de main?*" Promptly the reply came back: "The garrison at Harpers Ferry is under your orders. You can diminish or increase it as you think the circumstances justify."

Meanwhile the new commander had called on Hooker, who reacted to the order with as much apparent relief as Lincoln and Halleck had felt in issuing it. In fact, nothing in Fighting Joe's five-month tenure,

in the course of which the army had experienced much of profit as well
as pain, became him more than the manner in which he brought it to a
close. Conferring with Meade on his plans and dispositions, he was co-
operative and pleasant, except for one brief flare-up when Meade, looking over the situation map, remarked that the various corps seemed
"rather scattered." Then Hooker quieted down, issued a farewell address urging support for his successor — "a brave and accomplished officer, who has nobly earned the confidence and esteem of this army on
many a well-fought field" — and got into a spring wagon, alongside
Hardie, for the ride to the railroad station. Meade shook his hand, stood
for a moment watching the wagon roll away, then turned and entered
the tent Hooker had just vacated. Presently he was interrupted by Reynolds, who had put on his dress uniform to come over and congratulate
his fellow Pennsylvanian. This had a good effect on those who had
wondered what his reaction would be: the more so because those closest
to him knew that he had gone to Washington early that month, when
it was rumored that Fighting Joe was about to get the ax, to tell Lincoln
that he did not want the command — for which, with Couch gone, he
was next in line — unless he was allowed more freedom of action than
any of the army's five unfortunate chieftains had been granted up to
then. Now, if not before, Reynolds had his answer, and he took it with
aplomb. Sedgwick too arrived to offer congratulations and assurance of
support, having managed to assuage the burning in his bosom which the
announcement had provoked. News that it was Meade who would head
the army, and not himself, had reached Uncle John while he was out for
his morning ride. For him, as for most old soldiers, the tradition of
seniority was a strong one. Putting the spurs to his horse, he led his
staff on a hard gallop for some distance to relieve his agitation, then
rode over to shake the hand of the man who had passed him by.

That hand was a busy one just now, getting the feel of the controls even as the vehicle was headed for a collision. Meade's own elevation called for other promotions and advancements beyond those recently conferred in the wake of Chancellorsville, which in turn had
followed hard upon another extensive shake-up after bloody Fredericksburg. As a result, not one of the seven army corps was commanded now
by the general who had led it into battle at Antietam, and the same was
true of all but two of the nineteen infantry divisions — Humphreys' and
Alpheus S. Williams' — only four of which were commanded by major
generals: Doubleday, Birney, Newton, and Carl Schurz. Of the fifteen
brigadiers in charge of divisions, seven had been appointed to their
posts since early May: John C. Caldwell, Alexander Hays, James Barnes,
Romeyn B. Ayres, Samuel W. Crawford, Horatio G. Wright, and
Francis Barlow. Equally new to their positions were Hancock and
George Sykes, successors to Couch and Meade as corps commanders.
In fact, only Reynolds and Slocum had the same division commanders

they had had at Chancellorsville: Doubleday, James S. Wadsworth, and John C. Robinson with the former, Williams and John W. Geary with the latter. Other drawbacks there were, too. In contrast to Lee, all of whose corps and division commanders were West Pointers except for one V.M.I. man, Meade had only fourteen academy graduates among the twenty-six generals who filled those vital positions in the Army of the Potomac. This meant that nearly half were nonprofessionals, and of these a number were political appointees: Dan Sickles for example, for whom Meade had small use, either military or private. He had, how-ever, for whatever it was worth, a better geographical distribution among his generals than Lee had achieved. Eight were Pennsylvanians and seven were New Yorkers, while three were from Connecticut, two from Maine, two from Germany — Schurz and Adolf von Steinwehr, both of course in Howard's corps — and one each from Vermont, Mas-sachusetts, Maryland, and Virginia. The revised order of battle was as follows:

I. REYNOLDS	II. HANCOCK	III. SICKLES	V. SYKES
Wadsworth	Caldwell	Birney	Barnes
Doubleday	Gibbon	Humphreys	Ayres
Robinson	Hays		Crawford

VI. SEDGWICK	XI. HOWARD	XII. SLOCUM
Wright	Barlow	Williams
Howe	Steinwehr	Geary
Newton	Schurz	

Doubtful as were the qualities of a sizable proportion of these men, one third of whom had been assigned to their current posts within the past eight weeks, none was more of a military question mark than the man who had just been given the most responsible job of all. This doubt was not so much because of any lack of experience; Meade had performed well, if not brilliantly, in combat as the commander of a brigade, a divi-sion, and a corps. If at Chancellorsville, through no fault of his own, he had been denied an appreciable share in the battle, at Fredericksburg his had been the only division to achieve even a brief penetration of the rebel line, and surely this had been considered by Lincoln — along with Rey-nolds' unacceptable stipulation and Sedgwick's alleged poor showing in early May, of which Hooker had complained — in making his choice as to who was to become the army's sixth commander. The question, rather, was whether Meade could inspire that army when pay-off time came round, as it was now about to do. He seemed utterly incapable of provok-ing the sort of personal enthusiasm McClellan and Hooker could arouse by their mere presence; Burnside and Pope, even the hapless McDowell, seemed downright gaudy alongside Meade, who gave an impression of professorial dryness and lack of juice. What he lacked in fact was glamour, not only in his actions and dispatches, but also in his appearance, which a journalist said was more that of "a learned pundit than a soldier." Two birthdays short of fifty, he looked considerably older, with a "small and compact" balding head, a grizzled beard, and outsized pouches under eyes that were "serious, almost sad," and "rather sunken" on each side of what the reporter charitably described as "the late Duke of Wellington class of nose." The over-all effect, although "decidedly patrician and distinguished," was not of the kind that brought forth cheers or a wholesale tossing of caps, particularly when it was known to be combined with a hair-trigger temper and a petulance which tested in turn the patience of his staff. "What's Meade ever done?" was a common response among the men — those outside his corps, at least — when they heard that he was their new commander. The general himself had few delusions on this score. "I know they call me a damned old snapping turtle," he remarked.

Whatever other shortcomings he might have, in addition to lacking glamour, it presently was shown that indecision was not one of them: at least not now, in these first hours. "So soon as I can post myself up, I will communicate more in detail," he had closed an early-morning telegram accepting the appointment to command. By midafternoon, having studied Hooker's plans and dispositions, along with intelligence reports on Lee — reports which, incidentally, turned out to be extremely accurate; "The enemy force does not exceed 80,000 men and 275 guns," he was told by Maryland observers who kept tally on what passed through Hagerstown, and this was within 5000 men and 3 guns of agreement with Lee's own figures, which included his scattered cavalry — Meade had decided on a course of action and had already begun to issue orders that would put it into execution. "I propose to move this army tomorrow in the direction of York," he wired Halleck at 4.45 p.m. This meant that he had rejected Hooker's plan for a westward strike at Lee's supply line. Moreover, the decision was made irrevocable by dispatches, not only recalling the units that had gone in that direction, but also ordering French to march eastward to Frederick with 7000 men while the remainder of the garrison served as train guards for the Harpers Ferry stores, which were to be removed at once to the capital defenses. Meade thus was adopting what had seemed to him at the outset the only proper course for him to take in conformity with his orders from above: "I must move toward the Susquehanna, keeping Washington and Baltimore well covered, and if the enemy is checked in his attempt to cross the Susquehanna, or if he turns toward Baltimore, to give him battle." Reynolds was retained as commander of the three corps in the lead on the swing north, and a warning order went out soon after sundown for the whole army to "be ready to march at daylight tomorrow. . . . Strong exertions are required."

That meant early reveille and breakfast in the dark, but the men had grown accustomed to this in the two weeks they had spent on the road since leaving the Rappahannock. All the same, and even though they had taken what Lincoln called the "inside track," the pace had been killing — Slocum's corps, as an extreme example, had covered thirty-three hot dusty miles in a single day while moving up to Fairfax — with the result that straggling had been worse than at any time since the berry-picking jaunt to First Bull Run, just three weeks short of two full years ago. For the most part, those who fell out managed to catch up at night and start out with their units in the morning, but enough had dropped out permanently, skulking in barns along the way, to bring the army's total down to 94,974 effectives of all arms. Then — on June 28, by coincidence a Sunday — had come a day of rest, occasioned by the change of commanders, and now they were off again. Although they did not know just where they were going, at any rate they were glad it was not back to the Old Dominion. "We have marched through some beautiful country," a colonel wrote home. "It is refreshing to get out of the barren desert of Virginia and into this land of thrift and plenty." One thing was practically certain, however, and this was that the road they now were taking led to battle. But that was all right, too, apparently, despite the tradition of defeat which had been lengthened under Burnside and Hooker and was a part of Meade's inheritance. "We felt some doubt about whether it was ever going to be our fortune to win a victory in Virginia," another soldier afterwards recalled, "but no one admitted the possibility of a defeat north of the Potomac."

★ ★ ★

For Lee, this same Sunday had been a day of puzzlement, mounting tension, and frustration. He not only did not know of the early-morning switch in blue commanders; he did not even know that for the past two days the whole Federal army had been on the same side of the Potomac as his own. Such ignorance might have been expected to be the opposite of disturbing — a maxim even described it as "bliss"— except that, as he knew only too well, having had occasion to prove it to several opponents, a lack of information was all too often the prelude to disaster. A recent prime example of this was Hooker, of whom Jackson had said on the ride to Guiney Station: "He should not have sent away his cavalry. That was his great blunder. It was that which enabled me to turn him, without his being aware of it, and to take him by the rear." Now Lee himself was in somewhat the same danger, and for somewhat the same reason. For the better part of a week he had heard nothing at all from Stuart, on whom he had always depended for information, or from any of his six brigades. One was at Carlisle with Ewell, approaching the Susquehanna; two were guarding the Blue Ridge passes, far to the south; while the other three, presumably, were off on another of those circumferential "rides" that had brought fame to their plumed leader. This last was not in itself the reason for Lee's anxiety. After all, he himself had authorized the adoption of such a course. What bothered him was the silence, which was as complete as if a sound-proof curtain had been dropped between him and his one best source of information. Scarcely an officer who approached him there in Shetter's Woods today escaped the question: "Can you tell me where General Stuart is?" or: "Where on earth is my cavalry?" or even: "Have you any news of the enemy's movements? What is the enemy going to do?"

No one had ever heard him ask such things before, for the simple reason that he had never needed to ask them; Stuart had generally supplied the answers in advance. And now, for lack of answers, he was obliged — as most of his opponents, to their distress in the course of the past year, had been obliged — to fall back on uninformed conjecture. This summoned up a host of alarming possibilities, including the danger that the bluecoats might be contemplating an attack on thinly defended Richmond or on his even more thinly defended supply line in the Cumberland Valley: both of which maneuvers had in fact been proposed by Hooker and disallowed by Lincoln. One would be about as unwelcome to Lee as the other in the present dispersed condition of his army, one third of which was a good forty miles from Chambersburg, where the remaining two thirds were in profitless bivouac and so completely stripped of cavalry that the foraging was being done by soldiers mounted on horses from the artillery and the wagon train. However, for all his inward anxiety, which he masked as best he could behind a show of being calm and even cheerful, Lee not only let his dispositions stand; he sent word for Ewell to continue the advance on Harrisburg, and prepared to move the rest of his army in that direction the following day, first Longstreet and then Hill, both of whom were put on the alert. "If the enemy does not find us," he explained, "we must try to find him, in the absence of the cavalry, as best we can." So he said, continuing the attempt to mask his growing concern. But still he asked all comers: "Can you tell me where General Stuart is?" and "Where on earth is my cavalry?"

Perhaps it was just as well, so far at least as his temper was concerned, that no one within range of his voice could give him the answer, which was not of a nature to relieve his qualms. In fact, it might well have upset him more than did the tantalizing silence. For even as he inquired of various callers as to the whereabouts of his cavalry on this Sunday afternoon, Stuart and the more than 5000 troopers of his three best brigades were on the northeast fringe of Washington, some seventy miles away. That was as the crow flew, moreover, and for anyone but a crow it would have been considerably farther, not only because Jeb had no more notion of Lee's whereabouts than Lee had of his, but also because a good many of those intervening miles were occupied by the Federal army, which Lee mistakenly assumed to be still south of the Potomac but which in fact was being alerted even now for a resumption of its northward march at dawn. This meant that Stuart would face tomorrow the same frustration he had faced today, and indeed for the past three days as well, in attempting to carry out his instructions to make contact with the right flank of the Confederate army of invasion; Hooker had stood in his path, and so would Meade. It had been that way from the outset, just after midnight June 24, when he first left Salem and moved east, beyond the Bull Run Mountains, to find a heavy column of blue infantry marching squarely athwart the route he had chosen for what was intended to be not only the greatest of all his "rides," but also indemnity for the ugly things some of the southern papers had been saying about him ever since the surprise they claimed he had suffered a couple of weeks ago at Brandy Station.

His plan, based on information that the bluecoats were inactive in their camps east of the mountains and were scattered over so wide an area that he would be able to push his way between two of their corps in order to get beyond them for a crossing of the Potomac in their rear, had been workable the day before, when the information was true; but it was true no longer. By coincidence, Hooker began his northward march to the Potomac shortly before Stuart emerged from Glasscock's Gap on the morning of June 25, and that was how it happened that Jeb found his progress blocked by a whole corps of Federals in motion across his front. Promptly he unlimbered the six guns he had brought along and began to shell the passing column, which extended north and south for a greater distance than the eye could follow. He thus was mindful of Lee's instructions to do the enemy "all the damage you can," but the admonition included in the same letter, that he was not to attempt his favorite maneuver unless he found he could do so "without hindrance," was ignored. Turning off to the south, he camped for the night near Buckland, intending to swing wide around the enemy rear next morning. However, dawn showed the Federals gone, and he rode east through Bristoe and Brentsville, not sighting a single bluecoat all day long, to bivouac just south of Occoquan Creek, which he crossed at Wolf Run Shoals next morning, June 27. In better than fifty hours he had covered less than forty miles of road, and he was about as far from the nearest Potomac ford as he had been when he started. Moreover, horses and men were beginning to show how hard they had been worked these past two weeks, fending off the aggressive blue troopers at such places as Middleburg and Aldie before undertaking their present exertions deep in the enemy rear. Frequent halts were necessary for rest and feeding, no matter how Stuart chafed when he remembered that his orders had been to cross the Potomac as soon as practicable after the 24th, three days ago.

Pressing northward, first through Fairfax Station, where he captured most of a 100-man detachment of New York cavalry, and then to Fairfax Court House, where he called a halt to let his hungry troopers "go through" several sutler shacks and graze their horses, he struck the

Leesburg-Alexandria turnpike and turned left along it for Dranesville, which he reached soon after sundown. Smoldering campfires were evidence that Federal infantry had recently passed this way and were still in the vicinity, guarding the better Potomac fords upstream; so he swung due north for a crossing at Rowser's Ford, which was deep and wide and booming. "No more difficult achievement was accomplished by the cavalry during the war," a staff officer later declared. The guns went completely out of sight, and the ammunition was distributed among the men, who kept it above water by carrying it over in their arms. By 3 o'clock in the morning, June 28 — as Meade awoke to find Hardie standing beside his cot — the entire command, one member said, "stood wet and dripping on the Maryland shore." Stuart let his troopers sleep till dawn, then resumed the march, mindful of his orders to "take position on General Ewell's right, place yourself in communication with him, guard his flank, keep him informed of the enemy's movements, and collect all the supplies you can for the use of the army." The trouble was he did not know Ewell's position, any more than he knew Lee's, except that Ewell would "probably move toward the Susquehanna." Jeb's decision to move in that direction, too, was easily arrived at. The whole Union army was to the west; the heavily-manned Washington defenses were to the east; all that was left — unless he gave the project up and retraced his steps southward, which apparently never crossed his mind — was north, and that was the way he went.

By midday he was in Rockville, a town on the National Road, which ran from Washington through Frederick, present headquarters of the Army of the Potomac, and thence on out to Ohio. Rockville was thus on the main Federal supply route, and scouts reported a train of 150 mule-drawn wagons on the way there from the capital, whose outskirts were less than a dozen miles away. Soon they came in sight and the raiders bore down on them, whooping in hungry anticipation of a feast. "The wagons were brand new, the mules fat and sleek, and the harness in use for the first time," one trooper later wrote. "Such a train we had never seen before and did not see again." Though almost half were captured at that first swoop, the other teamsters got their wagons turned around and took off down the road at a hard trot. For a time it looked as if they might be able to outrun the weary rebel horses, but presently a wagon overturned and caused a pile-up, blocking the road for all but about two dozen of the others, whose drivers continued their race for safety, still pursued, until the gray riders came within full view of Washington itself and abandoned the chase. Even without the ones that got away, the spoils were rich, including 400 teamsters, 900 mules, and 125 wagons loaded with hams, bacon, sugar, hardtack, bottled whiskey, and enough oats to feed the 5000 half-starved mounts of the raiders for several days. Much time was spent at Rockville, paroling the prisoners, feeding the horses, and accepting the admiring glances of some young ladies from a local seminary, who came out waving improvised Confederate flags and requesting souvenir buttons. While all this was going on, Stuart toyed with the notion of making a quick dash into the northern capital, but then rejected it regretfully — for lack of time, he subsequently explained — and resumed his northward march at sundown, hampered somewhat by the "one hundred and twenty-five best United States model wagons and splendid teams with gay caparisons" which he was determined to turn over to Lee, as a sort of super trophy of the ride, when and if he managed to find him.

A twenty-mile night march brought the raiders into Cooksville, where they captured another detachment of blue cavalry on the morning of June 29 before pushing on to Hood's Mill, a station on the B&O about midway between Baltimore and Frederick. While further disrupting the Federal lines of supply and communication by tearing up the tracks there and burning a bridge at Sykeston, three miles east, Stuart inquired of friendly Marylanders as to Ewell's whereabouts. None of them could tell him anything, but newspapers just in from the north reported Confederate infantry at York and Carlisle, moving against Wrightsville and Harrisburg; so Jeb pressed on to Westminster, fifteen miles north, on the turnpike connecting Gettysburg and Baltimore. Arriving in the late afternoon, he gobbled up another mounted blue detachment and made camp for the night. Scouts brought word that Union cavalry was in strength at Littletown, twelve miles ahead and just beyond the Pennsylvania line. Next morning — it was now the last day of June, the sixth he had spent out of touch with the rest of the army — he took the precaution of placing Fitz Lee on the left of the column, assigned Hampton to guard the captured wagons, and rode in the lead with Colonel John R. Chambliss, successor to the wounded Rooney Lee. His immediate objective, another fifteen miles to the north, was Hanover, where he would be able to choose between two good roads, one leading northwest to Carlisle and the other northeast to York, for a hook-up with one or the other of Ewell's reported columns of invasion. What he encountered first at Hanover, however, was a fight. It was an unequal affair, the enemy force amounting to no more than a single brigade, but what the blue horsemen lacked in numbers they made up for in vigor. A sudden charge struck and shattered the head of the gray column, and Stuart himself was obliged to take a fifteen-foot ditch jump to avoid being captured along with his blooded mare Virginia. "I shall never forget the glimpse I then saw of this beautiful animal away up in midair over the chasm," a staff officer later wrote, "and Stuart's fine figure sitting erect and firm in the saddle." Bringing up reserves, Jeb drove off the attackers, who in turn were reinforced by another brigade. No serious fighting ensued, however, for while the Federals seemed content to block the road to Gettysburg, a dozen miles to the west, Stuart wanted only to take the road to York, twenty miles to the northeast.

After some desultory long-range firing, the two forces drew apart, the Confederates still hampered by the train of captured wagons and some 400 prisoners, taken here and elsewhere in the past two days since leaving Rockville, where the previous 400 had been paroled.

This called for another night march, and the riders who made it remembered it ever after as a nightmare. "It is impossible for me to give you a correct idea of the fatigue and exhaustion of the men and beasts," a lieutenant afterwards said. "Even in line of battle, in momentary expectation of being made to charge, [the men] would throw themselves upon their horses' necks, and even to the ground, and fall to sleep. Couriers in attempting to give orders to officers would be compelled to give them a shake and a word, before they could make them understand." Reaching Dover soon after dawn of the hot first day of July, Stuart learned to his chagrin that there were no Confederates at York, six miles east. They had been there, two days ago, but now they were gone and no one would say where. So he turned the head of the column hard left toward Carlisle, 25 miles northwest, supposing that Ewell had ordered a concentration there. He was wrong: as he discovered when he approached the town that afternoon and found it occupied by Pennsylvania militia, who peremptorily rejected his demand for a surrender. Jeb and his road-worn troopers were in no shape for a fight, even with raw home guardsmen, one of his officers frankly admitted. "Weak and helpless as we were," he wrote home later, "our anxiety and uneasiness were painful indeed. Thoughts of saving the wagons now were gone, and we thought only of how we, ourselves, might escape." Contenting himself with a token long-range shelling of the U.S. cavalry barracks, the plumed commander was at a loss for a next move until well after nightfall, when two scouts who had left the column near York, with instructions to search westward for signs of the army, reported back to Stuart outside Carlisle. They had found Lee and the main body that day at Gettysburg, where a battle was in progress, and Lee had sent them to find and summon the long-absent Jeb, who thus was placed in the unusual position of having the army commander report to him the location of the infantry he had been ordered to get in touch with and protect.

At 1 o'clock in the morning, July 2 — one week, to the hour, since he first set out on the ride that was designed, in part, to retrieve his slipping reputation — Stuart had his troopers on the march for Gettysburg, which was thirty miles away by the nearest road. This was their fifth night march in the past eight days, and it was perhaps the hardest of them all. Southward the weary horses plodded, over Yellow Breeches Creek, through Mount Holly Pass, and across the rolling farmland of Adams County, of which Gettysburg was the county seat. The riders were so exhausted, it was noted, that one who tumbled from his mount slept sprawled across the fence that broke his fall. At dawn they still had miles to go, and even the indefatigable Jeb, though he still clung tenaciously to the train of captured wagons as the one substantial trophy of his ride, could see that a rest halt had to be called if he was to arrive with more than a remnant of his three brigades. It was late afternoon before he reached the field of the greatest battle of the war, having missed all of the first day and most of the second. Lee received him with an iciness which a staff officer found "painful beyond description."

Reddening at the sight of his chief of cavalry, the gray commander raised one arm in a menacing gesture of exasperation. "General Stuart, where have you been?" he said. "I have not heard a word from you in days, and you the eyes and ears of my army." Jeb wilted under this unfamiliar treatment and became so flustered that he played his trump card at the outset. "I have brought you 125 wagons and their teams, General," he announced: only to have Lee reply, "Yes, General, but they are an impediment to me now." Then suddenly Lee softened. Perhaps it was Stuart's obvious dismay or his somewhat bedraggled appearance after eight days in the saddle; or perhaps it was a recollection of all the service this young man had done him in the past. At any rate, a witness recalled years later, Lee's manner became one "of great tenderness" as he added: "Let me ask your help now. We will not discuss this longer. Help me fight these people."

The reason Stuart had encountered none of Ewell's men at York or Carlisle the day before — a Wednesday — was that Lee, acting on information that reached him Sunday night, had recalled them Monday morning. As it was, the tail of Early's column, marching westward on the road through East Berlin and Heidlersburg, had been less than ten miles from the head of Stuart's own at the time he took the risky ditch jump near Hanover on Tuesday. In fact, the foot soldiers had heard the guns of that brief engagement, but had not investigated because Lee, despite his repeated warning to Stuart to be on the lookout for Ewell, had neglected to warn Ewell to be on the lookout for Stuart: with the result that the cavalry's roundabout hegira was prolonged for two more days, including some thirty-odd hours beyond the opening of the battle, which in turn resulted from Lee's groping his way across the Pennsylvania landscape, deprived of his eyes and ears, as he said, and with little information as to the enemy's whereabouts or intentions. Because that ten-mile gap had been ignored — not only ignored, but unsuspected — whatever Lee encountered, good or bad, was bound to come as a surprise, and surprise was seldom a welcome thing in war. And so it was. Coincidents refused to mesh for the general who, six weeks ago in Richmond, had cast his vote for the long chance. Fortuity itself, as the deadly game unfolded move by move, appeared to conform to a pattern of hard luck; so much so, indeed, that in time men would say of Lee, as Jael had said of Sisera after she drove the tent peg into his temple, that the stars in their courses had fought against him.

Such information as he had, and it was meager, had come to him not from Robertson or Jones, whom Stuart had left to guard the Blue Ridge passes, nor from Jenkins, who was off with Ewell, but from a spy — "scout" was the euphemistic word — sent out some weeks before by Longstreet, with instructions to pick up what useful tips he could in the lobbies and barrooms of Washington. His name was Harrison, and no one knew much about him except that he was a Mississippian, bearded and of average height, with sloping shoulders, pale hazel eyes, and an abiding dislike of all Yankees. Lee, for one, apparently considered him unsavory and declined at first to see him when he was brought to Shetter's Woods that Sunday night. "I have no confidence in any scout," he said. Informed by a staff officer, however, that Harrison claimed the Federal army had crossed the Potomac — which Lee could scarcely credit, in the absence of any such report from Stuart — he changed his mind and sent for him, shortly before midnight. Travel-stained and weary, the spy told Lee that

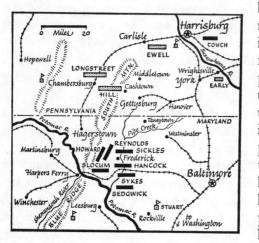

he had been in Frederick that morning, having heard in Washington that Hooker had transferred his headquarters to that place. Arriving he had found it true. At least two corps were there, he said, and others were in the vicinity, with two more pushed out toward South Mountain. After observing all this he had procured a horse and ridden hard for Chambersburg to report to Longstreet, who had sent him on to Lee. Incidentally, he remarked in closing, Hooker had been replaced that day by Meade.

Lee reacted fast — as well he might — to this news that the blue army had been for the past two days on the same side of the Potomac as his own, one of whose corps, in addition to being divided itself, was thirty-odd miles away from the other two, which were threatened in turn by a possible movement against their rear. It was not so much that he feared for his supply line; he was prepared to abandon contact with Virginia anyhow. The trouble was, if the Federals crossed South Mountain and entered the lower Cumberland Valley — as Harrison had claimed they were about to do, and as Hooker in fact had intended — they would force Lee to conform, in order to meet the threat to his rear, and thus deprive him of the initiative he had to retain if he was to conduct the sort of campaign he had in mind. In the absence of his cavalry, moreover, the dispersed segments of his army were in danger of being surprised and swamped by overwhelming numbers: Meade, in short, might do to him what he had planned to do to Hooker — defeat him in detail. What was called for, in the face of this, was a rapid concentration of all his forces, preferably east of the mountains so as to compel the enemy to abandon the threat to his rear. Orders designed to effect this went out promptly. Ewell was instructed to give up his advance on Harrisburg and return at once to Chambersburg with all three of his divisions. Hill and Longstreet, who had just been alerted for a northward march to the Susquehanna, were told to prepare instead for a move on Cashtown, eighteen miles to the east and just beyond South Mountain; the former would start today — it was morning by now, June 29 — the latter tomorrow, which would keep the single road from being clogged. On second thought, and for the same purpose of avoiding a jam, Lee sent a follow-up message to Ewell, suggesting that he remain on the far side of the mountains and march directly to Cashtown or Gettysburg, another eight miles to the east. Simultaneously, couriers hurried south to urge Robertson and Jones to leave the Blue Ridge and join the army in Pennsylvania as soon as possible. A seventh brigade of cavalry, under Brigadier General John B. Imboden, assigned to Lee for use on the invasion but so far only used to guard the western approaches to the lower Cumberland Valley, was also summoned, but since it would be at least two days before these horsemen could get to Chambersburg, Lee told Longstreet to leave one division behind to protect the trains until Imboden arrived. Meanwhile the rest of the army would converge on Cashtown, from which point it could threaten both Washington and Baltimore, thus retaining the initiative by forcing the enemy to turn back east or remain there, in order to keep between the gray invaders and those two vital cities.

All this had been arranged within eight hours of Harrison's report to Lee. But neither the spy nor anyone else could tell him anything of Stuart, who had vanished as if into quicksand. However, an officer who arrived from the south that morning reported that he had met two cavalrymen who told him they had left Stuart on June 27, all the way down in Prince William County, on the far side of Occoquan Creek. Lee was startled to hear this, having learned from Harrison that Hooker had begun to cross the Potomac two full days before that time. Though he kept up a show of confidence for the benefit of subordinates — "Ah, General, the enemy is a long time finding us," he told a division commander; "If he does not succeed soon, we must go in search of him" — Lee was obviously disturbed, and he kept asking for news of Stuart from all callers, none of whom could tell him anything. One more item concerned him, though few of his lieutenants agreed that it should do so. They were saying that Meade was about as able a general as Hooker, but considerably less bold, and they were exchanging congratulations on Lincoln's appointment of another mediocre opponent for them. Lee, who had known the Pennsylvanian as a fellow engineer in the old army, did not agree. "General Meade will commit no blunder on my front," he said, "and if I make one he will make haste to take advantage of it."

While Longstreet marked time at Chambersburg, waiting for Hill to clear the road on which his three divisions were proceeding east to Cashtown, Ewell began his southward march from Carlisle. Greatly disappointed by the cancellation of his plan to occupy the Pennsylvania capital, which he saw as a fitting climax to the campaign that had opened so auspiciously at Winchester and continued for the next two weeks as a triumphal procession through one of the most prosperous regions of the North, Old Bald Head was puzzled by the apparent indecisiveness of his chief. Jackson's orders, enigmatic though they often were, had always been precise and positive; whereas Lee had not only reversed himself by ordering a return to Chambersburg, he had also modified this further by changing the objective to Cashtown or Gettysburg and leaving it up to the corps commander to choose between the two. Unaccustomed to such leeway, which Jackson had never allowed him on any account, Ewell deferred making a final choice until next day, when he would reach Middletown, aptly named because it was equidistant from both of these alternative objectives. Sending word for Early to head west from York and taking up the southward march himself with Rodes while Johnson came along behind with the spoils-laden wagon train, he was also nettled by Lee's additional instructions that if at any point he encountered what he judged to be a large force of the enemy, he was to avoid a general engagement, if practicable, until the other two corps were at hand. This seemed to Ewell a plethora of ifs, and he fumed under the added burden of responsibility, not only for the safety of his corps, but also for the safety of the army, in a situation which, for him at least, was far from clear. Much as he missed his amputated leg, he missed even more the iron guidance of the man under whom he had been serving when he lost it.

Those same precautionary instructions had gone of course to Hill, who was known to have little caution in his make-up. His policy, throughout his year of service under Lee — beginning with the attack that opened the Seven Days offensive, which he had started rolling for the simple reason that he could no longer abide the strain of standing idle — had been to pitch into whatever loomed in his path, with little or no regard for its strength or composition. This had stood the Confederacy in good stead from time to time, especially at Cedar Mountain, where he had saved Stonewall from defeat, and at Sharpsburg, where he had done the same for Lee, whose reference to him in the official report of that battle, "And then A. P. Hill came up," had become a byword in the army. Little Powell was the embodiment of the offensive spirit, here in Pennsylvania as well as back home in Virginia, and so were the troops of his command, who took a fierce pride in the fact. Completing the march to Cashtown that first day, Heth's division went into camp while the other two were still on the road, and hearing that Early's men had overlooked a supply of shoes while passing through Gettysburg the week before, Heth sent his lead brigade forward next morning, June 30, to investigate the rumor. Its commander, Brigadier General Johnston Pettigrew, mindful of Lee's warning not to bring on a battle until the whole army was at hand, prudently withdrew when he encountered Federal troopers along a creekbank west of town, not knowing what number of blue soldiers of all arms might be lurking in rear of the cavalry outposts. He returned to Cashtown late that afternoon, having put his men into bivouac about midway between there and Gettysburg, and reported on the day's events. Heth did not think highly of such wariness. What was more, he wanted those shoes. So he took Pettigrew to Hill and had him repeat the account of what he had seen. Hill agreed with Heth. "The only force at Gettysburg is cavalry," he declared, "probably a detachment of observation." Meade's infantry forces were still down in Maryland, he added, "and have not struck their tents."

Heth was quick to take him up on that. "If there is no objection," he said, "I will take my division tomorrow and go to Gettysburg and get those shoes."

"None in the world," Hill told him.

★ ★ ★

One strenuous objector was there, however, in the person of John Buford, a tough, Kentucky-born regular with a fondness for hard fighting and the skill to back it up. And though Hill was strictly correct in saying that the only bluecoats now in Gettysburg were cavalry, Buford's two brigades were formidable in their own right, being equipped with the new seven-shot Spencer carbine, which enabled a handy trooper to get off twenty rounds a minute, as compared to his muzzle-loading adversary, who would be doing well to get off four in the same span. Moreover, in addition to having five times the firepower of any equal number of opponents, these two brigades were outriders for the infantry wing under Reynolds, whose own corps was camped to-night within six miles of the town, while those under Howard and Sickles were close behind him. Meade had set up army headquarters just south of the state line at Taneytown, about the same distance from Reynolds as Reynolds was from Gettysburg, and all but one of his seven corps — Sedgwick's, off to the east at Manchester — were within easy marching distance of the latter place. He was, in fact, about as well concentrated as Lee was on this last night of June. The Confederates had the advantage of converging on a central point — Ewell at Heidlersburg and Longstreet in rear of Cashtown were each about ten miles from Gettysburg, and Hill was closer than either — whereas the Federals would be marching toward a point that was beyond their perimeter, but Meade had the advantage of numbers and a less congested road net: plus another advantage which up to now, except for the brief September interlude that ended bloodily at Sharpsburg, had been with Lee. The northern commander and his soldiers would be fighting on their own ground, in defense of their own homes.

His march north, today and yesterday, after the day spent getting the feel of the reins, had been made with the intention, announced to Halleck at the outset, "of falling upon some portion of Lee's army in detail" with the full strength of his own. His "main point," he said, was "to find and fight the enemy," since in his opinion "the attitude of the enemy's army in Pennsylvania presents us the best opportunity we have had since the war began." But this morning, receiving information "that the enemy are advancing, probably in strong force, on Gettysburg," he had begun to doubt that that was really what he wanted after all. "Much oppressed with a sense of responsibility and the magnitude of the great interests intrusted to me," as he wrote his wife, he had begun to think that his best course would be to take up a strong defensive position, covering Washington and Baltimore, and there await attack. It was his intention, he declared in a circular issued that afternoon, "to hold this army pretty nearly in the position it now occupies until the plans of the enemy shall have been more fully developed," adding that it was "not his desire to wear the troops out by excessive fatigue and marches, and thus unfit them for the work they will be called upon to perform." He found what he considered an excellent position along the south bank of Pipe Creek, just to the rear of his present headquarters at Taneytown, and he had his engineers start laying it out on the morning of July 1, planning to rally his army there in case Lee came at him in dead earnest. "The commanding general is satisfied that the object of the movement of the army in this direction has been accomplished," he announced in another circular, "viz. the relief of Harrisburg, and the prevention of the enemy's intended invasion of Philadelphia, &c. beyond the Susquehanna. It is no longer his intention to assume the offensive until the enemy's movements or position should render such an operation certain of success." If this was reminiscent of Hooker in the Wilderness, Meade went Fighting Joe one better by making it plain that every corps commander was authorized to initiate a retirement to the Pipe Creek line, not only by his own corps but also by the others, in the event that the rebels made a lunge at him: "The time for falling back can only be developed by circumstances. Whenever such circumstances arise as would seem to indicate the necessity for falling back and assuming this general line indicated, notice of such movement will be at once communicated to these headquarters and to all adjoining corps commanders."

That was a long way from the intention expressed two days ago, "to find and fight the enemy." But the fact was, Meade had already lost control of events before he made this offer to abide by the decision of the first of his chief subordinates who took a notion that the time had come to backtrack. Even as the circular was being prepared and the engineers were laying out the proposed defensive line behind Pipe Creek, John Reynolds was committing the army to battle a dozen miles north of the headquarters Meade was getting ready to abandon. And Reynolds in turn had taken his cue from Buford, who had spread his troopers along the banks of another creek, just west of Gettysburg; Willoughby Run, it was called. "By daylight of July 1," he later reported, "I had gained positive information of the enemy's position and movements, and my arrangements were made for entertaining him until General Reynolds could reach the scene."

Buford was all business and hard action, now as always. A former Indian fighter, he drove himself as mercilessly as he did his men, with the result that he would be dead within six months, at the age of thirty-seven, of what the doctors classified as "exposure and exhaustion." Convinced now that the fate of the nation was in his hands, here on the outskirts of the little college town, the Kentuckian was prepared to act accordingly. A journalist had recently described him as being "of a good-natured disposition, but not to be trifled with," a "singular-looking party ... with a tawny mustache and a little, triangular gray eye, whose expression is determined, not to say sinister." The night before, when one of his brigade commanders expressed the opinion that the rebels would not be coming in any considerable strength and that he would be able to hold them off without much trouble, Buford had not agreed at all. "No, you won't," he said. "They will attack you in the morning and they will come booming — skirmishers three-deep. You will have to fight like the devil until supports arrive."

✗ 2 ✗

That was how they came, three-deep and booming; Heth was on his way to "get those shoes." In the lead today, by normal rotation of the honor, was the Alabama brigade of Maryland-born James Archer. A Princeton graduate who had discovered an aptitude for war in Mexico and had gone on to become a U.S. Army captain and now a Confederate brigadier at the age of forty-six, Archer had fought in every major battle under Lee, from the Seven Days through Chancellorsville, where he led the charge on Hazel Grove that broke the back of the Federal defense. Hill had fallen sick in the night and was confined to his tent in Cashtown this morning, too weak to mount a horse, but with Archer out front he would have all the aggressiveness even he could desire — as was presently demonstrated. Though Pettigrew had warned him the previous evening that he was likely to run into trouble short of

Gettysburg, Archer moved his Alabamians rapidly eastward, down the
Chambersburg Pike, until they topped a rise and came under fire, first
from the banks of a stream in the swale below and then from the slopes
of another north-south ridge beyond, on whose crest a six-gun battery
was in action at a range of three quarters of a mile. That was about 8
o'clock. Archer ordered up a battery of his own, and while it took up
the challenge of the guns across the way, he shook out a triple line of
skirmishers, textbook style, and prepared to continue the advance. But
Heth, who had come to the head of the column by now, decided to
make doubly sure there would be no further delay. He called up a
Mississippi brigade commanded by Brigadier General Joseph R. Davis,
put it on the left of Archer, north of the pike, and sent them forward
together, down into the shallow valley that was floored with the shimmering gold of ripened wheat fields. The two brigades started downhill through the standing grain, the skirmishers whooping and firing as
they went. Just as the Deep South had led the way to secession — Alabama had been fourth and Mississippi second among the original seven
states to leave the Union — so was it leading the way into the greatest
battle of the war that had been provoked by that withdrawal.

Buford's troopers, back across Willoughby Run by now and in
position on McPherson's Ridge, fired their carbines rapidly as the butternut riflemen came at them down the east side of Herr Ridge. But it
was obvious to their general, who had a good view of the scene from
the cupola of a Lutheran seminary on the crest of the next rearward
ridge, about midway between Gettysburg and the one they were defending a mile from town, that his two brigades of dismounted men, one
out of four of whom had to stay behind to hold the horses of the other
three, were not going to be able to hang on long in the face of all that
power. Moreover, reports had reached him from outposts he had established to the north, toward Heidlersburg, that substantial rebel forces
were advancing from there as well. Unless Federal infantry came up
soon, and in strength, he would have to pull out to avoid being swamped
from both directions. At about 8.30, however, as he started down the
ladder, perhaps to give the order to retire, he heard a calm voice asking
from below: "What's the matter, John?" It was Reynolds, whom many
considered not only the highest ranking but also the best general in the
army. Buford shook his head. "The devil's to pay," he said, and he
came on down the ladder. But when Reynolds asked if this meant that
he could not hang on till the I Corps got there, most likely within an
hour, the cavalryman said he reckoned he could; at any rate he would
try. That was enough for Reynolds. He sent at once for Howard and
Sickles, urging haste on the march to join him, then turned to an aide
and gave him a verbal message for Meade at Taneytown. "Tell him the
enemy are advancing in strong force, and that I fear they will get to the
heights beyond the town before I can. I will fight them inch by inch, and

if driven into the town I will barricade the streets and hold them back as long as possible."

He himself rode back to bring up Wadsworth's division, which was leading the march up the Emmitsburg Road, and guided it cross-country, over Seminary Ridge and up the Chambersburg Pike toward McPherson's Ridge, where by now, after two full hours of fighting, Buford's troopers were approaching both the crest of the ridge, uphill in their rear, and the limit of their endurance. Reynolds directed one of Wadsworth's two brigades to the right and the other to the left, to bolster the cavalry and oppose the rebel infantry coming at them. The race was close; he knew that unless he hurried he would lose it. Already the time was past 10 o'clock, and he could see Confederates among the trees of an apple orchard just to the left of where the pike went out of sight beyond the ridge. He turned in the saddle and called back over his shoulder to the infantry trudging behind him: "Forward, forward, men! Drive those fellows out of that! Forward! For God's sake, forward!" Those were his last words. He suddenly toppled from his horse and lay quite still, face-down on the soil of his native Pennsylvania. No one knew what had hit him — including Reynolds himself, most likely — until an aide saw the neat half-inch hole behind his right ear, where the rifle bullet had struck. When they turned him over he gasped once, then smiled; but that was all. He was dead at the age of forty-two, brought down by a rebel marksman in the orchard just ahead. "His death affected us much," a young lieutenant later wrote, "for he was one of the *soldier* generals of the army."

Beyond the ridge, Heth had decided by now that the time had come for him to press the issue with more than skirmishers. He passed the word and Davis and Archer went in with their main bodies, left and right of the turnpike, intending to overrun the rapid-firing blue troopers spread out on the slope before them. Archer's men were thrown into some disorder by a fence they had to climb just west of Willoughby Run, but at last they got over and splashed across the stream. As they started up McPherson's Ridge, however, the woods along the crest were suddenly filled with flame-stabbed smoke and the crash of heavy volleys. This was musketry, not sporadic carbine fire, and then they saw why. Not only were these new opponents infantry, but their black hats told the startled and stalled attackers that this was the Iron Brigade, made up of hard-bitten Westerners with a formidable reputation for hard fighting and a fierce pride in their official designation as the first brigade of the first division of the first corps of the first army of the Republic. Staggered by the ambush and outnumbered as they were, the butternut survivors perceived that the time had come to get out of there, and that was what they did. Splashing back across the stream, however, they piled up again at the high fence and were struck heavily on the outer flank by a Michigan regiment that had worked its way around through the woods to the south. Most got over, but about 75 Confederates were captured while awaiting their turn at the fence: including Archer, who was grabbed and mauled by a hefty private named Patrick Maloney. Exuberant over the size of his catch — as well he might be; no general in Lee's army had ever been captured before — Maloney turned Archer over to his captain, who refused to accept the sword that was offered in formal surrender. "Keep your sword, General, and go to the rear," he told him. "One sword is all I need on this line." A staff lieutenant who had taken no part in the fighting did not see it that way, however, and insisted on having the trophy even after the prisoner explained that it had been declined by the man who was entitled to it. Archer was furious, not only at this but also because of the roughing-up the big Irishman had given him; which accounted in part for his reaction when he was presented to Doubleday, who had succeeded Reynolds as corps commander. "Archer! I'm glad to see you," the New Yorker cried, striding forward with his hand out. They had been friends in the old army, but apparently that meant nothing to Archer now. "Well, I'm not glad to see you by a damn sight," he said coldly, and he kept his hand at his side.

North of the turnpike, the other half of Heth's attack had better success, at least at the start. Though Reynolds even in death had won his race on the Union left, where the Iron Brigade arrived in time to prepare for what was coming, the brigade on the right not only had a longer way to go, and consequently less time for getting set, it also found no covering woods along that stretch of McPherson's Ridge. Davis's men — five regiments scraped together from the Richmond defenses and the Carolina littoral, none of whom had worked together previously and only two of which had ever fought in Virginia — could see what lay before them, and they advanced with all the eagerness of green troops glad of a chance to demonstrate their mettle. One of the five was a North Carolina outfit whose colonel went down early in the charge, shot as he took up the fallen colors, and when another Tarheel officer bent over him to ask if he was badly hurt, he replied: "Yes, but pay no attention to me. Take the colors and keep ahead of the Mississippians." By then the whole line was going in on the double. On the crest ahead, the Federals wavered and then, as Wadsworth sought to forestall a rout by ordering a withdrawal, fell back hastily toward Seminary Ridge. Davis was elated. The President's nephew, he was aware of muttered complaints of nepotism, and he was happy to be proving his worth and his right to the stars on his collar. Yelling in anticipation of coming to grips with the fleeing bluecoats, the attackers swept over the crest of McPherson's Ridge and into the quarter-mile-wide valley beyond. There they funneled into the deep cut of an unfinished railroad bed, which seemed to offer an ideal covered approach to the Federal rear, but which in fact turned out to be a trap. Once in, they found the sides of the cut so high and steep that they could not fire out, and Doubleday, spotting the opportunity, quickly took advantage of it by sending two regiments over from south of the pike, where Archer had just been routed. "Throw down your muskets! Throw down your muskets!" the men in the cut heard voices calling from overhead, and they looked up into the muzzles of rifles slanted down at them from the rim above. Caught thus in a situation not unlike that of fish in a rainbarrel, some 250 graybacks surrendered outright, dropping their weapons where they stood, while casualties were heavy among those who chose to attempt escape by running the gauntlet westward. The reversal was complete. Davis and his survivors fell back across McPherson's Ridge, profoundly shaken by the sudden frown of fortune and considerably reduced from the strength they had enjoyed when they first came whooping over the crest, headed in the opposite direction. Here on the Confederate left, after so brave a beginning, the attackers had wound up with an even worse disaster than had been suffered on the right. Though Davis himself, unlike Archer, had avoided capture, a good half of his men had either been taken prisoner or shot, and the rest were too demoralized to be of any present use at all.

Doubleday was as elated as Davis had been, a short while back. Moreover, his hard-won feeling of security was strengthened by the arrival of the other two divisions of the corps, his own and Robinson's, and close on their heels came Howard, riding in advance of his own corps, which was coming fast and would be there within an hour. Eleven years younger than forty-four-year-old Doubleday, Howard assumed command of the field by virtue of his seniority. While the skirmishers of both armies kept up a racket down in the valley, banging away at each other from opposite banks of Willoughby Run, he reinforced Wadsworth on McPherson's Ridge and continued the long-range artillery duel with rebel batteries on Herr Ridge. It was noon by now; the XI Corps was arriving, under Schurz, and the lines were much the same as they had been four hours ago, when Buford's dismounted troopers were all that held them. Unquestionably, there were a great many butternut soldiers on the field — you could see them plainly across the valley, "formed in continuous double lines of battle," a staff man noted, adding that "as a spectacle it was striking" — but Howard believed he was ready for whatever came his way. Sickles ought to be arriving soon, and he had sent for Slocum as well; that would give him five more divisions, a total of eleven, perhaps by nightfall.... Just then, however, a shell burst in rear of the Union center, followed quickly by another and another, all with such startling accuracy that one regimental commander sent an angry complaint that the supporting guns were firing short. But those were not friendly shells, dropped in error; they were Confederate. A mile north of the Chambersburg Pike, the two eastern ridges merged at a dominant height called Oak Hill, and there an enemy battery was in action, signaling danger to the Federal right, which extended only about half that distance. Coming south across the fields around Oak Hill, directly toward the vulnerable flank, was another gray flood of rebel infantry. One-armed Howard, knowing he had to move fast to meet the threat, bent the north end of Doubleday's line back east, astride Seminary Ridge, and hurried the first two divisions of his own corps across the rolling farmland north of Gettysburg, with instructions for Schurz to form a new line there, at right angles to the first. They barely had time to arrive before the storm burst.

This new gray pressure was brought to bear by Rodes. Like Heth, he was going into battle for the first time as a major general, and just as his fellow Virginian had faced the test without his corps commander at hand to advise him, so too was Rodes on his own, not because Ewell lay sick in his tent, as had been the case with Hill, but because he preferred to ride near the tail of the column in his buggy. Old Bald Head was in a strange mood anyhow, confused by discretionary orders and aggrieved by the sudden abandonment of his advance on Harrisburg, just as he had the place within his grasp. At Middletown that morning, confronted with the necessity for choosing between his alternate objectives, he had had his mind made up for him at last by a note from Hill, informing him that the Third Corps was on its way to Gettysburg; so he had directed Rodes to take the left fork, which led there. Besides, that seemed a convenient point for a junction with Early who was marching from the west, while Johnson, off to the east with the train, could join them there by turning east when he reached Cashtown. By nightfall the corps would be reunited for the first time in a week, but until then Ewell preferred to allow all three division commanders to function independently. Rodes no doubt appreciated the confidence this implied. At any rate, hearing heavy firing up ahead at noon, he quickened the pace and reached Oak Hill about 1.30 to find a golden opportunity spread before him. On parallel ridges extending south from where he stood, Confederates and Federals were disposed in an attitude not unlike that of two animals who had just met and scrapped and then drawn back, still growling, for a better assessment of each other before coming to grips again. What attracted Rodes at first glance was the fact that the enemy flank, half a mile down the eastern ridge, was wide open to an oblique attack from the road along which his division was advancing. He would have to move fast, however, for already the near end of the Union line was beginning to curl back in response to his appearance, and reinforcements were pouring in large numbers from the streets of Gettysburg, taking up positions from which to defend it. This last was quite all right with Rodes. It was not the town he wanted, dead ahead; it was the blue force on the ridge to his right front. Accordingly, after posting one of his five brigades out to the left, with instructions to hold off the still-arriving defenders of the town in case they went over to the offensive — which they well might do; their number by now was larger than his own — he held another brigade in reserve and put the remaining three in line abreast, facing south, for a charge against the flank of the bluecoats on the ridge. All this was quickly done, with no time spared for a preliminary reconnaissance or even the advancement of a skirmish line. By 2 o'clock the alignment had been completed, and Rodes gave his three attack brigades the order to go forward.

They did go forward, but into chaos. Left on its own by the other two brigades — one stalled at the outset; the other drifted wide — the center brigade stepped in midstride into slaughter when a line of Federals, hidden till then, rose from behind a low stone wall, diagonal to the front, and killed or wounded about half of the advancing men with a series of point-blank volleys pumped directly into their flank. Such was the price they paid for the time Rodes saved by foregoing a reconnaissance. The survivors hit the ground alongside the fallen, some making futile attempts to return the decimating fire, while others began waving scraps of cloth in token of surrender. Observing this, their shaken commander, Brigadier General Alfred Iverson, sent word to Rodes that one whole regiment had raised the white flag and gone over to the enemy on first contact. Though Rodes did not credit the hysterical report, he saw only too clearly that he had the makings of a first-class disaster on his hands. Like Heth to the south, he had paid in disproportionate blood for the ready aggressiveness which in the past had been the hallmark of the army's greatest victories, but which now seemed mere rashness and the hallmark of defeat. It had been so for the captured Archer and for Davis, and now it was the same for Iverson, who was so demoralized by what he had seen, or thought he had seen, that he had to turn over to his adjutant the task of trying to extricate his shattered regiments.

It was at this critical juncture that Lee drew near. Riding through the mountains east of Chambersburg that morning, he had heard the rumble of guns in the distance and wondered what it meant. Hill, who had risen from his sickbed at the sound, pale and feeble though he was, and called for his horse in order to go forward and investigate, could tell Lee nothing more than he already knew — namely, that Heth had marched on Gettysburg, with Pender in support — nor could Anderson, whose division was just beyond Cashtown and within half a dozen miles of the ominous booming. Despite repeated warnings that a general engagement was to be avoided until the army was reunited, the noise up ahead was too loud, or anyhow too sustained, for a mere skirmish. Moreover, Lee was aware of Napoleon's remark that at certain edgy times a dogfight could bring on a battle, and it seemed to him that with his infantry groping its way across unfamiliar hostile terrain, in an attempt to perform the proper function of cavalry, this might well be one of those times. He was worried and he said so.

"I cannot think what has become of Stuart," he told Anderson. "I ought to have heard from him long before now. He may have met with disaster, but I hope not." As he spoke he gazed up the road, where the guns continued to rumble beyond the horizon. "In the absence of reports from him, I am in ignorance of what we have in front of us here. It may be the whole Federal army, or it may be only a detachment. If it is the whole Federal force, we must fight a battle here." For once, he did not seem pleased at the prospect of combat, and he spoke of a withdrawal before he knew what lay before him: "If we do not gain a victory, those defiles and gorges which we passed this morning will shelter us from disaster." And having used the word disaster twice within less than a minute, he hurried ahead, as Hill had done before him, to see for himself what grounds there might be for such forebodings.

About 2.30, after passing through Pender's division, which was formed for attack on both sides of the pike but was so far uncommitted, he ascended Herr Ridge to find the smoky panorama of a battle spread before him — a battle he had neither sought nor wanted. Heth had three brigades in line on the slope giving down upon Willoughby Run, and Lee now learned that he had attacked some three hours earlier, due east and on a mile-wide front, only to encounter Federal infantry whose presence he had not even suspected until he saw what was left of his two attack brigades streaming back from a bloody repulse. Since then, belatedly mindful of the warning not to bring on a battle, he had contented himself with restoring his shattered front while engaging the enemy guns in a long-range contest. Lee could see for himself the situation that had developed. Across the way, disposed along the two parallel ridges that intervened between the one on which he stood and Gettysburg, plainly visible two miles to the southeast, the Federals confronted Heth in unknown strength, their right flank withdrawn sharply in the direction of the town, from whose streets more bluecoats were pouring in heavy numbers, in order to meet a new Confederate threat from the north. This was Rodes, just arrived from Heidlersburg, Lee was told, and though his attack was opportune, catching the bluecoats end-on and almost unawares, he was making little headway because he had launched it in a disjointed fashion. At that point Heth came riding up, having heard that Lee was on the field. Anxious to make up for a slipshod beginning, he appealed to the commanding general to let him go back in.

"Rodes is heavily engaged," he said. "Had I not better attack?"

Lee was reluctant. "N-no," he said slowly, continuing to sweep the field with his glasses. It was not that he lacked confidence in Heth, who was not only a fellow Virginian and a distant cousin, but was also the only officer in the army, aside of course from his own sons, whom he addressed by his first name. It was because Lee still had no real notion of the enemy strength, except that it was obviously considerable, and he was by no means willing to risk the apparent likelihood of expanding a double into a triple repulse. "No," he said again, more decisively than before; "I am not prepared to bring on a general engagement today. Longstreet is not up."

But suddenly his mind was changed by what he saw before him. Rodes's right brigade, after drifting wide, came down hard on the critical angle where the Union line bent east, and his reserve brigade, committed after the wreck of Iverson, dislodged the Federals from their position behind the diagonal stone wall, while his left brigade recovered momentum and plunged into a quarter-mile gap between the two blue corps, north and west of Gettysburg. Assailed and outflanked, the eastward extension of Doubleday's line began to crumble as the men who had held it retreated stubbornly down Seminary Ridge. Simultaneously, Howard's two divisions under Schurz—his own, now led by Brigadier General Alexander Schimmelfennig, and Barlow's; the third, Von Steinwehr's, had been left in reserve on the other side of the town —were assaulted by a new gray force that came roaring down the Harrisburg Road—it was Early, arriving from York—to strike their right at the moment when Rodes was probing the gap beyond their left. As a result, this line too began to crumble, but much faster than the other.... On Herr Ridge, Lee saw much of this through his binoculars. Blind chance having reproduced in miniature the conditions of Second Manassas, with Chancellorsville thrown in for good measure, he dropped his unaccustomed cloak of caution and told Hill, who rode up just then, to send both Heth and Pender forward to sweep the field.

They did just that, but only after fierce and bloody fighting, particularly on McPherson's Ridge, south of the pike, where the Iron Brigade was posted. Unleashed at last, Heth's men went splashing across Willoughby Run and up the opposite slope, to and finally over the fuming crest. Heth himself did not make it all the way, having been unhorsed by a fragment of shell which struck him on the side of the head, knocked him unconscious, and probably would have killed him, too, except that the force of the blow was absorbed in part by a folded newspaper tucked under the sweatband of a too-large hat acquired the day before in Cashtown. Hundreds of others in both armies were not so fortunate. Told by Doubleday to maintain his position at all costs, Brigadier General Solomon Meredith, commander of the Iron Brigade, came close to following these instructions to the letter, although he himself, like Heth, was knocked out before the action was half over. The 24th Michigan, for example, had come onto the ridge with 496 officers and men; it left with 97. This loss of just over eighty percent was exceeded only by the regiment that inflicted it, Pettigrew's 26th North Carolina, whose two center companies set new records for battlefield losses that

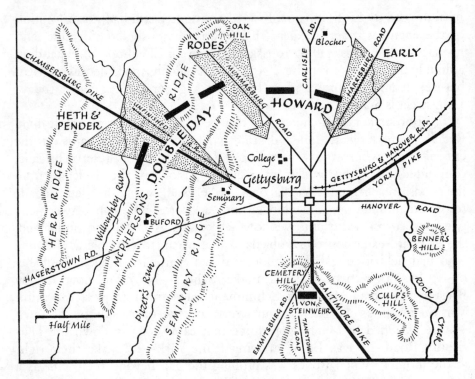

would never be broken, here or elsewhere; one took 83 soldiers into the fight and emerged with only 2 unhit, while the other went in with 91, and all were killed or wounded. Pender, sent forward by Hill as the struggle approached a climax, overlapped the south flank of the defenders and added the pressure that forced them off the ridge. The men of the Iron Brigade fell back at last — 600 of them, at any rate, for twice that many were casualties out of the original 1800 — ending the brief half hour of concentrated fury. "I have taken part in many hotly contested fights," Pettigrew's adjutant later declared, "but this I think was the deadliest of them all." Coming up in the wake of the attack he heard "dreadful howls" in the woods on the ridge, and when he went over to investigate he found that the source of the racket was the wounded of both sides. Several were foaming at the mouth, as though mad, and seemed not even to be aware that they were screaming. He attributed their reaction to the shock of having been exposed to "quick, frightful conflict following several hours of suspense."

  Across the way, Ewell's two divisions were having a much easier time than Hill's. While Rodes was pressing Doubleday steadily southward down Seminary Ridge, widening the gap on the left of the line Schurz had drawn north of the town, Early struck hard at the far right of the Union front, which was exposed to just such a blow as the one that had crumpled that same flank at Chancellorsville, two months ago tomorrow. Most of the men opposing him had been through that experience, and now that they foresaw a repetition of it, they reacted in the same fashion. They broke and ran. First by ones and twos, then by squads and platoons, and finally by companies and regiments, they forgot that they had welcomed the chance to refute in action the ugly things the rest of the army had been saying about them; instead, they took off rearward in headlong flight. Barlow, a twenty-nine-year-old New York lawyer who had finished first in his class at Harvard and volunteered at the start of the war as a private in a militia company, tried desperately to rally the division he had commanded for less than six weeks, but was shot from his horse and left for dead on the field his men were quitting. It was otherwise with Schimmelfennig. A former Prussian officer, ten years older than Barlow and presumably that much wiser, he went along with the rush of his troops, all the way into Gettysburg, until he too was unhorsed by a stray bullet while clattering down a side street, and took refuge in a woodshed, where he remained in hiding for the next three days.

Yelling with pleasure at the sight of the blue flood running backwards across the fields as if the landscape had been tipped, the rebel pursuers cut down and gathered in fugitives by the hundreds, all at comparatively small cost to themselves, since but little of their fire was being returned. "General, where are your dead men?" an elated young officer called to Brigadier General John B. Gordon, whose six Georgia regiments had led the charge that threw the bluecoats into retreat before contact was established. Still intent on the pursuit, Gordon did not pause for an answer. "I haven't got any, sir!" he shouted as he rode past on his black stallion. "The Almighty has covered my men with his shield and buckler."

Lee observed from atop Herr Ridge the sudden climax of this latest addition to his year-long string of victories. Riding forward in the wake of Pender's exultant attack, which was delivered with the cohesive, smashing power of a clenched fist, he crossed McPherson's Ridge, thickly strewn with the dead and wounded of both armies, and mounted the opposite slope just as the Federals abandoned a fitful attempt to make a stand around the seminary. Ahead of him, down the remaining half mile of the Chambersburg Pike, they were retreating pell-mell into the streets of Gettysburg, already jammed with other blue troops pouring down from the north, under pressure from Ewell, as into a funnel whose spout extended south. Those who managed to struggle free of the crush, and thus emerge from the spout, were running hard down two roads that led steeply up a dominant height where guns were emplaced and the foremost of the fugitives were being brought to a halt, apparently for still another stand; Cemetery Hill, it was called because of the graveyard on its lofty plateau, half a mile from the town square. Another half mile to the east, about two miles from where Lee stood, there was a second eminence, Culp's Hill, slightly higher than the first, to which it was connected by a saddle of rocky ground, similarly precipitous and forbidding. These two hills, their summits a hundred feet above the town, which in turn was about half that far below the crest of Seminary Ridge, afforded the enemy a strong position — indeed, a natural fortress — on which to rally his whipped and panicky troops, especially if time was allowed for the steadily increasing number of defenders to improve with their spades the already formidable advantages of terrain. Lee could see for himself, now that he had what amounted to a ringside view of the action, that his victory had been achieved more as the result of tactical good fortune than because of any great preponderance of numbers, which in fact he did not have. Prisoners had been taken from two Union corps, six divisions in all, and they reported that the rest of the blue army was on the march to join them from bivouacs close at hand. Some 25,000 attackers, just under half of Lee's infantry, had faced 20,000 defenders, just over one fourth of Meade's, and the resultant casualties had done little to change the over-all ratio of the two armies, on and off the field. Nearly 8000 Confederates had fallen or been captured, as compared to 9000 Federals, about half of whom had been taken prisoner. It was clear that if the tactical advantage was not pressed, it might soon be lost altogether, first by giving the rattled bluecoats a chance to recompose themselves, there on the dominant heights just south of town, and second by allowing time for the arrival of heavy reinforcements already on the way. Moreover, both of these reasons for continuing the offensive were merely adjunctive to Lee's natural inclination, here as elsewhere, now as always, to keep a beaten opponent under pressure, and thus off balance, just as long as his own troops had wind and strength enough to put one foot in front of the other.

Ill though he was, ghostly pale and "very delicate," as one observer remarked, A. P. Hill was altogether in agreement that the new Federal position had to be carried if the victory was to be completed. But when Lee turned to him, there on Seminary Ridge, and proposed that the Third Corps make the attack, Little Powell declined. Anderson's division was still miles away; Heth's was shattered, the commander himself unconscious, and Pender's blown and disorganized by its furious charge and wild pursuit. The survivors were close to exhaustion and so was their ammunition, which would have to be replenished from the train back up the pike. Regretfully Hill replied that his men were in no condition for further exertion just now, and Lee, knowing from past experience that Hill invariably required of them all that flesh could endure, was obliged to accept his judgment. That left Ewell. Rodes had been roughly handled at the outset, it was true, but Early was comparatively fresh, had suffered only light casualties in driving the skittish Dutchmen from the field, and was already on the march through the streets of the town, rounding up herds of prisoners within half a mile of the proposed objective; besides which, it seemed fitting that the Second Corps continue its Jacksonian tradition of hard-legged mobility and terrific striking power, demonstrated recently at Winchester, a month after Stonewall was laid to rest nearby in the Shenandoah Valley, and redemonstrated here today in Pennsylvania. Having made the decision, Lee gave a staff officer oral instructions to take Ewell. As usual, not being in a position to judge for himself the condition of the troops or the difficulties the objective might present when approached from the north, he made the order discretionary; Ewell was "to carry the hill occupied by the enemy, if he found it practicable" — so Lee paraphrased the instructions afterwards in his formal report — "but to avoid a general engagement until the arrival of the other divisions of the army."

That was about 4.30; barely an hour had passed since Hill threw Pender into the follow-up attack on Seminary Ridge, sweeping it clear of defenders within less than half an hour, and a good four hours of daylight remained for Ewell's follow-up attack on Cemetery Hill, which would complete the victory by annihilating or driving the survivors from the scene before Meade could accomplish his convergence there.

Presently, as Lee continued to search the field for signs that the intended attack was under way, Longstreet arrived, riding well in advance of his troops, who had marked time short of Cashtown all morning, under instructions to yield the single eastward road to Johnson, who was hurrying to join the other divisions of the Second Corps. While Lee explained what had happened so far today, and pointed out the hill aswarm with bluecoats across the valley, Old Peter took out his binoculars and made a careful examination of the front. A broad low ridge, parallel to and roughly three quarters of a mile east of the one on which he stood, extended two miles southward from Cemetery Hill to a pair of conical heights, the nearer of which, called Little Round Top, was some fifty feet taller than the occupied hill to the north, while the farther, called simply Round Top, was more than a hundred feet taller still. On the map, and in the minds of students down the years, this complex of high ground south of Gettysburg conformed in general to the shape of a fishhook, with Round Top as the eye, Cemetery Ridge as the shank, Cemetery Hill as the bend, and Culp's Hill as the barb. Neither of the dominant heights to the south appeared to have been occupied yet by the enemy, though it was fairly clear that either would afford the Federals another rallying point in the event of another retreat. However, if this bothered Lee, he did not show it as he stood waiting for Ewell to open the attack from the north. Certainly it did not bother Longstreet, who had the look of a man whose prayers had been answered. Completing his survey of the field, he lowered his glasses, turned to his chief, and declared with evident satisfaction that conditions were ideal for pursuing the offensive-defensive campaign on which he presumed they had agreed before they left Virginia.

"If we could have chosen a point to meet our plans of operation," he said, "I do not think we could have found a better one than that upon which they are now concentrating. All we have to do is throw our army around by their left, and we shall interpose between the Federal army and Washington. We can get a strong position and wait, and if they fail to attack us we shall have everything in condition to move back tomorrow night in the direction of Washington, selecting beforehand a good position into which we can place our troops to receive battle next day. Finding our object is Washington and that army, the Federals will be sure to attack us. When they attack, we shall beat them, as we proposed to do before we left Fredericksburg, and the probabilities are that the fruits of our success will be great."

The southern commander's reaction to this proposed surrender of the initiative to Meade was immediate and decisive. "No," he said, and gestured with his fist in the direction of Cemetery Hill as he spoke. "The enemy is there, and I am going to attack him there."

"If he is there," Old Peter countered, unimpressed, "it will be because he is anxious that we should attack him: a good reason, in my judgment, for not doing so."

Lee still did not agree. He had made an auspicious beginning on his plan for toppling the Federal units piecemeal as they came up, like a row of dominoes, and he was determined to go ahead with it. "No," he said again. "They are there in position, and I am going to whip them or they are going to whip me."

For the present, Longstreet let it go at that, observing that his chief "was in no frame of mind to listen to further argument," but he resolved to return to the subject as soon as Lee had simmered down. "In defensive warfare he was perfect," he wrote years later. "When the hunt was up, his combativeness was overruling."

Just then a courier arrived with a message from Ewell, sent before the one from Lee had reached him. Rodes and Early believed they could take Cemetery Hill, he reported, if Hill would attack it simultaneously from the west. Lee replied that he was unable to furnish this support, except by long-range artillery fire, and after repeating his instructions for Ewell to take the height alone, if possible, added that he would ride over presently to see him. Once more Longstreet spoke up. Minute by minute, he had watched the number of bluecoats increasing on the hill, while those already there were making the dirt fly as they worked at improving the natural strength of the position. He was still opposed to the attack, he said, but if it was going to be made at all, it had better be made at once. Lee did not reply to this immediately. Instead, after sending the courier back to Ewell, he asked where the First Corps divisions were by now. McLaws was a couple of miles this side of Cashtown, Old Peter replied, with Hood somewhere behind him, awaiting road space on the pike. When Lee explained that he could not risk a general assault until these fresh units arrived, Longstreet again fell silent — whether in agreement or disagreement, he did not say — and soon rode off, apparently to hasten the march of the column whose head was half a dozen miles away.

It was now past 5.30 and the guns had stopped their growling on both sides. The staff officer returned to report that he had delivered the hour-old message to Ewell, but there was no other evidence that it had been received. Down below, the streets of the town were still crowded with Confederates, busy flushing Union fugitives out of cellars and back alleys, and there was no sign whatsoever that Ewell was preparing to launch the attack he had twice been told to make if he believed it would be successful. Meantime, the sun was dropping swiftly down the sky and the survivors of the two blue corps were hard at work improving their defenses. One welcome interruption there was, in the form of a pair of Stuart's troopers who brought word to Seminary Ridge of the skirmish near Hanover the day before, the fruitless grope toward York, and the subsequent decision to push on to Carlisle. Relieved to learn that Jeb had managed to avoid personal disaster, whatever trouble he might have made for others, Lee told the horsemen to ride the thirty miles north at once, with orders for the cavalry to rejoin the army as soon as possible. That could not be sooner than tomorrow, of course, but at least he could anticipate removal of the blindfold he had worn throughout the week of Stuart's absence. Near 7 o'clock, with sunset half an hour away and full darkness a good hour beyond that — which left just time enough, perhaps, for launching the attack on Cemetery Hill — Lee mounted Traveller and rode toward Gettysburg, intending not only to pay Ewell the visit he had promised, but also to discover for himself the reason for the long delay.

★ ★ ★

At Taneytown, a dozen miles from the hill where the men of the two wrecked blue corps were plying their shovels in frantic anticipation of the overdue assault, Meade had heard nothing of the eight-hour battle aside from the note in which Reynolds announced that he would "fight [the rebels] inch by inch . . . and hold them back as long as possible." Not even the booming of the guns came through; for though the east wind carried their rumble as far as Pittsburgh, 150 miles to the west, it was not audible ten miles to the south, apparently having been absorbed by the Round Tops and the sultry air, which served as a soundproof curtain in that direction. In the early afternoon, however, a New York *Times* correspondent came riding back from Gettysburg on a lathered horse and requested the use of the army telegraph in order to file a story on the fighting. Taken at once to headquarters, he could only report that the conflict had been fierce, that the issue had been in doubt when he left, and that one among the many who had fallen was John Reynolds. All of this was a shock for Meade. Not only had he lost the officer on whom he had depended most for guidance during these first days of command, but one fourth of his army had been committed, perhaps beyond the possibility of disengagement, a hard day's march north of his chosen position along Pipe Creek, which the engineers were still mapping and preparing for occupation. Moreover, a 2 o'clock dispatch from Howard, confirming the newsman's statement and adding that he had sent for Sickles and Slocum — which would mean the commitment, once they arrived, of just over half the army — was followed by one from Buford, addressed to Pleasonton, announcing that two enemy corps — two thirds of the rebel army, it would seem — had made a junction on the heights northwest of town and seemed determined to press the issue to a conclusion, however bloody. Outnumbered and outflanked on the left and right, the defenders had been severely crippled, Buford added, by the untimely death of Reynolds and the resultant loss of co-ordination all along the line. "In my opinion," the cavalryman closed his dispatch, "there seems to be no directing person. . . . P.S. We need help now."

The note was headed 3.20 p.m., by which time help had been on the way for better than an hour: substantial help, moreover, though it consisted of only one general and his staff. Hancock's corps had reached Taneytown shortly before noon, and Meade had held it there while waiting to hear from Reynolds. When he heard instead of that general's death, he told Hancock to turn his corps over to Gibbon and ride to Gettysburg as a replacement for their fellow Pennsylvanian, with full authority to assume command of all units there and recommend whether to reinforce or withdraw them. He himself would remain in Taneytown, Meade said, to control the movements of the other corps and continue work on the Pipe Creek line, which would be needed worse than ever in the event of a northward collapse. Hancock was thirty-nine, a year older than Sickles and six years older than Howard; all three had been promoted to major general on the same day, back in November, but the other two had been made brigadiers before him and therefore outranked him still. When he suggested that this might make for trouble up ahead, Meade showed him a letter from Stanton, stating that he would be sustained in such arrangements by the President and the Secretary of War. So Hancock set out. He rode part of the way in an ambulance, thus availing himself of the chance to study a map of the Gettysburg area, which he had never previously visited though he was born and raised at Norristown, less than a hundred miles away. Coming within earshot of the guns, which swelled to a sudden uproar about 3.30, he shifted to horseback and rode hard toward the sound of firing. At 4 o'clock, the hour that Lee climbed Seminary Ridge to find a Confederate triumph unfolding at his feet, Hancock appeared on Cemetery Hill, a mile southeast across the intervening valley, to view the same scene in reverse. "Wreck, disaster, disorder, almost the panic that precedes disorganization, defeat and retreat were everywhere," a subordinate who arrived with him declared.

One-armed Howard was there by the two-story arched brick

gateway to the cemetery, brandishing his sword in an attempt to stay the rout, but he was doing little better now than he had done two months ago at Chancellorsville, under similar circumstances. Von Steinwehr, an old-line Prussian and a believer in fortifications, had put his troops to digging on arrival, and the work had gone well, even though one of his two brigades had been called forward when the line began to waver north of town. The trouble was, there were so few men left to hold the hilltop, intrenched or not. Out of the 20,000 on hand for the battle, nearly half had fallen or been captured, while practically another fourth were fugitives who had had their fill of fighting: as was indicated by the fact that the provost guardsmen of a corps that came up two hours later herded ahead of them some 1200 skulkers encountered on the Baltimore Pike, which was only one of the three roads leading south. Fewer than 7000 soldiers — the equivalent of a single Confederate division — comprised the available remnant of the two wrecked Union corps, including the brigade that had remained in reserve on the hilltop all along. With all too clear a view of the jubilant mass of rebels in the town and on the ridge across the way, Howard foresaw an extension of the disaster, the second to be charged against his name in the past two months. Anxious as ever to retrieve his reputation, which had been grievously damaged in the Wilderness and practically demolished north of Gettysburg today, he was chagrined to hear from Hancock that Meade had sent him forward to take charge. "Why, Hancock, you cannot give orders here," he exclaimed. "I am in command and I rank you." When the other repeated that such were Meade's instructions all the same, he still would not agree. "I do not doubt your word, General Hancock," he said stiffly, "but you can give no orders while I am here." Possessed of a self-confidence that required no insistence on prerogatives, Hancock avoided having the exchange degenerate into a public squabble by pretending to defer to Howard's judgment in deciding whether to stand fast or fall back. "I think this is the strongest position by nature on which to fight a battle that I ever saw," he said, looking east and south along the fishhook line of heights from Culp's Hill to the Round Tops, "and if it meets with your approbation I will select this as the battlefield." When Howard replied that he agreed that the position was a strong one, Hancock concluded: "Very well, sir. I select this as the battlefield."

Howard later protested that he had selected and occupied Cemetery Hill as a rallying point long before Hancock got there. This was true; but neither could there be any doubt, when the time came for looking back, that it was the latter who organized the all-round defense of the position, regardless of who had selected it in the first place. Meade had chosen well in naming a successor to the fallen Reynolds. Fourteen months ago, in the course of his drive up the York-James peninsula, McClellan had characterized Hancock as "superb," and the word stuck; "Hancock the Superb," he was called thereafter, partly because of his handsome looks and regal bearing — "I think that if he were in citizen's clothes, and should give commands in the army to those who did not know him," one officer observed, "he would be likely to be obeyed at once"— but also because of his military record, which was known and admired by those below as well as by those above him. The army's craving for heroes, or at any rate a hero, had not been diminished by the fact that so many who supposedly qualified as such had melted away like wax dolls in the heat of combat; Hancock seemed an altogether likelier candidate. A Maine artilleryman, for example, recalling the Pennsylvanian's sudden appearance on Cemetery Hill, later asserted that his "very atmosphere was strong and invigorating," and added: "I remember (how refreshing to note!) even his linen clean and white, his collar wide and free, and his broad wrist bands showing large and rolling back from his firm, finely molded hands." Carl Schurz, who might have been expected to side with Howard, his immediate superior, found Hancock's arrival "most fortunate" at this juncture. "It gave the troops a new inspiration," he declared. "They all knew him by fame, and his stalwart figure, his proud mien, and his superb soldierly bearing seemed to verify all the things that fame had told about him. His mere presence was a reinforcement, and everybody on the field felt stronger for his being there."

His first order was for the troops to push forward to the stone walls that ran along the northern face of the hill, in order to present a show of strength and thus discourage an advance by the rebels down below. "I am of the opinion that the enemy will mass in town and make an effort to take this position," he told the captain of a battery posted astride the Baltimore Pike at the rim of the plateau, "but I want you to remain here until you are relieved by me or by my written order, and take orders from no one." It was clear to all who saw him that he meant business, and though Howard had chosen to defend only a portion of the hill, Hancock soon extended the line to cover it from flank to flank; after which he turned his attention to Culp's Hill. Half a mile to the east and slightly higher than the ground his present line was drawn on, that critical feature of the terrain had not been occupied, despite the obvious fact that Cemetery Hill itself could not be held if this companion height was lost. He told Doubleday to send a regiment over there at once. "My corps has been fighting, General, since 10 o'clock," the New Yorker protested, "and they have been all cut to pieces." Hancock replied: "I know that, sir. But this is a great emergency, and everyone must do all he can." With that he turned away, as if there could be no question of not obeying, and when he came back presently he found that Doubleday, whose regiments had been reduced to the size of companies in the earlier fighting, had sent Wadsworth's whole division to occupy the hill and the connecting saddle of high ground. It was, in fact, the shadow of a division, no larger than a small brigade, but the position was a strong one, heavily timbered and strewn with rocks that varied in size, as one defender wrote, "from a chicken coop to a pioneer's cabin." Moreover, the lead division of Slocum's corps soon arrived and was posted there, too. Feeling considerably more secure, Hancock got off a message to Meade in which he stated that he believed he could hold his ground till nightfall and that he considered his present position an excellent one for fighting a battle, "although somewhat exposed to be turned by the left."

Across the way, on Seminary Ridge, Longstreet was expressing that same opinion even now. The difference was that Old Peter was a subordinate, whereas Hancock was in actual command and therefore in a position to do something about it. Weak though the line was on those two hills to the north, he saw that it could not be held, even in strength, if those two commanding heights to the south — the Round Tops — were occupied by the enemy, whose batteries then would enfilade all the rest of the fishhook. And having noted this, he acted in accordance with his insight. Slocum's second division (but still not Slocum himself; he refused to come forward in person and take command by virtue of his rank, judging that Meade's plans for the occupation of the Pipe Creek line were being perverted by this affair near Gettysburg, which seemed to be going very badly. He would risk his men, but not his career; heads were likely to roll, and he was taking care that his would not be among them) was approaching the field soon after 5 o'clock, when its commander reported to Hancock near the cemetery gate. "Geary, where are your troops?" he was asked, and replied: "Two brigades are on the road advancing." Hancock gestured south, down Cemetery Ridge. "Do you see this knoll on the left?" He was pointing at Little Round Top. "That knoll is a commanding position. We must take possession of it, and then a line can be formed here and a battle fought. . . . In the absence of Slocum, I order you to place your troops on that knoll."

This was promptly done, and with the continuing forbearance of the Confederates, who obligingly refrained from launching the attack Hancock had predicted, Federal confidence gradually was restored. Here and there, along the heights and ridges, men began to say they hoped the rebels would come on, because when they did they were going to get a taste of Fredericksburg in reverse. Arriving with his lead division about 6 o'clock, Sickles was posted on the northern end of Cemetery Ridge, just in rear of Howard's and Doubleday's position on Cemetery Hill, which thus was defended in considerable depth. His other division would arrive in the night, as would Hancock's three under Gibbon, if Meade released them, to extend the line southward along the ridge leading down to the Round Tops. Once this had been done, the fishhook would be defended from eye to barb, and if Meade would also send Sykes and Sedgwick, reserves could be massed behind the high ground in the center, where they would have the advantage of interior lines in

moving rapidly to the support of whatever portion of the convex front
might happen to be under pressure at any time. All this depended on
Meade, however, and when Slocum at last came forward at 7 o'clock
(apparently he had decided to risk his reputation after all, or else he had
decided that it was more risky to remain outside events in which his
soldiers were involved) Hancock transferred the command to him and
rode back to Taneytown to argue in person for a Gettysburg concentration of the whole army, nine of whose nineteen divisions were there
already, with a tenth one on the way.

He arrived at about 9.30 to find his chief already persuaded by the
message he had sent him four hours earlier. "I shall order up the troops,"
Meade had said, after brief deliberation, and orders had gone accordingly
to Gibbon, Sykes, and Sedgwick, informing them that the Pipe Creek
plan had been abandoned in favor of a rapid concentration on the heights
just south of Gettysburg, where the other half of the army was awaiting
their support. However, instead of going forward at once himself —
there would be no time for a daylight reconnaissance anyhow — Meade
decided to get some badly needed sleep. At 1 a.m. he came out of his
tent, mounted his horse, and rode the twelve miles north with his staff
and escort, a full moon floodlighting the landscape of his native Pennsylvania. At 3 o'clock, barely an hour before dawn, he dismounted at the
cemetery gate, through which there was a rather eerie view of soldiers
sprawled in sleep among the tombstones. Across the way, on the western
ridge and down in the moon-drenched town below, he saw another sobering sight: the campfires of the enemy, apparently as countless as the
stars. Slocum, Howard, and Sickles were there to greet him, and though
he had seen but little of the position Hancock had so stoutly recommended, all assured him that it was a good one. "I am glad to hear you
say so, gentlemen," Meade replied, "for it is too late to leave it."

By the time he had made a brief moonlight inspection of Culp's
and Cemetery hills, dawn was breaking and Hancock's three divisions
were filing into position on Cemetery Ridge, having completed their all-
night march from Taneytown. Sykes had reached Hanover and turned
west in the darkness; he would arrive within a couple of hours. Only
Sedgwick's corps was not at hand, the largest of the seven. Uncle John
had promised to make it from Manchester by 4 o'clock that afternoon,
and though it seemed almost too much to hope that so large a body of
men could cover better than thirty miles of road in less than twenty
hours, Meade not only took him at his word; he announced that he would
attack on the right, as soon as Sedgwick got there.

✘ 3 ✘

Lee's headquarters tents were pitched in a field beside the Chambersburg
Pike, on the western slope of Seminary Ridge. When he rose from sleep,

an hour before dawn — about the same time Meade drew rein beside the
gate on Cemetery Hill — his intention, like his opponent's, was to attack
on the right. He had arrived at this decision the previous evening, in the
course of a twilight conference north of Gettysburg with Ewell, whom
he found gripped by a strange paralysis of will, apparently brought on,
or at any rate intensified, by Lee's stipulation that an assault on the bluecoats attempting a rally on the hilltop south of town, though much desired, not only could not be supported by troops outside his corps, as
Ewell had requested, but also was to be attempted only if he found it
"practicable," which Ewell interpreted as meaning that he must be certain of success. It occurred to him that in war few things were certain,
least of all success; with the result that he refrained from taking any risk
whatever. First he waited for Johnson, whose division did not come onto
the field until past sundown, and finally he called the whole thing off,
finding by then that the heights beyond the town bristled with guns and
determined-looking infantry, deployed in overlapping lines, well dug in
along much of the front, and heavily reinforced.

Though it was not Lee's way to challenge an assessment made by
a general on ground which he himself had not examined, when he arrived for the conference he indicated his regret by expressing the hope
that Ewell's decision would not apply to next day's operations. "Can't
you, with your corps, attack on this front tomorrow?" he asked. Ewell
said nothing; nor did Rodes, whose accustomed fieriness had been subdued by his narrow escape from disaster in his first action as a major
general, and Johnson was not present. That left Early, who did not hesitate to answer for his chief that an offensive here on the left, after the
Federals had spent the night preparing for such a move, would be unwise. However, he added, indicating the Round Tops looming dimly in
the distance and the dusk, an attack on the right, with the mass of
bluecoats concentrated northward to meet the expected threat from
Ewell, offered the Confederates a splendid opportunity to seize the high
ground to the south and assail the Union flank and rear from there.
Ewell and Rodes nodded agreement, but when Lee replied: "Then perhaps I had better draw you around towards our right, as the line will be
very long and thin if you remain here, and the enemy may come down
and break through," Early again was quick to disagree. In his view, that
would spoil the whole arrangement by allowing the foe to turn and give
his full attention to the blow aimed at his rear. As for the integrity
of the present line, Lee need have no qualms; whatever its shortcomings
as a base from which to launch an offensive, the position was an excellent one for defense. Besides, Early went on to say, much captured material and many of the wounded could not be moved on such brief notice, not to mention the effect on morale if the troops were required to
give up ground they had won so brilliantly today.

Lee heard him out, then pondered, head bent **forward. The main** thing he disliked about the proposal was that it would require a change in his preferred style of fighting, typified by Manassas, where he had used the nimble Second Corps to set his opponent up for the delivery of a knockout punch by the First Corps, whose specialty was power. Early was suggesting what amounted to a change of stance, which was neither an easy nor a wise thing for a boxer to attempt, even in training, let alone after a match was under way, as it was now. Head still bowed in thought, Lee mused aloud: "Well, if I attack from the right, Longstreet will have to make the attack." He raised his head. "Longstreet is a very good fighter when he gets in position and gets everything ready, but he is so slow." The extent of his perplexity was shown by this criticism of one subordinate in the presence of another, a thing he would never have done if he had not been upset at finding the commander of the Second Corps, famed for its slashing tactics under Jackson, content to fall back on the defensive with a victory half won. However, when Early, still speaking for his chief, who seemed to have lost his vocal powers along with those employed to arrive at a decision, assured him that the three divisions would be prompt to join the action as soon as the attack was launched across the way, Lee tentatively accepted the plan and rode back through the darkness to Seminary Ridge.

Once he was beyond the range of Early's persuasive tongue, however, his doubts returned. He reasoned that the blow, wherever it was to be delivered — and he had not yet decided on that point — should be struck with all the strength he could muster. If Ewell would not attempt it on the left, he would bring him around to the right, thus shortening the line while adding power to the punch. Accordingly, he sent him instructions to shift his three divisions west and south at once if he was still of the opinion that he could launch no drive from where they were. This not only restored Ewell's powers of speech; it brought him in person to army headquarters. Dismounting with some difficulty because of his wooden leg, he reported that Johnson had examined the Federal position on Culp's Hill and believed he could take it by assault. This changed the outlook completely; for if Culp's Hill could be taken, so could the main enemy position on Cemetery Hill, which it outflanked. Happy to return to his accustomed style, which was to use his left to set his opponent up for the knockout punch he planned to throw with his right, Lee canceled Ewell's instructions for a shift and directed instead that he remain where he was, with orders to seize the high ground to his front as soon as possible. By now it was close to midnight; Ewell rode back to his own headquarters north of Gettysburg. Lee pondered the matter further. Since Longstreet, who would deliver the major blow, was not yet up, whereas Ewell was already in position, he decided to time the latter's movements by the former's, and sent a courier after Ewell with instructions for him not to advance against Culp's Hill until he heard Longstreet open with his guns across the way. This done, Lee turned in at last to get some sleep, telling his staff as he did so: "Gentle-men, we will attack the enemy as early in the morning as practicable."

Rising at 3 a.m. he ate breakfast in the dark and went forward at first light to the crest of the ridge, preceded by a staff engineer whom he sent southward, in the direction of the Round Tops, to reconnoiter the ground where the main effort would be made. To his relief, as he focused his glasses on the enemy position, though he saw by the pearly light of dawn that the Federals still held Cemetery Hill in strength, the lower end of the ridge to the south appeared to be as bare of troops as it had been at sunset. Longstreet soon arrived to report that McLaws and Hood were coming forward on the pike, having camped within easy reach of the field the night before — all but one of Hood's brigades, which was on the way from New Guilford, more than twenty miles to the west. Pickett too was on the march, having been relieved by Im-boden the day before at Chambersburg, but could scarcely arrive be-fore evening. Glad at any rate to learn that Hood and McLaws were nearby, Lee then was startled to hear Old Peter return to yesterday's proposal that the Confederates maneuver around the Union left and thus invite attack instead of attempting one themselves against so formidable a position as the enemy now held. While Longstreet spoke, the force of his words was increased by the emergence on Cemetery Ridge of brigade after brigade of blue-clad soldiers, extending the line southward in the direction of the Round Tops. However, Lee rejected his burly lieuten-ant's argument out of hand, much as he had done the previous afternoon, although by sunup it was apparent that his plan for a bloodless occupa-tion of the enemy ridge would have to be revised. Longstreet lapsed into a troubled silence, and at that point A. P. Hill came up, still pale and weak from illness. Except to report that his whole corps was at hand, Anderson having arrived in the night, he had little to say. Heth was with him, his head wrapped in a bandage, too badly shaken by yesterday's injury to resume command of his division, which was to remain in re-serve today under Pettigrew, the senior brigadier. Hood rode up soon afterwards, ahead of his men. As he watched the bluecoats cluster thicker on the ridge across the mile-wide valley, Lee told him what he had told his corps commander earlier. "The enemy is here," he said, "and if we do not whip him, he will whip us." Hood interpreted this to mean that Lee intended to take the offensive as soon as possible, but Longstreet took him aside and explained in private: "The general is a little nervous this morning. He wishes me to attack. I do not wish to do so without Pickett. I never like to go into battle with one boot off."

Hood could see that both men were under a strain; but whatever its cause, it was mild compared to what followed presently. As the sun climbed swiftly clear of the horizon, Lee worked out a plan whereby he would extend his right down Seminary Ridge to a point beyond the en-emy left, then attack northeast up the Emmitsburg Road, which ran diagonally across the intervening valley, to strike and crumple the Union flank on Cemetery Ridge. Though he said nothing of this to Longstreet, who had expressed his disapproval in advance, he explained it in some detail to McLaws when he rode up shortly after 8 o'clock. "I wish you to place your division across this road," Lee told him, pointing it out on the map and on the ground. "I wish you to get there if possible without being seen by the enemy. Can you do it?" McLaws said he thought he could, but added that he would prefer to take a close-up look at the terrain in order to make certain. Lee replied that a staff engineer had been ordered to do just that, "and I expect he is about ready." He meant that the officer was probably about ready to report, but McLaws understood him to mean that he was about ready to set out. "I will go with him," he said. Before Lee could explain, Longstreet broke in, having overheard the conversation as he paced up and down. "No, sir," he said emphatically, "I do not wish you to leave your division." As he spoke he leaned forward and traced a line on the map, perpendicular to the one Lee had indicated earlier. "I wish your division placed so," he said. Quietly but in measured tones Lee replied: "No, General, I wish it placed just opposite." When the embarrassed McLaws repeated that he would like to go forward for a look at the ground his division was going to occupy, Longstreet once more refused to permit it and Lee declined to intervene further. So McLaws retired in some bewilderment to rejoin his troops and await the outcome of this unfamiliar clash of wills.

Presently the staff engineer, Captain S. R. Johnston, returned from his early-morning reconnaissance on the right, and his report was everything Lee could have hoped for. According to him, the Federals had left the southern portion of Cemetery Ridge unoccupied, along with both of the Round Tops. When Lee asked pointedly, "Did you get there?" — for the information was too vital to be accepted as mere hearsay — Johnston replied that his report was based entirely on what he had seen with his own eyes, after climbing one of the spurs of Little Round Top. Lee's pulse quickened. This confirmed the practicality of his plan, which was for Longstreet to launch an oblique attack up the Emmitsburg Road, get astride the lower end of Cemetery Ridge, and then sweep northward along it, rolling up the Union flank in order to get at the rear of the force on Cemetery Hill, kept under pressure all this time by Ewell, who was to attack on the left, fixing the bluecoats in position and setting them up for the kill, as soon as he heard the guns open fire to the south. Moreover, while Lee was considering this welcome intelligence, Longstreet received a report that his reserve artillery, eight batteries which were to lend the weight of their metal to the assault, had just arrived. It was now about 9 o'clock. Except for Pickett's division and Brigadier General Evander Law's brigade, on the march respectively from Chambersburg and New Guilford, the whole First

Corps was at hand. Still, Lee did not issue a final order for the attack, wanting first to confer with Ewell and thus make certain that the Second Corps understood its share in the revised plan for the destruction of "those people" across the way.

Leaving Hill and Longstreet on Seminary Ridge, he rode to Ewell's headquarters north of Gettysburg, only to find that the general was off on a tour of inspection. Trimble was there, however, serving in the capacity of a high-ranking aide and advisor, and while they waited for Ewell to return he conducted Lee to the cupola of a nearby almshouse, which afforded a good view of the crests of Culp's and Cemetery hills, above and beyond the rooftops of the town below. Observing that the defenses on the two heights had been greatly strengthened in the course of the sixteen hours that had elapsed since Ewell first declined to attack the rallying Federals there, Lee said regretfully: "The enemy have the advantage of us in a short and inside line, and we are too much extended. We did not or could not pursue our advantage of yesterday, and now the enemy are in a good position." When Ewell at last returned, Lee repeated what he had told Trimble, stressing the words, "We did not or could not pursue our advantage," as if to impress Ewell with his desire that the Second Corps would neglect no such opportunity today. Though it was plain that the Union stronghold had been rendered almost impregnable to attack from this direction, he explained his overall plan in detail, making it clear that all three divisions here on the left were to menace both heights as soon as Longstreet's guns began to roar, and he added that the demonstration was to be converted into a fullscale assault if events disclosed a fair chance of success. This done, he rode back toward Seminary Ridge, along whose eastern slope two of Hill's divisions were already posted, well south of the Chambersburg Pike. Anderson's, which had not arrived in time for a share in yesterday's fight, was farthest south, under orders to join Longstreet's attack as it came abreast, rolling northward, and Pender's was to do the same in turn, simultaneously extending its left to make contact with the Second Corps southwest of Gettysburg. Heth's division, which was in about as shaken a state as its shell-shocked commander, would remain in reserve on the far side of Willoughby Run, not to be called for except in the event of the threat of a disaster.

It was just past 11 o'clock when Lee returned to Seminary Ridge, suffering en route from what an officer who rode with him called "more impatience than I ever saw him exhibit upon any other occasion," and gave Longstreet orders to move out. Observing his chief's disappointment at finding the two First Corps divisions still occupying the standby positions in which he had left them two hours earlier, Longstreet did not presume to suggest that he wait for Pickett — as he had told Hood he preferred to do, even though this would have postponed the attack until sundown at the soonest — but he did request a half-hour delay to allow for the arrival of Law, whose brigade was reported close at hand by now. Lee agreed, although regretfully, and when Law came up shortly before noon, completing a 24-mile speed march from New Guilford in less than nine hours, the two divisions lurched into motion, headed south under cover of Herr Ridge, which screened them from observation by enemy lookouts on the Round Tops. Apparently Meade had begun to rectify his neglect of those bastions, for signal flags were flapping busily from the summit of the nearer of the two. Lee was not disturbed by this, however. Now that the march was under way, his calm and confidence were restored. "Ah, well, that was to be expected," he said when scouts reported that the enemy left was being extended southward along Cemetery Ridge. "But General Meade might as well have saved himself the trouble, for we'll have it in our possession before night."

Longstreet's veterans agreed. The march was far from an easy one, the day being hot and water scarce, but they were accustomed to such hardships, which were to be endured as prelude to the delivery of the assault that would determine the outcome of the battle. Moreover, they considered it standard procedure that theirs was the corps selected for that purpose. "There was a kind of intuition, an apparent settled fact," one of its members later declared, "that after all the other troops had made their long marches, tugged at the flanks of the enemy, threatened his rear, and all the display of strategy and generalship had been exhausted in the dislodgment of the foe, and all these failed, then when the hard, stubborn, decisive blow was to be struck, the troops of the First Corps were called on to strike it." As it turned out, however, the march was a good deal harder and longer than they or anyone else, including Lee and Longstreet, had expected when they began it. The crow-flight distance of three miles, from their starting point near Lee's headquarters to their jump-off position astride the Emmitsburg Road just opposite the Round Tops, would be doubled by the necessity for taking a roundabout covered route in order to stay hidden from Meade, who would be able to hurry reinforcements to any portion of his line within minutes of being warned that it was threatened. Nor was that all. This estimated distance of six miles had to be redoubled in turn, at least for some of the marchers, when it was discovered that the movement eastward would be disclosed to the enemy if the butternut column passed over the crest of Herr Ridge here to the south where the woods were thin. Plainly upset by this sign of the guide's incompetence — but no more so than the guide himself, Captain Johnston of Lee's staff, who had neither sought nor wanted the assignment, who had not reconnoitered west of Seminary Ridge at all, and who later protested that he "had no idea that I had the confidence of the great General Lee to such an extent that he would entrust me with the conduct of an army corps moving within two miles of the enemy line" — Longstreet halted the

column and reversed its direction of march, back northward to a point
near the Chambersburg Pike again, where the ridge could be crossed
under cover of heavy woods. Some time was saved by giving the lead to
Hood, who had followed McLaws till then, but nearly two full hours
had been wasted in marching and countermarching, only to return to
the approximate starting point. Longstreet's anger soon gave way to sadness. A soldier who watched him ride past, "his eyes cast to the ground,
as if in deep study, his mind disturbed," recorded afterwards that Old
Peter today had "more the look of gloom" than he had ever seen him
wear before.

　　Southward the march continued, under cover of McPherson's
Ridge, then around its lower end, eastward across Pitzer's Run and
through the woods to Seminary Ridge, which here approached the Emmitsburg Road at the point desired. The head of the column — Law's
brigade, which by now had spent twelve blistering hours on the march
— got there shortly after 3 o'clock. This was not bad time for the distance hiked, but the better part of another hour would be required to
mass the two divisions for attack. Worst of all, as Hood's men filed in
on the far right, confronting the rocky loom of Little Round Top, they
saw bluecoats clustered thickly in a peach orchard half a mile to the
north, just under a mile in advance of the main Federal line on Cemetery
Ridge and directly across the road from the position McLaws had been
assigned. This came as a considerable surprise. They were not supposed
to be there at all, or at any rate their presence was not something that
had been covered by Lee's instructions.

★　★　★

　　Neither was their presence in the orchard covered by any instructions from their own commander. In fact, at the time Hood's men
first spotted them, Meade did not even know they were there, but supposed instead that they were still back on the ridge, in the position he
had assigned to them that morning. Since 9 o'clock — six hours ago, and
within six hours of his arrival — his dispositions for defense had been
virtually complete. Slocum's two divisions, reunited by shifting Geary
north from Little Round Top, occupied the southeast extremity of
Culp's Hill, while Wadsworth's I Corps division was posted on the summit and along the saddle leading west to Cemetery Hill. There Howard's
three divisions held the broad plateau, supported by the other two divisions of the First Corps, now under Virginia-born John Newton, whom
Meade had ordered forward from Sedgwick's corps because he mistrusted
Doubleday. Thus eight of the sixteen available divisions were concentrated to defend the barb and bend of the fishhook, with Sykes's three
in general reserve, available too if needed. South of there, along the
nearly two miles of shank, the five divisions under Hancock and Sickles
extended the line down Cemetery Ridge to the vicinity of Little Round

Top, though the height itself remained unoccupied after Geary's early-morning departure. Buford's cavalry guarded the left flank, Gregg's the right, and Kilpatrick's the rear, coming west from Hanover.

Meade had established headquarters in a small house beside the Taneytown Road, half a mile south of Cemetery Hill and thus near the center of his curved, three-mile line. Here, once the posting of his men and guns had been completed, he busied himself with attempts to divine his opponent's intentions. With Ewell's three divisions in more or less plain view to the north, he expected the rebel attack to come from that direction and he had massed his troops accordingly. However, as the sun climbed swiftly up the sky, the apparent inactivity of the other two enemy corps disturbed him, knowing as he did that Lee was seldom one to bide his time. It seemed to him that the Virginian must have something up his sleeve — something as violent and bloody, no doubt, as Chancellorsville, where Hooker had been unhorsed — and the more he considered this possibility, the less he liked the present look of things. At 9.30, thinking perhaps the proper move would be to beat his old friend to the punch, he asked Slocum to report from Culp's Hill on "the practicability of attacking the enemy in that quarter." When Slocum replied an hour later that the terrain on the right, though excellent for defense, was not favorable for attack, Meade abandoned the notion of taking the offensive when Sedgwick arrived. In point of fact, he already had his chief of staff at work in the low-ceilinged garret of his headquarters cottage, preparing an order for retirement. Not that he meant to use it unless he had to, he explained later; but with so large a portion of Lee's army on the prowl, or at any rate out of sight, he thought it best to be prepared for almost anything, including a sudden necessity for retreat. At 3 o'clock, still with no substantial information as to his adversary's intentions, he wrote Halleck that he had his army in "a strong position for defensive." He was hoping to attack, he said, but: "If I find it hazardous to do so, or am satisfied the enemy is endeavoring to move by my rear and interpose between me and Washington, I shall fall back to my supplies at Westminster. . . . I feel fully the responsibility resting upon me," he added, "and will endeavor to act with caution."

At least one of his corps commanders — Sickles, whose two divisions were on the extreme left of the line — had serious reservations about the defensive strength of the position, at least so far as his own portion of it was concerned. Cemetery Ridge lost height as it extended southward, until finally, just short of Little Round Top, it dwindled to comparatively low and even somewhat marshy ground. Three quarters of a mile due west, moreover, the Emmitsburg Road crossed a broad knoll which seemed to Sickles, though its crest was in fact no more than twelve feet higher than the lowest point of the ridge, to dominate the sector Meade had assigned him. The only cover out there was afforded by the scant foliage of a peach orchard in the southeast corner of a junction formed by a dirt road leading back across the ridge; artillery from either side could bludgeon, more or less at will, that otherwise bald hump of earth and everything on it. But to Sickles, gazing uphill at it from his post on the low-lying far left of the army, the situation resembled the one that had obtained when his enforced abandonment of Hazel Grove caused the Union line to come unhinged at Chancellorsville, and he reasoned that the same thing would happen here at Gettysburg unless something more than skirmishers were advanced to deny the Confederates access to that dominant ground directly to his front. As the morning wore on and Meade did not arrive to inspect the dispositions on the left, Sickles sent word that he was grievously exposed. Meade, concerned exclusively with the threat to his right and having little respect anyhow for the former Tammany politician's military judgment, dismissed he warning with the remark: "Oh, generals are apt to look for the attack to be made where they are." To Sickles this sounded more than ever like Hooker, and at midmorning he went in person to headquarters to ask if he was or was not authorized to post his troops as he thought best. "Certainly," Meade replied, "within the limits of the general instructions I have given you. Any ground within those limits you choose to occupy I leave to you." So Sickles rode back, accompanied by Henry Hunt, whom Meade sent along to look into the complaint, and though the artillerist rather agreed that it was valid, he also pointed out the danger of establishing a salient — for that was what it would amount to — so far in advance of the main line, so open to interdictory fire, and so extensive that the available troops would have to be spread thin in order to occupy it. In short, he declined to authorize the proposed adjustment, though he promised to discuss it further with the army commander and send back a final decision. As the sun went past the overhead and no word came from headquarters, Sickles continued to fume and fret. Learning finally that Buford's cavalry had been relieved from its duty of patrolling the left flank, which he believed exposed him to assault from that direction, he could bear it no longer. If Meade was blind to obvious portents of disaster, Sickles certainly was not. He decided to move out on his own.

At 3 o'clock, while Meade was writing Halleck that his position was a strong one "for defensive," the veterans of Hancock's corps, playing cards and boiling coffee along the northern half of Cemetery Ridge, taking it easy as the long hot day wore on and no attack developed, were surprised to hear drums rolling and throbbing, off to the left, and when they looked in that direction they saw Sickles' two divisions of better than 10,000 men advancing westward across the open fields in formal battle order, bugles blaring and flags aflutter, lines carefully dressed behind a swarm of skirmishers all across the front. "How splendidly they march!" one of the watchers cried, and another remarked in round-eyed admiration: "It looks like a dress parade, a review." The movement was so deliberate, so methodical in execution, that John Gibbon, sitting his horse alongside Hancock, who had dismounted, wondered if the II Corps had somehow failed to receive an order for a general advance. Hancock knew better. Leaning on his sword and resting one knee on the ground, he tempered his surprise with amusement at the sight of Old Dan Sickles leading his soldiers to the war. "Wait a moment," he said, and he smiled grimly as he spoke, "you'll see them tumbling back."

Some among Sickles' own officers were inclined to agree with this prediction: especially after they had reached and examined their new position, half a mile and more in front of the rest of the army. In ordering the maneuver, one brigadier observed, the corps commander had shown "more ardor to advance and meet the fight than a nice appreciation of the means to sustain it." Old soldiers reviewing the situation down the years expressed the same thought in simpler terms when they said that Sickles "stuck out like a sore thumb." Not only was there little cover or means of concealment, out here on the broad low hump of earth; there was also a half-mile gap between the extreme right of the salient and the left of Hancock's corps, back on the ridge. Moreover, Hunt's theoretical objection that Sickles did not have enough troops for the operation he proposed was sustained by the fact that his new line — extending from near the Cordori house, well up the Emmitsburg Road, to the peach orchard, where it bent sharply back to form an angle, and then across the southwest corner of a large wheat field, to end rather inconclusively in front of a mean-looking jumble of boulders known appropriately as the Devil's Den, just west of Little Round Top — was about twice the length of the mile-long stretch of ridge which now lay vacant in its rear. As a result, the position had little depth, practically no reserves or physical feature to fall back on, and was unsupported on both ends. To some, it seemed an outright invitation to disaster: an impression that was strengthened considerably, within half an hour of the march out, by a full-scale bombardment from rebel guns across the way, in the woods along the eastern slope of Seminary Ridge.

Riding down at last in response to the sudden uproar, Meade was appalled to see what Sickles had improvised here on the left. "General, I am afraid you are too far out," he said, understating the case in an attempt to keep control of his hair-trigger temper. Still in disagreement, Sickles insisted that he could maintain his position if he were given adequate support: a stipulation he had not made before. "However, I will withdraw if you wish, sir," he added. Meade shook his head as the guns continued to growl and rumble in the woods beyond the Emmitsburg Road. "I think it is too late," he said. "The enemy will not allow you." He was calculating his chances as he spoke. The situation had been greatly improved by the arrival of Sedgwick, whose three divisions now were filling up the Baltimore Pike, across Rock Creek, and onto the field, ending on schedule their long march from Manchester. They could replace Sykes in general reserve and thus free those three well-rested divisions to move in support of Sickles. "If you need more artillery, call on the reserve!" Meade shouted above the thunder of the bombardment. "The V Corps and a division of Hancock's will support you —"

But that was as far as he got. His horse reared in terror at the roar of a nearby gun and suddenly bolted, the bit in his teeth. For a moment all Meade's attention was on the fear-crazed animal, which seemed as likely to carry him into the enemy lines as to remain within his own, but presently he got him under control again and galloped off to order up supports for Sickles in the salient.

It was clear by now that they would be needed soon; for behind him, as he rode, he could hear above the uproar of the guns the unnerving quaver of the rebel yell, which signified all too clearly that Lee was launching another of those savage attacks that had won fame for him and his scarecrow infantry.

★ ★ ★

Although Lee's ready acceptance of the role of attacker seemed to indicate otherwise, the odds were decidedly with Meade. Sedgwick's arrival completed the concentration of the Army of the Potomac, which remained some 80,000 strong after deductions for stragglers and yesterday's casualties. Lee on the other hand, with Pickett's division and six of the seven cavalry brigades still absent, had fewer than 50,000 effectives on the field after similar deductions. Moreover, the tactical deployment of the two forces extended these eight-to-five odds considerably. Meade's 51 brigades of infantry and seven of cavalry were available for the occupation of three miles of line, which gave him an average of 27,000 men per mile, or better than fifteen to the yard — roughly twice as heavy a concentration as the Confederates had enjoyed at Fredericksburg — whereas Lee's 34 brigades of infantry and one of cavalry were distributed along a five-mile semicircle for an average of 10,000 men to the mile, or fewer than six per yard. As for artillery, Meade had 354 guns and Lee 272, or 118 to the mile, as compared to 54.

Nor were numbers the whole story. If the attacker enjoyed the advantage of being able to mass his troops for a sudden strike from a point of his choice along the extended arc, this was largely offset by the defender's advantage of being able to rush his ample reserves along the chord of that arc, first to bolster the threatened point and then to counterattack; so that the problem for Lee was not only to achieve a penetration, but also to maintain it afterwards in order to exploit it, which might prove an even greater difficulty. What was more, as he had warned Ewell the evening before, any thinning of the circumferential line to provide a striking force elsewhere would expose the weakened sector to being swamped and broken by the kind of powerful assault Meade could launch, more or less at will, from his interior lines. In short, if Sickles had exposed his two divisions to possible destruction by his occupation of the salient, the same might be said of Lee, in the light of all this, with regard to his whole army and the manner in which he had disposed it.

Longstreet had discerned a good deal of this at first glance; at any rate he had recognized the potentials of disaster, even though he had no access to figures comparing the tactical strengths of the two armies. The two positions were there to look at, Meade's and Lee's, and the only thing he liked about the latter was that it could be abandoned without much trouble. When Lee declined his suggestion that the Confederates move around the Federal left and take up a similar position of their own, thus reversing the present assignment of roles, Old Peter was dismayed. Failure by Hill and Ewell to complete the victory by driving the blue fugitives from the heights they had fallen back on, which was his second choice as a proper course of action, only increased his despondency. "It would have been better had we not fought at all than to have left undone what we did," he had said the night before, in response to a staff officer's exuberance over the day's success. Renewing his plea for a withdrawal this morning, the burly Georgian had been rebuffed again: whereupon he turned sulky. Though he had of course obeyed all orders given him, he had not anticipated them in the best tradition of the Army of Northern Virginia, with the result that he was partly to blame for the delays encountered in the course of the unreconnoitered flank march. As it approached its close, however, his spirits rose — as they always did in proximity to the enemy. Above all, by a sort of extension if not reversal of his native stubbornness, he was determined to carry out Lee's orders to the letter.

Just how determined Longstreet was in this respect was demonstrated to McLaws and Hood shortly after they halted their divisions in wooded jump-off positions due west of the Peach Orchard and the Devil's Den. McLaws rode forward, then dismounted and walked to the edge of the woods, about a quarter of a mile from the Emmitsburg Road, for a look at the ground over which his troops would be advancing. There in plain sight he saw two blue divisions, one posted north along the road and the other southeast in the direction of the Round Tops. "The view presented astonished me," he later recalled, "as the enemy was massed in my front, and extended to my right and left as far as I could see." Whatever validity they might have had when they were conceived, two miles away and something over five hours ago, Lee's plans for an attack up the Emmitsburg Road, in order to get astride the lower end of Cemetery Ridge, were obviously no longer practicable. Not only was the Union left not overlapped, as had been presupposed, but McLaws would be exposing his flank to end-on fire if he attacked in accordance with instructions. He notified Longstreet of this turn of events, only to be told that the orders were not subject to alteration. "There is no one in your front but a regiment of infantry and a battery of artillery," the staff man who brought this message informed him. McLaws replied that he knew better, having seen with his own eyes what was out there. But this had no effect. Three times he protested, and three times he was told to attack as ordered. And the same was true of Hood. Never in his military life had the sad-eyed blond young giant requested a modification of an order to attack, but he took one look at the situation and reacted much as McLaws was doing, half a mile to the north. Before protesting, however, he sent out scouts to search for an alternative to what appeared to him to be a suicidal venture. They promptly found one. All the country south of the Round Tops was unoccupied, they reported; Meade's far left was wide open to just such an attack as Lee had contemplated. So Hood sent word to Longstreet that it was "unwise to attack up the Emmitsburg Road, as ordered," and requested instead that he be allowed "to turn Round Top and attack the enemy in flank and rear."

Longstreet's reply — based, as he said later, on Lee's repeated earlier refusal to permit any maneuver around the enemy left — was brief and to the point: "General Lee's orders are to attack up the Emmitsburg Road." Supposing there must have been some misunderstanding, Hood repeated his request, and again his chief replied with that one sentence: "General Lee's orders are to attack up the Emmitsburg Road." By now Hood had been in position for nearly an hour, confronting the fissured tangle of the Devil's Den and the rocky frown of Little Round Top, and the longer he looked at what his men were being required to face, the more he became convinced that they were doomed. "In fact," he declared afterwards, "it seemed to me that the enemy occupied a position so strong — I may say impregnable — that, independently of their flank fire, they could easily repel our attack by merely throwing or rolling stones down the mountain side as we approached." Once more he urged Longstreet to grant him freedom to maneuver, only to have Old Peter deny him for still a third time: "General Lee's orders are to attack up the Emmitsburg Road." All that was lacking to complete the symbolism was a cockcrow. What came instead was a staff officer with peremptory instructions for him to go forward without delay, and while Hood was making last-minute adjustments in the alignment of his brigades, the corps commander himself rode up. It was 4 o'clock. With his troops already in motion, Hood made a fourth and final appeal for permission to maneuver around Round Top for a strike at the open flank and rear of the blue army. Longstreet still would not agree, though he did at least change the wording of his one-sentence reply. "We must obey the orders of General Lee," he said.

Lee's instructions called for the attack to be launched in echelon, from right to left, not only by divisions — first Hood, then McLaws, and finally Anderson, with Pender alerted to strike in turn if additional pressure was needed — but also by the brigades within those divi-

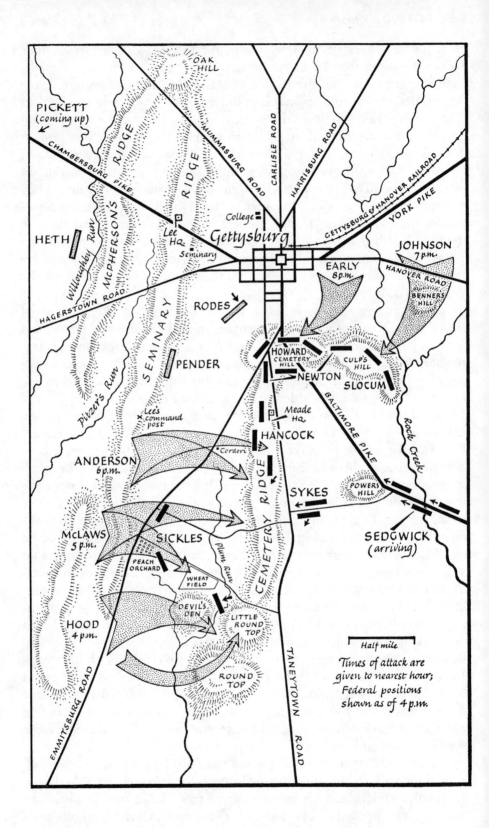

sions, so that the attack would gather strength as it rolled northward. This meant that Law, on Hood's and therefore the army's right, would be the first to step off. And so he did, promptly at 4 o'clock: but not as ordered. If Longstreet would not disregard or modify Lee's instructions, nor Hood Longstreet's, Law — a month short of his twenty-seventh birthday and next to the youngest of Lee's generals — had no intention of exposing first the flank and then the rear of his troops to the destructive fire of the Yankees in the Devil's Den, as would necessarily be the case if he advanced with his left aligned on the Emmitsburg Road. His unwillingness was not the result of any lack of courage, a quality he had demonstrated on field after field, beginning with Gaines Mill, where his brigade had charged alongside Hood's to break Fitz-John Porter's apparently unbreakable triple line and give the Army of Northern Virginia its first victory. He would make whatever sacrifice was called for, but he saw that to advance as ordered would be to spill the blood of his five Alabama regiments to little purpose and with no chance of return. Consequently, in flat disobedience of orders, he charged due east, in a frontal not an oblique attack on the Devil's Den and Little Round Top itself, which he saw as the key to control of the field.

Brigadier General J. B. Robertson's Texas brigade conformed, being next in line, and the result, as Lee's far right and Meade's far left came to grips in that vine-laced maze of boulders and ravines, "was more like Indian fighting," one participant would recall, "than anything I experienced during the war." By the time Hood's other two brigades, both from Georgia and under Georgians, Brigadier Generals Henry L. Benning and G. T. Anderson, joined the melee in the Devil's Den, they found the conflict quite as confused as it was fierce. Hood was down, unhorsed by a shell fragment much as Heth had been the day before, except that he was struck in the arm and carried out of the battle on a stretcher. Such control as remained was on the company level, or even lower. "Every fellow was his own general," a Texan later wrote. "Private soldiers gave commands as loud as the officers; nobody paying any attention to either."

While this highly individualistic struggle was building toward a climax half a mile west of Little Round Top, Law gave twenty-seven-year-old Colonel William Oates instructions to veer southward with two regiments and flush a troublesome detachment of Union sharpshooters out of some woods at the foot of the steep northwest slope of Round Top. It was done in short order, though not without galling casualties; after which the five hundred survivors continued their uphill charge, scrambling hand over hand around and across huge boulders and through heavy underbrush, to call a halt at last on the lofty summit, panting for breath and wishing fervently that they had not sent their canteens off to be filled just before they received the order to advance. Unlike the lower conical hill immediately to the north, which had been cleared of timber in the fall and thus afforded an excellent all-round view of the countryside, this tallest of all the heights in Adams County — sometimes called Sugarloaf by the natives — was heavily wooded from base to crown, a condition detracting considerably from its tactical usefulness. Through the trees due north, however, just over a hundred feet below and less than half a beeline mile away, Oates could see the barren, craggy dome of Little Round Top, deserted except for a handful of enemy signalmen busily wagging their long-handled flags, while off to the left, on lower ground, smoke boiled furiously out of the rocks where the fight for the Devil's Den was raging at the tip of the left arm of the spraddled V drawn by Sickles, its apex in the Peach Orchard and its right arm extended for the better part of a mile up the Emmitsburg Road, south and west of the main Federal position along the upper end of Cemetery Ridge and on the dominant heights to the north and east, bend and barb of the fishhook Meade had chosen to defend. All this lay before and below the young Alabama colonel, who continued to look it over while his troops were catching their breath on the crest of Round Top. Victory seemed as clear to him, in his mind's eye, as the town of Gettysburg itself, which he could see through the drifting smoke, and the green fields rolling northward out of sight. He believed that with his present force he could hold this hilltop stronghold against the whole Yankee army, if necessary, so steep were the approaches on all sides, and if a battery of rifled guns could somehow be manhandled up here, piece by piece and part by part if need be, not a cranny of Meade's fishhook line would be tenable any longer than it would take a detail of axmen to clear a narrow field of fire. So he believed. But just then a courier arrived from Law with instructions for him to push on and capture Little Round Top. Oates protested briefly, to no avail, then got his parched and weary men to their feet — feet that had covered no less than thirty miles of road and mountainside since 3 o'clock that morning at New Guilford — and started them down the northern face of Round Top, intent on carrying out the order.

It did not seem to him that this would be too difficult, particularly after he crossed the wooded valley between the Round Tops and was joined by a third regiment of Alabamians and two of Texans who had fought their way eastward through the lower fringes of the Devil's Den. Earlier, looking down from the taller of the two peaks, he had seen that the lower was not only undefended but also unoccupied, except by a handful of signalmen, and the confidence he derived from this was strengthened as the uphill march began and then continued without an indication that a single enemy rifleman stood or crouched among the rocks ahead. Two thirds of the way up, however, as the butternut skirmishers approached a ledge that formed a natural bastion around the southwest face of the hill, a heavy volley of musketry exploded in their faces. Oates knew at once, from the volume of fire — he afterwards described it as the most destructive he had ever encountered — that it had been delivered by nothing less than a brigade, and probably a veteran one at that. This meant that he had a fight on his hands, against troops in a position that afforded the same advantages he had contemplated enjoying in defense of the hilltop he had just abandoned under protest that he could hold it against all comers with two regiments of about 500 badly winded men and no artillery at all. It was obvious here on Little Round Top, though, that a good many more men than that were shooting at him from the rocky ledge ahead, and what was more they had artillery, two guns spraying canister from the crest above and beyond them. As soon as he could establish a firing line of his own, the three Alabama regiments on the right and the two Texas regiments on the left, Oates gave the order for an all-out uphill charge to drive the Federals back on their guns and off the mountaintop.

That the blue defenders had taken position on Little Round Top, even as Oates was on his way down from the companion height to seize it, was due to the vigilance and perception of one man, a staff brigadier who, strictly speaking, had no direct command over troops at all. Gouverneur K. Warren, the army's thirty-three-year-old chief engineer, a frail-looking New Yorker, thin-faced and clean-shaven except for a drooped mustache and a tuft of beard just below his lower lip, had ridden over to inspect the hill's defenses at about the same time Meade's brief talk with Sickles was being interrupted by his horse's antic reaction to the rebel cannonade. Disturbed to find the high ground all but unoccupied, despite its obvious tactical value, Warren told the signalmen to keep up their wigwag activity, simply as a pretense of alertness, whether they had any real messages to transmit or not — which was why Oates had found them so busy when he looked down at them from across the valley — and quickly notified Meade of the grave danger to his left. Meade passed the word to Sykes, whose corps by now was in motion to reinforce Sickles, and Sykes passed it along to Barnes. Barnes, who at sixty-two was the oldest division commander in the army, was not with his troops at the time, but Colonel Strong Vincent, who at twenty-six was the army's youngest brigade commander, responded by marching at once to occupy the hill. Arriving less than a quarter of an hour before the Texans and Alabamians, he advanced his brigade — four regiments from as many different states, Pennsylvania, New York, Maine, and Michigan — to the far side of the crest, well downhill in order to leave room for reinforcements, and took up a stout position in which to wait for what was not long in coming. Warren meanwhile had ordered up two guns of First Lieutenant Charles Hazlett's battery, helping to manhandle them up the rocky incline and onto the summit. This done, he went in search of infantry supports, which he could see were about to be needed badly, and found Brigadier General Stephen

H. Weed's brigade of Ayres's division marching west on the road leading out to the Peach Orchard. When the commander of the rear regiment, Colonel Patrick O'Rorke — by coincidence it was the 140th New York, which Warren himself had commanded before he moved up to staff — protested that he and his men were under orders to join Sickles, Warren did not waste time riding to the head of the column to find Weed. "Never mind that, Paddy," he said. "Bring them up on the double-quick, and don't stop for aligning. I'll take the responsibility." O'Rorke did as Warren directed, and Weed soon followed with his other three regiments, double-timing them as best he could up the steep, boulder-clogged incline and over the crest, to find the struggle raging furiously below him on the equally steep and rocky southwest face of the fuming hill.

　　　Vincent by then had fallen, shot through the heart as he ranged up and down the firing line. "Don't yield an inch!" was his last command, and though his men tried their hardest to do as he said, one officer was to recall that, under the influence of no less than five charges and countercharges, "the edge of the fight swayed back and forward like a wave." The conflict was particularly desperate on the far left, where the 20th Maine, made up of lumberjacks and fishermen under Colonel Joshua Chamberlain, a former minister and Bowdoin professor, opposed the 15th Alabama, Oates's own regiment, composed for the most part of farmers. Equally far from home — Presque Isle and Talladega were each 650 crowflight miles from Little Round Top, which lay practically on the line connecting them — the men of these two outfits fought as if the outcome of the battle, and with it the war, depended on their valor: as indeed perhaps it did, since whoever had possession of this craggy height on the Union left would dominate the whole fishhook position. "The blood stood in puddles in some places on the rocks," Oates said later. Losses were especially heavy among Federals of rank. O'Rorke, who was barely twenty-three and an officer of much promise, having been top man in the West Point class of '61, was killed along with more than two dozen of his men in the first blast of musketry that greeted his arrival. Weed, coming up behind him with the rest of the brigade, was shot in the head by a sniper down in the Devil's Den, and as Hazlett, who was standing beside him directing the fire of his two guns, bent forward to catch any last words the twenty-nine-year-old brigadier might utter, he too was dropped, probably by the same long-range marksman, and fell dead across Weed's body.

　　　Casualties on the Confederate side were as heavy, if not heavier, and increased steadily as blue reinforcements continued to come up, unmatched by any on the downhill side. With all but one of the field officers killed or wounded in the Texas regiments, and no replacements anywhere in sight, Major J. C. Rogers, who had succeeded to leadership of the 5th Texas by elimination, might have thought he had been forgotten by the high command, except that presently a courier from division came up the hillside, dodging from boulder to boulder among the twittering bullets and screaming ricochets. He brought no expected word of reinforcements, but he did have a message from the wounded Hood's successor. "General Law presents his compliments," he told Rogers, "and says to hold the place at all hazards." This was altogether too much for the hard-pressed major. "Compliments, hell!" he roared above the clatter of battle. "Who wants compliments in such a damned place as this? Go back and ask General Law if he expects me to hold the world in check with the 5th Texas regiment!"

Oates could see that the struggle could have but one end if it continued at this rate, five regiments fighting uphill against eight who were supported by artillery in defense of a position he had judged to be nearly impregnable in the first place. So long as there was a hope of reinforcements he would fight — "Return to your companies; we will sell out as dearly as possible," he told his captains — but presently, after the courier arrived with nothing more substantial than Law's compliments, he ordered a withdrawal. Just as the word was passed, the Maine men launched a bayonet attack. "When the signal was given we ran like a herd of wild cattle," Oates later admitted.

Near the base of the hill they rallied, being joined by the rest of Law's and Robertson's brigades, together with those of Anderson and Benning, who had succeeded by now in driving the Federals out of the Devil's Den, capturing three guns in the process. Not that the fighting had abated; Sykes had brought up two of his divisions in support of Sickles, with the result that the odds were as long down here as they had been above. There on the lower western slopes of Little Round Top the survivors began collecting rocks of all shapes and sizes, constructing a barricade to fight behind, and all the while the soldiers of both armies kept up a hot fire, banging away at whatever showed itself or perhaps at nothing at all. "Both sides were whipped," a Texas private explained afterwards, "and all were mad about it."

McLaws was also engaged by now, in part at least, and though this finally helped to relieve the pressure on the men who were fighting for their lives at the base of the rocky hill, the wait had been a long one, Longstreet having held him back in hopes that when he went forward at last he would find the enemy line greatly weakened by the shift of troops to meet Hood's attack on Little Round Top, which after all was not the assigned objective. Such withholding tactics had made possible the one-punch knockout Old Peter had scored at Second Manassas, a year ago next month, and he planned to repeat that coup today. If this was hard on Hood, whose men were thus required to absorb the single-minded attention of the entire Federal left wing for more than an hour, it was not easy on McLaws and his four brigade commanders, who were burning to advance: particularly Barksdale, whose thirst for glory was as sharp in Pennsylvania as it had been on his great day at Fredericksburg, where Lee to his delight had let him challenge the whole Yankee army. From the eastern fringe of the woods in which his troops awaited the signal to move out, the Mississippian could see bluecoats milling about in the Peach Orchard, as if they had it in mind to advance against him, and a battery posted temptingly at the apex of the salient, less than six hundred yards away. "General, let me go; General, let me charge," he kept begging McLaws, who declined, being under orders to wait for corps to inform him when the time was ripe. Soon Longstreet came riding northward through the woods and drew rein to talk with McLaws. Born within a week of each other, forty-two years ago, the two Georgians had been classmates at West Point. Equally burly of form and shaggy of hair and beard, they even resembled one another, not only in looks but also in their deliberative manner. Barksdale approached them and renewed his plea. "I wish you would let me go in, General," he appealed to the corps commander; "I will take that battery in five minutes." Longstreet looked out at the guns in the orchard, then back at the tall, white-maned Mississippian, who was trembling with excitement. Old Peter liked Barksdale, who was half a year his junior but looked older because of the prematurely gray hair worn shoulder-length, and greatly admired his spirit; but he would not be hurried. "Wait a little," he said in a calm, deep voice. "We are all going in presently."

It was near 5.30 before he gave the signal that opened the secondary attack. McLaws went in as Hood had done, his brigades committed in echelon from the right, which meant that Barksdale had some more waiting to do, being stationed on the left. South Carolinians under Brigadier General J. B. Kershaw — one of the five generals the town of Camden was to contribute to the Confederacy before the war was over — went forward with a shout, headed straight for the big wheat field north of the Devil's Den, about midway between Little Round Top and the Peach Orchard. Longstreet walked out with them as far as the Emmitsburg Road, where he stopped and waved them on with his hat, adding his own deep-throated version of the rebel yell to the tumult. They struck the center of Birney's division, which was posted behind a low stone wall along the near edge of the shimmering field of wheat, with Barnes's two remaining brigades in close support. As the fighting mounted swiftly toward a climax, Brigadier General Paul J. Semmes — younger brother of the *Alabama*'s captain — brought his Georgians out to join the stand-up fight, and behind them came the third brigade, still more Georgians, under Brigadier General W. T. Wofford, who had led them since the death of Tom Cobb in the sunken road at Fredericksburg. The Union line began to crumble under this added pressure, men dropping all along it and others scrambling rearward to get a head start in the race for safety.

Just then Semmes fell mortally wounded, which resulted in some confusion among his troops; but the loss was overbalanced at this critical point by one on the other side. Sickles was riding his line, erect on horseback, ignoring the whistle of bullets and the scream of shells, until one of the latter came along that could not be ignored because it struck his right leg, just above the knee, and left it hanging in shreds. He fell heavily to the ground, but kept cool enough to save his life by ordering a tourniquet improvised from a saddle strap. As he lay there, pale from the sudden loss of blood, his thigh bone protruding stark white against the red of mangled flesh, a staff officer rode up and asked solicitously, if superfluously: "General, are you hurt?" Normally, Sickles would have laughed at the simplicity of the question, but not now. "Tell General Birney he must take command," he replied. Lifted onto a stretcher, he heard through the waves of pain and shock that a rumor was being spread that he was dead; so he called the bearers to a halt while one of them lit a cigar for him, then rode the rest of the way to the aid station with it clenched at a jaunty angle between his teeth, puffing industriously at it by way of disproving the rumor that he had stopped breathing. Thus did Old Dan Sickles leave the war, to proceed in time to other fields of endeavor, including a well-publicized liaison with the deposed nymphomaniac Queen of Spain.

There was to be a great deal of discussion, beginning tonight and continuing down the years, as to whether his occupation of the salient, half a mile and more in front of the main Union line, had been a colossal blunder or a tactically sound maneuver. Whatever else it was or wasn't — and entirely aside from the fact that it helped to discourage Longstreet's men from attacking as Lee had ordered, straight up the Emmitsburg Road, which probably would have meant utter destruction for them if Sickles had stayed back on the ridge to tear their flank as they went by — the movement resulted at any rate in the wrecking of his corps, whose two divisions, formerly under Phil Kearny and Joe Hooker and therefore among the most famous in the army, were to suffer well over four thousand casualties in the two hours before sunset. The worst of the damage occurred when the line gave way at the western rim of the wheat field. "It is too hot; my men cannot stand it!" Barnes cried, and he ordered a retreat. Birney's were quick to follow, despite his efforts to stop them. But as the elated Confederates started forward, in close and hot pursuit, they were met by a fresh division under Caldwell, whom Hancock had alerted to stand by for trouble after predicting — quite accurately, as it turned out — that Sickles' troops would "come tumbling back" from the salient. Caldwell struck with all his strength, holding nothing in reserve. And now, though he lost three of his four brigade commanders, two of them killed on contact, it was the rebels who fell back through the trampled grain, the steam gone out of their drive. From Little Round Top to the northern edge of the wheat field, the fighting degenerated into a bloody squabble as regiment fought regiment, alternately driving and being driven. "What a hell is there down in that valley!" a Federal lieutenant exclaimed after viewing the carnage from up on Cemetery Ridge. Birney's men were out of it by then, such as remained uncaptured and alive, and now the turn had come of those with Humphreys in the orchard and strung out along the road northeast of there.

Longstreet's "presently" had begun to seem interminable to Barksdale and his soldiers, held under cover and straining at the leash all the time the other three brigades were taking on most of Birney's and Barnes's divisions and finally all of Caldwell's, which came in fresh to stop them short of the ridge. Though opinion was divided as to the distinguishing characteristics of these troops from the Deep South — a Virginia artilleryman, for example, having learned to feel secure whenever his battery had the support of the Mississippians, was to say that theirs was the brigade "I knew and loved best of all in Lee's army"; whereas a Chambersburg civilian, observing the various rebel outfits that passed through his town, decided quite to the contrary that "those from Mississippi and Texas were more vicious and defiant" than the rest — the men themselves not only would have considered both of these remarks complimentary, but also would have been hard put to say which compliment they preferred. Certainly their viciousness and defiance were apparent to the Federals in the orchard, just over a quarter-mile away, as they came running eastward out of the woods, unleashed at last and eager to come to grips. Barksdale was out in front of the whole line, his face "radiant with joy," as one observer remarked, to be leading what a Confederate lieutenant and a Union colonel referred to afterwards, respectively, as "the most magnificent charge I witnessed during the war" and "the grandest charge that was ever made by mortal man." His earlier assurance that he could "take that battery in five minutes" had sounded overconfident at the time, mainly because the stout rail fences on both sides of the Emmitsburg Road seemed likely to slow his advance while they were being torn down or climbed over. As it turned out, however, the fences were no deterrent at all. They simply vanished under the impact of the charging Mississippians, who reached the Peach Orchard even sooner than their general had predicted, whooping with delight as they swarmed over the battery and such of its defenders as had resisted the impulse to get out of the path of that savage assault. Four of the guns and close to a thousand prisoners were taken in one swoop, but that was only a part of what Barksdale was after. Still out front, hatless so that his long white hair streamed behind him as he ran, he shouted: "Forward, men! Forward!" pointing with his sword at the blue line half a mile ahead on Cemetery Ridge.

He did not make it that far, nor did any of his men. A Federal brigadier, watching the conspicuous figure draw nearer across the stony

floor of the valley, assigned a whole company of riflemen the task of
bringing him down; which they did. As for his men, the vigilant Hunt
had prepared a reception for them by massing forty guns along the crest
and down the slope of the ridge. Meade had seen to it that these batteries
had infantry support by shifting troops southward from his over-
crowded right, but the guns themselves, blasting the attackers wholesale
as they came within easy range, turned out to be enough. Still they came
on, overrunning the first line of artillery on the slope, where the cannoneers fought them with pistols and rammer staffs and whatever came
to hand, and all the while the guns on the crest flung canister point-
blank at them, mangling blue and gray alike. Finally, unsupported on
the left or right, Barksdale's men fell back westward to a line along
Plum Run, midway between the road and the ridge, leaving half their
number dead or wounded on the field, including their commander.
Scouts from a Vermont regiment were to bring him into their lines that
night, shot through both legs and the breast, and he would die by morning, his thirst for glory slaked at last.

Hood and McLaws had done their worst, and the 15,000 men in
their eight brigades, having taken on six full enemy divisions, together
with major portions of three others — a total of 22 Federal brigades,
disposed with all the advantages of the defensive and containing better
than twice as many troops as came against them — were fought to a
standstill along an irregular line stretching northward from the Round
Tops to the Peach Orchard, anywhere from half a mile to a mile beyond
the Emmitsburg Road, which had marked the line of departure. Proud
of what his soldiers had accomplished against the odds, though he knew
it was less than Lee had hoped for, Longstreet was to say: "I do not hesitate to pronounce this the best three hours' fighting ever done by any
troops on any battlefield." The cost had been great — more than a third
of the men in the two divisions had been hit; Hood would be out of
combat for some time, a grievous loss, and Semmes and Barksdale forever — but so had been the gain: not so much in actual ground, though
that had been considerable, as in its effect of setting the bluecoats up for
the kill. Meade had been stripping his center, along with his right, to
reinforce his left. And now the offensive passed to Hill, or more specifically to Richard Anderson, whose division was on the right, adjoining
McLaws, and who now took up his portion of the echelon attack from a
position directly opposite the weakened Union center.

In this as in the other two divisional attacks the brigades were to
be committed in sequence from the right, and it opened with all the
precision of a maneuver on the drill field. Nor was there any such delay
as there had been in the case of McLaws, held in check by Longstreet
while Hood's men were storming the Devil's Den and fighting for their
lives on Little Round Top. At 6.20, when Barksdale's survivors began

their withdrawal from the shell-swept western slope of Cemetery Ridge, Anderson sent Wilcox and his Alabamians driving hard for a section of the ridge just north of where the Mississippians had struck and been repulsed. Next in line, Colonel David Lang's small brigade of three Florida regiments followed promptly, supported in turn by Brigadier General Ambrose R. Wright's Georgians, who came forward on the left. But that was where the breakdown of the echelon plan began. Brigadier General Carnot Posey, having already committed three of his four Mississippi regiments as skirmishers, had not understood that he was to charge with the fourth, and his doubts became even graver when he discovered that his left would not be covered by Brigadier General William Mahone, who could not be persuaded that his Virginia brigade, posted all day in reserve, was intended to have a share in the attack. Wilcox by now had sent his adjutant back to ask for reinforcements, and Anderson had sent him on to Mahone with full approval of the request. But Mahone refused to budge. "I have my orders from General Anderson himself to stay here," he kept insisting, despite the staff man's protest that it was the division commander who had sent him. As a result, Posey advanced his single regiment only as far as the Emmitsburg Road, where he came under heavy artillery fire, and Wright, after pausing briefly to give the two laggard brigades a chance to catch up and cover his left, went on alone when he saw that the Mississippians would come no farther and that the Virginians had no intention of advancing at all.

The fault was primarily Anderson's. Missing the firm if sometimes heavy hand of Longstreet, under whom he had always fought before — except of course at Chancellorsville, where Lee himself had taken him in charge — he was unaccustomed to Hill's comparatively light touch, which allowed him to be less attentive to preparatory details. Furthermore, Hill had understood that his right division was more or less detached to Longstreet, whereas Longstreet had interpreted Lee's instructions merely to mean that Hill would be in support and therefore still in command of his own troops. Consequently, neither exercised any control over Anderson, who followed suit by leaving the conduct of the attack to his subordinates, with the result that it broke down in midcareer.

At this point, however, with Wilcox, Lang, and Wright driving hard for Cemetery Ridge, the question of blame seemed highly inappropriate. A more likely question seemed to concern a proper distribution of praise among the three attacking brigades for having pierced the Union center. Hancock certainly saw it in that light, and with good cause. Meade having placed him in command of the III Corps as well as his own when Sickles fell, he had sent one of his three divisions to reinforce the left an hour ago, and since then he had been using elements of the two remaining divisions to bolster the line along Plum Run, where McLaws was keeping up the pressure. As a result, he had found neither the time nor the means to fill the gap on his left, where Caldwell had been posted until his departure, and the even larger gap that had yawned beyond it ever since Sickles moved out to occupy the salient. To his horror, Hancock now saw that Wilcox was headed directly for this soft spot, driving the remnant of Humphreys' division pell-mell before him as he advanced, with Lang on his left and Wright on the left of Lang. Gambling that no simultaneous attack would be launched against his right, just below Cemetery Hill, Hancock ordered Gibbon and Hays to double-time southward along the ridge and use what was left of their commands to plug the gap the rebels were about to strike.

He hurried in that direction, ahead of his troops, and arrived in time to witness the final rout of Humphreys, whose men were in full flight by now, with Wilcox close on their heels and driving hard for the scantly defended ridge beyond. As he himself climbed back up the slope on horseback, under heavy fire from the attackers, Hancock wondered how he was going to stop or even delay them long enough for a substantial line of defense to be formed on the high ground. Gibbon and Hays "had been ordered up and were coming on the run," he later explained, "but I saw that in some way five minutes must be gained or we were lost." Just then the lead regiment of Gibbon's first brigade came over the crest in a column of fours, and Hancock saw a chance to gain those five minutes, though at a cruel price.

"What regiment is this?" he asked the officer at the head of the column moving toward him down the slope.

"First Minnesota," Colonel William Colvill replied.

Hancock nodded. "Colonel, do you see those colors?" As he spoke he pointed at the Alabama flag in the front rank of the charging rebels. Colvill said he did. "Then take them," Hancock told him.

Quickly, although scarcely a man among them could have failed to see what was being asked of him, the Minnesotans deployed on the slope — eight companies of them, at any rate; three others had been detached as skirmishers, leaving 262 men present for duty — and charging headlong down it, bayonets fixed, struck the center of the long gray line. Already in some disorder as a result of their run of nearly a mile over stony ground and against such resistance as Humphreys had managed to offer, the Confederates recoiled briefly, then came on again, yelling fiercely as they concentrated their fire on this one undersized blue regiment. The result was devastating. Colvill and all but three of his officers were killed or wounded, together with 215 of his men. A captain brought the 47 survivors back up the ridge, less than one fifth as many as had charged down it. They had not taken the Alabama flag, but they had held onto their own. And they had given Hancock his five minutes, plus five more for good measure.

Those ten minutes were enough. By the time Wilcox reached the foot of the ridge, with Lang bringing up his three regiments on the left, Gibbon's division had taken position on the crest and was pouring heavy volleys of musketry into the ranks of both brigades from dead ahead. Staggered by this, and torn on his unprotected right by fire from the massed batteries that had repulsed Barksdale half an hour before, Wilcox looked back across the valley and saw that his appeal for reinforcements had not been answered. Regretfully he ordered a retreat. So did Lang at the same time. And as the Alabamians and Floridians began their withdrawal from the base of the ridge, Wright's Georgians struck with irresistible force, some four hundred yards to the north. "On they came like the fury of a whirlwind," a Pennsylvania captain later recalled. The impetus of their drive carried them swiftly up the slope and into the breaking ranks of the defenders, then through the line of guns, whose cannoneers scattered, and onto the crest. They did not stay there long — Gibbon and Hays had them greatly outnumbered, as well as outflanked on the right and left, and Meade had already ordered another three divisions to converge on the threatened point from Cemetery Hill, three quarters of a mile to the north, and Culp's Hill, about the same distance across the eastern valley — but while they were there Wright believed that he had victory within his reach. On the reverse slope, bluecoats were streaming rearward across the Taneytown Road, and half a mile beyond it the Baltimore Pike was crowded with fugitives. Yet these were only the backwash of the battle. Nearer at hand, on the left and right, he saw heavy blue columns bearing down on him, and he saw too — like Wilcox and Lang before him, though they had achieved no such penetration of the main Union line — that to stay where he was, unsupported, meant capture or annihilation. He ordered a withdrawal, which was achieved only by charging a body of Federals who had gained his rear by now, and then fell back across the Emmitsburg Road, taking punishment all the way from the two dozen guns he had captured and then abandoned. Like Wilcox and Lang, Wright had lost nearly half his men in that one charge, and he found this a steep price to pay for one quick look at the Union rear, even though he believed ever after that the end of the war had been within his reach if only he had been supported while he was astride the crest of Cemetery Ridge, midway of the Yankee line and within plain sight of the cottage Meade was using as headquarters for his army.

The hard fact that no supports were at hand when the Georgians crested the ridge and stood poised there, silhouetted against the eastern sky for one brief fall of time as they pierced the enemy center, did not mean that none had been available. Though Posey and Mahone had hung back, declining for whatever reasons to go forward — the former calling a halt halfway across the valley and the latter refusing to budge from the shade of the trees on Seminary Ridge, directly behind Lee's command post — there still was Pender, whose division was to the Third Corps what Hood's and Johnson's were to the First and Second, the hardest-hitting and fiercest of the three. And yet Pender was not there after all: not Pender in person. Like Heth and Hood, at about the same time yesterday and earlier today, he had been unhorsed by a casual fragment of shell while riding his line to inspect and steady his men for their possible share in the attack then rolling northward. The wound in his leg, though ugly enough, was not thought to be very serious, or at any rate not fatal. But it was. Two weeks later the leg was taken off, infection having set in during the long ambulance ride back to Virginia, and he did not survive the amputation. "Tell my wife I do not fear to die," the twenty-nine-year-old North Carolinian said in the course of his suffering, which was intense. "I can confidently resign my soul to God, trusting in the atonement of our Lord Jesus Christ. My only regret is to leave her and our children." If this had the tone of Stonewall Jackson, under whom Pender had developed into one of the best of all Lee's generals despite his youth, his last words sounded even more like his dead chief: "I have always tried to do my duty in every sphere of life in which Providence has placed me." Few doubted afterwards that he would have done that duty here today at Gettysburg by leading his four brigades across the valley to assault the ridge just north of where Wright had struck it. There was in fact little to stop him once he got there. Not only had Hancock shifted his two divisions south to counter Anderson's attack; Meade had also moved Newton's two in that direction from their position supporting Howard on Cemetery Hill. But that was beside the point, as it turned out. The decision whether to join the charge had been discretionary anyhow, according to Lee's orders, and when Pender was hit and carried off the field, his temporary successor Brigadier General James Lane, having watched Anderson's two adjoining brigades falter, decided that it was no longer advisable for his troops to advance, since they would not be supported on the right. Moreover, A. P. Hill was not there at the time, having ridden northward to confer with Rodes, and did not urge Lane on.

With that, the three-hour-long assault on Cemetery Ridge broke down completely. Hood, McLaws, and Anderson — some 22,000 men in all, including the cannoneers — had tried their hands in sequence against a total of no less than 40,000 blue defenders. Better than 7000 of the attackers had fallen in the attempt, and all they had to show for this loss of one third of the force engaged was the Devil's Den, plus the Peach Orchard, which had been proved to be practically indefensible in the first place, and a few acres of stony ground on the floor of the valley between the ridges. "The whole affair was disjointed," a member of Lee's staff admitted later. "There was an utter absence of accord in the movements of the several commands."

The truth was, the army had slipped back to the disorganization of the Seven Days, except that here at Gettysburg there was no hard-core tactical plan to carry it through the bungling. There was in fact scarcely any plan at all, Lee's instructions for an attack up the Emmitsburg Road having been rejected out of necessity at the start. This, to-gether with the refusal of the Federals to panic under pressure, as they had done so often before when the graybacks came screaming at them, had stood in the way of victory. And yet, in light of the fact that each of the three attacking divisions in turn had come close to carrying the day, there was more to it than that. Specifically, there was Warren and there was Hancock, both of whom had served their commander in a way that none of Lee's chief lieutenants had served him. Warren had acted on his own to save Little Round Top and the battle, and Hancock had done the same to prevent a breakthrough, first at the lower end and then at the center of Cemetery Ridge; but no one above the rank of colonel — Oates, the exception, lacked the authority to make it count — had acted with any corresponding initiative on the other side. There was, as always, no lack of Confederate bravery, and the army's combat skill had been demonstrated amply by the fact that, despite its role as the attacker, it had inflicted even more casualties than it had suffered, yet these qualities could not make up for the crippling lack of direction from above and the equally disadvantageous lack of initiative just below the top.

Longstreet sensed a good part of this, of course — perhaps even his own share of the blame, at least to a degree — but once more his reaction was a strange one. Though he was saddened by the wounding of Hood and the death or capture of Barksdale, which he believed were the main reasons he had failed to break Meade's line, he was by no means as gloomy as he had been in the course of the roundabout march into position. "We have not been so successful as we wished," he told an in-quirer, and that was all he said. He seemed glad, for once, that his share of the fighting was over. If Hill had broken down, it was not his fault; he had small use for Little Powell anyhow. And now the battle passed to Ewell.

Stung by Lee's complaint that he had failed to "pursue our ad-vantage of yesterday," Ewell was eager to make a redemptive showing today, despite the difficulties of terrain on this northern quarter of the field. After Lee had departed he had kept busy, all through what was left of the morning and most of the afternoon, inspecting his three divi-sions, which were disposed along a convex arc on three sides of Gettys-burg, Rodes to the west, Early just south, and Johnson to the east, con-fronting the two dominant heights at the bend and barb of the Union fishhook. His instructions required him to guard the Confederate left, keeping as many bluecoats occupied there as possible, and to stage a vigorous demonstration, by way of insuring that effect, when Long-street's guns began to roar at the far end of the line. Moreover — and this was the prospect he found most attractive, in connection with his desire to make a showing — if Ewell decided that he could strike with a fair chance of success, he was to convert the demonstration into a real attack, driving the enemy from Cemetery and Culp's hills, which commanded the Taneytown Road and the Baltimore Pike, both vital to the Federals if they were thrown into retreat from these two northern heights and the ridge leading southward to the Round Tops. The wait was a long one, anxious as Ewell was, and some time after 4 o'clock, when the distant booming at last informed him that Longstreet's artillery preparation had begun, he decided to respond in the same fashion. Six batteries, held under cover till then by Major Joseph Latimer, Johnson's twenty-year-old chief of artillery, were sent to the crest of Benner's Hill, a solitary eminence one mile east of town, with orders to pummel Culp's Hill, half a mile southwest across the valley of Rock Creek. Ewell felt that this would not only serve as a "vigorous demonstration," fixing the blue defenders in position as required, but would also afford him an opportunity to study their reaction and thus determine the advisability of launching an all-out uphill infantry assault.

The answer was both sudden and emphatic, as might have been expected if a proper reconnaissance had been made. Benner's Hill was not only fifty feet lower than the height across the way; it was also bald, which meant that the two dozen guns found neither cover nor concealment when they went into action there, whereas the Federal cannoneers had spent the past twenty hours digging lunettes and piling up embankments to add to the security of their densely wooded battery positions. Lashing their teams up the reverse slope of the isolated hill, the Confederates opened fire from its crest soon after 5 o'clock, and within a few minutes of the prompt and wrathful response by the heavier guns directly across the valley, as well as by those a mile away on Cemetery Hill, it was obvious that there could be no doubt as to the outcome of the duel, but only as to how long it could be sustained against the odds. Starkly exposed on the naked summit, the gray gunners stood to their work under a deluge of hot metal and amid sudden pillars of smoke and flame reared by exploding caissons. After about an hour of this, Latimer, who was known as the "Boy Major" and was said to be developing fast into another Pelham, felt compelled to send word that his position was untenable, a thing he had never done before in the two years since he had interrupted his sophomore year at VMI to join the army. Johnson at once authorized him to withdraw all but four of the guns, which were to remain there in support of the attack Ewell had just ordered all three of his divisions to make, despite this graphic evidence of the fury they were likely to encounter as they approached the hilltop objectives he assigned them. Latimer's withdrawal was necessarily slow, his crews having been reduced to skeletons by the counterbattery fire, and he himself was mortally wounded before it was completed, a high price to pay for confirming what should have been apparent before the one-sided contest even began.

On the face of it, the infantry attempt seemed equally doomed. Actually this was not the case, however, for the paradoxical reason that Ewell had failed in his primary mission of holding the blue forces in position on his front. By 6 o'clock, when the attack order was issued, Meade had taken thorough alarm at the series of threats to his left and center, and by 7 o'clock, when the advance began against his right, he had shifted two of Newton's three divisions southward, together with all but a single brigade from the two divisions in Slocum's corps. All that remained by then on Cemetery Hill, which Early and Rodes were to assault in sequence from the north and the northwest, were the three battered divisions under Howard, while Culp's Hill was even more scantly held by Wadsworth's division of the I Corps, down to half its normal strength after yesterday's drubbing on Seminary Ridge, and the one brigade Slocum had left behind. That was where the paradox came in. If Ewell had succeeded in holding the departed bluecoats in position, as Lee had instructed him to do, the attack would have been as suicidal as any ever attempted by either army in the whole course of the war; but as it was, with the defenses manned only by Howard's jumpy Dutchmen, Wadsworth's thin line of survivors from the rout of the day before, and the single brigade from Geary's division, the chances of a Confederate breakthrough here on the north were considerably better than fair, despite the obvious difficulties of the terrain. For one thing, thanks to Meade's alarm at the unrelenting fury of the three-hour-long assault on the Round Tops and Cemetery Ridge, Ewell's troops outnumbered the defenders to their front, an advantage no other attacking force had enjoyed on any portion of the field today.

Johnson's division, which had arrived too late for a share in the battle yesterday, had remained in the same position for nearly twenty-four hours, a mile east of Gettysburg and north of the Hanover Road, its four brigades posted from right to left under Colonel J. M. Williams and Brigadier Generals John M. Jones, George H. Steuart, and James A. Walker. The men of the first were Louisianians, and the rest were nearly all Virginians, like Old Clubby himself, who took them forward at 7 o'clock, brandishing the post-thick hickory stick from which his nickname was derived. That left half an hour till sunset, but they had more than a mile to go and armpit-deep Rock Creek to cross before they came within musket range of their Culp's Hill objective. As a result, the sun was well down behind it by the time they came surging up the northeast slope, yelling fiercely as they approached the crest. They did not make it all the way; Wadsworth's troops, including the remnant of the Iron Brigade, were well dug in and quite as determined as they had been when they shattered Heth's attack the day before. Jones was wounded early in the fight, and his and Williams's men, unsupported because Walker and his famed Stonewall Brigade remained in reserve on the far side of the creek, had all they could do to keep from being driven off the hillside. Around to the left, Steuart had better luck, the trenches down the southern nose of the hill having yawned vacant ever since Slocum's departure, half an hour before the rebel advance got under way. The gray attackers swarmed into and along them, whooping as they swung northward in the twilight, apparently unopposed, only to strike a new line of fortifications, drawn at right angles to the old and occupied by the brigade Slocum had left behind. The struggle here was as bitter as on the right, and the defenders — five regiments of upstate New Yorkers under Brigadier General George S. Greene — fought with a determination every bit as grim as Wadsworth's.

Rhode-Island-born, with a seagoing son who had served as executive officer on the *Monitor*, Greene was sixty-two, a few months older than the ineffectual Barnes and therefore the oldest Federal on the field. "Old Man Greene," his soldiers called him, or sometimes merely "Pop," for though he had finished second in his class at West Point forty years ago, he affected an easy style of dress that made him look more like a farmer than a regular army man. What he was, in fact, was a civil engineer; he had left the service early to build railroads and design municipal sewage and water systems for Washington, Detroit, and several other cities, including New York, whose Central Park reservoir was his handiwork, along with the enlarged High Bridge across the Harlem River. Such experience, as he applied it now to laying out intrenchments, stood him and his 1300 men in good stead this evening on Culp's Hill. Rather than attempt to hold the empty trenches on his right with his one brigade, which would have stretched it beyond the breaking point, he had dug a traverse, midway of the line and facing south behind a five-foot-thick embankment of earth and logs. Here his troops fought savagely, holding their own against Steuart's frantic lunges, and were reinforced at last by two regiments Wadsworth was able to spare when the pressure eased on the north end of the hill. When the commander of the first of these reported to him on the firing line, the battle racket was so terrific that Greene had to give up trying to shout above the uproar, and instead wrote his name on a card which he handed to the colonel by way of identification. For two hours, from twilight well into darkness, the firing hardly slacked. Then gradually it did, dying away to a sputter of individual shots, as if by mutual agreement that the blind slaughter had grown pointless: as indeed it had. Johnson was forced to content himself with what was after all a substantial lodgment on the far Union right, and Greene was more or less satisfied that he had been able to keep it from being enlarged, though it was clear to the fighters on both sides that the lull would not last past daylight.

Although it started later and ended sooner, Early's attack on Cemetery Hill, launched when he heard Johnson open fire on the far left, not only accomplished a deeper penetration, but also came even closer than Wright's had done, two hours ago, to achieving a complete breakthrough and the consequent disruption of Meade's whole fishhook system of defense. His four brigades were from four different states, Virginia, Louisiana, North Carolina, and Georgia; Gordon commanded the last of these, and the other three were respectively under Brigadier Generals William Smith and Harry T. Hays and Colonel Isaac Avery. Smith had no share in the assault, having been posted two miles out the York Pike to fend off a rumored threat to the rear. Nor did Gordon, as the thing turned out; Early held him in reserve. But the North Carolinians and Louisianians did all they could, in fury and hard-handed determination, to make up for these subtractions. Hays advanced on the right and Avery on the left, headed straight for the steep northeast face of the hundred-foot hill, and neither brigade would be stopped. Avery fell at the outset, mortally wounded, but his men kept going, over and past three successive lines of bluecoats disposed behind stone walls, defying the frantic overhead fire of infantry and artillery massed on the summit. Hays, a Tennessee-born and Mississippi-raised New Orleans lawyer whose brigade had first won fame under Dick Taylor in the Shenandoah Valley, refused to be outdone, though he too had to contend with three successive blue lines, the first along the far side of a ravine at the foot of the hill, the second behind a stone wall halfway up, and the third in well-dug rifle pits just short of the crest, protected by an abatis of felled trees. Losses were surprisingly light, partly because the downhill-firing Federals tended to overshoot the climbing graybacks, but mostly, as Hays said later, because of "the darkness of the evening, now verging into night, and the deep obscurity afforded by the smoke." Another reason was that the defenders here were Howard's men, who had yesterday's disaster fresh in mind. Hays called no names, merely reporting that his troops, having taken the third Yankee line at small cost to themselves, "found many of the enemy who had not fled hiding in the pits for protection." While these were being rousted out and told to make their own way to the rear as prisoners, the two rebel brigades surged over the lip of the plateau, in hot pursuit of the fugitive survivors. One-armed Howard was there, again the unhappy witness of a scene that by now was becoming familiar. "Almost before I could tell where the assault was made," he afterwards declared, "our men and the Confederates came tumbling back together."

Once more, having failed to stem the rout, he was left with a choice of joining it or exposing himself to capture, along with the guns his cannoneers had abandoned when the attackers reached point-blank range. "At that time," Hays noted proudly, "every piece of artillery which had been firing upon us was silent." The Louisianians and Tarheels swarmed among them, in full possession of the Union stronghold at the bend of the three-mile fishhook. Like Wright before him, a mile to the south, though darkness permitted him no such view of the enemy rear, Hays experienced a feeling of elation as he looked about the plateau for the reinforcements he had been told to expect. For a moment he thought he saw them; heavy masses of infantry were coming up from the southwest in the gloom. He could not be sure they were not Federals, in which case he would take them under fire, but he had been "cautioned to expect friends" from that direction, either Longstreet or Hill, or Rodes from his own corps. Even when they fired at him, dropping a number of his men, he did not shoot back, not wanting to compound the error if they were Confederates. They fired again and kept coming on through the darkness; still he held his fire, perhaps remembering the fall of Jackson in the Wilderness, two months ago tonight. A third volley crashed, much nearer now, and he saw by the fitful glare of the muzzle flashes that the uniforms were blue. A close look even showed the trefoil insignia of the II Corps on the flat-top forage caps of the still advancing Federals, whose "Clubs Are Trumps" motto Hays and his men knew only too well from hard experience. They were, in fact, Colonel S. S. Carroll's brigade of Hancock's third division, and Hancock himself had sent them. He had been talking just now with Gibbon in the twilight, gazing westward from the point on Cemetery Ridge where Wright's breach had been sealed, when the racket of Early's attack erupted on the north slope of Cemetery Hill. "We ought to send some help over there," he told Gibbon, who was acting as corps commander while his chief undertook the larger duties Meade had assigned him. As the uproar drew nearer, signifying the progress of the attackers, Hancock added with rapid decision: "Send a brigade. Send Carroll."

Carroll it was. And Hays, already staggered by the three unanswered volleys — the third had been especially destructive, delivered as it was at such close range — gave the order at last for his men to return the fire. This they did, glad to be released from hard restraint, and kept it up as fast as they could ram cartridges and draw triggers, bringing the blue mass to a stumbling halt. Beyond it, however, Hays could see other such masses forming in the flame-stabbed darkness; Howard's fugitives were rallying to support the troops who had opened ranks to let them through and then gone on to stop the rebels in their tracks. Looking back over his shoulder for some sign that Gordon was advancing, and wishing fervently that at any moment he would see Rodes and his five brigades come charging across the plateau from the west, Hays held his own for a time against the odds, but then, abandoning all hope of support, gave the necessary commands for a withdrawal. Unpursued past the line of abandoned guns, the two brigades fell back in good order, firing as they went, and called a halt at the bottom of the hill, angry that neither Gordon nor Rodes had mounted the slope to help them exploit the greatest opportunity of the day.

This lack of support — which, if supplied, might well have made up for all the miscalculations and fumbled chances of the past two days — resulted from a series of interrelated hesitations and downright failures of nerve on the part of several men. Early had withheld Gordon because he saw at the last moment that Rodes was not advancing on his right, and Rodes had called off his attack for the same reason, with regard to Lane. In a sense, it all went back to the fall of Pender and the curious defection of Mahone; or perhaps it went even further back than that, to the near escape from disaster Rodes had experienced yesterday. Restrained at first by a fear of being involved in another fiasco if he charged unsupported up Cemetery Hill, he now was prodded by a desire to retrieve what his restraint had cost him. When he heard the clatter of gunfire on the overhead plateau, which signified unmistakably that the blue defenses had been breached, he repented his inaction and decided to go forward anyhow, with or without support. But by the time he got his troops in position to advance — most of them had been waiting all day in Gettysburg itself, which meant that they had to be disentangled from the complex of streets and houses before they could form for attack — the hilltop clatter had subsided; Hays had brought his two brigades back down the northeast slope. Rodes took a careful, close-up look at the objective, which bristled with guns, and decided — no doubt wisely, at this late hour — that "it would be a useless sacrifice of life to go on." However, instead of bringing his five brigades back to their various starting points, he put them in line along the hollow of an old roadbed southwest of town, a position, he later reported, "from which I could readily attack without confusion." He did not explain why he had not done this sooner, in order to be able to move promptly in support of Hays, but he added: "Everything was gotten ready to attack at daybreak."

So he said. But for now the fighting was over, all but the final stages of Johnson's blind assault on Old Man Greene's well-engineered intrenchments, a mile across the way. Presently this too sputtered into silence, and moonlight glistened eerily on the corpse-strewn valleys and hillsides, its refulgence no longer broken by the fitful and ubiquitous pinkish-yellow stabs of muzzle flashes. Here and there, the wounded troubled the stillness with their cries for water and assistance, but for the most part the veterans of both armies were inured to this by now; they slept to rest their minds and bodies for tomorrow.

Thus ended the second day of what was already the bloodiest battle of the war to date, with no one knew how much more blood still to be shed on this same field.

★   ★   ★

Their lines drawn helter-skelter in the darkness, the soldiers could sleep; but not the two commanders and their staffs, who had the task of assessing what had been done today, or left undone, in order to plan for tomorrow. In this, the two reacted so literally in accordance with their native predilections — Lee's for daring, Meade's for caution —

that afterwards, when their separate decisions were examined down the tunnel of the years — which provides a diminished clarity not unlike that afforded by a reversed telescope — both would be condemned for having been extreme in these two different respects.

Lee had spent the battle hours at his command post on Seminary Ridge, midway of that portion of the line occupied by Hill's two divisions, and though this gave him a clear view of most of the fighting in the valley below and on the ridge across the way, he had made no attempt to control or even influence the action once the opening attack had been launched on the far right. An observer who was with him recorded that he sent only one message and received only one all afternoon, despite what another witness described as "an expression of painful anxiety" on his face as the assault rolled north toward its breakdown — just at the point where he stood, between Anderson and Pender, with Mahone's brigade taking it easy in the woods directly behind the command post — then shifted across to Culp's Hill and moved back toward him through the gathering dusk, only to stall again when it got to Rodes. Both breakdowns were particularly untimely, since in each case they had occurred at the moment when the echeloned build-up of pressure resulted at last in a penetration of the enemy defenses, hard by the point that had been scheduled to be struck next. If there was bitter mockery in these two near-successes, which had had to be abandoned for lack of support, there was also much encouragement in the over-all results of the five-hour contest. All that had been lacking, Lee perceived and later reported, was "proper concert of action." Substantial lodgments had been effected and maintained by Hood and Johnson, on the far right and far left; Meade was clamped as in a vise. Moreover, high ground along the Emmitsburg Road had been taken by McLaws in the vicinity of the Peach Orchard, which afforded good positions for the massing of artillery to support an attack on the enemy center or left center. It was just at that point, shortly before sundown and directly opposite the command post, that Lee had focused his binoculars to watch Wright's Georgians storm Cemetery Ridge, driving off the defending infantry and cannoneers, and then stand poised on the crest for a long moment, as if balanced on a knife blade, before they had to fall back for want of support. What had almost been achieved today could be achieved tomorrow, Lee believed, with "proper concert of action" and artillery support.

Basically, what he intended was a continuation of the tactics employed today. Longstreet and Ewell would strike simultaneously on the right and left, driving for the Taneytown Road and the Baltimore Pike, just in rear of their primary objectives, while Hill stood by to assist either or both in exploiting whatever opportunities proceeded from the exertion of this double pressure on an enemy Lee presumed was badly shaken by the headlong routs and heavy losses of the past two days. Not that there was no room for doubt or occasion for hesitation. There was indeed. If the fighting today had shown nothing else, it certainly had shown that this was a difficult undertaking. However, the situation was not without its compensations and attractions from the Confederate point of view. In at least one sense, the very strength of the close-knit Federal position worked to the disadvantage of the men who occupied it, and this was that any collapse at all was likely to be total and disastrous. Lee could never forget the breakthrough Hood and Law had scored a year ago at Gaines Mill, where they had launched a frontal assault on Turkey Hill under conditions not unlike those the army faced at Gettysburg. What he hoped for, in short, was a repetition of that exploit tomorrow: by Pickett.

That general had marched his three Virginia brigades to within three miles of the field by 6 o'clock, an hour and a half before sunset; but when he notified Lee of his arrival and asked if he was to press on and join the battle he could hear raging toward its climax just ahead, Lee had sent him instructions to go into bivouac where he was, apparently wanting the men to be fully rested for the work he already had in mind for them tomorrow. These 5000 soldiers would come a good deal short of making up for the nearly 9000 who had fallen here today, not to mention the nearly 8000 who had fallen or been captured the day before, but there were others to be taken into account in comparing the force of the blow he planned to strike with the one he had struck already, which had failed. In addition to Pickett, whose newly arrived division would supply the extra power Lee believed would insure an initial breakthrough, two of Hill's divisions and one of Ewell's had taken little or no part in the fighting today, and the same could be said of two of Anderson's brigades, two of Early's, and one of Johnson's. Longstreet alone had put in all the men he had on hand. In point of fact, only 16 of the army's 37 infantry brigades had been seriously engaged today, which left 21 presumably well rested for tomorrow. Moreover, Stuart's three veteran brigades of cavalry would also be available — two had arrived by sundown and the third was expected before sunrise — to harry the retreat of whatever remnant of the blue army survived the collapse that would attend the rapid exploitation of Pickett's breakthrough. . . . Such then were the factors that contributed to Lee's decision to renew the attack next morning. All this seemed not only possible but persuasive to a man who had determined to stake everything on one blow and whose confidence in his troops — "They will go anywhere and do anything, if properly led" — had been strengthened by the sight of what they had accomplished, rather than weakened by the thought of what they had failed to accomplish because of a lack of "concert" on the part of their commanders. Just as yesterday's successes had led to a continuation of the offensive today, so did today's successes — such as they were — lead to a continuation of the offensive tomorrow. And both were a part of what would be meant, in the years ahead, when it came to be said of Lee that the stars had fought against him in Pennsylvania.

By midnight, when he retired to his tent to get some sleep, his plans had been developed in considerable detail. A message had gone to Ewell, instructing him to open the action on the left at daybreak, and another to Hill, directing him to detach two brigades from Rodes to reinforce Johnson on Culp's Hill for that purpose, while Pendleton had been told to advance the artillery, under cover of darkness, into positions from which to support the attack on the left and right and center. No orders reached Longstreet, however; nor was Pickett alerted for the night march he would have to make if he was to have any share in the daybreak assault. Perhaps this was an oversight, or perhaps Lee had decided by then to attack at a later hour and thus give his troops more rest, though if so he neglected to inform Ewell of the change. In any event, none of the three corps commanders visited headquarters that evening to discuss their assignments for tomorrow; Lee neither summoned them nor rode out to see them, and though he sent instructions to Ewell and Hill, he did not get in touch with Longstreet at all, apparently being satisfied that the man he called his old warhorse would know what was expected of him without being told.

Across the way, on Cemetery Ridge, the northern leader was taking no such chances. An hour before Lee retired for the night, Meade assembled his corps commanders for a council of war in the headquarters cottage beside the Taneytown Road. He sent for them not only because he wanted to make sure they understood their duties for tomorrow, but also because he wanted to confer with them as to what those duties should be. Moreover, he wanted their help in solving a dilemma in which he had placed himself earlier that evening, the unguarded victim of his own enthusiasm. Elated by Warren's success in holding Little Round Top, as well as by Hancock's subsequent ejection of the rebels who pierced his center near sundown, he had gotten off an exultant message to Halleck. "The enemy attacked me about 4 p.m. this day," he wrote, "and, after one of the severest contests of the war, was repulsed at all points." This last was untrue and he knew it, though he might contend that, strictly speaking, neither the Devil's Den nor the Peach Orchard was an integral part of his fishhook system of defense. In any case, he closed the dispatch with a flat assurance: "I shall remain in my present position tomorrow, but am not prepared to say, until better advised of the condition of the army, whether my operations will be of an offensive or defensive character."

The courier had scarcely left with the message — it was headed 8 p.m. — when Johnson's attack exploded on the right. His troops swarmed into and along the trenches Slocum had vacated half an hour before, and while their advance was being challenged by Wadsworth and

Greene, Early struck hard at Cemetery Hill, driving Howard's panicky Dutchmen from the intrenchments on the summit. Thanks to Hancock, the nearer of these two dangers was repulsed, at least for the time, but the graybacks maintained the lodgment they had effected at the far end of the line. To Meade, this meant that his position — already penetrated twice today, however briefly, first left, then right of center — was gravely menaced at both extremities: from the Devil's Den, hard against Little Round Top, and on Culp's Hill itself. The inherent possibilities were unnerving. Though he ordered Slocum to return to the far right with all his troops and prepare to oust the rebels at first light, Meade now began to regret the flat assurance he had given Halleck that he would not budge from where he was. He foresaw disaster, and not without cause. Five days in command, he already had suffered about as many casualties as the bungling Hooker had lost in five whole months, and it appeared fairly certain that he was going to suffer a good many more tomorrow. In fact, considering what Lee must have learned today from his exploratory probes of the Union fishhook, it was by no means improbable that he had plans for breaking it entirely. And if that happened, the chances were strong that the Army of the Potomac would be abolished right here in its new commander's own home state. The more he thought about it, the more it seemed to Meade that the best way to avoid that catastrophe would be to pull out before morning and retire to the Pipe Creek line, which had seemed to him much superior in the first place. By now, moreover, his chief of staff had completed the formal orders for withdrawal; they could be issued without delay. As for his untimely assurance to Washington — "I shall remain in my present position tomorrow" — it occurred to him that a negative vote on the matter by his corps commanders would release him from his promise. Accordingly, he sent word for them to come to headquarters at once for a council of war.

All seven came, and more. Pleasanton was off on cavalry business — he later testified that he had been ordered to prepare for covering the withdrawal — but since Hancock and Slocum had brought Gibbon and Williams along, nine generals were present in addition to Meade and two staff advisers, Butterfield and Warren. A dozen men made quite a crowd in the little parlor, which measured barely ten feet by twelve and whose furnishings included a deal table in the center, with a cedar water bucket, a tin cup, and a pair of lighted candles on it, a somewhat rickety bed in one corner, and five or six chairs. These last were soon filled, as was the bed, which served as a couch, leaving three or four of the late arrivers, or their juniors, with nothing to sit on but the floor. A witness remarked afterwards that, for all their rank, those in attendance were "as modest and unpretentious as their surroundings" and "as calm, as mild-mannered, and as free from flurry or excitement as a board of commissioners met to discuss a street improvement." By

11 o'clock all were there. Meade opened the council by announcing that he intended to follow whatever line of action was favored by a majority of those present. Then he submitted three questions for a formal vote: "1. Under existing circumstances, is it advisable for this army to remain in its present position, or to retire to another nearer its base of supplies? 2. It being determined to remain in present position, shall the army attack or wait the attack of the enemy? 3. If we wait attack, how long?" As was the custom in such matters, the junior officer voted first, the senior last. From Gibbon through Slocum, with Butterfield keeping tally, all nine agreed that the army should neither retreat nor attack. Only on the third question was there any difference of opinion, and this varied from Slocum's "Stay and fight it out" to Hancock's "Can't wait long," which perhaps was some measure of how much fighting each had done already. At any rate, Meade had his answer. His lieutenants having declined to take him off the hook, the assurance he had given Halleck remained in effect. "Well, gentlemen," he said when all the votes were in, "the question is settled. We will remain here."

By now it was midnight. On the far side of the valley, Lee had retired, and on this side the Union council of war was breaking up. As the generals were departing to rejoin their commands, along and behind the three-mile curve of line, Meade stopped Gibbon, whose troops were posted on the nearby crest of Cemetery Ridge, due west of the headquarters cottage. "If Lee attacks tomorrow, it will be in your front," he told him. Gibbon asked why he thought so. "Because he has made attacks on both our flanks and failed," Meade said, "and if he concludes to try it again it will be on our center." Nearly a quarter-century later Gibbon recalled his reaction to this warning that it was his portion of the fishhook line that Lee would strike at: "I expressed the hope that he would, and told General Meade, with confidence, that if he did we would defeat him."

❉ 4 ❉

July 3; Lee rose by starlight, as he had done the previous morning, with equally fervent hopes of bringing this bloodiest of all his battles to a victorious conclusion before sunset. Two months ago today, Chancellorsville had thundered to its climax, fulfilling just such hopes against longer odds, and one month ago today, hard on the heels of a top-to-bottom reorganization occasioned by the death of Stonewall Jackson, the Army of Northern Virginia had begun its movement from the Rappahannock, northward to where an even greater triumph had seemed to be within its reach throughout the past forty-odd hours of savage fighting. Today would settle the outcome, he believed, not only of the battle — that went without saying; flesh and blood, bone and sinew and nerve could only stand so much — but also, perhaps, of the war; which, after all, was why he had come up here to Pennsylvania in the first place. He woke to a stillness so profound that one of Gibbon's officers, rolled in his blankets near a small clump of trees on Cemetery Ridge, two thirds of the way up the shank of the Union fishhook, heard the courthouse clock a mile away in Gettysburg strike three. Lee emerged from his tent soon afterwards, fully dressed for the fight, and shared a frugal breakfast with his staff. Three miles northwest, Pickett's men were stirring, too, in a grove of oaks where they had made camp beside the Chambersburg Pike at sundown. Well rested though still a little stiff from yesterday's long march, which had ended not in battle, as they had expected, but in bivouac, they were the shock troops Lee would employ today in an ultimate attempt to achieve the breakthrough he had been trying for all along. It was for this reason, this purpose, that he had withheld them from the carnage they might otherwise have arrived in time to share the day before.

With sunrise only an hour away, however, it was obvious that he had abandoned his plan for a dawn attack. A good two hours would be required for Pickett to move his three brigades from their present bivouac area and mass them in a jump-off position well down Seminary Ridge. For them to have any share in an attack at dawn, they had to have been in motion at least an hour ago, and Lee not only had not sent Pickett or his corps commander any word of his intentions; he did not even do so now. Perhaps, on second thought, he had reasoned that more deliberate preparations were required for so desperate an effort, including another daylight look at the objective, which the enemy might have reinforced or otherwise rendered impregnable overnight. Besides, the assault would necessarily be a one-shot endeavor; late was as good as early, and maybe better, since it not only would permit a more careful study of all the problems, but also would lessen the time allowed the Federals for mounting and launching a counterattack in event of a Confederate repulse. Or perhaps it was even simpler than that. Perhaps Lee merely wanted time for one more talk with the man he called his warhorse, whose three divisions he had decided to use in the assault. At any rate, it was Longstreet he set out to find as soon as he mounted Traveller in the predawn darkness and rode eastward up the reverse slope of Seminary Ridge, delaying only long enough to send a courier to Ewell with word that the proposed attack, though still designed as a simultaneous effort on the right and the far left, would be delayed until 10 o'clock or later.

From the crest of the ridge, as he gazed southeast to where the first pale streaks of dawn had just begun to glimmer, he was greeted by a sudden eruption of noise that seemed to have its source in the masked valley beyond Cemetery Hill. It was gunfire, unmistakably, a cannonade mounting quickly to a sustained crescendo; but whose? In the ab-

sence of reports, Lee could not tell, but he knew at once that one of
two regrettable things had happened. Either his message had failed to
reach Ewell in time, in which case his plan for the synchronization of
the two attacks had gone awry, or else Meade had gotten the jump on
him in that direction, leaving Ewell no choice whatsoever in the matter
of when to fight.

In point of fact, it was something of both. The courier had not
yet reached Second Corps headquarters (indeed, he had not had time to)
and Meade *had* seized the initiative. Slocum, returning to the Federal
right with both of his divisions before midnight, had massed them along
the Baltimore Pike for the purpose of driving the Confederates from
the lower end of Culp's Hill, where they had effected a lodgment soon
after his sundown departure. At 3.45, accordingly, he opened with four
batteries he had posted along the northern slope of Powers Hill, blasting away at the rebels crouched in the trenches his own men had dug
the day before. For fifteen minutes he kept up the fire, taking care that
the guns did not overshoot and drop their shells on Greene's troops just
beyond, then paused briefly to survey the damage as best he could in the
dim light. Apparently unsatisfied, he resumed the cannonade, joined now
by a battery firing southeast from Cemetery Hill, and continued it for
the better part of an hour, after which he intended to launch an infantry assault.

This time, though, it was the Confederates who got the jump on
their opponents in this struggle for possession of the barb of the Union
fishhook. Unable to bring artillery over Rock Creek and the rough
ground he had crossed to gain the position he now held, Johnson had
his men lie low among the rocks and in the trenches while the shells
burst all around them. Then, as soon as the hour-long bombardment
ended, he sent them surging forward, determined to gain control of the
Baltimore Pike in accordance with last night's orders from Lee and
Ewell. In this he was unsuccessful, though he gave it everything he had,
including the added strength of the two brigades from Rodes, under
Brigadier General Junius Daniel and Colonel Edward O'Neal. Slocum's troops refused to yield, and now that the graybacks were out of
their holes the guns resumed their firing on the left and on the right,
their targets clearly defined for them against the risen sun. Presently
word arrived from Ewell that Lee had ordered a postponement of the
attack here on the left so that it might be co-ordinated with Longstreet's on the right, which had been delayed; but Old Clubby, fighting less by now in hope of gain than for survival — to attempt even to
disengage would be to invite destruction — no longer had any say-so in
the matter. Unrelentingly severe, the contest degenerated into a series
of brief advances and sudden repulses, first by one side, then the other.
For better than five hours this continued, Slocum being reinforced by a
brigade from Sedgwick's corps and Johnson adding Smith's brigade of

Early's division to his ranks, but neither could gain a decided advantage over the other, except in the weight of metal thrown. The unopposed Federal guns made the real difference, and they were what told in the end. By 10.30 the Confederates had been driven off Culp's Hill, approximately back to the line at its eastern base along Rock Creek, from which they had launched their attack the day before. Slocum, having recovered his lost trenches, was content to hold them, and Johnson was obliged to forgo any attempt to retake them. All he could do today he had done already, for the casualties in his seven brigades had been heavy and the survivors were fought to a frazzle. Whatever Longstreet was going to accomplish, around on the far side of the fishhook, would have to be accomplished on his own.

Lee had already taken this into account, however, and he had not seen in it any cause for cancellation of his plans. Ewell's share in them had been secondary anyhow, a diversionary effort designed to mislead his opponent into withholding reinforcements from that portion of the Federal line assigned to Longstreet for a breakthrough, with consequent disruption of the whole. If Meade had taken the offensive against Ewell, Lee's purpose might be served even better in that regard, since this would require the northern commander to employ more troops at the far end of his position than if he had remained on the defensive there. A more serious question was whether he could be prevented from turning the tables on the Confederates by scoring a breakthrough of his own, but Lee was no more inclined to worry about the possibility of such a mishap here at Gettysburg than Jackson had been at Fredericksburg, when he remarked of the soldiers now under fire on Culp's Hill, "My men have sometimes failed to take a position, but to defend one, never!" Lee might have said the same thing now, and he also might have added on Ewell's behalf, as Jackson had done on his own, "I am glad the Yankees are coming." At any rate, after pausing on the crest of Seminary Ridge to listen to the cannonade a mile across the way, he turned Traveller's head southward, noting with pleasure by the spreading light of dawn that Meade did not seem to have strengthened his center overnight, and continued his ride in search of Longstreet.

He found him shortly after sunrise, three miles down the line, in a field just west of Round Top. The burly Georgian had emerged at last from the gloom into which his heavy losses, following hard upon the rejection of his counsel, had plunged him the previous evening. Moreover, his first words showed the reason for this recovery of his spirits. "General," he greeted Lee, "I have had my scouts out all night, and I find that you still have an excellent opportunity to move around to the right of Meade's army and maneuver him into attacking us." Apparently he believed that yesterday's experience must have proved to the southern commander the folly of attempting to storm a position of great natural strength, occupied by a numerically superior foe who had demonstrated forcefully his ability to maintain it against the most violent attempts at dislodgment. But Lee was as quick to set Old Peter straight today as he had been the day before, and he did so with nearly the same words. "The enemy is there," he said, pointing northeast as he spoke, "and I am going to strike him." Longstreet's spirits took a sudden drop. He knew from Lee's tone and manner that his mind was quite made up, that no argument could persuade him not to continue the struggle on this same field. Accordingly, after giving instructions canceling the intended shift around the south end of the Federal line, Old Peter turned again to his chief to receive his orders for the continuation of the battle he did not want to fight, at least not here.

These orders only served to deepen his gloom still further. What Lee proposed was that Longstreet strike north of the Round Tops with his whole corps, now that Pickett was at hand, in an attempt to break the Union line on Cemetery Ridge. Essentially, this was what Old Peter had tried and failed to do the day before, after protesting to no avail, and he did not believe that his chances for success had been improved by the repulse already suffered, especially in view of the fact that all three of the attacking divisions had been fresh and up to full strength when they were committed yesterday, whereas two of the three Lee intended to employ today were near exhaustion and had lost no less than a third of their men by way of demonstrating that the attempt had been unwise in the first place. In opposing the selection of troops for the assault, Longstreet pointed out that to withdraw his two committed divisions from the vicinity of the Devil's Den and the Wheat Field would be to expose the right flank of the attacking column to assault by the bluecoats now being held in check in that direction. Lee thought this over briefly, then agreed. McLaws and Law would hold their ground; Pickett would be supported instead by two of Hill's divisions, and the point of attack would be shifted northward, from the left center to the right center of the enemy ridge, though this would afford the attackers less cover and a greater distance to march before they came to grips with the defenders on the far side of the nearly mile-wide valley.

Longstreet did some rapid calculations. Pickett had just under 5000 men, his division being the smallest in the army, and the chances were that Hill's would be no larger, if as large, after his losses of the past two days. That gave a rough total of 15,000 or less, and Longstreet did not believe this would be enough to do the job Lee had in mind. Perhaps he had reproached himself the night before for not having made a firmer protest yesterday against what he had believed to be an unwise assignment. If so, he made sure now, at the risk of being considered insubordinate, that he would have no occasion for self-reproach on that account tonight. "General," he told Lee in a last face-to-face endeavor to dissuade him from extending what he believed was an invitation to disaster, "I have been a soldier all my life. I have been with soldiers engaged in fights by couples, by squads, companies, regiments, divisions, and armies, and should know as well as anyone what soldiers can do. It is my opinion that no 15,000 men ever arrayed for battle can take that position."

Lee's reply to this was an order for Pickett to be summoned. He was to post his three brigades behind Seminary Ridge, just south of the army command post near the center of the line, and there await the signal to attack. Two of Anderson's brigades, those of Lang and Wilcox, already posted in the woods adjoining Pickett's assembly area, would be on call for his support if needed. On his left, north of the command post and also under cover of the ridge, Heth's four brigades — under Pettigrew, for Heth was still too jangled to resume command — would be massed for the same purpose, supported in turn by two brigades from Pender, who was also incapacitated. Longstreet was to be in over-all command of the attack, despite his impassioned protest that it was bound to fail, and would give the signal that would launch it, though only three of the eleven brigades involved were from his corps. The plan itself, as Lee explained it to his lieutenant while they rode northward for an inspection of the terrain and the units selected to cross it, had at least the virtue of simplicity. The objective was clearly defined against the skyline: a little clump of umbrella-shaped trees, four fifths of a mile away on Cemetery Ridge, just opposite the Confederate command post. Pickett and Pettigrew, each with two brigades in support, would align on each other as they emerged from cover and advanced, guiding on the distinctive landmark directly across the shallow valley from the point where their interior flanks would come together. By way of softening up the objective, the assault would be preceded by a brief but furious bombardment from more than 140 guns of various calibers: 80 from the First Corps, disposed along a mile-long arc extending from the Peach Orchard to the command post back on Seminary Ridge, and 63 from the Third Corps, strung out north of the command post, along the east slope of the ridge. This would be the greatest concentration of artillery ever assembled for a single purpose on the continent, and Lee appeared to have no doubt that it would pave the way for the infantry by pulverizing or driving off the batteries posted in support of the Union center.

Longstreet displayed considerably less confidence than did his chief as they rode north along the line McLaws had fallen back to in the darkness, after charging eastward across the wheat field and part way up the western slope of Cemetery Ridge. "Never was I so depressed as upon that day," Old Peter declared years later. Presently they came to Wofford, who proudly reported to Lee that his brigade had nearly reached the crest of the ridge the day before, just north of Little Round Top, in pursuit of the troops Dan Sickles had exposed. But when the army commander inquired if he could not go there again, the Georgian's jubilation left him.

"No, General, I think not," he said.

"Why not?" Lee asked, and Wofford replied:

"Because, General, the enemy have had all night to intrench and reinforce. I had been pursuing a broken enemy, and the situation now is very different."

Longstreet looked at Lee to see what effect this might have on him, but apparently it had none at all. The two men continued their ride northward, all the way to the sunken lane where Rodes's three remaining brigades were posted on the outskirts of Gettysburg, and then back south again. Twice they rode the full length of the critical front, and all this time Lee refused to be distracted by the clatter of Ewell's desperate back-and-forth struggle across the way, smoke from which kept boiling out of the hidden valley in rear of Lee's prime objective on Cemetery Ridge. He was leaving as little as possible to chance, including the posting of individual batteries for the preliminary bombardment.

Only once, in the three hours required for this careful examination of the ground over which the attack would pass, did he admit the possibility that it might not be successful, and this was when A. P. Hill, who joined him and Longstreet in the course of the reconnaissance, suggested that instead of using only eight of his thirteen brigades, as instructed, he be allowed to send his whole corps forward. Lee would not agree. "What remains of your corps will be my only reserve," he said, "and it will be needed if General Longstreet's attack should fail."

By now it was 9 o'clock; Pickett's three brigades of fifteen veteran regiments — 4600 men in all, and every one a Virginian, from the division commander down — were filing into position behind Seminary Ridge, there to await the signal which Longstreet, who would give it, believed would summon them to slaughter. Pickett himself took no such view of the matter. He saw it, rather, as his first real chance for distinction in this war, and he welcomed it accordingly, his hunger in that regard being as great as that of any man on the field, on either side. This was not only because he had missed the first two days of battle, marking time at Chambersburg, then eating road dust on the long march toward the rumble of guns beyond the horizon, but also because it had begun to appear to him, less than two years short of forty and therefore approaching what must have seemed the down slope of life, that he was in danger of missing the whole war. That came hard; for he had already had one taste of glory, sixteen years ago in Mexico, and he had found it sweet.

After a worse than undistinguished record at West Point — the class of 1846 had had fifty-nine members, including George McClellan and T. J. Jackson, and Pickett had ranked fifty-ninth — he went to war, within a year of graduation, and was the first American to scale the ramparts at Chapultepec, an exploit noted in official reports as well as in all the papers. Twelve years later he made news again, this time by defying a British squadron off San Juan Island in Puget Sound; "We'll make a Bunker Hill of it," he told his scant command; for which he was commended by his government and applauded by the press. Then came secession, and Pickett resigned his commission and headed home from Oregon. Arriving too late for First Manassas, he was wounded in the shoulder at Gaines Mill, just too early for a part in the charge that carried the day. That was a year ago this week, and he had seen no large-scale fighting since, not having returned to duty till after Second Manassas and Sharpsburg. At Fredericksburg his division had been posted in reserve, with scarcely a glimpse of the action and no share at all in the glory; after which, by way of capping the anticlimax, as it were, the Suffolk excursion had caused him to miss Chancellorsville entirely. But now there was Gettysburg, albeit the contest was two thirds over before he reached the field, and when he was offered this opportunity to deliver what Lee had designed as the climactic blow of the greatest battle of them all, he perceived at last what fate had kept in store for him through all these tantalizing months of blank denial. He grasped it eagerly, not only for his own sake, but also for the sake of the girl he called "the charming Sally," his letters to whom were always signed "Your Soldier."

So eager was he, indeed, that an English observer who saw him for the first time here today, just after Pickett learned of his assignment, described him as a "desperate-looking character." But the fact was he might have given that impression almost anywhere, on or off the field of battle, if only because of his clothes and his coiffure. Jaunty on a sleek black horse, he wore a small blue cap, buff gauntlets, and matching blue cuffs on the sleeves of his well-tailored uniform. Mounted or afoot, he carried an elegant riding crop. His boots were brightly polished and his gold spurs glinted sunlight, rivaling the sparkle of the double row of fire-gilt buttons on his breast. Of middle height, slender, graceful of carriage — "dapper and alert," a more familiar witness termed him, while another spoke of his "marvelous pulchritude" — he sported a curly chin-beard and a mustache that drooped beyond the corners of his mouth and then turned upward at the ends. To add to the swashbuckling effect, his dark-brown hair hung shoulder-length in ringlets which he anointed with perfume. There were those who alleged that he owed his rapid advancement to his friendship with the corps commander, which dated back to the peacetime army, rather than to any native ability, which in fact he had had little chance to prove. "Taking Longstreet's orders in emergencies," the corps adjutant would recall, "I could always see how he looked after Pickett, and made us give him things very fully; indeed, sometimes stay with him to make sure he did not go astray."

His three brigadiers were all his seniors in years, and one had been his senior in rank as well, until Pickett's October promotion to major general. James L. Kemper, the youngest, was just past his fortieth birthday. A former Piedmont lawyer and politician, twice elected speaker of the House of Delegates, he was the only nonprofessional soldier of the lot, and though he retained a fondness for high-flown oratory — "Judging by manner and conversation alone," an associate observed, "he would have been classed as a Bombastes Furioso" — his combat record was a good one, as was that of his troops, whose three previous commanders now commanded the three corps of the army. Kemper had been with the brigade from the outset, first at the head of a regiment, and had fought in all its battles, from First Manassas on. He and his men shared another proud distinction, dating back to what Southerners liked to refer to as the "earlier" Revolution; one of the five regiments was a descendant of George Washington's first command, and Kemper's grandfather had served as a colonel on the future President's staff. By contrast, though he too was of a distinguished Old Dominion family — one that had given the Confederacy the first of its seventy-seven general officers who would die of wounds received in action — Richard B. Garnett was a comparative newcomer to the division and had never led his present brigade in a large-scale battle. Forty-five years old, strikingly handsome, a West Pointer and a regular army man, he had advanced rapidly in the early months of the war and had succeeded Jackson as commander of the Stonewall Brigade. Then at Kernstown, where he ordered a withdrawal to avoid annihilation, had come tragedy; Jackson removed him from his post and put him in arrest for retreating without permission. Garnett promptly demanded a court-martial, convinced that it would clear him of the charge, but the case dragged on for months, interrupted by battle after battle — all of which he missed — until Lee took a hand in the matter, immediately after Sharpsburg, and transferred him to Longstreet's corps to take command of Pickett's brigade when that general, whom he had previously outranked, was promoted to command of the division. Neither Fredericksburg nor Suffolk brought Garnett the opportunity by which he hoped to clear his record of the Kernstown stain, and now in Pennsylvania he was not only limping painfully from an injury lately suffered when he was kicked in the knee by a horse; he was also sick with chills and fever. Medically speaking, he should have been in bed, not in the field, but he was determined to refute — with blood, if need be — the accusations Jackson had leveled against his reputation. The third and oldest of the three brigadiers, forty-six-year-old Lewis Armistead, was also something of a romantic figure, though less by circumstance than by inclination. A widower, twice brevetted for gallantry in Mexico, he was a great admirer of the ladies and enjoyed posing as a swain. This had earned him the nickname "Lo," an abbreviation of Lothario, which was scarcely in keeping with his close-cropped, grizzled beard or receding hairline. He had, however, a sentimental turn of mind and fond memories of life in the old army. For example, he and Hancock, who was waiting for him now across the way though neither knew it, had been friends. "Hancock, goodbye," he had said in parting, two years ago on the West Coast as he prepared to cross the continent with Albert Sidney Johnston; "you can never know what this has cost me." As he spoke he put both hands on his friend's shoulders, and tears stood in his eyes. Now he and Dick Garnett stood together on the crest of Seminary Ridge, looking out across the gently rolling valley toward the little clump of umbrella-shaped trees which had been pointed out to them as their objective, a mile away on Cemetery Ridge. Both men were experienced soldiers, and both knew at a glance the ordeal they and their brigades would be exposed to when the signal came for them to advance. Finally Garnett broke the silence. "This is a desperate thing to attempt," he said. Armistead agreed. "It is," he replied. "But the issue is with the Almighty, and we must leave it in His hands."

Completing what was described as "a shady, quiet march" of about five miles, southeast along the turnpike, then due south through the woods along the far bank of a stream called Pitzer's Run, Pickett's men were unaware of what awaited them beyond the screening ridge; or as one among the marchers later put it, "No gloomy forebodings hovered over our ranks." Not since Sharpsburg, nearly ten months ago, had the troops in these fifteen regiments been involved in heavy fighting, and this encouraged them to believe — quite erroneously, but after the custom of young men everywhere — that they were going to live forever. Near the confluence of Pitzer's and Willoughby Runs, they were halted and permitted to break formation for a rest in the shade of the trees. The sun had burned the early morning clouds away, and though the lack of breeze gave promise of a sultry afternoon, the impression here in this unscarred valley behind Seminary Ridge was of an ideal summer day, no different from any other except in its perfection. "Never was sky or earth more serene, more harmonious, more aglow with light and life," one among the loungers afterwards wrote. Presently they were called back into ranks, told to leave their extra gear in the care of a single guard from each regiment, and marched eastward over the crest of the ridge, then down its opposite slope and into a wooded swale a couple of hundred yards beyond, where they were halted. Here too they were shielded from hostile observers by the low bulge of earth extending northward from the Peach Orchard, along which they could see the corps artillery disposed in a slow curve from the right, the cannoneers silhouetted against the skyline directly in their front. Two brigades of infantry were up there, too, under Wilcox, but Pickett's orders were for his own troops to take it easy here in the swale, doing nothing that might attract the enemy's attention. Soon after they were in position, Lee arrived and began to ride along the lines of reclining men. Mindful of their instructions not to give away their presence, they refrained from cheering; but as the general drew abreast of each company, riding slowly, gravely past, the men rose and took off their hats in silent salute. Lee returned it in the same manner, the sunlight in his gray hair making a glory about his head.

If he seemed graver than usual this morning, he had cause. He had just come from making a similar inspection of the troops disposed northward along the densely wooded eastern slope of Seminary Ridge, where they too were waiting under cover for the signal to move out, and he had noticed that a good number of them wore bandages about their heads and limbs. "Many of these poor boys should go to the rear; they are not able for duty," he remarked. Drawing rein before one hard-hit unit, he looked more closely and realized, apparently for the first time, how few of its officers had survived the earlier fighting. "I miss in this brigade the faces of many dear friends," he said quietly. Riding away, he looked back once and muttered to himself, as if to fend off such tactical doubts as were provoked by personal sorrow: "The attack must succeed."

His choice of the half-dozen brigades that made up the left wing of the assault force — Heth's four, plus two from Pender — was doubly logical, in that all the troops so chosen were handy to the jump-off position and had not been engaged the day before, which not only lessened the chance of disclosing his intention to the enemy by their preliminary movements, but also was presumed to mean that they were fresh, or at any rate well rested, for the long advance across the valley and the subsequent task of driving the bluecoats off the ridge on the far side. What had not been taken into account, however — at least not until Lee saw for himself the thinned ranks and the bandaged wounds of the survivors — was the additional and highly pertinent fact that five of the six had suffered cruelly in the first day's fighting. Both division commanders were out of action, and only two of the six brigades were still under the leaders who had brought them onto the field. The one exception on both counts was Lane's brigade, which had not been heavily engaged and still had its original commander; but this was offset by the misfortune of the other brigade from Pender's division, which had lost its leader, Brigadier General Alfred Scales, together with all but two of its officers above the rank of captain and more than half of those of that rank or below. This was the unit Lee had paused in front of this morning to remark that he missed "the faces of many dear friends," and it was led now by Colonel William Lowrance, who never before had commanded anything larger than a regiment. Moreover, because Lee did not consider Lane experienced enough to succeed the wounded Pender, he had summoned old Isaac Trimble over from Ewell and put him in charge of the two brigades, though he too had never served in such a capacity before, despite his recent promotion to major general, and had

had no previous acquaintance, on or off the field of battle, with the troops he was about to lead across the valley in support of the four brigades under Pettigrew.

These last made up the first wave of the attack, here on the left, and they too had been more severely mauled in the earlier fighting than the army commander or his staff took into account. "They were terribly mistaken about Heth's division in the planning," Lee's chief aide declared afterwards. "It had not recovered, having suffered more than was reported on the first day." In point of fact, whether the planners knew it or not, the division had lost no less than forty percent of its officers and men. Ordinarily, this would have ruled out its employment as a fighting force, particularly on the offensive, until it had been reorganized and brought back up to strength; but in this case it had been selected to play a major role in the delivery of an attack designed as the climax of the army's bloodiest battle. Whether the choice proceeded from ignorance, indifference, or desperation (there was evidence of all three; Longstreet, while admitting his own profound depression, later said flatly that Lee had been "excited and off his balance") some measure of the condition of the division should have been perceived from the fact that only one of the original four commanders remained at the head of his brigade, and this was the inexperienced Davis, whose troops had lost so heavily when he led them into an ambush on the opening day. The captured Archer had been replaced by Colonel B. D. Fry, Colonel John M. Brockenbrough by Colonel Joseph Mayo, and Pettigrew by Colonel J. K. Marshall. All three were thus as new to command of their brigades as Pettigrew was to command of the division, which in turn had not been organized till after Chancellorsville and had gone into its first fight as a unit less than fifty hours ago. It had in all, after the cooks, the extra-duty men, and the lightly wounded were given rifles and brought forward into its ranks, about the same number of troops as Pickett had; that is, about 4600. Trimble had 1750 in the second line. If Wilcox and Lang added their 1400 to the assault, this Pickett-Pettigrew-Trimble total of just under 11,000 would be increased to roughly 12,500 effectives, a figure well below the 15,000 which the man in over-all command of the attack had already said would not be enough to afford him even the possibility of success.

In addition to Armistead and Garnett, who agreed that the maneuver was "a desperate thing to attempt," a good many other high-ranking officers had had a look at the ground in front by now, and their impressions were much the same. To a staff major, on a midmorning visit to the command post near the center, the long approach to the Union position across the shallow valley — more than half a mile out to the Emmitsburg Road, past a blue skirmish line "almost as heavy as a single line of battle," then another quarter-mile up the gradual slope of Cemetery Ridge, where the main enemy line was supported from the crest above by guns that could take the attackers under fire throughout most of their advance — resembled "a passage to the valley of death." Impressions mainly agreed, but reactions varied. For example, an artillerist observed that Pickett was "entirely sanguine of success in the charge, and was only congratulating himself on the opportunity," whereas Pettigrew seemed more determined than elated. Tomorrow would be his thirty-fifth birthday, and though his intellectual accomplishments were perhaps the highest of any man on the field — a scholar in Greek and Hebrew, fluent as well in most of the modern languages of Europe, he had made the best grades ever recorded at the University of North Carolina, where he had also excelled in fencing, boxing, and the single stick, then had traveled on the continent and written a book on what he had seen before returning to settle down to a brilliant legal career, only to have it interrupted by the war and the experience of being left for dead on the field of Seven Pines — he now was devoting his abilities to the fulfillment of his military duties. Slender and lithe of figure, with a neatly barbered beard, a spike mustache, and a dark complexion denoting his Gallic ancestry, Pettigrew was quite as eager as Pickett for distinction, but his eagerness was tempered by a sounder appreciation of the difficulties, since he had fought on this same field two days ago, against this newest version of the Army of the Potomac. Perhaps he recalled today what he had written after a visit to Solferino: "The invention of the Minié ball and the rifled cannon would, it was thought, abolish cavalry and reduce infantry charges within a small compass." On the other hand, if he was remembering his comments on that battle, fought four years ago in Italy, he might have drawn encouragement from the fact that in it the French had crushed the Austrian center, much as Lee intended to crush the Union center here today, with a frontal assault delivered hard on the heels of an intense bombardment.

The men themselves, though few of them had the chance to examine the terrain over which they would be advancing, knew only too well what lay before them; Lee and Longstreet had directed that they be told, and they had been, in considerable detail. "No disguises were used," one wrote afterwards, "nor was there any underrating of the difficult work at hand." They were told of the opportunities, as well as of the dangers, and it was stressed that the breaking of the Federal line might mean the end of the war. However, there were conflicting reports of their reaction. One declared that the men of Garnett's brigade "were in splendid spirits and confident of sweeping everything before them," while another recalled that when Mayo's troops, who were also Virginians, were informed of their share in the coming attack, "from being unusually merry and hilarious they on a sudden had become as still and thoughtful as Quakers at a love feast." Some managed to steal a look at the ground ahead, and like their officers they were sobered by what they saw. One such, a Tennessee sergeant from Fry's brigade, walked forward to the edge of the woods, looked across the wide open valley at the bluecoats standing toylike in the distance on their ridge, and was so startled by the realization of what was about to be required of him that he spoke aloud, asking himself the question: "June Kimble, are you going to do your duty?" The answer, too, was audible. "I'll do it, so help me God," he told himself. He felt better then. The dread passed from him, he said later. When he returned to his company, friends asked him how it looked out there, and Kimble replied: "Boys, if we have to go it will be hot for us, and we will have to do our best."

All this time, the waiting soldiers had been hearing the clatter of Ewell's fight beyond the ridge. By 10.30 it had diminished to a sputter and withdrawn eastward, indicating only too plainly how he had fared; Lee knew unmistakably, before any such admission reached him from the left, that what he had designed as a two-pronged effort had been reduced, by Ewell's failure, to a single thrust which the enemy would be able to oppose with a similar concentration of attention and reserves. However, he did not cancel or revise his plans in midcareer. That was not his way. Like Winfield Scott, on whose staff he had served in Mexico, he believed it "would do more harm than good," once the selected units were in position, for him to attempt to interfere. "It would be a bad thing if I could not rely on my brigade and division commanders," he told a Prussian observer three days later. "I plan and work with all my might to bring the troops to the right place at the right time. With that, I have done my duty." The same rule applied to a brisk skirmish that broke out, at 11 o'clock, around a house and barn on the floor of the valley, half a mile east-northeast of the command post and about midway between the lines. Confederate sharpshooters posted in the loft of the barn had been dropping Federal officers on the opposing ridge all morning, and finally two blue regiments moved out and drove the snipers back; whereupon Hill's guns opened thunderously with a half-hour bombardment. This in turn made the house and barn untenable for the new occupants, who set them afire and withdrew to their own lines, having solved the problem they had been sent to deal with. Lee watched from the command post and made no protest, either at the expenditure of ammunition, which was considerable, or at the resultant disclosure of the battery positions, which up to now the crews had been so careful to conceal. "I strive to make my plans as good as human skill allows," he told the Prussian inquirer, in further explanation of the hands-off policy he practiced here today, "but on the day of battle I lay the fate of my army in the hands of God."

By now it was noon, and a great stillness came down over the field and over the two armies on their ridges. Between them, the burning house and barn loosed a long plume of smoke that stood upright in the hot and windless air. From time to time some itchy-fingered picket would fire a shot, distinct as a single handclap, but for the most part the silence was profound. For the 11,000 Confederates maintaining their mile-wide formation along the wooded slope and in the swale, the heat was oppressive. They sweated and waited, knowing that they were about to be launched on a desperate undertaking from which many of them would not be coming back, and since it had to be, they were of one accord in wanting to get it over with as soon as possible. "It is said, that to the condemned, in going to execution, the moments fly," a member of Pickett's staff wrote some years later, recalling the strain of the long wait. "To the good soldier, about to go into action, I am sure the moments linger. Let us not dare say, that with him, either individually or collectively, it is that 'mythical love of fighting,' poetical but fabulous; but rather, that it is nervous anxiety to solve the great issue as speedily as possible, without stopping to count the cost. The Macbeth principle — *'Twere well it were done quickly* — holds quite as good in heroic action as in crime."

Colonel E. P. Alexander, a twenty-eight-year-old Georgian and West Pointer, had been up all night and hard at work all morning, supervising the movement into position of the 80 guns of the First Corps. By noon the job had been completed; the batteries were disposed along their mile-long arc, southward from the command post to the Peach Orchard and beyond, and the colonel, having taken time to breakfast on a crust of cornbread and a cup of sweet-potato coffee, was awaiting notification to fire the prearranged two-gun signal that would open the 140-gun bombardment. Young as he was, he had been given vital assignments from the outset of the war and had fought in all the army's major battles, first as Beauregard's signal officer, then as Johnston's chief of ordnance, and later as commander of an artillery battalion under Longstreet. Serving in these various capacities, he had contributed largely to the curtain-raising victory at Manassas, as well as to the subsequent effectiveness of Confederate firepower, and since his transfer from staff to line he had been winning a reputation as perhaps the best artillerist in Lee's army, despite the flashier performances of men like Latimer and Pelham. His had been the guns that defended Marye's Heights at Fredericksburg and accompanied Jackson on the flank march at Chancellorsville. However, his most challenging assignment came today from Longstreet, who instructed him to prepare and conduct the First Corps' share of the bombardment preceding the infantry attack. When the objective was shifted northward along Cemetery Ridge, after the early morning conference between Lee and Longstreet, Alexander rearranged his dispositions "as inoffensively as possible," seeking to hide his intentions from enemy lookouts on the heights, and took care to keep his crews from "getting into bunches." He listened with disapproval as Hill's 60-odd guns began their premature cannonade, northward along Seminary Ridge, and would not allow his own to join the action, lest they give away the positions he had taken such pains to conceal. As the uproar subsided and was followed by the silence that came over the field at noon, he received an even greater shock from his own corps commander, who informed him that he would be required to make the decision, not only as to when the infantry attack was to begin, but also as to whether it was to be launched at all. "If the artillery fire does not have the effect to drive off the enemy or greatly demoralize him, so as to make our effort pretty certain," Longstreet wrote in a message delivered by an aide, "I would prefer that you should not advise Pickett to make the charge. I shall rely a great deal upon your judgment to determine the matter and shall expect you to let General Pickett know when the moment offers."

Alexander experienced a violent reaction to this sudden descent of command responsibility. "Until that moment, though I fully recognized the strength of the enemy's position," he recalled years later, "I had not doubted that we would carry it, in my confidence that Lee was ordering it. But here was a proposition that *I* should decide the question. Overwhelming reasons against the assault at once seemed to stare me in the face." He replied at some length, declining the heavy burden Old Peter appeared to be attempting to unload. "General," he protested, "I will only be able to judge of the effect of our fire on the enemy by his return fire, for his infantry is but little exposed to view and the smoke will obscure the whole field. If, as I infer from your note, there is any alternative to this attack, it should be carefully considered before opening our fire, for it will take all the artillery ammunition we have left to test this one thoroughly, and if the result is unfavorable, we will have none left for another effort. And even if this is entirely successful it can only be so at a very bloody cost." Longstreet's answer was not long in coming. Having failed to persuade the colonel to join him in resubmitting his protest that the charge was bound to fail — which was what he had been suggesting between the lines of his rather turgid note — he merely rephrased the essential portion of what he had said before. "Colonel," he wrote, "The intention is to advance the infantry if the artillery has the desired effect of driving the enemy's off, or having other effect such as to warrant us in making the attack. When that moment arrives advise General P., and of course advance such artillery as you can use in aiding the attack."

This left one small loophole — "*if* the artillery has the desired effect" — and Alexander saw it. No cannonade had ever driven Union batteries from a prepared position, and he certainly had no confidence that this one would accomplish that result. But before he replied this second time he decided to confer with two men of higher authority than his own. The first was his fellow Georgian A. R. Wright, who had stormed the enemy ridge the day before, achieving at least a temporary penetration, and could therefore testify as to the difficulty involved.

"What do you think of it?" Alexander asked him. "Is it as hard to get there as it looks?" Wright spoke frankly. "The trouble is not in going there," he said. "I was there with my brigade yesterday. There is a place where you can get breath and re-form. The trouble is to stay there after you get there, for the whole Yankee army is there in a bunch." Alexander took this to mean that the attack would succeed if it was heavily supported, and he assumed that Lee had seen to that. Thus reassured, he went to see how Pickett was reacting to the assignment. He not only found him calm and confident, but also gathered that the ringleted Virginian "thought himself in luck to have the chance." So the colonel returned to his post, just north of the Peach Orchard, and got off a reply to Old Peter's second message. "When our fire is at its best," he wrote briefly, even curtly, "I will advise General Pickett to advance."

Word came soon afterwards from Longstreet: "Let the batteries open. Order great care and precision in firing."

By prearrangement, the two-gun signal was given by a battery near the center. According to a Gettysburg civilian, a professor of mathematics and an inveterate taker of notes, the first shot broke the stillness at exactly 1.07, following which there was an unpropitious pause, occasioned by a misfire. Nettled, the battery officer signaled the third of his four pieces and the second shot rang out. "As suddenly as an organ strikes up in church," Alexander would recall, "the grand roar followed from all the guns."

★ ★ ★

The firing was by salvos, for deliberate precision, and as the two-mile curve of metal came alive in response to the long-awaited signal, the individual pieces bucking and fuming in rapid sequence from right to left, a Federal cannoneer across the valley was "reminded of the 'powder snakes' we boys used to touch off on the Fourth of July." To a man, the lounging bluecoats, whose only concern up to then had been their hunger and the heat, both of which were oppressive, knew what the uproar meant as soon as it began. "Down! Down!" they shouted, diving for whatever cover they could find on the rocky forward slope of Cemetery Ridge. By now the rebel fire was general, though still by salvos within the four-gun units, and to Hunt, who was up on Little Round Top at the time, the sight was "indescribably grand. All their batteries were soon covered with smoke, through which the flames were incessant, whilst the air seemed filled with shells, whose sharp explosions, with the hurtling of their fragments, formed a running accompaniment to the deep roar of the guns." That was how it looked and sounded to a coldly professional eye and ear, sited well above the conflict, so to speak. But to Gibbon, down on the ridge where the shots were landing, the bombardment was "the most infernal pandemonium it has ever been my fortune to look upon." One of his soldiers, caught like him in the sudden deluge of fire and whining splinters, put it simpler. "The air was all murderous iron," he declared years later, apparently still somewhat surprised at finding that he had survived it.

In point of fact, despite the gaudiness of what might be called the fireworks aspect of the thing, casualties were few among the infantry. For the most part they had stone walls to crouch behind; moreover, they were disposed well down the slope, and this, as it turned out, afforded them the best protection of all. At first the fire was highly accurate, but as it continued, both the ridge and the batteries at opposite ends of the trajectory were blanketed in smoke, so that the rebel gunners were firing blind, just as Alexander had foretold. As the trails dug in, the tubes gained elevation and the shellbursts crept uphill, until finally almost all of the projectiles were either landing on the crest, where most of the close-support artillery was posted, or grazing it to explode in the rearward valley. "Quartermaster hunters," the crouching front-line soldiers called these last, deriving much satisfaction from the thought that what was meant for them was making havoc among the normally easy-living men of the rear echelon.

Havoc was by no means too strong a word, especially in reference to what was occurring around and in army headquarters. The small white cottage Meade had commandeered, immediately in rear of that portion of the ridge on which the rebels had been told to mass their hottest fire, became untenable in short order. Its steps were carried away by a direct hit at the outset, along with the supports of the porch, which then collapsed. Inside the house, a solid shot crashed through a door and barely missed the commanding general himself, while another plowed through the roof and garret, filling the lower rooms with flying splinters. Meade and his staff retired to the yard, where sixteen of their horses lay horribly mangled, still tethered to a fence; then moved into a nearby barn, where Butterfield was nicked by a shell fragment; and finally transferred in a body all the way to Powers Hill, where Slocum had set up the night before. Here at last they found a measure of the safety they had been seeking, but they were about as effectively removed from what was happening back on Cemetery Ridge, or was about to happen, as if they had taken refuge on one of the mountains of the moon.

Meanwhile, other rear-area elements had been catching it nearly as hard. Down and across both the Taneytown Road and the Baltimore Pike, fugitives of all kinds — clerks and orderlies, ambulance drivers and mess personnel, supernumeraries and just plain skulkers — were streaming east and south to escape the holocaust, adding greatly to the panic in their haste and disregard for order. Nor were such noncombatants the only ones involved in the confusion and the bloodshed. Returning to its post on the left, the VI Corps brigade that had been lent to Slocum that morning to assist in the retaking of Culp's Hill — he had not had to use it, after all — was caught on the road and lost 23 killed and wounded before it cleared the zone of fire. More important still, tactically speaking, the parked guns of the reserve artillery and the wagons of the ammunition train, drawn up in assumed safety on the lee side of the ridge, came under heavy bombardment, losing men and horses and caissons in the fury of the shellbursts, and had to be shifted half a mile southward, away from the point where they would be needed later. All in all, though it was more or less clear already that the gray artillerists were going to fail in their attempt to drive the blue defenders from the ridge, they had accomplished much with their faulty gunnery, including the disruption of army headquarters, the wounding of the chief of staff, and the displacement of the artillery reserve, not to mention a good deal of incidental slaughter among the rearward fugitives who had not intended to take any part in the fighting anyhow. Unwittingly, and in fact through carelessness and error, the Confederates had invented the box barrage of World War One, still fifty-odd years in the future, whereby a chosen sector of the enemy line was isolated for attack.

Awaiting that attack, crouched beneath what seemed a low, impenetrable dome of screaming metal overarching the forward slope of their isolated thousand yards of ridge, were three depleted divisions under Hancock, six brigades containing some 5700 infantry effectives, or roughly half the number about to be sent against them. This disparity of forces, occupying or aimed at the intended point of contact, was largely the fault of Meade, whose over-all numerical superiority was offset by the fact that his anticipations did not include the threat which this small segment of his army was about to be exposed to. Despite his midnight prediction to Gibbon that today's main rebel effort would be made against "your front," he not only had sent him no reinforcements; he had not even taken the precaution of seeing that any were made immediately available by posting them in proximity to that portion of the line. Daylight had brought a change of mind, a change of fears. He no longer considered that the point of danger, partly because his artillery enjoyed an unobstructed field of fire from there, but mostly because he recollected that his opponent was not partial to attacks against the center. As the morning wore on and Ewell failed to make headway on the right, Meade began to be convinced that Lee was planning to assault his left, and he kept his largely unused reserve, the big VI Corps, massed in the direction of the Round Tops. At 12.20, when Slocum sent word that he had "gained a decided advantage on my front, and hope to be able to spare one or two brigades to help you on some other part of the line," the northern commander was gratified by the evidence of staunchness, but he took no advantage of the offer. Then presently, under the distractive fury of the Confederate bombardment, which drove him in rapid, headlong sequence from house to yard, from yard to barn, and then from barn to hilltop, he apparently forgot it. Whatever defense of that critical thousand yards of ridge was going to be made would have to be made by the men who occupied it.

They amounted in all to 26 regiments, including two advanced as skirmishers, and their line ran half a mile due south from Ziegler's Grove, where Cemetery Hill fell off and Cemetery Ridge began. Gibbon held the center with three brigades, flanked on the left and right by Doubleday and Hays, respectively with one and two brigades; Gibbon had just over and Hays just under 2000 infantry apiece, while Doubleday had about 1700. For most of the long waiting time preceding the full-scale Confederate bombardment, these 5700 defenders had been hearing the Slocum-Johnson struggle for Culp's Hill, barely a mile away. At first it made them edgy, occurring as it did almost directly in their rear, but as it gradually receded and diminished they gained confidence. Finally it sputtered to a stop and was succeeded by a lull, which in turn was interrupted by the brief but lively skirmish for possession of the house and barn down on the floor of the western valley. The half-hour rebel cannonade that followed accomplished nothing, one way or the other, except perhaps as a bellow of protest at the outcome of the fight. By contrast, hard on the heels of this, the midday silence was profound. "At noon it became as still as the Sabbath day," a blue observer later wrote. He and his fellows scarcely knew what to make of this abrupt cessation, in which even the querulous skirmishers held their fire. "It was a queer sight to see men look at each other without speaking," another would recall; "the change was so great men seemed to go on tiptoe not knowing how to act." This lasted a full hour, during which they tried to improvise shelter from the rays of the sun and sought relief from the pangs of hunger. There was precious little of either shade or food, there on the naked ridge, but shortly after 1 o'clock, when the curtain of silence was suddenly ripped to tatters by the roar of what seemed to be all the guns in the world, they forgot the discomforts of heat and hunger, acute as these had been, and concentrated instead on a scramble for cover behind the low stone walls. However, as the pattern of shellbursts moved up the slope and stayed there — except for an occasional round, that is, that tumbled and fell short — they found that, once they grew accustomed to the whoosh and flutter of metal just overhead, the bombardment was not nearly so bad as it seemed. "All we had to do was flatten out a little thinner," one of the earth-hugging soldiers afterwards explained, "and our empty stomachs did not prevent that."

Despite the feeling of security that came from lying low, it seemed to another crouching there "that nothing four feet from the ground could live." Presently, however, he and his companions all along that blasted thousand yards of front were given unmistakable proof that such was not the case, at least so far as one man was concerned. As the bombardment thundered toward crescendo, they were startled to see Hancock, mounted on a fine black horse and trailed by most of his staff, riding the full length of his line amid the hiss and thud of plunging shells and solids. He rode slowly, a mounted orderly beside him displaying the swallow-tailed corps guidon. Resisting the impulse to weave or bob when he felt the breath of near misses on his face, the general only stopped once in the course of his excursion, and that was when his horse, with less concern for show than for survival, became unmanageable and forced him to take over the more tractable mount of an aide, who perhaps was not unhappy at the exchange since it permitted him to retire from the procession. Hancock resumed his ride at the same deliberate pace, combining a ramrod stiffness of backbone with that otherwise easy grace of manner expected of top-ranking officers under fire — a highly improbable mixture of contempt and disregard, for and of the rebel attempt to snuff out the one life he had — whereby the men under him, as one of them rather floridly explained, "found courage to endure the pelting of the pitiless gale." Intent on giving an exemplary performance, he would no more be deterred by friendly counsel than he would swerve to avoid the enemy shells that whooshed around him. When a brigadier ventured a protest: "General, the corps commander ought not to risk his life that way," Hancock replied curtly: "There are times when a corp commander's life does not count," and continued his ride along the line of admiring soldiers, who cheered him lustily from behind their low stone walls, but were careful, all the same, to remain in prone or kneeling positions while they did so.

Another high-ranking Federal was riding better than three times that length of line at the same time, but he did so less by way of staging a general show, as Hancock was doing to bolster the spirits of the men along his portion of the front, than by way of assuring conformity with Army Regulations. "In the attack," these regulations stated, "the artillery is employed to silence the batteries that protect the [enemy] position. In the defense, it is better to direct its fire on the advancing troops." It was the second of these two statements that here applied, and no one knew this better than Henry Hunt, who had been an artillery instructor at West Point and had spent the past two years in practical application, on the field of battle, of the theories he had expounded in the classroom. On Cemetery Hill, on Little Round Top, and along the ridge that ran between them, he had twenty batteries in position, just over one hundred guns that could be brought to bear on the shallow western valley and the ridge at its far rim. Just now there were no "advancing troops" for the long line of Union metal "to direct its fire on," but Hunt was convinced there soon would be, and his first concern — after observing, from his lofty perch at the south end of the line, the "indescribably grand" beginning of the Confederate bombardment — was that his cannoneers not burn up too much of their long-range ammunition in counterbattery fire, lest they run short before the rebel infantry made its appearance. Accordingly, after instructing Lieutenant B. F. Ritten-house to keep up a deliberate fire with his six-gun battery on Little Round Top, Hunt rode down onto the lower end of Cemetery Ridge and ordered Lieutenant Colonel Freeman McGilvery, commanding seven batteries of 37 guns from the artillery reserve, to refrain from taking up the enemy challenge until the proper time. The same in-structions went to Captain John G. Hazard, commanding the six II Corps batteries whose 29 guns were posted north of there, above and below the little umbrella-shaped clump of trees. On Cemetery Hill, completing the two-mile ride from Little Round Top, Hunt repeated what he had told Rittenhouse at the outset; Major T. W. Osborn was to keep up a deliberate counterbattery fire with the 29 guns of his six XI Corps batteries. By this arrangement, one third of the 101 guns were to do what they could to disconcert the rebel gunners by maintaining a crossfire from the high-sited extremities of the Federal position, while the remaining two thirds kept silent along the comparatively low-lying ridge that ran between them. However, it did not work out that way entirely. Completing his slow ride along his thousand-yard portion of the front, Hancock observed that his cannoneers were idle (if idle was quite the word for men who were hugging the earth amid a deluge of shells) and promptly countermanded Hunt's instructions. He did so, he explained afterwards, because he believed that his infantry needed the deep-voiced encouragement of the guns posted in close support on the crest of the ridge directly in their rear. Whatever comfort the blue foot soldiers derived from the roar and rumble in response to the fire of the rebel guns down in the valley, Hunt watched with disapproval as the half-dozen II Corps batteries came alive, but there was nothing he could do about it, since the corps commander had every right to do as he thought best with his own guns, no matter what any and all staff special-ists might advise.

All this time the Confederates kept firing, exploding caissons, dis-mounting guns, and maiming so many cannoneers — particularly in those batteries adjacent to the little clump of trees — that replacements had to be furnished from nearby infantry outfits, supposedly on a vol-unteer basis, but actually by a hard-handed form of conscription. "Vol-unteers are wanted to man the battery," a Massachusetts captain told his company. "Every man is to go of his own free will and accord. Come out here, John Dougherty, McGivern, and you Corrigan, and work those guns." For a solid hour the bombardment did not slacken, and when another half hour was added to this, still with no abatement, Mc-Gilvery ordered his seven batteries to open fire at last, convinced that by now the rebels must be getting low on ammunition and would have to launch their infantry attack, if they were going to launch it at all, before his own supply ran low. That was about 2.30; all the surviving

Union guns were in action, bucking and roaring along the whole two miles of line. From down in the valley, Alexander peered through the billowing smoke and it seemed to him that both enemy heights and the connecting ridge were "blazing like a volcano." On Cemetery Hill, where he availed himself of the excellent observation post established by the XI Corps chief of artillery, Hunt watched with gratification this tangible proof that, for all its prolonged fury, the rebel cannonade had failed to drive his gun crews from their pieces or the guns themselves from their assigned positions. It occurred to him, however, that in the light of this evidence, as plain from below as from above, the Confederates might not attempt their infantry assault at all, and he considered this regrettable. Standing beside him, Osborn suddenly asked: "Does Meade consider an attack of the enemy desirable?" When Hunt replied that the army commander had expressed a fervent hope that the rebels would try just that, "and he had no fear of the result," the major added: "If this is so, why not let them out while we are all in good condition? I would cease fire at once, and the enemy could reach but one conclusion, that of our being driven from the hill."

Hunt thought this over briefly, then agreed. Moreover, while the batteries on the hill fell silent one by one, he rode down onto Cemetery Ridge to increase the effectiveness of the ruse by passing the word along to the remaining two thirds of his guns. At closer range, however, he found the II Corps batteries so badly mauled by the rebel cannonade and so low on ammunition that he decided they might as well use up what few long-range rounds were still on hand. For example, Lieutenant Alonzo Cushing's battery, posted just north of the clump of trees, had only three of its six guns still in working order and only two of these in action, casualties having reduced the number of cannoneers to barely enough for two slim crews; Cushing himself, a twenty-two-year-old West Pointer from Wisconsin, had twice been hit by fragments of exploding shells, one of which had struck him in the crotch and groin. Despite the pain, he refused to leave the field or relinquish his command, and Hunt let him stay, together with his handful of survivors. A Rhode Island battery just south of the clump was in even worse shape, its ammunition practically exhausted, all of its officers dead or wounded, and barely enough men left to serve the three remaining guns; Hunt took a quick look at the wreckage and gave the survivors permission to withdraw, which they did in a rather helter-skelter fashion, being leaderless, but took their three guns with them. Riding on south, Hunt passed the cease-firing order along to McGilvery, down near the far end of the ridge, and finally to Rittenhouse, whose six guns had been firing all the while from Little Round Top. When the weary and badly cut-up batteries of the II Corps had gotten off their few remaining rounds, thus adding to the effectiveness of the pretense by giving the impression that the guns were being knocked out group by group, spasmodically, the whole Union line fell silent under the continuing rain of rebel projectiles.

That was about 2.45, and it soon became apparent that the ruse had worked, at least in part. Within another five or ten minutes, the Confederates also stopped firing, and what Osborn later referred to as "a singularly depressing silence" settled over the field. Whether the ruse had worked entirely would not be known until the enemy infantry started forward across the valley, but the Federal cannoneers were taking no chances that it had failed. The cooling tubes were swabbed to remove the gritty residue of powder and thus prepare them for the rapid-fire work that lay ahead, while in those batteries that had used up all their long-range ammunition, the pieces were carefully loaded with canister. Forty-four-year-old Alex Hays, a Pennsylvanian like his corps and army commanders, was certain that the rebs would soon be coming through the screening smoke. "Now, boys, look out; you will see some fun!" he called to the men of his two brigades, posted north of the clump of trees. In confirmation of his prediction, shortly after 3 o'clock, Warren wigwagged a message from the Little Round Top signal station, which afforded a clear view beyond the hump of earth that Sickles had claimed and lost the day before: "They are moving out to attack." Presently, all along the bend and shank of the Union fishhook, the waiting troops could see for themselves, through or below the rifting, lifting smoke, that what Warren had signaled was true. "Here they come!" men exclaimed as they caught sight of the long gray lines moving toward them across the shallow basin inclosed by the two ridges.

Reactions to this confrontation varied. "Thank God! Here comes the infantry!" one exuberant bluecoat cried. Though it was obvious at a glance that the attackers, moving steadily forward under their red and blue flags, outnumbered the defenders by no less than two to one, he and others like him looked forward to the slaughter, anticipating a Fredericksburg in reverse. A New Yorker, on the other hand, remembering the sight two days later, wrote in a home letter: "Beautiful, gloriously beautiful, did that vast array appear in the lovely little valley." Then he and his fellows — first the cannoneers, who took up their work with a will, and then the foot soldiers, no less eager — settled down to the task of transforming those well-dressed long gray lines into something far from beautiful.

There they came. And for them, advancing eastward over the gently undulating floor of the shallow valley, the relief of tension was as great as it was for the men awaiting their arrival on the ridge just under a mile across the way. In fact, if a comparison of losses was any measure of the strain, it was probably greater. The Federal infantry had suffered a good deal less from the bombardment than the Federal

artillery had done, but for the Confederates, whose infantry was posted
behind instead of in front of their fuming line of metal, it was the other
way around. Both sides were overshooting, with the unequal result that
the eastbound "overs" spared the bluecoats on the forward slope of
their ridge, whereas a high proportion of their long shots landed squarely
in the ranks of the gray soldiers drawn up to await the order to advance. Fewer than 200 of the former were hit, while the latter suffered
approximately twice that number of casualties in the course of the
nearly two-hour-long exchange. "Such a tornado of projectiles it has
seldom been the fortune or misfortune of anyone to see," one of Pickett's
veterans declared. It seemed to go on forever, he recalled, under a high
hard hot blue sky that soon became "lurid with flame and murky with
smoke," until presently the sun was in a red eclipse, "shadowing the
earth as with a funeral pall," though this gave little relief from the heat,
which was even more oppressive here in the swale than it was for the
blue soldiers on the high ground in the distance. "Many a poor fellow
thought his time had come," another grayback wrote. "Great big, stout-
hearted men prayed — loudly, too." Stretcherbearers were kept on the
run, answering the sudden, high-pitched yells of the wounded up and
down the sweaty, mile-long formation. One of Kemper's men, attempting later to describe what he had been through, finally gave it up and
contented himself with a four-word description of his ordeal by fire:
"It was simply awful." Even so, not all the accustomed butternut
risibility was suppressed. Near one badly pounded company, when a
rabbit suddenly broke from a clump of bushes and went bounding for
the rear: "Run, old hare," a man called after him. "If I was a old hare,
I'd run too."

Officers of rank, commanders of the nine brigades and three divisions, kept moving among the waiting troops, seeking to encourage them
by example, much as Hancock was doing at the same time across the
way. However, the response was somewhat different on this side of the
valley. When Longstreet rode along the front of Pickett's division and a
round shot plowed the ground immediately under his horse's nose, the
general kept the startled animal under control, "as quiet as an old farmer
riding over his plantation on a Sunday morning, and looked neither to
the right or left." Thus an admiring captain described the scene; but the
men themselves, apparently resentful of the implication that they
needed steadying, had a different reaction. "You'll get your old fool
head knocked off!" one of them called out to him, while others shouted
angrily: "We'll fight without you leading us!" Similarly, in Armistead's
brigade, where the troops had been instructed to remain prone throughout the bombardment, there was resentment that their commander felt
it necessary to move erect among them with encouraging remarks and a
showy disregard for the projectiles whooshing past him. One soldier
rose in protest, and when Armistead ordered him to lie back down,

pointed out that he was only following his general's example. Armistead, however — like Hancock on the ridge across the valley — had a ready answer. "Yes, but never mind me," he said. "We want men with guns in their hands."

Out front, on the low bulge of earth crowned by the peach orchard Barksdale's men had seized the day before, Alexander had been watching all this time for evidence that the cannonade was accomplishing its mission, which was to wreck the enemy batteries or drive them from the ridge that was the infantry's objective. So far, although an hour had elapsed since his guns first opened, the young colonel had seen little that encouraged him to believe that he was going to succeed in his assignment. Volcano-like, the enemy ridge and its two flanking heights not only continued to return the fire directed at them, but presently that return fire grew more furious than ever, despite an occasional burst of flame and the sudden resultant erection of a pillar of smoke whose base marked the former location of a caisson. Earlier, Wright and Pickett had persuaded him that all Lee intended would be accomplished in short order. After more than an hour of steady firing, however, Alexander's doubts returned in strength. Moreover, the pressure of command responsibility grew heavier by the minute, until at last, as he wrote later, "It seemed madness to order a column in the middle of a hot July day to undertake an advance of three fourths of a mile over open ground against the center of that line." What was worse, another half hour reduced the ammunition supply to the point where the attack would have to be launched without delay if it was to have artillery support. Shortly after 2.30, with the counterbattery fire approaching crescendo, Alexander dispatched a courier with a note informing Pickett of the situation. "If you are to come at all, you must come at once, " he told him, "or we will not be able to support you as we ought. But the enemy's fire has not slackened materially and there are still 18 guns firing from the cemetery." This last had reference to the little clump of trees, which the colonel had been told was a cemetery, and though he was mistaken in this, his estimate as to the number of guns still active in that vicinity was accurate enough. And presently, as he kept peering through the smoke to catch the slightest encouraging reaction by the blue gunners in the distance, he observed with gratification that the Federals had ceased firing on the hill to the left, and soon afterwards he spotted a rearward displacement by some guns near the critical center. It was the battered Rhode Islanders, whom Hunt had given permission to withdraw their three surviving pieces, but in his elation — for the enemy fire continued to slacken all along the ridge and on both adjoining heights — Alexander persuaded himself that the withdrawal had been considerably more substantial than it was in fact. In other words, the blue ruse had worked far better than its authors would have any way of knowing until they saw the long gray lines of infantry advancing. He got off a second note to Pickett, hard on the heels of the first: "For God's sake come quick. The 18 guns have gone. Come quick or my ammunition will not let me support you properly."

Pickett by then had already acted on the first of the two dispatches. Glad to receive anything that might end the strain of waiting, he mounted his horse and rode at once to Longstreet, whom he found sitting on a snake rail fence out front, observing the bombardment. Dismounting, he handed him the note. Old Peter read it deliberately, but said nothing. "General, shall I advance?" Pickett asked eagerly. Longstreet, who later explained: "My feelings had so overcome me that I could not speak, for fear of betraying my want of confidence," responded with a silent nod. That was enough for the jaunty long-haired Virginian. "I am going to move forward, sir," he said. Then he saluted, remounted, and rode back to join his men.

Front and center of his division, he delivered from horseback what one of his officers called "a brief, animated address" which only those soldiers nearest him could hear but which ended on a ringing note: "Up, men, and to your posts! Don't forget today that you are from old Virginia!" There was, however, no disconcerting haste as the troops were placed in attack formation. For the most part, they simply rose to their feet and began to dress their regimental lines while their colonels passed among them repeating the instructions received from above: "Advance slowly, with arms at will. No cheering, no firing, no breaking from common to quick step. Dress on the center." In at least one outfit, a survivor would recall, one of the captains led in the singing of a hymn and a white-haired chaplain offered prayer. Nor was the step-off itself unduly precipitate. Pettigrew gave the signal on the left to the new leader of his old brigade: "Now, Colonel, for the honor of the good Old North State, forward!" The advance was somewhat ragged at first, as if the Virginians, Mississippians, Alabamians, and Tennesseans of his division supposed that the spoken order only applied to the Carolinians, but the laggard brigades soon restored the alignment by double-timing to catch up. Meanwhile, in the wooded swale to the south, others had taken up the cry. Armistead, whose brigade comprised the supporting line on the right, as Trimble's two did on the left, did not neglect the opportunity afforded for another display of determination. "Sergeant, are you going to plant those colors on the enemy works today?" he asked a nearby colorbearer, and when the sergeant gave the staunch expected answer, "I will try, sir, and if mortal man can do it, it shall be done," the general removed his wide-brimmed black felt hat, placed it on the point of his sword, and raised it high for all to see, shouting in a voice that carried from flank to flank of his brigade: "Attention, 2d Battalion, the battalion of direction! Forward, guide centerrr, *march!*" and led the way. Beyond the left, within the lower limits of the town of Gettysburg, onlookers from Rodes's division, seeing Pettigrew's troops emerge from the woods and begin their downhill march into the valley, called out to the Federal surgeons who had remained behind to tend the captured wounded of their army: "There go the men who will go through your damned Yankee line for you!"

Longstreet had preceded them out to the line of guns and was conferring with Alexander. Pleased though he had been at seeing the enemy artillery first slack then cease its fire, he was anything but pleased when he saw his own guns follow suit immediately after he gave Pickett the nod that would send him forth to what he himself had predicted would be slaughter. But his greatest surprise was at Alexander's explanation that he had suspended firing in order to save ammunition, being doubtful whether enough remained on hand for proper support of the infantry on its way across the valley. Old Peter was plainly horrified, despite the colonel's earlier statement that the supply was limited. "Go and stop Pickett right where he is, and replenish your ammunition!" he exclaimed. Now it was Alexander's turn to be surprised. "We can't do that, sir," he protested. "The train has but little. It would take an hour to distribute it, and meanwhile the enemy would improve the time." Longstreet made no reply to this. For a long moment he stood there saying nothing. Then he spoke, slowly and with deep emotion. "I do not want to make this charge," he said; "I do not see how it can succeed. I would not make it now but that General Lee has ordered it and expects it."

With that he stopped, gripped by indecision and regret, though in point of fact he had been given no authority to halt the attack even if he had so chosen. The young artillerist volunteered nothing further. Just then, however, the issue was settled for once and all by the appearance of Garnett's and Kemper's brigades from the swale behind the guns. Garnett was mounted, having been granted special permission to ride because of his injured knee and feverish condition, and Alexander went back to meet him; they had been friends out on the plains in the old army. Apparently the Virginian was experiencing a chill just now, for he wore an old blue overcoat buttoned close to his throat despite the July heat. Alexander walked beside the horse until they reached the slope leading down to the Emmitsburg Road and the Union ridge beyond. There he stopped and watched his friend ride on. "Goodbye," he called across the widening gap, and he added, as if by afterthought: "Good luck."

★   ★   ★

By now — some twenty or thirty minutes after the Union guns stopped firing, and consequently about half that long since Alexander followed suit — much of the smoke had been diffused or had drifted off, so that for the attackers, many of whom had stepped at a stride from the dense shade of their wooded assembly areas into the brilliant sunlight that dappled the floor of the valley, the result was not only dazzling to their eyes but also added to their feeling of elation and release. "Before us lay bright fields and fair landscape," one among them would recall.

It was not until the effect of this began to wear off, coincidental with the contraction of their pupils, that they saw at last the enormity of what was being required of them, and by then, although the vista afforded absolute confirmation of their direst apprehensions, the pattern of exhilaration had been set. Under the double influence of secondary inertia and terrific deliberation, the long gray lines came on, three brigades to the south under Pickett and six to the north under Pettigrew and Trimble, with a quarter-mile gap between the interior flanks of the two formations, the former composed of fifteen and the latter of twenty-seven regiments, all with their colors flying at more or less regular intervals along the rows of nearly 11,000 striding men. Harvey Hill was to say of the individual Confederate, as he had observed him in offensive action: "Of shoulder-to-shoulder courage, spirit of drill and discipline, he knew nothing and cared less. Hence, on the battlefield, he was more of a free-lance than a machine. Whoever saw a Confederate line advancing that was not crooked as a ram's horn? Each ragged rebel yelling on his own hook and aligning on himself." But Hill, though he was to see about as much combat as any general on either side before the war was over, was not at Gettysburg. If he had been, he would have had to cite it as the exception. Forbidden to step up the cadence or fire their rifles or even give the high-pitched yell that served at once to steady their own nerves and jangle their opponents', the marchers concentrated instead on maintaining their alignment, as if this in itself might serve to awe the waiting bluecoats and frighten them into retreat. And in point of fact, according to one among the watchers on the ridge across the way — a colonel commanding a brigade adjacent to the little clump of trees — it did at least produce the lesser of these two reactions. For him, the advancing graybacks had "the appearance of being fearfully irresistible," while a foreign observer, whose point of vantage was on the near side of the valley, used the same adjective to communicate the impression the attackers made on him: "They seemed impelled by some irresistible force." Out front with the rebel skirmishers, a captain had a closer view of the troops as they strode down the slope toward where he crouched, and he remembered ever afterwards the "glittering forest of bayonets," the two half-mile-wide formations bearing down "in superb alignment," the "murmur and jingle" of trouser-legs and equipment, and the "rustle of thousands of feet amid the stubble," which stirred up dust and chaff beneath and before them "like the dash of spray at the prow of a vessel."

They came on at a steady rate of about one hundred yards a minute, and before they had been three minutes in the open — barely clear of the line of friendly guns, whose cannoneers raised their hats in salute and wished them luck as they passed through — the Union batteries, as if in quick recovery from the shock of seeing them appear thus, massed for slaughter, began to roar. The gray lines dribbled rag-doll shapes, each of which left a gap where it had been while still in motion. Flags plunged with sudden flutters in the windless air, only to be taken up at once as the fallen colorbearers were replaced. This happened especially often in the regiments on the flanks, which came under galling long-range fire delivered in enfilade from the two heights, Cemetery Hill on the left and Little Round Top on the right. Pettigrew's troops had farther to go, since they had begun their march from Seminary Ridge itself, but this had been foreseen and allowed for; Pickett had been charged with closing the quarter-mile interval between the two formations, which would lengthen the distance his three brigades would have to cover in the course of their advance. Accordingly, once they were clear of the line of guns, in plain view of the little clump of trees just over half a mile ahead, he gave his troops the order, "Left oblique!" They obeyed it neatly, executing in midstride a half-face to the north, which, at every full step of their own, brought them half a step closer to the flank of the undeviating marchers on their left. All this time, both groups were taking losses, a more or less steady leakage of killed and wounded, who lay motionless where they fell or turned and hobbled painfully up the slope they had descended. Coming presently to a slight dip, about midway of the valley — a swale not deep enough to hide them from the enemy gunners, but conveniently parallel to the ridge that was their objective — Pickett's men received their second order, which was to halt, close up the gaps their casualties had left, and dress the line. They did so, once more with the deliberate precision of the drill field, but with the difference that such gaps continued to appear at an even more alarming rate as the Union gunners, delighted with this sudden transformation of a moving into a stationary target, stepped up their rate of fire. The result was the first evidence of confusion in the Confederate ranks. A soldier would look toward the comrade on his right, feeling meanwhile with his extended hand for the shoulder of the comrade on his left, and there would be a constant sidling motion in the latter direction, as men continued to fall all down the line, leaving additional gaps that had to be closed. This might have gone on indefinitely, or at any rate until there were no survivors left to dress or dress on, but at last the order came for them to continue the advance, still on the oblique.

This they did, to the considerable relief of most of the bluecoats on the ridge ahead, whose reaction to the maneuver was one of outrage, as if they had been exposed to a blatant indecency, such as the thumbing of a nose, though for others the feeling of revulsion was tempered by awe and incredulity. "My God, they're dressing the line!" some among the waiting infantry exclaimed, more by way of protest than applause. In the course of the ten- or fifteen-minute lull allowed by the enemy guns before the attackers first appeared on the far side of the valley, the defenders had improved the time by repairing what little damage had been done to their improvised earthworks by the rebel cannonade. Now there was nothing left to do but wait, and in some ways that was the hardest thing of all. In fact, some among them found it downright impossible. Despite the renewed Confederate bombardment, they stood up behind their low stone walls or their meager scooped-up mounds of dirt and began to shoot at the graybacks half a mile away, only to have their officers tell them gruffly to hold their fire until the Johnnies came within decent range. Hays, who was jumpy enough himself, being of an excitable nature, found a way to pass the time for the men of his two brigades; he put them through a few stiff minutes of drill in the manual of arms, despite the overhead hiss and flutter of going and coming projectiles. Meanwhile the Union cannoneers kept busy, at any rate those who had husbanded their long-range ammunition for the opportunity now at hand, including the men in a six-gun battery that came up with full limbers just as the lull was ending and replaced the departed Rhode Islanders in the position directly south of the clump of trees. Rittenhouse and Osborn had the best of it in this respect, slamming their shells in at angles that caught the advancing lines almost end-on, but others were by no means idle. "We had a splendid chance at them," one of McGilvery's captains later testified, "and we made the most of it." Watching the effects of this — the gnawed flanks and the plunging flags, the constantly recurring gaps all up and down the long gray front — the bluecoats cheered, and from time to time a man would holler "Fredericksburg!" elated by the thought that he was seeing, or was about to see, a repetition of that fiasco, though with certain welcome differences. On that field, for example, only the last four hundred yards of the attack had been made in full view of the defenders behind their wall of stone and dirt, yet not a single one of the attackers had come within twenty yards of the objective. Here the critical distance was more than three times as great, and the waiting soldiers took much consolation in the fact that the respective roles of the two armies, as attackers and defenders, had been reversed. "Come on, Blue Belly!" the rebs had yelled, but now it was the other way around; now it was the Federals who were yelling, "Come on, Johnny! Keep on coming!" even though the Confederates were bringing no blankets or overcoats along and their worn-out shoes would not be worth stripping from their corpses.

On Pickett's right, Kemper's brigade was taking cruel punishment from the half-dozen guns on Little Round Top, whose gunners tracked their victims with the cool precision of marksmen in a monstrous shooting gallery, except that in this case the targets were displayed in depth, which greatly increased the likelihood of hits. Moreover, the slightest excess in elevation landed their shots in Garnett's ranks "with fearful effect," as one of his officers would report, "sometimes as many as ten men being killed [or] wounded by the bursting of a single shell." But worse by far was the predicament of the troops on Pettigrew's left. Here Mayo's brigade — Virginians too, but fewer by half in number; their heavy losses at Chancellorsville had never been made up, and they had been under a series of temporary commanders for nearly a year, with the result that their morale had been known to be shaky even before the bloody action two days ago had taken its further toll — caught the end-on fire, not of six but of 29 high-sited guns, with correspondingly greater suffering and disruption. As they tottered forward under the merciless pounding from the batteries on Cemetery Hill, these unfortunates had all they could do to maintain their alignment and keep their four flags flying. Whereupon, about two hundred yards short of the Emmitsburg Road, having passed the still-hot ashes of the house and barn set afire by the forenoon bombardment, they were struck on the flank by a regiment of Ohioans from the Union skirmish line, whose colonel massed and launched them in an assault as unexpected as it was bold. The reaction of the Virginians — it was they who "on a sudden had become as still and thoughtful as Quakers at a love feast" when they first learned that the attack was to be made and that they were to have a share in it — was immediate and decisive. Despite their four-to-one numerical advantage and their well-earned heritage of valor, they took off rearward at a run, flags and all, to the considerable dismay of the onlookers who had told the Federal surgeons, "There go the men who will go through your damned Yankee line for you," and did not stop until they regained the cover of Seminary Ridge. By quick subtraction, four of Pettigrew's regiments, nearly one fourth of the total in his division, thus were removed from his calculations as effectively as if they had stepped into bottomless quicksand. Osborn's gunners, observing the flight of the brigade which up to now had been their sole concern, cheered lustily and swung their muzzles without delay along a short arc to the left. Their first shell burst in the midst of Davis's brigade, killing five men in one of his Mississippi regiments.

Nothing quite like this abrupt defection had ever happened before, at least not in Lee's army, though the sight had been fairly common in the ranks of its opponents over the past two years, beginning at First Manassas and continuing through Second Winchester. Most Confederate witnesses reacted first with unbelief and then with consternation; but not Longstreet, who had steeled himself at the outset by expecting the very worst. Still seated on the snake rail fence at the far end of the field, he moved at once to counteract what he had seen through the shellbursts to the north, sending word for Anderson to commit his three remaining brigades — Wright's and Posey's and Mahone's; Lang and Wilcox had already been instructed to furnish such help for Pickett if it was needed — in support of the line thus weakened. No one could know whether the sudden collapse of this one brigade was indicative of what the others would do when the pressure intensified, but there was always the danger, even in quite sound units, that when a flank started to crumble, as this one had done, the reaction would continue all down the line. And in fact it did continue in one regiment under Davis, some of whose green troops took off rearward in the wake of the Virginians, but the other three held steady, taking in turn the end-on pounding from the batteries on the height as they kept up their steady progress across the valley. By now the interior flanks of Pettigrew and Pickett had come together on the near side of the fence-lined Emmitsburg Road, beyond which the blue skirmishers fired a volley or two before hurrying back to their own line, some four hundred yards up the slope behind them. The resultant crowding of Fry's and Garnett's brigades, which occurred before the latter received the order that brought its marchers off the oblique, presented a close-packed target the Union gunners did not neglect from point-blank range on the ridge ahead. "Don't crowd, boys!" a rebel captain shouted, his voice as lackadaisical amid the bursting shells as that of a dancing master. There was in fact a certain amount of formal politeness as the two brigades came together, Tennesseans on the one hand and Virginians on the other, under circumstances designed to favor havoc. Southern courtesy had never been more severely tried, yet such protest as was heard was mild in tone. It was here that the classic Confederate line was spoken: "Move on, cousins. You are drawing the fire our way."

Armistead was hard on Garnett's heels by now, and Kemper's men had drifted left, not only in an attempt to keep in touch with the latter's contracting line, but also in obedience to a natural inclination to flinch from the increasingly effective fire directed at their exposed flank from Little Round Top as well as from the south end of the Federal ridge, where McGilvery's seven batteries were massed. From close in rear of his advancing troops, Pickett saw his and Pettigrew's lead brigades, crowded into a blunted wedge perhaps five hundred yards in width, surge across the road and its two fences, taking severe losses from the opening blasts of canister loosed by guns that had been silent until now, and begin their climb up the slope toward the low stone wall behind which the blue infantry was crouched. He saw that his men were going to make it, a good part of them anyhow; but he saw, too — so heavy had their casualties been on the way across the valley, and so heavy were they going to be in storming the wall itself, which extended the length of the front and beyond — that unless the survivors were stoutly reinforced, and soon, they would not be able to hold what they were about to gain. Accordingly, he sent a courier to inform Longstreet of this close-up estimate of the situation. The courier, a staff captain, galloped fast to find Old Peter, but even so he took time to draw rein in an attempt to rally some stragglers he found trotting toward the rear. "What are you running for?" he demanded, glaring down at them.

One of the men looked up at him as if to say the question was a foolish waste of breath, though what he actually said was: "Why, good gracious, Captain, aint you running yourself?" Too flustered to attempt an answer, the courier gave his horse the spur and continued on his mission, feeling rather baffled by the encounter.

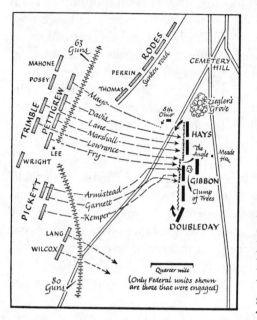

He found Old Peter still perched atop the snake rail fence, observing through his binoculars the action on the ridge. The general listened attentively to Pickett's message, but before he could reply a distinguished British visitor rode up: Lieutenant Colonel Arthur Fremantle, of Her Majesty's Coldstream Guards. Despite his high rank in a famous regiment, this was his first experience of battle. "General Longstreet," he said, breathless with excitement, "General Lee sent me here, and said you would place me in a position to see this magnificent charge." Then, observing for himself the struggle in progress on the ridge across the way, he exclaimed: "I wouldn't have missed this for anything!" Old Peter laughed, an incongruous sound against that backdrop of death and destruction. "The devil you wouldn't!" he said; "I would like to have missed it very much. We've attacked and been repulsed. Look there." All the colonel could see, amid swirls of smoke on the slope at which the general was pointing, half a mile in the distance, was that men were fighting desperately; but Longstreet spoke as if the issue was no longer in doubt. "The charge is over," he said flatly. And then, having attended in his fashion to the amenities due a guest, he turned to the courier and added: "Captain Bright, ride to General Pickett and tell him what you have heard me say to Colonel Fremantle." The courier started off, but the general called after him: "Captain Bright!" Drawing rein, Bright looked back and saw Old Peter pointing northward. "Tell General Pickett that Wilcox's brigade is in that orchard, and he can order him to his assistance."

The courier galloped off at last, and the burly Georgian returned to watching the final stages of the action, pausing only to countermand his recent order for Anderson's three reserve brigades to be committed. Wilcox and Lang could go forward, in accordance with Lee's original arrangements — Longstreet's final instructions, shouted after the courier when he first started back to Pickett, were more in the nature of a reminder than a command — but if what was happening on the ridge was only the prelude to a repulse, as he believed, then Anderson's three and Pender's two uncommitted brigades would be needed to meet the counterattack Meade would be likely to launch in the wake of the Confederates as they fell back down the slope and recrossed the valley. Fremantle marveled at his companion's self-possession under strain, remarking afterwards that "difficulties seem[ed] to make no other impression on him than to make him a little more savage." In point of fact, though Old Peter kept his binoculars trained on the flame-stabbed turmoil halfway up the enemy ridge, he watched the fighting not so much in suspense as to the outcome — for that had been settled already, at least to his own disgruntled satisfaction — as to study the manner in which it came about. Convinced that the attack had failed, even before the first signs of retreat were evident, he was mainly interested in seeing how many of his soldiers would survive it.

But they themselves had no such detached view of the holocaust in which they were involved. Massed as they were on a narrow front, flailed by canister from both flanks and dead ahead, the men of the five lead brigades were mingled inextricably; few of them had any knowledge of anything except in their immediate vicinity, and very little of that. "Everything was a wild kaleidoscopic whirl," a colonel would recall. Fry, for one, thought victory was certain. "Go on; it will not last five minutes longer!" he shouted as he fell, shot through the thigh while urging his brigade to hurry up the slope. Nearby a lieutenant waved his sword and exulted as if he saw the end of the war at hand. "Home, boys, home!" he cried. "Remember, home is over beyond those hills!" Sheets of flame leaped out at the charging graybacks as the blue infantry opened fire along the wall, but they held their own fire until Garnett passed the word, which was taken up by officers all up and down the front: "Make ready. Take good aim. Fire low. *Fire!*" Uphill sheets of flame flashed in response and blue-capped heads dropped from sight beyond the wall. "Fire! Fire!" they could hear the Federal officers shouting through the smoke and muzzle-flashes. Still wrapped in his old army overcoat, Garnett rocked back in the saddle and fell heavily to the ground, dead, the Kernstown stain removed at last. Kemper meanwhile had turned and called to Armistead, who was close in his rear: "Armistead, hurry up! I am going to charge those heights and carry them, and I want you to support me!" His friend called back, "I'll do it!" and added proudly: "Look at my line. It never looked better on dress parade." But Kemper by then was in no condition to observe it; he had fallen, shot in the groin as he ordered the final assault. Pickett thus was down to a single brigade commander, and Pettigrew was in the same condition on the left, where only Davis remained, Marshall having been killed at about the same time Fry went down. Unhorsed by a shell on his way across the valley, Pettigrew had crossed the Emmitsburg

Road on foot and then had been wounded painfully in the hand as he began to climb the ridge. He remained in command, though his troops were mingled beyond the possibility of over-all control, even if he could have managed to make himself heard above the tremendous clatter of firing and the high screams of the wounded. Nevertheless, like Pickett's leaderless two on the right, his three brigades continued their uphill surge, eager to come to grips with their tormentors beyond the wall, and for the first time on this field today the rebel yell rang out.

On the Union right, near Ziegler's Grove, Hancock watched with admiration as Hays, whose northern flank considerably overlapped the enemy left, swung his end regiment forward, gatelike, to make contact with the Ohioans who had halted after routing Mayo and had taken up a position facing southwest with their left on the Emmitsburg Road. As a result of this pivoting maneuver, which was accompanied by two brass Napoleons firing double-shotted canister, some 450 men who otherwise would have had no share in the fighting after the rebels actually struck the blue defenses, well down the line and beyond their angle of sight, were placed where they could and did pump heavy volleys into the mangled flank of the attackers, adding greatly to the confusion and the carnage. Hancock shouted approval of this happy improvisation and took off southward at a gallop, intending to see whether the same could not be done at the opposite end of the position, which likewise extended well beyond the huddled mass of graybacks driving hard against his center. He rode fast, but even so he had cause to fear he would be too late. The stone wall along which his five brigades were deployed ran due south for a couple of hundred yards from Ziegler's Grove, then turned sharply west for eighty yards, thus avoiding the clump of umbrella-shaped trees, before it made as sharp a turn again to resume its former direction. The jog in the wall — described thereafter as The Angle — had caused Gibbon's men to be posted eighty yards in advance of Hays's, which meant that they would be struck first: as indeed they were. Galloping southward along the ridge, Hancock was hailed by Colonel Arthur Devereux, who commanded one of two regiments Gibbon had placed in reserve, well up the slope behind his center. "See, General!" Devereux cried, pointing. "They have broken through; the colors are coming over the stone wall. Let me go in there!" Reining his horse in so abruptly that he brought the animal back on its haunches, Hancock looked and saw that the report was all too true. Less than two hundred yards away, due west and northwest of the clump of trees, which partly obscured his view, he saw a host of butternut soldiers, led by a gray-haired officer who brandished a sword with a black hat balanced on its point, boiling over the wall in hot pursuit of a blue regiment that had bolted. Some two hundred undefended feet of the south leg of the angle had been overrun. "Go in there pretty God-damned quick!" the general shouted, and spurred on southward to order Doubleday to repeat the flanking maneuver that was working so well at the far end of the line. That way, the breakthrough might at least be limited in width, and if Devereux got there in time it might even be contained.

Arriving, Hancock found that Doubleday, or anyhow the commander of the one I Corps brigade attached for defense of the Union center, had anticipated the order; Brigadier General G. J. Stannard, a former Vermont dry-goods merchant and militia officer, had already begun the pivot maneuver and was wheeling two of his three regiments into an advance position from which to tear the flank of the attackers pressing forward to exploit their narrow penetration of the south leg of the angle, directly in front of the clump of trees and less than two hundred yards north of the point where Stannard's gatelike swing was hinged. Vermonters all, the 900 men of these two outsized regiments were nine-month volunteers; "nine monthlings hatched from $200 bounty eggs," scornful veterans had dubbed them on their recent arrival from the soft life of the Washington defenses. They had seen their first action yesterday and their army time was almost up, but they were determined to give a good account of themselves before returning home. Now the opportunity was at hand. Company by company, they opened fire as they wheeled into line, blasting the rebel flank, and as they delivered their murderous volleys they continued to move northward, closing the range until their officers were able to add the fire of their revolvers to the weight of metal thrown into the writhing mass of graybacks. "Glory to God! Glory to God!" Doubleday shouted, swinging his hat in approval as he watched from up the slope. "See the Vermonters go it!"

Hancock too was delighted, but while he was congratulating Stannard on the success with which his green troops had executed the difficult maneuver, a bullet passed through the pommel of his saddle and buried itself in the tender flesh of his inner thigh, along with several jagged bits of wood and a bent nail. Two officers caught him as he slumped, and when they had lowered him to the ground Stannard improvised a tourniquet — a knotted handkerchief wound tight with a pistol barrel — to stanch the flow of blood from the ugly wound. Hancock himself extracted the saddle nail unaided, though he mistook its source. "They must be hard up for ammunition when they throw such shot as that," he said wryly. Stretcherbearers came on the run, but he refused to be carried off the field just yet. He insisted on staying to watch the action, which now was mounting swiftly toward a climax.

The gray-haired Confederate officer he had glimpsed through the screen of trees as he rode southward in rear of the center was his old friend Armistead, whom he had seen last in California and did not recognize now because of the distance and the smoke. Working his way forward to assume command of the frantic press of troops after Garnett and Kemper had fallen, Armistead found himself at the stone wall, midway of the 200-foot stretch from which a regiment of Pennsylvanians had bolted to avoid contact with the charging rebels. There the gray advance had stopped, or anyhow paused, while those in front knelt behind its welcome cover and poured a heavy fire into the secondary blue line up the slope. He saw, however, that it would not do to lose momentum or allow the Federals time to bring up reinforcements. "Come on, boys! Give them the cold steel!" he cried, and holding his saber high, still with the black hat balanced on its tip for a guidon, he stepped over the wall, yelling as he did so: "Follow me!" Young Cushing's two guns were just ahead, unserved and silent because Cushing himself was dead by now, shot through the mouth as he called for a faster rate of fire, and Gibbon had been taken rearward, a bullet in his shoulder. Then Armistead fell too, killed as he reached with his free hand for the muzzle of one of the guns, and the clot of perhaps 300 men who had followed him over the wall was struck from the right front by the two regiments Devereux had brought down "pretty God-damned quick" from the up-hill slope beyond the clump of trees. The fight was hand to hand along the fringes, while others among the defenders stood back, left and front and right, and fired into the close-packed, heaving mass of rebel troops and colors. "Every man fought on his own hook," a bluecoat would recall, with little regard for rank or assignment, high or low. Even Hunt was there, on horseback, emptying his revolver into the crush. "See 'em! See 'em!" he cried as he pulled trigger. Then his horse went down, hoofs flailing, with the general underneath. Men on both sides were hollering as they milled about and fired, some cursing, others praying, and this, combined with the screams of the wounded and the moans of the dying, produced an effect which one who heard it called "strange and terrible, a sound that came from thousands of human throats, yet was not a commingling of shouts and yells but rather like a vast mournful roar."

Neither on the left nor on the right of the shallow penetration of the center, assailed as they were from north and south by the double envelopment Hays and Stannard had improvised, could the Confederates make real headway. Pettigrew's troops, advancing up their additional eighty yards of slope, which one of them noted incongruously was "covered with clover as soft as a Turkish carpet," were in fact outnumbered by the defenders of the two hundred yards of wall above the angle. Fry's brigade and part of Marshall's having gone in with the Virginians to the south, all that remained were Davis's brigade and Marshall's remnant, and though they kept coming on, torn by rifle fire and canister from the flank and dead ahead, they had not the slightest chance of scoring a breakthrough and they knew it. The most they could hope to accomplish was to keep the enemy units in their front from being shifted to meet the threat below the angle, and this they did, though at a cruel cost. A Mississippi regiment — including the University Greys, a company made up exclusively of students from the state university, which suffered a precisely tabulated loss of 100% of its members killed or wounded in the charge — managed to plant its colors within arm's length of the Union line before it was blasted out of existence, and a sergeant from a North Carolina outfit, accompanied by one man bearing the regimental colors, got all the way up to the wall itself, but only because the admiring defenders held their fire as they drew near. "Come over to this side of the Lord!" a bluecoat shouted: whereupon the two surrendered and crossed over with their flag. Some others availed themselves of the same mercy at various points along the line, but these were all. Except as captives, or as corpses tumbling headlong under pressure from the rear, not an attacker got over the wall north of the angle.

Blood dripping from his wounded hand, Pettigrew sent word for Trimble to bring his two supporting brigades forward and add their weight to the attack. Trimble did so, ordering Lowrance to the right, against the angle, and Lane to reinforce the battered left. Mounted, he watched with pride as they swung past him. "Charley, I believe those fine fellows are going into the enemy's line," he told an aide. But he was wrong. Moreover, as he watched them waver and recoil under the impact of the heavy fire the Federals brought to bear, he was hit a bonesplintering blow in the leg he had nearly lost at Manassas, just over ten months back, from a wound that had kept him all those fretful months out of combat. He passed the command to Lane, whom he had succeeded only four hours ago, but stayed to watch the outcome of the action. Discouraged by what he saw, the sixty-one-year-old Marylander, whose reputation for hard-handed aggressiveness was unsurpassed by any man in either army, went rapidly into shock from pain and loss of blood, and declined to permit his aide to attempt to rally the troops for a renewal of the assault, which he now perceived could not succeed. "No," he said slowly, sadly, in response to the aide's request. "The best thing the men can do is get out of this. Let them go."

They did go, here and on the right and in the center — at any rate, those who had not surrendered and were still in any condition, either physical or mental, to undertake the long walk back across the shell-torn valley. This was harder for those within the angle, not only because they had to run the longest gauntlet between the two converging wings under Hays and Stannard, but also because they were the last to realize that the assault had failed. For them, the let-down was abrupt and sickening. "I looked to the right and left," a Virginia lieutenant would recall, "and felt we were disgraced. . . . We had, for the first time, failed to do our duty." It was only after he started back and saw for himself that the friends he missed were casualties, not skulkers, that he began to comprehend the nature of the failure, and "felt that after all we were not disgraced." He made it back across, as did June Kimble, the

Tennessee sergeant who had resolved to do his duty and had done it, but who now admitted frankly: "For about a hundred yards I broke the lightning speed record." Once more, however, his conscience intervened. With a horror of being shot in the back, he turned to face the bluecoats firing downhill at him and walked backwards until he was out of musket range, then turned again and plodded uphill amid shellbursts that plowed the farther reaches of what a Federal observer called "a square mile of Tophet." Fortunately, the final stages of the withdrawal were favored somewhat by the advance of Wilcox and Lang, who came forward in response to calls from Pickett. Although Wilcox later reported that by the time he emerged from cover "not a man of the division that I was ordered to support could I see," his limited advance had at least the effect of causing Stannard, who was wounded too by now, to order his Vermonters back into line to meet this new menace to their flank, thus easing the pressure on those Confederates who were last to leave the angle and the more stubbornly defended portions of wall above and below it.

Even so, barely more than half of the 11,000 men in the nine-brigade assault force — including Mayo's defectors, whose losses had been comparatively light, and those disabled stalwarts who managed to hobble or crawl the westward distance across the valley — returned to the ridge they had left with such high hopes an hour ago. The rest, some 5000 in all, were either killed or captured. Further allowance for the wounded among the survivors, as well as for those who were killed or injured during the preliminary bombardment and in the belated advance of Lang and Wilcox, raised the total to about 7500 casualties, which amounted to sixty percent of the 12,500 Confederates engaged from first to last. In the five leading brigades under Pickett and Pettigrew the ratio of losses was considerably higher, no less indeed than seventy percent; so that it was no wonder that the former, writing five days later to his fiancée, spoke of "my spirit-crushed, wearied, cut-up people," especially if he had reference to his subordinate commanders. Not only had he lost all three of his brigadiers, but of his thirteen colonels eight were killed and all the rest were wounded. In fact, of his thirty-five officers above the rank of captain only one came back unhit, a one-armed major, and Pettigrew's losses were almost as grievous in that regard. In Fry's brigade two field officers escaped, in Marshall's only one, and in Davis's all were killed or wounded. Moreover, the Union infantry force, with half as many troops as came against them, suffered no more than 1500 casualties, barely one fifth of the number they inflicted while maintaining the integrity of their position. "We gained nothing but glory," a Virginia captain wrote home before the week was out; "and lost our bravest men."

The gloom that settled over the western ridge was more than

matched, at least in intensity, by the elation of the victors on the one across the way. On Cemetery Hill, watching as the rebel lines began to come unhinged, a captain shouted: "By God, boys, we've got 'em now. They've broke all to hell!" And down on the blood-splotched ridge below, when it became apparent that such was indeed the case, a wild celebration got under way before the gunfire stopped. Hays, who had had two horses shot from under him and had lost all but six of his twenty orderlies, was so exuberant that he grabbed and kissed young David Shields, a lieutenant on his staff. "Boys, give me a flag!" he cried. "Get a flag, Corts, get a flag, Dave, and come on!" There was no shortage of such trophies; for of the 38 regimental flags that had been brought within musket range of the wall, here on the right and on the left, no less than 30 had been captured. Hays and the two staff officers he had invited to join him in a horseback victory dance rode up and down the division line, each trailing a stand of rebel colors in the dust behind his mount, cheered by those of their grinning soldiers who were not still busy taking pot shots at the butternut figures retreating in disorder across the valley. Recalling his excitement, Shields wrote later: "My horse seemed to be off the ground traveling through the air." His impression was that if he could survive what he had just been through, he could survive almost anything, in or out of the catalogue of war. He was going to live forever. "I felt though a shot as large as a barrel should hit me in the back, it would be with no more effect than shooting through a fog bank."

Meanwhile the nearly 4000 rebel prisoners, wounded and unwounded, were being rounded up and sent to the rear. "Smart, healthy-looking men," one Federal called them, adding: "They move very quick, walk like horses." It was strange to see them thus, close up and de-fanged, without their guns and yells. They had a simple dignity about them which their ragged clothes served more to emphasize than lessen. Nor were all of them in rags. "Many of their officers were well dressed, fine, proud gentlemen," another observer wrote soon afterwards, "such men as it would be a pleasure to meet, when the war is over. I had no desire to exult over them, and pity and sympathy were the general feelings of us all upon the occasion." This last was not entirely true. At least one Union officer was alarmed by the thought that the prisoners — who, after all, numbered only a few hundred less than the surviving defenders of the ridge — might take it into their heads to renew the fight with the discarded weapons thickly strewn about the ground at their feet. There was, as it turned out, no danger of this; but the commander of a reserve battery, galloping forward in response to belated orders to reinforce the badly pounded guns along the center, received a different kind of shock. As he came up the reverse slope of the ridge he saw a mass of gray-clad men come over the crest ahead, and his first thought was that the position had been overrun. He signaled a halt and was about to give the order to fall back, when he saw that the Confederates bore no arms and were under guard.

Meade had much the same original reaction. Arriving at last from Powers Hill, he too mistook the drove of prisoners for evidence of a breakthrough. Then, as he realized his mistake and rode on past them toward the crest, he encountered a lieutenant from Gibbon's staff. "How is it going here?" he asked eagerly, and received the reply: "I believe, General, the enemy's attack is repulsed." Meade could scarcely credit the information, welcome though it was. "What!" he exclaimed. "Is the assault already repulsed?" By that time he had reached the crest, however, and the lieutenant's assurance, "It is, sir," was confirmed by what he saw with his own eyes: more captives being herded into clusters along the left and right and center, his own troops cavorting with abandoned rebel flags, and the fugitives withdrawing amid shellbursts on the far side of the valley, all unmistakable evidence of a victory achieved. "Thank God," he said fervently. The lieutenant observed that Meade's right hand jerked involuntarily upward, as if to snatch off his slouch hat and wave it in exultation, but then his concern for dignity prevailed. Instead he merely waved his hand, albeit rather self-consciously, and cried, just once: "Hurrah!" This done, he gave the staffer instructions for the posting of reinforcements expected shortly, "as the enemy might be mad enough to attack again." Adding: "If the enemy does attack, charge him in the flank and sweep him from the field," he rode on down the ridge, where he was greeted with cheers of recognition and tossed caps. A band had come up by now from somewhere, and when it broke into the strains of "Hail to the Chief" a correspondent remarked, not altogether jokingly: "Ah, General Meade, you're in very great danger of being President of the United States."

Despite the evidence spread before him that the Confederates were in a state of acute distress, and therefore probably vulnerable to attack, the northern commander's words had made it clear that he had no intention of going over to the offensive. No one on the other side of the valley had heard those words, however. If they had, their surprise and relief would have been at least as great as his had been on learning that their attempt to pierce his center had been foiled. This was especially true of Longstreet. A counter-puncher himself, he expected Meade to attack without delay, and he moved at once to meet the threat as best he could, sending word for Wright, whom he had halted when he saw the charge must fail, to collect and rally the fugitives streaming back toward the center, while he himself attended to that same function on the right. Now that the painful thing he had opposed was over, he recovered his bluff and hearty manner. He rode among the returning troops and spoke reassuringly to them, meantime sending word for Mc-

Laws and Law to pull back to the line they had taken off from yesterday and thus place their divisions in position to assist in the defense of the weakened center. When one commander protested that his men could not be rallied, Old Peter mocked at his despair. "Very well; never mind then, General," he told him. "Just let them remain where they are. The enemy's going to advance, and will spare you the trouble." Fremantle thought the Georgian's conduct "admirable," and when he paused at one point to ask if the colonel had anything to drink, the Britisher not only gave him a swig of rum from a silver flask but also insisted that he keep the rest, together with its container, as a token of his esteem. Longstreet thanked him, put the flask in his pocket for future reference, and continued to move among the fugitives with words of cheer and encouragement, preparing to meet the counterattack which he believed Meade would be delivering at any moment now.

But most of the survivors came streaming back the shortest way, straight across the valley toward the command post midway of its western rim, like hurt children in instinctive search of solace from a parent: meaning Lee. There the southern commander had remained throughout their advance and their brief, furious struggle on the distant ridge, until he saw them falter and begin their slow recoil; whereupon he rode forward to meet them coming back, to rally them with words of reassurance, and to share with them the ordeal of the counterattack he believed would soon be launched. Nor did he disappoint them in their expectations of solace and sustainment. "All this will come right in the end," he told them. "We'll talk it over afterwards. But in the meantime all good men must rally. We want all good and true men just now." He made it clear to all he met that he considered the failure of the charge not their fault, but his, for having asked of them more than men could give. To Fremantle, who had ridden over from the right, he said: "This has been a sad day for us, Colonel. A sad day. But we can't always expect to win victories." After advising the visitor to find a safer point for observation, he continued to move among his soldiers in an attempt to brace them for the storm he thought was coming. "Very few failed to answer his appeal," Fremantle noted, "and I saw many badly wounded men take off their hats and cheer him."

One among the fugitives most in need of encouragement was Pickett, who came riding back with an expression of dejection and bewilderment on his face. Leading his division into battle for the first time, he had seen two thirds of it destroyed. Not only had his great hour come to nothing; tactically speaking, it added up to considerably less than nothing. Lee met him with instructions designed to bring him back to the problem now at hand. "General Pickett, place your division in rear of this hill," he told him, "and be ready to repel the advance of the enemy should they follow up their advantage." At least one bystander observed that in his extremity Lee employed the words "the enemy" rather than his usual "those people." But Pickett was in no state to observe anything outside his personal loss and mortification.

"General Lee, I have no division now," he said tearfully; "Armistead is down, Garnett is down, and Kemper is mortally wounded —"

"Come, General Pickett," Lee broke in. "This has been my fight, and upon my shoulders rests the blame. The men and officers of your command have written the name of Virginia as high today as it has ever been written before. . . . Your men have done all that men can do," he added after a pause for emphasis. "The fault is entirely my own."

He repeated this as he rode from point to point about the field: "It's all my fault," "The blame is mine," and "You must help me." To Wilcox, who was about as unstrung as Pickett in reporting that he was not sure his troops would stand if the Federals attacked, Lee was particularly solicitous and tender. "Never mind, General," he told him, taking his hand as he spoke. "All this has been my fault. It is I who have lost this fight, and you must help me out of it the best way you can." Fremantle, who had not followed his advice to find a place of safety, thought it "impossible to look at him or listen to him without feeling the strongest admiration," and when he rode forward to the line of guns, the Britisher found the cannoneers ready to challenge any blue attack on the disrupted center. They had much the same reaction as his own to Lee's appeal. "We've not lost confidence in the old man," they assured him, speaking defiantly, almost angrily, as if someone had suggested otherwise. "This day's work will do him no harm. Uncle Robert will get us into Washington yet. You bet he will."

By no means all responded in that fashion, however — especially among the troops who had been all the way to the enemy ridge and back, as the artillerists had not — and even concerning those who did there was considerable doubt as to whether they would stand their ground, this soon after their delivery from chaos, if they were exposed to more than the possibility of further danger. In point of fact, there was strong evidence that they would not. When some officers managed to form a line along the forward slope of Seminary Ridge, still in plain view of the Union batteries, the rallied fugitives broke badly under the long-range fire their concentration drew. "Then commenced a rout, that increased to a stampede," an indignant witness later wrote. Fleeing rearward over the crest, the mass of several hundred fear-crazed men was funneled into a ravine along the western slope, and there, without regard for orders or appeals from their officers, who were swept along in the crush, they "pushed, poured, and rushed in a continuous stream, throwing away guns, blankets, and haversacks," until at last a straggler line, composed of the more stalwart few among them, was thrown across their path and "dammed [them] up."

Lee did not reproach them even then, knowing as he did that time alone could heal the wounds their morale had suffered in the hour just past. What was more, his ready acceptance of total blame for the failure of the assault was not merely a temporary burden he assumed for the sake of encouraging his troops to resist the counterattack he believed Meade was about to launch at them; he continued to say the same things in the future, after the immediate need for them was past and the quite different but altogether human need for self-justification might have been expected to set in. "It's all my fault. I thought my men were invincible," he told Longstreet the next day, perhaps by way of making specific admission that he had been wrong in overruling his chief lieutenant's objection that the charge was bound to fail. And in his official report to the President, forwarded on the last day of the month, he repeated for the record his assertion that such fault as might be found could not properly be applied to the men who had bled and died to sustain his pride in them. "The conduct of the troops was all that I could desire or expect," he wrote, "and they deserved success so far as it can be deserved by heroic valor and fortitude. More may have been required of them than they were able to perform, but my admiration of their noble qualities and confidence in their ability to cope successfully with the enemy has suffered no abatement from the issue of this protracted and sanguinary conflict."

✠ 5 ✠

Protracted the conflict had certainly been, and sanguinary too, three days of fighting having produced a combined total of about 50,000 casualties North and South. Nor was it quite over yet. Although Lee could not and Meade would not renew the infantry action, two indecisive and as it were extraneous cavalry engagements — one three miles east of Gettysburg, deep in the Federal right rear, and the other just west of Round Top, on the Confederate right flank — were, respectively, still to be ended and begun. The former, which reached a climax at about the time Pickett and Pettigrew surged up Cemetery Ridge, was the result of Jeb Stuart's attempt to carry out his instructions for placing his troopers in a position from which to harry the expected, or at any rate hoped-for, blue retreat; whereas the latter, fought about an hour after the gray attackers fell back across the valley, was the result of Judson Kilpatrick's attempt, in the absence of instructions, to strike while the tactical iron was hot and thus not only throw the rebels into retreat but also provoke a panic that would prevent them from achieving a getaway. Neither Stuart nor Kilpatrick, quite different in makeup and ability, but altogether similar in their thirst for action and applause, succeeded in accomplishing what he set out to do. In fact, as the two things turned out, both generals would have done better to remain within their respective lines, together with all their men: especially Kilpatrick.

At midday Stuart rode eastward out the York Pike with the brigades of Chambliss and Jenkins, the latter now under Colonel M. J. Ferguson since its regular commander had been wounded the day before; Hampton and Fitz Lee followed at a distance, bringing the total to just over 6000 sabers. One night's rest could scarcely have restored either the men or their mounts after a week on the go, but Jeb was eager for a fight. On Evelington Heights a year ago this morning, by way of providing the just-concluded drama of the Seven Days with an upbeat epilogue, he had opened fire with a single howitzer on McClellan's blue host encamped at Harrison's Landing, and though he had been criticized for flushing the game in this fashion, he would have liked nothing better today than another such opportunity, especially after the chilling reception his chief had given him yesterday when he rejoined the army that had been groping blindfold in his absence. For more than two miles, however, he did not sight a single enemy soldier. The Pennsylvania countryside looked altogether peaceful, its rolling farmlands untouched by war, despite the thunder of the great cannonade behind him, south of Gettysburg, which began soon after 1 o'clock and continued to rumble without diminution as he turned south about 2.30 along Cress Ridge, which extended down to the Hanover Road and the Baltimore Pike beyond. Presently he spotted horsemen a mile to the east on the Low Dutch Road, a lane that paralleled the ridge, and promptly decided to defeat or drive them off, thus clearing his path to the Union rear. Accordingly, after posting Chambliss behind a screen of woods, he dismounted Ferguson's men and sent them forward to take position around a large barn on the farm of a family named Rummel. They would serve as bait to draw the Federals, whose strength was so far undisclosed, after which Stuart planned to attack with Chambliss, then sweep the field with Hampton and Lee, whom he warned by courier to remain under cover of the ridge as they came up, thereby adding the shock of surprise to the weight of their horseback assault on the unsuspecting bluecoats whose attention would be fixed on the dismounted and presumably vulnerable band of graybacks in the Rummel barnyard.

It did not work out quite that way, for several reasons. For one, the blue riders were in much greater numbers than he knew. Two brigades of David Gregg's division, reinforced by one brigade from Kilpatrick's, were at hand, 5000 strong, armed with repeating carbines, and apparently as eager for a clash as Stuart was. This by itself would have been all right — the Confederates still had the numerical advantage — but it presently developed that Ferguson's men, through a misinterpretation of instructions, had drawn only ten rounds of ammunition each, with the result that they ran out of bullets almost as soon as the fight got started. Stuart had to send in Chambliss prematurely, in order to keep the bait from being gobbled before he was set to spring the trap. Even this was not too bad, or anyhow it need not have been, if Hampton and Lee had come up as planned; but they did not. Disclosing their presence while still too far away to achieve surprise, they gave the Federals time to fall back from the melee around the barn and form their ranks to receive the charge. In fact, a good many of the bluecoats did a great deal more than that. They moved to meet it. The brigade attached from Kilpatrick included four Michigan regiments commanded by a recently promoted brigadier named George A. Custer, bottom man in the West Point class of '61, which had lost its top man yesterday on Little Round Top. Custer, whose love of combat was only exceeded by his ache for glory, saw the rebel column approaching and moved fast. "Come on, you Wolverines!" he shouted, four lengths in front of the lead regiment, his long yellow ringlets streaming in the wind. A Federal witness described what followed. "As the two columns approached each other, the pace of each increased, when suddenly a crash, like the falling of timber, betokened the crisis. So sudden and violent was the collision that many of the horses were turned end over end and crushed their riders beneath them. The clashing of sabers, the firing of pistols, the demands for surrender and cries of the combatants now filled the air."

Gregg dealt ably with the situation that developed, sending in other units to strike the flanks of the gray column which Custer had brought to a standstill by meeting it head-on, and while the saber-to-saber conflict was in progress, cannoneers on both sides threw in shell and canister whenever they could do so without too great risk of hitting their own men. Hampton went down with a deep gash in his head, but was brought off the field in time to prevent his capture. Stuart, perhaps reasoning that it was not after all his mission to stage a cavalry fight at this stage of the battle — which he had no way of knowing was now at its climax, back on Cemetery Ridge, with Armistead crying "Follow me!" as he stepped over the low stone wall along Meade's center — withdrew his troopers to the ridge from which they had charged, and Gregg, who had cause to be well satisfied, was content to let them go. The artillery exchange continued till past sundown, at which time the Confederates retired northward and went unmolested into bivouac alongside the York Pike, near the point where they had left it six hours back. Gregg reported 254 casualties, most of them Custer's, whose Michiganders would suffer, before the war was over, a larger number of killed and wounded than any other cavalry brigade in the Union army. Stuart listed 181, but since this was exclusive of Ferguson's brigade and the artillery, the losses probably were about equal on both sides. Jeb made the most of the affair in his report, praising the conduct of some of his regiments by saying that "the enemy's masses vanished before them like grain before the scythe." Yet the fact remained that, for once, he had failed to drive an outnumbered foe from a fair field of fight. "Defeated at every point, the enemy withdrew," Gregg declared, and while Stuart objected strenuously to the claim — he had withdrawn when he got good and ready, he maintained — there could be no denying that he had failed in his purpose of reaching the Union rear, even though it later developed that there was no retreat for him to harry and therefore no real work for him to do if he had been there.

Four miles southwest of the Rummel farm, the other cavalry action was over too by now. Beginning some two hours later, it ended some two hours earlier, and if, despite this brevity, its potential fruits were greater — the intention had been to throw Lee's right into confusion, hard on the heels of the Pickett-Pettigrew repulse, and thus set him up for a crumpling assault to be launched by the blue infantry from the western slopes of the Round Tops — so too was the failure, which amounted to nothing more or less than a fiasco. Kilpatrick's remaining brigade, commanded by twenty-six-year-old Brigadier General Elon J. Farnsworth, was in position on the rebel flank, opposed by a skirmish line of Texans from Law's division, which extended from the base of Round Top west to the Emmitsburg Road. A year older than Farnsworth, and four years older than Custer, who had been a West Point classmate, Kilpatrick rode back and forth among his troopers, expressing what one of them called "great impatience and eagerness for orders." There was nothing unusual in this, for that was his accustomed manner, all the way back to his boyhood in New Jersey. "A wiry, restless, undersized man with black eyes [and] a lantern jaw," as a fellow officer described him, he had stringy blond side whiskers, bandy legs that gave him a rolling gait, and a burning ambition which he attempted to assuage and advance with constant aggressiveness and bluster. The result was not uncomical, at least to some observers; Sherman, for one, was to call him "a hell of a damned fool," and a member of Meade's staff remarked that "it was hard to look at Kilpatrick without laughing." But this last was not always the case for those who served under him — "Kill Cavalry," they had dubbed him, somewhat ruefully — and it was especially not the case today, so far as Farnsworth was concerned; for Kilpatrick kept insisting that he make horseback probes at the rebel skirmish line, despite the boulder-strewn terrain, which was highly unsuitable for cavalry operations, and the renowned marksmanship of the Texans, who had emptied a good many saddles by now and were backed up, moreover, by Law's old brigade of Alabamians, whose skill was scarcely less in that respect. However, the worst was still to come for Farnsworth and his men.

It came shortly before 5 o'clock, when an orderly arrived on a lathered horse from Cemetery Ridge, shouting as he drew near: "We turned the charge! Nine acres of prisoners!" That was enough for Kilpatrick. Though he had no instructions to go over to the offensive, he assumed that Meade was on the lookout for a chance to strike at the rebel line, especially if some part of it could be thrown into confusion beforehand, and he quickly determined to provide such an opportunity for the forces gazing down from the slopes of Round Top. Turning to Farnsworth, he told him to commit a West Virginia regiment at once, with orders to hack a gap in the butternut skirmish line, then go for the Confederate main body, deployed along the base of the height beyond Plum Run, opposing the blue infantry above. The West Virginians tried it and were repulsed, losing heavily when the Texans rose from behind a rail fence and slammed massed volleys at them. They tried it again — and again, by way of demonstration that the terrain was unsuited to horseback maneuver, were driven back. But Kilpatrick was not satisfied. Having often maintained that cavalry could "fight anywhere except at sea," he was out to prove it here today. He told Farnsworth to send in a second regiment, this time one of Vermonters who had suffered cruelly in the earlier skirmishing. Farnsworth had shown his mettle in some forty engagements since the first days of the war, and only four days ago he had been promoted from captain to brigadier in recognition of his bravery under fire. There could scarcely be any question of his courage, but after what they had both just seen he could not believe he had heard his chief aright. "General, do you mean it?" he asked. "Shall I throw my handful of men over rough ground, through timber, against a brigade of infantry? The 1st Vermont has already been fought half to pieces. These are too good men to kill." But Kilpatrick not only meant it; he wanted it done without question or delay. "Do you refuse to obey my orders?" he snapped. "If you are afraid to lead this charge, I will lead it." Farnsworth rose in his stirrups, flushed with anger. "Take that back!" he cried, and an observer thought the tall young man "looked magnificent in his passion." Kilpatrick bristled back at him for a moment, but then repented and apologized. "I didn't mean it. Forget it," he said. Farnsworth's anger subsided as quickly as it had risen. "General, if you order the charge, I will lead it," he replied; "but you must take the responsibility." Kilpatrick nodded. "I take the responsibility," he said.

The Texans were even readier now than they had been before. Posted within earshot, they had overheard the hot exchange between the two young brigadiers: with the result that they not only had time to brace themselves for what was coming, but also time to pass the word along to Law that his rear would be threatened if the troopers managed to punch a hole in the widespread skirmish line. The Vermonters were prepared to do just that, though one of them later wrote: "Each man felt, as he tightened his saber belt, that he was summoned to a ride to death." Farnsworth having massed them in depth, they broke through on a narrow front about midway of the line, taking losses along both flanks as they made their penetration, then swung hard east to strike the rear of the rebel infantry on the far side of Plum Run, which was bone dry at this season. They crossed, still at a gallop, but it would have been far better for them if they had not. As they approached what they thought was the Confederate rear, their drawn sabers flashing sunlight, it was as if the head of the column struck a trip wire. Oates, forewarned, had faced his Alabamians about, ignoring the enemy infantry uphill, and presented a solid front to the blue riders. The survivors turned sharply north again, in an attempt to avoid a second volley; but that too was a mistake, since it carried them directly along the line of marksmen who did not neglect the rare opportunity for point-blank firing at cavalry in profile. For some, indeed, it was like a return to happier days. A company commander, seeing a horse collapse in midstride with a bullet through the brain, heard a private alongside him shout: "Captain, I shot that black!" Asked why he had not aimed for the rider instead of the horse, the Alabamian grinned. "Oh, we'll get him anyhow," he said. "But I'm a hunter, and for two years I haven't looked at a deer's eye. I couldn't stand it."

By that time Law had reinforced the skirmishers with another regiment; so that when the blue survivors turned back west and south, they found the entry gap resealed. What had been intended as a havoc-spreading charge now degenerated into a sort of circus, Roman style, with the penned-in horsemen riding frantically in large circles, ricocheting from cluster to cluster of whooping rebels as they tried to find a way out of the fire-laced coliseum. Farnsworth had his mount shot from under him, took another from a trooper who was glad to go afoot, and in final desperation — perhaps with Kilpatrick's taunt still ringing in his ears — made a suicidal one-man charge, saber raised, against a solid mass of Confederates who brought him down with five mortal wounds. Some 65 of his men had fallen with him by the time the remnant found an exit and regained the safety of the Union lines. No earthly good had been accomplished, except by way of providing a show for the spectators, blue and gray, who had watched as in an amphitheater. Still, Kilpatrick did not regret having ordered the attempt; he only regretted that the infantry onlookers, high on the slopes of Round Top, had failed to seize the advantage offered them by the Vermonters on the plain below; in which case, he reported, "a total rout would have ensued." As for Farnsworth: "For the honor of his young brigade and the glory of his corps, he gave his life. . . . We can say of him, in the language of another, 'Good soldier, faithful friend, great heart, hail and farewell.' " Thus Kilpatrick, who had sent him to his death with words of doubt as to his courage.

The infantry had not come down to join the mix-up in the valley for the sufficient reason that it had received no instructions to do so, although there were those who urged this course on Meade in no uncertain terms. One such was Pleasonton, who was quite as cocky as his lieutenants. "I will give you half an hour to show yourself a great general," he told his chief, soon after the latter's arrival on Cemetery Ridge. "Order the army to advance, while I take the cavalry and get in Lee's rear, and we will finish the campaign in a week." But Meade was having no part of such advice. Six days in command, he had spent the last three locked in mortal combat, all of it defensive on his side, and he had no intention of shifting to the offensive on short notice, even if that had been possible, simply because another in the sequence of all-out rebel assaults on his fishhook line had been repulsed. Besides, he was by no means convinced that this was the last of them. "How do you know Lee will not attack me again?" he replied. "We have done well enough." Pleasonton continued to press the point, maintaining that the Confederates, low on supplies by now and far from base, would be obliged to surrender if nailed down; to which Meade's only response was an invitation for the cavalryman to accompany him on the triumphal ride along the ridge to Little Round Top. It seemed to Pleasanton that the cheers of the troops "plainly showed they expected the advance," but the army commander did not swerve from the opinion he had just expressed: "We have done well enough."

Hancock made a similar appeal, with similar results. Lifted into an ambulance after the charge had been repulsed, he ordered the vehicle halted as soon as it reached the Taneytown Road, where shells from long-range Whitworths north of Gettysburg were still landing, and began to dictate a message to be delivered at once to Meade. After explaining that he had been "severely but I trust not seriously wounded," he made it clear that he had not left his troops "so long as a rebel was to be seen upright." Interrupted by the attending surgeon, who protested against the delay, especially under enfilading fire from the rebels, the wounded general replied testily: "We've enfiladed *them*, God damn 'em," and went on with his dictation. He urged his chief to hurl Sedgwick and Sykes at Seminary Ridge without delay — if, indeed, this had not been done already. "If the VI and V corps have pressed up, the enemy will be destroyed," he predicted, and he added, by way of reinforcing his claim that Lee was in no condition to withstand a determined attack: "The enemy must be short of ammunition, as I was shot with a tenpenny nail." However, all he heard from Meade was a verbal message that avoided the central issue altogether. "Say to General Hancock," his fellow Pennsylvanian replied, "that I regret exceedingly that he is wounded, and that I thank him for the country and for myself for the service he has rendered today."

By this time McLaws had begun the withdrawal Longstreet ordered, and when the Federal skirmishers followed the graybacks out to the Emmitsburg Road, reclaiming the salient lost the day before, they were met by heavy volleys from guns and rifles; which tended to confirm the wisdom of Meade's decision, as he afterwards explained, not to advance on Seminary Ridge "in consequence of the bad example [Lee] had set for me, in ruining himself attacking a strong position." Nor was the northern commander alone in this belief. Henry Hunt, who had been pulled from under his toppled horse at the climax of the rebel assault and suffered only minor aches and pains from the injuries received, sided absolutely with his chief. "A prompt counter-charge after combat between two small bodies of men is one thing," the artillerist later wrote; "the change from the defensive to the offensive of an army, after an engagement at a single point, is quite another. To have made such a change to the offensive, on the assumption that Lee had made no provision against a reverse, would have been rash in the extreme." Warren thought so, too. It was generally felt, he subsequently declared, "that we had saved the country for the time and that we had done enough; that we might jeopardize all that we had done by trying to do too much." Such were the opinions of the two surviving members of the quartet of generals — the dead Reynolds and the wounded Hancock were the other pair — who were commonly given credit, then and later, for having done most to prevent another defeat from being added to the Union record: a defeat, moreover, which, given the time and place, some would maintain the Union could not have survived.

    In point of fact, the greatest deterrent was the mute but staggering testimony of the casualty lists. Including Reynolds, Sickles, and Hancock, the three most aggressive of its corps commanders, a solid fourth of the Federal army had been killed or wounded or captured, and well over half again as many skulkers and stragglers had simply wandered off or been knocked loose from their units. A head count next morning would show 51,414 present of all ranks. Of the more than 38,000 men who thus were absent, the actual casualties numbered 23,049 — precisely tabulated a few days later at 3155 killed, 14,529 wounded, 5365 captured — which left some 15,000 not accounted for, just now at least, and encouraged the belief that the losses had been even greater than they were in fact. Moreover, they were quite unevenly distributed. Of Meade's seven infantry corps, the four led into action by Reynolds, Hancock, Sickles, and Howard had suffered almost ninety percent of the casualties, and if this had its brighter aspect — Sedgwick's corps, the largest in the army, had scarcely been engaged at all, and might therefore be considered available for delivery of the counterstroke urged by Pleasonton and Hancock — it also cast a corresponding gloom over those who had done the bleeding. All in all, when they became available, these figures did much to support the judgment of the responsible commander that, notwithstanding the tactical desirability of launching an immediate mass assault, which was as clear to him as it was to any man on the field, the troops were in no condition to sustain it.

    On the other hand there was testimony from Lee's own ranks that the Confederates were in no condition to resist an assault if one had

been made against them. "Our ammunition was so low," Alexander confessed, "and our diminished forces at the moment so widely dispersed
along the unwisely extended line, that an advance by a single fresh corps,
[Sedgwick's] for instance, could have cut us in two." Few on that same
side of the line agreed with this, however. After all, it was not Lee's army
that had been shattered in the desperate charge that afternoon, but only
eight of his thirty-seven brigades, five of which — Anderson's other
three and Pender's two: the same number that had stood fast for Meade
across the way — were on hand to defend his center. Moreover, all his
cavalry was up by now, including Imboden's 2000 troopers who had arrived at midday, and not one piece of artillery had been lost. Far from
being depressed by the repulse, many along the rebel line had been angered by what they had seen and were eager for revenge; they asked for
nothing better than a chance to serve the blucoats in the same manner,
if they could be persuaded to attack. "We'll fight them, sir, till hell freezes
over," one grayback told an observer, "and then, sir, we will fight them
on the ice." Indeed, adversity seemed to knit them closer together as a
family, which was what they had become in the past year under Lee,
and brought out the high qualities that would stand them in good stead
during the downhill months ahead. Longstreet, for example, riding out
after dark to inspect his skirmish line, found a battery still in position
near the Peach Orchard, though he had ordered all his artillery withdrawn to the cover of the western ridge some time before. "Whose are
these guns?" he demanded; whereupon a tall man with a pipe in his
mouth stepped out of the shadows. "I am the captain," he said quietly,
and when the general asked why he had stayed out there in front of the
infantry, the artilleryman replied: "I am out here to have a little skirmishing on my own account, if the Yanks come out of their holes."
Amused by the prospect of a skirmish with 12-pounder howitzers, and
heartened by such evidence of staunchness in a time of strain, Old Peter
threw back his head and let his laugh ring out once more across that
somber field.

Incongruous as his laughter had seemed that afternoon, just before the 11,000-man assault wave broke and began to ebb, it sounded
even stranger now in the darkness, under cover of which the extent of
the army's losses could begin to be assessed. From the top down, they
were unremittingly grievous. Of the 52 Confederate generals who had
crossed the Potomac in the past three weeks, no less than 17 — barely
under one third — had become casualties in the past three days. Five
were killed outright or mortally wounded: Semmes and Barksdale,
Pender, Armistead and Garnett. Two were captured: Archer, who had
been taken on the first day, and Trimble, who had not been able to
make it back across the valley today with a shattered leg: and this figure
would be increased to three when the army began its withdrawal, since
Kemper was too badly injured to be moved. Nine more were wounded:

some lightly, such as Heth and Pettigrew, others gravely, such as Hood, whose arm might have to be taken off, and Hampton, who had received not one but two head cuts and also had some shrapnel in his body. When the list was lengthened by 18 colonels killed or captured, many of them officers of high promise, slated for early promotion, it was obvious that the Army of Northern Virginia had suffered a loss in leadership from which it might never recover. A British observer was of this opinion. He lauded the offensive prowess of Lee's soldiers, who had marched out as proudly as if on parade in their eagerness to come to grips with their opponents on the ridge across the way; "But they will never do it again," he predicted. And he told why. He had been with the army since Fredericksburg, ticking off the illustrious dead from Stonewall Jackson down, and now on the heels of Gettysburg he asked a rhetorical question of his Confederate friends: "Don't you see your system feeds upon itself? You cannot fill the places of these men. Your troops do wonders, but every time at a cost you cannot afford."

That might well be. Certainly there was no comfort in a comparison of the representation on the list of those of less exalted rank. Here, too, no less than a third had fallen — and possibly more, for the count was incomplete. Lee recorded his losses as 2592 killed, 12,709 wounded, and 5150 captured or missing, a total of 20,451: which was surely low, for a variety of reasons. For one, a few units that had fought made no report, and for another he had directed in mid-May that troops so lightly wounded that they could remain with their regiments were not to be listed as casualties, although such men were included in the Federal tabulations. Moreover, his figure for the number captured or missing could not be reconciled with the prisoner-of-war records in the Adjutant General's office at Washington, which bore the names of 12,227 Confederates captured July 1-5. The true total of Lee's losses in Pennsylvania could hardly have been less than 25,000 and quite possibly was far heavier; 28,063 was the figure computed by one meticulous student of such grisly matters, in which case the butcher's bill for Gettysburg, blue and gray together, exceeded 50,000 men. This was more than Shiloh and Sharpsburg combined, with Ball's Bluff and Belmont thrown in for good measure. And while there was considerably less disparity of bloodshed among the several corps of the attackers — Hill had suffered most and Ewell least, but both were within a thousand of Longstreet, who had lost perhaps 8500 — this was by no means true of smaller units within the corps. Gordon's exultation, "The Almighty has covered my men with his shield and buckler," could scarcely have been echoed by any commander of the eight brigades that went up Cemetery Ridge, and even within these there was a diversity of misfortune. Most regiments came back across the valley with at least a skeleton cadre to which future recruits or conscripts could be attached; but not all. The 14th Tennessee, for example, had left Clarksville in 1861 with 960 men on its muster roll, and in the past two years, most of which time their homeland had been under Union occupation, they had fought on all the major battlefields of Virginia. When Archer took them across Willoughby Run on the opening day of Gettysburg they counted 365 bayonets; by sunset they were down to barely 60. These five dozen survivors, led by a captain on the third day, went forward with Fry against Cemetery Ridge, and there — where the low stone wall jogged west, then south, to form what was known thereafter as the angle — all but three of the remaining 60 fell. This was only one among the forty-odd regiments in the charge; there were others that suffered about as cruelly; but to those wives and sweethearts, parents and sisters and younger brothers who had remained at its point of origin, fifty miles down the Cumberland from Nashville, the news came hard. "Thus the band that once was the pride of Clarksville has fallen," a citizen lamented, and he went on to explain something of what he and those around him felt. "A gloom rests over the city; the hopes and affections of the people were wrapped in the regiment. . . . Ah! what a terrible responsibility rests upon those who inaugurated this unholy war."

No one felt the responsibility harder than Lee, though, far from inaugurating, he had opposed the war at the outset, when some who now were loudest in their lamentations had called for secession or coercion, whatever the consequences, and had allowed themselves to be persuaded that all the blood that would be shed could be mopped up with a congressman's pocket handkerchief; whereas it now turned out that, at the modest rate of a gallon for every dead man and a pint for each of the wounded, perhaps not all the handkerchiefs in the nation, or both nations, would suffice to soak up the blood that had been spilled at Gettysburg alone. Such macabre calculations might be of particular interest down the years — a fit subject, perhaps, for a master's thesis when centennial time came round — but Lee's tonight were of a different nature. From the moment he saw the shattered brigades of Pickett and Pettigrew begin their stumble back across the valley, it was obvious that what was left of his army, low on food and with only enough ammunition on hand for one more day of large-scale action, would have to retreat. After riding forward to help rally the fugitives and thus present as bold a front as possible to discourage a counterattack, he went to his tent and there, by candlelight, resumed his study of the maps over which he had pored throughout the hectic week preceding the blindfold commitment to battle. If his problems now were no less difficult, they were at least much simpler, having been reduced to the logistics of withdrawing his survivors, together with his wounded, his supply train, and his prisoners, from the immediate front of a victorious opponent deep in hostile territory. He chose his routes, decided on the order of march, and then, despite the lateness of the hour and his bone-deep weariness after three days of failure and frustration, went in person to make certain that his plans were understood by the responsible commanders. By dawn, Ewell and Longstreet were to have their troops disposed along Seminary Ridge, north and south of Hill's present position in the center. All day tomorrow, whether Meade attacked or not, they were to hold their ground and thus afford a head start for the wounded, as well as for the supply train and the captives; after which they were to take up the march themselves, under cover of darkness, with Hill in the lead, followed by Longstreet, and Ewell bringing up the rear. Pickett's remnant — a scant 800 of his badly shaken men would be on hand at daylight — was assigned to guard the 5000-odd Federal prisoners on the return, and Imboden's troopers would escort the miles-long column of ambulances and forage wagons loaded with such of the wounded as the surgeons judged could survive the long ride home. By this arrangement, the last infantry division to reach the field, as well as the last cavalry brigade, would be the first to depart. Before leaving his tent, Lee sent word for Imboden to report to headquarters and wait for his return, intending to give him detailed instructions for the conduct of the march. Then he went out into the night.

Unlike the vague and discretionary orders he had issued throughout the week leading up to battle and even during the past three days of fighting, in the course of which his messages had been verbal and for the most part tentative, his instructions now were written and precise, allowing no discretion whatsoever to anyone at all. In Hill's case, moreover, since his was the corps that would mark the route and set the pace, Lee took the added precaution of conferring with him in person, tracing for him the line of march on the map and making certain there was no possibility of a misunderstanding. This might have waited for morning; the infantry movement would not begin until the following evening at the earliest; but evidently Lee felt that he should not, or could not, sleep until the matter had been disposed of to his satisfaction. Delegation of authority, under orders that not only permitted but encouraged a wide degree of latitude in their execution by subordinates, had been the basis for his greatest triumphs, particularly during the ten months he had had Jackson to rely on; Second Manassas and Chancellorsville were instances in point. But at Gettysburg, with Stonewall just seven weeks in his grave, the system had failed him, and his actions tonight were an acknowledgment of the fact. Though he would return to the system in time, out of necessity as well as from choice, on this last night of his greatest and worst-fought battle he abandoned it entirely. He relied on no one but himself.

It was late, well after midnight, by the time he left Hill and rode back through the quiet moonlit camps along Seminary Ridge to his headquarters beside the Chambersburg Pike. Imboden was waiting for him there, as instructed, though no one else was stirring; his staff had gone to sleep so tired that not even a sentry had been posted. Lee drew rein and sat motionless for a time, apparently too weary to dismount, but as the cavalryman stepped forward, intending to assist him, he swung down and leaned for another long moment against Traveller, head bowed and one arm thrown across the saddle for more rest. Imboden watched him, awed by the tableau — "The moon shone full upon his massive features and revealed an expression of sadness that I had never before seen upon his face" — then, hoping, as he said later, "to change the silent current of his thoughts," ventured to speak of his obvious fatigue: "General, this has been a hard day on you." Lee raised his head, and his fellow Virginian saw grief as well as weariness in his eyes. "Yes, this has been a sad, sad day to us," he replied, emphasizing the word he had used that afternoon in speaking to Fremantle. Again he fell silent, but presently he "straightened up to his full height" and spoke "with more animation and excitement" than Imboden had ever seen him display: "I never saw troops behave more magnificently than Pickett's division of Virginians did today in that grand charge upon the enemy. And if they had been supported as they were to have been — but, for some reason not yet fully explained to me, were not — we would have held the position and the day would have been ours." This last was a strange thing for him to say, for he himself had denied Hill permission to throw his whole corps into the assault. However, there was no mistaking the extent of his regret. "Too bad; too bad," he groaned; "Oh, too bad!"

Suppressing his emotion, he invited Imboden into his tent for a study of the map and the long road home, which he was about to take. "We must now return to Virginia," he said.

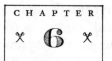

Unvexed to the Sea

★ ✗ ☆

ALL NEXT MORNING, HAVING COMPLETED THE perilous nighttime disengagement of both wings in order to form a continuous line of defense along Seminary Ridge, from Oak Hill on the north to the confronting loom of Round Top on the south, the Confederates awaited the answer to the question that was uppermost in their minds: Would the Federals attack? Apparently they would not. "What o'clock is it?" Longstreet finally asked an artillerist standing beside him. "11.55," the officer replied, and ventured a prediction: "General, this is the 'Glorious Fourth.' We should have a salute from the other side at noon." Noon came and went but not a gun was fired. Old Peter believed he knew why. "Their artillery was too much crippled yesterday to think of salutes," he said with satisfaction. "Meade is not in good spirits this morning."

Presently there was evidence that he was wrong. Across the way, in the vicinity of the Peach Orchard, a Union brigade was seen deploying for battle. Nothing came of this, however; for just at that time — about 1 o'clock — rain began to fall, first a drizzle, then a steady downpour; the bluecoats jammed their fixed bayonets into the ground to keep the water from running down their rifle barrels, then squatted uncomfortably beside them, shoulders hunched against the rain. Obviously they had abandoned all notion of attack, if indeed they had had any such real intention in the first place. On their separate ridges, an average mile apart, the men of both armies peered at one another through the transparent curtain of rain as it sluiced the bloodstains from the grass and rocks where they had fought so savagely the past three days, but would not fight today.

Lee appeared calm and confident as he watched the departure of the long column of wounded at the height of the afternoon rainstorm and continued his preparations for the withdrawal of the infantry and artillery that night. Beneath the surface, however, he was testy: as was shown by his response to a well-meant pleasantry from one of Ewell's young staff officers who came to headquarters with a report from his chief. "General," he said encouragingly, "I hope the other two corps are in as good condition for work as ours is this morning." Lee looked at him hard and said coldly, "What reason have you, young man, to suppose they are not?" Even before it became evident that the Federals were not going to attack he proposed, by means of a flag of truce, a man-for-man exchange of prisoners, thus risking a disclosure of his intentions in hope of lightening his burden on the march. Nothing came of this; Meade prudently declined, on grounds that he had no authority in such matters, and Lee continued his preparations for the withdrawal, prisoners and all. Imboden and the wounded were to return by way of Cashtown and Chambersburg, Greencastle and Hagerstown, for a Potomac crossing near Williamsport, a distance of forty-odd miles, while the infantry would follow a route some dozen miles shorter, southwest through Fairfield to Hagerstown for a crossing at the same point, its left flank protected by units of Stuart's cavalry on the road to Emmitsburg. Though he felt confident that his opponent would be restricted in maneuver by the continuing obligation to cover Baltimore and Washington, Lee recognized the impending retrograde movement as probably the most hazardous of his career. His troops did not seem greatly dispirited by the failure of the campaign, but their weariness was apparent to even a casual eye and a good third of those who had headed north with such high hopes a month ago would not be returning. Including the walking wounded who remained with their commands, he had fewer than 50,000 effectives of all arms. Moreover, Meade by now must have received heavy reinforcements from the surrounding northern states, as well as from his nearby capital: whereas Lee could expect no such transfusions of strength until he crossed the Potomac, if at all.

Leaving his campfires burning on the ridge, Hill began the withdrawal soon after nightfall. Longstreet followed, still in a driving rain that served to muffle the sound of the army's departure from its opponent across the valley. There were delays, however, and it was 2 o'clock in the morning before Ewell began his march. By now the roads were troughs of mud, which made for heavy going: so heavy, indeed, that it was 4 o'clock in the afternoon by the time the lead elements of the Second Corps plodded into Fairfield, only nine miles from the now deserted ridge just west of Gettysburg. Part of the delay was caused by free-swinging Union troopers, who got among the trains and captured a number of wagons, together with their guards and drivers. Old Bald Head was so outraged by this development that he was for facing about and fighting, then and there. But Lee would not agree. "No, no, General Ewell," he said; "we must let those people alone for the present. We will try them again some other time." Hill and Longstreet, well beyond Fairfield before sundown, had no such difficulties. The latter, in fact, was in high good spirits when he called a halt that evening, conveniently near a roadside tavern where his staff had arranged for dinner to be served. Apparently the troops outside were getting theirs, too, for in the course of the meal there was a sound of scuffling in the adjoining chamber, followed by the appearance of a hard-faced farmwife who pushed her way into the dining room, exclaiming as she advanced: "Which is the General? Where is the great officer? Good heavens, they are killing our fat hogs! Our milk cows now are going!" On the march northward, such a complaint would have brought sudden and heavy reprisal on the offenders, but not now. "Yes, Madam," Old Peter told her, shaking his head in disapproval, "it's very sad; very sad. And this sort of thing has been going on in Virginia for more than two years. Very sad."

He took over the lead from Hill next day, July 6, and though the rain continued to fall and the mud to deepen, the men stepped out smartly once they were clear of Monterey Pass and beyond South Mountain. "Let him who will say it to the contrary," a Texan wrote home, "we made Manassas time from Pennsylvania." At 5 p.m. Longstreet entered Hagerstown, and Lee, who rode with him as usual, was relieved to learn that the train of wounded had passed through earlier that day and should have reached the Potomac by now, half a dozen miles away. Imboden had made good speed with his 17-mile-long column, though at the cost of much suffering by the wounded, whose piteous cries to be left by the road to die were ignored by the drivers in obedience to orders that there were to be no halts for any reason whatever, by day or night. Many of the injured men had been without food for thirty-six hours, he later wrote, and "their torn and bloody clothing, matted and hardened, was rasping the tender, inflamed, and still oozing wounds. Very few of the wagons had even a layer of straw in them, and all were without springs. . . . From nearly every wagon as the teams trotted on, urged by whip and shout, came such cries and shrieks as these: 'Oh, God! Why can't I die?' 'My God, will no one have mercy and kill me?' 'Stop! Oh, for God's sake, stop just for one minute; take me out and let me die on the roadside!' 'I am dying, I am dying!' . . . During this one night," the cavalryman added, "I realized more of the horrors of war than I had in all the two preceding years." Bypassing Chambersburg in the darkness, the lead escort regiment rode through Greencastle at dawn, and when the troopers were a mile beyond the town, which had offered no resistance at all in the course of the march north the week before, some thirty or forty citizens rushed out of their houses and "attacked the train with axes, cutting the spokes out of ten or a dozen wheels and dropping the wagons in the streets." Imboden sent a detachment of troopers back, and this put an end to the trouble there. Beyond Hagerstown, however, the Union cavalry appeared in strength from Frederick and began to harass the column. At Williamsport, finding the pontoon bridge destroyed by raiders from downstream on the opposite bank, Imboden called a halt and deployed his men and vehicles in the style employed by wagon trains when attacked by Indians on the plains. Arming his drivers with spare rifles and placing his 23 guns at regular intervals along the half-circle of wagons, he faced northeast, the river at his back, and managed to hold off the attackers until Fitz Lee arrived and drove them away.

The army commander got there the following morning, still riding with Longstreet at the head of the infantry column, and though he was pleased to learn that Imboden and his nephew Fitz had staved off the immediate threat by the blue horsemen, who had greatly outnumbered the defenders until now, he could see for himself that his predicament, here on the north bank of the river he had marched so hard to reach, was worse by far than the one in which he had found himself three days ago at Gettysburg, after the failure of his final attempt to break the Union fishhook. Not only was the pontoon bridge destroyed, but the recent torrential rains had swollen the Potomac well past fording. Low on food, as well as ammunition for its guns, the army was cut off from Virginia, together with its prisoners and its wounded. Lee's first thought was for these last; he directed that all the ferryboats in the region were to be collected and used in transporting the injured men to the south bank; the wagons, like the infantry and the artillery, would have to wait until the river subsided or the bridge could be rebuilt. Meanwhile, if Meade attacked, the Confederates, with small chance to maneuver and none at all to retreat, would have to give him battle under conditions whereby victory would yield but little profit and defeat would mean annihilation.

Accordingly, the engineers began their task of laying out a system of defense that extended some three miles in each direction, upstream and down from Williamsport, where in normal times a man could wade across. Both of its extremities well covered, the six-mile curve of line was anchored north on Conococheague Creek and south on the Potomac below Falling Waters, the site of the wrecked bridge. As at Gettysburg, Hill took the center and Ewell and Longstreet the left and right — they had by now about 35,000 effectives between them, including the cannoneers whose limber chests were nearly empty — while Stuart's troopers reinforced the flanks and patrolled the front. By next day, July 8, the dispositions were complete, though the men continued to improve them with their shovels, and Lee received the welcome news that ammunition for his guns was on the way from Winchester; it would arrive tomorrow and could be brought across by the ferries already hard at work transporting the wounded to the Virginia bank. Foam-flecked and swollen, the river was still on the boom, however, farther than ever past fording and with no decrease predicted. So far, Meade's infantry had not appeared, but Lee did not believe it would be long in coming — and in strength much greater than his own. He kept up a show of calmness, despite a precarious shortage of food and the personal strain of having been informed that his son Rooney, taken to Hanover County to recover from his Brandy Station wound, had been captured by raiders and hauled off to Fort Monroe, where he was being held as a hostage to insure the safety of some Federal prisoners charged with various crimes against the people of the Old Dominion. Despite the fret of such distractions, Lee wrote that night to the President, proposing once more that Beauregard's "army in effigy" march at once for the Rappahannock and thus create a diversion in his favor through this anxious time of waiting for the Potomac to subside.

"I hope Your Excellency will understand that I am not in the least discouraged," he added, somewhat apologetic over this second appeal for help from outside his department, "or that my faith in the protection of an all-merciful Providence, or in the fortitude of this army, is at all shaken. But, though conscious that the enemy has been much shattered in the recent battle, I am aware that he can be easily reinforced, while no addition can be made to our numbers. The measure, therefore, that I have recommended is altogether one of a prudential nature."

Learning from scouts the following evening that the Federal main body was on the march from Frederick, he was convinced that his army would soon have to fight for its survival, which in turn meant the survival of the Confederacy itself. In this extremity he occupied himself with the inspection and improvement of his defenses, the distribution of the newly arrived ammunition for his batteries, and the nerving of his troops for the shock he believed was coming. Though the river continued to rise in his rear and food and forage were getting scarcer by the hour — the men were now on half rations and the horses were getting nothing to eat but grass and standing grain — he kept up a show of confidence and good cheer. Only those who knew him best detected his extreme concern: Alexander, for example, who later testified that he had never seen his chief so deeply anxious as he appeared on July 10, one week after the guns of Gettysburg stopped roaring. This did not show, however, in a dispatch the general sent Davis that night from his still bridgeless six-mile bridgehead on the north bank of the still unfordable Potomac. "With the blessing of Heaven," he told the President, "I trust that the courage and fortitude of the army will be found sufficient to relieve us from the embarrassment caused by the unlooked-for natural difficulties of our situation, if not to secure more valuable and substantial results. Very respectfully, your obedient servant, R. E. LEE."

In all this time, Sunday through Saturday, no two opposing infantrymen had looked at one another along the barrels of their rifles, and the source of this week-long lethargy on the part of those who should have been pursuers lay in the make-up of the man who led them. His caution, which had given the blue army its first undeniable large-scale victory to balance against the five major defeats it had suffered under as many different leaders in the past two years, was more enlarged than reduced by the discovery, on the morning of July 5, that the Confederates were no longer in position on the ridge across the way; so that while the first half of Lee's prediction — "General Meade will commit no blunder on my front" — had been fulfilled, the second half — "If I make one, he will make haste to take advantage of it" — had not. Not that there was no occasion for this increase of caution. The defenders had suffered heavily in the three-day conflict, particularly in the loss of men of rank. Schimmelfennig, who emerged from his woodshed hiding place when Gettysburg was reoccupied on the 4th, was meager compensation for the sixteen brigade and division commanders killed or wounded in the battle, let alone for the three corps commanders who had fallen. Besides, avoidance of risk having gained him so much so far, Meade had no intention of abandoning that policy simply because the winds of chance appeared to have shifted in his favor for the moment.

Whether they had in fact shifted, or had merely been made to seem to, was by no means certain. Lee was foxy, as Meade well knew from old acquaintance. He was known to be most dangerous when he appeared least so: particularly in retreat, as McClellan had discovered while pursuing him under similar circumstances, back in September, after presuming to have taken his measure at South Mountain. Moreover, he was not above tampering with the weather vane, and there was evidence that such was the case at present. Francis Barlow, who had been wounded and captured on the opening day of battle while commanding one of Howard's overrun divisions north of town, was left behind in Gettysburg when the rebels withdrew to their ridge on the night of July 3. He got word to headquarters next morning that Lee's plan, as he had overheard it from his sick-bed, was to feign retreat, then waylay his pursuers. Meade took the warning much to heart and contented himself that afternoon, at the height of the sudden rainstorm, with issuing a congratulatory order to the troops "for the glorious result of the recent operations." That those operations had not ended was evident to all, for the graybacks were still on Seminary Ridge, less than a mile across the rain-swept valley. "Our task is not yet accomplished," the order acknowledged, "and the commanding general looks to the army for greater efforts to drive from our soil every vestige of the presence of the invader."

It was read to all regiments that evening. In one, when the reading was over, the colonel waved his hat and called for three cheers for Meade. But the men were strangely silent. This was not because they had no use for their new chief, one of them afterwards observed; it was simply because they did not feel like cheering, either for him or for anyone else, rain or no rain. Many of them had been engaged all day in burying the dead and bringing in the wounded of both armies, and this was scarcely the kind of work that put them in the frame of mind for tossing caps and shouting hurrahs. Mostly though, as the man explained, the veterans, "with their lights and experiences, could not see the wisdom or the occasion for any such manifestation of enthusiasm." They had done a great deal of cheering over the past two years, for Hooker and Burnside and Pope and McDowell, as well as for Little Mac, and in the course of time they had matured; or as this witness put it, their "business sense increased with age." Someday, perhaps, there would be a reason for tossing their caps completely away and cheering themselves hoarse, but this did not seem to them to be quite it. So they remained silent, watching the colonel swing his hat for a while, then glumly put it back on his head and dismiss them.

That evening the corps commanders voted five to two to hold their present ground until it was certain that Lee was retreating. Next morning — Sunday: Meade had been just one week in command — they found that he was indeed gone, but there was doubt as to whether he was retreating or maneuvering for a better position from which to renew the contest. Sedgwick moved out in the afternoon, only to bog down in the mud, and fog was so heavy the following morning that he could determine nothing except that the Confederates had reached Monterey Pass, southwest of Fairfield. "As soon as possible," Meade wired Halleck, "I will cross South Mountain and proceed in search of the enemy." On second thought, however, and always bearing in mind his instructions to "maneuver and fight in such a manner as to cover the capital and Baltimore," he decided that his best course would be to avoid a direct pursuit, which might necessitate a costly storming of the pass, and instead march south into Maryland, then westward in an attempt to come up with Lee before he effected a crossing near Williamsburg, where French's raiders had wrecked the pontoon bridge the day before. In Frederick by noon of July 7, fifty-odd hours after finding that his opponent had stolen away from his front under cover of darkness, the northern commander indulged himself in the luxury of a hot bath in a hotel and put on fresh clothes for the first time in ten days. This afforded him considerable relief, but it also provided a chance for him to discover how profoundly tired he was. "From the time I took command till today," he wrote his wife, "I . . . have not had a regular night's rest, and many nights not a wink of sleep, and for several days did not even wash my face and hands, no regular food, and all the time in a state of mental anxiety. Indeed, I think I have lived as much in this time as in the last thirty years."

The men, of course, were in far worse shape from their exertions. Four of the seven corps had been shot almost to pieces, and some of the survivors had trouble recognizing their outfits, so unequal had been the losses in the various commands, including more than 300 field and company grade officers lost by the quick subtractive action of shells and bullets and clubbed muskets. III Corps veterans, who were among the hardest hit in this respect, sardonically referred to themselves as "the III Corps as we understand it." Their uniforms were in tatters and their long marches through dust and mud, to and from the three-day uproar, had quite literally worn the shoes off their feet. Meade's regular army soul was pained to see them, though the pain was salved considerably by a wire received that afternoon from Halleck: "It gives me pleasure to inform you that you have been appointed a brigadier general in the Regular Army, to rank from July 3, the date of your brilliant victory." This welcome message was followed however by two more from Old Brains that were not so welcome, suggesting as they did a lack of confidence in his aggressive qualities. "Push forward and fight Lee before he can cross the Potomac," one directed, while the other was more specific: "You have given the enemy a stunning blow at Gettysburg. Follow it up, and give him another before he can reach the Potomac. . . . There is strong evidence that he is short of artillery ammunition, and if vigorously pressed he must suffer." Meade wanted it understood that the suffering was unlikely to be as one-sided as his superior implied. He too was having his troubles and he wanted them known to those above him, who presumed to hand down judgments from a distance. "My army is assembling slowly," he replied, still in Frederick on July 8. "The rains of yesterday and last night have made all roads but pikes almost impassable. Artillery and wagons are stalled; it will take time to collect them together. A large portion of the men are barefooted. . . . I expect to find the enemy in a strong position, well covered with artillery, and I do not desire to imitate his example at Gettysburg and assault a position where the chances were so greatly against success. I wish in advance to moderate the expectations of those who, in ignorance of the difficulties to be encountered, may expect too much. All that I can do under the circumstances I pledge this army to do."

Apparently Halleck did not like the sound of this, for he replied within the hour: "There is reliable information that the enemy is crossing at Williamsport. The opportunity to attack his divided forces should not be lost. The President is urgent and anxious that your army should move against him by forced marches." Meade had not heard a word from Lincoln, either of thanks for his recent victory or of encouragement in his present exertions, and now there was this indirect expression of a lack of confidence. Forced marches! The Pennsylvanian bristled. "My army is and has been making forced marches, short of rations and barefooted," he wired back, pointing out in passing that the information as to a rebel crossing differed from his own, and added: "I take occasion to repeat that I will use my utmost efforts to push forward this army." Old Brains protested that he had been misconceived. "Do not understand me as expressing any dissatisfaction," he replied; "on the contrary, your army has done most nobly. I only wish to give you opinions formed from information received here." But having entered this disclaimer he returned to his former tone, ignoring Meade's denial that any appreciable part of the rebel force had crossed the Potomac, either at Williamsport or elsewhere. "If Lee's army is so divided by the river," he persisted, "the importance of attacking the part on this side is incalculable. Such an opportunity may never occur again.... You will have forces sufficient to render your victory certain. My only fear now is that the enemy may escape."

At Middletown on July 9, having replaced Butterfield with Humphreys as chief of staff and thus got rid of the last reminder of Hooker's luckless tenure, Meade was pleased that no rain had fallen since early the day before. Though the Potomac remained some five feet above its normal level and therefore well past fording, the roads were drying fast and permitted better marching. Moreover, Halleck was keeping his word as to reinforcements. The army had 85,000 men present for duty and 10,000 more on the way, which meant that its Gettysburg losses had been made good, although a number of short-term militia and grass-green conscripts were included. "This army is moving in three columns," Meade informed Halleck before midday, "the right column hav-

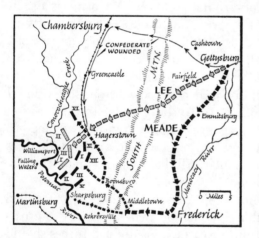

ing in it three corps.... I think the decisive battle of the war will be fought in a few days. In view of the momentous consequences, I desire to adopt such measures as in my judgment will tend to insure success, even though these may be deemed tardy." Delighted to hear that Meade was in motion again, however tardy, the general-in-chief was careful to say nothing that might cause him to stop and resume the telegraphic argument. "Do not be influenced by any dispatch from here against your own judgment," he told him. "Regard them as suggestions only. Our information here is not always correct." In point of fact, now that contact seemed imminent, it was Old Brains who was urging caution. More troops were on the way, he wired next day, and he advised waiting for them. "I think it will be best for you to postpone a general battle till you can concentrate all your forces and get up your reserves and reinforcements.... Beware of partial combats. Bring up and hurl upon the enemy all your forces, good and bad."

Meade agreed. He spent the next two days, which continued fair, examining the curved shield of Lee's defenses and jockeying for a position from which to "hurl" his army upon them. By early afternoon of

July 12 — Sunday again: he now had been two full weeks in command — he was ready, though the skies again were threatening rain. Selected divisions from the II, V, and VI Corps confronted a rebel-held wheat field, pickets out, awaiting the signal to go forward, when a Pennsylvania chaplain rode up to the command post and protested the violation of the Sabbath. Couldn't the battle be fought as well tomorrow? he demanded. For once Meade kept his temper, challenged thus by a home-state man of the cloth, and explained somewhat elaborately that he was like a carpenter with a contract to construct a box, four sides and the bottom of which had been completed; now the lid was ready to be put on. The chaplain was unimpressed. "As God's agent and disciple I solemnly protest," he declared fervently. "I will show you that the Almighty will not permit you to desecrate his sacred day.... Look at the heavens; see the threatening storm approaching!" Whereupon there were sudden peals of thunder and zigzags of lightning, as in a passage from the Old Testament, and rain began to pour down on the wheat field and the troops who were about to move against it. Meade canceled the probing action, returned to his quarters, and got off a wire to Halleck. "It is my intention to attack them tomorrow," he wrote; but then — perhaps with the chaplain's demonstration in mind — he added, "unless something intervenes to prevent it."

So he said. But a council of war he called that evening showed that his chief subordinates were opposed to launching any attack without a further examination of Lee's position. Only Wadsworth, commanding the I Corps in the absence of Newton, who was sick, agreed with Meade wholeheartedly in favoring an assault, although Howard, anxious as always to retrieve a damaged reputation, expressed a willingness to go along with the plan. Despite reports that the Potomac was falling rapidly after four days of fair weather, Meade deferred to the judgment of five of his seven corps commanders, postponed the scheduled advance, and spent the next day conducting a further study of the rebel dispositions. Informing Halleck of the outcome of the council of war, he told him: "I shall continue these reconnaissances with the expectation of finding some weak point upon which, if I succeed, I shall hazard an attack." Old Brains was prompt to reply that he disapproved of such flinching now that the two armies were once more face to face. "You are strong enough to attack and defeat the enemy before he can effect a crossing," he wired. "Act upon your own judgment and make your generals execute your orders. Call no council of war. It is proverbial that councils of war never fight. Reinforcements are pushed on as rapidly as possible. Do not let the enemy escape."

It was plain that the advice as to councils of war amounted to an attempt to lock the stable after the pony had been stolen. And so too did the rest of it, as the thing turned out. When Meade at last went forward next morning, July 14, he found the rebel trenches empty and all but a rear-guard handful of graybacks already on the far bank of the Potomac. Aside from a number of stragglers picked up in the rush, together with two mud-stalled guns — the only ones Lee lost in the whole campaign — attacks on the remnant merely served to hasten the final stages of the crossing, after which the delivered Confederates cut their rebuilt pontoon bridge loose from the Maryland shore and looked mockingly back across the swirling waters, which were once more on the rise as a result of the two-day rainstorm the chaplain had invoked.

Meade was not greatly disappointed, or at any rate he did not seem so in a dispatch informing Halleck of Lee's escape before it had even been completed. The closing sentence was downright bland: "Your instructions as to further movements, in case the enemy are entirely across the river, are desired."

For Lee, threatened in front by twice his number and menaced within the perimeter by starvation, the past three days had been touch and go, all the time with the receding but still swollen Potomac mocking his efforts to escape. In the end it was Jackson's old quartermaster, Major John Harman, who managed the army's extraction and landed it safe on the soil of Virginia, having improvised pontoons by tearing down abandoned houses for their timbers and floating the finished products down to Falling Waters, where they were linked and floored; "a good bridge," Lee called the result, and though a more critical staff officer termed it a "crazy affair," it served its purpose. Its planks overlaid with lopped branches to deaden the sound of wheels and boots, it not only permitted the secret withdrawal of the guns and wagons in the darkness; it also made possible the dry-shod crossing of the two corps under Longstreet and Hill, while Ewell managed to use the ford at Williamsport, his tallest men standing in midstream, armpit deep, to pass the shorter waders along. By dawn the Second Corps was over, but the First and Third were still waiting for the trains to clear the bridge. At last they did, and Longstreet crossed without interference, followed by Hill's lead division: at which point guns began to roar.

"There!" Lee exclaimed, turning his head sharply in the direction of the sound. "I was expecting it — the beginning of the attack."

He soon learned, however, that Heth, who had recovered from his head injury and returned to the command of his division, had faced his men about and was holding off the attackers while Hill's center division completed the crossing; whereupon Heth turned and followed, fighting as he went. It was smartly done. Despite an official boast by Kilpatrick that he captured a 1500-man Confederate brigade, only about 300 stragglers failed to make it over the river before the bridge was cut loose from the northern bank, and the loss of the two stalled guns, while regrettable, was more than made up for by the seven that had been taken in Pennsylvania and brought back. Another loss was more grievous.

On Heth's return to duty, Johnston Pettigrew had resumed command of what was left of his brigade, which served this morning as rear guard. He had his men in line, awaiting his turn at the bridge, when suddenly they were charged by a group of about forty Union cavalrymen who were thought at first to be Confederates brandishing a captured flag, so foolhardy was their attack. Pettigrew, one of whose arms was still weak from his Seven Pines wound, while the other was in a sling because of the hand that had been hit at Gettysburg, was tossed from his startled horse. He picked himself up and calmly directed the firing at the blue troopers, who were dashing about and banging away with their carbines. Eventually all of them were killed — which made it difficult to substantiate or disprove the claim that they were drunk — but meantime one took a position on the flank and fired so effectively that the general himself drew his revolver and went after him in person. Determined to get so close he could not miss, Pettigrew was shot in the stomach before he came within easy pistol range. He made it over the bridge, refusing to be left behind as a prisoner, and lived for three days of intense suffering before he died at Bunker Hill, Virginia, the tenth general permanently lost to the army in the course of the invasion. The whole South mourned him, especially his native North Carolina, and Lee referred to him in his report as "an officer of great merit and promise."

Saddened by this last-minute sacrifice of a gallant fighter, but grateful for its delivery from immediate peril, the army continued its march that day and the next to Bunker Hill, twenty miles from the Potomac, and there it went into camp, as Lee reported, for rest and recruitment. "The men are in good health and spirits," he informed Richmond, "but want shoes and clothing badly. . . . As soon as these necessary articles are obtained we shall be prepared to resume operations." That he was still feeling aggressive, despite the setback he had suffered, was shown by his reaction on July 16 to information that the enemy was preparing to cross the river at Harpers Ferry. "Should he follow us in this direction," Lee wrote Davis, "I shall lead him up the Valley and endeavor to attack him as far from his base as possible."

Meade's exchanges with his government, following his laconic report of a rebel getaway, were of a different nature. Halleck was plainly miffed. "I need hardly say to you," he wired, "that the escape of Lee's army without another battle has created great dissatisfaction in the mind of the President, and it will require an active and energetic pursuit on your part to remove the impression that it has not been sufficiently active before." This was altogether more than Meade could take, particularly from Lincoln, who still had sent him no word of appreciation or encouragement, by way of reward for the first great victory in the East, but only second-hand expressions of doubt and disappointment. The Pennsylvanian stood on his dignity and made the strongest protest within his means. "Having performed my duty conscientiously and to the best of my ability," he declared, "the censure of the President conveyed in your dispatch ... is, in my judgment, so undeserved that I feel compelled most respectfully to ask to be immediately relieved from the command of this army." There Halleck had it, and Lincoln too. They could either refrain from such goadings or let the victorious general depart. Moreover, Meade strengthened his case with a follow-up wire, sent half an hour later, in which he passed along Kilpatrick's exuberant if erroneous report of capturing a whole rebel brigade on the near bank of the Potomac. Old Brains promptly backtracked, as he always seemed to do when confronted with vigorous opposition from anyone, blue or gray, except Joe Hooker. "My telegram, stating the disappointment of the President at the escape of Lee's army, was not intended as a censure," he replied, "but as a stimulus to an active pursuit. It is not deemed a sufficient cause for your application to be relieved."

In the end Meade withdrew his resignation, or at any rate did not insist that it be accepted, and on July 17, 18, and 19 — the last date was a Sunday: he now had been three weeks in command — he crossed the Potomac at Harpers Ferry and Berlin, half a dozen miles downstream, complying with his instructions to conduct "an active and energetic pursuit," although he was convinced that such a course was overrisky. "The proper policy for the government would have been to be contented with driving Lee out of Maryland," he wrote his wife, "and not to have advanced till this army was largely reinforced and reorganized and put on such a footing that its advance was sure to be successful." In point of fact, however, he had already been "largely reinforced." His aggregate present on July 20 was 105,623 men, including some 13,500 troopers, while Lee on that same date, exclusive of about 9000 cavalry, had a total of 50,178, or barely more than half as many infantry and cannoneers as were moving against him. Confronted with the danger of being cut off from Richmond, he abandoned his plan for drawing the enemy up the valley and instead moved eastward through Chester Gap. On July 21 — the second anniversary of First Manassas, whose twice-fought-over field lay only some thirty miles beyond the crest of the Blue Ridge — Federal lookouts reported dust clouds rising; the rebels were on the march. Lee reached Culpeper two days later, and Meade, conforming, shifted to Warrenton, from which point he sent a cavalry and infantry column across the Rappahannock on the last night of the month. Gray horsemen opposed the advance, but Lee, aware of the odds against him and unwilling to take the further risk of remaining within the V of the two rivers, decided to fall back beyond the Rapidan. This was accomplished by August 4, ending the sixty days of marching and fighting which comprised the Gettysburg campaign. Both armies were back at their approximate starting points, and Meade did not pursue.

He had at last received from Washington the accolade that had been withheld so long, though the gesture still was not from Lincoln. "Take it altogether," Halleck wrote, "your short campaign has proved your superior generalship, and you merit, as you will receive, the confidence of the government and the gratitude of your country." But Meade had already disclaimed such praise from other sources. "The papers are making a great deal too much fuss about me," he wrote home. "I claim no extraordinary merit for this last battle, and would prefer waiting a little while to see what my career is to be before making any pretensions. ... I never claimed a victory," he explained, "though I stated that Lee was defeated in his efforts to destroy my army." Thin-skinned and testy as he was, he found it hard to abide the pricks he received from his superiors. He doubted, indeed, whether he was "sufficiently phlegmatic" for the leadership of an army which he now perceived was commanded from Washington, and he confided to his wife that he would esteem it the best of favors if Lincoln would replace him with someone else. Who that someone might be he did not say, but he could scarcely have recommended any of his present subordinates, whose lack of energy he deplored. Most of all, he missed his fellow Pennsylvanians, the dead Reynolds and the convalescing Hancock. "Their places are not to be supplied," he said.

With nine of his best generals gone for good, and eight more out with wounds of various depth and gravity, Lee had even greater cause for sadness. Just now, though, his energies were mainly confined to refitting his army, preparing it for a continuation of the struggle he had sought to end with one hard blow, and incidentally in putting down a spirit of contention among his hot-tempered subordinates as to where the blame for the recent defeat should go. Few were as frank as Ewell, who presently told a friend that "it took a dozen blunders to lose Gettysburg and [I] committed a good many of them," or as selfless as Longstreet, who wrote to a kinsman shortly after the battle: "As General Lee is our commander, he should have the support and influence we can give him. If the blame, if there is any, can be shifted from him to me, I shall help him and our cause by taking it. I desire, therefore, that all the responsibility that can be put upon me shall go there, and shall remain there." Later he would vigorously decline the very chance he said he hoped for, but that was in the after years, where there was no longer any question of sustaining either the army commander or the cause. Others not only declined it now but were quick to point out just where they thought the blame should rest: Pickett, for instance, whose report was highly critical of the other units involved in the charge tradition would give his name to. Lee returned the document to him with the suggestion that it be destroyed, together with all copies. "You and your men have covered yourselves with glory," he told him, "but we have the enemy to fight and must carefully, at this critical moment, guard against dissensions which the reflections in your report would create. . . . I hope all will yet be well."

His own critique of the battle, from the Confederate point of view, was given five years later to a man who was contemplating a school history. Referring the writer to the official accounts, Lee avoided personalities entirely. "Its loss was occasioned by a combination of circumstances," he declared. "It was commenced in the absence of correct intelligence. It was continued in the effort to overcome the difficulties by which we were surrounded, and [a success] would have been gained could one determined and united blow have been delivered by our whole line. As it was, victory trembled in the balance for three days, and the battle resulted in the infliction of as great an amount of injury as was received and in frustrating the Federal campaign for the season." Reticent by nature in such matters, he was content to let it go at that, except for once when he was out riding with a friend. Then he did speak of personalities, or anyhow one personality. "If I had had Stonewall Jackson with me," he said, looking out over the peaceful fields, "so far as man can see, I should have won the battle of Gettysburg."

That was still in the future, however. For the present he reserved his praise for the men who had been there. "The army did all it could," he told one of his numerous cousins in late July. "I fear I required of it impossibilities. But it responded to the call nobly and cheerfully, and though it did not win a victory it conquered a success. We must now prepare for harder blows and harder work."

✗ 2 ✗

Having failed in his effort to "conquer a peace" by defeating the principal Union army north of its capital, Lee had failed as well in his secondary purpose, which had been to frighten the Washington authorities into withdrawing Grant and Banks from their strangle-hold positions around Vicksburg and Port Hudson, thereby delivering from danger not only those two critical locations but also the great river that ran between them, the loss of which would cut the South in two. But Lee's was not the only attempt to forestall that disaster. In addition to Joe Johnston, whose primary assignment it was, Kirby Smith too had plans for the relief of Pemberton and Gardner, on whose survival depended his hope of remaining an integral part of the Confederacy. Though these included nothing so ambitious as an intention to end the war with a single long-odds stab at the enemy's vitals, they were at least still in the course of execution when Pickett's and Pettigrew's men came stumbling back from Cemetery Ridge, leaving the bodies of their comrades to indicate the high-water mark of Lee's campaign, which now was on the

ebb. Nor were these Transmississippi plans without the element of boldness. Encouraged by Magruder's success in clearing Texas of all trace
of the invader, Smith hoped his other two major generals, Holmes in
Arkansas and Taylor in West Louisiana, might accomplish as much in
their departments. If so, he might attain the aforementioned secondary
purpose of causing the Federal high command to detach troops from
Grant and Banks, in an attempt to recover what had been lost across the
river from their respective positions, and thus lighten the pressure on
Vicksburg and Port Hudson. At any rate Smith thought it worth a
try, and in mid-June, being frantically urged by Richmond to adopt
some such course of action — Davis and Seddon by then had begun losing
confidence that anything was going to come of their increasingly strident appeals to Johnston along those lines — he instructed Taylor and
Holmes to make the effort.

Taylor, who had just returned disgruntled to Alexandria after
his strike at Milliken's Bend — a tactical success, at least until Porter's
gunboats hove onto the scene, but a strategic failure, since the objective
turned out to be little more than a training camp for the Negro recruits
Grant had enlisted off the plantations roundabout — was pleased to be
ordered back onto what he considered the right track, which led down
to New Orleans. His plan, as he had outlined it before the fruitless excursion opposite Vicksburg, was to descend the Teche and the Atchafalaya, recapture Berwick Bay and overrun the Bayou Lafourche region,
which lay between Grand Lake and the Mississippi, deep in Banks's rear,
interrupting that general's communications with New Orleans and threatening the city itself; whereupon Banks would be obliged to raise his
siege of Port Hudson in order to save New Orleans, whose 200,000 citizens he knew to be hostile to his occupation, and Gardner then could
march out to join Johnston for an attack on Grant's rear and the quick
delivery of beleaguered Vicksburg. Such at least were Taylor's calculations — or more properly speaking, his hopes; for his resources were
admittedly slim for so ambitious a project. He had at Alexandria three
small cavalry regiments just arrived from Texas under Colonel J. P.
Major, a twenty-seven-year-old Missouri-born West Pointer whose
peacetime army career had included service in Albert Sidney Johnston's
2d Cavalry, which already had provided the South with eight and
the North with two of their leading generals. Awaiting instructions on
the upper Teche, to which they had returned in the wake of Banks's
withdrawal in mid-May, were five more such mounted regiments under
Thomas Green, the Valverde hero who had been promoted to brigadier
for his share in the New Year's triumph at Galveston, along with three
regiments of Louisiana infantry under Brigadier General Alfred Mouton, thirty-four years old and a West Pointer, a Shiloh veteran and native of nearby Vermilionville, son of the former governor and brother-
in-law to Frank Gardner, whose rescue was the object of the campaign.

The combined strength of the three commands was about 4000 effectives, barely one tenth of the force available to Banks, but Taylor intended to make up in boldness for what he lacked in numbers.

The advance was made in two widely divided columns. While Mouton and Green swung down the west bank of the Teche, marching unopposed through Opelousas and New Iberia, Taylor rode with Major across the Atchafalaya, then down Bayou Fordoche to within earshot of the guns of Port Hudson. At that point he left him, on June 18, with orders to move rapidly to the rear of Brashear City, the objective upon which the two forces were to converge for a simultaneous attack five days later. The distance was one hundred miles, entirely through occupied territory, but Major made it on schedule. Skirmishing briefly that afternoon with the bluecoats on guard at Plaquemine, a west-bank landing below Baton Rouge, he bypassed fortified Donaldsonville after nightfall and set off next morning down Bayou Lafourche, which left the Mississippi just above the town. Some thirty miles below on the 20th, he rode into Thibodaux, whose garrison had fled at the news of his approach, and next day he struck the railroad at Terrebonne, thirty miles east of Brashear, then turned due west to complete his share of the convergence Taylor had designed. Moving crosscountry with relays of quick-stepping mules hitched to his ambulance, that general had joined Mouton and Green on their unopposed march through Franklin to Fort Bisland. By nightfall of June 22 they were at Berwick and were poised for an amphibious attack, having brought with them a weird collection of "small boats, skiffs, flats, even sugar-coolers," which they had gathered for this purpose during their descent of the Teche. Batteries were laid under cover of darkness for a surprise bombardment in support of the scheduled dawn assault on the Brashear fortifications, just eastward across the narrow bay. Taylor's old commander in the Shenandoah Valley doubtless would have been proud to see how well his pupil, whose preparatory work had been done not at West Point but at Yale, had learned the value of well-laid plans when the object was the capture or destruction of an enemy force in occupation of a fixed position.

Old Jack's pride would have swelled even more next morning, when the Louisianian gathered the fruits of his boldness and careful planning. While some 300 dismounted Texans manned the 53 boats of his improvised flotilla — it was fortunate that there was no wind, Taylor said later, for the slightest disturbance would have swamped them — Green's cannoneers stood to their pieces. At first light they opened fire, and as they did so the sea-going troopers swarmed ashore, encouraged by the echoing boom of Major's guns from the east. Flustered by the sudden bombardment, which seemed to erupt out of nowhere, and by the unexpected assault from both directions, front and rear, the blue defenders milled about briefly, then surrendered. The take was great, for here at the western terminus of the railroad Banks had cached the ord-

nance and quartermaster supplies he intended to use in his planned return up the Teche and the Red. In addition to 1700 prisoners, a dozen
heavy-caliber guns and 5000 new-style Burnside repeaters and Enfield
rifles were captured, together with two locomotives and their cars,
which were unable to get away eastward because Major had wrecked
the bridge at Lafourche Crossing, and commissary and medical stores in
such abundance that they brought to more than $2,000,000 the estimated
profit from Taylor's well-engineered strike. The general's pleasure was
as great as that of his men, who wasted no time before sitting down to
gorge themselves on the spoils. Their main concern was food, but his was
the acquisition of the implements with which to continue his resistance
to the invasion of his homeland. "For the first time since I reached western Louisiana," he exulted afterwards, "I had supplies."

All in all, it was the largest haul any body of Confederates had
made since Stonewall followed up his raid on Manassas Junction with
the capture of Harpers Ferry, back in September. Like his mentor, however, Taylor did not allow his exultation to delay his plans for the further discomfiture of his adversary. Next morning, leaving one regiment
to sort the booty and remove it to Alexandria for safekeeping, he
pressed on north and east, once more in two columns. While Green and
Major marched for Donaldsonville, near which they were to establish
batteries for the purpose of disrupting traffic on the Mississippi and thus
sever the main line of supply and communications available to the besiegers of Port Hudson, Mouton's infantry went by rail to Thibodaux,
from which point he sent pickets down the line to Bayou des Allemands,
within twenty-five miles of New Orleans. It was during the early morning hours of June 28 that Taylor encountered his first setback, though
not in person. Approaching Donaldsonville the night before, Green had
meant to bypass it, as Major had done on his way south, but the existence
of an earthwork at the junction of the Lafourche and the Mississippi
proved irresistible, perhaps in part because the Yankees had given it a
hated name: Fort Butler. He disposed 800 dismounted troopers for attack and sent them forward two hours before dawn. The result was a
bloody repulse, administered by the 225 defenders and three gunboats
that arrived in time to support them. Green, who had suffered 261 casualties and inflicted only 24, pulled back, chagrined, and went about his
proper business of establishing his three batteries on the west bank of the
river, some ten miles below the town. He opened fire on July 7 and for
three days not only kept the Mississippi closed to transports and unarmored supply boats, but also sent out mounted patrols as far downstream
as Kenner, barely a dozen miles from the heart of New Orleans, which
was already in a turmoil of expectancy as a result of Mouton's continued
presence at Thibodaux and nearby Bayou des Allemands.

Secessionists were joyously predicting the imminent entry of the
graybacks who were knocking at the gates, and William Emory, with

fewer than 1000 men to oppose a rebel host he reckoned at 13,000, was altogether in agreement that the place was the Confederacy's for the taking. What was more, as we have seen already, he had said as much to Banks. "It is a choice between Port Hudson and New Orleans," he informed him on July 4, adding: "You can only save this city by sending me reinforcements immediately and at any cost." Dick Taylor thus had accomplished the preliminary objective of his campaign; that is, he had brought the pressure he intended upon Banks, who now would be obliged to withdraw from Port Hudson, permitting Gardner to join Johnston for the delivery of Pemberton by means of an attack on Grant's intrenchments from the rear. So much Taylor had planned or anyhow hoped for. But Banks, as we have also seen, refused to cooperate in the completion of the grand design. If New Orleans fell, he told Halleck, he would retake it once the business at hand was completed and his army was free to be used for that purpose; but meantime he would hang on at Port Hudson till it surrendered, no matter what disasters threatened his rear. Observing this perverse reaction, Taylor was obliged to admit that once again, as at Milliken's Bend a month ago, though his tactics had been successful his strategy had failed. He had gained much in his brief campaign — particularly at Brashear City, whose spoils would greatly strengthen his future ability to resist the blue invaders — but he had not accomplished the recapture of New Orleans, which he saw as a cul-de-sac to be avoided, or the raising of the siege at Port Hudson.

Theophilus Holmes, though neither as energetic nor as inventive as Zachary Taylor's son and Stonewall Jackson's pupil, was also under compunction to do something toward relieving their hemmed-in friends across the way. Since the turn of the year, when Marmaduke made his successful raid into Missouri, burning the Springfield supply base and bringing a hornetlike swarm of guerillas out of the brush and canebrakes, all the elderly North Carolinian had attempted in this regard was a repeat performance by that same general in late April, this time with twice as many men and instructions to put the torch to the well-stocked military depots along the west bank of the Mississippi north of Cairo, particularly Cape Girardeau, from which Grant was drawing much of his subsistence for the campaign far downriver. Little came of this, however. Marmaduke and his 5000 troopers — the largest body of horsemen ever assembled in the Transmississippi — struck and routed an inferior blue force at Fayetteville on April 18, then crossed the line into his native state and rode eastward across it in two columns, one through Fredericktown and the other through Bloomfield, driving Yankee outpost garrisons before him as he advanced. Secessionists, many of whom had kinsmen riding with him, greeted their favorite with cheers. His father had been governor before the war and he himself would be governor after it, a bachelor just past thirty now, tall and slender, quick-tempered and aristocratic in manner, with a full beard, delicate hands and feet, and fine hair brushed smooth on top and worn long in back so that it flared in a splendid ruff behind his head. His eyes were kindly and intelligent, though they had a disconcerting squint that came from his being at once near-sighted and unwilling to disfigure himself with glasses. He had studied both at Harvard and Yale before his graduation from West Point six years ago, but neither this formal preparation nor his success on the similar mission back in January stood him in much stead on April 25, when he completed his investment of Cape Girardeau with a demand for an immediate surrender; to which Brigadier General John McNeil, a fifty-year-old former Boston hatter and St Louis insurance agent, who had increased the strength of the garrison to 1700 by bringing in his brigade the day before, replied with an immediate refusal. Marmaduke attacked and found the resistance stiff, all the approaches being covered by well-served artillery. Not only was he repulsed, but scouts reported steamers unloading reinforcements from St Louis at the Cape Girardeau dock. So he withdrew next morning, after launching one more attack designed to discourage pursuit. It failed in its purpose, however, and the retreat southward across the St Francis bottomlands of the Missouri boot heel required all his skill to avoid being intercepted by the now superior forces of the enemy. By May Day he was back in Arkansas, having suffered 161 casualties, and though he claimed that Federal losses "must have been five times as great as mine in killed and wounded" — McNeil and the others who had opposed him admitted a scant 120, combined — all he had to show for his pains, aside from some 150 recruits picked up in the course of the 400-mile-long ride, was "a great improvement in the number and quality of horses" in his command.

Grant was over the river by then, hard on the march for Jackson, but Holmes attempted nothing more in the way of interference until he received in mid-June an excerpt from a letter the Secretary of War had written Johnston in late May, after Pemberton was besieged, suggesting that he urge the Transmississippi commanders to "make diversions for you, or, in case of the fall of Vicksburg, secure a great future advantage to the Confederacy by the attack on, and seizure of, Helena, while all the available forces of the enemy are being pushed to Grant's aid." Seddon added that, though he was cut off from those commanders and therefore had no means of ordering the adoption of his suggestion, its tactical soundness was "so apparent that it is hoped it will be voluntarily embraced and executed." He was right, so far at least as concerned its being "embraced," for Holmes had already conferred with Sterling Price on the same notion, and Price, who had taken command in early June of two brigades of infantry, not only declared that his men were "fully rested and in excellent spirits," but also expressed confidence that if Holmes would bring up two more brigades, together they could "crush the foe" at Helena. He had, moreover, an up-to-the-minute report from "an intelligent lady" just arrived from the west-bank Arkansas town, in which she described the enemy garrison as "exceedingly alarmed," much reduced by downriver calls for reinforcements, "and apprehensive that you will attack them daily." Seddon's suggestion reached Holmes at Little Rock on June 14, together with a covering letter from Kirby Smith, who left its adoption or rejection up to him. Holmes was eager, for once, being greatly encouraged by Price's coincidental approval of the project. "I believe we can take Helena. Please let me attack it," he replied next day, and Smith consented promptly. "Most certainly do it," he told him. That was on June 16. Two days later Holmes issued orders for a concentration of his forces, preparatory to launching the attack.

He had available for the effort just under 5000 infantry in Price's two brigades and a third under Brigadier General James Fagan, a thirty-five-year-old Kentucky-born Arkansan who was a veteran of the Mexican War as well as of Shiloh and Prairie Grove, and just over 2500 cavalry in the two brigades remaining with Marmaduke — two others had been detached since his repulse at Cape Girardeau — and a third under Brigadier General Lucius Walker, who was thirty-three, a nephew of Tennessee's James K. Polk and a West Point graduate, though he had abandoned army life to enter the mercantile business in Memphis until Sumter put him back in uniform. Holmes's instructions called for a cavalry screen to be thrown around Helena as soon as possible, in order to conceal from its blue defenders the infantry concentration scheduled for June 26 across the St Francis River at Cotton Plant and Clarendon, within fifty miles of the objective. Walker and Marmaduke moved out promptly, followed by Price and Fagan. Anxious to get back onto the victory trail that had led to Wilson's Creek and Lexington, up in his home state, before he was sidetracked into defeat at Pea Ridge and more recently at Iuka and Corinth, Price had announced to his troops that they would "not only drive the enemy from our borders, but pursue him into his own accursed land." The men, who idolized him and affectionately called him Pap, cheered at the news that these words were about to be translated into action, and Fagan likewise reported that his brigade was "ready and in high condition and spirit" as the march got under way. Those spirits were soon dampened, however, by torrents of rain that turned the roads to quagmires and flooded the unbridged streams past fording. As a result, it was June 30 before the infantry reached the areas designated. Holmes remained calm, despite the strain of a four-day wait, and engaged in no useless criminations. "My dear general," he wrote Price while the former Missouri governor was still on the march through calf-deep mud, "I deeply regret your misfortune." Revising his schedule accordingly, he moved

out from Clarendon and Cotton Plant on July 1, arrived within five
miles of Helena on the evening of July 3, and issued detailed instructions
for an attack at dawn next morning. Much depended on concert of action, for the Union position featured mutually supporting earthworks
and intrenchments, but Holmes counted also on his assumed superiority
in numbers. His strength was 7646 effectives, and he reckoned that of
the enemy at "4000 or 5000" at the most.

It was in fact much closer to the lower than to the higher figure;
4129 bluecoats were awaiting him in the Helena defenses. But what he
did not know was that they had been warned of his coming and had
made special preparations to receive him, including arrangements for
the support of the gunboat *Tyler*, whose 8-inch guns had helped to save
the day at Shiloh under similar circumstances. The post commander,
Benjamin M. Prentiss, had done even stouter service on that bloody field
by holding the Hornets Nest until he and his division were overrun and
captured. Exchanged in October, the Virginia-born Illinois lawyer had
won promotion to major general and assignment to command of the
District of East Arkansas — meaning Helena, since this was the only
Union-occupied point in the region below Memphis. For the past four
days, disturbed by the rebel cavalry thrashing about in the brush outside
his works, Prentiss had had the garrison up and under arms by 2.30
each morning, and just yesterday he had issued an order forbidding a
Fourth of July celebration his officers had planned for tomorrow. However, the most effective preparation of all had begun in late December,
when Fred Steele went downriver with Sherman and three fourths of
his corps, leaving the remnant exposed to a sudden thrust such as Holmes
was launching now. At that time, six months ago, the total defense consisted of a single bastioned earthwork, called Fort Curtis for the then
commander of the department, whose guns could sweep the gently
rising ground of the hills that cradled the low-lying town beside the
river, but since then Prentiss had constructed breastworks and dug rifle
pits along the brow of the ridge, an average half mile beyond the fort,
overlooking the timber-choked terrain of its more precipitous eastern
slopes, and on the three dominant heights, Rightor Hill on the right,
Graveyard Hill in the center, and Hindman Hill on the left, he had in-
stalled batteries which he designated, north to south, as A, B, C, D.
Stoutly emplaced and mutually supporting, so that if one fell those adjoining could turn their fire on it, those four batteries and their protective intrenchments, which linked them into an iron chain of defense,
covered the six roads that passed over the semicircular ridge and converged on Fort Curtis like so many spokes on the hub of half a
wheel, and the cannoneers who manned them could feel secure — especially after a look back over their shoulders at the *Tyler* riding at anchor beyond the town — in the knowledge that Prentiss and his engineers had made the most of what nature had placed at their disposal,

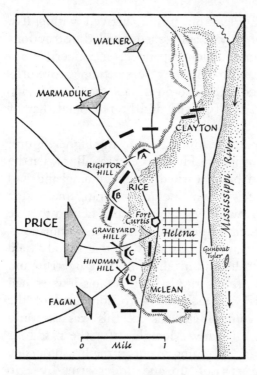

Brigadier General Frederick Salomon commanded the division Steele had left behind. One of four immigrant brothers who served the Union through this crisis — three of them as colonels and brigadiers and the fourth as wartime governor of Wisconsin, to which they had fled from their native Prussia to avoid the consequences of having fought on the losing side in the Revolution of 1848 — he had three small brigades, each led by a colonel: two of infantry, under William McLean and Samuel Rice, and one of cavalry under Powell Clayton. Like Salomon, these three officers were all in their middle or early thirties, nonprofessionals who had risen strictly on merit if not in action, and their troops were Westerners to a man, mostly farm boys out of Missouri, Iowa, and Wisconsin. Except for a single regiment of Hoosiers who had served with Pope in the taking of New Madrid and Island Ten, some fifteen months ago, the total field experience of the garrison had been the recent Yazoo Pass fiasco, in which they had been matched primarily against gnats and mosquitoes while the navy tried in vain to reduce Fort Pemberton. Still irked by the memory of that unhappy experience, and in accordance with Prentiss's standing instructions, they turned out of their bunks and took their posts at 2.30, an hour before dawn and a good two hours before sunrise of this Independence Day. Clayton's troopers were on the far right, guarding the river road north of town; McLean's and Rice's cannoneers and riflemen were disposed along the hilltop chain of batteries and intrenchments. Half an hour after they were in position, Holmes's attack opened against the left center. At first it was rather tentative, driving the Federal outpost pickets back up the rugged western slopes of Hindman and Graveyard hills, but presently it exploded in full fury as the butternut pursuers came yelling after them, massed shoulder to shoulder in a solid drive for possession of the two high-sited batteries Prentiss had labeled C and D.

Their repulse was not as sudden as their eruption, but it was equally emphatic. In part this was because they had found the last five miles of road, which they covered after dark, in even worse shape than the hundred-odd they had traversed so painfully during the past week:

with the result that they had been unable to bring their guns along and therefore had to attack without artillery support, of which the Federals had plenty. Fagan's brigade struck first, storming Hindman Hill — so called because it was here that the former Confederate commander had built the fine brick house Curtis had taken for his headquarters soon after occupying the town the year before. Three successive lines of half-bastions were rapidly penetrated and seized, but not the hilltop battery itself, which met the attackers with volleys of grape that shattered their formation, sent them scrambling for cover, and pinned them down so effectively that they could not even retreat. Price's two brigades did better, at least at first. Battery C was taken in a rush, the graybacks swarming over Graveyard Hill and whooping among the captured guns. The weaponless rebel artillerymen came up, prepared to turn the pieces on their late owners, only to find that the retreating cannoneers had carried off all the friction primers, which left the guns about as useless to their captors as so much scrap iron. Moreover, they came under enfilade fire from the two adjoining batteries and took a pounding as well from Fort Curtis, dead ahead at the foot of the gradual eastern slope. Nor was that all. Receiving word that Hindman Hill was under assault, Prentiss had signaled Lieutenant Commander J. M. Prichett of the *Tyler:* "Open fire in that direction." Now Prichett did, and with a vengeance, the fuzes of his 8-inch shells cut at ten and fifteen seconds. So demoralized were the attackers by the sudden deluge of heavy-caliber projectiles that, according to one blue officer, two groups of about 250 men each responded "by hoisting a white flag, their own sharpshooters upon the ridge in their rear firing from cover upon and cursing them as they marched out prisoners of war."

Holmes did what he could to expand the lodgment, sending one of Price's brigades to co-operate with Fagan in the stalled drive on Battery D. But to no avail; McLean and Rice held steady, backed up stoutly by Fort Curtis and the *Tyler*, whose bow and stern guns were firing north and south, respectively, while her ponderous broadside armament tore gaps in the rebel center. The early morning coolness soon gave way to parching heat; men risked their lives for sips of water from the canteens of the dead. Around to the north, Marmaduke had even less success against the defenders of Rightor Hill, and though he later complained vociferously that Walker had not supported him on his vulnerable left flank, the fact was he had already found Batteries A and B too hot to handle. He and Walker together lost a total of 66 men, only a dozen of whom were killed. As usual, it was the infantry that suffered, and in this case most of the sufferers wore gray. Including prisoners, the three brigades under Price and Fagan lost better than 1500 men between them. Holmes was not only distressed by the disproportionate losses, which demonstrated the unwisdom of his unsupported assault on a fortified opponent; he also saw that the attack would have been a mistake even if it had been successful, since the force in occupation would have been at the mercy of the *Tyler* and other units of the Federal fleet, which would make the low-lying river town untenable in short order. By 10.30, after six hours of fighting, all this was unmistakably clear; Holmes called for a withdrawal. By noon it had been accomplished, except for some minor rear-guard skirmishing, although better than one out of every five men who had attacked was a casualty. His losses totaled 1590, nearly half of them captives pinned down by the murderous fire and unable to retreat.

Prentiss lost 239: less than six percent of his force, as compared to better than twenty percent of the attackers. However, even with the odds reduced by this considerable extent, he still had too few men to risk pursuit. Reinforcements arrived next day from Memphis, together with another welcome gunboat, but he was content to break up a rebel cavalry demonstration which he correctly judged to be nothing more than a feint designed to cover a general retirement. By dawn of July 6 the only live Confederates around Helena were captives, many of them too gravely wounded to be moved. In praising his troops for their stand against nearly twice their number, Prentiss did not neglect his obligation to the *Tyler*, whose skipper in time received as well a letter of commendation from the Secretary of the Navy. "Accept the Department's congratulations for yourself and the officers and men under your command," the Secretary wrote, "for your glorious achievement, which adds another to the list of brilliant successes of our Navy and Army on the anniversary of our nation's independence."

✗ 3 ✗

It was indeed a Glorious Fourth, from the northern point of view; Gideon Welles did not exaggerate in speaking wholesale of a "list of brilliant successes" scored by the Union, afloat and ashore, on this eighty-seventh anniversary of the nation's birth. For the South, however, the day was one not of glory, but rather of disappointment, of bitter irony, of gloom made deeper by contrast with the hopes of yesterday, when Lee was massing for his all-or-nothing attack on Cemetery Ridge and Johnston was preparing at last to cross the Big Black River, when Taylor was threatening to retake New Orleans and Holmes was moving into position for his assault on Helena. All four had failed, which was reason enough for disappointment; the irony lay in the fact that not one of the four, Lee or Johnston, Taylor or Holmes, was aware that on this Independence Eve, so far at least as his aspirations for the relief of Vicksburg or Port Hudson were concerned, he was too late. At 10 o'clock that morning, July 3, white flags had broken out along a portion of Pemberton's works and two high-ranking officers, one a colonel, the other a major general, had come riding out of their lines and into those of the besiegers, who obligingly held their fire. The senior bore a letter from his commander, addressed to Grant. "General," it began: "I have the honor to propose to you an armistice for several hours, with a view to arranging terms for the capitulation of Vicksburg."

Pemberton's decision to ask for terms had been reached the day before, when he received from his four division commanders, Stevenson, Forney, Smith, and Bowen, replies to a confidential note requesting their opinions as to the ability of their soldiers "to make the marches and undergo the fatigues necessary to accomplish a successful evacuation." After forty-six days and forty-five nights in the trenches, most of the time on half- and quarter-rations, not one of the four believed his troops were in any shape for the exertion required to break the ring of steel that bound them and then to outmarch or outfight the well-fed host of bluecoats who outnumbered them better than four to one in effectives. Forney, for example, though he expressed himself as "satisfied they will cheerfully continue to bear the fatigue and privation of the siege," answered that it was "the unanimous opinion of the brigade and regimental commanders that the physical condition and health of our men are not sufficiently good to enable them to accomplish successfully the evacuation." There Pemberton had it, and the other three agreed. "With the knowledge I then possessed that no adequate relief was to be expected," the Pennsylvania Confederate later wrote, "I felt that I ought not longer to place in jeopardy the brave men whose lives had been intrusted to my care." He would ask for terms. The apparent futility of submitting such a request to a man whose popular fame was based on his having replied to a similar query with the words, "No terms except an unconditional and immediate surrender can be accepted," was offset — at least to some extent, as Pemberton saw it — by two factors. One was that the Confederates had broken the Federal wigwag code, which permitted them to eavesdrop on Grant's and Porter's ship-to-shore and shore-to-ship exchanges, and from these they had learned that the navy wanted to avoid the troublesome, time-consuming task of transporting thousands of grayback captives far northward up the river. This encouraged the southern commander to hope that his opponent, despite his Unconditional Surrender reputation, might be willing to parole instead of imprison the Vicksburg garrison if that was made a condition of avoiding at least one more costly assault on intrenchments that had proved themselves so stout two times before. The other mitigating factor, at any rate to Pemberton's way of thinking, was that the calendar showed the proposed surrender would occur on Independence Day. Some among the defenders considered a capitulation on that date unthinkable, since it would give the Yankees all the more reason for crowing, but while Pemberton was aware of this, and even agreed that it would involve a measure of humiliation, he also counted it an advantage. "I am a northern man," he told the objectors on his staff. "I know my people. I know their peculiar weaknesses and their national vanity; I know we can get better terms from them on the Fourth of July than on any other day of the year. We must sacrifice our pride to these considerations."

One other possible advantage he had, though admittedly it had not been of much use to Buckner at Donelson the year before. John Bowen had known and befriended Grant during his fellow West Pointer's hard-scrabble farming days in Missouri, and it was hoped that this might have some effect when the two got down to negotiations. Although Bowen was sick, his health undermined by dysentery contracted during the siege — he would in fact be dead within ten days, three months short of his thirty-third birthday — he accepted the assignment, and that was how it came about that he was the major general who rode into the Union lines this morning, accompanied by a colonel from Pemberton's staff. However, it soon developed that the past seventeen months had done little to mellow Grant in his attitude toward old friends who had chosen to do their fighting under the Stars and Bars. He not only declined to see or talk with Bowen, but his reply to the southern commander's note, which was delivered to him by one of his own officers, also showed that he was, if anything, even harsher in tone than he had been in the days when Buckner charged him with being "ungenerous and unchivalrous." Pemberton had written: "I make this proposition to save the further effusion of blood, which must otherwise be shed to a frightful extent." Now Grant replied: "The useless effusion of blood you propose stopping by this course can be ended at any time you may choose, by an unconditional surrender of the city and garrison.... I do not favor the proposition of appointing commissioners to arrange terms of capitulation, because I have no terms other than those indicated above."

There were those words again: Unconditional Surrender. But their force was diminished here at Vicksburg, as they had not been at Donelson, by an accompanying verbal message in which Grant said that he would be willing to meet and talk with Pemberton between the lines that afternoon. Worn by strain and illness, Bowen delivered the note and repeated the off-the-record message, both of which were discussed at an impromptu council of war, and presently — by then it was close to 3 o'clock, the hour Grant had set for the meeting — he and the colonel retraced in part the route they had followed that morning, accompanied now by Pemberton, who spoke half to himself and half to his two companions as he rode past the white flags on the ramparts. "I feel a confidence that I shall stand justified to my government, if not to the southern people," they heard him say, as if he saw already the scapegoat role in which he as an outlander would be cast by strangers and former friends for whose sake he had alienated his own people, including two brothers who fought on the other side. First, however, there came a ruder shock. Despite the flat refusal expressed in writing, he had interpreted Grant's spoken words, relayed to him through Bowen, as an invitation to parley about terms. But he soon was disabused of this impression. The three Confederates came upon a group of about a dozen Union officers awaiting them on a hillside only a couple of hundred yards beyond the outer walls of the beleaguered city. Ord, McPherson, Logan, and A. J. Smith were there, together with several members of Grant's staff and Grant himself, whom Pemberton had no trouble recognizing, not only because his picture had been distributed widely throughout the past year and a half, but also because he had known him in Mexico, where they had served as staff lieutenants in the same division. Once the introductions were over, there was an awkward pause as each waited for the other to open the conversation and thereby place himself in somewhat the attitude of a suppliant. When Pemberton broke the silence at last by remarking that he understood Grant had "expressed a wish to have a personal interview with me," Grant replied that he had done no such thing; he had merely agreed to such a suggestion made at second hand by Bowen.

Finding that this had indeed been the case, though he had not known it before, Pemberton took a different approach. "In your letter this morning," he observed, "you state that you have no other terms than an unconditional surrender." Grant's answer was as prompt as before. "I have no other," he said. Whereupon the Pennsylvanian — "rather snappishly," Grant would recall — replied: "Then, sir, it is unnecessary that you and I should hold any further conversation. We will go to fighting again at once." He turned, as if to withdraw, but fired a parting salvo as he did so. "I can assure you, sir, you will bury many more of your men before you will enter Vicksburg." Grant said nothing to this, nor did he change his position or expression. The contest was like poker, and he played it straight-faced while his opponent continued to sputter, remarking, as he later paraphrased his words, that if Grant "supposed that I was suffering for provisions he was mistaken, that I had enough to last me for an indefinite period, and that Port Hudson was even better supplied than Vicksburg." Grant did not believe there was much truth in this, but he saw clearly enough from Pemberton's manner that his unconditional-surrender formula was not going to obtain without a good deal more time or bloodshed. So he unbent, at least to the extent of suggesting that he and Pemberton step aside while their subordinates talked things over. The Confederate was altogether willing — after all, it was what he had proposed at the outset, only to be rebuffed — and the two retired to the shelter of a stunted oak nearby. In full view of the soldiers on both sides along this portion of the front, while Bowen and the colonel talked with the other four Union generals, the blue and gray commanders stood together in the meager shade of the oak tree, which, as Grant wrote afterwards, "was made historical by the event. It was but a short time before the last vestige of its body, root and limb had disappeared, the fragments taken as trophies. Since then the same tree has furnished as many cords of wood, in the shape of trophies, as 'The True Cross.'"

But that was later, after the souvenir hunters had the run of the field. For the present, the oak remained as intact as almost seven weeks of bullets and shells from both sides had allowed, and Grant and Pemberton continued their pokerlike contest of wills beneath its twisted branches. If the Confederate played a different style of game, that did not necessarily mean that he was any less skillful. In point of fact — at any rate in the limited sense of getting what he came for — he won; for in the end it was the quiet man who gave way and the sputterer who stood firm. In the adjoining group, Bowen proposed that the garrison "be permitted to march out with the honors of war, carrying with them their arms, colors, and field batteries," which was promptly denied, as he no doubt had expected; whereupon Pemberton, after pointing out that his suggestion for the designation of commissioners had been rejected, observed that it was now Grant's turn to make a counteroffer as to terms. Grant agreed; Pemberton would hear from him by 10 o'clock that evening, he said; and with that the meeting broke up, though it was made clear that neither opponent was to consider himself "pledged." Both returned to their own lines and assembled councils of war to discuss what had developed. Pemberton found that all his division commanders and all but two of his brigade commanders favored capitulation, provided it could be done on a basis of parole without imprisonment. Grant found his officers of a mind to offer what was acceptable, although he himself did not concur; "My own feelings are against this," he declared. But presently, being shielded in part from the possible wrath of his Washington superiors by the overwhelming vote of his advisers, he "reluctantly gave way," and put his terms on paper for delivery to Pemberton at the designated hour. Vicksburg was to be surrendered, together with all public stores, and its garrison paroled; a single Union division would move in and take possession of the place next morning. "As soon as rolls can be made out, and paroles signed by officers and men," he stipulated, "you will be allowed to march out of our lines, the officers taking with them their side-arms and clothing, and the field, staff, and cavalry officers one horse each. The rank and file will be allowed all their clothing, but no other property." Remembering Pemberton's claim that he had plenty of provisions on hand, Grant added a touch that combined generosity and sarcasm: "If these conditions are accepted, any amount of rations you may deem necessary can be taken from the stores you now have, and also the necessary cooking utensils for them. . . . I am, general, very respectfully, your obedient servant, U. S. GRANT, Major General."

Now that he had committed his terms to paper, he found them

much more satisfactory than he had done before. "I was very glad to give the garrison of Vicksburg the terms I did," he afterwards wrote. To have shipped the graybacks north to Illinois and Ohio, he explained, "would have used all the transportation we had for a month." Moreover, "the men had behaved so well that I did not want to humiliate them. I believed that consideration for their feelings would make them less dangerous foes during the continuance of hostilities, and better citizens after the war was over." So he said, years later, making a virtue of necessity and leaving out of account the fact that he had begun with a demand for unconditional surrender. For the present, indeed, he was so admiring of the arrangement, from the Union point of view, that he did what he could to make certain Pemberton could not reject it — as both had reserved the right to do — without risking a mutiny by the beleaguered garrison. He had Rawlins send the following note to his corps commanders: "Permit some discreet men on picket tonight to communicate to the enemy's pickets the fact that General Grant has offered, in case Pemberton surrenders, to parole all the officers and men and to permit them to go home from here."

He could have spared himself the precaution and his courier the ride. "By this time," a Confederate declared, "the atmosphere was electric with expectancy, and the wildest rumors raced through camp and city. Everyone had the air of knowing something vital." What was more, a good deal of back-and-forth visiting had begun on both sides of the line. "Several brothers met," a Federal remarked, "and any quantity of cousins. It was a strange scene." Whatever the blue pickets might say, on whatever valid authority, was only going to add to the seethe of speculation within and without the hilltop fortress which was now about to fall, just under fourteen months after its mayor replied to the first demand for surrender, back in May of the year before: "Mississippians don't know, and refuse to learn, how to surrender to an enemy. If Commodore Farragut and Brigadier General Butler can teach them, let them come and try." The upshot was that Grant had come and tried, being so invited, and now Pemberton had been taught, although it galled him. Assembling his generals for a reading of the 10 o'clock offer, he remarked — much as his opponent had done, an hour or two ago, across the way — that his "inclination was to reject these terms." However, he did not really mean it, any more than Grant had meant it, and after he had taken the all but unanimous vote for capitulation, he said gravely: "Gentlemen, I have done what I could," then turned to dictate his reply. "In the main, your terms are accepted," he told Grant, "but in justice both to the honor and spirit of my troops, manifested in the defense of Vicksburg, I have to submit the following amendments, which, if acceded to by you, will perfect the agreement between us. . . ." The added conditions, of which there were two, were modest enough in appearance. He proposed to march his soldiers out of the works, stack arms, and then move off before the Federals took possession, thus avoiding a confrontation of the two armies. That was the first. The second was that officers be allowed "to retain their . . . personal property, and [that] the rights and property of citizens . . . be respected." But Grant declined to allow him either, and for good cause. As for the first, he replied, it would be necessary for the troops to remain under proper guard until due process of parole had been formally completed, and as for the second, while he was willing to give all citizens assurance that they would be spared "undue annoyance or loss," he would make no specific guarantees regarding "personal property," which he privately suspected was intended to include a large number of slaves, freed six months ago by Lincoln's Proclamation. "I cannot consent to leave myself under any restraint by stipulations," he said flatly. Denial of the proposed amendments was contained in a dispatch sent before sunrise, July 4. Pemberton had until 9 a.m. to accept the original terms set forth in last night's message; otherwise, Grant added, "I shall regard them as having been rejected, and shall act accordingly."

Now it was Pemberton's turn to bend in the face of stiffness, and this he did the more willingly since the morning report — such had been the ravages of malnutrition and unrelieved exposure — showed fewer than half his troops available for duty as effectives. "General," he answered curtly about sunrise: "I have the honor to acknowledge the receipt of your communication of this day, and in reply to say that the terms proposed are accepted." The rest was up to Grant, and it went smoothly. At 10 o'clock, in response to the white flags that now fluttered along the full length of the Confederate line, John Logan marched his division into the works. Soon afterwards the Stars and Stripes were flying over the Vicksburg courthouse for the first time in two and a half years. If the victors were somewhat disappointed professionally that seven weeks of intensive shelling by 220 army cannon, backed up by about as many heavier pieces aboard the gunboats and the mortar rafts, had done surprisingly little substantial damage to the town, it was at least observed that the superficial damage was extensive. Not a single pane of glass remained unbroken in any of the houses, a journalist noted. It was also observed that, despite the southern commander's claim that he had ample provisions, the gauntness of the disarmed graybacks showed only too clearly, not only that such was not the case, but also that it apparently had not been so for some time. One Federal quartermaster, bringing in a train of supplies for the troops in occupation, was so affected by the hungry looks on the faces of the men of a rebel brigade that he called a halt and began distributing hardtack, coffee, and sugar all around. Rewarded by "the heartfelt thanks" of the butternut scarecrows, he said afterwards that when his own men complained that night about the slimness of their rations, "I swore by all the saints in the calendar that the wagons had broken down and the Johnny Rebs had stolen all the grub." Not only was there little "crowing," which some Confederates had feared would be encouraged and enlarged by a Fourth of July surrender, but according to Grant "the men of the two armies fraternized as if they had been fighting for the same cause." Though that was perhaps an overstatement of the case, there was in fact a great deal of mingling by victors and vanquished alike — "swapping yarns over the incidents of the long siege," as one gray participant put it — and even some good-natured ribbing back and forth. "See here, Mister; you man on the little white horse!" a bluecoat called out to Major Lockett, whose engineering duties had kept him on the move during lulls in the fighting. "Danged if you aint the hardest feller to hit I ever saw. I've shot at you more'n a hundred times." Lockett took it in good part, and afterwards praised his late adversaries for their generosity toward the defeated garrison. "General Grant says there was no cheering by the Federal troops," he wrote. "My recollection is that on our right a hearty cheer was given by one Federal division 'for the gallant defenders of Vicksburg!'"

Pemberton did not share in the fraternization, not only because of his present sadness, his sense of failure, and his intimation of what the reaction of his adoptive countrymen would be when they got the news of what had happened here today, but also because of his nature, which was invariably distant and often forbidding. For him, congeniality had been limited mainly to the family circle he had broken and been barred from when he threw in with the South. Even toward his own officers he had always been stiffly formal, and now toward Grant, who came through the lines that morning on his way to confer with Porter at the wharf, he was downright icy; indeed, rude. Perhaps it was the northern commander's show of magnanimity, when he knew that such concessions as had been granted — parole of the garrison, for example, instead of a long boat ride to prison camps in Ohio and Illinois — had been the result of hard bargaining and a refusal to yield to his original demand for unconditional surrender. In any event, one of his staff found Pemberton's manner "unhandsome and disagreeable in the extreme." No one offered Grant a seat when he called on Pemberton in a house on the Jackson road, this officer protested, and when he remarked that he would like a drink of water, he was told that he could go where it was and help himself. He did not seem perturbed by this lack of graciousness, however; he went his way, taking no apparent umbrage, content with the spoils of this Independence Day, which were by far the greatest of the war, at any rate in men and materiel. Confederate casualties during the siege had been 2872 killed, wounded, and missing, while those of the Federals totaled 4910; but now the final tally of captives was being made. It included 2166 officers, 27,230 enlisted men, and 115 civilian employees, all paroled except one officer and 708 men, who preferred to go north as prisoners rather than risk being exchanged and required to fight again. In ordnance, too, the harvest was a rich one, yielding 172 cannon, surprisingly large amounts of ammunition of all kinds, and nearly 60,000 muskets and rifles, many of such superior quality that some Union regiments exchanged their own weapons for the ones they found stacked when they marched in.

One additional prize there was, richer by far than all the rest combined and to which they had served as no more than prologue. The Mississippi would return to its old allegiance as soon as one remaining obstruction had been removed, and that allegiance would be secure as soon as one continuing threat had been abolished. The obstruction — Port Hudson — was not really Grant's concern except for the dispatching of reinforcements, which he could now quite easily afford, to help Banks get on with the job. He kept his attention fixed on Joe Johnston — the threat — who continued to hover, off to the east, beyond the Big Black River. Conferring with Porter, Grant requested his co-operation in flushing out the rebels up the Yazoo, re-established there by Johnston while the Federals were concentrating on the reduction of Vicksburg. As usual, the admiral was altogether willing; he assigned an ironclad and two tinclads the task of escorting 5000 infantry upstream to retake Yazoo City, which the Confederates had refortified since their flight from the approaching gunboats back in May. But the northern army commander's main concern was Johnston himself and the force he was assembling west of Jackson. Yesterday, while surrender negotiations were under way, Grant had notified Sherman, whose troops were already faced in that direction, that he was to strike eastward as soon as Vicksburg fell. "I want Johnston broken up as effectually as possible, and roads destroyed," he wired. This message was followed shortly by another, in which he was more specific as to just what breakage was expected. "When we go in," he told his red-haired lieutenant, "I want you to drive Johnston from the Mississippi Central Railroad, destroy bridges as far as Grenada with your cavalry, and do the enemy all the harm possible. You can make your own arrangements and have all the troops of my command, except one corps — McPherson's, say. I must have some troops to send to Banks, to use against Port Hudson."

As it turned out, there was no need for more troops at Port Hudson. All that was required was valid evidence that its companion bluff 240 miles upriver was in Union hands, and this arrived before the reinforcements: specifically, during the early hours of July 7. That evening Gardner received from one of his three brigade commanders — Miles, whose position on the far right afforded him a view of the river, as well as of the extreme left of the Federal intrenchments — a report of strange doings by the enemy, ashore and afloat: "This morning all his land batteries fired a salute, and followed it immediately [by another] with shotted guns, accompanied by vociferous yelling. Later in the day the fleet fired a salute also. What is meant we do not know. Some of them hallooed over, saying that Vicksburg had fallen on the 4th instant. My own impression is that some fictitious good news has been given to his troops in order to raise their spirits; perhaps with a view of stimulating them to a charge in the morning. We will be prepared for them should they do so."

The colonel's men shared his skepticism as well as his resolution, even when confronted with documentary evidence in the form of a "flimsy" tossed into their lines, bearing the signature of the Federal adjutant-general and announcing Pemberton's surrender three days ago. "That's another damned Yankee lie!" a butternut defender shouted back. But Gardner himself was not so sure. He had fought well, inflicting 4363 casualties at a cost of only 623 of his own, and though by now the trenches were less than twenty feet apart in places and the enemy was obviously about to launch another massive assault, which was likely to succeed at such close range, he was prepared to fight still longer if need be. On the other hand, it was no part of his duty to sacrifice the garrison for no purpose — and obviously Port Hudson's purpose, or anyhow its hope of survival, was tied to that of Vicksburg. If the Mississippi bastion had fallen, so must the Louisiana one, exposed as it would be to the possible combination of both Union armies. So Gardner adopted the logical if somewhat irregular course of inquiring of his opponent, by means of a flag of truce next morning, as to whether the report of Vicksburg's fall was true. And when Banks supplied confirming evidence, in the form of a dispatch Grant had sent on the surrender date, Gardner decided that the time for his own capitulation was at hand. Final details were not worked out until the following day, July 9, when the besiegers marched in and took possession, but a train of wagons had already entered Port Hudson the previous afternoon, loaded with U.S. Army rations for the half-starved garrison. Banks combined firmness and generosity. Though his terms had been unconditional, he paroled his 5935 enlisted captives and sent only their 405 officers to New Orleans to await exchange or shipment north. Moreover, having acquired some 7500 excellent rifles and 51 light and heavy guns, he closed the formal surrender ceremony with "a worthy act, well merited." Thus his adjutant characterized the gesture in describing it years later. "By General Banks's order, General Gardner's sword was returned to him in the presence of his men, in recognition of the heroic defense."

If there was haste in the northern commander's method, including parole of all his enlisted prisoners, there was also method in his haste. Albeit they were the sweeter, being his first, Banks was no more inclined than Grant to sit down and enjoy the fruits of his victory; for just as the latter took out after Joe Johnston as soon as Vicksburg fell, so did the former concern himself with Dick Taylor as soon as Port Hudson followed suit. Faced as he was with the departure of the nine-month volunteers who made up a considerable portion of his army, Banks had to choose between using the remainder as guards for the captured garrison or as a mobile force for driving out the reported 13,000 Confederates who had moved into his rear and were threatening New Orleans from Bayou Lafourche and Berwick Bay. Quite aside from the pleasure he derived from being generous to a defeated foe, that was why he paroled nearly 6000 of his 6340 prisoners: to get them off his hands and thus be free to deal with Taylor. Having decided, he wasted no time. While the surrender ceremony was in progress he put Weitzel's and Grover's divisions aboard transports and sent them at once to Donaldsonville, where they would begin their descent of the Lafourche, disposing of infiltrated rebels as they went. The debarkation was completed on July 11; next afternoon the two blue divisions began their advance down opposite banks of the bayou. Early the following morning, however — July 13 at Koch's Plantation, six miles from Donaldsonville — Weitzel's two west-bank brigades, and indirectly Banks himself, were given a cruel demonstration of the fact that haste sometimes made waste, even in pursuit.

Tom Green, with his own and Major's brigade of mounted Texans, had been having a fine time disrupting traffic on the Mississippi with the guns he had established on its right bank, ten miles below the town. Though they could do no real damage to the *Essex*, which came down to challenge them, they did succeed in driving the ironclad off and puncturing the steam-drums of several less heavily armored vessels. A battery commander referred to the 12-foot levee as "the best of earthworks," and Green was prepared to stay there indefinitely, finding balm in his present success for the sting of the recent setback at Fort Butler. After three days of such fun, however, he learned of the arrival of ten transports at Donaldsonville and the debarkation of two blue divisions with better than five times his number of men. Determined not to leave without a fight, whatever the odds, he pulled back from the river, crossed the Lafourche, and lay in wait for what was coming. What was coming was Weitzel, supported by Grover across the way. Green struck hard, soon after sunrise of July 13, caught the bluecoats off guard, and threw them into such hasty retreat that they abandoned three of their guns to their pursuers. They lost 50 killed, 223 wounded, and 186 captured or missing, while Green lost 9 killed and 24 wounded. He withdrew westward, unmolested, and rejoined Taylor at Vermilionville, that general having retired with all his spoils from Brashear City when he learned of Gardner's surrender and the intended return downriver of the besieging army. By no means strong enough for a full-scale battle with the greatly superior forces of the Federals near their base, he was content to wait for them to attempt a second ascent of the Teche. They would find him better equipped for resistance than he had been before his recent brief but profitable drive to the outskirts of New Orleans.

Banks accepted the Koch's Plantation check with his usual easy grace, even setting aside a court-martial's findings that one of Weitzel's brigade commanders had been guilty of drunkenness on duty and misconduct in the presence of the enemy. The former Speaker was looking for no scapegoat; he would take whatever blame there was, along with the praise, as designer and director of the campaign from start to finish. And of praise there was much. It was Banks, after all, who had removed the final obstruction to Union control of the Mississippi, following Grant's extraction of "the nail that held the South's two halves together." On July 16, one week after the fall of Port Hudson, the unarmed packet *Imperial* tied up at New Orleans and began unloading cargo she had brought unescorted from St Louis. For the first time in thirty months, the Father of Waters was open to commerce from Minnesota to the Gulf.

Meanwhile Porter and Sherman had gone about their assignments, though for both there had been irksome delays followed by mishaps for which irksome was all too mild a word; Porter's, in fact, had occurred on the same day as Weitzel's, and while it had been considerably less bloody it was also a good deal more expensive. Originally intended as reinforcements for Banks, since they had spent less than a month in the Vicksburg trenches, 5000 men of Herron's division were shifted to lighter-draft transports on July 11, when news of the fall of Port Hudson arrived, and set out up the Yazoo next morning, escorted by two 6-gun tinclads and the 14-gun ironclad *Baron de Kalb*, formerly the *St Louis* but rechristened when it developed that the navy already had a warship by that name. One of the original seven built by James Eads in the fall of '61 and a veteran of all the major engagements on the Tennessee, the Cumberland, and the Mississippi north of Vicksburg, she had carried the flag eight weeks ago on a similar expedition to Yazoo City and beyond, which had resulted in much damage to the enemy at no cost to the fleet. This last was not to be the case this time, however. Isaac Brown, who had sunk the *De Kalb's* sister ship *Cairo* with a demijohn of powder up this same winding river in December, was back again with forty survivors of the crew from his lost ram *Arkansas*, and he had plans for a repeat performance. His navy artillerists managed to drive the ironclad back around the bend when she appeared below the town at noon of July 13, but a Tarheel regiment assigned to the place by Johnston withdrew on learning that Herron had landed three of his own with instructions to bag the defenders. Obliged to pull back for lack of support, Brown and his sailors left something behind them in addition to their guns: as Porter and Herron presently discovered. The two were on the bridge of the flagship, steaming slowly upstream toward the undefended town, when — just after sunset, abreast of the yards where, about this time a year ago, the *Arkansas* had acquired her rusty armor — one of Brown's improvised torpedoes exploded directly under her bow.

As she began to settle, another went off under her stern, which hastened her destruction. Within fifteen minutes, though all aboard managed to escape with nothing worse than bruises, she was on the muddy bottom, providing a multichambered home for gars and catfish. Herron, having survived this violent introduction to one of the dangers involved in combined operations, went ashore to complete his share of the mission, afterwards reporting the destruction of the Yazoo City fortifications and five of the nine rebel steamboats found lurking in the vicinity, together with the capture of some 300 prisoners, six guns, and about 250 small-arms, as well as 2000 bales of cotton and 800 horses and mules which he commandeered from the planters roundabout. He was enthusiastic; no less than 50,000 more bales were awaiting discovery and seizure in the region, he declared. Porter, on the other hand, summed up the operation somewhat ruefully. "But for the blowing up of the *Baron de Kalb*, it would have been a good move," he informed his superiors, and he added, by way of extenuating this loss of his fourth ironclad since December: "While a rebel flag floats anywhere the gunboats must follow up. The officers and men risk their lives fearlessly on these occasions, and I hope the Department will not take too seriously the accidents which happen to the vessels when it is impossible to avoid them."

Sherman made no such apology, though his particular mishap had occurred the day before and had been preceded by a week of hot and profitless activity. Grant's instructions for him to "do the enemy all the harm possible," accompanied as they were by the prospect of having close to 50,000 troops with which to carry them out, had put the red-haired Ohioan in what he liked to call "high feather," and when they were followed next day — July 4 — by the news that Vicksburg had fallen, his excitement reached fever pitch. "I can hardly restrain myself," he replied. Nor did he: adding, "This is a day of jubilee, a day of rejoicing to the faithful. . . . Already are my orders out to give one big huzza and sling the knapsack for new fields." Those new fields lay on the far side of the Big Black, however, which was now past fording because of a sudden four-foot rise resulting from heavy rains upstate. Sherman spent two days throwing bridges at Birdsong's Ferry and Messinger's Ford and due east of Bovina, thus providing a crossing for each of his three corps, and on July 6 the "Army of Observation," so called from the days of the siege, passed over the river in pursuit of Johnston, who had retired toward Jackson the day before, on learning of Pemberton's surrender. As the rebels withdrew eastward along roads that were ankle-deep in dust — no matter how many inches of rain had fallen upstate, not a drop had fallen here in weeks — they made things difficult for their pursuers by leading animals into such few ponds as had not dried in the heat, then killing them and leaving their carcasses to pollute the water. It was Johnston's intention not only to delay his opponent by such devices, but also to goad him into attempting a reckless, thirst-crazed assault on the

Jackson intrenchments, which the Confederates had repaired and improved since Grant's departure and in which they had taken refuge by the time the superior Federal force completed its crossing of the Big Black, twenty-five miles away.

The crafty Virginian's attempt to discourage and torment his pursuers with thirst was unsuccessful, however, for several reasons. For one, the siege-toughened bluecoats simply dragged the festering carcasses from the ponds, gave the water a few minutes to settle, then brushed the scum aside and drank their fill, apparently with no ill effects at all. For another, the rain soon moved down from the north, sudden thunderous showers under which the marchers unrolled their rubber ponchos and held them so that the water trickled into their mouths as they slogged along. Lifted so recently by the greatest victory of the war, their spirits were irrepressible, whether the problem was too little moisture or too much. "The dirt road would soon be worked into a loblolly of sticky yellow mud," one veteran was to recall. "Thereupon we would take off our shoes and socks, tie them to the barrel of our muskets, poise the piece on the hammer on either shoulder, stock uppermost, and roll up our breeches. Splashing, the men would swing along, singing 'John Brown's Body,' or whatever else came handy." They gloried in their toughness and took pride in the fact that they never cheered their generals, not even "Uncle Billy" Sherman. A surgeon wrote home that they were "the noisiest crowd of profane-swearing, dram-drinking, card-playing, song-singing, reckless, impudent daredevils in the world." They would have accepted all this as a compliment, second only to one Joe Johnston had paid them in warning his Richmond superiors not to underrate Grant's Westerners, who in his opinion were "worth double the number of northeastern troops." They thought so, too, and were ready to prove it on July 10 when their three columns converged on the rebel intrenchments outside Jackson and took up positions before them, Ord's four divisions to the south, Steele's three in the center, and Parke's two on the north.

Within the semicircular works — which, as usual, he considered "miserably located" — Johnston had four divisions of infantry confronting the Union nine, plus a small division of cavalry which he used to patrol the flanks along Pearl River, above and below the town. He made several brief sorties in an attempt to provoke the bluecoats into attacking, but Sherman, though he enjoyed a better than two-to-one numerical advantage, had had too much experience with earthworks these past eight weeks to be tempted into rashness. Instead, he spent two days completing his investment, meantime sending raiders north and south to break the Mississippi Central and thus cut Jackson off from any possible rail connection with the outside world, the bridge in its rear not having been rebuilt since its destruction back in May. Then on July 12, despite his admonitions as to caution, the mishap came. On Ord's front, Lauman was advancing his division through an area obscured by trees and brush, when the lead brigade of 880 veterans suddenly found itself exposed to a withering crossfire from guns and rifles, losing 465 men and three stands of colors, as well as most of the cannoneers and horses of a section of artillery, before the remnant could recover from the shock and back-pedal. "I am cut all to pieces," Lauman lamented; Ord relieved him of command. Sherman approved the brigadier's removal, but refused to be disconcerted by the affair, which had at least confirmed his assumption that Joe Johnston was a dangerous man when cornered: so much so, in fact, that the Ohioan began to wish the Virginian gone. "I think we are doing well out here," he informed Grant two days later, "but won't brag till Johnston clears out and stops shooting his big rifle guns at us. If he moves across Pearl River and makes good speed, I will let him go."

That was just what Johnston had in mind, now that Sherman had the capital invested on three sides. "It would be madness to attack him," he wired Richmond that same day. "In the beginning it might have been done, but I thought then that want of water would compel him to attack us." By next morning, July 16, he was convinced that his only hope for survival lay in retreat. "The enemy being strongly reinforced, and able when he pleases to cut us off," he notified Davis, "I shall abandon this place, which it is impossible for us to hold." Accordingly, after nightfall, he proceeded to carry out the most skillful of his withdrawals so far in the war. Previously — at Manassas and Yorktown, as well as here at Jackson two months ago yesterday, on the day after his arrival from Tennessee — it had been his practice to leave guns and heavy equipment in position lest their removal, which was likely to be noisy, warn the enemy of his intention; but not now. Silently the guns were withdrawn by hand from their forward emplacements while the sick and wounded were being sent eastward across the river, followed by brigade after brigade of soldiers who had been kept busy with picks and shovels till after midnight, drowning out the sounds of the evacuation. Breckinridge's Orphans, who had accomplished Lauman's discomfiture four days ago, went last. The lines of the aborted siege, which had cost the Federals 1122 casualties and the Confederates 604, yawned empty in the darkness and remained so until daylight brought a blue advance and the discovery that Johnston had escaped across the Pearl, much as Lee had done across the Potomac three nights earlier with somewhat less success.

He took with him everything movable but he could not take the railroad or the town. Undefended, Jackson was reoccupied — and reburned. That task was assigned to Sherman's old corps, primarily to Blair's division, which was fast becoming proficient in such work, while Ord moved south with instructions to break up the Mississippi Central "absolutely and effectually" for a distance of ten miles, and Parke did the same in the opposite direction. Steele's men did a thorough job on the capital, sparing little except the State House and the Governor's Mansion. Pettus had departed, but the victorious generals held a banquet in his mansion on the second night of the occupation, and when one brigadier was missing next morning he was found asleep beneath the table, so freely had the wine flowed. "You can return slowly to Black River," Grant replied to news that the town had fallen, but Sherman stayed on for a week, supervising the extensive demolition his chief had prescribed at the outset. Added to what had been done in May, this new damage converted the Mississippi capital into what he referred to as "one mass of charred ruins." (Blair's exuberant veterans had a briefer, more colorful description of the place; "Chimneyville," they called it.) Though he found the stripping of the countryside by his foragers for fifteen miles around "terrible to contemplate," Sherman thought it proper to add that such was "the scourge of war, to which ambitious men have appealed rather than [to] the judgment of the learned and pure tribunals which our forefathers have provided for supposed wrongs and injuries." Characteristically, however, before his departure he distributed supplies to civilian hospitals and turned over to a responsible committee enough hard bread, flour, and bacon to sustain five hundred people for thirty days, his only condition being that none of this food was to be converted "to the use of the troops of the so-called Confederate states." Despite the damage to their pride, the committeemen were glad to accept the offer, whatever the condition. "The inhabitants are subjugated. They cry aloud for mercy," Sherman informed his commander back at Vicksburg.

How lasting the damage would be, either to their pride or to their property, was open to some question. Up to now, particularly in regions where the occupation had been less than constant, the rebels had shown remarkable powers of recovery from blows about as heavy. On the march eastward from the Big Black, for example, one of the Federal columns had crossed a portion of the field that took its name from Champion Hill, which the shock of battle had left all torn and trampled, scorched and scored by shells and strewn with wreckage. That was how the marchers remembered the scene from their passage this way a little less than two months back; but now, to their considerable surprise, they found that much of the field had been plowed and planted and corn stood four feet tall in neat, lush rows, not only as if the battle had never been fought, but also as if, except for the reappearance of the soldiers, there had never been a war at all, either here or anywhere else. It was in a way discouraging. This time, though, as Johnston faded back before them without fighting, they were less distracted and could give their full attention to the destruction which had been more or less incidental on the western march. They blazed a trail of devastation; gins, barns, farmhouses, almost everything burnable went up in flames and smoke; rearward the horizon was one long smudge. Looting took on new dimensions, sometimes of absurdity. One officer, watching a cavalryman stagger along with a grandfather's clock in his arms, asked what on earth he planned to do with it, and the trooper explained that he was going to take it apart "and get a pair of the little wheels out of it for spur rowels." There was time, too, for bitterness. A colonel viewing a porticoed mansion set back from the road in a grove of trees, neatly fenced and with a well-kept lawn and outbuildings, including slave quarters, burst out hotly: "People who have been as conspicuous as these in bringing this thing about *ought* to have things burned! I would like to see those chimneys standing there without any house." That his troops had taken his words to heart was evident on the return from Jackson, when the regiment passed that way again. His wish had been fulfilled. All that remained of the plantation house was its blackened chimneys. "Sherman monuments," they were called; or, perhaps more aptly, "Sherman tombstones."

Some among the Confederates in and out of uniform, but most particularly Richmond friends of Davis and Seddon, put the blame for much of this on Johnston, whose policy it had ever been to sacrifice mere territory, the land and all it nourished, rather than risk avoidable bleeding by any soldier in his charge. Always, everywhere in this war except at Seven Pines — which battle, poorly fought as it was, had done more to sustain than refute his theory: especially from the personal point of view, since it had cost him two wounds and command of the South's first army — he had backed up after a minimum of fighting, leaving the civilians of the evacuated region to absorb the shocks he evaded. So some said, angered by his apparent lack of concern for the fate of Vicksburg, which he had been sent to save. Others not only disagreed; they even pointed to the recent campaign as an example of his superior generalship. Unlike Pemberton, who had lost his army by accepting risks Johnston had advised him to avoid, the Virginian had saved his men to fight another day, and in the process had inflicted nearly twice as many casualties as he suffered. Mainly such defenders were members of his army, who not only had good cause to feel thankful for his caution, but also had come under the sway of his attractive personality. A genial companion, as invariably considerate of subordinates as he was critical of superiors, he won the affection of associates by his charm. There were, however, a few who were immune, and one among them was Pemberton, though this was only recently the case. At the outbreak of the war they had been friends; Johnston in fact had chosen the Pennsylvanian as his adjutant before the northern-born officer's transfer to South Carolina. But that was far in the past, in the days before the siege one friend had waited in vain for the other to raise.

Soon afterwards, in mid-July and in accordance with Grant's instructions for the paroled lieutenant general to report to his immediate superior, Pemberton found the Virginian "sitting on a cleared knoll on a moonlight night surrounded by members of his staff." Thus a witness described the scene, adding that when Johnston recognized the "tall, handsome, dignified figure" coming toward him up the slope, he sprang from his seat and advanced to meet him, hand outstretched.

"Well, Jack old boy," he cried. "I'm certainly glad to see you!"

Pemberton halted, stood at attention, and saluted.

"General Johnston, according to the terms of parole prescribed by General Grant, I was directed to report to you."

The two men stood for a moment in silence as Johnston lowered his unclasped hand. Then Pemberton saluted once more, punctiliously formal, and turned away.

They never met again.

✗ 4 ✗

News that Meade had stopped Lee at Gettysburg sent Lincoln's expectations soaring; he foresaw the end of the war, here and now, if only the victory could be pressed to its logical conclusion with "the literal or substantial destruction" of the rebel host before it recrossed the Potomac. Then came the letdown, first in the form of the northern commander's Fourth of July congratulatory order to his troops, calling for still "greater efforts to drive from our soil every vestige of the presence of the invader." Lincoln's spirits took a sudden drop. "My God, is that all?" he exclaimed, and presently he added: "This is a dreadful reminiscence of McClellan. . . . Will our generals never get that idea out of their heads? The whole country is our soil." His fears were enlarged the following day by word that Lee had stolen away in the night, and no dispatch from Meade, that day or the next, gave any assurance of a vigorous pursuit. Lincoln fretted as much *after* as he had done before or during the three-day battle, so high were his hopes and so great was his apprehension that they would be unfulfilled. At a cabinet meeting on July 7 his expression was one of "sadness and despondency," according to Welles, "that Meade still lingered at Gettysburg, when he should have been at Hagerstown or near the Potomac, in an effort to cut off the retreating army of Lee." That afternoon he was conferring with Chase and a few others in his office, pointing out Grant's progress to date on a map of Mississippi, when Welles came running into the room with a broad smile on his face and a telegram from Porter in his hand. The admiral had sent a fast boat up to Cairo, the Memphis wirehead having broken down, and beat the army in getting the news to Washington: "I have the honor to inform you that Vicksburg has surrendered to the U.S. forces on this 4th day of July."

Lincoln rose at once. "I myself will telegraph this news to General Meade," he said, then took his hat as if to go, but paused and turned to Welles, throwing one arm across the shoulders of the bearer of good tidings. "What can we do for the Secretary of the Navy for this glorious intelligence? He is always giving us good news. I cannot in words tell you my joy over this result. It is great, Mr Welles; it is great!" The Secretary beamed as he walked to the telegraph office with his chief, who could not contain his pleasure at the outcome of Grant's campaign. "This will relieve Banks. It will inspire me," he said as he strode along. He thought it might also inspire Meade, and he had Halleck pass the word to him that Vicksburg had surrendered; "Now if General Meade can complete his work so gloriously prosecuted thus far . . . the rebellion will be over."

A wire also went to Grant: "It gives me great pleasure to inform you that you have been appointed a major general in the Regular Army, to rank from July 4, the date of your capture of Vicksburg." Moreover, on Grant's recommendation, Sherman and McPherson soon were made permanent brigadiers, the reward that had gone to Meade at Frederick that same day. The following day, however, when Grant's own announcement of Pemberton's capitulation came limping in behind Porter's — which had said nothing about terms — there was cause to think that his victory was by no means as complete as had been supposed before details of the surrender were disclosed. Surprise and doubt were the reaction to the news that practically all of the nearly 30,000-man garrison had been paroled. Halleck, for instance, protested by return wire that such terms might "be construed into an absolute release, and that the men will immediately be placed in the ranks of the enemy." Grant had already noted that the arrangement left his and Porter's "troops and transports ready for immediate service" against Johnston and Gardner, which otherwise would not have been the case, and when he explained that the parolees had been turned over to an authorized Confederate commissioner for the exchange of prisoners, which made the contract strictly legal, Old Brains was mollified. So was Lincoln, who was a lawyer himself and knew the dangers that lurked in informalities, though what appealed to him most was Grant's further contention that the surrendered troops were "tired of the war and would get home just as soon as they could." There, he believed, they would be likely to create more problems for the Confederacy than if they had been lodged in northern prison camps, a headache for the Union, which would be obliged to feed and guard them while awaiting their exchange.

Others not only disagreed, but some among them formed a delegation to call on Lincoln with a protest against Grant's dereliction and a demand for his dismissal from command. What rebel could be trusted? they asked, and predicted that within the month Pemberton's men would violate their parole and be back in the field, once again doing their worst to tear the fabric of the Union. Referring to his callers as "crossroads wiseacres," though they must have included some influential dignitaries, Lincoln afterwards described to a friend his handling of the situation. "I thought the best way to get rid of them was to tell the story of Sykes's dog. Have you ever heard about Sykes's yellow dog? Well, I must tell you about him. Sykes had a yellow dog he set great store by —" And he went on to explain that this affection was not shared by a group of boys who disliked the beast intensely and spent much of their time "meditating how they could get the best of him." At last they hit upon the notion of wrapping an explosive cartridge in a piece of meat, attaching a long fuze to it, and whistling for the dog. When he came out and bolted the meat, cartridge and all, they touched off the fuze, with spectacular results. Sykes came running out of the house to investigate the explosion. "What's up? Anything busted?" he cried. And then he saw the dog, or what was left of him. He picked up the biggest piece he could find, "a portion of the back with part of the tail still hanging to it," and said mournfully: "Well, I guess he'll never be much account again — as a dog." Lincoln paused, then made his point. "I guess Pemberton's forces will never be much account again as an army." He smiled, recalling the reaction of his callers. "The delegation began looking around for their hats before I had got quite to the end of the story," he told his friend, "and I was never bothered any more after that about superseding the commander of the Army of the Tennessee."

Now as always he shielded Grant from the critics who were so quick to come crying of butchery, whiskey, or incompetence. "I can't spare this man. He fights," he had said after Shiloh, and more than a month before the surrender of Vicksburg he had called the campaign leading up to the siege "one of the most brilliant in the world." In a sense, this latest and greatest achievement was a vindication not only of Grant but also of the Commander in Chief who had sustained him. Perhaps Lincoln saw it so. At any rate, though previously he had corresponded with him only through Halleck, even in the conferring of praise and promotions, this curious hands-off formality, which had no counterpart in his relations with any of the rest of his army commanders, past or present, ended on July 13, when he wrote him the following letter:

> My dear General
> I do not remember that you and I ever met personally. I write this now as a grateful acknowledgment for the almost inestimable service you have done the country. I wish to say a word further. When you first reached the vicinity of Vicksburg, I thought you should do what you finally did — march the troops across the neck, run the batteries with the transports, and thus go below; and I never had any faith, except a general hope that you knew better than I, that the Yazoo Pass expedition and the like could succeed. When you got below and took Port Gibson, Grand Gulf, and vicinity, I thought you should go down the river and join General Banks; and when you turned north-

ward, east of the Big Black, I feared it was a mistake. I now wish to make the personal acknowledgment that you were right and I was wrong.

Yours very truly
A. LINCOLN

Though in time, when news of the fall of Port Hudson arrived, a congratulatory dispatch also went to Banks, expressing Lincoln's "thanks for your very successful and very valuable military operations this year" — "The final stroke in opening the Mississippi never should, and I think never will, be forgotten," he wrote — no such letter went to Meade, nor did Lincoln mention him by name in responding to a White House serenade on the evening of July 7, tendered in celebration of the double victory. "These are trying occasions," he said, adding a somber note to the tone of jubilation, "not only in success, but also for want of success." He withheld personal praise of Meade because he was waiting for a larger occasion that did not come, though he kept hoping against hope. Finally, his hopes dwindling, he turned cynical. On July 12, when the general wired that he would attack the flood-stalled Confederates next day "unless something intervenes to prevent it," Lincoln ventured a prediction: "They will be ready to fight a magnificent battle when there is no enemy there to fight." Nevertheless, the news two days later that Lee had made a getaway came as an awful shock to him. "We had them in our grasp," he groaned. "We had only to stretch forth our hands and they were ours. And nothing I could say or do could make the army move." He told his son Robert, home from Harvard: "If I had gone up there, I could have whipped them myself." So great was his distress, he adjourned a cabinet meeting on grounds that he was in no frame of mind for fit deliberation. Nor was he. In his extremity — having passed in rapid succession from cynicism, through puzzlement and exasperation, to the edge of paranoia — he questioned not only the nerve and competence of Meade and his subordinates, but also their motives. "And that, my God, is the last of this Army of the Potomac!" he cried as he walked out with the Secretary of the Navy. "There is bad faith somewhere. Meade has been pressed and urged, but only one of his generals was for an immediate attack, was ready to pounce on Lee; the rest held back. What does it mean, Mr. Welles? Great God, what does it mean?"

Halleck did not exaggerate in wiring Meade of Lincoln's "great dissatisfaction" on that day; Welles recorded in his diary that "on only one or two occasions have I ever seen the President so troubled, so dejected and discouraged." Meade's request to be relieved of command, submitted promptly in response to Halleck's wire, shocked Lincoln into recovering his balance. For this was more than a military matter; it was a downright political threat, with sobering implications. The Administration simply could not afford to be placed in the position of having forced the resignation of the man who, in three hard days of fighting, had just turned back the supreme Confederate effort to conquer a peace: an effort, moreover, launched hard on the heels of Union defeats at Fredericksburg and Chancellorsville, which had been fought under leaders now recognized as hand-picked incompetents, both of whom had been kept in command for more than a month after their fiascos. No matter what opinion the citizenry might have as to whether or not the rebels had been "invaders," politically it would not do to make a martyr of the hero who had driven them from what he called "our soil." After instructing Old Brains to decline the general's request to be relieved, Lincoln sat down and wrote Meade a letter designed to assuage the burning in his breast. So great was his own distress, however, that the words came out somewhat differently from what he had intended. In the end it was Lincoln's burning that was assuaged, at least in part. For example, yesterday's letter to Grant had begun: "My dear General," whereas today's bore no salutation at all, merely the heading: "Major General Meade." He opened by saying, "I am very — *very* — grateful to you for the magnificent success you gave the cause of the country at Gettysburg, and I am sorry now to [have been] the author of the slightest pain to you. But I was in such deep distress myself that I could not restrain some expression of it." Whereupon he proceeded to extend that expression of dissatisfaction in a review of the events of the past ten days. Meade had "fought and beat the enemy," with losses equally severe on both sides; then Lee's retreat had been halted by the swollen Potomac, and though Meade had been substantially reinforced and Lee had not, "yet you stood and let the flood run down, bridges be built, and the enemy move away at his leisure, without attacking him." The words were cutting, but those that followed were sharper still. "Again, my dear general, I do not believe you appreciate the magnitude of the misfortune involved in Lee's escape. He was within your easy grasp, and to have closed upon him would, in connection with our other late successes, have ended the war. As it is, the war will be prolonged indefinitely.... It would be unreasonable to expect, and I do not expect you can now effect much. Your golden opportunity is gone, and I am distressed immeasurably because of it."

He ended with a further attempt at reassurance: "I beg you will not consider this a prosecution or persecution of yourself. As you had learned that I was dissatisfied, I have thought it best to kindly tell you why." But on reading the letter over he could see that it was perhaps not so "kindly" after all; that, in fact, rather than serve the purpose of soothing the general's injured feelings, it was more likely to provoke him into resubmitting his request to be relieved of his command. So Lincoln put the sheets in an envelope labeled "To General Meade, never sent or signed," filed it away in his desk, and having thus relieved his spleen contented himself with issuing next day a "Proclamation of Thanksgiving," expressing his gratitude, not to Grant or Meade or Banks or Prentiss, but to Almighty God for "victories on land and on the sea so signal and so effective as to furnish reasonable grounds for augmented confidence that the Union of these States will be maintained, their Constitution preserved, and their peace and prosperity permanently restored." He further besought the public to "render the homage due to the Divine Majesty, for the wonderful things He has done in the nation's behalf, and invoke the influence of His Holy Spirit to subdue the anger which has produced and so long sustained a needless and cruel rebellion, to change the hearts of the insurgents, to guide the counsels of the Government with wisdom adequate to so great a national emergency, and to visit with tender care and consolation throughout the length and breadth of our land all those who, through vicissitudes of marches, voyages, battles, and sieges, have been brought to suffer in mind, body, or estate, and finally to lead the whole nation, through the paths of repentance and submission to the Divine Will, back to the perfect enjoyment of Union and fraternal peace. In witness whereof," the Proclamation ended, "I have hereunto set my hand and caused the seal of the United States to be affixed."

Though it was in large part a reaction to the knowledge that the suffering and bloodshed of the past two years would continue indefinitely past the point at which he believed they could have been stopped, Lincoln's extreme concern over the fact that one of his two great victories had been blunted was also based on fear that if he did not win the war in the field, and soon, he might lose it on the home front. There appeared to be excellent grounds for such apprehension. Ever since the fall elections, which had gone heavily against him in certain vital regions of the country, the loyal and disloyal opposition had been growing, not only in size but also in boldness, until now, in what might have been his hour of triumph, he was faced with the necessity for dealing with riots and other domestic troubles, the worst of which reached a climax in the nation's largest city on the day he issued his Proclamation of Thanksgiving. Though he could assign a measure of the blame to Meade, whose timidity had cost him the chance, as Lincoln saw it, of ending the war with a single stroke, he knew well enough that the discontent had been cumulative, the product of an almost unbroken seven-month sequence of military reverses, a good many of which he had engineered himself, and that the failure might be defined more reasonably as one of leadership at the top. Indeed, many did so define it, both in speeches and in print. During the past two years, while healing the split in his cabinet and winning the respect of those who were closest to him, he had grown in the estimation of the great mass of people who judged him solely from a distance, by his formal actions and utterances and by the gathering aura of his honesty and goodness. There were, however, senators and congressmen, together with other federal and state officials of varying importance, who saw him only occasionally and were offended by what they saw.

"The lack of respect for the President in all parties is unconcealed," Richard Dana, a U.S. district attorney from Massachusetts, had written home from the national capital at the beginning of a visit in late February. Author of *Two Years Before the Mast,* a founder of the Free Soil party and now a solid Republican, Dana spent two weeks looking and listening, then delivered himself of a still harsher judgment based on what he had seen and heard: "As to the politics of Washington, the most striking thing is the absence of personal loyalty to the President. It does not exist. He has no admirers, no enthusiastic supporters, none to bet on his head. If a Republican convention were to be held tomorrow, he would not get the vote of a State. He does not act, or talk, or feel like the ruler of a great empire in a great crisis. This is felt by all, and has got down through all the layers of society. It has a disastrous effect on all departments and classes of officials, as well as on the public. He seems to me to be fonder of details than of principles, of tithing the mint, anise, and cummin of patronage, and personal questions, than of the weightier matters of empire. He likes rather to talk and tell stories with all sorts of persons who come to him for all sorts of purposes than to give his mind to the noble and manly duties of his great post. It is not difficult to detect that this is the feeling of his cabinet. He has a kind of shrewdness and common sense, mother wit, and slipshod, low-leveled honesty, that made him a good Western jury lawyer. But he is an unutterable calamity to us where he is. Only the army can save us."

If there was some perception here, there was also much distortion, and in any event the judgment was merely personal. More serious were the signs of organized obstruction. "Party spirit has resumed its sway over the people," Seward had lamented in the wake of the fall elections, and Sumner had written a friend soon after the turn of the year: "The President tells me that he now fears 'the fire in the rear' — meaning the Democracy, especially at the Northwest — more than our military chances." When the Bay State senator spoke of "the Democracy" he meant the Democrats, particularly that wing of the party which opposed the more fervent innovations of his own: Emancipation, for example, and the draft. At any rate Lincoln's anxiety seemed well founded. "I am advised," Governor Oliver P. Morton of Indiana had wired the Secretary of War, "that it is contemplated when the Legislature meets in this State to pass a joint resolution acknowledging the Southern Confederacy and urging the States of the Northwest to dissolve all constitutional relations with the New England States. The same thing is on foot in Illinois." The same thing, or something resembling it, was indeed on foot in the President's home state, where the legislature had likewise gone Democratic in the fall. However, though the Illinois house passed resolutions praying for an armistice and recommending a convention of all the states North and South to agree upon some adjustment of their differences, the senate defeated by a few votes the proposal to discuss the matter; Governor Richard Yates was not obliged to exercise the veto. On the other hand, Morton did not allow matters to progress even that far in Indiana. He had spies in the opposition ranks, and when he saw what he believed was coming he dissolved the legislature by the simple expedient of advising the Republican minority to withdraw, which left the body without a quorum. The trouble with this was that it also left the Hoosier governor without funds for running the state for the next two years. But he solved the dilemma by strenuous and unconstitutional efforts. After obtaining loans from private sources and the counties, amounting to $135,000 in all, he appealed to Lincoln for the necessary balance. Lincoln referred him to Stanton, who advanced him $250,000 from a special War Department fund. Morton had what he needed to keep Indiana loyal and going, though it bothered him some that the law had been severely bent if not broken in the process. "If the cause fails, you and I will be covered with prosecutions, imprisoned, driven from the country," he told Stanton, who replied: "If the cause fails I do not wish to live."

Stanton believed in rigorous methods, especially when it came to dealing with whatever seemed to him to smack or hint of treason, and he had been given considerable sway in that regard. Perceiving at the outset that the septuagenarian Bates was unequal to the task, Lincoln had put Seward in charge of maintaining internal security, which included the power to arrest all persons suspected of disloyalty in those regions where habeas corpus had been suspended despite the protest of the courts, including the Supreme Court itself. The genial New Yorker did an effective job, particularly in Maryland and Kentucky during their periods of attempted neutrality; judges and legislators, among others who seemed to the government or the government's friends to favor the government's enemies, were haled from their benches and chambers, sometimes from their beds, and clapped into prisons, more often than not without being told of the charges or who had preferred them. When protests reached Lincoln he turned them aside with a medical analogy, pointing out that a limb must sometimes he amputated to save a life but that a life must never be given to save a limb; he felt, he said, "that measures, however unconstitutional, might become lawful by becoming indispensable to the preservation of the Constitution, through the preservation of the nation." After Seward came Stanton, who assumed the security duties soon after he entered the cabinet in early '62. In addition to the fierce delight he took in crushing all advocates of disunion, he enjoyed the exercise of power for its own sake. "If I tap that little bell," he told a visitor, obviously relishing the notion, "I can send you to a place where you will never hear the dogs bark." Apparently the little bell rang often; a postwar search of the records disclosed the names of

13,535 citizens arrested and confined in various military prisons during Stanton's tenure of office under Lincoln, while another survey (not concerned with names, and therefore much less valid) put the total at 38,000 for the whole period of the war. How many, if indeed any, of these unfortunates had been fairly accused — and, if so, what their various offenses had been — could never be known, either then or later, since not one of all those thousands was ever brought into a civil court for a hearing, although a few were sentenced by military tribunals.

One of these last was Ohio's Vallandigham, who had continued to fulminate against the abuses of the minority by the majority, including the gerrymandering of his district by the addition of a Republican county, which had resulted in his defeat in the fall election. "I learned my judgment from Chatham: 'My lords, you cannot conquer America.' And you have not conquered the South. You never will. . . . The war for the Union is, in your hands, a most bloody and costly failure," he told his fellow congressmen during the following lame duck session. His main targets were the Emancipation Proclamation and the Conscription Act. With the former, he declared, "war for the Union was abandoned, war for the Negro openly begun, and with stronger battalions than before. With what success? Let the dead at Fredericksburg and Vicksburg answer. . . . Will men enlist now at any price? Ah, sir, it is easier to die at home. I beg pardon, but I trust I am not 'discouraging enlistments.' If I am, then first arrest Lincoln, Stanton, and Halleck and some of your other generals, and I will retract; yes, I will recant. But can you draft again? Ask New England, New York; ask Massachusetts; [but] ask not Ohio, the Northwest. She thought you were in earnest, and gave you all, all — more than you demanded. Sir, in blood she has atoned for her credulity, and now there is mourning in every house and distress and sadness in every heart. Shall she give you any more? Ought this war to continue? I answer, no; not a day, not an hour. What then? Shall we separate? Again I answer, no no, no! What then? . . . Stop fighting, Make an armistice."

So he counseled, and though a Republican member wrote in his diary that this was "a full exhibition of treason" and downright "submission to the rebels," Vallandigham and others like him considered themselves dedicated rather to opposing men like Thaddeus Stevens, whose avowed intent it was to "drive the present rebels as exiles from this country" and to "treat those states now outside of the Union as conquered provinces and settle them with new men." Democrats knew only too well who these "new men" would be: Republicans. To ask them to support this redefined conflict was asking them to complete the stripping of their minority of its former greatest strength, the coalition with conservatives of the South, and thus assure continuing domination by the radical majority down the years. Faced with this threat of political extinction, and having seen their friends arrested by thousands in defiance of their rights, diehard anti-Republicans banded together in secret organizations, especially in Ohio, Indiana, and Illinois, where a prewar society known as "Knights of the Golden Circle," so called because it had been founded to promote the advancement of national interests around the sun-drenched rim of the Caribbean, was revived and enlarged; "Order of American Knights," its new members called it, and later changed the name again to "Sons of Liberty." Their purpose was to promote the success of the Democratic party — first in the North, while the war was on, and then in the South when it was over, which they hoped would be soon — and to preserve, as they said, "the Constitution as it is, the Union as it was." By way of identification to one another, in addition to such intricate handclasps and unpronounceable passwords as were common in secret fraternities, they wore on their lapels the head of Liberty cut from an old-style penny; "Copperheads," their enemies called them, in scornful reference to the poisonous reptile by that name.

Vallandigham was their champion, and when Congress adjourned in March he came home and addressed them from the stump, along the same lines he had followed in addressing his former colleagues. A tall man in his early forties, handsome and gifted as a speaker, with clear gray eyes, a mobile mouth, and a dark fringe of beard along his lower jaw and chin, he found his words greeted with more enthusiasm here than they had received in Washington, where one or another of his opponents had threatened from time to time to cut his throat. On May Day, with Hooker stalled in the Wilderness and Grant on the march across the Mississippi, the Ohioan addressed a crowd of thousands assembled in his home state for a mass Democratic meeting at Mount Vernon. He made a rousing speech, asserting that the war could be concluded by negotiation but that the Republicans were prolonging the bloodshed for political purposes. The Union had gone by the board as a cause, he added; what was being fought for now, he said, was liberation of the blacks at the cost of enslaving the whites. This brought him more than the cheers of the crowd, which included a large number of men wearing copper Liberty heads in their buttonholes. It also resulted, four days later — or rather three nights later, for the hour was 2.30 a.m. May 5 — in his arrest by a full company of soldiers at his home in Dayton, by order of Major General Ambrose Burnside, commander of the Department of the Ohio.

Still smarting from the whips and scorns that followed Fredericksburg and the Mud March, the ruff-whiskered general had established headquarters in Cincinnati in late March and, outraged by Copperhead activities in the region, issued on April 13 a general order prescribing the death penalty for certain overt acts designed to aid or comfort the Confederacy. Moreover, he added, "the habit of declaring sympathy for the enemy will not be allowed. . . . It must be distinctly understood that treason, expressed or implied, will not be tolerated in this department."

Then on May Day had come Vallandigham's speech at Mount Vernon, reported to Burnside by two staff captains he had sent there in civilian clothes to take notes. Clearly this was a violation of the general order, and on May 4, without consulting his superiors or subordinates or even an attorney, he instructed an aide-de-camp to proceed at once to Dayton and arrest the offender. The aide boarded a special train, taking a company of soldiers along, and by 2.30 next morning was banging on Vallandigham's door. Refused admittance, the soldiers broke it down, seized the former congressman in his bedroom, and carried him forthwith to prison in Cincinnati. Brought before a military commission eight days later — though he declined to plead, on grounds that the tribunal had no jurisdiction over a civilian — he was given a two-day trial, at the close of which he was found guilty of violating the general order and was sentenced to close confinement for the duration of the war. Burnside approved the findings and the sentence that same day, May 16, and designated Fort Warren in Boston Harbor as the place of incarceration.

From the outset, though he promptly assured the general of his "firm support," Lincoln had doubted the wisdom of the arrest. Now his doubts were abundantly confirmed. Vallandigham had declined to plead his case before the tribunal, but he did not hesitate to plead it before the public in statements issued from his cell in Cincinnati. Denouncing Burnside as the agent of a despot, he asserted: "I am here in a military bastille for no other offense than my political opinions." Newspapers of various shades of opinion were quick to champion his basic right to freedom of speech, war or no war. As a result, he progressed overnight from regional to national prominence, his cause having been taken up by friends and sympathizers who sponsored rallies for him all across the land. Vallandigham in jail was a far more effective critic of the Administration than he had been at large; Lincoln was inclined to turn him loose, despite his previous assurance of "firm support" for Burnside and his subsequent reply to a set of resolutions adopted at a protest meeting in Albany, New York: "Must I shoot a simple-minded soldier boy who deserts, while I must not touch a hair of a wily agitator who induces him to desert? . . . I think that in such a case to silence the agitator and save the boy is not only constitutional but withal a great mercy." However, this was leaving out of account the fact that the soldier and the agitator came under different codes of law, and the last thing Lincoln wanted just now was for the legality of Burnside's general order to be tested in the civil courts. He cast about, and as usual he came up with a solution. Burnside had warned that offenders might be sent "beyond our lines and into the lines of their friends." Early the previous year, moreover, Jefferson Davis had done just that to Parson Brownlow, arrested under suspicion of treasonous activities in East Tennessee. Wherever the notion came from, Lincoln found in it the solution to his problem of what to do with Vallandigham, and on May 26 commuted his sentence to banishment, thereby creating the prototype for "The Man Without a Country." Soon afterwards, south of Murfreesboro, the Ohioan was delivered by a detachment of Federal cavalry, under a flag of truce, to a Confederate outpost north of Tullahoma. Informed that he could not remain in the South if he considered himself a loyal citizen of the Union, he made his way to Wilmington, where he boarded a blockade-runner bound for the West Indies. On July 5, two months after his arrest, he turned up in Nova Scotia. Ten days later — having been nominated unanimously for governor by the state Democratic convention, which had been held at Columbus in mid-June — he opened his campaign for election to that high office with an address to the people of Ohio, delivered from the Canadian side of the border at Niagara Falls. Under the British flag, he said, he enjoyed the rights denied him by "usurpers" at home, and he added that he intended to "return with my opinions and convictions . . . not only unchanged, but confirmed and strengthened."

In time he did return, wearing false hair on his face and a large pillow strapped beneath his waistcoat. Presently he threw off these Falstaffian trappings and campaigned openly, despite the warning that the original sentence would be imposed if he broke the terms of his commutation. Lincoln did not molest him this time, however, nor would he allow the military to do so, having learned from the experience in May. Moreover, he had acted by then to prevent further unnecessary roiling of the citizenry by Burnside. In early June, encouraged by his apparent success in suppressing freedom of speech in his department, the general moved against the press in a similar heavy-handed manner. At 3 o'clock in the morning, June 3, cavalry vedettes rode up to the offices of the Chicago *Times*, which he had charged with "repeated expression of disloyalty and incendiary statements." Reinforced an hour later by two companies of infantry from Camp Douglas, they stopped the presses, destroyed the papers already printed, and announced that the *Times* was out of business. The reaction was immediate and uproarious. A noon meeting of prominent Chicagoans, presided over by the mayor, voted unanimously to request the President to revoke the suppression, and in Court House Square that evening a crowd of "20,000 loyal citizens," including many Republicans, gathered to hear speeches against such arbitrary seizures of power by the military and to cheer the news that in Springfield that afternoon the legislature had denounced the general for his action. Confronted with such outbursts of indignation, which seemed likely to spread rapidly beyond his home-state borders, much as the Vallandigham affair had spread beyond the borders of Ohio, Lincoln rescinded Burnside's order the following morning. What was more, he followed this up by having Stanton direct his over-zealous subordinate to arrest no more civilians and suppress no more newspapers without first securing the approval of the War Department.

In all conscience, he had troubles enough on his hands without the help or hindrance of the fantastically whiskered general in Cincinnati, whose brief foray against the Illinois paper was by no means an isolated example of all-out censorship. From start to finish, despite Lincoln's instructions for department commanders to exercise "great caution, calmness, and forbearance" in the matter, no less than 300 newspapers large and small, including such influential publications as the New York *World,* the Louisville *Courier,* the New Orleans *Crescent,* the Baltimore *Gazette,* and the Philadelphia *Evening Journal* — Democratic all — were suppressed or suspended for a variety of offenses, ranging from the usual "extension of aid or comfort to the enemy" to the release of a bogus proclamation which had the President calling for "400,000 more." In thus increasing the public's apprehension of an extension of the draft, he was treading on dangerous ground — dangerous to the government, that is — for nothing so inflamed resentment as did the Conscription Act which Congress had passed in early March and which had begun to be placed in operation by early summer. This resentment was directed less against the draft itself, which was plainly necessary, than it was against the way the act was written and administered. Actually, though it provoked a good deal of volunteering by men who sought to avoid the stigma of being drafted and the discomfort of not being able to choose their branch of service, it was far from effective in accomplishing its avowed purpose, as postwar records would show; 86,724 individuals escaped by paying the $300 commutation fee, while of the 168,649 actually drafted, 117,986 were hired substitutes, leaving a total of 50,663 men personally conscripted, and of these only 46,347 went into the ranks. Though barely enough to make up the losses of two Gettysburgs, draftees and substitutes combined amounted to less than ten percent of the force the Union had under arms in the course of the war; in fact, they fell far short of compensating for the 201,397 deserters, many of whom had been drafted in the first place. However, the popular furor against conscription was provoked not by its end results, which of course were unknown at the time, but rather by the vexations involved in its enforcement, which brought the naked power of military government into play on the home front and went very much against the national grain. While provost marshals conducted house-to-house searches, often without the formality of warrants, boards of officers sentenced drafted boys as deserters for failing to report for induction, and troops were used without restraint to break up formal protest meetings as well as rowdy demonstrations. In retaliation, conscription officials were roughed up on occasion, a few being shot from ambush as they went about their duties, and others had their property destroyed by angry mobs, all in the good old American way dating back to the Revolution. So-called "insurrections," staged at scattered points throughout the North, invariably met with harshness at the hands of soldiers who did not always bother to discriminate between foreign and domestic "rebels," especially when brought back from the front to deal with this new home-grown variety. In mid-June, for example, an uprising in Holmes County, Ohio, was quelled so rigorously by the troops called in for that purpose that their colonel felt obliged to account for their enthusiasm when he made his report of the affair. "The irregularities committed by some of the men," he wrote, "were owing more to their having campaigned in the South than to any intention on their part of violating my express orders to respect private property."

This rash of draft disturbances, which broke out during the long hot summer leading up to and continuing beyond the two great early-July victories, was by no means limited to the Old Northwest or the Ohio Valley, where secret societies were most active in opposition to the Administration and its measures. Boston and Newark had their clamorous mobs, as did Albany and Troy, New York, and Columbia and Bucks counties, Pennsylvania. There were uprisings in Kentucky and New Hampshire, and the governor of Wisconsin had to call out the state militia to deal with demonstrations in Milwaukee and Ozaukee County, where immigrants from Belgium, Holland, and Germany, especially vigorous in resisting what they had left Europe to escape, attacked the draft headquarters with guns and clubs and stones. By far the greatest of all the riots, however, was the one that exploded in New York City, hard on the heels of Vicksburg and Gettysburg, while Lincoln was writing his sent and unsent letters to Grant and Meade. Partly the trouble was political; protests had been made by party orators that Democratic districts were being required to furnish more than their fair share of conscripts and that ballot boxes were being stuffed with imported Republican soldier votes. Partly, too, it was racial; charges were also made that Negro suffrage was a device for overthrowing the white majority, including Tammany Hall, and that Negroes were being shipped in from the South to throw the Tammany-loyal workers, mostly Irish, out of work. Whatever began it, the three-day riot soon degenerated into violence for its own sake. On Monday, July 13, a mob wrecked the draft office where the drawing of names had begun two days before, then moved on to the Second Avenue armory, which was seized and looted, along with jewelry stores and liquor shops. By nightfall, with the police force overpowered, much of the upper East Side had been overrun. Segments of the mob were reported to be "chasing isolated Negroes as hounds would chase a fox," and the chase generally ended beneath a lamppost, which served conveniently as a gibbet. All next day this kind of thing continued, and nearly all of the next. A colored orphanage was set afire and the rioters cheered the leaping flames, seeing the Negroes not only as rivals for their jobs but also as the prime cause of the war. According to one witness of their fury, "three objects — the badge of a defender of the law, the uniform of the Union army, the skin of a helpless and outraged race — acted upon these madmen as water acts upon a rabid dog." By morning of the third day, however, representatives of all three of these hated categories were rare. The mob had undisputed control of the city.

In Washington, Lincoln and Stanton reacted to news of the violence by detaching troops from Meade to deal with the situation. They arrived on Wednesday evening and got to work at once. "We saw the grim batteries and weatherstained and dusty soldiers tramping into our leading streets as if into a town just taken by siege," another witness recorded in his diary. According to him, the action was brief and bloody. "There was some terrific fighting between the regulars and the insurgents; streets were swept again and again by grape, houses were stormed at the point of the bayonet, rioters were picked off by sharpshooters as they fired on the troops from housetops; men were hurled, dying or dead, into the streets by the thoroughly enraged soldiery; until at last, sullen and cowed and thoroughly whipped and beaten, the miserable wretches gave way at every point and confessed the power of the law." Estimates of the casualties ranged from less than 300 to more than 1000, though some Democrats later protested that the figures had been enlarged by Republican propagandists and that there was "no evidence that any more than 74 possible victims of the violence of the three days died anywhere but in the columns of partisan newspapers." Whether the dead were few or many, one thing was clear: Lincoln was determined to enforce the draft. "The government will be able to stand the test," Stanton had replied by wire to Mayor George Opdyke's request for troops at the height of the trouble, "even if there should be a riot and mob in every ward of every city."

Conscription resumed on schedule, August 19, and though there was grumbling, there was no further violence in the nation's largest city; the Secretary had seen to the fulfillment of his prediction by sending in more troops, with orders to crack down hard if there was any semblance of resistance. Lincoln stood squarely behind him, having denied Governor Horatio Seymour's plea for a suspension of the draft. "Time is too important," he told the Democratic leader, and while he agreed to look into the claim that the state's quota was unfair, he made it clear that there would be no delay for that or any other purpose. "We are contending with an enemy who, as I understand, drives every able-bodied man he can reach into his ranks, very much as a butcher drives bullocks into a slaughter pen. No time is wasted, no argument is used. This produces an army ... with a rapidity not to be matched on our side if we first waste time to re-experiment with the volunteer system." His intention, he said in closing, was to be "just and constitutional, and yet practical, in performing the important duty with which I am charged, of maintaining the unity and free principles of our common country." And so it was. Under Lincoln there was Stanton, and under Stanton there

was Provost Marshal General James B. Fry, who headed a newly created bureau of the War Department. Under Fry, in charge of enrollment
districts corresponding roughly to congressional districts all across the
land, were the provost marshals, who were responsible not only for the
functioning of the conscription process but also for the maintenance of
internal security within their individual districts. Each could call on his
neighboring marshals for help in case of trouble, as well as on Fry in
Washington, and Fry in turn could call on Stanton, who was prepared to
lend the help of the army if it was needed and the Commander in Chief
approved. Lincoln's long arm now reached into every home in the
North, as well as into every home in the South that lay in the wake of
his advancing armies, east and west.

Now that he had had time to absorb the shock Lee's getaway had
given him, he felt better about the outcome of the battle in Pennsylvania
and the capacity of the general who had won it. Though he was still
regretful — "We had gone through all the labor of tilling and planting
an enormous crop," he complained, "and when it was ripe we did not
harvest it" — he was also grateful. That was the word he used: saying,
"I am very grateful to Meade for the service he did at Gettysburg," and
asking: "Why should we censure a man who has done so much for his
country because he did not do a little more?" All the same, he could
scarcely help contrasting the eastern victory with the western one,
which had left him not even "a little more" to wish for. Nor could he
avoid comparing the two commanders. More and more, he was coming
to see Grant as the answer to his military problem: not only because of
his obvious talent, demonstrated in the capture of two rebel armies intact, but also because of his attitude toward his work. For example,
when Lorenzo Thomas was sent to Mississippi to direct the recruiting
of Negro troops, Grant had been instructed to assist him, and though he
said quite frankly, "I never was an abolitionist, not even what could
be called anti-slavery," he had replied forthrightly: "You may rely upon
it I will give him all the aid in my power. I would do this whether
the arming the negro seemed to me a wise policy or not, because it is an
order that I am bound to obey and I do not feel that in my position I
have a right to question any policy of the government."
Lincoln liked the tone of that. In contrast to the petulance he had
encountered in his dealings with five of the six commanders of the eastern army (McDowell, the exception, had also turned sour in the end,
after two months of service under Pope) Grant had the sound of a man
he could enjoy working closely with, and apparently he had the notion
of bringing him East, although Halleck and Charles Dana, who had returned to Washington shortly after the fall of Vicksburg, were certain
that the general would prefer to continue his service in the West. Presently there was first-hand evidence that such was indeed the case; for

Dana wrote to Grant in late July, telling him what was afoot, and got a reply in early August. "General Halleck and yourself were both very right in supposing that it would cause me more sadness than satisfaction to be ordered to the command of the Army of the Potomac. Here I know the officers and men and what each general is capable of as a separate commander. There I would have all to learn. Here I know the geography of the country and its resources. There it would be a new study. Besides, more or less dissatisfaction would necessarily be produced by importing a general to command an army already well supplied with those who have grown up, and been promoted, with it. . . . While I would disobey no order, I should beg very hard to be excused before accepting that command." This too was forthright; the President, if he saw the letter, was left in no doubt as to Grant's own preference in the matter. At any rate Lincoln decided to stick with Meade for the time being, much as he had done with Burnside and Hooker after telling a friend that "he was not disposed to throw away a gun because it missed fire once; that he would pick the lock and try it again." Grant would keep, Grant would be there in case he was needed; Grant was his ace in the hole.

Meanwhile there was the war to get on with, on the political front as well as on the firing line. In mid-June out in Illinois, at the height of the Vallandigham controversy and two weeks after Burnside's suppression of the Chicago *Times,* a monster protest rally had been staged in Lincoln's own home town; Copperhead orators had whipped the assembly into frenzies of applause, and the meeting had closed with the adoption of peace resolutions. Now, with the fall elections drawing near, Republicans were calling for loyal Democrats to join them, under the banner of a "National Union" party, in campaigning for support of the Administration's war aims. They planned a record-breaking turnout at Springfield in early September, to offset whatever effect the previous gathering might have had on voters of the region, and the arrangements committee invited Lincoln to come out and speak. He considered going — after all, except for military conferences, he had not left Washington once in the thirty months he had been there — but found the press of business far too great. Instead, he decided in late August to write a letter to the chairman of the committee, James Conkling, to be read to the assembly and passed on to the rest of the country by the newspapers, giving his views on the conflict at its present stage. He began by expressing his gratitude to those "whom no partizan malice, or partizan hope, can make false to the nation's life," then passed at once, since peace seemed uppermost in men's minds nowadays, to a discussion of "three conceivable ways" in which it could be brought about. First, by suppressing the rebellion; "This I am trying to do. Are you for it? If you are, so far we are agreed." Second, by giving up the Union; "I am against this. Are you for it? If you are, you should say so plainly." Third, by negotiating some sort of armistice based on compromise with the Confederates; but "I do not believe any compromise, embracing the maintenance of the Union, is now possible. All I learn leads to a directly opposite belief."

After disposing thus, to his apparent satisfaction, of the possibility of achieving peace except by force of arms, he moved on to another matter which his opponents had lately been harping on as a source of dissatisfaction: Emancipation. "You say you will not fight to free negroes. Some of them seem willing to fight for you; but no matter. Fight you, then, exclusively to save the Union. I issued the Proclamation on purpose to aid you in saving the Union. Whenever you shall have conquered all resistance to the Union, if I shall urge you to continue fighting, it will be an apt time then for you to declare you will not fight to free negroes. I thought that in your struggle for the Union, to whatever extent the negroes should cease helping the enemy, to that extent it weakened the enemy in his resistance to you. Do you think differently? I thought that whatever negroes can be got to do, as soldiers, leaves just so much less for white soldiers to do in saving the Union. Does it appear otherwise to you? But negroes, like other people, act upon motives. Why should they do anything for us if we will do nothing for them? If they stake their lives for us, they must be prompted by the strongest motive — even the promise of freedom. And the promise, being made, must be kept."

And having progressed so far in what an associate called a "stump speech" delivered by proxy, Lincoln passed to the peroration. Here he broke into a sort of verbal buck-and-wing:

> The signs look better. The Father of Waters again goes unvexed to the sea. Thanks to the great Northwest for it. Nor yet wholly to them. Three hundred miles up, they met New England, Empire, Keystone, and Jersey, hewing their way right and left. The Sunny South, too, in more colors than one, also lent a hand. On the spot, their part of the history was jotted down in black and white. The job was a great national one, and let none be banned who bore an honorable part in it. And while those who have cleared the great river may well be proud, even that is not all. It is hard to say that anything has been more bravely and well done than at Antietam, Murfreesboro, Gettysburg, and on many fields of lesser note. Nor must Uncle Sam's web-feet be forgotten. At all the watery margins they have been present. Not only on the deep sea, the broad bay, and the rapid river, but also up the narrow muddy bayou, and wherever the ground was a little damp, they have been and made their tracks. Thanks to all. For the great republic, for the principle it lives by and keeps alive, for man's vast future — thanks to all.
>
> Peace does not appear so distant as it did. I hope it will come soon, and come to stay, and so come as to be worth the keeping in all future time. It will then have been proved that among free men there

can be no successful appeal from the ballot to the bullet, and that they who take such appeal are sure to lose their case and pay the cost. And then there will be some black men who can remember that, with silent tongue and clenched teeth and steady eye and well-poised bayonet, they have helped mankind on to this great consummation, while I fear there will be some white ones unable to forget that, with malignant heart and deceitful speech, they have strove to hinder it.

Still, let us not be over-sanguine of a speedy final triumph. Let us be quite sober. Let us diligently apply the means, never doubting that a just God, in his own good time, will give us the rightful result.

✗ 5 ✗

In their first reports of Gettysburg, southern newspapers hailed the battle as a climactic triumph. "A brilliant and crushing victory has been achieved," the Charleston *Mercury* exulted on July 8, and two days later the Richmond *Examiner* informed its readers that the Army of Northern Virginia, with upwards of 30,000 prisoners in tow, was on the march for Baltimore. Presently, when it was learned that the graybacks had withdrawn instead to the Potomac, these and other southern journals assured the public that there was "nothing bad in this news beyond a disappointment"; Lee, whose "retrograde movement" had been "dictated by strategy and prudence," was "perfectly master of the situation." Though the victory "had not been decisive" because of "the semblance of a retreat," the outcome of the Pennsylvania conflict remained "favorable to the South." Not until the last week of the month did the *Examiner* refer to the "repulse at Gettysburg." By that time, however, the *Mercury*'s editor had also come full circle and like his Richmond colleague had recovered, through hindsight, his accustomed position as an acid critic of the Administration's conduct of the war. "It is impossible for an invasion to have been more foolish and disastrous," he pronounced.

For the most part, Lee's weary soldiers were content to leave such public judgments to the home-front critics, but privately there were some who agreed with the angry Carolinian. They had been mishandled and they knew it. "The campaign is a failure," a Virginia captain wrote home on his return to native soil, "and the worst failure the South has ever made. Gettysburg sets off Fredericksburg. Lee seems to have become as weak as Burnside. And no blow since the fall of New Orleans had been so telling against us." News of the loss of Vicksburg, which the strike across the Potomac had been designed in part to prevent, served to deepen the gloom, especially for those whose lofty posts afforded them a long-range view of the probable consequences. Longstreet, for example, wrote years later, looking back: "This surrender, taken in connection with the Gettysburg defeat, was, of course, very discouraging to our superior officers, though I do not know that it was felt as keenly by the rank and file. For myself, I felt that our last hope was gone, and that it was now only a question of time with us." Officials in Richmond also were staggered by the double blow, and of these perhaps the hardest hit was Seddon, who had put his faith in Johnston. Nowadays, according to a War Department clerk, the Secretary resembled "a galvanized corpse which has been buried two months. The circles around his eyes are absolutely black." Others about the office were as grim, particularly after reading the preliminary reports of the commanders in the field. "Gettysburg has shaken my faith in Lee as a general," R. G. H. Kean, chief of the Bureau of War, recorded in his diary on July 26. "To fight an enemy superior in numbers at such terrible disadvantage of position in the heart of his own territory, when the freedom of movement gave him the advantage of selecting his own time and place for accepting battle, seems to have been a great military blunder. [Moreover] the battle was worse in execution than in plan. . . . God help this unhappy country!" Two days later another high-placed diarist, Chief of Ordnance Josiah Gorgas, who had worked brilliantly and hard to provide the enormous amounts of matériel lost or expended, west and east, confessed an even darker view of the situation. "It seems incredible that human power could effect such a change in so brief a space," he lamented. "Yesterday we rode on the pinnacle of success; today absolute ruin seems to be our portion. The Confederacy totters to its destruction."

The one exception was Davis, who neither contributed to nor shared in the prevailing atmosphere of gloom that settled over the capital as a result of the triphammer blows struck by the Federals east and west. It was not that he failed to appreciate the gravity of the situation, the extent and intensity of the danger in both directions. He did. "We are now in the darkest hour of our political existence," he admitted in mid-July. Rather, it was as if defeat, even disaster, whatever else it brought, also brought release from dread and a curious inverse lift of the spirit after a time of strain which had begun with Grant's crossing of the Mississippi River and the death of Stonewall Jackson. Visitors to the White House in mid-May found him "thin and frail and gaunt with grief," and the tension increased tremendously when Vicksburg was besieged and Lee started north on June 3, the President's fifty-fifth birthday. Mrs Davis said afterwards that throughout this time her husband was "a prey to the acutest anxiety": so much so, indeed, that he found it nearly intolerable to have to wait deskbound in Richmond while his and the nation's fate was perhaps being decided in Pennsylvania and far-off Mississippi. He yearned for the field, a return to his first profession, and like Lincoln — who would declare somewhat later, under a similar press of anxiety: "If I had gone up there I could have whipped them myself" — he considered personal intervention. At any rate he expressed such a hope aloud, if only to his wife. "If I could take one wing and Lee the other," she heard him say one hot June night, "I think we could between us wrest a victory from those people." But that was not to be, either for him or his opponent, though presently there was disquieting news from Bragg and Buckner that Rosecrans and Burnside were on the march in Middle and East Tennessee, and hard on the heels of this came the first vague reports of Lee's retreat and Pemberton's surrender. Moreover, on July 10, when Vicksburg's fall was officially confirmed and Lee reported his army marooned on the hostile northern bank of the Potomac, bad news arrived from still another quarter. Beauregard wired that the enemy had effected a sudden lodgment on Morris Island; Fort Wagner had not been taken, the Creole declared, but the build-up and the pressure were unrelenting. Three days later, however, with Bragg in full retreat and the possible loss of Charleston increasing the strain on the President's frayed nerves, word came from Lee that his army was over the swollen river at last and back on the soil of Virginia, unpursued. Davis seized upon this one gleam of brightness in the gloom, and the clerk who had noted the black circles around Seddon's eyes recorded in his diary: "The President is quite amiable now. The newspaper editors can find easy access and he welcomes them with a smile."

There was more to this than a grasping at straws, though of course there was that as well; nor was his smile altogether forced, though of course it was in part. Davis saw in every loss of mere territory a corresponding gain, if only in the sense that what had been lost no longer required defending. Just as the early fall of Nashville and New Orleans had permitted a tighter concentration of the Confederacy's limited military resources and had given its field commanders more freedom of action by reducing the number of fixed positions they were obliged to defend, so might the loss of the Mississippi make the defense of what remained at once more compact and more fluid. What remained after all was the heartland. Contracted though its borders were, from the Richmond apex south through the Carolinas to Savannah on the Atlantic and southwest through East Tennessee and Alabama to Mobile on the Gulf, the nation's productive center remained untouched. There the mills continued to grind out powder, forge guns, weave cloth; there were grown the crops and cattle that would feed the armies; there on the two seaboards were the ports into which the blockade-runners steamed. In the final analysis, as Davis saw it, everything else was extra — even his home state, which now was reduced to serving as a buffer. Besides, merely because the far western portion of the country had been severed from the rest, it did not follow that the severed portion would die or even, necessarily, stop fighting. In point of fact, some of the advantages he saw accruing to the East as a result of the amputation might also obtain in the Transmississippi, if only the leaders there were as determined as he himself was. Accordingly, after making himself accessible to the Richmond editors so that they might spread these newest views among the defenders of the heartland, he took as his first task next day, July 14, the writing of a series of letters designed to encourage resolution among the leaders and people whose duties and homes lay beyond the great river just fallen to the Union.

Of these several letters the first went to Kirby Smith, commander of that vast region which in time would be known as Kirby-Smithdom. "You now have not merely a military, but also a political problem involved in your command," Davis told him, and went on to suggest that necessity be made a virtue and a source of strength. Cut off as it was, except by sea, the Transmississippi "must needs be to a great extent self-sustaining," he wrote, urging the development of new plants in the interior to manufacture gun carriages and wagons, tan leather for shoes and harness, and weave cloth for uniforms and blankets, as well as the establishment of a rolling mill for the production of ironclad vessels, "which will enable you in some contingencies to assume the offensive" on the Arkansas and the Red. In any case, he added, "the endurance of our people is to be sorely tested, and nothing will serve more to encourage and sustain them than a zealous application of their industry to the task of producing within themselves whatever is necessary for their comfortable existence. And in proportion as the country exhibits a power to sustain itself, so will the men able to bear arms be inspired with a determination to repel invasion. . . . May God guide and preserve you," the long letter ended, "and grant to us a future in which we may congratulate each other on the achievement of the independence and peace of our country." This was followed by almost as long a letter to Theophilus Holmes, the only one of Smith's three chief subordinates who had suffered a defeat. Far from indulging in criminations for the botched assault on Helena, the details of which were not yet known in Richmond, Davis chose rather "to renew to you the assurance of my full confidence and most friendly regards. . . . The clouds are truly dark over us," he admitted, but "the storm may yet be averted if the increase of danger shall arouse the people to such a vigorous action as our situation clearly indicates." Nor were the military leaders the only ones to whom the President wrote in this "darkest hour." He also addressed himself, in a similar vein of encouragement, to Governors Harris Flanagin of Arkansas, Francis R. Lubbock of Texas, and Thomas C. Reynolds of Missouri. And having received from Senator R. W. Johnston a gloomy report of dissatisfaction in Arkansas, including some talk of seceding from the sundered Confederacy, he replied on this same July 14: "Though it was well for me to know the worst, it pained me to observe how far your confidence was shaken and your criticism severe on men who I think deserve to be trusted. In proportion as our difficulties increase, so must we all cling together, judge charitably of each other, and strive to bear and forbear, however great may be the sacrifice and bitter the trial. . . . The sacrifices of our people have been very heavy both of blood and of treasure; many like myself have been robbed of all which the toil of many years had gathered; but the prize for which we strive — freedom, and independence — is worth whatever it may cost. With union and energy, the rallying of every man able to bear arms to the defense of his country, we shall succeed, and if we leave our children poor we shall leave them a better heritage than wealth."

In urging these Westerners to "judge charitably of each other, and strive to bear and forbear," he was preaching what he practiced in the East in regard to Lee and Pemberton. Both had come under a storm of criticism: especially the latter, who not only had suffered a sounder defeat, but also had no earlier triumphs to offset it. So bitter was the feeling against him in the region through which he marched his Vicksburg parolees on their way to Demopolis, Alabama — a scarecrow force, severely reduced by desertions which increased with every mile it covered — that the President was obliged in mid-July to detach Hardee from Bragg, despite the touch-and-go situation in Tennessee, and send him to Demopolis to gather up the stragglers and assume the task of remolding them into a fighting unit. This left Pemberton without a command, though he had been exchanged and was available for duty. In early August, Davis wrote him a sympathetic letter: "To some men it is given to be commended for what they are expected to do, and to be sheltered, when they fail, by a transfer of the blame which may attach. To others it is decreed that their success shall be denied or treated as a necessary result, and their failures imputed to incapacity or crime. . . . General Lee and yourself have seemed to me to be examples of the second class, and my confidence has not been diminished because 'letter writers' have not sent forth your praise on the wings of the press. I am no stranger to the misrepresentation of which malignity is capable, nor to the generation of such feeling by the conscientious discharge of duty." However, it was no easy thing to find employment for a discredited lieutenant general. Bragg at first expressed a willingness to take him, but presently, having conferred with his officers, reported somewhat cryptically that it "would not be advisable." Pemberton returned to Richmond, and after waiting eight months for an assignment, appealed to the Commander in Chief to release him for service "in any capacity in which you think I may be useful." Davis replied that his confidence in him was unimpaired — "I thought and still think that you did right to risk an army for the purpose of keeping command of even a section of the Mississippi River. Had you succeeded none would have blamed; had you not made the attempt, few if any would have defended your course" — but ended, two months later, by accepting the Pennsylvanian's resignation as a lieutenant general, at which rank he was unemployable, and by presenting him with a commission as a lieutenant colonel of artillery, the rank he had held in that same branch when he first crossed over and threw in with the South. In this capacity Pemberton served out the war, often in the thick of battle, thereby demonstrating a greater devotion to the cause he had adopted than did many who had inherited it as a birthright.

To Lee, too, went sustaining letters expressive of the President's confidence after the late reverse in Pennsylvania. "I have felt more than ever before the want of your advice during the recent period of disaster," Davis wrote in late July, closing "with prayers for your health, safety and happiness," and in early August, after assuring the general that he could "rely upon our earnest exertions to meet your wants," he offered the opinion that the Virginian might do well to withdraw his army closer to Richmond and thus encourage the enemy to attack him in a position that could be reinforced more readily; but he made it clear that now as always he was leaving the final decision to the commander in the field, who might prefer to defend the line of the Rappahannock, as he had done so successfully twice before. In closing, Davis spoke again of how sorely Lee had been missed throughout the fourteen months since he had left his post as presidential adviser: "I will not disturb your mind by reciting my troubles about distant operations. You were required in the field and I deprived myself of the support you gave me here. I need your counsel, but must strive to meet the requirements of the hour without distracting your attention at a time when it should be concentrated on the field before you. . . . As ever, truly your friend, Jeffn Davis."

No such letter went to Joe Johnston, though the correspondence between the Chief Executive and this other top-ranking Virginian was a good deal more voluminous. When a friend remarked, one day amid these troubles, that Vicksburg had fallen "apparently from want of provisions," Davis replied scathingly: "Yes, from want of provisions inside, and a general outside who wouldn't fight." First his anger and then his scorn had been aroused by efforts on the part of Johnston and his friends to free the general of all responsibility for the loss not only of Vicksburg and Port Hudson, but even of Jackson, their claim being based on a renewal of the complaint that he had not been allowed enough authority to permit decisive action. Davis replied on July 15 with a fifteen-page letter in which he reviewed the entire case, order by order, dispatch by dispatch, showing that Johnston had been given unlimited authority to act as he thought best, and he concluded in summation: "In no manner, by no act, by no language, either of myself or of the Secretary of War, has your authority . . . been withdrawn, restricted, or modified." Johnston's response was a request that he be relieved of all responsibility for the disaster that seemed to be shaping up for Bragg, and Davis was prompt to comply. On July 22 the Department of Tennessee was removed from the Virginian's control. However, the apparent effect of this was to afford the general and his staff more time for self-justification.

There now began to appear, in various anti-Administration journals throughout the South, excerpts from a 5000-word "letter" written by Dr D. W. Yandell, Johnston's medical director, ostensibly to a fellow physician in Alabama. Secret dispatches and official orders were quoted, certain evidence that the writer had had access to the general's private files, and Johnston was praised extravagantly at the expense of Pemberton and the Commander in Chief, who were charged with indecision and lack of foresight. On August 1 Davis sent a copy of this "article-letter," which was being passed around in Richmond, directly to Johnston with a covering note that combined irony and contempt: "It is needless to say that you are not considered capable of giving countenance to such efforts at laudation of yourself and detraction of others, and the paper is sent to you with the confidence that you will take the proper action in the premises." The effect, of course, was to widen the rift between the two leaders, whose rupture was soon complete. An acquaintance observed that from this time forward Johnston's "hatred of Jeff Davis became a religion with him." Davis, on the other hand, was content to restrict himself to slighting references such as those he had made while the latest of the Virginian's "retrograde adjustments" was still in progress. "General Johnston is retreating on the east side of Pearl River," he informed Lee on the second anniversary of Manassas, "and I can only learn from him of such vague purposes as were unfolded when he held his army before Richmond." A week later the veil lifted a bit, but only to descend again. "General Johnston, after evacuating Jackson, retreated to the east, to the pine woods of Mississippi," Davis wrote Lee on July 28, "and if he has any other plan than that of watching the enemy, it has not been communicated."

Meanwhile Johnston, having advised the War Department of his intention "to hold as much of the country as I can and to retire farther only when compelled to do so," was enjoying a brief vacation in Mobile with his wife, who told a friend in early August that she had found her husband looking well and in "tolerable spirits, as cheerful as if Jeff was throwing rose leaves at him, instead of nettles and thorns."

"Misfortune often develops secret foes," Davis had said in a letter written earlier that week to Lee, "and oftener still makes men complain. It is comfortable to hold someone responsible for one's discomfort." Lee could testify to the truth of this, having seen it demonstrated first on his return from western Virginia, back in the rainy fall of '61, and now again on his return from Pennsylvania, when some of the same irate critics took him to task for blunders in the field. But the President had something else to say, of which Lee, concerned almost exclusively with army matters throughout the past year, was perhaps much less aware. Convinced that "this war can only be successfully prosecuted while we have the cordial support of the people," Davis had been pained to observe what he set down next: "In various quarters there are mutterings of discontent, and threats of alienation are said to exist, with preparation for organized opposition.... If a victim would secure the success of our cause," he added in closing, "I would freely offer myself."

This last was scarcely necessary, however, since a good many influential men had already singled him out for that distinction. In Charleston, for instance, the Robert Barnwell Rhetts, Senior and Junior, stepped up their attacks against him in the columns of their *Mercury*, and the father was in Columbia even now, suggesting as a member of the South Carolina convention, still in session, that Davis be impeached. There was considerable disagreement as to whether his sins were mainly ones of omission or commission, but his critics agreed that, whichever they were, he had them to a ruinous extent. Old Edmund Ruffin, Virginia's secession leader who had gone down to Sumter to fire the first shot of the war, referred contemptuously nowadays to "our tender conscienced and imbecile President," while James L. Alcorn, a fellow Mississippian of doubtful loyalty to the Confederacy, pulled out all the stops in calling him a "miserable, stupid, one-eyed, dyspeptic, arrogant tyrant." Two of his more vehement opponents, W. L. Yancey and seventy-year-old Sam Houston, were removed from the political scene by death before the end of July — the former as a result of a kidney ailment, though some editors hostile to Davis claimed the Alabamian died of a broken heart and acute regret at having presented "the man and the hour" to the inaugural crowd thirty months ago in Montgomery — but plenty of others remained: Robert Toombs, for example, whose wounded pride continued to fester down in Georgia. "Toombs is ready for another revolution," a diarist observed, "and curses freely everything Confederate from the President down to a horse boy." North Carolina's Governor Zebulon Vance, who had fought against secession as a Unionist and then against the Yankees as an officer of the line, was equally ready to take on the Richmond government as a champion of States Rights. "I can see but little good, but a vast tide of inflowing evil from these inordinate stretches of military powers which are fast disgracing us equally with our northern enemies," he told his constituents, and he was so zealous in his concern for their comfort and welfare that he was said to have in his warehouses, on the chance they might be needed some day, more uniforms than were on the backs of the ragged soldiers in Lee's army, to which he himself had belonged until he resigned and came home to campaign for the election he had won last fall.

How a nation which at the outset had been practically without industrial facilities for warfare, which had lost more than half its harbors and had the remaining few blockaded, which was penetrated from the landward side by large and well-organized columns of invasion, and which was outnumbered worse than five to one in available manpower for its armies, could hope to survive unless its people were united in die-hard resistance Vance did not say. His concern at that particular time had been the suspension of habeas corpus during a crisis, and apparently his concern stopped there, whatever concomitant problems loomed alongside it or lurked in the background. Other leaders had other concerns as exclusive. Georgia's Joe E. Brown — "Joseph the Governor of all the Georgias," a home-state editor dubbed him; another said that he suffered from delusions in which he was "alternately the State of Georgia and the President of the Confederate States" — saw conscription as the great evil to be feared and fought. "The people of Georgia will refuse to yield their sovereignty to usurpation," he had notified Davis in October, and since then he had done much to prove he meant it, beginning with an executive order forbidding the taking or shipment of firearms from the state. Under his guidance the legislature elected Herschel V. Johnson, Stephen Douglas's 1860 running mate, to the Confederate senate on a program of opposition to the central government. Its members cheered wildly an address Johnson delivered before his departure, protesting the concentration of power in Richmond, and were joined in their applause by a fellow Georgian in whose hands a good part of that power had supposedly been placed: Vice President Alexander Stephens. There was nothing unusual in his presence at Milledgeville on this occasion, for he had early become disenchanted with the republic he had helped to establish and now he spent more time at home in nearby Crawfordville than he did at his duties in the national capital. Nor was there anything unusual, by now, in his indorsement of a speech against the Administration of which he was nominally a part. Like his friend Toombs, he was "ready for another revolution" whose cause would be the same as the First and Second, staged respectively in 1776 and 1861: both of which, as Stephens saw it, had since been betrayed. What he feared most, whether it was dressed in red or blue or gray, was what he later termed "the Demon of Centralism, Absolutism, Despotism!" That was the true enemy, and with it there could be no compromise whatever. "Away with the idea of getting independence first, and looking after liberty afterward," he declared. "Our liberties, once lost, may be lost forever."

Such opinions, voiced by such leaders — "impossiblists," they would be called one day — made waverers of many among their listeners who had been steadfast up to then, and defeatists of those who were wavering already. Moreover, their influence ranged well beyond the halls and stumps from which they spoke, for their words were broadcast far and wide by newspapers whose editors shared their views. The Rhetts and Edward Pollard of the *Examiner*, who referred to Davis as "a literary dyspeptic [with] more ink than blood in his veins, an intriguer busy with private enmities," were only three among the many, including the editors and owners of the Lynchburg *Virginian*, the Atlanta *Southern Confederacy*, the Macon *Telegraph* and *Intelligencer*, the Columbus *Sun*, and the Savannah *Republican*. Georgians were thus predominant, but the most blatant in his approach to downright treason was William Holden of the Raleigh *Standard*. Unsuppressed (for the Confederate government never censored so much as a line in a single paper throughout the war) Holden continued to rail against the Administration and all it stood for, uninterrupted except for one day in September when a brigade from Lee's army, passing through the North Carolina capital, indignantly wrecked the office of the *Standard*. Holden resumed publication without delay; but meanwhile, the soldiers having departed, a crowd of his admirers marched in retaliation on the plant of the rival *State Journal*, a Davis-loyal paper just up the street, and destroyed its type, presses, and machinery. Despite a presidential warning that those who sowed "the seeds of discontent and distrust" were preparing a "harvest of slaughter and defeat," hostile editors not only continued their attacks on the government, but also carried in their news columns the identification of military units in their areas, plans of yet unfought battles and campaigns, the arrival and departure times of blockade-runners, descriptions and locations of vital factories and munition works, all in such detail, a diarist remarked, that the North had no need for spies; "Our newspapers tell every word there is to be told, by friend or foe." Helpful though all this was to the enemy, the worst effect on the nation's chances for survival lay in the undermining of the public's confidence in eventual victory. Profoundly shaken by the double defeat of Gettysburg and Vicksburg, the people looked to their leaders for reassurance. From some they got it, while from others all they got was "I told you so" — as indeed they had, with a stridency that increased with every setback. All too often, as a result, enthusiasm was replaced by apathy. "They got us into it; let them get us out," men were saying nowadays, and by "them" they meant the authorities in Richmond.

In point of fact, if the public's faith in its government's paper money was a fair reflection of its attitude in general, the decline of confidence had begun much earlier. For the first two years of the war — that is, through April of the present year — the dollar had fallen gradually, if steadily, to a ratio of about four to one in gold. This was not too bad; the Federal greenback had fallen to about three to one in the same period. However, in the next four months, while Union money not only held steady but even rose a bit, Confederate notes declined nearly twice as much in value as they had done in the course of the past two years. In May, despite the splendid victory at Chancellorsville, the dollar fell from 4.15 to 5.50, the worst monthly drop to date. In June, moreover, with Lee on the march in Pennsylvania to offset Grant's progress in Mississippi, it took an even greater drop, from 5.50 to 7. In July, with Vicksburg lost and Lee in retreat, it tumbled to 9, and by the end of August, with the full impact of the two defeats being felt by all the people, one gold dollar was worth an even dozen paper dollars. To some extent, though the figures themselves could not be argued with, their effect could be discounted; men — some men; particularly money men — were known to be more touchy about their pocketbooks than they were about their lives, withholding the former while risking the latter for a cause. Davis, for one, could maintain that the shrinking of the dollar, even though the damage was to a large extent self-inflicted, was only one more among the hardships to be endured if independence was to be achieved. "Our people have proven their gallantry and patriotic zeal," he had written Lee; "their fortitude is now to be tested. May God endow them with all the virtue which is needed to save a suffering country and maintain a just cause."

Beyond the northern lines, as we have seen, there were many who agreed with Davis that his cause was just; who at any rate were willing to have the Confederates depart in peace. Similarly, or conversely, there were many behind the southern lines who disagreed with him; who were also for peace, but only on Union terms. Some had lost heart as a result of the recent reverses, while others had had no heart for the war in the first place. The latter formed a hard core of resistance around which the former gathered in numbers that increased with every Federal success. It was these men Davis had in mind when, after referring to "mutterings of discontent," he spoke of downright "threats of alienation" and "preparation for organized opposition." Such preparations had begun more than a year ago, but only on a small scale, as when some fifty men in western North Carolina raised a white flag and marched slowly around it praying for peace. Since then, the movement had grown considerably, until now the South too had its secret disloyal societies: Heroes of America, they called themselves, or Sons of America, or sometimes merely "Red Strings," from the identifying symbol they wore pinned to their lapels. While neither as numerous nor as active as their counterparts in the North, they too had their passwords, their signs and grips and their sworn objectives, which were to discourage enlistment, oppose conscription, encourage desertion, and agitate for an early return to the Union. Mostly the members were natives of a mountainous peninsula more than a hundred miles in width and six hundred miles in length, extending from the Pennsylvania border, southwest through western Virginia and eastern Tennessee, down into northern Georgia and Alabama. Owning few or no slaves, and indeed not much of anything else in the way of worldly goods, a good portion of these people wanted no part of what they called "a rich man's war and a poor man's fight." War or fight, its goals were those of the Piedmont and Tidewater regions, not their own, and they contributed substantially to the total of 103,400 Confederate desertions computed to have occurred in the course of the war. So far, they had amounted more to a potential than to an actual danger; Streight's raid across North Alabama, for example, had been planned with their support in mind, but they had not been of much use to him with Forrest close in his rear. However, the coming months would show that Davis had been quite right to give them his attention in late July, when they made their first significant gains outside the fastness of the Appalachian chain.

Reverses in the field, increasingly forthright opposition to the central government by regional States Rights leaders, the formation and expansion of societies dedicated to sabotage of the entire Confederate effort, all combined to increase the discouragement natural to the hour. If not convictions of defeat, then anyhow widespread doubts of ultimate victory took root for the first time. In the present "gloom of almost despondency," a Richmond editor wrote in mid-August, "many faint-hearted regard all as lost." This was Pollard, who tended to exaggerate along these lines for reasons of his own; but even so staunch a supporter of the Administration as Congressman Dargan of Alabama — who had proved his mettle, if not his effectiveness, by making an unsuccessful bowie knife attack on his opprobrious colleague Henry Foote — fell into a midsummer state of desperation. "We are without doubt gone up; no help can be had," he wrote Seddon from Mobile in late July. "The failure of the Government to reinforce Vicksburg, but allowing the strength and flower of the Army to go north when there could be but one fate attending them, has so broken down the hopes of our people that even the little strength yet remaining can only be exerted in despair." He pinned his own hopes, such as they were, on foreign intervention, and since he believed that what stood in the way of this was slavery, he favored some form of Confederate emancipation. "So would the country," he declared, if the people were given the choice between abolition and defeat — especially in light of the fact that defeat would mean abolition anyhow. At any rate, he told his friend the Secretary of War, "If anything can be done on any terms in Europe, delay not the effort. If nothing can, God only knows what is left for us."

Dargan would perhaps have done better to write to the Secretary whose proper business was diplomacy. But it was as well he did not; Benjamin's department was having the least success of all this summer, both at home and abroad. In June, for example, Davis had had a letter from the Vice President down in Georgia, suggesting that he be sent on a mission to Washington, ostensibly to alleviate the sufferings of prisoners and humanize the conduct of the war, but actually, once negotiation on these matters was under way, to treat for peace on a basis of "the recognition of the sovereignty of the States and the right of each in its sovereign capacity to determine its own destiny." Just what he meant by this was not clear, and anyhow his disapproval of the government was too well known to permit his use as a spokesman, particularly at a conference on peace with the government's enemies. But Davis too was distressed by the growth of what he considered barbarism in the conflict, and he wired for Stephens to come to Richmond at once. Though he had no intention of allowing the Georgian any large authority — "Your mission is one of humanity, and has no political aspects," he informed him — he thought it might be advantageous to have an emissary on northern soil, whatever his basic persuasion, when Lee delivered the knockout blow he planned as a climax to the invasion about to be launched. Armed with two identical letters, one from Commander in Chief Davis to Commander in Chief Lincoln, the other from President Davis to President Lincoln — his instructions were to deliver whichever was acceptable — Stephens set off down the James, July 3, on the flag-of-truce steamer *Torpedo*. His hopes were high, despite the imposed restrictions, for he and Lincoln had been fellow congressmen and friends before the war. Off Newport News next morning, however, he submitted to the Union commander a request that he be allowed to proceed to Washington, only to be kept sweltering for two days aboard the motionless *Torpedo* while waiting for an answer. At last it came, in the form of a wire from Stanton on July 6: "The request is inadmissible. The customary agents and channels are adequate for all needful military communications and conference between the United States forces and the insurgents." Back at Richmond next day, the frail and sickly Georgian, who was barely under average height but weighed less than one hundred pounds with his boots on, learned that Gettysburg had been fought and lost — which explained, as a later observer remarked, why "Lincoln could afford to be rude" — and that evening the first reports of the fall of Vicksburg arrived. Discomfited and disgruntled, Stephens remained in Richmond for a couple of months, then returned to Crawfordville before Congress reconvened. A guidebook to the capital, listing the office and home addresses of government officials, contained the note: "The Vice President resides in Georgia."

Events abroad had taken a turn no more propitious than those on the near side of the Atlantic, although this too came hard on the heels of revived expectations. Despite the North's flat rejection of Mercier's offer to mediate a truce in February, friends of the Confederacy had been encouraged since then by what seemed to them an increasing conviction in Europe that the South could never be conquered. Chancellorsville had served to confirm this impression, even in the minds of men unwilling to admit it, and the London *Times* on May 2, unaware that the Wilderness battle was in mid-career, had noted that the Union was "irreparably divided." Looking back on the earlier Revolution, the editor said of the former Colonies: "We have all come to the conclusion that they had a right to be independent, and it was best they should be. Nor can we escape from the inference that the Federals will one day come to the same conclusion with regard to the Southern States." James Mason drew much solace from such remarks. Observing the hard times the cotton shortage had brought to the British spinning industry, he found himself emerging from the gloom into which more than a year of diplomatic unsuccess had plunged him. "Events are maturing which must lead to some change in the attitude of England," he informed Benjamin. Across the way in Paris, John Slidell was even more hopeful. "I feel very sanguine," he wrote, "that not many months, perhaps not many weeks, will elapse without some decided action on Napoleon's part." Grant's slam-bang May campaign in Mississippi offset considerably the brilliance of Lee's triumph over Hooker, but when it was followed by the determined resistance of Vicksburg under siege, with Johnston supposedly closing on Grant's rear, the Confederate flame of independence burned its brightest. Moreover, it was at this point that Lee set out on his second invasion of the North. The first, launched just under ten months ago, had come closer to securing foreign intervention than anyone outside the British cabinet knew; now if ever, with the second invasion in progress, was the time for an all-out bid for intervention. To ease the way, Benjamin assured a distinguished English visitor — Arthur Fremantle, who passed through Richmond in mid-June on his way to join Lee in Pennsylvania — that the South's demands were modest. To draw up a treaty of peace acceptable to the Confederacy, he said, it would only be necessary to write the word "self-government" on a blank sheet of paper. "Let the Yankees accord that," he told the colonel, "and they might fill up the paper in any manner they choose. . . . All we are struggling for is to be let alone."

There were those in the British Parliament who not only saw the opportunity as clearly as did anyone in the Confederate State Department, but also were willing to act. Two such were William S. Lindsay and John A. Roebuck, opposition stalwarts who, perceiving their chance for action after months of forced delay, crossed the Channel for an interview with Napoleon on June 20. Informed of his views that the time was ripe for joint intervention in the war across the sea, they hastened back to present them in a motion Roebuck brought before the house on June 30, requesting the Queen to enter into negotiations with foreign powers for the purpose of welcoming the Confederacy into the family of nations. They hoped thereby to place the government in a dilemma between recognition and resignation; however, they had neglected in their enthusiasm to make sure of their forces. When the ministry replied that no such proposal had been received from France, Napoleon failed to confirm their account of the interview, and thus exposed their veracity to question. John Bright and W. E. Forster, long-time Liberal proponents of the Union, both made powerful speeches against the motion, laced with sarcastic remarks on Roebuck's efforts to represent the Emperor on the floor of Parliament. What was more, as the debate wore on it developed that other pro-Confederate members did not approve of such overzealous methods, and Benjamin Disraeli, the Conservative leader, declined to commit the party to what amounted in the popular mind to a defense of slavery. Finally, on July 13, after waiting two weeks in vain for word of a victory won by Lee on northern soil, Roebuck — a diminutive individualist of somewhat ridiculous aspect; "Don Roebucco," *Punch* had dubbed him, "the smallest man 'in the House' " — admitted defeat by moving the discharge of his motion. Three days later the first reports of Gettysburg reached London, followed within the week by news of the fall of Vicksburg; after which there was no hope of a revival of the motion, either by Roebuck or anyone else. In fact, the ill-managed debate had done a good deal more to lower than to raise the Confederacy's chances of securing foreign recognition, particularly in England, where some of the ineptness and downright absurdity of its champions was connected, as a general impression, with the cause they had sought to further.

Benjamin perceived in this another instance of the attitude he had complained of earlier: "When successful fortune smiles on our arms, the British cabinet is averse to recognition because 'it would be unfair to the South by the action of Great Britain to exasperate the North to renewed efforts.' When reverses occur ... 'it would be unfair to the North in a moment of success to deprive it of a reasonable opportunity of accomplishing a reunion of the States.' " Davis agreed with this bleak assessment of the situation. " 'Put not your trust in princes,' " he had told his people before New Year's, "and rest not your hopes on foreign nations. This war is ours; we must fight it out ourselves." All the same, he had kept Mason in London all this time, suffering under snubs, on the off-chance that something would occur, either on this or that side of the water, to provoke a rupture between the Unionists and the British, who in that case would be glad to find an ally in the South. But this latest development, with its tarnishing absurdities, was altogether too much for him to bear. The game was no longer worth the candle, and he had Benjamin notify Mason of his decision. On August 4 the Secretary wrote as follows to the Virginian in England: "Perusal of the recent debates in the British Parliament satisfies the President that the government of Her Majesty has determined to decline the overtures made through you for establishing, by treaty, friendly relations between the two governments, and entertains no intention of receiving you as the accredited minister of this government near the British court. Under these circumstances, your continued residence in London is neither conducive to the interests nor consistent with the dignity of this government, and the President therefore requests that you consider your mission at an end, and that you withdraw, with your secretary, from London."

A private letter accompanied the dispatch, authorizing the envoy to delay his departure "in the event of any marked or decisive change in the policy of the British cabinet." But Mason too had had all he could bear in the way of snubs by now. Before the end of the following month he gave up his fashionable West End residence, removed the diplomatic archives, and took his leave of England, sped on his way by a hectoring editorial in the *Times* on the South's folly in demanding recognition before it had earned it. Despite the high hopes raised at the start of his mission by the *Trent* Affair, all he had to show for twenty months of pains was a note in which the foreign minister, Lord John Russell, after explaining that his reasons for declining the Virginian's overtures were "still in force, and it is not necessary to repeat them," expressed "regret that circumstances have prevented my cultivating your personal acquaintance, which, in a different state of affairs, I should have done with much pleasure and satisfaction." Joining Slidell in Paris, only a day away from London by train and packet, Mason kept himself and his staff in readiness for a return to England on short notice. Moreover, he believed he knew what form, if any, this notice was likely to take. Translating his diplomatic problems into British political terms, he pinned his remaining hopes on a Tory overthrow of Palmerston's coalition government, whose continuance in power he felt depended on the survival of the elderly Premier, and his correspondence with friends he had left behind, across the Channel, was peppered from this time forward with anxious inquiries as to the octogenarian's health. But Lord Palmerston — who, in point of fact, had been friendlier to the South than Mason knew — had a good two years of life left in him, and those two, as it turned out, were six months more than quite enough.

The shock felt by Davis at this all but final evidence that the Confederacy would have to "fight it out," as he had said, without the hope of foreign intervention — for it was generally understood that France could not act without England, and Russia had been pro-Union from the start — was lessened somewhat, or at any rate displaced, by an even greater shock which he received on reading a letter the South's first soldier had written him four days after Benjamin wrote Mason. From Orange Courthouse, his new headquarters south of the Rapidan, Lee sent the President on August 8 what seemed at first to be some random musings on the outcome of the Gettysburg campaign. His tone was one of acceptance and resolution, of confidence in what he called "the virtue of the whole people. . . . Nothing is wanting," he declared, "but that their fortitude should equal their bravery to insure the success of our cause. We must expect reverses, even defeats. They are sent to teach us wisdom and prudence, to call forth greater energies, and to prevent our falling into greater disasters. Our people have only to be true and united, to bear manfully the misfortunes incident to war, and all will come right in the end." Davis agreed. In fact he had spent the past month saying much the same thing, not only to the public at large, but also, more specifically, to the heads of the nation's armies, including Lee. Nor did he disagree with what came next, having heard it before from his dead friend and hero Albert Sidney Johnston, who had been the subject of far more violent attacks by the press in another time of crisis. "I know how prone we are to censure," Lee continued, "and how ready [we are] to blame others for the non-fulfillment of our expectations. This is unbecoming in a generous people, and I grieve to see its expression. The general remedy for want of success in a military commander is his removal. This is natural, and in many instances proper. For no matter what may be the ability of the officer, if he loses the confidence of his troops disaster must sooner or later ensue." For all his basic agreement with the principle here expressed, Davis was by no means prepared for the application Lee made in the sentence that followed: "I have been prompted by these reflections more than once since my return from Pennsylvania to propose to Your Excellency the propriety of selecting another commander for this army."

There was where the shock came in. Davis read on with mounting apprehension as Lee explained what had brought him to make this request. Moreover, the care with which he had chosen his words indicated plainly that the letter had not been written as a mere gesture, but rather with publication in mind, as the closing document of a career that had ended in failure and sadness, but not in bitterness or despair:

I have seen and heard of expression of discontent in the public journals at the result of the expedition. I do not know how far this feeling extends in the army. My brother officers have been too kind to report it, and so far the troops have been too generous to exhibit it. It is fair, however, to suppose that it does exist, and success is so necessary to us that nothing should be risked to secure it. I therefore, in all sincerity, request Your Excellency to take measures to supply my place. I do this with the more earnestness because no one is more aware than myself of my inability for the duties of my position. I cannot even accomplish what I myself desire. How can I fulfill the expectations of others? In addition I sensibly feel the growing failure of my bodily strength. I have not yet recovered from the attack I experienced the past spring. I am becoming more and more incapable of exertion, and am thus prevented from making the personal examinations and giving the personal supervision to the operations in the field which I feel to be necessary. I am so dull that in making use of the eyes of others I am frequently misled. Everything, therefore, points to the advantages to be derived from a new commander, and I the more anxiously urge the matter upon Your Excellency from my belief that a younger and abler man than myself can readily be obtained. . . .

I have no complaints to make of anyone but myself. I have received nothing but kindness from those above me, and the most considerate attention from my comrades and companions at arms. To Your Excellency I am specially indebted for uniform kindness and consideration. You have done everything in your power to aid me in the work committed to my charge, without omitting anything to promote the general welfare. I pray that your efforts may at length be crowned with success, and that you may long live to enjoy the thanks of a grateful people.

    With sentiments of great esteem,

I am very respectfully and truly yours,
R. E. LEE, General

Davis was dismayed. He had by now become reconciled to the permanent loss of some 15,000 of the South's best fighting men at Gettysburg, but if that defeat was also going to cost him Lee, who had held the North's main army at bay for more than a year and had provoked the removal of four of its commanders in the process, the loss might well be insupportable. Moreover, recent adversity East and West had drawn the two men even closer to one another, in their service to an imperiled cause, than they had been fifteen months ago in Richmond during a similar time of strain. Whether the nation could survive without Lee at the head of its first-line army Davis did not know, but he doubted that he himself could. "I need your counsel," he had written him earlier that week. Besides, for Davis, loyalty rendered was invariably returned, and Lee was not only personally loyal, he was also modest, magnanimous, and unselfish. Contrasting these qualities with those lately encountered in that other Virginian, that other Johnston — Joe — Davis could tell his ranking field commander: "Were you capable of stooping to it, you could easily surround yourself with those who would fill the press with your laudations, and seek to exalt you for what you had not done rather than detract from the achievements which will make you and your army the subject of history and object of the world's admiration for generations to come." Such words might serve to ease the sting of the lashings the journalists had been handing out. As for the general's failing health, this too could be set aside as no valid reason for resigning, Davis believed, even without the example of his own debilitation, which included loss of sight in one eye and searing pain that sometimes made the other almost useless. "I am truly sorry to know that you still feel the effects of the illness you suffered last spring, and can readily understand the embarrassment you experience in using the eyes of others, having been so much accustomed to make your own reconnaissances. Practice will however do much to relieve that embarrassment, and the minute knowledge of the country which you have acquired will render you less dependent for topographical information."

    These things he could and did say, along with much else, in an attempt to dissuade Lee from resigning and thus spare the nation the calamitous loss of his service in the field. Fully conscious of the importance of choosing the proper tone and phrasing, he spent two days studying the general's letter and composing his own thoughts by way of rebuttal. Then on August 11, incorporating the sentences quoted above, he wrote his answer:

> General R. E. Lee,
> Commanding Army of Northern Virginia:
> Yours of the 8th instant has been received. I am glad to find that you concur so entirely with me as to the want of our country in this trying hour, and am happy to add that after the first depression consequent upon our disasters in the West, indications have appeared that our people will exhibit that fortitude which we agree in believing is alone needful to secure ultimate success.
> It well became Sidney Johnston, when overwhelmed by a senseless clamor, to admit the rule that success is the test of merit, and yet there has been nothing which I have found to require a greater effort of patience than to bear the criticisms of the ignorant, who pronounce everything a failure which does not equal their expectations or desires, and can see no good result which is not in the line of their own imaginings. I admit the propriety of your conclusions, that an officer who loses the confidence of his troops should have his position changed, whatever may be his ability; but when I read the sentence I was not at all prepared for the application you were about to make. Expressions of discontent in the public journals furnish but little evidence of the sentiment of an army. . . .
> But suppose, my dear friend, that I were to admit, with all their implications, the points which you present, where am I to find that new commander who is to possess the greater ability which you believe to be required? I do not doubt the readiness with which you would give way to one who could accomplish all that you have wished, and you will do me the justice to believe that if Providence should kindly offer such a person for our use, I would not hesitate to avail of his services.
> My sight is not sufficiently penetrating to discover such hidden merit, if it exists, and I have but used to you the language of sober earnestness when I have impressed upon you the propriety of avoiding all unnecessary exposure to danger, because I felt our country could not bear to lose you. To ask me to substitute you by someone in my judgment more fit to command, or who would possess more of the confidence of the army or of the reflecting men in the country, is to demand of me an impossibility.
> It only remains for me to hope that you will take all possible care of yourself, that your health and strength may be entirely restored, and that the Lord will preserve you for the important duties devolved upon you in the struggle of our suffering country for the independence which we have engaged in war to maintain.
>
> As ever, very respectfully and truly yours,
> JEFFERSON DAVIS

After this, there was no more talk of Lee resigning. As long as the Army of Northern Virginia existed he would remain at its head.

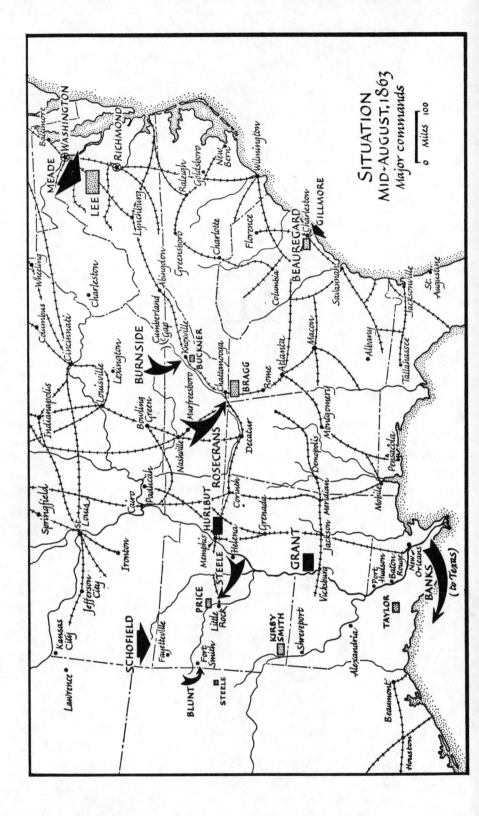

SITUATION
MID-AUGUST, 1863
Major commands

0 ___ 100 Miles

Riot and Resurgence

★ ✗ ☆

AS JUNE WORE ON, ROSECRANS AND HIS ARMY of the Cumberland approached the end of their six-month convalescence from the rigors of Stones River. The narrowness of his escape from total disaster on that field having convinced him more than ever of the wisdom of meticulous preparation — which, as he saw it, had made the hairbreadth difference between victory and defeat — he would no more respond to prodding now than he had done in the months leading up to that horrendous New Year's confrontation just short of Murfreesboro. Directly or indirectly, but mostly directly, Lincoln and Stanton and Halleck all three had tried their hand at getting him to move: to no avail. He would not budge, though he would sometimes agree blandly, as if for the sake of prolonging the argument, that an advance was highly desirable.

Immediately after Chancellorsville, for instance, when Stanton reported — quite erroneously — that Hooker had inflicted as many casualties as he suffered, Rosecrans replied: "Thanks for your dispatch. It relieves our great suspense. What we want is to deal with their armies. Piece for piece is good when we have the odds. We shall soon be ready here to try that." So he said. But May went by, and still he would not budge. "I would not push you to any rashness," Lincoln wrote, "but I am very anxious that you do your utmost, short of rashness, to keep Bragg from getting off to help Johnston against Grant." The Ohioan's answer was both prompt and brief: "Dispatch received. I will attend to it." But he did not. June came in, and still he would not budge. "If you can do nothing yourself," Halleck wired, "a portion of your troops must be sent to Grant's relief." Old Rosy was unperturbed by this threat of amputation. "The time appears now nearly ripe," he responded, "and we have begun a movement, which, with God's blessing, will give us some good results." He omitted, however, a definition of "nearly." June wore on; he would not budge. By June 16 Lincoln's patience was exhausted, and he had the general-in-chief put a point-blank question to the Middle Tennessee commander: "Is it your intention to make an immediate movement forward? A definite answer, yes or no, is required." Halleck asked for a yes or a no, but Rosecrans gave him both. "In reply to your inquiry," he wired back, "if immediate means tonight or tomorrow, no. If it means as soon as all things are ready, say five days, yes."

At any rate this fixed the jump-off day; Washington settled back to wait for word, June 21, that the Army of the Cumberland was in motion. What came instead, by way of anticlimax on that date, was another wire, so little different in substance from the many received before that the whole sheaf might have been shuffled and refiled, indiscriminate of sequence, with little or no disturbance of its continuity, since in point of fact it had none. Bulky though it was — Old Brains had already complained to Rosecrans of the strain his frequent telegrams had placed on the military budget — the file was not so much a series of pertinent dispatches as it was a loose collection of secondhand maxims designed to strengthen his brief for refusing to expose his troops to bloodshed. "We ought to fight here," he wired, "if we have a strong prospect of winning a decisive battle over the opposing force, and upon this ground I shall act. I shall be careful" he added, "not to risk our last reserve without strong grounds to expect success." It was exasperating, to say the least; for it was becoming increasingly apparent, on evidence supplied by himself, that what Old Rosy was doing was fighting a verbal holding action, not so much against the rebels in his front as against his own superiors in his rear. Lincoln's patience almost snapped again. Three days later, however — on June 24, in a telegram headed barely two hours after midnight — the longed-for word came through: "The army begins to move at 3 o'clock this morning. W. S. Rosecrans, Major General."

The "strong grounds" on which he based his expectation of success were twofold, logistical and tactical, and he had neglected no detail in either category. Logistically he had adopted what might be called a philosophy of abundance. His requisitions, submitted practically without remission, reflected a conviction that there simply could not be too much of anything. As long ago as mid-April, for example, one of his brigadiers had been awed by the sight, at the Murfreesboro depot, of 40,000 cases of hard bread stacked in a single pile, while there were also gathered roundabout, in orderly profusion, such quantities of flour, salt pork, vinegar, and molasses as the brigadier had never seen before; he marveled at the wealth and prodigality of the government he was defending. Nor was food by any means the commander's sole or even main concern. Operating as he would be in a region that called for long supply trains and numerous cavalry to guard them and protect the flanks and front of the infantry line-of-march, he had put in for and received since December 1 no fewer than 18,450 horses and 14,067 mules. Exclusive of culls, this gave him — or should have given him, according to the quartermaster general, when combined with the number shown on hand — a total of 43,023 animals, or about one for every two men in his army. Rosecrans did not consider this one beast too many, especially since he had evacuated some 9000 of them as unserviceable and was complaining even then that over a fourth of those remaining were worn out. So it went; he kept demanding more of everything. The same applied to men. He had, as of mid-June, a total of 87,800 effectives, a considerable preponderance when compared to his estimated total for Bragg of 41,680 of all arms. However, this left out of account the necessary garrisons for Nashville, Donelson, Clarksville, and other such vital places in his rear — including Murfreesboro itself, when move-out time came round — which reduced, or would reduce, his total to 65,137 strictly available for the offensive. That was still a preponderance, but it was scarcely a man too many, as he saw it, to assure him what he called "a strong prospect of winning a decisive battle over the opposing force." Moreover, to this would be added, as he had complained soon after the bloodletting at Stones River, multiple difficulties of terrain. "The country is full of natural passes and fortifications," he informed the impatient Washington authorities, "and demands superior forces to advance with any success."

Lacking what he considered strength enough to assure a victory as the result of any direct confrontation, he had decided to depend instead on guile, and with this approach to the problem he began to perceive that the tricky terrain of which he had complained in January could be employed to his advantage. Bragg had his infantry disposed along the near side of Duck River, two divisions at Shelbyville under Polk and two at Wartrace under Hardee, about twenty miles from Murfreesboro and roughly half that far from Tullahoma, his headquarters and supply base on the Nashville & Chattanooga Railroad leading down across Elk River and the Tennes-see, respectively twenty-five and sixty miles in rear of the present line of intrenchments north of the Duck. Just to the front of this line, and occupied by rebel outpost detachments, an almost mountainous ridge, broadening eastward into a high plateau, stood in the path of a direct advance by the superior blue force. Formerly Rosecrans had seen this as a barrier, further complicating the tactical problem Bragg had set for him, but presently he began to conceive of it

as a convenient screen, behind which he could mass his army for a surprise maneuver designed to turn the graybacks out of the works they had
spent the past five months improving. Four main passes, each accommo-
dating a road, pierced the ridge and gave access to the lush valley just beyond. In the center were Bellbuckle Gap, through which the railroad
ran, and Liberty Gap, a mile to the east, with a wagon road also leading
down to Wartrace. The remaining two gaps, Guy's and Hoover's, were
respectively six miles west and east of the railroad, the former accommo-
dating the Shelbyville pike and the latter the macadamized road from
Murfreesboro to Manchester, which was sixteen miles east of Wartrace
and twelve miles northeast of Tullahoma. It was in this tangled pattern
of gaps and roads, so forbidding at first inspection, that Rosecrans found
the answer to the problem Bragg had posed him.

He had no intention of advancing due south, through Bellbuckle
or Liberty Gap, for a frontal assault on the Confederate intrenchments,
which presumably was just what Bragg was hoping he would do. Nor
was it any part of his design to launch an isolated attack on either of the
rebel corps alone, since their positions were mutually supporting. His
plan was, rather, to outflank them, thereby obliging the graybacks to
come out into the open for a fight against the odds — or, better yet, to
throw them into headlong retreat by threatening their rear, either at
Tullahoma, where their supplies were stored, or somewhere else along
the sixty brittle miles of railroad leading down past the Alabama line.
This could be done, he figured, by forcing one of the outer gaps, Guy's
or Hoover's, and swinging wide around the western or eastern flank of
the rebel infantry. The western flank was favored by the terrain, which
was far more rugged to the east; but it also had the disadvantage of being
the more obvious, and therefore expected, approach. Then too, Polk's
was the stronger of the two enemy corps, Hardee's having been weakened by detachments sent to Johnston in Mississippi. Rosecrans weighed
the alternatives, one against the other, and chose the eastern flank. He
would send his main body, the two corps of Thomas and McCook,
southeastward through Hoover's Gap, then down the macadamized
road to Manchester, from which place he could lunge at Tullahoma, in
case the rebels remained in position north of the Duck, or continue his
march southeastward for a strike at some point farther down. By way of
initial deception, however, he would feint to the west, sending Granger's
corps through or around Guy's Gap and down the pike toward Shelbyville, thus encouraging his opponent to believe that it was there the
blow would land. Simultaneously — and here was where the deepest
guile and subtlety came in — he would feint to the east with Crittenden's
corps, through Bradyville toward McMinnville: with the difference that
this supplementary feint was intended to be recognized as such, thereby
convincing Bragg (who, he knew, took great pride in his ability to "see
through" all such tactical deceptions) that the main effort was certainly

in the opposite direction. . . . Looking back over the plan, now that he had matured and refined it during months of poring over maps and assembling supplies, meantime resisting impatient and unscientific proddings from above, Old Rosy was delighted with his handiwork. And indeed he had good cause to be pleased by the look of the thing on paper. If he reached the unfordable Tennessee before the rebels did, he would be between them and Chattanooga, his true goal, the capture of which he knew was one of Lincoln's fondest hopes; he could turn on the outnumbered and probably demoralized Bragg, who would be confined by necessity to the north bank of the river, and destroy him at his leisure. Or at its worst, if the Confederates somehow avoided being cut off from a crossing, he still would have driven them, brilliantly and bloodlessly, out of Middle Tennessee.

Secrecy being an all-important element of guile, he played his cards close to his vest. He said nothing of the particulars of his plan to either his subordinates or his superiors when, on June 16, he confided to the latter — prematurely, as it turned out — that he would advance in "say five days." Not even on June 24, in the telegram sent at 2.10 in the morning to announce that the army would be on the march within fifty minutes, did he say in what direction or strength the movement would be made. He was taking no chance on a Washington leak, even at that late hour, though of course his corps and division commanders had been informed of their share in the grand design and told to have their units deployed on schedule. Gordon Granger, with the one division remaining in his reserve corps after heavy detachments for garrison duty at Nashville and other points, began his march down the pike toward Shelbyville, preceded by a full division of cavalry, with instructions to kindle campfires on a broad front every night in order to encourage Polk, and therefore Bragg, to believe that this was the Federal main effort. Crittenden, one of whose three divisions remained on guard at Murfreesboro, began to execute the transparent feint eastward in the direction of McMinnville with the other two, preceded by a brigade of cavalry. George Thomas, whose four-division corps was much the largest in the army, took up the march for Hoover's Gap and Manchester, followed by Alex McCook, who had been told to make a disconcerting attack on Liberty Gap with one of his three divisions, thereby fixing Hardee in position at Wartrace, just beyond the gap, while Thomas circled his flank to threaten his rear. As usual, with Old Rosy in charge, no detail had been neglected. The foot soldiers were massed in their respective assembly areas, all ten divisions of them under carefully briefed commanders, and staff officers checked busily to see that all was as it should be, not only among the combat elements, but also in the rear echelon, including the various supply trains loaded with rations for twelve days. Nothing that could be calculated had been overlooked. Half the beef had been salted, for example, and loaded in wagons for ready distribution, while the other half was on the hoof: self-propelled, so to speak, for speed and ease of transportation.

Whereupon, just as the troops stepped out in the predawn darkness, beginning to weave the network of marches designed to accomplish Bragg's discomfiture, something uncalculated — indeed, incalculable — occurred. What Rosecrans later described as "one of the most extraordinary rains ever known in Tennessee at that period of the year" began to fall; "no Presbyterian rain, either," an Illinois soldier called it, "but a genuine Baptist downpour."

That was only the beginning. Crittenden afterwards maintained that, from this day forward, it "rained incessantly for fifteen days," and reports by lesser commanders bore witness to the difficulties involved. "Rain poured in torrents the entire night"; "Train not up in consequence of difficult traveling"; "Wet weather all day"; "Troops and animals much jaded." There was small comfort in knowing that the rain also fell on the rebels, but the men derived a kind of bitter satisfaction from the knowledge that they could learn to put up with almost anything. "It rained so much and so hard," one declared, "that we ceased to regard it as a matter of any consequence and simply stood up and took it, without attempting to seek shelter or screen ourselves in the least. Why should we, when we were already wet to the skin?" Besides, they had been heartened at the outset, before the fields and secondary roads were churned shin-deep in mud, by reports of a solid achievement that opened the way for the column under Thomas, who had been given the leading role in the present act of the drama Rosecrans was directing. More specifically, the accomplishment had been scored by Colonel John T. Wilder's brigade of Major General J. J. Reynolds' division.

It had been Wilder, a former Indiana industrialist, who surrendered Munfordville to Bragg, together with more than 4000 soldiers and 10 guns, as an incident of the Confederate advance into the Bluegrass region of Kentucky the previous September. The memory of that still rankled, and Wilder and his command, two regiments of fellow Hoosiers and two from Illinois, exchanged soon after their captors released them on parole — though not in time to fight at Perryville — were determined to make the rebels pay for that indignity. Just now they were in an excellent position to do so, for they were the lead element of the column that would deliver the main effort intended to throw Bragg into confusion. Moreover, they were superbly equipped for the work at hand, both in mobility and firepower, partly as a result of efforts by Rosecrans and partly as a result of efforts of their own. Short of cavalry, the army commander had mounted two of his infantry brigades, and one of these was Wilder's, who had also seen to it that his troops were armed with seven-shot Spencer carbines, the first unit in the West to be so accoutered. He had done this by signing a personal note upon which security bankers in his home town of Greensburg had advanced funds for purchase of the Spencers, the men having agreed to periodic deductions from their pay in order to reimburse their commander, pending their own reimbursement by the army once the red tape had been cleared away. So armed and mounted, 2000 strong, they left their camps above Murfreesboro at exactly 3 a.m. and by midmorning were herding enemy pickets into the northern mouth of Hoover's Gap, the prompt seizure of which was prerequisite to the success of the whole campaign. Wilder did not hesitate in fear of a trap or ambush, but plunged straight ahead through the three-mile-long pass with all the strength and speed he could muster, his mounted infantry driving the graybacks before them with the considerable help of their rapid-fire weapons. The works at the southern end of the gap were taken in a rush, together with the silk-embroidered colors of the 1st Kentucky Infantry, an elite Confederate outfit. Unlimbering their six guns, the Hoosiers and Prairie Staters broke up a savage counterattack and held the pass alone until the other two brigades of the division came plodding up to reinforce them, swinging their caps and cheering despite the rain. As a result of Wilder's daring and resolution, and at a relatively minor cost of 14 killed and 47 wounded, the way now lay open for an advance by Thomas around Hardee's flank and into his rear.

Bragg personally was not in good shape, either physically or mentally, for resisting the strain his opponent was about to apply as a test of his staunchness and perception. He had weathered the criticisms leveled at him by his chief subordinates, the steady depletion of his army by detachments ordered to Pemberton and Johnston, and the near-fatal illness of his wife, only to undergo a siege of boils which, by his own admission, had culminated in "a general breakdown" of his health by early summer. None of these troubles, particularly the last, had had the effect of sweetening his temper, lengthening his patience, or enabling him to abide the shortcomings of his associates, most of whom he considered unfit for their present duties. Unfortunately, too, these various woes and discomforts had served to increase, if anything, his accustomed savagery of looks and reflexes. "This officer in appearance is the least prepossessing of the Confederate generals," the ubiquitous Colonel Fremantle had recorded in his diary when he visited Bragg that spring, en route from Texas to Richmond. "He is very thin; he stoops; and has a sickly, cadaverous, haggard appearance; rather plain features, bushy black eyebrows which unite in a tuft on the top of his nose, and a stubby, iron-gray beard; but his eyes are bright and piercing. He has the reputation of being a rigid disciplinarian, and of shooting freely for insubordination. I understand he is rather unpopular on this account, and also by reason of his occasional acerbity of manner."

Not that the Tennessee commander lacked grounds for pride in what he and his men had accomplished during their sojourn in the lush

Duck River Valley. After all — though admittedly it was with the determined co-operation of an adversary who resisted all urgings to advance — he had held his ground and managed to feed and refit his badly outnumbered army in the process. "Our transportation is in fine condition," Polk was writing home, "horses and mules all fat, and battery horses and batteries in fine condition. The troops have plenty of clothes and are well shod. We have plenty of food also, and so far as the fields before us are any indication, there never was such a wheat harvest." Moreover, despite the permanent loss of some 6000 men at Murfreesboro and the detachment since of at least that many more, including Breckinridge's whole division, Bragg's mid-June strength of 46,250 effectives (for once in this war, at any rate, a Union commander had underestimated the force arrayed against him) was appreciably greater than it had been before New Year's. Primarily he had accomplished this by rigid enforcement of the conscription laws in the region threatened by a Federal advance, for he knew only too well that this might be his last chance to get at this particular reservoir of manpower, Davis having given him permission beforehand to fall back across the Tennessee as soon as he judged the pressure against his front to be insupportable. Rosecrans, however, for all his underestimation of Bragg's strength, had exerted almost no pressure at all in the past five months; so that Bragg had had ample opportunity to drill and condition his soldiers for the work that lay ahead. This was the sort of thing he did best, and the results had been gratifying. Even Fremantle, a product of the most rigid sort of training, admitted that the citizen soldiers "drilled tolerably well, and an advance in line was remarkably good." That was high praise indeed from an officer of the Coldstream Guards, though he could not repress a shudder on observing that some of the men had removed their jackets because of the heat and marched past the reviewing stand in shirt sleeves. When he expressed a desire to see them "form squares," he was told by his host that they had not been taught this maneuver, since "the country does not admit of cavalry charges, even if the Yankee cavalry had the stomach to attempt it." Similarly, he noted that the absence of the bayonet as a standard piece of equipment was a matter of small concern to the troops, "as they assert that they have never met any Yankee who would wait for that weapon." This last, of course, was far from true — as any stormer of the Hornets Nest or the Round Forest could have testified — but it was a measure of the men's high spirits that they made the claim to the credulous Englishman, who closed the account of his visit by remarking that "the discipline in this army is the strictest in the Confederacy."

    In round numbers, 32,000 infantry and artillery were with Polk and Hardee on the Shelbyville-Wartrace line, while 14,000 cavalry were with Wheeler and Forrest, strung out for thirty miles east and west, respectively, with headquarters at McMinnville and Columbia.

These 46,000 effectives, comprising the Army of Tennessee, did not include some 15,000 under Buckner, who was charged with the defense of Knoxville against Burnside. That general, what time he was not fulminating against the Copperheads in his rear, was known to be preparing for an advance by the Army of the Ohio, though he had been crippled even more sorely than Bragg by detachments sent to Mississippi. To help discourage the threat in that direction, and also to continue the harassment of his Middle Tennessee opponent's lines of supply, Bragg had recently agreed to a proposal by John Morgan that he stage another of his famous "rides" into Kentucky with his 2500 Bluegrass troopers. Nettled by the defeats suffered in late March and early April at Milton and Liberty — he had in fact accomplished nothing significant since his spectacular Christmas Raid, hard on the heels of his marriage to Mattie Ready — Morgan had sought permission to extend his field of operations beyond the Ohio River, for the double purpose of carrying the scourge of war into the heartland of the North and restoring the glitter to his somewhat tarnished reputation; but Bragg (unlike Lee, who assented, though with misgivings, to a somewhat similar proposal by Jeb Stuart that same week in Virginia, preliminary to his crossing of the Potomac) had withheld approval of this extension of the raid, not wanting the Kentuckian and his men to be too far away in case Rosecrans lurched into motion in their absence. As it turned out, however, when he received word from his outposts on June 24 that the Federals were indeed in motion, not only on the left and right but also against his center, Morgan was already beyond reach, and Bragg did not discover until some weeks later, along with news of the disastrous consequences, that the freewheeling cavalryman had simply disobeyed the restrictive portion of the orders he had received.

Just now, though, Bragg had troubles enough on his hands, without looking afield for others. Correctly identifying the movements on Bradyville and Guy's Gap as feints, he left Crittenden and Granger to the attention of Forrest and Wheeler, and concentrated instead on opposing with his infantry the more immediate danger to his front. On the 25th he counterattacked at Liberty Gap, which had fallen to McCook the previous evening. Hardee failed to drive the bluecoats from the pass but he did succeed in holding them there, and Bragg, encouraged by this, sent orders for Polk to advance next day through Guy's Gap, then swing east for a descent on the rear of the troops opposing Hardee. Polk, as usual, protested, and Bragg as usual insisted. He reversed himself that night, however, on learning that the column under Thomas was approaching Manchester, still preceded by Wilder's rapid-firing horseback infantry and followed by Crittenden, who had abandoned his feint toward McMinnville and turned south at Bradyville. There was nothing for it now, as Bragg assessed the situation, but to call off the proposed attack on Liberty Gap and fall back on Tullahoma to protect his base and his present flank and rear. This he did with all possible speed, though the going was heavy; Polk left Shelbyville early on the 27th and did not reach Tullahoma, eighteen muddy miles away, until late next afternoon, soon after Hardee completed his march down the railroad in the rain. At any rate Bragg's army now was concentrated, protected by works prepared in advance, and he was determined to give the Yankees battle there.

Once more Rosecrans was unco-operative. Having reached Manchester the day before, June 27, he spent a day replenishing supplies brought forward on the hard-surfaced pike, and then resumed his march, not toward Tullahoma, as Bragg expected, but southeastward as before, toward Hillsboro and Pelham, still threatening the railroad on which his adversary depended for subsistence. At a council of war held on the night of the 28th, when Polk expressed some uneasiness that the Federals would continue their previously successful tactics by circling the right flank, Bragg taunted him by asking: "Then you propose that we shall retreat?" The bishop did indeed. "I do," he said firmly, "and that is my counsel." Hardee was less positive; he thought perhaps protection of the rear could be left to the cavalry while the infantry fought in its present intrenched position, outflanked or not; Rosecrans might gain the Confederate rear only to find the Confederates in his own. Bragg adjourned the council without making any definite decision. He would await developments, he said.

Developments were not long in coming. Granger and McCook had occupied Shelbyville and Wartrace that same day, moving in behind the departed graybacks, and though Rosecrans had no intention of attacking Tullahoma from the north, the presence of these two divisions at the crossings of the Duck was a menace Bragg could not ignore. Meanwhile Thomas, with McCook's other two divisions in support and Crittenden close behind, continued his march from Manchester to Hillsboro, a dozen miles due east of Bragg's right flank, and sent Wilder's hard-riding foot soldiers — already dubbed "The Lightning Brigade" as a result of their rapid seizure of Hoover's Gap on the opening day of the campaign — ahead to Pelham for an independent crossing of Elk River and a strike at the railroad near Decherd or Cowan, twenty miles in rear of the rebel works at Tullahoma. High trestles over gorges along this mountainous stretch of the line presented inviting targets, since the destruction of even one of them would be about as effective, so far as the flow of supplies was concerned, as the destruction of them all. Wilder's men rode fast and hard, anticipating further revenge for the Munfordville indignity. Reaching Decherd on June 28, they attacked a small detachment of rebel guards and drove them from a stockade: only to discover that a railroad might be vulnerable in some ways, yet still be highly defensible in others. No less than six gray regiments of infantry, responding to a telegraphic summons from the guards, arrived suddenly aboard cars from up the line. The blue raiders had barely time to get away on their horses, avoiding capture by the superior force and contenting themselves with the wrecking of an alternate trestle near Winchester, on the branch line to Fayetteville. Next morning, after a fireless bivouac in the brush, they tried the main line again, this time below Cowan, but with similar results; the ultramobile Confederate infantry once more drove them off before they could inflict any serious damage. Wilder fell back toward Pelham, pausing near Sewanee to wreck another trestle on the branch line to Tracy City, then continued his withdrawal, hastened by the interception of information that Forrest was on his trail. Aided by a driving rain, which obliterated his tracks, he eluded his pursuers and rode back into Manchester at noon of the 30th. Though he had failed to carry out his primary assignment, which had been to interrupt traffic on the Nashville & Chattanooga by destroying one of its main-line trestles, he had at any rate demolished one on each of the two branch lines, east and west, and he reported proudly that he had done so without the loss of a single man on the three-day expedition deep in the enemy rear. Thankful for what he had done, rather than critical for what he had not done, both Thomas and Rosecrans praised him highly for his resourcefulness and daring.

So did Bragg, though indirectly, not so much in words as by reaction. Wilder's strike, deep in his rear, plus the presence of Thomas on his flank with eight divisions, convinced him at last that retreat was the wisest policy at this juncture. The two-day wait having gained him time for removal of his stores and heavy equipment, he issued orders on the last night of June for a withdrawal. At Decherd next day he asked his corps commanders for advice: "The question to be decided instantly [is] shall we fight on the Elk or take post at the foot of the mountain at Cowan?" Polk favored Cowan, but Hardee was more explicit. "Let us fight at the mountain," he advised. Bragg did neither. The retreat being under way, he preferred to continue it rather than risk a long-odds battle with the unfordable Tennessee immediately behind him. While the infantry plodded southward under the unrelenting rain, Forrest guarded the rear. On July 3, with Polk and Hardee safely across Sewanee Mountain and out of the unsprung trap Old Rosy had devised, Federal cavalry in heavy numbers forced the pass near Cowan, and as the rear-guard Confederate troopers fell back rapidly through the streets of the town a patriotic lady came out of her house and began reviling them for leaving her and her neighbors to the mercy of the Yankees. "You great big cowardly rascal!" she cried, singling out Forrest himself for attack, not because she recognized him (it presently was made clear that she did not) but simply because he happened to be handy; "why don't you turn and fight like a man instead of running like a cur? I wish old Forrest was here. He'd make you fight!" Old Forrest, as she called him, did not pause for either an introduction or an explanation, though later he joined in the laughter at his expense, declaring that he would rather have faced an enemy battery than that one irate female.

Bragg could find nothing whatever to laugh about in his present situation. He had saved his army, but at the cost of abandoning Middle Tennessee. Moreover, with every horseback mile a torture to his boils, he was nearer than ever to the physical breakdown of which he had spoken earlier, and when a solicitous chaplain remarked from the road-side that he seemed "thoroughly outdone," he replied: "Yes, I am ut-terly broken down." Nor did he deny that he had been outdone tacti-cally as well. "This is a great disaster," he confided dolefully, leaning from his saddle to whisper the words into the chaplain's ear.

Beyond Cowan he transferred to a railway car for less discomfort and more speed. After pausing at Bridgeport to send a dispatch notifying the Adjutant General of his retreat, he reached Chattanooga early on July 4, at about the same time his telegram reached Richmond, where it served as a forecast of even darker ones that followed at staggered in-tervals with the staggering information of what had occurred on that same day at Gettysburg, Helena, and Vicksburg. Meantime his army continued its withdrawal. Descending the slopes of the Cumberland Pla-teau, it entered the lovely Sequatchie Valley, then turned south along the right bank of the Tennessee for a crossing downstream at Bridge-port, just beyond the Alabama line. Here Forrest gave over his rear-guard duties to a brigade from Cheatham's division, which was charged with maintaining a temporary bridgehead to discourage pursuit, and crossed the river in the wake of the rest of the army on the night of July 6, just three days short of the anniversary of his crossing northward as the spearhead of the advance into Kentucky. After a year of march-ing nearly a thousand miles and fighting two great battles, both of which he claimed as victories though both were preludes to retreat, Bragg was back where he started.

Rosecrans was willing to leave him there for the present. At a cost of 570 casualties, including less than a hundred dead and barely a dozen missing, the Federals had captured no fewer than 1634 prisoners — many of them Middle Tennessee conscripts who came into the north-ern lines of their own accord, wanting no more of the war now that their homeland was no longer being fought for — and had inflicted, despite their role as attackers, about as many wounds as they had suffered. They were proud of themselves and proud of the chief who had planned and supervised the campaign that ended, so far as the foot soldiers were concerned, with Bragg's retreat across the Elk on July 2. On that day, having moved into the abandoned rebel works at Tullahoma, they set-tled down for the first true rest they had enjoyed since setting off in their predawn marches from Murfreesboro, nine days back. Rain and mud, short rations, and all too little sleep had been their portion all this time; "It would be hard to find a worse set of used-up boys," an Indiana infantryman confessed. But they were well enough rested, a few days later, to cheer heartily at the news of Vicksburg's fall. Tremendously set up by their own recent success in a campaign which even the enemy newspapers were already calling "masterful" and "brilliant," they figured that Chattanooga was next on the list, and they were ready to take it whenever Old Rosy gave the word.

✗ 2 ✗

In Washington, too, there was delight that the campaign had gone so well, although the fact that so much had been accomplished with so little bloodshed seemed rather to validate the opinion, urged for months, that the issue could have been forced much sooner to the same conclusion with a corresponding gain in time. The first discordant note, struck amid the general rejoicing, was sounded by Stanton on July 7 in a telegram informing Rosecrans that Vicksburg had fallen and that the Gettysburg attackers were in full retreat. "Lee's army overthrown; Grant victorious," the Secretary wired. "You and your noble army now have the chance to give the finishing blow to the rebellion. Will you neglect the chance?" Nettled that the goading thus was resumed almost before his weary men had time to catch their breath and scrape the mud from their boots and clothes — not to mention that the taunt preceded any official congratulations for an achievement which even the enemy had begun to refer to as masterful — Rosecrans managed, as was usual in such verbal fencing matches with his superiors, to give as good as, if not better than, he got. "You do not appear to observe the fact that this noble army has driven the rebels from Middle Tennessee," he replied on that same day. "I beg in behalf of this army that the War Department may not overlook so great an event because it is not written in letters of blood." Four days later, in hope of avoiding further prods and nudges of this kind, he listed for Halleck some of the difficulties he faced. These included the necessary replacement of a 350-foot railroad bridge across Duck River, as well as a long trestle south of there, the relaying of several miles of track, both on the main line down to Tullahoma and on the branch line out to Manchester and McMinnville, and the construction of new corduroy roads in order to get his wagon trains across the seas of mud. Then too, he noted, there was the problem of Burnside and his delayed advance on Knoxville, which would not only protect the flank of the Army of the Cumberland when move-out time came round, but would also complicate matters for the enemy on the opposite bank of the Tennessee. In short, Rosecrans wanted it understood by the general-in-chief and those with whom he was in daily contact, meaning Stanton and Lincoln, that "the operations now before us involve a great deal of care, labor, watchfulness, and combined effort, to insure the successful advance through the mountains on Chattanooga."

The result was that Halleck stepped up the prodding. "You must not wait for Johnston to join Bragg," he wired on July 24, "but must move forward immediately. . . . There is great dissatisfaction felt here at the slowness of your advance. Unless you can move more rapidly, your whole campaign will prove a failure." A confidential letter written that same day put the issue even more bluntly: "The patience of the authorities here has been completely exhausted, and if I had not repeatedly promised to urge you forward, and begged for delay, you would have been removed from your command." This was a familiar threat, and Rosecrans met it much as he had done before. "I say to you frankly," he replied on August 1, "that whenever the Government can replace me by a commander in whom they have more confidence, they ought to do so, and take the responsibility of the result." He followed this with an expanded list of the difficulties in his path, but once more with results quite different from the ones he had hoped to bring about. "Your forces must move forward without further delay," Halleck snapped back at him three days later. "You will daily report the movement of each corps till you cross the Tennessee River." Rosecrans could scarcely believe his eyes. But when he inquired, by return wire, "if your order is intended to take away my discretion as to the time and manner of moving my troops," Old Brains replied that this was precisely his intention: "The orders for the advance of your army, and that its movements be reported daily, are peremptory." On August 6, a Thursday, the Middle Tennessee commander started a dispatch with what seemed a definite commitment — "My arrangements for beginning a continuous movement will be completed and the execution begun by Monday next" — only to proceed at once to enlarge on the difficulties and to request either that the order be modified or else that he be relieved of his command. He may or may not have been bluffing; in any case it did not work. Halleck was relentless. "I have communicated to you the wishes of the Government in plain and unequivocal terms," he replied next day. "The object has been stated, and you have been directed to lose no time in reaching it. The means you are to employ, and the roads you are to follow, are left to your own discretion. If you wish to promptly carry out the wishes of the Government, you will not stop to discuss mere details."

Old Rosy had one string left to his bow: an out-of-channels appeal made early that month to Lincoln, in hopes that he would intervene on the side of the field commander. "General Halleck's dispatches imply that you not only feel solicitude for the advance of this army but dissatisfaction at its supposed inactivity," he had written, thus extending to the Commander in Chief an invitation to step into the argument with a denial that this was so. On August 10 — the "Monday next" which Rose-

crans had set as the date on which he would march, though he did not —
Lincoln replied at length. "I have not abated in my kind feeling for and
confidence in you," the letter began encouragingly, but then went into a
review of the anxiety the writer had felt because of the Middle Tennessee general's immobility while Bragg was sending troops to Johnston
for the relief of Vicksburg. As strategy, Lincoln added, this "impressed
me very strangely, and I think I so stated to the Secretary of War and
General Halleck." In the present case, moreover, he had doubts about
the wisdom of accumulating such vast amounts of food and equipment
as a prelude to the move on Chattanooga. "Does preparation advance at
all? Do you not consume supplies as fast as you get them forward? . . .
Do not misunderstand," he said in closing. "I am not casting blame
upon you. I rather think, by great exertion, you can get to East Tennessee. But a very important question is, Can you stay there? I make no
order in the case — that I leave to General Halleck and yourself." In other
words, he would not intervene. Old Rosy's bow was quite unstrung,
even though the President ended his letter with further expression of
his personal good will. "And now, be assured that I think of you in all
kindness and confidence, and that I am not watching you with an evil
eye. Yours very truly, A. Lincoln."

Having lost this ultimate appeal for a delay, Rosecrans finally
began his march on August 16. This time, the recuperative halt had lasted
not six months, as at Murfreesboro, but six weeks. It was time enough,
however, for his purpose. Now as then, once he got moving he moved
fast, with much attention to detail and much dependence on deception.

Burnside had begun his march on Knoxville the day before, after
similar difficulties with the Washington authorities were brought to a
head by a similar direct order for him to get moving, ready or not. In
point of fact, despite the impatience of those above him, he had had
excellent reasons for delay. First, when he was about to move in early
June he was stripped of his veteran IX Corps, which went to Vicksburg
under Parke. While waiting for its return he began assembling another,
composed of inexperienced garrison troops brought forward from such
places as Cincinnati, and sent a mixed brigade of 1500 cavalry and
mounted infantry under Colonel William P. Sanders to look into conditions beyond the mountainous bulge of the horizon. Sanders, a thirty-
year-old Kentucky-born West Pointer, set out on June 14, and in the
course of the next nine days he not only disrupted rebel communications
throughout East Tennessee, but also destroyed a number of bridges
along the vital Tennessee & Virginia Railroad, including a 1600-foot
span across the Holston River. He returned on June 23, elated by his success, which he reported was due in large part to the friendliness of natives
whose loyalty to the Union had not been shaken by more than two years
of waiting in vain for deliverance from Confederate oppression. Much

encouraged, Burnside might have set out then and there with his green corps — thus matching Old Rosy's advance on Tullahoma, which got under way next morning — except that it was at this point that John Hunt Morgan exploded in his rear, necessitating the employment of all his cavalry in a chase through the Copperhead-infested region north of the Ohio, which the raiders crossed near Brandenburg on the night of July 8 after a wild ride northward through Kentucky, capturing blue detachments as they went and provoking alternate reactions of fear and elation in the breasts of the loyal and disloyal in their path.

On July 2, about midway between Nashville and Barbourville, Morgan crossed the upper Cumberland with eleven regiments, 2460 men in all, and a section of rifled guns. Four of his five brothers rode with him, Calvin, Richard, Charlton, and Thomas, and his brother-in-law Colonel Basil Duke commanded the larger of his two brigades; so that the raid was in a sense a family affair. Indeed, in an even more limited sense, it was a private affair. His disobedience of Bragg's orders regarding a crossing of the Ohio, which he had intended from the start, was based on the conviction that no mere "ride," even if the itinerary included Louisville, Frankfort, and Lexington, would accomplish his objective of stopping Rosecrans or Burnside, who would simply let the Bluegrass region look out for itself while they marched south, respectively, through Middle and East Tennessee. On the other hand, a strike into Indiana and Ohio could not so easily be ignored, either by them or by their superiors, for political as well as military reasons. As for the danger, though admittedly it was great, Morgan thought it might not prove so extreme as it appeared. Boldness was sometimes its own best protection, as he had demonstrated often in the past, and this was the epitome of boldness. Once across the Ohio he intended to ride east, through or around Cincinnati, always keeping within reach of the river, which was reported to be seasonally low, for a recrossing into Kentucky whenever the pressure on the north bank grew too great. Or at the worst, if this maneuver proved impractical, he would continue east and north for a juncture with Lee in Pennsylvania and a return by easy stages to his proper theater of the war. This would be an affair not only for the history books and tactics manuals of the future, but also for the extension and enlargement of the legends and songs already being told and sung in celebration of earlier, lesser horseback exploits by Morgan and his "terrible" men: an inheritance, in short, to be handed down to Confederate patriots yet unborn, including the child his young wife was about to bear him down in Tennessee. And so it was; so it became; though not precisely in the form intended.

At least the beginning was propitious, the entry into Kentucky despite the presence of some 10,000 soldiers Burnside had posted along the Cumberland with instructions to prevent just that. The raiders penetrated the screen without encountering anything more substantial than a small detachment of cavalry beyond Burkesville, which they easily brushed aside. Late the following night, however, while taking a rest halt at Columbia, they heard bluecoats on the north bank of the Green preparing earthworks from which to challenge any attempt to cross the bridge. They were five companies of Michigan infantry, and next morning, not wanting to leave them active in his rear, Morgan sent in a demand for their surrender. "On any other day I might," the Federal colonel replied, smiling, "but on the Fourth of July I must have a little brush first." By way of testing his earnestness and the strength of his position, the raiders gave him what he sought: to their regret, for they were repulsed with a loss of 80 killed and wounded, out of less than 600 engaged, having inflicted fewer than 30 enemy casualties, most of whose hurts were superficial. Morgan crossed the river elsewhere, convinced by now that he should have done so in the first place, and pressed on through Campbellsville to camp that night near Lebanon, where he had his second fight next day. Here the challengers were a regiment of Union-loyal Kentuckians, whose colonel replied in the Wolverine vein to a note demanding instant capitulation. "I never surrender without a struggle," he said grimly. This time the attack was made by both Confederate brigades for a quick settlement of the issue, however bloody. After some savage house-to-house fighting, the Federals fell back to the railroad station, where they finally yielded under assault. More than 400 prisoners were taken, along with valuable medical supplies, again at a cost of about 80 casualties for the attackers. But for Morgan personally the price was steeper than any comparison of cold figures could possibly indicate. Tom, the youngest of the brothers with him, was killed in the final volley fired before the white flag went up. The four surviving brothers buried him in the garden of a sympathetic Lebanon preacher, then resumed their ride northward, though with much of the glory and all of the gladness already gone from the raid for them.

In Bardstown on July 6, hoping to throw his pursuers off his trail, Morgan feinted simultaneously north and east by sending fast-riding columns toward Louisville and Harrodsburg, but swung the main body westward through Garnettsville to Brandenburg, where an advance detachment seized two small steamers for crossing the wide Ohio. This was accomplished between noon and midnight, July 8, despite some interference from a prowling Union gunboat that hung around, exchanging shots with the two rebel guns, till it ran out of ammunition. Their crossing completed, the raiders burned the steamers against the Indiana bank and pushed on six miles northward before halting for what little was left of the night. As they approached the town of Corydon next morning they found a sizable body of Hoosier militia drawn up to contest their entrance. Not wanting to take time to go around them, Morgan decided to go through them; which he did, scattering the home guardsmen in the process — they suffered a total of 360 casualties, of whom 345 were listed as missing — but at a cost to himself of 8 men killed and 33 wounded. Nor was that the worst of it. Taking the midday meal at a Corydon hotel, he learned from the innkeeper's daughter that Lee had been whipped six days ago at Gettysburg and was on his way back to Virginia. This meant that Morgan's alternate escape plan, involving a hookup with the invaders in Pennsylvania, was no longer practical, if indeed it had ever been. Apparently undaunted, he pressed on northward, that day and the next, through Palmyra to Salem, just over forty air-line miles from the Ohio and less than twice that far from Indianapolis. The Indiana capital was in a turmoil, its celebration of the great double victory at Gettysburg and Vicksburg brought to an abrupt and woeful end by news that Morgan was over the river with 10,000 horsemen and on his way even now to capture and sack the city. Church and fire bells rang the alarm, and a crowd turned out in front of the Bates House to hear Governor Morton read the latest dispatches. More than 60,000 citizens responded throughout the state to his appeal for militia volunteers, as many as possible of those who were immediately available being posted along the southern outskirts of the capital, toward Martinsville and Franklin, with orders to stop the gray raiders at all costs.

But they were not coming that way after all. Morgan had veered east from Salem on July 10, through Vienna to Lexington, where he allowed himself, if not his companions, the luxury of a night's rest in a hotel — and narrowly avoided, as it turned out, the ignominy of being captured in bed by a detachment of blue troopers who rode up to the building while he slept, then fell back hastily when his orderly gave the alarm, never suspecting the prize that lay within their grasp. Doubling the column to regain the lead, the Kentucky brigadier took up a zigzag course next day, through Paris and Vernon, for a small-hours halt at Dupont. Back in the saddle by dawn of the 12th, he rode that night into Sunman, fifteen miles short of the Indiana-Ohio line, which he crossed next day into Harrison, barely twenty miles from downtown Cincinnati. With Vicksburg lost, Lee defeated, and Bragg in full retreat, his purpose was no longer to cut railroads, wreck supply dumps, or even disrupt communications — except, of course, to the extent that such depredations would serve to confuse his pursuers — but simply to stretch out the expedition and thus prolong the inactivity of Burnside, who could not advance on Knoxville, in conjunction with Rosecrans' advance on Chattanooga, until his cavalry rejoined him. Morgan's proper course, in line with this reduced objective, was to move rapidly, appear suddenly at unexpected points, and then slip away before the superior forces combined against him could involve him in time-consuming fights that would only serve to exhaust his men and horses. Yet there was the rub. In the past ten days he had covered nearly 400 miles, including the crossing of three major rivers, at a cost of some 500 casualties and stragglers. Men and horses were beginning to break down at an alarming rate, just as he was about to call on them for even more strenuous exertions. However, he had no choice in the matter. What had begun as a raid, a foray as of a fox upon a henhouse, had turned into a foxhunt — and, hunting or hunted, Morgan was still the fox. He pressed on, southeastward now, in the direction of Cincinnati and the Ohio, which he was obliged to keep close on his right for a crossing in case he was cornered.

Down to fewer than 2000 men, he rode fast that night through the northeast suburbs of Cincinnati, not wanting to risk their dispersion in the labyrinth of its streets or to expose them to the temptations of its downtown bars and shops, overburdened as some of them were already with plunder they had gathered along the way. He did not call a halt for sleep until the column reached Williamsburg late that afternoon, some two dozen miles beyond the city, having covered no less than ninety miles in the past day and a half. Next morning, July 15, Morgan was feeling confident and expansive as his troopers took up the march. "All our troubles are now over," he told his staff, anticipating a three-day ride by easier stages to the fords upstream from Buffington, which he had had reconnoitered by scouts before he left Tennessee and which had been reported as an excellent point for a crossing back into Kentucky. While he traversed the southern tier of Ohio counties, through or around Locust Grove, Jasper, and Jackson, newspaper editors in his rear recovered sufficiently from their fright to begin crowing. "John Morgan's raid is dying away eastward," the Chicago *Tribune* exulted, "and his force is melting away as it proceeds. Their only care is escape and their chances for that are very slight." This was on July 16, and two days later the editor felt spry enough to manage a verbal sally. "John Morgan is still in Ohio," he wrote, "or rather is in Ohio without being allowed to be still."

It was true; Morgan was still in Ohio, delayed by militiamen quite as determined as the Hoosiers he had encountered on his first day on northern soil. Bypassing Pomeroy that morning, 150 miles east of Cincinnati, he had had to call a halt at Chester, just beyond, to wait for stragglers: with the result that the head of the column did not approach the river above Buffington until well after dark. Here he received his worst shock to date. Swollen by two weeks of rain, the Ohio was on an unseasonal boom, and the fords — if they could be called that, deep as they were — were guarded by 300 enemy infantry who had been brought upstream on transports, together with two guns which they had emplaced on the north bank, covering the approaches to the shallowest of the fords. Moreover, if transports could make it this far upriver, so could gunboats; which was something the general had not counted on. Deciding to wait for daylight before attacking, he gave his men some badly needed sleep, then sent two regiments forward at dawn, only to discover that the bluecoats had abandoned their position in the darkness, tumbling their guns into the river unobserved and leaving the crossing unguarded for most of the night. However, there was no time for crimination or even regret for this lack of vigilance on the part of the scouts; for just then two things happened, both calamitous. A gunboat rounded the lower bend, denying the raiders access to the ford, and heavy firing broke out at the rear of the long gray line of weary men on weary horses. Two heavy columns of Federal cavalry, 5000 strong and well rested, had come up from Pomeroy after an overnight boat ride from downstream and had launched an immediate all-out attack on the raiders, who were wedged in a mile-long valley beside the swollen river, awaiting their turns at a ford they could not use. Morgan reacted with his usual quick intelligence, leading the head of the column out of the unblocked northern end of the narrow valley while the rear guard did what it could to fight off the attackers. But resistance quickly crumpled and the withdrawal became a rout. He was fortunate, under the circumstances, to lose no more than half of his command, including 120 killed or wounded and some 700 captured — Duke and two more of the Morgan brothers, Richard and Charlton, were among the latter — together with both of his guns and such of his wagons as had managed to keep up. One of these belonged to an old Tennessee farmer who had intended to trade for a load of salt at Burkesville, then return to his home on Calf-killer Creek, near Sparta. Unable to turn back for lack of an escort, he had stayed with the column, and now he found himself in far-off Ohio, beside an alien river, with Yankee troopers charging full-tilt at him and shooting as they came. Exhausted though he was, and badly frightened, he delivered extemporaneously one of the great, wistful speeches of the war. "Captain," he said to an officer standing beside him amid the twittering bullets, "I would give my farm in White County, Tennessee, and all the salt in Kentucky, if I had it, to stand once more safe and sound on the banks of Calf-killer Creek."

So would the thousand survivors who got away from Buffington with Morgan have liked to be back on their farms in Tennessee and Kentucky; but that was not to be, at least not soon, except for some 300 who made it across the river that afternoon at Blennerhassett's Island, a few miles below Parkersburg, West Virginia. The ford was deep, the current swift, and a number of riders and their mounts were swept away and drowned. Moreover, the crossing had scarcely begun when the gunboat reappeared from below, guns booming, and slammed the escape hatch shut. In midstream aboard a powerful horse, Morgan himself could have made it across, yet he chose instead to return to the north bank and stay with the remaining 700 to the bitter end of what, from this point on, was not so much a raid as it was a frantic attempt to avoid capture by the greatly superior forces converging from all points of the compass upon the dwindling column of graybacks. Northward they rode, through Eagleport and across the Muskingum River, twisting and turning for six more days, still following the right bank of the Ohio in search of another escape hatch. But there was none; or at any rate there was none that was not blocked. On July 26, down to fewer than 400 now because of the increasing breakdown of their horses, the survivors were brought to bay at Salineville, on Beaver Creek, near New Lisbon, and there — just off the tip of West Virginia's tiny panhandle, less than a hundred miles from Lake Erie and only half that far from Pittsburgh — Morgan and the 364 troopers still with him laid down their arms. In the thirty days since leaving Sparta on June 27, they had ridden more than 700 miles, averaging twenty hours a day in the saddle from the time they crossed the Ohio, and though they met with disaster in the end, they had at least accomplished their primary objective of preventing an early march southward by Burnside, in conjunction with Rosecrans' advance on Tullahoma, which would have made Bragg's retreat across the Tennessee a far more difficult maneuver than the unharassed withdrawal it actually was.

Morgan and his chief lieutenants, captured at Salineville and elsewhere, were brought in triumph back to Cincinnati, where Burnside pronounced them ineligible for parole. Nor was that the worst of it. Acting on misinformation that Abel Streight had been so treated after his capture in Alabama three months earlier, the authorities ordered that the Ohio raiders were to be confined in the State Penitentiary at Columbus for the duration of the war. And there they were lodged before the month was out. "My sleep was very much disturbed," a Kentuckian recorded in his diary, "by the terrible impression made upon my mind by our confinement in such a place." It was, he said, "enough to shock the sensibilities of any refined gentleman." Now that Burnside had his hands on Morgan he was taking no chance whatever of his escaping. All visitors were denied access to the prisoners, even the general's mother, presumably on the suspicion that she might smuggle in a bustle full of hacksaws. Hardest of all for them to bear, however, was the indignity of being dressed in convict clothes and shorn of their hair and beards. This last was the ultimate in inhumanity, according to one of the four reunited Morgan brothers, who had the full horror of war brought home to him by the loss of his mustache and imperial. Presently Governor Tod himself tendered what one of the captives called "a most untimely apology for an outrageous and disgraceful act." The shearing had been an administrative error, the governor explained, but Morgan's brother Charlton expressed a harsher opinion of the action. "The entire world will stamp it as disgraceful to this nation and the present age," he fervently protested.

Pleased with the capture and prompt disposition of the raiders — and encouraged as well, although it scarcely bore out his previous contention that they had been waiting for just such a treacherous chance, by the failure of the Copperheads to come to the aid of these outlaws deep in his rear — Burnside ordered his cavalry to rejoin the three divisions of infantry marking time all this while on the line of the Cumberland, gave them a couple of weeks to rest and get their horses back in shape, and then came forward himself in mid-August to direct in person the maneuver he had devised, under pressure from Washington, for delivering East Tennessee from the grip of the rebels under Buckner. Like Rosecrans, who was to advance simultaneously on his right, he counted heavily on deception to offset the disadvantages of terrain, and in this connection, by way of increasing his opponent's confusion and alarm, he had resolved to make his approach march in four columns. Two were of cavalry, one to advance on the left through Big Creek Gap and the other on the right through Winter's Gap, while the third, made up of two divisions of infantry, marched between them on Kingston, which lay at the confluence of the Clinch and Tennessee rivers, forty miles below Knoxville, the objective of all three columns. The fourth, composed of the remaining infantry division, would move directly on Cumberland Gap, which the Federals had taken in June of 1862 and then been obliged to abandon when Bragg and Kirby Smith outflanked it on their way to Kentucky, a year ago this month, and which was occupied now by a garrison of about 2500 graybacks, well entrenched, heavily armed, and amply supplied with provisions for a siege. Burnside had some 24,000 effectives in all, a comfortable preponderance; but the way was long, the roads steep, and the adversary tricky. Consequently, he planned carefully and gave his full attention to details, substituting pack mules for wagons in his trains, for instance, and mounting the lead regiments of both infantry columns so that they would set a fast pace for the troops who slogged along behind them. Learning at the last minute that his long-lost IX Corps veterans were finally on the way to rejoin him, though sadly decreased by casualties and sickness in the Mississippi lowlands — the two divisions, in fact, were down to about 6000 men between them — he decided not to wait. They could join him later, after they had rested, got the fever out of their bones, and been brought back up to strength. Besides, having planned without them and waited all this time in vain for their return, he preferred to move without them. And once he got moving he moved fast, with a march that matched the mid-November performance of the Army of the Potomac when he shifted it from the upper to the lower Rappahannock by way of preparation for the mid-December nightmare at Fredericksburg, which had haunted him, waking or sleeping, ever since.

This time it was otherwise. Though the two marches were alike in the sense that he encountered no opposition en route, this one differed profoundly in that he encountered none at the end, either. Reaching Kingston on September 1, unchallenged, he entered Knoxville with the infantry main body two days later, to find that the mounted column that had proceeded by way of Winter's Gap had arrived the day before.

Buckner had pulled out, bag and baggage, abandoning everything east of Loudon and west of Morristown, except Cumberland Gap, which the one-division column was attacking from the north. Delighted by his first large-scale victory since Roanoke Island, nineteen months ago, Burnside made a triumphal entrance at the head of the two-division column, September 3, and was hailed by the joyous citizens as their deliverer from oppression; "a rather large man, physically," an observer noted, "about six feet tall, with a large face and a small head, and heavy side-whiskers." These last added considerably to the over-all impression of the general as "an energetic, decided man, frank, manly, and well educated." He was, in brief, what was called a show officer. "Not that he *made* any show," the witness added; "he was naturally that."

Discontent with anything less than the whole loaf, he left two thirds of his infantry and cavalry to maintain his grip on Knoxville and that vital stretch of the only railroad directly connecting the rebel East and West, and set out three days later with the rest for Cumberland Gap, where the garrison still held out. He covered sixty miles of mountainous road in two days and four hours, completing the investment from the south as well as the north, and on the day of his arrival, September 9, forced the unconditional surrender of the 2500 defenders, together with all their equipment and supplies, including fourteen guns. Hearing next day from Rosecrans that Bragg was in full retreat upon Rome, Georgia, Burnside assumed that everything was under control in that direction; he turned his attention eastward instead, intending to complete his occupation of East Tennessee, to and beyond the North Carolina line, and to seize, by way of lagniappe, the important Confederate saltworks near Abingdon, Virginia. After a long season of blight and personal disappointment, he had rediscovered the heady delight of victory, and he was hard after more of the same.

With as little bloodshed — which, in effect, meant none at all — Rosecrans had marched on as rigid a schedule, over terrain no less forbidding, to accomplish as much against more seasoned defenders of an even tougher objective. For him too, once he got started, speed and dexterity were the keynotes. His army completed its crossing of the Tennessee on September 4, the day after Burnside rode into Knoxville, and five days later — September 9, the day Cumberland Gap came back into Union hands — he occupied Chattanooga, long recognized as the gateway to the heartland of the South, whose seizure Lincoln had said a year ago was "fully as important as the taking and holding of Richmond." Not only were many Confederates inclined to agree with this assessment, but they also considered the fall of one to be quite as unlikely as the fall of the other. On the face of it, in fact, the western bastion seemed to them the stronger of the two. Though it lacked the protective genius of Lee, it had its geographical compensations, such as the Tennessee

River to serve as a moat and the surrounding mountains and ridges to serve as ramparts in its defense, both of them the gift of God himself. "I tell you," a high-ranking Deep South officer later told a Federal correspondent, "when your Dutch general Rosencranz commenced his forward movement for the capture of Chattanooga, we laughed him to scorn. We believed that the black brow of Lookout Mountain would frown him out of existence, that he would dash himself to pieces against the many and vast natural barriers that rise all around Chattanooga, and that then the northern people and the government at Washington would perceive how hopeless were their efforts when they came to attack the real South."

In determining a solution to the problem during his six-week halt at Tullahoma and McMinnville, on the northwest side of the Cumberland Plateau, Rosecrans had reached deeper than ever into the bag of tricks that was always part of his military luggage. Bragg had Polk's corps disposed for a close-up defense of the city and Hardee's off to the east, protecting the railroad to Cleveland and beyond, while Wheeler's cavalry guarded the river crossings below and Forrest's those above. The obvious Federal strategy called for a movement toward the left, the better to make contact with Burnside. But this would not only take the army across the Sequatchie River and over Walden's Ridge, away from its railroad supply line back to Nashville; it also had the disadvantage of being expected, with Bragg already half deployed to meet it. The alternative was a move to the right for a crossing downstream, in the vicinity of the new forward supply base at Stevenson, and this was the one Old Rosy chose. It too would have its drawbacks, once he was over the river, since it would give him a longer way to go and three steep ridges to cross before he got to Chattanooga; but the reward would be correspondingly great. That way, with skill and luck, he might trap Bragg's whole army in its city fortress beside the river to the north, much as Grant had trapped Pemberton's at Vicksburg. Or if Bragg grew alert to the danger in his rear and fell back southward, down the line of the Western & Atlantic Railroad to Dalton or Rome, Rosecrans might catch him badly strung out and destroy him. However, if either of these aims was to be accomplished, it was necessary meanwhile to keep his opponent's attention fixed northward or northeastward, for the double purpose of making an undelayed crossing well downstream and a rapid march eastward, across the ridges in Northwest Georgia, to gain the rebel commander's rear before he became aware of what was looming. And here again was where guile and deception came in.

Keeping his main body well back from the river to screen his true intention, he demonstrated upstream with three brigades. Every night they lighted bonfires in rear of all possible crossings, from opposite Chattanooga itself clear up to Washington, a distance of forty miles, and while special details sawed the ends from planks and threw the scraps into creeks flowing into the Tennessee, others pounded round the clock on empty barrels in imitation of shipyard workers, thereby encouraging rebel scouts across the way to report that boats were being constructed for an amphibious assault somewhere along that stretch of the river. On August 21, by way of adding punch to the show, a battery went into action on Stringer's Ridge, directly across from the city, throwing shells into its streets and scoring hits on two steamboats at its wharf, one of which was sunk and the other disabled. Bragg's reaction was to withdraw the brigade from the north-bank bridgehead he had been holding all this time near Bridgeport, fifty miles downstream, and before the week was out a crossing by the mass of the blue army was underway in that vicinity: by Thomas at Bridgeport itself, where pontoons were thrown in replacement of the burned railroad bridge: by McCook, twelve miles below at Caperton's Ferry: and by Crittenden, ten miles above at Shellmound, which was twenty air-line miles due west of Chattanooga and twice that far by river. None of the three met any substantial resistance, so well had the upstream deception served its purpose. Except for Granger's one-division reserve corps, on guard at the Stevenson depot of supplies, and the three detached brigades, which kept making threatening gestures to fix Bragg's attention northward, Rosecrans had his whole army across the Tennessee by September 4, including all his artillery and trains loaded with ammunition enough for two great battles and rations for better than three full weeks, in case he remained that long out of touch with his base on the north bank. The main thing, as he saw it, was to keep moving and move fast. And that he did.

It took some doing, for the terrain was rugged; but Old Rosy had planned for that as well, directing the formation of company-sized details equipped with long ropes for hauling guns and wagons up difficult grades when the mules faltered. Perpendicular to his line of march, the three lofty ridges — actually long, narrow mountains, with deep valleys intervening — were Raccoon Mountain, Lookout Mountain, and Missionary Ridge. Lookout, which extended all the way to the bend of the river just below Chattanooga, was penetrated by only two gaps: Stevens Gap, 18 miles southwest of the city, and Winston Gap, 24 miles farther down. Rosecrans planned to use them both for a fast march eastward, sending Crittenden directly along the railroad, around the sheer north face of the mountain and into the city, which Bragg would probably evacuate when he learned that the other two corps were moving through the passes in his rear — McCook by way of Winston Gap, then around the lower end of Missionary Ridge, toward Alpine and Summerville, and Thomas by way of Stevens Gap, which also pierced Missionary Ridge within a dozen miles of LaFayette — for a blow at his vital and vulnerable rail supply line from Atlanta. Here again there were drawbacks, theoretical ones at any rate. The two outer columns, Crittenden's and McCook's, would be more than forty miles apart, and neither would be within a day's march of Thomas in the center; Bragg might concentrate and strike at any one of the isolated three. But this too had been foreseen and guarded against by sending all but one brigade of the cavalry with McCook — who seemed most susceptible in that regard, being on the remoter flank — while the remaining brigade preceded Crittenden, ready to give warning in case such a threat developed. The main thing was speed, and this assured just that. Rosecrans rode with the trooperless middle column, not only to keep in closer touch with all three of his chief lieutenants, but also to act as a goad to Thomas, who had many admirable qualities but was known to be somewhat lethargic on occasion.

Proud in the knowledge that they were the first Federals to penetrate this region since the beginning of the war, the men reacted with enthusiasm to the march, particularly when they saw spread out before them such vistas as the one unrolled from atop Raccoon Mountain. "Far beyond mortal vision extended one vast panorama of mountains, forests, and rivers," an Illinois veteran later wrote. "The broad Tennessee below us seemed like a ribbon of silver; beyond rose the Cumberlands, which we had crossed. The valley on both sides was alive with the moving armies of the Union, while almost the entire transportation of the army filled the roads and fields along the Tennessee. No one could survey the grand scene on that bright autumn day unmoved, unimpressed with its grandeur and the meaning conveyed by the presence of that mighty host." Presently word came from Crittenden that Bragg had apparently had a similar reaction to the presence of all those bluecoats in his rear; for when the Kentuckian drew near Chattanooga on September 8 he learned that the Confederates were in mid-evacuation, and next morning, as the tail of the gray column disappeared through Rossville Gap and behind the screen of Missionary Ridge, the city fell without the firing of a shot. Rosecrans passed the word to the troops of the central column, who did their best to rock Lookout with their cheers as they slogged through Stevens Gap.

Simultaneously, scores of butternut deserters began to filter into the Union lines with reports of Bragg's demoralization. He was in full flight for Rome or perhaps Atlanta, they declared, quite unmanned by this latest turning movement and in no condition to resist an attack if one could be thrown at him before he got there. Convinced that he had acted wisely in accepting the risk of dispersion for the sake of speed, Old Rosy urged his cheering soldiers forward, intent on giving the panic-stricken rebels what the deserters said would amount to a coup de grâce.

★   ★   ★

Rosecrans was partly right about Bragg, but only up to a point a good way short of the whole truth. The Confederate commander had been outsmarted, and he had fallen back in haste, even in some disorder, to escape the closing jaws of the Federal trap; but that was as far as it went. He was not retreating now, nor was he avoiding a fight. Rather, he was in search of one, although on different terms, having by now devised a trap of his own. As for the butternut scarecrows who had come stumbling into the northern lines, peering nervously over their shoulders and babbling of demoralization in the fleeing press of comrades left behind, Old Rosy would have done well to bear in mind some words one of his young staffers wrote years later: "The Confederate deserter was an institution which has received too little consideration.... He was ubiquitous, willing, and alto-

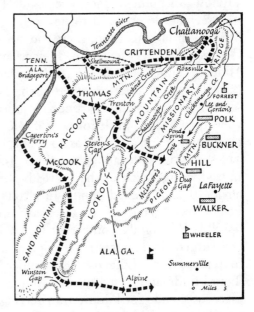

gether inscrutable. Whether he told the truth or a lie, he was always equally sure to deceive. He was sometimes a real deserter and sometimes a mock deserter. In either case he was sure to be loaded." In the present instance, a considerable number of them were indeed "loaded," being scouts sent forth by Bragg himself, who had chosen them for their ability to be convincing in misrepresentation of the true state of affairs in the army that lay in wait for the exuberant bluecoats, just beyond the last of the screening ridges.

Bragg's present aggressiveness had come only after six weeks of uncertainty and confusion following his retreat across the Tennessee. Hearing from Adjutant General Cooper on August 1 that the government was anxious to reinforce him with most of Johnston's army, on condition that he recross the river for an attack on Rosecrans, he replied next day that he was willing, provided "a fight can be had on equal terms." But three days later he withdrew the offer. "After fully examining all resources," he wired, "I deem them insufficient to justify a movement across the mountains." He meant the Cumberland Plateau, which he had just traversed and which by then was serving Rosecrans as a screen to hide his preparations for pursuit. He did not like having it there at all; he wished it could be abolished. "It is said to be easy to defend a mountainous country," he complained to one of his corps commanders, "but mountains hide your foe from you, while they are full of gaps through which he can pounce upon you at any time. A mountain is like the wall of a house full of rat holes. The rat lies hidden at his hole, ready to pop out when no one is watching. Who can tell what lies hidden behind that wall?" Respectfully, while in this frame of mind, he informed Richmond that he declined to plunge his army into "a country rugged and sterile, with a few mountain roads only by which to reach a river difficult of passage. Thus situated," he explained, "the enemy need only avoid battle for a short time to starve us out." But he added, by way of final encouragement: "Whenever he shall present himself on this side of the mountains the problem will be changed."

On the strength of this last, though disappointed that Bragg was unwilling to take the offensive, the authorities decided to reinforce him anyhow. In point of fact, even aside from the evidence that Joe Johnston seemed determined to do nothing with the troops standing idle in Mississippi all this time, they had no choice; repulses or surrenders at Gettysburg and Vicksburg, Helena and Port Hudson, plus the loss of Middle Tennessee and Morgan's raiders, all within a single month, had caused them to question whether the South could survive another large-scale defeat this soon, particularly one that would swing ajar the gateway to its heartland. Informed of Richmond's decision, Bragg set about reorganizing his army so as to incorporate without delay the new brigades and divisions about to join or rejoin him from various directions. Indeed, reorganization had already begun on a limited scale. Hardee having been detached in mid-July to take over the mutinous remnant of Pemberton's band of parolees awaiting exchange at Demopolis, the irascible and highly competent D. H. Hill, promoted to lieutenant general subject to congressional approval, had come from North Carolina to replace him. Likewise the dapper and experienced, if disgruntled, Tom Hindman arrived in mid-August from the Transmississippi, and a place was made for him by transferring the less distinguished Withers to an administrative post in his native Alabama. Soon afterwards Buckner was ordered to evacuate Knoxville, and having moved southwest to Loudon, where he burned the railroad bridge across the Tennessee, he continued his march to the Hiwassee, less than forty miles from Chattanooga. There he stopped, for the time being, under orders to contest an advance by Burnside, if one developed, and stand ready to join Bragg on short notice if one did not. By that time Breckinridge had arrived with the first of two divisions being sent from Mississippi. He rejoined his old corps, formerly Hardee's, and Major General A. P. Stewart's division was detached from Hill to be combined with Buckner's and thus form a new third corps under the Kentuckian, who was summoned from the Hiwassee, Burnside having turned his attention elsewhere. When W. H. T. Walker joined Bragg with the second of the two divisions from Johnston, another division was organized by detaching and combining brigades from divisions already present, thus providing a fourth corps under his command. Practically overnight — that is, within a ten-day period extending from late August into early September — the Army of Tennessee had grown from two to four corps, each with two divisions, and a total strength of about 55,000 effectives, including cavalry.

Having in these eight infantry divisions 26 brigades with which to oppose 33 brigades in the eleven Federal divisions — considerably better odds, after all, than the ones he had prevailed against at Murfreesboro — Bragg developed, in the course of the reorganization of his expanded army, strong hopes of being able to defeat his adversary in pitched battle. He was not so sure, however, that this was what it would come to here, any more than it had at Tullahoma, where he had been outmaneuvered and given no real chance to defend a position he had been determined not to yield without a fight. In fact, there were signs that it would not. All this time Rosecrans had been demonstrating as if for a crossing well above Chattanooga, a repetition of the strategy that had won him Middle Tennessee, and Bragg had been reacting fretfully. Harvey Hill, for one, was quite unfavorably impressed. The junior lieutenant in Bragg's battery a dozen years ago in Texas — George Thomas, now commanding a blue corps across the way, and John Reynolds, recently killed at Gettysburg, were the other two lieutenants — Hill had looked forward to the reunion at Chattanooga, but was received with none of the warmth he had expected from his chief. "He was silent and reserved and seemed gloomy and despondent," Hill said later of his fellow North Carolinian. "He had grown prematurely old since I saw him last, and showed much nervousness." Moreover, as the newcomer learned from those who had been with the army all along, this was not entirely due to worry about his opponent on the far side of the river. "His relations with his next in command (General Polk) and with some others of his subordinates were known to be not pleasant. His many retreats, too, had alienated the rank and file from him, or at least had taken away that enthusiasm which soldiers feel for the successful general, and which makes them obey his orders without question." Fresh from the East, where he had been impressed by Lee's great daring, always based on sound knowledge of the enemy's dispositions, Hill was shocked by Bragg's apparent ignorance of the enemy's whereabouts and movements, which resulted in his maintaining a supine attitude while waiting for Rosecrans to show his hand. It was Hill to whom he described the Cumberlands as "the wall of a house full of rat holes," and Hill afterwards recorded that he "was most painfully impressed with the feeling that it was to be a haphazard campaign on our part."

However that might be, and it was as yet no more than an impression, it presently developed that Bragg had been quite right to suspect that Old Rosy was groping elbow-deep in his bag of tricks. No sooner was the Confederate reorganization completed than Bragg learned that the Federals were not only over the river, well downstream, but were also far in his rear, crossing Lookout and the other north-south Georgia ridges for a strike at the rail supply line whose loss would mean starvation for the defenders of Chattanooga. Determined not to be trapped as Pemberton had been at Vicksburg, he promptly evacuated the city and fell back southward through Rossville Gap to a position from which to block the continued advance of the three blue columns when they came around and over Missionary Ridge. His left was at LaFayette, two dozen miles from Chattanooga, and his right at Lee & Gordon's Mill, twelve miles north, where the road from Rossville crossed Chickamauga Creek. Walker held the former, Polk the latter, and Hill and Buckner were posted in between, confronting the westward loom of Pigeon Mountain, a crescent-shaped spur of Lookout Mountain which inclosed the lower end of Missionary Ridge and its eastern valley, a cul-de-sac known locally as McLemore's Cove. Bragg saw in this the trap he had been seeking, the trap he had encouraged Rosecrans to enter by sending out loaded deserters to dispel the Ohioan's native caution and hasten his march with the promise of an easy triumph over a demoralized opponent. Wheeler and Forrest, who had been called in and now were operating respectively on the immediate left and right, toward Alpine and Rossville, were instructed to impede the advance of McCook and Crittenden from Winston Gap and Chattanooga. This would leave the balance of the army, some 40,000 infantry and artillery, free to concentrate against Thomas, who had a total of 23,000 effectives, and destroy him there in the fastness of McLemore's Cove; after which the victors would turn on either or both of the remaining enemy columns, still well beyond supporting distance of each other, and administer the same annihilation treatment. Bragg so ordered on the evening of September 9, shortly after receiving from his scouts, civilian as well as military, reports that Thomas's lead division had entered the cove that afternoon and made a sundown camp on upper Chickamauga Creek.

His plan combined the virtues of simplicity and power, and his orders were issued with the coolness of a gambler holding four aces against a splurger whose overconfidence had been nurtured by an inordinate run of luck. While Cleburne's division of Hill's corps attacked due west through Dug Gap, corking the Pigeon Mountain outlet and fixing the bluecoats in position, Hindman's division of Polk's corps would move southwest from Lee & Gordon's Mill, up Chickamauga Creek, sealing the mouth of the cul-de-sac and striking the enemy flank and rear. Basically, the operation was intended to be like that of a meatgrinder, and if Thomas reinforced his lead division in the cove, so much the better; Breckinridge would be in support of Cleburne, Cheatham of Hindman, and the Federal reinforcements would only give them that much more meat to grind. Hindman set out an hour after midnight, September 10, and halted at dawn, four miles short of contact, waiting to hear from Cleburne. He had a long, tense wait. Finally a message came from Hill, protesting that he had not received his orders till after daylight, that Cleburne himself was sick in bed, with four of his best regiments absent on other duties, and that the proposed attack was risky in the first place, since Thomas had probably sent his lead division forward "as a bait to draw us off from below." In short, Cleburne would not be coming; not this morning at any rate. Later in the day, while still maintaining his indecisive position short of contact, Hindman received a message from Bragg, urging him to finish up his work in the cove as quickly as possible, because Crittenden's corps was on the march from Chattanooga by way of Rossville Gap, directly in his rear. This added fright to confusion, and after remaining all night in a position which he judged perilous in the extreme, the veteran of Prairie Grove decided next morning to withdraw the way he had come. By now, though, Bragg had sent Buckner to his support, with orders to force the issue promptly, and Cleburne was through Dug Gap; so Hindman returned southward. But when the two gray forces came together that afternoon in McLemore's Cove there was nothing blue between them. Thomas at last had spotted the danger, despite his lack of cavalry, and withdrawn to the far side of Missionary Ridge.

Bragg was furious, blaming the lost opportunity on Hindman's indecisiveness and Hill's "querulous, insubordinate spirit," while they in turn put the blame on him, claiming that their orders had been permissive rather than peremptory. However, he resolved to try again, in a different direction and with different commanders. Thomas had withdrawn to safety, but Crittenden had not. Polk having retired toward LaFayette at his approach, the Kentuckian had sent one of his three divisions to occupy Lee & Gordon's Mill while the other two moved against Ringgold, a station on the railroad between Chattanooga and Dalton, in accordance with his orders to break the rebel supply line. Learning of this next morning from Forrest, who was patrolling that flank of the army, Bragg directed Polk to return to his former position with his own reunited corps and Walker's, and attack the isolated Federals there at dawn, September 13. "This division crushed and the others are yours," he told him. The bishop protested that Crittenden, taking alarm, had recalled the two divisions from their march on Ringgold and now had his whole corps posted for defense behind the Chickamauga at that point. This was quite true, as it turned out, but Bragg replied that it was no matter; Polk had four divisions to the enemy's three, and he would send Buckner's two to assist him in case they were needed, which seemed unlikely; the attack was to be launched on schedule, as directed. But when he reached the field at 9 o'clock next morning he found Polk on the defensive, still unwilling to advance lest he be swamped. Madder than ever, the terrible-tempered Confederate commander finally got Polk and Walker and Buckner into assault formation by noon and sent them forward — only to discover that Crittenden, after the manner of Thomas two days ago in McLemore's Cove, had escaped the trap by withdrawing undetected beyond Missionary Ridge. In a rage of frustration and regret for the two rare chances he had lost in the past three days, Bragg pulled his whole army once more back to LaFayette, the best position from which to counter a thrust at his vital supply line by any one or all three of the blue columns across the way.

But there was small likelihood of any such thrust by then. The scales having fallen at last from his eyes, Rosecrans was doing all he could to get the three isolated segments of his army back together before they were abolished, one by one, by a rebel army which he now knew was not only not retreating in disorder, but also had been heavily reinforced. And now there followed a three-day interlude during which neither commander knew much of what the other was doing, although the graybacks at least had the physical advantage of standing still while their opponents tramped the dusty hills and valleys that lay between them and concentration. Presently the blue movements took on a new urgency, a new franticness, with the circulation of reports that Bragg was about to be even more substantially reinforced by troops already on the way by rail from Lee in Virginia; three divisions of them, rumor had it, under Longstreet. Old Rosy and his staff began to curse Burnside, who had turned east by now from Knoxville and Cumberland Gap instead of in their direction for the intended hookup: with the result, as they believed, that now it was they who were in grievous danger of being cut off from their base, exposed to the threat of starvation, and swamped by superior numbers, including a whole corps of hardbitten killers from the far-off eastern theater.

Meanwhile at LaFayette, where the Confederates were recovering from their recent fruitless exertions in McLemore's Cove and near Lee & Gordon's Mill, Harvey Hill marveled at the apparent casualness with which these Westerners, blue and gray alike, accepted the proximity of their adversaries just on the opposite side of the intervening ridge. It was quite unlike what he had known before, back in Virginia under Lee. "When two armies confront each other in the East, they get to work very soon," he remarked to one of his veteran brigadiers. "But here you look at one another for days and weeks at a time." The brigadier, a cockfight enthusiast, laughed. "Oh, we out here have to crow and peck straws awhile before we use our spurs," he said.

All the same, as Hill, observed long afterwards in recording the exchange, "the crowing and pecking straws were now about over." A dozen to twenty miles north of there, above Lee & Gordon's Mill, the woods-choked field of Chickamauga awaited the confrontation that would result, within the week, in what would not only be the greatest battle of the West, but would also be, for the numbers engaged, the bloodiest of the war.

✕ 3 ✕

Reports that Longstreet was en route were true, but once more only up to a point, the difference being that this time the exaggeration was in the opposite direction, serving rather to deepen the blue commander's fears than to heighten his expectations. Old Peter was coming with two, not three divisions; Pickett's was still in no shape for another headlong commitment, and though it too had been detached from Lee, it was left behind to assist in the close-up defense of Richmond when the other two, under McLaws and Law — or Hood, as it turned out — passed through the capital on the first stage of their long ride to Northwest Georgia. The decision to send them to join Bragg had been arrived at during a White House conference in late August and early September, a conference not unlike the one that had preceded the march into Pennsylvania, except that this time the gray-bearded commander of the Army of Northern Virginia carried much less weight in council than he had done before his defeat at Gettysburg, which had been the direct result of the weight he exerted then in overriding the objections of Reagan. Besides, since that and the other early-July reverses in Mississippi, Arkansas, Louisiana, and Middle Tennessee, additional threats to the national existence had developed, including not only the menace to East Tennessee — which was lost while the conference was in progress — but also on the Atlantic seaboard, particularly at Charleston, and in the far-off Transmississippi. These too had served to strengthen the conviction that the country simply could not afford another defeat in the vital central theater, and therefore the decision had been to reinforce Bragg at the expense of all the others, including Lee, who would be left to face the victorious Meade with a greatly reduced force, and Beauregard, who was calling urgently for assistance in resisting an all-out Union amphibious effort to rock and wreck the cradle of secession.

Du Pont's repulse, back in April, had resulted in some sour-grapes talk on the part of Gideon Welles to the effect that Charleston, "a place of no strategic importance," had not been worth taking in the first place; but the failure rankled badly over the span of the next two months, with the result that he decided to try again with a more determined commander. Rear Admiral Andrew H. Foote, apparently recovered from the wound he had suffered while clearing the lower Tennessee and the Cumberland, as well as the Mississippi down to Memphis, was the logical choice for the job and was appointed despite his reluctance to supersede his old friend Samuel Du Pont. He died in New York in late June, however, while on the way to his new post, and the position went instead to Rear Admiral John A. Dahlgren, head of the Bureau of Ordnance, inventor of the bottle-shaped gun that had done so much to give the Union its victories afloat, and an intimate friend of Lincoln's during his command of the Washington Navy Yard in the first two years of the war. Described by a correspondent as "a light complexioned man of perhaps forty years of age," though he was in fact in his mid-fifties, Dahlgren was "slight and of medium height, [with] pale and delicate features. His countenance is exceedingly thoughtful and modest . . . while his eye is inevitably keen, and his thin nostrils expand as he talks, with a look of great enthusiasm." Welles believed this last proceeded from less admirable qualities than those the reporter discerned. "He is intensely ambitious," the Secretary noted in his diary, "and, I fear, too selfish. He has the heroism which proceeds from pride, and would lead him to danger and death; but whether he has the innate, unselfish courage of the genuine sailor and soldier, remains to be seen." Despite these doubts on the part of his superior, based in part on personal observation and in part on the fact that he had never been in action, Dahlgren was given command of the South Atlantic Blockading Squadron, which he took over as Du Pont's successor in early July, together with special instructions covering the employment of his patched-up ironclads to effect the reduction of the South Carolina city, defiant behind the guns and obstructions around and in its harbor.

This time there was no plea from the Department that the army not be allowed to "spoil" the show by having a vital part in it. Rather, the admiral was to work in conjunction with Brigadier General Quincy Gillmore, who had arrived three weeks earlier to assume command of the 15,000 infantrymen, artillerists, and engineers assigned to take the lead in the opening phase of the combined attack. Fort Sumter was seen as the key to control of Charleston harbor, and Gillmore, a thirty-eight-year-old Ohio-born West Pointer — top man in the otherwise undistinguished class of 1849 — had been called in, as a fortifications expert and a master of siege operations, to give an opinion on whether the army could reduce it. He replied that this could best be done by mounting heavy guns on the north end of Morris Island, held at present by the Confederates, and using them to knock the famed pentagonal fort to pieces; after which, as Gillmore saw it, the ironclads would be able to steam in and administer the same treatment to the city itself, on the far side of the harbor, until such time as the white flag went up. His plan approved, he got to work as soon as he arrived in mid-June, and by the time Dahlgren took over from Du Pont he was ready to launch his opening attack from Folly Island, where he had secretly massed a 3000-man assault force, against the adjoining southern end of Morris Island, preparatory to a drive up its narrow four-mile length to Cummings Point, which was less than 1500 yards from Sumter. On July 10, encouraged by a promotion to major general, he sprang a dawn attack which caught the rebels so thoroughly off guard that by noon he had the lower three fourths of the island in his grip. All that remained was Battery Wagner, dead ahead, and Battery Gregg, 1300 yards farther along on Cummings Point. His loss so far had amounted to scarcely more than a hundred men, only fifteen of whom were dead. Wasting no time, he ordered another all-out assault next morning. This too was launched with verve and determination, but with considerably less satisfactory results. The first wave made it up to Wagner's parapet, only to be shattered by heavy volleys of grape and musketry, while the support formations were scattered by high-angle fire from Gregg. Within an hour the attackers lost 49 killed, 167 captured or missing, and 123 wounded, and so far as the repulsed survivors could see, these 339 casualties had been expended without any effect whatever on either the earthwork or its defenders, who kept up a deadly sniping at everything blue that showed above the level of the sandy ground out front.

Undaunted, Gillmore spent a week bringing up another 3500 soldiers and emplacing 41 guns for counterbattery work; then at noon of July 18 he opened fire, which was also the signal for Dahlgren's monitors to close the range and pound both rebel works from the seaward flank. This continued for more than seven hours, and presently Battery Wagner ceased to reply, its cannoneers driven from their guns. Then at 7.30 — the attack hour had been set for twilight so that the defenders would not be able to take careful aim — the Union guns fell silent too, ashore and afloat, and the 6000 Federals started forward on a necessarily narrow front of less than 200 yards. In the lead was a Massachusetts regiment, all-Negro except for its officers, who were mostly Boston bluebloods, including its young colonel, Robert Gould Shaw, whose mother had wept for joy at the sight of her boy leading black men forth to war; "What have I done, that God has been so good to me!" she cried at the grand farewell review staged in Boston in late May. In less than seven weeks, however, it developed that God had not been so good to her after all, unless what she wanted in place of her son was a fine bronze statue on the Common. The 1000-man rebel garrison came out of the bombproof to which it had retired at the height of the cannonade and met the attackers as it had done the week before, with even more spectacular results. Here in the East, on Morris Island just outside Charleston harbor, as formerly in the West, at Milliken's Bend and Port Hudson, Negro troops proved that they could stop bullets and shell fragments as well as white men; but that was about all. When flesh and blood could stand no more, the survivors fell back from the ditch and parapet, black and white alike, and returned to the trenches they had left an hour ago. Casualties had been heavy; 1515 of the attackers had fallen, as compared to 174 of the defenders, and next morning when the latter peered out of their sight slits they saw live and dead men strewn in piles and windrows, their bodies horribly mangled by close-up artillery fire, while detached arms and legs and heads were splattered all about. A brief truce sufficed for removal of the wounded and disposal of the slain, including the twenty-six-year-old Shaw, who had taken a bullet through the heart and was buried in a common grave with his Negro soldiers, nearly half of whom had been lost in the repulse.

Somewhat daunted, but still determined, Gillmore decided to settle down to regular siege operations and take Sumter under fire from where he was, the range being only about 3000 yards. From close up, he would batter Wagner and Gregg into submission, meanwhile bringing eighteen heavy guns to bear in a round-the-clock attempt to breach the fort less than a mile across the water from the inaccessible north end of the island. By mid-August three parallels had been drawn and advanced, preparatory to launching a sudden, swamping rush upon the stubborn earthwork dead ahead, and Sumter was being bombarded at a rate of nearly 5000 shells a week, its brick walls cracking and crumbling under the impact of 300-pound projectiles, the heaviest ever employed by rifled field artillery up to then. Another innovation was the use of calcium lights, which threw the ramparts of Battery Wagner into stark relief and helped to prevent the rebels from making nighttime sorties against the gunners and diggers in their immediate front. Still a third innovation was the establishment in the marshes between Morris and James islands, off to the left and about 8000 yards from downtown Charleston, of an 8-inch Parrott rifle — promptly dubbed the "Swamp Angel" by the engineers who sweated and floundered in the salty mud to place the big gun on its platform — for the purpose of heaving its 200-pound shells, specially filled for the occasion with liquid and solidified Greek Fire, into the city's streets and houses. On August 21 the monster weapon was reported ready, and Gillmore sent a note across the lines demanding the immediate evacuation of Morris Island and Fort Sumter; otherwise, he warned, he would open fire "from batteries already established within easy and effective range of the heart of the city." No answer having been received by midnight, he sent word for the gun to go into action. At 1.30 a.m. the first shell was on the way. The sound of alarm bells and whistles, which reached them faintly across the nearly five miles of marsh and water, told the crew that the percussion-fuzed shell had found its mark, and they followed this with fifteen others, equally accurate, before dawn. At that time Gillmore received a message signed G. T. Beauregard, protesting his barbarity and rejecting his ultimatum that Wagner and Gregg and Sumter be abandoned. "It would appear, sir, that despairing of reducing these works, you now resort to the novel measure of turning your guns against the old men, the women and children, and the hospitals of a sleeping city," the Creole hotly accused his adversary, and he predicted that this "mode of warfare, which I confidently declare to be atrocious and unworthy of any soldier . . . will give you 'a bad eminence' in history, even in the history of this war." Gillmore replied that the city had had forty days' notice, this being the length of time he had been battering at its gates, and despite the added protests of the Spanish and British consuls he ordered the bombardment resumed on August 23. Twenty more incendiary shells were fired, six of which exploded prematurely in the tube with spectacular pyrotechnical effects, and though no member of the crew was hurt by these sudden gushes of flame from the vent and muzzle, the gun itself was probably weakened. At any rate, on the twentieth shot the breech of the piece blew out of its jacket, just behind the vent, and the Swamp Angel ended her brief career of thirty-six rounds, thirty of which had landed squarely on target in the birthplace of secession, whatever "bad eminence" she might have gained for Gillmore in the process.

He made no attempt to replace the ruined cannon, believing as he did that he soon would have possession of Cummings Point, where the ground was firmer and the range to Charleston shorter. By August 26 his sappers were within 200 yards of Battery Wagner, and within another week the distance was half that. All this time, the bombardment of Fort Sumter had continued, with gratifying results. Most of its southern wall was down, and both the western and eastern walls were badly cracked. Practically every casemate had been breached. On the first night in September, when six of the monitors gave the crumbling fort a five-hour pounding, not a shot was fired from the rubble in reply. Gillmore stepped up the action against Wagner. On September 5 he began a relentless 42-hour cannonade during which no less than 3000 shells were rained upon the earthwork, preparatory to the final assault. But when the guns stopped firing in the predawn darkness of September 7, so that the infantry could rush forward and end the 58-day siege — in the course of which the Federals had suffered a total of 2318 casualties and inflicted 641 — it was discovered that the Confederates had evacuated both Wagner and Gregg the night before, despite the constant deluge of metal, and withdrawn in rowboats to James Island. Once more, Beauregard's uncanny sense of timing had not failed him. Advancing to emplace his heaviest guns on Cummings Point, from which he could resume his shelling of the city, Gillmore passed the word to Dahlgren that the army's share of the operation had been accomplished. Morris Island had been occupied entirely and Fort Sumter had been neutralized; now the navy's turn had come to take the lead. Proud Charleston would be brought to its knees if the ironclads would only steam across the harbor and bring it under the muzzles of their guns.

But could they? Dahlgren was far from certain: so little so, in fact, that he was unwilling to make the attempt until Sumter had not only been "neutralized," as the army claimed, but taken. Moreover, he wanted the honor of doing the taking, and he believed he saw how this could be done without exposing his valuable monitors to sudden destruction by a torpedo or by point-blank fire from a gun kept hidden amid the rubble for that purpose. Constant shelling had tumbled the bricks of the south wall down to the water's edge, affording an incline which, though steep and rugged, could be scaled without the delay the use of ladders would involve. If a surprise landing could be accomplished, a storming party would be into the place before its defenders even had time to sound the alarm. So at least the naval commander believed, or reasoned, when he called on September 7 — the same day Morris Island fell to the army — for 500 naval volunteers to make a small-boat landing by the dark of the moon the following night. By way of preamble he sent in a demand for the fort's surrender and received, at second hand, Beauregard's reply: "Tell Admiral Dahlgren to come and take it." That was just what he was preparing to do, and when the officer he had placed in charge of the venture expressed some doubts that it would succeed, Dahlgren scoffed at his fears. "You have only to go and take possession," he assured him. "You will find nothing but a corporal's guard." Accordingly, the volunteers were loaded into some thirty assault boats and towed within half a mile of Sumter before moonrise the next night. No lights were shown and the oars were muffled, but the rebel lookouts spotted them anyhow and gave the alarm, including the firing of rockets, which was the signal for batteries on James and Sullivan's islands to open fire on the waters near the fort. Caught under the resultant two-way barrage, the marines and sailors hurried ashore and were received by the 300-man garrison lying in wait for them with rifles, fire-balls, hand grenades, and brickbats, which combined to make conditions even worse on the beach than on the water. Five of the boats were captured, along with more than a hundred men and thirteen officers. The rest got away as best they could through the ring of fire, bringing their wounded with them. "Nobody hurt on our side," Beauregard reported.

Dahlgren took the check as proof that he had been wise not to risk his iron flotilla in any such challenge to the alert and tricky rebels, but he could not escape the depression that proceeded from the knowledge that he had done no better, so far, than the man he had replaced. The enervating heat, plus long confinement in the poorly ventilated monitors, had impaired his health; moreover, he was often seasick, which caused him to lose caste with his sailors and perhaps with himself as well. Worst of all, though, was the gnawing sense of failure. Victory was the cure, he knew, but he would not risk the alternative, defeat, which in this case would be utterly disastrous, not only to his ships and men, but also to his career. Nothing helped, or even seemed to. "I am better today," he confided in his journal, "but the worst of this place is that one only stops getting weaker. One does not get stronger." Torn between desire and fear, ambition and indecision, he reacted physically to the mental strain. "My debility increases, so that today it is an exertion to sit in a chair. I do not see well. How strange — no pain, but so feeble. It seems like gliding away to death. How easy it seems! Why not, to one whose race is run?" It was scarcely to be expected, with the admiral in this frame of mind, that the navy would press matters beyond the point that had been reached when Morris Island fell. Nor did it. Dahlgren perceived that Sumter had become little more than an infantry outpost, its heaviest guns having been removed in secret to Sullivan's Island during the two-month siege of Battery Wagner; Fort Moultrie was now the real obstacle to a penetration of the harbor, and the only way to close with it was by steaming through the torpedo-infested channel, which was something he was by no means willing to attempt. Meanwhile — illogically, but for lack of anything better in the way of employment for his vessels and their crews — he maintained an intermittent bombardment of Sumter. Formerly a brick masonry fort, it was now a powerful earthwork; the shells it absorbed only served to make it more impervious by stirring up and adding to the rubble any attackers would have to climb and cross, dodging fire-balls and grenades, in order to come to grips with the defenders. He had tried that once, however, and he had no intention of trying it again.

Gillmore at least had the satisfaction of knowing that he had carried out his primary assignment by securing possession of Morris Island, but even if he had had another intermediary objective in mind — which he did not — he would have had no way to get there, shipless as he was, with bottomless marshes on one flank, open sea on the other, and the mine-strewn harbor dead ahead. Like Dahlgren, he contented himself with lobbing projectiles into Sumter, barely 1400 yards away, or into Moultrie, twice that distance across the harbor mouth. By way of diversion he sometimes threw a long-range salvo or two at Charleston, which was about half a mile closer to Cummings Point than it was to the platform that had kept the ill-fated Swamp Angel out of the mud. None of these seemed to accomplish much, however. Sumter merely continued to squat there, defiant and misshapen — "a noble mass of ruins," Beauregard called it, "over which still float our colors" — responding to hits by sending up puffs of brickdust, but otherwise appearing as indifferent as an elephant to flea bites. Moultrie did not even do that much, so far as the Federal spotters could see from a range of 2800 yards, and presently they left off shooting at it. As for Charleston itself, while banks moved their resources from the lower to the upper part of town and hospitals were evacuated in the impact zone, the chief complaint of those citizens who had recovered from their early panic and returned to their homes, keeping tubs of water handy in all the rooms for fighting fires, was that the scream of the Yankee shells disturbed their sleep. They were proud of themselves, proud of their defenders out on the firing line, and proudest of all of Beauregard, their original hero, to whom Congress afterwards tendered a joint resolution of thanks for "a defense which, for the skill, heroism, and tenacity displayed during an attack scarcely paralleled in warfare ... is justly entitled to be pronounced glorious by impartial history and an admiring country."

. . .

But that was later. The Richmond conference ended on September 7, a day that seemed more the occasion for alarm than for high-flown congratulations, least of all to Beauregard, since it was then that Morris Island fell and the Charleston commander stepped up his plea for reinforcements, predicting graver disasters unless the odds he faced were shortened. All the statesmen and generals knew, as they studied the situation from their council room in the White House, was that events appeared to be mounting rapidly toward an unwelcome climax — not only down the Atlantic seaboard, but also along the opposite end of the thousand-mile frontier. In that far-western quarter the odds were even longer and the enemy had mounted a two-pronged offensive designed to restore the northern two thirds of Arkansas, including its capital, to the domain of the Union. The Confederacy having been sundered by the loss of Vicksburg and Port Hudson, the Federals seemed to be losing no time in getting to work on the disconnected halves, particularly the one that lay beyond what Lincoln called the "unvexed" Mississippi.

One prong was being driven eastward from Indian Territory, with Fort Smith as its immediate goal, and the other was being driven westward from Helena, whose garrison, flushed by its success in breaking up the Independence Day assault, had been strengthened by the return of Frederick Steele's division, which had gone downriver eight months ago with Sherman and now came back with the names of the many engagements of the Vicksburg campaign proudly stitched to its battle flags. Much to the disgruntlement of Prentiss, who submitted his resignation as a result, command of the inland expedition went to Steele, together with instructions to "break up Price and occupy Little Rock," a hundred crow-flight miles away in the heart of the state. To do this he had two divisions of infantry, totaling only about 6000 effectives — "The sick list is frightful," he reported — plus one division of cavalry, as large as the two of infantry put together, detached from Schofield. This mounted force, led by Brigadier General John W. Davidson, a forty-year-old Virginia-born West Pointer, left Bloomfield, Missouri, and proceeded south down Crowley's Ridge to Clarendon, Arkansas, which it reached on August 8, to be joined nine days later by Steele, who marched his foot soldiers from Helena and took command of the combined 12,000. Shifting his base to De Valls Bluff, a dozen miles northwest, he spent another two weeks making final preparations and then on September 1, in accordance with his instructions, set out for the capital, just under fifty miles due west. By that date the opposite prong — a scratch collection of seven regiments, three composed of Union-loyal Indian volunteers and one of Negroes, all under James Blunt, the former Ohio doctor who had been promoted to major general as a reward for Prairie Grove — had attained its initial objective with a bloodless occupation of Fort Smith, 125 miles from Little Rock and just short of the western border. Back in mid-July, Blunt had prepared the way for this maneuver with an attack on the Confederates to his front at Honey Springs, fifty miles west of his goal, driving them south in disorder and destroying the stores they had collected for subsistence in that barren region of Indian Territory. Commanded by Brigadier General William Steele, a forty-year-old New Yorker and West Pointer who had married South, the rebel force of nine regiments, six of them Indian, was actually larger than Blunt's; but when the action was joined the graybacks found to their dismay that their powder, imported from Europe by way of Texas, had turned to paste in their cartridge boxes. They ran and kept on running. Satisfied merely to have them out of the way for the time being, Blunt did not pursue. He returned instead to the Arkansas River to rest and refit his victorious 3000 multicolored troops, then turned east in late August to occupy Fort Smith on September 1, the day the other Steele started west from De Valls Bluff.

About this time, while events were heading up for the recovery of most of Arkansas, word came of a "raid" some 300 miles to the north, across the Missouri-Kansas line, that provoked more excitement and indignation throughout the country than any that had been staged in the course of the nearly four years since John Brown struck at Harpers Ferry. The difference was that this one, launched against the region where Brown had got his start, was not only a good deal bloodier, and therefore more atrocious, but was also as complete a success as the other had been a failure. Heavy detachments of troops from Schofield to Grant and Steele, well downriver, had emboldened

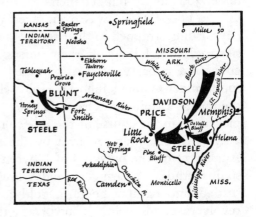

the guerillas lurking in the Missouri brush: particularly Charles Quantrill, who had secured a captain's commission from Richmond and was eager to justify his bars, as well as to pay off old scores from the prewar border troubles, by leading his irregulars on a more daring expedition than any they had attempted up to now. He favored a strike at Lawrence, an old-time abolitionist settlement forty miles beyond the Kansas line. At first his men would not agree, believing that the prize, though fat, would not be worth the risk; but two developments which occurred in rapid succession in mid-August changed their minds, adding a thirst for revenge to their already strong desire for loot. For the past three months the Federal commander of the District of the Border, Brigadier General Thomas Ewing, had been arresting women charged with giving encouragement and assistance to guerillas, many of whom were their sons and brothers and husbands. This had enraged the men in the brush, who, whatever their excesses in other directions, had invariably maintained a hands-off attitude toward the mothers and sisters and wives of their Jayhawk adversaries. The prisoners were confined in certain buildings in Kansas City, and on August 14 one of these, a dilapidated three-story brick affair with a liquor shop on the ground floor, collapsed — as Ewing had been warned it might do — killing four of the women outright and seriously injuring several others. When news of this reached Quantrill's men they promptly reconsidered their chief's proposal for a raid on Lawrence. "We can get more revenge and more money there than anywhere else in the state of Kansas," he told them. Then four days later Ewing announced in a general order that not only would more such arrests be made, but that "the wives and children of known guerillas, and also women who are heads of families and are willfully engaged in aiding guerillas, will be notified . . . to remove out of this district and out of the State of Missouri forthwith." The order was dated August 18; "We could stand no more," a guerilla who had lost a sister in the Kansas City tragedy wrote later. Next day Quantrill set out from Blackwater Creek in Johnson County, headed west for Lawrence with a column of just under 300 bloody-minded men.

The distance was over seventy miles and they made it in two days, riding strapped to their saddles the second night so that they could sleep without falling off their horses. While still in Missouri they encountered a party of 104 mounted Confederate recruits proceeding south under Colonel John D. Holt, who decided to take them along on the raid as a training exercise. These, plus a number of other volunteers picked up in the course of the ride to the border, brought the column to a strength of about 450 men by the time it drew rein at daybreak of August 21 on the outskirts of Lawrence. Three weeks past his twenty-sixth birthday, wearing a gaudy, low-cut guerilla shirt, gray trousers stuffed into cavalry boots, a gold-corded black slouch hat, and four revolvers in his belt, Quantrill assigned each unit its special mission, then led the howling charge that swept from the southeast into the streets of the sleeping town. Long since warned to expect no quarter, the raiders intended to give none. With the exception of a single adult male civilian — the hated Jayhawk chieftain Senator James H. Lane, who was to be taken back to Missouri alive, if possible, for a semi-public hanging — Quantrill's orders called for the killing of "every man big enough to carry a gun." First to fall, in accordance with these instructions, was the Reverend S. S. Snyder, sometimes lieutenant of the 2d Kansas Colored Infantry, shot dead under the cow he was milking in his yard. Next were seventeen recruits encountered in the otherwise deserted camp of the 14th Cavalry, several of them pistoled before they emerged from their blankets. Thus began a three-hour orgy of killing, interspersed with drinks in commandeered saloons and exhibitions of fancy riding. Men were chased and shot down as they ran; others were dragged from their homes and murdered in front of their wives and children; still others were smothered or roasted alive when the houses in which they hid were set afire. Holt and other less bloodthirsty members of the band managed to protect a few of the fugitives, but not many; Quantrill, who had lived for a time in Lawrence before the war, had prepared a vengeance list beforehand, and all who were on it and in town this morning wėre disposed of, except for the man whose name was at its head. Wily Jim Lane took flight in his nightshirt, warned by the first thunder of hooves as the guerillas swept in across the prairie, and hid out undetected in a cornfield until they rode away, leaving 80 new widows and 250 fatherless children weeping in the ruins of the town. Nearly 200 buildings had been wrecked or burned, including all three newspaper offices and most of the business district, for a property loss amounting to about two million dollars. In all, though not one woman was physically harmed, no less than 150 Kansans were killed, fewer than twenty of whom were soldiers and several of whom were scarcely more than boys. Not one of them sold his life dearly, however, for the only casualty the raiders suffered was a former Baptist preacher who got drunk, passed out, and was killed and scalped by an Indian when he was discovered, shortly after his friends had ridden away. His body was dragged through the streets behind a horse by a free Negro until it was stripped naked, and the grieving citizens pelted it with stones by way of revenge.

Loaded with booty, the rest of the guerillas had pulled out southward about 9 o'clock that morning, shortly after lookouts on Mount Oread reported a heavy column of troopers approaching from the north and west, beyond the Kansas River. Setting ambushes to delay his pursuers, who converged from all points of the compass as the news from Lawrence spread across the plains, and swerving aside in the twilight to avoid a blue garrison lying in wait for him at Paola, Quantrill made it back across the Missouri line next morning with nearly all of his command. At this point the order was "Every man for himself," and the raiders faded into the brush by a hundred different trails to resume their various disguises as farmers, parolees, and Union-loyal residents of the scattered towns and hamlets. All who were detected subsequently were executed on the spot, as those had been who were caught up with when their horses went lame or collapsed from exhaustion during the chase across the prairie. "No prisoners have been taken, and none will be," Ewing informed Schofield, and four days after what became known as the Lawrence Massacre he issued, at Jim Lane's insistence, his famous General Order Number 11, directing the forcible removal of all persons, male or female, child or adult, loyal or disloyal, who lived more than a mile from a Federal post in the four Missouri counties south of the Missouri River and adjacent to the border. The time limit was fifteen days from the date of issue, August 25. By mid-September the order had been so effectively enforced that Cass County, which had had a population of 10,000 before the war, was occupied by fewer than 600 civilians; Bates County, directly south, had even less. Moreover, the vengeance-minded 15th Kansas Cavalry, delighted at having been given the assignment of seeing that Ewing's order was obeyed, went through the region so enthusiastically with torch and sword, leaving nothing but chimneys to show where houses and cabins once had stood, that it was known for years thereafter as the Burnt District. Not that Quantrill was deterred. He collected his scattered guerillas, continued his depredations, including attacks on wagon trains and steamboats on the Missouri, and finally withdrew south in early October to winter in Texas with a force of 400 hard-bitten men, most of whom had been with him on the raid that nearly wiped Lawrence from the map.

By then the issue had been settled in central Arkansas, and though Steele had failed to "break up Price," he had succeeded admirably in carrying out the rest of his assignment. In temporary command of the district after Holmes fell sick in late July, Price concentrated his 8000 effectives at Little Rock, squarely between the menacing blue prongs of Blunt and Steele, the former in occupation of Fort Smith, just under 150 miles to the west, and the latter advancing from De Valls Bluff, one third that distance to the east. Bracing to meet the nearer and heavier threat — Blunt had only about 4000 men, while Steele had three times as many — the bulky but agile Missourian intrenched a line three miles in length on the north bank of the Arkansas, protected by swamps in front and anchored to the river below the capital in his rear, access to which was provided by three pontoon bridges. Though he took the precaution of sending his accumulated stores to Arkadelphia, sixty miles southwest, he reported that his troops were "in excellent condition, full of enthusiasm, and eager to meet the enemy." So was he, despite the known disparity in numbers, if the bluecoats would only attack him where he was. But Steele, as it turned out, had a different notion. Maneuvering as if for a frontal assault, he sent Davidson's 6000 troopers on a fast ride south to strike the river well downstream from the Confederate position.

This was begun on September 6, and Price on that same day lost one of his two cavalry brigadiers, not by enemy action, but rather as the result of a quarrel between them. For the past two months Marmaduke had been openly critical of Lucius Walker's failure to support him in the attack at Helena; now as they skirmished with the advancing Federals and the Tennessean gave ground under pressure, the hot-tempered Missourian accused him of outright cowardice. Walker replied, as expected, with a challenge which was promptly accepted, the terms being "pistols at ten paces to fire and advance," and the former Memphis businessman fell mortally wounded at the second fire. The conditions of honor having been satisfied in accordance with the code — which, presumably, was one of those things the South was fighting to preserve as part of its "way of life" — presently, after a period of intense suffering by the loser, the Confederacy had one general less than it had had when the two men took position, ten paces apart, and began to walk toward one another, firing as they advanced.

Within four days of this exchange the South also had one state capital the less. Assisted no doubt by the resultant confusion across the way, Davidson got his horsemen over the river at dawn of September 10, moved them rapidly up the scantly defended right bank toward Little Rock, and after forcing a crossing of Bayou Fourche, five miles below the town, received its formal surrender by the civil authorities shortly after sundown. Price had reacted fast: as indeed he had had need to do, if he was to save his army. Outflanked by the cavalry while Steele kept up the pressure against his front, he withdrew from his north-bank intrenchments, set his pontoons afire to prevent the blue infantry from following in his wake, and put his troops on the march for Arkadelphia, to which point he had prudently removed his stores the week before. There on the south bank of the Ouachita he took up a new position extending fifty miles downstream to Camden, with detachments posted as far east as Monticello, about midway between the latter place and the Federal gunboats prowling unchallenged up and down the Mississippi. Steele did not pursue.

Casualties had been light on both sides in both operations — 137 for Steele, 64 for Price; 75 for Blunt, 181 for Steele — but they were no adequate indication of what had been won and lost in the double-pronged campaign. "If they take Fort Smith, the Indian country is gone," Holmes had remarked in February, and now in September his prediction had been unhappily fulfilled. Similarly, the loss of Little Rock — fourth on the list of fallen capitals, immediately following Jackson, which had been preceded the year before by Baton Rouge and Nashville — extended the Union occupation to include three fourths of Arkansas, a gain for which the victors presumably would have been willing to pay ten or even one hundred times the actual cost.

This too was included in the Richmond assessment of the over-all situation. Although, like Chattanooga and Cumberland Gap, Little Rock had not fallen by the time the White House conference ended on September 7 — it fell three and the others two days later — its loss, like theirs, could be anticipated as a factor to be placed in the enemy balance pan alongside Fort Smith, Knoxville, and Morris Island, all of which passed into Federal possession while the council was considering what could best be attempted to offset the reverses lately suffered at Tullahoma, Gettysburg, Vicksburg, Helena, and Port Hudson. Within that same horrendous span, late June through early September, only two events occurred which might have been considered as adding weight to the South's high-riding opposite pan, one the New York draft riot and the other the Quantrill raid on Lawrence. However, both of these were not only comparatively slight, they were also of doubtful character as assets: especially the latter, which, if claimed, would expose the Confederacy to charges of land piracy, or worse, before the bar of world opinion. In strategic terms, moreover, the outlook was no less clear for being bleak. Rosecrans was over the Tennessee River, and unless Bragg could stop him — as, apparently, he could not — the Army of the Cumberland would be free to march southeast through Georgia to the coast, which would mean that the eastern half of the nation, already severed from the western half by the loss of the Mississippi, would itself be cut in two. In that event, nothing would remain to be governed from Richmond but the Carolinas and so much of Virginia as lay south of the Rappahannock, a political and geographical fragment whose survival was already threatened from the north by the Army of the Potomac, from the west by the troops now in occupation of Knoxville and East Tennessee, and from the east by the amphibious force holding Charleston under siege, all three of which had lately been victorious, to various degrees, under Meade, Burnside, and Gillmore.

Despite the fact that it now had some 20,000 fewer effectives than it had had three months ago when its commander urged a similar course of action under similar circumstances, Davis had warmed at first to Lee's proposal, submitted at the outset of the strategy conference, that the Army of Northern Virginia once more take the offensive against Meade. On the last day of August Lee sent word to Longstreet, who had been left in charge on the Rapidan, to "prepare the army for offensive operations." Old Peter replied that he would of course obey his chief's instructions and had already passed them on to Ewell and A. P. Hill, but "I do not see that we can reasonably hope to accomplish much" by continuing to fight a war of stalemate and attrition. "I am inclined to the opinion that the best opportunity for great results is in Tennessee," he asserted. "If we could hold the defensive here with two corps and send the other to operate in Tennessee with [Bragg's] army, I think that we could accomplish more than by an advance from here." This was written on September 2, the day Burnside's cavalry rode into Knoxville, and two days later Rosecrans completed his crossing of the Tennessee River, posing the intolerable threat of a march through Georgia to the sea. Davis and Seddon — to whom Longstreet had written earlier, by invitation, renewing his pre-Gettysburg claim "that the only hope of reviving the waning cause was through the advantage of interior lines" — reacted with a sudden shift from approval of Lee's proposal to approval of his lieutenant's, except that they preferred that the Virginian himself go west to deliver in person the blow designed to bring Old Rosy to his knees. Lee demurred, asserting that the general already on the scene and familiar with the terrain could do a better job. Davis reluctantly acquiesced, and the final plan to reinforce Bragg from

Virginia, though not to supersede him, was approved. On September 6 Lee sent word for his quartermaster to arrange for transportation by rail to Northwest Georgia for two of Longstreet's divisions. Next morning the Richmond council adjourned, and he returned to Orange. By the following day, September 8, the designated troops were on the move.

Longstreet rode over to headquarters to bid his gray-bearded commander farewell. They talked for a while in the latter's tent and then emerged. Lee said nothing more until the burly Georgian had one foot in the stirrup, prepared to mount. "Now, General, you must beat those people out in the West," he told him. Old Peter took his foot from the stirrup and turned to face his chief. "If I live," he said. "But I would not give a single man of my command for a fruitless victory." This was a rather impolitic thing to say to a commander whose greatest victories had been "fruitless" in the sense that Longstreet meant, but Lee either missed or ignored the implication. He merely repeated that arrangements had been made and orders issued to assure that any success would be exploited. Then he watched the man he called "my old warhorse" mount and ride away, leaving him barely more than 45,000 troops with which to block or parry an advance by an army that lately had whipped him with nearly equal numbers and now had almost twice the strength of his own.

"Never before were so many troops moved over such worn-out railways," a First Corps staff officer later wrote, though not quite accurately, since he left out of account (as most veterans of the eastern theater, together with most eastern-born or -trained historians, were prone to do in matters pertaining to the western theater) Bragg's transfer of his whole army from Tupelo to Chattanooga by way of Mobile the previous year. "Never before were such crazy cars — passenger, baggage, mail, coal, box, platform, all and every sort wobbling on the jumping strap-iron — used for hauling good soldiers," the staffer went on. "But we got there nevertheless." Here too a degree of inaccuracy crept in; for out of a total of 12,000 men in the two divisions, only about 7500 reached the field in time for a share in the fighting that had begun before the first of them arrived. Primarily this was because the fall of Knoxville, just the week before, denied them use of the East Tennessee & Virginia Railroad, which up till then had afforded a direct 550-mile route from Gordonsville to Dalton. As a result, a roundabout route had to be taken — first by way of southern Virginia, then down through both of the Carolinas, and finally across the width of Georgia, with no possibility of using through trains because of the varying gauges of track on the dozen different lines — for a total distance of nearly 1000 miles from Orange Courthouse to Catoosa Station, which was within earshot of the battle they heard raging as they approached the end of their long journey through the heartland.

For the troops themselves — Deep Southerners to a man, except the Texans and Arkansans, now that Pickett's Virginians had been detached — the trip had all the elements of a lark, despite the cramped accommodations, the thrown-together meals, and the knowledge that possible death and suffering awaited them at its end. Many of the Carolinians and Georgians — South Carolinians, that is; for there were no North Carolinians in Longstreet's corps — passed through home towns they had not visited in two years, and though guards were posted at all the stops to assure that no unauthorized furloughs were taken, it was good to see that the old places were still there, complete with pretty girls who passed out delicacies and blushed at the whoops of admirers. For Hood's men there was an added bonus in the form of their commander, who rejoined them when they passed through Richmond, where he was recuperating from his Gettysburg wound. Though his arm was still useless in a sling, he was unable to resist the impulse to come along when he saw, as he said later, that "my old troops, with whom I had served so long, were thus to be sent forth to another army — quasi, I may say, among strangers." They cheered at the news that he was aboard and was going to Georgia with them. At Weldon, North Carolina, alternate routes — one via Raleigh, Charlotte, and Columbia, the other via Goldsboro, Wilmington, and Florence — relieved the strain on the overworked roads until they combined again at Kingsville, South Carolina, where a matron diarist watched the overloaded trains chuff past in what seemed a never-ending procession. "God bless the gallant fellows," she wrote; "not one man intoxicated, not one rude word did I hear. It was a strange sight. What seemed miles of platform cars, and soldiers rolled in their blankets lying in rows with their heads all covered, fast asleep. In their gray blankets packed in regular order, they looked like swathed mummies. . . . A feeling of awful depression laid hold of me. All those fine fellows going to kill or be killed, but why? A word took to beating about my head like an old song, 'The Unreturning Brave.' When a knot of boyish, laughing young creatures passed, a queer thrill of sympathy shook me. Ah, I know how your homefolks feel. Poor children!"

From Branchville, immediately south of there, the route extended due west, via Augusta, to Atlanta, where it turned northwest and ran the final 125 miles northwest to the unloading point, four miles short of Ringgold and 965 circuitous miles from Orange. McLaws and Hood had four brigades each. Two of the former's and one of the latter's would not reach the field until the action had ended — neither would McLaws himself, who was charged with hurrying the last infantry elements northward from Atlanta; nor would a single piece of the corps artillery with which Alexander, still back in the Carolinas, was bringing up the rear — but the five brigades that did arrive in time were to play a significant part in the battle that was in progress when they got there. Hood arrived on September 18, had his horse unloaded from a boxcar, then mounted, still with his arm in its sling, and rode toward the sound of firing, some half a dozen miles away along the banks of a sluggish, meandering, tree-lined creek whose name he now heard for the first time: Chickamauga, an Indian word that meant "stagnant water" or, more popularly, "River of Death." Before nightfall he and his three brigades had a share, by Bragg's direction, in forcing a crossing of the stream at a place called Reed's Bridge, near which they were joined next day by the two brigades from McLaws' division.

Longstreet reached Catoosa Station the following afternoon, September 19, but found no guide waiting to take him to Bragg or give him news of the battle he could hear raging beyond the western screen of woods. When the horses came up on a later train, he had three of them saddled and set out with two members of his staff to find the headquarters of the Army of Tennessee. He was helped in this, so far as the general direction was concerned, by the rearward drift of the wounded, although none of these unfortunates seemed to know exactly where he could find their commander. Night fell and the three officers continued their ride by moonlight until they were halted by a challenge out of the darkness just ahead: "Who comes there?" "Friends," they replied, promptly but with circumspection, and in the course of the parley that followed they asked the sentry to identify his unit. When he did so by giving the numbers of his brigade and division — Confederate outfits were invariably known by the names of their commanders — they knew they had blundered into the Union lines. "Let us ride down a little way to find a better crossing," Old Peter said, disguising his southern accent, and the still-mounted trio withdrew, unfired on, to continue their search for Bragg. It was barely an hour before midnight when they found him — or, rather, found his camp; for he was asleep in his ambulance by then.

He turned out for a brief conference, in the course of which he outlined, rather sketchily, what had happened up to now in his contest with Rosecrans, now approaching a climax here at Chickamauga, and passed on the orders already issued to the five corps commanders for a dawn attack next morning. Longstreet, though he had never seen the field by daylight, was informed that he would have charge of the left wing, which contained six of the army's eleven divisions, including his own two fragmentary ones that had arrived today and yesterday from Virginia. For whatever it might be worth, Bragg also gave him what he later described as "a map showing prominent topographical features of the ground from the Chickamauga River to Mission Ridge, and beyond to the Lookout Mountain range." Otherwise he was on his own, so far as information was concerned.

✗ 4 ✗

Before the close of the Sunday that presently was dawning — September 20; the sun both rose and set at approximately straight-up 6 o'clock, for this was the week of the autumnal equinox — Old Peter was to discover that he was on his own in other ways as well. He was up and about at first light, correcting the faulty alignment of his wing and alerting his troops for their share in the attack Bragg had ordered to be opened "at day-dawn" on the far right, where Polk was in command, and then to be taken up in sequence by the divisions posted southward along the four-mile line of battle. Sunlight dappled the topmost leaves of the trees, then moved down the branches, but there was no sound of the firing Longstreet had been told to expect from the right as the signal for his own commitment on the left. An hour he waited, then another and another, and still there was no crash of guns from the north or word from headquarters of a postponement or cancellation of the attack. Like Lee at Gettysburg, where the shoe had been on the other foot, the burly Georgian scarcely knew what to make of this, except as an indication that such things were not ordered well in the western army. However, he was not of an excitable or even impatient nature, being rather inclined, as a matter of course, to take things as they came. Besides, whatever its cause, the present delay gave him time to examine and improve his dispositions, to familiarize himself at least to some extent with the heavily wooded terrain, and to learn a good deal more than Bragg had taken the trouble to tell him of what had happened, so far, on this confusing field where the two armies had come together for the fourth of their bloody confrontations, a year and a half after Shiloh, a year after Perryville, and nine months after Murfreesboro, all three of which it gave promise of exceeding, both in fury and in bloodshed, despite the apparent — and indeed, in the light of this indication of suffering to come, quite natural — reluctance of the two forces to resume what had got started here the day before.

Bragg now had on hand all the troops he was going to have for the battle. Each of his five corps had two divisions, except Longstreet's, now under Hood, which had three or anyhow parts of three: Hood's own under Law, McLaws' under Kershaw, and one created the previous week, when two more brigades arrived from Mississippi and were combined with Brigadier General Bushrod Johnson's brigade, detached from Stewart's division of Buckner's corps, to form a new provisional division under his command. Longstreet massed this three-division corps, the bulk of which had come with him from Virginia and comprised his Sunday punch, at the right center of his portion of the line, alongside Hindman's division, which had been detached from Polk the day before. On the left and right, respectively on the outer and interior flanks, were Buckner's two divisions under Preston and Stewart. Exclusive of Wheeler's cavalry, patrolling southward beyond an eastward bend of the creek on which his left was anchored, Old Peter had some 25,000 effectives. Polk had roughly the same number in his wing, exclusive of Forrest's cavalry on his right. Hill's two divisions, under Breckinridge and Cleburne, were on the outer flank, and next to them, massed in depth along the center, were the two divisions of Walker's corps, commanded by Brigadier Generals St John Liddell and States Rights Gist. Cheatham's division was posted on the interior flank, adjoining Longstreet. All eleven of these divisions, six in the left and five in the right wing, had three brigades each, with the exception of Cheatham's, which had five, and Liddell's and Kershaw's, which had two apiece; Polk had 16, Longstreet 17 brigades. Bragg's total of 33 infantry brigades was thus the same as the number Rosecrans had in his eleven divisions, but the average blue division was somewhat larger than the average gray division, with the result that the Federals had some 56,000 infantry and artillery, as compared to the Confederate 50,000. However, this disparity was offset by the fact that Rosecrans had only just over 9000 troopers, while Bragg had nearly 15,000, so that the total for each of the opposing forces was approximately 65,000 of all arms. A further disparity in guns, 170 Federal and 200 Confederate, made little tactical difference on terrain so densely wooded that visibility seldom extended for more than fifty yards in any direction; Chickamauga was by no means an artillery contest. On the other hand, Rosecrans had the decided advantage of commanding an army he had trained and fought as a unit for nearly a year now, whereas a good third of Bragg's had joined him during the past few weeks, including five brigades that had arrived in the past two days and a wing commander who had never seen the field by daylight until dawn of the second day of battle.

Already the effect of this had seemed likely to prove fatal. To judge from the poor showing the Confederates had made in failing to spring the trap on Thomas, nine days ago in McLemore's Cove, and then again on Crittenden, two days later at Lee & Gordon's Mill — both as a result of breakdowns along the unfamiliar chain of command — the evident inability of Bragg's subordinates to work in harmony, either with him or with each other in the execution of carefully laid plans, certainly did not promise well for the outcome of future confrontations, which were unlikely to afford them any such lopsided numerical and tactical advantages as they had twice neglected. Bragg was so put out by this turn of events that he fell back on LaFayette and sulked for three whole days: during which time Rosecrans, thoroughly alarmed though unmolested, got his three divergent columns approximately back together and brought his reserve corps forward from Stevenson to Rossville. Crittenden remained at the foot of Missionary Ridge, near Lee & Gordon's Mill, and Thomas shifted to Pond Spring, midway between Crittenden and his own former post at Stevens Gap, while McCook

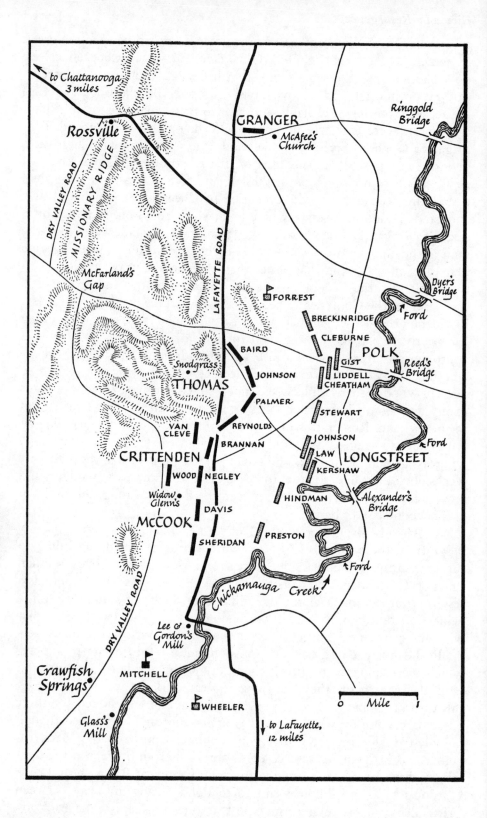

made a long march northward, in rear of Lookout Mountain, to take up the position Thomas had just vacated. By sundown, September 17, all this had been accomplished; Granger, Crittenden, Thomas, and Mc-Cook had their corps respectively in bivouac near Rossville Gap, Lee & Gordon's Mill, Pond Spring, and Stevens Gap, each within about six miles of the next one up or down the line that more or less followed the course of Chickamauga Creek, just east of Missionary Ridge. Rosecrans could draw his first easy breath since his discovery, four days back, that the rebels, far from fleeing in fear and disorder, as they had encouraged him to believe, had been intent on destroying his divided army.

He would have breathed less easily, however, if he had known what his opponent was planning, and had in fact begun to do that day, by way of accomplishing his further discomfiture. Encouraged by word that Longstreet was close at hand with reinforcements from Virginia, Bragg had emerged Achilles-like from his sulk and put his troops in motion, once more with Old Rosy's destruction as his goal. Marching north from LaFayette that morning, he massed his army before nightfall on the east side of Chickamauga Creek, his left at Glass's Mill, a mile above (that is, south of) Lee & Gordon's, and his right near Reed's Bridge, five miles downstream. Polk advised a rapid march on Rossville Gap, the seizure of which would cut the Federals off from their new base at Chattanooga and thus oblige them to attack the Confederates in a position selected in advance; but Bragg had something more ambitious in mind, involving the cul-de-sac in which Thomas had nearly come to grief a week ago tomorrow. According to orders written late that night and issued before daylight, Polk would demonstrate on the left, fixing Crittenden in position, while Buckner and Walker — supported by Hood, who was scheduled to arrive in the course of the day — crossed by fords and bridges, well below, with instructions to "sweep up the Chickamauga, toward Lee & Gordon's Mill." As they approached that point, Polk was to force a crossing and assist in driving the outflanked blue-coats southward into McLemore's Cove for another try at the meat-grinder operation. Wheeler's horsemen would plug the gaps in Pigeon Mountain, preventing a breakout, and Forrest's would guard the outer flank of the two corps — three, if Hood arrived in time — charged with executing the gatelike swing that was designed to throw Crittenden into retreat by bringing them down hard on his flank and rear. Meanwhile, opposite Glass's Mill, Hill would hold the pivot and stand ready to strike at any reinforcements from Thomas, moving north from Pond Spring toward the mouth of the cove, and pack them back into the grinder. The attack was to open in the far right at Reed's Bridge, and the jump-off hour was set for sunrise. Remembering what had happened near here a week ago, when a similar maneuver was attempted on a smaller scale, Bragg closed his field order with an admonition: "The above movements will be executed with the utmost promptness, vigor, and persistence."

Perhaps, after all that had gone wrong before, this was more an expression of hope than an expectation. At any rate he was sorely disappointed. Already nervous about his left — "It is of utmost importance that you close down this way to cover our left flank," he had wired Burnside yesterday, adding (though in vain, as it turned out) "I want all the help we can get promptly" — Rosecrans had taken alarm at sundown reports from scouts that there were rebels on the march in large numbers in the woods across the creek, and he had begun, accordingly, to sidle his army northward in the darkness. Moving Crittenden beyond Lee & Gordon's to cover the Chattanooga-LaFayette road, he advanced Thomas to Crawfish Springs, a hamlet just in rear of Glass's Mill, and McCook to the position Thomas had vacated at Pond Spring. By sunrise, as a result of these three shifts, his four corps — Granger had stayed put at Rossville Gap — were not only more tightly concentrated, the intervals between them having been reduced by half or better, but his left was also about two miles north of where it had been at sunset, when the southern commander made his calculations for an attack which thus was based on faulty or outdated information as to the blue dispositions. Then too, despite the closing admonition, there was the habitual lack of promptness in the movement of the various gray columns, plus what Bragg later referred to, rather charitably, as "the difficulties arising from the bad and narrow country roads," not to mention the stinging opposition of Federal mounted units with their rapid-fire weapons. In any event, though crossings were effected late in the day — by Hood, who arrived with his three brigades about 4 o'clock, and Walker — Buckner, Polk, and Hill were still on the east side of the creek at nightfall, with six of the ten divisions now on the field. Buckner crossed in the darkness, as did one of Polk's divisions; so that by daylight, September 19, Bragg had all of his infantry on the west bank except Hindman's division and the two with Hill. He had scarcely accomplished a fraction of all he intended today, but at any rate he was at last in a position to launch the turning movement he had designed two nights ago.

Or so he thought, still basing his calculations on a belief that the Union left was at Lee & Gordon's Mill. Actually, however, he was even wronger now than he had been the day before. Still concerned about his flank and his lines of supply and communication leading back to Chattanooga, Rosecrans had continued his sidling movement along the road toward Rossville Gap. Again leaving his position to be filled by McCook, Thomas marched across the rear of Crittenden in the darkness and extended the left another two miles north. By dawn, although Negley had not yet vacated Crawfish Springs and Reynolds was still en route, the Union-loyal Virginian's other two divisions, under Brigadier Generals Absalom Baird and J. M. Brannan, were in position at the intersection of the LaFayette Road and the road leading east to Reed's Bridge and west to McFarland's Gap, two miles south of Rossville. Consequently — though Bragg not only failed to suspect it, but in fact continued to base his attack plan on a belief that the reverse was true — the Federal left extended beyond the Confederate right. As Harvey Hill said later, with all the wisdom of hindsight, "While our troops had been moving up the Chickamauga, the Yankees had been moving down, and thus out-flanked us."

The first real indication that this was so came in the emphatic form of an attack that struck and nearly crumpled the northern extrem-ity of the Confederate line before it could begin the movement Bragg had ordered. Informed at sunup by an outpost colonel that the rebels had only a single brigade across the creek at Reed's Bridge, directly to his front, Thomas decided, on the basis of this misinformation, to attack and abolish it then and there. Brannan's division, advancing eastward, soon encountered Forrest's cavalry, out on a prowl. Dismounting his troopers, Forrest skirmished briskly to delay the bluecoats while Walker was sending Gist to his assistance. Surprised and thrown into sudden re-treat when the gray infantry struck, Brannan managed to rally on Baird, sent forward by Thomas to bolster the line; but not for long. Walker threw Liddell into the conflict alongside Gist, and the two of them, with Forrest still tearing at the blue flank, drove the Federals back on their line of departure, one mile east of the LaFayette Road. Finding himself with a good deal more of a fight on his hands than he had expected, Thomas by now had called for reinforcements, and Rosecrans, still con-cerned about his left, responded promptly by sending Palmer of Crit-tenden's corps and Johnson of McCook's. The latter got there first and went in hard, stemming the near rout that had developed. Once more the line of battle swayed indecisively until the weight of numbers told. Then the graybacks began to give ground, until they in turn were rein-forced by two brigades from Cheatham and the balance was restored.

That was the pattern, here and elsewhere along the four-mile line today. Always the weight of numbers decided the issue at every point in what was patently a battle not of generals but of soldiers. ("All this talk about generalship displayed on either side is sheer nonsense," Wilder declared long afterwards, looking back on the Chickamauga nightmare. "There was no generalship in it. It was a soldier's fight purely, wherein the only question involved was the question of endur-ance. The two armies came together like two wild beasts, and each fought as long as it could stand up in a knock-down and drag-out encounter. If there had been any high order of generalship displayed, the disasters to both armies might have been less.") What mainly distinguished the conflict from the outset was its fury. An Alabamian described the racket as "one solid, unbroken wave of awe-inspiring sound . . . as if all the fires of earth and hell had been turned loose in one mighty effort to destroy each other." Fighting deep in the woods, with visibility strictly limited to his immediate vicinity, each man seemed to take the struggle as a highly personal matter between him and the blue or butternut figures he saw dodging into and out of sight, around and behind the clumps of brush and trunks of trees. "By the holy St Patrick, Colonel," a Tennessee private replied when told to pick up the flag that had fluttered down when the color-bearer fell, "there's so much good shooting around here I haven't a minute's time to waste fooling with that thing." All such interruptions, or attempts at interruption, were resented, sometimes even by men of rank. Bedford Forrest, for example, flew into a towering rage at an infantry brigadier for distracting him with messages expressing concern for his flanks. When the first of these was brought to him by an aide — "General Forrest, General Ector directed me to say to you that he is uneasy about his right flank" — the cavalryman, who wore a linen duster over his uniform today with his sword and pistol buckled outside, replied laconically: "Tell General Ector that he need not bother about his right flank. I'll take care of it." Presently, though, the staffer was back with word that his chief was uneasy again, this time about his left. Forrest, who was busy directing the fire of a battery of horse artillery, gave a roar of exasperation. "Tell General Ector that by God I am here," he shouted above the din of the guns, "and will take care of his left flank as well as his right!"

He did as he promised, but only by the hardest. All morning, here on the Confederate right, the struggle was touch and go, until the beginning was unrememberable and no end seemed possible. All there was was now, a raging fury. When an owl flew up, startled out of a tree by the battle racket, some crows attacked it in flight between the lines. "Moses, what a country!" a soldier exclaimed as he watched. "The very birds are fighting."

By now it was past midday. Rosecrans came up from Crawfish Spring about 1 o'clock, riding toward the sound of guns, and established headquarters in a small log house belonging to Mrs Eliza Glenn, the widow of a Confederate soldier. Located on a commanding elevation a bit under two miles north of Lee & Gordon's Mill and half a mile west of the road along with his army was deployed, this afforded him an excellent site, just south of the center of his line, from which to give close attention to his right, while the ablest of his corps commanders took charge of the left, which extended to the intersection not quite three miles to the north. Neatly dressed in black trousers, a white vest, and a plain blue coat, Old Rosy was in fine spirits, and with cause; Thomas had gotten the jump on the rebels this morning and seemed to be holding them handily with the reinforcements sent in prompt response to his request. Not even the capture, in the course of an early afternoon skirmish in the woods about a mile due east of headquarters, of some prisoners from Hood's division — conclusive evidence that part at least of Longstreet's corps, with an estimated strength of 17,000 effectives, was already on the scene — served to diminish the confidence displayed in the northern commander's bearing. A reporter, observing the general's flushed cheeks and sparkling eyes, considered him "very handsome," Roman nose and all, as he went over the growing collection of dispatches from subordinates, brought by couriers from all quarters of the field, and studied a rather sketchy map unrolled on the Widow Glenn's parlor table. He was in such good spirits, in fact, that he took the occasion to indulge in one of his favorite pastimes, the interrogation of a prisoner.

The man selected was a Texas captain, taken just now in the skirmish on the far side of the LaFayette Road. Rosecrans invited him to step outside, and the two sat together, apart from the officers of the staff, on a log in the side yard. Whittling as he spoke, the Ohioan conversed pleasantly for a time, then casually inquired about the Confederate dispositions.

"General, it has cost me a great deal of trouble to find your lines," the captain answered. "If you take the same amount of trouble you will find ours."

Smiling, Rosecrans went on whittling and asking questions, but to small avail. The prisoner, though he readily admitted that he was from Bragg's army, could not recall what corps or division he belonged to.

"Captain," Rosecrans said at last, "you don't seem to know much, for a man whose appearance seems to indicate so much intelligence."

Now it was the Texan's turn to smile.

"Well, General," he replied, "if you are not satisfied with my information, I will volunteer some. We are going to whip you most tremendously in this fight."

Soon after the rebel captain had been taken to the rear — alternately reticent and voluble, but about as irksome one way as the other — there was evidence that his parting remark might well turn out to be an accurate prediction. Moreover, the evidence was not only promptly presented; it was also repeated twice in the course of the next four hours, in the form of three extremely savage attacks launched against as many parts of the Federal line by Stewart, Hood, and Cleburne, three of the hardest-hitting commanders in Bragg's army.

So far, except for some minor skirmishing between the lines, there had been no action on the Union right with anything like the violence of the fighting that had continued all this time on the left, where Thomas was engaged with four of the eight blue divisions now on hand. Bragg had sent for Stewart's division of Buckner's corps, intending to throw it into the seesaw battle raging on the Confederate right; but Stewart — a forty-two-year-old Tennessean called "Old Straight" by his men, partly because of his ramrod posture, but mostly because he had taught mathematics at West Point, where he had acquired the nickname, and afterwards at Cumberland University — as he marched downstream through the woods, took a sudden turn to the west at about 2.30, either by design or error, and lunged instead at the enemy center, a mile south of where Bragg had intended to commit him. He struck Van Cleve's division of Crittenden's corps, which had seen no combat so far in the campaign and was unbraced for the shock. Having recently come into line after making their second night march in the past two days, Van Cleve and his men were not only considerably worn but were also as thoroughly confused as the Illinois soldier who later remarked wryly that "the reassembling of his three corps by Rosecrans was a tactical proceeding that even the privates could not make heads or tails of." At any rate, the three brigades broke badly under the impact of a host of screaming rebels, hurled at them from the dense woods in their front. Crittenden himself and Van Cleve, who at fifty-four was the oldest Federal brigadier — a New-Jersey-born Minnesotan and a member of the West Point class of 1831, he had been twenty-five years out of uniform when the war came — did what they could to stay the rout, though with little or no success. Stewart's troops made it up to and across the LaFayette Road to where the Glenn house, its yard crowded with staff orderlies and couriers and their mounts, was in plain view across the rolling landscape. But so, by now, was something else; two somethings else, in fact. Thomas's two remaining divisions under Reynolds and Negley, hard on their way north to join him, were halted in their tracks, still in column and nearly a mile apart, then faced right and thrown without delay into the breach, which Thomas had already begun to narrow by sending Brannan's troops — recovered by now, in part at least, from the mauling they had taken on the left — against its northern lip. As these three blue divisions converged upon his isolated gray one, Stewart fell sullenly back from contact, firing as he went. Half a mile east of the road he called a halt, and there, under cover of the woods he had emerged from, laid down a mass of fire that discouraged pursuit.

Hood was in position on the left of Stewart, due west of Alexander's Bridge. At the height of the uproar to his right front, though he was without orders, he put his two divisions in line abreast, Johnson on the left of Law, and started them forward at about 4 o'clock, by which time the racket up ahead had begun to subside. Tramping westward through the woods and brush, the Texas brigade, on the far right, went past one of Stewart's Tennessee regiments, which had just returned, blown and bloody, from its brief penetration of the Union line. "Rise up, Tennesseans," one of the advancing soldiers called, "and see the Texans go in!" Too weary to reply, let alone stand, Stewart's fought-out infantry lay there panting and watching as Hood's men swept past them, first the skirmishers, then the solid ranks of the main body, the pride of the Army of Northern Virginia, Lee's hard hitters who had shattered many a Yankee line, from Gaines Mill to the Devil's Den. Holding their attack formation as best they could in the heavy woods, these stalwarts broke into the clear near the LaFayette Road, a mile south of where Stewart had crossed it an hour ago, and went with a shout for a blue division drawn up to receive them on the west side of the road, apparently without supports on either flank.

It was Davis, of McCook. His three brigades were struck by the rebel six with predictable results; for though the bluecoats stood for a time, firing nervously but rapidly into the long line of attackers, the limit of their endurance was soon reached. Both overlapped flanks gave way at once, as if on signal, and the center promptly buckled under the strain. Once more, however, as the unstrung Federals fled westward and the Confederates pursued them to within plain view of the Widow Glenn's, yelling for all they were worth, a pair of blue divisions — the last two of the ten that would reach the field today — arrived most opportunely from the south, with all the patness of the cavalry in light fiction. Wood's division of Crittenden's corps was in the lead, coming down from Lee & Gordon's Mill, and now it was the rebels who were outflanked; Johnson had to call a halt to meet the menace to his left, as did Law, beyond him on the right. Davis rallied and led his fugitives back into the fight at about the same time Sheridan's division arrived from Crawfish Springs to tip the balance in favor of the Union. Halted, Johnson had to yield to this new pressure, and Law was obliged to conform: especially when Wilder's Lightning Brigade, still detached from Reynolds and held by Rosecrans in reserve for such emergencies, added the weight of its multishot carbines to the fray. The two butternut divisions fell back to the east side of the road, which then became and remained the dividing line between the Confederate left and the Federal right. Sheridan, in accordance with his instinct for aggression, tried to press matters with a charge, but was repulsed, and Hood settled into a new line about a mile in advance of his old one. On the right, as the men of the Texas brigade retired through the woods, badly cut up by Wilder's rapid-fire weapons in the final stage of their withdrawal, they came back to where they had called on Stewart's blown and bloody Tennesseans to "rise up ... and see the Texans go in." The regiment was still there, fairly well rested from its exertions, and one of its members did not neglect the opportunity thus afforded. "Rise up, Tennesseans," he called, "and see the Texans come out!"

By now it was sunset and the third in this sequence of savage attacks was about to be launched at the far end of the line. Summoned for one more go at the Federal left, where the fighting had slacked as if by common consent though the issue was still in doubt, Cleburne left his position opposite Lee & Gordon's at about the time Stewart's drive on the enemy center was being repulsed and Hood's was getting started against the right. Fording the Chickamauga well above Alexander's Bridge, the use of which would have delayed their march, his men found the spring-fed water icy cold and armpit deep. Wet and chilled, they continued northward through the woods for another four miles to reach their jump-off position just after sundown. Across the way, Thomas now had five divisions, Reynolds having come on to join him while Negley stayed behind to plug the gap created when Van Cleve was driven rearward. "Old Pap," as the solidly built Virginian's soldiers liked to call him, had seen to it that Baird and Johnson, who were posted at the extremity of his line, were braced for the assault he was convinced would be renewed before the day was over, while Palmer, Reynolds, and Brannan, who continued his line southward in that order, were warned to be ready to lend a hand. When the sun went down behind Missionary Ridge and no new attack had developed, they began to tell each other he was wrong; until Cleburne exploded out of the darkling woods, directly in front of Baird and Johnson, and proved him emphatically right. The three gray brigades were in line abreast, covering more than a mile from flank to flank, with Cheatham in close support. Though little could be seen in the gathering darkness, the immediate impression was one of absolute chaos as Cleburne's 5000 screaming men bore down on roughly twice that many defenders in the two blue divisions in their path. They charged with a clatter of musketry so tremendous that they seemed to be trying to make up for the disparity in numbers by the rapidity of their fire. That was in fact the case; Cleburne placed great stock in fast, well-aimed fire, and had drilled his troops relentlessly in rifle tactics, in and out of normal work hours, with just the present effect in mind. An Indiana captain later recorded that the advancing graybacks were "loading and firing in a manner that I believe was never surpassed on any battlefield during the rebellion," and Cleburne himself declared soon afterwards that "for half an hour [the firing] was the heaviest I ever heard."

This time there was no last-minute outside help; unlike Crittenden and McCook, Thomas had to fight with what he had when he was hit. After all, however, what he had was half the army, and though he lost a pair of guns, three stands of colors, some 400 captured men, and nearly a mile of ground on his outer flank, it was enough to stave off disaster. When full darkness put an end to what another Hoosier called "a display of fireworks that one does not like to see more than once in a lifetime," the blue line was severely contracted but unbroken. Baird and Brannan were forced back to the LaFayette Road on the left and right, but the three divisions between them maintained an eastward bulge of about 600 yards at its deepest. Cleburne's men, bedding down wherever they happened to be when the order reached them to stop firing, could hear the Federals hard at work beyond the curtain of night, felling trees to be used in the construction of breastworks along the contracted bulge of their new line. Shivering in their still-wet clothes, for the night was unseasonably cold for September, the listening Confederates knew only too well that they would have to try to overrun those breastworks in the morning.

Back at his campfire near Alexander's Bridge, Bragg was telling his corps commanders — all but Longstreet, who would get his instructions when he arrived near midnight, and Hill, who afterwards explained that he had not been able to locate the command post in the darkness — that the army's objective remained the same as yesterday: "to turn the enemy's left, and by direct attack force him into McLemore's Cove." Kershaw arrived after dark with his two brigades, completing a fast march from the Ringgold railhead, and was sent at once to Hood. By way of final preparation, Breckinridge was ordered to take position on Cleburne's right, extending the gray line northward in an attempt to outflank Thomas, while Hindman made a shorter march to get between Hood and Preston on the left. These three divisions, so far uncommitted, would complete the order of battle for tomorrow's attack, which Polk was scheduled to open at dawn on the far right and which would then be taken up in sequence, corps by corps, all down the line.

Hill would later refer caustically to the disjointed sequence of attacks, in which he himself had taken no part except to detach one of his divisions, as "the sparring of the amateur boxer, not the crushing blows of the trained pugilist," and Bragg in turn would describe the action, so far, as nothing more than "severe skirmishing" engaged in by his various corps and division commanders, for the most part on their own, "while endeavoring to get into line of battle." But no one knew better than Rosecrans, across the way in the Widow Glenn's lamp-lighted parlor, how near a thing it had been for him at times. In addition to the day-long pounding his left had managed to absorb — including the blood-curdling twilight assault by what sounded like tens of thousands of fiends equipped with the latest style rapid-fire weapons — two rebel penetrations, one of his center and one of his right, had surged to within plain view of army headquarters, and of these the second had come so close that he and members of his staff had had to shout at one another in order to be heard above the din.

Some measure of his mounting concern could be seen in a series of telegrams sent to the War Department in the course of the day by Charles Dana, who had arrived from Vicksburg the week before to continue his services as a behind-the-scenes observer for Stanton. "Rosecrans has everything ready to grind up Bragg's flank," he reported from Crawfish Springs that morning, and at 1 p.m. he followed this up — or, rather, he failed to follow it up — with a somewhat less encouraging or at any rate less emphatic message, sent as he left for the scene of the fighting three miles north: "Everything is going well, but the full proportions of the conflict are not yet developed." By 2.30 the telegraph line had been extended to the Glenn house, and Dana kept the operator busy. "Fight continues to rage," he wired. "Decisive victory seems assured." At 3.20 he passed along a report from Thomas "that he is driving rebels, and will force them into Chickamauga tonight." Though the center was being assailed by then, and the right was about to be, Dana was not fazed. "Everything is prosperous. Sheridan is coming up," he announced at 4 o'clock. A near commitment at 4.30 as to the outcome — "I do not yet dare to say our victory is complete, but it seems certain" — was modified in the dispatch that followed at 5.20: "Now appears to be undecided contest, but later reports will enable us to understand more clearly."

So it went; so it had gone all day. Despite his show of heartiness, what he mainly communicated was his confusion in attempting to follow a battle which, as he said, was "fought altogether in a thick forest, invisible to outsiders." In that sense, even the army commander was an outsider. Except for a rearward trickle of reports, most of them about as disconcerted as Dana's to Stanton, no one at headquarters could do much more than guess at what was happening in the smoky woods beyond the LaFayette Road. Rosecrans tried for a time, with the help of Mrs Glenn, to follow the progress of the fight by ear. She would make a guess, when a gun was heard, that it was "nigh out about Reed's Bridge" or "about a mile fornenst John Kelly's house," and he would try to match this information with the place names on the map. But it was a far from satisfactory procedure, for a variety of reasons. The map was a poor one in the first place, and after a while the roar was practically continuous all along the front. A reporter thought he had never witnessed "anything so ridiculous as this scene" between Old Rosy and the widow. Presently, when Stewart's men broke through the Federal center, she had to be removed to a place of greater safety, but Rosecrans, "fairly quivering with excitement," continued to pace back and forth, rubbing his palms rapidly together as the sound of firing swelled and quickened. "Ah! there goes Brannan!" he exclaimed with obvious satisfaction. He might have been right; besides, the noise was about all he had to go on; but it did not seem to the reporter that the general understood the situation any better than the departed countrywoman had done. Still, he kept pacing and exclaiming, perhaps in an attempt to ease the tension on his nerves and keep his spirits up. "Ah — there goes Brannan!" he would say; or, "That's Negley going in!"

Out on the line, when darkness finally put an end to the long day's fighting, the troops had a hard time of it. "How we suffered that night no one knows," a veteran was to recall. "Water could not be found; the rebels had possession of the Chickamauga, and we had to do without. Few of us had blankets and the night was very cold. All looked with anxiety for the coming of the dawn; for although we had given the enemy a rough handling, he had certainly used us very hard."

Under such conditions, despite much loss of sleep both nights before, work on the construction of breastworks was welcome as a means of keeping warm, as well as a diversion from thoughts of tomorrow. For Rosecrans, however, there could be no release from the latter; it was his job. He could take pride in the fact that his line, though obliged to yield an average mile of ground throughout its length today, was not only intact but was also considerably shorter than it had been when this morning's contest opened. Then too, word had come that Halleck at last was doing all he could to speed reinforcements to North Georgia; urgent appeals had gone from Washington to Burnside and Grant, at Knoxville and in Mississippi, directing them to send troops to Chattanooga in all haste, and similar messages had been dispatched to Hurlbut at Memphis, Schofield in Missouri, and John Pope in far-off Minnesota. It was a comfort to Rosecrans to know that in time there would be these supports to fall back on. Meanwhile, though, he had to fight with what he had on hand, and he was by no means sure that this would be enough, since prisoners had been taken from no less than a dozen regiments known to have arrived just yesterday from Virginia. How many others had come or were arriving tonight he did not know, for the captives were nearly as close-mouthed under interrogation as the Texas captain had been this afternoon, but intelligence officers had little trouble identifying these "Virginians" by their standard gray uniforms, which were in natty contrast to the "go-as-you-please" garments worn in the western armies. Occasionally, too, a scrap of information could be extracted by goading the prisoners into anger. "How does Longstreet like the western Yankees?" one was asked in a mocking tone, and he replied with a growl: "You'll get enough of Longstreet before tomorrow night."

This might be nothing more than wishful rebel thinking. On the other hand it might be an informed and accurate prediction. At any rate, whichever it was, Rosecrans decided — as he had done under similar circumstances on New Year's Eve almost nine months ago — that he would do well to call a council of war for the triple purpose of briefing his principal subordinates on the over-all situation, of obtaining their recommendations as to a proper course of action, and of enabling him, at some later date, to shift at least a share of the blame in event of a defeat. Besides, he had a natural fondness for conference discussions, especially late-at-night ones, whether the subject was strategy or religion. The council accordingly convened at headquarters at 11 o'clock that evening. Most of those present, including the three corps commanders, had attended the conference held at the close of the first day's fighting in the last great battle; the difference was in the staff. "Poor Garesché," as Rosecrans had referred to the previous chief of staff after his head was blown off by a cannonball, had been replaced in January by Brigadier General James A. Garfield, a thirty-two-year-old former Ohio schoolteacher, lawyer, lay preacher, and politician, whose warm handclasp seemed to one observer to convey the message, "Vote early. Vote right," and whose death, at the hands of an assassin who voted both early and right and then failed to get the appointment to which he believed this entitled him, would occur exactly eighteen years from today, partly as a direct result of what was going to happen here tomorrow. Big-headed, with pale eyes and a persuasive manner — like Hooker, he was a protégé of Secretary Chase's, and up to now his most notable service in the war had been as a member of the court-martial that convicted Fitz-John Porter — Garfield opened the council by displaying for the assembled generals a map with the positions of all the Union divisions indicated, along with those of the Confederates so far as they were known; after which Rosecrans called for individual opinions as to what was to be done. McCook and Crittenden — the Ohioan, according to an obviously unfriendly fellow officer, had "a weak nose that would do no credit to a baby" and a grin that gave rise to "suspicion that he is either still very green or deficient in the upper story," while the Kentuckian was characterized more briefly as "a good drinker," one of those men, fairly common in the higher echelons of all armies, who "know how to blow their own horns exceedingly well" — had little to contribute in the way of advice, each perhaps being somewhat chagrined by the loss of one of his three divisions, detached that morning to reinforce the left, and somewhat subdued by the near-destruction of one of his remaining two in the course of the afternoon. Not so Thomas, who differed as much from them in outlook, or anyhow in the emphatic expression of his outlook, as he did in appearance. Ponderous and phlegmatic, he was described by another observer as "not scrimped anywhere, and square everywhere — square face, square shoulders, square step; blue eyes with depths in them, withdrawn beneath a pent-house of a brow, features with legible writing on them, and the whole giving the idea of massive solidity, of the right kind of man to 'tie to.' " Though he slept through much of the conference — not only because it was his custom (he had done the same at Stones River) but also because he had spent the last two nights on the march and most of today under heavy attack — he repeated the same words whenever he was called on for a tactical opinion: "I would strengthen the left." But when Rosecrans replied, as he did each time, "Where are we going to take it from?" there was no answer; Thomas would be back asleep by then, propped upright in his chair.

At the council held nine months ago in the rain-lashed cabin beside the Nashville pike, the discussion had centered mainly on whether the army should retreat; but here tonight, in the small log house on the field of Chickamauga, the word was used only in connection with the rebels. The decision, committed to paper for distribution as soon as it was reached, was that the Federals would hold their ground. Unless

Bragg withdrew under cover of darkness — there was some conjecture that he might, though it was based more on hope than on tangible evidence, of which there was not a shred that indicated a change in his clear intention to destroy them — they would offer him battle tomorrow, on the same terms as today. At this late hour, in point of fact, that seemed not only the bravest but also the safest thing to do, considering the risk a retreating army would run of being caught, trains and all, strung out on the roads leading back through Rossville and McFarland's gaps to Chattanooga, which was a good ten miles from the Widow Glenn's. There would be minor readjustments, though not of Granger's three-brigade reserve force, which was instructed to remain where it was, covering Rossville Gap and holding that escape hatch open in case of a collapse. To lessen the chances of this last, which would be most likely to occur as a result of a rebel breakthrough, Rosecrans directed that his ten-division line of battle along the LaFayette Road was to be strengthened by further contraction. Thomas would hold his five divisions in their present intrenched position on the left, and McCook would move his two northward to connect with Negley's division, on Thomas's right, while Crittenden withdrew his two for close-up support of the center or a rapid shift in whichever direction they were needed, north or south. When all this had been discussed and agreed on, Garfield put it in writing and read it back, and when this in turn had been approved it was passed to the headquarters clerks for copying. By now it was midnight. While the generals were waiting for the clerks to finish their task, Rosecrans provided coffee for a social interlude, the principal feature of which was a soulful rendition by "the genial, full-stomached McCook," as one reporter called him, of a plaintive ballad entitled "The Hebrew Maiden."

Possibly Thomas slept through this as well; possibly not. In any event, it was 2 o'clock in the morning before he returned to his position on the left, where he found a report awaiting him from Baird, who warned that his division, posted on the flank, could not be extended all the way to the Reed's Bridge road, as ordered, and still be strong enough to hold if it was struck again by anything like the twilight blow that had sent it reeling for more than a mile until darkness ended the fighting. Thomas made a quick inspection by moonlight and arrived at the same conclusion, then sent a message back to headquarters, explaining the trouble and requesting that Negley, who had been halted and thrown in to shore up the crumbling center while on his way to the left that afternoon, be ordered to resume his northward march and rejoin his proper corps, the critical outer flank of which was in danger of being crushed for lack of support or turned for lack of troops to extend it. Rosecrans promptly agreed by return messenger, as he had done to all such specific requests from his senior corps commander; Negley would march at dawn. Reassured, Thomas at last bedded down under a large oak, one of whose protruding roots afforded a pillow for his head, and there resumed the sleep that had been interrupted, if not by McCook's singing, then at any rate by the breakup of the council of war, some time after midnight.

He woke to Sunday's dawn, already impatient for Negley's arrival. The sun came up blood red through the morning haze and the smoke of yesterday's battle, which still hung about the field. "It is ominous," the chief of staff was saying, back at the Widow Glenn's, as he pointed dramatically at the rising sun. "This will indeed be a day of blood." Thomas needed no sign to tell him that, but he was growing increasingly anxious about his unsupported flank, which the army commander had assured him would be reinforced without delay. The sun rose higher. Presently it was a full hour above the land-line, and still Negley had not arrived. Rosecrans himself came riding northward about this time, however, and though his face was drawn and puffy from strain and lack of sleep, he spoke encouragingly as he drew rein from point to point along the line. "Fight today as well as you did yesterday," he told his troops, "and we shall whip them!" This had a somewhat mixed effect. "I did not like the way he looked," a soldier later recalled, "but of course felt cheered, and did not allow myself to think of any such thing as defeat."

✗ 5 ✗

Bragg and his staff were up and mounted before daylight, waiting for the roar of guns that would signal Polk's compliance with his orders, received in person the night before, "to assail the enemy on our extreme right at day-dawn of the 20th." Perhaps by now, after the repeated frustrations of the past two weeks, the Confederate commander might have been expected to accept delay, if not downright disobedience, as more or less standard procedure on the part of his ranking subordinates — particularly Polk and Hill, the wing and corps commanders directly in charge of the troops who would open the attack — but such was not the case. Even if he had learned to expect it, he had by no means learned to take it calmly. Three months later, when he submitted his official account of the battle, his anger was still apparent. "With increasing anxiety and disappointment," he wrote then, "I waited until after sunrise without hearing a gun, and at length dispatched a staff officer to Lieutenant General Polk to ascertain the cause of the delay and urge him to a prompt and speedy movement."

By the time the aide located Polk, delivered the message, and returned, the sun was more than an hour high and Bragg's impatience had been mounting with it. Not a gun had yet been fired, and across the way the Yankees were hard at work improving by daylight the breastworks they had constructed in the darkness. The thought of this was enough to sour a far sweeter disposition than Bragg would ever be able to lay claim to. Moreover, what the staff officer had to report on his return brought his chief's wrath to what might be called full flower. He had found the bishop, he declared, "at a farm house three miles from the line of his troops, about one hour after sunrise, sitting on the gallery reading a newspaper and waiting, as he said, for his breakfast." Hearing this, Bragg did something rare for him. He cursed — "a terrible exclamation," the aide termed the outburst — then rode to Polk's headquarters, intending no doubt to rebuke the wing commander in person, but found that he had just left for the front, remarking as he did so: "Do tell General Bragg that my heart is overflowing with anxiety for the attack. Overflowing with anxiety, sir."

It was close to 8 o'clock by then, better than two hours past the hour scheduled for an advance on the far right, and Bragg learned from one of the bishop's aides, who had remained behind, something of what had caused the mix-up and delay. Hill had not only failed to find army headquarters last night; he had also failed to locate Polk, who in turn had been unable to find him. As a result, unlike Cheatham and Walker, who had reported to headquarters the evening before, Hill had neither received his orders to attack nor been led to suspect that Bragg or anyone else had any such plans in mind for the two divisions on the northern flank. Learning of this for the first time from the courier who returned that morning from an unsuccessful all-night search for Hill, Polk sent orders directly to Breckinridge and Cleburne, bypassing the fugitive corps commander, for them to "move and attack the enemy as soon as you are in position." Hill was with them when the message was delivered, and when they protested that their men were not only not "in position," but had not had time to eat their morning rations, he backed them up with a note in which he blandly informed the wing commander that it would be "an hour or so" before the two divisions would be ready to go forward. It was this reply, received at about 7.30, that had caused the bishop — whose overflowing heart by now outweighed his empty stomach — to interrupt his breakfast on the farmhouse gallery, or perhaps not even wait any longer for it to be served, and set out instead for the front and a conference with Hill.

Bragg got there first, however, apparently by taking a shorter route. Trailed by his staff, he rode up to where Hill had established headquarters between Breckinridge and Cleburne, whose troops had still not been placed in attack formation and were just now being fed. When Bragg inquired testily why he had not attacked at daylight in accordance with last night's order, Hill replied coolly and with obvious satisfaction, as he afterwards recalled, "that I was hearing then for the first time that such an order had been issued and had not known whether we were to be the assailants or the assailed." Bragg's anger and impatience had no discernible effect on him whatever. He would not be hurried. Miffed at having been cast in a role subordinate to that of the other two lieutenant generals, who had been made wing commanders while all he had under him was the corps he had brought onto the field, he was unmistakably determined, in the words of a later observer, "to assert to the limit what authority he retained." Soon Polk arrived, but neither he nor Bragg, scarcely on speaking terms by now with one another, was able to get their fellow North Carolinian to hurry things along; Hill's claim was that he could scarcely be held responsible for not obeying instructions that had not reached him. He took his time, and what was more he saw to it that his two division commanders took theirs as well. The troops were aligned punctiliously under cover of the woods, and all was re-ported ready, down to the final round in the final cartridge box, before Hill gave the nod that sent Breckinridge forward at 9.30, followed within fifteen minutes by Cleburne on his left, a full four hours past the time Bragg had set for the attack to open on the far right of the army.

Across the way, Rosecrans too had been having his troubles dur-ing the long delay, and though he began the day in a frame of mind that seemed cheerful enough for a man who had had but little sleep to ease the built-up tension on his nerves, he completely lost his temper before he returned to headquarters from his early morning ride along his still-contracting line of battle. Greeted by Thomas when he reached the left, he found him in high spirits over his successful resistance to yes-terday's frantic rebel attempts to drive him from the field. "Whenever I touched their flanks they broke, General; they broke!" he exclaimed. In point of fact, as the long silence continued on through sunrise and beyond, it had become increasingly apparent that they had learned their lesson; they seemed to want no more of it today. Still, it was strange to see the phlegmatic Virginian display such exuberance, even though it lasted only until he spotted a newsman riding with the staff; whereupon he flushed and withdrew at once into the habitual reserve which he used as a shield between himself and such people. He spoke instead of possible danger to his left. Scouts had reported that the Confederates, out beyond the screening woods and thickets, were continuing to shift in that direction. "You must move up, too, as fast as they do," Rosecrans told him. Thomas agreed, but he also pointed out that this required more troops. There was the rub; Negley had not arrived. Rosecrans assured him that Negley was on the way by now, for he himself had seen to it in the course of his ride north along the line. Thomas was relieved to hear this, though he repeated that he would not consider his flank secure until reinforcements got there to extend and shore it up.

But when the Union commander rode back south, retracing his steps but not stopping now for speeches, he found to his chagrin that the reinforcements he had just assured Thomas were already on their way had not budged from their position in the center, where he had left them an hour ago with orders to march north. However, Negley had an excellent reason for his apparent insubordination. McCook still had not closed the gap created by Crittenden's withdrawal in compliance with last night's instructions, so that if Negley had pulled out in turn, as ordered, he would have left a mile-wide hole in the Federal center; which plainly, at a time when an all-out rebel assault was expected at any minute almost anywhere along the front, would not do. Nettled — as well he might be, for the sun was two hours high by now — Rosecrans hurried rearward and told Crittenden to return Wood's division to the line in place of Negley's, which then could be released to join Thomas, two miles away on the unshored northern flank. Next he rode south in search of McCook, whose slowness was at the root of the present trouble. Finding him, he stressed the need for haste and an early end to the grumbling confusion into which his two divisions had been thrown by a renewal of their sidling movement toward the left. All this time, though only by the hardest, Old Rosy had managed to keep a grip on his temper. But when he returned to the center and found Negley still in position, with Wood nowhere in sight, he lost it entirely. Pausing only long enough to order Negley to send one of his three brigades to Thomas at once, even though no replacements had arrived, he galloped rearward and presently came upon Wood, who was conferring with his staff about the unexpected and still pending movement back into line. "What is the meaning of this, sir?" Rosecrans barked at him. "You have disobeyed my specific orders. By your damnable negligence you are endangering the safety of the entire army, and by God I will not tolerate it! Move your division at once, as I have instructed, or the consequences will not be pleasant for yourself." Wood, a forty-year-old Kentuckian, flushed at being upbraided thus in the presence of his staff, but as a West Pointer, a regular army man, and a veteran of all the army's fights, from Shiloh on, he knew better than to protest. Choking back his resentment, he saluted and put his three brigades in motion.

The lead brigade was just coming into line, at about 9.45, when an uproarious clatter broke out on the far left, fulfilling Thomas's prediction that his would be the flank the rebels would assault. From the sound of it, as heard by Rosecrans at the Widow Glenn's, to which he had returned after venting his spleen in the encounter with Wood, they were putting in all they had.

They were indeed putting in all they had at that end of the line: not all at once, however, as the sudden eruption seemed to indicate by contrast with the silence which it shattered, but rather in a series of divisional attacks, as Bragg had ordered. Breckinridge struck first, on the far right. Though his left brigade came up against the north end of the mile-long curve of breastworks and was involved at once in an unequal fire fight, standing in the open to swap volleys with an adversary under cover, the other two found no such obstacle in their path. Thomas had prolonged his line by shifting one of Johnson's brigades from his center, and the brigade detached in haste from Negley had just arrived to extend the left still farther, but there had not been time enough for felling trees, much less for the heavy task of snaking and staking the trunks into position to fight behind. As a result, the two gray brigades advancing southward down the LaFayette Road met and fought the two blue ones on equal terms, first with a stand-up exchange of volleys, face to face, and then, as the defenders began to waver, with a charge that drove them rearward in a rush. However, Thomas had made good use of the time afforded him by the delaying action. Two more brigades were at hand by then, one from Brannan, which he brought over from his right, and one from Van Cleve, which Rosecrans had sent double-timing to the left when the attack first exploded in that direction. Together they stalled the advance of the jubilant graybacks, and then with the help of the other two brigades, which rallied when the pressure was relieved, drove them back northward, restoring the flank that had crumbled under assault. There was, of course, the danger that they might be reinforced to try again in greater strength; in which case Thomas would be hard put to find reinforcements of his own, for Cleburne's attack had been launched by now, due south of and adjoining Breckinridge, with such persistent savagery that not a man could be spared from the close-up defense of the long line of breastworks in order to meet a new threat to the left. All Thomas could do was continue what he had been doing ever since he reached the field; that is, call on Rosecrans for more troops from the right and center, which had been stripped to less than four divisions, as compared to the more than six already concentrated here.

Events would show that this was rather beside the point, however, for though the old one would continue with much of its original fury all morning, there was not going to be any new end-on threat to the Union left. Bragg had called for a definite series of attacks, beginning on his far right and continuing in sequence down the full length of his line, and neither Polk nor Hill (if, indeed, they were even aware of the Chancellorsville-like opportunity — which apparently they were not) was in any frame of mind to make suggestions, let alone appeals, to a commander who was already in a towering rage because his instructions had not been followed to the letter. Instead, they continued to hammer unrelentingly at the long southward curve of enemy breastworks, encouraged from time to time by reports such as one sent back by Brigadier General Lucius Polk, the bishop's thirty-year-old nephew, whose brigade of Cleburne's division smashed through the Federal outpost works, just in front of the center of the bulge, and drove the blue pickets back on their main line of resistance. Elated, he turned in mid-career to an officer on his staff. "Go back and tell the old general," he said, meaning his uncle, "that we have passed two lines of breastworks; that we have got them on the jump, and I am sure of carrying the main line." By the time this reached the wing commander, who was conferring with Cheatham, the brigade had been repulsed. But that was no part of the report, and Polk was as elated by the message as his nephew had been when he gave it to the aide. "General," he told Cheatham, "move your division and attack at once." The Tennessean, who had massed his five brigades in anticipation of the order, was prompt to comply. "Forward, boys, and give them hell!" he shouted, much as he had done nine months ago at Murfreesboro, and the bishop approved now, as he had then, of the spirit if not of the words his friend had chosen to express it. "Do as General Cheatham says, boys!" he called after the troops as they moved out.

But Cheatham had no greater success than Hill had had before him. His men went up to within easy range of the breastworks, which seemed to burst into flame at their approach, then recoiled, all in one quick involuntary movement like that of a hand testing the heat of a still-hot piece of metal. Walker's two divisions, held in reserve till then, had much the same reaction when they were committed at about 10.45, shortly after Cheatham had been repulsed. By now the entire right wing was engaged, including Forrest's dismounted horsemen, who went in with Breckinridge. "What infantry is that?" Hill asked in the course of a tour of inspection on the right. He had never seen troops like these in the East. "Forrest's cavalry," he was told. Presently, when Forrest himself came riding back to meet him, the North Carolinian removed his hat in salutation. "General Forrest," he said, "I wish to congratulate you and those brave men moving across that field like veteran infantry upon their magnificent behavior. In Virginia I made myself extremely unpopular with the cavalry because I said that so far I had not seen a dead man with spurs on. No one could speak disparagingly of such troops as yours." Whether the Tennessean blushed at this high praise could not be told, for in battle his face always took on the color of heated bronze. "Thank you, General," he replied, then wheeled his horse and with a wave of his hand galloped back into the thick of the fight that had excited Hill's admiration.

At no one point along the Confederate right had the issue been pressed to its extremity by the mass commitment of reserves to achieve a breakthrough. Rather, the pressure had been equally heavy on all points at once, as if what Bragg intended to accomplish was not so much a penetration as a cataclysm, a total collapse of the whole Union left, like that of a dam giving way to an unbearable weight of water. This was in fact what he was after, and at times it seemed to some among the defenders that he was about to get it. "The assaults were repeated with an impetuosity that threatened to overwhelm us," according to John Palmer,

whose division was on loan to Thomas from Crittenden. Except on the
extended flank, however, where there had been no time to throw up
breastworks, casualties had been comparatively light for the Federals,
who were protected by the stout log barricade they had constructed
overnight and improved during the four daylight hours which Hill's
delay had afforded them this morning. It was not so for the attackers;
their losses had been heavy everywhere. "The rebs charged in three
distinct lines," an Ohio captain wrote, "but each time they charged they
were driven back with fearfully decimated ranks." Some measure of
the truth of this was shown in the loss of those who led the frantic
charges. Breckinridge, Cleburne, and Gist each had a brigade commander
killed or mortally wounded in the course of this one hour: Brigadier
Generals Ben Hardin Helm, who had married Mary Lincoln's youngest
sister and recently succeeded to command of the Orphan Brigade, and
James Deshler, who had been exchanged, promoted, and transferred east
after his discomfiture by Sherman at Arkansas Post, and Colonel Peyton
Colquitt, who had taken over Gist's brigade when that general was
put in charge of the division Walker brought from Mississippi. Moreover, another of Breckinridge's brigadiers, Daniel W. Adams, an accident-
prone or perhaps merely unlucky Kentucky-born Louisianan who had
lost an eye at Shiloh and been severely wounded again at Murfreesboro,
was shot from his horse and captured when the attack that crumpled the
Union flank was repulsed by reinforcements whose arrival was unmatched by any of his own. It had gone that way, with varying degrees
of success, but nowhere with complete success, all along the front of the
Confederate right wing. Still, with the evidence of the casualty lists before him, Bragg could scarcely complain of any lack of determination in
the fighting, no matter how disappointed he was at the outcome so far
of his attempt to smash Old Rosy's left as a prologue to rolling up his
entire line and packing it southward into McLemore's Cove for destruction.

By 11 o'clock all five of Polk's divisions had been committed.
Now Longstreet's turn had come. Bragg passed the word for Stewart to
go in, and in he went, driving hard for the enemy breastworks at the
point where they curved back to the LaFayette Road immediately opposite his position on the right of the Confederate left wing.

★ ★ ★

There Reynolds was posted, with Brannan on his right, one east
and the other west of the road, the latter having pulled his division
back about a hundred yards in order to take advantage of the cover afforded by some heavy woods in rear of a cleared field which would have
been much harder to defend. Stewart hit them both, attacking with all
the fury of yesterday, when he had shattered the blue line half a mile to

the south and penetrated to within sight of the Widow Glenn's before he was expelled. Today, though, there were breastworks all along the front, and he achieved nothing like his previous success. He was, in fact, flung back before he made contact, just as most of Polk's attackers had been, and had to be content, like them, with laying down a mass of fire that seemed to have little effect on the defenders beyond obliging them to keep their heads down between shots. There was, however, a good deal more to it than that, even though the result would not be evident for a while. What Stewart mainly accomplished was a further encouragement of Thomas's conviction that Bragg was throwing everything he had at the Union left, and this caused the Virginian to intensify his appeal for still more troops from the right and center, an appeal that had been communicated practically without letup, ever since the first attack exploded on his flank, by a steady procession of couriers who came to headquarters with messages warning that the left would surely be overwhelmed if it was not strengthened promptly.

Rosecrans still was quite as willing to do this as he had been earlier, when he said flatly that Thomas would be sustained in his present position "if he has to be reinforced by the entire army." In point of fact, that was what it was fast coming to by now. Shortly after 10 o'clock, with Van Cleve's remaining brigades already on their way north, McCook had been told to alert his troops for a rapid march to the left "at a moment's warning," and half an hour later the order came, directing him to send two of Sheridan's brigades at once and to follow with the third as soon as the corps front had been contracted enough for Davis to hold it alone. This would put eight divisions on the left, under Thomas, and leave only two on the right, one under Crittenden and one under McCook, but Rosecrans was preparing to send still more in that direction if they were needed. His calculations — "Where are we going to take it from?" — were interrupted at this point, however, by another of Thomas's couriers, a staff captain who, in addition to the accustomed plea for reinforcements, brought alarming news of something he had observed (or failed to observe) in the course of his ride from the left. Passing in rear of Reynolds, he had not seen Brannan's troops in the woods to the south; consequently, he reported "Brannan out of line and Reynolds' right exposed." The same opinion, derived from the same mistake, was expressed in stronger terms by another Thomas aide, who arrived on the heels of the captain and declared excitedly that there was "a chasm in the center," between the divisions of Reynolds and Wood, who had replaced Negley in the position on Brannan's right. Apparently convinced by the independent testimony of two eyewitnesses, Rosecrans did not take time to check on a report which, if true, scarcely allowed time for anything but attempting to repair an extremely dangerous error before it was discovered and exploited by the rebels. Instead, he turned

to a staff major — Garfield, he later explained, "was deeply engaged in
another matter" — and told him to send an order to Wood at once, correcting the situation. The major did so, heading the message 10.45 a.m.

> Brigadier General Wood, Commanding Division:
> The general commanding directs that you close up on Reynolds as
> fast as possible, and support him. Respectfully, &c.
> FRANK S. BOND, Major and Aide-de-Camp.

Wood received it at 10.55, barely more than an hour after the
vigorous dressing-down Old Rosy had given him for slowness in obeying a previous order. This time he did not delay execution, although
there was a degree of contradiction in the terms "close up on" and "support." Nor did he take time to find and confer with Crittenden, who had
been bypassed as if in emphasis of the need for haste expressed in the
phrase, "as fast as possible." McCook happened to be with him, though,
when the message was delivered, and on receiving his assurance that
Davis would sidle northward to fill the gap that would be left, the Kentuckian promptly began the shift the order seemed to require. There being no way to close on Reynolds without going around Brannan, who
was in position on Reynolds' right, Wood did just that. He pulled his
division straight back out of line and set out, across Brannan's rear, for
the hookup with Reynolds. Riding ahead to scout the route, he encountered Thomas, told him of the order, and asked where his brigades should
be posted in compliance. To his surprise, Thomas declared that Reynolds
was in no need of support — he and Brannan had just repulsed Stewart
without much trouble — but that Baird needed it badly, up at the far end
of the line. Wood said that he was willing to go there if Thomas would
take the responsibility for changing his instructions, and when the Virginian, duly thankful for a windfall that had plumped a full division of
reinforcements into his empty lap, replied that he would gladly do so,
Wood rode back to pass the word to his brigade commanders.

 That was how it came about that in attempting to fill a gap that
did not exist, Rosecrans created one; created, in fact, what Thomas's
overexcited aide had referred to, half an hour ago, as "a chasm in the
center." The aide had been mistaken then, but his words were now an
accurate description of what lay in the path of Longstreet, who was preparing, under cover across the way, to launch an all-out assault directly
upon the quarter-mile stretch of breastworks Wood's departure had left
unmanned.

 Old Peter had followed the progress of the fight with mounting
dissatisfaction. Up to now, the piecemeal nature of the attacks had given
the battle an all-too-familiar resemblance to Gettysburg, and he wanted
no more of that than he could possibly avoid. At 11 o'clock, with Polk's
wing unsuccessfully committed, he ventured a suggestion to the army

commander, of whom he had seen nothing since the night before, "that my column of attack could probably break the enemy's line if he cared to have it go in." In referring thus to his entire wing as a "column of attack," he was recommending that the attack in echelon, which in alley-fight terms amounted to crowding and shoving and clawing and slapping, be abandoned in favor of a combined assault, which amounted in those same terms to delivering one hard punch with a clenched fist. Just then, however, Stewart moved out alone on direct orders from Bragg, who had thrown caution to the winds — and science, too — by sending word for all the division commanders to go forward on their own in a frantic, headlong, unco-ordinated effort to overrun the Federal defenses. This was altogether too much for Longstreet. Though his admiration for the naked valor of the Confederate infantry was as large as any man's, he had recently seen the South's greatest single bid for victory turned into its worst defeat by a similar act of desperation in Pennsylvania, and he was determined not to have the same thing happen here in his home state if he could help it. He rode to the front at once to restrain Hood, whom he knew to be impetuous, from committing his corps before all three of his divisions, Johnson's and Law's and Kershaw's, were massed to strike as a unit, together with Hindman's on his left.

He got there just in time; Hood already had Johnson deployed, with Law in close support, and was about to take them forward. Longstreet had him wait for Kershaw, who formed a third line behind Law, and for Hindman, who dressed in a double line on Johnson, extending the front southward for a total width of half a mile. With Stewart engaged on Hood's right and Preston held in reserve on Hindman's left, Old Peter thus had four of his six divisions, eleven of his seventeen brigades, and some 16,000 of his 25,000 soldiers massed for the delivery of his clenched-fist blow. This was roughly half again more than he had had for the "charge" on the third day at Gettysburg, and not only were the troops in better condition here in Georgia than the ones had been in Pennsylvania, where four of the nine brigades had been shot to pieces in earlier actions, but they also had less than half as far to go before making contact, as well as excellent concealment during most of their approach. Longstreet apparently had no doubt whatsoever that the attack would be successful. Earlier that morning, speaking with what Hood described as "that confidence which had so often contributed to his extraordinary success," he had assured the tawny-bearded young man "that we would *of course* whip and drive [the Yankees] from the field," and Hood said afterwards: "I could not but exclaim that I was rejoiced to hear him so express himself, as he was the first general I had met since my arrival who talked of victory." However, for all his confidence, Old Peter did not forget the dangers that lurk in military iotas. He saw to it, in person and with the help of his staff, that his preliminary instructions were followed to the letter. Then and only then, shortly before 11.15, he gave the order for the column to go forward, due west through the dense woods that had screened his preparations.

With barely a quarter mile to go before they reached it, Bushrod Johnson's lead brigades crossed the LaFayette Road within ten minutes of receiving Longstreet's nod. As they surged across the dusty road and the open field beyond — the field that Wood had recessed his line to avoid — they encountered galling fire from the left and right, where Hindman and Law were hotly engaged, but almost none from directly ahead. Welcome though this was, they thought it strange until they found out why. Entering the woods on the far side, they scrambled over the deserted breastworks and caught sight, dead ahead and still within easy reach, of the last of Wood's brigades in the act of carrying out the order to "close up on and support" Reynolds. Yelling, the Confederates struck the vulnerable blue column flank and rear, sitting-duck fashion, and, as Johnson described the brief action, "cast the shattered fragments to the right and left." Still on the run, the butternut attackers crashed on through the forest and soon emerged into another clearing, larger than the first, with Missionary Ridge looming westward beyond the tops of intervening trees. Here at last, after their half-mile run, they paused to recover their breath and alignment, and Johnson later communicated something of the elation he and those around him felt, not only at what they had accomplished so far, but also at what lay spread before them, stark against the backdrop of the green slopes of the ridge. "The scene now presented was unspeakably grand," he declared in his report. "The resolute and impetuous charge, the rush of our heavy columns sweeping out from the shadow and gloom of the forest into the open fields flooded with sunlight, the glitter of arms, the onward dash of artillery and mounted men, the retreat of the foe, the shouts of the hosts of our army, the dust, the smoke, the noise of firearms — of whistling balls and grapeshot and of bursting shell — made up a battle scene of unsurpassed grandeur."

There was little time for admiring the view, however, since it included, in addition to the items mentioned, a number of hostile guns in furious action along a low ridge half a mile away, some firing southeast, some northeast, and some due east at him. Hood rode up amid the shellbursts, managing his horse with one hand because the other still hung useless in its sling. "Go ahead," he told Johnson, who was realigning his three brigades, "and keep ahead of everything." The Ohio-born Tennessean did just that. His men had taken a six-gun Federal battery soon after they crossed the road, but this had only sharpened their appetite for more. Resuming the advance, they quickly overran a position from which nine guns were firing, then plunged ahead to seize four more whose crews did not limber them in time for a getaway, as several others managed to do along that ripple of high ground overlooking a scene of moiling confusion in the enemy rear. Here Johnson called a halt at last, having accomplished a mile-deep penetration of the Union center, the destruction or dispersal of a whole brigade of bluecoats, and the capture of nineteen pieces of artillery, all between 11.15 and noon. Bracing his troops for a possible shock, he threw out skirmishers and sent word back to Longstreet of his need for reinforcements in case the enemy launched a counterattack at his isolated division, which had lost about one fourth of its strength in the course of its long advance. Such an attack did not seem likely, though, if he could judge by what he saw from where he stood. The blue army seemed to have come apart at the seams under the impact of that one savage blow, and its fugitives were streaming in disorder up the Dry Valley Road, which curved north and west across their rear, toward Missionary Ridge and the solitary notch that indicated McFarland's Gap and possible deliverance from the terror that had suddenly come on them, less than an hour ago, after a morning of taking it easy while the battle raged at the far end of the line.

Hindman had had much to do with the creation of the blue confusion. Though he encountered a far greater number of Federals in the course of his advance on Johnson's left, and thus was limited to a shallower penetration, this gave him the chance to inflict a far greater number of casualties, and that was what he did. Johnson had struck and shattered a single brigade, but Hindman served two whole divisions in that manner within the same brief span of time, converting McCook's supposed defense of the Union right into the headlong race for safety which Johnson observed with such elation when he called a halt soon afterward on the ridge overlooking the Dry Valley Road, a mile beyond the point where he had pierced the enemy center. Much as the unmanned breastworks in his front had facilitated the Tennessean's breakthrough, so did the Arkansan have the good fortune to find both Sheridan and Davis in motion when he hit them. The former, in compliance with his orders to reinforce the left, was marching north across the latter's rear, and the latter was sidling in the same direction, under instructions to close the gap created by Wood's abrupt departure, when they were assailed by Hindman's yelling graybacks, who came swarming out of the woods before the pickets along the LaFayette Road had time to do more than get off a few wild shots by way of sounding the alarm. Davis's men scattered rearward in a panic that soon infected Sheridan's two lead brigades, whose ranks were overrun by the fugitives as a prelude to being struck by their pursuers, with the result that the two divisions were mingled in flight. "McCook's corps was wiped off the field without any attempt at real resistance," an Illinois colonel later testified, adding that he had seen artillerists cut the traces and abandon their guns in order to make a faster getaway, while others on foot, including some who might otherwise have been willing to stand their ground, were swept along by the mob, "like flecks of foam upon a river." McCook himself was one of those flecks, and Sheridan and Davis were two more; but Brigadier

General William H. Lytle was not. Commanding Sheridan's third brigade, which had been left behind as a covering force southeast of the Widow Glenn's, he ordered a countercharge in an attempt to stem the rout, but fell at the first rebel volley and died soon after his men ran off and left him, the only Union general, out of thirty of that rank on the field, to be killed or captured or even touched by metal in this bloodiest of all the western battles.

One check there was, and a bloody one at that, though not from McCook or either of his two division commanders. Detached from Reynolds, the Lightning Brigade was still posted in support of the Union right, and when Hindman routed the foot soldiers there, capturing guns and colors on the run, Wilder brought his mounted troops in hard on the rebel flank and opened fire with his repeaters. That tore it. The southernmost gray brigade lost its momentum, then collapsed in a rush as frantic as any on the other side, falling back all the way to the LaFayette Road and beyond. On the alert for some such reverse, however, Longstreet promptly threw in a brigade from Preston's reserve division, restored the line with the help of the rallied brigade, and forced the mounted bluecoats westward in the wake of their companions, who had not paused to take advantage of this respite, but had used it rather to increase their lead in the race for McFarland's Gap. Struck by an exploding shell, the Glenn house was afire by now, burning briskly under the noonday sun, with no sign of Rosecrans or his staff. Hindman called a halt, put his cannoneers to work shelling the throng of fugitives to the north and west on the Dry Valley Road, and began to reckon the fruits of his triumph, which were rich. He had taken 17 guns, ten of them abandoned, 1100 prisoners, including three full colonels, 1400 small arms, together with 165,000 rounds of ammunition, and five stands of colors, all within less than an hour and against a force considerably larger than his own.

Law and Kershaw had made similar gains, along with the infliction of a similar disruption, against much stiffer resistance by the defenders of the Union center. Watching Johnson's cheering soldiers hurdle the unmanned breastworks in their front, Law saw that they were taking cruel punishment from the bluecoats on their northern flank as they poured through the gap; so with soldierly instinct he obliqued his three brigades to the right, intending to accomplish a double purpose, first of relieving the pressure on Johnson, by drawing at least a part of the fire, and then of widening the gap by dislodging Brannan, whose own flank had been exposed by Wood's departure. Both of these objectives were attained in rapid order. Turning from the breakthrough on their right to meet this sudden menace to their front, the Federals divided their fire and wavered in the face of what seemed to them a limited choice of falling back or being ground between two rebel millstones. They chose the former course, and chose it with an individual urgency in direct ratio to each regiment's proximity to the threatened flank. Brannan's line swung gatelike, hinged on its left at the juncture with Reynolds, who held firm despite a renewal of Stewart's attack. Now it was Law's troops who were hurdling unmanned breastworks. Moreover, just as Johnson had found one of Wood's brigades defenseless in his path, so now did Law find one of Van Cleve's in that predicament as a result of having been delayed in setting off on its march to reinforce Thomas. It too was struck and shattered, quite as abruptly as the other had been: except that this time there was retribution. Hearing the uproar in its rear, which signified the destruction of its companion brigade, Wood's middle brigade was halted by its commander, Colonel Charles G. Harker, New Jersey-born, only five years out of West Point, and at twenty-five a veteran of all the western battles from Shiloh on. He faced his men about and launched a savage counterattack, not at Johnson, who had pressed on westward out of reach, but at Law, who had just knocked Brannan's gate ajar and shattered Van Cleve's sitting-duck brigade. Boldness paid off for the youthful colonel. Not only was Law stopped in his tracks by Harker's unexpected lunge, but the Texas brigade on the open flank was driven rearward in what for a time had the makings of a large-scale repulse.

Returning from his hurried conference with Johnson, midway of that general's exuberant advance, Hood arrived to find his old brigade in full retreat. This was a rare sight at any time, despite the reverse that had ended its brief penetration of the enemy line the day before, but it was particularly unwelcome in this apparent hour of victory. Blond and gigantic, though his useless arm prevented him from gesturing with his sword by way of emphasis, he rode among the fleeing Texans, exhorting them to stand their ground. They stopped in time to catch him as he toppled from the saddle, shot through the upper thigh by a rifle bullet that shattered the bone and necessitated a field amputation that would leave him barely enough of a stump to accommodate an artificial leg. As he fell he muttered incongruously, repeating in shock what he had said a few minutes ago to Johnson: "Go ahead, and keep ahead of everything." These were thought at the time to be his dying words, a fitting valedictory to battle — such wounds were all too often fatal — but that was not to be the case, and besides he had the satisfaction, as he was being taken away on a stretcher, of knowing that the line had been restored by Kershaw. Bringing up his two brigades at the critical moment of the corps commander's fall, the South Carolinian not only stemmed the incipient rout; he also resumed the advance, driving the resurgent bluecoats west and north with the help of the rallied Texans, who were eager now to get revenge for what had been done to them and their beloved Hood.

At this point, some time after noon, Longstreet rode up from the south, where he had repaired a similar reverse by sending in one of Preston's brigades to shore up Hindman's collapsed flank, and expressed great

satisfaction at finding that all three elements of his clenched-fist blow —
Hindman on the left, Johnson in the center, and Law and Kershaw on
the right — had succeeded admirably, so far, in fulfilling his prediction that "we would of course whip and drive [the Yankees] from the
field." Up to now, this only applied to about one third of the blue army,
including two complete divisions and portions of three others, but Old
Peter believed he had solved the problem of how best to press the issue
to its desired conclusion: "As our right wing had failed of the progress
anticipated, and had become fixed by the firm holding of the enemy's
left, we could find no practicable field for our work except by a change
of the order of battle from [a] wheel to the left, to a swing to the
right." Instead of pivoting on Preston, as originally intended, he proposed to pivot on Stewart, in the opposite direction. In other words,
Bragg's plan was not only to be abandoned; it was to be reversed. Pursuit of the remnant of the Union right, in flight for McFarland's Gap
across the way, could be left to Wheeler, whose troopers, after exchanging
shots all morning with enemy vedettes across the creek below Lee &
Gordon's, had just forced a crossing at Glass's Mill and driven the Federal horsemen southward, away from the battle which was then approaching its climax three miles north. Couriers were sent at once to
have him take up the chase of the fugitives on the Dry Valley Road,
which passed through nearby Crawfish Springs, while the gray infantry
turned sharp right to complete — with the aid of Polk's wing, which
would have little to do but keep up the pressure it had been applying for
better than three hours now, although without conspicuous success —
the destruction of the remaining two thirds of the blue army. Law and
Kershaw had faced in that direction already, drawn by the retirement of
Brannan's right, but instructions had to be sent to Johnson and Hindman, as well as to Preston, who was still holding the abandoned pivot,
to form their three divisions on the left of Law and Kershaw, along a
new east-west line from which Longstreet intended to launch one last
clenched-fist blow that would result in a knockout victory over an adversary who presumably was groggy from the effects of the punch just
landed in his midriff.

However desirable it might have been, there was no question of
an immediate jump-off. Preparations involving a right-angle variation in
the direction of attack for an entire wing of the army, as well as changes
in the posting of practically all of the elements that composed it, would
of course take time, since they would require not only a great deal of
shifting of units, large and small, over considerable distances — Preston,
the extreme example, had nearly three miles to go before his troops
would be in position — but also a prerequisite restoration of control
within the five divisions themselves, most of which had been severely
disorganized by the mingling of regiments and brigades in the course of
their furious breakthrough and their long advance over difficult terrain.

Besides, Old Peter had never been one to begrudge time spent in preparation for the delivery of an assault, particularly in a situation such as the one that now obtained, with a good six hours of daylight still remaining and a single, well-co-ordinated effort being counted on to accomplish the objective. Orders had to be drawn up and distributed before they could be obeyed, and limber chests and cartridge boxes had to be refilled. Nor did he believe in neglecting the inner man; stomachs needed refilling, too, and that included his own. Before leaving on a tour of inspection, he directed that a lunch be spread for him to eat on his return. Dodging snipers, he reconnoitered the new defensive line the Federals had established, perpendicular to their old one along the LaFayette Road, along the irregular slopes of an eastern spur of Missionary Ridge; Snodgrass Hill was its name, according to Bushrod Johnson, whom he encountered in the course of his ride along the front. The Tennessean pointed out what he believed was "the key of the battle," a point where the bluecoats clustered thickly on the wooded slope ahead. Longstreet looked at it carefully. "It was a key, but a rough one," he said later. For the present, he instructed Buckner to establish a twelve-gun battery at the junction of the two wings, explaining that this would give him the advantage of enfilade fire down both segments of the Union line: the old one extending north, which had resisted Polk's attacks all day, and the new one extending west, which he himself was about to test for the first time. Now as before, he seemed to have little doubt as to the outcome. "They have fought their last man, and *he* is running," he said jovially, despite the evidence he had just seen to the contrary, when he returned to headquarters and sat down to his lunch of Nassau bacon and Georgia sweet potatoes. The former was an all-too-familiar item on the diet of all Confederates, East and West; "nausea bacon," it was sometimes called; but not the latter — anyhow not in the theater in which Old Peter had done all his fighting up to now. "We were not accustomed to potatoes of any kind in Virginia," he would remark more than thirty years later, still remembering the meal, "and thought we had a luxury."

There were two interruptions, both of them drastic though only the first was violent. It came in the form of a shell that burst in the woods nearby, one of whose jagged splinters ripped through a book a mounted courier was reading and struck a staff colonel, knocking him from his place at the table and to the ground, where he lay gasping as if in the throes of death. Startled, his fellow staffers leaped up to staunch the expected flow of blood, but they could not find the wound. Reacting with his usual calm, Longstreet saw that the gasping was caused by a large bite of sweet potato, which had become lodged in the colonel's windpipe when the iron fragment grazed him, and "suggested that it would be well to first relieve him of the potato and give him a chance to breathe. This done, he revived," the general recalled; "his breath came freer, and he was soon on his feet." That was the first interruption. The second came soon after the other officers rejoined their chief at the table, and if it was less violent it was also a good deal more alarming in the end. It came in the form of a message from Bragg, from whom the commander of the left wing had heard nothing since the night before, requesting his attendance at a conference a short distance in rear of the new mile-long line that was being formed in the woods to the west of the LaFayette Road. Longstreet promptly rode to meet him amid the wreckage of what had been the Union right, and after giving him a brief description of the rout that had resulted in the capture of some forty guns, together with thousands of small arms and prisoners and no less than two square miles of ground, explained his decision to wheel right instead of left, as originally instructed, in order to complete the destruction of what remained of the blue army.

Bragg did not seem to share his lieutenant's enthusiasm, and when the latter went on to suggest that the left wing be reinforced from the right, which would have little more to do than hold its ground once the attack was resumed on the south, the North Carolinian broke in testily: "There is not a man in the right wing who has any fight in him." Taken aback, Longstreet at last saw what the trouble was. Bragg was miffed because his design for herding the bluecoats into McLemore's Cove had gone astray; or as the Georgian later put it, "He was disturbed by the failure of his plan and the severe repulse of his right wing, and was little prepared to hear suggestions from subordinates for other moves or progressive work." In other words, if he could not win in just the way he wanted, he did not care about winning at all, or anyhow he wanted no personal share in such a victory. So at any rate it seemed. This fairly incredible impression was strengthened, moreover, by the manner in which Bragg brought the conference to a close. "If anything happens, communicate with me at Reed's Bridge," he said curtly, and he turned his horse and rode in that direction, which would place him well in rear of the stalled right, as far as possible from the scene of the critical attack about to be launched by Longstreet on the left.

Old Peter scarcely knew what to make of his chief's reaction. "From accounts of his former operations, I was prepared for halting work," he afterwards wrote, understating the case in an attempt to bring in a touch of humor that was altogether lacking at the time, "but this, when the battle was at its tide and in partial success, was a little surprising." However, as he returned to his new-drawn line to give the signal that would launch the assault designed to complete his half-won triumph, he soon recovered his aplomb, if not his accustomed heartiness. "There was nothing for the left wing to do but work along as best it could," he said.

Thus Bragg, in effect, removed himself from management of the battle, but only after his opponent had removed himself, in fact and person, not only from the battle but also from the field on which it was being fought. Whether out of petulance or panic, each of the two leaders reacted in accordance with his nature and his lights, for while the southern commander appeared to doubt that the contest was half won, Rosecrans had not seemed to question the evidence that it was considerably more than half lost. Not that he was a coward: Rich Mountain, Iuka, Corinth, and above all Stones River were sufficient refutation of the charge, and moreover his gloomy assessment was shared by those around him. With the exception of Lytle, whose sudden death was taken as confirmation of the majority opinion, no one with stars on his shoulders and a close-up look at the proportions of the rebel breakthrough failed to share the abrupt and general conviction that all was lost. Not only the army commander, but also his chief of staff, two of his three corps commanders, and four of his ten division commanders — in short, every man in charge of anything larger than a brigade on that quarter of the field — agreed that in the present instance, with the choice narrowed to flight or death or capture, discretion was the better part of valor. Practically of one accord, they all turned tail and ran and their troops ran with them, flecks of foam on the blue stream rushing northward up the Dry Valley Road and westward through McFarland's Gap, eager to put the bulletproof mass of Missionary Ridge between themselves and their screaming gray pursuers.

Soon after getting off the order to Wood, Rosecrans had ridden to the right, accompanied by Dana and Garfield and several other members of his staff, intending to hurry the sidling movement that would thicken the thinned center. He was sitting his horse directly in rear of Davis, whose division was in motion, when Longstreet's attack exploded dead ahead and to the immediate left front. Dana, who was badly in need of sleep, had dismounted for a nap in the grass; the first he knew of the impending breakthrough was when he was awakened by what he afterwards called "the most infernal noise I ever heard." Startled — "Never in any battle had I witnessed such a discharge of cannon and musketry" — he looked up and saw something that alarmed him even more. Old Rosy was crossing himself. "Hello!" he thought. "If the general is crossing himself, we are in a desperate situation." Sure enough, when he looked around he "saw our lines break and melt away like leaves before the wind. . . . The whole right of the army had apparently been routed." Rosecrans by then had reached the same conclusion, for he turned to his staff and said in a voice surprisingly calm amid the confusion of the headlong rush which Dana would compare to melting leaves: "If you care to live any longer, get away from here." His advice was so quickly taken that Dana did not even attempt a description of the dispersal or employ a single additional metaphor, mixed or otherwise. He simply remarked that "the headquarters around me disappeared."

Others "disappeared" as rapidly, even though they were out of earshot of their chief's advice. McCook's third great battle was also his third rout, and the greatest of the three. Like Davis and Sheridan, he made a brief attempt to stem the tide, then took off rearward, a leader in the race for safety, and those of his men who had not already bolted were quick to follow his example. Crittenden, too, was a part of the crush, but strictly on an individual basis. He had no troops left under him anyhow, the last of his three divisions having been detached to Thomas by midmorning, though Van Cleve himself was swept from the field with the remnant of the brigade that was wrecked by Law. Similarly, Negley became a fugitive when he led his rear brigade off on a tangent, then found his way to the left blocked by Johnson's mile-deep penetration of the center. A few among the responsible commanders, such as Wilder, maintained control of their units, but they were the exception. "Many of the officers of all ranks," according to another Indiana colonel, "showed by their wild commands and still wilder actions that they had completely lost their heads and were as badly demoralized as the private soldiers."

One among the exceptions was a young officer from McCook's staff, who managed to skirt the confusion and get through to Thomas on the left. The Virginian told him to return the way he had come and bring up Davis and Sheridan to support his dangling right. He made it back to the Dry Valley Road, and as he rode westward alongside it — for the road itself was jammed with fugitives crowding it shoulder-to-shoulder and raising a waist-high cloud of dust — he appealed to various officers in the fleeing column, but to small avail. Although the rebel pursuit had broken off by now, they either would not believe him when he said so, or else they could not see in this any reason for slowing the pace of their retreat. "See Jeff, Colonel," they told him, or "See Phil." Appeals to the men themselves were even less successful. "We'll talk to you, my son, when we get to the Ohio River!" one veteran replied, much to the amusement of his fellow trudgers. Finally, in McFarland's Gap, the young staffer overtook Davis and Sheridan, and though the former expressed a doubtful willingness to give the thing a try, the latter wanted nothing further to do with the mismanaged contest he had just put behind him. "He had lost faith," the colonel observed as he pushed on to gain the head of the column, up toward Rossville.

There where the road forked, one branch leading northwest to Chattanooga, the other east through Rossville Gap, then south to the field on whose opposite flank the scramble had begun — the distance in each case was about four miles — Rosecrans and the remnant of his staff drew rein to breathe their horses. By now the battle racket had died down, screened by the loom of Missionary Ridge, and though by dismounting and putting their ears to the ground they could hear the rattle of small arms, which signified that Thomas was still in action with at least a part of his command, the lack of any rumble from his guns seemed to indicate that the left wing had not fared much better than the right. If this was so, the thing to do was establish a straggler line on the outskirts of Chattanooga, where the two sundered portions of the army could be reunited and rallied for a last-ditch stand with the deep-running Tennessee River at its back. For his own part, Old Rosy was determined to return to the field and share with whatever troops were left the final stages of their withdrawal, leaving to his chief of staff the task of bringing the fugitives to a halt and putting them into a new defensive position before the gray wave of attackers swept over them again. However, when he turned to Garfield and began to tell him all that would have to be done — the selection of proper ground, the assignment of units to their places in line, the opening of new channels of supply and communication, and much else — the chief of staff, confused by the complexity of what he termed "the great responsibility," made a suggestion: "I can go to General Thomas and report the situation to you much better than I can give those orders." Rosecrans thought this over briefly, then reluctantly agreed. "Well," he said, "go and tell General Thomas my precautions to hold the Dry Valley Road and secure our commissary stores and artillery. [Tell him] to report the situation to me and to use his discretion as to continuing the fight on the ground we occupy at the close of the afternoon or retiring to a position in the rear near Rossville."

So while Garfield set out eastward on a ride that would take him in time to the White House — though not for long; the assassin's bullet would find him before he had been four months in office — Rosecrans took the left-hand fork that led to Chattanooga. But now the shock set in. The nearer he drew to the city the more depressed he became, as if some sort of ratio obtained between his distance from the battlefield and his realization of the enormity of his position as a commander who had deserted his army in its bloodiest hour of crisis. When he pulled rein at last, about 3.30, in front of the three-story residence where departmental headquarters had been established eleven days ago, he was so exhausted in body and broken in spirit that he had to be assisted to dismount. "The officers who helped him into the house did not soon forget the terrible look of the brave man, stunned by sudden calamity," an observer remarked, and added: "In later years I used occasionally to meet Rosecrans, and always felt that I could see the shadow of Chickamauga upon his noble face."

Dana arrived immediately behind him, having become separated from the others in what he called "the helter-skelter of the rear." That he too was much depressed by what he had seen, though his depression took a different form, was obvious from the wire he got off to Stanton at 4 o'clock, as soon as he had had time to catch his breath. "My report today is of deplorable importance," he informed the Secretary. "Chickamauga is as fatal a name in our history as Bull Run." Still badly shaken, he described the onslaught of the rebels, which was unlike anything he had seen at Vicksburg, his one previous experience of war. "They came through with resistless impulse, composed of brigades formed in divisions. Before them our soldiers turned and fled. It was wholesale panic. Vain were all attempts to rally them." He was as uncertain of what would happen next as he was of the army's losses up to now, but he ventured a guess or two in both directions. "Davis and Sheridan are said to be coming off at the head of a couple of regiments in order, and Wilder's brigade marches out unbroken. Thomas, too, is coming down the Rossville road with an organized command, but all the rest is confusion. Our wounded are all left behind, some 6000 in number. We have lost heavily in killed today. The total of our killed, wounded, and prisoners can hardly be less than 20,000, and may be much more. . . . Enemy not yet arrived before Chattanooga. Preparations making to resist his entrance for a time."

★ ★ ★

Some of this was useful to the Washington authorities as an estimate of the situation resulting from the sudden turn of fortune — surprisingly so, in light of the fact that it amounted to little more than guesswork by a rattled nonprofessional who had seen only a portion of the field — but much of it was about as inaccurate as might have been expected. This last applied in particular to the reference to Thomas. Not only was he not "coming down the Rossville road," as Dana claimed, but even as the telegrapher clicked away at the doleful message composed in haste and panic, the Virginian was fighting hard, resisting the combined assaults of both Confederate wings in a climactic struggle to maintain the integrity of the position he had held all morning against one. In the end — that is, before nightfall — his skill and determination in continuing this odds-on fight with what remained of the blue force after its commander had fled with a full third of the troops who had composed it at the outset, would win him the name by which he would be known thereafter: "The Rock of Chickamauga."

Indeed, there was much about him that was rocklike, not alone in the sense of being "the right kind of man to tie to," but also in appearance, especially when viewed from up close. According to a soldier observer, his "full rounded, powerful form," six feet in height and well over two hundred pounds in weight, "gradually expands upon you, as a mountain which you approach." Moreover, in addition to sheer bulk, he gave an impression of doggedness and imperturbability. "This army doesn't retreat," he had said in a similar crisis at Stones River, despite the evidence to the contrary, and it was obvious from his manner that the same thing applied here, so far at least as concerned the two thirds of the army still on the field and in his charge. Brannan's gatelike swing had ended on the rising ground in his left rear; there he posted his division, extending his right westward along the convenient eastern spur of Mis-

sionary Ridge. Single brigades
from the variously shattered and
scattered commands of Wood,
Van Cleve, and Negley, combined with those of Brannan,
provided the equivalent of two
divisions for the defense of this
new line, and Thomas reinforced it further by detaching
one brigade each from Johnson
and Palmer, who stood at the
bulging center of the north-
south line confronting Polk.
The east-west position was one
of great natural strength, heavily
wooded and uphill for attackers,

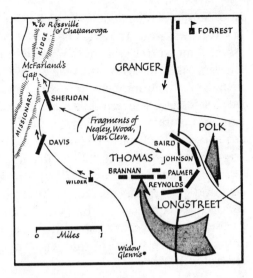

but whether or not it could be held against as savage a fighter as Longstreet would depend in the final analysis on the troops who occupied it.
Thoroughly aware of this, as he also was of the fact that they had already
backpedaled once today under pressure from the same gray veterans
who were massing now for a follow-up assault, Thomas moved among
them in an attempt to stiffen their resolution for what he knew was coming. "This hill must be held and I trust you to do it," he told Harker,
who replied: "We will hold it or die here." Thomas rode on, and presently came to one of Harker's regimental commanders, Colonel Emerson
Opdycke. "This point must be held," he told him. The Ohio colonel
agreed. "We will hold this ground," he said, "or go to heaven from it."
Opdycke's men nodded approval of his words, but whether they really
meant it remained to be seen.

They meant it. About 2 o'clock, while Longstreet was returning
from his unprofitable conference with Bragg, Kershaw assaulted the left
of the new Federal position with the demidivision composed of his own
South Carolina brigade and Barksdale's Mississippians, now under Brigadier General Ben G. Humphreys. "Ranks followed ranks in close order,
moving briskly and bravely against us," a defender later wrote. These
were the men who had taken the Wheat Field and the Peach Orchard,
eighty days ago at Gettysburg, and they were determined to do as well
this afternoon at Chickamauga. They did not; not yet, at any rate. Harker's troops, together with those in Brannan's left brigade and the brigade from Palmer, under Brigadier General William Hazen, fired their
rifles with such steadiness and precision that the gray ranks faltered,
withered, and fell back. Kershaw, who had thought one hard rap would
cause the bluecoats to continue their withdrawal, was unwilling to admit
that this had been disproved so quickly. After a pause for realignment he
again sent his two brigades forward against the Union there. The result

was the same. They surged up the slope, then fell back down it, having taken losses quite as heavy as before. Still unconvinced, he tried a third assault, and suffered a third repulse. Such uphill work was about as exhausting as it was bloody. One regimental commander reported that his men were "panting like dogs tired out in the chase." In the course of the last charge, he would recall, he had seen a fifteen-year-old soldier lagging behind and weeping, and when he told him that this was no time for hanging back out of fear, the boy explained that his trouble was not fright but exasperation. "That aint it, Colonel," he wailed between sobs. "I'm so damned tired I can't keep up with my company." Convinced at last, and perceiving that even his full-grown men were winded, Kershaw called a halt at the base of the hill to watch for some sign that the Federals were weakening their left to meet the attack that was being launched by now against their right by Johnson and Hindman, off at the far end of the line.

Thomas might well have weakened his embattled left to reinforce his threatened right, outnumbered and overlapped as it was by the two butternut divisions being massed in the woods below, except that he received unexpected help at just this critical juncture. All morning, up near McAfee's Church, which was two miles east of Rossville and about twice that distance from the hilly spur where Brannan staged his rally, Gordon Granger had fretted because his one-division Reserve Corps, charged with guarding the Rossville Gap in case it was needed as an escape hatch, was being kept from the battle he could hear raging to the south. About 11 o'clock — an hour and a half after Polk began his delayed attack and shortly before Longstreet scored the breakthrough that threw Davis and Sheridan off the field and swung Brannan out of his place in the disintegrating center of the Union line — he and his chief of staff climbed a haystack in an attempt to see something of what was going on. All they saw, far down the LaFayette Road, was a boiling cloud of dust and smoke with the fitful yellow flash of batteries mixed in at its base, but Granger soon arrived at a decision. "I am going to Thomas, orders or no orders!" he declared, snapping his glasses back in their case. The staffer was more cautious. "And if you go," he warned, "it may bring disaster to the army and you to a court martial." Granger was a career man, West Point '45, and normally an avoider of such risks; but not now. "There's nothing in our front but ragtag, bobtail cavalry," he said. "Don't you see Bragg is piling his whole army on Thomas? I am going to his assistance." And with that he climbed down off the haystack and ordered Steedman to prepare to march at once with two of his brigades, leaving the third behind to continue holding the Rossville escape hatch open in the event of a collapse by the main body, which he would soon be joining, four miles south.

Within half an hour the march was under way. Granger's remark that Bragg was "piling his whole army on Thomas" had been in error at the time he made it; Longstreet had not yet gone in. But now that the remaining half of the Confederate force had been committed, with the resultant abolition of the Federal right, the statement was in the rapid process of becoming quite literally true; so that Granger's decision, though based in part on an erroneous assumption, turned out to be militarily sound; Thomas was indeed in need of help, and it was fortunate for him that Granger began his four-mile march before the need existed, let alone before it became acute. Even so, there were delays. About noon, a mile down the LaFayette Road, the lead brigade was taken under fire by a pair of batteries in position on the flank. Steedman was obliged to go from column of march into line of battle, facing east to meet this threat from what turned out to be a sizable detachment of Forrest's men. Blue skirmishers, moving against the guns, caused the rebel troopers to give ground; yet when the skirmishers returned the graybacks followed, resuming their harassing tactics. Finally, in exasperation — for he was a short-tempered man at best — Granger sent for the third brigade to come down from McAfee's Church and hold the troublesome horsemen off while he took up his march, southwest now across the fields and through the woods in order to approach the nearly beleaguered Thomas from the rear. A mile short of the blue flank the second delay occurred; but it was brief, consisting of nothing more than a short wait for part of Negley's division to get out of the way, which it soon did, being hard on the go for Rossville and deliverance from chaos. The two columns passed each other, one headed into and the other out of the battle, and Granger rode ahead to report that his two brigades were close at hand.

He was a hard-mannered regular, originally from upper New York State, a veteran of Mexico and the Indian wars, shaggy in looks, brusque in speech, and not much liked — either by his troops, who resented a strictness that sometimes prescribed horsewhipping for minor camp offenses, or by his fellow officers, who found him uncongenial — but Thomas had seldom been as glad to see anyone as he was to see Granger, whom he greeted with a handshake and a smile that was all the broader because he had thought the column approaching his rear was hostile. That would indeed have been the final straw; for Kershaw's attack was in full career on his left by now, and Hindman and Johnson were massing their divisions for an advance on the right, which they overlapped. When they began to move forward, out of the woods and onto an intervening ridge, Granger saw the problem at a glance. "Those men must be driven back," he said. Thomas agreed. "Can you do it?" he asked. Granger nodded grimly. "Yes," he said. "My men are fresh, and they are just the fellows for that work. They are raw troops and they don't know any better than to charge up there."

Whether the basis for their conduct was ignorance, sheer heroism, or a combination of both, the men of the reserve corps were indeed "the fellows for that work." Steedman, who was forty-seven, Pennsylvania born, a former printer, Texas revolutionist, and Ohio legislator — "a great, hearty man, broad-breasted [and] broad-shouldered," whose face, according to an admirer, was "written all over with sturdy sense and stout courage" — brought them up on the double and committed them with no more delay that it took to tell a staff officer to see that his name was spelled correctly in the obituaries. Leading the charge on horseback, he saw his green troops waver at their first sight of the enemy up ahead; whereupon he grabbed the regimental colors from an Illinois bearer alongside him and waved the rippling silk to draw their attention. "Go back, boys, go back," he roared, "but the flag can't go with you!" They did not go back; they went forward, still with Steedman in the lead, but now on foot; for the rippling blue of the colors had attracted the attention of the rebels, too, with the result that his horse had been shot from under him. Badly shaken by the fall, the general got up and hobbled forward, still brandishing the flag and roaring, "Follow me!" Ahead, the graybacks gave ground before such fury and determination, then rallied and counterattacked. However, the bluecoats had the ridge by then and held it, though at the cost of losing one fifth of their number within their first twenty minutes of combat. And that was only the beginning; they would lose as many more in the next three hours. In fact, of the 3700 men in the two brigades, nearly half — 1788 — would be casualties by sundown.

Steep though the price was, the gain was great. Not only had they shored up and prolonged Brannan's overlapped western flank; they also had brought with them from McAfee's Church a hard-hitting battery of three-inch rifles, which added the weight of their metal to the blue resistance, and no less than 95,000 rounds of small-arms ammunition. This last was in particular demand, because the army's main ordnance supply train had been involved in McCook's collapse and flight, and Thomas's soldiers were burning up what they had on hand at a fearful rate; an Ohio regiment of 535 men, for example, would expend nearly 45,000 rounds of rifle ammunition before the day was over. In the face of such fiery opposition — an average expenditure of better than 80 rounds per man, including casualties — it was no wonder that Longstreet pronounced Johnson's "key of the battle," by which the Tennessean meant the hilly spur along whose slopes the east-west Union line was drawn, "a rough one."

Returning from his conference with the disgruntled Bragg, Old Peter arrived to find Kershaw checked on the right and Johnson and Hindman just going in on the left. Like them, he had thought it probable that a determined nudge would persuade the bluecoats to continue their retreat, but when the second attack was repulsed — disclosing, as he said later, that the defenders were "full of fight, even to the aggressive" — he knew he was in for trouble. Hindman, who had been struck in the neck by a fragment of shell but declined to quit the field, agreed with this revised assessment, subsequently reporting that while he "never saw Confederate soldiers fight better," he had "never known Federal troops to fight so well." However, Longstreet wasted no time on regret that Kershaw had jumped the gun, committing his two brigades before the six at the far end of the line were ready, or that Johnson, conversely, had not swept around the open flank before Granger arrived to brace it. Instead, he sent word for them to keep up the pressure on the two extremities while Preston was massing his three brigades, only one of which had seen any action so far in the battle, for an assault on the blue center. Then at last, with Law coming in on Kershaw's left and Stewart on his right, the second of Old Peter's clenched-fist blows would dispose of what had survived the devastation of the first.

Shortly before 4 o'clock, Preston — "genial, gallant, lovable William Preston," Longstreet called the forty-six-year-old Kentuckian, whom he met for the first time this afternoon — got his troops in position, two brigades advanced in echelon and one held in reserve, and sent them forward against the center of Brannan's line. By now the defenders had improvised breastworks from stones and fallen trees, anything at all that would stop a bullet, so that when the attackers emerged from the woods at the foot of the slope they were met by heavy, well-aimed fire directed confidently at them from the crest ahead. They did not stop or attempt to return this fire until they were within eighty yards of the flame-stabbed smoke that obscured the enemy position. There they halted, exposed as they were, and engaged in a deadly exchange of volleys with the sheltered bluecoats for nearly an hour. "Only new troops could accomplish such a wonderful feat," a general who opposed them declared; which perhaps was true (Hood's Texans, for example, prided themselves on knowing when to stand and when to run, and in point of fact had chosen the latter course twice already on this same field, today and yesterday) except that it left out of account the determined example of the officers who led them. The two brigades were commanded by a pair of Alabamians, Brigadier General Archibald Gracie and Colonel John H. Kelly, both of whom had had considerable experience under fire. New York born — he had distinguished kinsmen in the Union ranks — Gracie was thirty, a graduate of Heidelberg and West Point and a merchant in Mobile before secession returned him to the profession for which he had been trained, while Kelly was only twenty-three, having left West Point as a cadet to go with his native state when the war began. Both had risen fast and far, but strictly on ability, beginning respectively as an infantry captain and an artillery lieutenant; Kelly, who had soldiers under him better than twice his age, had commanded a battalion at Shiloh, a regiment at Perryville and Murfreesboro, and now a brigade at Chickamauga, which would earn him a wreath for his three stars and make him the youngest general in the army. So led, Preston's two committed brigades stood their ground and took their punishment, losing 1054 of their 2879 effectives in the process, but fixing the Federals in position while the divisions on their left and right were heartened by their example and Breckinridge finally got the twelve-gun battery posted near the junction of the two wings. Even Polk, across the way, came alive at last in response to the sustained uproar of the volleys Gracie's and Kelly's men were exchanging with their opponents, and sent word for his division commanders to match the pressure, there on the east, that Longstreet was exerting from the south.

No one knew better than Thomas, wedged as it were between anvil and sledge, that once the Confederates achieved this concert of action, east and south, the issue could not long remain in doubt. Moreover, though the two armies had begun the day with equal numbers and though each would suffer casualties of about one third its total strength before the battle ended, another third of the blue army had fled the field by early afternoon, which left Thomas with only about one third of the original Union force, as compared to Bragg's two thirds; in short, after succeeding by default to the command, the Virginian faced odds of roughly two to one, with the additional disadvantage of being pressed from two directions, in each of which the enemy strength was about equal to both Federal wings combined. He knew that under these circumstances he would have to withdraw eventually, but he hoped to prolong the struggle until he could do so under cover of darkness. As late as 4 o'clock, when Garfield arrived with his absent chief's suggestion for "retiring to a position in the rear," Thomas declined even to consider a retreat by daylight. "It will ruin the army to withdraw it now," he said. "This position must be held until night." Before another hour had passed, however, with Preston clawing at him from below and the other rebel divisions of both wings increasing the tempo of their action and inching closer to his lines, he saw that to attempt a much longer delay would be to risk a breakthrough which would be even more costly to him than a daylight disengagement, dangerous though such a maneuver was said to be in all the tactics manuals. Accordingly, about 5 o'clock, while the sun was still an hour high, he settled on a plan for withdrawal, first on the left, where the pressure was less severe, and then on the right. The divisions along the north-south line would pull out in reverse order, first Reynolds, then Palmer, then Johnson, each passing in rear of the unit on its left; Baird would be last and would serve as rear guard on the march to McFarland's Gap and Rossville, where a new line of battle would be formed to discourage pursuit beyond that point. Similarly, Brannan and Steedman, together with the brigades that had been used to reinforce them, would fall back in sequence from the east-west line, following the same route to comparative safety.

Or so at any rate Thomas hoped, knowing full well that the execution of the orders designed to bring this about would be difficult at best.

Reynolds began the movement at 5.30, and for the next two hours, from broad daylight into darkness, the battle raged with a new intensity, a new sense of urgency, as various units of both armies, obliged by the attendant confusion to operate more or less on their own, attempted on the one hand to achieve, and on the other to forestall, deliverance from slaughter. Thomas had improvised well, but in a situation so fluid that orders no longer applied by the time they were issued, let alone received, success or failure depended almost entirely on the naked valor of his infantry and the ability of his subordinate commanders to maintain control of troops who, after all, were running for their lives. In this regard, Reynolds was outstanding. Marching north on the LaFayette Road, in rear of the other three divisions, he reached the extreme left to find that Liddell had outflanked Baird and was about to strike the Union line end-on. Instead of turning west for McFarland's Gap, as ordered, the Kentucky-born Hoosier launched a savage counterattack that drove the would-be flankers back and kept open the path of retreat for the other three divisions, who were themselves under mounting pressure from Breckinridge and Cleburne. Though they lost heavily in the withdrawal, being obliged to abandon their wounded along with their dead, the four divisions managed to effect a disengagement by moving rapidly westward, outstripping their pursuers in the race for Missionary Ridge, behind which the sun had set by now. Brannan and Steedman had a harder time of it: particularly the former, who was required to hold his ground while the latter began his withdrawal in the wake of the left-wing divisions which had passed across his rear. When Steedman pulled back, Hindman's and Johnson's men boiled over the ridge in close pursuit, and Preston committed his third brigade, which plunged through the newly opened breach and then turned right to fall on Brannan's unprotected flank. Three regiments were captured in one swoop, two from Michigan and one from Ohio, and the battle abruptly disintegrated, here on the right as it had on the left, into a race. That Brannan's survivors won it was due in large part to a pair of Indiana regiments from Reynolds' division. Coming upon a broken-down ammunition wagon, abandoned by a teamster who had fled with his mules in the earlier rout, the Hoosiers filled their empty cartridge boxes and countermarched, under direct orders from Thomas himself, to serve as rear guard and cover the final stage of the retreat. This they did, checking the butternut pursuers with volleys fired blind in the gathering darkness; after which they once more faced about and took up their westward march, the last blue troops to leave the field.

In some ways, though, the hardest part of the battle still lay before them; for they marched now, down the dark valley from McFarland's Gap to Rossville, with the taste of defeat bitter in their mouths and a great weariness in their limbs. Perryville and Stones River had been bad enough, but the fact that they had remained in control of both those fields when the smoke lifted had given their generals and journalists the basis for a claim to victory. Not so here. This was absolute, unarguable defeat, and as such it was depressing beyond anything they had ever known. "Weary, worn, tired and hungry," a captain in a veteran regiment later wrote, "we sullenly dragged ourselves along, feeling a shame and disgrace that had never been experienced by the Old Sixth before." Those who fell out of the column because of wounds or exhaustion were left to their own inadequate devices by those who had the strength to keep going. Behind them, beyond the intervening ridge, they could hear the rebels celebrating their triumph with loud yells. Another officer in the retreating column, First Lieutenant Ambrose Bierce, a topographical engineer with Hazen, thought the sound "the ugliest any mortal ever heard." Presently, however, there was a stretch of road well down the valley "across which that horrible yell did not prolong itself," he added, "and through that we finally retired in profound silence and dejection, unmolested."

Back on the field of Chickamauga, their spirits lifted by the release of tension, the Confederates kept yelling, despite an almost equal physical weariness, long after their adversaries were out of earshot. As Longstreet put it, "The Army of Tennessee knew how to enjoy its first grand victory," beginning at the moment when the two wings came together, there on the reverse slopes of the hilly spur from which the Yankees had just been driven, and continuing into the night with "a tremendous swell of heroic harmony that seemed almost to lift from their roots the great trees of the forest." Harvey Hill declared years later that the cheers "were such as I had never heard before, and shall not hear again." In point of fact, along strictly practical lines, the victors had more to whoop about than anyone yet knew. Afterwards, when the field had been gleaned, Bragg would report the capture of more than 8000 prisoners, 51 guns, and 23,281 small arms, together with 2381 rounds of artillery ammunition and 135,000 rifle cartridges. The multipaged scavenger list, certified by the chief of ordnance, would include such items as 35 pounds of picket rope, 365 shoulder straps, and 3 damaged copper bugles, as well as "wagons, ambulances, and teams, medicines, hospital stores, &c., in large quantities." It was, in brief, the largest haul ever made by either side on a single field of battle. For the present, however, all the exultant graybacks knew was that they had scored a triumph of considerable proportions, and they did not delay their celebration to wait for the particulars of its scope.

Nor did others who were not there to see for themselves. After the recent and apparently interminable sequence of knee-buckling reverses, soldiers and civilians throughout the nation were elated by the news from North Georgia, which seemed to them to bear out earlier predictions that the northern armies would find what true resistance meant when they approached the southern heartland. "The effects of this great victory will be electrical," a Richmond clerk recorded in his diary. "The whole South will be filled again with patriotic fervor, and in the North there will be a corresponding depression. . . . Surely the Government of the United States must now see the impossibility of subjugating the Southern people, spread over such a vast expanse of territory, and the European governments ought now to interpose and put an end to this cruel waste of blood and treasure."

★ ★ ★

In war, as in love — indeed, as in all such areas of so-called human endeavor — expectation tended to outrun execution, particularly when the latter was given a head start in the race, and nowhere did this apply more lamentably, at any rate from the Richmond point of view, than in the wake of Chickamauga, probably the greatest and certainly the bloodiest of all the battles won by the South in its fight for the independence it believed to be its birthright. Harvey Hill said later that he had "never seen the Federal dead lie so thickly on the ground, save in front of the sunken wall at Fredericksburg." In point of fact, though Hill may not have seen them on his quarter of the field, the Confederate dead lay even thicker; but in any case, now that the Yankees were on the run, he and the other two lieutenant generals, commanding the two wings, were altogether in favor of a rapid and slashing pursuit of the beaten foe. Though Longstreet called a halt in the dusk that followed his second breakthrough, it was for the same purpose as the halt that had followed his first at midday; namely, to consolidate his forces for the delivery of another heavy blow. "As it was almost dark," he afterwards reported, "I ordered my line to remain as it was, ammunition boxes to be filled, stragglers to be collected, and everything [placed] in readiness for the pursuit in the morning." Polk, perhaps aware that he had done less to win the victory up to now, prepared to do more by sending out scouts to look into the possibility of continuing the slaughter of the vanished enemy. Later, when the scouts returned to report that the bluecoats had not slacked their headlong retreat, the bishop rode to headquarters and informed Bragg — whom he roused from bed, much as Old Peter had done at about the same hour the night before — "that the enemy was routed and flying precipitately from the field, and that then was the opportunity to finish the work by the capture or destruction of [Rosecrans'] army, by prompt pursuit, before he had time to reorganize or throw up defenses at Chattanooga." So an aide who rode with him testified: adding, however, that "Bragg could not be induced to look at it in that light, and refused to believe that we had won a victory."

It was true that the commanding general had received no formal

notification of the outcome of the battle, but only because this had
seemed to his subordinates a highly superfluous gesture. ("It did not occur to me on the night of the 20th to send Bragg word of our complete
success," Longstreet explained years later. "I thought that the loud
huzzas that spread over the field just at dark were a sufficient assurance
and notice to anyone within five miles of us.") On the other hand, if
what he wanted was an eyewitness who could testify to the behavior of
the Federals after they reached the far side of Missionary Ridge — beyond which, conceivably, they might rally and lie in wait for him to
commit some act of rashness — that too was available, soon after first
light next morning, in the form of a Confederate private who had been
captured the previous day, then escaped amid the confusion of the blue
retreat, and made his way back to his outfit before dawn. When he told
his captain of what he had seen across the way — for instance, that the
Unionists were abandoning their wounded as they slogged northward,
intent on nothing but their flight from fury — he was taken at once to
repeat his story, first to his regimental and brigade commanders, then to
Bragg himself. The stern-faced general heard him out, but was doubtful,
if not of the soldier's capacity for accurate observation, then at any rate
of his judgment on such a complicated matter. "Do you know what a retreat looks like?" he asked sharply, fixing the witness with a baleful
glare. Irked by his commander's mistrust, the man replied with words
that endeared him to his comrades, then and thereafter, when they were
repeated, as they often were, around campfires and at future veteran
gatherings. "I ought to, General," he said; "I've been with you during
your whole campaign."

Whatever effect this may have had on the irascible general's disposition, a look at the field by daylight quickly convinced him that his
army was in no condition for the pursuit his chief subordinates were
urging him to undertake. The dead of both sides, stiffened by now in
agonized postures, and the wounded, many of them with their hurts
yet untended, seemed to outnumber the unhit survivors, and while this
was true in the case of a dozen regiments under Longstreet — who afterwards computed his losses at 44 percent — it was of course an exaggeration in the main, proceeding from shock at the grisly scene. The fact was
that the two armies had suffered a combined total of nearly 35,000
casualties, and most of them were Bragg's. Though the Federals had
some 2500 more men killed and missing than the Confederates (6414, as
compared to 3780) the latter had about 5000 more wounded (9756 in
blue, 14,674 in gray) so that the butcher's bill, North and South, came to
16,170 and 18,454 respectively. The combined total of 34,624 was exceeded only by the three-day slaughter at Gettysburg and by the week-
long series of five battles known collectively as the Seven Days, in both
of which considerably larger numbers of troops had been engaged. In
all the other battles of the war so far — including Chancellorsville,

which lasted one day longer and also involved about 50,000 more troops — the losses had been less than at Chickamauga, where they were greater by about 10,000 than at Shiloh, Second Manassas, or Murfreesboro, the three next bloodiest two-day confrontations. These statistics could not yet be broken down in any such manner, being as yet unknown, but they were suggested plainly enough by a tour of the field and a talk with unit commanders along the way. Nine Confederate generals had been killed or wounded, as compared to only one in the Federal ranks, and the loss of artillery horses, as a result of fighting at such close quarters, had been so heavy as to cripple that vital arm. "In one place down in the woods," a soldier wrote of a walk he took that morning, "I counted sixteen big artillery horses lying in one heap. A little way off was another heap of twelve more. And that was the way it was all through there." Without horses, Bragg could not haul his guns, and without guns he did not believe that his men could force Rossville Gap or assault the prepared defenses between there and Chattanooga. "How can I?" he replied to urgings that he press northward without delay. "Here is two-fifths of my army left on the field, and my artillery is without horses." He still felt that way about it, some weeks later, when he touched on the matter in his official report of the campaign. "Any immediate pursuit by our infantry and artillery would have been fruitless," he declared, "as it was not deemed practicable with our weak and exhausted force to assail the enemy, now more than double our numbers, behind his intrenchments."

One who did not feel that way about it, then or later, was Bedford Forrest. Early that morning, pressing forward on his own with 400 troopers, the Tennessean charged an outpost detachment of Federals who fired one volley and fled so rapidly that their lookouts had no time to desend from an observation platform they had constructed in the top of a tree on the crest of Missionary Ridge. Forrest's horse had been struck, a large artery severed in its neck, but the general staunched the spurt of blood by thrusting a finger into the bullet hole and thus gave chase. Pulling rein at last beneath the improvised tower atop the ridge, he withdrew his finger and dismounted before the animal collapsed, then summoned his prisoners down from their high perch, questioned them sharply, and climbed up to see for himself what he could see. That he could see a great deal — including the blue army, feverishly active in his front, and the gray army, immobile in his rear — was shown by a dispatch he dictated to a staff officer on the ground:

> We are in a mile of Rossville. Have been on the point of Missionary Ridge. Can see Chattanooga and everything around. The enemy's trains are leaving, going around the point of Lookout Mountain.
> The prisoners captured report two pontoons thrown across [the Tennesee River] for the purpose of retreating.
> I think they are evacuating as hard as they can go.

They are cutting timber down to obstruct our passage.
I think we ought to press forward as rapidly as possible.

The message was addressed to Polk, commander of the nearer wing,
and ended with the words, "Please forward to Genl Bragg." Anticipating the response he believed this information would provoke, Forrest
continued his policy of "keeping up the scare" by penetrating to within
three miles of Chattanooga from the south, meanwhile shifting his guns
northward along the ridge to engage the batteries posted in close defense
of the town below. All this time, according to one of his troopers, the
general was "almost beside himself at the delay." Finally he learned that
the infantry would not be coming as he had advised; Bragg was holding
it east of Missionary Ridge and near the railroad, shifting Polk to Chickamauga Station and army headquarters to Ringgold Bridge, while Longstreet remained in position to police the field and wait for McLaws, who
arrived in the late afternoon with the rest of his division. Nettled by
what seemed to him flagrant neglect of an opportunity gained at the
cost of much suffering and bloodshed, Forrest rode back to protest in
person, only to be told that the army could not move far from the railroad because of its critical lack of supplies. "General Bragg, we can get
all the supplies our army needs in Chattanooga," he replied. But this too
was rejected: Bragg's mind was quite made up. Forrest returned to his
men, exasperated and outdone. "What does he fight battles for?" he
fumed.

That was Monday. On Tuesday, unmolested even by Forrest,
whose handful of troopers had been recalled, Rosecrans completed the
concentration of his army within the Chattanooga defenses, and Bragg
ordered the occupation of Missionary Ridge and Lookout Mountain,
as well as the establishment of a line of posts across the valley that lay
between them. By Wednesday, September 23, the date of the autumnal
equinox, all of these abandoned points had been seized, and the Federal
works, which rose and thickened hour by hour as shovels flashed along
the intrenched perimeter, were under long-range fire from the surrounding heights. Three courses of action — or, rather, two of action and one
of inaction — were open to the Confederates. 1.) They could attempt to
turn the bluecoats out of their position by crossing the river above or
below the town, thus gaining their rear and breaking their tenuous supply line. 2.) They could leave a small force to observe the enemy trapped
in Chattanooga, and move with the greater part of the army against
Burnside, who would then be obliged to evacuate Knoxville or fight
against long odds. 3.) They could concentrate on the present investment,
hoping to starve the defenders into surrender. Longstreet favored a combination of the first two — "The hunt was up and on the go," he afterwards explained, "when any move toward [the enemy's] rear was safe,

and a speedy one encouraging of great results" — but Bragg, much to Old Peter's disgust and over his vigorous objections, chose the third.

This was by no means as impractical as Longstreet seemed to think. By extending his left to include the crest of Raccoon Mountain, Bragg denied his adversary use of the rail and wagon roads not only on the south but also on the immediate north bank of the Tennessee, which lay well within reach of his high-sited batteries, and thus obliged Rosecrans to haul supplies from Stevenson and Bridgeport by a roundabout and barren route, first across the bridgeless Sequatchie River, then up and over Walden's Ridge, and finally down to the steamboat landing opposite Chattanooga, a distance of some sixty tortuous miles which would become increasingly difficult when the fall rains set in and the mud deepened. Unwilling to leave the harassment entirely to the elements, Bragg on September 30, one week after getting his infantry and artillery into their interdictory positions, ordered Wheeler over the river on a raid. The diminutive Alabamian crossed next morning near Muscle Shoals with 4000 cavalry and eight guns, and on the following day he intercepted a train of 400 heavily loaded wagons at Anderson's Crossroads, deep in the Sequatchie Valley. After burning the wagons and sabering the mules, he moved north to McMinnville, then west to Shelbyville, both of which he captured, together with their supply depots, which he destroyed. By now, though, the rains had come in earnest and he was involved in a running fight with superior blue forces that converged upon him from all directions. Repulsed at Murfreesboro, he turned back south, losing four of his guns and more than a thousand of his men before he recrossed the Tennessee near Rogersville on October 9. Despite his considerable success in the execution of his mission — a Union observer afterwards declared that the disruptive and destructive strike was nearly fatal to the army besieged in Chattanooga — the cost had been high, and Wheeler did not suggest that he attempt another such raid, deep in the enemy rear. Nor did Bragg require one of him, apparently being content to watch and wait.

The fact was, he had troubles enough with his own supply lines, unmolested though they were, without concerning himself unduly about those across the way. No matter how hungry the bluecoats might be getting, down in the town, his own troops were convinced that they themselves were hungrier on the heights. "In all the history of the war," a Tennessee infantryman was to write, "I cannot remember of more privation and hardships than we went through at Missionary Ridge. . . . The soldiers were starved and almost naked, and covered all over with lice and camp itch and filth and dirt. The men looked sick, hollow-eyed, and heart-broken, living principally upon parched corn which had been picked out of the mud and dirt under the feet of officers' horses." There was, as usual, much bitterness over Bragg's apparent reluctance to gather the fruits of a victory they had won, but this time it was intensified by resentment of his attempts to shift the blame to other shoulders than his own. Within two days of the battle, with the army at last on the march, Polk had received a stiff note demanding an explanation of why his attack had been delayed on the morning of the 20th, and when his reply reached headquarters on the last day of September, Bragg pronounced it "unsatisfactory" and relieved the bishop of his command. Hindman received the same treatment for his conduct earlier that month at McLemore's Cove, dispite his acknowledged contribution to the triumph that followed ten days later. Hill too came under fire from the army chieftain, who complained of his former lieutenant's "critical, captious, and dictatorial manner," as well as of his "want of prompt conformity to orders," and recommended to Richmond that he be suspended, like the others, from duty with the Army of Tennessee.

All three were incensed: particularly the two lieutenant generals, who in point of fact had taken care to register their protests beforehand, after a secret meeting on September 26 with Longstreet, who outranked them both. Intent on doing to Bragg what he was about to do to them — that is, accomplish his removal — they urged Old Peter to join them, in his semi-independent capacity, in complaining to Richmond of their commander's "palpable weakness and mismanagement manifested in the conduct of the military operations of this army." Polk wrote privately to his friend the President along these lines, though not in time to forestall the blow which he described as "part of [Bragg's] long-cherished purpose to avenge himself on me for the relief and support I have given him in the past. . . . The truth is, General Bragg has made a failure, notwithstanding the success of the battle, and he wants a scapegoat." Figuratively, but with dignity, the bishop gathered his robes about him for the train ride to Atlanta, where he was sent to await the disposition of his case. "I feel a lofty contempt for his puny effort to inflict injury upon a man who has dry-nursed him for the whole period of his connection with him, and has kept him from ruining the cause of the country by the sacrifice of its armies." So he complained in private, after the blow fell. But Longstreet had already made a stronger statement to the Secretary of War, adopting Prayer Book phraseology to add weight to his words. "Our chief has done but one thing that he ought to have done since I joined his army," Old Peter informed Seddon on the day of his meeting with Polk and Hill. "That was to order the attack upon the 20th. All other things that he has done he ought not to have done. I am convinced that nothing but the hand of God can save us or help us as long as we have our present commander."

Such was the unhappy state of affairs in the Army of Tennessee, the men hungry and disgruntled and the generals bitterly resentful, on the morrow of what Longstreet, in his letter to Richmond, called "the most complete victory of the war — except, perhaps, the first Manassas," he added, remembering past glory and gladder times.

Beyond the semicircular rim of earthworks, down in the town and off at the far end of the chain of command leading back to Washington, a scapegoat hunt was also under way. McCook and Crittenden had already been relieved, ostensibly for flight in time of danger, yet it had not escaped notice that the winner in the headlong race for safety was the man who consented to their removal. Stanton, for one, observed caustically that the two corps commanders had "made pretty good time away from the fight, but Rosecrans beat them both."

Moreover, the reverse had come in sudden and sharp contrast to expectations Old Rosy himself had aroused. "The army is in excellent condition and spirits," he had telegraphed soon after darkness ended the first day's fighting, "and by the blessing of Providence the defeat of the enemy will be total tomorrow." Lincoln did not like the sound of this, finding it reminiscent of Joe Hooker, and when he learned next evening that the army had been routed, he claimed to have foreseen such a turn of events. "Well, Rosecrans has been whipped, as I feared," he said. "I have feared it for several days. I believe I feel trouble in the air before it comes." Nor was the general's immediate reaction of a kind to encourage hope that he would make an early recovery from the setback. "We have met with a serious disaster," he notified Halleck soon after he reached Chattanooga; "extent not yet ascertained. Enemy overwhelmed us, drove our right, pierced our center, and scattered troops there." Despite his own gloom, which was heavy, Lincoln tried to lift the Ohioan's. "Be of good cheer," he wired him late that night. "We have unabated confidence in you and in your soldiers and officers. . . . We shall do our utmost to assist you. Send us your present posting." But the general, in his reply the following morning, gave no indication that he would attempt to stay in the town he had fallen back on. In fact, he expressed some doubt that he could do so, even if he tried: "Our loss is heavy and our troops worn down. . . . We have no certainty of holding our position here." Such irresolution was disturbing in a commander. What was more, when the President asked him next day to "relieve my anxiety as to the position and condition of your army," Rosecrans replied in effect that his faith was not so much in himself or his army as it was in Providence. "We are about 30,000 brave and determined men," he wired; "but our fate is in the hands of God, in whom I hope."

Lincoln soon emerged from his gloom. The important thing, as he saw it, was not that Rosecrans had been whipped at Chickamauga, but that he still held Chattanooga. As long as he did so, he could keep the Confederates out of Tennessee and also deny them use of one of their most important railroads. "If he can only maintain this position,

without [doing anything] more," the President told Halleck, "the rebellion can only eke out a short and feeble existence, as an animal sometimes may with a thorn in its vitals." By now, after three days' rest and
no pursuit, Rosecrans had recovered a measure of his resolution. "We
hold this point, and cannot be dislodged except by very superior numbers," he wired on September 23, although he made it clear that this depended on "having all reinforcements you can send hurried up." Lincoln had been doing his best in this respect, instructing Halleck to order
troops to Chattanooga from Vicksburg and Memphis, while he himself
undertook to prod Burnside into marching fast from Knoxville. When
Burnside replied that he was just then closing in on Jonesboro, which lay
in the opposite direction, the President lost his temper. "Damn Jonesboro," he said testily, and returned to his efforts to get the ruff-
whiskered general to swing west. This proved so difficult, however, that
he decided in the end to leave him where he was, covering Knoxville;
Rosecrans would have to be reinforced from elsewhere. And that same
night, September 23, Lincoln met with Stanton, Halleck, Chase, and
Seward, together with several lesser War Department officials, in an attempt to determine just where such reinforcements could be found.

Stanton, having heard that evening from Dana that the Army of
the Cumberland, outnumbered, dejected, and under fire from the heights
inclosing Chattanooga on the south and east, could not hold out for
more than a couple of weeks unless it was promptly and substantially reinforced, had called the midnight conference to suggest a solution to
the problem. Since Burnside apparently could not be budged, and since
the troops ordered from Vicksburg and Memphis would have to make
a slow overland march for lack of any means of transportation, the
Secretary proposed that Rosecrans be sent a sizable portion of the Army
of the Potomac, which could make the trip by rail. Lincoln and Halleck objected that this would prevent Meade from taking the offensive,
but Stanton replied: "There is no reason to expect General Meade will
attack Lee, although greatly superior in force, and his great numbers
where they are are useless. In five days 30,000 could be put with Rosecrans." The President doubted this last, offering to bet that no such number of men could even be brought to Washington within that span of time.
Still, it was clear that something had to be done, and when Seward and
Chase sided with their fellow cabinet member Lincoln allowed himself
to be persuaded. Unless Meade intended to launch an immediate offensive, two of his corps would be detached at once and sent to Chattanooga. These would be Howard's and Slocum's, and they would be commanded by Joe Hooker, who was conveniently at hand and unemployed.
Aside from this reduction of the force proposed and this choice of a
leader, which rather galled him, Stanton was given full charge of the
transfer operation, with instructions to arrange it as he saw fit. He flew
into action without delay. The meeting broke up at about 2 o'clock in

the morning, and at 2.30 he got off a wire to Meade, directing him to have the two corps ready to load aboard northbound trains by nightfall, and another to Dana, informing him that the reinforcements would be sent. "[We] will have them in Nashville in five or six days from today," he declared, "with orders to push on immediately wherever General Rosecrans wants them."

Telegrams were also sent — in fact had been sent beforehand, so confident was the Secretary that the council would approve his plan — to officials of three of the several railroads involved, requesting them to "come to Washington as quickly as you can." By noon of the 24th they were in Stanton's office, poring over maps and working out the logistical details required for transporting four divisions, together with their guns and wagons, from the eastern to the western theater, 1200 circuitous miles across the intervening Alleghenies. Four changes of cars were necessary, two at unbridged crossings of the Ohio, near Wheeling and Louisville, and two more at Washington and Indianapolis, where there were no connecting tracks between the roads that must be used. Hooker was authorized to commandeer all the cars, locomotives, plants, and equipment that he deemed necessary, but no such action had to be taken, so complete was the co-operation of all the lines. Before sundown of the following day, just forty-four hours after Dana's warning reached the War Department, the first trainload of soldiers pulled into Washington from Culpeper, the point of origin down in Virginia. By the morning of the 27th, two days later, 12,600 men, together with 33 cars of field artillery and 21 of baggage, had passed through the capital, and at 10 o'clock that evening Stanton wired former Assistant Secretary Thomas A. Scott, who had returned to his prewar duties with the Pennsylvania Railroad and was posted at Louisville to regulate the operation west of the mountains: "The whole force, except 3300 of the XII Corps, is now moving." Within another two days Scott reported trains pulling regularly out of Louisville, and at 10.30 the following night — September 30 — the first eastern troops reached Bridgeport, precisely on the schedule announced at the outset, six days back. By October 2, nearly 20,000 men, 10 six-gun batteries with their horses and ammunition, and 100 carloads of baggage had arrived at the Tennessee railhead. "Your work is most brilliant," Stanton wired Scott. "A thousand thanks. It is a great achievement."

It was indeed a great achievement, this swiftest of all the mass movements of troops in history, and most of the credit belonged to the Secretary of War, who had worked feverishly and efficiently to accomplish what many, including the Commander in Chief, had said could not be done. Under his direction, the North had given its answer to the South's strategic advantage of occupying the interior lines; for though the Confederates had stolen a march and thereby managed, in Forrest's phrase, to "get there first with the most men," the Federals had promptly upped the ante by moving farther and faster with still more. In the final stages of the operation, Wheeler's raiders delayed some of the supply trains by tearing up sections of track, but all got through safely in the end. "You may justly claim the merit of having saved Chattanooga," Hooker wired Stanton on October 11, after posting his four divisions to prevent a rebel crossing below the town and a descent on the hungry garrison's rear. The Secretary was pleased to hear so, just as he had been pleased the week before at the evidence that he had been right in rejecting doleful objections that Lee would attack if Meade's army was weakened by any substantial detachment of troops to Rosecrans. " 'All quiet on the Potomac,' " he had informed the Chattanooga quartermaster on October 4. "Nothing to disturb autumnal slumbers. . . . All public interest is now concentrated on the Tennessee."

Bragg's complaint that the Federals had "more than double our numbers" was untrue in regard to the time he made it his excuse for not rapidly following up the advantage gained at Chickamauga. In fact, when McLaws arrived — with two of his own and one of Hood's brigades, plus the First Corps artillery, which soon was posted atop Lookout Mountain — the Confederates became numerically superior. But now that Hooker had crossed the Alleghenies with nearly 20,000 reinforcements, the situation was reversed. It was the besiegers who were outnumbered. This novel condition, rarely paralleled in military annals, was about to become more novel still; Sherman was on the way from Vicksburg, via Memphis, with another five divisions. Even when he reached Chattanooga, the Army of the Cumberland would not have "more than double" the number of troops in the Army of Tennessee, but it already had a considerable preponderance without him. Although there was still the menace of starvation — an Illinois private was complaining, tall-tale style, that since Chickamauga he and his comrades had eaten "but two meals a day, and one cracker for each meal" — Rosecrans at least could relax his fears that Bragg was going to drive him into the river with a sudden, downhill infantry assault. The rebels lacked the strength, and no one knew this better than their chief. A graver danger, so far as the northern commander was personally concerned, lurked at the far end of the telegraph wires linking his headquarters to those of his superiors in Washington. This applied in particular to the headquarters of the Secretary of War, whose original mistrust of his fellow Ohioan was being confirmed almost daily in the confidential reports he received from Dana, his special emissary on the scene.

Immediately after the battle, the former Brook Farmer had been glad to "testify to the conspicuous and steady gallantry of Rosecrans on the field"; he put the blame for the defeat on "that dangerous blunderhead McCook" and on Crittenden, whom he considered derelict and incompetent. Before the month was out, however, he had begun to sour on Old Rosy. "He abounds in friendliness and approbativeness," Dana wired on the 27th, "[but] is greatly lacking in firmness and steadiness of will. He is a temporizing man. . . . If it be decided to change the chief commander" — there had been no intimation that such a thing was being considered; Dana brought it up of his own accord — "I would take the liberty of suggesting that some Western general of high rank and great prestige, like Grant, for instance, would be preferable as his successor." Three days later he favored Thomas for the post, saying: "Should there be a change in the chief command, there is no other man whose appointment would be so welcome to this army." As for the present leader, Dana informed Stanton "that the soldiers have lost their attachment for [him] since he failed them in the battle, and that they do not now cheer him until they are ordered to do so." In the course of the next two weeks, the first two in October, the Assistant Secretary's conviction became even more pronounced in this regard. "I have never seen a public man possessing talent with less administrative power, less clearness and steadiness in difficulty, and greater practical incapacity than General Rosecrans. He has inventive fertility and knowledge, but he has no strength of will and no concentration of purpose. His mind scatters; there is no system in the use of his busy days and restless nights. . . . Under the present circumstances I consider this army to be very unsafe in his hands." Thus Dana, on the 12th. Six days later, after passing along a report that the soldiers were shouting "Crackers!" at staff officers who moved along them to inspect the fortifications, he added the finishing touches to his word portrait of a man in control of nothing, least of all himself: "Amid all this, the practical incapacity of the general commanding is astonishing, and it often seems difficult to believe him of sound mind. His imbecility appears to be contagious. . . . If the army is finally obliged to retreat, the probability is that it will fall back like a rabble, leaving its artillery, and protected only by the river behind it."

He might have spared himself and the telegrapher the labor of composing and transmitting this last in his series of depositions as to the general's unfitness for command; for by now, although he would not find it out until the following day, the purpose he intended had been achieved. Stanton had been passing his dispatches along to the Commander in Chief, who had found in them a ready confirmation of his own worst suspicions. Despite this, and because he had not yet decided on a replacement, Lincoln had continued his efforts to stiffen Old Rosy's resolution. On October 12, for instance, while Dana was observing the "scattered" condition of the Ohioan's mind, Lincoln wired: "You and Burnside now have [the enemy] by the throat, and he must break your hold or perish." Rosecrans replied that afternoon, complaining that the corn was ripe on the rebel side of the Tennessee, while "our side is barren." Nevertheless, and in spite of this evidence of divine displeasure, he closed by remarking, much as before, that "we must put our trust in God, who never fails those who truly trust." Commendable though such faith was, particularly after all the Job-like strain that had been placed on it of late, the President would have preferred to see it balanced by a measure of self-reliance. And not only did this quality appear to be totally lacking in the commander of the army now holed up in Chattanooga, but it had begun to seem to Lincoln that ever since Chickamauga, as he told his secretary, Rosecrans had been acting "confused and stunned, like a duck hit on the head."

Ridicule by the President was often the prelude to a general's dismissal, and this was no exception; Rosecrans was about to go, as Buell and McClellan had gone before him. But there was still the question of a successor to be settled before he went. Dana's recommendation of Thomas appealed to Lincoln, who had said of the Virginian shortly after the battle that earned him the sobriquet, "The Rock of Chickamauga": "It is doubtful whether his heroism and skill, exhibited last Sunday afternoon, has ever been surpassed in the world." Stanton felt much the same way about him. "It is not my fault that he was not in chief command months ago," he replied to Dana's observation that there was "no other man whose appointment would be so welcome to this army." However, there was also Grant, who had been comparatively idle since the fall of Vicksburg, fifteen weeks ago. This was plainly a waste the nation could ill afford. What was most desirable was some arrangement that would employ the full abilities of both, and it took Lincoln until mid-October to arrive at a solution that did just that.

CHAPTER

8

The Center Gives

★ ✗ ☆

FOR GRANT, THE THREE-MONTH PERIOD THAT
followed the fall of Vicksburg — more specifically, the ninety days
that elapsed between Sherman's recapture of Jackson in mid-July and
Lincoln's mid-October solution to the western command problem —
had been a time of strain not unlike the one that followed Shiloh and the
occupation of Corinth the year before, in which his counsel was rejected
and he felt himself to be more or less a supernumerary in the conduct
of the war. Now as then, he saw his army dismembered and dispersed,
its various segments dispatched to critical theaters, while he himself was
confined with the mere remnant to the quiet backwater which he had
created along his particular stretch of the Mississippi. He did not consider submitting his resignation, as he had done before, but he suffered,
as the result of a horseback accident midway of this season of frustration, an injury which for a term seemed likely to produce the same effect by removing him entirely from the scene, flat on his back on a
stretcher. It was indeed a period of tension, of strain of the kind he had
always borne least well, and it was attended, as all such times had been
for him, by rumors of his drinking, which was said to be his only relief
from the boredom that invariably descended when there was no fighting
to be done and his wife was not around.

Not, of course, that he and the troops who remained with him
had been completely idle all this time. While Herron was conducting his
foray up the Yazoo, which had cost Porter the *De Kalb*, and Sherman
was closing in on Jackson, the price of which was to run him just over
1100 casualties, Grant sent one of McPherson's brigades down to
Natchez to look into a report that there was heavy rebel traffic there in
goods moving to and from the otherwise cut-off Transmississippi.
Brigadier General T. E. G. Ransom, who commanded the expedition,
found the report to be altogether true. Moreover, by sending mounted
pursuers east and west he made the simultaneous capture of a wagon

train bound for Alexandria with half a million rounds of rifle and artillery ammunition and a drove of 5000 Texas cattle bound for Alabama, both of which had crossed the river the day before, headed in opposite directions. This was a sizable haul, achieved without the loss of a man, and one month later, at nearly as cheap a price, Grant made a considerably larger one at Grenada, the railroad junction south of the Yalobusha where the Confederates had collected most of the rolling stock of the Mississippi Central, trapped there since May by Johnson's precipitate burning of the bridge across the Pearl when he evacuated Jackson. The raid was two-pronged, one cavalry column sent south from Memphis by Hurlbut while another was sent north by Sherman. On August 17 they converged upon the junction, which so far had resisted all efforts to take it — including Grant's, back in December — and after a brief skirmish with the outnumbered garrison, which fled to avoid capture, went to work on the huge conglomeration of engines and cars "so closely packed as to make a small town of themselves." An elated trooper described them so, and afterwards the official tally listed no fewer than 57 locomotives and more than 400 freight and passenger cars wrecked and burned, together with depot buildings and machine shops containing a wealth of commissary and ordnance supplies. The total bill of destruction was set at $4,000,000, which made the raid one of the most profitable of the war. Presently, however, this figure had to be scaled down a bit. Learning that the Confederates had returned to Grenada in the wake of the departed bluecoats and were frugally carting away the precious locomotive driving wheels, removed from the rubble and ashes, Hurlbut advised in his report that, next time they went out on such a venture, the raiders use sledges to crack off the flanges of the wheels and thus render them unsalvageable.

Both Natchez and Grenada were satisfactory accomplishments, so far as they went, but after all they were only raids. Grant wanted something more: something comparable, in its influence on the outcome of the war, to the recent reduction of Vicksburg and the attendant opening of the Mississippi: something, in short, that would knock the flanges off the whole Confederate machine. Banks had suggested, soon after the fall of Port Hudson, an operation against Mobile, and so had Sherman, who proposed that the coastal city be taken as prelude to an advance up the Alabama River to Selma and beyond, threatening Bragg's rear while Rosecrans, who had maneuvered his adversary back across the Tennessee, brought pressure against his front. Grant approved and passed the word to Halleck. "It seems to me now that Mobile should be captured," he wired on July 18, "the expedition starting from some point on Lake Pontchartrain." Halleck replied that the plan had merit, but added characteristically that it would not do to hurry. "I think it will be best to clean up a little," he advised. "Johnston should be disposed of; also Price, Marmaduke, &c., so as to hold the line of the Arkansas River . . .

[and] assist General Banks in cleaning out Western Louisiana. When these things are accomplished there will be a large available force to operate either on Mobile or Texas." Just when this would be he did not say. Banks meanwhile had continued to recommend the same objective, though with no better success, and on the last day of the month he left New Orleans aboard a fast packet to confer with Grant at Vicksburg, which he reached the following morning. After putting their heads together both generals continued to urge Halleck to order the reduction of the Confederacy's only remaining Gulf port east of the Mississippi. "I can send the necessary force," Grant offered. Whereupon the general-in-chief suddenly cut the ground from under their feet by flatly rejecting the Mobile proposal in favor of an all-out effort against coastal Texas. "There are important reasons why our flag should be restored to some part of Texas with the least possible delay," he wired on August 6. He did not say what those reasons were, but three days later Lincoln himself got in touch with Grant on the matter. "I see by a dispatch of yours that you incline strongly toward an expedition against Mobile," he wrote. "This would appear tempting to me also, were it not that, in view of recent events in Mexico, I am greatly impressed with the importance of re-establishing the national authority in Western Texas as soon as possible."

Personally considerate though this was, it was not very enlightening; nor was Halleck's explanation, which he made in a covering letter to Banks, that the decision in favor of a Lone Star expedition had been "of a diplomatic rather than of a military character, and resulted from some European complications, or, more properly speaking, was intended to prevent such complications." In point of fact, the matter was more complex than anyone outside the State Department knew, including Old Brains himself, who was a student of international affairs. Benito Juárez, elected head of the Mexican government in the spring of 1861, coincident with the crisis over Sumter, had announced at the time of First Bull Run a two-year suspension of payments to foreign creditors for debts contracted by his predecessor; in response to which Spain, France, and England concluded a convention looking toward a forcible joint collection of their claims and sent some 10,000 troops to Mexico by way of proof that they meant business. By May of the following year, in the period between Shiloh and the Seven Days, while Stonewall Jackson was on the rampage in the Shenandoah Valley, England and Spain had obtained satisfaction from Juárez on the debt, and they withdrew their soldiers. France did not; Napoleon III, attracted by Mexico's wealth and weakness, had plans designed to rival in the New World those of his illustrious uncle in the Old. He stepped up his demands, including insistence on indemnity and payment of certain shady claims advanced by Swiss-French bankers, rapidly increased his occupation force to 35,000 men, and began a march inland from Vera Cruz and Tampico, which was resisted fitfully and ineffectually by guerillas operating much as they had done against Cortez and Winfield Scott, over the same route of conquest. In June of 1863, with Lee on the march for Pennsylvania and Vicksburg under siege, Mexico City fell to the invaders and a pro-French government was set up.

Such was the situation Lincoln faced when Banks and Grant proposed the Mobile expedition the following month. Entirely aside from the violation of the Monroe Doctrine, which he was willing to overlook until the present larger troubles on his hands were cleared away, he knew only too well the pro-Confederate sympathies Napoleon embraced for his own reasons. If foreign intervention came, as the Emperor had been urging for the past two years, Lincoln wanted to be ready to defend the line of the Rio Grande against the imperial forces now in occupation of the capital to the south. That, in brief, was why Mobile had gone by the board; he wanted Union troops in Texas, where none now were, and he did not believe that Banks and Grant were strong enough to accomplish both objectives at the same time. Banks was down to about 12,000 men, the enlistment period of no fewer than twenty-two of his nine-month regiments having expired since the fall of Port Hudson, and the borrowed segments of the army Grant commanded in the taking of Vicksburg were needed now by the generals who had lent them—Burnside in East Tennessee, for instance, Prentiss in Northeast Arkansas, and Schofield in guerilla-torn Missouri — as well as by Rosecrans, who claimed that a farther advance against Bragg was dependent, among other things, on reinforcements being sent him from the army lying idle in Mississippi. "On this matter," Halleck summed up in a wire to Banks on August 12, "we have no choice, but must carry out the views of the Government."

Grant was disappointed, having been convinced that the taking of Mobile, followed by a drive northward into the Confederate heartland to dispose of Bragg and put the squeeze on Lee, would have shortened the war by months — or even years, if that was what it came to — but he accepted the rejection of his counsel in good part, aware that the command decision was based on considerations beyond his ken. In any event there was little he could do about it now, even if the decision were reversed. The dismemberment of his army had begun, and it proceeded with such rapidity that within one month, mid-August to mid-September, his strength was reduced from better than five corps to less than two. Parke's IX Corps left first, dispatched to Burnside, who was marking time in Kentucky. Then Steele's division of Sherman's XV Corps was sent to Helena for the offensive against Price, followed by J. E. Smith's division of McPherson's XVII Corps. Washburn's XVI Corps also returned upriver, one division continuing on to strengthen Schofield in Missouri, while the other two debarked at Memphis to rejoin Hurlbut. Meantime, in order to beef up Banks for the top-priority Texas undertaking, Ord's XIII Corps, with Herron's division attached, proceeded downriver to New Orleans, the staging area for the drive that was intended to secure the line of the Rio Grande against Napoleon's new world dream of conquest and expansion. All that remained by then at Vicksburg were the two reduced corps of Sherman and McPherson. They were quite enough, however, in consideration of the fact that there was practically nothing left for them to do. And now there began for Grant, who was otherwise unemployed, what might be called a social interlude, a time of unfamiliar relaxation and apparent gladness, though it ended all too abruptly with the general confined to a bed of pain in a New Orleans hotel room.

He had a good deal to be glad about at the outset, both for his own sake and his friends'. His appointment as a regular army major general had lifted him almost to Halleck's level as one of the only two men of that rank on active duty. Nor had the government delayed approval of his suggestion that Sherman and McPherson be made regular brigadiers, the reward that had gone to Meade for Gettysburg. Thanks to him, moreover, seven of his colonels now wore stars on their shoulder straps, and so did Rawlins, who was jumped from lieutenant colonel to brigadier general at his chief's solicitation. "He comes the nearest being indispensable to me of any officer in the service," Grant had said of his fellow townsman in the letter of recommendation, and he added, though he must have been aware that this was spreading it rather thick: "I can safely say that he would make a good corps commander." In addition to official recognition, which included the unprecedented You-were-right-I-was-wrong letter from the President, he soon was given cause to know how much his latest victory had raised him in the public's estimation. On August 26 he attended in Memphis the first of many banquets that would be tendered in his honor over the course of the next twenty years. In front of his place at table in the Gayoso House there was a pyramid inscribed with the names of all his battles, beginning with Belmont, and he was presented to the two hundred guests with the toast, "Your Grant and my Grant," in which his reopening of the Mississippi to commerce was compared to the exploits of two other heroes much admired along the river that ran past Memphis, Hernando de Soto and Robert Fulton. He responded with an attractively awkward speech of two brief sentences, thanking the citizens for their kindness and promising to do all he could for their prosperity, then sat down amid loud, prolonged applause. Three days later, after stopping off at Vicksburg for a quick inspection of headquarters, he was in Natchez, where he found the wealthy planters entirely co-operative in their concern for the survival of their fine mansions on the bluff. Proceeding downriver to pay Banks a return visit, he reached New Orleans on September 2.

Banks knew how to entertain a guest; moreover he had all the resources of a high-living Creole society at his disposal. Two days later he staged a grand review at nearby Carrollton in honor of his visitor, who, mounted on a spirited charger procured for him on this occasion as a tribute to his horsemanship, watched Ord's veterans swing past with the names of their and his recent upriver victories on their banners. It was a stirring moment for them and him, a last reunion before they set off for new fields; but the day was grievously marred before it ended. Returning from the suburb to the heart of the city, Grant's borrowed mount shied at a hissing locomotive and, bolting, collided with a carriage that was coming from the opposite direction. Horse and rider went down hard. The animal rose from the cobblestones unassisted, but not Grant, who had suffered a badly dislocated hip, as well as a possible fracture of the skull, and was unconscious; in which condition he was carried on a litter to the nearby St Charles Hotel. Almost at once the story that he had been drinking began to make the rounds, gathering details as it went. Years later William Franklin, who had been transferred from the East to command a corps on the Texas expedition, testified in private that he "*saw* Grant tumble from his horse drunk." It even began to be said that the fall had occurred in the course of the review, which had been brought thereby to an unceremonious end, and that the general had been knocked out not so much by the blow on his head as by the whiskey in his stomach. Grant knew nothing of this at the time, nor indeed of anything else. In fact, the first he knew of having been hurt was when he regained consciousness, somewhat later, to find "several doctors" hovering over him. "My leg was swollen from the knee to the thigh," he afterwards wrote, "and the swelling, almost to the point of bursting, extended along the body up to the armpit. The pain was almost beyond endurance. I lay at the hotel something over a week without being able to turn myself in bed."

★　★　★

While Grant was laid up, confined to a world of pain whose limits were described by the four walls of his hotel room, Banks opened the campaign designed to carry out the instructions of his superiors to restore the flag of the Union "to some part of Texas with the least possible delay." As it turned out, however, he encountered something worse than delay in the execution of his plans, the first results of which were about as abruptly disastrous as his fellow general's fall on horseback, drunk or sober.

Halleck had advised an amphibious movement "up Red River to Alexandria, Natchitoches, or Shreveport, and the military occupation of northern Texas. . . . Nevertheless," he added, "your choice is left unrestricted." Banks replied with numerous logistical objections, not the least of which was that the Red was nearly dry at this season of the year. He favored a sudden descent on the coast, specifically at Sabine Pass, to be followed by an overland march on Galveston and other points beyond.

Accordingly, having been given his choice, he ordered Franklin to load a reinforced division onto transports and proceed to Sabine Pass, where he would rendezvous with a four-gunboat assault force. The rebel defenses were said to be weak, despite the reverse the navy had suffered here in January; once these had been subdued by the warships, Franklin was to put his troops ashore and move inland to the Texas & New Orleans Railroad, linking Houston and Beaumont and Orange, and there await the arrival of the balance of his corps, which by then would have been brought forward by the unloaded transports. It was all worked out in careful detail, and on September 7, three days after Grant's accident, Franklin arrived before the pass and was joined that evening by the gunboat flotilla under Lieutenant Frederick Crocker, U.S.N. Fort Griffin, the rebel work protecting Sabine City, mounted half a dozen light guns and was garrisoned by less than fifty men; Crocker attacked it the following afternoon, having six times the number of heavier guns in his four warships. The engagement was brief and decisive. Within half an hour one gunboat was hit in the boiler, losing all her steam, and a few minutes later a second ran aground in the shallow bay and was given the same treatment by the marksmen in the fort. Both vessels struck their colors, surrendering with their crews of about 300 men, including 50 killed or wounded and the luckless lieutenant in command, while the third retired out of range with the fourth, which had not engaged. Still aboard the transports with his soldiers, whom the navy was unable to put ashore, Franklin felt there was nothing to do but turn around and go back to New Orleans, and that was what he did, reporting a total loss of six men, who had been aboard the surrendered gunboats as observers, together with 200,000 rations thrown overboard to lighten a grounded transport and 200 mules served likewise when the steamer on which they were loaded lost her stack in a heavy sea on the way home.

So feeble had the attack been that Magruder at first could not believe it was anything more than a feint, designed to distract his attention from the main effort somewhere else along the coast. When no such blow was delivered in the course of the next few days, Prince John contented himself with what had been accomplished; a "brilliant victory," he called the fight, a "gallant achievement," and finally, in an excess of pride at what his gunners had done in the face of long odds, "the most extraordinary feat of the war." Congress eventually passed a resolution of thanks, "eminently due, and hereby cordially given," to the two officers and the 41 men of the garrison who had stood to their outranged guns and outfought the Yankee warships.

On the other hand, Banks assigned the reason for the failure to the "ignorance" of the naval officers involved; one of his chief regrets, no doubt, was that Farragut was not around to blister them a bit, having returned to New York for badly overdue repairs to his flagship *Hartford* in the Brooklyn Navy Yard. In any case, on Franklin's return the Massachusetts general decided that the line of advance up the Red to Northeast Texas, suggested previously by Old Brains, was probably the best invasion route after all, and he informed Lincoln that while the army was "preparing itself" for the execution of this larger plan, which would have to be delayed until rain had swelled the river, he would continue his efforts to move in directly from the Gulf against the Lone Star beaches — or, anyhow, some beach; for he left himself plenty of latitude as to just where he would strike next time, merely remarking that he proposed "to attempt a lodgment upon some point on the coast from the mouth of the Mississippi to the Rio Grande."

By then the year was well into October, and two other Federal commanders in the Transmississippi region, James Blunt and John Schofield, had unexpected problems on their hands in the departments of the Frontier and Missouri. William Steele and Pap Price had been driven from Fort Smith and Little Rock, the former deep into Indian Territory and the latter beyond the line of the Arkansas. Schofield could breathe easier; so he thought — until Jo Shelby came riding northward, all the way to the Missouri River, and Quantrill, while crossing the southeast corner of Kansas on his way to winter in Texas, gave Blunt an opportune demonstration that he had a talent for something more than murdering civilians in or under their beds.

From Arkadelphia, where he ended his retreat in mid-September, Price launched Shelby on a raid into his home state, hoping thus to discourage Schofield from reinforcing Fred Steele for a follow-up push from the Arkansas River to the Ouachita. Three months short of his thirty-third birthday, the Missouri cavalryman was still a colonel despite outstanding service in practically every major engagement fought in the region since Wilson's Creek; even now he was nursing an unhealed wound he had suffered in his sword arm during the Helena repulse, twelve weeks ago. Though, like Jeb Stuart, he took his nickname from his initials and wore a foot-long plume on his hat, there was a hard, practical core to his daring, a concentration more on results than on effect, which afterwards caused Alfred Pleasonton, who rode for three years against Stuart before transferring to the far western theater — although it perhaps should be noted in passing that he never came up against Forrest — to say flatly, after a year of fighting there as well, that "Shelby was the best cavalry general of the South." Part of the evidence in support of this contention was put on record during the present raid, which lasted longer and covered a greater distance than any undertaken by any body of horsemen from either army in the whole course of the war, including Morgan's famous raid into Ohio, which ended in disaster, whereas Shelby returned with a stronger force than he had had at the outset. He set out with 600 troopers on September 22, passing next day through Caddo Gap, forty miles northwest of Arkadelphia, and five days later crossed the Arkansas River a hundred miles above Little Rock, midway between Clarksville and Fort Smith. Riding north through Huntsville and Bentonville, he crossed the state line to reach Neosho on October 4 and promptly forced the surrender of 400 Union cavalry who had holed up in the stout brick courthouse, former capitol of the short-lived Confederate-allied Republic of Missouri, which the bluecoats had converted into a fort and were determined to hold, at any rate until the rebel cannon started knocking it to pieces. Along with the men, the victors took their horses, their fine Sharps rifles and navy revolvers, and their clothes, which were used as an effective disguise, so far at least as they went round, by the former gray-clad raiders. Next day the ride north continued, still with the stockily built and heavily bearded colonel in the lead.

His goal was Jefferson City; he had it in mind to raise the Stars and Bars over the statehouse, not only as a sign that Missouri was by no means "conquered," but also as a gesture to discourage the Union high command from detaching troops from here to exploit its recent gains in Arkansas or to shore up Rosecrans, who had been whipped two weeks ago at Chickamauga and now was under siege in Chattanooga; in furtherance of which intention Shelby sent out parties, left and right of his line of march, to cut telegraph wires, burn installations and depots of supply, attack outlying strong points, and in general spread confusion as to his strength and destination. On north he rode, through Sarcoxie and Bowers Mill, Greenfield and Stockton, Humansville and Warsaw, to Tipton on the Missouri Pacific, which he struck on October 10. Jefferson City was less than forty miles away, due east on the railroad, but his enemies were thoroughly aroused by now, expecting him to move in that direction. Instead, after tearing up track on both sides of Tipton, burning the depot, and setting fire to a large yard of freight cars, he pressed on north to Booneville, where he was greeted next day by the mayor and a delegation of citizens who came out to assure him of their southern loyalty and ask that he spare their property. This he did, except for the new $400,000 bridge across the nearby Lamine River, which he wrecked. "Now the broad bosom of the grand old Missouri lay unveiled before us in the red beams of the autumn sun," his adjutant later wrote, "and the men, forgetting all their privations and dangers, broke out in one long, loud, proud hurrah." The hurrah could indeed have been a loud one, for Shelby's strength had grown by now to more than a thousand troopers by the addition of recruits who had flocked to join him on the way. Moreover, the column was lengthened by three hundred captured wagons, drawn not by mules or draft horses, but by the hundreds of cavalry mounts he had taken in the series of surrenders that had marked his line of march, surrenders or flights which had netted him no fewer than forty stands of colors and ten "forts" of one kind or another. If the blue-clad graybacks cheered themselves hoarse with pride as they stood on the south bank of the wide Missouri, just under four hundred air-line miles from the nearest Confederate outpost, it was not without reason.

Their problem now was escape from the greatly superior Federal columns rapidly converging on them from the south and east and north. Shelby led them west along the south bank of the Missouri, in the direction of his prewar home at Waverly. Before they got there, however, they had their one full-scale engagement of the raid, October 13 near Arrow Rock, where the enemy columns finally brought them to bay, outnumbered five to one. Splitting his command in two, Shelby dismounted the larger half and fought a savage defensive action in which he lost about one hundred men while the smaller half made a mounted getaway by punching a hole in the line of the attackers; whereupon he remounted the remainder and did the same at another point, taking a different escape route to confuse and split his pursuers. On through Waverly he rode that night, still accompanied by his train, which he had brought out with him. At nearby Hawkins Mill, however, he was later to report, "finding my wagons troublesome, and having no ammunition left except what the men could carry, I sunk them in the Missouri River, where they were safe from all capture." This done he turned south. Bypassing Lexington, Harrisonville, and Butler to skirt the Burnt District, he reached Carthage on October 17 and turned east next day through Sarcoxie, which he had visited two weeks before, on his way north. Laying ambushes all the while to delay pursuers, he re-entered Arkansas on October 19 and was joined next day on the Little Osage River by the smaller force that had split off at Arrow Rock a week ago. From the Little Osage he moved by what he called "easy stages" to Clarksville, where he recrossed the Arkansas River on October 26 and made his way south through the Ouachita Mountains to Washington. There at last he called a halt, November 3, forty miles southwest of his starting point at Arkadelphia. In the forty-one days he had been gone he had covered a distance of 1500 miles, an average of better than thirty-six miles a day, and though he had suffered a total loss of about 150 killed and wounded, he had also picked up 800 recruits along the way, so that he returned with twice the number of men he had had when he set out. He listed his gains — 600 Federals killed or wounded, 500 captured and paroled; 6000 horses and mules taken, together with 300 wagons, 1200 small arms, and 40 stands of colors; $1,000,000 in U. S. Army supplies destroyed, plus $800,000 in public property — then laconically closed his report, which was addressed to Price's adjutant: "Hoping this may prove satisfactory, I remain, major, very respectfully, your obedient servant, Jo. O. Shelby, Colonel." Highly pleased — as well it might be; for there was also substance to his claim that the raid had kept 10,000 Missouri bluecoats from being sent to assist in raising the siege at Chattanooga — the government promoted him to brigadier the following month.

Quantrill by now was calling himself a colonel, too, and had even acquired a uniform in which he had his picture taken wearing three stars on the collar, a long-necked young man with hooded eyes, a smooth round jaw, and a smile as faint as Mona Lisa's. But the government — much to its credit, most historians were to say — declined to sanction his self-promotion, even after he scored a second victory in Kansas, one far more impressive, militarily, than the first, which he had scored six weeks before at Lawrence. While Shelby was preparing to set out from Arkadelphia, Quantrill was reassembling his guerillas on familiar Blackwater Creek, intending to take them to Texas for the winter. In early October the two columns passed each other, east and west of Carthage, Shelby and his 600 going north, Quantrill with about 400 going south, neither aware of the other's presence, some twenty miles away. On October 6, when the former passed through Warsaw, the latter drew near Fort Baxter, down in the southeast corner of Kansas at Baxter Springs, which was held by two companies of Wisconsin cavalry and one of Kansas infantry. Quantrill decided to take it. While the attack was in progress, however, he learned that a train of ten wagons was approaching from the north, attended by two more companies of Wisconsin and Kansas troops; so he pulled back half his men, and went to take that too. His luck was in. The train and troops were the baggage and escort of James Blunt, lately appointed commander of the District of the Frontier, on his way to establish headquarters at Fort Baxter. When Blunt saw the horsemen in line across the road ahead, he assumed they were an honor guard sent out from the fort to meet him. He halted to have his escort dress its ranks, then proceeded at a dignified pace to receive the salute of the waiting line of horsemen.

He received instead a blast of fire at sixty yards, followed promptly by a screaming charge that threw his hundred-man escort first into milling confusion and then, when they recognized what they were up against — the guerillas, having been warned to expect no quarter, certainly would extend none — into headlong flight. This last availed all but a handful of them nothing; 79 of the hundred were quickly run down and killed, including Major Henry Curtis, Blunt's adjutant and the son of the former department commander. Blunt himself made his escape, though he was nearly unhorsed in taking a jump across a ravine. Thrown from his saddle and onto his horse's neck by the rebound, he clung there and rode in that unorthodox position for a mile or more, outdistancing his pursuers, who turned back to attend to the business of dispatching the prisoners and the wounded. Quantrill called off the attack on the fort — its garrison had suffered 19 casualties to bring the Federal total to 98, as compared to 6 for the guerillas — and proceeded to rifle the abandoned wagons. Included in the loot was all of Blunt's official correspondence, his dress sword, two stands of colors, and several demijohns of whiskey. Quantrill was so pleased with his exploit that he even took a drink or two, something none of his companions had seen him do before. Presently he became talkative, which was also quite unusual. "By God," he boasted as he staggered about, "Shelby couldn't whip Blunt; neither could Marmaduke; but *I* whipped him." He went on south to Texas, as he had intended when he left Johnson County the week before, and Blunt was removed not long thereafter from the command he had so recently acquired.

But Holmes and Price, reduced by sickness and desertion to a force of 7000, had not been greatly helped by either Shelby or Quantrill; Steele still threatened from Little Rock, and though he had not been reinforced, he outnumbered them two to one. On October 25, the day before Shelby recrossed the Arkansas River on his way back from Missouri, Holmes ordered a withdrawal of the troops left at Pine Bluff, thus loosening his last tenuous grasp on the south bank of that stream in order to prepare for what Kirby Smith believed was threatening, deep in his rear: Banks had begun another ascent of the Teche and the Atchafalaya, which could take him at last to the Red and into Texas. Once this happened, Smith's command, already cut off from the powder mills and ironworks of the East, would be cut off from the flow of goods coming in through Mexico. "The Fabian policy is now our true policy," he declared, and he advised that if further retreat became necessary, Holmes could move "by Monticello, along Bayou Bartholomew to Monroe, through a country abundant in supplies."

★ ★ ★

Grant by then had left for other fields. In mid-September, after ten days of confinement to the New Orleans hotel room, unable even to sit up in bed, he had himself carried aboard a steamboat bound for Vicksburg, and there, although as he said later he "remained unable to move for some time afterwards," he was reunited with his wife and their four children, who came down to join him in a pleasant, well-shaded house which his staff had commandeered for him on the bluff overlooking the river. Under these circumstances, satisfying as they were to his uxorious nature, his convalescence was so comparatively rapid that within a month he was hobbling about on crutches.

McPherson kept bachelor quarters in town, boarding with a family in which, according to Sherman, there were "several interesting young ladies." Not that his fellow Ohioan had neglected his own comfort. Like Grant, Sherman had his family with him — it too included four children — camped in a fine old grove of oaks beside the Big Black River, near the house from whose gallery, several weeks ago, the dozen weeping women had reviled him for the death of one of their husbands at Bull Run. He had been discomfited then, but that was all behind him now, together with his doubts about the war and his share in it. Grant had given his restless spirit a sense of direction and dedication; he could even abide the present idleness, feeling that he and his troops had earned a decent period of rest. "The time passed very agreeably," he would recall years later, "diversified only by little events of not much significance." That he was in favor of vigorous efforts at an early date, however, was shown in a letter he wrote Halleck on September 17 — the day after Grant's return from New Orleans — in response to one from the general-in-chief requesting his opinions as to "the question of reconstruction in Louisiana, Mississippi, and Arkansas. . . . Write me your views fully," Halleck urged him, "as I may wish to use them with the President."

Never one to require much encouragement for an exposition of his views, the red-haired general replied with a letter that was to fill eight close-spaced pages in his memoirs. He had done considerable thinking along these lines, based on his experiences in the region before and during the war, and if by "reconstruction" Halleck meant a revival of "any civil government in which the local people have much say," then Sherman was against it. "I know them well, and the very impulses of their nature," he declared, "and to deal with the inhabitants of that part of the South which borders on the great river, we must recognize the classes into which they have divided themselves." First, there were the planters. "They are educated, wealthy, and easily approached. . . . I know we can manage this class, but only by *action*," by "pure military rule." Second were "the smaller farmers, mechanics, merchants, and laborers. . . . The southern politicians, who understand this class, use them as the French do their masses — seemingly consult their prejudices, while they make their orders and enforce them. We should do the same." Third, there were "the Union men of the South. I must confess that I have little respect for this class. . . . I account them as nothing in this great game of war." Fourth and last, he narrowed his sights on "the young bloods of the South: sons of planters, lawyers-about-town, good billiard players and sportsmen, men who never did work and never will. War suits them, and the rascals are brave, fine riders, bold to rashness, and dangerous subjects in every sense. They care not a sou for niggers, land, or any thing." His solution to the problem they posed as "the most dangerous set of men that this war has turned loose upon the world" was easily stated: "These men must all be killed or employed by us before we can hope for peace." Just how they were to be employed by the government they were fighting Sherman did not say, but having sketched the various classes to be dealt with, he proceeded to give his prescription for victory over them all. "I would banish all minor questions, assert the broad doctrine that as a nation the United States has the right, and also the physical power, to penetrate to every part of our national domain, and that we will do it — that we will do it in our own time and in our own way; that it makes no difference whether it be in one year, or two, or ten, or twenty; that we will remove and destroy every obstacle, if need be, take every life, every acre of land, every particle of property, everything that to us seems proper; that we will not cease till the end is attained; that all who do not aid us are enemies, and that we will not account to them for our acts." Lest there be any misunderstanding, he summed up what he meant. "I would not coax them, or even meet them half way, but make them so sick of war that generations would pass away before they would again appeal to it. . . . The only government needed or deserved by the States of Louisiana, Arkansas, and Mississippi now exists in Grant's army." He closed by asking Halleck to "excuse so long a letter," but in sending it to Grant for forwarding to Washington, he appended a note in which he added: "I would make this war as severe as possible, and show no symptoms of tiring till the South begs for mercy. . . . The South has done her worst, and now is the time for us to pile on our blows thick and fast."

Halleck presently wired that Lincoln had read the letter and wanted to see it published, but Sherman declined, preferring "not to be drawn into any newspaper controversy" such as the one two years ago, in which he had been pronounced insane. "If I covet any public reputation," he replied, "it is as a silent actor. I dislike to see my name in print." Anyhow, by then he was on the move again; his troops had "slung the knapsack for new fields," and he himself had experienced a personal tragedy as deep as any he was ever to know in a long life.

Rosecrans had been whipped at Chickamauga while Sherman's letter was on its way north, and before it got to Washington the wires were humming with calls for reinforcements to relieve Old Rosy's cooped-up army. On September 23 Grant passed the word for Sherman to leave at once for Memphis with two divisions, picking up en route the division McPherson had recently sent to Helena, and move toward Chattanooga via Corinth on the Memphis & Charleston Railroad, which he was to repair as he went, thus providing a new supply line. Drums rolled in the camps on the Big Black; for the next four days the roads to Vicksburg were crowded with columns filing onto transports at the wharf. The steamer *Atlantic* was the last to leave, and on it rode Sherman and his family. He was showing the two girls and the two boys his old camp as the boat passed Young's Point, when he noticed that nine-year-old Willy, his first-born son and namesake — "that child on whose future I based all the ambition I ever had" — was pale and feverish. Regimental surgeons, summoned from below deck, diagnosed the trouble as typhoid and warned that it might be fatal. It was. Taken ashore at Memphis, the boy died in the Gayoso House, where Grant's banquet had been staged five weeks ago. Sherman was disconsolate, though he kept busy attending to details involved in the eastward movement while his wife and the three remaining children went on north to St Louis with the dead boy in a sealed metallic casket. "Sleeping, waking, everywhere I see poor Willy," he wrote her, and he added: "I will try to make poor Willy's memory the cure for the defects which have sullied my character — all that is captious, eccentric and wrong."

His grief seemed rather to deepen than to lift. A week after his son's death he was asking, "Why was I not killed at Vicksburg and left Willy to grow up and care for you?" By that time, though, his troops were all in motion, some by rail and some on foot, and on October 11 he started for Corinth aboard a train that carried his staff and a battalion of regulars. At Collierville, twenty miles out of Memphis, the train and depot, which had been turned into a blockhouse and surrounded by shallow trenches, were attacked by rebel cavalry under Chalmers, an old Shiloh adversary, whose strength he estimated at 3000. He himself had fewer than 600 and no guns, whereas the raiders had four. To gain time, he received and after some discussion declined a flag-of-truce demand for unconditional surrender, meanwhile disposing his few troops for defense and sending a wire for hurry-up assistance. The fight that followed lasted four hours, at the end of which time the rebels withdrew to avoid contact with a division marching eastward in response to the wire that, after the manner of light fiction, had got through just before the line was cut. Though it had not really been much of a fight, as such things went at this stage of the war — he had lost 14 killed, 42 wounded, and 54 captured, while Chalmers had lost 3 killed and 48 wounded — Sherman was tremendously set up. Five staff horses had been taken, including his favorite mare Dolly, and the graybacks had also confiscated his second-best uniform, but these seemed a small price to pay for the recovery of his accustomed spirits. He had escaped from gloom.

By October 16 he had his entire corps — increased to five divisions by the addition of two from Hurlbut — past Corinth, and three days later the head of the column reached Eastport to find a fleet of transports awaiting its arrival, loaded with provisions and guarded by two of Porter's gunboats. The establishment of this supply route on the Tennessee enabled Sherman to abandon the railroad west of there, but he still had 161 miles of track to rebuild and maintain, in accordance with Halleck's orders, from Iuka to Stevenson. This too he took in stride; for he was again in what he liked to call "high feather." He encouraged his men to live off the country, having decided that the best way to keep raiders out of Kentucky was to cut an arid swath across northern Mississippi and Alabama. The men took to the notion handily, not only because it agreed with their own, but also because their appetites had sharpened with the advent of early fall weather and days of working on the railroad. Sherman could scarcely contain his delight at their performance. "I never saw such greedy rascals after chicken and fresh meat," he exulted in a letter home. "I don't believe I will draw anything for them but salt. I don't know but it would be a good plan to march my army back and forth from Florence and Stevenson to make a belt of devastation between the enemy and our country."

"My army," he said, and truly; for by that time Lincoln's solution of the western command problem had been announced. On October 10, the day before Sherman left Memphis to make his spirit-restoring defense of the Collierville blockhouse, Grant received at Vicksburg a badly delayed order from Halleck directing him to report without delay to Cairo for instructions. The order, dated October 3, had taken a full week to reach him. He left at once, though he was still on crutches, and stopped off at Columbus, Kentucky, six days later — the guerilla-cut telegraph line had been restored to that point by then, only one day short of two weeks after the date on Halleck's order — to report that he was on his way upriver. Perhaps he wondered if he was to be disciplined for not keeping in touch and going off to New Orleans, as he had been after Donelson for not keeping in touch and going off to Nashville, though he could not see that he deserved any more blame in the present instance than he had deserved then. At any rate he was not much enlightened when he reached Cairo next morning, October 17, and was handed a wire directing him to proceed at once to the Galt House in Louisville, where he would receive further instructions from an officer of the War Department. He boarded a train that would take him there by way of Indianapolis. But that afternoon, as the train was pulling out of the station at the latter place, an attendant came hurrying out and flagged it to a halt. Behind him, bustling up the platform on short legs, came the Secretary of War, Edwin M. Stanton himself, whom Grant had never met. He swung aboard the last car, wheezing asthmatically, and worked his way forward, as the train gathered speed, to the car occupied by the general and his staff. "How are you, General Grant?" he said, grasping the hand of Dr Edward Kittoe, the staff surgeon. "I knew you at sight from your pictures."

This was quickly straightened out; Kittoe did not look much like his chief anyhow, though he wore a beard and a campaign hat and was also from Galena. After the amenities, exchanged while the train rocked on toward Louisville, Stanton presented Grant with two copies of a War Department order dated October 16, both of which had the same opening paragraph:

> By direction of the President of the United States, the Departments of the Ohio, of the Cumberland, and of the Tennessee, will constitute the Military Division of the Mississippi. Major General U. S. Grant, United States Army, is placed in command of the Military Division of the Mississippi, with his headquarters in the field.

In brief, this was Lincoln's unifying solution to the western command problem. With the exception of the troops in East Louisiana under Banks, who outranked him, Grant was put in charge of all the Union forces between the Allegheny Mountains and the Mississippi River. That was all there was to one of the copies of the order, but the other had an added paragraph, relieving Rosecrans from duty with the Army of the Cumberland and appointing Thomas in his place. The choice was left to Grant, who had no fondness for Old Rosy; "I chose the latter," he remarked dryly, some years afterward. Sherman of course would succeed to command of the Army of the Tennessee, and Burnside would continue, at least for the present, as head of the Army of the Ohio.

At Louisville, which they reached that night, Grant and the Secretary spent the following day together at the Galt House discussing the military outlook, mostly from the Washington point of view. That evening — by which time, the general said later, "all matters of discussion seemed exhausted" — Grant and his wife, who had come from Vicksburg with him by boat and train, left the hotel to call on relatives, while Stanton retired to his room with an attack of asthma. It had been decided to defer issuance of the War Department order until the general and his staff had had time to attend to various preparatory details. Presently, however, a messenger arrived with the latest dispatch from Dana, announcing that Rosecrans intended to evacuate Chattanooga and predicting utter disaster as a result. Highly agitated, Stanton sent bellboys and staff officers to all parts of the city in a frantic search for Grant. None of them could find him until about 11 o'clock, when they all found him at once. As he returned to the hotel from his call on relatives, it seemed to him that "every person [I] met was a messenger from the Secretary, apparently partaking of his impatience to see me." Upstairs, he found Stanton pacing about in his dressing gown and clutching the fatal dispatch, which he insisted called for immediate action to prevent the loss of Chattanooga and the annihilation of the troops besieged there. Grant agreed, and at once sent two dispatches of his own: one informing Rosecrans that he was relieved of command, the other instructing Thomas to hold onto Chattanooga "at all hazards." Thomas replied promptly with a message that indicated how aptly he had been characterized as the Rock of Chickamauga. "We will hold the town till we starve," he told Grant.

❌ 2 ❌

" 'All quiet on the Potomac.' Nothing to disturb autumnal slumbers," Stanton had wired the Chattanooga quartermaster on October 4, proud of his management of the transfer west of two corps from the army down in Virginia, which apparently had been accomplished under Lee's very nose without his knowledge, or at any rate without provoking a reaction on his part. Three days later, however, Meade's signalmen intercepted wigwag messages indicating that the rebels were preparing for some sort of movement in their camps beyond the Rapidan, and two days after that, on October 9, word came from the cavalry outposts that Lee was on the march, heading west and north around Meade's flank, much as he had done when he maneuvered bold John Pope out of a similar position, fourteen months ago, and brought him to grief on the plains of Manassas. Presently things were anything but quiet on the Potomac, deep in the Federal rear; for Meade was headed in that direction, too, and the indications were that there was going to be a Third Bull Run.

Lee had been wanting to take the offensive ever since his return from Pennsylvania. "If General Meade does not move, I wish to attack him," he told Davis in late August. The detachment of Longstreet soon afterward had seemed to rule this out, however, since it reduced Lee's strength to less than 50,000, whereas the Federals had nearly twice that number in his immediate front. Also there was the problem of his health, a recurrence of the rheumatic malady that had racked him in early spring. Then had come the news of Chickamauga, which was like a tonic to him. "My whole heart and soul have been with you and your brave corps in your late battle," he wrote Old Peter. "It was natural to hear of Longstreet and Hill charging side by side, and pleasing to find the armies of the East and West vying with each other in valor and devotion to their country. A complete and glorious victory must ensue under such circumstances. . . . Finish the work before you, my dear general, and return to me. I want you badly and you cannot get back too soon." Glorious the victory had been, but he presently learned that it was a long way from complete, which meant that the detached third of his army would not be rejoining him anything like as soon as he had hoped. Then came a second tonic-like report. Two of Meade's corps had been sent west to reinforce Rosecrans, with the result that the odds against Lee were reduced from two-to-one to only a bit worse than eight-to-five. He had taken the offensive against longer odds in the past, and now he prepared to do so again, not only for the same reasons — to relieve the pressure on Richmond, to break up enemy plans in their formative stage, and to provide himself with more room for maneuver — but also by much the same method. What he had in mind, when reports of the Union reduction were confirmed in early October, was a repetition of the tactics he had employed against Pope in a similar confrontation on this same ground; that is, a march around the enemy flank, then a knockout blow delivered as the blue mass drew back to avoid encirclement.

Once he had decided he moved quickly. On October 9 the two

corps of the Army of Northern Virginia began their march up the south bank of the Rapidan, westward beyond the Union right, then north across the river. The last time Lee had done this, just over a year ago, he had also had only two corps in his army. Longstreet and Jackson had led them then; now it was Ewell and A. P. Hill, two very different men. Another difference was in Lee himself. He had ridden Traveller then; now he rode in a wagon, so crippled by rheumatism that he could not mount a horse.

Stuart's cavalry had been organized into two divisions, one under Wade Hampton and the other under Fitzhugh Lee, both of whom were promoted to major general. Hampton was still recuperating from his Gettysburg wounds; Stuart led his division himself, covering the right flank of the infantry on the march, and left Fitz Lee to guard the river crossings while the rest of the army moved upstream. After two days of swinging wide around Cedar Mountain — rich with memories for A. P. Hill, not only because he was a native of the region and had spent his boyhood in these parts, but also because it was here that he had saved Jackson from defeat in early August, a year ago — the gray column entered Culpeper from the southwest on the 11th. Meade had had his headquarters here, and three of his corps had been concentrated in the vicinity, with the other two advanced southward to the north bank of the Rapidan. Now he was gone, and his five corps were gone with him. Like Pope, he was falling back across the Rappahannock to avoid being trapped in the constricting apex of the V described by the confluence of the rivers. Beyond Culpeper, however, Stuart came upon the cavalry rear guard, drawn up at Brandy Station to fight a delaying action on the field where most of the troopers of both armies had fought so savagely four months before. In the resultant skirmish, which he called Second Brandy, Jeb had the satisfaction of driving the enemy horsemen back across the Rappahannock, only failing to bag the lot, he declared, because Fitz Lee did not arrive in time after splashing across the unguarded Rapidan fords. At any rate, he felt that the question of superior abilities, which some claimed had not been decided by the contest here in June, was definitely settled in his favor by the outcome of this second fight on the same ground. Elated though he was, he did not fail to show that he had learned from his mistakes on the recent march into Pennsylvania. Not that he admitted that he had made any; he did not, then or now or later; but he kept in close touch with the commanding general, sending a constant stream of couriers to report both his own and the enemy's position. "Thank you," Lee said to the latest in the series, who had ridden back to inform him that the blue cavalry was being driven eastward. "Tell General Stuart to continue to press them back toward the river. But tell him, too," he added, "to spare his horses — to spare his horses. It is not necessary to send so many messages." Turning to Ewell, whom he was accompanying today, he said of this staff officer and another who had reported a few minutes earlier: "I think these two young gentlemen make *eight* messengers sent me by General Stuart."

He was in excellent spirits, partly because of this evidence that his chief of cavalry had profited from experience; for whatever profited Stuart also profited Lee, who depended heavily on his former cadet for the information by which he shaped his plans. Then too, the pains in his back had let up enough to permit him to enter Culpeper on his horse instead of on the prosaic seat of a wagon, and though he preferred things simple for the most part, he also liked to see them done in style. Moreover, there had been an exchange which he had enjoyed in the course of the welcome extended by the old men and cripples and women and children who turned out to cheer the army that had delivered them from this latest spell of Federal occupation. Not, it seemed, that the occupation had been entirely unpleasant for everyone concerned. At the height of the celebration, one indignant housewife struck a discordant note by informing the general that certain young ladies of the town had accepted invitations to attend band concerts at John Sedgwick's headquarters, and there, according to reports, they had given every sign of enjoying not only the Yankee music, but also the attentions of the blue-coated staff officers who were their escorts. Lee heard the superpatriot out, then looked sternly around at several girls whose blushes proved their guilt of this near-treason. "I know General Sedgwick very well," he replied at last, replacing his look of mock severity with a smile. "It is just like him to be so kindly and considerate, and to have his band there to entertain them. So, young ladies, if the music is good, go and hear it as often as you can, and enjoy yourselves. You will find that General Sedgwick will have none but agreeable gentlemen about him."

Whatever effect these words had on the woman who lodged the complaint — and whose fate, after the general's departure, can only be guessed at — they served, by their vindication of youth, to heighten the gaiety of the occasion. Nor was Culpeper the only scene of rejoicing for deliverance. Bragg's great victory in North Georgia, Lee's northward march, the repulse of the Union flotilla at Sabine Pass, the apparent disinclination of the Federals to follow up their Vicksburg conquest, Beauregard's continuing staunchness under amphibious assault: all were hailed in the Richmond *Whig* on this same October 11, under the heading "The Prospect," as evidence that the South, whose resilience after admittedly heavy setbacks had now been demonstrated to all the world, could never be defeated by her present adversary. "As the campaigning season of the third year of the war approaches its close," the editor summed up, "the principal army of the enemy, bruised, bleeding, and alarmed, is engaged with all its might [at Chattanooga] digging into the earth for safety. The second largest force, the once Grand Army of the Potomac, is fleeing before the advancing corps of General Lee. The third, under Banks, a portion of which has just been severely chastised by a handful of men, is vaguely and feebly attempting some movement against Texas. The fourth, under Grant, has ceased to be an army of offense. The fifth, under Gillmore, with a number of ironclads to aid him, lays futile siege to Charleston. Nowhere else have they anything more than garrisons or raiding forces. At all points the Confederate forces are able to defy them."

Lee had it in mind to brighten his share of the prospect still further by intercepting Meade's withdrawal up the Orange & Alexandria Railroad. He could not divide his army, as he had done against Pope, using half of it to fix the enemy in place while the other half swung wide for a strike at the rear; he lacked both the transport and the strength, and besides, with the bluecoats already in motion, there wasn't time. But he could attempt a shorter turning movement via Warrenton, along the turnpike paralleling the railroad to the east, in hope of forcing Meade to halt and fight in a position that would afford the pursuers the chance, despite the disparity in numbers, to inflict what the dead Stonewall had called "a terrible wound." Accordingly, the Culpeper pause was a brief one; Little Powell had time for no more than a quick look at his home town as he passed through in the wake of Ewell, who in turn pushed his men hard to close the gap between them and the cavalry up ahead, beyond Brandy and the Rappahannock crossings. Stuart skirmished with the blue rear guard all the rest of that day and the next, banging away with his guns and gathering stragglers as he went. Lee, still riding with Ewell, reached Warrenton on the 13th to receive a report from Jeb that the Federals were still at Warrenton Junction, due east on the main line, burning stores. There seemed an excellent chance of cutting them off, somewhere up the line: perhaps at Bristoe Station, where Jackson had landed with such explosive effect that other time. Next morning Hill's lean marchers took the lead. Remembering the rewards of that other strike, they put their best foot forward, if for no other reason than the hope of getting it shod. Shoes, warm clothes, food, and victory: all these lay before them, fifteen miles away at Bristoe, if they could only arrive in time to forestall a Yankee getaway.

As they marched their hopes were heightened by the evidence that Meade, though clearly on the run, had no great head start in the race. "We found the campfires of the enemy still burning," one of Hill's men would recall. "Guns, knapsacks, blankets, etc. strewn along the road showed that the enemy was moving in rapid retreat, and prisoners sent in every few minutes confirmed our opinion that they were fleeing in haste." Another of the marchers, cheered at the outset because he had eaten a whole pot of boiled cabbage for breakfast — perhaps by way of distending his stomach for the feast he hoped to enjoy before nightfall — recorded the satisfaction he and his comrades felt at reliving the glad August days of 1862, when they had tramped these roads with the same goal ahead. "We all entered now fully into the spirit of the movement," he declared. "We were convinced that Meade was unwilling to face us, and we therefore anticipated a pleasant affair, if we should succeed in catching him." Little Powell, it was observed, had put on his red wool hunting shirt, as he generally did at the prospect of a fight, and that seemed highly appropriate today, on a march which the first soldier said "was almost like boys chasing a hare."

Meade had been prodded, these past three months since his re-crossing of the Potomac, more by the superiors in his rear than by the rebels in his front. Lincoln was giving Halleck strategy lectures, and Old Brains was passing them along with interlinear comments which, to Meade at least, were about as exasperating as they were banal. As a result he had become more snappish than ever. Staff officers quailed nowadays at his glance. If Lee had caught him somewhat off balance in his reaction to the sudden advance across the Rapidan, it was small wonder.

Back in September, for instance, when he asked what the government wanted him to do — he could drive Lee back on Richmond, he said, but he failed to see the advantage in this, since he lacked the strength to mount a siege — Halleck referred the question to the President, who replied that Meade "should move upon Lee at once in the manner of general attack, leaving to developments whether he will make it a real attack." The general-in-chief rephrased and expanded this. "The main objects," he told Meade, "are to threaten Lee's position, to ascertain more certainly the condition of affairs in his army, and, if possible, to cut off some portion of it by a sudden raid." Then he, like Lincoln, stressed that these were suggestions, not orders. Meade replied that this last was precisely the trouble, so far as he was concerned. He saw no profit to be gained from the proposed endeavor, whereas he discerned in it the possibility of a good deal of profitless bloodshed, and he was therefore "reluctant to run the risks involved without the positive sanction of the government." Lincoln remained unwilling to accept the responsibility it seemed to him the general was trying to unload; "I am not prepared to order or even advise an advance in this case," he told Halleck. But he added that he saw in the present impasse "matter for very serious consideration in another aspect." If Lee's 60,000 could neutralize Meade's 90,000, he went on, why could not Meade, at that same two-three ratio, detach 50,000 men to be used elsewhere to advantage while he neutralized Lee's 60,000 with his remaining 40,000? "Having practically come to the mere defensive," Lincoln wrote, "it seems to be no economy at all to employ twice as many men for that object as are needed." And having come so far in the way of observation, he went further: "To avoid misunderstanding, let me say that to attempt to fight the enemy slowly back into his intrenchments at Richmond, and there to capture him, is an idea I have been trying to repudiate for quite a year. My judgment is so clear against it that I would scarcely allow the attempt to be made if the general in command should desire to make it. My last attempt upon Richmond was to get McClellan, when he was nearer there than the enemy was, to run in ahead of him. Since then I have constantly desired the Army of the Potomac to make Lee's army, and not Richmond, its objective point. If our army cannot fall upon the enemy and hurt him where he is, it is plain to me it can gain nothing by attempting to follow him over a succession of intrenched lines into a fortified city."

Meade perceived that he had fallen among lawyers, men who could do with logic and figures what they liked. Moreover the President, in his conclusion with regard to the unwisdom of driving Lee back into the Richmond defenses, had merely returned to the point Meade himself had made at the outset, except that now the latter found it somehow used against him. The technique was fairly familiar, even to a man who had never served on a jury, but it was no less exasperating for that, and Meade was determined that if he was to go the way of Mc-Dowell and McClellan, of Pope and McClellan again, of Burnside and Hooker, he would at least make the trip to the scrap heap under his own power. In the absence of orders or "sanction" from above, he would accept the consequences of his own decisions and no others, least of all those of which he disapproved; he would fall, if fall he must, by following his own conscience. Thus, by a reaction like that of a man alone in dangerous country — which Virginia certainly was — his natural caution was enlarged. In point of fact, he believed he had reasons to doubt not only the intentions of those above him, but also the present temper of the weapon they had placed in his hands three months ago and had recently diminished by two-sevenths. Of the five corps still with him, only two were led by the generals who had taken them to Gettysburg, and these were Sykes and Sedgwick, neither of whom had been seriously engaged in that grim struggle. Of the other three, the badly shot-up commands of Reynolds and Sickles were now under Newton and French, who had shown little in the way of ability during or since the return from Pennsylvania, and Warren, who had replaced the irreplaceable Hancock, was essentially a staff man, untested in the exercise of his new, larger duties. This too was part of what lay behind Meade's remarks, both to his wife in home letters and to trusted members of his staff in private conversations, that he disliked the burden of command so much he wished the government would relieve him.

So when Lee came probing around his right, October 9 and 10, though he knew that Lincoln and Halleck would not approve, he did as Pope had done: pulled out of the constricting V to get his army onto open ground that would permit maneuver. Unlike Pope, however, he did not stop behind the Rappahannock to wait for an explosion deep in his rear. Instead, he kept moving up the Orange & Alexandria Railroad — bringing his rear with him, so to speak. His aim was basically the same as

Lee's: the infliction of some "terrible wound," if Lee and Providence afforded him the opportunity. Meanwhile he took care to see that he afforded none to an adversary whose considerable fame had been earned at the expense of men who either had been negligent in that respect or else had been overeager in the other. He kept his five corps well closed up, within easy supporting distance of one another as they withdrew northeast along the railroad.

Not all who were with him approved of his cautious tactics; a volunteer aide, for example, considered them about as effective as trying "to catch a sea gull with a pinch of salt"; but Meade was watching and waiting, from Rappahannock Station through Warrenton Junction, for the chance he had in mind. Then suddenly on October 14, just up the line at Bristoe Station, he got it. The opportunity was brief, scarcely more indeed than half an hour from start to finish, but he made the most of it while it lasted. Or anyhow the untried Warren did.

Approaching Bristoe from the west at high noon, after a rapid march of fifteen miles, Hill saw northeastward, beyond Broad Run and out of reach, heavy columns of the enemy slogging toward Manassas Junction, a scant four miles away. He had not won the race. But neither had he lost it, he saw next; not entirely. What appeared to be the last corps in the Federal army was only about half over the run, crossing at a ford just north of the little town on the railroad, which came in arrow-straight from the southwest, diagonal to the Confederate line of march. The uncrossed half of the blue corps, jammed in a mass on the near bank of the stream while its various components awaited their turn at the ford, seemed to Little Powell to be his for the taking, provided he moved promptly. This he did. Ordering Heth, whose division was in the lead, to go immediately from march to attack formation, he put two of his batteries into action and sent word for Anderson, whose division was in column behind Heth's, to come forward on the double and reinforce the attack. Fire from the guns did more to hasten than to impede the crossing, however, and Hill told Heth, though he had only two of his four brigades in line by now, to attack at once lest the bluecoats get away. Heth obeyed, but as his men started forward he caught a glint of bayonets to their right front, behind the railroad embankment. When he reported this to Hill, asking whether he would not do better to halt for a reconnaissance, Hill told him to keep going: Anderson would be arriving soon to cover his flank. So the two brigades went on. It presently developed, however, that what they were going on to was by no means the quick victory their commander had intended, but rather a sudden and bloody repulse at the hands of veterans who had stood fast on Cemetery Ridge, fifteen weeks ago tomorrow, to serve Pickett in much the same fashion, except that here the defenders had the added and rare advantage of surprise.

They made the most of it. Behind the embankment, diagonal to the advancing line, was the II Corps under Warren, the former chief of engineers, who, demonstrating here at Bristoe as sharp an eye for terrain as he had shown in saving Little Round Top, had set for the unsuspecting rebels what a later observer called "as fine a trap as could have been devised by a month's engineering." His — not Sykes's, as Hill had supposed from a hurried look at the crowded ford and the heavy blue columns already beyond Broad Run — was the last of the five Federal corps, and when he saw the situation up ahead he improvised the trap that now was sprung. As the two gray brigades came abreast of the three cached divisions, the bluecoats opened fire with devastating effect. Back up the slope, Little Powell watched in dismay as his troops, reacting with soldierly but misguided instinct, wheeled right to charge the embankment wreathed in smoke from the enfilading blasts of musketry. This new attempt, by two stunned brigades against three confident divisions, could have but one outcome. The survivors who came stumbling back were pitifully few, for many of the startled graybacks chose surrender, preferring to remain with their fallen comrades rather than try to make the return journey up the bullet-torn slope they had just descended. Elated, the Federals made a quick sortie that netted them five pieces of artillery and two stands of colors, which they took with them when they drew off, unmolested, across the run. The worst loss to the Confederates, though, was men. Both brigade commanders were shot down, along with nearly 1400 killed or wounded and another 450 captured. The total thus was close to 1900 casualties, as compared to a Union total of about 300, only fifty of whom were killed. In the particular, the results were even sadder from the southern point of view. A North Carolina regiment on the exposed flank lost 290 of its 416 enlisted men, or just under seventy percent, plus all but three of its 36 officers. Here too fell Carnot Posey, who was struck in the thigh by a fragment of shell when he brought up his Mississippi brigade near the close of the action. The wound, though ugly, was not thought to be grave, but infection set in and he died one month later.

Indignation swept through the gray army when the rest of it arrived in the course of the afternoon and learned of what had happened at midday, down in the shallow valley of Broad Run. No segment of the Army of Northern Virginia had suffered such a one-sided defeat since Mechanicsville, which had also been the result of Little Powell's impetuosity. "There was no earthly excuse for it," a member of Lee's staff declared, "as all our troops were well in hand, and much stronger than the enemy." One North Carolinian, still angered years later by the sudden and useless loss of so many of his friends, said flatly: "A worse managed affair than this . . . did not take place during the war." Hill's only reply to such critics was included in the report he submitted within two weeks. "I am convinced that I made the attack too hastily," he wrote, "and at the same time that a delay of half an hour, and there would have been no enemy to attack. In that event I believe I should equally have blamed myself for not attacking at once." Seddon and Davis both endorsed the report. "The disaster at Bristoe Station seems due to a gallant but over-hasty pressing on of the enemy," the former observed, while the latter added: "There was a want of vigilance." These comments stung the thin-skinned Virginian, but worse by far had been Lee's rebuke next morning when Hill conducted him over the field, where the dead still lay in attitudes of pained surprise, and explained what had occurred. Lee said little, knowing as he did that his auburn-haired lieutenant's high-strung impetuosity, demonstrated in battle after battle — but most profitably at Sharpsburg, of which he himself had written: "And then A. P. Hill came up" — had gained the army far more than it cost.

"Well, well, General," he remarked at last, "bury these poor men and let us say no more about it."

He was distracted by the possibility of much heavier bloodshed, four miles up the line, where so much blood had been shed twice already. It seemed to him that Meade, encouraged by Warren's coup the day before, would call a halt and prepare to fight a Third Manassas. That was very much what Lee himself wanted, despite the disparity in numbers, and when someone expressed regret that so historic a field should be widely known by the unromantic name "Bull Run," he replied that with the blessings of God they would "make it another Cowpens." Others had a different reason for wanting to push on at once to the famed junction. According to one of Stuart's men, "We were looking forward to Manassas with vivid recollections of the rich haul we had made there just prior to the second battle of Manassas, and everybody was saying, 'We'll get plenty when we get to Manassas.' " As it turned out, though, Meade wanted no part of a third fight on that unlucky ground. He marched rapidly beyond it, without even a rest halt for his army. There was no battle, and there was no "rich haul" either. "We were there before we knew it," the hungry trooper wrote. "Everything was changed. There was not a building anywhere. The soil, enriched by debris from former camps, had grown a rich crop of weeds that came halfway up the sides of our horses, and the only way we recognized the place was by our horses stumbling over the railroad tracks."

This dreary vista was repeated all around. "Never have I witnessed as sad a picture as Prince William County now presents," a young staff colonel noted in a letter home. " 'Tis desolation made desolate indeed. As far as the eye can reach on every side, there is one vast, barren wilderness; not a fence, not an acre cultivated, not a living object visible, and but for here and there a standing chimney, on the ruins of what was once a handsome and happy home, one would imagine that man was never here and that the country was an entirely new one, without any virtue except its vast extent." Under such circumstances, with an inadequate wagon train and the railroad inoperable because the Federals had blown the larger bridges as they slogged northward, for Lee to remain where he was meant starvation for his men and horses. Nor could he attack, except at a prohibitive disadvantage; Meade had taken a position of great natural strength, which he promptly

improved with intrenchments, along the Centerville-Chantilly ridge. Lee was confident he could turn him out of this, but that would be to drive him back on Washington with its 50,000-man garrison and its 589 guns (Richmond, by contrast, had just over 5000 men in its defenses and 42 guns); which plainly would not do, even if the poorly shod and thinly clad Confederates had been in any condition for pursuit, now that the weather was turning colder, along the rocky pikes of Fairfax County. Next day, October 16, a heavy rain seemed more or less to settle the question of any movement, in any direction whatever, by drenching the roads and fields, swelling the unbridged streams, and confining the southern commander to his tent with an attack of what was diagnosed as lumbago. His decision, reached before the downpour stopped that night, was to withdraw as he had come, back down the railroad, completing the destruction his opponent had begun. The march south got under way next morning, despite the mud. Stuart, assigned the task of covering the rear, did so with such zest and skill that he won another of those handy and sometimes laugh-provoking victories by which he justified his plume and his fox-hunt manner.

Meade did not pursue, except with his cavalry, and he soon had cause to regret that he had done even that much. Stuart withdrew by way of Gainesville, down the Warrenton pike, Fitz Lee by way of Bristoe, down the railroad; the arrangement was that the two would combine if either was faced with more than he could handle. Pressed by superior numbers of blue troopers — Pleasonton had three divisions, under Buford, Gregg, and Kilpatrick — Jeb fell back across Broad Run on the night of the 18th and, sending word for Fitz to reinforce him, took up a position on the south bank to contest a crossing at Buckland Mills. He was having little trouble doing this next morning, banging away with his guns at the bridge he had purposely left intact as a challenge, when a courier arrived with a suggestion from Fitz Lee, who had heard the firing and ridden ahead to assess the situation. If Stuart would fall back down the turnpike, pretending flight in order to draw the Yankees pellmell after him, the courier explained, Fitz would be able to surprise them when they came abreast of a hiding place he would select for that purpose, some distance south, behind one of the low ridges adjoining the pike; whereupon Jeb could turn and charge them, converting the blue confusion into a rout. Stuart liked the notion and proceeded at once to put it into effect. The bluecoats — Judson Kilpatrick's division, with Custer's brigade in the lead — snapped eagerly at the bait, pounding across the run in close pursuit of the fleeing graybacks, who led them on a five-mile chase to Chestnut Hill. At that point, only two miles short of Warrenton, the "chase" ended. Hearing Fitz Lee's guns bark suddenly from ambush, Jeb's horsemen whirled their mounts and charged the head of the now halted and badly rattled column in their rear. There followed another five-mile pursuit — much like the first, except that it was in the opposite direction and was not a mock chase, as the other had been, but a true flight for life — all the way back to Buckland Mills, where Stuart finally called a halt, laughing as he watched the Federals scamper across to the north bank of Broad Run. He had captured something over two hundred of them, along with several ambulances, Custer's headquarters wagon, and a good deal of dropped equipment. One regret he had, however, and this was that Kilpatrick had not kept his artillery near the front, as prescribed by the tactics manual; in which case, Jeb was convinced, "it would undoubtedly have fallen into our hands."

Lee congratulated his chief of cavalry, along with his nephew Fitz, for achieving "this handsome success" — an action known thereafter to Confederates as the "Buckland Races" — though he was also prompt to deny the permission sought by Stuart, in his elation at the outcome of the ruse, to undertake a raid behind Meade's lines while the blue troopers were trying to pull themselves together. In truth, Jeb and his men had done quite enough in the past ten days. Not only did the Buckland farce help to restore the army's morale, damaged five days ago by the Bristoe fiasco, but at a cost of 408 casualties, most of them only slightly injured, he had inflicted 1251 on the enemy cavalry, all but about three hundred of them killed or captured, and had assisted in the taking of some 600 infantry prisoners, mostly stragglers encountered during the movement north. Meade's losses totaled 2292, which was only a bit lower than Lee's for the same period, including those suffered at Bristoe. Except for that unfortunate engagement, the gray army could congratulate itself on another highly successful, if necessarily brief, campaign. With no more than 48,402 effectives, as compared to Meade's 80,789, Lee had maneuvered his adversary into a sixty-mile withdrawal, from the Rapidan to beyond Bull Run. And now, though he himself was obliged to withdraw in turn for lack of subsistence, he did what he could to insure that the inevitable Union follow-up would be a slow one. Meade had burned only the bridges on the Orange & Alexandria; now Lee burned the crossties, too, and warped the rails beyond salvation by piling them atop the burning ties. The Federals, unable to feed themselves without the use of the railroad now that the autumnal rains were turning the roads to quagmires, would advance no faster than their work gangs could lay track. Recrossing the Rappahannock, Lee called a halt and gave his men some badly needed rest while waiting for the blue army to arrive.

This took even longer than he had supposed it would do: not only because of the thorough job the blue and butternut wreckers had done on the Orange & Alexandria, but also because the Federal commander was involved again in a distractive telegraphic skirmish with the authorities in his rear. The President had been distressed by what seemed to him the supine attitude of Meade in falling back under pressure from Lee's inferior force, and this distress was increased on October 15, when the general, announcing Warren's repulse of the rebels at Bristoe Station, passed along information gleaned from prisoners "that Hill's and Ewell's corps, reinforced to a reported strength of 80,000, are advancing on me, their plan being to secure the Bull Run field in advance of me." He supposed, he said, that Lee would "turn me again, probably by the right . . . in which case I shall either fall on him or retire nearer Washington." Lincoln presumed from past performances that Meade would certainly choose the latter course, and when it did not come to that, since Lee advanced no farther than Bull Run, he took this as evidence that the Confederates were by no means as strong as the prisoners had claimed. Irked by what seemed to him a superfluity of caution, he risked a near commitment. "If Gen. Meade can now attack [Lee] on a field no worse than equal for us," he wrote Halleck next day, "and will do so with all the skill and courage which he, his officers, and men possess, the honor will be his if he succeeds, and the blame may be mine if he fails." Perhaps Meade noted the "may" in the copy Halleck sent him that same day, or perhaps he recalled that other such letters had preceded other downfalls. In any event, since neither of his superiors was willing to put the suggestion in the form of a direct order, he chose rather to continue the policy he had been following all along. Besides, he protested, this policy was no different from the one being urged on him. "It has been my intention to attack the enemy, if I can find him on a field no more than equal for us," he replied. "I have only delayed doing so from the difficulty of ascertaining his exact position, and the fear that in endeavoring to do so my communications might be jeopardized."

It seemed to Halleck that what Meade was in fear of jeopardizing was his reputation. Accordingly, with the encouragement of their Commander in Chief, he decided to crack down harder, apparently in the belief that more pressure from above might stiffen the reluctant general's backbone. Two days later, on October 18, Meade reported that Lee was again in motion, and though he did not know what the Virginian had in mind, he thought he might be headed for the Shenandoah Valley, as he had done after Chancellorsville. Halleck replied that this might be so, but he added tauntingly: "If Lee has turned his back on you to cross the mountains, he certainly has seriously exposed himself to your blows, unless his army can move two miles to your one." By evening, moreover, the general-in-chief had decided there was nothing to the report. "Lee is unquestionably bullying you," he wired. "If you cannot ascertain his movements, I certainly cannot. If you pursue and fight him, I think you will find out where he is. I know of no other way." Sooner or later, all subordinates — even the placid Grant — bridled under this kind of treatment from Old Brains, and the short-tempered Meade was by no means an exception. "If you have any orders to give me, I am prepared to receive and obey them," he shot back, "but I must insist on being spared the infliction of such truisms in the guise of opinions as you have recently honored me with, particularly as they were not asked for." By way of emphasis he added: "I take this occasion to repeat what I have before stated, that if my course, based on my own judgment, does not meet with approval, I ought to be, and I desire to be, relieved from command." This was his trump card, never played without overriding effect; for who was there in the Army of the Potomac to replace him? ("What can I do, with such generals as we have?" Lincoln had asked, some weeks ago, in response to urgings that the Pennsylvanian be relieved. "Who among them is any better than Meade?") Snail-like, Halleck pulled his horns in — as, in fact, it was his custom to do whenever they encountered resistance. "If I have repeated truisms," he wired the general next morning, "it has not been to give offense, but to give you the wishes of the government. If, in conveying these wishes, I have used words which were unpleasing, I sincerely regret it." Now it was Meade's turn to be high-handed. "Your explanation of your intentions is accepted," he replied, "and I thank you for it."

Privately, however — when he found out, as he presently did, that the Confederates were not headed for the Valley but were withdrawing as they had come, back down the railroad — he admitted that Lee had indeed bullied him, though he did not use that word. He perceived now that it had never been his adversary's real intention to come between him and Washington at all, as he had supposed, but simply to maneuver him rearward, sixty miles or more, and thus forestall a continued Union advance during the brief period of good weather that remained. Lee's had been "a deep game," Meade wrote his wife on October 21, "and I am free to admit that in the playing of it he has got the advantage of me." Accordingly, after his cavalry failed to intercept or indeed scarcely even trouble the retiring enemy, he put his repair gangs to work on the wrecked supply line and followed with his infantry. The advance was necessarily slow, being regulated to the speed with which the rails were laid and the bridges reconstructed. There was even time for a quick visit to the capital, at Halleck's urging, for a conference with the President. This was held on October 23, and Meade reported to his wife that he found Lincoln kind and considerate, though obviously disappointed that he had not got a battle out of Lee. At one point, though, the talk shifted to Gettysburg and the touchy subject of the pursuit of the rebels to the Potomac. "Do you know, General, what your attitude toward Lee for a week after the battle reminded me of?" Lincoln asked, and when Meade replied, "No, Mr President, what is it?" Lincoln said: "I'll be hanged if I could think of anything else than an old woman trying to shoo her geese across a creek."

For once, Meade kept his temper under control, but he was glad to return next day to his army, away from the Washington atmosphere. Though the advance was proceeding about as fast as could be expected with the railroad as thoroughly smashed as it was, he dispensed with none of his previous caution, wanting no part of a battle on such terms as he believed Lee (not Lincoln) would be willing to offer him. Finally, by the end of the month, he was back on the Rappahannock, whose crossings he found defended. He had been reinforced to a strength of 84,321 effectives, whereas Lee was down to 45,614 as a result of sickness brought on by exposing his thin-clad veterans to cold and rainy weather on the march. Unaware that the odds had lengthened again to almost two-to-one, Meade took a long look at the rebel defenses and, finding them formidable — Lee's soldiers had apparently been as hard at work as his own, but with shovels rather than sledges — proposed on November 2 a change of base downstream to Fredericksburg, which he said would not only put him back on the direct route to Richmond, but would also avoid the need for crossing a second river immediately after the first.

Lincoln was prompt to disapprove. He had been willing to have the army fight a Third Bull Run, but it seemed to him only a little short of madness to invite a Second Fredericksburg. So Meade looked harder than ever at what faced him here on the upper Rappahannock, where, if anywhere, he would have to do his fighting.

Despite the nearly two-to-one odds his army faced in its risky position within the constricting V of the rivers, Lee awaited Meade's advance with confidence and as much patience as his ingrained preference for the offensive would permit. "If I could only get some shoes and clothes for the men," he said, "I would save him the trouble." In electing to stand on the line of the Rappahannock — shown in the past to be highly vulnerable at Kelly's Ford, where the south bank was lower than the north — he had evolved a novel system of defense. Massing his troops in depth near the danger point, he prepared to contest a crossing there only after the blue infantry had moved beyond the effective range of its artillery on the dominant north bank, and in furtherance of this plan (patterned, so far, after the one he had used with such success at Fredericksburg, just short of eleven months ago) he maintained at Rappahannock Station, five miles upstream, a bridgehead on the far side of the river, fortified against assault by the labor-saving expedient of turning the old Federal works so that they faced north instead of south. A pontoon bridge near the site of the wrecked railroad span, safely beyond the reach of enemy batteries, made possible a quick withdrawal or reinforcement of the troops who, by their presence, were in a position to divide Meade's forces or attack him flank and rear in case he massed them for a downstream crossing. Ewell's corps guarded all these points, with Early in occupation of the tête-de-pont, Rodes in rear of Kelly's Ford, and Johnson in reserve; Hill's was upstream, beyond Rappahannock Station. For more than two weeks, October 20 to November 5, Lee waited in his Brandy headquarters for Meade's arrival. On the latter date his outpost scouts sent word that blue reconnaissance patrols were probing at various points along the river, and two days later the whole Union army was reported to be approaching in two main columns, one headed for the north-bank bridgehead, the other for Kelly's Ford.

This report, which was just what he had expected and planned for, reached him about noon. After notifying Hill to be on the alert for orders to reinforce Ewell, he rode from Brandy to Early's headquarters near the south end of the pontoon bridge affording access to the works on the north bank. When Early explained that he was sending another of his brigades to join the one already across the river, Lee approved but he also took the precaution of ordering Hill to shift his right division over to the railroad so that it would be available as an additional reserve. Similarly, when he learned a bit later that the bluecoats had crossed in force at Kelly's Ford, he instructed Edward Johnson to move in closer support of Rodes. Old Jubal went over to the north bank late in the afternoon and returned to report that the Yankees had made so little impression there that one of his brigade commanders had assured him that, if need be, he could hold the position against the whole Federal army. Dusk came down, and presently, in the gathering darkness beyond the river, Lee and Early saw muzzle flashes winking close to the works on the north bank. A south wind carried the noise away, and anyhow the pinkish yellow flashes soon went out. Convinced that this brief twilight action had been no more than a demonstration, probably to cover the advance on Kelly's Ford — in any event, no enemy had ever made a night attack on his infantry in a fortified position — Lee rode back to Brandy under the growing light of the stars, well satisfied with the results so far of the reception he had planned for Meade along the Rappahannock.

Unwelcome news awaited him at headquarters, in the form of a dispatch from Ewell. The greater part of two regiments assigned by Rodes to picket duty at Kelly's Ford had been gobbled up by the Federals, who then had laid a pontoon bridge and were sending substantial reinforcements across to the south bank. A loss of 349 veterans was not to be taken lightly, but aside from this the situation was about what Lee had expected. The thing to do now was make threatening gestures from within the bridgehead, which should serve to hold a major portion of Meade's force on the north bank, and shift two divisions of Hill's corps eastward to strengthen Rodes and Johnson for an all-out fight in rear of Kelly's Ford. That was the preconceived plan, whereby Lee intended to fall on a segment of the blue army, as he had done so often in the past, with the greater part of his own. Before this could be ordered, however, still worse news — indeed, almost incredible news — arrived from Early. Massing heavily at close range in the darkness before moonrise, the Federals had stormed and overrun the north-bank intrenchments, killing or capturing all of the troops in the two Confederate brigades except about six hundred who had swum the river or run the gauntlet over the pontoon bridge. The loss would come to 1674 men: and with them, of course, went the bridgehead itself, upon which the plan for Meade's discomfiture depended. Nor was it only the offensive that had been wrecked. Obviously the army could not remain in its present position after daylight, exposed on a shallow extended front with the Rapidan in its rear. Lee was upset but he kept his poise, thankful at any rate that Early had set the floating bridge afire to prevent a crossing by the bluecoats now in occupation of Rappahannock Station. Orders went out for Hill to retire by crossing the railroad between Culpeper and Brandy, while Ewell fell back toward Germanna Ford, contesting if necessary the advance of the blue force from Kelly's. For two days the movement continued. On November 9, when the bluecoats drew near, both corps halted and formed for battle, still within the V, but when Meade did not press the issue Lee resumed his withdrawal and crossed the Rapidan next morning. The army was back in the position it had left, marching west and north around the enemy right, a month ago yesterday.

The blue-clad veterans were elated; their 461 casualties amounted to less than a fourth of the number they had inflicted. French had moved with speed and precision on the left, seizing Kelly's Ford before the rebel pickets even had time to scamper rearward out of reach, and Uncle John Sedgwick, on the right with his own and Sykes's corps, had performed brilliantly, improvising tactics which resulted in the capture not only of the fortified tête-de-pont, supposed impregnable by its defenders, but also of the largest haul of prisoners ever secured by the army in one fell, offensive swoop. Meade's stock rose accordingly with the men in the ranks, who began to say that Bobby Lee had better look to his laurels, though there was presently some grumbling that the coup had not been followed by another, equally vigorous and even more profitable, while the rebs were on the run. Conversely, there was chagrin in the Confederate ranks. The double blow had cost a total of 2033 men: more, even, than Bristoe Station and in some ways even worse than that fiasco, which at least had not been followed by an ignominious retreat. Now it was Ewell's turn to be excoriated, as Hill had been three weeks before. "It is absolutely sickening," one of his young staff officers, a holdover from Stonewall's day, lamented. "I feel personally disgraced . . . as does everyone in the command. Oh, how each day is proving the inestimable value of General Jackson to us!" Early and Rodes were both intensely humiliated, and though Lee did not berate them or their corps commander, any more than he had berated Little Powell in a similar situation, neither did he attempt to reduce their burden of guilt by assigning any share of the blame to the men who had been captured and were now on their way to prison camps in the North. Quite the contrary, in fact; for he observed in his report to Richmond that "the courage and good conduct of the troops engaged have been too often tried to admit of question."

Both the elation on the one hand and the chagrin on the other were soon replaced by a sort of mutual boredom on both sides of the familiar Rapidan, where the two armies returned to their old occupation of staring at one another from the now leafless woods on its opposite banks — what time, that is, they were not engaged in the informal and illegal exchange of coffee, tobacco, and laugh-provoking insults. If there was less food on the south bank, there was perhaps more homesickness on the north, the majority of the soldiers there having come a longer way to save the Union than their adversaries had come to save the Confederacy. Presently there was rain and more rain, chill and dripping, which served to increase the discomfort, as well as the boredom, despite the snug huts put up as a sign that the armies had gone into winter quarters. A northern colonel, a staff volunteer, spoke for both sides in giving his reaction to his surroundings. "The life here is miserably lazy," he wrote home; "hardly an order to carry, and the horses all eating their heads off. . . . If one could only be at home, till one was *wanted*, and then be on the spot. But this is everywhere the way of war; lie still and lie still; then up and maneuver and march hard; then a big battle; and then a lot more lie still."

✗ 3 ✗

Rosecrans was relieved on the day of the Buckland Races, exactly one month after the opening day of Chickamauga, whose loss had resulted

first in his retreat, then in his besiegement, and finally in his removal
from command. Grant left Louisville by rail next morning, October 20,
spent the night in Nashville, and went on the following day to Stevenson, Alabama, for an early evening conference with Rosecrans, who had
left Chattanooga the day before, promptly on receipt of Grant's wire,
because he had not wanted to encourage by his presence any demonstrations of regret at his departure from the army he would have commanded for a full year if he had lasted one week longer. It was untrue
that he had intended to evacuate the beleaguered town, as Dana had told
Stanton he had it in mind to do; in point of fact, he had been hard at work
for the past ten days with his chief of engineers on plans for solving the
acute supply problem as a prelude to resuming the offensive. Moreover,
though he disliked Grant and knew quite well that Grant returned the
feeling, his devotion to their common cause enabled him not only to
share with the incoming general, who had just ordered his removal, his
recently worked-out plans for lifting the siege, but even to do so cordially. "He came into my car," Grant subsequently wrote, "and we held
a brief interview, in which he described very clearly the situation at
Chattanooga, and made some excellent suggestions as to what should be
done. My only wonder was that he had not carried them out."

After the conference, Old Rosy took up his journey north and
Grant proceeded to Bridgeport, where he spent the night. Next morning, with his crutches strapped to the saddle like a brace of carbines —
for he still could not manage afoot without them — he began the sixty-
mile horseback trek up the Sequatchie Valley and over Walden's Ridge,
made necessary by the long-range rebel guns on Raccoon Mountain
commanding the direct approach to Chattanooga, which was less than
half the roundabout distance the army trains were obliged to travel if
they were to maintain a trickle of supplies for the hungry bluecoats
cooped up in the town. At Jasper, ten miles out, the party stopped for a
visit with Oliver Howard, who had established his corps headquarters
there soon after his arrival from Virginia two weeks before. In the
course of their talk Howard saw Grant looking intently at an empty
whiskey bottle on a nearby table. "I never drink," the one-armed general said hastily, anxious lest his reputation for sobriety be doubted by
his new commander, whatever shortcomings the latter himself might
have in that regard. "Neither do I," Grant replied, straight-faced, as he
rose and hobbled out on his crutches to be lifted back onto his horse.
Beyond Jasper — particularly around Anderson's Crossroads, the halfway point, where Wheeler had wrought such havoc twenty days ago —
he began, like Browning's Childe Roland, to get an oppressive firsthand
notion of the difficulties in store for him ahead. Rain had turned low-
lying stretches of the road into knee-deep bogs, and other stretches
along hillsides had been made almost impassable by washouts; the crippled general had to be carried over the worst of these, which were too

unsafe to cross on horseback. Ten thousand mules and horses had died by
now, either by rebel bayonets or from starvation, and a great many of
their carcasses were strewn along the roadway, offensive alike to eye
and nose and conscience, especially for a man who loved animals as
much as Grant did. Perhaps not even the field of Shiloh, with its grisly
two-day harvest still upon it, offended him more than what he encountered in the course of the present two-day ride up that quiet valley
and over that barren ridge, which he descended late on October 23 to
regain the north bank of the Tennessee, immediately opposite the town
that was his goal.

In some ways Chattanooga itself was worse; for there, in addition to more dead and dying horses, you saw the faces of the soldiers,
which showed the effects not only of their hunger — "One of the regiments of our brigade," a Kansas infantryman was to testify, "caught,
killed, and ate a dog that wandered into camp" — but also the dejection
proceeding from their month-old defeat at Chickamauga and the apparent hopelessness of their present tactical situation, ringed as they were by
the rebel victors on all the surrounding heights. Grant crossed the river
just before dark, riding carefully over the pontoon bridge, and went at
once to see Thomas, who had promised four days ago to "hold the
town till we starve." This was something quite different, Grant now
discerned, from saying that the army would be able to live there, let
alone come out of the place victorious. "I appreciated the force of this
dispatch ... when I witnessed the condition of affairs which prompted
it," he afterwards declared. The night was cold and rainy. He could
see the campfires of the Confederates, gleaming like stars against the
outer darkness, above and on three sides of him, as if he stood in the pit
of a darkened amphitheater, peering up and out, east and west and
south.

Chattanooga was said to be an Indian word meaning "mountains
looking at each other," and next morning Grant perceived the aptness of
the name. He saw on the left the long reach of Missionary Ridge, a solid
wall that threw its shadow over the town until the sun broke clear of its
rim, and on the right the cumulous bulge of Raccoon Mountain. Dead
ahead, though, was the dominant feature of this forbidding panorama.
Its summit 1200 feet above the surface of the river at its base, Lookout
Mountain rose, a Union correspondent had remarked, "like an ever-
lasting thunder storm that will never pass over." Seen as Grant saw it
now, wreathed in mist, the journalist continued, "it looms up ... and
recedes, but when the sun shines strongly out it draws so near as to
startle you." Grant was to see it that way too, in time, but for the
present what impressed him most were the guns posted high on the
slopes and peaks and ridges, all trained on the blue army here below.
With the help of glasses he could even see the cannoneers lounging about

in careless attitudes, as if to emphasize by their idleness the advantage they enjoyed. "I suppose," he said years later, "they looked upon the garrison of Chattanooga as prisoners of war, feeding or starving themselves, and thought it would be inhuman to kill any of them except in self-defense."

With two thirds of his practically useless cavalry sent away, Thomas had about 45,000 effectives in his Army of the Cumberland, and though nothing had yet been done to relieve the most pressing of their problems — the hunger that came from trying to live on quarter-rations — Dana at least had been quick to inform Stanton, on the day of Grant's arrival "wet, dirty, and well," that "the change at headquarters here [under Thomas] is already strikingly perceptible. Order prevails instead of universal chaos." For one thing, there had been a complete reorganization, a top-to-bottom shake-up, in the course of which regiments were consolidated, brigades re-formed, and divisions redistributed. Formerly there had been eleven of these last; now there were six, assigned three each to two instead of the previous four corps. Palmer had succeeded Thomas, and Granger had been placed at the head of a new corps formed by combining his own with those of the departed Crittenden and McCook. Sheridan, Wood, and Brigadier General Charles Cruft, Palmer's successor, commanded the three divisions under Palmer; Johnson, Davis, and Baird the three under Granger. The other five division commanders had been disposed of or employed in various ways; Negley was sent North, ostensibly for his health, while Steedman and Van Cleve were made post commanders of Chattanooga and Murfreesboro, and Reynolds and Brannan were respectively appointed to be chiefs of staff and artillery, directly under Thomas. Grant approved of all these arrangements, some of which had been effected by Rosecrans, but as he examined the tactical situation confronting the reorganized army — including the alarming discovery that there was not enough ammunition for one hard day of fighting — he found it altogether bleak. "It looked, indeed, as if but two courses were open," he afterwards remarked: "one to starve, the other to surrender or be captured."

Not only did the Confederates have the tactical advantage of gazing down on their opponents with something of the complacency of marksmen contemplating fish in a rain barrel; they also had a numerical advantage. Bragg had close to 70,000 veterans on those heights and in the intervening valleys. This would be considerably overmatched, of course, when and if the Federal reinforcements arrived. Hooker was already standing by, near Bridgeport, with some 16,000 effectives — exclusive, that is, of service personnel — in the four divisions he had brought from the Army of the Potomac, while Sherman was working his way east along the Memphis & Charleston Railroad with another 20,000 in the five divisions of his Army of the Tennessee, and Burnside

had about 25,000 around Knoxville in the four divisions of his Army
of the Ohio. This gave a total of well over 100,000 men in the four
commands. Even without Burnside, who now definitely was not coming — though he was strategically useful where he was, as a bait or a
menace, hovering eastward off Bragg's flank — the combination of
Thomas, Hooker, and Sherman would give Grant nearly half again as
many troops as stood in the ranks of his gray besiegers. First, though, he
must get them into Chattanooga, and before he could do that he would
have to find a way to feed them when they got there, since otherwise
they would only increase the number of hungry mouths and speed the
garrison's already rapid progress toward starvation. That was what it
came to every time, no matter how many angles the problem was seen
from: the question of how to open a new supply line, supplementing or
replacing the inadequate, carcass-littered one that led back over Walden's Ridge and down the Sequatchie Valley to the railhead depots
bulging with food and ammunition at Stevenson and Bridgeport.

  The answer came out of a conference with Thomas and his chief
engineer, W. F. Smith, who had served in the same capacity under Rosecrans. This was that same "Baldy" Smith who had led a corps at Fredericksburg but had been transferred out of the Virginia army — as a result,
it was said, of his inability to get along with Hooker any better than he
had with Burnside — and had commanded the Pennsylvania militia that
stood off Jeb Stuart at Carlisle during the Gettysburg campaign, after
which he had been given his present assignment with the army down in
Tennessee. A Vermont-born West Pointer, short and portly, thirty-
nine years old and described by a fellow staffer as having "a light-brown
imperial and shaggy mustache, a round, military head, and the look of a
German officer, altogether," Smith was still a brigadier, despite the lofty
posts he had filled, because Congress refused to confirm his promotion
on grounds that he had been deeply involved in the machinations against
Burnside: as indeed he had, for he was by nature contentious, ever quick
to spot and carp at the shortcomings of his superiors. Grant had not
seen him since their Academy days, twenty years before, but he was
greatly taken with him on brief reacquaintance, mainly because Smith
had arrived, on his own and in conferences with Rosecrans, at what he
believed was the answer to the question of how to open a new and
better supply line back to Bridgeport. It was based of course on geography, but it was also based on daring. The Tennessee River, which flowed
due west past Chattanooga, turned abruptly south just beyond the town,
then swung back north as if by rebound from the foot of Lookout
Mountain. Two miles upstream, on the western side of the point of land
inclosed by this narrow bend — Moccasin Point, it was called, from its
resemblance, when seen from above, to an Indian shoe — was Brown's
Ferry, an excellent site for a crossing because it was beyond the reach
of all but the longest-range guns on Lookout and only a mile from the

pontoon bridge already in use north of the town. From Brown's Ferry
the river flowed on north, then turned south again, around the long
northwestern spur of Raccoon Mountain, to describe a second and
longer bend, along whose base a road led westward through Cummings
Gap to another Tennessee cross-
ing known as Kelley's Ferry,
and from there along the right
bank of the river down to
Bridgeport.

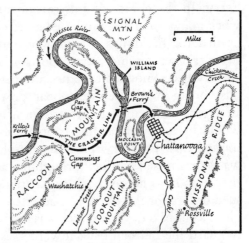

Here then was the ideal
route: save for one drawback.
The rebels held it. They had
guns emplaced on Raccoon
Mountain and pickets advanced
to the river itself, squarely
athwart the coveted approaches
to the gap through which the
road connecting the two ferries
ran. But Smith had the answer to this as well, a tactical solution employing the principles of speed and stealth to achieve surprise and, with surprise, success. Crossing at Bridgeport, a force from Hooker would follow
the railroad east around the south flank of the mountain, then move north
under cover of darkness, still following the railroad through Wauhatchie, to close upon Brown's Ferry from the rear. Meanwhile, and also
under cover of darkness, a force from Thomas would advance on the
same point in two columns, one marching overland, first across the pontoon bridge at Chattanooga, then west across the narrow base of Moccasin Point, and the other floating noiselessly downriver in pontoon
boats, past the sheer north face of Lookout, to spearhead the crossing at Brown's Ferry, capture the gray outpost there, and hold on
while the boats were being anchored and floored over by an engineer
detachment so that the column approaching by land could cross as reinforcements; whereupon the two forces, one from Hooker and one
from Thomas, would combine for mop-up operations, opening Cummings Gap to clear the road leading west to Kelley's Ferry and dislodging the enemy guns on Raccoon Mountain. Once this was done, the new
supply route — half the length of the old one over Walden's Ridge, and a
good deal less than half as tortuous — would be securely in Federal
hands; the troops in Chattanooga could go back on full rations, refill
their cartridge boxes and limber chests, and prepare to deal with the
graybacks still on Lookout Mountain and Missionary Ridge.

Grant liked the sound of this — particularly the notion of the silent run past Lookout, reminiscent as it was of the maneuver that opened
the final phase of the Vicksburg campaign — afterwards saying of
Smith: "He explained the situation of the two armies and the topography

of the country so plainly that I could see it without an inspection." All the same, on the day after his arrival he rode out with Thomas and his chief engineer, back to the north bank of the Tennessee and across the base of Moccasin Point for a look at the lay of the land around Brown's Ferry. In the course of this reconnaissance Smith also showed him the work going on at a sawmill he had established for getting out the lumber needed for building the pontoons and flooring the bridge they would support after serving as transports and assault boats. Fifty of these had already been knocked together and caulked, and the workmen were also busy on an improvised steamboat, powered, as the sawmill itself was, by an engine commandeered from a nearby cotton gin. This last, Smith said, would be used for hauling supplies, once the river had been opened to traffic below the ferry. He seemed to have thought of everything. Grant was so impressed by the thoroughness and ingenuity of these preparations that as soon as he got back to Chattanooga that evening he not only issued orders for the plan to be adopted; he also directed that it was to begin within two days. Hooker was instructed to leave one division behind to guard the railroad back toward Nashville and to cross with the other three at Bridgeport on October 26, marching fast through Wauhatchie to approach Brown's Ferry from the south. Thomas was told to move the following morning, before daylight, thus allowing Hooker time to come within reach of their common objective. Grant further stipulated that Smith was to be in direct charge of the two-pronged approach from Chattanooga, later explaining that the staff engineer "had been so instrumental in preparing for the move, and so clear in his judgment about the manner of making it, that I deemed it but just to him that he should have command of the troops detailed to execute the design."

His trust was not misplaced; there was no better example, in the whole course of the war, of what the combination of careful planning, ingenuity, and great daring could accomplish under intelligent leadership. Hooker crossed on schedule at Bridgeport, leaving Slocum and one of his divisions behind to guard the Nashville & Chattanooga Railroad against saboteurs and raiders, and proceeded eastward along the Memphis & Charleston with Slocum's other division and Howard's two, a force of about 11,000 effectives. That night Smith set out across Moccasin Point with two brigades of infantry and a battalion of engineers, numbering in all about 3500 men, and at 3 o'clock the following morning, October 27, a selected group of 1500 others, who had been loaded aboard the improvised fleet of sixty pontoon-transports, cast off and started downstream from the Chattanooga wharves, two dozen men and one officer in each boat. The current was strong; there was no need for oars, except to steer with, during the nearly circuitous six-mile run. Screened by a light mist, they hugged the right bank and made the trip in just two hours, undetected by rebel lookouts despite the frantic cries of one unfortunate soldier who fell overboard and was left to drown, as he had been warned beforehand would be done if he got careless. Reaching Brown's Ferry at 5 o'clock, half an hour before dawn, the troops in the first boats swarmed ashore and captured the drowsy pickets, while oarsmen in the unloaded transports began their task of ferrying Smith's overland marchers across from the right bank, where they had waited all this time under cover of the brush and darkness.

One dispersed brigade of Confederates — for, as it turned out, this was all the force the enemy had west of Lookout Mountain — attempted to assault the beachhead in the gray dawn, but was quickly thrown into retreat by the superior blue force, which then proceeded to fortify and intrench a defensive perimeter while the engineers went hard to work on the bridge. By midmorning the pontoons had been moored and floored; reinforcements from Thomas could march across in almost any numbers Smith or Grant decided might be needed. Few would be, apparently, for those graybacks who had not been captured at the time of the landing, or knocked out during the quick repulse that followed, had withdrawn eastward across Lookout Valley, leaving Raccoon Mountain and Cummings Gap in Federal hands. Moreover, dispatches sent forward that afternoon by Hooker announced that he was approaching Wauhatchie and would arrive in person the next day. This he did, together with two of his divisions, the third having been posted as a rear guard at Wauhatchie. And now for the first time, here on the south bank of the Tennessee River, near Brown's Ferry, Union soldiers of the East and West shook hands and congratulated each other on the success of their combined operation, by which a new supply route into besieged Chattanooga was about to be opened; "The Cracker Line," they dubbed it.

Hooker had had no share in anything so obviously exciting as a six-mile run downriver through misty darkness. But the fact was, he and his troops had had perhaps the most nerve-racking time of all, if only because of the duration of the strain; and in the end they did the only real fighting involved in the operation. As he marched eastward by daylight on his first and second days away from Bridgeport, Lookout Mountain loomed nearer and taller with every mile. Rebels up there in untold numbers were watching him, alone so to speak in their own back yard, and he knew it. He counted himself fortunate when he reached Wauhatchie without being attacked, and he took the precaution of dropping John Geary's division off at that point, as a safeguard for his rear, while he continued his march north with Howard's two divisions under von Steinwehr and Carl Schurz. Presently, though, on the night of the day he made contact with Smith at Brown's Ferry — October 28 — Fighting Joe had cause to believe that what he had thought was a precautious act had in fact been an extremely rash one that might cost him no less than one third of the force he had brought across the Tennessee, and possibly much more. A sudden midnight booming of guns, loud not only at the ferry but also in the town across the way, informed him that Geary was under assault in his isolated position, three miles off. What was worse, if the attack was in sufficient force it might be launched for the purpose of overwhelming the bridgehead, in which case there would be nothing for Howard's men to do but retreat with Smith's across the river and into Chattanooga, where they would have to share the hungry garrison's meager rations and thus hasten its progress toward starvation or surrender. Determined to do what he could to avert such a fate, along with further damage to the reputation he had been given a chance to retrieve in a new theater, Hooker put Schurz on the march to reinforce the embattled Geary, the flashes of whose guns were playing fitfully on the southern horizon despite the brightness of a moon only two nights past the full, and alerted Steinwehr to stand ready to come, too, if he was needed.

The trouble, as it turned out, was by no means as serious as he had feared: not only because Geary's men gave an excellent account of themselves in defending the position at Wauhatchie, but also because the Confederates — four brigades from the absent Hood's division — became confused in their first attempt at a night attack and were unable to co-ordinate their efforts. Though the soldiers on both sides had traveled a thousand miles or more from Virginia to come to grips here in the darkness near the Tennessee-Georgia line, neither could distinguish the presence of the other except by the flashes of the shots they fired. In this sort of situation the advantage lay with the defenders, who remained in one place and at least knew where they themselves were, whereas the attackers did not even know that much for a good part of the time. Moreover, the element of surprise was by no means altogether with the latter. Geary's teamsters, for example, became frightened by the uproar and deserted their picketed mules; whereupon the mules, left to their own devices in the flame-stabbed pandemonium, broke loose from their tethers and stampeded toward the rebels, who in turn became frightened, thinking a cavalry charge had been launched at them, and stampeded too. (Just as Southerners liked to celebrate such affairs as the Buckland Races with rollicking verses, generally in parody of something at once hackneyed and heroic, so did an anonymous Ohio infantryman immortalize this "Charge of the Mule Brigade":

> *Half a mile, half a mile,*
> *Half a mile onward,*
> *Right toward the Georgia troops*
> *Broke the two hundred.*
> *"Forward, the Mule Brigade;*
> *Charge for the rebs!" they neighed.*

Straight for the Georgia troops
Broke the two hundred.

Five stanzas later came the envoy:

When can their glory fade?
O the wild charge they made!
All the world wondered.
Honor the charge they made;
Honor the Mule Brigade,
Long-eared two hundred.)

In any event — aside, that is, from the disconcerting, not to say unnerving effect on the graybacks of having some two hundred fear-crazed mules come bearing down on them out of the clattering darkness — Schurz came up soon to even the odds, and the confused engagement broke off about as suddenly as it had begun. By 4 o'clock, two hours before sunrise, the Confederates had withdrawn across Lookout Creek, leaving the field to the men who had held it in the first place, and Bragg made no further attempt to interfere with the opening of the new Federal supply line. At a cost of well under five hundred casualties — 420 for Hooker, 37 for Smith — Grant had inflicted perhaps twice as many, including the prisoners taken at Brown's Ferry and picked up later on Raccoon Mountain, and had delivered the Chattanooga garrison from the grim threat of starvation, the most urgent of the several problems he had found waiting for him on his arrival, five days back. On October 30, exactly one week after he rode into town, "wet, dirty, and well," the little steamboat Smith had built tied up at Kelley's Ferry, completing a run from Bridgeport with a cargo of 40,000 rations for the troops at the opposite end of Cummings Gap. According to an officer aboard her, an orderly sent on horseback to announce the steamer's arrival returned to report "that the news went through the camps faster than his horse, and the soldiers were jubilant and cheering, 'The Cracker Line's open. Full rations, boys! Three cheers for the Cracker Line,' as if we had won another victory; and we had."

So far as Grant himself was concerned, the issue had been decided as soon as the pontoon bridge was thrown and the bridgehead secured at Brown's Ferry. His mind had moved on to other matters, even before the night action at Wauhatchie seemed for a moment to threaten the loss of what had been won. "The question of supplies may now be regarded as settled," he wired Halleck that evening, four hours before Geary came under attack. "If the rebels give us one week more time I think all danger of losing territory now held by us will have passed away, and preparations may commence for offensive operations."

✗ 4 ✗

Pleased though he was by the prospect, as he saw it from his Chattanooga headquarters now that the Cracker Line was open, Grant would have felt even more encouraged if he somehow had been able to sit in on the councils across the way, on Lookout Mountain and Missionary Ridge, and thus acquire firsthand knowledge of the bitterness that had prevailed for the past month in the camps of his adversaries. Bragg's dissatisfaction with several of his ranking lieutenants for their shortcomings during the weeks that preceded Chickamauga — willful ineptitudes, as he saw it, which had cost him the opportunity to destroy the Federal army piecemeal, in McLemore's Cove and elsewhere — was matched, if not exceeded, by their dissatisfaction with his failure, as they saw it, to gather the fruits of their great victory during the weeks that followed. Resentment bred dissension; dissension provoked criminations; recriminations led to open breaks. Polk and Hindman had departed and Harvey Hill was about to follow, relieved of duty by the army commander; while still another top subordinate — more nearly indispensable, some would say, than all the rest combined — had left under his own power. This was Forrest.

His contention that "we ought to press forward as rapidly as possible" having been ignored on the morning after the battle, the Tennessee cavalryman was sent northwest with his division, four days later, to head off or delay a supposed Union advance from Knoxville. No such threat existed, but Forrest did encounter enemy cavalry hovering in that direction and drove them helter-skelter across the Hiwassee, then through Athens and Sweetwater, slashing at their flanks and rear, to Loudon, where the survivors managed to get beyond his reach by crossing the Tennessee, eighty miles above Chattanooga and less than half that far from Knoxville. Having determined that no bluecoats were advancing from the latter place, he was on his way back across the Hiwassee, September 28, when he received a dispatch signed by an assistant adjutant on Bragg's staff. "The general commanding desires that you will without delay turn over the troops of your command previously ordered to Major General Wheeler." There was no explanation, no mention of the raid that Wheeler was about to make on the Federal supply line: just the peremptory order to "turn over the troops of your command." Forrest complied, of course, but then, having done so, dictated and sent through channels a fiery protest. "Bragg never got such a letter as that before from a brigadier," he told the staffer who took it down. A couple of days later, during an interview with the army commander, he was assured that he would get his men back as soon as they returned from over the river, and he was granted, in the interim, a ten-day leave to go to La Grange, Georgia, to see his wife for the first time since his visit to Memphis to recuperate from his Shiloh wound, a year and a half ago.

While he was at La Grange, sixty miles southwest of Atlanta, he received an army order issued just after his interview with Bragg, assigning Wheeler "to the command of all the cavalry in the Army of Tennessee." Since his oath — taken in early February, after the Donelson repulse and their near duel — that he would never again serve under Wheeler was well known at headquarters, this amounted to a permanent separation of Forrest and the troopers he had raised on his own and seasoned, shortly afterward, on his December strike at Grant's supply lines in West Tennessee. Moreover, he took the order as a personal affront and he reacted in a characteristically direct manner. Interrupting his leave, he went at once to see the commanding general, accompanied by his staff surgeon as a witness.

Bragg received him in his tent on Missionary Ridge, rising and offering his hand as the Tennessean entered. Forrest declined it. "I am not here to pass civilities or compliments with you, but on other business," he said, and he launched without further preamble into a heated denunciation, which he punctuated by stabbing in Bragg's direction with a rigid index finger: "I have stood your meanness as long as I intend to. You have played the part of a damned scoundrel, and are a coward, and if you were any part of a man I would slap your jaws and force you to resent it. You may as well not issue any more orders to me, for I will not obey them . . . and I say to you that if you ever again try to interfere with me or cross my path it will be at the peril of your life." And having thus attended to what he had called his "other business," he turned abruptly and stalked out of the tent. "Well, you are in for it now," his doctor companion said as they rode away. Forrest disagreed. "He'll never say a word about it; he'll be the last man to mention it. Mark my words, he'll take no action in the matter. I will ask to be relieved and transferred to a different field, and he will not oppose it."

Forrest was right in his prediction; Bragg neither took official notice of the incident nor disapproved the cavalryman's request for transfer, which was submitted within the week. He was wrong, though, in his interpretation of his superior's motives. Braxton Bragg was no coward; he was afraid of no man alive, not even Bedford Forrest. Rather, he was willing to overlook the personal affront — as the hot-tempered Tennessean, with far less provocation, had not been — for the good of their common cause. He knew and valued Forrest's abilities, up to a point, and by not pressing charges for insubordination — which would certainly have stuck — he saved his services for the country. Partly, no doubt, this was because he saw him as primarily a raider, not only a nonprofessional but an "irregular," and as such less subject to discipline for irregularities, even ones so violent as this. Others of higher rank in his army were less direct in their denunciations, but he exercised no such forbearance where they were concerned. Polk and Hindman and Hill, for instance; these he saw as regulars, and he treated them as such, writing directly to the Commander in Chief of their "want of prompt conformity to orders," as well as of their "having taken steps to procure my removal in a manner both unmilitary and un-officerlike."

He had particular reference to Hill in this, and he was right. In fact, there existed in the upper echelon of his army a cabal whose purpose was just that, to "procure [his] removal," and to do so by much the same method he himself had been employing; that is, by complaining individually and collectively to the President and the Secretary of War. Davis had received by now Polk's letter stigmatizing Bragg for "palpable weakness and mismanagement," and had also read Longstreet's note to Seddon, protesting "that nothing but the hand of God can save us or help us as long as we have our present commander." These he sought to deal with indirectly, on October 3, by explaining at some length to Bragg why he had recommended that the charges against the departed Polk not be pressed. "It was with the view of avoiding a controversy, which could not heal the injury sustained and which I feared would entail further evil," he wrote, adding that to persist would involve a full-scale investigation, "with all the crimination and recrimination there to be produced. . . . I fervently pray that you may judge correctly," he said in closing, "as I am well assured you will act purely for the public welfare." He hoped that this appeal to Bragg for a reduction of the pressure from above would serve to lessen the tension elsewhere along the chain of command; but he received a document, two days later, which showed that tension to be even greater than he had supposed. It came in the form of a round robin, a petition addressed to the President and signed by a number of general officers, including Hill and Buckner. While admitting "that the proceeding is unusual among military men," the petitioners contended that "the extraordinary condition of affairs in this army, the magnitude of the interests at stake, and a sense of the responsibilities under which they rest to Your Excellency and to the Republic, render this proceeding, in their judgment, a matter of solemn duty, from which, as patriots, they cannot shrink."

Their grounds for concern were stated at some length. "Two weeks ago this army, elated by a great victory which promised to be the most fruitful of the war, was in readiness to pursue the defeated enemy. That enemy, driven in confusion from the field, was fleeing in disorder and panic-stricken. . . . Today, after having been twelve days in line of battle in that enemy's front, within cannon range of his position, the Army of Tennessee has seen a new Sebastopol rise steadily before its view. The beaten enemy, recovering behind its formidable works from the effects of his defeat, is understood to be already receiving reinforcements, while heavy additions to his strength are rapidly approaching him. Whatever may have been accomplished heretofore, it is certain that the fruits of the victory of the Chickamauga have now escaped our grasp. The Army of Tennessee, stricken with a complete paralysis, will in a few days' time be thrown strictly on the defensive, and may deem itself fortunate if it escapes from its present position without disaster." Having thus stated the problem, the generals then went on to propose a solution that was at once tactful and explicit. "In addition to reinforcements, your petitioners would deem it a dereliction of the sacred duty they owe the country if they did not further ask that Your Excellency assign to the command of this army an officer who will inspire the army and the country with undivided confidence. Without entering into a criticism of the merits of our present commander, your petitioners regard it as a sufficient reason, without assigning others, to urge his being relieved, because, in their opinion, the condition of his health totally unfits him for the command of an army in the field."

Authorship of the document was afterwards disputed. Some said Buckner wrote it, others Hill. Bragg, for one, believed he recognized the hand of the latter in the phrasing, but Hill denied this; "Polk got it up," he said. Whoever wrote it, Davis decided that what it called for — particularly in a closing sentence: "Your petitioners cannot withhold from Your Excellency the expression of the fact that, as it now exists, they can render you no assurance of the success which Your Excellency may reasonably expect" — was another presidential journey west. "I leave in the morning for General Bragg's headquarters," he wired Lee, who was preparing to cross the Rapidan that week, "and hope to be serviceable in harmonizing some of the difficulties existing there."

He left Richmond aboard a special train, October 6, accompanied by two military aides, Colonels William P. Johnston and Custis Lee — sons of Albert Sidney Johnston and R. E. Lee — his young secretary, Burton Harrison, and the still-disconsolate John Pemberton, for whom no commensurate employment had been found in the nearly three months since his formal release from parole. Personally this saddened Davis almost as much as it did the unhappy Pennsylvanian, whom he admired for his firmness under adversity. But the truth was, there was much of sadness all around them as they traveled through the heartland of the South, in the faces of the people in their shabby towns and on their neglected farms, in the condition of the roadbeds and the cars, and even in the itinerary the presidential party was obliged to follow. The Confederacy's shrinking fortunes were reflected all too plainly in the fact that this second western journey was necessarily far more roundabout than the first had been in December, when Davis had gone directly to Chattanooga by way of Knoxville. Now the compass-boxing route led south through Charlotte and Columbia, then westward to Atlanta, and finally north, through Marietta and Dalton, to Chickamauga Station. That other time, moreover, he had extended his trip to include what he called "the further West," but this would not be possible now, the area thus referred to having fallen, like Knoxville and Chattanooga itself, under Federal occupation. Reaching Bragg's headquarters on Missionary

Ridge, October 9, he conferred in private with the general, who unburdened himself of a great many woes by placing the blame for them on
his subordinates; regretfully declined the proffered services of Pemberton as a replacement for Polk, though he was still unwilling to restore
the latter to duty; and, in conclusion, submitted his resignation as commander of the Army of Tennessee. This Davis refused, not wanting to
disparage the abilities of the only man under whom a Confederate army
had won a substantial victory since the death of Stonewall Jackson, back
in May. That evening he presided over a council of war attended by
Bragg and his corps commanders, Longstreet, Hill, Buckner, and
Cheatham, who had taken over from Polk, pending the outcome of the
bishop's current set-to with his chief. After what Davis later described
as "a discussion of various programmes, mingled with retrospective remarks on the events attending and succeeding the battle of Chickamauga" — in the course of which he continued his efforts "to be serviceable in harmonizing some of the difficulties" — he inquired whether
anyone had any further suggestions. Whereupon Longstreet spoke up.
Bragg, he said, "could be of greater service elsewhere than at the head of
the Army of Tennessee."

An embarrassing silence followed: embarrassing at any rate to
Bragg, who looked neither left nor right, as well as to Davis, who after
all had come here to compose differences, not to create scenes that would
enlarge them. After a time, however, he asked the other generals how
they felt about the matter, and all replied that they agreed with what
had just been said — particularly Hill, who seemed to relish the opportunity this afforded for an airing of his views. Bragg sat immobile
through the painful scene, his dark-browed face expressionless. Without
giving any opinion of his own, Davis at last adjourned the council. But
next day, when he sounded Longstreet on his willingness to accept the
command in place of Bragg, the Georgian declined. "In my judgment,"
he explained later, "our last opportunity was gone when we failed to follow the success at Chickamauga, and capture or disperse the Union
army, and it could not be just to the service or myself to call me to a position of such responsibility." He had, however, a suggestion: Joseph E.
Johnston. Davis bridled at the name, which Longstreet said "only served
to increase his displeasure, and his severe rebuke." This in turn caused
Old Peter to tender his resignation, but Davis, as he said, "was not
minded to accept that solution to the premise." At the close of the interview, Longstreet afterwards wrote, "the President walked as far as the
gate, gave me his hand in his usual warm grasp, and dismissed me with
his gracious smile; but a bitter look lurking about its margin, and the
ground-swell, admonished me that the clouds were gathering about
headquarters of the First Corps even faster than those that told the doom
of the Southern cause."

If Davis was pained, if a bitter look did lurk in fact about the

margin of his smile, it was small wonder; for he was being required to
deal with a problem which came more and more to seem insoluble.
Though Bragg's subordinates, or former subordinates, all agreed that he
should be removed, none of those who were qualified was willing to take
his place. First Longstreet, then Hardee, on being questioned, replied
that they did not want the larger responsibility, while Polk and Hill,
Buckner and Cheatham, either through demonstrated shortcomings in
the case of the former pair or lack of experience in the latter, were
plainly unqualified. Lee had been suggested, but had made it clear that he
preferred to remain in Virginia, where there could be no doubt he was
needed. Joe Johnston, on the other hand, had once been offered the command and once been ordered to it, and both times had refused, protesting
that Bragg was the best man for the post. Besides, if past performance
was any indication of what could be expected from a general, to appoint
Johnston would be to abandon all hope of an aggressive campaign
against the cooped-up Federals. . . . Davis thought the matter over for
three days, and then on October 13 announced his decision in the form
of a note to Bragg: "Regretting that the expectations which induced the
assignment of that gallant officer to this army have not been realized, you
are authorized to relieve Lieutenant General D. H. Hill from further
duty with your command." It had been obvious from the outset that one
of the two North Carolinians would have to go. Now Davis had made
his choice. Bragg would remain as commander of the army, and Hill —
an accomplished hater, with a sharp tongue he was never slow to use on
all who crossed him, including now the President — would return to his
home state.

In addition to concerning himself with this command decision, in
which Bragg emerged the winner more by default than by virtue of his
claim, Davis also inspected the defenses, reviewed the troops, and held
strategy conferences for the purpose of learning what course of action
the generals thought the army now should take. Basically, Bragg was in
favor of doing nothing more than holding what he had; that is, of keeping the Federals penned up in the town until starvation obliged them to
surrender. He felt sure that this would be the outcome, and he said so,
not only now but later, in his report. "Possessed of the shortest road to
the depot of the enemy, and the one by which reinforcements must reach
him," he would still maintain in late December, "we held him at our
mercy, and his destruction was only a question of time." When Davis
expressed dissatisfaction with his apparent lack of aggressiveness, Bragg
came up with an alternate plan, suggested to him earlier that week in a
letter from Beauregard, who, as was often the case when he had time
on his hands — Gillmore and Dahlgren were lying idle just then, licking
the wounds they had suffered in the course of their recent and nearly
fruitless exertions, outside and just inside Charleston harbor — had
turned his mind to grand-scale operations. In Virginia and elsewhere the

Confederates should hold strictly to the defensive, he said, so that Bragg could be reinforced by 35,000 troops, mainly from Lee, in order to cross the Tennessee, flank the bluecoats out of Chattanooga, and crush them in an all-out showdown battle; after which, he went on, Bragg could assist Lee in administering the same treatment to Meade, just outside Washington. He suggested, though, that the source of the plan be kept secret, lest the President be prejudiced against it in advance by his known dislike of its originator. "What I desire is our success," Old Bory wrote. "I care not who gets the credit." So Bragg at this point, being pressed for aggressive notions, offered the program as his own, expanding it slightly by proposing that a crossing be made well upstream for a descent on the Federal rear by way of Walden's Ridge. Davis listened with interest, Bragg informed Beauregard, finding merit in the suggestion; he "admitted its worth and was inclined to adopt it, only" — here was the catch; here the Creole's spirits took a drop — "he could not reduce General Lee's army." That disposed of the scheme Bragg advanced as his own, and the true author's hopes went glimmering.

Longstreet too had an alternate plan, however, which was not greatly different except that it involved no reinforcements and called for a move in the opposite direction. He proposed a change of base to Rome, for added security, and a crossing in force at Bridgeport; a move, he said, "that would cut the enemy's rearward line, interrupt his supply train, put us between his army at Chattanooga and the reinforcements moving to join him, and force him to precipitate battle or retreat." Davis liked the sound of this much better, largely because it had the virtue of economy in attempting the same purpose. Besides, he knew only too well the danger inherent in waiting idly outside the town while Yankee ingenuity went to work on the very problems for which it was best suited. Bragg concurring, albeit with hesitation, the President hopefully ordered the adoption of Old Peter's proposal and adjourned the conference.

So far, he had not addressed the troops. In fact he had declined to do so on his arrival five days ago, when he was welcomed at Chickamauga Station by a crowd of soldiers who called for a speech as he mounted his horse for the ride to army headquarters. "Man never spoke as you did on the field of Chickamauga," Davis told them, lifting his hat in return salute, "and in your presence I dare not speak. Yours is the voice that will win the independence of your country and strike terror to the heart of a ruthless foe." Now that he had toured their camps, however, and had seen for himself how rife the discontent was, he changed his mind and did what he had said he dared not do. Referring to the men before him as "defenders of the heart of our territory," he assured them that "your movements have been the object of intensest anxiety. The hopes of our cause greatly depend upon you, and happy it is that all can securely rely upon your achieving whatever, under the blessing of Providence, human power can effect." This said, he returned to his primary task of pouring oil on troubled waters, speaking not only to the troops themselves, but also to their officers, particularly those of lofty rank. "When the war shall have ended," he declared, "the highest meed of praise will be due, and probably given, to him who has claimed least for himself in proportion to the service he has rendered, and the bitterest self-reproach which may hereafter haunt the memory of anyone will be to him who has allowed selfish aspiration to prevail over the desire for the public good. . . . He who sows the seeds of discontent and distrust prepares for the harvest of slaughter and defeat. To zeal you have added gallantry; to gallantry, energy; to energy, fortitude. Crown these with harmony, due subordination, and cheerful support of lawful authority, that the measure of your duty may be full." He ended with a prayer "that our Heavenly Father may cover you with the shield of his protection in the hours of battle, and endow you with the virtues which will close your trials in victory complete."

These words were spoken on October 14, the date of A. P. Hill's sudden and bloody repulse at Bristoe Station. Davis stayed on for three more days, continuing his efforts to promote "harmony, due subordination, and cheerful support of lawful authority" at all levels in the strife-torn Army of Tennessee; then on October 17 — the date Stanton overtook Grant at Indianapolis — ended his eight-day visit by reboarding the train to continue his journey south for an inspection of the Mobile defenses. As he left he was assured by Bragg that Longstreet's plan for a crossing of the Tennessee on the Federal right at Bridgeport would be undertaken as soon as the troops could be gotten ready to advance.

Two days later, after inspecting a cannon foundry and other manufacturing installations at Selma, Alabama, he addressed a large crowd from his hotel balcony, asserting that if the "non-conscripts" would volunteer for garrison duty, and thus release more regular troops for service in the field, "we can crush Rosecrans and be ready with the return of spring to drive the enemy from our borders. The defeat of Rosecrans," he added, swept along by the enthusiasm his words had aroused — and unaware, of course, that Rosecrans would be relieved that day by a wire from Grant in Louisville — "will practically end the war." From Selma he proceeded to Demopolis, where he crossed the Tombigbee River and continued west across the Mississippi line to Meridian for a visit with his septuagenarian brother at nearby Lauderdale Springs. The war had been hard on Joseph Davis. Formerly one of the state's wealthiest planters, he had had to move twice already to escape the advancing Federals, not counting refugee stops along the way, and now his wife lay dying in a dilapidated house, having conserved her ebbing strength for one last glimpse of "Brother Jeff." The weary President was distressed by what he saw here, for to him it represented what was likely to happen to all his people, kin and un-kin, if the South failed in its bid for independence. Nevertheless he managed, in the course of his stay in Meridian, to work out a solution to another thorny problem of command. On October 23 — while Grant rode south down Walden's Ridge to enter Chattanooga before nightfall — he wired instructions for Bragg and Johnston, in their now separate departments, to have Polk and Hardee swap jobs and commanders, the latter to take charge of the former's corps in the Army of Tennessee, while the bishop took over the Georgian's duties at the camp for recruitment and instruction near Demopolis. This done, Davis left next morning for Mobile. After a tour of inspection with Major General Dabney H. Maury, commander of the city's defenses, he returned to the Battle House and spoke as he had done at Selma the week before, emphasizing that "those who remain at home, not less than those in arms, have their duties to perform. Each of all can encourage the spirit which can bring success," he told his listeners, adding that "men using the opportunities given by war to make fortunes will be detested by their posterity." A local reporter, impressed by the Chief Executive's "remarkably clear enunciation," observed that, though he spoke "without the slightest apparent effort, his words penetrated far down the street and were heard distinctly by most of the vast crowd gathered on the occasion."

Davis remained in Mobile over Sunday, October 25 — cheered by news of the Buckland Races, which Stuart had staged on Monday, but disappointed by Bragg's report that rain had delayed his preparations for a crossing at Bridgeport, as well as by the returns from Ohio's second-Tuesday elections, held just under two weeks ago, which showed that Lincoln's hard-war candidates had defeated Vallandigham and his Golden Circle friends — then left the following day for Montgomery, where he had arranged to have Forrest board the train for a conference en route to Atlanta. Valuing the Tennessean's abilities, the Commander in Chief not only approved his transfer to North Mississippi, where he would have authority "to raise and organize as many troops for the Confederate service as he finds practicable," but also directed that Bragg send the cavalryman a two-battalion cadre of his veteran troopers, plus Morton's battery, and recommended to Congress his promotion to major general. Forrest left the train at Atlanta, pleased to be taking up new duties as an independent commander in a region he knew well; but for his erstwhile traveling companion there was disturbing news from the Chattanooga theater. While Bragg had been waiting for the weather to clear before he moved against the enemy right, the Federals, with no apparent concern for mud and rain, had anticipated him in that direction by crossing the river themselves. Aggressive as always, Davis saw in this a chance for offensive action. "It is reported here that the enemy are crossing at Bridgeport," he wired Bragg on the 29th. "If so it may give you the opportunity to beat the detachment moving up to reinforce Rosecrans as was contemplated. . . . You will be able to anticipate him, and strike with the advantage of fighting him in detail." It had become increasingly evident, though, that weather was a pretense; that Bragg was favoring his preference for the defensive, despite a presidential warning, repeated today, that "the period most favorable for actual operations is rapidly passing away, and the consideration of supplies presses upon you the necessity to recover as much as you can of the country before you." Anxious that something be done at once, in Middle or East Tennessee, to justify Longstreet's prolonged absence from Virginia — where Lee was facing grievous odds, having fallen back to the line of the Rappahannock, and might need him at any moment — Davis added: "In this connection it has occurred to me that if the operations on your left should be delayed, or not be of prime importance, that you might advantageously assign General Longstreet with his two divisions to the task of expelling Burnside and thus place him in position, according to circumstances, to hasten or delay his return to the army of General Lee."

Much might come of either of these suggestions: the destruction of the blue column that had ventured across the river, within easy reach of the Confederate left, or the expulsion of Burnside from Knoxville and East Tennessee, far upstream on the right, "to recover that country and re-establish communications with Virginia." But for the present, with whatever patience he could muster while waiting for Bragg to make up his mind and move in one direction or the other, Davis resumed his journey back to the capital by way of Savannah and Charleston, neither of which he had visited since the outbreak of the war. He was welcomed to the former place on Halloween with an exuberant torchlight procession, followed by a reception at the Masonic Hall. A young matron who stood in line for a handshake wrote her soldier brother that she and her friends "were much pleased with the affability of the President. He has a good, mild, pleasant face," she added, "and, altogether, looks like a President of our struggling country *should* look — careworn and thoughtful, and firm, and quiet."

His affability came under a strain next morning, however, when Bragg announced the failure of the attempted counterstroke on his left, three nights ago at Wauhatchie, and placed the blame on Old Peter for having used an inadequate force ineptly. "The result related is a bitter disappointment," Davis replied, "as my expectations were sanguine that the enemy, by throwing across the Tennessee his force at Bridgeport, had ensured the success of the operation suggested by General Longstreet, and confided to his execution." In any case, the way was still open for an advance around the Federal right, and he hoped it would be taken, though he was obliged as always to leave the final decision to the commander on the scene. As for himself, he faced an ordeal of his own the following day in Charleston, where Beauregard was in command and the Rhetts had been attacking him, almost without remission, for the past two years in their *Mercury*. As his train drew near the station, November 2, he heard the booming of guns being fired in his honor, and when the

presidential car lurched to a stop beside the platform a welcoming committee came aboard. In the lead were Beauregard, his aide and amanuen-
sis Colonel Thomas Jordan, and Robert Barnwell Rhett, a colonel too. As
a later observer put it, Davis must have "wondered how the visit would
turn out when the first three hands raised in salute to him belonged to
three enemies." Perhaps it was this that threw him off his stride for the
first time in the course of the autumn journey he had undertaken in the
hope of harmonizing discord. At any rate, inadvertently or on purpose,
here today in South Carolina he did his office, his country, and his cause
the worst disservice he had done since he sent the curt, slashing note in
reply to Joe Johnston's six-page letter of protest at being ranked behind
Lee and the other Johnston, more than two years ago in Virginia. What
made it worse in this case was that he not only passed up an easy chance
to heal, he actually widened a dangerous rift, and he did so with nearly as
curt a slash as he had used before, except that this time the technique
involved omission.

　　Not that the citizens themselves were cold or unfriendly. "The
streets along the line of procession were thronged with people anxious to
get a look at the President," a *Courier* reporter wrote. "The men cheered
and the ladies waved their handkerchiefs in token of recognition." Proud
of their resistance to Du Pont's and Dahlgren's iron fleet, as well as of
their standing up to Gillmore's long-range shelling — which had recently begun anew, after a respite of about a month — they were
pleased that the Chief Executive had come to praise their valor and share
their danger. Flags were draped across the fronts of homes and buildings,
and garlands of laurel stretched from the city hall to the courthouse,
supporting a large banner that bid him welcome. This was Davis's first
Charleston visit since the spring of 1850, when he had accompanied the
body of John C. Calhoun from Washington to its grave in St Philip's
churchyard, and he recalled that sad occasion when he spoke today from
the portico of the city hall. In saluting the defenders of Sumter, he had
special praise for the fort's commander, Major Stephen Elliott, and predicted that if the Federals ever took the city they would find no more
than a "mass of rubbish," so determined were its people in their choice of
whether to "leave it a heap of ruins or a prey for Yankee spoils."
("Ruins! Ruins!" the crowd shouted.) "Let us trust to our commanding
general, to those having the charge and responsibilities of our affairs,"
Davis said, with a sidelong glance at Beauregard, and he added a note of
caution, as he had done in all his speeches this past month: "It is by
united effort, by fraternal feeling, by harmonious co-operation, by casting away all personal considerations . . . that our success is to be
achieved. He who would now seek to drag down him who is struggling,
if not a traitor, is first cousin to one; for he is striking the most deadly
blows that can be [struck]. He who would attempt to promote his own
personal ends . . . is not worthy of the Confederate liberty for which we

are fighting." In closing, he thanked the people and assured them of his prayers "for each and all, and above all for the sacred soil of Charleston."

At the reception held afterwards in the council chamber, people inquired of one another whether they had noticed that the President, after singling out Major Elliott for praise, not only had failed to congratulate Beauregard for his skillful defense of the city by land and water, but also had not mentioned him by name. Indeed, except for that one sidelong reference to "our commanding general," when the crowd was advised to put its trust in those in charge, Old Bory might as well not have been in Charleston at all, so far as Davis was concerned. Most of those present had noted this omission, which could scarcely have been anything but intentional, it seemed to them, on the part of a man as attentive to the amenities as the President normally was. Certainly Beauregard himself had felt the slight, and it was observed that he did not attend a dinner given that evening in Davis's honor by former governor William Aiken in his house on Wragg's Square. In point of fact, the general had already declined an invitation two days earlier. "It would afford me much pleasure to dine with you," he had told Aiken, "but candor requires me to inform you that my relations with the President being strictly official, I cannot participate in any act of politeness which might make him suppose otherwise." However, even if he had accepted earlier, he most likely would not have attended a dinner honoring a man who had just given him what amounted to a cut direct. Hard on the heels of the brief reference to him in the speech, moreover, had come the allusion to complainers as cousins to traitors, and this perhaps infuriated the Creole worst of all, touching him as it did where he was tender. Unburdening his feelings to a friend, he protested that Davis had "done more than if he had thrust a fratricidal dagger into my heart! he has *killed* my *enthusiasm* for our holy cause! ... May God forgive him," he added; "I fear I shall not have charity enough to pardon him."

Although Davis saw little or nothing of the general out of hours, according to a friendly diarist he spent a pleasant week as the former governor's house guest, "Beauregard, Rhetts, Jordan to the contrary notwithstanding. ... Mr Aiken's perfect old Carolina style of living delighted him," the diarist noted, not only because of "those old grey-haired darkies and their automatic, noiseless perfection of training," but also because it afforded him the leisure, while resting from the rigors of his journey, to hear firsthand accounts of the unsuccessful but persistent siege-in-progress. Gillmore had resumed his bombardment from Cummings Point a week ago, on October 26, and while at first it had been as furious as before, it presently slacked off to an intermittent shelling. An occasional big incendiary projectile was flung at Charleston, but mostly he concentrated his attention on Sumter, chipping away at the upper casemates until it began to seem to observers that the fort, daily reduced in height as debris from the ramparts slid down the outer walls, was sinking slowly beneath the choppy surface of the harbor. The defenders were on the alert for another small-boat assault, but none was attempted; Gillmore and Dahlgren, it was said, were unwilling to risk a recurrence of the previous fiasco, though each kept insisting that the other should try his hand at reducing the ugly thing. To the Confederates, however, the squat, battered pentagon was a symbol of their long-odds resistance, and as such it took on a strange beauty. An engineer captain wrote home of the feelings aroused by the sight of its rugged outline against the night sky, lanterns gleaming in unseen hands as work crews piled sandbags on the rubble, sentinels huddled for warmth over small fires in the casemates. "That ruin is beautiful," he declared, and added: "But it is more than this, it is emblematic also. . . . Is it not in some respects an image of the human soul, once ruined by the fall, yet with gleams of beauty and energetic striving after strength, surrounded by dangers and watching, against its foes?"

Nor, as might have been expected with the resourceful Beauregard in charge, had the garrison's efforts been limited entirely to the defensive. Using money donated for the purpose by Charlestonians, the general had had designed and built a cigar-shaped torpedo boat, twenty feet long and five feet wide, powered by a small engine and equipped with a ten-foot spar that had at its bulbous tip a 75-pound charge of powder, primed to explode when one of its four percussion nipples came in contact with anything solid, such as the iron side of a ship. Manned by a crew of four — captain and pilot, engineer and fireman — she was christened *David* and sent forth after sunset, October 5, to try her luck on the blockading squadron just across the bar. Her chosen Goliath was the outsized *New Ironsides*, the Yankee flagship that had escaped destruction back in April when the boiler-torpedo, over which Du Pont unwittingly stopped her during his attack, failed to detonate. Undetected by enemy lookouts, the *David* made contact with her spar-tip charge six feet below the *Ironsides'* waterline, but the resultant explosion threw up a great column of water that doused the little vessel's fires when it came down and nearly swamped her. As she drifted powerless out to sea, the jolted bluejackets on the ironclad's deck opened on her with a heavy fire of musketry and grape, prompting all four of her crew to go over the side. Two of these were picked up by the Federals, the captain as he paddled about in the darkness and the fireman when he was found clinging next morning to the *Ironsides'* rudder; they were clapped in irons and later sent North by Dahlgren to be tried for employing a weapon not sanctioned by civilized nations. Nothing came of that, however; they presently were exchanged, for the captain and a seaman from a captured Union gunboat, and sent back to Charleston. The other two had been there all along. Returning to the half-swamped *David* after the firing stopped, the pilot found that the engineer had been clinging to her all this time because he could not swim. They relighted her fires with a bull's-eye lantern and, eluding searchers on all sides, steamed back into the harbor before dawn. As for the *New Ironsides,* she had not been seriously damaged, the main force of the underwater explosion having fortunately been absorbed by one of her inner bulkheads. After a trip down to Port Royal for repairs to a few leaky seams, she soon returned to duty with the squadron — though from this time on, it was observed, her crew was quick to sound the alarm and open fire whenever a drifting log or a floating patch of seaweed, or less comically an incautious friendly longboat, happened near her in the dark.

Firsthand knowledge of such events as this brief sortie by the *David,* even though it failed in its purpose, and of such reactions to destruction as those of the engineer captain to the ruins of Sumter, even though no response could be made to the diurnal pounding, served to strengthen Davis's conviction that the South could never be subdued, no matter how much of its apparently limitless wealth and strength the North expended and exerted in its attempt to bring her to her knees; Charleston, for him, was proof enough that the unconquerable spirit of his people could never be humbled, despite the odds and the malignity, as it seemed to him, with which they were brought to bear. He stayed through November 8 — his fifth Sunday away from the national capital and his wife and children — then returned the following day to the Old Dominion. Lee, he learned on arrival, was falling back across the Rapidan, having suffered a double reversal two nights ago at Kelly's Ford and Rappahannock Bridge. Davis did not doubt that the Virginian would be able to hold this new river line, whatever had happened along the old one; his confidence in Lee was complete. His concern was more for what might happen around Chattanooga, for he now was informed that Bragg, while continuing to maintain that the weather prevented a strike at the newly opened Federal supply line on his immediate left, had been quick to adopt the suggestion that Longstreet be sent against Burnside, far off on his right, thereby reducing his army by one fourth.

On the face of it, that did not seem too risky, considering the great natural strength of his position, but others as well as Davis saw the danger in that direction, not only to Bragg but also to the authority that had backed him in the recent intramural crisis. Davis had everywhere been "received with cheers" on his journey, a War Department diarist observed. "His austerity and inflexibility have been relaxed, and he has made popular speeches wherever he has gone. . . . The press, a portion rather, praises the President for his carefulness in making a tour of the armies and forts south of us; but as he retained Bragg in command, how soon the tune would change if Bragg should meet with a disaster!" No one understood this better than Davis, who still believed that the best defense against a Federal assault, even upon so impregnable a position as the one held by the Army of Tennessee, would be for Bragg to knock the enemy in his immediate front off balance with an offensive of his own, and this seemed all the more the proper course now that it was known that the man in command at Chattanooga was Grant, who had made the worst sort of trouble for the Confederacy almost everywhere he had been sent, so far in the war. Accordingly, two days after his return to Richmond, being still immersed in a mass of paperwork collected in his absence, Davis had Custis Lee send Bragg a reminder of this point of view. "His Excellency regrets that the weather and condition of the roads have suspended the movement [on your left]," Lee wired, "but hopes that such obstacles to your plans will not long obstruct them. He feels assured that you will not allow the enemy to get up all his reinforcements before striking him, if it can be avoided." The President, Lee added, stressing by repetition the danger in delay, "does not deem it necessary to call your attention to the importance of doing whatever is to be done before the enemy can collect his forces, as the longer the time given him for this purpose, the greater will be the disparity in numbers."

★ ★ ★

Unlike Davis, who twice in the past eleven months had visited every Confederate state east of the Mississippi except Florida and Louisiana, addressing crowds along the way and calling for national unity in them all, Lincoln in two and one half years — aside, that is, from four quick trips on army business: once to confer with Winfield Scott at West Point, twice to see McClellan, on the James and the Antietam, and once to visit with Joe Hooker on the Rappahannock line — had been no farther than a carriage ride from the White House. He had made no speeches on any of the exceptional occasions, being strictly concerned with military affairs, and for the most part even the citizens of Washington had not known he was gone until after he returned. This was not to say that he had not concerned himself with national unity or that he had made no appeals to the people in his efforts to achieve it; he had indeed, and repeatedly, in messages to Congress, in proclamations, and in public and private letters to individuals and institutions. One of the most successful of these had been his late-August letter to James Conkling, ostensibly an expression of regret that he was unable to attend a rally of "unconditional Union men" in his home town of Springfield, but actually a stump speech to be delivered by proxy at the meeting. John Murray Forbes, a prominent Boston businessman, had been so impressed with the arguments therein advanced in support of the government's views on the Negro question — "a plain letter to plain people," he called it — that he wrote directly to Lincoln in mid-September, suggesting that he also set the public mind aright on what Forbes considered the true issue of the war. "Our friends abroad see it," he declared; "John Bright and his glorious band of European republicans see that we are fighting for Democracy, or (to get rid of the technical name) for liberal institutions. ... My suggestion then is that you should seize an early opportunity, and any subsequent chance, to teach your great audience of plain people that the war is not North against South, but the *People* against the *Aristocrats*. If you can place this in the same strong light that you have the Negro question, you will settle it in men's minds as you have that."

Lincoln filed the letter in his desk and in his mind, and seven weeks later, on November 2, acting on the suggestion that he "seize an early opportunity," accepted an invitation to attend the dedication of a new cemetery at Gettysburg for the men who had fallen there in the July battle. The date, November 19, was less than three weeks off, and the reason for this lateness on the part of the committee was that he had been an afterthought, its original intention having been to emphasize the states, which were sharing the expenses of the project, not the nation. Besides, even after the thought occurred that it might be a good idea to invite the President, some doubt had been expressed "as to his ability to speak upon such a grave and solemn occasion." However, since the principal speaker, the distinguished orator Edward Everett of Massachusetts, had been chosen six weeks earlier, it was decided — as Lincoln was told in a covering letter, stressing that the ceremonies would "doubtless be very imposing and solemnly impressive" — to ask him to attend in a rather minor capacity: "It is the desire that after the oration, you, as Chief Executive of the nation, formally set apart these grounds to their sacred use by a few appropriate remarks." Duly admonished to be on his good behavior, to avoid both length and levity, Lincoln accepted the invitation, along with these implied conditions, on the day it was received.

He had not intended to crack any jokes in the first place, at least not at the ceremony itself, though in point of fact he was in higher spirits nowadays than he had been for months. For one thing, the military outlook — badly blurred by the effects of the heavy body blow Bragg landed at Chickamauga in mid-September — had improved greatly in the past ten days: specifically since October 23, when Grant rode into Chattanooga and set to work in his characteristic fashion, opening the Cracker Line and sustaining it with a victory in the night action at Wauhatchie, all within a week of his arrival, then wound up by notifying Halleck that "preparations may commence for offensive operations." If Banks had been thwarted so far in his designs on coastal Texas, that might be taken as a temporary setback, amply balanced in the far-western theater by Steele's success, on the heels of his Little Rock triumph, in driving the rebels out of Pine Bluff on October 25. Similarly, in the eastern theater, though Gillmore and Dahlgren had made but a small impression down in Charleston harbor, the news from close at hand in Virginia was considerably improved. Lee was on the backtrack from Manassas, presumably chastened by his repulse at Bristoe Station, and Meade was moving south again, rebuilding the wrecked railroad as he went. Lincoln now felt a good deal kindlier toward the Pennsylvanian than he had done in the weeks immediately following Gettysburg. If Meade had much of the exasperating caution that had characterized McClellan in the presence of the enemy, at least he was no blusterer like Pope or blunderer like Burnside, and despite his unfortunate snapping-turtle disposition he did not seem to come unglued under pressure, as McDowell and Hooker had tended to do and done. All in all, though it was evident that he was not the killer-arithmetician his Commander in Chief was seeking, the impression was that he would do till the real thing came along, and this estimate was heightened within another week, when he overtook Lee on the line of the Rappahannock, administered a double dose of what he had given him earlier at Bristoe, and drove him back across the Rapidan. "The signs look better," Lincoln had said in closing his letter to Conkling in late August. Now in November, reviewing the over-all military situation that had been disrupted by Chickamauga and readjusted since, he might have amended this to: "The signs look even better."

But it was on the political front that the news was best of all. Last year's congressional elections had been a bitter pill to swallow, but in choking it down, the Administration had learned much that could be applied in the future. For one thing, there was the matter of names. "Republican" having come to be something of an epithet in certain sections of the country, the decision was made to run this year's pro-Lincoln candidates under the banner of the National Union Party, thus to attract the votes of "loyal" Democrats. For another, with the enthusiastic co-operation of Stanton in the War Department, there were uses to which the army could be put: especially in doubtful states, where whole regiments could be furloughed home to cast their ballots, while individual squads and platoons could be assigned to maintain order at the polls and assist the local authorities in administering oaths of loyalty, past as well as present, required in several border states before a citizen could enter a voting booth. New England had gone solidly Republican in the spring. Then in August, with the help of considerable maneuvering along the lines described above, the President was pleased to note that his native Kentucky had "gone very strongly right." Tennessee followed suit, and so, presently, did all but one of the rest of the states that held elections in the fall. Only in New Jersey, where the organization was weak, did the "unconditional Unionists" lose ground. Everywhere else the outcome exceeded party expectations, particularly in Pennsylvania, Massachusetts, New York, and Maryland, in all of which the situation had been judged to be no better than touch-and-go. Ohio, where Vallandigham was opposed by John Brough in the race for governor, balloted on October 13; Lincoln said that he felt more anxious than he had done three years ago, when he himself had run. He need not have worried. With the help of 41,000 soldier votes, as compared to 2000 for Vallandigham, Brough won by a majority of 100,000. "Glory to God in the highest," Lincoln wired; "Ohio has saved the Nation." Four days later, having got this worry out of the way, he celebrated substantially by issuing another call for "300,000 more." The states were to raise whatever number of troops they could by volunteering, then complete their quotas by drafting men "to reinforce our victorious armies in the field," as the proclamation put it, "and bring our needful military operations to a prosperous end, thus closing forever the fountains of sedition and civil war."

News that the President would appear at Gettysburg reached the papers soon after his acceptance of the tardy invitation, and their reactions varied from bland to indignant, hostile editors protesting that a ceremony intended to honor fallen heroes was no proper occasion for what could only be a partisan appeal. Certain prominent Republicans, on the other hand, professed to believe it was no great matter, one way or the other, since Lincoln was by now a political cipher anyhow, a "dead card" in the party deck. "Let the dead bury the dead," Thaddeus Stevens quipped when asked for an opinion on what was about to happen just outside the little college town where he once had practiced law and still owned property. Lincoln held to his intention to attend the ceremonies, despite the quips and adverse comments in and out of print. He was, he remarked in another connection this week, not much upset by anything said about him, especially in the papers. "These comments constitute a fair specimen of what has occurred to me through life. I have endured a great deal of ridicule without much malice, and have received a great deal of kindness not quite free from ridicule. I am used to it." Meanwhile, in the scant period between the tendering of the invitation and the date for his departure, there was not much time for composing his thoughts, let alone for setting them down on paper. In addition to the usual encroachments by job- and favor-seekers, there was the wedding of Chase's sprightly daughter Kate to wealthy young Senator William Sprague of Rhode Island, the most brilliant social affair to be held in Washington in the nearly three years since the Southerners left the District; there was an urgent visit by the high-powered New York politician Thurlow Weed, who came with a plan for ending the war by means of a ninety-day armistice, a scheme that had to be heard in full and then rejected tactfully, lest Weed be offended into an enmity the cause could not afford; there was the necessity for day-to-day work on the annual year-end message to Congress, which it would not do to put off till the last minute, though the last minute was in fact about at hand already. All this there was, and more, much more: with the result that by the time the departure date came round, November 18, Lincoln had done little more than jot down a few notes on what he intended to say next day in Pennsylvania. Worst of all, in the way of distraction, Tad was sick with some feverish ailment the doctors could not identify, and Mrs Lincoln was near hysterics, remembering Willie's death, under similar circumstances, twenty months ago in this same house. But Lincoln did not let even this interfere with his plans and promise. The four-car special, carrying the President and three of his cabinet members — Seward, Blair, and Usher; the others had declined, pleading the press of business — his two secretaries, officers of the army and navy, his friend Ward Lamon, and the French and Italian ministers, left the capital around noon. Lincoln sat for a time with the others in a drawing room at the back of the rear coach, swapping stories for an hour or so, and then, as the train approached Hanover Junction, excused himself to retire to the privacy of his compartment at the other end of the car. "Gentlemen, this is all very pleasant," he said, "but the people will expect me to say something to them tomorrow, and I must give the matter some thought."

Arriving at sundown, he went to the home of Judge David Wills, on the town square, where he and Everett and Governor Curtin would spend the night. The streets and all the available beds were crowded, visitors having come pouring in for tomorrow's ceremonies, notables and nondescripts alike, many of them with no place to sleep and most of them apparently past caring. Accompanied by a band, a large group roamed about in the early dark to serenade the visiting dignitaries, including the President. He came out at last and gave them one of those brief speeches, the burden of which was that he had nothing to say. "In my position it is somewhat important that I should not say foolish things," he began. "— If you can help it!" a voice called up, and Lincoln took his cue from that: "It very often happens that the only way to help it is to say nothing at all. Believing that is my present condition this evening, I must beg you to excuse me from addressing you further." Unsatisfied, the crowd proceeded next door and called for Seward, who did better by them, though this still was evidently far from enough, since they serenaded five more speakers before calling it a night. Lincoln by then had completed the working draft of tomorrow's address and gone to bed, greatly relieved by a wire from Stanton passing along a message from Mrs Lincoln that Tad was much improved.

By morning the crowd had swelled to 15,000, most of whom were on the prowl about the town in search of breakfast or about the surrounding fields in search of relics, an oyster-colored minnie ball, a tarnished button, a fragment of shell that might or might not have killed a man. In any event, whatever disappointments there were for the hungry, the pickings were good for the souvenir hunters, for it was later calculated that 569 tons of ammunition had been expended in the course of the three-day battle. Coffins were much in evidence, too, though the work of reinterring the dead — at $1.59 a body — had been suspended for the solemn occasion now at hand. At 10 o'clock the procession began to form on the square, marshaled by Lamon and led by the President on horseback. An hour later it began to move, in what one witness referred to as "an orphanly sort of way," toward Cemetery Hill, where the ceremonies would be held. Lincoln sat erect at first, wearing a black suit, a high silk hat, and white gloves, but presently he slumped in the saddle, arms limp and head bent forward in deep thought, while behind him rode or walked the governors of six of the eighteen participating states, several generals, including Doubleday and Gibbon, and a number of congressmen, as well as the officials who had come up with him on the train. Within fifteen or twenty minutes these various dignitaries had taken their places on the crowded platform, and after a wait for Everett, who was late, the proceedings opened at noon with a prayer by the House chaplain, following which the principal speaker was introduced. "Mr President," he said with a bow, tall and white-haired, just under seventy years of age, a former governor of Massachusetts, minister to England for John Tyler, president of Harvard, successor to Daniel Webster as Secretary of State under Millard Fillmore, and in 1860 John Bell's running mate on the Constitutional Union ticket, which had carried Virginia, Kentucky, and Tennessee. "Mr Everett," Lincoln replied, and the orator launched forthwith into his address.

"Standing beneath this serene sky," with "the mighty Alleghenies dimly towering" before him, Everett raised his "poor voice to break the eloquent silence of God and Nature." He did so for two hours by the clock, having informed the committee beforehand that the occasion was "not to be dismissed with a few sentimental or patriotic commonplaces." Nor was it. He outlined the beginning of the war, reviewed the furious three-day action here, discussed and denounced the doctrine of state sovereignty, lacing his eloquence with historical and classical allusions, and came at last to a quotation from Pericles: "The whole earth is the sepulchre of illustrious men." Recognizing the advent of the peroration because he had been given advance proofs of the address, Lincoln took from his coat pocket a fair copy he had made of his own speech that morning, put on his steel-bowed spectacles, and read it through while Everett drew to a close, head back-flung, and pronounced the final sentence in a voice that had not faltered once in the whole two hours: "Down to the latest period of recorded time, in the glorious annals of our common country there will be no brighter page than that which relates the Battles of Gettysburg." Amid prolonged applause he took his seat, and after the Baltimore Glee Club had sung an ode composed for the occasion, Lamon pronounced the words: "The President of the United States." Lincoln rose, and as a photographer began setting up his tripod and camera in front of the rostrum, delivered — in what a reporter called "a sharp, unmusical treble voice," but with what John Hay considered "more grace than is his wont" — the "few appropriate remarks" which the committee had said it desired of him "after the oration."

"Fourscore and seven years ago our fathers brought forth upon this continent a new nation, conceived in liberty and dedicated to the proposition that all men are created equal. Now we are engaged in a

great civil war, testing whether that nation, or any nation so conceived
and so dedicated, can long endure. We are met on a great battlefield of
that war. We are met to dedicate a portion of it as the final resting
place of those who here gave their lives that that nation might live. It
is altogether fitting and proper that we should do this. But in a larger
sense we cannot dedicate, we cannot consecrate, we cannot hallow this
ground. The brave men, living and dead, who struggled here, have consecrated it far above our poor power to add or detract." A polite scattering of applause was overridden at this point as Lincoln continued.
"The world will little note, nor long remember, what we say here, but
it can never forget what they did here. It is for us, the living, rather,
to be dedicated here to the unfinished work that they have thus far so
nobly carried on. It is rather for us to be here dedicated to the great task
remaining before us, that from these honored dead we take increased devotion to that cause for which they here gave the last full measure of
devotion; that we here highly resolve that these dead shall not have died
in vain; that the nation shall, under God, have a new birth of freedom;
and that government of the people, by the people, for the people, shall
not perish from the earth."

He finished before the crowd, a good part of whose attention had
been fixed on the photographer anyhow, realized that he was fairly
launched on what he had to say. In reaction to what a later observer described as the "almost shocking brevity" of the speech, especially by contrast with the one that went before, the applause was delayed, then scattered and barely polite. Moreover, the photographer missed his picture.
Before he had time to adjust his tripod and uncap the lens, Lincoln had
said "of the people, by the people, for the people" and sat down, leaving
the artist with a feeling that he had been robbed. Apparently many of
those present felt the same, agreeing in advance with what the Chicago
Times would say tomorrow about the President's performance here
today: "The cheek of every American must tingle with shame as he
reads the silly, flat and dishwatery utterances of the man who has to be
pointed out to intelligent foreigners as the President of the United
States." In fact, as he resumed his seat alongside his friend Lamon and
heard the perfunctory spatter of applause whose brevity matched his
own, the speaker himself was taken with a feeling of regret that he had
not measured up to what had been expected of him. Recalling a word
used on the prairie in reference to a plow that would not clean itself
while shearing through wet soil, he said gloomily: "Lamon, that speech
won't *scour*. It is a flat failure and the people are disappointed."

In time — for not all editors were as scathing as the one in his
home state; a Massachusetts paper, for example, printed the address in
full and remarked that it was "deep in feeling, compact in thought and
expression, and tasteful and elegant in every word and comma" — Lincoln revised not only his opinion of what he called "my little speech,"

but also the text itself, improving on what a Cincinnati editor had already described as "the right thing in the right place, and a perfect thing in every respect." When Everett remarked in a letter next day, "I should be glad if I could flatter myself that I came as near the central idea of the occasion, in two hours, as you did in two minutes," he replied: "In our respective parts yesterday, you could not have been excused to make a short address, nor I a long one. I am pleased to know that, in your judgment, the little I did say was not entirely a failure." Subsequently, when the orator asked for a copy of the speech, Lincoln gladly sent him one incorporating certain workshop changes. The second "We are met" became "We have come"; "a portion of it" became "a portion of that field"; "resting place of" became "resting place for"; "the unfinished work that they have thus far so nobly carried on" became "the unfinished work which they who fought here have thus far so nobly advanced"; "the nation shall, under God," became "this nation, under God, shall." Two later drafts he also made as presentation copies, with only two additional changes, one in the first sentence, where "upon" was shortened to "on," and one in the last, where "here" was dropped from the phrase "they here gave." The final draft — only two words longer than the one he had part-read, part-improvised at the Gettysburg ceremony, though he had altered, to one degree or another, half of its ten sentences — would be memorized in the future by millions of American school children, including those of the South, despite his claim that a victory by their forebears, in their war for independence, would have meant the end of government by and for the people. That speech did indeed scour, even in dark and bloody ground.

After the ceremonies on Cemetery Hill, Lincoln returned to the Wills house for lunch, after which he held an unscheduled reception, shaking hands for about an hour, then went to a patriotic rally at the Presbyterian church, where he listened to an address by the new lieutenant governor of Ohio. Finally at 6.30 he boarded the train for Washington. Much of the time that afternoon he had seemed gloomy and listless, and now on the train he gave way to weariness and malaise, lying stretched out on one of the side seats in the drawing room, a wet towel folded across his eyes and forehead. Back in the capital by midnight, he found good news awaiting him at the White House: Tad had been up and about today, apparently as well as if he had never been sick at all. Presently it developed however that the first family still had an invalid on its hands, only this time the member who fell ill was the President himself and the doctors had no trouble identifying the ailment. It was varioloid, a mild form of smallpox. Placed in isolation by order of his physician, Lincoln for once was free of the importunities of the office-seekers who normally hemmed him in.

"There is one thing good about this," he said with a somewhat rueful smile. "I now have something I can give everybody."

✗ 5 ✗

When Grant learned on November 5 that Bragg had detached Longstreet's two divisions the day before to send them and Wheeler's cavalry against Burnside, thus reducing the strength of the besiegers of Chattanooga by one fourth, he fairly ached to attack him, then and there, despite the semicircular frown of all those guns on all those heights. Indeed, there seemed to be sore need for haste: not only because the Confederates had rail transportation as far as Loudon, two thirds of the way to Knoxville — which meant that Old Peter might be able to return within a week or ten days, including the time it would take him to defeat and capture the bluecoats there or drive them from the region they had held for two months now, thereby reopening the Tennessee & Virginia Railroad for the use of such reinforcements as the Richmond government might take the notion to send him or Bragg on an overnight ride from Lynchburg — but also because Lincoln, who was known to be touchy about East Tennessee and the protection of its Union-loyal residents, might be tempted for political reasons to disrupt the plans of the commander of the newly created Military Division of the Mississippi. Sure enough, as Grant said later, the Washington authorities no sooner heard of Longstreet's departure from his immediate front than they became "more than ever anxious for the safety of Burnside's army, and plied me with dispatches faster than ever, urging that something should be done for his relief."

He was altogether willing, but he could not see that sending part of his army to Knoxville, at this stage of the campaign, would do anything more than add to Burnside's supply problem, which was nearly as grievous as his own had been on his arrival, two weeks back. What he had in mind, instead, was to attack Bragg's right. If successful, this would break his grip on Chattanooga by dislodging him from Missionary Ridge, and even if it failed it would be likely, if it was pressed with vigor, to alarm him into recalling Longstreet. In either case, as Grant saw it, Burnside would be relieved far more effectively than by the addition of several thousand hungry mouths to his command. On November 7, however, when he suggested the attack to Thomas, whose troops would have to make it, he was told that the thing could not be done. The Cracker Line had been open barely a week, and though the men were already back on full rations, no replacements for the starved artillery horses had yet come through. The few survivors, wobbly as they were, were not enough to move the guns out of the parks, according to Thomas, much less to pull them forward in support of the advancing infantry, and without them the attack was bound to fail. Unwilling to let it go at that, Grant proposed that mules or officers' mounts be used to haul the pieces, but the Virginian explained that the former, though superb in draft, were undependable under fire, while the latter would not work in traces and lacked the heft required of gun teams anyhow. Regretfully, in the light of this, the general whose arm was infantry felt obliged to defer to the old-line artilleryman. "Nothing was left to be done," he afterwards observed, "but to answer Washington dispatches as best I could; urge Sherman forward, although he was making every effort to get forward, and encourage Burnside to hold on, assuring him that in a short time he should be relieved."

His red-haired successor in command of the Army of the Tennessee was indeed making every effort to get forward, for he had received at Iuka ten days ago an order delivered by "a dirty, black-haired individual with mixed dress and strange demeanor" — thus Sherman later described the messenger — who had left Chattanooga on the day after Grant's arrival and paddled a canoe down the Tennessee, over treacherous Muscle Shoals, to find him. The instructions were for him to leave the railroad work to one division and press on at once with the other four to Bridgeport, where he would be in position to block an attempt by Bragg to turn the Federal right, disrupt the new supply line, and flank the defenders out of Chattanooga. (Though it might have been inferred from this that Grant had been reading his opponent's mail, he did not actually know that Bragg — or, more properly speaking, Longstreet — had any such plan in mind. It just had seemed to him wise to forestall so logical a move on the part of an adversary reputed to be as bold as he was tricky.) Furthermore, as an added logistical precaution, Grant directed Sherman to abandon work on the Memphis & Charleston, west of Decatur, so that the division left behind could concentrate on repairing the Tennessee & Alabama, which ran north of there, through Columbia, to Nashville, and thus provide him with two lines connecting his railhead supply base at Stevenson with his main depot back at the capital. That way, he would not only have a spare all-weather line in case raiders broke through to the Nashville & Chattanooga; he would also be able to keep up his stocks of ammunition and food when the opportunity came for him to forward supplies to Burnside, who at present had no rail connection with the outside world. . . . This was a large order, for the line north of Decatur had been thoroughly wrecked by cavalry and saboteurs, but the commander of the division assigned to the task was Brigadier General Grenville M. Dodge. A capable soldier, with a wound and a promotion dating from Pea Ridge to prove it, the thirty-two-year-old New Englander was also an experienced railroad builder, civil engineer, and surveyor; "Level Eye," the Indians had dubbed him, watching him at work out on the plains before the war. Grant figured that if anyone could do the job it was Dodge, and his confidence was not misplaced. Working without a base of supplies from which to draw either rations or equipment, without skilled labor of any kind, except such as he could find in the ranks of his 8000-man division, and with nothing but axes, picks, and spades for tools, he completed the job within forty days, al-

though it required the rebuilding of no fewer than 182 bridges and about
as many culverts while re-laying 102 miles of track northward across the
lowlands and uplands of North Alabama and Middle Tennessee. His
troops would get none of the glory in the campaign that now was about
to open in earnest, but no division in any of the three blue armies involved worked harder or deserved more credit for the outcome.

But that was still in the future. For the present, Sherman pushed
on eastward, crossing the Tennessee at Eastport to reach Florence by
November 1, at which point, after three weeks on the go, he was about
midway between Memphis and Chattanooga. To avoid the delay that
would be involved in ferrying four divisions across Elk River, wide and
bridgeless this far down, he marched up its north bank for a crossing by
the bridge near Decherd, then followed the railroad down to Stevenson. He reached Bridgeport in advance of his troops on the night of November 13 to find a dispatch awaiting him from Grant, urging him to
hurry ahead to Chattanooga for a conference. This he did the following
day, proceeding via the Cracker Line, and rode into town that evening
to be greeted by the superior he had not seen since he left him on crutches
at Vicksburg in September. He was pleased to see that by now the
crutches had been discarded; but when they rode out together next
morning on a tour of inspection, finding himself confronted by the awesome loom of Lookout Mountain on the south, while to the east, against
the long, shadowy backdrop of Missionary Ridge, "rebel sentinels, in a
continuous chain, were walking their posts in plain view, not a thousand yards off," Sherman was amazed. He had been told what to expect,
but what he saw came as such a shock to him that he involuntarily exclaimed: "Why, General Grant, you are besieged!" Grant nodded. "It's
too true," he said. And then he told him what he had in mind to do
about it.

Thomas's troops, he said — according to Sherman's recollection
of the briefing — "had been so demoralized by the Battle of Chickamauga that he feared they could not be got out of their trenches to assume the offensive." That was where Sherman came into the picture;
"he wanted my troops to hurry up, to take the offensive *first;* after
which, he had no doubt the Cumberland army would fight well." The
attack was to be launched against Bragg's extreme right, Grant explained: specifically against the northern end of Missionary Ridge, which
he had reconnoitered and found unfortified. After crossing at Brown's
Ferry, Sherman would press on under cover of darkness and throw a
pontoon bridge across the Tennessee four miles above Chattanooga, just
below the mouth of Chickamauga Creek, for a surprise assault designed
to strike the enemy ridge end-on and then sweep down it from the north,
dislodging rebels as he went; Thomas meanwhile would fix them in position by threatening from the west, and Hooker would stand ready with
his Easterners to lend a hand in whatever direction he was needed. Sher-

man liked the sound of this, particularly his assignment to the leading role, but said that he would prefer to take a look at the terrain by daylight. So he and Grant, accompanied by Baldy Smith, crossed over to the north bank of the river, then up it to a hill overlooking the scene of the proposed attack on the opposite bank. He studied it as carefully as distance allowed, then returned before dark, well pleased by what he had seen. There was, however, a need for haste; Longstreet had been gone for better than ten days now and might get back before Sherman's men were in position, in which case they would encounter that much more resistance. Accordingly, the Ohioan did not spend another night in Chattanooga, but returned instead to Bridgeport, again by way of the Cracker Line, to brief his four division commanders on the plan of attack and see that they got their troops on the march without delay.

He had hoped to have them in jump-off position within five days; that is, by November 20 for a dawn attack next morning; but, as he explained later, "the condition of the roads was such, and the bridge at Brown's so frail, that it was not until the 23d that we got three of my divisions behind the hills near the point indicated above Chattanooga for crossing the river."

He need not have fretted about those three lost days. They gained him much, as the thing turned out, and Grant as well. In fact, if he had been delayed one day longer, he not only would have profited still more; he would have been spared the considerable mortification he was to suffer two days later at the hands of Pat Cleburne, who in that case would not have been there. For Bragg had decided, only the day before Sherman got into his jump-off position unobserved, to double the strength of Longstreet's 11,000-man infantry column by detaching another two divisions from the lines around Chattanooga to join him for the suppression of Burnside, under siege by then at Knoxville, and one of the two was Cleburne's.

Old Peter had protested his own detachment in the first place, on the double grounds that he would not be strong enough to deal quickly with Burnside and that his departure would leave the main body, strung out along six miles of line, dangerously exposed to an assault by Grant, who already had been reinforced by Hooker and presumably would soon be joined as well by the even larger force marching eastward under Sherman. But Bragg, with what Longstreet described as a "sardonic smile," declined either to cancel or strengthen the movement against Knoxville, and "intimated that further talk was out of order." He had his reasons: largely personal ones, apparently, dating from the conference three weeks ago, at which the Georgian had volunteered the opinion that the Army of Tennessee would benefit from a change of commanders. Informing Davis, who had suggested the detachment in his letter two days earlier from Atlanta, that "the Virginia troops will move in the direction indicated as soon as practicable," Bragg had added: "This will be a great relief to me." That was on the last day of October, and four days later, despite his protest, Longstreet was detached. He took with him the divisions of McLaws and Hood — the latter now under Brigadier General Micah Jenkins, who was senior to Law and had superseded him on his arrival after Chickamauga — Alexander's artillery, and Wheeler's three brigades of cavalry. This gave him a total of about 15,000 effectives of all arms. His assignment was "to destroy or capture Burnside's army," which in turn had just over 25,000 troops in occupation of East Tennessee.

It was Longstreet's belief that his best chance for success, under the circumstances, lay in striking before his adversary had time to concentrate his forces. But that turned out to be impossible, for a variety of reasons. Not the least of these was that he lacked the means of moving his pontoons except on flatcars, which meant that he had to cross the Holston River at Loudon, where the railroad ended because the bridge was out, rather than at some point closer than thirty air-line miles from his objective. To add to his woes, not only did the trains run badly off schedule, but he found no rations on hand when he reached Sweetwater, as he had been assured they would be, and had to mark time there while they were being brought in from the country roundabout. "The delay that occurs is one that might have been prevented," he wired Bragg on November 11, "but not by myself.... As soon as I find a probability of moving without almost certain starvation, I shall move, provided the troops are up." Bragg retaliated in kind. "Transportation in abundance was on the road and subject to your orders," he shot back next day. "I regret it has not been energetically used. The means being furnished, you were expected to handle your own troops, and I cannot understand your constant applications for me to furnish them." Old Peter pushed forward on his own, crossing at Loudon on the 13th, but reviewing the situation years later he remarked: "It began to look more like a campaign against Longstreet than against Burnside."

In point of fact, although their methods differed sharply, the blue commander to his front was no less skillful an opponent than the gray one in his rear. Warned by Grant that a heavy detachment was headed in his direction, Burnside was not only on the alert for an attack; he was also mindful of his instructions to keep the enemy from returning to Chattanooga as long as possible. "Sherman's advance has reached Bridgeport," Grant wired on the day after the rebels crossed the Holston. "If you can hold Longstreet in check until he gets up, or by skirmishing and falling back can avoid serious loss to yourself and gain time, I will be able to force the enemy back from here and place a force between Longstreet and Bragg that must inevitably make the former take to the mountain passes by every available road." Accordingly, Burnside did not seriously contest the Confederate advance. Abandoning Kingston, he called his scattered forces in from all points except Cumberland Gap, thus keeping that escape hatch open in the event of a disaster, and aside from a brief delaying action at Campbell Station on the 14th, about midway between Loudon and Knoxville, did not risk a sudden termination of the contest, either by a victory or a defeat. He had some 20,000 soldiers with him; more, he knew, than were in the column advancing on him. But it was not a battle he was after. It was time.

He got it, too. Arriving before Knoxville on November 17, Longstreet found the bluecoats skillfully disposed and well dug in. "We went to work, therefore," he afterwards reported, "to make our way forward by gradual and less hazardous measures, at the same time making examinations of the enemy's entire position." For the better part of a week this continued, his caution enlarged by the knowledge that Burnside had more men inside the place than he himself had outside. Then on November 23 he received a message Bragg had written the day before, informing him that "nearly 11,000 reinforcements are now moving to your assistance." Old Peter was to go ahead and defeat Burnside now, "if practicable"; otherwise he could wait for the additional strength already on the way. Having looked the situation over carefully for the past six days, without finding a single chink in the Federal armor, Longstreet decided that the "practicable" thing to do was wait a couple more.

Bragg's decision to add weight to the blow aimed at Knoxville, seeking thereby to hasten the return of the detachment by giving it the strength to settle the issue there without additional delay, was based in part on a growing suspicion that Old Peter had been right, after all, when he warned of the danger involved in any prolonged weakening of the force in occupation of the six-mile line of intrenchments drawn around two sides of Chattanooga. Longstreet had been gone for nearly three weeks now, and all sorts of things had been happening down in the town, indicative of the fact that the blue commander had something violent in mind. Moreover, Sherman had reached Bridgeport the week before, then suddenly, after crossing at Brown's Ferry, had disappeared as mysteriously as if the earth had swallowed up all four of his divisions. Bragg inferred that the Ohioan must have marched over Walden's Ridge: in which case he was probably headed for Knoxville, with the intention not only of raising the siege but also of swamping the already outnumbered Longstreet. If this was so, the thing to do was beat him to the punch, using the speed made possible by the railroad, and settle the issue before he got there. Accordingly, having reorganized what was left of his army into two large corps of four divisions apiece — one under Hardee, who had replaced Polk, and one under Breckinridge, who had replaced Hill — Bragg decided to dispatch one division from each, Cleburne from Hardee, Buckner from Breckinridge, and send them to Knoxville at once. He no sooner reached this decision than he acted on it. Buckner being absent sick, and Preston having been called to Richmond, his troops were placed under Bushrod Johnson, who pulled them out of line on November 22 and shifted them rearward to Chickamauga Station, where they boarded the cars for a fast ride to Loudon and a march beyond the Holston. Cleburne followed next day to wait for the return of the cars that had carried Johnson up the line.

Consolidation of Walker's two small divisions had reduced the army's total from eleven to ten divisions, and of these, with Johnson and Cleburne gone, Bragg now had a scant half dozen, containing fewer than 40,000 effectives of all arms. Hardee held the left of the semicircular line, with Stevenson posted on the crest of Lookout and eastward across the valley as far as Chattanooga Creek, Walker across the rest of the valley, and Cheatham on his right, occupying the south end of the line on Missionary Ridge, the rest of which was held by Breckinridge, with Stewart adjoining Cheatham and the other two divisions — Breckinridge's own and Hindman's, respectively under William Bate and Patton Anderson, the senior brigadiers — disposed along the northern extension of the ridge, but not all the way to the end overlooking the confluence of Chickamauga Creek and the Tennessee River, where the ground was so rough that Bragg had decided a few outpost pickets would suffice to hold it. The fact was, he had need to conserve his forces, especially since the latest of his two considerable detachments. Sidling left and right to fill the gaps created by the departure of Johnson and Cleburne, the troops disposed in three lines down the western face of the ridge were a good two lateral yards apart, not even within touching distance of each other. Admittedly this was a dangerous situation, but their chief depended on the natural strength of the position to compensate for what he lacked in numbers.

However, on the afternoon of the day Cleburne pulled back to follow Johnson up to Knoxville, Bragg was given cause to believe that his judgment was about to be challenged in the stiffest kind of way. Grant advanced a large body of troops — apparently Thomas's whole army — due east from Chattanooga, as if he intended to have an all-out try at breaking the thin-spread center of the rebel line. Though the mass of bluecoats called a halt about midway across the plain and began to intrench a new line just beyond range of the batteries on Missionary Ridge, Bragg was alarmed into recalling Cleburne, whose men were loading onto the cars when the summons reached him. Early next morning, November 24, the southern commander received a still greater shock in the form of a dispatch from an outpost on the right. Four blue divisions were crossing the Tennessee River immediately below the mouth of Chickamauga Creek, apparently for an assault on the practically undefended north end of the ridge. It was Sherman, the dispatch added, and Bragg knew at last that the Ohioan had not gone off to Knoxville, as he had supposed, but rather had gone into hiding behind the hills above Chattanooga, massing for the attack now being launched.

Hastily, he passed the word for Cleburne, whose troops had returned overnight from Chickamauga Station, to double-time his division northward and repulse if he could the four-division assault which, if successful, would flank the Confederates off the ridge their commander had believed to be impregnable: until now.

★ ★ ★

As was his custom when confronted with delays, long or short — including the four-month delay above Vicksburg, early this year — Grant used the three days, spent waiting for Sherman to get into position, to polish up the plan he had designed for Bragg's discomfort, improvising variations which he believed would make it at once more certain and complete. Such strain as there was, and admittedly there was much, was not so much on his own account as on Burnside's, and perhaps less on Burnside's account than on the reaction of the Washington authorities to the news that Knoxville was besieged, cut off from telegraphic communication with the outside world. "The President, the Secretary of War, and General Halleck were in an agony of suspense," Grant afterward recalled. "My own suspense was also great, but more endurable," he added, "because I was where I could do something to relieve the situation."

What he specifically had in mind to do, as he had told Burnside the week before, was to "place a force between Longstreet and Bragg" by throwing the latter into retreat and cutting the rail supply line in his rear, thus obliging Old Peter to raise his siege and "take to the mountain passes by every road" in search of food. At that time he had intended to leave the real work to Sherman and his Army of the Tennessee, with the Cumberland and Potomac troops more or less standing by to lend such help as might be needed. Thomas, for instance, was to menace but not attack the enemy center, while Hooker — reduced to a single division by the subtraction of Howard's two, which crossed at Brown's Ferry to be available as a reserve for the forces north and east of Chattanooga — stood guard at the foot of Lookout Valley, below Wauhatchie, to prevent a rebel counterstroke from there. But now, as he waited for Sherman to come up, Grant perceived that if Fighting Joe were strengthened a bit he might take the offensive on the right, against Lookout itself, and thus discourage Bragg from reinforcing his assailed right from his otherwise unmolested left. Accordingly, Thomas was ordered to send Cruft's division from Granger's corps to Hooker, and when Sherman's rear division, under Osterhaus, was kept from crossing by a breakdown of the pontoon bridge at Brown's Ferry, it too was sent to Hooker and replaced by another from Thomas, under Davis, who was detached from Palmer's corps. Thomas thus was reduced from six to four divisions, while Sherman still had four, Hooker three, and Howard two. Such a distribution seemed ideal, considering the assignments of the three commanders and the fact that the last was available as a reinforcement for the first.

These thirteen blue divisions, containing in all about 75,000 effectives, were to be employed by Grant in the following manner against the 43,000 effectives in Bragg's seven divisions. Sherman's effort on the left was still to be the main one, his orders being "to secure the heights on the northern extremity [of Missionary Ridge] to about the railroad tunnel before the enemy can concentrate against him," then drive southward down the crest, dislodging graybacks as he went. To assist in this, Thomas would menace the rebel center, fixing the defenders in position, and Howard would hold his corps "in readiness to act either with [Thomas] or with Sherman." Hooker meanwhile would deliver a secondary attack on the far right, and if successful — although this seemed unlikely, considering the difficulties of terrain on that quarter of the field — was to cross Lookout Mountain and Chattanooga Valley for a descent on Rossville, where he would turn sharp left and, matching Sherman's effort from the opposite direction, sweep northward up Missionary Ridge; at which point in the proceedings, with the rebel army clamped firmly between the two attackers north and south, Thomas's feint against the center might be converted into a true assault that would mean the end of Bragg.

One possible source of difficulty was a growing bitterness between the Federal armies, especially those of the East and West. "The

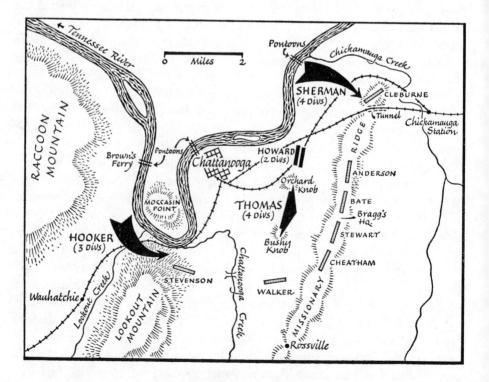

Potomac men and ours never meet without some very hard talk," one of Sherman's veterans wrote home. Westerners jeered at Easterners as paper-collar soldiers. "Bull Run!" they hooted, as if they themselves had never been whipped in battle. Resentful of the fact that the "Virginians," as they sometimes referred to these transfers from the eastern theater, had always had first call on new equipment and such luxuries as the quartermaster afforded, they would remark as they slogged past Hooker's bivouacs: "Fall back on your straw and fresh butter," and they would add, looking rearward over their shoulders: "What elegant corpses they'll make in those fine clothes!" After this would come the ultimate insult, delivered *sotto voce* from the roadside as the Easterners minced by: "All quiet on the Potomac." The latter in turn were disdainful, looking down their noses at the western soldiers, who preferred Confederate-style blanket rolls to knapsacks, walked with the long, loose-jointed stride of plowmen, and paid their officers little deference. "Except for the color of their uniforms, they looked exactly like the rebels," a New Yorker observed with unconcealed distaste. Individual confrontations were likely to produce at least a verbal skirmish. One of Blair's men, for example, wandering over for a look at Slocum's camps, was surprised to see the corps insignia — a five-pointed star — sewn or glued or stenciled onto practically everything in sight, from the flat crowns of forage caps to the tailgates of wagons. "Are you all brigadier generals?" he inquired, in real or feigned amazement. An Easterner explained that this was their corps badge, and asked: "What's yours?" The Westerner bristled. No such device had been known out here before, but he was unwilling to be outdone. "Badge, is it?" he snorted. For emphasis, he slapped the leather ammunition pouch he wore on his belt, just over his liver. "There, by Jesus! Forty rounds in the cartridge box and twenty in the pocket." In time, that would become his own XV Corps insignia — a cartridge box inscribed "Forty Rounds" — but tempers were not sweetened by such exchanges, in which neither antagonist took any care to disguise his low opinion of the other as a dude or a backwoodsman.

Nor were matters improved when the men of the three armies learned of their respective assignments in Grant's plan for lifting the siege of Chattanooga. This applied in particular to members of the Army of the Cumberland, whose role it was to stand on the defensive, merely bristling, while the other two armies "rescued" them by attacking on the left and right. Perhaps, too, they had heard by now of Grant's expressed concern that "they could not be got out of their trenches to assume the offensive." On top of all this, Thomas himself was hopping mad: not at Grant, though doubtless he masked some resentment he must have felt in that direction, but at Bragg, whose headquarters were plainly visible on the crest of the ridge across the way. A letter had arrived from the North for a Confederate officer, and Thomas, having determined that it was harmless from the security point of view, sent it through the lines with a note attached, requesting his one-time battery commander to pass it along. The letter came back promptly, with a curt indorsement on the note: "Respectfully returned to General Thomas. General Bragg declines to have any intercourse with a man who has betrayed his State." Thomas was incensed. "Damn him," he fumed; "I'll be even with him yet." Sherman, who was present, observed that the Virginian's poise, reputed to be impervious to shock, was shakable after all, at least when he was touched where he was tender. "He was not so imperturbable as the world supposes," the Ohioan testified years later, recalling Old Pap's reaction to the snub from his former superior and friend.

Hooker felt considerably better after Grant's revision of the attack plan, which changed his role from defensive to offensive, but the only change for Thomas was the loss of one third of his command, detached left and right to where the battle would be fought while he and his remaining four divisions stood by as spectators. Presently there was a further change, however, whereby they were given at least the chance for a ringside seat, a closer view of the action they were more or less barred from. On November 22 a rebel deserter reported that Bragg was about to evacuate his present lines. Though Grant mistrusted evidence so obtained, knowing how often those who imparted it were "loaded," this was altogether too serious to be ignored; Bragg might have plans for an all-out move against Burnside, availing himself of the railroad for a sudden descent on Knoxville, in which case Grant would be left holding the bag at Chattanooga. Moreover, the report gained credence when Buckner's division pulled out that afternoon, followed next morning by Cleburne's. Accordingly, Grant instructed Thomas to make a pretense of attacking Missionary Ridge by advancing his army, or what was left of it, about half the distance across the intervening plain. If he could do this, he would not only test the extent of the Confederate withdrawal, which might be greater than had been observed, and perhaps frighten Bragg into recalling the troops already detached; he would also secure a better location from which to demonstrate against the enemy center next day, November 24, when Sherman and Hooker — the former at last was moving into his jump-off position opposite the mouth of Chickamauga Creek — were scheduled to open their attacks against the flanks.

Thomas received his orders at 11 o'clock in the morning, and by 12.30 — so anxious were he and they for a share in the work — he had begun to maneuver his 25,000 veterans into positions from which to advance. In full view of their rivals from the Virginia and Mississippi theaters, as well as of the rebels out on the plain ahead and the tall ridge beyond, these soldiers of the Cumberland army made the most of this opportunity to refute the taunts that they had been permanently cowed by their defeat nine weeks ago. Granger's corps, with Wood in the lead and Sheridan in support, was the first to move out into the open. "It was an inspiring sight," a staff observer would recall. "Flags were flying; the quick, earnest steps of thousands beat equal time. The sharp commands of hundreds of company officers, the sound of drums, the ringing notes of the bugles, companies wheeling and countermarching and regiments getting into line, the bright sun lighting up ten thousand polished bayonets till they glistened and flashed like a flying shower of electric sparks, all looked like preparations for a peacetime pageant, rather than for the bloody work of death." Across the way, the Confederates thought so, too. They emerged from their trenches and stood on the parapets, calling to one another to come watch the Yankees pass in review. Palmer's corps followed Granger's; Johnson and Baird went through similar convolutions to get into line on the right. For the better part of an hour this continued. Then at about 1.30 the drums and bugles stepped up their tempo and changed their tone, beating and blaring the charge. That was the first the butternut watchers knew of the attack that was in mid-career before they got back into their trenches to resist it. Orchard Knob and Bushy Knob, fortified rebel outposts about in the center of the plain, were taken in a rush as the blue wave — flecked with shellbursts now, as if with foam — swept over them, engulfing those defenders who had not broken rearward in time for a getaway to the safety of the main line, back on Missionary Ridge. Promptly, or at any rate as soon as their officers could persuade them to leave off cheering and tossing their caps, the victors got to work with picks and shovels, turning the just-won intrenchments to face the other way, and there they settled down for the night, having taken their ringside seats for the fight which, now that the preliminaries were over and Sherman had his four divisions cached in their jump-off position on the left, was scheduled to begin soon after first light next morning.

A mile or more in advance of the line they had taken off from shortly after midday, Thomas and his Cumberlanders had drawn and shed the first blood after all, despite Grant's original intention to exclude them from any leading part in the accomplishment of their own deliverance. Their losses amounted to about 1100 killed and wounded, but they had inflicted nearly as many casualties as they suffered, including the prisoners they took. Perhaps by now, moreover, Grant had been disabused of his notion as to their reluctance to leave their trenches without the example of Sherman's men to inspire them. At any rate he seemed pleased: as well he might. Afterwards he told why. "The advantage was greatly on our side now," he wrote, "and if I could only have been assured that Burnside could hold out ten days longer" — this being the length of time he figured it would take him to finish whipping Bragg and then, if necessary, get reinforcements up to Knoxville — "I should have rested more easily. But we were doing the best we could for him and the cause."

Gathered about their campfires on the ridge, where they were disposed in three separate lines — one along its base, another about halfway up its steep western slope, and a third along its crest, four hundred feet above the plain — the Confederates admitted they had been surprised by the sudden conversion this afternoon of a two-corps "review" into an irresistible assault, but they still were not alarmed. Orchard Knob and Bushy Knob were merely outposts, no more integral to the defense of the main line of resistance than was the sheer bastion of Lookout Mountain, off on the distant left. What counted was Missionary Ridge itself. That was where the strength was, and the bluecoats, still beyond reach of all but the heaviest guns emplaced along the crest, would find a quite different reception awaiting them, when and if — although that seemed unlikely — they moved against it from their newly taken positions on the hilly plain below. "We feel we can kill all they send after us, notwithstanding our line is so thin that we are two yards apart," one of Breckinridge's Orphans wrote in his journal that night, looking down at the fires the Federals had kindled on the floor of the valley, as myriad as the stars they seemed to reflect. In this he was expressing the opinion of his army commander, who was convinced, as he said later, that Missionary Ridge could be "held by a line of skirmishers against any assaulting column."

A message wigwagged from Lookout after sundown, warning that a blue force seemed to be massing in the valley beyond for an uphill attack, gave Bragg no evident concern. Though the mountain was defended by only one brigade on its western flank and another on its summit, detached from Cheatham, he made no attempt to strengthen or adjust his dispositions there, apparently because he did not want to discourage the Federals, if they were indeed reckless enough to make the attempt, from breaking their heads against its rocky sheerness. Neither this new threat to his left, nor Thomas's advance that afternoon against his center, seemed to him sufficient cause for recalling either Johnson or Cleburne, who had pulled out yesterday and today. However, a message that reached him early next morning from the far right, warning that a sizable body of the enemy was crossing the Tennessee near the mouth of Chickamauga Creek, was quite another matter. He rode north at once to see for himself what this amounted to, and when he learned that what it amounted to was Sherman, whose troops he had thought were on their way to Knoxville, he reacted fast with a dispatch calling Cleburne back from Chickamauga Station. "We are heavily engaged," he told him, stressing the need for haste. "Move up rapidly to these headquarters."

There was in fact less need for haste than the southern commander knew. Sherman would not constitute an actual threat for some time now, though even he did not yet know that it would not be the rebels who would delay still further the opening of his carefully planned attack on the scantly defended northern end of Missionary Ridge, but geography, an unsuspected trick of the terrain. For the better part of the past week the red-haired Ohioan had been made nervously ill by the knowledge that he was falling behind the schedule Grant had set. "I feel as if I had a 30-pound shot in my stomach," he told a friend in the course of his muddy approach march. Today, though, all that was changed. Everything went smooth as clockwork. He had a thousand-man assault force over the river in boats by daylight, and behind them a pontoon bridge was thrown for a crossing by the main body before noon. Unopposed, except by a handful of butternut pickets who fled at their first sight of no less than four blue divisions coming at them, Sherman pushed forward onto the high ground he had examined nine days ago from the far side of the river. By late afternoon he had the position completely occupied: only to learn, to his acute dismay, that what he had taken was a detached hill, not actually even a part of Missionary Ridge, which lay beyond it, across a rocky valley. Red-faced, though he blamed the error on the inadequate map he had been given, he notified Grant of what had happened and instructed his troops to dig in for the night. They would continue — or, more properly speaking, begin — their assault on the enemy ridge at first light tomorrow, even though they had lost the element of surprise, which he and they had taken such precautions to achieve.

Seven miles away on the far right, southwest across the plain where the Cumberlanders occupied the ringside seats they had taken yesterday — "Thomas having done on the 23d what was expected of him on the 24th," Grant explained, "there was nothing for him to do this day except to strengthen his position" — a quite different kind of action was in progress, one in which the so-called "fog of war" prevailed in fact, not merely in the mind of the blue commander. Lookout had been wreathed in mist all morning and afternoon, except for tantalizing moments when the curtain would lift or part, only to descend or close again, affording the watchers little more than fleeting reassurance that the sheer bulk of the mountain was still there. Hooker's progress, if any, could not be determined by the eye, although, as Grant remarked from the command post shifted forward to Orchard Knob, "the sound of his artillery and musketry was heard incessantly." What was in progress, there beyond the gauzy screen, was what later would be called the "Battle Above the Clouds," despite objections by a correspondent that "there were no clouds to fight above, only heavy mist," and by Grant himself, who scoffed long afterwards: "The Battle of Lookout Mountain is one of the romances of the war. There was no such battle and no action even worthy to be called a battle on Lookout Mountain. It is all poetry."

Poetry it may have been, but if there were no clouds and no battle fought above them, there was at least some bleeding done, along with a great deal of hard work, in the course of this day-long skirmish in the mist. Hooker had about 12,000 troops, one division from each of the three armies on the field, with which to oppose the 1200-man brigade that stood between him and the crest of the mountain, where a second gray brigade was posted. Spread out along the east bank of Lookout Creek, with instructions to "fall back fighting over the rocks" if attacked, the Confederates did just that when the greatly superior Union mass forced a crossing near Wauhatchie and moved forward on a wide front, overlapping them on both flanks. Gun crews on the rearward heights were active at this stage of the attack, firing with precision into the blue ranks toiling upward, but this became increasingly difficult as the range decreased and it became necessary to raise the trails of the pieces higher and higher, until finally the tubes could not be depressed enough to keep them from overshooting; at which point the guns became only so much useless metal, so far as the defense of Lookout was concerned, and had to be removed to save them from being overrun. As they withdrew, the second gray brigade came down the rugged western slope to reinforce the first, and presently Stevenson sent a third brigade from the far side of the mountain. The three attempted to form a line among the rocks, but they soon found it was no use; the three blue divisions had caught the spirit of the chase and would not be denied. Supported by fire from batteries massed on Moccasin Point, just across the river, Geary's "paper collar" Easterners rounded the gray right flank and threatened to cut the defenders' line of retreat. There was a brief, hard fight near a farmhouse on a craggy bench about midway up the otherwise almost sheer north face of the mountain, and then once more the weight of numbers told. Again the Confederates fell back hastily, and this time Fighting Joe called a halt to consolidate his gains. Though he continued to probe upward, on through what was left of daylight into dusk — "I could see the whole thing," a rebel peering down from the crest was to say of the final stage of the contest; "It looked like lightning bugs on a dark night" — Hooker thought it best, except for a few patrols sent out to keep the enemy off balance, to rest his leg-weary men for tomorrow, which he expected to be as strenuous as today. He had suffered, or would suffer in the course of the three-day action, a total of 629 casualties, including 81 dead and 8 missing, but this seemed rather a bargain price for nearly half a mountain that practically everyone, blue or gray, had judged to be impregnable.

In point of fact he had won the whole mountain, though he would not know this until morning. Shortly after midnight, the Federal patrols having long since bedded down, Stevenson received instructions from Bragg to fall back across the eastern valley, in concert with Walker's division, and join in the defense of Missionary Ridge, where it was evident by now that the main Union effort would be centered. This he did, burning the single bridge over Chattanooga Creek as soon as his battered soldiers had crossed it in a darkness made profound by a total eclipse of the moon. Fighting Joe remained in full but isolated control of the "ever-lasting thunder storm" for which he had fought so hard today and was preparing to fight tomorrow, not knowing that it was entirely his already. Grant, of course, did not know this either, though in a wire he got off to Halleck, shortly after sundown, he sounded as if he did: "The fighting today progressed favorably. Sherman carried the end of Missionary Ridge, and his right is now at the tunnel, and his left at Chickamauga Creek. Troops from Lookout Valley carried the point of the mountain, and now hold the eastern slope and a point high up. Hooker reports two thousand prisoners taken, besides which a small number have fallen into our hands from Missionary Ridge."

Assuming from this, as well he might, that little remained to be accomplished around Chattanooga, Lincoln himself replied next morning with congratulations, gratitude, and a reminder: "Well done. Many thanks to all. Remember Burnside."

★ ★ ★

Little if any of the information Grant reported in his telegram to Halleck after sundown of November 24 had been true at the time he put it on the wire. Sherman not only had not "carried the end of Missionary Ridge," he had not even reached it; nor had Hooker, whose troops were still on the western, not the eastern slope of Lookout, "carried the point of the mountain." As for prisoners, Fighting Joe had inflicted fewer casualties than he suffered; the figure 2000 was a good deal closer to the total number of Confederates he encountered than it was to the number he had captured, which in fact was less than a tenth of the figure Grant passed on to Washington. However, before Lincoln's "Well done. Many thanks" arrived next morning, a part at least of what had been distorted was confirmed. The sun came up in a cloudless sky about 6.40; Lookout loomed with startling clarity, its curtain of mist dispelled. Watching from Orchard Knob, the Federal commander saw the rippling glitter of the Stars and Stripes break out on the 1200-foot peak, raised there by a patrol in proof that Geary's kid-glove Easterners had indeed "carried the point of the mountain" after all. Down on the plain, the Cumberland watchers broke into cheers at the sight, and Grant settled back, albeit impatiently, to wait for Hooker to complete his assignment, which was to proceed southeast across the intervening valley for a strike at Rossville and a drive northward up Missionary Ridge to meet Sherman driving south.

The wait, as it turned out, was a long one. Though the eastern slope of Lookout was less difficult than the western, and even afforded a winding road for the descent, the three divisions entered the valley below to find the bridge over fordless Chattanooga Creek destroyed and few materials at hand for constructing another; with the result that they were delayed some four hours in their advance on Rossville. Neither Grant nor the Cumberlanders, who knew that he did not intend to unleash them until the rebs intrenched to their front were firmly clamped between the two blue forces driving north and south along the ridge, took kindly to this evidence of Fighting Joe's ineptness, even though they had more or less anticipated it because of the blow-hard reputation he had brought with him from the East. This delay was mild in its effect, however, compared to the one on the far left, where no such failure had been expected of Grant's star general in command of his star army, whose reputation lately had become one of unfailing success and whose complaint had been that they could no longer get the Johnnies to fight them in the open.

Sherman went forward at dawn, as ordered, but found Cleburne in his path and was stopped cold. Rocked back — quite literally; for the defenders heaved boulders down on the heads of the attackers when their guns could no longer be brought to bear — he charged again and again, and again and again he was repulsed. "You may go up the hill if you like," he had rather casually instructed his brother-in-law Brigadier General Hugh Ewing, who commanded his lead division, adding: "Don't call for help until you actually need it." Ewing actually needed it about as soon as he got started, and Sherman not only supplied it, in the form of his three remaining divisions; he also threw in Howard's two, which were ordered to join him before midday. Yet nothing he could do would serve to move these six divisions over or around the one gray division in their path. About 3 o'clock, after eight hot hours of fighting, no appreciable gain, and more than 1500 casualties, including 261 captured when the Confederates made an unexpected sortie, Sherman admitted he had done all he could on this line. "Go signal Grant," he told a staff major. "The orders were that I should get as many as possible in front of me, and God knows there are enough. They've been reinforcing all day."

Those had not been his orders at the outset; nor were they now. "Attack again," Grant promptly replied, and Sherman did so, though with no better success. He was wrong, too, about enemy reinforcements. All he had had in his immediate front all day was Cleburne, whose five brigades had moved into position late the day before and organized it for defense by working most of the night, their task rendered more difficult by the eclipse of the moon, which for a time had made it necessary to work by sense of touch, including the spotting of the fourteen guns they employed today against the forty emplaced on the hill the Federals had occupied yesterday, off the nose of Missionary Ridge. Cleburne suffered a total of 222 casualties, less than one sixth the number he inflicted, and captured eight stands of colors, six of which were picked up from the ground where they had fallen in front of his line. Shortly before 4 o'clock Bragg sent him the first and only reinforcements of the day, the Orphan Brigade, detached from Bate to extend the right. The Kentuckians saw little action, since Sherman had desisted by then from his attempt to drive southward down the ridge, but one of them went up on his own for a look at what Cleburne's men had been doing all this time. "They had swept their front clean of Yankies," he wrote in his journal; "indeed, when I went up about sundown the side of the ridge in their front was strewn with dead yankies & looked like a lot of boys had been sliding down the hill side, for when a line of the enemy would be repulsed, they would start down hill & soon the whole line would be rolling down like a ball, it was so steep a hill side there."

While Cleburne and his troops were enjoying the respite they had earned, a message arrived from Hardee, directing him, as he afterwards reported, "to send to the center all the troops I could spare, as the enemy were pressing us in that quarter." Detaching two of his brigades, he accompanied them part of the way southward down the ridge to see that they made good time. "Before I had gone far, however," he added, still shocked by this development though his report was written some weeks later, "a dispatch from General Hardee reached me, with the appalling news that the enemy had pierced our center."

It was true; the Confederate center had been pierced. Bluecoats were clustered thick by now on Missionary Ridge, whooping and yelling in raucous celebration of a sudden, incredible victory scored less than three miles south of Sherman's all-day no-gain fight for Tunnel Hill, and hundreds of butternut prisoners were already on their way across the westward plain, taunted by their captors as they went: "You've been wanting to get there long enough. Now charge on Chattanooga!" Appalling as the news was, at least to gray-clad hearers, it became far more so when they learned of the manner in which it had come to pass. What one division had done against six, all morning and most of the afternoon on the far right, five divisions had not managed to do against four in resisting an attack that had lasted barely an hour from start to finish. Rephrasing the news only made it rankle more. Confronted by no worse than equal numbers in the vicinity of his own army headquarters, where he enjoyed positional advantages superior to those that enabled Cleburne's greatly inferior force to stand fast at the north end of the line, the vaunted southern fighting man had lost a soldiers' battle.

Joyous though the outcome was from the Union point of view, the slow hours leading up to it had been anything but pleasant for the overall Federal commander, who had stood by all this time on Orchard Knob and watched his carefully worked-out plans go by the board, or at any rate awry. After sending Howard's two divisions to Sherman, in futile hope that they would provide the added weight that would enable his old Army of the Tennessee to achieve the breakthrough on which those plans depended, Grant had Thomas detach Baird's division from his right and send it northward too. Thomas did so, but word came from

the unhappy Sherman that he already had more troops than he could find
room for on his present narrow front. So Baird was halted and put back
into line where he then was, on Thomas's left. That was about 2
o'clock, and except for this minor rearrangement — Granger's two divisions now were flanked by Palmer's — the Army of the Cumberland
had done nothing all day long; or all day yesterday either, for that matter. An hour later, two dispatches arrived from opposite directions.
One was from Hooker, reporting that he had finally reached Rossville,
where he had captured a quantity of supplies after driving the rebel outpost guards from the gap, and was sending Cruft's division north along
the crest of Missionary Ridge, supported on the left and right by Geary
and Osterhaus, who were deployed respectively on the western and
eastern slopes. The other dispatch was from Sherman and was far less
welcome, since what it said, in effect, was that he had shot his wad.
Disgruntled, Grant clamped down tighter on his unlit cigar. With
Fighting Joe at last where he wanted him, he had no intention of relax-
ing the pressure on either end of the enemy line. "Attack again," he signaled his red-haired lieutenant in reply, though with no different results,
as we have seen.

All this time he had been getting increasingly restless, and when
he saw what he took to be reinforcements moving northward along the
ridge, he began to worry in earnest that Bragg — whose headquarters he
could see plainly on the 400-foot crest, a mile and a half away, with
couriers arriving and departing — was about to go over to the offensive
against the stalled attackers off the north end of his line. Since Hooker
was still a good three miles off and could scarcely be expected to get
there before sunset, Grant figured that the quickest way to counteract
the danger would be for Thomas to menace the rebel center. He did not
like to order this, however, not only because it was an extremely hazardous undertaking, but also because the conditions he had insisted were
necessary before the movement could be attempted had not been
achieved; Bragg, unclamped, could give his full attention to any threat
against his center. At last, although reluctantly, he inquired of the Virginian standing beside him: "Don't you think it's about time to advance
against the rifle pits?" Instead of replying, Thomas continued to examine
the enemy ridge through his binoculars, as if to show that he was not
here to agree or disagree with opinions, but to execute orders. If Grant
wanted him to move forward against that bristling triple line of intrenchments, in the face of all those guns frowning down from the crest,
let him say so. Finally, at about 3.30, Grant did say so; whereupon
Thomas at once passed the word to his corps commanders. Wood and
Sheridan had their divisions in the center, with Baird supporting the
former on the left and Johnson supporting the latter on the right. The
signal for the attack would be the firing of six guns in quick succession,
at which time the Cumberlanders, kept idle all day yesterday and up to

now today, would advance and seize the rifle pits at the base of the ridge on the far side of the plain. At 3.40, ten minutes after Grant told Thomas to move out, the first of the six signal guns was fired under the personal direction of the ebullient and high-strung Gordon Granger, who stood on the Orchard Knob parapet, lifting and lowering his right arm in rapid sequence as he shouted: "Number One, *fire!* Number Two, *fire!* Number Three, *fire!* Number Four, *fire!* Number Five, *fire!*"

Before the sixth gun roared the leading elements were off. "Forward, guide center, march!" sixty regimental commanders shouted, and the 25,000 infantry in the four blue divisions began their plunge of nearly a mile across the wooded, hilly plain. "Number Six, *fire!*" Granger cried.

At first the only reaction on the part of the defenders was a scattering of shots from the gray pickets, who fell back hastily to gain the cover of the earthworks in their rear. Presently, though, as if recovering from the shock of unbelief that what they saw spread out below was real, the Confederate artillerists came alive. Bragg had 112 guns, and most of these were trained on the mile-wide formation of bluecoats moving toward them. "A crash like a thousand thunderclaps greeted us," one Federal was to remember, while a second observed that "the whole ridge to our front had broken out like another Ætna." The effect of this rain of projectiles, bursting over and among the close-packed ranks of the attackers, was like that of a sudden shower on a crowd of pedestrians; they quickened the pace, and those in the lead broke into a run. Well rested from their last previous advance, just over fifty hours ago, the men of the two center divisions caught something of the excitement of a race, each wanting to be first to reach the objective. Then too there was the knowledge that they were advancing in full view of their rivals on the left and right, who had been brought here from Mississippi and Virginia to extract them from the trap that had been devised to complete their defeat and destruction, but whose failure to carry out the required preliminaries had resulted in the unleashing of what had plainly been regarded, up to then, as the second team. Now the roles were more or less reversed; the second team had become the first, and those who had been intended to be saved were being called upon to do the saving. That was a pleasant thing to contemplate. Moreover there was the motive of revenge, a private matter strictly between them and the butternut soldiers just ahead. "Chickamauga! Chickamauga!" the Cumberlanders were yelling as they charged.

As they drew near the works at the base of the ridge they saw there could be no doubt they were going to take them. Already the defenders had begun to waver, flinching from the threat of contact, and presently, when the attackers closed to within pistol range, they broke. "A few rushed to the rear, and with frantic eagerness began to climb the slope," a Kansas infantryman would recall, "but nearly all, throwing down their muskets and holding up their hands in token of surrender, leaped to our side of the intrenchments and cowered behind them, for the hail of bullets raining down from the hill was as deadly to them as to us. The first line was won."

Winning it and holding it were different things, however: as the victors soon found out. Almost at once, though they were in full control of the lower works and though the ridge was so steep that few of the guns on its crest could be brought to bear on them, the position took on the aspect of a trap. Graybacks in the second line, midway up the slope, were pouring in a murderous, plunging fire, and cannoneers were rolling shells with sputtering fuzes down the hillside to explode in the lost rifle pits below. Amid all this confusion, company officers were brandishing their sabers and shouting for the new occupants to get to work with shovels, bayonets, anything that would help to reverse the parapets and throw some dirt between themselves and the marksmen overhead; but the principal reaction was a sort of aimless milling about, combined with a good deal of ducking and dodging, and a rapidly growing realization that the only practical solution was for them to get out of this untenable position as quickly as possible, either by retreating or continuing the charge. They chose the latter course, wanting more than anything to come to grips with their tormentors. By twos and threes, then by squads and platoons as the conviction took hold, blue-clad figures began to push forward, crouching low for traction on the slope.

At first their officers called after them to stop, but they paid no attention to this, and the lieutenants and captains, affected by the spirit of the men, rushed to join them, still gesturing with their swords and yelling, superfluously and illogically, out of habit: "Follow me!" Soon even the colonels and brigadiers had caught the spirit of the advance, and presently whole regiments were surging up the ridge, aligning as best they could on the colors while calling for the bearers to climb faster.

Down at the command post on Orchard Knob, this unexpected development — plainly visible, though reduced to miniature by distance — provoked the same reaction of stunned disbelief the rebel gunners had evinced when the blue mass first began its advance across the plain. Grant, for one, saw that he might have a first-class disaster on his hands if the Confederates repulsed the Cumberlanders, then followed through with a counterattack as the demoralized bluecoats tumbled down the slope and into the valley, where no reserves had been withheld to form a straggler line on which to rally. "Thomas, who ordered those men up the ridge?" he said angrily. Thomas replied in his usual quiet way: "I don't know. *I* did not." Grant turned to Granger, whom he had just reproached sharply for spending time with the guns instead of tending to his larger duties as a corps commander. "Did you order them up, Granger?" The New Yorker denied it, emphatically but enthusiastically, for he too had caught the spirit of the charge by now.

"No; they started up without orders," he said, and he added happily: "When those fellows get started all hell can't stop them." Grant turned his attention back to the action in front, remarking as he did so that somebody was going to suffer professionally if the men who had taken the bit in their teeth were repulsed.

At first that seemed altogether likely, considering the difficulties of terrain and Bragg's reputation as a counterpuncher; but not for long. Watching the upward progress of the sixty regiments as they engaged in a gallant rivalry to see which would be first to reach the crest, a staff colonel observed that "at times their movements were in shape like the flight of migratory birds, sometimes in line, sometimes in mass, mostly in V-shaped groups, with the points toward the enemy. At these points regimental flags were flying, sometimes drooping as the bearers were shot, but never reaching the ground, for other brave hands were there to seize them." That was how it looked in small from Orchard Knob. Up close, there was the gritty sense of participation, the rasp of heavy breathing, the drum and clatter of boots on rocky ground, and always the sickening thwack of bullets entering flesh and striking bone. Phil Sheridan saw and heard it so as he stood at the base of the ridge, watching his troops in their attempt to outstrip the rivals on their left in Wood's division, and accepted a drink from a silver flask held out by a staff captain. Before he drank he lifted the flask in salute to a group of gray-clad officers he saw in front of Bragg's headquarters, directly up the slope. "Here's to you!" he called. This may have failed to attract the attention of those for whom it was intended, but it certainly did not fail in the case of a pair of gunners in a nearby rebel battery. Swinging their pieces in his direction, they returned the salute with two well-placed rounds that kicked dirt over Sheridan and the captain standing beside him. "Ah, that is ungenerous!" he replied as he brushed off his uniform; "I shall take those guns for that." First, though, he took the drink, and then he started forward, necessarily on foot because his horse had been shot from under him during the advance across the plain.

There seemed an excellent chance that he would carry out his threat, for by now the second line had been overrun, midway up the slope, and his men were driving hard for the crest beyond. They had been helped considerably in advance by the Confederate dispositions, which were faulty in several respects, probably because the natural strength of the terrain had made the defenders overconfident to the point of not believing that their preparations would be tested. For example, standing orders that the troops in the lower rifle pits were to fire no more than a couple of massed volleys when the attackers came within effective range, then fall back to the intermediate position just uphill, had not been made clear to the troops involved; with the demoralizing result that while some had attempted to hold their ground, others had seemed to flee, infecting uninformed comrades with their apparent panic. Worst of all, perhaps, the officers who laid out the upper line had erred in placing it on the geographic, rather than on the "military" crest — literally along the topmost line, that is, rather than along the highest line from which the enemy could be seen and fired on — so that many of the Federal climbers found themselves protected by defilade practically all the way to the top, and once they were there they were able to take rebel strong-points under fire from the flank, distracting the attention of the defenders from the attackers coming straight at them up the ridge. Threatened thus, the graybacks here did what those below had done already; they broke and they broke badly, despite the pleas and curses of their officers, including Bragg himself, who rode among them in a desperate, last-minute effort to persuade them to rally and drive the winded enemy troops back down the slope. "Here is your commander!" he called to them. But they either ignored him, intent as they were on getting beyond the reach of the rapid-firing bluecoats, or else they taunted him with the army catch phrase: "Here's your mule!"

When the Federals crested the ridge they saw spread out below them on the reverse slope what one of them called "the sight of our lives — men tumbling over each other in reckless confusion, hats off, some without guns, running wildly." Too blown to cheer, the victors swung their caps and gestured for the laggards to hurry forward and share the view. "My God, come see them run!" a Hoosier private shouted over his shoulder. A Kansan, writing years later, relived the excitement provoked by the tableau. This beat Bull Run, Wilson's Creek, and the opening phases of Perryville and Stones River. This beat Chickamauga. "Gray clad men rushed wildly down the hill and into the woods, tossing away knapsacks, muskets, and blankets as they ran. Batteries galloped back along the narrow, winding roads with reckless speed, and officers, frantic with rage, rushed from one panic-stricken group to another, shouting and cursing as they strove to check the headlong flight. Our men pursued the fugitives with an eagerness only equaled by their own to escape; the horses of the artillery were shot as they ran; squads of rebels were headed off and brought back as prisoners, and in ten minutes all that remained of the defiant rebel army that had so long besieged Chattanooga was captured guns, disarmed prisoners, moaning wounded, ghastly dead, and scattered, demoralized fugitives. Mission Ridge was ours."

Bragg himself had barely escaped capture, as had Breckinridge, but not their two adjutants or some 3000 other prisoners, who were taken along with 7000 abandoned small arms and 37 cannon, one third of all Bragg had. One of these last was claimed by Sheridan in person, who came running up and leaped astride one of the two guns that had fired at him a few minutes ago. Wrapping his bandy legs around the tube, he swung his hat and cheered. Harker, who commanded his third brigade, followed suit by mounting a nearby gun in a similar fashion, but scorched his seat on the hot metal and could not sit a horse for the next two weeks. In this he was less fortunate than his division commander, who either was made of sterner stuff or else had chosen a cooler piece; at any rate Sheridan stayed astride the gun and continued to cheer and swing his hat, exultant over the reversal of what had happened two months ago at Chickamauga, where he had been among those in headlong flight from fury. All round him now the men were cheering, too, having caught their breath, and Granger rode up from Orchard Knob at the height of the celebration to engage in a sort of victory dance on horseback. "I'm going to have you all court-martialed!" he shouted, laughing. "You were ordered to take the works at the foot of the hill and you've taken those on top! You have disobeyed orders, all of you, and you know that you ought to be court-martialed!"

Not that the position had been taken without cost. In fact, the cost had been about as steep as the grade up which the attack was launched: particularly to the two divisions in the center. Wood suffered 1035 casualties, as compared to a combined total of 789 for Baird and Johnson, in support on the left and right; whereas Sheridan lost 1346, a bit over twenty percent of the 6500 infantry he had had when he started forward. Moreover, there was a good deal of variation in the losses by smaller units within the larger ones, depending on the luck of the draw in their assault on different portions of the ridge. Some had cover most of the way up and therefore contributed little to the amount of blood that was shed on the slope, while others had to pass through a continuous hail of bullets and were grievously battered in the process. An Indiana regiment, for instance, started its climb with 337 effectives and lost 202 of them, or nearly sixty percent, killed and wounded in the forty-five minutes required to reach the crest. After such bleeding and exertion by the infantry, and in the absence of cavalry, which was still beyond the river because of a continuing lack of forage on the south bank, it was small wonder no true pursuit was undertaken within the brief remaining span of daylight that followed the collapse of the rebel center. Sheridan, once he had come down off his perch astride the cannon, was eager to take up the chase, but the other division commanders were not, even though they had suffered fewer casualties, and Granger declined to unleash him.

Meanwhile the Confederates made good use of the respite thus allowed them. Continuing to hold off Sherman with one hand — no difficult task, since he attempted no renewal of his attack — Cleburne prevented a widening of the breakthrough with the other, and Stewart served Hooker in much the same fashion north of Rossville. Sunset was at 4.50; Hardee rallied his and Breckinridge's fugitives on the near side of Chickamauga Creek and began a withdrawal across it under cover of darkness, one hour later. The moon rose full, drenching the fields and the lost ridge with a glistening yellow light almost bright enough to read by, if anyone had been of a mind to read. "By 9 p.m. everything was across," according to Cleburne, "except the dead and a few stragglers lingering here and there under the shadows of the trees for the purpose of being captured, faint-hearted patriots succumbing to the hardships of the war and the imagined hopelessness of the hour."

Next morning Bragg continued the withdrawal southeast into Georgia, attempting to gain the cover of Taylor's Ridge, just beyond Ringgold, and leaving a trail of charred supply dumps and broken-down wagons, as well as four more cannon, to mark the line of his retreat. He had lost, in the course of the three-day action, November 23-25, fewer than half as many killed and wounded as his adversary — 361 and 2160, as compared to 753 and 4722 in those two doleful categories — but his 4146 captured and missing, in contrast to Grant's 349, raised the Confederate total of 6667 above the Federal 5824. But that was by no means all there was to the outcome of the fighting, nor was it fitting as a yardstick by which to measure the extent of the disaster. Bragg had lost a great deal more than the scant fifteen percent of his army which these figures indicated, and a great deal more than the 41 guns his cannoneers had abandoned, even though they amounted to more than a third of all he had. Guns and men could be replaced; Chattanooga, on the other hand, was now what a northern journalist called "a gateway wrenched asunder." The road lay open into the heartland of the South, and all that stood between the bluecoats and a rapid penetration was the battered and dispirited remnant of the force they had just driven from a position its commander had deemed impregnable. And in fact he was still of that opinion, believing that all it had lacked was men determined to defend it. Unlike Lee, who at Gettysburg had said, "It's all my fault," Bragg at this stage was not inclined to shoulder even a fraction of the blame for the outcome of the contest. The burden of his official report, submitted later, was that the flaw had been in his soldiers. "No satisfactory excuse can possibly be given for the shameful conduct of the troops ... in allowing their line to be penetrated. The position was one which ought to have been held by a line of skirmishers against any assaulting column." So he said, making no reference to the faulty dispositions or the unclear orders, both of which were his responsibility.

Not many agreed with him, however, either in his own army or in the one now in control of what he had lost. An Ohio infantryman, for example, coming forward on the morning after the battle for a walk along the northern end of Missionary Ridge, encountered the body of one of the men who had fought here under Cleburne. In the course of the recent siege he himself had learned something of privation, of the effects of hunger and exposure on the human spirit in its will to persevere against the odds, and this had given him a better understanding of the problems that had been so much a part of daily living for this dead soldier and others like him, whose own commander even now was blaming him and them, along with the bolters, for the loss of a position he and they had died in an attempt to save. Bending down for a closer look at the dead Confederate, the Ohioan afterwards told of what he saw. "He was not over fifteen years of age, and very slender in size. He was clothed in a cotton suit, and was barefooted; barefooted, [in] that cold and wet . . . November. I examined his haversack. For a day's ration there was a handful of black beans, a few pieces of sorghum, and a half dozen roasted acorns. That was an infinitely poor outfit for marching and fighting, but that Tennessee Confederate had made it answer his purpose."

Ultimately, if only in wry comment, at least one man on the Federal side agreed with Bragg as to the strength of the position, and that was Grant. Miffed by fortune's upset of his plans for Sherman's glorification, if not his own — on the first day, Thomas had played the leading role because Sherman was late in getting into position; on the second, Hooker had stolen the thunder from "above the clouds" while Sherman was attacking an undefended hill, just short of his true objective; on the third, Thomas once more occupied the limelight after Sherman was fought to a standstill by an opponent greatly his inferior in numbers — the over-all Union commander had sought to disassociate himself from a contest decided in outright violation not only of his wishes but also of his orders. "Damn the battle!" he was quoted as saying in that first fit of pique; "I had nothing to do with it." He recovered from this within a couple of hours, however, and got off a wire to Washington in which he had no reservations "in announcing a complete victory over Bragg." In time, he was even able to joke about it. Asked some years later whether he did not agree that his adversary had made a serious mistake in detaching Longstreet, he said he did, and when it was further suggested that Bragg must have considered his position impregnable, Grant agreed with that also, though his comment was accompanied by a smile and a shrewd look. "Well, it *was* impregnable," he said.

At any rate the Chattanooga gateway had been wrenched asunder, and what would come of this no man could say for certain, although some believed they knew, including members of the army now on the muddy and disconsolate retreat for Ringgold.

"Captain, this is the death knell of the Confederacy," a junior officer had remarked to his company commander as the withdrawal got under way from Missionary Ridge. "If we cannot cope with those fellows with the advantages we had on this line, there is not a line between here and the Atlantic Ocean where we can stop them."

"Hush, Lieutenant," the captain told him, slogging rearward through the darkness. "That is treason you are talking."

☆ ☆ ☆

Depressed by the necessity for withdrawal and retreat, following hard upon the collapse of the Confederate center, the lieutenant overlooked the effectiveness with which Cleburne, outnumbered four or five to one, had "coped" with Sherman all day on the right. Two days later at Taylor's Ridge, as if by way of a reminder, the Arkansan repeated his performance, this time with even greater success, against Hooker and odds no worse than three to one. Moreover, this repetition of his exploit was the outcome of what had been thought to be a suicide assignment. Bragg made it to Ringgold by nightfall of November 26, fifteen miles down the railroad linking Chattanooga and Atlanta, and though so far he was more or less intact, he knew the Federals were closing on him rapidly. Encumbered as he was, and they were not, by a slow-moving wagon train hub-deep in mud, they would be certain to overtake him tomorrow unless he could do something to halt or anyhow delay them long enough to give him a new head start in the race for Dalton, another fifteen miles down the track. Accordingly, as he pressed on beyond the town and through the gap in Taylor's Ridge, he sent peremptory orders for a last-ditch stand at that point by the division guarding his rear. This was Cleburne's. It seemed hard to sacrifice good soldiers for no other purpose than to gain a little time, but Bragg believed he had no choice if he was to avoid the total destruction that would be likely to ensue if he was overtaken in his present condition, strung out on the muddy roads. "Tell General Cleburne to hold this position at all hazards," he instructed the staff officer who delivered the message, "and keep back the enemy until the artillery and transportation of the army are secure."

Though he had been told to cross in the darkness and thus avoid being overtaken by the superior blue force closing on his rear, Cleburne had stopped for the night on the west side of bridgeless East Chickamauga Creek, two miles short of the town, so his men could sleep in dry clothes before resuming the march next morning. Such concern for their welfare was characteristic of him, but it was practical as well, since he was convinced that a rear-guard action, even with a deep-running stream at their backs, would cost them fewer casualties than would lengthen the sick lists after a crossing of the waist-deep ford and a chilly halt on the east bank with no sun or exercise to warm them. Bragg's orders for a stand beyond Ringgold "at all hazards" reached him shortly before midnight, and he rode ahead to reconnoiter the position by moonlight, leaving instructions for the troops to be roused and started forward three hours later. At daybreak, having crossed the creek and filed through the streets of the Georgia hamlet, they found him waiting for them at the mouth of the narrow gorge through which the railroad plunged on its way to Atlanta. After about an hour, which he spent posting them and his two guns in accordance with a plan he had worked out while they were asleep, an enemy column emerged from the nearby eastern limits of the town, the bluecoats marching four abreast, preceded by a line of skirmishers, textbook style. Cleburne had his 4100 brush-masked graybacks hold their fire until the unsuspecting skirmishers were practically upon them, then open up with everything they had, including pistols. The head of the blasted column drew back snakelike on the writhing body, which coiled itself into attack formation and then came on again, 12,000 strong. This time there was no surprise, but the repulse was as complete. Hooker — for that was who it was, and he still had the three divisions with which he had seized Lookout Mountain three days ago — paused to take stock, then probed on the right, attacking uphill, well south of the gap, in an attempt to outflank the defenders; only to find that they had shifted a portion of their force to meet him. Repulsed, he feinted again at the center and launched another uphill assault, this time on the left of the gap; but with the same result. Fighting Joe once more took stock, and decided to wait for his guns, which were toiling slowly eastward through the churned-up mud of the road from Chattanooga Valley, where they had been stalled until late yesterday for lack of a bridge strong enough to support them over Chattanooga Creek. By the time they arrived, the morning was gone and Cleburne had carried out his mission; Bragg's leading elements were in Dalton by then, safely beyond the craggy loom of Rocky Face Ridge, and the rest were not far behind, having been given the head start they needed. At a cost of 221 casualties — one less than he had suffered at Tunnel Hill — Cleburne had inflicted 442 by Hooker's admission. This was exactly double the number of his own, including more than a hundred prisoners he had taken along with three stands of colors, but Confederates were convinced the Federal losses were much larger than Fighting Joe admitted. A straggler from Walker's division, for example, watching the lop-sided contest from a grandstand seat on the ridge, pronounced it "the doggondest fight of the war." Down there below, he would recall years later, "the ground was piled with dead Yankees; they were piled in heaps. The scene looked unlike any battlefield I ever saw," he added. "From the foot to the top of the hill was covered with the slain, all lying on their faces. It had the appearance of the roof of a house shingled with dead Yankees."

Cleburne and his division, which he kept in position till well past noon and then withdrew unmolested, later received a joint resolution of thanks from Congress "for the victory obtained by them over superior forces of the enemy at Ringgold Gap, in the State of Georgia," but all that Hooker got from the engagement was a snub from his commander and an unceremonious return to inaction. When Grant came to write his report of the campaign, Ringgold Gap was referred to briefly as "a severe fight, in which we lost heavily in valuable officers and men," and he added an indorsement to Fighting Joe's own report that must have stung the glory-hungry general deeply: "Attention is called to that part of the report giving . . . the number of prisoners and small arms captured, which

is greater than the number really captured by the whole army." Grant
was an accomplished undercutter when he chose to be, and in Hooker's
case he did so choose, both now and down the years. For the present, he
directed him to hold his ground, "but to go no farther south at the expense of a fight." Cast once more in a supporting role, the unhappy
Easterner was told next day: "The object in remaining where you are is
to protect Sherman's flank while he is moving toward Cleveland and Loudon."

Once more the volatile redhead was the star, this time in a production entitled "The Relief of Knoxville," where Longstreet was still
hanging on and keeping Burnside under siege, despite Grant's prediction
that he would "take to the mountain passes" once the Chattanooga Federals came between him and Bragg and stood astride the rail supply line
in his rear. Sherman was altogether willing to try another turn at playing the role of savior, but he took care to have it understood that he did
not want to be left stranded in the backwater region once he had wound
up what he was being sent there to accomplish. He was utterly opposed to tying up masses of troops, least of all his own, for the purpose of
protecting a handful of civilians, many of whom he considered of doubtful loyalty anyhow, while the main stream of the war ran on to slaughter
elsewhere. "Recollect that East Tennessee is my horror," he wrote
Grant on December 1 from the near bank of the Hiwassee, while preparing to set out next day for Loudon and Knoxville. "That any military
man should send a force into East Tennessee puzzles me. Burnside is there
and must be relieved, but when relieved I want to get out, and he
should come out too."

Burnside's men were in complete agreement; in fact, they had
been so all along. "If this is the kind of country we are fighting for," one
of them had declared on completing the southward march across the
barrens, "I am in favor of letting the rebs take their land and their niggers
and go to hell, for I wouldn't give a bit an acre for all the land I have seen
in the last four days." The trouble was that Lincoln very much wanted
them there, for precisely the reason Sherman derided: to protect the
Union-loyal citizens and relieve them of their long-borne yoke of Confederate oppression. Moreover, cooped up as they now were in Knoxville, under siege by Longstreet's two divisions plus a third that had arrived under Bushrod Johnson, the problem was not so much how to get
out as it was how to survive on meager rations. They were no longer
fighting for East Tennessee — which in point of fact they had abandoned, except for Knoxville itself and Cumberland Gap, the now inaccessible escape hatch fifty air-line miles due north — but for their lives.

Old Peter and his soldiers were about as unhappy outside the
town — and incidentally, what with the wretched supply conditions,
about as hungry — as the Federals hemmed inside it. He had probed for

chinks in the blue defenses and, finding none, had waited for the reinforcements Bragg had said were on the way. Fewer than half of the
promised 11,000 arrived, but at least they brought him up to a strength
nearly equal to that of the force besieged. He continued to search for
weak spots, though with no better success. By November 27 — the
date of Cleburne's fight at Ringgold — coincident with the issuance of
orders for accomplishing a breakthrough at a point he had selected, a
rumor had begun to spread that Bragg had been whipped at Chattanooga. How much truth there was in this, Longstreet did not know, but
in reply next day to a suggestion from McLaws that the thing to do was
abandon the siege without further delay and return at once to Virginia,
lest they be caught between two superior Union forces, he persisted in
his belief that the best solution, if the rumor of Bragg's defeat was true,
was a quick settlement of the issue here at Knoxville. His reasons were
twofold: first because it would not do to leave a fellow commander in
the lurch, no matter how little regard he had for him personally, and second because a victory over Burnside would dispose of at least one of the
two menaces to a successful withdrawal if such a course became unavoidable. That is, if he stayed where he was, at least for a time, he might
draw off a portion of the blue horde rumored to be in pursuit of Bragg,
and he might also simplify his own problems, when and if the time came
for him to retire eastward over the primitive mountain roads. "It is a
great mistake to suppose that there is any safety for us in going to Virginia if General Bragg has been defeated," he told his fellow Georgian,
"for we leave him at the mercy of his victors, and with his army destroyed our own had better be also, for we will be not only destroyed,
but disgraced. There is neither safety nor honor in any other course than
the one I have chosen and ordered. . . . The assault must be made at the
time appointed, and must be made with a determination which will insure success."

The time appointed was dawn next morning, November 29, and
the point selected for assault was Fort Loudon, a bastioned earthwork
previously established by the Confederates at the tip of a long salient extended westward from the main line of intrenchments to include a hill
1000 yards beyond the limits of the town; Fort Sanders, the Federals had
renamed it, in memory of the young cavalry brigadier who had made a
successful bridge-burning raid through the region, back in June, but had
been mortally wounded two weeks ago at Campbell Station, supposedly
by a civilian sniper, while resisting the gray advance on Knoxville. Originally Longstreet had intended to use Alexander's artillery to soften up
the objective before the infantry moved in; then later he decided to stake
everything on surprise, which would be sacrificed if he employed a preliminary bombardment, and on the sheer weight of numbers massed on a
narrow front. Assigning two brigades from McLaws to the assault, with
a third in support from Jenkins — a total of about 3000 effectives, as

compared to fewer than 500 within the fort, including the crews of its twelve guns — he posted the first wave of attackers within 150 yards of the northwest corner of the works in the cold predawn darkness of the night whose end would be the signal for the jump-off. The advance was to be conducted in columns of regiments, the theory being that such a deployment in depth would give added power to the thrust and insure that there would be no wait for reinforcements in case unexpected resistance developed in the course of the attack. It was stressed that there was to be no pause for anything whatever, front or rear, and that the main thing was to keep moving. Once the position had been overrun, the surviving remnant of the garrison, if any, was to be driven eastward through the town, so that other strongpoints along the line could be taken in reverse, thus effecting a quick reduction of the whole.

Longstreet had planned carefully, with close attention to such details as had occurred to him and the specialists on his staff. But so had Burnside: as the butternut attackers discovered when they rushed forward through the dusk of that frosty Sunday morning. The first thing they struck was wire — not barbed wire; that refinement was achieved by a later generation; but telegraph wire — looped and stretched close to the ground between stakes and stumps, which not only tripped the men at the heads of the columns and sent them sprawling and cursing, but also served as an unmistakable warning to the garrison that an assault was being launched. Nor was this innovation by any means the worst of what the Confederates encountered in the course of the next hour. Continuing through and over the wire, laced in a network knee- and ankle-high, they gained the ditch to find that it was nine feet deep — not five, as they had been informed by the staffers who had done their reconnoitering with binoculars at long range — while the parapet just beyond it, slippery with half-frozen mud and a powdering of sleet, was crowded along its crest with blue defenders, ranked shoulder to shoulder and thoroughly alert, who delivered steady blasts of musketry into the packed gray mass a dozen feet below. Without scaling ladders, which no one had thought would be needed, some men tried to get up and over the wall by standing on the shoulders of their comrades, but were either hurled back or captured. One color bearer, hoisted in this fashion, was grabbed by the neck and snatched from sight, flopping like a hooked fish being landed, and though three others managed to plant their standards on the rim of the parapet, a succession of replacements was required to keep them there. All this time, two triple-shotted guns on the flank were raking the trench with a fire that dropped the dead and injured of the two assault brigades beneath the feet of the men of the third, who came sliding down the counterscarp to add to the wedged confusion. By now, with the Federals heaving lighted shells into the ditch, where they exploded with fearful effect at such close quarters, it had become apparent, at least to the troops immediately concerned, that the only result of continuing the attack — if, indeed, it could still be called that at this stage — would be to lengthen the already considerable list of casualties. When Longstreet, coming forward with two more brigades which he intended to throw into the uproar, learned from McLaws of the woeful state of affairs up ahead, he rejected pleas by Jenkins and Johnson that they be allowed to try their hand, and ordered the recall sounded. Dazed and panicky, the survivors of the three committed brigades, or anyhow so many of them as did not prefer surrender to the further risk of catching a bullet in the back, returned through the wire they had encountered at the outset.

Generous as ever in such matters, Burnside promptly sent out a flag of truce and offered his old friend permission to remove his dead and injured from the ditch. Longstreet gratefully accepted, then requested and received an extension of the truce when this turned out to be a heavier task than he had supposed without a close-up view of the carnage. He had suffered 813 casualties — 129 killed, 458 wounded, and 226 captured — in contrast to his adversary, who lost, out of 440 effectives in Fort Sanders at the time of the attack, a total of 8 killed and 5 wounded. Thirteen was a decidedly lucky number in this instance; moreover, the high proportion of dead among the scant handful of Union casualties resulted from the fact that the defenders had exposed no more than their heads to the rattled fire of the attackers, and even then for only so long as it took them to take aim, which was scarcely necessary at that range and with a target of that size. Up to now, the Federal losses for the whole campaign had been higher than those of the besiegers, but today's losses brought the over-all totals, North and South, respectively to 693 and 1142. What was more, these figures were approximately final; for while the work of removing Old Peter's unfortunates was in progress he received a message informing him that Bragg had fallen back from Chattanooga, thirty miles down the railroad toward Atlanta, and advising him to do the same from Knoxville, either toward Georgia or Virginia, but in any case to have Wheeler report to Dalton as soon as possible with his three brigades. Having complied with the instructions for the cavalry to move out, Longstreet decided to hold his ground until he could discover whether the road to Dalton was open. He remained in front of Knoxville until he learned from a captured dispatch, two days later, that Sherman was on the way from Loudon with six divisions, which would give the Federals ten in all, as compared to the Confederate three. Accordingly, on the night of December 3 he put his trains in motion, not toward Dalton but northeast, in the direction of Virginia, and followed shortly after dark next evening with his infantry, unobserved. "Detached from General Lee, what a horrible failure is Longstreet!" an eastern diarist exclaimed, forgetful of his great day at

Chickamauga and unaware that he had been sent to East Tennessee not only against his wishes but also over his protest that the expedition was tactically unwise, both from Bragg's point of view and his own.

Sherman arrived next day, riding in ahead of the relief column, which he had stopped at Maryville, eighteen miles to the south, when he learned that the Confederates had pulled back from Knoxville. Notified that the siege had been lifted, Grant proposed that Longstreet be pursued and driven across the Blue Ridge, thus to assure his removal as a hovering threat; but the redhead wanted no part of such an assignment. "A stern chase is a long one," he protested, determined to resist all efforts to shift him farther eastward from the Mississippi Valley, which he still saw as the cockpit of the war. Now that the big river had been cleared and reclaimed from source to mouth, he preferred to deal with the rebels down in Georgia, intending to complete their destruction by driving them back on the rail transportation hub eighty air-line miles across the mountains in their rear. "My troops are in excellent heart," he declared, "ready for Atlanta or anywhere." Instructed to detach two divisions to strengthen the Knoxville garrison — in case Longstreet attempted a comeback from Rogersville, where he had ended his unpursued retreat, sixty-odd miles up the Holston — Sherman had Granger proceed north from Maryville with Sheridan and Wood, while he himself returned by easy stages to Chattanooga with his own four divisions. There he found Thomas and Hooker taking a well-earned rest from their recent exertions. Now that blustery weather had arrived, the Cumberland and ex-Potomac troops were already settling down in winter camps. Similarly, Grant had transferred his headquarters back to Nashville, and presently Sherman joined him there, enjoying such relaxations as the Tennessee capital afforded outside work hours, which the two friends spent designing further troubles for the Confederacy, to be undertaken in various directions as soon as the weather cleared.

That would not be for some time, however. Meanwhile Thomas was occupying himself with the establishment of a military cemetery on Orchard Knob. The thought had occurred to him, on the day he took it, that this would make a lovely burying ground for the Union soldiers who had fallen or were still to fall in the battles hereabout, and almost before the smoke of his involuntary assault on Missionary Ridge had cleared he had a detail at work on the project. When the chaplain who was to be in charge inquired if the dead should be buried in plots assigned to the states they represented — as was being done at Gettysburg, where Lincoln had spoken a couple of weeks ago — the Virginian lowered his head in thought, then shook it decisively and made a tumbling gesture with both hands. "No, no; mix 'em up, mix 'em up," he said; "I'm tired of states rights." Increased responsibility, accompanied by a growing and reciprocal fondness for the men in the army he now led, had brought a new geniality to the stolid Rock of Chickamauga. He had even begun to tell stories on himself: as, for example, of the soldier who had come to him recently asking for a furlough. "I aint seen my old woman, General, for four months," the man explained. If he thought this could not fail in its persuasiveness he was wrong. "And I have not seen mine for two years," Thomas replied. "If a general can submit to such privation, surely a private can." Evidently the soldier had not previously considered this connection between privates and privation. At any rate he looked doubtful. "I don't know about that, General," he said. "Me and my wife aint made that way."

No doubt the Virginian's jovial mood was also due in part to the fulfillment of his vow to be "even" with his former battery commander for the insult he had received in the course of the siege that had been lifted when his Cumberlanders took the bit in their teeth and charged, "against orders," up Missionary Ridge. What was more, his satisfaction was enlarged by the knowledge that he had obtained it despite the department commander's attempt to limit his participation in the action that had finally put revenge within his reach. In that double sense, as the outcome applied to both commanders, past and present, his gratification was doubly sweet.

As for Bragg, the reconsolidation of his army behind Rocky Face Ridge — completed on November 28 with the arrival of Cleburne, who was greeted with cheers for his rebuff of Hooker at Ringgold Gap the day before — brought with it not only a sense of relief at having been delivered from destruction, but also a certain added ruefulness, a letdown following hard upon the relaxation of tension. He knew now just how narrow his escape had been and, what was worse, how unlikely he was to be so fortunate in another contest with the foe who had just flung him out of a position he had judged impregnable. Worst of all, perhaps, was the attitude of the troops, then and since. "Here's your mule!" they had hooted in response to his attempt to rally them with "Here is your commander," and he took it as a bad sign that, far from being despondent over their disgrace, many of them were grinning at the memory of their headlong break for safety. "Flicker, flicker!" they called to one another in their camps, that being their accustomed cry when they saw a man whose legs would not behave in combat. "Yaller-hammer, Alabama! Flicker, flicker, yaller-hammer!" they would shout, adding by way of reprise: "Bully for Bragg! He's hell on retreat!" Though this might be no more than their way of shrugging off embarrassment, it did not seem to him to augur well for the outcome of the next blue-gray confrontation, wherever that might be. "We hope to maintain this position," he wired Richmond the following day, "[but] should the enemy press on promptly we may have to cross the Oostenaula," another fifteen miles to the south, beyond Resaca. "My first estimate of our disaster was not too large," he continued, "and time only can restore order and morale. All possible aid should be pushed on to Resaca." And having gone so far in the way of admission, he went one step further. "I deem it due to the cause and to myself," he added, "to ask for relief from command and an investigation into the causes of the defeat."

Perhaps this last was no more than a closing flourish, such as he had employed at the end of the letter sent out after Murfreesboro, wherein he invited his lieutenants to assess his military worth. In any event, just as they had taken him at his word then, whether he meant it or not, so did Davis now. "Your dispatches of yesterday received," the adjutant general replied on the last day of November. "Your request to be relieved has been submitted to the President, who, upon your representation, directs me to notify you that you are relieved from command, which you will transfer to Lieutenant General Hardee, the officer next in rank and now present for duty."

There he had it. Or perhaps not quite; perhaps the flourish — if that was what it was — could be recalled. At any rate, if he was thus to be brought down, he would do what he could to assure that his was not a solitary departure. In sending next day, by special messenger, "a plain, unvarnished report of the operations at Chattanooga, resulting in my shameful discomfiture," he included a letter addressed to his friend the Commander in Chief, who had sustained him invariably in the past. "The disaster admits of no palliation," he wrote, "and is justly disparaging to me as a commander. I trust, however, you may find upon full investigation that the fault is not entirely mine. . . . I fear we both erred in the conclusion for me to retain command here after the clamor raised against me. The warfare has been carried on successfully, and the fruits are bitter. You must make other changes here, or our success is hopeless. . . . I can bear to be sacrificed myself, but not to see my country and my friends ruined by the vices of a few profligate men." Specifically he charged that Breckinridge had been drunk throughout the three-day battle and "totally unfit for any duty" on the retreat, while Cheatham was "equally dangerous" in that regard. As for himself, he said in closing, "I shall ever be ready to do all in my power for our common cause, but feel that some little rest will render me more efficient than I am now. Most respectfully and truly, yours, Braxton Bragg, General, &c."

Still in Dalton the following day, December 2, he tried a different tack in a second letter — still headed "Headquarters Army of Tennessee" and still signed "General, Commanding" — in which he assessed the tactical situation and made an additional suggestion: "The enemy has concentrated all his available means in front of this army, and by sheer force of numbers has triumphed over our gallant little band. No one estimates the disaster more seriously than I do, and the whole responsibility and disgrace rest on my humble head. But we can redeem the past. Let us concentrate all our available men, unite them with this gallant little army, still full of zeal and burning to redeem its lost character and prestige, and with our greatest and best leader at its head — yourself, if practicable — march the whole upon the enemy and crush him in his power and his glory. I believe it practicable, and I trust that I may be allowed to participate in the struggle which may restore to us the character, the prestige, and the country which we have just lost."

Whatever might come of this in the future, and he knew how susceptible to flattery Davis was in that respect, there was nothing for him to do now, after waiting two whole days for them to be rescinded, but carry out the instructions he had received. Painful though the parting was, at least for him — "The associations of more than two years, which bind together a commander and his trusted troops, cannot be severed without deep emotion," he remarked in the farewell address he issued that same day — he turned his duties over to Hardee, as ordered, and took his leave. In the seventeen months he had been at its head the Army of Tennessee had fought four great battles, three of which had ended in retreat though all save the last had been claimed as victories. Similarly, in the equal span of time ahead, it would fight a great many more battles that would likewise be claimed as victories although they too — once more with a single exception, comparatively as bloody as Chickamauga — would end in retreat; but not under Bragg. His tenure had ended. "I shall proceed to La Grange, Georgia, with my personal staff," he notified Richmond, "and there await further orders."

CHAPTER

✗ **9** ✗

Spring Came on Forever

★ ✗ ☆

NEWS OF THE GREAT CHATTANOOGA VICTORY, which had begun on Monday and ended on Wednesday, spread throughout the North on the following day, November 26. By coincidence, in a proclamation issued eight weeks earlier at the suggestion of a lady editor, Lincoln had called upon his fellow citizens "to set apart and observe the last Thursday of November next, as a day of thanksgiving and praise to our beneficent Father who dwelleth in the Heavens." Instituted thus "in the midst of a civil war of unequaled magnitude and severity," this first national Thanksgiving was intended not only as a reminder for people to be grateful for "the blessings of fruitful fields and healthful skies," but also as an occasion for them to "implore the interposition of the Almighty Hand to heal the wounds of the nation and to restore it, as soon as may be consistent with the Divine purposes, to the full enjoyment of peace, harmony, tranquillity, and Union." Now that word of what had happened yesterday on Missionary Ridge was added to the "singular deliverances and blessings" for which the public was urged to show its gratitude today, it seemed to many that the Almighty Hand had interposed already, answering a good part of their prayers in advance, and that the end so fervently hoped for might be considerably nearer than had been supposed when the proclamation was issued in early October, not quite two weeks after the shock of Chickamauga caused those hopes to take a sudden drop. "This is truly a day of thanksgiving," Halleck wired Grant as the news of his latest triumph went out across the land and set the church bells ringing as wildly as they had rung after Donelson and Vicksburg.

Moreover, just as Thomas had taken his revenge for Chickamauga, so had Banks obtained by now at least a degree of recompense for the drubbing he had suffered in September, when he opened his campaign against coastal Texas with Franklin's botched attack on Sabine Pass. Revising his plan by reversing it, end for end, he decided to start with a landing near the Mexican border, then work his island-hopping way back east. It was true the pickings would be much slimmer at the outset, for there was little that far down the coast that was worth taking; but the objectives were unlikely to be as stoutly defended, and he would be moving toward, rather than away from, his New Orleans base of supplies, which should serve to encourage his men to fight harder and move faster, if for no other reason than to hasten their return. Accordingly, after sending Franklin's unhappy soldiers to Berwick for a renewed ascent of the Teche — an ascent that would end abruptly on November 3 at Grand Coteau, ten miles short of Opelousas, where the column was assaulted and driven back through Vermilionville to New Iberia by Richard Taylor and Tom Green, who lost 180 and inflicted 716 casualties, including the 536 fugitives they captured — he loaded aboard transports a 3500-man division, commanded by a Maine-born major general with the resounding name of Napoleon Jackson Tecumseh Dana, who set out from New Orleans on October 26, escorted by three gunboats. This time Banks went along himself, presumably to guard against snarls and hitches. At any rate there were none. On November 2 — the day before Franklin was thrown into sudden reverse at Grand Coteau — Dana put his troops ashore at Brazos Santiago, off the mouth of the Rio Grande, and though he encountered practically no resistance, the gray-backs having been withdrawn to thicken the defenses in East Texas, Banks did not let this tone down the announcement of his achievement. "The flag of the Union floated over Texas today at meridian precisely," he notified Washington. "Our enterprise has been a complete success." Four days later he occupied Brownsville, just under thirty miles inland, opposite Matamoros, and sent for the puppet governor Andrew Hamilton, who had been waiting off-stage all this time and who was established there at the southernmost tip of the state and the nation, along with his gubernatorial staff of would-be cotton factors, before the month was out. Meanwhile Banks had followed up his initial success with a series of landings on Mustang and Matagorda islands, thus gaining control of Aransas Pass and Matagorda Bay. But that was all; that was as far as he got on his way back east. Galveston and the mouth of the Brazos River were too strongly held for him to attack them with Dana's present command, reduced as it was by garrison detachments, and Halleck could not be persuaded to accede to requests for reinforcements. All Banks had gained for his pains these past three months, including the drubbing at Sabine Pass, was a couple of dusty border towns and a few bedraggled miles of Texas beach, mostly barren dunes, which he described as "inclement and uncomfortable, in consequence of the sterility of the soil and the violence of the northers."

Despite the flamboyance with which they were announced — "My most sanguine expectations are more than realized," Banks had proclaimed after occupying Brownsville; "Everything is now as favorable

as could be desired" — the authorities in Washington were not inclined
to include these shallow coastal lodgments, amounting in fact to little
more than pinpricks along one leathery flank of the Texas elephant,
among those things for which the nation should be thankful on its first
Thanksgiving. Hamilton governed far too small and remote an area for
his claims to be taken seriously, inside or outside the state, and it seemed
to Lincoln, although he later thanked Banks politically for his "successful and valuable operations," that all the general had really done was
shift some 3500 of his soldiers off to the margin of the map, where they
were of about as much tactical value as if their transports had gone to the
bottom of the Gulf with them aboard. Halleck expressed an even dim-
mer view of the proceedings. "In regard to your Sabine and Rio Grande
expeditions," he protested to the Massachusetts general, "no notice of
your intention to make them was received here till they were actually
undertaken." Old Brains was especially irked by the setback at Grand
Coteau, which he saw as the result of an unwise division of force, occasioned by the unauthorized excursion down the coast. In his opinion, the
Teche, the Atchafalaya, and the Red afforded the best approach to the
Lone Star State, and though he understood that these streams were at
present unusable even as supply routes, being practically dry at this season of the year, he wanted the entire command standing by for the early
spring rise that would convert them into arteries of invasion. For this
reason, as well as for the more general one that none were available, he
flatly refused to send reinforcements for an attack on Galveston by the
amphibious force which by now had worked its way back east to Matagorda, explaining testily that even if such an attack were successful —
and even if the place did not turn out to be a trap, as it had done before
— it still would be no more than a diversion from the true path of conquest.

Besides, there were nearer and larger frets, invoking more immediate concern; Knoxville, for example. "Remember Burnside," Lincoln had wired yesterday in response to Grant's announcement that victory was within reach at Chattanooga. He could breathe easier now, for
while Longstreet's siege was apparently still in progress he knew that
Grant, relieved of the presence of Bragg, was free to turn his attention
to East Tennessee. But there was a still nearer fret, not sixty miles southwest of Washington, and though in this case the Union force was on the
offensive, the Commander in Chief had learned from long experience
that the strain of waiting for news of an expected success was quite as
great as waiting for news of an expected failure — particularly since experience had also taught him, all too often, that anticipated triumphs
had a way of turning into the worst of all defeats; Chancellorsville, for
instance. Meade at last had resumed his movement southward, having
taken a two-week rest from the exertion of crossing the Rappahannock,
and on this Thanksgiving morning the leading elements of his army were

over the Rapidan, entering the gloomy western fringe of the Wilderness in whose depths Joe Hooker had come to grief in early May, just short of seven months ago.

His decision to cross and come to grips with Lee on that forbidding ground was based in part on a growing confidence proceeding from the fact that he had whipped him rather soundly in both of their recent face-to-face encounters, first at Bristoe Station and then at Rappahannock Bridge and Kelly's Ford. Moreover, there had come to hand on November 21 a detailed intelligence report which put the enemy strength at less than 40,000 effectives, as compared to his own 84,274 on that date. Actually, Lee's total was 48,586; Meade had just under, not just over, twice as many troops as his opponent. But in any case the preponderance was encouraging, and after four days of studying the figures and the map, he distributed on November 25 a circular directing his five corps commanders to be ready to march at 6 o'clock next morning, half an hour before sunrise. Lee's two corps were strung out along the south bank of the river, one east and the other west of Clark's Mountain, their outer flanks respectively at Mine Run and Liberty Mills, some thirty miles apart; Meade's plan called for a crossing by the downstream fords, well beyond the Confederate right, and a fast march west, along the Orange Turnpike, for a blow at the rebel east flank before Lee could bring up his other corps in support. Unlike Hooker, Meade designed no feints or diversions, preferring to concentrate everything he had for the main effort. He relied entirely on speed, which would enable him to strike before his adversary had time to get set for the punch, and on the known numerical advantage, which would be far greater than two to one if he could mass and commit his fifteen infantry divisions before the rebel six achieved a concentration. All this was explained to the responsible subordinates, whose marches began on schedule from their prescribed assembly areas near Ely's and Germanna fords, well downstream from the apparently unsuspecting graybacks in their works across the way. Aside from a heavy morning fog, which screened the movement from enemy lookouts on Clark's Mountain — more evidence, it would seem, of the interposition of the Almighty Hand in favor of the Union on this Thanksgiving Day — the weather was pleasant, a bit chilly but all the more bracing for that, and the blue troops stepped out smartly along the roads and trails leading down to the various fords that had been assigned them so that a nearly simultaneous crossing could be made by the several columns. That too had been part of the design combining speed and power.

As always, there were hitches: only this time, with speed of such vital importance, they were even more exasperating than usual. What was worse, they began to crop up almost at the outset. Meade had planned with elaborate care, issuing eight-day rations to the men, for instance, to avoid the need for a slow-rolling wagon train that would take

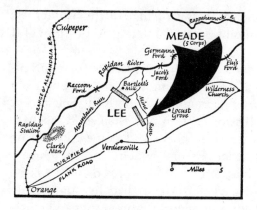

up a lot of road space and require a heavy guard; but he had neglected the human factor. In the present case, as it turned out, that factor was embodied in the person of William French, successor to Sickles as chief of the III Corps, which had been enlarged to three divisions, the same as the other four. A Maryland-born West Pointer nearing fifty, French was a tall, high-stomached man with an apoplectic look and a starchy manner, a combination that led an unadmiring staffer to remark that he resembled "one of those plethoric French colonels who are so stout, and who look so red in the face, that one would suppose someone had tied a cord tightly around their necks." So far in the war, though he had taken part in all the army's major fights except the two Bull Runs and Gettysburg, he had not distinguished himself in action. Today — and tomorrow too, for that matter, as developments would show — his performance was a good deal worse than undistinguished. Assigned to cross at Jacob's Ford, which meant that he would have the lead when the five corps turned west beyond the river, since it was the nearest of the three fords being used, he was not only late in arriving and slow in crossing, but when he found the opposite bank too steep for his battery horses to manage, he sent his artillery down to Germanna Ford and snarled the already heavy traffic there. It was dusk before he completed his crossing and called a halt close to the river, obliging those behind him to do likewise. Next morning he stepped off smartly to make up for the time lost, then promptly took the wrong fork in the road and had to countermarch. By the time he got back on the right track, the sun was past the overhead and the movement was a full day behind schedule. Red-faced and angry, for Meade was prodding him hard by now, French set out once more through the woods that screened his approach to the rebel flank, supposedly a mile away, only to run into butternut skirmishers who obliged him to call a halt and deploy his lead division. Having done so, he started forward again; but not for long. Well short of the point he had been due to reach before he encountered anything more than an outpost handful of gray pickets, the firing stepped up and he found himself involved in a full-scale engagement with what seemed to be most of the rebels in the world. Apparently Lee had made good use of the time afforded him yesterday and today by the hitches that had slowed and stalled the greatly superior mass of bluecoats closing upon him through the woods on his downstream flank.

The southern commander had indeed made use of the time so

generously allowed him. Informed by a scout on Thanksgiving Eve of the issue of eight-day rations across the way, he alerted his outposts to watch for a movement, upstream or down, and sat back to await developments. If the length of the numerical odds disturbed him, he could recall the victory he had scored against even longer odds, seven months ago, on practically this same ground. "With God's help," a young officer on his staff wrote home that night, "there shall be a Second Chancellorsville as there was a Second Manassas." Next morning, when Stuart reported the Federals crossing in force by the lower fords, Lee sent word for Hill to take up the march from beyond Clark's Mountain to join Ewell, whose corps was on the right, and shifted army headquarters the following day from Orange to Verdiersville, a dozen miles east on the plank road. He did not know yet whether Richmond or the Army of Northern Virginia was Meade's objective, but in any case he decided that his best course was to move toward him, either for an interception or for a head-on confrontation. In the absence of Ewell, who was sick, the Second Corps was under Early; Lee told him to move eastward, down the pike toward Locust Grove, and keep going until he encountered something solid. That was how it came about that French, once he recovered his sense of direction and got back on the track that afternoon, found the woods a-boil with graybacks and was obliged to engage in an unscheduled and unwanted fight, one mile short of his immediate objective. Dusk ended the brief but savage action, in which each side lost better than 500 men, and Lee had Early fall back through the darkness to a previously selected position on the far side of Mine Run, which flowed due north into the Rapidan. Hill would arrive tomorrow and extend the line southward, taking post astride the turnpike and the plank road east of Verdiersville, while Early covered the approaches to Bartlett's Mill on the far left, near the river. Anticipating with satisfaction his first purely defensive full-scale battle since Fredericksburg, just two weeks short of a full year ago, Lee instructed his men to get busy with their shovels, preparing for a repetition of that butchery.

Coming up next day through a driving rain, which made for heavy marching, the bluecoats found themselves confronted by a seven-mile line of intrenchments whose approaches had been cleared for over-lapping fields of fire. They took one look at the rebel works, sited for-biddingly along a ridge on the dominant west bank of the boggy stream, and decided that for the high command to send down orders for an assault would amount to issuing death warrants for most of the troops involved. Their generals rather thought so, too, when they came forward to reconnoiter, Warren and Sedgwick on the left and right, French in the center, and Sykes and Newton in reserve. By sundown the rain had slacked and stopped, giving way to a night so cold that the water froze in the men's canteens. All next day the reconnaissance continued, and so did the spadework across the run. Meade was determined to try for a breakthrough, if one of his corps commanders would only find him a weak spot in the gray defenses. That night, when Sedgwick and Warren reported that they had found what he wanted on both flanks of the position, he issued instructions for an attack next morning. Sedgwick would open with his artillery at 7 o'clock on the right, attracting the enemy's attention in that direction, and Warren would launch an assault one hour later at the far end of the line, supported by French, who would feint at the rebel center, and by Newton, who would mass in his rear to help exploit the breakthrough. Similarly, Sykes would move up in close support of Sedgwick, whose bombardment was to be followed by an assault designed to shatter the Confederate left. With both flanks crumpled and no reserves on hand to shore them up, Lee would fall back in disarray and the blue reserves would hurry forward to complete his discomfort and destruction.

So ordered, so attempted; Uncle John opened on schedule with all his guns, while down the line the troops assigned to the assault grew tenser by the minute as the time drew near for them to go forward. Whatever the generals back at headquarters might be thinking, the men themselves, crouched in the brush and peering out across the slashings at the icy creek which they would have to cross to get within reach of the butternut infantry — dug in along the ridge to await their coming and probably smiling with anticipation as they fondled their rifles or stood by their double-shotted cannon — did not like any part of the prospect now before them. For one thing, a man even lightly hit, out there in the clearing where no stretcher bearers could get to him, would probably die in this penetrating cold. For another, they judged that their deaths would be purposeless, for they did not believe that the assault could possibly succeed. Waiting for the guns to stop their fuming, some of the soldiers passed the time by writing their names and addresses on bits of paper or chips of wood, which they fastened inside their clothes; "Killed in action, Nov. 30, 1863," a few of the gloomier or more cynical ones among them added. However, just as the artillery left off roaring and they were about to step forward into chaos, a message arrived from army headquarters: "Suspend the attack until further orders." Later they found out why. On the far left, after discovering by daylight that the rebel defenses had been greatly strengthened overnight, Warren sent word that the assault he had deemed feasible yesterday would be suicidal today. Meade rode down to see for himself, found that he agreed with this revised assessment, and canceled the attack, both left and right. Grinning, the reprieved troops discarded their improvised dogtags and thought higher than ever of Warren, who they were convinced had done the army as solid a service, in avoiding a disaster here today, as he had performed five months ago at Little Round Top or last month at Bristoe Station. What he had done, they realized, took a special kind of courage, and they were grateful not only to him but also to the commander who sustained him. Moreover, since supplies were getting low and a thaw would soften the crust of frozen mud without which no movement would be possible on the bottomless roads, Meade decided next day to withdraw the army over the same routes by which it had crossed the Rapidan, five days back, and entered this luckless woodland in the first place. So ordered, so done; the rearward movement began shortly after sunset, December 1, and continued through the night.

Glad as the departing bluecoats were to escape the wintry hug of the Wilderness, they were more fortunate than they knew. On November 30, the expected assault not having been launched against his intrenchments, Lee had been summoned to the far right by Wade Hampton, who, recovered from his Gettysburg wounds and returned to duty, had discovered an opening for a blow at the Union left, not unlike the one Hooker had received in May on his opposite flank, a few miles to the east. Looking the situation over, the southern commander liked what he saw, but decided to wait before taking advantage of it. He felt sure that Meade would attack, sooner or later, and he did not want to pass up the near certainty of another Fredericksburg, even if it meant postponing a chance for another Chancellorsville. By noon of the following day, however, with the Federals still immobile in his front, he changed his mind. "They must be attacked; they must be attacked," he muttered. Accordingly, he prepared to go over to the offensive with an all-out assault on the flank Hampton had found dangling. Sidling Early's men southward to fill the gap, Lee withdrew two of Hill's divisions from the trenches that evening and massed them south of the plank road, in the woods beyond the vulnerable enemy left, with orders to attack at dawn. Early would hold the fortified line overlooking Mine Run, while Hill drove the blue mass northward across his front and into the icy toils of the Rapidan. This time there would be no escape for Meade, as there had been for Hooker back in May, for there would be twelve solid hours of daylight for pressing the attack, not a bare two or three, as there had been when Jackson struck in the late afternoon, under circumstances otherwise much the same.

"With God's blessing," the young staffer had predicted six nights ago, "there shall be a Second Chancellorsville." But he was wrong; God's blessing was withheld. When the flankers went forward at first light they found the thickets empty, the Federals gone. Chagrined (for though he had inflicted 1653 casualties at a cost of 629 — which brought the total of his losses to 4255 since Gettysburg, as compared to Meade's 4406 — he had counted on a stunning victory, defensive or offensive), Lee ordered his cavalry after them and followed with the infantry, marching as best he could through woods the bluecoats had set afire in their wake. It was no use; Meade's head start had been substantial, and he was back across the Rapidan before he could be overtaken. In the Confederate ranks there was extreme regret at the lost opportunity, which grew in estimation, as was usual in such cases, in direct ratio to its inaccessibility. Early and Hill came under heavy criticism for having allowed the enemy to steal away unnoticed. "We miss Jackson and Longstreet terribly," the same staff officer remarked. But Lee, as always, took the blame on his own shoulders: shoulders on which he now was feeling the weight of his nearly fifty-seven years. "I am too old to command this army," he said sadly. "We should never have permitted those people to get away."

★ ★ ★

Although Davis shared the deep regret that Meade had not been punished more severely for his temporary boldness, he did not agree with Lee as to where the blame for this deliverance should rest. Conferring with the general at Orange on the eve of the brief Mine Run campaign, two weeks after his return from the roundabout western journey — it was the Commander in Chief's first visit to the Army of Northern Virginia since its departure from Richmond, nearly sixteen months before, to accomplish the suppression of Pope on the plains of Manassas — he had not failed to note the signs that Lee was aging, which indeed were unmistakable, but mainly he was impressed anew by his clear grasp of the tactical situation, his undiminished aggressiveness in the face of heavy odds, and the evident devotion of the veterans in his charge. Davis's admiration for this first of his field generals — especially by contrast with what he had observed in the course of his recent visit to the Army of Tennessee — was as strong as it had been four months ago, when he listed his reasons for refusing to accept Lee's suggestion that he be replaced as a corrective for the Gettysburg defeat. By now though, as a result of what had happened around Chattanooga the week before, he had it once again in mind to shift him to new fields. Directed to take over from Bragg, who was relieved on the day Meade began his withdrawal from the Wilderness, Hardee replied as he had done when offered the command two months ago. He appreciated "this expression of [the President's] confidence," he said, "but feeling my inability to serve the country successfully in this new sphere of duty, I respectfully decline the command if designed to be permanent." Davis then turned, as he had turned before, to Lee: with similar results. The Virginian replied that he would of course go to North Georgia, if ordered, but "I have not that confidence either in my strength or ability as would lead me of my own option to undertake the command in question."

It was Lee's opinion that Beauregard was the logical choice for the post he had vacated a year and a half ago; but Davis liked this no better than he did the notion, advanced by others, that Johnston was the best man for the job. He had small use for either candidate. Deferring action on the matter until he had had a chance to talk it over with Lee in person, he wired for him to come to Richmond as soon as possible.

Meantime the Chief Executive kept busy with affairs of state. Congress met for its fourth session on December 7, and the President's year-end message was delivered the following day.

"Gloom and unspoken despondency hang like a pall everywhere," a diarist noted on that date, adding: "Patriotism is a pretty heavy load to carry sometimes." Davis no doubt found it so on this occasion, obliged as he was to render a public account of matters better left unreviewed, since they could only thicken the gloom and add to the despondency they had provoked in the first place. In any case he made no attempt to minimize the defeats of the past fall and summer. Congress had adjourned in May; "Grave reverses befell our arms soon after your departure," he admitted at the outset. Charleston and Galveston were gleams in the prevailing murk, but they could scarcely relieve the fuliginous shadows thrown by Gettysburg and Vicksburg, along with other setbacks in that season of defeat, and the bright flame of Chickamauga had been damped by Missionary Ridge, which he confessed had been lost as the result of "misconduct by the troops." So it went, throughout the reading of the lengthy message. Gains had been slight, losses heavy. Nor did Davis hold out hope of foreign intervention, as he had done so often in the past. Diplomatically, with recognition still withheld by the great powers beyond the Atlantic, the Confederacy was about as near the end of its rope as it was financially, with $600,000,000 in paper — "more than threefold the amount required by the business of the country" — already issued by the Treasury on little better security than a vague promise, which in turn was dependent on the outcome of a war it seemed to be losing. He could only propose the forcible reduction of the volume of currency; which in itself, as a later observer remarked, amounted to "a confession of bankruptcy." The end of the contest was nowhere in sight, he told the assembled legislators, and he recommended a tightening and extension of conscription as a means of opposing the long numerical odds the Federals enjoyed. "We now know that the only reliable hope for peace is the vigor of our resistance," he declared, "while the cessation of their hostility is only to be expected from the pressure of their necessities." In closing he came back to the South's chief asset, which had won for her the sometimes grudging admiration of the world. "The patriotism of the people has proved equal to every sacrifice demanded by their country's need. We have been united as a people never were united under like circumstances before. God has blessed us with success disproportionate to our means, and under His divine favor our labors must at last be crowned with the reward due to men who have given all they possessed to the righteous defense of their inalienable rights, their homes, and their altars."

Lincoln's year-end message to the Federal Congress, which also convened on the first Monday in December, was delivered that same

Tuesday, thus affording the people of the two nations, as well as those of the world at large, another opportunity for comparing the manner and substance of what the two leaders had to say in addressing themselves to events and issues which they viewed simultaneously from opposite directions. The resultant contrast was quite as emphatic as might have been expected, given their two positions and their two natures. Not only was there the obvious difference that what were admitted on one hand as defeats were announced as victories on the other, but there was also a considerable difference in tone. While Davis, referring defiantly to "the impassable gulf which divides us," denounced the "barbarous policy" and "savage ferocity" of an adversary "hardened in crime," the northern President spoke of reconciliation and advanced suggestions for coping with certain edgy problems that would loom when bloodshed ended. He dealt only in passing with specific military triumphs, recommending the annual reports of Stanton and Halleck as "documents of great interest," and contented himself with calling attention to the vast improvement of conditions in that regard since his last State of the Union address, just one week more than a year ago today. At that time, "amid much that was cold and menacing," he reminded the legislators, "the kindest words coming from Europe were uttered in accents of pity that we were too blind to surrender a hopeless cause"; whereas now, he pointed out, "the rebel borders are pressed still further back, and by the opening of the Mississippi the country dominated by the rebellion is divided into distinct parts, with no practical communication between them." A share of the credit for this accomplishment was due to the Negro for his response to emancipation, Lincoln believed. "Of those who were slaves at the beginning of the rebellion, full one hundred thousand are now in the United States military service, about one half of which number actually bear arms in the ranks; thus giving the double advantage of taking so much labor from the insurgent cause, and supplying the places which otherwise must be filled with so many white men. So far as tested, it is difficult to say they are not as good soldiers as any."

Having said so much, and reviewed as well such divergent topics as the budget, foreign relations, immigration, the homestead law, and Indian affairs, he passed at once to the main burden of his message, contained in an appended document titled "A Proclamation of Amnesty and Reconstruction." Lately, in answer to a letter in which Zachariah Chandler, pleased by the outcome of the fall elections but alarmed by reports that the moderates were urging their views on the President during the preparation of this report on the State of the Union, had warned him to "stand firm" against such influences and pressures — "Conservatives and traitors are buried together," the Michigan senator told him; "for God's sake don't exhume their remains in your Message. They will smell worse than Lazarus did after he had been buried three days" — Lincoln had sought to calm the millionaire drygoods merchant's fears. "I am glad the elections this autumn have gone favorably," he replied, "and that I have not, by native depravity, or under evil influences, done anything bad enough to prevent the good result. I hope to 'stand fast' enough not to go backward, and yet not to go forward fast enough to wreck the country's cause." The appended document, setting forth his views on amnesty for individuals and reconstruction of the divided nation, was an example of what he meant. In essence, it provided that all Confederates — with certain specified exceptions, such as holders of public office, army generals and naval officers above the rank of lieutenant, former U.S. congressmen and judges, and anyone found guilty of mistreating prisoners of war — would receive a full executive pardon upon taking an oath of loyalty to the federal government, support of the Emancipation Proclamation, and obedience to all lawful acts in reference to slavery. Moreover, as soon as one tenth of the 1860 voters in any seceded state had taken the oath prescribed, that state would be readmitted to the Union and the enjoyment of its constitutional rights, including representation in Congress.

Reactions varied, but whether its critics thought the proclamation outrageous or sagacious, a further example of wheedling or a true gesture of magnanimity, there were the usual objections to the message as proof of Lincoln's ineptness whenever he tried to come to grips with the English language. "Its words and sentences fall in heaps, instead of flowing in a connected stream, and it is therefore difficult reading," the *Journal of Commerce* pointed out, while the Chicago *Times* was glibly scornful of the backwoods President's lack of polish. "Slipshod as have been all his literary performances," the Illinois editor complained, "this is the most slovenly of all. If they were slipshod, this is barefoot, and the feet, plainly enough, never have been shod." However, the New York *Times* found the composition "simple and yet perfectly effective," and Horace Greeley was even more admiring. He thought the proclamation "devilish good," and predicted that it would "break the back of the Rebellion," though he stopped well short of the *Tribune*'s White House correspondent's judgment that "no President's message since George Washington retired into private life has given such general satisfaction as that sent to Congress by Abraham Lincoln today."

Just how general that satisfaction might be, he did not say, but one person in emphatic disagreement was Charles Sumner, who, as he sat listening to the drone of the clerk at the joint session, favored visitors and colleagues with a demonstration of the inefficacy of caning as a corrective for infantile behavior. Watching as he "gave vent to his half-concealed anger," a journalist observed that, "during the delivery of the Message, the distinguished Senator from Massachusetts exhibited his petulance to the galleries by eccentric motions in his chair, pitching his documents and books upon the floor in ill-tempered disgust."

Sumner's disgust with this plan for reconstruction was based in part on his agreement with the New York *Herald* editor who, commenting on the proposal that ten percent of the South's voters be allowed to return the region to the Union, stated flatly that he did not believe there were "that many good men there." Besides, the Bay State senator had his own notion of the way to deal with traitors, and it was nothing at all like Lincoln's. In a recent issue of the *Atlantic Monthly* he had advocated the division of the Confederacy, as soon as it had been brought to its knees, into eleven military districts under eleven imported governors, "all receiving their authority from one source, ruling a population amounting to upward of nine millions. And this imperial domain, indefinite in extent, will also be indefinite in duration . . . with all powers, executive, legislative, and even judicial, derived from one man in Washington." Although he admitted that "in undertaking to create military governors, we reverse the policy of the Republic as solemnly declared by Jefferson, and subject the civil to the military authority," he thought such treatment no worse than was deserved by cane-swinging hotheads who had brought on the war by their pretense of secession. So far as he was concerned, though he continued to deny the right of secession, he was willing to accept it as an act of political suicide. Those eleven states were indeed out of the Union, and the victors had the right to do with them as they chose, including their resettlement with good Republican voters and the determination of when and under what conditions they were to be readmitted. Most of the members of his party agreed, foreseeing a solid Republican South.

Lincoln wanted that too, of course, but he did not believe that this was the best way to go about securing it. For one thing, such an arrangement was likely to last no longer than it took the South to get back on its feet. For another, he wanted those votes now, or at any rate in time for next year's presidential and congressional elections, not at the end of some period "indefinite in duration." Therefore he considered it "vain and profitless" to speculate on whether the rebellious states had withdrawn or could withdraw from the Union, even though this was precisely the issue on which most people thought the war was being fought. "We know that they were and we trust that they shall be in the Union," he said. "It does not greatly matter whether in the meantime they shall be considered to have been in or out."

This was a rift that would widen down the years, but for the present the Jacobins kept their objections within bounds, knowing well enough that when readmission time came round, it would be Congress that would sit in judgment on the applicants. Southward, however, the reaction was both violent and sudden. Lincoln's ruthlessness — an element of his political genius that was to receive small recognition from posthumous friends who were safe beyond his reach — had long been apparent to his foes. For example, in addition to the unkept guarantees he had given slaveholders in his inaugural address, he had declared on revoking Frémont's emancipation order that such matters "must be settled according to laws made by law-makers, and not by military proclamations," and he had classified as "simply 'dictatorship' " any government "wherein a general, or a President, may make permanent rules of property by proclamation." Thus he had written in late September of the first year of the war, exactly one year before he issued his own preliminary emancipation proclamation, which differed from Frémont's only in scope, being also military, and which showed him to be a man who would hold to principles only so long as he had more to gain than lose by them. Observing this, Confederates defined him as slippery, mendacious, and above all not to be trusted.

Certainly Davis saw him in that light, increasingly so with the passing months, and never more so than in this early-December amnesty offer. "That despot," he now called Lincoln, whose "purpose in his message and proclamation was to shut out all hope that he would *ever* treat with us, on *any* terms." Acceptance would amount to unconditional surrender, Davis asserted, and by way of showing what he meant he paraphrased the offer: "If we will break up our government, dissolve the Confederacy, disband our armies, emancipate our slaves, take an oath of allegiance binding ourselves to him and to disloyalty to our states, he proposes to pardon us and not to plunder us of anything more than the property already stolen from us. . . . In order to render his proposals so insulting as to secure their rejection, he joins to them a promise to support with his army one tenth of the people of any state who will attempt to set up a government over the other nine tenths, thus seeking to sow discord and suspicion among the people of the several states, and to excite them to civil war in furtherance of his ends."

Thus Davis reflected a reversed mirror-image of his adversary's offer, saying: "I do not believe that the vilest wretch would accept such terms." Without exception southern editors agreed. "We who have committed no offense need no forgiveness," they protested, quoting Benjamin Franklin's reply to a British offer of amnesty. "How impudent it is," the Richmond *Sentinel* observed of Lincoln, "to come with our brothers' blood upon his accursed hands, and ask us to accept his forgiveness! But he goes further. He makes his forgiveness dependent on terms." Congress was more vigorous in its protest. Resolutions were introduced denouncing "the truly characteristic proclamation of amnesty issued by the imbecile and unprincipled usurper who now sits enthroned upon the ruins of Constitutional liberty in Washington City," while others made it abundantly clear that the people of the Confederacy, through their elected representatives, did "hereby, solemnly and irrevocably, utterly deny, defy, spurn back, and scorn the terms of amnesty offered by Abraham Lincoln in his official proclamation." All such resolutions were tabled, however, upon the protest by one member that they "would appear to dignify a paper emanating from that wretched and detestable abortion, whose contemptible emptiness and folly will only receive the ridicule of the civilized world." It was decided, accordingly, that "the true and only treatment which that miserable and contemptible despot, Lincoln, should receive at the hands of the House is silent and unmitigated contempt."

Unmitigated this contempt might be, but silent was the one thing it was not. In fact, as various members continued to plumb and scale the various depths and heights of oratory, it grew more strident all the time. Evidently they had been touched where they were sore. And indeed, in its review of Lincoln's message, the New York *World* had warned that such would be the case. Violence was a characteristic of the revolutionary impulse, the *World* declared; "You can no more control it than a flaxen hand can fetter flame"; so that if what the President was really seeking was reconciliation — or even, as Davis claimed, division within the Confederate ranks — he could scarcely have chosen a worse approach. "If Mr Lincoln were a statesman, if he were even a man of ordinary prudence and sagacity, he would see the necessity for touching the peculiar wound of the South with as light a hand as possible." What the editor had in mind was slavery, and so did the frock-coated gentlemen in Richmond, along with much else which they believed was endangered by this war of arms and propaganda. In the course of their two-month session they gave the matter a great deal of attention, and before it was over they produced a joint resolution, issued broadcast as an "Address of Congress to the People of the Confederate States." Specifically an attack on the Lincoln administration for its policies and conduct of the war, the resolution was also an exhortation for the southern people to continue their resistance to northern force and blandishments, including the recent amnesty proclamation.

> It is absurd to pretend that a government really desirous of restoring the Union would adopt such measures as the confiscation of private property, the emancipation of slaves, the division of a sovereign state without its consent, and a proclamation that one tenth of the population of a state, and that tenth under military rule, should control the will of the remaining nine tenths. The only relation possible between the two sections under such a policy is that of conqueror and conquered, superior and dependent. Rest assured, fellow citizens, that although restoration may still be used as a war cry by the northern government, it is only to delude and betray. Fanaticism has summoned to its aid cupidity and vengeance, and nothing short of your utter subjugation, the destruction of your state governments, the overthrow of your social and political fabric, your personal and public degradation and ruin, will satisfy the demands of the North.

About midway through the lengthy document, after charging that the Federals had provoked the war and were "accountable for the

blood and havoc and ruin it has caused," the legislators presented a catalogue of "atrocities too incredible for narration."

> Instead of a regular war, our resistance to the unholy efforts
> to crush out our national existence is treated as a rebellion, and the
> settled international rules between belligerents are ignored. Instead
> of conducting the war as betwixt two military and political organiza-
> tions, it is a war against the whole population. Houses are pillaged
> and burned. Churches are defaced. Towns are ransacked. Clothing of
> women and infants is stripped from their persons. Jewelry and me-
> mentoes of the dead are stolen. Mills and implements of agriculture
> are destroyed. Private saltworks are broken up. The introduction of
> medicines is forbidden. Means of subsistence are wantonly wasted to
> produce beggary. Prisoners are returned with contagious diseases....

The list continued, then finally broke off. "We tire of these indignities
and enormities. They are too sickening for recital," the authors confessed, and passed at once to the lesson to be learned from them. "It is
better to be conquered by any other nation than by the United States.
It is better to be a dependency of any other power than of that.... We
cannot afford to take steps backward. Retreat is more dangerous than
advance. Behind us are inferiority and degradation. Before us is everything enticing to a patriot." As for how the war was to be won, the
answer was quite simple: by perseverance.

> Moral like physical epidemics have their allotted periods, and
> must sooner or later be exhausted and disappear. When reason re-
> turns, our enemies will probably reflect that a people like ours, who
> have exhibited such capabilities and extemporized such resources, can
> never be subdued; that a vast expanse of territory with such a popu-
> lation cannot be governed as an obedient colony. Victory would not
> be conquest. The inextinguishable quarrel would be transmitted "from
> bleeding sire to son," and the struggle would be renewed between
> generations yet unborn.... There is no just reason for hopelessness or
> fear. Since the outbreak of the war the South has lost the nominal
> possession of the Mississippi River and fragments of her territory; but
> Federal occupation is not conquest. The fires of patriotism still burn
> unquenchably in the breasts of those who are subject to foreign dom-
> ination. We have yet in our uninterrupted control a territory which,
> according to past progress, will require the enemy ten years to over-
> run.

In conclusion — though the words came strangely from the lips
of men who, despite their nominal membership in a single national party,
comprised perhaps the most fractious, factious political assembly in the
western world to date — the legislators recommended "unfaltering

trust," on the part of the southern people in their leaders, as the surest guide if they would tread "the path that leads to honor and peace, although it lead through tears and suffering and blood."

> Let all spirit of faction and past party differences be forgotten in the presence of our cruel foe.... We entreat from all a generous and hearty co-operation with the government in all branches of its administration, and with the agents, civil or military, in the performance of their duties. Moral aid has the "power of the incommunicable," and, by united efforts, by an all-comprehending and self-sacrificing patriotism, we can, with the blessing of God, avert the perils which environ us, and achieve for ourselves and children peace and freedom. Hitherto the Lord has interposed graciously to bring us victory, and in His hand there is present power to prevent this great multitude which come against us from casting us out of the possession which He has given us to inherit.

Such were the first bitter fruits of Lincoln's proclamation, offering amnesty to individuals and seeking to establish certain guidelines for the future reconstruction of the South.

★ ★ ★

Receiving on December 9 the President's instructions for him to come to Richmond, Lee supposed a decision had been reached to send him to North Georgia as Bragg's successor, despite his expressed reluctance to leave the Old Dominion and the army whose fame had grown with his own in the eighteen months since Davis placed him at its head. With Longstreet in East Tennessee, Ewell absent sick, and A. P. Hill as usual in poor health, the summons came at what seemed to him an unfortunate time, particularly since the latter two, even aside from their physical debility, had not fulfilled his expectations in their present subordinate positions. But orders were orders; he left at once. "My heart and thoughts will always be with this army," he said in a note to Stuart as he boarded at Orange a train that had him in the capital before nightfall.

He found to his relief, however, that no decision had been made regarding his transfer to the western theater. The President, in conference with his Cabinet on the matter of selecting a new leader for the army temporarily under Hardee, had merely wanted his ranking field commander there to share in the discussion. Lee's reluctance having been honored to the extent that it had removed him from consideration for the post, the advisers found it difficult to agree on a second choice. Not only were they divided among themselves; Davis withheld approval of every candidate proposed. Some were all for Beauregard, for instance, but the Commander in Chief had even less confidence in the Creole than he had in Joe Johnston, who was being recommended warmly in the press, on the floor of Congress, in letters from friends, and by Seddon.

While the Secretary admitted that he had been disappointed by his fellow Virginian's "absence of enterprise" in the recent Mississippi operations, he believed that "his military sagacity would not fail to recognize the exigencies of the time and position, and so direct all his thoughts and skill to an offensive campaign." Davis was doubtful. He rather agreed with Benjamin, who protested that during his six-month tenure as Secretary of War he had found in Johnston "tendencies to defensive strategy and a lack of knowledge of the environment." Others present inclined to the same view. On the evidence, Old Joe's talent seemed primarily for retreat: so much so, indeed, that if left to his own devices he might be expected to wind up gingerly defending Key West and complaining that he lacked transportation for a withdrawal to Cuba in the event that something threatened one of his flanks. Finally, however, at the close of a full week of discussion, Johnston was favored by a majority of those present, and the minority, though still unreconciled to his appointment, confessed that it had no one else to offer. According to Seddon, "the President, after doubt and with misgiving to the end, chose him ... not as with exaltation on this score, but as the best on the whole to be obtained." He wired him at Meridian that same day, December 16, two weeks after Bragg had been relieved: "You will turn over the immediate command of the Army of Mississippi to Lieutenant General Polk and proceed to Dalton and assume command of the Army of Tennessee.... A letter of instructions will be sent to you at Dalton."

Requested to inspect the capital defenses, Lee stayed on for another five days, during which time he was lionized by the public and invited by the House of Representatives to take what was infelicitously called "a seat on the floor." After the Sunday service at Saint Paul's he was given a silent ovation as he passed down the aisle, bowing left and right to friends in the congregation, and forty-year-old Mrs Chesnut, who prided herself on her sophistication, confessed in her diary that when the general "bowed low and gave me a smile of recognition, I was ashamed of being so pleased. I blushed like a schoolgirl." A four-day extension of the visit would have allowed him to spend his first Christmas with his family since two years before the war, but he would not have it so; he was thinking of his army on the Rapidan and the men there who were far from home as this gayest of holidays drew near. For their part, while they envied, they did not resent his good fortune. In point of fact, they doubted that he would take advantage of it. "It will be more in accordance with his peculiar character," a staff major wrote from Orange to his sweetheart on December 20, "if he leaves for the army just before the great anniversary; he is so very apt to suppress or deny his personal desire when it conflicts with the performance of his duty." The young officer was right. Lee returned next day, having sacrificed a Richmond Christmas with his wife in order to be with his troops and share in their frugal celebration of what had always been for Southerners a combination of all that was best in the gladdest days of the departing year.

All was quiet in the camps along the Rapidan, but the cavalry had been kept busy in his absence — and fruitlessly busy, at that — attempting to head off or break up a raid into Southwest Virginia, deep in the army's rear, by a column of hard-riding horsemen under Averell, who had been given an independent brigade after Hooker relieved him of duty amid the fury of Chancellorsville. Regaining the safety of his own lines on the day Lee returned to Orange, Averell proudly reported that in the past two weeks his troopers had "marched, climbed, slid, and swum 355 miles," avoided superior combinations of graybacks sent to scatter or capture them, and cut the Tennessee & Virginia Railroad at Salem (just west of a hamlet called Big Lick, which twenty years later would change its name to Roanoke and grow to be a city) where three depots crammed with food and equipment on consignment to the Army of Northern Virginia were set afire. At a cost of 6 men drowned, 5 wounded, and 94 missing, he had captured some 200 of the enemy, 84 of whom he brought back with him, together with about 150 horses. This time he left no sack of coffee for his friend Fitzhugh Lee, who commanded one of the columns that failed to intercept him, but he could say, as he had said before: "Here's your visit. How do you like it?" Fitz liked it no better now than he had done in March, after Kelly's Ford. Nor did Stuart, who was presented with further evidence of the decline of the advantage he had enjoyed in the days when his superior riders were mounted on superior, well-fed horses.

Meanwhile the foot soldiers took it easy, blue and gray alike. Meade's withdrawal from Lee's formidable Mine Run front — accomplished with such skill and stealth that his opponent's resultant attitude resembled that of a greenhorn lured into the Wilderness by pranksters who left him holding the bag on a "snipe hunt" — had ended all infantry operations for the year. On both sides of the river the two armies went into winter quarters, beginning what would be a five-month rest. On the north bank, for Meade despite his crankiness was liberal in such matters, generals, colonels, majors, even captains were able to bring their wives into camp on extended visits. One witness considered their presence greatly beneficial, and not only to their husbands. "Their influence softens and humanizes much that might otherwise be harsh and repulsive," he declared. "In their company, at least, officers who should be gentlemen do not get drunk." On the other hand, a high-toned Massachusetts staff man was a good deal less enthusiastic about these army ladies. "Such a set of feminine humans I have not seen often," he wrote home. "It was Lowell's factories broken loose and gone wild." However, except on the off chance that a few orderlies got lucky, all this meant little to the enlisted men, who were obliged to depend on their own resources and limit the count of their blessings to the fact that they were not to be shot at for a while. "The troops burrowed into the earth and built their little shelters," a Federal brigadier was to recall, "and the officers and men devoted themselves to unlimited festivity, balls, horse races, cockfights, greased pigs and poles, and other games such as only soldiers can devise."

For most of the people of Richmond, women and old men and children, politicians and officeholders of high and low degree, as well as for the maimed and convalescent veterans in private homes and hospitals on the city's seven hills, this holiday season was scarcely gayer than it was for their friends and kinsmen on the Rapidan with Lee. For some few others, however, owners of plantations down the country, not yet taken over by invaders, provisions had been forwarded for laying out a meal that had at least a resemblance to the feasts of olden times. Christmas dinner at Colonel and Mrs Chesnut's, for example, included oyster soup, boiled mutton, ham, boned turkey, wild duck and partridges, plum pudding, and four kinds of wine to wash it down with. "There is life in the old land yet!" the diarist exclaimed.

Among her guests that day was John Bell Hood, the social catch of the town. Taken a few miles south of the field where he lost his leg, he had spent a month in bed on a North Georgia farm and then, because it was feared he might be captured so near the enemy lines, continued his convalescence in Atlanta for another month before coming on to Richmond in late November. With his left arm still in a sling and his right trouser leg hanging empty, his eyes deep-set in a pain-gaunted face above the full blond beard of a Wagnerian hero, the thirty-two-year-old bachelor general had the ladies fluttering around him, his hostess said, "as if it would be a luxury to pull out their handkerchiefs and have a good cry." Instead, they brought him oranges and peeled and sliced them for him, prompting another guest to remark that "the money value of friendship is easily counted now," since oranges were selling in the capital markets for five Confederate dollars each. Shortly after Chickamauga, Longstreet had recommended the Kentucky-born Texan's promotion to lieutenant general "for distinguished conduct and ability in the battle of the 20th instant." Moreover, although Hood was nearly six years younger than A. P. Hill, the present youngest officer of that rank, there was little doubt that the promotion would be confirmed; for he was now an intimate of the President's and accompanied him on carriage rides and tours of inspection, in and about the city.

Another Kentuckian was being talked about on all sides this Christmas, here and elsewhere, and did much to lift the gloom resulting from the reverses lately suffered, including his own. On November 28 word flashed across the North and South that John Morgan and six of his captains, taken with him in the course of the raid that ended near Salineville four months back, had escaped the night before from the Ohio

Penitentiary by tunneling out of their cell block and scaling the outer wall. That was all that was known for the time being, except that Buckeye posses bent on his recapture were combing the region and searching the cellars and attics of all suspected Copperheads. In mid-December, two weeks later, he turned up on the near bank of the Tennessee River, below Kingston, and soon afterwards crossed the Great Smoky Mountains to Franklin, North Carolina, well beyond reach of the searchers in his rear. The particulars of his flight were as daring as the wildest of his raids. Dressed as civilians, he and his companions had boarded a fast night express at Columbus, just outside the prison walls, and reached Cincinnati before the morning bed check showed them missing from their cells. By that time they were over the Ohio, riding south on borrowed horses — there was little in the Bluegrass that John Morgan could not have for the asking — to cross the Cumberland near Burkesville. Two of the party had been lost just outside Louisville, picked up by a Federal patrol, but the others made it all the way. Morgan himself reached Danville, Virginia, in time for Christmas dinner with his wife, who was recuperating there from a miscarriage, brought on it was said by worry about her husband and resentment of Ohio's vindictive treatment of him as a felon. Now he was with her again, and soon he would be back with the army, too. He had been summoned to Richmond, where a public reception was being planned in his honor, he was informed, "thusly [to] say to the despicable foe that in their futile efforts to degrade you before the world they have only elevated you in the estimation of all Confederate citizens, and the whole civilized world."

Anticipation of his arrival, which was scheduled for January 2, gave a lift to the spirits of the people of the capital. But for many, unable to draw on such resources as were available to the Chesnuts and their guests, the holiday itself was depressing in its contrast to the ones they had enjoyed last year and the year before, when the festivities were heightened by recent victories at Fredericksburg and Ball's Bluff. No such occasions warranted celebration now. "It is a sad, cold Christmas, and threatening snow," a government clerk recorded in his diary. "The children have a Christmas tree, but it is not burdened. Candy is held at $8 per pound." Nor did he find much evidence of merriment among his fellow townsmen when he went out for a walk that afternoon. "Occasionally an *exempt*, who has speculated, may be seen drunk. But a somber heaviness is in the countenances of men as well as in the sky above." Although, like candy, a Christmas turkey was beyond his means, "[I] do not covet one. This is no time for feasting," he declared. Presently, if only out of surfeit, Mrs Chesnut was inclined to agree. "God help my country!" she exclaimed on New Year's Day, looking back somewhat ruefully on the round of holiday parties she had given or attended. "I think we are like the sailors who break into the spirits closet when they find out the ship must sink." Reviewing her correspondence for the year now past, she came upon an early draft of a letter she had written Varina Davis during a September visit to the South Carolina plantation that furnished so many delicacies for her table. It had seemed to her then, she told the first lady, that the people were divided into two main groups, one made up of enthusiasts whose "whole duty here consists of abusing Lincoln and the Yankees, praising Jeff Davis and the army of Virginia, and wondering when this horrid war will be over," while the other included "politicians and men with no stomach for fighting, who find it easier to cuss Jeff Davis and stay at home than to go to the front with a musket. They are the kind who came out almost as soon as they went into the war, dissatisfied with the way things were managed. Joe Johnston is their polar star, the redeemer!"

Polar star and redeemer he might be to the disaffected Carolinians, as well as to the western soldiers once more in his charge, but to his superiors in Richmond he was something else again. Receiving the President's telegram of December 16, the general spent a few days putting his affairs in order, including the transfer of his present command to Polk, and then on December 22 set out by rail for North Georgia. Two days after Christmas he reached Dalton, where he took over from Hardee without further delay. Awaiting him there were the instructions promised in the wire received ten days ago in Mississippi, one set from the Commander in Chief and another from the Secretary of War, both urging an early campaign against the Federals in his front. While admitting that "the army may have been, by recent events, somewhat disheartened," Seddon believed that Johnston's presence would restore its "discipline, prestige, and confidence" in preparation for the recovery of all that had been lost. "As soon as the condition of your forces will allow," the Secretary added, "it is hoped that you will be able to assume the offensive." Davis wrote in a similar vein. Information lately received encouraged "a not unfavorable view of the material of the command," he said, and "induces me to hope that you will soon be able to commence active operations against the enemy. . . . You will not need to have it suggested that the imperative demand for prompt and vigorous action arises not only from the importance of restoring the prestige of the army, and averting the dispiriting and injurious results that must attend a season of inactivity, but also from the necessity of reoccupying the country upon the supplies of which the proper subsistence of the armies materially depends." The general on the scene could best determine "the immediate measures to be adopted in attaining this end," the President remarked, and he urged him to "communicate fully and freely with me concerning your proposed plan of action, that all the assistance and co-operation may be most advantageously afforded that it is in the power of the government to render. Trusting that your health may be preserved, and that

the arduous and responsible duties you have undertaken may be successfully accomplished, I remain very respectfully and truly yours, Jeffn
Davis."

      Whereupon — in response to these conciliatory statements of
confidence in the general's ability, these offers to replace past bitterness
with cordiality — the old trouble rose anew, bringing with it apparent
confirmation of the doubts expressed by Benjamin and others at the series of high-level conferences leading to the choice of a new commander
for the Army of Tennessee. Johnston had not thought he would get the
post; "The temper exhibited toward me makes it very unlikely that I
shall ever again occupy an important position," he told a friend in mid-
September; but when he learned of his new assignment, three months
later, he was delighted. This reaction lasted no longer, however, than it
took him to reach Dalton and read the letters of instruction. As always,
he bridled at what he considered prodding, especially from these two,
who all through June had tried to persuade him to wreck his army for
no purpose, so far as he could see, except as a gesture of sympathy for
the garrison penned up in Vicksburg as a result of their unwisdom. Now
here they were, at it again, trying to nudge him into rashness and disaster! His reply to Seddon was edged with irony. "The duties of military
administration you point out to me shall be attended to with diligence,"
he said. But he added flatly: "This army is now far from being in condition to 'resume the offensive.' " A similar reply went to Davis. "Your
Excellency well impresses upon me the importance of recovering the
territory we have lost. I feel it deeply; but difficulties appear to me in
the way." These he listed in considerable detail, including a shortage of
transportation and subsistence, the long numerical odds the Federals enjoyed, and the poor condition of the roads because of recent heavy
rains. He might be able to resist an attack in his present position, he declared, but under the conditions now prevailing he could not even entertain the notion of delivering one. In short: "I can see no other mode of
taking the offensive here than to beat the enemy when he advances, and
then move forward."

      There they had it — as, indeed, they had had it so often before,
wherever Johnston commanded in this war. The Manassas region beyond the Rappahannock, the York-James peninsula, the Mississippi
heartland, all had been given up by him on the heels of similar protests at
suggestions that he "assume the offensive" or merely stand his ground.
Seddon and Davis saw their worst fears realized. If past performance was
any indication of what to expect, Johnston would backpedal in response
to whatever pressure the enemy brought against him in North Georgia,
and this time it would be the *national* heartland that would pass into
Federal possession as a result. Their inclination was to remove him before that happened, but this would mean a return to the problem of
finding another commander for the army, which was no more soluble

now than it had been in mid-December. They had him; they would have to live with him. The result, as they continued to plead for an advance and he continued to bridle at the prodding, was increased dissatisfaction and petulance at both ends of the telegraph wires connecting Richmond and Dalton.

Whatever second thoughts his superiors might be having as to their wisdom in appointing this new commander of the Army of Tennessee, the men under him were delighted. In fact, the pleasure they had experienced on hearing of Bragg's departure was redoubled by the news that Johnston was to take his place, and according to one veteran's recollection, civilians reacted in a similar manner: "At every bivouac in the field, at every fireside in the rear, the joyous dawn of day seemed to have arisen from the night." Rations improved with the Virginian's arrival; the clothing issue was liberalized; even a system of furloughs was established. Moreover, whereas Bragg had kept to his tent between campaigns — confined there, more often than not, by dyspepsia — Johnston not only made it a point to pay frequent visits to all the camps, he also did not limit his attention to men with bars or stars on their collars. "He passed through the ranks of the common soldiers, shaking hands with every one he met," a private was to recall years later. "He restored the soldier's pride; he brought the manhood back to the private's bosom; he changed the order of roll-call, standing guard, drill, and such nonsense as that. The revolution was complete. He was loved, respected, admired; yea, almost worshipped by his troops. I do not believe there was a soldier in his army but would gladly have died for him."

This last was based in part no doubt on their knowledge that he would ask of them no dying he could spare them; that he believed, as they did, in a minimum of bloodshed, and would always sacrifice mere terrain if the price of holding it seemed to him excessive. But there was a good deal more to it than that. Veneration was deepened by affection, and the affection was returned. No matter how touchy Johnston might be in his relations with superiors, he was invariably friendly to those below him on the military ladder, considerate of their needs and never seeming to fear that this might lessen his dignity or cost him any measure of their respect. One day soon after his arrival in Dalton, for example, Cheatham brought a number of men from his division over to army headquarters in a body, accompanied by a band with which to serenade the new commander. Presently Johnston stepped hatless from his tent to thank them for the music and the visit; whereupon Cheatham performed a highly informal ceremony of introduction. "Boys," he said, affectionately patting the general's bald head two or three times as he spoke, "this is Old Joe."

✗ 2 ✗

In all seasons and all weathers, stifling heat or numbing cold, the men aboard the Federal blockaders kept their stations, stood their watches, and patrolled their designated segments of the highly irregular three thousand miles of coastline between Old Point Comfort and Matamoros. Not for them had been the thunderous runs by the frigates and gunboats under Farragut and Porter, during which the world seemed turned to flame and a man's heart pounded as if to break the confines of his ribs, or the exhilarating chases by the raiders under Semmes and Maffitt, staged hundreds of miles from the sight of land and punctuated with coaling stops in sinful foreign ports. A sailor who managed to secure a leave from one of the river fleets was sure to receive at home a hero's welcome for his share in the humbling of Vicksburg or Port Hudson, and since her sinking of the *Hatteras*, off Galveston a year ago, the *Alabama* had added an even three dozen Yankee ships and barks and schooners to her string of prizes, while the *Florida*, after her nimble sprint out of Mobile Bay, had taken just over two dozen such merchant vessels in that same span. The men on blockade duty envied blue and gray alike, not only for the stormy present but also for the future still to come. Someday perhaps, if they survived the boredom and saltpeter, there would be the question: "What did you do, Father, in the war?" Within the limitations of the truth, about the only satisfactory answer they could give — satisfactory to themselves, that is — would be: "I'd rather not talk about it."

Nor were conditions any better in that regard for the crews of ships assigned to add offensive punch to the four blockading squadrons. In contrast to 1862, when it had appeared that no salt water attack could fail, whatever the objective, the year just past had seen no fort subdued, no harbor seized, except along the scantly defended lower coast of Texas, where the year-end gains were far outweighed by the reverses suffered earlier at Galveston and Sabine Pass. If such efforts on the Gulf amounted to little, those on the Atlantic came to less. Du Pont's repulse at Charleston, and Dahlgren's protracted frustration since, had served no purpose the men could discern except to make them thankful that the brass had not seen fit to test the defenses of Wilmington or Mobile. There were dangers enough outside such places, it seemed to them, without venturing any closer: as the *Ironsides* could testify, having had her timbers shivered by the unscathed *David*. Two months later, on December 6, the monitor *Weehawken* — leader of the nine-boat iron column that had steamed into Charleston harbor back in April — met a harsher and still more ignominious fate, without an enemy in sight. Tied up to a buoy inside the bar, she had taken on an extra load of heavy ammunition which so reduced her freeboard that the ebb tide flooded an open hawse pipe and a hatch, foundering her so rapidly that she carried 31 of her crew with her on her sudden plunge to the bottom. There was small glory here for either the dead or the survivors, who were promptly transferred to other vessels to keep up the work of raising puffs of brick dust from the defiant ruin of Sumter. Morale was not helped, either, when they learned of Father Gideon's response to a request from Dahlgren — who knew something of the strain on their nerves because of the jangled state of his own — that a whiskey ration be distributed under medical supervision. Welles did not approve. He recommended that iced coffee or oatmeal mixed with water be used as a pick-me-up instead.

Boredom was the main problem, especially for the crews of the blockaders, who could not see that their day-in day-out service had much to do with fighting at all, let alone with speeding the victory which hard-war politicians and editors kept saying was just around the corner. Off Cape Fear, where the sleek gray runners steaming in from Nassau and Bermuda found cover under the unchallenged guns of Fort Fisher, a bluejacket wrote home to his mother (as the letter was paraphrased years later by a student of the era) that she could get some notion of blockade duty if she would "go to the roof on a hot summer day, talk to a half dozen degenerates, descend to the basement, drink tepid water full of iron rust, climb to the roof again, and repeat the process at intervals until she was fagged out, then go to bed with everything shut tight." Individual reactions to this monotony, which was scarcely relieved by an unbroken diet of moldy beans, stale biscuits, and sour pork, varied from fisticuffs and insubordination to homosexuality and desertion. Officers fraternized ashore with Negro women, a practice frowned on by the Navy, and mess crews specialized in the manufacture of outlaw whiskey distilled from almost any substance that would ferment in the southern heat — as in fact nearly everything would, including men. Rheumatism and scurvy kept the doctors busy, along with breakbone fever, hemorrhoids, and damage done by knuckles. These they could deal with, after their fashion, but there was no medicine for the ills of the spirit, brought on by the strain of monotony, poor food, and unhealthy living conditions, which produced much longer casualty lists than did rebel shells or torpedoes. "Give me a discharge, and let me go home," a distraught but articulate coal heaver begged his skipper after months of duty outside Charleston. "I am a poor weak, miserable, nervous, half crazy boy. . . . Everything jars upon my delicate nerves."

Inside the harbor, Beauregard was about as deep in the doldrums as were the blue-clad sailors beyond the bar. Disappointed that he had not been ordered west to resume command of the army Bragg had inherited from him, privately he was telling friends that his usefulness in the war had ended, and he predicted defeat for the Confederacy no later than spring or summer. He gave as the cause for both of these disasters "the persistent inability and obstinacy of our rulers." Primarily he meant Davis, of whom he said: "The curse of God must have been on our people when we chose him out of so many noble sons of the South, who would have carried us safely through this Revolution."

In addition to the frustration proceeding from his belief that presidential animosity, as evidenced by slights and snubs, had cost him the western command he so much wanted, the Creole's gloom was also due to the apparent failure of a new weapon he had predicted would accomplish, unassisted, the lifting of the Union blockade by the simple process of sinking the blockaders. There had arrived by rail from Mobile in mid-August, disassembled and loaded on two flatcars, a cigar-shaped metal vessel about thirty feet in length and less than four feet wide and five feet deep. Put back together and launched in Charleston harbor, she resembled the little *David*-class torpedo boats whose low silhouette made them hard for enemy lookouts to detect. Actually, though, she had been designed to carry this advantage a considerable step further, in that she was intended to travel under as well as on the water, and thus present no silhouette at all. She was, in short, the world's first submarine. Christened the *H. L. Hunley* for one of her builders, who had come from Alabama with her to instruct the Carolinians in her use, she was propeller-driven but had no engine, deriving her power from her eight-man crew, posted at cranks along her drive shaft, which they turned on orders from her coxswain-captain. Water was let into ballast tanks to lower her until she was nearly awash; then her two hatches were bolted tight from inside, and as she moved forward the skipper took her down by depressing a pair of horizontal fins, which were also used to level and raise her while in motion. To bring her all the way up, force pumps ejected the water from her tanks, decreasing her specific gravity; or in emergencies her iron keel could be jettisoned in sections by disengaging the bolts that held it on, thus causing her to bob corklike to the surface. A glass port in the forward hatch enabled the steersman to see where he was going while submerged, and interior light was supplied by candles, which also served to warn of the danger of asphyxiation by guttering when the oxygen ran low. Practice dives in Mobile Bay had demonstrated that the *Hunley* could stay down about two hours before coming up for air, and she had proved her effectiveness as an offensive weapon by torpedoing and sinking two flatboats there. Her method of attack was quite as novel as her design. Towing at the end of a 200-foot line a copper cylinder packed with ninety pounds of powder and equipped with a percussion fuze, she would dive as she approached her target, pass completely under it, then elevate a bit and drag the towline across the keel of the enemy ship until the torpdo made contact and exploded, well astern of the submarine, whose crew would be cranking hard for a getaway, still underwater, and a return to port for a new torpedo to use on the next victim. Beauregard looked the strange craft over, had her workings explained to him by Hunley, and predicted an end to the

Yankee blockade as soon as her newly volunteered crew learned to handle her well enough to launch their one-boat offensive against the U. S. Navy.

Such high hopes were often modified by sudden disappointments, and the *Hunley* was no exception to the general application of the rule. Certain drawbacks were soon as evident here as they had been at Mobile earlier: one being that she was a good deal easier to take down than she was to bring back up, particularly if something went wrong with her machinery, and something often did. She was, in fact — as might have been expected from her combination of primitive means and delicate functions — accident-prone. On August 29, two weeks after her arrival, she was moored to a steamer tied to the Fort Johnson dock, resting her "engine" between dives, when the steamer unexpectedly got underway and pulled her over on her side. Water poured in through the open hatches, front and rear, and she went down so fast that only her skipper and two nimble seamen managed to get out before she hit the bottom. This was a practical demonstration that none of the methods providing for her return to the surface by her own devices would work unless she retained enough air to lift the weight of her iron hull; a started seam or a puncture, inflicted by chance or by enemy action while she was submerged, would mean her end, or at any rate the end of the submariners locked inside her. If this had not been clear before, it certainly was now. Still, there was no difficulty in finding more volunteers to man her, and Hunley himself, as soon as she had been raised and cleared of muck and corpses, petitioned Beauregard to let him take command. He did so on September 22 and began at once a period of intensive training to familiarize his new crew with her quirks. This lasted just over three weeks. On October 15, after making a series of practice dives in the harbor, she "left the wharf at 9.25 A.M. and disappeared at 9.35. As soon as she sank," the official post-mortem continued, "air bubbles were seen to rise to the surface of the water, and from this fact it is supposed the hole at the top of the boat by which the men entered was not properly closed." That was the end of Hunley and all aboard, apparently because someone had been careless. It was also thought to be the end of the vessel that bore his name, for she was nine fathoms down. A diver found her a few days later, however, and she was hauled back up again. Beauregard was on hand when her hatch lids were removed. "The spectacle was indescribably ghastly," he later reported with a shudder of remembrance. "The unfortunate men were contorted into all sorts of horrible attitudes, some clutching candles . . . others lying in the bottom tightly grappled together, and the blackened faces of all presented the expression of their despair and agony."

Despite this evidence of the grisly consequences, a third crew promptly volunteered for service under George E. Dixon, an army lieutenant who transferred from an Alabama regiment to the *Hunley* and was also a native of Mobile. Trial runs were renewed in early November, but the method of attack was not the same. Horrified by what he had seen when the unlucky boat was raised the second time, Beauregard had ordered that she was never again to function underwater, and she was equipped accordingly with a spar torpedo like the one her rival *David* had used against the *Ironsides,* ten days before she herself went into her last intentional dive. A surface vessel now like all the rest, except that she was still propelled by muscle power, she continued for the next three months to operate out of her base on Sullivan's Island, sometimes by day, sometimes by night. But conditions were never right for an attack; tide and winds conspired against her, and at times the underpowered craft was in danger of being swept out to sea because of the exhaustion of the men along her crankshaft. Finally though, in the early dusk of February 17, with a near-full moon to steer her by, a low-lying fog to screen her, and a strong-running ebb tide to increase her normal four-knot speed, Dixon maneuvered the *Hunley* out of the harbor and set a course for the Federal fleet, which lay at anchor in the wintry darkness, seven miles away.

At 8.45 the acting master of the 1200-ton screw sloop *Housatonic* — more than two hundred feet in length and mounting a total of nine guns, including an 11-inch rifle — saw what he thought at first was "a plank moving [toward us] in the water" about a hundred yards away. By the time he knew better and ordered "the chain slipped, engine backed, and all hands called to quarters" in an attempt to take evasive action and bring his guns to bear, it was too late; "The torpedo struck forward of the mizzen mast, on the starboard side, in line with the magazine." Still trembling from the shock, the big warship heeled to port and went down stern first. Five of her crew were killed or drowned, but fortunately for the others the water was shallow enough for them to save themselves by climbing the rigging, from which they were plucked by rescuers before the stricken vessel went to pieces.

There were no Confederate witnesses, for there were no Confederate survivors; the *Hunley* had made her first and last attack and had gone down with her victim, either because her hull had been cracked by the force of the explosion, only twenty feet away, or else because she was drawn into the vortex of the sinking *Housatonic.* In any case, searchers found what was left of the sloop and the submarine years later, lying side by side on the sandy bottom, just beyond the bar.

★ ★ ★

Quincy Gillmore had been about as unhappy outside Charleston as Beauregard was inside the place, although for different reasons. Six months of siege, of suffering far greater losses than he inflicted, had gained him nothing more than Morris Island, out on the rim of the harbor, and the chance to heave an occasional long-range shell into the city — a practice which his adversary had predicted would win him "a bad eminence in history." That might be, but what bothered Gillmore most was that it seemed to increase rather than lessen the resolution of the defenders. Besides, the next step was up to the navy, and Dahlgren would not take it. The result was stalemate and frustration, a sharp regret on Gillmore's part that he had come down here in the first place. He wanted to be up and doing; he wanted room for maneuver, a chance to fight an enemy he could see; none of which was available to him here. Then in mid-January a letter from the Commander in Chief relieved his claustrophobia by opening vistas to the south. He was to undertake, without delay, the conquest of Florida.

The letter was not sent through regular channels, but was delivered in person by the President's twenty-five-year-old private secretary John Hay, who arrived wearing a brand-new pair of major's leaves on the shoulders of a brand-new uniform. Moreover, the document he brought with him made it clear that he had been commissioned to play a leading role in the show about to open down the coast. If Gillmore thought it strange at first that the choice for so important a post had been based exclusively on political qualifications — for the young man had had little experience in any other line — he soon perceived, from reading the instructions, that the proposed campaign was intended to be at least as much a political as a military endeavor. "I wish the thing done in the most speedy way possible," Lincoln wrote, "so that, when done, it [will] lie within the range of the late proclamation on the subject." It was the month-old Proclamation of Amnesty and Reconstruction he meant. He already had agents at work in Louisiana and Arkansas, attempting within the framework of its provisions to establish in them the ten-percent governments he maintained would entitle them to representation in Congress, where their gratitude was expected to prove helpful to the Administration, and it had occurred to him that Florida would make a convenient addition to the list. Hay had Unionist friends there who had written to him, he informed his diary and his chief, "asking me to come down . . . and be their Representative." Lincoln thought it a fine idea. Useful as the young Hoosier was in his present job, he might be even more so in the House. Accordingly, after commissioning him a major and making sure that he was equipped with enough oath-blanks to accommodate the ten percent of Floridians who presumably were weary of rebellion, he gave him the letter of instructions to pass along to Gillmore and wished him success in his venture into an unfamiliar field. "Great good luck and God's blessing go with you, John," he said.

Arriving in South Carolina, Hay assured Gillmore that it was not the President's intention to disrupt his current operations against Charleston, that all he wanted was "an order directing me to go to Florida and open my books of record for the oaths, as preliminary to future proceedings." He soon found, however, that the general was not touchy on that point. Far from considering Lincoln's project an intrusion, Gillmore saw it as an indorsement and extension of a proposal he himself had made in letters to Stanton and Halleck that same week, unaware that Hay was on the way from Washington. "I have in contemplation the occupation of Florida, on the west bank of the Saint Johns River, at a very early day," he announced, requesting their approval. He had it in mind to extend his coastal holdings a hundred miles inland to the Suwannee River, which he explained would enable him: 1) "To procure an outlet for cotton, timber, lumber, turpentine, and other products"; 2) "To cut off one of the enemy's sources of commissary supplies"; 3) "To obtain recruits for my colored regiments"; and 4) — appended after receiving Lincoln's instructions, which amounted to the approval he was seeking —"To inaugurate measures for the speedy restoration of Florida to her allegiance." In addition to these four "objects and advantages," as he called them, he was also attracted to the venture by the knowledge that the Confederacy had none of its regular troops assigned to the state's defense. The only graybacks there were militia, and Gillmore believed he could walk right over them with a single veteran division from his army lying idle outside Charleston and at Hilton Head, waiting for the navy to take the step it would not take. Now that the President's letter had unleashed him, he was eager to be off, and he fretted because Hay was held up by last-minute administrative details. "There will not be an hour's delay after the major is ready," he informed Lincoln on January 21, and he added: "I have every confidence in the success of the enterprise."

It was another two weeks before the preliminaries had been attended to. Then finally, on February 6, Brigadier General Truman Seymour's division, composed of three brigades of infantry, two regiments of cavalry, and four batteries of artillery — a force of about 8000 in all, mostly Regulars, New Englanders, and Negroes — got aboard twenty transports at Hilton Head and set off down the coast, escorted by two gunboats. Next morning the flotilla steamed into the St Johns estuary and docked unopposed at Jacksonville, which had been reduced to little more than ruins by the two previous Federal occupations and deserted by all but about two dozen of its prewar families. Hay went ashore and set up shop, beginning with a line-up at the guardhouse. He explained to the captive rebels that if they took the prescribed oath they would be given certificates of loyalty and allowed to return home; otherwise they would be sent North to prison camps. "There is to be neither force nor persuasion used in this matter," he told them. "You decide for yourselves." Most signed promptly, about half making their marks, and took their leave. Hay turned next to the civilians, and though they were less eager to signify repentance for their transgressions, he succeeded in getting the signatures of a number whom he described as "men of substance and influence," presumably meaning those who still had something left to lose. Encouraged, he looked forward to lengthening the list as soon as the army extended its occupation and demonstrated that it was here to stay. Meantime he made a $500 investment in Florida real estate, partly because he knew a hard-times bargain when he saw one, but also by way of establishing residence for the political race that would follow close upon his securing the signatures of ten percent of the qualified electors.

He had reason to believe this would not take long. Gillmore and the navy had been as active in their fields of endeavor as Hay had been in his, and they had also been as successful, if not more so; at least at the outset. Steaming on past Jacksonville after debarking most of the force they had escorted down the coast, the two warships trained their guns on Picolata and Palatka, respectively thirty and fifty miles upstream, and put troops ashore to garrison them, thus establishing firm (and, as it turned out, permanent) control of a coastal region twenty to thirty miles in width and seventy miles in length, east from the St Johns River to the Atlantic and south from Fernandina, near the Georgia line, to below Saint Augustine, which had been reoccupied in late December. What was more, while the navy was consolidating these gains, Gillmore had his troops in motion westward, intent on extending the conquest inland all the way to the Suwannee, as he had said he would do when he first announced his plans.

Florida had two railroads, one running southwest from Fernandina, through Gainesville, to Cedar Key on the Gulf of Mexico, the other due west from Jacksonville to Tallahassee. He took the latter as his route of march, the Atlantic & Gulf Central, his primary objective being Lake City, about sixty miles away. Setting out on February 8, the day after his debarkation, by the following morning he had his cavalry in Baldwin, at the crossing of the two railroads and one third of the way to his goal. His infantry marched in next day, still preceded by the troopers, who pressed on ten miles down the line to Barber's and then another ten to Sanderson, only twenty miles from Lake City. But after advancing half that distance, the cavalry commander, Colonel Guy V. Henry, learned on reaching Olustee that rebel militia were massing in sizable numbers for resistance up ahead; so he turned back. It was well for him and his three small regiments that he did, if he had been counting on infantry support in case of trouble; for when he re-entered Sanderson on the 12th he found that Gillmore was withdrawing to Jacksonville, leaving Seymour to backtrack in his wake and hold Baldwin with the major part of his division while he himself returned to Hilton Head to make further arrangements he had not known were needed, until now.

He too had learned of the rebels massing at Lake City to contest a farther blue advance, and this had served to give him pause. However, his main concern was logistics: meaning supplies, primarily food and ammunition, and how to get them forward to the troops as they slogged westward across a sandy waste of stunted oaks, pine trees, and palmettos. He lacked wagons and mules to draw them, having counted on using the railroad, and though he had plenty of boxcars, captured by Henry's fast-riding troopers before they could be withdrawn beyond the Suwannee, the only locomotive he had on hand was one he had brought with him, which had promptly nullified his foresight by breaking down. So he turned back, better than halfway to his goal, not so much in fear of the gray militia up ahead — although they were reported to be numerous — as in anticipation of what would happen to his soldiers once they had eaten up the six-day rations they carried with them on their march through this barren, inland region. Before returning to Hilton Head to correct in person his miscalculation in logistics, he told Seymour to hold Baldwin at all costs, thus to cover Jacksonville in case the enemy moved against him, but otherwise to be content with consolidating rather than extending his occupation of the coastal region east of the St Johns. That was Gillmore's second miscalculation: not taking sufficiently into account the temperament of his chief subordinate, who would assume command while he himself was up the coast.

A forty-year-old Vermont-born West Pointer, Seymour had seen about as much action as any man on either side in the war, including service as an artillery captain at Sumter when the opening shots were fired. Earlier he had been brevetted twice for bravery in Mexico and the Seminole War, and he had risen about as rapidly as he could have wished in the first two years of the contest still in progress, succeeding to the command of a division in the course of the Seven Days, after which had come Second Bull Run, South Mountain, and Antietam. In all these battles, whether his job was staff or line, he had demonstrated ability; yet somehow, while earning an additional three brevets, he had missed distinction. Then had come a transfer to the Carolina coast, and there too he had performed with credit, especially in the taking of Battery Wagner, where he was severely wounded as a result of his practice of exposing himself under fire. Somehow, though, distinction still eluded him at every turn. And now there was this fruitless westward march across the barrens of North Florida, ended in midcareer by a withdrawal and followed by peremptory instructions for him to remain strictly on the defensive in the absence of a superior whose outstanding characteristic seemed to him to be an unwillingness to assume the risks that went with gain and were in fact the handholds to distinction. Gillmore left Jacksonville on February 13; Seymour managed to endure four days of inactivity in his nominal, if temporary, position as commander of the Florida expedition. Then on the fifth day he went over to the offensive.

He did this strictly on his own, ostensibly because of a report that the rebels were about to remove the rails from the Atlantic & Gulf

Central, which he knew would upset Gillmore's plans for a resumption of the advance to the Suwannee. It was not that he was unaware of the risks involved; he was; the question later was whether he had welcomed or ignored them. For example, garrison detachments had reduced his mobile strength to about 5500 effectives, and though he suspected that the Confederates had more troops than that around Lake City, he knew they were militia to a man and apt therefore to flinch from contact

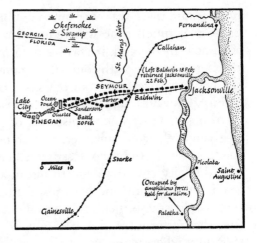

with anything that came at them in a determined manner, which was precisely what he had in mind. Moreover, he intended to make up for the possible disparity in numbers by seizing the initiative and moving with celerity once he had it. "I wish the thing done in the most speedy way possible," Lincoln had said, and Seymour demonstrated his agreement with this approach when he left Jacksonville on February 18 and cleared Baldwin before nightfall. By sundown of the following day his infantry was beyond Barber's, having covered better than thirty miles of sandy road, and his orders were for the march to be resumed at dawn. For added speed, he advanced in three columns, keeping close on the heels of the cavalry to avoid the delay of having to probe the front or shield the flanks with skirmishers detached from his three infantry brigades. All morning, February 20, he kept his soldiers on the go, slogging through Sanderson and on to Olustee without a rest halt, intent on reaching Lake City before the graybacks had time to get set for the strike. Blown, hungry, and considerably strung out, the three columns converged as they approached Ocean Pond, a swamp just beyond Olustee, around whose southern reaches the road and the railroad passed together along a narrow neck of firm ground with bogs on the left and right. It was here, barely a dozen miles from Lake City and on terrain that was scarcely fit for fighting — at any rate, not the kind of fighting he had in mind — that Seymour first encountered resistance in the form of butternut skirmishers who rose from hiding and took the heads of the three blue columns under fire, then faded back into the palmetto thickets. Recovering as best he could from the surprise, which came all the harder because he had expected to be the inflictor, not the victim, he gave orders for the pursuit to be pressed without delay. It was; but not for long. Within five minutes and two hundred yards, he found himself involved in the battle known thereafter as Olustee or Ocean Pond.

The contest lasted from shortly after noon until about 4 o'clock,

not because there was ever much doubt as to the outcome, but simply because that much time was required to make Seymour admit he'd been
whipped. In the end, it was his own men who convinced him, although
the Confederates, with four guns against his sixteen, had been highly persuasive in this regard from the start. Brigadier General Joseph Finegan,
a thirty-nine-year-old Irish-born Floridian, had about the same number
of troops as his opponent, just over or under 5500, and though they were
as green as their commander, an unblooded prewar lumberman and rail-
roader, they were by contrast rested and forewarned, having moved out
of Lake City two days ago to dig in along the near end of the swamp-
bound neck of land and there await the arrival of the bluecoats on terrain
that would cramp their style and limit their artillery advantage. As a result, the butternut militia had only to stand more or less firm and keep
shooting, whereas the attackers were obliged to try to maneuver, which
was practically impossible, hemmed in as they were on the left and right
by spongy ground and blasted from the front by masses of graybacks
who also enjoyed the protection of intrenchments. The fighting consisted mainly of a series of breakdowns and disintegrations which occurred when a number of blue regiments, exposed to such obvious tactical
disadvantages, wavered and finally came apart under pressure. A New
Hampshire outfit was the first to give way, followed by another of Negro regulars who fled when their colonel was shot down, and total collapse was only forestalled by Seymour's belated permission for the rest
to withdraw. They did so in considerable haste and disorder, leaving six
of their guns behind them on the field. Early darkness ended the pursuit,
which had been delayed by another Negro regiment assigned to rear-
guard duty. Casualties totaled 1861 for the Federals, including more than
700 killed or captured, while the Confederates lost 946, with fewer than
100 dead or missing. Seymour had at last achieved distinction, but not at
all of the kind for which he yearned, since it resulted from the addition
of his name to the list of those commanders, North and South, who suffered the soundest thrashings of the war.

Slogging rearward under cover of darkness, the whipped and bleeding survivors were as bitter as they were footsore. "This moment of
grief is too sacred for anger," an officer wrote home. But that was by
no means the general reaction, which was not unlike the one displayed
on the similar withdrawal from the field of Chickamauga, five months
ago tonight. If this retreat was on a smaller scale, as far as concerned the
number of troops involved, it was at any rate much longer, and it was
harder in still other ways. Without nearly enough ambulances or wagons
to accommodate the wounded, crude litters had to be improvised, with
results that were not only painful for the men being jolted but also exhausting for the bearers. Still, they made good time: better, indeed, than
they had made on the speedy outward march. By moonrise they were
at Sanderson, ten miles from the scene of their defeat, and they passed

through Barber's before daybreak. The second of these two segments was even grimmer than the first, partly because the marchers were wearier, partly too because they lacked by then the disconcerting spur of pursuit, the rebels having halted far in the rear. Now they had time for comprehending what had happened back there at Olustee, and that had perhaps the grimmest effect of all. "Ten miles we wended or crawled along," a participant afterwards said of the small-hours trek from Sanderson to Barber's, "the wounded filling the night air with lamentations, the crippled horses neighing in pain, and the full moon kissing the cold, clammy lips of the dying." Moreover, there was no halt on the 21st at Baldwin, despite previous instructions for holding that vital crossing at all costs, and by sunup of the following morning the head of the column was in Jacksonville, which it had left four days and a hard hundred miles ago.

Gillmore's dismay, on learning of what had happened in his absence and against his orders, was increased by information that the Confederates had advanced beyond Baldwin and were intrenching a line along McGirt's Creek, midway between that place and Jacksonville. Whether this was in preparation for defense or attack he did not know, though it might well be for the latter, since they were reported to have been heavily reinforced from Georgia. In any case, the question was no longer whether he could advance to the Suwannee, as he had formerly intended, but whether he could hold the coastal strip he had seized within a week of his arrival; Beauregard had outfoxed him again, he admitted to his superiors in Washington. "The enemy have thrown so large a force into Florida," he informed Halleck on February 23, "that I judge it to be inexpedient to do more at the present time than hold the line of the Saint Johns River."

One thing he could and did do, however, and that was to relieve Seymour of the command he had abused. But this was plainly a case of locking the stable after the pony was stolen. Certainly it was no help to Hay, who was finding it much harder now to obtain signatures for his oath-blanks. In fact, many who had signed appeared to regret that they had done so; while others, as he noted in his diary, "refused to sign, on the ground that they were not repentant." It was becoming increasingly clear, with the spread of news of the recent Union defeat, that he and his chief had miscalculated the temper of the people. Florida, the least populous of the Confederate states, had furnished the smallest number of troops for the rebel armies; but that was by no means a fit basis on which to determine her zeal for the secessionist cause, which was indicated far better by the fact that she had given a larger proportion of her eligible men than had any other state. On March 3, within twelve days of the rebel victory at Olustee, Hay frankly confessed: "I am very sure that we cannot now get the President's 10th." This being so, there was little point in his remaining. Nor did he. After a side excursion to Key West

— where he went in hope of picking up a few more signatures, but found instead "a race of thieves and a degeneration of vipers" — he returned somewhat crestfallen to the capital, intending to resume his former duties if his chief would overlook the unhappy events of the past month and take him back.

He found the hostile papers in full bay, charging Lincoln with having "fooled away 2000 men in a sordid attempt to manufacture for himself three additional votes in the approaching Presidential election." Nor did Hay escape their censure as a party to the conspiracy to overawe Florida, not for any true military purpose, but merely to win himself a seat in Congress and deliver a set of committed delegates to the Republican convention. This last, they said, explained the reckless haste that had brought Seymour to defeat; for the convention would be held in June, and the hapless general had been obliged to expose his troops to slaughter in an attempt to carry out his orders to complete the intended conquest of that waste of sand in time for a new government to be formed and delegates to be chosen who would cast their votes for Lincoln's renomination. Returning at the height of the scandal aroused by the failure of his mission, Hay armed himself with extenuating documents for the confrontation with his chief. He expected at least a grilling — for there was enough unpleasant truth in the opposition's charges to make them sting far worse than the usual fabrications — but he was wrong; Lincoln assumed that the young man had done his best in a difficult situation, and did not blame him for the trouble the journalists were making. "There was no special necessity of my presenting my papers," Hay wrote in his diary that night, "as I found he thoroughly understood the state of affairs in Florida and did not seem in the least annoyed by the newspaper falsehoods about the matter."

Others received a different impression of the President's reaction to this latest in the series of attacks designed to expose him as a master of deceit, an unprincipled opportunist, a clod, a tyrant, a bawdy clown, a monster. Earlier that month a White House visitor observed that Lincoln seemed "deeply wounded" by the allegation that he had been willing to pay in blood for votes. As usual, however, even as he was ringed by critics flinging charges at his head, he could see at least one touch of humor in the situation. He told in this connection of a backwoods traveler who got caught one night in a violent storm and who floundered about in the blackness, his sense of direction lost amid blinding zigzags of lightning and deafening peals of thunder, until finally a bolt crashed directly overhead, awesome as the wrath of God, and brought him to his knees, badly frightened. By ordinary not a praying man, he kept his petition brief and to the point. "O Lord," he cried, "if it's all the same to you, give us a little more light and a little less noise!"

★ ★ ★

While Gillmore and Hay, with Seymour's manic assistance, were failing to bring Florida back into the Union under the terms of the Proclamation of Amnesty and Reconstruction, another quasi-military project which had to do with that document, and which likewise had the President's enthusiastic approval, was moving into its final preparatory stages in Virginia. Aimed at nothing so ambitious as the overnight return of the Old Dominion to its former allegiance, this second venture along those lines was an attempt to see that the people there were acquainted at first hand, rather than through the distorting columns of their local papers or the vituperative speeches of their leaders, with the terms of Lincoln's offer; in which case, it was presumed, a good many of them would be persuaded to see the wisdom of acceptance and the folly of delay. Even if the project fell a long way short of accomplishing the most that could be hoped for, it would at least create doubt and provoke division in the enemy ranks, its authors believed, at a time when the struggle was about to enter its most critical phase. Just as the Florida venture mixed war and politics, so was this Virginia expedition designed to combine a military and a propaganda effort. Lincoln had warned his adversaries that he would not leave "any available card unplayed," and this — though it would go considerably further in bloody intent, before it was over, than he had realized when he approved it — was another example of the fact that he meant exactly what he said.

Designed strictly as a cavalry operation, the project had its beginning in the mind of Judson Kilpatrick, who conceived the notion of launching a bold strike at the Confederate capital, sixty miles in Lee's rear, for the triple purpose of crippling and snarling the lines of supply and communication between the Rapidan and the James, disrupting the rebel government by jangling the nerves of the people who functioned at its center, and freeing the Union captives being held there in increasingly large numbers since the breakdown of the system of exchange. Like his purpose, his motivation was threefold: love of action, desire for acclaim, and envy. Averell having recently been applauded for his successful year-end raid into southwest Virginia, the New Jersey cavalryman planned to win far more applause by striking, not with a lone brigade, but with his whole division, and not at some remote objective on the fringes of the map, as Averell had done, but at the very solar plexus of rebellion. Such a blow would outdo all the horseback exploits that had gone before it, including the highly touted "rides" by Stuart in his heyday. Besides, Kilpatrick did not believe the hit-and-run operation would be nearly as risky, or anyhow as difficult, as it sounded. His information was that Richmond was scantly protected by inexperienced home guardsmen who would not be able to offer serious resistance to an approximately equal number of veteran troopers armed with seven-shot repeaters, not to mention the fact that his strength would be more than doubled, once he broke through the rim of the city's defenses, by the liberation and addition of some 5000 bluecoats reported to be at Libby and on Belle Isle. A more difficult problem, just now, was how to go about securing the approval he had to have before he could take off southward on the venture he was sure would bring him fame. He had little caution in his makeup, but at any rate he knew better than to propose his scheme to Pleasonton, who might hog it, or to the overcautious Meade, who would be certain to see it as harebrained and reject it in short order. Instead, he took care to communicate in private with certain persons known to be close to the highest authority of all. That was in late January, and the result was about as prompt as he expected. On February 11 a high-priority telegram clicked off the wire from Washington, addressed to the commander of the Army of the Potomac: "Unless there be strong reasons to the contrary, please send Gen. Kilpatrick to us here, for two or three days. A. Lincoln."

"Us" included Stanton, who shared with his chief a staunch, perhaps an extravagant admiration for military boldness, a quality sadly lacking in the upper echelons of the eastern theater, as they saw it, but personified by the bandy-legged general known to the army as "Kill Cavalry." The latter arrived in the capital next morning — the President's fifty-fifth birthday — and was received in private by the Secretary of War. Stanton liked the proposition even better at first hand than he had by hearsay, seeing in it, in addition to the fruits predicted by its author, the possibility of affording a real boost to morale on the home front when the news went out that Federal horsemen had clattered through the streets of Richmond, striking terror into the hearts of rebel leaders and freeing thousands of blue-clad martyrs from a durance worse than vile. Moreover, having applauded the young brigadier's conception, which was much in line with his own belief as to the manner in which this war should be fought, the Secretary passed along a suggestion from Lincoln that would give the raid an added dimension, and this was that each trooper carry with him a hundred or so copies of the recent amnesty proclamation for distribution along the way. Kilpatrick pronounced this a splendid notion, then presently, the details having been agreed on, returned to the Rapidan, encouraged and flattered by the confidence thus shown by the head of the War Department — who made it clear that he spoke as well for the Commander in Chief — in a twenty-seven-year-old subordinate, less than three years out of West Point. Hard in his wake, orders came to Culpeper directing that his division be reinforced to a strength of about 4000 for the raid he proposed and that he be given all the assistance he required, including diversionary actions by other units, foot and horse.

Meade was not happy about the project, of which he had known nothing until now. Nor was Pleasonton, who recalled the ill-fated Stoneman raid, which had been similar in purpose and conception, but which had accomplished little except "the loss to the government [of] over 7000 horses, besides the equipments and men left on the road." In short, the chief of cavalry said flatly, the expedition was "not feasible at this time." As for the proposed distribution of the President's proclamation, he suggested that this could be done better, and far cheaper, by undercover agents, and he offered "to have it freely circulated [by this method] in any section of Virginia that may be desired." But nothing came of these objections by the New Jersey cavalryman's immediate superiors. In fact, they were received in Washington as further evidence of the timidity which had crippled the eastern army from the outset. The orders were peremptory, Meade was told; Kilpatrick was to be given a free rein.

About the time of Washington's Birthday, which came ten days after Lincoln's, bales of leaflets reprinting the amnesty proclamation arrived for distribution to the raiders, who were to scatter them broadcast on the way to Richmond. There also arrived from Washington, four days later and only two days short of the jump-off date, a twenty-one-year-old colonel who came highly recommended for his "well-known gallantry, intelligence, and energy" — this last despite a wooden leg and a manner described by an admirer as "soft as a cat's." Ulric Dahlgren was his name. He was the admiral's son, but he preferred the cavalry to the navy because he believed the mounted arm would afford him more and better chances for adventure and individual accomplishment. Commissioned a captain at nineteen by Stanton himself before the war was a year old, he had served in rapid succession on the staffs of Sigel, Burnside, Hooker, and Meade, all of whom had found him useful as well as ornamental, and it had been near Boonsboro, during the pursuit of Lee after Gettysburg, that he received the wound that resulted in the amputation. Once he was able to get about on crutches he went down the coast and convalesced aboard his father's flagship outside Charleston; after which he returned to Washington, where he was jumped three ranks to colonel, reportedly the youngest in the army, and fitted for an artificial leg. While there, he learned of the preparations then in progress for the horseback strike about to be launched against the rebel capital, and he went at once to cavalry headquarters near Brandy to appeal to Pleasonton for permission to go along, despite his crippled condition. Pleasonton sent him to Kilpatrick, who not only acceded to his plea, but also gave him the all-important assignment of leading the way across the Rapidan at the head of a special 500-man detachment, with other hazardous tasks to follow in the course of the ride from that river to the James. "If successful," he wrote his father, delighted to be back in the war at all, let alone with such a daredevil role to play, "[the raid] will be the grandest thing on record; and if it fails, many of us will 'go up.' I may be captured or I may be 'tumbled over,' but it is an undertaking that if I were not in I should be ashamed to show my face again." He was especially taken with the notion that he would be riding into the very heart of the rebellion, and he added: "If we do not return, there is no better place to 'give up the ghost.' "

Jump-off was set for an hour before midnight, February 28, and proceeded without a hitch, partly because Lee was pulled off balance by Sedgwick, who had shifted his corps upstream that day, as if for a crossing in that direction, while Kilpatrick was massing his 3585 troopers under cover of the woods in rear of Ely's Ford, twenty miles downriver. At the appointed hour they splashed across, mindful of their instructions to "move with the utmost expedition possible on the shortest route past the enemy's right flank." So well did it go that by dawn the column reached Spotsylvania, fifteen miles beyond the Rapidan, unchallenged; at which point, as had been prearranged, Dahlgren and his 500 veered slightly right, while the main body continued to move straight ahead for Richmond, less than fifty miles away. The plan was for the smaller column to cross the James near Goochland, well upstream, so as to approach the rebel capital from the southwest at the same time Kilpatrick came upon it from the north, thereby causing the home-guard defenders to spread thinner and thus expose themselves to the breakthrough that would result in the clatter of Federal hoofs in the streets of their city and the release of 5000 captives from Libby and Belle Isle. Dahlgren's was the longer ride; he would have to avoid delay to arrive on schedule. Kilpatrick saw him off from Spotsylvania, wished him Godspeed as he disappeared into the misty dawn of leap-year day, then continued on his own route, south-southeast, which would bring him and his 3000 to the northern gates of Richmond, if all went as planned, at the same time the young colonel and his detached 500 came knocking at the western gates.

Speed was the watchword; Kilpatrick rode hard and fast, unopposed and apparently unpursued. This last was due in part to a second diversion, back on the Rapidan line. While Sedgwick was feinting westward, George Custer was shifting his 1500-man cavalry brigade even farther in that direction for a dash southward into Albemarle County, a movement designed to attract still more of Lee's attention away from the heavier column rounding his opposite flank. Custer, like Kilpatrick, had certain peculiarities of aspect ("This officer is one of the funniest-looking beings you ever saw," a colonel on Meade's staff wrote home, "and looks like a circus rider gone mad! He wears a huzzar jacket and tight trousers, of faded black velvet trimmed with tarnished gold lace. His head is decked with a little gray felt hat; high boots and gilt spurs complete the costume, which is enhanced by the general's coiffure, consisting in short, dry, flaxen ringlets!") but these gaudy trappings, coupled with a flamboyant personality and a reputation as a glory-hunter, did not interfere with his effectiveness when sheer courage was what was called for — as it was here, off on his own in Lee's left rear, with the task of drawing as many of Stuart's horsemen after him as possible, away from the main effort to the east. He could scarcely have done a better job, as it turned out. Crossing the river that same Sunday night, some forty miles upstream from Ely's Ford, he threatened Charlottesville next day and returned to the north bank of the Rapidan on Tuesday, March 1, having ridden more than a hundred miles through hostile territory, burned three large grist mills filled with flour and grain, and captured about fifty graybacks and 500 horses, all without the loss of a man and only a few wounded. So well indeed had he carried out his mission, particularly with regard to attracting the rebel cavalry's attention, that he was notified on his return, officially and in writing, of Pleasonton's "entire satisfaction . . . and gratification . . . at the prompt manner in which the duties assigned to you have been performed."

Before Custer returned to the Union lines Kilpatrick was knocking at the gates of Richmond. Across the North Anna by noon of February 29, he had paused astride the Virginia Central at Beaver Dam Station, midway to his objective, and after setting fire to the depot and other installations, thus to discourage any pursuit by rail once Lee found out that some 4000 blue raiders were menacing the capital in his rear, pressed on to make camp near the South Anna by nightfall. An hour past midnight he roused his sleeping troopers and was off again through the darkness, undeterred by an icy rainstorm or the fact that he had received no answering signal when he sent up rockets to indicate his position to Dahlgren, whose detachment was somewhere off to the west. "No rockets could be seen for any distance on such a night as that," an officer was to note, recalling that the "sharp wind and sleet forced men to close their eyes" as they rode southward, their wet clothes frozen stiff as armor. By daylight they were over the Chickahominy near Ashland, and at 10 o'clock in the morning, having covered sixty miles of road in the past thirty-five hours, they came jogging down the Brook Pike to within sight of Richmond and range of its outer fortifications, five miles from the heart of town. No sooner did they appear than they were taken under fire. Kilpatrick brought up his six guns for counterbattery work and prepared to overrun the defenders, "believing that if they were citizen soldiers" — by which he meant home guardsmen — "I could enter the city." So he reported some weeks later, in the calmness of his tent. One thing that bothered him now, though, was that the boom and clatter of his engagement had drawn no reply from Dahlgren, who should have arrived simultaneously on the far side of the James, there to create the prearranged diversion, but who had either been delayed or gobbled up. Another matter for concern was that the rebels up ahead were doing a highly professional job of defending their position. They were in fact part-time volunteers — government clerks, old men, and boys, considerably fewer in number than the bluecoats to their front, and serving antiquated or worn-out guns long since replaced by new ones in Lee's army — but they handled their pieces with such precision that Kilpatrick began to believe that they had been reinforced by regulars. "They have too many of those damned guns!" he fumed, riding his line amid shell-bursts and withholding the order to charge until he could better determine what stood between him and the breakthrough he intended; "they keep opening new ones on us all the time."

It was strange, this sudden transformation in a hell-for-leather commander who up to now had fairly ached to put his troopers inside Richmond. He had worked all the angles to circumvent his immediate superiors, whose timidity he had seen as the main obstacle to an undertaking that simply could not fail once it got past their disapproval, and had ridden a hard sixty miles through hostile country, bristling with aggressiveness and chafing with impatience all the way. Yet now that he had come within plain view of his goal — the goal, for that matter, of every blue-clad soldier in the eastern theater — he declined to risk the last brief sprint, half a mile down the turnpike, then past or through or over "those damned guns," which were all that stood between him and the completion of the mission he had designed with his own particular talents in mind, or anyhow his notion of those talents. It was unquestionably strange, but perhaps it was not as sudden as it seemed; perhaps it had been this way all along, behind the swagger and the blustering impatience. In any case he limited his aggressiveness, here on the outskirts of his objective, to a tentative sparring match, keeping one ear cocked for some indication that Dahlgren and his daredevil 500 were knocking at the gates beyond the James. After six or seven hours of this, the rebel guns had indeed grown in numbers, along with their infantry support, as reinforcements were hustled to the threatened sector from others undisturbed along the defensive rim, and Kilpatrick finally arrived at a decision. "Feeling confident that Dahlgren had failed to cross the river, and that an attempt to enter the city at that point would but end in a bloody failure," he later reported, "I reluctantly withdrew." He fell back northeastward, recrossing the Chickahominy at Meadow Bridge to give his men and horses some badly needed sleep in the sodden fields around Mechanicsville, where Lee had opened his Seven Days offensive, just over twenty months ago.

There had been no fighting here since then, but presently there was. At 10 o'clock, unable to sleep or rest — in part because of the wet and the cold, in part because of his fret at having failed — Kilpatrick remounted his troopers and prepared to launch a night attack down the Mechanicsville road, avoiding the stoutly held pike to the west, in order to achieve a penetration that would last no longer than it took to free the prisoners and come back out again. Before he could get his weary men in line, however, he was himself attacked by rebel horsemen who came at him from the direction of Yellow Tavern, out of the darkness in his rear. Though he managed to beat off this assault, all thoughts of resuming the offensive gave way at once to the problem of survival: especially when he learned, as he soon did, that the attackers were not "citizen soldiers," which were all he had faced till now, but regulars from Wade Hampton's division, who had taken up the belated pursuit from the Rapidan line and then had narrowed the gap between him and them while he was sparring with Richmond's defenders this afternoon. His concern was no longer with the liberation of the prisoners in the city; it was rather how to keep from joining them as a prisoner himself. Once more his decision was to withdraw northeastward, and this he did, effecting a skillful disengagement to make camp at dawn near Bethesda Church, midway between the Chickahominy and the Pamunkey. Here he remained all morning, March 2, fighting off regular and irregular Confederates who were gathering in ever larger numbers all around him in the woods and swamps. He kept hoping to hear from Dahlgren, but he did not. At noon he abandoned his vigil, together with all hope of entering Richmond, and withdrew to make camp at Tunstall's Station, near McClellan's old base at White House. There at last he was joined that night by a captain and 260 men from Dahlgren's detachment. They had a gloomy tale to tell, though they did not know the even gloomier ending, which was occurring at about that same time, some dozen air-line miles to the northeast.

Despite the almost constant rain, which made for heavy going, Dahlgren had set a rapid pace after he and his picked 500 turned off from the main body at Spotsylvania before sunup, leap-year morning. Proceeding south through Fredericks Hall, where he called a midday halt to feed the horses, he crossed the South Anna late that night and rode into Goochland, thirty miles up the James from the rebel capital, as March 1 was dawning. Here he picked up a young Negro named Martin Robinson, a slave from a nearby plantation, who offered to show him a place where the bridgeless river could be forded. The colonel was in excellent spirits, for he had kept to a difficult schedule and was about to get his troopers into position for the final dash that would put them in southside Richmond before noon, just as he had promised Kilpatrick he would do. So he thought; but not for long. Arriving at the intended crossing — Jude's Ford, it was called — he found the river on the boom, swollen by the two-day rain and running too swift to be breasted; whereupon the handsome young colonel, whose manner was said to be "soft as a cat's," showed his claws. Although the guide appeared to be quite as surprised as he himself was at the condition of the ford, Dahlgren suspected treachery, and in his anger at having been thwarted — for it was clear now, if nothing else was, that he could not reach his objective either on time or from the appointed direction — ordered him hanged. This was accomplished with dispatch there by the river, one end of a picket rope being flung across a convenient limb while the other was fastened snugly about the neck of the Negro, whose protests were cut short when he left the ground. Without further delay, and almost before the suspended man had ended his comic-dreadful jig, the blue column was back in motion, trotting eastward down the north bank of the James, its commander watching intently for some sign of a ford shallow enough to be used.

Finding none he paused occasionally to set fire to a grist mill or damage a lock in the left-bank canal, which delayed him still more. It was late afternoon by the time he cleared Short Pump, eight miles from Richmond, and heard the boom of guns in the misty northeast distance. He quickened the pace, but presently he too encountered resistance, with the result that by the time he got close to the city Kilpatrick had withdrawn. So far as Dahlgren could tell, alone in the gathering dusk with rebel militia all around him, his horses sagging with fatigue and a hard rain coming down, the main body had simply vanished. His instructions in such a case — that is, once the raid was over: as it now definitely was, though not at all in the manner Kilpatrick had predicted — called for a return to the Union lines, either by way of Fredericksburg or down the York-James peninsula. He chose the former route, turning off to the north, away from Richmond and across the Chickahominy, well above Meadow Bridge. His troopers had had little sleep in the past three nights, and by now the column had split in two, some 300 of the men becoming separated from the rest in the gloom and confusion. These were the ones — 260 of them, at any rate; about forty were captured or shot from their saddles next day — who joined the main body at Tunstall's the following night. Meanwhile, Dahlgren and the remaining 200 managed to cross the Pamunkey, a few miles north of there, and continued on through the darkness to the Mattaponi, exchanging shots with roving bands of rebels all the way. This stream too they crossed, but they got only a bit farther. Approaching King and Queen Courthouse, just beyond the river, they stumbled into an ambush laid in their path by Fitz Lee's regulars, who had also arrived from the Rapidan by now. Dahlgren, riding point, decided to brazen or bluff his way through; or perhaps he recalled that he had told his father there was no better place to die. "Surrender, you damned rebels," he cried, flourishing his revolver, "or I'll shoot you!" The answering volley unhorsed him with four bullets in his body, and witnesses afterwards testified that before he struck the ground he had already given up what he had called the ghost.

Most of those with him were likewise killed or captured, a number being flushed from hiding next morning by pursuers who put bloodhounds on their trail. Kilpatrick was incensed when he heard of this unchivalrous practice from a dozen of Dahlgren's men who managed to get through to him a few days later at Yorktown, where he ended his withdrawal down the Peninsula, safe within the Union lines. He spoke, in his official report, of the colonel's death as "murder" — a curious charge for a professional to make — but he did not hesitate, in that same document, to blame the dead man for the unhappy outcome of the project he himself had planned and led. "I am satisfied that if Colonel Dahlgren had not failed in crossing the river," he declared, ". . . I should have entered the rebel capital and released our prisoners." As it was, instead of decreasing the prison population of Richmond, he had increased it by some 300 veteran troopers (his total loss was 340, but a good many of them were killed) and in addition had lost 583 horses in the course of the ride, plus another 480 too broken down to be of any further use when it was over. About the only profit he could point to was the incidental damage inflicted on various installations along the way, together with the claim that "several thousand of the President's amnesty proclamations were scattered throughout the entire country."

In point of fact, a sizable proportion of these last had been unloaded as dead weight, heaved overboard into roadside ditches when the project degenerated into a race for survival, and whatever of propaganda value was derived from the scattering of Lincoln's amnesty offer had been considerably offset by the hard-handed excesses of the blue troopers engaged in an expedition whose most lamented casualty, according to a Richmond editor, was "a boy named Martin, the property of Mr David Meems, of Goochland." Even so, the resentments stirred up in the course of the raid were mild indeed, compared to those that developed on both sides when it was over: particularly in regard to Ulric Dahlgren, whose zeal was even more in evidence after his death than it had been before he toppled from his horse near King and Queen. His body was subjected to various indignities, including the theft of his artificial leg, the clumsy removal of one of his fingers to get at a ring he was wearing, and the scavenging of other of his private possessions, such as his watch, his boots, and even his clothes. News of these atrocities created a stir of outrage in the North, but this in turn was overmatched by the furor that followed in the South upon the publication of certain papers found among his personal effects. These included the draft of an address to his command and a detailed set of instructions for what he called "a desperate undertaking." "We will cross the James River into Richmond," he had written, "destroying the bridges after us and exhorting the released prisoners to destroy and burn the hateful city; and do not allow the rebel leader Davis and his traitorous crew to escape." Thus the proposed address, though there was no evidence that it had been delivered. The instructions were more specific. "The men must keep together and well in hand," he urged, "and once in the city it must be destroyed and Jeff Davis and cabinet killed. Pioneers will go along with combustible material."

To Southerners, when these exhortations to arson and assassination were released in print, it appeared that this amounted to hoisting the black flag, and they called bitterly for emulation of the example set — conveniently forgetting, it would seem, Quantrill's previous excesses out in Kansas. One of the angriest among them was Seddon, who sent copies of the documents to Lee, stating that in his opinion their "diaboli-cal character" required "something more than a mere informal publica-tion in our newspapers. My own inclinations are toward the execution of at least a portion of those captured at the time. . . . I desire to have the benefit of your views and any suggestions you may make." Lee re-plied that he too was shocked by the details of this "barbarous and inhu-man plot," but that execution of the captured troopers would bring re-taliation, and he wanted no part of a hanging-match with the Yankees. Besides, he told the Secretary, "I do not think that reason and reflection would justify such a course. I think it better to do right, even if we suffer in so doing, than to incur the reproach of our consciences and posterity." Instead he sent the inflammatory documents across the lines to Meade, together with a note inquiring "whether the designs and in-structions of Colonel Dahlgren, as set forth in these papers . . . were authorized by the United States Government or by his superior officers, and also whether they have the sanction and approval of those authori-ties." Meade investigated the matter and replied "that neither the United States Government, myself, nor General Kilpatrick authorized, sanc-tioned, or approved the burning of the city of Richmond and the killing of Mr Davis and cabinet, nor any other act not required by military necessity and in accordance with the usages of war." He also included, for whatever it was worth, a letter from Kilpatrick, impugning the au-thenticity of the papers. "But I regret to say," Meade privately informed his wife, "Kilpatrick's reputation, and collateral evidence in my posses-sion, rather go against this theory."

There the matter rested, so far at least as Meade and Lee were concerned. As for Lincoln, he too was willing to let it lie, if it only would, and he did not call, as he had done after the frustration of the first of his two attempts to extend the influence of his amnesty proclama-tion, for "more light"; there had been quite enough of that by now. Both failures were depressing for him to look back on, especially the second. The Florida expedition had been merely a fiasco, a military em-barrassment, but the Kilpatrick raid was that and more, adding as it did a deeper bitterness to a fratricidal struggle which, in all conscience, was bitter enough already. It was as if Lincoln, in attempting to soothe and heal the national wounds, had reached blindly into the medicine chest and mistaken an irritant for a salve. That this had been the effect was shown in part by the reaction of newspapers North and South. Calling hotly for reprisal, the Richmond *Examiner* now saw the conflict as "a war of extermination, of indiscriminate slaughter and plunder," while the New York *Times* exulted in the damage done by the raiders in Vir-ginia and gloated over reports brought back of "the large number of dilapidated and deserted dwellings, the ruined churches with windows out and doors ajar, the abandoned fields and workshops, the neglected plantations." As for the slave Martin Robinson, whose body had been left dangling beside unusable Jude's Ford, he had met "a fate he so richly deserved," according to the *Times*, because he had "dared to trifle with the welfare of his country."

That was what they had come to, South and North, as the war moved toward and into its fourth and bloodiest spring.

✕ 3 ✕

For Grant, the three-month span of comparative idleness that came after the storming of Missionary Ridge was nothing like the one that had followed his earlier triumph at Vicksburg. His manner then had been that of a man not only uncertain of the future, but also doubtful about the present, with time on his hands and no notion of how to use it. Lacking in effect an occupation, what he mainly had been, through that difficult time — after as well as before the New Orleans horseback accident, which had added pain without distraction and immobility without relaxation — was bored. That was by no means the case now. For one thing, there was his vast new department to be inspected, most of which he had had no chance to visit, even briefly, until the Chattanooga siege was lifted. After a well-earned Christmas rest, he went in early January to Knoxville, then up through Cumberland Gap to Barbourville, from there by way of Lexington to Louisville, and finally back down through Nashville to his starting point, with the added satisfaction of having solved a number of supply and security problems all along the route. He had always enjoyed travel, especially when it took him to new places, and what was more the trip presented many of the aspects of a triumphal tour. "All we needed was a leader," a wounded private had told him when he climbed Missionary Ridge in the wake of the men who had carried it, and that was the reaction wherever he went on his swing through East Tennessee and Central Kentucky. "*Hail to the Chief*, both words and air, greeted him at every stopping place," an associate was to recall.

Nor was this enthusiasm by any means limited to those in uniform. Called to St Louis immediately afterwards by the supposedly dangerous illness of one of his children (a false alarm, as it turned out, for the crisis was past when he arrived) he had no sooner checked into the Lindell Hotel — "U.S.Grant, Chattanooga," he signed the register — than he was besieged by admirers with invitations, including one to a banquet tendered in his honor by two hundred leading citizens, determined to outdo in lavishness the affair put on five months ago by their commercial rivals down in Memphis. This he accepted, along with a resolution of thanks from the Common Council. If he was modest in his demeanor at such functions, and brief in his response to speeches of praise, that did not mean that he enjoyed them any less. The fact was, he enjoyed them very much, comparing the treatment accorded him now with the attitude he had encountered in prewar days, a brief five years ago, when he tried his hand at selling real estate in this same city and hardscrabble farming just outside it, and failed at both so thoroughly that he had been reduced to peddling firewood in its streets. This he knew was the way of the world, but he enjoyed the drama of the contrast between then and now, especially here in his wife's home state, where the opinion once had been fairly unanimous, not only that she had married beneath her station, but also that she had saddled herself with a husband who turned out to be a failure in his chosen line of work and a ne'er-do-well in several others.

In addition to these honors done him at first hand, others came from a distance, including three that arrived in rapid order from the seat of government before the year was out. When, amid salutes and illuminations celebrating the Chattanooga triumph, news spread throughout the North that Knoxville too had been delivered, the President coupled his announcement of the victory with a recommendation that the people gather informally in their churches to pay homage to the Almighty "for this great advancement of the national cause," and he followed this next day, December 8, with a personal message to Grant, who passed it along in a general order: "Understanding that your lodgment at Chattanooga and Knoxville is now secure, I wish to tender you, and all under your command, my more than thanks — my profoundest gratitude — for the skill, courage, and perseverance with which you and they, over so great difficulties, have effected that important object. God bless you all." Congress, not to be outdone, passed before Christmas a joint resolution thanking the Illinois general and his men "for their gallantry and good conduct in the battles in which they have been engaged" and providing for "a gold medal to be struck, with suitable emblems, devices, and inscriptions, to be presented to Major General Grant ... in the name of the people of the United States of America." In time the medal was forwarded as directed, bearing on one side a profile of the general, surrounded by a laurel wreath and a galaxy of stars, and on the other a figure of Fame holding a trumpet and a scroll inscribed with the names of his victories. The motto was "Proclaim liberty throughout the Land." Meantime a bill was offered to revive the grade of lieutenant general — previously held only by George Washington and Winfield Scott, the former briefly, the latter merely by brevet — for the purpose of assuring that Grant, for whom alone it was intended, would assume by virtue of that lofty rank the post now occupied by Halleck, who stood above him on the list of major generals. Senator James Doolittle of Wisconsin, for one, was specific in his reasons for supporting the proposal. So far in the war, he declared with an enthusiasm that avoided understatement, Grant had won 17 battles, captured 100,000 prisoners, and taken 500 pieces of artillery; "He has organized victory from the beginning, and I want him in a position where he can organize *final* victory and bring it to our armies and put an end to this rebellion."

Doolittle's colleagues wanted final victory, too, and agreed that the probable way to get it would be to apply the western formula in the East; but a majority shared two objections to the course proposed. One was that Grant was needed in the field, not behind a desk in the capital — even if the desk was that of the general-in-chief — and the other was an ingrained fear of creating a military Grand Lama who might someday develop political ambitions and use the army to further them. As a result, the bill failed to pass.

On the face of it, this seemed no great loss, since Grant by then had already offered the government his solution to the problem of how to win the war, only to have it rejected out of hand. Reverting to the proposal he had made soon after the fall of Vicksburg, he sent Charles Dana to Washington in mid-December to lay before his superiors a plan for holding the line of the Tennessee with a skeleton force while the rest of his troops steamed down the Mississippi to New Orleans, from which point they would move against Mobile and reduce it, then march through Alabama and across Georgia, living off the abundance of the Confederate heartland as they went. Meantime the Virginia army would pin Lee down by taking the offensive, and in this connection he suggested that Meade be replaced by Sherman or Baldy Smith, who could better appreciate the need for co-ordinating the eastern and the western efforts. . . . Presently Dana wired Grant that he had explained the scheme to Lincoln, Stanton, and Halleck, all three of whom had seen considerable merit in it: aside, that is, from the risk to which it would expose the weakened Union center while the bulk of the troops from there were on the way downriver. That drawback made it sound to them like something devised by McClellan; which plainly would not do. Besides, they wanted no more Chickamaugas, especially none that would be followed up by the victors, who presumably would do just that if they were given the second chance this seemed to offer. In short — except for that part of it favoring Meade's replacement by Smith, which all three chiefs applauded as an excellent idea, despite some misgivings about Baldy's "disposition and personal character" — Grant's proposal was turned down. Dana added, though, that the trio had welcomed his suggestions and had said that they would like to hear more of them, if he had any more of them in mind.

He did indeed. Still with his eye on Mobile, he then proposed a dual offensive against that place and Atlanta, the two drives to be launched simultaneously from New Orleans and Chattanooga, while the eastern army gave up its weary attempt to capture Richmond from the north and landed instead on the North Carolina coast in order to approach the rebel capital from the south, astride its lines of supply and communication. He said nothing more about replacing Meade with

Sherman — probably because he had decided he would need him to lead one of the two western columns — or with Smith, who by now had begun to exercise the talent for contention that had kept him in hot water most of his military life and would in time cause Grant, who once had seemed to think he hung the moon, to refer to him as "a clog." In his reply, which incorporated Lincoln's and Stanton's views as well as his own, Halleck did not mention Baldy either, no doubt assuming that Grant had confirmed their misgivings about the Vermonter's "disposition," but limited himself to an assessment of the strategy involved in the proposal for a double-pronged offensive, East and West. It would not do. Not only did it commit the cardinal sin of attempting two big things at once in each of the two theaters; it also required more troops than were available in either. If attempted, it would expose both Washington and Chattanooga to risks the government simply could not run, and moreover it showed the flawed conception of a commander who made enemy cities his primary objective, rather than enemy armies, as the President had lately been insisting must be done if this war was ever to be won. In Halleck's opinion, Grant would do better to concentrate on the problems at hand in Tennessee and North Georgia, and leave the large-scale thinking to those who were equipped for it. Just as Meade's objective was Lee's army, Grant's was Johnston's, and both were to keep it firmly in mind that neither Washington nor Chattanooga — nor, for that matter, East Tennessee, the region of Lincoln's acutest concern — was to be exposed to even the slightest danger while they attempted to carry out their separate missions of destroying the rebel masses in the field before them.

Sherman had returned by now from Knoxville. Grant informed him that the spring campaign, which would open as soon as the roads were fit for marching, would be southward against Joe Johnston and Atlanta, and every available man in both his and Thomas's armies would be needed for what promised to be the hardest fighting of the war. The redhead was all for it; but first he wanted to put an end to disruptions that had developed in the department he had left to come to Tennessee. In his absence, guerillas had taken to firing at steamboats from the banks of the big river, north and south of Vicksburg, and he did not intend to abide this outrage. "To secure the safety of the navigation of the Mississippi River," he declared, "I would slay millions. On that point I am not only insane, but mad. . . . I think I see one or two quick blows that will astonish the natives of the South and will convince them that, though to stand behind a big cottonwood and shoot at a passing boat is good sport and safe, it may still reach and kill their friends and families hundreds of miles off. For every bullet shot at a steamboat, I would shoot a thousand 30-pounder Parrotts into even helpless towns on Red, Ouachita, Yazoo, or wherever a boat can float or soldier march." To those who objected to this as war against civilians, he made the point that if rebel snipers could "fire on boats with women and children in them, we can fire and burn towns with women and children." Angry, he grew angrier by the week. Taking dinner at the home of a Union-loyal Nashville matron, for example, he turned on his hostess when she began to upbraid him for the looting his troops had done on the march to Knoxville. "Madam," he replied, "my soldiers have to subsist themselves even if the whole country must be ruined to maintain them. There are two armies here. One is in rebellion against the Union; the other is fighting for the Union. If either must starve to death, I propose it shall not be the army that is loyal." This said, he added in measured tones: "War is cruelty. There is no use trying to reform it. The crueler it is, the sooner it will be over."

His main fear just now was that the guerillas along the Lower Mississippi, emboldened by the example of the snipers, would band together in sufficient strength to attack the reduced garrisons at various river ports and thus undo much that had been accomplished, at a considerable expense of Federal blood and ingenuity, in the past year. It was Sherman's notion — a notion made more urgent by the need for reducing those garrisons still further in order to furnish additional troops for the campaign scheduled to open in North Georgia in late March or early April — to return to Mississippi between now and then, rather than keep his veteran soldiers lying idle in their winter camps, and nip this threat of renewed obstruction in the bud. As he put it in mid-December, after discussing the problem with Grant, "I think in all January and part of February I can do something in this line." He did not propose to waste his energies in running down individual snipers, which would be like trying to rid a swamp of mosquitoes by swatting them one by one, but rather to destroy the economy — the society, even, if need be — that afforded them subsistence. The way to do this, he maintained, was to wreck their production and transportation facilities so thoroughly that they would have nothing left to defend and nothing left to live on if they attempted resistance for its own sake. What was more, the situation there seemed made to order for the execution of such a project. Less than two hundred miles east of Jackson was Selma, Alabama, whose cannon foundry and other manufacturing installations Jefferson Davis had admired on his October visit, and roughly midway between them was Meridian, where three vital railroads intersected and which served as a storage and distribution center, not only for industrial products from the east, but also for grain and cattle from the fertile Black Prairie region just to the north. A rapid march by a sizable force, eastward from Vicksburg, then back again for a total distance of about five hundred miles, could be made within the two available months, he believed, and the smashing of these two major objectives, together with the widespread destruction he intended to accomplish en route, would assure a minimum of trouble for the skeleton command he would leave behind when he came back upriver to rejoin Grant for the drive on Atlanta — which Johnston, incidentally, would be much harder put to defend without the rations and guns now being sent to him from Meridian and Selma. That was what the Ohioan had had in mind when he spoke of "one or two blows that will astonish the natives."

There were, as he saw it, three main problems, each represented by an enemy commander who would have to be dealt with in launching this massive raid, first across the width of Mississippi and then beyond the Tombigbee to a point nearly halfway across Alabama. One was Polk, who had in his camps of instruction at Demopolis, between Meridian and Selma, the equivalent of two divisions with which to oppose him. Another was Johnston, who might send heavy detachments rearward by rail to catch him far from base and swamp him. The third was Forrest, who by now had attracted a considerable number of recruits to the cavalry division he was forming in North Mississippi and could be expected to investigate, in his usual slashing manner, any blue activity within reach. Discussing these problems with Grant, Sherman arrived at answers to all three. As for the first, he would employ no less than four divisions in his invasion column — two from McPherson's corps at Vicksburg and two from Hurlbut's at Memphis, which he would pick up on his way downriver — for a total of 20,000 infantry, plus about 5000 attached cavalry and artillery. That should take care of Polk, who could muster no better than half that many: unless, that is, he was reinforced by Johnston, and Grant agreed to discourage this by having Thomas menace Dalton. Forrest, the remaining concern, was to be attended to by a special force under W. Sooy Smith, recently placed at the head of all the cavalry in the Army of the Tennessee. At the same time the main body started east from Vicksburg, Smith was to set out south from West Tennessee, with instructions to occupy and defeat Forrest on the way to a link-up with Sherman at Meridian, from which point he and his troopers would take the lead on the march to Selma. His superiors saw, of course, that his more or less incidental defeat of Forrest, en route to the initial objective, was a lot to ask; but to make certain that he did not fail they arranged for him to be reinforced to a strength of 7000, roughly twice the number Forrest had in his green command. In any case, having arrived at this solution to the third of the three problems, Grant and his red-haired lieutenant parted company for a time, the latter to enjoy a Christmas leave with his family in Ohio while the former set out, shortly afterward, on the triumphal inspection tour through East Tennessee and Kentucky, followed by what turned out to be a pleasant visit to St Louis, where he was dined and toasted by civic leaders who once had looked askance at him as a poor catch for a Missouri girl.

In Memphis by mid-January, Sherman found Hurlbut busy carrying out instructions he had sent him to prepare two divisions for the trip downriver and the long march that would follow. While there, he also conferred with Smith, stressing the need for promptness and a vigorous celerity if his horsemen, with nearly twice the distance to cover from their starting point at nearby Collierville, were to reach Meridian at the same time as the foot soldiers, who would set out simultaneously from Vicksburg. Something else he stressed as well, which if neglected could bring on a far direr result than being thrown off schedule. This was what he referred to as "the nature of Forrest as a man, and of his peculiar force," a factor he first had learned to take into account at Fallen Timbers, after Shiloh, where his attempt at a pursuit had been brought to a sudden and unceremonious halt by one of the Tennessean's headlong charges, delivered in defiance not only of the odds, but also of the tactics manuals he had never read. "I explained to him," Sherman said afterwards of this conference with his chief of cavalry, "that in his route he was sure to encounter Forrest, who always attacked with a vehemence for which he must be prepared, and that, after he had repelled the first attack, he must in turn assume the most determined offensive, overwhelm him and utterly destroy his whole force." Without scoffing at the danger, Smith exhibited a confidence in the numerical advantage his superior's foresight had assured him for the impending confrontation with the so-called Wizard of the Saddle. Meantime Hurlbut completed his preparations. On the 25th he embarked with his two divisions, and Sherman followed two days later. By February 1 — the date set for Smith to begin his nearly 250-mile ride from Collierville, southeast to Okolona, then down the Mobile & Ohio to Meridian, wrecking and burning as he went — all the appointed elements of the infantry column were on hand at Vicksburg.

Sherman spent another two days making certain that all was in order for the march, which necessarily would be made without a base of supplies, and assessing the latest intelligence from spies beyond the lines. Polk by now had shifted his headquarters westward across the Tombigbee, from Demopolis to Meridian, and had posted his two divisions at Canton and Brandon, respectively under Loring and Sam French, twenty miles north and twelve miles east of Jackson, while his cavalry, under Stephen Lee, patrolled the region between the Pearl and the Big Black. Far from being alarmed by this, the northern commander was pleased to find his adversaries nearer than he had supposed; for they numbered barely half his strength, with 28 guns opposing 67 in the blue column, and the sooner he came to grips with them, the sooner they would be disposed of as a possible deterrent to his eastward progress and the destruction of everything of value in his path. Intending to move light, without tents or baggage even for corps commanders or himself, he had prescribed a minimum of equipment — "The expedition is one of celerity," he said, "and all things must tend to that"—but, even so, the twenty-day supply of such essentials as hardtack, salt, and coffee, together with ammunition and medical stores, required a 1000-wagon train. On February 3, having assured himself that all was as he had required, he passed the order that put his four divisions in motion for the Big Black River, one third of the way to Jackson, which in turn was a third of the way to Meridian, where Smith was to join him for the march on Selma, another hundred miles along the railroad he would follow all the way.

The march was in two columns, a corps in each, and so rapid that by nightfall both were over the river, trains and all, covering mile after eastward mile of ground for which they had fought in May, while headed in the opposite direction. Now as then, the weather was bright, the roads firm, and the soldiers in high spirits. They reached Edwards next day, swung past Champion Hill to end the third day's march at Bolton, and camped near Clinton the fourth night, within a dozen miles of the Mississippi capital. So far, the only resistance they had encountered was from small bands of cavalry; Lee was trying to slow their advance, and thus gain time for the two Confederate divisions to concentrate beyond the Pearl and there dispute a crossing. But Sherman saw through the design. Refusing to be delayed, he brushed the horsemen aside with his guns and kept his veterans slogging with such speed that Lee had no opportunity to destroy the pontoons of a large bridge, thrown across the river just beyond Jackson, before the Federals marched in on February 7. Twice already, in the past nine months, the torch had been put to this unfortunate town; now Sherman re-re-burned it, meantime pressing on for an uncontested crossing of the Pearl. Loring and French were in retreat by then, on opposite sides of the river — the former scuttling northward and the latter to the east, back to the places they had advanced from — having failed to get together in time to challenge the invaders at the only point where the terrain gave them a chance to prevail against the odds. Sherman kept moving. He reached Brandon the following evening — his forty-fourth birthday — and Morton on the 9th. In less than a week, he had not only covered better than half the distance between Vicksburg and Meridian; he had also scattered his opposition so effectively that now there was nothing between him and his initial objective except one badly rattled gray division, in flight from the four blue ones in its rear.

He pressed on, spurred by fear that he would be late for his rendezvous with Smith, who was due to reach Meridian tomorrow, after ten days on the road. The march was single column now, to provide a more compact defense against Lee's still-probing horsemen, and while McPherson paused for a day of destructive work on the railroad around Morton, Hurlbut made such good time that by sundown of the 12th he had passed through Decatur, northeast of Newton Station, and was less than thirty miles from Meridian. Sherman decided to wait there for McPherson, who was expected within a couple of hours. Detaching a regiment from Hurlbut's rear to serve as a guard, he and his staff unsaddled their horses in the yard of a house where an aide had arranged for supper; after which the general lay down on a bed to get some sleep. He was awakened by shouts and shots, and looked out of a window to find butternut cavalry "dashing about in a cloud of dust, firing their pistols." It developed that the colonel of the regiment detached to guard him, mistaking a front-riding group of staff officers for the head of McPherson's column, had considered himself relieved and pushed on eastward in an attempt to overtake his division before dark. When Sherman learned that this was what had happened, he sent an aide to order the regiment back on the double, while he himself prepared to retire with his companions to a corncrib for a blockhouse-style defense. Fortunately, the rebel troopers were giving their attention to some straggler wagons, never suspecting the larger prize within their reach, and before the townspeople could call it to their attention, the red-faced colonel returned on the run and drove them off, delivering the army commander from the gravest personal danger he had experienced since his near-capture at Collierville, four months ago yesterday. Presently McPherson did in fact come up, and Sherman went back to bed for a full night's sleep.

Another two days of marching brought the head of the blue column into Meridian by midafternoon of February 14. Polk had left by rail with the last of his troops that morning, retiring beyond the Tombigbee to Demopolis. After pleading in vain for reinforcements, he had concerned himself with the removal of an estimated $12,000,000 in military property, south to Mobile or east to Selma, together with the rolling stock of the three railroads; so that when Sherman marched in on Valentine's Day he found the warehouses yawning empty and the tracks deserted in all four directions. Furious at the loss, he put the blame on Smith, who should have arrived four days ago, in time to prevent the removal of the spoils, but who had neither come himself nor sent a courier to account for his departure from the schedule he had agreed to, three weeks back, in Memphis. Determined to make the most of the situation as he found it — for though the military property had been hauled away, the facilities were still there, and there was civilian property in abundance — the red-haired Ohioan gave his men a well-earned day of rest, then distributed the tools he had brought along to assure the efficient accomplishment of the object of his raid. "For five days," he subsequently reported, "10,000 men worked hard and with a will in that work of destruction, with axes, crowbars, sledges, clawbars, and with fire, and I have no hesitation in pronouncing the work as well done. Meridian, with its depots, store-houses, arsenal, hospitals, offices, hotels, and cantonments, no longer exists."

While the rest of the soldiers in the two corps were attending to the railroads — Hurlbut north and east of town, McPherson south and west, burning trestles, smashing culverts, and warping rails over bonfires fed by crossties — Sherman kept peering through the smoke for some sign of Smith and his 7000 troopers, who were to lead the march on Selma as soon as the present demolition work was finished. But there was none. "It will be a novel thing in war," he complained testily, between puffs on a cigar, "if infantry has to await the motions of cavalry."

His impatience was due in large part to the disappointing con-trast between his present situation, in which the nonarrival of his cavalry left him marking time in Meridian — albeit vigorously, to a tempo set by pounding sledges and crackling flames — and the pros-pect that had seemed to lie before him, three weeks ago in Memphis, at the time of his conference with the commander of the mounted column. Smith not only had been eager to undertake the assignment, but had shown a ready appreciation of what was required to make it a success. He was to ride southeast to Okolona, visiting such destruction upon the inhabitants of this 100-mile swath across North Mississippi as his schedule would permit, and then turn south along the Mobile & Ohio, scourging the heart of the Black Prairie region with fire and sword, all the way to his projected link-up with the infantry, an-other 130 miles below, for the combined march eastward across the Tombigbee. As for the tactical danger, the cavalryman declared that the best procedure would be "to pitch into Forrest wherever I find him." He did not say this boastfully, but rather in accordance with his instructions, which advised him to do just that.

Neither a greenhorn nor a braggart, Smith was a West Pointer like his commander and fellow Ohioan, who was ten years his senior, and had risen on ability in the army to which he returned on the out-break of war, interrupting what had promised to be (and later was) a distinguished career as a civil engineer. Graduating with Sheridan and McPherson, he had commanded a brigade at Shiloh while these other two Ohioans were still low-ranking staffers, and he led a division with such proficiency throughout the Vicksburg campaign that Grant soon afterwards made him his chief of cavalry. What was more, in the case of his present assignment, his confidence in his combat-tested ability as a leader was greatly strengthened by a look at the composition of the force he would be leading. In addition to five regiments he brought with him from Middle Tennessee, he would have at his disposal a Memphis-based division under Ben Grierson, who had ridden to fame over nearly the same route nine months before, and a veteran brigade already ordered to join him from Union City, up near the Kentucky line. Out of this total of better than 12,000 cavalry, he would select the 7000 he was to have in his hard-riding column, armed to a man with breech-loading carbines and accompanied by twenty pieces of artillery, double-teamed for speed. This would give him not only three times as many guns and twice as many troopers as were with Forrest, whose newly recruited division was all that stood between Smith and his objective, but also the largest and best-equipped body of Federal horsemen ever assembled in the western theater. It was small wonder he expressed no doubt that he could accomplish all that was asked of him at the late-January conference.

But Sherman had no sooner gone downriver than Smith learned that the 2000-man brigade from Union City, nearly one third of his intended force, was being delayed by floods and washouts all along the way. "Exceedingly chagrined," he informed the army commander that he thought it "wisest, best, and most promising" to postpone his departure until the brigade's arrival brought his column up to the strength assured him beforehand. He still felt "eager to pitch into [Forrest]," he said, "but I know that it is not your desire to 'send a boy to the mill.'" This was written on February 2, the day after he was supposed to have left Collierville and the day before Sherman left Vicksburg. As it turned out, moreover, the brigade did not reach Memphis until the 8th, and Smith found its horses so worn by their exertions that he felt obliged to give them a two-day rest. Then at last, on February 11 — one day after he was to have reached his initial objective, 230 miles away — he set out. He would "push ahead with all energy," he declared in a follow-up dispatch to Sherman, reporting that his men and their mounts were "in splendid condition" for the rigorous march. "Weather beautiful; roads getting good," he added. In a companion message to Grant, however, he sounded less ebullient. Earlier he had informed the department commander that his troopers were "well in hand, well provided with everything, and eager for the work," but now he confessed that the last-minute delay — already prolonged one day beyond the ten he was to have spent riding southward for the link-up at Meridian — had been "so long and so vexatious that I have worried myself into a state of morbid anxiety, and fear that I will be entirely too late to perform my part of the work."

Even though he was traversing, southeast of Collierville, what one of his lieutenants called a "rough, hopeless, God-forsaken" country, despoiled by nearly two years of contention and hard-handed occupation, his spirits rose in the course of the early stages of the march, partly because the tension of waiting had finally been relieved and partly because his prediction that Forrest would "show fight between the Coldwater and the Tallahatchie" was not borne out. He crossed the former stream near Holly Springs on the 12th and the latter at New Albany two days later — simultaneously, although he did not know it, with Sherman's arrival in Meridian — "without firing a shot." By now the column was badly strung out, however, and he was obliged to call a halt while the rear elements caught up; with the result that he did not reach Okolona until February 18. His schedule required a march rate of about twenty-five miles a day, but in this first week he had not averaged half that, despite the fact that he had encountered no opposition more formidable than a "rabble of State troops" near Pontotoc, which he brushed aside with ease, and had spent little time on the destructive work that was so much a part of his assignment. This last was because, so far, all he had run across that was worth destroying were a few outlying barns and gins. Now that he was astride the M&O, however, the opportunity for such labor was considerably enlarged: so much so, indeed, that from Okolona to West Point, a distance of about thirty miles, his troopers spent more time ripping up track and setting fires than they did in the saddle. "During two days," a brigade commander later wrote, "the sky was red with the flames of burning corn and cotton."

The sky was red with more flames than these; for the blue horsemen — especially those who were off on their own, as stragglers or outriders; "bummers," they would be called a bit later in the conflict — did not neglect the chance to scorch the holdings of secessionists in their path. What was more, a Federal colonel added, slaves on plantations roundabout, "driven wild with the infection, set the torch to mansion houses, stables, cotton gins, and quarters," and "came en masse to join our column, leaving only fire and absolute destruction behind them." Smith, for one, was "deeply pained" to find his command "disgraced by incendiarism of the most shocking kind. I have ordered the first man caught in the act to be shot," he notified Grierson, "and I have offered $500 reward for his detection." As for the Negroes, though he had encouraged them to join him as a means of increasing the disruption of the region and decreasing its future contribution to the Confederate war effort, he now had some 3000 of them on his hands and was finding them a severe encumbrance to his so-called "flying column," just at a time when he seemed likely to have to move his fastest. Despite his relief that Forrest had failed to "show fight" in the early stages of the march, it had begun to occur to him that the Tennessean might be postponing his attack until he reached a position "where he could concentrate a larger force, and where we would be to some extent jaded and farther from home."

By way of confirmation for these fears, a recently captured Indiana trooper managed to escape and rejoin his outfit on February 19, south of Okolona, with information that "Forrest's whole force was reported to be in the vicinity of West Point," barely a dozen miles ahead, and was "said to be 8000 or 9000 strong." Consequently when his lead elements ran into stiffer resistance next morning in that direction, Smith paused for thought. It seemed to him that his adversary, with the unexpected advantage of superior numbers, was laying a trap for him just down the line. He thought about this long and hard, and that evening his adjutant replied to a dispatch from one of his brigade commanders: "The general is very sick tonight."

His information was partly wrong, but his conclusion was entirely right. Though Forrest had a good deal less than half the number of men reported by the slippery Hoosier, he was indeed laying a trap for the blue column moving toward him down the Mobile & Ohio: a trap whose springing, incidentally, would commit his green command to its first concerted action. He had come to Mississippi in mid-November with fewer than 300 veterans from his old brigade, and two weeks later he took them northward, deep into West Tennessee, on a month-long tour of recruiting duty behind the Union lines, from which he returned by New Year's with some 3500 effectives, a sizable drove of hogs and cattle, and forty wagonloads of bacon. As here applied, the term "effectives" was questionable, however, since his recruits were mostly absentees and deserters, men who had skedaddled at least once before and could be expected to do so again at the first chance. "Forrest may cavort about that country as much as he pleases," Sherman had said when he heard what the rebel cavalryman was up to, north of Memphis. "Every conscript they now catch will cost a good man to watch." That this was a quite reasonable assertion no one knew better than the newly promoted major general who had this jumpy, unarmed mass in charge. But he depended on rigorous training and stern discipline — along with a few summary executions, if they were what was needed — to discourage the fulfillment of the Ohioan's prediction; after which would come the fighting that would knit what he now referred to as "my force of raw, undrilled, and undisciplined troops" into a cohesive unit, stamped with the aggressive personality of its leader and filled with a fierce pride in itself and him. With this in mind, he began in early January a program of unrelenting drill, mounted and dismounted, combined with a system of sharp-eyed inspections to assure compliance with his directives. This had been in progress barely a month when he received word at his headquarters, north of Panola, that Sherman was on the march from Vicksburg, 150 miles to the south, evidently intending to strike at Meridian and possibly also at Selma or Mobile. Eight days later, Smith left Collierville, 50 miles to the north, and Forrest made this second column his concern, determined to prevent a junction of the two, though even the smaller one had twice his strength and was infinitely superior in experience and equipment.

While Smith was moving southeast, from Holly Springs to Okolona, Forrest paralleled the blue march by shifting from Panola to Starkville. Outnumbered two to one, he could not risk an all-out attack in open country; nor could he lie in wait for the invaders until he knew where they were headed and what route they would take to get there. They might, for example, cross the Tombigbee east of Tupelo for a link-up with Sherman at Demopolis or Selma, leaving the graybacks crouched in a useless ambush far behind, or they might turn abruptly southwest and make for Jackson, passing in rear of the butternut column hurrying eastward. So Forrest bided his time and awaited developments, keeping his four undersized brigades spread out to counter an advance from any one of several directions. Then on February 19, when Smith began his wrecking descent of the M&O, it was plain that he intended to follow the railroad all the way to Meridian, and Forrest was free to develop a specific plan to stop him. Which he did. Sending one brigade to West Point as a bait to lure the bluecoats on, he ordered the others to take up a position three miles below, in a swampy pocket enclosed on the west and south by Sakatonchee and Oktibbeha creeks and on the east by the Tombigbee. That was the trap. The bait brigade, commanded by Colonel Jeffrey Forrest, the general's twenty-six-year-old brother, fell back next day as ordered, skirmishing lightly to draw the Federals through West Point and into the pocket prepared for their destruction. They followed cautiously, into and just beyond the town; but there they stopped, apparently for the night. Believing that they would come on again next morning, February 21, Forrest continued his preparations to receive them with a double envelopment.

He was wrong. Although there was an advance, which brought on a brief engagement, it soon became evident that this was a mere feint — a rear-guard action, designed to cover a withdrawal. Nearly two thirds of the way to his objective, Smith had given up trying to reach it; had decided, instead, to backtrack. Ahead were swamps and an enemy force reported to be larger than his own, while he was already ten full days behind schedule, still with eighty-odd miles to go and some 3000 homeless Negroes on his hands. "Under the circumstances," he afterwards declared, "I determined not to move my encumbered command into the trap set for me by the rebels."

Forrest, having gained what he called the "bulge," reacted fast. If the Yankees would not come to him, then he would go to them. And this he did, with a vengeance. Being, as he said later, "unwilling they should leave the country without a fight," he ordered his entire command to take up the pursuit of the retreating bluecoats. Moreover, the rearguard skirmish had no sooner begun than he attended to another matter of grave concern: namely, the behavior of his "raw, undrilled, and undisciplined" troopers in their reaction to being shot at, many of them for the first time. As he approached the firing line he met a panic-stricken Confederate stumbling rearward, hatless and gunless, in full flight from his first taste of combat. Forrest dis-

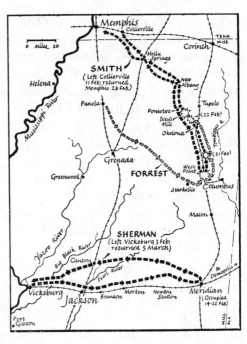

mounted to intercept him, flung him face-down by the roadside, then took up a piece of brush and administered what a startled witness described as "one of the worst thrashings I have ever seen a human being get." This done, he jerked the unfortunate soldier to his feet, faced him about, and gave him a shove that sent him stumbling in the direction of the uproar he had fled from. "Now, God damn you, go back to the front and fight!" he shouted after him. "You might as well be killed there as here, for if you ever run away again you'll not get off so easy." Still raw and undrilled, but by no means undisciplined, the man rejoined his comrades on the firing line, and the story quickly spread, not only through the division — as the general no doubt intended — but also through both armies, until finally it was made the subject of a *Harper's Weekly* illustration titled "Forrest Breaking in a Conscript."

For the next two days he handled Smith in much the same fashion. After driving the rear-guard Federals through West Point, he came upon them again, three miles beyond the town, stoutly posted along a timbered ridge approachable only by a narrow causeway. His solution was to send one regiment galloping wide around the enemy flank, with orders to strike the rear, while the others dismounted to attack in front. Admittedly, this was a lot to ask of green troops, but Forrest employed a method of persuasion quite different from the one he had used a while ago on the panicked conscript. "Come on, boys!" he roared, and led the way, thus setting an example which caused one of his men to recall, years later, that "his immediate presence seemed to inspire everyone with his terrible energy, more like that of a piece of

powerful steam machinery than of a human being." So led, they drove
the bluecoats from the ridge, then remounted and continued the pursuit until nightfall, when their commander called a halt, midway between West Point and Okolona, in a hastily abandoned bivouac area,
stocked not only with rations and forage, but also with wood for the
still-burning campfires. While the graybacks bedded down and slept beside the cozy warmth provided by their foes, Smith kept his main
body plodding northward and did not stop until well past midnight,
within four miles of Okolona. Burdened with captured stock and run-
away slaves, and weary as they were from their long march — since
sunup, they had covered better than twice the distance they had managed on any one of the other nine days since they left Collierville —
his men got a late start next morning. By that time Forrest, who had
had his troopers up and on the go by dawn, well rested and unencum-
bered, had closed the ten-mile gap and was snapping again at the tail
and flanks of the blue column.

Smith was learning, as Streight had learned before him, that
it could be even more dangerous to run from the Tennessean than it
was to stand and fight him. However, instead of turning on him with
all he had, he dropped off a couple of regiments just beyond Okolona
and a full brigade at Ivey's Hill, five miles farther along on the road
to Pontotoc, still intent on saving his train and protecting the Negroes
in his charge. After a running fight through the town, hard on the heels
of the rear guard, the gray pursuers came upon the first of these two
prepared positions and were brought to a halt by fire from the superior
Federal weapons. At this point Forrest arrived. "Where is the enemy's
whole position?" he asked Colonel Tyree Bell, whose brigade had the
lead this morning. "You see it, General," Bell replied, and added:
"They are preparing to charge." "Then we will charge them," Forrest said: and did. The result was a blue rout. Five guns were abandoned shortly thereafter by an artillery lieutenant who complained
hotly in his report that his battery had been forced off the road and
into a ditch by Union troopers who overtook him "in perfect confusion," hallooing: "Go ahead, or we'll be killed!" The chase continued
to Ivey's Hill, where the defenders, allowed more time to get set, gave
a considerably better account of themselves. Opening ranks to let the
fugitives through, they took under well-aimed fire the two brigades advancing toward them across the prairie. At the first volley the commanders of both were shot, one in the hand, the other through the
throat. The second of these was Jeffrey Forrest, and though the general reached him immediately after he fell — this youngest of his five
brothers, posthumously born and sixteen years his junior, whom he
had raised as a son and made into a soldier — he found him dead. He
remained bent over him for a minute or two, then rose and ordered

his bugler to sound the charge. The fighting that followed was savage and hand-to-hand. Within the next hour, Forrest had two horses killed under him and accounted in person for three enemy soldiers, shot or sabered.

Thus assailed, the Federals once more fell back to try another stand in a position ten miles from Pontotoc; which was also lost, along with another gun, but which at any rate ended the relentless chase that had begun two days ago, nearly fifty miles away, below West Point. "Owing to the broken down and exhausted condition of men and horses, and being almost out of ammunition," Forrest presently reported, "I was compelled to stop pursuit." Smith was unaware of this, however, and kept going even harder than before. Judging the rebel strength by Forrest's aggressiveness, he believed that Stephen Lee had arrived to join the chase, though in point of fact he now had nothing on his trial but the "rabble of state troops" he had brushed aside when he passed this way the week before, headed in the opposite direction. In Pontotoc by midnight, he resumed the march at 3 a.m. and cleared New Albany that afternoon, February 23, destroying in his rear the bridges across the Tallahatchie. All next day he kept moving, unwilling to risk another stand, and rode at last into Collierville on the 25th, having covered in five days the same distance he had required ten days to cover while going south. Not even then did he call a halt, however; he kept going all the following day, through Germantown to Memphis, there ending at last what one brigade commander described as "a weary, disheartened, almost panic-stricken flight, in the greatest disorder and confusion."

His loss in men had not been great (it amounted to 388 in all, including 155 missing, as compared to a total of 144 for his opponent — a disparity which Forrest, as the attacker, could only account for by "the fact that we kept so close to them that the enemy overshot our men") but the cost in horseflesh had been cruel. Smith returned with no more than 2200 riders who could be described as adequately mounted; the other 4800 were either on foot or astride horses no longer fit for service in the field. A corresponding loss in cavalry morale, so lately on the rise in all the Union armies, was indicated by an unhappy colonel's remark that "the expedition filled every man connected with it with a burning shame." Nor was that by any means the worst of it from the northern point of view. The worst was still to come, resulting not so much from Federal losses as from Confederate gains. Practically overnight, by this victory over twice their number — and the capture, in the process, of six guns and several stands of colors — Forrest's green recruits had acquired a considerable measure of that fierce pride which in time would enable their commander to prevail against even longer odds and for much larger stakes. Already he was preparing to go over to the offensive, beginning with a return to West Tennessee and the accomplishment there of a great deal more than the mere enlargement of his now veteran division.

Though Sherman had been doubtful of Smith's competence from the start, deeming him "too mistrustful of himself for a leader against Forrest," this took none of the sting from his censure of his fellow Ohioan for "allowing General Forrest to head him off and defeat him with an inferior force." But that was later, after he learned the gloomy particulars of the cavalry excursion, and in any case he had waited for Smith no longer than it took him to wipe the appointed meeting place off the map. By the time the frazzled horsemen returned to Memphis, Sherman had recrossed the Pearl and gone into bivouac at Canton, north of Jackson, still with no knowledge of what, if anything, had happened to the mounted column, which in fact had begun its retreat from West Point on the day he ended his five-day stay in Meridian and abandoned his proposed advance on Selma.

Not that he considered his own part in the campaign anything less than "successful in the highest degree," both on the outward march and the return, which he made along a different route, twenty-odd miles to the north, so as to avoid the grainless, cowless, hogless trail his twelve brigades of infantry had blazed while slogging eastward. "My movement to Meridian stampeded all Alabama," he informed Halleck three days later, on February 29. "Polk retreated across the Tombigbee and left me to smash things at pleasure, and I think it is well done. . . . We broke absolutely and effectually a full hundred miles of railroad . . . and made a swath of desolation fifty miles broad across the State of Mississippi which the present generation will not forget." After listing his spoils, which included "some 500 prisoners, a good many refugee families, and about ten miles of negroes," he announced that the destruction he had wrought "makes it simply impossible for the enemy to risk anything but light cavalry this side of Pearl River; consequently, I can reduce the garrisons of Memphis, Vicksburg, and Natchez to mere guards, and, in fact, it will set free 15,000 men for other duty. I could have gone on to Mobile or over to Selma," he added, "but without other concurrent operations it would have been unwise." Privately, however, in a companion letter to his wife, he confessed his regret that Smith's nonarrival had prevented him from applying what his foes were calling "the Sherman torch" to Alabama. "As it was," he chuckled, for he always enjoyed a small joke on the clergy, "I scared the bishop out of his senses."

It was Polk he meant, of course, and he was right; the bishop had indeed been frightened, not only for Meridian, Demopolis, and Selma, but also for Mobile, a greater prize than any of those others in his care. His fears for the Confederacy's only remaining Gulf port east of the Mississippi had been enlarged in late January when Farragut — who had just returned from a New York holiday, taken while the *Hartford* was being refitted in the Brooklyn Navy Yard — appeared before the place with a squadron of multigunned warships, evidently intending to launch another of his all-out attacks, not one of which had ever failed with him on hand to see that it was pressed to the required extremity. In point of fact, the admiral was only there to heighten Polk's fears for the loss of the port and to discourage him from drawing reinforcements from its garrison when Sherman began his march. There was no need to attack; he accomplished his purpose merely by his month-long presence, just outside the bay, and gained in the process much valuable information which he would put to substantial use when he came back again, not for a feint or diversion, but in earnest. As a result, when Sherman set out from Vicksburg in early February, Polk was convinced that his goal was Mobile and that what was intended was a combined assault, by land and water, designed to remove that vital port from the list of the South's assets in continuing its struggle to maintain its national existence. Outnumbered two to one, or worse, the bishop called loudly on Richmond for assistance, and Richmond passed his appeal to Johnston, the only possible source for reinforcements in a hurry. Whereupon there was staged in North Georgia a grim comedy involving a balking contest between the two commanders, blue and gray.

Johnson protested for all he was worth. In the first place, he did not believe the proposed reinforcements could reach Polk in time to head off Sherman; and what was more he was convinced that any substantial reduction of his already outnumbered force, which was being required to maintain a position that had "neither intrinsic strength nor strategic advantage," would not only expose Atlanta to capture by the blue mass in his front, but would also be likely to result in the destruction of what would remain of the army charged with its defense. This chilling presentation to the government of a choice between losing one or the other of two of its principal cities had the effect of delaying, though not of forestalling, a peremptory order requiring the immediate detachment of Hardee's corps to Polk for the purpose of covering Mobile. Received on February 16, the order began to be carried out four days later — by coincidence, on the day Sherman began his return march from Meridian — when the three divisions boarded the cars at Dalton for the long ride to Demopolis. Arriving next day they found they were unneeded; Sherman had withdrawn. Polk put them promptly back aboard the cars to rejoin Johnston, who by now was sending up distress signals of his own. His worst fears had been realized; Thomas was advancing. The Union-loyal Virginian had also received peremptory orders, and he too had delayed their execution. Instructed on February 14 to make a "formidable reconnaissance" of

Johnston's position, he took a week to get ready, then started forward from Ringgold on the eighth day, February 22, two days after Hardee departed with the divisions under Cheatham, Walker, and Cleburne. Grant's hope was that Thomas would catch his adversary off balance and thus be able to drive him back from Rocky Face Ridge and beyond Dalton, in order to "get possession of the place and hold it as a step toward a spring campaign."

With three of his seven divisions 350 roundabout miles away, Johnston was something worse than merely off balance when Thomas moved against him. Palmer's corps made the opening thrust at Tunnel Hill. Formerly occupied by Cleburne, this western spur of Rocky Face Ridge was now held only by Wheeler, whose horse artillery raised such a clatter that the bluecoats were discouraged from attacking until the following day, February 24. By then the rebel troopers had fallen back through Buzzard Roost Gap to cover the flanks of the infantry disposed along the ridge. Thomas probed the passes on the 25th, making some progress against the wide-spread defenders — especially at Dug Gap, immediately southwest of Dalton — but when Palmer launched a co-ordinated assault next morning he found that Hardee's three divisions, having completed their round-trip journey to Demopolis, were in position on the ridge; Cleburne, in fact, was on the flank of the flankers. Accordingly, Thomas withdrew as he had come, returning to Ringgold on the same day Sooy Smith rode back into Memphis and Sherman descended on Canton. His "formidable reconnaissance" had cost him 345 casualties and had failed in its larger purpose of seizing Dalton "as a step toward a spring campaign"; but he, like Farragut outside Mobile, had learned much that would be useful when he returned in earnest. As for Johnston, he was agreeably surprised. He had expected to be thrown into precipitate retreat; whereas his men had not only maintained the integrity of a position which he declared had "little to recommend it," but had inflicted better than twice the 167 casualties they suffered. Even more heartening than the bare tactical result was the contrast between the army's present frame of mind, here on Rocky Face Ridge, and the one that had been evidenced a dozen weeks ago on Missionary Ridge. Unquestionably its spirit had been lifted: perhaps indeed a bit too much, at least in one respect, to suit Old Joe. For in congratulating his troops on their work, he was critical of the artillery officers for having "exhibited a childish eagerness to discharge their pieces."

By now the Confederates had returned to Meridian, or at any rate to the desolation Sherman had created in its place. Speaking in Jackson on his first western visit, just over a year ago, Jefferson Davis had warned that the invaders had it in mind to handle Mississippi "without gloves," and now his words had been borne out; Meridian was an example of what the men he referred to as "worse than vandal hordes" could accomplish when their commander turned them loose with the admonition that "vigorous war . . . means universal destruction." In addition to the damage inflicted on the town itself, a total of twenty-four miles of railroad track, extending an average half dozen miles in all four directions, had been demolished, the crossties burned, the rails heated and twisted into what were known as "Sherman neckties." Beyond this circumference of utter destruction, for a distance of nearly fifty miles north and south, not a bridge or a trestle had been left unwrecked on the Mobile & Ohio. Already, in the course of their march from Jackson, the raiders had disposed of fifty-one bridges on the Southern, together with an even larger number of trestles and culverts, and they had extended their work eastward, nine miles beyond the junction, to add three more bridges and five trestles to the tally. Yet, sad as it was to survey the charred remains of what once had passed for prosperity in this nonindustrial region, sadder by far were the people of those counties through which the blue column had slogged on its way to and from the town that now was little more than a scar on the green breast of earth. They had the stunned, unbelieving look of survivors of some terrible natural disaster, such as a five-day hurricane, a tidal wave, or an earthquake: with the underlying difference that their grief had been inflicted by human design and was in fact a deliberate product of a new kind of war, quite unlike the one for which they had bargained three years ago, back in that first glad springtime of secession. It was, moreover, a war that was still in progress, and somehow that was the strangest, most distressful aspect of all. Their deprivation was incidental to the large design. They were faced with the aftermath before the finish.

Polk took no such gloomy view of the prospect. Though he could scarcely deny the all-too-evident validity of Sherman's boast of having "made a swath of desolation fifty miles broad across the State of Mississippi which the present generation will not forget," he did not agree with his adversary's further assertion that the east-central portion of the state could be written off as a factor in the conflict. "I have already taken measures to have all the roads broken up by him rebuilt," the bishop notified Richmond two days after the raiders turned back in the direction they had come from, "and shall press that work vigorously." Press it he did. Summoning to his Demopolis headquarters President Samuel Tate of the Memphis & Charleston Railroad, he put him in general charge of the restoration, with full authority to requisition both property and labor. Tate was a driver. Despite a crippling shortage of rails and spikes — not to mention the inevitable objections of planters to the impressment of such of their Negroes as had not gone off with Smith and Sherman — within twenty-six days he had the Mobile & Ohio back in operation, from Tupelo south to Mobile Bay, along with the Alabama & Mississippi, from Meridian to the Tombigbee. The Southern took longer, mainly because of administrative complications, but within another five weeks it too was open, all the way to the Pearl.

But that was later. At the time he made it, February 28, Sherman's pronouncement: "My movement cleared Mississippi at one swoop, and with the railroad thus destroyed the Confederacy cannot maintain an army save cavalry west of Tombigbee," seemed to him irrefutable. He was back in Vicksburg by then, having come on ahead of the infantry, which he left marking time in Canton, as he said afterwards, "with orders to remain till about the 3d of March" — he was still hoping Sooy Smith would turn up — "and then come into Vicksburg leisurely." Pleased by the added destruction of several miles of the Mississippi Central, north of Jackson — together with 19 locomotives, 28 cars, and 724 carwheels, which helped to ease his disappointment that Polk had managed to save the rolling stock on the other roads within his reach — he proudly announced: "Everything with my command was successful in the highest degree." That this was hardly an overstatement was evidenced by the anguished protests of his opponents and victims, soldiers and civilians, some of whom reported the damage at a larger figure than his own. Stephen Lee, for one, charged the raiders with "burning 10,000 bales of cotton and 2,000,000 bushels of corn and carrying off 8000 slaves, many mounted on stolen mules." He estimated the over-all loss at five million dollars, of which "three fourths was private property," and asked rhetorically: "Was this the warfare of the nineteenth century?" Sherman was not inclined to dispute the statistics, and he had already given his answer to Lee's question. This was indeed the warfare of the nineteenth century, at any rate as he intended to practice it, and he was not only proud of what had been accomplished by this first large-scale application of the methods that had aroused the South Carolinian's moral indignation; he was also looking forward to the time when he could apply those methods elsewhere, perhaps even in the angry young cavalryman's native state, where the provocation had begun.

First though would come Georgia; Mississippi had been something of a warm-up, a practice operation in this regard, just as perhaps Georgia in turn would be a warm-up for the Carolinas. In any case Sherman had composed at Vicksburg, by way of further preparation while waiting to set out across Mississippi, a letter to the assistant adjutant general of his army, most of whose members were in camps around Chattanooga waiting for him to return from his current excursion and lead them against Joe Johnston and Atlanta. Ostensibly addressed to Major R. M. Sawyer, the letter was in fact a warning to the civilians in his southward path, as well as a legalistic justification for military harshness, since it dealt primarily with his intention regarding "the treatment of inhabitants known or suspected to be hostile or 'secesh.'" His policy up to now, he said, had been to leave the question to local commanders of occupation forces, "but [I] am willing to give them the benefit of my acquired knowledge and experience," and though he admitted that it was "almost impossible to lay down rules" for their guidance in such matters, he proceeded to do precisely that, and more.

"In Europe, whence we derive our principles of war, as developed by their histories," he began, "wars are between kings or rulers, through hired armies, and not between peoples. These remain as it were neutral, and sell their produce to whatever army is in possession. . . . Therefore the rule was, and is, that wars are confined to the armies and should not visit the homes of families or private interests." Little or none of this applied in the present instance, however, any more than it had done in the case of the Irish insurrection against William and Mary, who dispossessed the rebels of their property, sent them forthwith into exile, and gave their lands to Scottish emigrants. The same could be done with justice here, Sherman declared, but he preferred to withhold such measures for a time, on grounds that the guilt was not entirely restricted to the guilty. "For my part," he explained, "I believe this war is the result of false political doctrine, for which we all as a people are responsible . . . and I would give all a chance to reflect and when in error to recant. . . . I am willing to bear in patience that political nonsense of slave rights, States rights, freedom of conscience, freedom of the press, and such other trash as have deluded the Southern people into war, anarchy, bloodshed, and the foulest crimes that have disgraced any time or any people." He would bear all this in patience, but only for a season; meanwhile he would have the occupation commanders "assemble the inhabitants and explain to them these plain, self-evident propositions, and tell them that it is now for them to say whether they and their children shall inherit the beautiful land which by the accident of nature had fallen to their share." After this, if they persisted in the error of their ways, would come the thunder. "If they want eternal war, well and good; we accept the issue, and will dispossess them and put our friends in their places." Moreover, the longer they delayed recanting, the sterner their fate would be. "Three years ago, by a little reflection and patience, they could have had a hundred years of peace and prosperity, but they preferred war; very well. Last year they could have saved their slaves, but now it is too late. All the powers of earth cannot return to them their slaves, any more than their dead grandfathers. Next year their lands will be taken; for in war we can take them, and rightfully, too, and in another year they may beg in vain for their lives." He warmed as he wrote, assuming the guise of an avenging angel — even the Archangel Michael — to touch on eschatology in the end. "To those who submit to the rightful law and authority, all gentleness and forbearance; but to the petulant and persistent secessionists, why, death is mercy, and the quicker he or she is disposed of the better. Satan and the rebellious saints of Heaven were allowed a continuous existence in hell merely to swell their just punishment. To such as would rebel against a Government so mild and just as ours was in peace, a punishment equal would not be unjust."

A copy went to his senator brother, with the request that it be printed for all to read, along and behind the opposing lines of battle. "It's publication would do no harm," he said, "except to turn the Richmond press against me as the prince of barbarians." Actually he was of the opinion that it would do much good, especially Southward, and he urged his adjutant to see that his views were presented to "some of the better people" of the region already occupied, with the suggestion that they pass them along to friends in whose direction he would be moving in the spring. "Read to them this letter," he wrote, "and let them use it so as to prepare them for my coming."

✖ 4 ✖

Sherman's notion of how the war could be won was definite enough, but whether it would be fought that way — with stepped-up harshness, to and through the finish — depended in no small measure on who would be directing it from the top. This was a presidential election year; the armies might have a new Commander in Chief before the advent of the victory which not even the ebullient Ohioan, in his days of highest feather, predicted would occur within the twelve-month span that lay between his return from Meridian, having demonstrated the effectiveness of his method, and the inauguration of the winner of the November contest at the polls. Moreover, the Republican convention was barely three months off, and though Lincoln had expressed a cautious willingness to stand for re-election — "A second term would be a great honor and a great labor," he had told Elihu Washburne in October, "which together, perhaps, I would not decline if tendered" — whether he would be renominated appeared doubtful. For one thing, recent tradition was against it; none of the other eight Presidents since Andrew Jackson had served beyond a single term. Besides, whatever his popularity with the people, the men who controlled the convention seemed practically unanimous in their conviction that a better candidate could be found. "Not a Senator can be named as favorable to Lincoln's renomination," the Detroit *Free Press* had reported, and the claim went uncontradicted. Nor was this opinion limited to his enemies. David Davis, who had managed his 1860 nomination, and who had been duly rewarded with a seat on the Supreme Court, declared in private: "The politicians in and out of Congress, it is believed, would put Mr Lincoln aside if they dared." Lyman Trumbull, an associate from early days and now a power in the Senate, believed however that it was not so much a question of daring as of tactics. Writing to a constituent back in Illinois, he presented the reasons behind this opposition and suggested that those who held them were merely biding their time between now and early June, when the delegates would convene in Baltimore. "The feeling for Mr Lincoln's re-election *seems* to be very general," he said, "but much of it I discover is only on the surface. You would be surprised, in talking with public men we meet here, to find how few, when you come to get at their real sentiment, are for Mr Lincoln's re-election. There is a distrust and fear that he is too undecided and inefficient to put down the rebellion. You need not be surprised if a reaction sets in before the nomination, in favor of some man supposed to possess more energy and less inclination to trust our brave boys in the hands and under the leadership of generals who have no heart in the war. The opposition to Mr L. may not show itself at all, but if it ever breaks out there will be more of it than now appears."

It broke out sooner than expected, though not from an unpredictable direction, the source of the explosion being Salmon Chase, or at any rate the men around or behind him, who saw in the adverse reaction to the overlenient Amnesty Proclamation an opportunity too fruitful to be neglected. Chase had been sobered by the Cabinet crisis of mid-December, fourteen months ago, but renewed ambition apparently caused him to forget his extreme discomfort at that time. In any case, in an attempt to influence various state conventions soon to be in session, a group of the Secretary's friends banded together and sent out in early February a "strictly private" letter afterwards known as the Pomeroy Circular. So called because it was issued over the signature of the group chairman, Senator Samuel C. Pomeroy of Kansas, a prominent Jacobin and old-line abolitionist, the document charged that "party machinery and official influence are being used to secure the perpetuation of the present Administration," asserted that "those who believe in the interests of the country and of freedom demand a change in favor of vigor and purity," and then went on to present five main points all delegates would do well to bear in mind. The first two were against Lincoln, whose re-election was not only "practically impossible" but also undesirable, since under him "the war may continue to languish" and "the cause of human liberty, and the dignity of the nation, suffer proportionately." The third point found "the 'one-term principle' absolutely essential to the certain safety of our republican institutions." The final two were devoted to Chase, who not only had "more of the qualities needed in a President during the next four years than are combined in any other candidate," but had developed, as well, "a popularity and strength ... unexpected even to his warmest admirers." Finally, each recipient was urged to "render efficient aid by exerting yourself at once to organize your section of the country" and to enter into correspondence with the undersigned chairman "for the purpose either of receiving or imparting information."

Lincoln was told of the "strictly private" circular as soon as it appeared. On February 6, Ward Lamon wrote from New York that a prominent banker there had received in his mail that morning, under the frank of an Ohio congressman, "a most scurrilous and abominable pamphlet about you, your administration, and the succession." Copies arrived from other friends on the lookout, but got no farther than Nicolay's desk; Lincoln would not read them. "I have determined to shut my eyes, so far as possible, to everything of that sort," he explained. "Mr Chase makes a good Secretary, and I shall keep him where he is. If he becomes President, all right. I hope we shall never have a worse man." He knew, of course, of the Ohioan's machinations, which were strengthened by the dispensation of some ten thousand jobs in his department, and he said of his activities as an inside critic, "I suppose he will, like the bluebottle fly, lay his eggs in every rotten spot he can find." But to some who advised that the "perfidious ingrate" be fired he replied: "I am entirely indifferent to his success or failure in these schemes, so long as he does his duty at the head of the Treasury Department." To others he maintained that "the Presidential grub" had much the same effect on the Secretary as a horsefly had on a balky plow horse; he got more work out of him when he was bit. Or perhaps it was even simpler than that. Perhaps Lincoln enjoyed watching the performance Chase gave. It was, after all, pretty much a repeat performance, and he already knew the outcome, agreeing beforehand with Welles, who predicted in his diary that the Pomeroy Circular would be "more dangerous in its recoil than its projectile." His adversaries had bided their time; now he was biding his. A Massachusetts congressman, returning from a visit to the White House at the height of this latest Chase-for-President boom, informed a colleague that Lincoln was only waiting for the Treasury chief to put himself a little more clearly in the wrong. "He thinks that Mr C. will sufficiently soon force the question. In the meantime I think he is wise in waiting till the pear is ripe."

The pear ripened over the weekend of Washington's Birthday. On Saturday, February 20, the *Constitutional Union* printed in full the text of the circular, and when it was picked up on Monday by the *National Intelligencer*, Chase could no longer pretend to be unaware of what his friends were doing in his behalf. Writing to Lincoln that same day, he declared however that he had "had no knowledge of the existence of this letter before I saw it in the *Union*." Some weeks ago, he went on, "several gentlemen" had called on him "in connection with the approaching election of Chief Magistrate," and though he had not felt that he could forbid them to work as they chose, he had "told them distinctly that I could render them no help, except what might come incidentally from the faithful discharge of public duties, for these must have my whole time"; otherwise, he knew nothing of what had been done by these gentlemen. "I have thought this explanation due to you as well as to myself," he told Lincoln. "If there is anything in my action or position which in your judgment will prejudice the public interest in my charge, I beg you to say so. I do not wish to administer the Treasury Department one day without your entire confidence. For yourself," he continued, appending a sort of amiable tailpiece to his tentative resignation, "I cherish sincere respect and esteem; and, permit me to add, affection. Differences of opinion as to administrative action have not changed these sentiments; nor have they been changed by assaults upon me by persons who profess to spread representations of your views and policy. You are not responsible for acts not your own; nor will you hold me responsible except for what I do or say myself. Great numbers now desire your re-election. Should their wishes be fulfilled by the suffrages of the people, I hope to carry with me into private life the sentiments I now cherish, whole and unimpaired."

He received next day a one-sentence reply, as inconclusive as it was brief. "Yours of yesterday in relation to the paper issued by Senator Pomeroy was duly received; and I write this note merely to say I will answer a little more fully when I can find the leisure to do so. Yours truly, A. Lincoln."

Chase out would be considerably more formidable than Chase in; Lincoln had no intention of accepting a resignation which, by splitting the party, might well lose the Republicans the election, whoever the candidate was. He did wait six full days, however, before he found "the leisure" to compose his promised answer. This may have been done primarily to allow the Ohioan plenty of time to squirm, but it also afforded others a chance to contribute to the squirmer's discomfort by heating up the griddle. When Chase spoke of "assaults upon me by persons who profess to spread representations of your views," it was the Blairs he meant: specifically, Montgomery and Frank. Back in the fall, as principal speaker at a Maryland rally, the Postmaster General had referred to the Jacobins as "co-adjutors of Presidential schemers," making it clear that he had the Treasury head in mind as the chief schemer, and since then he had been castigating his fellow Cabinet member at practically every opportunity. Even so, he was not as harsh in this regard as his brother Frank, the soldier member of the family of whom it was said, "When the Blairs go in for a fight they go in for a funeral." Soon after his corps went into winter quarters near Chattanooga, Frank Blair came to Washington as a Missouri congressman. This had required the surrender of his commission as a major general, but Lincoln had promised to take care of that. He wanted Blair to stand for Speaker of the House, a post at which so stout a fighter could be of even more use to the Administration than on the field of battle, and he agreed that if this did not work out he would restore the commission and Blair could return to his duties as a corps commander under Sherman. But the plan fell through. By the time the Missourian reached the capital in early January, Indiana's Schuyler Colfax, strongly anti-Lincoln in persuasion, had been elected Speaker. Nevertheless, since his corps was still lying idle down in Tennessee, Blair took his seat and stayed on in Washington, alert for a chance to strike at the President's enemies and his own. A chance was not long in coming. On February 5, the day the Pomeroy Circular began to go out across the land, Blair rose in the House to speak in defense of the Administration's policies on amnesty and reconstruction, opposition to which he declared had been "concocted for purposes of defeating the renomination of Mr Lincoln" in order to open the way for "rival aspirants." Everyone knew it was Chase he meant, and three weeks later, on February 27 — four days into the six allowed for squirming — he made the charge specific, along with several others. Referring to the circular, he said of the candidate favored therein: "It is a matter of surprise that a man having the instincts of a gentleman should remain in the Cabinet after the disclosure of such an intrigue against the one to whom he owes his position. [However] I suppose the President is well content that he should stay; for every hour that he remains sinks him in the contempt of every honorable mind." Beyond this, Blair asserted that "a more profligate administration of the Treasury Department never existed under any government," and that investigation would show that "the whole Mississippi Valley is rank and fetid with the frauds and corruptions of its agents . . . some of [whom] I suppose employ themselves in distributing that 'strictly private' circular which came to light the other day."

Such charges hurt badly. Damage to Chase's reputation was damage to his soul, and though he thought of himself as a scrupulous administrator of the nation's funds, he knew quite well that for political reasons he had made agents of men who could by no means be said to measure up to his own high standards. In any case — perhaps out of pity, for the punishment was heavy — Lincoln ended at least a part of the Secretary's torment, two days later, by declining his resignation. "On consideration," he declared, "I find there is really very little to say. My knowledge of Mr. Pomeroy's letter having been made *public* came to me only the day you wrote; but I had, in spite of myself, known of its *existence* several days before. I have not yet read it, and I think I shall not. I was not shocked or surprised by the appearance of the letter, because I had had knowledge of Mr. Pomeroy's committee, and of secret issues which I supposed came from it, and of secret agents who I supposed were sent out by it, for several weeks." He was saying here that if he could know so much of what was going on behind his back, Chase must have known about it too, despite his fervent denial. However that might be, Lincoln continued, "I have known just as little of these doings as my friends have allowed me to know . . . and I assure you, as you have assured me, that no assault has been made upon you by my instigation or with my countenance." Then came the close, the answer he had promised: "Whether you shall remain at the head of the Treasury Department is a question which I will not allow myself to consider from any stand-point other than my judgment of the public service, and, in that view, I do not perceive occasion for a change."

Chase was both relieved and pained: relieved to learn that he would remain at his post, which the long wait had taught him to value anew by persuading him that he was about to lose it, and pained because, as he plaintively observed, "there was no response in [the President's] letter to the sentiments of respect and esteem which mine contained." All this was rather beside the original point, however. Welles's prediction as to the "recoil" of the Pomeroy maneuver had already been borne out, its principal effect having been to rally Lincoln's friends to his support. And of these, as events had shown, there were many. By the time of his belated reply to Chase on Leap Year Day, no less than fourteen states, either by formal action of their legislatures or by delegates in convention, had gone on record in favor of a second term for the man in office. Among them were New Hampshire, where the Secretary had been born, Rhode Island, where his new son-in-law was supposedly in political control, and finally — unkindest cut — Ohio. In fact, Chase was advised by men from his home state to disentangle himself from the embarrassment into which his ambition had led him, and this he did in a letter to a Buckeye supporter, requesting that "no further consideration be given my name." He also made it clear, however, that he was only asking this from a sense of duty to the cause, which must not be endangered, even though he was still convinced that "as President I could take care of the Treasury better with the help of a Secretary than I can as Secretary without the help of a President. But our Ohio folks don't want me enough." There was the rub; there was what had given him his quietus. "I no longer have any political side," he presently was saying, "save that of my country, and there are multitudes who like me care little for men but everything for measures."

The upshot of this pose of "honorable disinterestedness," as one of the newspapers reprinting the letter called it, was a general impression that he was merely awaiting a more favorable chance to get back in the running. A member of the Pomeroy group referred to the withdrawal as "a word of declination diplomatically spoken to rouse [our] flagging spirits," and David Davis likened its author to Mr Micawber waiting for something to "turn up." Chase had dreamed too long and too grandly for those who knew him to believe that he had stopped, even though it had been demonstrated conclusively, twice over, that his dreams would not come true. "Mr Chase will subside as a presidential candidate after the nomination is made, not before," the chairman of the Republican National Committee remarked, while the New York *Herald* ventured a comparison out of nature: "The Salmon is a queer fish, very wary, often appearing to avoid the bait just before gulping it down."

Whether Chase continued to dream and scheme made little difference now, though; Lincoln — with the Ohioan's unintentional assistance — had the nomination cinched. The election, however, was quite another matter. Despite the encouragement Republicans could draw from their successes at the polls in the past season, the outcome of the contest in November would depend even more on military than on political events of the next eight months, through spring and summer and into fall. For one thing, the fighting would be expensive both in money and blood, and the voters, as the ones who would do the paying and the bleeding, were unlikely to be satisfied with anything less than continuous victory at such prices. The past year had been highly satisfactory in this regard; Vicksburg and Missionary Ridge, even Gettysburg and Helena, were accomplishments clearly worth their cost. But the new year had started no better than the old year had ended. Sherman's destruction of Meridian could scarcely be said to offset Meade's unhappy stalemate at Mine Run or Seymour's abrupt defeat at Olustee, let alone Kilpatrick's frustration outside Richmond or the drubbing Sooy Smith had suffered at Okolona or the unprofitable demonstration Thomas had attempted against Dalton. A good part of the trouble seemed to proceed from mismanagement at the top, and the critics were likely to hold the top man responsible: especially in light of the fact that he had had a direct hand in a good proportion of these failures, all of which had been undertaken with his permission and some of which had been launched against the judgment of those below him on the military ladder. Now a reckoning time was coming, when the voters would have their say.

Congress, too, would have to face the voters: enough of it, at any rate, for defeat to cost the party now in power its comfortable majority, the loss of which would involve the surrender of committee chairmanships, the say-so in how and by whom the conflict would be pressed, easy access to much the largest pork barrel the nation had ever known, and finally the seizure and distribution of such spoils as would remain, two or three years from now, when the South was brought to its knees and placed at the disposal of the winners of the election this November. With so much at stake, it was no wonder the congressmen were jumpy at the prospect. Moreover, their nervousness was intensified by a presidential order, dated February 1, providing for the draft, on March 10, of "five hundred thousand men to serve for three years or during the war." This call for "500,000 more" — made necessary by the heavy losses in battle this past year, as well as by the pending expiration of the enlistments of those volunteers who had come forward, two and three years ago, with all the fervor Sumter and McClellan had aroused — was graphic evidence of what the campaigns about to open were expected to cost in blood and money, and as such it presented the electorate with a yardstick by which to measure the height and depth of victories and defeats. The former, then, had better be substantial if they were to count for much at the polls, and by the same token the latter had better be minor, especially if they were anything like the recent setbacks, which were so obviously the result of miscalculations at the top and for which the voters could take their revenge by the way they marked their ballots. With this danger in mind, the lawmakers had returned to considering the previously rejected bill providing for a revival of the grade of lieutenant general, which in turn would provide for a man at the top who, by a combination of professional training and proven ability in the field, could operate within a shrinking margin for error that was already too narrow for the amateur who had been in unrestricted control these past three years.

Although Congress had no power to name the officer to whom the promotion would go in the event the bill went through, it was understood that Grant was the only candidate for the honor. Besides, Lincoln would do the naming, and by now the Illinois general was as much his favorite as anyone's. Far from being resentful of what another in his place — Jefferson Davis, for example — would have considered an encroachment by the legislative branch, he welcomed the relief the bill proposed to afford him from a portion of his duties as Commander in Chief. Above all, he was prepared to welcome Grant, who had applied at Donelson, Vicksburg, and Chattanooga the victory formula Lincoln had been seeking all these years. Others had sought it, too, of course, and like him they now believed they had found it in the western commander. So many of them had done so by now, in fact, that they had provoked the only doubts he had about the general's fitness for the post. Like his friend McClernand, Lincoln was thoroughly aware that this war would produce a military hero who eventually would take up residence in the White House, and Grant's appeal in this respect had already reached the stage at which he was being wooed by prominent members of both political parties. They knew a winner when they saw one, and so did Lincoln; and that was the trouble. Involved as he was at the time in disposing of Chase, he was not anxious to promote the interests of a more formidable rival, which was precisely what he would be doing if he brought Grant to Washington as general-in-chief.

Nor was that the only drawback. There might be another even more disqualifying. "When the Presidential grub once gets in a man, it hides well," Lincoln had said of himself, and he thought this might apply as well to Grant, whose generalship would scarcely be improved by the distractive gnawing of the grub. However, when he inquired in that direction about such political aspirations, he was told the general had said in January that he not only was not a candidate for any office, but that as a soldier he believed he had no right to discuss politics at all. Pressed further, he relented so far as to add that, once the war was over, he might indeed run for mayor of Galena — so that, if elected, he could have the sidewalk put in order between his house and the railroad station. Lincoln could appreciate the humor in this (though not the unconscious irony which others would perceive a few years later, when this view of the primary use of political office would be defined as "Grantism") but he was not entirely satisfied. For one thing, that had been several weeks ago, before the would-be kingmakers had begun to fawn on Grant in earnest. Adulation might have turned his head. So Lincoln called in a friend of Grant's and asked him point-blank if the general wanted to be President. The man not only denied this; he produced a letter in which Grant said flatly that he had no political interests whatever. No doubt the statement was similar to one he made about this time in a letter to another friend, in which he declared: "My only desire will be, as it has been, to whip out rebellion in the shortest way possible, and to retain as high a position in the army afterwards as the Administration then in power may think me suitable for." Clearly, if this had been honestly said, it had not been said by a man who nurtured political ambitions. Lincoln's doubts were allayed. If Congress opened the way by passing the bill, he would see that the promotion went to the general for whom it was obviously intended.

Relief in any form would be most welcome, for the strain of frustration these past three years had brought him all too often to the verge of exhaustion and absolute despair. There was, after all, a limit to how many Fredericksburgs and Chancellorsvilles, how many Gettysburgs and Chickamaugas, even how many Olustees and Okolonas a man could survive. Mostly, though, the strain resulted from the difficulty of measuring up to private standards which he defined for a visitor whose petition he turned down, saying: "I desire to so conduct the affairs of this Administration that if, at the end, when I come to lay down the reins of power, I have lost every other friend on earth, I shall at least have one friend left, and that friend shall be deep down inside of me." Public critics he could abide or ignore, even those who called him clod or tyrant, clown or monster — "What's the harm in letting him have his fling?" he remarked of one of the worst of these; "If he did not pitch into me, he would into some poor fellow he might hurt" — but the critic lodged in his own conscience was not so easily lived with or dismissed. Some men appeared to have little trouble muffling that self-critic: not Lincoln, who saw himself "chained here in this Mecca of office-seekers," like Prometheus to his rock, a victim of his own dark-souled nature. "You flaxen men with broad faces are born with cheer, and don't know a cloud from a star," he once told a caller who fit this description; "I am of another temperament." It sometimes seemed to him, moreover, that each recovery from gloom was made at the cost of future resiliency. "Nothing touches the tired spot," he had confessed the year before, and lately he had come back to this expression. Returning from a horseback ride that had seemed to lift his spirits, he was urged by a companion to find more time for rest and relaxation. "Rest?" he said. He shook his head, as if the word was unfamiliar. "I don't know. . . . I suppose it is good for the body. But the tired part is *inside,* out of reach."

If Grant was the man who could bring this inner weariness some measure of relief, Lincoln was not only willing to call him East to try his hand; he intended to wait no longer, before he did so, than the time required by Congress to pass the necessary legislation.

★   ★   ★

Opposing the Federal war of conquest (for, rebellion or revolution, that was what it would have to come to if the North was going to win) the Confederacy was fighting for survival. This had been, and would continue to be, Davis's principal advantage over his opponent in their respective capacities as leaders of their two nations: that he did not have to persuade his people of the reality of a threat which had been only too apparent ever since the first blue-clad soldier crossed the Potomac, whereas Lincoln was obliged to invoke a danger that was primarily theoretic. In the event that the Union broke in two, democracy might or might not "perish from the earth," but there could be no doubt at all — even before Sherman created, by way of a preview, his recent "swath of desolation" across Mississippi's midriff — about what would happen to the South if its bid for independence failed. However, this was only one face of a coin whose down side bore the inscription *States Rights.* Flip the coin and the advantage passed to Lincoln.

By suspending *habeas corpus,* or by ignoring at will such writs as the courts issued, the northern President kept his left hand free to deal as harshly as he pleased with those who sought to stir up trouble in his rear. It was otherwise with Davis. Denied this resource except in such drastic instances as the insurrection two years ago in East Tennessee, he had to meet this kind of trouble with that hand fettered. Often he had claimed this disadvantage as a virtue, referring by contrast to the North as a land where citizens were imprisoned "in utter defiance of all rights guaranteed by the institutions under which they live." Now though, with the approach of the fourth spring of the war, obstruction and defeatism had swollen to such proportions that conscription could scarcely be enforced or outright traitors prosecuted, so ready were hostile judges to issue writs that kept them beyond the reach of the authorities. Davis was obliged to request of Congress that it permit him to follow procedures he had scorned. "It has been our cherished hope," he declared in a special message on February 3, "that when the great struggle in which we are engaged was past we might exhibit to the world the proud spectacle of a people . . . achieving their liberty and independence, after the bloodiest war of modern times, without a single sacrifice of civil right to military necessity. But it can no longer be doubted that the zeal with which the people sprang to arms at the beginning of the contest has, in some parts of the Confederacy, been impaired by the long continuance and magnitude of the struggle. . . . Discontent, disaffection, and disloyalty are manifested among those who, through the sacrifices of others, have enjoyed quiet and safety at home. Public meetings have been held, in some of which a treasonable design is masked by a pretense of devotion to State sovereignty, and in others is openly avowed. . . . Secret leagues and associations are being formed. In certain localities, men of no mean position do not hesitate to avow their hostility to our cause and their advocacy of peace on the terms of submission." All this was painful to admit, even in secret session, but Davis foresaw still greater problems unless the trend was checked. "Disappointment and despondency will displace the buoyant fortitude which animates [our brave soldiers] now. Desertion, already a frightful evil, will become the order of the day." He knew how sacred to his hearers the writ was, and he assured them that he would not abuse the license he was asking them to grant him. "Loyal citizens will not feel the danger, and the disloyal must be made to fear it. The very existence of extraordinary powers often renders their exercise unnecessary." In any case, he asserted in conclusion, "to temporize with disloyalty in the midst of war is but to quicken it to the growth of treason. I therefore respectfully recommend that the privilege of the writ of *habeas corpus* be suspended."

After twelve days of acrimonious debate — highlighted by an impassioned protest from the Vice President, who sent word from Georgia that if Davis was given the power he sought, "constitutional liberty will go down, never to rise again on this continent" — Congress agreed, though with profound misgivings, to a six-month suspension of the writ. However, the fight did not end there by any means. Stephens and his cohorts merely fell back to prepared positions, ranged in depth along the borders of their several sovereign states, and there continued their resistance under the banner of States Rights. "Georgians, behold your chains!" an Athens newspaper exhorted in an editorial printed alongside the newly passed regulations, which were appropriately framed in mourning borders. "Freemen of a once proud and happy country, contemplate the last act which rivets your bonds and binds you hand and foot, at the mercy of an unlimited military authority." An Alabama editor demanded the names of those congressmen "who, in secret conclave, obsequiously laid the liberties of this country at the feet of the President," so that they could be defeated if they had the gall to stand for re-election. Henry Foote, having long since warned that he "would call upon the people to rise, sword in hand, to put down the domestic tyrant who thus sought to invade their rights," proceeded to do just that. Nor was this defiance limited to words. Under the leadership of such men, Mississippi and Georgia passed flaming resolutions against the act; Louisiana presently did so, too, and North Carolina soon had a law on its books nullifying the action of the central government. Not even these modifications, crippling as they were to the purpose for which the writ had been suspended, allayed the fears of some that the rights of the states were about to be lost in "consolidation." If such a catastrophe ever came to pass, a Virginian declared, "it would be a kind boon in an overruling Providence to sweep from the earth the soil, along with the people. Better to be a wilderness of waste, than a lasting monument of lost liberty."

A wilderness of waste was what was all too likely to result from this nonrecognition of the fact that the South's whole hope for independence was held up by the bayonets of her soldiers, who in turn required the support of a strong central government if they were to be properly employed — or even, for that matter, clothed and fed — in a years-long conflict so costly in blood and money, at the stage it now had reached, that its demands could only be met by the enactment and rigid enforcement of laws which did in fact, as those who opposed them charged, involve the surrender of basic "rights" hitherto reserved to the states and the individual. Yet this was the one sacrifice the "impossiblists," who valued their rights above their chance at national independence, could not make. "Away with the idea of getting independence first, and looking after liberty afterwards," Stephens had said. "Our liberties, once lost, may be lost forever." "Why, sir," a Georgia congressman exclaimed, "this is a war for the Constitution! It is a *constitutional* war." It was also, and first, a war for survival; but the ultraconservatives, including the fire-eaters who had done so much to bring it on, had been using the weapon of States Rights too long and with too much success, when they were members of the Union, to discard it now that they had seceded. They simply would rather die than drop that cudgel, even when there was no one to use it on but their own people and nothing to strike at except the solidarity that was their one hope for victory over an adversary whose reserves of men and wealth were practically limitless. It was in this inflexibility that the bill came due for having launched a conservative revolution, and apparently it was necessarily so, even though their anomalous devotion to an untimely creed amounted to an irresistible death-wish. But that was precisely their pride. They had inherited it and they would hand it down, inviolate, to the latest generation; or they would pray God "to sweep from the earth the soil, along with the people."

No more than a casual glance at the map sufficed to show the gravity of the military situation they would not relax their civil vigilance to face. Shaded, the Federal gains of the past two years resembled the broad shadow of a bird suspended in flight above the Mississippi Valley, its head hung over Missouri, its tail spread down past New Orleans, and its wings extended from Chesapeake Bay to Texas. What shape the pres-

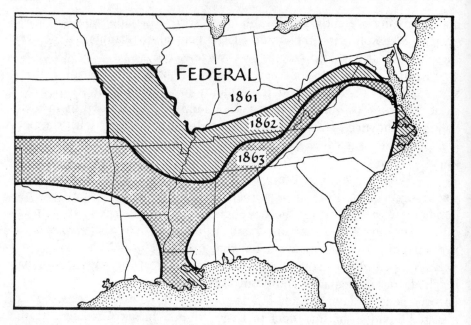

ent year would give this shadow was far from clear to those who lived in its penumbra, but they saw clearly enough that the creature who cast it could not be driven back into the land from which it had emerged; at any rate, not to stay there. R. E. Lee, after two expensive attempts to do just that, admitted as much to Davis in early February. "We are not in a condition, and never have been, in my opinion, to invade the enemy's country with a prospect of permanent benefit," he wrote, although he added that he hoped, by means of a show of force in East Tennessee or Virginia, to "alarm and embarrass him to some extent, and thus prevent his undertaking anything of magnitude against us."

Davis agreed that the South was limited by necessity to the strategic defensive. Indeed, that had been his policy from the start, pursued in the belief that Europe would intervene if the struggle could be protracted. The difference now lay in the object of such protraction. Foreign intervention was obviously never going to come, but he still hoped for intervention of another kind. In the North, a presidential election would be held in November, and he hoped for intervention by a majority of the voters, who then would have their chance to end the bloodshed by replacing Lincoln with a man who stood for peace. Peace, no matter whether it was achieved in the North or the South, in the field or at the polls, meant victory on the terms the Confederate leader had announced at the outset, saying, "All we ask is to be let alone." In the light of this possibility, the South's task was to add to the war weariness of the North; which meant, above all, that the enemy was to be allowed no more spirit-lifting triumphs — especially none like Vicksburg or Missionary Ridge, which had set all the church bells ringing beyond the Potomac and the Ohio — and that whatever was lost, under pressure of the odds, must not only be minor in value, but must also be paid for in casualties so heavy that the gain would be clearly disproportionate to the cost, particularly in the judgment of those who would be casting their ballots in November.

On the face of it — by contrast, that is, with the two preceding years, each of which had included the added burden of launching an invasion that had failed — this did not appear too difficult a task. In the past calendar year, moreover, while the Federal over-all strength was declining from 918,211 to 860,737 men, that of the Confederates increased from 446,622 to 463,181. This was not only the largest number of men the South had had under arms since the war began; it was also nearly 100,000 more than she had had two years ago, on the eve of her greatest triumphs. However, such encouragement as Davis might have derived from a comparison of these New Year's figures, showing the North-South odds reduced to less than two to one, was short-lived. One month later, Lincoln issued his call for "500,000 more."

That was better than ten times the number Lee had on the Rapidan, covering Richmond, or Johnston had around Dalton, covering Atlanta, and since the loss of either of these cities, in addition to being a strategic disaster for the South, would provide the North with a triumph that would be likely to win Lincoln the election, Davis was faced at once with the problem of how to match this call with one of his own. But the hard truth was that nothing like half that many troops — the number required if the current odds were not to be lengthened intolerably for the savage fighting that would open in the spring — could be raised under the present conscription laws, even though these had been strengthened in December by the passage of legislation that modified exemptions, put an end to the hiring of substitutes, and provided for the replacement of able-bodied men, in noncombatant jobs, with veterans who had been incapacitated by wounds or civilians who previously had been passed over for reasons of health. The bottom of the manpower barrel was not only in sight; it had been scraped practically clean to provide the army with every available male within the conscription age-range of eighteen to forty-five. One possibility, unpleasant to contemplate since it would expose the government more than ever to the charge that it was "robbing the cradle and the grave," would be to extend the range in either or both directions. Another possibility, far more fruitful, was suggested by Pat Cleburne; but it was worse than unpleasant, it was unthinkable. In early January the Irish-born former Helena lawyer prepared and read to his fellow generals in the Army of Tennessee a paper in which he examined the sinking fortunes of the Confederacy and proposed to deal simultaneously with what he conceived to be the two main problems blocking the path to independence: the manpower shortage, which was growing worse with every victory or defeat, and slavery, which he saw as a millstone the nation could no longer afford to carry in its effort to stay afloat on the sea of war. In brief, Cleburne's proposal was that the South emancipate its Negroes — thus making a virtue of necessity, since in his opinion slavery was doomed anyhow — and enlist them in its armies. This would "change the race from a dreaded weakness to a [source] of strength," he declared, and added: "We can do this more effectually than the North can now do, for we can give the Negro not only his own freedom, but that of his wife and child, and can secure it to him in his old home." Moreover, he said, such an action "would remove forever all selfish taint from our cause and place independence above every question of property. The very magnitude of the sacrifice itself, such as no nation has ever voluntarily made before, would appall our enemies . . . and fill our hearts with a pride and singleness of purpose which would clothe us with new strength in battle."

Recovering presently from the shock into which the foreign-born general's views had thrown them, the corps and division commanders were unanimous in their condemnation of the proposal, which they saw as a threat to everything they held dear. "I will not attempt to describe my feelings on being confronted by a project so startling in its character," one wrote in confidence to a friend. He labeled the paper a "monstrous proposition . . . revolting to Southern sentiment, Southern pride, and Southern honor," and predicted that "if this thing is once openly proposed to the army the total disintegration of that army will follow in a fortnight." Advised by Johnston and the others to proceed no further with the matter, Cleburne did not insist that the paper be forwarded, but another general considered it so "incendiary" in character that he took the trouble to get a copy and send it on to Richmond. There the reaction was much the same, apparently, as the one it had provoked in Dalton. Johnston received, before the month was out, a letter from the Secretary of War, expressing "the earnest conviction of the President that the dissemination or even promulgation of such opinions under the present circumstances of the Confederacy, whether in the army or among the people, can be productive only of discouragement, distraction, and dissension." The army commander was instructed to see to "the suppression, not only of the memorial itself, but likewise of all discussion and controversy respecting or growing out of it." Johnston replied that Cleburne, having observed the manner in which it was received, had already "put away his paper," and that he himself had had "no reason since to suppose that it made any impression." In point of fact, the suppression Richmond called for was so effective that nothing further was heard of the document for more than thirty years, when it finally turned up among the posthumous papers of a staff officer. One possible effect it had, however, and that was on Cleburne himself, or in any case on his career. Although Seddon had assured Johnston that "no doubt or mistrust is for a moment entertained of the patriotic intents of the gallant author of the memorial," and though the Arkansan was considered by many to be the best division commander in either army, South or North, he was never assigned any larger duties than those he had at the time he proposed to emancipate the slaves of the South and enlist them in her struggle for independence.

Davis had not been as shocked by the proposal as Seddon's letter seemed to indicate. For one thing, he agreed with the underlying premise that slavery was doomed, no matter who won or lost the war, and had said as much to his wife. What alarmed him was the reaction, the "distraction and dissension," that would follow the release of what one of its hearers had called "this monstrous proposition." Knowing, as he did, how much more violent than the generals the politicians would be in their denunciation of such views — particularly the large slaveholders among them, such as Howell Cobb, who said flatly: "If slaves will make good soldiers, our whole theory of slavery is wrong" — he foresaw that the result would be calamitous in its effect on the fortunes of the Confederacy, which would be so torn internally by any discussion of the issue that, even though the army could be doubled in size by adoption of the plan, there would be nothing left for that army to defend but discord. Even so, Davis did not completely reject the notion. He kept it — much as Lincoln had kept the Emancipation Proclamation — as an ace in the hole, to be played if all else failed.

Meantime he still was faced with the necessity for matching, at least to some degree, his adversary's call for more additional troops than there were at present in all the southern armies. Left with the alternative of extending conscription, he moved to do so in a message to Congress suggesting 1) that all industrial exemptions be abolished and 2) that the upper and lower age-range limits be raised and reduced, respectively, to fifty and seventeen. The first of these two suggestions kicked up the greater furor. Newspaper editors, who feared (groundlessly, as it turned out) that they would lose their printers if the law was strengthened to this extent, protested that freedom of the press was threatened. For others, the fear was more general. A Virginia congressman, for example, asserted that such legislation would "clothe the President with the powers of an autocrat" and invest him with "prerogatives before which those of Napoleon sink into insignificance," while Foote rose up again in his wrath to declare that "Others may vote to extend this man's power for mischief; I hold in contempt him and his whole tribe of servitors and minions." There were, however, enough of the "tribe" — or, in any case, enough of Foote's colleagues of all persuasions who saw the need for keeping the army up to a strength that would enable it to challenge the blue host that would be advancing with the spring — for the proposed measure to be adopted on February 17, the day Congress adjourned. Word went out at once to the conscription agents of the enlargement of the harvest they would be gleaning. No drawing of lots, no "wheels of fortune," such as were used in the North to select candidates for induc-

tion, were required in the South. From this time forward, it was simply the task of the agents to enroll or exempt every white male in the
Confederacy between the ages of seventeen and fifty.

Davis's reaction to this granting of his request was mixed. Pleased
though he was to have the measure passed, and though he himself had
asked for what had been given, he was saddened by the widening of the
age-range: not by the raising of the upper limit, which brought it within
five years of his own age, but by the reduction of the lower limit, which
seemed to him a spending of future hopes. The old and the middle-aged
could be spared. The young were another matter. The South would
have great need, in the years ahead, of all the talent she could muster —
as much, perhaps, if she lost the war, as if she won it — yet there was no
telling how much of that talent, still undeveloped at seventeen, would be
destroyed and left behind, packed into shallow burial trenches on the
fields of battles still unfought. It grieved him that the mill of war, as he
remarked, was about to "grind the seed corn of the nation."

While the young and the old were thus being gathered in camps
of instruction, where they would be converted into material fit for use
in chinking what he once had called "our wall of living breasts," Davis
gave his attention to strengthening and replacing the men who would
lead them. The appointment in early January of George Davis of North
Carolina to succeed Attorney General Watts, who had left Richmond
the month before to be inaugurated as governor of Alabama, marked the
first change in the Cabinet since Seddon took over the War Department,
more than a year ago. Little attention was paid to this, for the post en-
tailed few duties; but the same could not be said of two changes that followed, for they were military, and anything that involved the army was
always of consuming interest. Before adjourning, Congress had authorized the President to appoint a sixth full general, thus to allow a freer
hand to the commander of the Transmississippi, cut off as he was from
either the direction or assistance of the central government. Davis's
prompt award of the promotion to Kirby Smith, for whom of course it
had been intended, was applauded by everyone, in or out of the army,
except Longstreet, whose name headed the list of lieutenant generals, on
which Smith's had stood second. "A soldier's honor is his all," Old Peter
afterwards protested, "and of that they would rob him and degrade him
in the eyes of his troops." Piqued at having thus been overleaped — and
unhappy as he was anyhow, because of his late repulse at Knoxville and
the disaffection that had spread through his corps in its mountainous
camps around Greeneville, seventy miles to the east — his first reaction
was that "the occasion seemed to demand resignation." But on second
thought he decided that this "would have been unsoldierly conduct.
Dispassionate judgment suggested, as the proper rounding of the soldier's life, to stay and go down with faithful comrades of long and
arduous service."

Painful though the burning was in Longstreet's ample bosom, it was no more than a pinpoint gleam compared to the fires of resentment lighted by the announcement, a few days later, of the second military change. On February 22, the second anniversary of his inauguration as head of the permanent government, Davis summoned Lee to the capital for another conference. There were matters of strategy to be discussed, and something else as well. The Virginian's former post as advisor to the Commander in Chief had been vacant for more than twenty months; now Davis proposed to name Bragg as his successor. This was certain to surprise and dismay a great many people who saw the North Carolinian as the author of most of their present woes, but Davis believed that Bragg's undeniable shortcomings as a field commander — particularly his tendency to convert drawn battles into defeats by retreating, and victories into stalemates by failing to pursue — were not disqualifications for service in an advisory capacity; whereas his equally undeniable virtues, as an administrator and a strategist — his northward march into Kentucky, for example, undertaken on his own initiative at a time of deepest gloom, had reversed the whole course of the war in the western theater, and he had also proved himself (all too often, some would say) a master in the art of conducting tactical withdrawals — would be of great value to the country. Lee agreed, and the appointment was announced two days later, on February 24: "General Braxton Bragg is assigned to duty at the seat of government, and, under the direction of the President, is charged with the conduct of the military operations in the armies of the Confederacy."

Surprise and dismay, private and public, were indeed the reactions to the terrible-tempered general's elevation, coming as it did only one day short of three months since his rout at Missionary Ridge. "No doubt Bragg can give the President valuable counsel," a War Department diarist observed, but in his opinion Davis — whom he described as being "naturally a little oppugnant" — derived "a secret satisfaction in triumphing thus over popular sentiment, which just at this time is much averse to General Bragg." The sharpest attacks, as might have been expected, were launched by the editors of the Richmond *Whig* and the *Examiner*. Both employed irony in their comments, ignoring the advisory nature of Bragg's assignment by pretending to believe that Davis had given his pet general direct command over Lee and Johnston. "When a man fails in an inferior position," the *Whig* declared, "it is natural and charitable to conclude that the failure is due to the inadequacy of the task to his capabilities, and wise to give him a larger sphere for the proper exertion of his abilities." Pollard of the *Examiner* struck with a heavier hand, though his pen was no less sharp. "The judicious and opportune appointment of General Bragg to the post of commander-in-chief of the Confederate armies will be appreciated," he noted wryly, "as an illustration of that strong common sense which forms the basis of the President's character." He managed to sustain this tone for half a column, then dropped it in midsentence: "This happy announcement should enliven the confidence and enthusiasm reviving among the people like a bucket of water poured on a newly kindled grate."

Davis went his way, as he had done from the beginning. "If we succeed we shall hear nothing of these malcontents," he had told his wife three years ago in Montgomery. "If we do not, then I shall be held accountable by friends as well as foes. I will do my best." That was as much his guiding principle now as ever. He believed that Bragg would serve him and the country well in this new assignment, and so far as he was concerned the decision as to whether to use him ended there. "Opposition in any form can only disturb me inasmuch as it may endanger the public welfare," he had said. For all his aristocratic bearing and his apparent indifference to the barbs flung at him by men like Foote and Pollard, which gave rise to the persistent myth that he was deficient in feeling, he trusted the people far more than he did the politicians and journalists who catered to their weaknesses and fears, and he knew only too well the hardness of their lot in this season of lengthening death lists and spiraling inflation. Ten Confederate dollars would buy a yard of calico or a pound of coffee; bacon was $3.50 a pound, butter $4; eggs were $2 a dozen, chickens $6 a pair. Such prices made for meager living, particularly for city dwellers who had no vegetable gardens to tend or harvest. But even these were fortunate, so far at least as food was concerned, in comparison with the soldiers. The daily ration in the Army of Northern Virginia this winter was four ounces of bacon or salt pork and one pint of unbolted cornmeal, and though a private was free to scrounge what he could in his off hours, including wild onions and dandelion greens, his pay of $11 a month would not go far toward the purchase of supplements, even when they were available, which was seldom. Still, there were those who seemed to make out well enough from time to time: as a hungry infantryman, out on a greens hunt, discovered one day when he came upon a group of commissary officers enjoying an al fresco luncheon in the shade of a clump of trees. He approached the fence surrounding the grove, put his head through the palings, and gazed admiringly at the spread of food. "I say, misters," he called to the diners at last, "did any of you ever hearn tell of the battle of Chance'lorsville?"

This irrepressibility, which sustained him in adversity, this overriding sense of the ridiculous, uncramped even by the pangs of hunger, was as much a part of what made the Confederate soldier "terrible in battle" as was the high-throated yell he gave when he went into a charge or the derisive glee with which he tended to receive one, anticipating a yield of well-shod corpses. Davis counted heavily on this spirit to insure the survival of the armies and the nation through the harder times he knew would begin when the present "mud truce" ended. He was too much a military realist not to take into account the lengthening odds, but

he included the imponderables in his calculations. To have done otherwise would have been to admit defeat before it came; which was not at
all his way. "I cultivate hope and patience," he said, "and trust to the
blunders of our enemy and the gallantry of our troops for ultimate
success."

★ ★ ★

In the North, as spring drew nearer and some perspective was
afforded for a backward look at the season approaching its end, there was
the feeling that such minor reverses as Olustee and Okolona, disappointing though they had been at the time, were no true detractions from the
significant victories scored at the outset at Rappahannock Bridge and
Chattanooga. These were the pattern-setters, the more valid indications
of what was to come when winter relaxed its grip and large-scale fighting was resumed. Along with this, there was also the growing belief
that the nation had found in Lincoln, despite his occasional military
errors, the leader it needed to see it through what remained of its fiery
trial. "The President is a man of convictions," *Harper's Weekly* had declared more than a year ago, combining these two impressions. "He has
certain profound persuasions and a very clear purpose. He knows what
the war sprang from, and upon what ground a permanent peace can be
reared. He is cautious, cool, judicial. [While] he knows that great revo-
lutions do not go backward, he is aware that when certain great steps in
their prosecution are once taken, there will be loud outcries and apprehension. But the ninth wave touches the point to which the whole sea
will presently rise, although the next wave, and the next, should seem to
show a falling off."

What *Harper's* had had in mind at the time was the Emancipation
Proclamation, but people rereading this now could see that Missionary
Ridge had been just such a ninth wave, lapping far up the military shin-
gle, and though "the next wave, and the next," had shown a falling off,
the tide would soon be at the full. Or anyhow they could believe they
saw this, and they reacted accordingly. During the current interim of
comparative inaction, the home-front war had taken on what would be
known in the following decade as a Chautauqua aspect, a revival of the
waning lyceum movement, which combined the qualities of the camp
meeting and the county fair, yet added a sophistication those old-time
activities had lacked. They assembled in churches, halls, and theaters to
enjoy in mass the heady atmosphere of pending victory. Primarily, such
gatherings were militant in tone — meaning abolitionist, for the anti-
slavery element had always been the militant wing of the party now in
power — with the result that those who attended could feel that they
were being strengthened and uplifted at the same time they were being
entertained. There was, for example, the Hutchinson family: singers
who could electrify an audience with their rendition of Whittier's "Hymn
of Liberty," sung to the tune of Luther's *Ein' feste Burg ist unser Gott.*

The thought might be muddled, the rhymes atrocious, but the sweetness
of the singers' voice and the fervor of their delivery gave the words a
power that swept the hearers along as part of the broad surge toward
that same freedom for which blue-clad soldiers were giving their lives,
beyond the roll of the horizon:

> *What gives the wheat-field blades of steel?*
> *What points the rebel cannon?*
> *What sets the roaring rabble's heel*
> *On the old star-spangled pennon?*
> *What breaks the oath*
> *Of the men o' the South?*
> *What whets the knife*
> *For the Union's life?*
> *Hark to the answer: Slavery!*

Or there was the Boston lecturer Wendell Phillips, who assured a New
York audience of its moral superiority over a foe whose only role in life
was to block the march of progress. He pictured the young man of the
South, "melted in sensuality, whose face was never lighted up by a purpose since his mother looked into his cradle," and declared that for such
men "War is gain. They go out of it, and they sink down." Whipped,
they would return "to barrooms, to corner groceries, to chopping straw
and calling it politics. [Laughter.] You might think they would go back
to their professions. They never had any. You might think they would
go back to the mechanic arts. They don't know how to open a jackknife.
[Great merriment.] There is nowhere for them to go, unless we send
them half a million of emancipated blacks to teach them how to plant
cotton." His solution to the problem of how to keep the beaten South
from relapsing "into a state of society more cruel than war — whose
characteristics are private assassination, burning, stabbing, shooting,
poisoning" — lifted the North's grim efforts to the height of a crusade:
"We have not only an army to conquer. We have a state of mind to annihilate."

Phillips could always fill a hall, but the star attraction this season,
all agreed, was the girl orator Anna E. Dickinson, who had begun her
career on the eve of her twentieth birthday, when she lost her job at the
mint in her native Philadelphia for accusing McClellan of treason at
Ball's Bluff. Since then, she had come far, until now she was hailed alternately as the Joan of Arc and the Portia of the Union. Whether she spoke
at the Academy of Music in her home city, at New York's Cooper
Union, or at the Music Hall in Boston, the house was certain to be packed
with those who came to marvel at the contrast between her virginal
appearance — "her features well chiseled, her forehead and upper lip of
the Greek proportion, her nostrils thin" — and the "torrent of burning,
scathing, lightning eloquence," which she released in what the same reviewer called "wonderfully lengthened sentences uttered without break

or pause." Hearing Anna was a dramatic experience not easily forgotten, though what you brought away with you was not so much a remembrance of what she had said as it was of the manner in which she had said it: which was how she affected Henry James, apparently, when he came to portray her, more than twenty years later, as Verena Tarrant. Her hatred of Southerners, especially Jefferson Davis, whom she compared to a hyena, was not so all-consuming that none was left for northern Democrats, who were without exception traitors to the cause of human freedom — as, indeed, were all who were not of the most radical persuasion, including such Republicans as Seward, "the Fox of the White House." She loved applause; it thrilled her, and her style became more forward as her listeners responded; so that her addresses were in a sense a form of intercourse, an exchange of emotions, back and forth across the footlights.

Quite different, but curious too in her effect on those who came to hear and see her, was another platform artist, the former slave Sojourner Truth. Tall and gaunt, utterly black, and close to eighty years of age, she made her appearances in a voluminous, floor-length, long-sleeved dress, a crocheted shawl, and the calico turban or headrag that was practically a badge of office for house servants in the South, particularly children's nurses; which was what she had been, before she won her freedom and came North. Battle Creek was now her home, and she journeyed not only through Michigan, but also through Illinois and Indiana and Ohio, including the Copperhead regions of those states, to plead for the extension of freedom to all her race, north as well as south of the Proclamation line. She spoke in a deep, musical voice, with natural grace and simple dignity, and vended as a side line, to help cover her travel expenses, photographs of herself in her speaking costume; "selling the shadow to sustain the substance," she explained. Her most valued possession, despite her illiteracy, was an autograph book containing the signatures of famous men and women she encountered along her way, one of whom would presently be the Great Emancipator himself. "For Aunty Sojourner Truth, A. Lincoln," he wrote, and she gave him one of her photographs, remarking that she sold them for her livelihood, "but this one is for you, without money and without price." She was much admired, though for the most part as an exotic, and was generally welcome wherever she went, although not always. Once in an Indiana town, for instance, when she was introduced to deliver an antislavery address to a large audience, a local Copperhead rose to repeat the rumor that she was a man, disguised in women's clothes, and to suggest that she permit a committee of ladies to examine her in private. She answered the challenge, then and there, by unfastening her dress and showing the crowd her shrunken, hound's-ear breasts. These had fed many black children, she said, but still more white children had nursed at them. By now the Copperheads — who had come to watch her, or his, exposure as a fraud — were filing out of the auditorium, a look of disgust on their faces, and Sojourner Truth shook her breasts at one of them, inquiring after him in her low contralto: "You want to suck?"

Wendell Phillips, Anna Dickinson, Sojourner Truth were only three among the many who were riding the wave of confidence that the worst was over, that the war could have but one ending now, and that it would come as soon as the South could be made to see what already was apparent in the North. Moreover, there had come with this belief a lessening of discord, not only among the people, but also in the conduct of affairs in Washington. "Never since I have been in public life has there been so little excitement in Congress," Sumner wrote on New Year's Day to a friend in England. "The way seems, at last, open. Nobody doubts the result. The assurance of the future gives calmness." This did not mean that the legislators were willing to take chances. Knowing as they did that the public's blame for any failure would be in ratio to the height of its expectations, they were in fact less willing to take chances than they had been at any time before. And it was for this reason that the bill to revive the grade of lieutenant general had itself been revived: to reduce the likelihood of military blunders at the top. "Give us, Sir, a live general!" a Michigan senator exclaimed in the course of the debate. He meant by this a man who would follow a straight path to victory, "and not let us be dragging along under influences such as have presided over the Army of the Potomac for these last many tedious and weary months; an army oscillating alternately between the Rappahannock and the Potomac, defeated today and hardly successful tomorrow, with its commanders changed almost as frequently as the moon changes its face. Sir, for one I am tired of this, and I tell [the] senators here that the country is getting weary of it."

Some proponents were in favor of naming Grant specifically in the bill, while others believed that this would be setting a dangerous precedent. Besides, Fessenden of Maine rose to ask, to whom could the promotion go if not to Grant? and then went on to point out that the honor would be greater if no name was mentioned, since to do so would be to imply that there had been a choice: "When the President says to us, as he will say unquestionably, 'I consider that General Ulysses S. Grant is the man of all others, from his great services, to be placed in this exalted position,' and when we, as we shall unquestionably, unanimously say 'Ay' to that and confirm him, have we not given him a position such as any man living or who ever lived might well be proud of, without putting his name in our bill originally and thus saying to the President, 'Sir, we cannot trust you to act on this matter unless we hint to you that we want such a man appointed'?" Lengthy and thorough the debate was, but there was never much doubt as to the outcome. Introduced on the first day of February, the measure was passed on the last, and the procedure Fessenden had outlined followed swiftly. Receiving the bill on March 1, Lincoln promptly signed it and named Grant for the honor next day. The Senate confirmed the appointment without delay, and on March 3 the general was ordered by telegraph to report at once to Washington, where he would receive his commission directly from the President.

Lincoln had been disappointed too often, over the course of the past three years, for him to allow his hopes to soar too high. He remembered McDowell and McClellan. He remembered Burnside and Hooker. Above all, he remembered Pope, who had also come East with western laurels on his brow. And there at hand, in case memory failed, was Halleck; Old Brains, too, had arrived from that direction, supposedly with a victory formula in his knapsack, and had wound up "a first-rate clerk." Still, after making all proper discounts, it seemed likely to Lincoln that now at last, in this general who had captured two rebel armies and routed a third, he had found the killer-arithmetician he had been seeking from the start.

✗ 5 ✗

Returning to Vicksburg on the last day of February, Sherman took no time out to recuperate from the rigors of the Meridian campaign, for he found there a week-old dispatch from Grant instructing him to cooperate with Banks in order to assure the success of the expedition up the Teche and the Red, which the Massachusetts general and Halleck had designed to accomplish the return of West Louisiana and East Texas to the Union, along with an estimated half million bales of hoarded cotton. Sherman himself was to rejoin Grant at Chattanooga in time to open the spring drive on Atlanta; he would therefore not participate in the Louisiana-Texas venture, save for making a short-term loan of some 10,000 troops to strengthen it; but he decided to confer in person with Banks, before he himself went back to Tennessee, on the logistical details of getting the reinforcements to him somewhere up the Red. Accordingly, he left Vicksburg that same day aboard the fast packet *Diana,* and arrived in New Orleans two days later, on March 2.

He found Banks in high spirits: not only because of the military outlook, which was considered excellent — Franklin had recovered from his early November repulse at Grand Coteau and had three divisions massed at Opelousas, ready to advance — but also because of political developments in accordance with Lincoln's reconstruction policy, whereby a Union-loyal candidate, one Michael Hahn, a native of Bavaria, had been elected governor of Louisiana by the necessary ten percent of the voters on February 22 and was to be inaugurated at New Orleans on March 5. Sherman's logistical problems were settled within two days, the arrangement being that the Vicksburg reinforcements would join Franklin at Alexandria on March 17 for the farther ascent of the Red, but Banks urged his visitor to stay over another two days for Hahn's in-

auguration, which he assured him would be well worth the delay. A
chorus of one thousand voices, accompanied by all the bands of the army,
would perform the "Anvil Chorus" in Lafayette Square, while church
bells rang and cannon were fired in unison by electrical devices. Sherman
declined the invitation. He had already gone on record as opposing such
political procedures, and what was more, he said later, "I regarded all
such ceremonies as out of place at a time when it seemed to me every
hour and every minute were due to the war." His mind on destruction,
not reconstruction, he reboarded the *Diana*, and three days later, on
March 6, was back in Vicksburg, to which by now the destroyers of
Meridian had returned, well rested from their week-long stay in Canton
and the additional spoliation they had accomplished at that place.

Remaining in Vicksburg only long enough to pass on to Mc-
Pherson the details of the arrangement he had made for reinforcing
Banks at Alexandria on St Patrick's Day, Sherman set off upriver again
the following morning, impatient to rejoin the troops he had left
poised near Chattanooga, waiting alongside those under Thomas and
Hooker for Grant to give the nod that would start them slogging southward, over or around Joe Johnston, into and through the heart of
Georgia. "Prepare them for my coming," he had told his adjutant, in
reference to the hapless civilians in his path, and now at last he was on
his way. On the second day out, however, the *Diana* was hailed by a
southbound packet which, to the Ohioan's surprise, turned out to have
one of Grant's staff captains aboard, charged with the delivery of a
highly personal letter his chief had written four days ago, on March 4, at
Nashville. "Dear Sherman," it read: "The bill reviving the grade of
lieutenant general in the army has become a law, and my name has been
sent to the Senate for the place. I now receive orders to report to Washington immediately, in person, which indicates either a confirmation or a
likelihood of confirmation. I start in the morning to comply with the
order, but I shall say very distinctly on my arrival there that I shall accept no appointment which will require me to make that city my headquarters. This, however, is not what I started out to write about. . . .
What I want is to express my thanks to you and McPherson as the men
to whom, above all others, I feel indebted for whatever I have had of
success. How far your advice and suggestions have been of assistance,
you know. How far your execution of whatever has been given you to
do entitles you to the reward I am receiving, you cannot know as well as
I do. I feel all the gratitude this letter would express, giving it the most
flattering construction. The word *you* I use in the plural, intending it for
McPherson also," the letter concluded. "I should write to him, and will
some day, but starting in the morning I do not know that I will find time
just now. Your friend, U. S. Grant."

Sherman vibrated with three conflicting reactions as he read the
first three sentences Grant had written: first, delight that his friend was

about to be so honored: second, alarm that he had been summoned to the fleshpots of the capital: third, relief that he did not intend to stay there. However, as the boat continued to push its way slowly upriver against the booming current, the third emotion gave way in turn to the second, which came back even stronger than at first. The fact was, though he idolized his friend and superior, he had never really trusted his judgment in matters concerning his career, and though he admired his simplicity of character, seeing it in the quality that perhaps had contributed most to his success, he was forever supposing that it would get him in trouble, especially if he fell into the hands of wily men who would know how to use him for their sordid ends. "Your reputation as a general is now far above that of any man living, and partisans will maneuver for your influence," he had warned him in a letter written during the Christmas visit to Ohio, at a time when the Grant-for-President drums were beginning to rumble. He counseled him earnestly to "Preserve a plain military character and let others maneuver as they will. You will beat them not only in fame, but in doing good in the closing scenes of this war, when somebody must heal and mend up the breaches." Nowhere were the wily more in evidence than in Washington, and the more he thought about it, the more he was convinced that "Grant would not stand the intrigues of the politicians a week," even though he went there with no intention of remaining any longer than it took to get a third star tacked on each shoulder of his weathered blouse. What was more, Sherman had a mystical feeling about the Mississippi River, which he called "the great artery" of America. "I want to live out here and die here also," he wrote to another friend this week, as the *Diana* chugged upstream, "and I don't care if my grave be like De Soto's in its muddy waters." He seemed to fear that if Grant wandered far from the banks of the big river, his reaction would be like that of Antaeus when he lost contact with the earth.

Accordingly, after two days of fretting and fuming, as the boat drew near Memphis on March 10 he dashed off an answer to Grant's "more than kind and characteristic letter," thanking him in McPherson's name and his own, but protesting: "You do yourself injustice and us too much honor in assigning us so large a share of the merits which have led to your high advancement.... At Belmont you manifested your traits, neither of us being near. At Donelson also you illustrated your character; I was not near, and General McPherson [was] in too subordinate a capacity to influence you. Until you had won Donelson, I confess I was almost cowed by the terrible array of anarchical elements that presented themselves at every point; but that victory admitted the ray of light which I have followed ever since.... The chief characteristic in your nature is the simple faith in success you have always manifested, which I can liken to nothing else than the faith a Christian has in his Saviour. This faith gave you victory at Shiloh and Vicksburg. Also, when you have completed your best preparations, you go into battle without hesitation, as at Chattanooga; no doubts, no reserve; and I tell you that it was this that made us act with confidence. I knew wherever I was that you thought of me, and if I got in a tight place you would come — if alive. My only points of doubt were as to your knowledge of grand strategy and of books of science and history, but I confess your common-sense seems to have supplied all this."

Having disposed thus of the disclaimers and the amenities, the volatile redhead passed at once to the main burden of his letter. If Grant stayed East, Sherman almost certainly would be given full charge of the West, and yet, although personally he wanted this above all possible assignments, he was unwilling to secure it at the cost of his friend's ruin, which was what he believed would result from any such arrangement. "Do not stay in Washington," he urged him. "Halleck is better qualified than you are to stand the buffets of intrigue and policy. Come out West; take to yourself the whole Mississippi Valley. Let us make it dead sure, and I tell you the Atlantic slope and Pacific shores will follow its destiny as sure as the limbs of a tree live or die with the main trunk. We have done much; still much remains. . . . For God's sake and your country's sake, come out of Washington! I foretold to General Halleck, before he left Corinth, the inevitable result to him, and I now exhort you to come out West. Here lies the seat of the coming empire, and from the West, when our task is done, we will make short work of Charleston and Richmond and the impoverished coast of the Atlantic."

Within a week he found his warning had been too late. Arriving in Memphis next day he received on March 14 a message from Grant arranging a meeting in Nashville three days later. If Sherman took this as evidence that his chief did not intend to make his headquarters in the East, he soon learned better. In Nashville on the appointed date, invested with the rank of lieutenant general and command of all the armies of the Union, Grant informed him that the Virginia situation required personal attention; he would be returning there to stay, and Sherman would have full charge of the West. However, what with the press of visiting dignitaries, all anxious for a look at a man with three stars on each shoulder, there was so little time for a strategy conference that it was decided the two generals would travel together as far as Cincinnati on Grant's return trip east. That way, it was thought, they could talk on the cars; but the wheels made such a clatter, they finally gave up trying to shout above the racket and fell silent. In Cincinnati they checked into the Burnet House, and there at last, in a private room with a sentry at the door, they spread their maps and got to work.

"Yonder began the campaign," Sherman was to say a quarter century later, standing before the hotel on the occasion of a visit to the Ohio city. "He was to go for Lee and I was to go for Joe Johnston. That was his plan."

List of Maps

Bibliographical Note

Index

LIST OF MAPS

*Maps drawn by George Annand, of Darien, Connecticut,
from originals by the author. All are oriented north.*

BIBLIOGRAPHICAL NOTE

In the course of this second of three intended five-year stints, the third of which will bring me to defeat and victory at Appomattox, my debt has grown heavier on both sides of the line where the original material leaves off, but most particularly on the near side of the line. Although the *Official Records*, supplemented by various other utterances by the participants, remain the primary source on which this narrative is based, the hundredth anniversary has enriched the store of comment on that contemporary evidence with biographies, studies of the conflict as a whole, examinations of individual campaigns, and general broodings on the minutiae — all of them, or anyhow nearly all of them, useful to the now dwindling number of writers and readers who, surviving exposure to the glut, continue to make that war their main historical concern. So that, while I agree in essence with Edmund Wilson's observation that "a day of mourning would be more appropriate," the celebration of the Centennial has at least been of considerable use to those engaged, as I am, in the process Robert Penn Warren has referred to as "picking the scab of our fate."

Not that my previous obligations have not continued. They have indeed, and they have been enlarged in the process. Kenneth P. Williams, Douglas Southall Freeman, J. G. Randall, Lloyd Lewis, Stanley F. Horn, Carl Sandburg, Bell I. Wiley, Bruce Catton, T. Harry Williams, Allan Nevins, Robert S. Henry, Jay Monaghan, E. Merton Coulter, Clifford Dowdey, Burton J. Hendrick, Margaret Leech are but a handful among the many to whom I am indebted as guides through the labyrinth. Without them I not only would have missed a great many wonders along the way, I would surely have been lost amid the intricate turnings and the uproar. Moreover, the debt continued to mount as the exploration proceeded: to Hudson Strode, for instance, for the extension of his *Jeffer-*

son Davis at a time when the need was sore, and to Mark Mayo Boatner for his labor-saving *Civil War Dictionary*. Specific accounts of individual campaigns, lately published to expand or replace the more or less classical versions by Bigelow and others, have been of particular help through this relentless stretch of fighting. Edward J. Stackpole's *Chancellorsville*, for example, was used in conjunction with two recent biographies of the hero of that battle, Frank E. Vandiver's *Mighty Stonewall* and Lenoir Chambers' *Stonewall Jackson*. Similarly, for the Vicksburg campaign, there were Earl Schenck Miers's *The Web of Victory* and Peter F. Walker's *Vicksburg, a People at War*, plus biographies of the two commanders, *Pemberton, Defender of Vicksburg* and *Grant Moves South*, by John C. Pemberton and Bruce Catton. For Gettysburg, there were Clifford Dowdey's *Death of a Nation*, Glenn Tucker's *High Tide at Gettysburg*, and George R. Stewart's *Pickett's Charge*. For the battles around Chattanooga, there were Glenn Tucker's *Chickamauga* and Fairfax Downey's *Storming of the Gateway*. James M. Merrill's *The Rebel Shore*, Fletcher Pratt's *Civil War on Western Waters*, and Clarence E. Macartney's *Mr. Lincoln's Admirals* contributed to the naval actions, as Benjamin P. Thomas' and Harold M. Hyman's *Stanton* did to events in Washington. These too were only a few of the most recent among the many, old and new, which I hope to acknowledge in a complete bibliography at the end of the third volume, *Red River to Appomattox*. Other obligations, of a more personal nature, were carried over from the outset: to the John Simon Guggenheim Memorial Foundation, which extended my fellowship beyond the norm: to the National Park Service, whose guides helped me (as they will you) to get to know so many confusing fields: to the William Alexander Percy Memorial Library, in my home town Greenville, Mississippi, which continued its loan of the *Official Records* and other reference works: to Robert D. Loomis of Random House, who managed to keep both his temper and his enthusiasm beyond unmet deadlines: to Memphis friends, who gave me food and whiskey without demanding payment in the form of talk about the war. To all these I am grateful: and to my wife Gwyn Rainer Foote, who bore with me.

Other, less specific obligations were as heavy. The photographs of Mathew Brady, affording as they do a gritty sense of participation — of being in the presence of the uniformed and frock-coated men who fought the battles and did the thinking, such as it was — gave me as much to go on, for example, as anything mentioned above. Further afield, but no less applicable, Richmond Lattimore's translation of the *Iliad* put a Greekless author in close touch with his model. Indeed, to be complete, the list of my debts would have to be practically endless. Proust I believe has taught me more about the organization of material than even Gibbon has done, and Gibbon taught me much; Mark Twain and Faulkner would also have to be included, for they left their sign on all they touched, and in the course of this exploration of the American scene I often found that they had been there before me. In a quite different sense, I am obligated also to the governors of my native state and the adjoining states of Arkansas and Alabama for helping to lessen my sectional bias by reproducing, in their actions during several of the years that went into the writing of this volume, much that was least admirable in the position my forebears occupied when they stood up to Lincoln. I suppose, or in any case fervently hope, it is true that history never repeats itself, but I know from watching these three gentlemen that it can be terrifying in its approximations, even when the reproduction — deriving, as it does, its scale from the performers — is in miniature.

As for method, it may explain much for me to state that my favorite historian is Tacitus, who dealt mainly with high-placed scoundrels, but that the finest compliment I ever heard paid a historian was tendered by Thomas Hobbes in the foreword to his translation of *The Peloponnesian War*, in which he referred to Thucydides as "one who, though he never digress to read a Lecture, Moral or Political, upon his own Text, nor enter into men's hearts, further than the Actions themselves evidently guide him ... filleth his Narrations with that choice of matter, and ordereth them with that Judgement, and with such perspicuity and efficacy expresseth himself that (as Plutarch saith) he maketh his Auditor a Spectator. For he setteth his Reader in the Assemblies of the People, and in their Senates, at their debating; in the Streets, at their Seditions; and in the Field, at their Battels." There indeed is something worth aiming at, however far short of attainment we fall.

— S.F.

Index

COMPREHENSIVE TABLE OF CONTENTS

The Civil War: A Narrative

Volume I, *Fort Sumter to Perryville*

"A stunning book full of color, life, character and a new atmosphere of the Civil War, and at the same time a narrative of unflagging power. Eloquent proof that an historian should be a writer above all else." —BURKE DAVIS

"This is historical writing at its best....It can hardly be surpassed." —*Library Journal*

"Anyone who wants to relive the Civil War, as thousands of Americans apparently do, will go through this volume with pleasure....Years from now, Foote's monumental narrative most likely will continue to be read and remembered as a classic of its kind."
—*New York Herald Tribune Book Review*

"There is, of course, a majesty inherent in the subject. Some sense of that ineluctable fact, however reluctant its expression, is evident in every honest consideration of our history. But the credit for recovering such majesty to the attention of our skeptical and unheroic age will hereafter belong peculiarly to Mr. Foote." —M. E. BRADFORD, *The National Review*

The Civil War: A Narrative

Volume III, *Red River to Appomattox*

"Foote is a novelist who temporarily abandoned fiction to apply the novelist's shaping hand to history: his model is not Thucydides but *The Iliad* and his story, innocent of notes and formal bibliography, has a literary design. Not by accident...but for cathartic effect is so much space given to the war's unwinding, its final shudders and convulsions....To read this chronicle is an awesome and moving experience. History and literature are rarely so thoroughly combined as here; one finishes this volume convinced that no one need undertake this particular enterprise again." —*Newsweek*

"I have never read a better, more vivid, more understandable account of the savage battling between Grant's and Lee's armies....Foote stays with the human strife and suffering, and unlike most Southern commentators, he does not take sides. In objectivity, in range, in mastery of detail, in beauty of language and feeling for the people involved, this work surpasses anything else on the subject. Written in the tradition of the great historian-artists—Gibbon, Prescott, Napier, Freeman—it stands alongside the work of the best of them." —*New Republic*

"The most written-about war in history has, with this completion of Shelby Foote's trilogy, been given the epic treatment it deserves." —*Providence Journal*

ABOUT THE AUTHOR

Although he now makes his home in Memphis, Tennessee, SHELBY FOOTE comes from a long line of Mississippians. He was born in Greenville, Mississippi, and attended school there until he entered the University of North Carolina. During World War II he served in the European theater as a captain of field artillery. In the period since the war, he has written five novels: *Tournament, Follow Me Down, Love in a Dry Season, Shiloh* and *Jordan County*. He has been awarded three Guggenheim fellowships.